Mexico

THIS EDITION WRITTEN AND RESEARCHED BY

John Noble,

Kate Armstrong, Stuart Butler, John Hecht, Beth Kohn,
Tom Masters, Josephine Quintero, Adam Skolnick,
Iain Stewart, Phillip Tang, Lucas Vidgen

PLAN YOUR TRIP

ON THE ROAD

Contents

LAND'S END, CABO ST LUCAS P732

ON THE ROAD

ALAN TOBEY/GETTY IMAGES ©

FOLK ART P826

Contents

UNDERSTAND

SURVIVAL GUIDE

SPECIAL FEATURES

Welcome to Mexico

Jungles, deserts; teeming cities, one-street pueblos; fiesta fireworks, Frida's angst: Mexico conjures up so many vivid images. And the reality lives up to the expectation.

An Outdoor Life

From the southern jungles to the smoking, snowcapped volcanoes and the cactus-dotted northern deserts, all surrounded by 10,000km of coast strung with sandy beaches and wildlife-rich lagoons, Mexico is an endless adventure for the senses. A climate that ranges from temperate to hot almost everywhere makes for a life spent largely in the open air. Take it easy lying on a beach, dining alfresco or strolling pretty streets, or get out and snorkel warm Caribbean reefs, hike mountain cloud forests or take a boat in search of dolphins or whales.

Art & Soul of a Nation

Mexico is packed with culture and history. Its pre-Hispanic civilizations built some of the world's great archaeological monuments, while the Spanish colonial era left beautiful towns full of tree-shaded plazas and richly sculpted stone churches and mansions. Modern Mexico has seen a surge of great art from the likes of Diego Rivera and Frida Kahlo. Top-class museums and galleries around the country document Mexico's fascinating history and its endless creative verve. Popular culture is just as vibrant, from the underground dance clubs of Mexico City to the wonderful handicrafts of the indigenous population.

Travel for All

Travel in Mexico is what you make it and the country caters to all types of visitor. Stay in pampering resorts, budget beach huts or colonial mansions. Eat cutting-edge fusion food in chic gourmet restaurants or grandmothers' recipes at a busy market *comedor* (food stall). Getting from A to B is easy thanks to comfortable buses that run almost anywhere and an extensive domestic flight network. Or try renting a car: Mexico has some excellent roads, and outside the cities traffic is mostly light.

Los Mexicanos

At the heart of your Mexican experience will be the Mexican people. A super-diverse crew from city hipsters to shy indigenous villagers, they're justly renowned for their love of color and frequent fiestas but are also philosophical folk, to whom timetables are less important than *simpatía* (empathy). You will rarely find Mexicans less than courteous; they're often positively charming, and they know how to please their guests. They're fiercely proud of Mexico, their one-of-a-kind homeland with its tight-knit family networks, beautiful-ugly cities, deep-rooted traditions, unique agave-based liquors and sensationally tasty, chili-laden food. It doesn't take long to understand why.

Why I Love Mexico

By John Noble, Author

I first felt Mexico's pull when reading, as a teenager, the barely credible story of Cortés and the Aztecs. My first visit was three months backpacking from the US border to the Guatemalan border, and I found a kind of spiritual home in the green highlands of Chiapas. Since then I've wandered over most parts of Mexico on 12 extended trips, and come to love its deserts, coasts, jungles and volcanoes too – and its endless variety of tasty foods, the spectacular evidence of its ancient civilizations, its inspired art and handicrafts, and, most of all, its charming, hospitable people.

For more about our authors, see page 896

Above: Hierve El Agua (p449)

Mexico

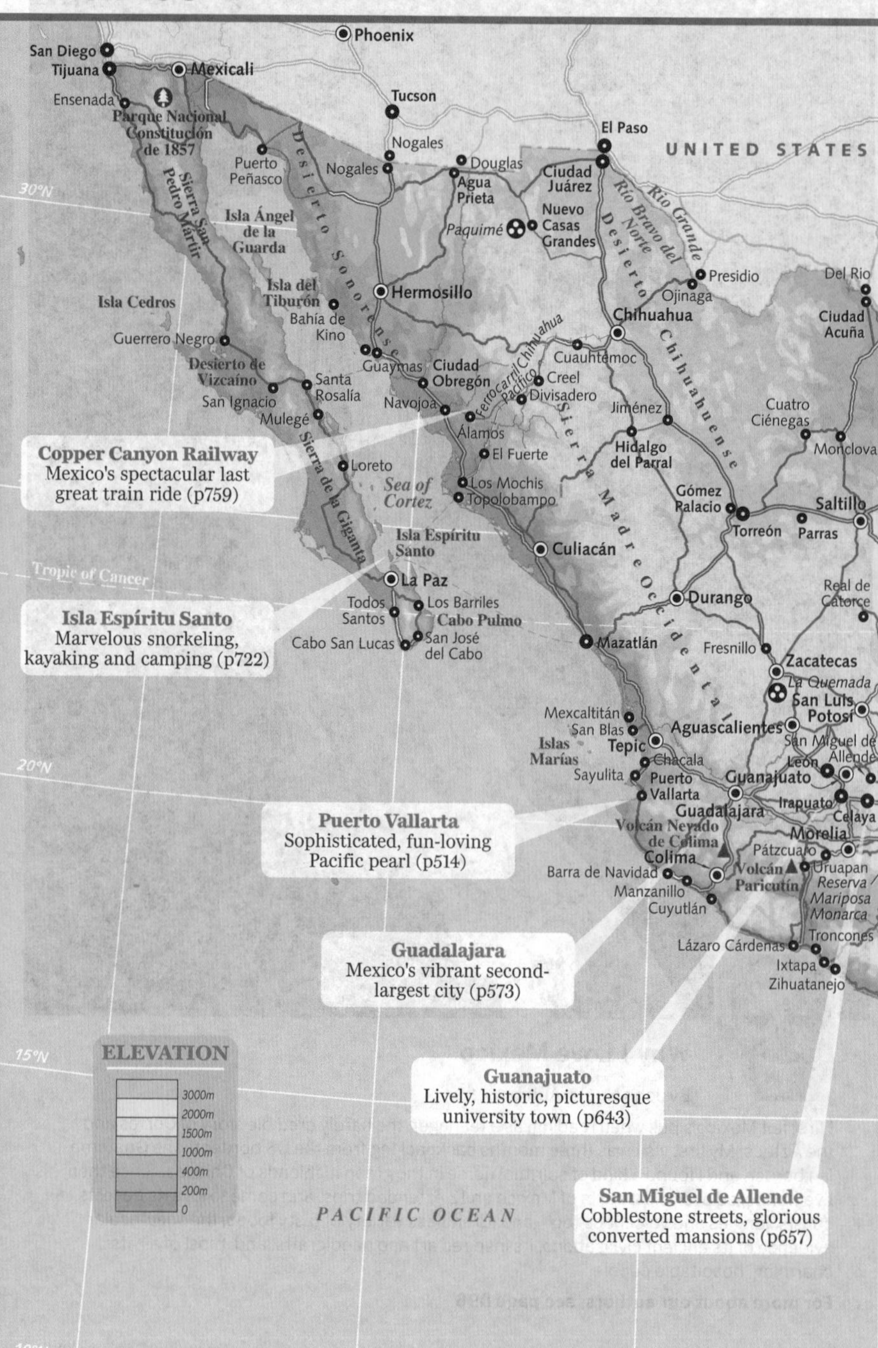
Phoenix
San Diego
Tijuana
Mexicali
Ensenada
Parque Nacional Constitución de 1857
Tucson
El Paso
UNITED STATES
Nogales
Nogales
Puerto Peñasco
Douglas
Agua Prieta
Ciudad Juárez
Desierto Sonorense
Sierra San Pedro Mártir
Isla Ángel de la Guarda
Nuevo Casas Grandes
Paquimé
Río Bravo del Norte
Río Grande
Desierto Chihuahuense
Presidio
Ojinaga
Del Rio
Ciudad Acuña
Hermosillo
Isla del Tiburón
Bahía de Kino
Isla Cedros
Chihuahua
Guerrero Negro
Ferrocarril Chihuahua Pacífico
Cuauhtémoc
Desierto de Vizcaíno
Guaymas
Ciudad Obregón
Creel
Divisadero
San Ignacio
Santa Rosalía
Navojoa
Mulegé
Jiménez
Cuatro Ciénegas
Monclova
Álamos
Hidalgo del Parral
El Fuerte
Sierra de la Giganta
Loreto
Sea of Cortez
Los Mochis
Topolobampo
Sierra Madre Occidental
Gómez Palacio
Torreón
Saltillo
Parras
Isla Espíritu Santo
Culiacán
Tropic of Cancer
La Paz
Todos Santos
Los Barriles
Cabo Pulmo
Durango
Real de Catorce
Cabo San Lucas
San José del Cabo
Mazatlán
Fresnillo
Zacatecas
La Quemada
San Luis Potosí
Mexcaltitán
San Blas
Aguascalientes
Islas Marías
Tepic
San Miguel de Allende
Chacala
León
Sayulita
Puerto Vallarta
Guanajuato
Irapuato
Guadalajara
Celaya
Volcán Nevado de Colima
Morelia
Colima
Pátzcuaro
Volcán Paricutín
Uruapan
Barra de Navidad
Manzanillo
Cuyutlán
Reserva Mariposa Monarca
Troncones
Lázaro Cárdenas
Ixtapa
Zihuatanejo
ELEVATION
3000m
2000m
1500m
1000m
400m
200m
0
PACIFIC OCEAN
30°N
20°N
15°N
10°N
115°W
110°W
105°W
Copper Canyon Railway
Mexico's spectacular last great train ride (p759)
Isla Espíritu Santo
Marvelous snorkeling, kayaking and camping (p722)
Puerto Vallarta
Sophisticated, fun-loving Pacific pearl (p514)
Guadalajara
Mexico's vibrant second-largest city (p573)
Guanajuato
Lively, historic, picturesque university town (p643)
San Miguel de Allende
Cobblestone streets, glorious converted mansions (p657)

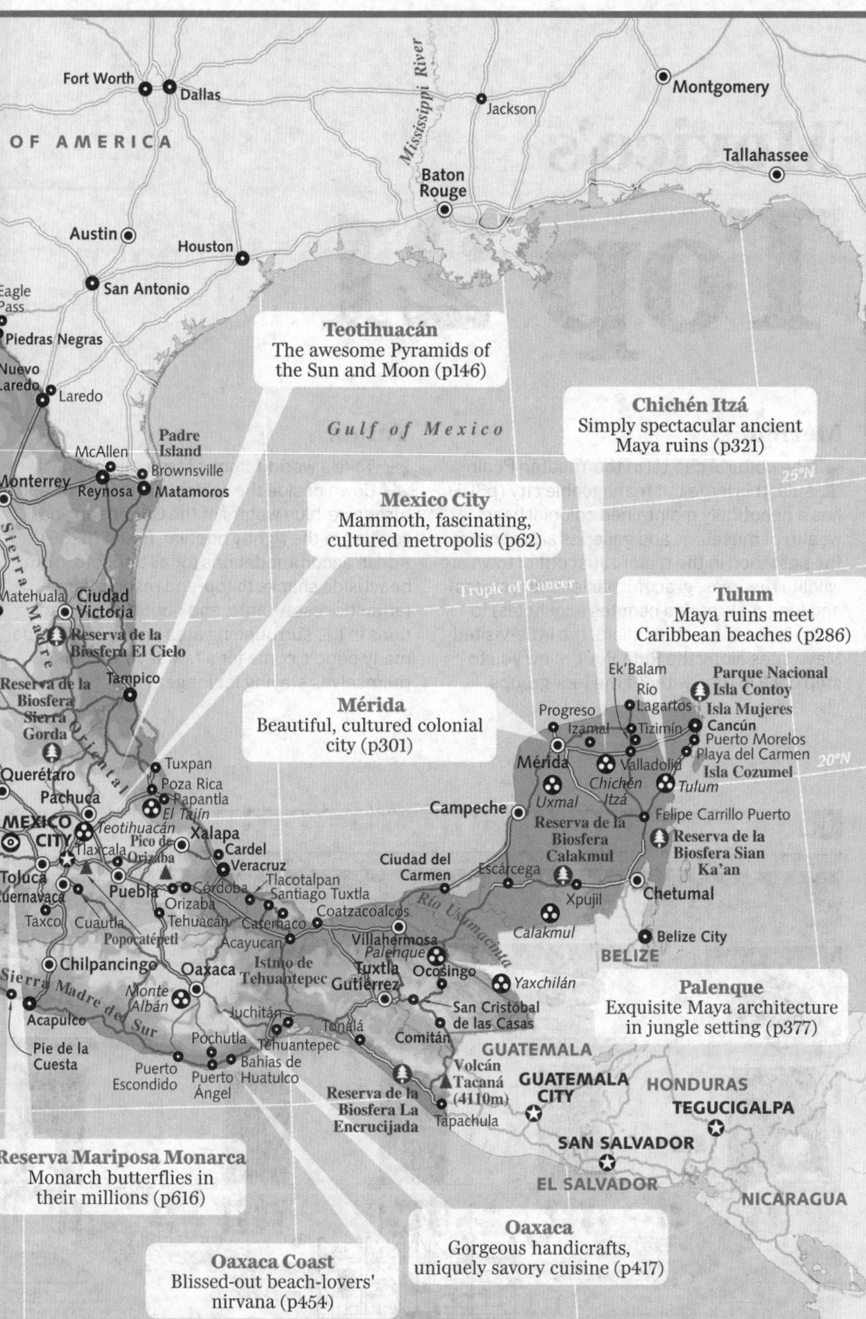
0 300 km
0 150 miles
Teotihuacán
The awesome Pyramids of the Sun and Moon (p146)
Chichén Itzá
Simply spectacular ancient Maya ruins (p321)
Mexico City
Mammoth, fascinating, cultured metropolis (p62)
Tulum
Maya ruins meet Caribbean beaches (p286)
Mérida
Beautiful, cultured colonial city (p301)
Palenque
Exquisite Maya architecture in jungle setting (p377)
Reserva Mariposa Monarca
Monarch butterflies in their millions (p616)
Oaxaca
Gorgeous handicrafts, uniquely savory cuisine (p417)
Oaxaca Coast
Blissed-out beach-lovers' nirvana (p454)
Fort Worth
Dallas
Jackson
Montgomery
OF AMERICA
Mississippi River
Tallahassee
Baton Rouge
Austin
Houston
San Antonio
Eagle Pass
Piedras Negras
Nuevo Laredo
Laredo
Gulf of Mexico
Padre Island
McAllen
Brownsville
Monterrey
Reynosa
Matamoros
25°N
Sierra Madre Oriental
Matehuala
Ciudad Victoria
Reserva de la Biosfera El Cielo
Tropic of Cancer
Reserva de la Biosfera Sierra Gorda
Tampico
Ek'Balam
Río Lagartos
Parque Nacional Isla Contoy
Isla Mujeres
Progreso
Izamal
Tizimín
Cancún
Puerto Morelos
Playa del Carmen
20°N
Mérida
Valladolid
Isla Cozumel
Querétaro
Tuxpan
Poza Rica
Papantla
El Tajín
Uxmal
Chichén Itzá
Tulum
Pachuca
Felipe Carrillo Puerto
MEXICO CITY
Teotihuacán
Xalapa
Campeche
Reserva de la Biosfera Calakmul
Reserva de la Biosfera Sian Ka'an
Tlaxcala
Pico de Orizaba
Cardel
Veracruz
Ciudad del Carmen
Toluca
Escárcega
Cuernavaca
Puebla
Córdoba
Tlacotalpan
Santiago Tuxtla
Orizaba
Xpujil
Chetumal
Taxco
Cuautla
Tehuacán
Catemaco
Coatzacoalcos
Río Usumacinta
Popocatépetl
Acayucan
Villahermosa
Palenque
Calakmul
Belize City
BELIZE
Chilpancingo
Oaxaca
Istmo de Tehuantepec
Tuxtla Gutiérrez
Ocosingo
Yaxchilán
Sierra Madre del Sur
Monte Albán
Juchitán
San Cristóbal de las Casas
Acapulco
Tonalá
Comitán
Pochutla
Tehuantepec
GUATEMALA
Pie de la Cuesta
Puerto Escondido
Puerto Ángel
Bahías de Huatulco
Volcán Tacaná (4110m)
GUATEMALA CITY
HONDURAS
TEGUCIGALPA
Reserva de la Biosfera La Encrucijada
Tapachula
SAN SALVADOR
EL SALVADOR
NICARAGUA
100°W
95°W
90°W

Mexico's Top 21

Mérida

1 The cultural capital of the Yucatán Peninsula, this large but manageable city (p301) has a beautifully maintained colonial heart, a wealth of museums and galleries and some of the best food in the region. Just out of town are wildlife reserves, graceful haciendas (estates) and jungle-shrouded cenotes (sinkholes) to swim in. A little further afield, the little-visited Maya sites along the Ruta Puuc allow you to step back in time without the tour groups.

Tulum

2 Take a world-famous Maya ruin, plonk it down beside the achingly white sands and turquoise-blue waters of the Caribbean and you've got the rightly popular Tulum (p286). Add in accommodations for all budgets, from beachside shacks to top-end resorts, some fantastic restaurants, and numerous attractions in the surrounding area and it's no wonder many people come for a few days and find themselves staying far longer.

MARK O'CALLAGHAN/GETTY IMAGES ©

2

The Pacific Coastline

3 Running from the desert islands of Baja California to verdant coves backed by lush tropical mountains, and from untrammeled expanses of sand to mangrove-fringed lagoons teeming with birdlife, Mexico's Pacific coastline is stunning in its natural beauty. Punctuating this primordial grandeur is a series of lively resort towns – Mazatlán, Puerto Vallarta, Manzanillo, Ixtapa, Zihuatanejo and Acapulco – interspersed with world-class surf spots such as Barra de Nexpa, Boca de Pascuales, Troncones and Puerto Escondido. Below: Beachside forest, Manzanillo

Relax on the Oaxaca Coast

4 After a few days on this 550km sequence of sandy Pacific beaches (p454) you'll be so relaxed you may not be able to leave. Head for the surf mecca and fishing port of Puerto Escondido, the low-key resort of Bahías de Huatulco, or the ultra-laid-back hangouts of Zipolite, San Agustinillo or Mazunte. Soak up the sun, eat good food, imbibe in easygoing beach bars, and, when the mood takes you, have a surf or snorkel, or board a boat to sight turtles, dolphins, whales, crocs or birdlife. Below: Playa Carrizalillo, Puerto Escondido

3

4

Chichén Itzá

5 Sure, it's on every tour-bus itinerary and you're never going to have the place to yourself, but there's a reason why this Maya site (p321) was declared one of the new Seven Wonders of the World – it is simply spectacular. From the imposing, monolithic El Castillo pyramid (where the shadow of the plumed serpent god Kukulcán creeps down the staircase during the spring and autumn equinoxes) to the Sacred Cenote and curiously designed El Caracol, you don't have to be an archaeologist to have an amazing time here.

Mexico City

6 The nation's long-standing political capital (p62) stands at the forefront of Mexico's cultural scene as well. This is where many of the country's top muralists left behind their most important works, such as Diego Rivera's cinematic murals in the Palacio Nacional and the social realism work of José Clemente Orozco in the Palacio de Bellas Artes. Art, music, dance and theater are everywhere – even a gondola ride along the ancient canals of Xochimilco wouldn't be complete without a fervent mariachi ballad. Above: Palacio de Bellas Artes

7

ANGUS OBORN/GETTY IMAGES ©

8

ANNE RIPPY/GETTY IMAGES ©

9

YVETTE CARDOZO/GETTY IMAGES ©

Monarchs in their Millions

7 Canopies of golden-orange butterflies cover the forests and hillsides in the Reserva Mariposa Monarca (Monarch Butterfly Reserve; p616), perhaps Mexico's most astonishing yearly natural phenomenon. It's the kind of annual event to plan your trip around – between November and March the migrant monarchs cover every surface, weighing down tree branches and changing the landscape into a permanent sunset as they winter far from the freezing Great Lakes during one of the planet's most spectacular migrations.

Puerto Vallarta

8 Tucked between jungle-clad mountains and North America's second-largest bay, Mexico's most appealing Pacific resort (p514) combines its dazzling setting with a fun-loving atmosphere that welcomes everyone from foodies and shopping devotees to outdoors enthusiasts and the international gay and lesbian community. Travel an hour out of town and you can be basking on a secluded beach, horseback riding in the Sierra Madre, whale-watching, diving or reeling in a giant fish worthy of a tall tale at happy hour. Zona Romántica, Puerto Vallarta

Shopping for Artisan Crafts

9 Mexico's super-bright, infinitely varied *artesanías* (handicrafts) are today's successors to the lavish costumes and beautiful ceramics of the pre-Hispanic nobility, and to the everyday handcrafted clothes, baskets and pots of their humbler subjects. Everywhere you go – whether browsing city stores, wandering through markets or visiting artisans in their village workshops – the skill, creativity and color sense of potters, weavers, metalsmiths, carvers and leatherworkers delights the eye and tempts the pocket.

Land's End, Baja California

10 Whether the beautiful rock formation El Arco (The Arch) comes as one stop of a cruise itinerary or at the end of a 1700km road trip, Land's End (p733) is a spectacular sight. Pelicans dive into the blue-green water, beach-goers lounge on Lover's Beach, *pangas* (skiffs) tootle around the sea-lion colony, and when the sun sets behind the arch the scenery is just magic. It's as beautiful under the water as above too – moray eels and multiple fish species await those who don flippers and a mask. Below: El Arco

Isla Espíritu Santo

11 Espíritu Santo island (p722) is spectacular in every way. Pink sandstone has been eroded by wind and waves into fingerlike protrusions, each harboring a beautiful cove. And if scenic beauty wasn't enough then there's snorkeling with gentle whale sharks, unparalleled diving, camping under a canopy of stunning stars, and kayaking along myriad azure bays on offer too. There's even a sea-lion colony.

Guanajuato

12 The glorious World Heritage–listed city of Guanajuato (p643) packs plenty into its narrow valley. This former mining town turned colorful university city is a feast of plazas, museums, opulent colonial mansions and pastel-hued houses. Snake along pedestrian alleyways, people-watch in the squares, mingle with marvelous mariachi groups, or party hard at *estudiantinas* (traditional street parties) and in the many student bars. The underground tunnels – the town's major transport routes – make for a particularly quirky way to get around.

The Pyramids of Teotihuacán

13 Once among Mesoamerica's greatest cities, Teotihuacán (p146) is now a popular day trip from the capital. The awesomely massive Pirámide del Sol (Pyramid of the Sun) and Pirámide de la Luna (Pyramid of the Moon) dominate the remains of the metropolis which, even centuries after its collapse in the 8th century AD, remained a pilgrimage site for Aztec royalty. Today it's a magnet for those who come to soak up the mystical energies that are believed to converge here. Bottom: Pirámide del Sol

12

RANDY PLETT/GETTY IMAGES ©

13

CHRISTIAN KOBER/GETTY IMAGES ©

DENNIS WALTON/GETTY IMAGES ©

PETER VON FELBERT/GETTY IMAGES ©

DENNIS WALTON/GETTY IMAGES ©

Oaxaca City

14 This highly individual southern city (p420) basks in bright upland light and captivates visitors with its gorgeous handicrafts, frequent fiestas and handsome colonial architecture. A uniquely savory cuisine is served at restaurants and market stalls, and the finest mezcal is distilled in nearby villages. Within easy reach are the superb ancient Zapotec capital, Monte Albán; dozens of indigenous craft-making villages with busy weekly markets; and the cool, forested hills of the Sierra Norte, perfect for hikers, mountain bikers and horseback riders. Above: Museo de las Culturas de Oaxaca

Mexico's Last Train Journey

15 Mexico's national passenger train network is dead but the Ferrocarril Chihuahua Pacífico (Copper Canyon Railway; p759) remains alive and kicking as one of Latin America's best rail trips. Trains climb from sea level at Los Mochis up to Chihuahua's high desert plains, via the sensational rocky landscapes of the Copper Canyon. Vistas from your window include alpine forests, subtropical valleys and glimpses of some of the world's deepest canyons. Alight at a photogenic stop for 15 minutes – or stay on for days of exciting exploring, hiking and biking.

San Miguel de Allende

16 After a hard morning of hitting the shops, churches and galleries along the cobblestone colonial streets of San Miguel de Allende (p657), there's nothing better than enjoying a luxurious respite at one of the thermal pools outside town – one of the most relaxing experiences in the region. After your soak, head to the nearby Santuario de Atotonilco, a fascinating magnet for Mexican pilgrims, then return to town for dinner in one of its many excellent restaurants. Above: Santuario de Atotonilco

BRUCE YUANYUE BI / GETTY IMAGES ©

DANITA DELIMONT/GETTY IMAGES ©

WIN-INITIATIVE/GETTY IMAGES ©

Mexican Art

17 If there's one art form that expresses Mexicans' emotions best, it's painting. The country's artistic creativity has ranged from vividly colorful pre-Hispanic murals and the revolutionary epics of Diego Rivera, to the tortured canvases of Frida Kahlo and edgy contemporary installations. Mexico City, Oaxaca and Monterrey are the three main hubs of Mexico's art world, but every city worth its salt has museums displaying the best from the past, as well as commercial galleries showcasing the creative currents of the present. Above: Detail of Diego Rivera mural, Palacio Nacional, Mexico City

Savor the Flavors

18 Mexican cuisine is like no other, and every part of the country has its own regional specialties, based on local ingredients and what's fresh on the day. For the tastiest travels, try local dishes from restaurants and busy market and street stalls – you'll lose count of the delicious culinary experiences you encounter. And when it's time for fine dining, seek out some of the legion of creative contemporary chefs who concoct amazing flavor combinations from traditional and innovative ingredients.

Palenque

19 Gather all your senses and dive headfirst into the ancient Maya world at exquisite Palenque (p377), where pyramids rise above jungle treetops and furtive monkeys shriek and catapult themselves through dense canopy. Wander the maze-like El Palacio (Palace), gazing up at its iconic tower, then scale the stone staircase of the Templo de las Inscripciones (Temple of the Inscriptions) the lavish mausoleum of Pakal (Palenque's mightiest ruler), and survey the sprawling ruins from its summit. Above: Detail of carving, Templo de la Calavera (Temple of the Skull), Palenque

Guadalajara

20 Mexico's second-largest city (p573) manages to dazzle despite being more a collection of pueblos than a great metropolis. This charmer gets under your skin with colonial buildings, awesome public spaces and wonderful craft shopping in the arty suburbs of Tlaquepaque and Tonalá. The young and middle-class party all weekend in smart bars and heaving dance clubs, and there's nowhere better in western Mexico to eat out. Below: Instituto Cultural de Cabañas

San Cristóbal de las Casas

21 Saunter the cobblestone streets of San Cristóbal de las Casas (p356), the high-altitude colonial city in the heart of indigenous Chiapas. A heady mix of modern and Maya, with cosmopolitan cafes and traditional culture, it's also a jumping-off point for Chiapas' natural attractions and fascinating Tzotzil and Tzeltal villages. Spend days exploring its churches and markets or horseback riding through pine forest, and chilly evenings by the fireplace of a cozy watering hole. Bottom: Iglesia de Guadalupe

20

21

Need to Know

For more information, see Survival Guide (p841)

Currency

Peso (M$)

Language

Spanish; also about 70 indigenous languages

Visas

Every tourist must have a tourist permit, available on arrival. Some nationalities also need visas.

Money

ATMs and money-changing offices widely available. Credit cards accepted in many midrange and top-end hotels.

Cell Phones

Many US and Canadian cellular carriers offer Mexico roaming deals. Mexican SIM cards can only be used in unlocked phones.

Time

Most of Mexico is on Hora del Centro (GMT/UTC minus six hours). Six northern and western states are on GMT/UTC minus seven or eight hours.

When to Go

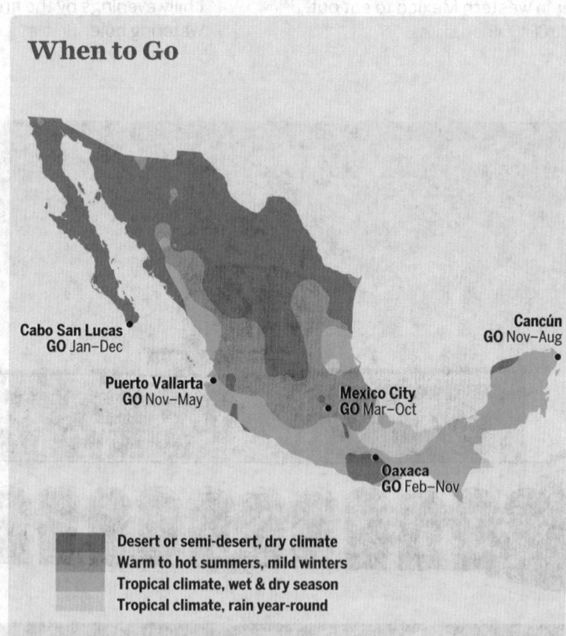

High Season

(Dec–Apr)

➡ December to April, the driest months over most of Mexico, bring winter escapees from colder countries.

➡ Christmas and Easter are Mexican holiday times, with transportation and coastal accommodations very busy.

Shoulder

(Jul & Aug)

➡ This is vacation time for many Mexicans and foreigners. It's hot almost everywhere, and very wet on the Pacific coast.

Low Season

(May, Jun, Sep–Nov)

➡ May and June see peak temperatures in many areas.

➡ September is the heart of the hurricane season, which doesn't always bring hurricanes but does bring heavy rains on the Gulf and Pacific coasts.

Useful Websites

Mexico Cooks! (mexicocooks.typepad.com) Excellent blog on Mexican life.

Lonely Planet (www.lonelyplanet.com/mexico) Destination information, hotel bookings, traveler forum, videos and more.

México (www.visitmexico.com) Official tourism site with plenty of helpful ideas.

Planeta.com (www.planeta.com) Great articles, listings, links, photos and more.

The Mexico Report (www.themexicoreport.com) Blog with travel and tourism news.

Is Mexico Safe? (www.ismexicosafe.org) The answer is 'yes'.

Important Numbers

Country code	✆52
Emergency	✆066 ✆088
International access code	✆00
National tourist assistance	✆078

Exchange Rates

Australia	A$1	M$12.08
Belize	BZ$1	M$6.51
Canada	C$1	M$11.86
Euro zone	€1	M$17.83
Japan	¥100	M$12.60
New Zealand	NZ$1	M$11.20
UK	UK£1	M$21.57
USA	US$1	M$13.01

For current exchange rates, see www.xe.com.

Daily Costs

Budget: Less than M$600

- Hostel dorm bed: MS$150
- Double room in budget hotel: M$350 to M$450
- *Comida corrida* (fixed-price lunch) in economical restaurant: M$50 to M$70
- 250km bus trip: M$200

Midrange: M$600–M$1800

- Double room in midrange hotel: M$500 to M$1100
- Good dinner with drinks: M$150 to M$250
- Museum admission: M$20 to M$60
- City taxi ride: M$25 to M$50
- Hiking/rafting/mountainbike day trip M$700 to M$1300

Top End: more than M$1800

- Double room in top-end hotel: M$1200 to M$5000
- Fine dinner with drinks: M$200 to M$500
- Personalized one-day tour: M$1000
- Two-hour horseback ride: M$600 to M$1000

Opening Hours

Opening hours given in this book are for high season. Some hours may be shorter in shoulder and low seasons. Hours vary widely but the following are typical:

Banks 9am-4pm Mon-Fri, 9am-1pm Sat

Stores/Shops 9am-8pm Mon-Sat (supermarkets and department stores 9am-10pm daily)

Restaurants 9am-11pm

Cafes 8am-10pm

Bars 1pm-midnight

Arriving in Mexico

Mexico City airport (p136) Authorized taxis, with ticket offices inside airport, cost M$205 to central areas. Metro (M$3) operates from 5am (6am Saturday, 7am Sunday) to midnight; Terminal Aérea station is 200m from Terminal 1.

Cancún airport (p284) Airport shuttles M$150 per person to downtown; taxis M$600 to downtown or hotel zone (or around M$250 from outside airport). ADO buses to downtown Cancún (M$52) and Playa del Carmen (M$124).

Getting Around

Bus Mexico's efficient, comfortable and reasonably priced inter-city bus network is generally the best option for moving around the country: on average you pay about M$1 per kilometer on 1st-class buses, covering around 75km per hour. Services are frequent on main routes.

Car A convenient option giving maximum independence: roads are serviceable, with speeds generally slower than north of the border or in Europe. Rental rates start around M$500 to M$600 per day including basic insurance.

Air More than 60 cities are served by domestic flights, which are well worth considering for longer inter-city trips. Fares vary widely depending on the airline and how far in advance you pay.

For much more on **getting around**, see p855

First Time Mexico

For more information, see Survival Guide (p841)

Checklist

- Check that your passport will be valid at least until you leave Mexico
- Check the airline baggage restrictions
- Organize travel insurance
- Make any bookings (for hotels, travel, sights)
- Inform your credit/debit card company
- Check if you can use your cell phone
- Get immunizations well in advance
- Check your government's Mexico travel information

What to Pack

- International electrical adaptor (for non-North Americans)
- Swimming and beach gear
- Flashlight (torch)
- Driver's license and other paperwork (if you're driving)
- Sun hat, shades, sunscreen
- A waterproof garment for rainy season
- Warm clothing for higher-elevation areas
- A sense of adventure

Top Tips for Your Trip

- Expect the unfamiliar – in food, language, climate, manners. In case the strangeness of a foreign land starts to get to you, stay somewhere where you feel comfortable, and remember that international cuisine is available in almost any town.
- Spend some time getting out of the cities and coastal resorts into the often dramatic countryside and some smaller towns and villages, where you'll see a side of Mexican life that many tourists miss.
- Mexico's much-reported drug-gang violence happens mostly in a small number of places, chiefly in the north, and tourists have rarely been victims. The country's most visited areas, such as the Yucatán Peninsula, have barely been touched by the violence.

What to Wear

Casual and comfortable is the key. In beach towns, shorts and short skirts are very common; sleeveless tops are fine, too. Take some sleeves and long pants/skirts to protect against sun and mosquitoes, or for evenings or non-beach towns. Dress conservatively when visiting churches. You'll want at least a sweater or light jacket for cooler inland areas and air-conditioned buses or planes. A hat for sun protection is essential; you can buy good, inexpensive ones in Mexico.

Sleeping

It's a good idea to reserve accommodations for your first night in Mexico, or if you're arriving somewhere at night, and for any lodgings during busy seasons. See p842 for more accommodations information.

- **Hotels** These cover the spectrum from basic budget establishments to chic boutique hotels and luxurious five-star resorts.
- **Hostels** There are hostels in most budget-traveler destinations. Many have good facilities and often have private rooms and dorms.
- **Cabañas** Cabins and huts, mostly found at beach destinations, ranging from very basic to positively luxurious.
- **Camping & hammocks** In the more budget-oriented beach spots, you can often sleep in a hammock or pitch a tent for very few pesos.

Money

Plan on making cash purchases with pesos; few businesses accept US dollars. It's easy to get pesos from ATMs using a major credit or debit card (Visa, MasterCard, American Express). Take a small reserve of cash (US dollars or euros) to exchange at banks or *casas de cambio* (exchange offices) if ATMs aren't available. You can make purchases with major credit and debit cards at many airlines, travel agencies, midrange and top-end hotels, restaurants and stores.

For more information, see p848.

Bargaining

It's often worth asking if any discount is available on room rates, especially if it's low season or you plan to stay more than two nights. In markets a little haggling is expected. Drivers of unmetered taxis, too, will often shave some pesos off their initial asking price.

Tipping

Some service workers depend on tips to supplement miserable wages.

➡ **Restaurants** Tip 10% to 15% unless service is included in the check.

➡ **Hotels** It's nice (though optional) to leave 5% to 10% of your room costs for cleaners.

➡ **Taxis** Drivers don't expect tips unless they provide some extra service.

➡ **Porters** Airport and hotel porters usually get M$50 to M$100.

➡ **Attendants** Car-parking and gas-station attendants expect M$5 or M$10.

Language

Mexico's main language is Spanish. Many Mexicans in the world of tourism also speak some English, often good English. In any accommodations catering to international travelers, you can get by with English. Still, it's useful and polite to know at least a few words of Spanish – Mexicans appreciate being greeted with '*Buenos días*' or some other phrase in their own tongue, even if they then break into fluent English. See Language (p862) for more information.

1 **Where can I buy handicrafts?**
¿Dónde se puede comprar artesanías?
don·de se *pwe*·de kom·*prar* ar·te·sa·*nee*·as

Star buys in Mexico are the regional handicrafts produced all over the country, mainly by the indigenous people.

2 **Which *antojitos* do you have?**
¿Qué antojitos tiene? ke an·to·*khee*·tos *tye*·ne

'Little whimsies' (snacks) can encompass anything – have an entire meal of them, eat a few as appetisers, or get one on the street for a quick bite.

3 **Not too spicy, please.**
No muy picoso, por favor. no mooy pee·*ko*·so por fa·*vor*

Not all food in Mexico is spicy, but beware – many dishes can be fierce indeed, so it may be a good idea to play it safe.

4 **Where can I find a *cantina* nearby?**
¿Dónde hay una cantina cerca de aquí?
don·de ai *oo*·na kan·*tee*·na *ser*·ka de a·*kee*

Ask locals about the classical Mexican venue for endless snacks, and often dancing as well.

5 **How do you say ... in your language?**
¿Cómo se dice ... en su lengua?
ko·mo se *dee*·se ... en su *len*·gwa

Numerous indigenous languages are spoken around Mexico, primarily Mayan languages and Náhuatl. People will appreciate it if you try to use their local language.

Etiquette

Mexicans are not huge sticklers for etiquette: their natural warmth takes precedence.

➡ **Greetings** '*Mucho gusto*' (roughly 'A great pleasure') is a polite thing to say when you're introduced to someone, accompanied by a handshake; if it's a woman and a man, the woman offers her hand first.

➡ **Pleasing people** Mexicans love to hear that you're enjoying their country. As a rule, they are slow to criticize or argue, expressing disagreement more by nuance than by blunt contradiction.

➡ **Visiting homes** An invitation to a Mexican home is an honor for an outsider; you will be treated very hospitably. Take a small gift if you can, such as flowers or something for the children.

What's New

Yucatán Maya Museums

The excellent Museo Maya de Cancún (p258) and Mérida's Gran Museo del Mundo Maya (p304) give the fascinating ancient Maya culture a welcome contemporary showcase in the Yucatán Peninsula's two most-visited cities.

Pico de Orizaba Cable Car

The Teleférico de Orizaba opened in 2014, whisking visitors from Orizaba city right up to the side of Mexico's highest mountain, the dormant volcano Pico de Orizaba, for incredible views and easy access to hiking routes. (p233)

Museo Jumex, Mexico City

Great news for art lovers: the Colección Jumex, one of Latin America's most important contemporary art collections, has a new home in Mexico City at the Jumex Museum. (p88)

San Francisco

San Francisco, aka San Pancho, is what nearby Sayulita once was – a down-home Pacific pueblo with a relaxed surfing scene and a light gringo footprint. The sea and beach are breathtaking. (p511)

José Cuervo Express

Travel the rails in sedate and classy style on this train ride from Guadalajara to one of the world's most famous tequila distilleries. (p598)

Centro de Textiles del Mundo Maya, San Cristóbal de las Casas

Over 500 hand-woven garments and other items gathered from throughout Mexico and Central America are on display at this excellent, recently opened museum. (p357)

Maximo Bistrot Local

New star of Mexico City's exciting culinary scene, with an ever-changing fusion menu drawing on European and Mexican recipes with fresh, seasonal ingredients, and a totally unpretentious atmosphere. (p115)

Atzompa, Oaxaca

This newly excavated ancient Zapotec site makes a scenic and fascinating counterpoint to nearby Monte Albán, and is nicely complemented by a community museum displaying exciting finds from the site. (p447)

Casa de los Venados, Valladolid

One of the most impressive collections of Mexican folk art in the country, made all the more impressive for being set in an award-winning renovated colonial mansion. (p328)

Museo de Sitio, Cantona

The well-preserved Mesoamerican city of Cantona is now even more attractive with its modern new museum showing around 600 pre-Hispanic objects, with a special focus on the volcanic glass, obsidian. (p173)

El Cielo, Valle de Guadalupe

El Cielo is typical of Baja California's sophisticated new wineries with its upmarket tasting facility, contemporary restaurant and boutique hotel. (p703)

For more recommendations and reviews, see lonelyplanet.com/

If You Like...

Pyramids & Temples

Teotihuacán Mexico's biggest ancient city, with the giant Pyramids of the Sun and Moon, and mural-decked palaces. (p146)

Palenque Exquisite Maya temples backed by steamy, jungle-covered hills. (p377)

Chichén Itzá A monument to ancient Mexico's obsession with time and death. (p321)

Uxmal Large Maya site with a riot of carved-stone ornamentation. (p312)

Yaxchilán Impressive temples in a wonderful Chiapas jungle setting, reached only by river. (p394)

Monte Albán Ancient Zapotec capital sits on a peerless hilltop site outside Oaxaca. (p442)

Tulum These late Maya temples and pyramids sit right on a beautifully rugged stretch of Caribbean coast. (p286)

Calakmul High pyramids in a huge, remote Maya city, still largely hidden in protected rainforest. (p341)

Historic Colonial Towns

Guanajuato The opulent mansions and narrow, winding streets of this lively university town are squeezed into a picturesque, steep valley. (p643)

San Miguel de Allende Charming, artsy town of cobblestone streets and lovely stone architecture, given an international dimension by its many foreign (mainly US) residents. (p657)

Oaxaca Gorgeous southern city with an indigenous flavor and stunning art and artisanry. (p420)

Zacatecas The magnificent cathedral of this city built on silver is the ultimate expression of colonial baroque. (p686)

Mérida Beautiful plazas and palaces adorn the Yucatán Peninsula's cultural capital. (p301)

Álamos Remote silver town in the lush Sierra Madre foothills, full of restored mansions, some of which are now atmospheric lodgings. (p752)

Beach Resorts

Puerto Vallarta A sophisticated Pacific resort with dazzling beaches, stylish restaurants and hot nightlife; also Mexico's gay beach capital. (p514)

Playa del Carmen The hip resort of the Caribbean coast, with a European style of chic. (p276)

Mazatlán Uniquely combines an attractive old colonial center and cultural attractions with classic fun in the sun. (p491)

Zihuatanejo This easygoing Pacific town has beautiful beaches and accommodations for all budgets and is still a fishing town. (p546)

Cancún The mother of Mexican resorts, an unabashed party town for international tourists with a 15km Caribbean beach. (p258)

Luxury Spas & Hotels

Mar de Jade, Chacala Idyllic Pacific mini-resort with yoga classes, temascal (pre-Hispanic sauna), vegetarian-friendly food and regular meditation and wellness retreats. (p510)

La Casa Que Canta, Zihuatanejo This superdeluxe clifftop

IF YOU LIKE... SWIMMING UNDERGROUND

Take a dip, and even a snorkel or dive, in some of the Yucatán Peninsula's cenotes (limestone sinkholes) such as Cristalino Cenote or Cenote Xlacah. (p278)

hotel has exquisite decor, superb service, no TVs and no kids under 16. (p551)

Casa Oaxaca, Oaxaca Boutique city hotel dedicated to art and handicrafts, with large rooms in stunning contemporary style and a beautiful colonial patio. (p433)

Casa Dulce Vida, Puerto Vallarta Seven sumptuous suites, leafy gardens and delicious privacy. (p522)

Present Moment Retreat, Troncones This Pacific spa resort, with thatched-roof bungalows in beautiful gardens, offers yoga, meditation and massage. (p543)

Posada La Poza, Todos Santos Wonderful Pacific-side retreat with lush gardens, saltwater pool and Jacuzzi, superb restaurant and no TVs. (p737)

Shopping

Mexico's star buys are the wonderful, colorful handicrafts – textiles, jewelry, ceramics, masks, woodwork, metalwork, leatherwork – made predominantly by indigenous people.

Mexico City The capital is a shopper's treasure trove, from craft stores to boutiques to flea, flower and food markets. (p127)

Oaxaca The city is full of markets and stores offering an array of the most inventive and colorful handicrafts. (p439)

San Miguel de Allende A mind-boggling array of craft shops, selling folk art from all over Mexico. (p667)

Guadalajara The artisans' suburbs of Tlaquepaque (upscale: p592) and Tonalá (down to earth: p584) are replete with classy ceramics, furniture, glassware and much more.

Top: Cenote Ik Kil (p326), near Chichén Itzá
Bottom: Maya masks

Indigenous village markets Weekly markets are bustling occasions full of local atmosphere; some of the most fascinating happen in villages around Oaxaca (p446) and San Cristóbal de las Casas (p371).

Getaway Beaches

Oaxaca coast International budget travelers make a beeline for the blissed-out beach villages of Mazunte (p474), San Agustinillo (p472) and Zipolite (p469).

Xcalak No cruise ships, no gas station, no bank, no grocery store, just a wonderful barrier reef – the Caribbean coast as it once was. (p296)

Playa Maruata Tranquil, low-budget Michoacán fishing village beloved by beach bums and sea turtles. (p539)

Barra de Potosí Palm-fringed white sands, calm waters, a lagoon full of birds and crocs, and a handful of guesthouses. (p556)

Isla Holbox Escape the hubbub of the Riviera Maya and wander the sandy roads of this palm-fringed Gulf coast getaway. (p272)

Mexican Cuisine

Mexico City The capital cooks up an unrivaled range of fare from all around Mexico, with upscale fusion restaurants serving creative *nueva cocina mexicana* (Mexican nouvelle cuisine), the world's best collection of taco stands, and everything in between. (p108)

Seafood Mexicans love their seafood and, naturally, it's at its most delicious on the coasts, from Baja California's beloved fish tacos to Veracruz' famed *huachinanago a la veracruzana* (snapper in a tomato-based sauce). (p726)

Oaxaca Famed for its seven varieties of *mole* (type of chili sauce), a peak of Mexican culinary art. (p434)

Cooking classes Prepare your own Mexican feasts under expert guidance in Oaxaca, Zihuatanejo, Tepoztlán, Tlaxcala or a dozen other towns.

Beef Northwest Mexico is ranching territory: carnivores will love its ubiquitous *carne asada* (marinated grilled beef), served in a taco or on a plate.

Antojitos An essential Mexican eating experience, ubiquitous *antojitos* ('little whims') are light dishes and snacks using *masa* (corn dough) – tacos, quesadillas, enchiladas, tamales and more.

IF YOU LIKE... SCENIC TRAIN RIDES

The Copper Canyon Railway climbs more than 2400m as it traverses the northwest's spectacular canyon country. (p759)

Museums & Galleries

Museo Nacional de Antropología, Mexico City The National Anthropology Museum is chock-full of stupendous relics from pre-Hispanic Mexico. (p83)

Museo Frida Kahlo, Mexico City The poignant home of the haunted artist. (p93)

Palacio Nacional, Mexico City Diego Rivera's famous Mexican history murals. (p70)

Museo Rafael Coronel, Zacatecas Wonderful collection of Mexican folk art. (p687)

Museo Nacional de la Muerte, Aguascalientes All things related to death, but far from macabre. (p671)

Museo de Antropología, Xalapa A superbly designed space with a marvelous archaeological collection. (p218)

Museo Jumex, Mexico City One of Latin America's leading contemporary art collections. (p88)

Horno3, Monterrey Outstanding museum on the history of Mexican steel-making, in the gigantic shell of a former blast furnace. (p794)

Diving & Snorkeling

Mexico's Caribbean coast, with the world's second-largest barrier reef, is world-famous for its warm, translucent waters full of wonderful corals and tropical fish.

Banco Chinchorro Off the southern end of the Caribbean coast, this is the northern hemisphere's largest coral atoll, with many wrecks. (p295)

Isla Cozumel Surrounded by 65 reefs with stunning coral formations, Cozumel has diving and snorkeling for everyone from beginners to the most experienced. (p280)

Isla Mujeres This island off Cancún has some lovely dives, with plenty of coral and some spectacular marine creatures. (p267)

ETHAN WELTY/GETTY IMAGES ©

Urique (p736), Barranca de Urique, Copper Canyon region

Bahías de Huatulco A string of beautiful Pacific bays with several coral plates and over 100 dive sites. (p480)

Xel-Há This commercial eco-park on the Riviera Maya offers easy snorkeling in a beautiful natural aquarium. (p275)

Surfing

Countless spots along the Pacific coast are bombarded with superb waves from April/May to October/November. Beginners can learn the craft almost year-round.

Puerto Escondido The Mexican Pipeline is one of the world's heaviest and scariest beach breaks; the Punta Zicatela point break works almost daily, and there are beginners' waves, too. (p454)

Boca de Pascuales Legendary hollow, hard-breaking barrels – strictly for experts. (p537)

Troncones A long, strong, world-class left point break and some excellent beach breaks, too. (p542)

Sayulita Dependable, medium-sized waves, good for practising or learning, and a mellow party vibe. (p512)

Barra de Nexpa One of several spots with healthy waves along the little-touched Michoacán coast. (p540)

Ensenada There's a wonderful point break at San Miguel. (p706)

San Blas Good for intermediates and beginners, with many beach and point breaks, and one of the world's longest waves. (p505)

Hiking, Mountain Biking & Horseback Riding

Best seasons vary from place to place and a guide is advisable on some routes.

Copper Canyon The northwest's spectacular canyon country is great for exploring on foot, horse or mountain bike, for a few hours or a couple of weeks. (p757)

Pueblos Mancomunados These Oaxacan mountain villages are linked by a scenic trail network, with horses, mountain bikes and good rural lodgings available. (p451)

Oaxaca Outstanding short- or long-distance rides with Horseback Mexico (p426) and, by bike, with Bicicletas Pedro Martínez (p426).

Rancho El Charro Horse treks into jungle-covered mountains behind Puerto Vallarta. (p519)

Volcanoes Dormant volcanoes that you can summit without technical climbing include Nevado de Toluca (p198), Paricutín (p631), Nevado de Colima(p606) and Tacaná (p410).

Bici-Burro Great mountain-bike outings from San Miguel de Allende. (p662)

Real de Catorce Head out into the desert hills on foot, bike or horse from this magical, crumbling old silver town in the Sierra Madre Oriental. (p682)

Wildlife

Whales From December/January to March, watch whales in Baja California's lagoons, off Mazatlán, Puerto Vallarta or Puerto Escondido. (p495)

Butterflies The trees of Michoacán's Reserva Mariposa Monarca (p616) turn bright orange when millions of huge monarch butterflies flutter in every winter.

Sea turtles Mexican beaches are major sea-turtle breeding grounds – enjoy up-close turtle experiences at Cuyutlán (p538), Playa Colola (p539), Playa Escobilla (p468), Tecolutla (p242), Xcacel-Xcacelito (p284) and elsewhere.

Whale sharks Swim with the world's biggest fish at Isla Contoy or Espíritu Santo. (p722)

Howler monkeys Spot these noisy primates in the jungle canopy at Palenque (p380), Yaxchilán (p394) or Laguna Miramar (p396).

Birds Mexico's forests and coastal lagoons thrill bird lovers, and bird-watching trips are available in dozens of places. For bright pink clouds of flamingos head to Río Lagartos or Celestún. (p332)

Kayaking & Rafting

Sea of Cortez Long or short trips around the islands, beaches and estuaries of Baja California's east coast, from bases like Mulegé (p717) or La Paz (p723), are the stuff of which sea kayakers' dreams are made.

Pacific Coast Many spots along the Pacific will rent you a kayak or take you on a kayak tour of the coasts, lagoons or islands. Top locations include Puerto Vallarta (p520) and Troncones (p542).

Veracruz rafting Veracruz state, with rivers plunging down from the Sierra Madre Oriental, is Mexico's white-water rafting center. The main bases are Jalcomulco (p223) and Tlapacoyan (p243).

Oaxaca rafting Rivers near Bahías de Huatulco have waters suitable for everyone from beginners (including children) to experienced rafters. (p480)

Tequila & Mezcal

Los Amantes Savor top mezcals from the local agave fields at this quaint Oaxaca tasting room. (p436)

Bósforo Duck into this Mexico City hideaway and enjoy some of the finest mezcals in town. (p119)

Atotonilco El Alto A highland Jalisco town producing what's considered the smoothest, sweetest tequila; tours available at Siete Leguas distillery. (p598)

Tequila The Jalisco town that the drink is named for: you can come by train from Guadalajara and visit distilleries. (p598)

Month by Month

TOP EVENTS

Día de Muertos, November

Carnaval, February

Día de la Independencia, September

Monarch butterfly season, February

Guelaguetza, July

January

It's warm to hot in coastal and lowland areas, cool in the highlands, and dry everywhere, attracting flocks of foreign tourists. The first week is Mexican holiday season, making transportation and coastal resorts busy.

Día de los Santos Reyes

January 6 (Three Kings' Day or Epiphany), rather than Christmas, is the day when Mexican children traditionally receive presents, commemorating the Three Kings' gifts for the baby Jesus. Mexicans eat *rosca de reyes*, a large oval sweetbread decorated with candied fruit.

Migratory Bird Season

January is the peak season for migratory birds along Mexico's Pacific coast, so it's a top time for vacationing twitchers. Lagoons and rivers at places such as Laguna Manialtepec (p464)and Lagunas de Chacahua (p465) are packed with fowl, and San Blas even holds an International Migratory Bird Festival. (p506)

February

Temperatures are marginally higher than in January, but it remains dry, making this a great month to be in most of Mexico, though it can still be cold in the north and at high altitudes.

Whale-Watching Season

Magnificent gray whales calve in bays and lagoons around Baja California (p696) from mid-December to mid-April. Whales can also be spotted along the whole Pacific coast during this period. Best months for Baja whale-watching are February and March.

Día de la Candelaria

Candlemas (February 2), commemorating the infant Jesus' presentation in the temple, is widely celebrated. In Tlacotalpan several days of festivities feature bull-running in the streets and a flotilla of boats following an image of the Virgin down the Río Papaloapan. (p246)

Carnaval

A big bash preceding the 40-day penance of Lent, Carnaval happens during the week leading up to Ash Wednesday (February 18, 2015; February 10, 2016). It's wildest in Veracruz (p209), La Paz (p723) and Mazatlán (p496), with parades and plenty of music, drinking, dancing, fireworks and fun.

Monarch Butterfly Season

From about mid-November to March the forests of the Reserva Mariposa Monarca (Monarch Butterfly Reserve) turn bright orange as millions of large monarch butterflies winter here. The best time to watch them is on a warm, sunny afternoon in February. (p616)

Top: Danza de los Voladores at Papantla's Feria de Corpus Christi (p238)
Bottom: Guelaguetza Festival (p430)

March

It's getting steadily warmer all over Mexico, but it's still dry, and the winter season for foreign tourism continues.

Festival de México

Mexico City's historic center hosts music, theater, dance and literary events featuring talent from Mexico and abroad – the capital's biggest cultural bash of the year. (p101)

Vernal Equinox

Visitors mob ancient Chichén Itzá for the spring (March 20–21) and autumnal (September 21–22) equinoxes, when patterns of light and shadow resemble a serpent ascending or descending El Castillo pyramid. Almost the same effect happens every day for a week preceding and following each equinox. (p321)

Festival Internacional del Cine

Mexico's biggest film event of the year draws top international actors and directors to Guadalajara for 10 days each March, with more than 250 films screened to over 100,000 viewers. (p584)

Spring Break

US students get a week's break in late February or March (dates vary between colleges) and many head to Mexican resorts such as Cancún, Puerto Vallarta, Cabo San Lucas or Acapulco for days of over-the-top partying. Be in it, or steer well clear!

April

Temperatures continue to increase but it stays dry. Semana Santa (Easter Week), which can be in March or April, is Mexico's major holiday week of the year, with tourist accommodations and transportation packed.

Semana Santa

Semana Santa (Holy Week) is the week from Palm Sunday to Easter Sunday (April 5, 2015; April 27, 2016). Good Friday sees solemn processions in many places, and enormous crowds attend a re-enactment of the Crucifixion in Iztapalapa, Mexico City. (p101)

Feria de San Marcos

Millions of people attend the exhibitions, bullfights, cockfights, rodeos, concerts and other events of Mexico's biggest state fair, in the city of Aguascalientes. It lasts about three weeks from mid-April, with the biggest parade on April 25. (p674)

May

Temperatures reach annual peaks in cities such as Mérida (average daily high 35°C), Guadalajara (31°C), Oaxaca (30°C) and Mexico City (26°C). It's low season for tourism, meaning cheaper prices for many accommodations.

Feria de Morelia

This three-week fair sees regional dance performances, bullfights, agricultural and handicraft exhibitions, fireworks and plenty of partying in the Michoacán capital. (p611)

Feria de Corpus Christi

Papantla's big bash features spectacular *voladores* (fliers) performances and indigenous dances, plus *charreadas* (Mexican rodeos), parades and bullfights. (p238)

June

The rainy season has started, bringing heavy downpours in the southeast, in some places along the Pacific coast and in the central highlands. Tourist numbers remain low, as do hotel prices.

Festival del Mole Poblano

Puebla celebrates its most famous contribution to Mexican cuisine, the chocolatey sauce *mole poblano,* in early June. (p158)

Surf's Up

Countless spots along the Pacific coast, including Puerto Escondido with its legendary Mexican Pipeline (p455), enjoy superb swells from April/May to October/November. June, July and August generally see the biggest waves. Beginners can learn the craft almost year-round at numerous spots.

July

It's still rainy in the southeast, central highlands and along the Pacific coast, but this is a summer vacation month for both foreigners and Mexicans, bringing busy times at many tourist destinations, and higher prices at some.

Guelaguetza

Oaxaca is thronged for this fantastically colorful feast of regional dance on the first two Mondays after July 16, with plenty of other celebratory events accompanying it. (p430)

Swimming with Whale Sharks

Massive whale sharks congregate to feed on plankton off Isla Contoy between mid-May and mid-September. The best time to swim with these gentle giants is July. (p272)

August

The summer holiday season continues, as do the rains, although they're less intense in most areas. June to August are brutally hot in the north.

Feria de Huamantla

Huamantla, east of Mexico City, lets rip over a few days and nights during its mid-August fair. On August 14 the streets are carpeted with flowers and colored sawdust; a few days later there's a Pamplona-esque running of the bulls. (p173)

La Morisma

Zacatecas stages a spectacular mock battle with 10,000 participants, commemorating the triumph of the Christians over the Moors in old Spain, usually on the last weekend of August. (p691)

September

Summer's over and it's the height of the hurricane season on the Yucatán Peninsula and Mexico's coasts. Hurricanes strike erratically, but it's a rainy month everywhere, and visibility for Caribbean divers is poor.

Día de la Independencia

On Independence Day (September 16), patriotic celebrations mark the anniversary of Miguel Hidalgo's 1810 call to rebellion against Spain, the Grito de Dolores: on the 15th, the Grito is repeated from every Mexican town hall, followed by fireworks. The biggest celebrations are in Mexico City. (p101)

October

Low season for tourism, and the possibility of hurricanes continues, but the rains have eased off everywhere except the Yucatán Peninsula.

Fiestas de Octubre

Guadalajara's big bash fills the whole month with free entertainment, livestock shows, art exhibitions and sporting events. Thousands of passionate pilgrims crawl on their knees behind a statue of the Virgin Mary carried to the city's Basílica de Zapopan. (p585)

Festival Internacional Cervantino

Guanajuato's two- to three-week arts festival, dedicated to Spanish writer Miguel de Cervantes, is one of the biggest cultural happenings in Latin America, with performances by music, dance and theater groups from around the world. (p649)

Copper Canyon Season

October, along with November and March, is one of the best months to visit northwest Mexico's spectacular canyon country (p757), with temperatures not too hot at the bottom of the canyons nor too cold at the top.

November

A quiet month for tourism. The weather is mostly dry and temperatures are subsiding. Snow tops the high peaks of the central volcanic belt.

Día de Muertos

(Day of the Dead; November 2) Cemeteries come alive as families decorate graves and commune with their dead, some holding all-night vigils. Special altars appear in homes and public buildings and sugar skulls and toy skeletons appear on market stalls. Associated events may start days before, notably around Pátzcuaro (p622) and Oaxaca (p430). See also p817.

Festival Gourmet International

Guest chefs from around Mexico and the world descend on the Pacific resort of Puerto Vallarta for this 10-day feast of the culinary arts. (p520)

Feria de la Plata

Some of Mexico's best silverwork is on show during the week-long national silver fair in Taxco in late November or early December. *Charreadas*, concerts, dances and donkey races add to the fun. (p192)

December

A dry month almost everywhere, and as cool as it gets. International winter tourism gets going, and the Christmas–New Year period is Mexican holiday time, with accommodations busy and prices often raised.

Día de Nuestra Señora de Guadalupe

Several days of festivities throughout Mexico lead up to the feast day of the Virgin who is the country's religious patron – the Day of Our Lady of Guadalupe (December 12). Millions converge on Mexico City's Basílica de Guadalupe, some traveling the final meters to t he shrine on their knees. (p99)

Christmas

Christmas is traditionally celebrated with a feast in the early hours of December 25, after midnight Mass. Pre- or post-Christmas events in some towns include *pastorelas* (nativity plays), as in Tepotzotlán (p141) and Pátzcuaro (p623), and *posadas* (candlelit processions), as in Taxco (p193).

Plan Your Trip
Itineraries

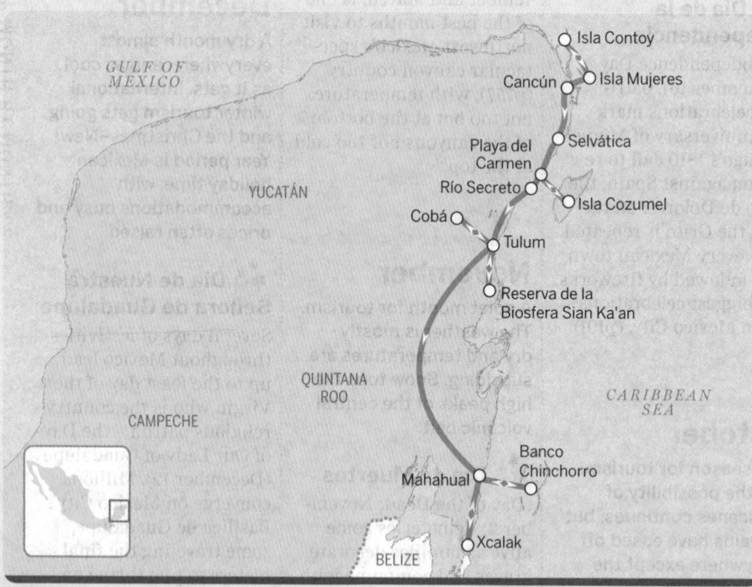

Riviera Maya & Costa Maya Getaway

Fly into **Cancún** and head straight for relaxed **Isla Mujeres'** beaches and snorkeling, taking a side-trip to **Isla Contoy**, a national park with excellent bird-watching and, June to September, the chance to swim with whale sharks.

Alternatively opt for hip **Playa del Carmen**, with its own fine beaches, underwater activities and lively nightlife. 'Playa' is also the jumping-off point for the world-famous dive sites of **Isla Cozumel**. If you have kids, spend a day at the nearby 'eco-parks' such as **Selvática** with its 12 jungle zip-lines, or **Río Secreto** where you hike and swim through a 600m-long cave. Next stop: **Tulum**, with one of Mexico's most perfect beaches and most spectacularly located Maya sites. Nearby are the pyramids and temples of **Cobá**, as well as the wildlife-rich **Reserva de la Biosfera Sian Ka'an**. South of Tulum the Costa Maya is less developed and touristed than the 'Riviera Maya' to the north. Head to **Mahahual**, a laid-back village with snorkeling and diving at the coral atoll **Banco Chinchorro**, or the tiny fishing town of **Xcalak**, another excellent water sports base. After three nights chilling at either of these, either opt for a fourth, or, if you're worried that you missed out on **Cancún's** nightlife, spend your last night there.

Flock of Magnificent Frigatebirds, Reserva de la Biosfera Sian Ka'an (p294)

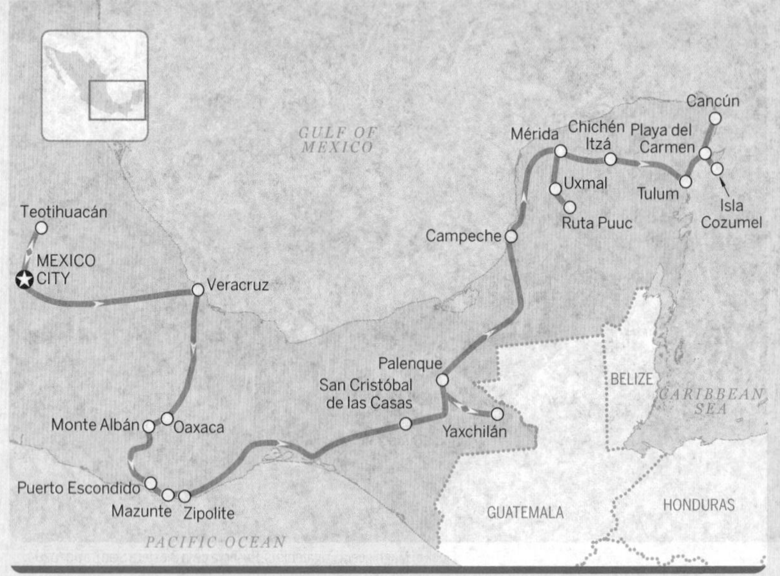
GULF OF MEXICO
Cancún
Mérida
Chichén Itzá
Playa del Carmen
Uxmal
Tulum
Isla Cozumel
Ruta Puuc
Teotihuacán
Campeche
MEXICO CITY
Veracruz
Palenque
BELIZE
San Cristóbal de las Casas
CARIBBEAN SEA
Monte Albán
Oaxaca
Yaxchilán
Puerto Escondido
Mazunte
Zipolite
GUATEMALA
HONDURAS
PACIFIC OCEAN

STOCKCAM/GETTY IMAGES ©

ANTONIO BUSIELLO/GETTY IMAGES ©

Beaches & Temples of Mexico's South

This classic journey leads south from Mexico's central heartland to its glorious Caribbean beaches, and gives a superb sampling of what makes the country so fascinating.

Start by exploring the exciting megalopolis of **Mexico City**, key to any understanding of Mexico the country. Take a side-trip to the awesome pyramids at **Teotihuacán**, capital of ancient Mexico's biggest empire. Then head east to the fun-loving port city of **Veracruz**, before crossing the mountains southward to **Oaxaca**. This cultured colonial city, with Mexico's finest handicrafts, sits at the heart of a beautiful region with a large indigenous population. Don't miss the ancient Zapotec capital, **Monte Albán**, nearby.

Head down to one of the relaxed beach spots on the Oaxaca coast, such as **Puerto Escondido**, **Mazunte** or **Zipolite**, for a few days' sun, surf and sand, before continuing east to **San Cristóbal de las Casas**, a beautiful highland town surrounded by intriguing indigenous villages. Move on to **Palenque**, perhaps the most stunning of all ancient Maya cities, with its backdrop of emerald-green jungle, and **Yaxchilán**, another marvelous Maya city, accessible only by river.

Head northeast to **Campeche**, an attractive mix of colonial city and bustling modern town, then move on to colonial **Mérida**, the Yucatán Peninsula's lively cultural capital and the base for visiting the superb ruins of **Uxmal** and the **Ruta Puuc**. Next stop: **Chichén Itzá**, the most celebrated of all the Yucatán's Maya sites. From here, it's on to **Tulum** on the Caribbean coast, another spectacular Maya site set beside a glorious beach. Finally make your way northward along the Riviera Maya to the hip beach town of **Playa del Carmen**, with a side trip to **Isla Cozumel** for world-class snorkeling and diving, to end at Mexico's most popular and unabashed coastal resort, **Cancún**.

Top: Pirámide de la Luna (p148), Teotihuacán
tom: Sea turtle and queen angelfish, Isla Cozumel (p280)

3 WEEKS Colonial Cities of Mexico's Heartland

The nation's capital is ringed by colonial cities blessed with gorgeous architecture of carved stone and colorful tiles, broad plazas, splashing fountains and lively contemporary cultural scenes. Trying to visit them all runs the risk of monument fatigue, but you can do justice to the region on this eight-stop route.

Mexico City itself has much grand colonial architecture, starting with its central plaza, the Zócalo, and the cathedral and National Palace that flank it. The colonial center is interestingly spiced with plenty of more modern, and a bit of pre-Hispanic, architecture and art, and there are masses of great places to eat and go out at night after a day of culture.

Head east to **Puebla**, which has the country's densest concentration of restored colonial churches and mansions – many of the latter now housing interesting museums – and is still one of the most Spanish-influenced cities in Mexico. Over 1000 buildings are adorned with the colorful *azulejos* (painted ceramic tiles) for which the city is famed.

Go west to Michoacán's lively capital **Morelia**, home to an inspiring cathedral, many other well-preserved colonial buildings and some great cafes and bars, but curiously ignored by most foreign tourists. **Pátzcuaro** is a handsome, low-rise, much smaller highland town where the indigenous Purépecha sell their wares around one of Mexico's loveliest central plazas.

Move northward up to prosperous **Zacatecas**, a stylish silver city with a stupendous baroque cathedral, fascinating art museums, and even a colonial silver- and gold-mine that you can tour. Heading back toward Mexico City you reach El Bajío, the region famed as the Cuna de la Independencia (Cradle of Independence) for its vital role in the 19th-century independence movement that put an end to Mexico's colonial era. Here, lively **Guanajuato** awaits with quixotic *callejones* (alleys), a vibrant student life and historical reminders galore, while the festive and charming expat capital **San Miguel de Allende** is full of beautifully restored colonial buildings, including many homes. Before you hit Mexico City again, don't neglect handsome **Querétaro**, which has several fine museums and a very walkable historic center.

GLOW IMAGES/GETTY IMAGES ©

DE AGOSTINI/S. GUTIERREZ/GETTY IMAGES ©

Top: Palacio Nacional (p70), Mexico City
Bottom: Catedral (p155), Puebla

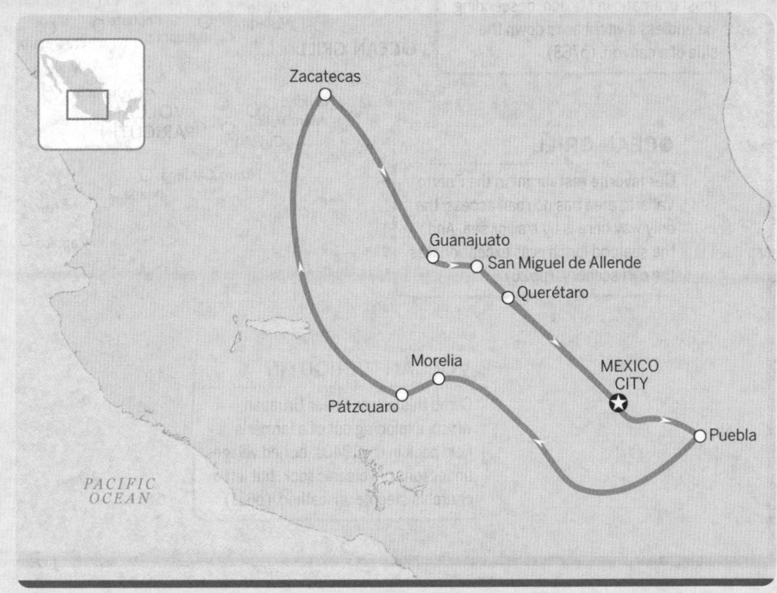
Zacatecas
Guanajuato
San Miguel de Allende
Querétaro
MEXICO CITY
Puebla
Morelia
Pátzcuaro
PACIFIC OCEAN

Off the Beaten Track: Mexico

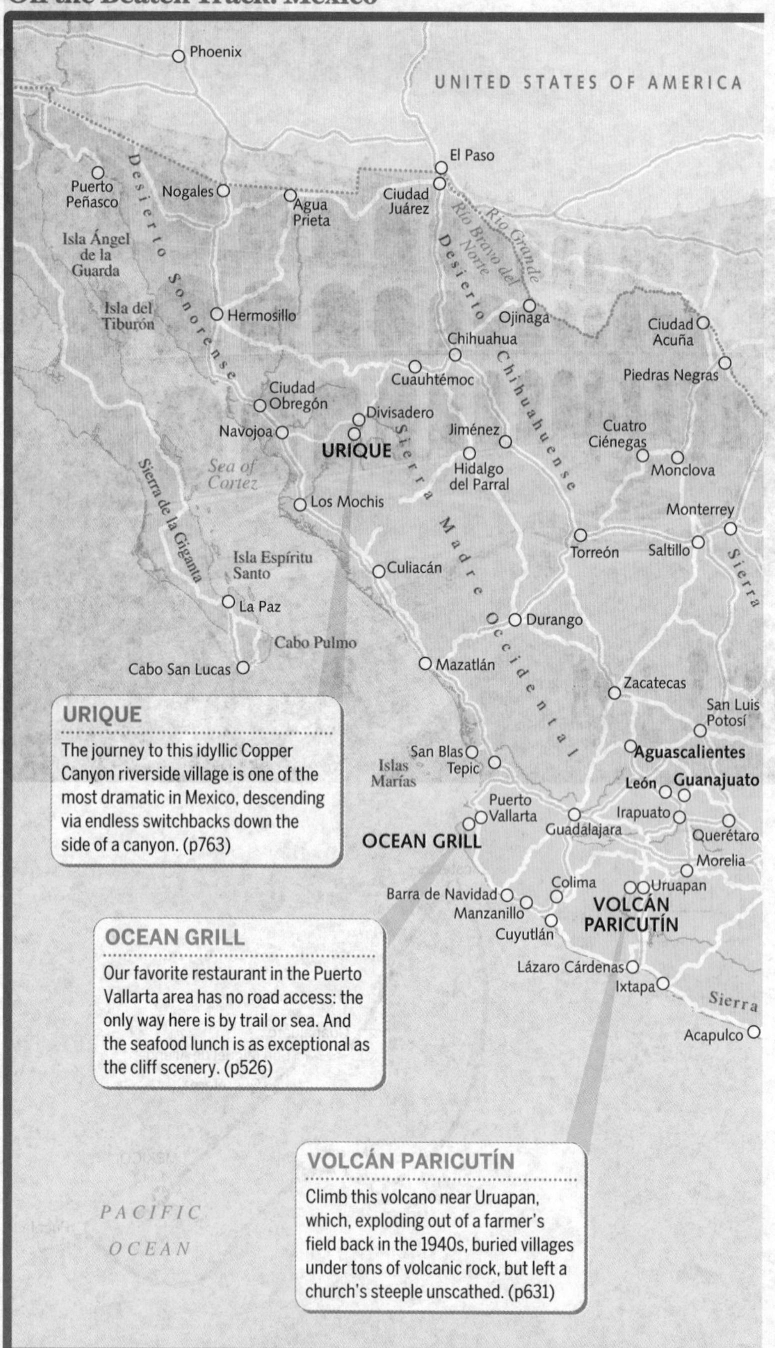

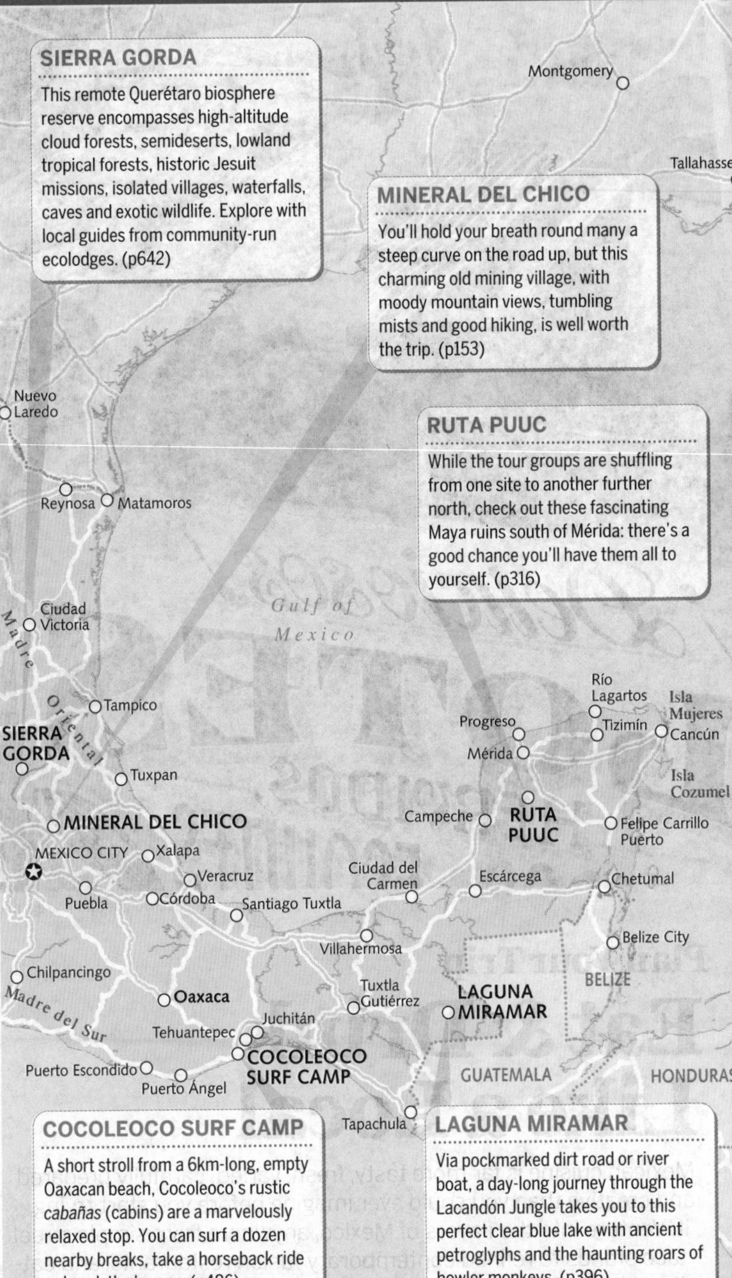
0 500 km
0 300 miles
SIERRA GORDA
This remote Querétaro biosphere reserve encompasses high-altitude cloud forests, semideserts, lowland tropical forests, historic Jesuit missions, isolated villages, waterfalls, caves and exotic wildlife. Explore with local guides from community-run ecolodges. (p642)
MINERAL DEL CHICO
You'll hold your breath round many a steep curve on the road up, but this charming old mining village, with moody mountain views, tumbling mists and good hiking, is well worth the trip. (p153)
RUTA PUUC
While the tour groups are shuffling from one site to another further north, check out these fascinating Maya ruins south of Mérida: there's a good chance you'll have them all to yourself. (p316)
COCOLEOCO SURF CAMP
A short stroll from a 6km-long, empty Oaxacan beach, Cocoleoco's rustic cabañas (cabins) are a marvelously relaxed stop. You can surf a dozen nearby breaks, take a horseback ride or kayak the lagoon. (p486)
LAGUNA MIRAMAR
Via pockmarked dirt road or river boat, a day-long journey through the Lacandón Jungle takes you to this perfect clear blue lake with ancient petroglyphs and the haunting roars of howler monkeys. (p396)
Montgomery
Tallahassee
Nuevo Laredo
Reynosa
Matamoros
Gulf of Mexico
Ciudad Victoria
Madre Oriental
Tampico
SIERRA GORDA
Tuxpan
MINERAL DEL CHICO
MEXICO CITY
Xalapa
Veracruz
Puebla
Córdoba
Santiago Tuxtla
Ciudad del Carmen
Villahermosa
Chilpancingo
Madre del Sur
Oaxaca
Tuxtla Gutiérrez
Juchitán
Tehuantepec
COCOLEOCO SURF CAMP
Puerto Escondido
Puerto Ángel
Tapachula
LAGUNA MIRAMAR
GUATEMALA
HONDURAS
BELIZE
Belize City
Chetumal
Escárcega
Campeche
RUTA PUUC
Felipe Carrillo Puerto
Mérida
Progreso
Río Lagartos
Tizimín
Isla Mujeres
Cancún
Isla Cozumel

Corn on the cob for sale at a street cart

Plan Your Trip

Eat & Drink Like a Local

Mexican cuisine is far more tasty, fresh, varied, carefully prepared and creative than you could ever imagine before you start trying it. Venture into the flavors of Mexico, anywhere from simple street taco stands to refined contemporary fusion restaurants, and eating will be a highlight of your trip.

The Year in Food

April

The start of the rainy season brings out the first *huitlacoche*, a corn fungus considered one of Mexico's greatest delicacies.

May to August

Mid-year festivals celebrate cheese and wine (Tequisquiapan), the famous chocolate-based sauce *mole poblano* (Puebla), mushrooms (Cuajimoloyas, Oaxaca) and wine again (Ensenada and Parras).

September

Fresh walnuts and pomegranates make Independence Day (September 16) the peak time for the patriotic dish, *chiles en nogada* (its green chilies, red pomegranate and white walnut sauce are the colors of the Mexican flag).

November

Día de Muertos (Day of the Dead, November 2) brings colorful candy skulls and chocolate coffins to street stalls. Uruapan attempts the world's-biggest-guacamole record during its Avocado Fair.

Food Experiences

Meals of a Lifetime

➡ **Pujol** (p116), **Mexico City** A multiple-course tasting extravaganza of contemporary Mexican cuisine: reserve weeks ahead.

➡ **Ocean Grill** (p526), **Puerto Vallarta** Stellar seafood lunches at a cliffside bistro reached by boat.

➡ **La Providencia** (p471), **Zipolite** Sophisticated fusion fare on a back lane in a budget beach hangout.

➡ **Kinich** (p321), **Izamal** Fresh, handmade Yucatán cuisine at its best.

➡ **Restaurante Lu** (p614), **Morelia** Pre-Hispanic ingredients turned into Mexican *alta cocina* (haute cuisine).

➡ **Finca de Vaqueros** (p466), **Pochutla** A ranch-style grilled-meat feast you won't quickly forget.

➡ **Las Mercedes** (p652), **Guanajuato** Traditional grandmother-style dishes with contemporary presentation that take hours to prepare.

Cheap Treats

Mexico has one of the world's great street-food cultures. All over the country, street stands, markets and small eateries dole out endless supplies of filling and nutritious snacks and light meals, morning, noon and night. The busiest stands usually have the tastiest offerings and freshest ingredients.

Foremost are the many varieties of *antojito* ('little whim'), light dishes using *masa* (corn dough). The quintessential *antojito* is the taco – meat, fish or vegetables wrapped in a tortilla (Mexico's ubiquitous corn or wheat-flour flatbread). Delicious varieties include *tacos al pastor* (with spit-cooked pork), *tacos de carne asada* (with grilled beef) and *tacos de pescado* (fish tacos, a favorite on the Pacific coast). There are many more types of *antojito* and an infinite variety of ingredients that can go into them. The most popular types include:

➡ *quesadillas* – a tortilla folded in half with a filling of cheese and/or other ingredients

➡ *enchiladas* – lightly fried tortillas with fillings, and covered in a chili sauce

➡ *tamales* – a wodge of *masa* mixed with lard, with stewed meat, fish or veggies in the middle, steamed in corn husks or banana leaf

Other common street foods:

➡ *tortas* – sandwiches (hot or cold) using a white bread roll

➡ *elotes* – freshly steamed or grilled corn on the cob, usually coated in mayonnaise and often sprinkled with chili powder

Dare to Try

Grasshoppers *(chapulines)* Fried with chili powder and garlic, they make a surprisingly munchable snack, especially accompanying a glass of mezcal. Plentiful in Oaxaca.

Corn fungus *(huitlacoche)* The black mold that grows on some cobs of corn (maize) has a truffle-like texture and has been considered a delicacy since pre-Hispanic times. Available during the mid-year rainy season at Mexico City's Mercado San Juan (p127) and as a sauce or stuffing ingredient at restaurants such as Axitla (p178), Tepoztlán.

Cow's-eye tacos *(tacos de ojos)* Yes that's right. Cows' eyes chopped up, steamed and put into tacos. Soft enough but not especially flavorsome and can be a bit greasy. Found at taco stands around the country and at Los Cocuyos (p108) restaurant in Mexico City.

Grubs and worms Ant larvae *(escamoles)* and maguey worms *(gusanos de maguey)* are seasonal fare from about March to June in the Puebla-Tlaxcala area. At Tlaxcala's Tirol (p170) you can share an insect tasting-plate with your friends for just M$450.

GREG ELMS/GETTY IMAGES ©

Birria, a goat stew

Local Specialties

Central Mexico

Guadalajara is famed for its *birria* (chili-spiced goat stew wrapped in agave leaves) and *tortas ahogadas* (drowned *tortas*) – sandwiches of *carnitas* (braised pork) and beans, soaked in a very spicy sauce. Not far away is Tequila, the town that gave Mexico its most famous drink, where you can visit distilleries, or even take the Tequila Express excursion train from Guadalajara. The city of Puebla has a proudly distinctive cuisine including perhaps Mexico's single most famous dish – *mole poblano*, a thick sauce of chilies, fruits, nuts, spices and chocolate, usually served over chicken.

Mexico City

The great melting pot of Mexican people and Mexican food, the capital has a vibrant street-food culture, with *antojitos* everywhere – at street stands, markets and thousands of taco stands. At the other end of the culinary scale top chefs create fantastic fusion dishes in ultra-contemporary

COOKING CLASSES

➡ **Estela Silva's Mexican Home Cooking School** (p169) Long-established school near Tlaxcala focusing on local cuisine. Courses run several days and include accommodations.

➡ **La Casa de los Sabores** (p429) Classes in Oaxacan and other Mexican meals at one of the best schools in Oaxaca.

➡ **La Villa Bonita** (p176) Courses of several days including accommodations, run by celebrated chef Ana García.

➡ **Little Mexican Cooking School** (p274) Classes on the Riviera Maya, preparing menus from seven different Mexican regions.

➡ **Zihuatanejo Cooking School** (p552) Highly recommended classes in local and national favorites.

Freshly grilled crab

restaurants melding haute-cuisine techniques with traditional Mexican ingredients, especially in the neighborhoods of Condesa, Roma and Polanco.

Oaxaca

This southern state is famed throughout Mexico for its unique dishes. Greatest renown belongs to its many *moles* – rich, thick sauces made with chilies, spices, nuts and often tomatoes, that go over meats. Oaxaca is also the world capital of mezcal, a potent sipping liquor made from agave plants, which is enjoying an upsurge in popularity.

Pacific Coast

Naturally, fresh fish and seafood are great here. *Pescado zarandeado* – fish grilled inside a wooden grill called a *zaranda* – is a specialty in the more northerly parts. Ceviches (marinated raw seafood cocktails) find a natural home in the hotter southern regions. Mazatlán, Sayulita, Puerto Vallarta and Zihuatanejo are all foodie havens, and Vallarta has attracted a good number of international chefs to open gourmet fusion restaurants, which play a big part in its November Festival Gourmet International.

The North

Beef, from this region's extensive ranches, and seafood in the coastal areas, are the specialties here. In Monterrey the signature dish is *cabrito asado* (kid goat roasted on skewers over an open fire).

Yucatán Peninsula

Caribbean flavors and indigenous Maya recipes influence the cuisine of Mexico's southeast corner. The most famous dish is *cochinita pibil* – suckling pig marinated in citrus juices and *achiote* (a spice made from red seeds) and traditionally roasted in a pit in the ground. A staple is the fiery *chile habanero* – *habanero* sauce goes very well on *papadzules* (tacos stuffed with hard-boiled eggs and pumpkin-seed sauce). Don't miss *sopa de lima*, a soup made from turkey, lime and tortilla pieces.

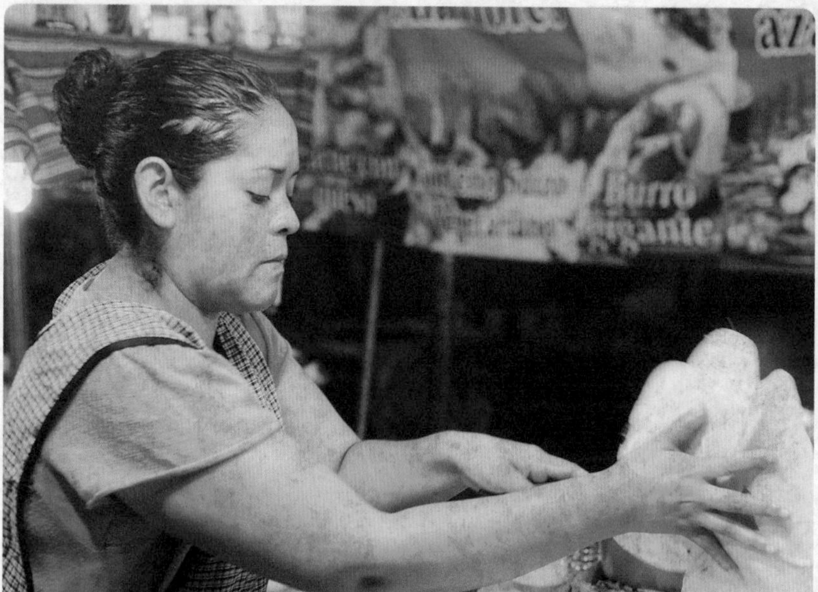

COSMO CONDINA/GETTY IMAGES ©

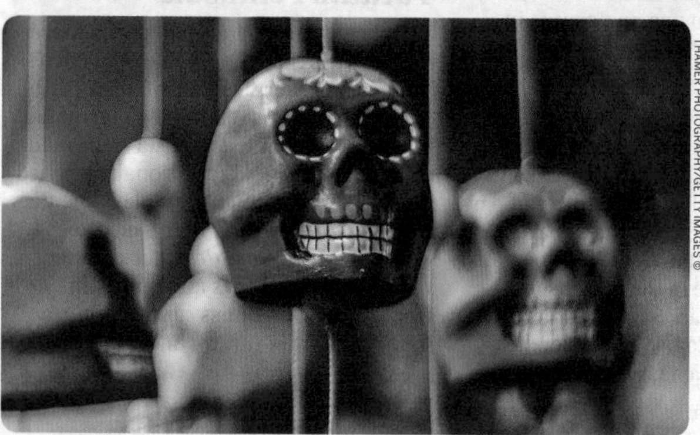

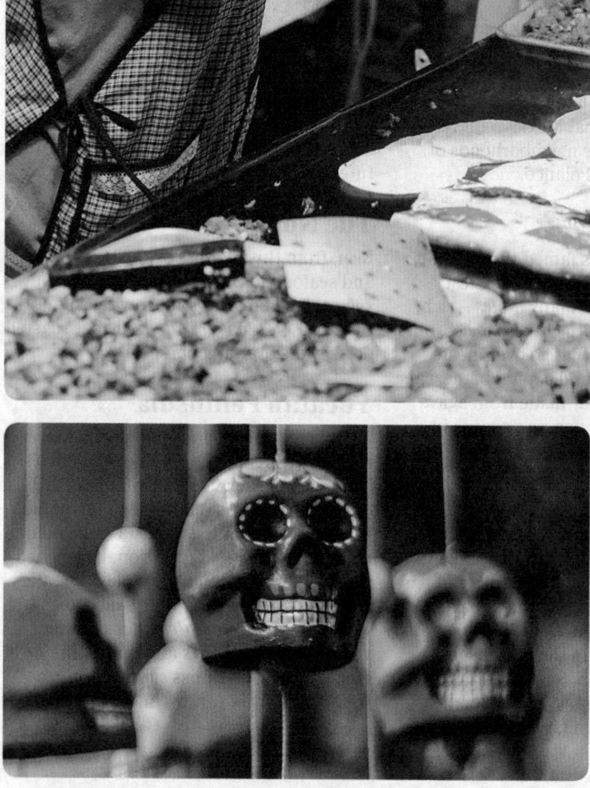

THAMER PHOTOGRAPHY/GETTY IMAGES ©

Above: Traditional Mexican food being prepared at a food stand

Left: Display of hanging sugar skulls

How to Eat & Drink

Chiles en nogada

When to Eat

Desayuno (breakfast) Usually served from 8:30am to 11am, it tends to be on the hearty side. Egg dishes are popular and some Mexicans down serious meaty platefuls.

Comida (lunch) The main meal of the day, usually served between 2pm and 4:30pm and comprising a soup or other starter, main course (typically meat, fish or seafood) and small dessert. *Comida corrida*, also known as *menú del día*, is an inexpensive fixed-price lunch menu.

Cena (dinner) For Mexicans, dinner is a lighter meal than lunch and often not eaten till 9pm. Nearly all restaurants serving dinner open from as early as 7pm though, offering full menus for those who want them.

Snacks At almost any time of day you can grab an *antojito* or *torta* at a cafe or street or market stall. You can also get sandwiches (toasted) in some cafes.

Where to Eat

In general *restaurantes* (restaurants) have full, multi-course menus and a range of drinks to accompany meals, while cafes and *cafeterías* offer shorter menus of lighter dishes and their drinks may focus on coffee, tea and soft drinks. Other types of eatery:

➡ *comedor* – 'eating room'; usually refers to economical restaurants serving simple, straightforward meals

➡ *fonda* – small, frequently family-run eatery, often serving *comida corrida*

➡ *mercado* (market) – many Mexican markets have *comedor* sections where you sit on benches eating economical, home-style food cooked up on the spot

➡ *taquería* – stall or eatery specializing in tacos

Menu Decoder

For an explanation of dishes you'll find on Mexican menus, see p871; for names of basic foods, p863.

➡ **a la parrilla** grilled on a barbecue grill

➡ **a la plancha** grilled on a metal plate

➡ **al carbón** cooked over open coals

➡ **aves** poultry

➡ **bebidas** drinks

➡ **carnes** meats

➡ **empanizado** fried in breadcrumbs

➡ **ensalada** salad

➡ **entradas** starters

➡ **filete** fillet

➡ **frito** fried

➡ **huevos** eggs

➡ **jugo** juice

➡ **legumbres** pulses

➡ **mariscos** seafood (not fish)

➡ **menú de degustación** tasting menu

➡ **mole** rich, thick sauce made with chilies, spices, nuts, often tomatoes and sometimes chocolate, that goes over meats

➡ **pescado** fish

➡ **plato fuerte** main dish

➡ **postre** dessert

➡ **salsa** sauce

➡ **sopa** soup

➡ **verduras** vegetables

Entrance to Tomb 105, Monte Albán (p442)

Plan Your Trip

Exploring Mexico's Ancient Ruins

Mexico's ancient civilizations were the most sophisticated and formidable in North or Central America. Towering pyramids, sculpted temples and gruesome sacrificial sites have amazed outsiders since the Spanish arrived in 1519. Today these sites are a national and global treasure: visiting some of them is an experience not to be missed.

Where & When

Top Five & Best Times to Visit

Most of Mexico's major pre-Hispanic sites are scattered around the center, south and southeast of the country. Here's our top five, along with the best time of year to visit them. Most sites open daily 9am to 5pm (some close Monday) – arriving early means fewer visitors and lower temperatures.

Teotihuacán, Central Mexico August, October to April

Chichén Itzá, Yucatán Peninsula November to April

Uxmal, Yucatán Peninsula November to April

Palenque, Chiapas October to May

Monte Albán, Oaxaca October to March

Mexico's Ancient Civilizations

Archaeologists have been uncovering Mexico's ancient ruins since the 19th century. Many impressive sites have been restored and made accessible to visitors, others have been explored in part, and thousands more remain untouched, buried beneath the earth or hidden in forests. The major civilizations were these:

➡ **Olmec** Mexico's 'mother culture' was centered on the Gulf coast, from about 1200 BC to 400 BC. It's famed for the giant stone sculptures known as Olmec heads.

➡ **Teotihuacán** Based at the city of the same name with its huge pyramids, 50km from Mexico City, the Teotihuacán civilization flourished in the first seven centuries AD, and ruled the biggest of the ancient Mexican empires.

➡ **Maya** The Maya, in southeast Mexico and neighboring Guatemala and Belize, flowered most brilliantly in numerous city-states between AD 250 and AD 900. They're famed for their exquisitely beautiful temples and stone sculptures. Maya culture lives on today among the indigenous population of these regions.

➡ **Toltec** A name for the culture of a number of central Mexican city-states, from around AD 750 to AD 1150. The warrior sculptures of Tula are the most celebrated monuments.

➡ **Aztec** With their capital at Tenochtitlán (now Mexico City) from AD 1325 to AD 1521, the Aztecs came to rule most of central Mexico from the Gulf coast to the Pacific. The best known Aztec site is the Templo Mayor in Mexico City.

Site Practicalities

➡ The most famous sites are often thronged with large numbers of visitors (arrive early). Others are hidden away on remote hilltops or shrouded in thick jungle, and can be the most exciting and rewarding to visit, for those with an adventurous spirit.

➡ Admission to archaeological sites costs from nothing up to around M$250, depending on the site (but only a handful of places, all in Yucatán state, cost more than around M$60).

➡ Go protected against the sun and, at jungle sites, against mosquitoes.

➡ Popular sites have facilities such as cafes or restaurants, bookstores, souvenir stores, audio guides in various languages, and authorized (but not fixed-price) human guides.

➡ Little-visited sites may have no food or water available.

➡ Guided tours to many sites are available from nearby towns, but public transportation is usually available, too.

➡ Major sites are usually wheelchair accessible.

➡ Explanatory signs may be in Spanish only, or in Spanish and English, or in Spanish, English and a local indigenous language.

Resources

- **Colecciones Especiales Street View** (www.inah.gob.mx/especial-street-view) Take virtual tours of 30 sites in Google Street View.
- **Instituto Nacional de Antropología e Historia** (INAH; www.inah.gob.mx) Mexico's National Institute of Anthropology and History administers 187 archaeological sites and 129 museums.
- **Mesoweb** (www.mesoweb.com) A diverse resource on ancient Mexico, especially the Maya.
- **An Archaeological Guide to Central and Southern Mexico** Joyce Kelly's book was published in 2001 and is still the best of its kind, covering 70 sites.

Top Museums

Some archaeological sites have their own museums, but there are also important city and regional museums that hold many of the most valuable and impressive pre-Hispanic artifacts and provide fascinating background on ancient Mexico.

- **Museo Nacional de Antropología, Mexico City** (p83) The superb National Museum of Anthropology has sections devoted to all the important ancient civilizations, and includes such treasures as the famous Aztec sun stone and a replica of King Pakal's treasure-laden tomb from Palenque.
- **Museo de Antropología, Xalapa** (p218) Mainly devoted to Gulf coast cultures, this excellent museum contains seven Olmec heads and other masterly sculptures among its 25,000-piece collection.

Sculptures of Quetzalcóatl, Chichén Itzá (p321)

- **Parque-Museo La Venta, Villahermosa** (p414) This outdoor museum-cum-zoo holds several Olmec heads and other fine sculptures from the site of La Venta, moved here in the 1950s when La Venta was under threat from petroleum exploration.
- **Museo Maya de Cancún** (p258) One of Mexico's most important collections of Maya artifacts, assembled from sites around the Yucatán Peninsula.

PRE-HISPANIC NUMBERS

Ancient Mexicans loved numbers. We've assembled some of our own:

- **25 million** – estimated Ancient Mexican population
- **8km** of tunnels dug by archaeologists beneath Cholula's Tepanapa Pyramid
- **70m** – the height of Teotihuacán's Pyramid of the Sun
- **100km** – the length of the *sacbé* (stone-paved avenue) from Cobá to Yaxuna
- **120** mural-covered walls in Teotihuacán's Tetitla Palace
- **300** masks of Chac, the rain god, at Kabah's Palace of Masks
- **6500** buildings at Calakmul
- **15,000** ritual ball-game courts found in Mexico (so far)
- **20,000** human hearts ripped out for the rededication of Tenochtitlán's Templo Mayor in 1487

Mexico's Ruins

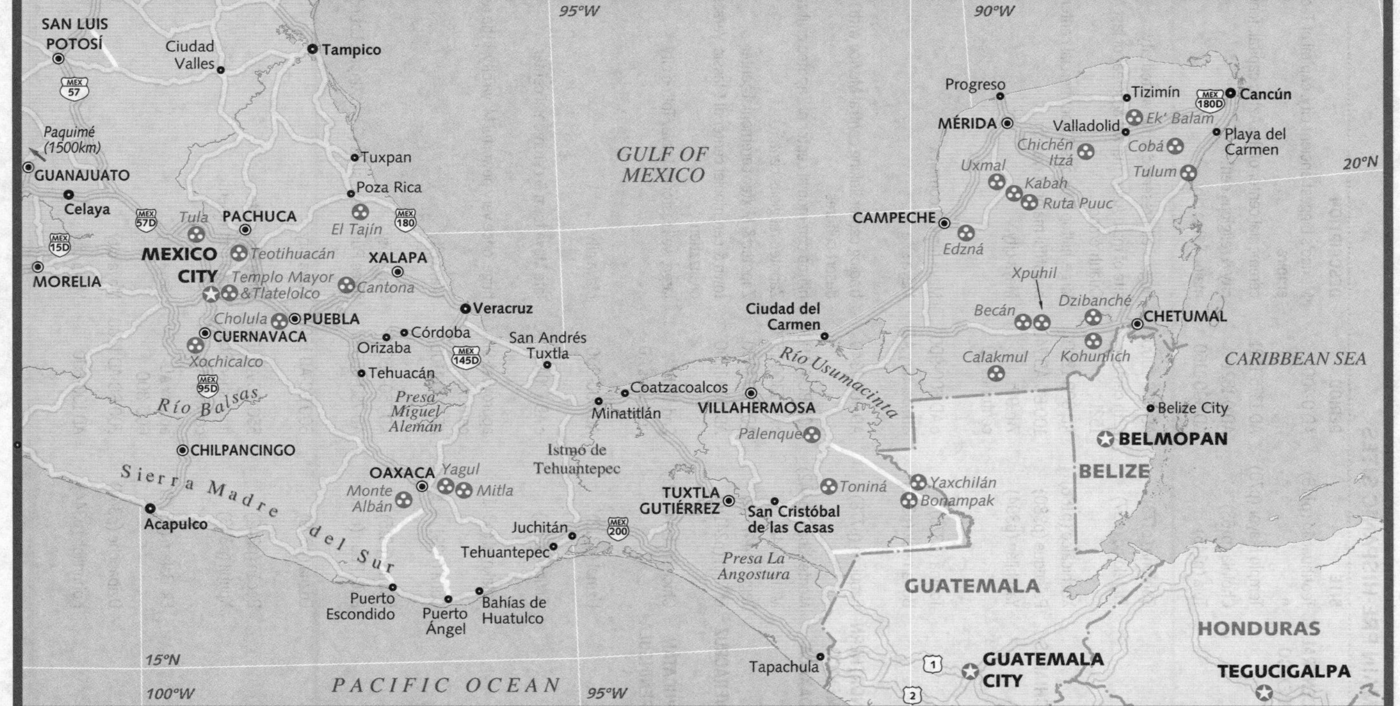

MAIN PRE-HISPANIC SITES

	SITE	PERIOD	DESCRIPTION
CENTRAL MEXICO	Teotihuacán (p146)	AD 0-700	Mexico's biggest ancient city, capital of Teotihuacán empire
	Templo Mayor (p70)	AD 1375-1521	ceremonial center of the Aztec capital, Tenochtitlán
	Cholula (p163)	AD 0-1521	city & religious center
	Tula (p145)	AD 900-1150	major Toltec city
	Cantona (p173)	AD 600-1000	huge, well-preserved, little-visited city
	Tlatelolco (p97)	12th century-1521	site of main Aztec market & defeat of last Aztec emperor Cuauhtémoc
	Xochicalco (p186)	AD 600-1200	large, hilltop religious & commercial center
CHIAPAS	Palenque (p380)	100 BC-AD 740	beautiful major Maya city
	Yaxchilán (p394)	7th-9th centuries AD	Maya city
	Toniná (p376)	c AD 600-900	Maya temple complex
	Bonampak (p391)	8th century AD	Maya site
NORTHERN MEXICO	Paquimé (p778)	AD 900-1340	trading center linking central Mexico with northern desert cultures
OAXACA	Monte Albán (p442)	500 BC-AD 900	hilltop ceremonial center of Zapotec civilization
	Mitla (p448)	c AD 1300-1520	Zapotec religious center
	Yagul (p447)	AD 900-1400	Zapotec & Mixtec ceremonial center
VERACRUZ	El Tajín (p241)	AD 600-1200	town & ceremonial center of Classic Veracruz civilization
YUCATÁN PENINSULA	Chichén Itzá (p321)	2nd-14th centuries AD	large, well restored Maya/Toltec city
	Uxmal (p312)	AD 600-900	Maya city
	Tulum (p286)	c AD 1200-1600	late Maya town & ceremonial center
	Calakmul (p341)	approx 1st-9th centuries AD	huge, once very powerful Maya city, little restored
	Cobá (p291)	AD 600-1100	Maya city
	Kabah (p315)	AD 750-950	Maya city
	Ruta Puuc (p316)	AD 750-950	three Puuc Maya sites (Sayil, Xlapak, Labná)
	Edzná (p339)	600 BC-AD 1500	Maya city
	Becán (p342)	550 BC-AD 1000	large Maya site
	Xpuhil (p343)	flourished 8th century AD	Maya settlement
	Ek' Balam (p331)	approx AD 600-800	Maya city
	Dzibanché (p344)	200 BC-AD 1200	Maya city
	Kohunlich (p344)	AD 100-600	Maya city

HIGHLIGHTS	LOCATION/TRANSPORTATION
Pyramids of Sun and Moon, Calzada de los Muertos, palace murals	50km northeast of Mexico City; frequent buses
ceremonial pyramid	downtown Mexico City
world's widest pyramid	8km west of Puebla; frequent buses
stone pillars carved as warriors	80km north of Mexico City; 1km walk or taxi from Tula bus station
24 ball courts, unique street system	90km northeast of Puebla; taxi or *colectivo* from Oriental
Aztec temple-pyramid	northern Mexico City; trolleybus or metro
Pyramid of Quetzalcóatl	35km southwest of Cuernavaca; bus
exquisite temples with jungle backdrop	7km west of Palenque town; frequent combis
temples & other buildings in riverside jungle setting	beside Río Usumacinta, 15km northwest of Frontera Corozal; van from Palenque to Frontera Corozal (170km), boat from Frontera Corozal to Yaxchilán
temples & pyramids on hillside	14km east of Ocosingo; combis from Ocosingo
superb, if weathered, frescoes	150km southeast of Palenque; van or bus to San Javier (140km), then taxi and van
adobe walls & buildings, clay macaw cages, rare geometric pottery	Casas Grandes village; buses from Nuevo Casas Grandes, 7km north
pyramids, observatory, panoramas	6km west of Oaxaca; bus
unique stone mosaics	46km southeast of Oaxaca; bus or *colectivo*
large ball court, rock 'fortress'	35km southeast of Oaxaca; bus or *colectivo*, then 1.5km walk
rare niched pyramids, 17 ball courts, *voladores* ('fliers') performances	6km west of Papantla; bus
El Castillo 'calendar temple', Mexico's biggest ball court, El Caracol observatory, Platform of Skulls	117km east of Mérida, 2km east of Pisté village; buses from Mérida, Pisté & Valladolid
pyramids, palaces, riotous sculpture featuring masks of rain god Chac	80km south of Mérida; buses from Mérida
temples & towers on superb Caribbean-side site	130km south of Cancún; taxi, walk or cycle from Tulum town
high pyramids with views over rainforest	60km south of Escárcega-Chetumal road; car, tour from Campeche or Chicanná, taxi from Xpujil
towering pyramids in jungle setting	Cobá village, 50km northwest of Tulum; buses from Tulum & Valladolid
Palace of Masks, with 300 Chac masks	104km south of Mérida; buses from Mérida & Uxmal
palaces with elaborate columns & sculpture, including Chac masks	113-122km south of Mérida; car, until bus from Mérida is reinstated
five-story pyramid-palace, Temple of Masks	53km southeast of Campeche; minibuses & shuttle service from Campeche
towered temples	8km west of Xpujil; taxi or car
three-towered ancient 'skyscraper'	Xpujil town, 123km west of Chetumal; buses from Campeche, buses & *colectivos* from Chetumal
huge Acrópolis & high pyramid with unusual carving	23km north of Valladolid by taxi or *colectivo*
semiwild site with palaces & pyramids	85km west of Chetumal; car, or tour from Xpujil
Temple of the Masks	72km west of Chetumal; car, tour from Xpujil, or bus & 8.5km walk/hitchhike

Plan Your Trip

Travel with Children

Best Regions for Kids

Yucatán Peninsula

Cancún, the Riviera Maya and nearby islands are geared to giving vacationers fun. The area is full of great beaches offering every imaginable aquatic activity, hotels designed to make life easy, and attractions from jungle zip-lines to swimming in underwater rivers. Other parts of the peninsula are great if your kids will enjoy exploring Maya ruins.

Central Pacific Coast

The Pacific coast offers all conceivable types of fun in, on and under the ocean and lagoons, and a vast range of places to base yourself, from sophisticated Puerto Vallarta to easygoing Zihuatanejo and countless smaller spots where your time is just yours and your family's.

Mexico City

The capital keeps kids happy with a hands-on children's museum, a first-rate zoo, dedicated kids' entertainment, and parks and plazas full of space and fun.

The sights, sounds and colors of Mexico excite kids just as they do adults – and Mexicans love children. There are lots of child-friendly attractions and activities, and with very few exceptions, children are welcome at all accommodations and almost any cafe or restaurant.

Mexico for Kids

Eating

Children may be less keen to experiment with exciting Mexican flavors than their parents are, but fortunately Mexico has plenty of places serving up familiar international fare. Italian restaurants are plentiful, foods like eggs, steaks, bread, rice and cheese are available everywhere, and fresh fruit is abundant. Simpler Mexican snacks like quesadillas, burritos and tacos, or steaming corn cobs straight from a street cart, are good ways of trying out local flavors. Restaurant staff are accustomed to children and can usually provide high chairs if needed, and prepare something that's not on the menu, if requested.

Sleeping

Mexico has some excitingly different places to stay that will please most kids – anything beachside is a good start, and rustic *cabañas* (cabins) provide a sense of adventure (but choose one with good mosquito nets!). Many hotels have a rambling layout and open-air space – courtyards, pool areas, gardens. The most family-oriented hotels tend to be found on the coasts.

Family rooms are widely available, and most hotels will put an extra bed or two in a room at little extra charge. Baby cots may not be available in budget accommodations. Most accommodations now have wi-fi access, and in the midrange and top end there will often be child-friendly channels on the TV for when your kids just need to flop down in front of a screen.

In this guide the symbol identifies places with particularly family-friendly facilities.

Getting Around

Try to do your traveling in smallish chunks of a few hours. The majority of Mexican buses show nonstop movies on video screens, most of which are family-friendly and help distract kids from a dull trip. Children under 13 pay half-price on many long-distance buses, and if they're small enough to sit on your lap, they usually go for free. If you're traveling with a baby or toddler, consider investing in deluxe buses for the extra space and comfort. Car rental and, on some routes, flying, are alternatives to buses: if you want a car with a child safety seat, the major international rental firms are the most reliable providers.

Children's Highlights

On & in the Water

➡ **Learn to surf** Kids as young as five can take classes at many spots with gentler waves along the Pacific coast, including Mazatlán, Sayulita, Ixtapa, Puerto Escondido and San Agustinillo.

➡ **Spot turtles, dolphins and whales** Boat trips head out from many places along the Pacific coast.

➡ **Snorkel in the Caribbean** Many beaches on the Caribbean coast and islands provide calm waters and colorful marine life for beginners.

➡ **Ride a gondola** Cruise ancient Aztec canals at Xochimilco, Mexico City (p88).

Multi-Adventure

➡ **Parque de Aventuras Barrancas del Cobre** The Copper Canyon Adventure Park's spine-tingling seven zip-lines carry you halfway to the canyon floor from its lip at 2400m. There's rappelling, climbing and a cable car too. (p765)

➡ **Selvática** Award-winning 12-zip-line circuit through the jungle near Cancún, with its own cenote (sinkhole) for swimming. (p275)

➡ **Boca del Puma** Zip-lining, horseback riding and a cenote to dip into, near Puerto Morelos. (p274)

➡ **Hidden Worlds** Zip-lines, sky cycles, rappelling and cenote snorkel tours, 25km south of Playa del Carmen. (p275)

➡ **Cuajimoloyas** Horseback riding, mountain-biking, hiking and a spectacular 900m zip-line, in the mountains near Oaxaca. (p451)

Animals

➡ **Baja whale-watching** See massive gray whales and their calves off the coasts of Baja California (January to March) – usually requires several hours in a boat, so best for older kids. (p714)

➡ **Zoológico de Chapultepec** Mexico City's large zoo has a wide range of the world's creatures in sizable enclosures, including two pandas. (p87)

➡ **La Ventanilla** Take a boat ride through a lagoon full of crocs and release baby turtles into the ocean at this Oaxaca ecotourism scheme. (p477)

➡ **El Refugio de Potosí** Pet a porcupine, hold snakes and tarantulas, and observe parrots, hummingbirds and armadillos. (p556)

➡ **Zoomat** Tuxtla Gutiérrez' zoo has 180 species, all from the state of Chiapas, including several types of big cat. (p348)

➡ **Playa Escobilla** See thousands of turtles crawl out of the ocean in a single night to lay eggs on this Oaxaca beach. (p468)

➡ **Acuario de Veracruz** At Veracruz' aquarium you'll be surrounded by sharks, rays and turtles, and can be lowered in a transparent cage into a pool of feeding sharks. (p208)

Museums & Mines

➡ **Papalote Museo del Niño** There are two of these fun, hands-on, children's museums – one in Mexico City (p87), one in Cuernavaca (p184). Good for kids up to about 11 years old.

HEALTH & SAFETY

Children are more easily affected than adults by heat, disrupted sleeping patterns, changes in altitude and strange food. Take care that they don't drink tap water, be careful to avoid sunburn, cover them up against insect bites, and ensure you replace fluids if a child gets diarrhea.

Don't hesitate to go to a doctor if you think it may be necessary. In general, privately run hospitals and clinics in Mexico offer better facilities and care than public ones. Adequate travel insurance will cover the cost of private medical care.

- **Museo Interactivo de Xalapa** (www.mix.org.mx; Av Murillo Vidal 1735; adult/child M$70/50; ⏲9am-5pm Mon-Fri, 10am-7pm Sat & Sun; 🚸) Themed rooms on science, ecology, art, and an IMAX cinema.
- **Mina El Edén** Take a miniature train into this colonial-era silver mine, then walk past old mineshafts and over subterranean pools. (p689)

Spectacles

- **Voladores (Fliers)** This indigenous Totonac rite involves men climbing up a 30m-high pole, then casting themselves off backward, attached only by ropes. Performed regularly at El Tajín. (p242)
- **Pirate Show** Campeche recalls its pirate-battered past with Disney-esque spectaculars in an old city gate. (p338)
- **Folk dance** Highly colorful, entertaining shows are given regularly by the Ballet Folklórico de México in Mexico City (p124)and several Guelaguetza groups in Oaxaca (p438).

Planning

- When planning your itinerary, bear in mind that few kids like traveling all the time; they're usually happier if they can settle into a place for a while, make friends and get on with some of the things they like doing back home.
- See a doctor about vaccinations at least one month – preferably two – before your trip.
- It's a good idea to book accommodations for at least the first couple of nights.
- Diapers (nappies) and sunscreen are widely available, but you may not easily find wet wipes, other creams, baby foods or familiar medicines outside larger cities and tourist towns.
- Lonely Planet's *Travel with Children* has lots of practical advice on the subject, drawn from firsthand experience.

Documents for Under-18 Travelers

Mexican law requires all minors (under-18s) traveling in or out of Mexico without one or both of their parents to carry notarized written permission from the absent parent(s). At the time of writing, this was only being enforced for Mexican minors leaving the country by air or sea, including those with dual nationality traveling on Mexican documentation such as a Mexican passport. The situation may change, however, and you should check with a Mexican consulate well in advance of travel. The US and Canadian governments recommend that minors traveling without both parents should carry a notarized consent letter in any case.

Regions at a Glance

Mexico City

Museums
Architecture
Food

Museum Mecca

You name it, Mexico City probably has a museum for it: from cutting-edge contemporary art to pre-Hispanic artifacts and antique toys. Make sure to visit the world-class National Anthropology Museum and Frida Kahlo's famed blue house.

Architecture Overload

Few other cities in the world can offer gleaming skyscrapers, colonial palaces and pre-Hispanic ruins all in one fell swoop. In the Centro Histórico alone, more than 1500 buildings are classified as historic monuments.

Focus on Food

Regional Mexican cuisine gets top billing in the capital. As expected in such an extraordinary culinary melting pot, everyone here seems to have an opinion on where you can find, say, the best Guerrero-style *pozole* (a hearty hominy, meat and veg soup) or the tastiest Yucatecan *cochinita pibil* (slow-roasted marinated pork).

p62

Around Mexico City

Food
Ruins
Small-Town Escapes

Regional Specialties

An incredible variety of indigenous ingredients and imported culinary influences combine in complex regional cuisines. Many towns have their own specialty, such as the pasties from the mining villages above Pachuca or Puebla's famed *mole poblano*.

Ancient Architecture

Some of Mexico's most awe-inspiring ruins stand within a few hours of the capital. Teotihuacán, with its stunning Pyramids of the Sun and Moon, is the most famous, but fascinating sites such as Cacaxtla, Xochitécatl, Xochicalco and Cantona can be explored in virtual solitude.

Pueblos Mágicos

With their leafy plazas, traditional crafts and gorgeous colonial edifices, remarkably well-preserved 'magical towns' such as Cuetzalan, Real del Monte, Malinalco and Valle de Bravo provide a perfect escape from the thick air and crowds of the capital.

p140

Veracruz

Archaeological Sites
Ecotourism
Food

Ancient Cultures

Several distinct pre-Hispanic cultures graced Mexico's Gulf coast, and all have left a weighty legacy. Examine the Classic Veracruz ruins of El Tajín with its curious 'niche' pyramid, and the magnificence of Totonac Zempoala, and see the genius of the region's ancient sculptors in Xalapa's Museo de Antropología.

Going Green

A geographic anomaly of rugged volcanoes and unsullied rainforest, the Los Tuxtlas region is working hard to promote Mexico's green credentials with rustic accommodations, off-the-beaten-track hiking opportunities and a nascent tourist infrastructure.

Fish, Glorious Fish

Thanks to the state's 690km-long coastline, fish headlines most Veracruz menus, in particular the spicy mélange known as *huachinango a la veracruzana*. Lining up behind it are the distinctive *moles* of Xico and the gourmet coffee of Coatepec.

p203

Yucatán Peninsula

Diving & Snorkeling
Maya Ruins
Beaches

Into the Blue

With hundreds of kilometers of Caribbean coastline bounded by the world's second-largest barrier reef, the Yucatán is a magnet for divers and snorkelers. Banco Chinchorro is the superstar and the underwater sculpture garden off Cancún provides another unique experience.

Oldies but Goodies

From world-famous Chichén Itzá to virtually unheard-of sites like Ek' Balam, the Yucatán is dotted with spectacular pyramids and temples. Many have a resonating atmosphere that even the loudest tour groups can't diminish.

A Day at the Beach

Finding the right beach for you is simply a matter of hopping on a bus (or boat). From the debauchery of Cancún to lonely Costa Maya beaches like Xcalak, the region's bleach-white sand and beautiful warm water must not be missed.

p255

Chiapas & Tabasco

Culture
Activities
Nature

Temples & Tradition

The world of the Maya lives on everywhere you turn here, from the preserved stone temples of Classic Maya civilization to the persistence of dramatic pre-Hispanic religious rituals and the intricate handwoven textiles and clothing still worn by many.

In Motion

Whether you're rappelling down into a jungle sinkhole, bouncing over a stretch of white water in a rubber raft, or climbing a 4000m volcano, Chiapas has multiple ways to raise your adrenaline levels.

Birds & Beasts

Nesting turtles, roaring monkeys and flashes of rainbow plumage are standard fare in the jungles and on the misty mountains and sandy beaches of this biodiverse region that's full of rare and endangered wildlife.

p345

Oaxaca

Culture
Beaches
Outdoor Activities

Cultural Hub

Oaxaca state is a hub of culture in so many senses: from Oaxaca City's vibrant arts scene and beautiful colonial buildings to the distinctive Oaxacan cuisine and the endlessly inventive handicrafts of the state's indigenous peoples. It all wraps up in a unique and proud Oaxacan regional identity.

Beach Life

With 550km of sandy Pacific strands and wildlife-rich lagoons, Oaxaca's coastline has it all – the pumping surf of Puerto Escondido, the blissed-out traveler scene of Zipolite and Mazunte, and the resort attractions of low-key Bahías de Huatulco.

The Great Outdoors

Hike or ride a horse or mountain bike through the Sierra Norte's mountain forests; surf the Pacific swells; raft rivers from the hills to the sea; snorkel or dive the beautiful Huatulco bays.

p417

Central Pacific Coast

Beaches
Food
Outdoor Activities

Surf & Sand

Conjure up the beach of your dreams and you'll find it here, whether wiggling your toes in the sand with margarita in hand, or chasing perfect waves along an endless ultramarine horizon.

Seafood Heaven

Sidle up to a beachside table at sunset, grab a cold beer and a fresh-cut lime, and settle into a plateful of *pescado zarandeado* (char-broiled fish stuffed with vegetables and spices), *tiritas* (citrus-and-chili-marinated raw fish slivers) or shrimp and red snapper cooked a dozen different ways.

Natural Highs

Kayak across a lagoon at dawn, ride horses into the Sierra Madre, swim among flitting butterflies in a boulder-strewn river, watch pelicans and whales parade through the waves or scan the nighttime sands for nesting mama turtles.

p489

Western Central Highlands

Food
Scenery
Culture

Culinary Feast

There's nowhere better to get a taste of Mexico's amazingly diverse culinary culture: delicious *sopitas* in Colima, pre-Hispanic ingredients brought to life as *alta cocina* (haute cuisine) in Morelia, and Guadalajara's diverse array of contemporary Mexican gourmet restaurants.

Dramatic Scenery

Tiny Colima state packs more of a scenic punch than almost anywhere in the region, with its dramatic twin volcanoes. For more glorious scenery don't miss the modern marvel, Volcán Paricutín, in Michoacán.

Cultural Offerings

The western central highlands groan with indigenous culture, most notably that of the thriving Purépecha people whose arts and crafts are sold around Pátzcuaro. You'll find superb art galleries and history museums in Guadalajara and Morelia, and great shopping for arts and crafts in Tlaquepaque.

p572

Northern Central Highlands

Museums
Food
Towns & Cities

Monumental Museums

Home to fascinating indigenous cultures and most of the silver that brought opulence to colonial grandees, this region was also the birthplace of Mexican independence from Spain. Excellent museums highlight everything from traditional artisanry and historical heroes to contemporary art.

Street & Table Food

The region's cities all have their own takes on classic Mexican bites, whether a trusty tortilla or a 'traditional' taco. Celebrated chefs, especially in San Miguel de Allende and San Luis Potosí, now offer cutting-edge, contemporary and international cuisine.

Pedestrian Paradise

Cobblestone colonial-era streets make for fascinating exploration on foot. Towns here are made for getting lost in – up narrow *callejones* (alleys) or down steep steps. Without doubt, you'll eventually end up on a pretty, laurel-tree-filled plaza.

p632

Baja California

Water Sports
Wine
Scenery

Surfing & Diving

Baja is a paradise for surfers of all levels, with beach, point and reef breaks up and down the Pacific coastline. Divers can do a two-tank dive in the Pacific and be at the natural aquarium of the Sea of Cortez in time for a night dive.

Ruta del Vino

The Valle de Guadalupe is producing the best wines in Mexico and this 'Napa Sur' is now garnering international acclaim. Its Wine Route makes for a great day (or two) out.

Majestic Mountains, Tropical Paradise

Where else in the world is desert just steps away from turquoise lagoons? At every corner are vistas that seem pulled from the pages of a vacation calendar.

p696

Copper Canyon & Northern Mexico

Outdoor Adventures
Cultures
Museums

Great Outdoors

The north is all about topographical overload. An idyllic coastline, vast deserts and dramatic canyons with climates from alpine to subtropical all contribute to a wealth of wildlife and tantalizing hiking and biking options.

Singular Cultures

The mysterious Tarahumara inhabit the Copper Canyon, and the Pacific coast is home to the Seri with their distinctive handicrafts. Chihuahua state is the center of Mexico's largest group of Mennonites, who produce delectable foodstuffs.

Museum Scene

Monterrey's spectacular Parque Fundidora is replete with cultural interest, particularly the Horno3 Museum devoted to steelmaking. In Saltillo you'll find museums focusing on the desert environment, *sarape* textiles and birdlife, while Chihuahua's many impressive offerings include the former residence of Pancho Villa.

p740

On the Road

Mexico City

☎55 / POP 20.1 MILLION / ELEV 2240M

Includes ➡

Best Places to Eat

➡ Pujol (p116)
➡ El Hidalguense (p114)
➡ Maximo Bistrot Local (p115)
➡ Los Cocuyos (p108)
➡ Hostería de Santo Domingo (p109)

Best Places to Stay

➡ Red Tree House (p105)
➡ Casa San Ildefonso (p102)
➡ Villa Condesa (p106)
➡ Casa Comtesse (p105)
➡ Chalet del Carmen (p107)

Why Go?

Much-maligned Mexico City is cleaning up its act these days. Revamped public spaces are springing back to life, the culinary scene is exploding and a cultural renaissance is flourishing. And here's the kicker: by somehow managing to distance itself from the drug war, the nation's capital has emerged as a 'safe haven' of sorts.

Remember that Mexico City is, and has ever been, the sun in the Mexican solar system. A stroll through the buzzing downtown area reveals the capital's storied history, from its pre-Hispanic underpinnings and colonial-era splendor to its contemporary edge. Organized chaos rules in this high-octane megalopolis, yet rest assured that the city offers plenty of escape valves in the way of old-school cantinas, intriguing museums, dramatic murals and boating excursions along ancient canals. With all that and so much more going on, you just might be swayed to scrap those beach plans.

When to Go

Mexico City

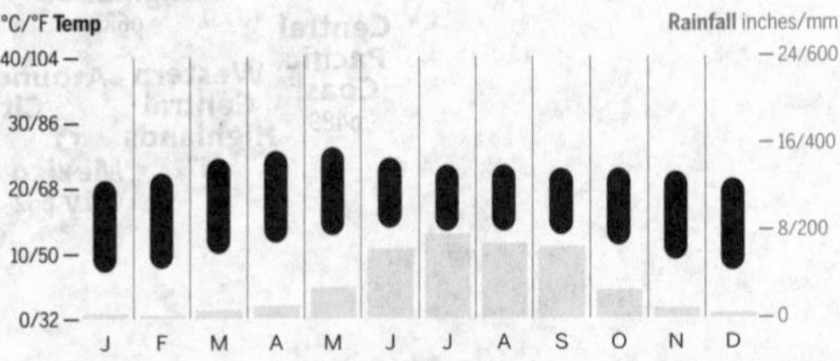

Late Mar–Apr Vacationing *chilangos* clear out for Easter, leaving the city remarkably calm.

Mar The *centro*'s streets become lively stages for cultural events during the Festival de México.

Nov Rainy season ends and the month begins with colorful Day of the Dead festivities.

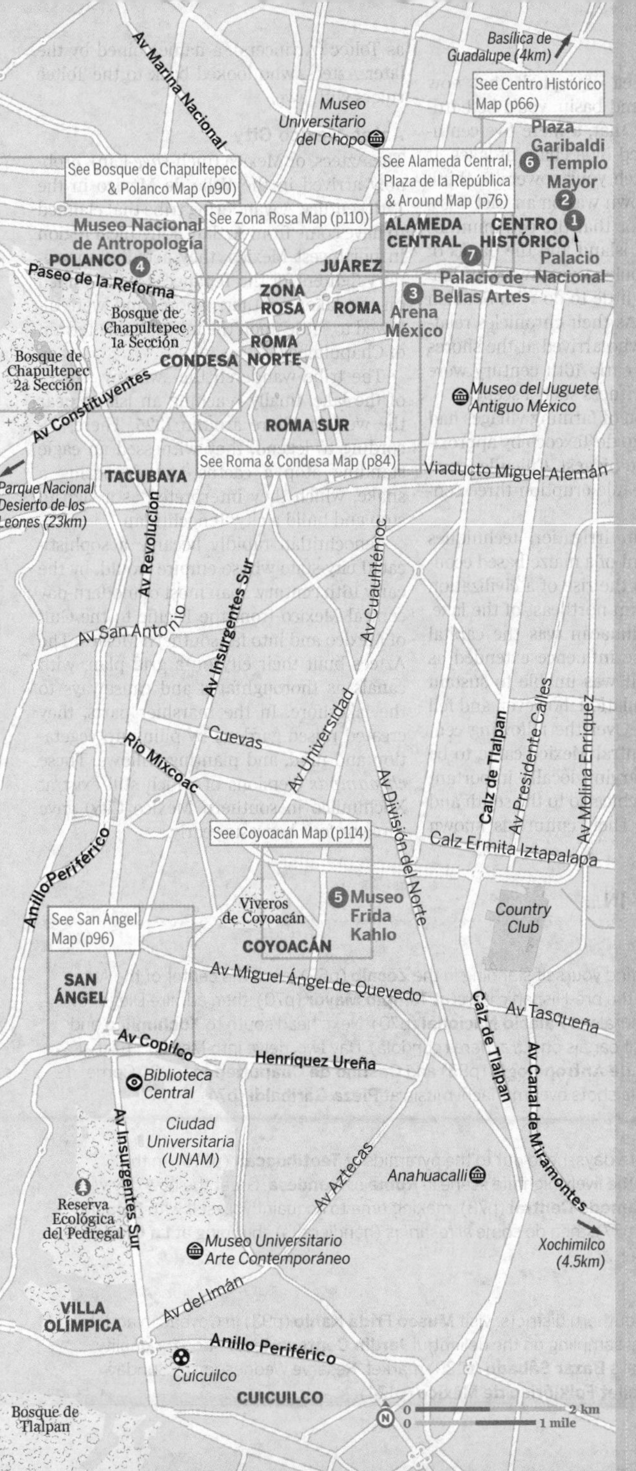

Mexico City Highlights

1. Study Diego Rivera's tableau of Mexican history at **Palacio Nacional** (p70)
2. Marvel at Aztec ruins in the heart of downtown at **Templo Mayor** (p70)
3. Cheer on the masked heroes at the *lucha libre* bouts of **Arena México** (p126)
4. Gaze upon the Aztec sun stone and other superb pre-Hispanic relics at **Museo Nacional de Antropología** (p83)
5. Share Frida's pain at her birthplace, Casa Azul in Coyoacán, now home to the **Museo Frida Kahlo** (p93)
6. Sing along to mariachi ballads in the soulful **Plaza Garibaldi** (p74)
7. Feast your eyes on colorful murals and folkloric dance performances at **Palacio de Bellas Artes** (p77)

History

Driving over the sea of asphalt that now overlays this highland basin, you'd be hard-pressed to imagine that, a mere five centuries ago, it was filled by a chain of lakes. It would further stretch your powers to think that today's downtown was on an islet crisscrossed by canals, or that the communities who inhabited this island and the banks of Lago de Texcoco spoke a patchwork of languages that had as little to do with Spanish as Malay or Urdu. As their chronicles related, the Spaniards who arrived at the shores of that lake in the early 16th century were just as amazed to witness such a scene.

A loose federation of farming villages had evolved around Lago de Texcoco by approximately 200 BC. The biggest, Cuicuilco, was destroyed by a volcanic eruption three centuries later.

Breakthroughs in irrigation techniques and the development of a maize-based economy contributed to the rise of a civilization at Teotihuacán, 40km northeast of the lake. For centuries Teotihuacán was the capital of an empire whose influence extended as far as Guatemala. It was unable to sustain its burgeoning population, however, and fell in the 8th century. Over the following centuries, power in central Mexico came to be divided between varying locally important cities, including Xochicalco to the south and Tula to the north. Their culture is known as Toltec (Artificers), a name coined by the later Aztecs, who looked back to the Toltec rulers with awe.

Aztec Mexico City

The Aztecs, or Mexica (meh-*shee*-kah), probably arrived in the Valle de México in the 13th century. A wandering tribe that claimed to have come from Aztlán, a mythical region in northwest Mexico, they acted as mercenary fighters for the Tepanecas, who resided on the lake's southern shore, and were allowed to settle upon the inhospitable terrain of Chapultepec.

The tribe wandered the swampy fringes of the lake, finally reaching an island near the western shore around 1325. There, according to legend, they witnessed an eagle standing atop a cactus and devouring a snake, which they interpreted as a sign to stop and build a city, Tenochtitlán.

Tenochtitlán rapidly became a sophisticated city-state whose empire would, by the early 16th century, span most of modern-day central Mexico from the Pacific to the Gulf of Mexico and into far southern Mexico. The Aztecs built their city on a grid plan, with canals as thoroughfares and causeways to the lakeshore. In the marshier parts, they created raised gardens by piling up vegetation and mud, and planting willows. These *chinampas* (versions of which still exist at Xochimilco in southern Mexico City) gave three or four harvests yearly.

MEXICO CITY IN...

Two Days

Day one and you find yourself standing in the **Zócalo** (p69), once the center of the Aztec universe. Explore the pre-Hispanic ruins at **Templo Mayor** (p70), then admire Diego Rivera's cinematic murals at **Palacio Nacional** (p70). Next, head south to **Xochimilco** and glide along ancient canals on a *trajinera* (gondola). Day two, delve into Mexico's past at **Museo Nacional de Antropología** (p83) and **Castillo de Chapultepec** (p83). Come nightfall, do tequila shots over mariachi music at **Plaza Garibaldi** (p74).

Four Days

With a couple more days, head out to the pyramids at **Teotihuacán** (p146). In the evening plug into the lively nightlife scene in **Roma** or **Condesa**. Greet the new day with a stroll around **Alameda Central** (p78), making time to acquaint yourself with **Palacio de Bellas Artes** (p77), then do some *artesanías* (handicrafts) shopping at **La Ciudadela** (p79).

One Week

Get to know the southern districts: visit **Museo Frida Kahlo** (p93) in Coyoacán and do dinner and mezcal sampling on the delightful **Jardín Centenario**; or shop for quality crafts at San Ángel's **Bazar Sábado** (p129) market. Reserve Wednesday or Sunday evening for the **Ballet Folklórico de México** (p124).

When the Spanish arrived in 1519, Tenochtitlán's population was between 200,000 and 300,000, while the entire Valle de México had perhaps 1.5 million inhabitants, making it one of the world's densest urban areas.

Capital of Nueva España

So assiduously did the Spanish raze Tenochtitlán that only a handful of structures from the Aztec period remain visible today. Having wrecked the Aztec capital, they set about rebuilding it as their own. Conquistador Hernán Cortés hoped to preserve the arrangement whereby Tenochtitlán siphoned off the bounty of its vassal states.

Ravaged by disease, the Valle de México's population shrank drastically – from 1.5 million to under 100,000 within a century of the conquest. But the city emerged as the prosperous, elegant capital of Nueva España, with broad streets laid over the Aztec causeways and canals.

Building continued through the 17th century, but problems arose as the weighty colonial structures began sinking into the squishy lake bed. Furthermore, lacking natural drainage, the city suffered floods caused by the partial destruction in the 1520s of the Aztecs' canals. One torrential rain in 1629 left the city submerged for five years.

Urban conditions improved in the 18th century as new plazas and avenues were installed, along with sewage and garbage-collection systems. This was Mexico City's gilded age.

Independence

On October 30, 1810, some 80,000 independence rebels, fresh from victory at Guanajuato, overpowered Spanish loyalist forces west of the capital. However, they were ill-equipped to capitalize on this triumph, and their leader, Miguel Hidalgo, chose not to advance on the city – a decision that cost Mexico 11 more years of fighting before independence was achieved.

Following the reform laws established by President Benito Juárez in 1859, monasteries and churches were appropriated by the government, then sold off, subdivided and put to other uses. During his brief reign (1864–67), Emperor Maximilian laid out the Calzada del Emperador (today's Paseo de la Reforma) to connect Bosque de Chapultepec with the center.

Mexico City entered the modern age under the despotic Porfirio Díaz, who ruled Mexico for most of the years between 1876 and 1911. Díaz ushered in a construction boom, building Parisian-style mansions and theaters, while the city's wealthier residents escaped the center for newly minted neighborhoods toward the west.

Modern Megalopolis

After Díaz fell in 1911, the Mexican Revolution brought war, hunger and disease to the streets of Mexico City. Following the Great Depression, a drive to industrialize attracted more money and people.

Mexico City continued to mushroom in the 1970s, as the rural poor sought economic refuge in its thriving industries, and the metropolitan area population surged from 8.7 to 14.5 million. Unable to contain the new arrivals, Mexico City spread beyond the bounds of the Distrito Federal (DF; Federal District) and into the adjacent state of México. The result of such unbridled growth was some of the world's worst traffic and pollution. At last count, the Greater Mexico City area had more than 20 million inhabitants.

For seven decades, the federal government ruled the DF directly, with presidents appointing 'regents' to head notoriously corrupt administrations. Finally, in 1997, the DF gained political autonomy. In 2000 Andrés Manuel López Obrador, of the left-leaning PRD (Party of the Democratic Revolution), was elected mayor. *Capitalinos* (capital-city residents) approved of 'AMLO.' His initiatives included an ambitious makeover of the *centro histórico* and the construction of an overpass for the city's ring road.

While López Obrador was narrowly defeated in the presidential election of 2006 (an outcome he fiercely contested based on fraud allegations), his former police chief Marcelo Ebrard won a sweeping victory in Mexico City, consolidating the PRD's grip on the city government. The PRD has passed a flood of progressive initiatives, including same-sex marriage and the legalization of abortion and euthanasia. In 2012 Ebrard passed the reins to his former attorney general, Miguel Ángel Mancera, who won the Mexico City mayoral race with more than 60% of the vote. Mancera supports a proposal to decriminalize and regulate marijuana consumption, a measure that is gaining traction in the DF.

Sights

You could spend months exploring all the museums, monuments, plazas, colonial buildings, monasteries, murals, galleries,

Centro Histórico

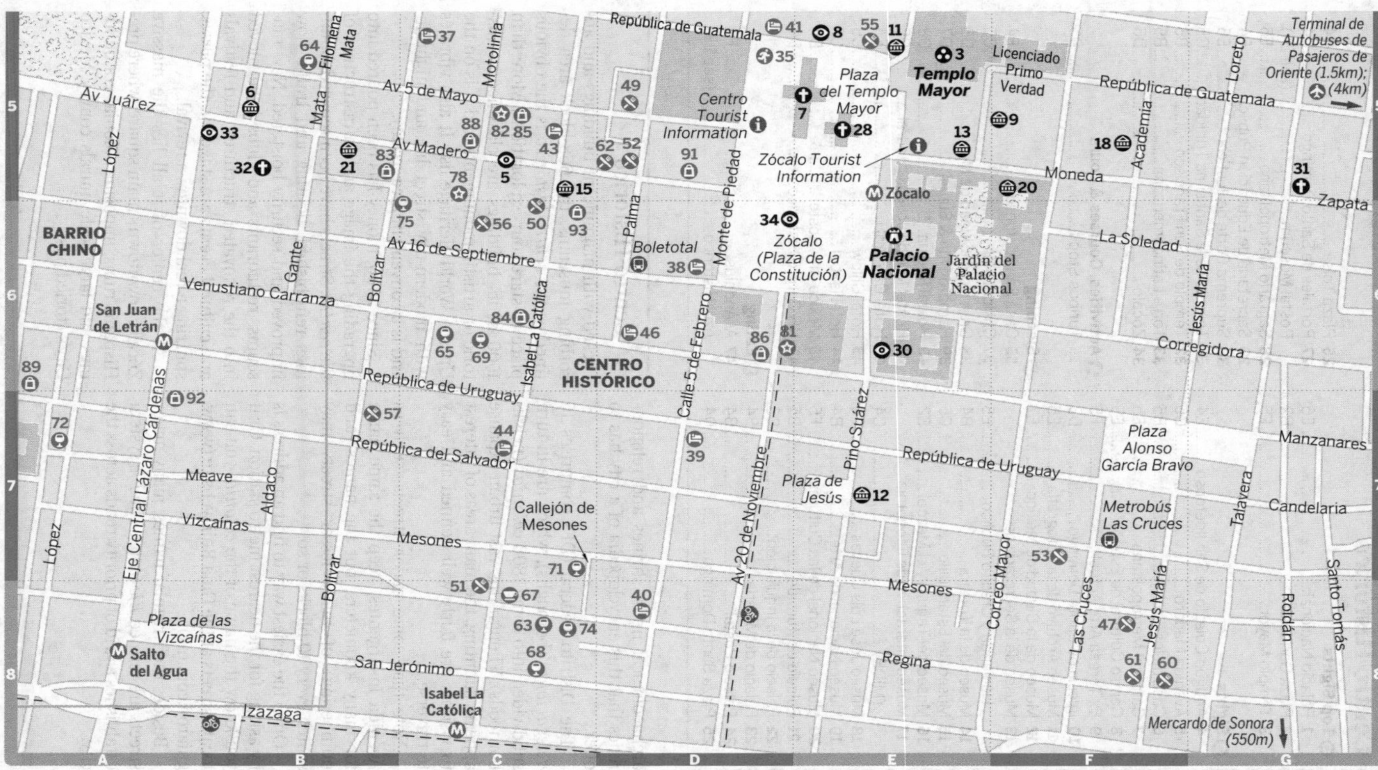
República de Guatemala
Terminal de Autobuses de Pasajeros de Oriente (1.5km); (4km)
Licenciado Primo Verdad
Templo Mayor
Plaza del Templo Mayor
Centro Tourist Information
Zócalo Tourist Information
Loreto
Academia
Moneda
Zapata
Av Juárez
Av 5 de Mayo
Motolinía
Filomena Mata
Mata
López
Av Madero
Palma
Monte de Piedad
Zócalo
Zócalo (Plaza de la Constitución)
Palacio Nacional
Jardín del Palacio Nacional
La Soledad
BARRIO CHINO
Av 16 de Septiembre
Boletotal
Gante
Bolívar
Venustiano Carranza
Isabel La Católica
San Juan de Letrán
Calle 5 de Febrero
Jesús María
Corregidora
CENTRO HISTÓRICO
República de Uruguay
República del Salvador
Pino Suárez
Plaza Alonso García Bravo
Manzanares
Eje Central Lázaro Cárdenas
Meave
Aldaco
Callejón de Mesones
Av 20 de Noviembre
Plaza de Jesús
Metrobús Las Cruces
Talavera
Candelaria
Vizcaínas
Mesones
Correo Mayor
Las Cruces
Roldán
Santo Tomás
Plaza de las Vizcaínas
Salto del Agua
San Jerónimo
Regina
Isabel La Católica
Izazaga
Mercardo de Sonora (550m)
A
B
C
D
E
F
G
5
6
7
8

Centro Histórico

Top Sights
1 Palacio Nacional ... E6
2 Plaza Garibaldi ... B2
3 Templo Mayor ... E5

Sights
4 Antiguo Colegio de San Ildefonso ... E4
5 Avenida Madero ... C5
6 Casa de los Azulejos ... B5
7 Catedral Metropolitana ... E5
8 Centro Cultural de España ... E5
9 Ex Teresa Arte Actual ... F5
10 Iglesia de Santo Domingo ... D3
11 Museo Archivo de la Fotografía ... E5
12 Museo de la Ciudad de México ... E7
13 Museo de la Secretaría de Hacienda y Crédito Público ... E5
14 Museo de la Tortura ... B4
15 Museo del Estanquillo ... C5
16 Museo del Tequila y el Mezcal ... B2
17 Museo Interactivo de Economía (MIDE) ... C4
18 Museo José Luis Cuevas ... F5
19 Museo Nacional de Arte ... B4
20 Museo Nacional de las Culturas ... F5
21 Palacio de Iturbide ... B5
22 Palacio de la Inquisición ... D3
23 Palacio de Minería ... B4
24 Palacio Postal ... B4
25 Plaza Santo Domingo ... D4
26 Plaza Tolsá ... B4
27 Portales de Santo Domingo ... D4
Postal Museum ... (see 24)
28 Sagrario Metropolitano ... E5
29 Secretaría de Educación Pública ... E4
30 Suprema Corte de Justicia ... E6
31 Templo de la Santísima Trinidad ... G5
32 Templo de San Francisco ... B5
33 Torre Latinoamericana ... B5
34 Zócalo ... D6

Activities, Courses & Tours
35 Turibús Stop ... D5

Sleeping
36 Casa San Ildefonso ... F4
37 Chillout Flat ... C5
38 Gran Hotel Ciudad de México ... D6
39 Hampton Inn & Suites ... D7
40 Hostal Regina ... D8
41 Hostel Mundo Joven Catedral ... D5
42 Hotel Catedral ... E4
43 Hotel Gillow ... C5
44 Hotel Isabel ... C7
45 Mexico City Hostel ... D4
46 NH Centro Histórico ... D6

Eating
47 Al Andalus ... F8
Azul Histórico ... (see 93)

archaeological finds, shrines and religious relics that this encyclopedia of a city has to offer.

The Distrito Federal (DF) comprises 16 *delegaciones* (boroughs), which are in turn subdivided into some 1800 *colonias* (neighborhoods). Though this vast urban expanse appears daunting, the main areas of interest to visitors are fairly well defined and easy to traverse.

Note that some major streets, such as Avenida Insurgentes, keep the same name for many kilometers, but the names (and numbering) of many lesser streets may switch every 10 blocks or so.

Often the easiest way to find an address is by asking for the nearest metro station. Or if you know the name of the *colonia*, you can locate streets at the Guia Roji website (www.guiaroji.com.mx).

Besides their regular names, many major streets are termed *Eje* (axis). The *Eje* system establishes a grid of priority roads across the city.

Centro Histórico

Packed with magnificent buildings and absorbing museums, the 668-block area defined as the *centro histórico* is the obvious place to start your explorations. More than 1500 of its buildings are classified as historic or artistic monuments and it is on the Unesco World Heritage list. It also vibrates with modern-day street life and nightlife, and is a convenient area to stay.

Since 2000, money has been poured into upgrading the image and infrastructure of the *centro*. Streets have been repaved, buildings refurbished, lighting and traffic flow improved and security bolstered. New museums, restaurants and clubs have moved into the renovated structures, and festivals and cultural events are staged in the plazas, spurring a real downtown revival.

At the center of it all lies the massive Zócalo, downtown's main square, where pre-Hispanic ruins, imposing colonial-era buildings and large-scale murals convey Mexico City's storied past.

48 Café de Tacuba C4
49 Café El Popular D5
50 Casino Español C6
51 Coox Hanal C8
52 El Cardenal D5
53 Helus F7
54 Hostería de Santo Domingo D3
55 La Casa de las Sirenas E5
56 La Casa del Pavo C6
57 Los Cocuyos B7
58 Los Girasoles B4
59 Mercado San Camilito B2
60 Restaurante Chon F8
61 Taquería Los Paisas F8
62 Vegetariano Madero D5

Drinking & Nightlife

63 Al Andar C8
64 Bar La Ópera B5
65 Bar Mancera C6
66 Bar Oasis B3
67 Café Jekemir C8
Downtown Mexico .... (see 93)
68 Hostería La Bota C8
69 La Faena C6
70 La Purísima B4
71 La Risa C7
72 Las Duelistas A7
73 Marrakech Salón B4
74 Mexicano C8
75 Salón Corona C6

Entertainment

76 Arena Coliseo D3
Centro Cultural de España .... (see 8)
77 La Perla C4
78 Pasagüero + La Bipo C5
79 Salón Tenampa B2
80 Teatro de la Ciudad C4
81 Ticketmaster Liverpool Centro D6
Ticketmaster Mixup Centro .... (see 15)
82 Zinco Jazz Club C5

Shopping

83 American Bookstore B5
84 Casasola Fotografía C6
85 Dulcería de Celaya C5
86 El Palacio de Hierro D6
87 Galería Eugenio C2
88 Gandhi C5
89 La Europea A6
90 La Lagunilla C1
Liverpool .... (see 81)
91 Mumedi D5
92 Plaza de la Computación y Electrónica A7
93 Plaza Downtown Mexico C6
94 Tepito F1

Zócalo PLAZA

(Map p66; Plaza de la Constitución, Colonia Centro; Ⓜ Zócalo) The heart of Mexico City is the Plaza de la Constitución. Residents began calling it the Zócalo, meaning 'base,' in the 19th century, when plans for a major monument to independence went unrealized, leaving only the pedestal. Measuring 220m from north to south, and 240m from east to west, it's one of the world's largest city squares.

The ceremonial center of Aztec Tenochtitlán, known as the Teocalli, lay immediately northeast of the Zócalo. In the 1520s Cortés paved the plaza with stones from the ruins of the complex. In the 18th century, the Zócalo was given over to a maze of market stalls until it was dismantled by Santa Anna, who placed the unfinished monument in its center.

Today, the Zócalo is home to the powers that be. On its east side is the Palacio Nacional (the presidential palace), on the north the Catedral Metropolitana, and on the south the city government offices. Jewelry shops and extravagant hotels line the arcade known as the Portal de Mercaderes on the plaza's west side.

As you emerge from metro Zócalo onto the vast central plaza, you may hear the booming of drums from the direction of the cathedral – the Aztec dancers are doing their thing. Wearing snakeskin loincloths, elaborately feathered headdresses and shell ankle bracelets, they move in a circle and chant in Náhuatl. At the center, engulfed in a cloud of fragrant copal smoke, drummers bang on the congalike *huehuetl* (indigenous drum) and the barrel-shaped, slitted *teponaztli*.

Variously known as Danzantes Aztecas, Danza Chichimeca or Concheros, the dancers perform their ritual daily in the plaza. It is meant to evoke the Aztec *mitote*, a frenzied ceremony performed by pre conquest Mexicans at harvest times. Yet scant evidence exists that the dancers' moves bear any resemblance to those of their forebears.

The square has variously served as a forum for mass protests, free concerts, a human chessboard, a gallery of spooky Día de Muertos (Day of the Dead) altars and an ice-skating rink. It's even been a canvas for photo artist Spencer Tunick, who filled the square with 18,000 nude Mexicans in May 2007.

The huge Mexican flag flying in the middle of the Zócalo is ceremonially raised at 8am by soldiers of the Mexican army, then lowered at 6pm.

★Templo Mayor ARCHAEOLOGICAL SITE

(Map p66; ☎55-4040-5600; www.templomayor.inah.gob.mx; Seminario 8; admission M$57, audio guide M$80; ⏲9am-5pm Tue-Sun; Ⓜ Zócalo) Before the Spaniards demolished it, the Teocalli of Tenochtitlán covered the site where the cathedral now stands, as well as the blocks to its north and east. It wasn't until 1978, after electricity workers happened on an 8-ton stone-disc carving of the Aztec goddess Coyolxauhqui, that the decision was taken to demolish colonial buildings and excavate the Templo Mayor.

The temple is thought to be on the exact spot where the Aztecs saw their symbolic eagle, perching on a cactus with a snake in its beak – the symbol of Mexico today. In Aztec belief this was, literally, the center of the universe.

Like other sacred buildings in Tenochtitlán, the temple was enlarged several times, with each rebuilding accompanied by the sacrifice of captured warriors. What we see today are sections of the temple's seven different phases. At the center is a platform dating from about 1400; on its southern half, a sacrificial stone stands in front of a shrine to Huizilopochtli, the Aztec war god. On the northern half is a chac-mool (a Maya reclining figure) before a shrine to the water god, Tláloc. By the time the Spanish arrived, a 40m-high double pyramid towered above this spot, with steep twin stairways climbing to shrines of the two gods.

The entrance to the temple site and museum is east of the cathedral, across the hectic **Plaza del Templo Mayor**. Authorized tour guides (with Sectur ID) offer their services by the entrance. Alternatively, rent an audio guide – available in English.

The on-site **Museo del Templo Mayor** (included in the site's admission price) houses a model of Tenochtitlán and artifacts from the site, and gives a good overview of Aztec, aka Mexica, civilization. Pride of place is given to the great wheel-like stone of Coyolxauhqui (She of Bells on her Cheek), best viewed from the top-floor vantage point. She is shown decapitated, the result of her murder by Huizilopochtli, her brother, who also killed his 400 brothers en route to becoming top god.

Ongoing excavation continues to turn up major pieces. Just west of the temple, a monolithic stone carved with the image of Tlaltecuhtli, the goddess of earth fertility, was unearthed in October 2006 and is now prominently displayed on the museum's 1st floor.

Another key find was made in 2011 when a ceremonial platform dating from 1469 was uncovered. Based on historical documents, archaeologists believe the 15m structure was used to cremate Aztec rulers. A recent dig also turned up what may be the trunk of a sacred tree found at a newly discovered burial site at the foot of the temple. Now more than ever, researchers feel they are inching closer to the first discovery of an Aztec emperor's tomb.

★Palacio Nacional PALACE

(National Palace; Map p66; ☎55-3688-1255; www.historia.palacionacional.info; Plaza de la Constitución; ⏲10am-5pm; Ⓜ Zócalo) FREE Inside this grandiose colonial palace you'll see Diego Rivera murals (painted between 1929 and 1951) that depict Mexican civilization from the arrival of Quetzalcóatl (the Aztec plumed serpent god) to the post-revolutionary period. The nine murals covering the north and east walls of the first level above the patio chronicle indigenous life before the Spanish conquest.

The Palacio Nacional is also home to the offices of the president of Mexico and the Federal Treasury.

The first palace on this spot was built by Aztec emperor Moctezuma II in the early 16th century. Cortés destroyed the palace in 1521, rebuilding it as a fortress with three interior courtyards. In 1562 the crown purchased the building from Cortés' family to house the viceroys of Nueva España, a function it served until Mexican independence.

As you face the palace, high above the center door hangs the **Campana de Dolores**, the bell rung in the town of Dolores Hidalgo by Padre Miguel Hidalgo in 1810 at the start of the War of Independence. From the balcony underneath it, the president delivers the *grito* (shout) – ¡Viva México! – on the evening of September 15 to commemorate independence.

Catedral Metropolitana CATHEDRAL
(Metropolitan Cathedral; Map p66; Plaza de la Constitución; bell tower admission M$20; ⏲cathedral 8am-8pm, bell tower 10:30am-6pm; Ⓜ Zócalo) FREE Mexico City's most iconic structure, this cathedral is a monumental edifice: 109m long, 59m wide and 65m high. Started in 1573, it remained a work in progress during the entire colonial period, thus displaying a catalog of architectural styles, with successive generations of builders striving to incorporate the innovations of the day.

Original architect Claudio Arciniega modeled the building after Seville's seven-nave cathedral, but after running into difficulties with the spongy subsoil he scaled it down to a five-nave design of vaults on semicircular arches. The baroque portals facing the Zócalo, built in the 17th century, have two levels of columns and marble panels with bas-reliefs. The central panel shows the Assumption of the Virgin Mary, to whom the cathedral is dedicated. The upper levels of the towers, with unique bell-shaped tops, were added in the late 18th century. The exterior was completed in 1813, when architect Manuel Tolsá added the clock tower – topped by statues of Faith, Hope and Charity – and a great central dome.

The first thing you notice upon entering is the elaborately carved and gilded Altar de Perdón (Altar of Forgiveness). There's invariably a line of worshippers at the foot of the Señor del Veneno (Lord of the Poison), the dusky Christ figure on the right. Legend has it that the figure attained its color when it miraculously absorbed a dose of poison through its feet from the lips of a clergyman to whom an enemy had administered the lethal substance.

The cathedral's chief artistic treasure is the gilded 18th-century **Altar de los Reyes** (Altar of the Kings), behind the main altar. Fourteen richly decorated chapels line the two sides of the building, while intricately carved late-17th-century wooden choir stalls by Juan de Rojas occupy the central nave. Enormous painted panels by colonial masters Juan Correa and Cristóbal de Villalpando cover the walls of the sacristy, the first component of the cathedral to be built.

Visitors may wander freely, though you're asked not to do so during Mass. A donation

MEXICO CITY FOR CHILDREN

As with elsewhere in Mexico, kids take center stage in the capital. Many theaters, including the Centro Cultural del Bosque (p124), stage children's plays and puppet shows on weekends and during school holidays. Animated movies are a staple at cinemas around town, though keep in mind that children's films are usually dubbed in Spanish.

Museums frequently organize hands-on activities for kids. The Museo de la Secretaría de Hacienda y Crédito Público (p74) often stages puppet shows on Sunday.

Mexico City's numerous parks and plazas are usually buzzing with kids' voices. **Bosque de Chapultepec** is the obvious destination, and then there are the Papalote Museo del Niño (p87), La Feria (p87) and the Zoológico de Chapultepec (p87), not to mention several lakes with rowboat rentals. Also consider Condesa's **Parque México**, where kids can rent bikes, and where Sunday is family activities day. Plaza Hidalgo (p94) in Coyoacán is another fun-filled spot with balloons, street mimes and cotton candy.

In **Xochimilco** kids find riding the gondolas through the canals as magical as any theme park. Also in this part of town is the Museo Dolores Olmedo (p89), where peacocks and pre-Hispanic dogs occupy the gardens, and children's shows are performed in the patio on Saturday and Sunday at 1pm. The museum also offers workshops for children.

Another great option is the Museo del Juguete Antiguo México (p104), a fascinating toy museum with more than 60,000 collectibles on display.

For more on activities for children, see the 'Infantiles' section at the Conaculta website (www.mexicoescultura.com).

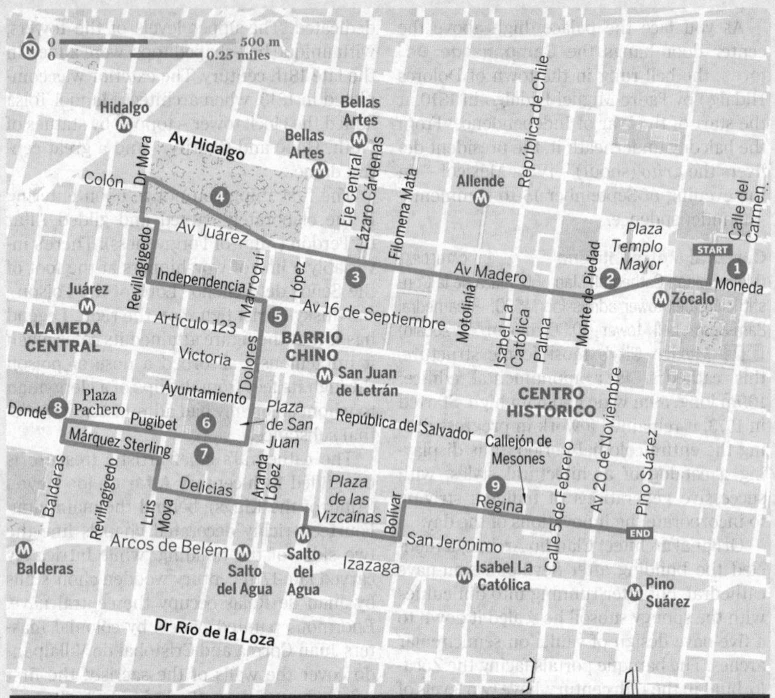

City Walk
Goin' Downtown

START EX TERESA ARTE ACTUAL
END REGINA CORRIDOR
LENGTH 5KM; THREE HOURS

Nothing beats wandering to fully appreciate the *centro*'s rich history.

Kick things off in the 17th-century **1 Ex Teresa Arte Actual** (p74) building. If there's one place that can put the whole sinking-city phenomenon into perspective, it's here.

As you cross the **2 Zócalo** (p69), one of the world's largest squares, stop and contemplate that the surrounding buildings sit atop Aztec temples, and that some of the imposing colonial structures were built with materials from the pre-Hispanic ruins.

Continue walking west along the bustling Avenida Madero to reach the iconic **3 Torre Latinoamericana** (p75) skyscraper. To get a feel for just how far Mexico City's concave valley spans, take in the panoramic view from the observation deck.

Next spend time strolling **4 Alameda Central** (p78), downtown's newly renovated park with fun fountains and a famous Diego Rivera mural on the west end.

Cut across Avenida Juárez to Calle Dolores and drop by **5 El Tío Pepe** for a beer or tequila. It's one of the city's oldest cantinas.

Head south along Dolores to **6 Mercado San Juan** (p127), a 60-year-old market frequented by chefs and devout foodies. Inside, look for **7 Gastrónomico San Juan** for wonderful deli treats and complimentary wine.

Exit the market on Pugibet and go west to Balderas to find **8 Centro de Artesanías la Ciudadela** (p127), a large crafts market with decent prices and great variety.

Return to the heart of downtown walking east until you hit the **9 Regina corridor**, a happening pedestrian thoroughfare. There you can rest at one of several sidewalk *mezcalerías*. Or if you prefer, cap off the walk at a nearby *pulque* joint on the corner of Mesones and Callejón de Mesones, a soulful little spot that's been pouring the viscous fermented beverage for more than a century. ¡*Salud*!

is requested to enter the sacristy or choir, where docents provide commentary, and you can climb the **bell tower**. Mexico City's archbishop conducts Mass at noon on Sundays.

Adjoining the east side of the cathedral is the 18th-century **Sagrario Metropolitano** (Map p66; ⏲8am-6:30pm). Originally built to house the archives and vestments of the archbishop, it is now the city's main parish church. Its front entrance and mirror-image eastern portal are superb examples of the ultradecorative Churrigueresque style.

Centro Cultural de España CULTURAL BUILDING
(Spanish Cultural Center; Map p66; www.ccemx.org; República de Guatemala 18; ⏲cultural center 10am-9pm Tue-Sun, museum 11am-7pm; Ⓜ Zócalo) FREE Always has a variety of cutting-edge art exhibitions going on. In the basement you'll find the **Museo de Sitio**, an interesting museum with the remains of 'El Calmécac,' a school where children of Aztec nobility received religious and military training during the reigns of Emperors Ahuízotl and Moctezuma II. It was built between 1486 and 1502.

Also in the museum are various artifacts unearthed as the cultural center was being expanded between 2006 and 2008, including several 2.4m-tall pre-Hispanic *almenas* (spiral-shaped decorative pieces), colonial-era ceramic objects and a weathered 20th-century handgun.

The cultural center's splendidly restored colonial building, which conquistador Hernán Cortés once awarded to his butler, has a cool terrace bar that stages live music and DJ sets Wednesday to Saturday from 10pm.

Museo Archivo de la Fotografía MUSEUM
(Photographic Archive Museum; Map p66; ☎55-2616-7057; www.cultura.df.gob.mx/index.php/recintos-menu/museos/maf; República de Guatemala 34; ⏲10am-6pm Tue-Sun; Ⓜ Zócalo) FREE Occupying a 16th-century colonial building, the city's photo museum hosts changing exhibits focusing on all things Mexico City. Additionally, the museum has amassed a vast archive comprising a century's worth of urban images.

Plaza Tolsá PLAZA
(Map p66; Ⓜ Bellas Artes) Several blocks west of the Zócalo is this handsome square, named after Manuel Tolsá, the late-18th-century sculptor and architect who completed the Catedral Metropolitana. He also created the bronze equestrian statue of the Spanish king Carlos IV (who reigned from 1788 to 1808), which is the plaza's centerpiece. It originally stood in the Zócalo.

Unfortunately, a botched restoration job using a nitric acid solution recently left part of the statue's surface badly damaged. King Carlos rides in front of the **Museo Nacional de Arte** (National Art Museum; Map p66; ☎55-5130-3400; www.munal.gob.mx; Tacuba 8; admission M$37, Sun free; ⏲10am-5:30pm Tue-Sun; Ⓜ Bellas Artes). Built around 1900 in the style of an Italian Renaissance palace, the museum holds collections representing every school of Mexican art until the early 20th century. A highlight is the work of José María Velasco, depicting the Valle de México in the late 19th century.

Opposite is the **Palacio de Minería** (Palace of Mining; Map p66; ☎55-5623-2982; www.palaciomineria.unam.mx; Tacuba 5; tours M$30; ⏲tours 11am & 1pm Sat & Sun; Ⓜ Bellas Artes), where mining engineers were trained in the 19th century. Today it houses a branch of the national university's engineering department. A neoclassical masterpiece, the palace was designed by Tolsá and built between 1797 and 1813. Visits are by guided tour only. The palace contains four meteorites that struck northern Mexico, one weighing more than 14 tons. There's also a museum on Tolsá's life and work.

Palacio Postal HISTORIC BUILDING
(Map p66; www.palaciopostal.gob.mx; Tacuba 1; ⏲8am-8pm Mon-Fri, 9am-3pm Sat & Sun; Ⓜ Bellas Artes) FREE More than just Mexico City's central post office, this early-20th-century palace is an Italianate confection designed by the Palacio de Bellas Artes' original architect, Adamo Boari. The beige stone facade features baroque columns and carved filigree around the windows; the bronze railings on the monumental staircase inside were cast in Florence.

The small **Postal Museum** (Map p66; ⏲9am-6pm Tue-Fri, to 3pm Sat & Sun; Ⓜ Bellas Artes) FREE, on the 1st floor, is where philatelists can ogle at a design of the first stamp ever issued in Mexico.

Museo Interactivo de Economía (MIDE) MUSEUM
(Interactive Museum of Economics; Map p66; ☎55-5130-4600; www.mide.org.mx; Tacuba 17; admission M$60; ⏲9am-6pm Tue-Sun; Ⓜ Allende) The former hospital of the Bethlehemites religious order has been the home of this museum since 2006. A slew of hands-on

exhibits are aimed at breaking down economic concepts. For coin connoisseurs, the highlight is the Banco de México's numismatic collection.

Museo de la Tortura MUSEUM

(Museum of Torture; Map p66; Tacuba 15; admission adult/child 7-13yr M$60/45; ⏲10am-6pm Mon-Fri, to 7pm Sat & Sun; Ⓜ Allende) Displaying European torture instruments from the 14th to 19th centuries, including a metal-spiked interrogation chair and the menacing skull splitter, this museum has surefire appeal to the morbidly curious.

Museo de la Secretaría de Hacienda y Crédito Público MUSEUM

(Finance Secretariat Museum; Map p66; ☎55-3668-1657; www.facebook.com/culturashcp; Moneda 4; ⏲10am-5pm Tue-Sun; Ⓜ Zócalo) FREE Sure, the name is a tough sell (yay, let's go to the Finance Secretariat Museum!), but it's actually a very interesting place. The museum shows off works from its collection of more than 30,000 pieces of Mexican art, much of it contributed by painters and sculptors in lieu of paying taxes.

Built in the 16th century, this former colonial archbishop's palace also hosts a full program of cultural events (many free), from puppet shows to chamber music recitals. The building sits atop the Templo de Tezcatlipoca, a temple dedicated to an Aztec god often associated with night, death and change through conflict. You'll see the temple's stairs just off the recently renovated main patio.

★**Plaza Garibaldi** PLAZA

(Map p66; cnr Eje Central Lázaro Cárdenas & República de Honduras; mariachi song M$130-150; Ⓟ; Ⓜ Garibaldi) Every night the city's mariachi bands belt out heartfelt ballads in this festive square. Wearing silver-studded outfits, they toot their trumpets and tune their guitars until approached by someone who'll pay for a song. Also roaming Garibaldi are white-clad *son jarocho* groups, hailing from Veracruz, and *norteño* combos, who bang out northern-style folk tunes.

The notoriously seedy Garibaldi got a recent makeover that included heightened security, but it's still rough around the edges. The latest addition to the plaza is the **Museo del Tequila y el Mezcal** (Map p66; www.mutemgaribaldi.mx; Plaza Garibaldi; admission M$50; ⏲1-10pm Sun-Wed, to 11:30pm Thu-Sat; Ⓜ Garibaldi), which has exhibits explaining the origins and production process of Mexico's two most popular distilled agave drinks. The tour ends with a tasting on a rooftop bar overlooking the plaza. An on-site store sells some decent, albeit overpriced, tequilas and mezcals.

Ex Teresa Arte Actual MUSEUM

(Map p66; www.exteresa.bellasartes.gob.mx; Licenciado Verdad 8; ⏲10am-5pm; Ⓜ Zócalo) FREE Mexico City was built atop a sloshy lake bed and it's sinking fast, as evidenced by this teetering former convent. The 17-century building now serves as a museum for performance art, contemporary exhibits, concerts and the occasional movie screening.

Avenida Madero STREET

This stately avenue west of the Zócalo boasts a veritable catalog of architectural styles.

Housed in a gorgeous neoclassical building two blocks from the square, **Museo del Estanquillo** (Map p66; ☎55-5521-3052; www.museodelestanquillo.com; Isabel La Católica 26; ⏲10am-6pm Wed-Mon; Ⓜ Allende) FREE contains the vast pop-culture collection amassed over the decades by DF essayist and pack rat Carlos Monsivais. The museum illustrates various phases in the capital's development by means of the numerous photos, paintings and movie posters from the collection.

Palacio de Iturbide (Palacio de Cultura Banamex; Map p66; ☎55-1226-0091; www.fomentoculturalbanamex.org; Av Madero 17; ⏲10am-7pm; Ⓜ Allende) FREE, with its late-18th-century baroque facade, is a few blocks westward. Built for colonial nobility, in 1821 this became the residence of General Agustín Iturbide, a Mexican independence hero who was proclaimed emperor here in 1822. (He abdicated less than a year later, after General Santa Anna announced the birth of a republic.) Also known as Palacio Cultural Banamex, it hosts exhibits drawn from the bank's extensive art collection.

Half a block past the pedestrian corridor Gante stands the amazing **Casa de los Azulejos** (House of Tiles; Map p66; ☎55-5512-9820; Av Madero 4; ⏲7am-1am; Ⓜ Allende). Dating from 1596, it was built for the Condes (Counts) del Valle de Orizaba. Most of the tiles that adorn the outside walls were produced in China and shipped to Mexico on the Manila *naos* (Spanish galleons used until the early 19th century). The building now houses a Sanborns restaurant in a covered courtyard around a Moorish fountain. The staircase has a 1925 mural by Orozco.

Across the way, the **Templo de San Francisco** (Map p66; Av Madero 7; ⊙8am-8pm) is a remnant of the vast Franciscan monastery erected in the early 16th century over the site of Moctezuma's private zoo. In its heyday it extended two blocks south and east. The monastic complex was divvied up under the postindependence reform laws; in 1949 it was returned to the Franciscan order in a deplorable state and subsequently restored. The elaborately carved doorway is a shining example of 18th-century baroque. Open-air art exhibitions are held in the adjoining atrium.

Rising alongside the monastery, the **Torre Latinoamericana** (Latin American Tower; Map p66; ☎55-5518-7423; www.torrelatino.com; Eje Central Lázaro Cárdenas 2; admission adult/child M$70/60; ⊙9am-10pm; Ⓜ Bellas Artes) was Latin America's tallest building when constructed in 1956. Thanks to the deep-seated pylons that anchor the building, it has withstood several major earthquakes. If you want to learn more about the construction of the tower and downtown's centuries-long development, a museum on the 38th floor houses a permanent photo exhibit. Up above, views from the 41st-floor lounge bar and the 44th-floor observation deck are spectacular, smog permitting. Admission is free if you're just visiting the bar.

Museo Nacional de las Culturas MUSEUM
(National Museum of Cultures; Map p66; ☎55-5512-7452; www.museodelasculturas.mx; Moneda 13; ⊙10am-5pm Tue-Sun; Ⓜ Zócalo) FREE Constructed in 1567 as the colonial mint, this renovated museum exhibits art, dress and handicrafts of the world's cultures; however, there's no explanatory text in English.

Templo de la Santísima Trinidad CHURCH
(Map p66; cnr Santísima & Zapata; Ⓜ Zócalo) The profusion of ornamental sculpture on the facade – including ghostly busts of the 12 apostles and a representation of Christ with his head in God's lap – is the main reason to visit the Church of the Holy Sacrament, five blocks east of the Zócalo as you walk along Calle Moneda. Most of the carving was done by Lorenzo Rodríguez from 1755 to 1783.

Suprema Corte de Justicia MURAL
(Supreme Court; Map p66; ☎55-4113-1000; Pino Suárez 2; ⊙9am-5pm Mon-Fri; Ⓜ Zócalo) FREE In 1940 muralist José Clemente Orozco painted four panels around the second level of the Supreme Court's central stairway, two dealing with the theme of justice. A more contemporary take on the same subject, *La historia de la justicia en México* (The History of Justice in Mexico), by Rafael Cauduro, unfolds over three levels of the building's southwest stairwell.

Executed in his hyper-realist style, Cauduro's series (aka *The Seven Worst Crimes*) catalogs the horrors of state-sponsored crimes against the populace, including the ever-relevant torture-induced confession. On the southeast corner of the building's interior, Ismael Ramos Huitrón's *La busqueda de la justicia* (The Search for Justice) reflects on the Mexican people's constant struggle to obtain justice, as does the social realism work *La justicia* (Justice), by Japanese-Mexican artist Luis Nishizawa, on the northwest stairwell. On the first level of the main stairway, American artist George Biddle painted *La guerra y la paz* (War and Peace) shortly after WWII ended. Photo ID required.

Museo de la Ciudad de México MUSEUM
(Museum of Mexico City; Map p66; ☎55-5542-0083; www.cultura.df.gob.mx/index.php/recintos-menu/museos/mcm; Pino Suárez 30; admission M$25, Wed free; ⊙10am-6pm Tue-Sun; Ⓜ Pino Suárez) Formerly a palace of the Counts of Santiago de Calimaya, this 18th-century baroque edifice now houses a museum with exhibits on city history and culture. Upstairs is the former studio of Joaquín Clausell, considered Mexico's foremost impressionist. The artist used the walls as an ongoing sketchbook during the three decades that he worked here until his death in 1935.

Plaza Santo Domingo PLAZA
(Map p66; cnr República de Venezuela & República de Brasil; 🚌 República de Argentina) Smaller and less hectic than the nearby Zócalo, this plaza has long served as a base for scribes and printers. Descendants of those who did the paperwork for merchants using the customs building (now the Education Ministry) across the square, the scribes work on the west side beneath the **Portales de Santo Domingo** (Map p66), aka Portales de Evangelistas.

To the north stands the maroon stone **Iglesia de Santo Domingo** (Map p66), a beautiful baroque church dating from 1736. The three-tiered facade merits a close look: statues of St Francis and St Augustine stand in the niches alongside the doorway. The middle panel shows St Dominic de Guzmán receiving a staff and the Epistles from St Peter

Alameda Central, Plaza de la República & Around

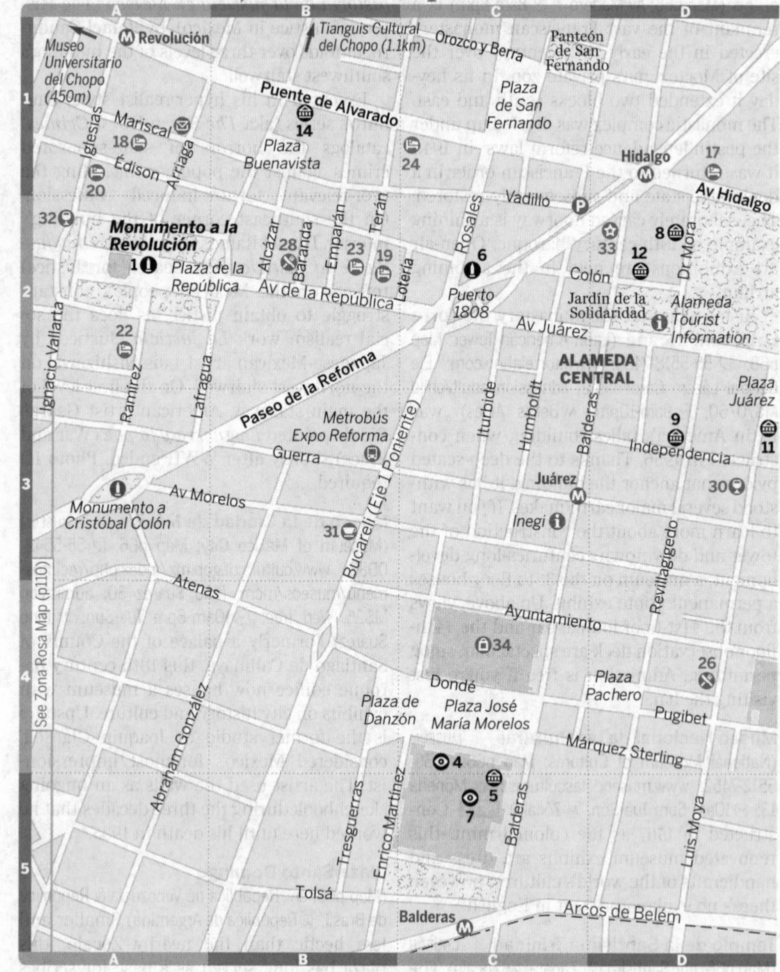

and St Paul, respectively. At the top is a bas-relief of the Assumption of the Virgin Mary.

East of the church, the 18th-century **Palacio de la Inquisición** (Map p66) was headquarters of the Holy Inquisition in Mexico until Spain decreed its closure in 1812. Its official shield is at the top of the facade.

Secretaría de Educación Pública MURAL
(Secretariat of Education; Map p66; ☎55-3601-1000; República de Brasil 31; ⏲9am-6pm Mon-Fri; República de Argentina) **FREE** The two front courtyards (on the opposite side of the building from the entrance off Plaza Santo Domingo) are lined with 120 fresco panels painted by Diego Rivera in the 1920s. Together they form a tableau of 'the very life of the people,' in the artist's words.

Each courtyard is thematically distinct: the one on the east end deals with labor, industry and agriculture, while the interior one depicts traditions and festivals. On the latter's top level is a series on proletarian and agrarian revolution, underneath a continuous red banner emblazoned with a Mexican *corrido* (folk song). The likeness of Frida Kahlo appears in the first panel as an arsenal worker.

Antiguo Colegio de San Ildefonso MUSEUM

(Map p66; ☎55-5702-2834; www.sanildefonso.org.mx; Justo Sierra 16; admission M$45, Tue free; ⏲10am-6pm Tue-Sun; Ⓜ Zócalo) Diego Rivera, José Clemente Orozco and David Siqueiros painted murals here in the 1920s. Most of the work on the main patio is by Orozco; look for the portrait of Hernán Cortés and his lover La Malinche underneath the staircase. The amphitheater, off the lobby, holds Rivera's first mural, *La creación,* undertaken upon his return from Europe in 1923.

A former Jesuit college built in the 16th century, San Ildefonso now hosts outstanding temporary art exhibitions.

Museo José Luis Cuevas MUSEUM

(Map p66; ☎55-5522-0156; www.museojoseluiscuevas.com.mx; Academia 13; admission M$20, Sun free; ⏲10am-6pm Tue-Sun; Ⓜ Zócalo) This museum showcases the works of artist Cuevas, a leader of the 1950s Ruptura movement, which broke with the politicized art of the post-revolutionary regime. Cuevas' **La Giganta**, an 8m-tall bronze female figure with some male features, dominates the central patio.

Alameda Central & Around

Emblematic of the downtown renaissance, the rectangular park immediately northwest of the *centro histórico* holds a vital place in Mexico City's cultural life. Surrounded by historically significant buildings, the Alameda Central has been the focus of ambitious redevelopment over the past decade. In particular, the high-rise towers on the Plaza Juárez have transformed the zone south of the park, much of which was destroyed in the 1985 earthquake. Metro stations Bellas Artes and Hidalgo are located on the Alameda's east and west sides, respectively. The north–south Eje Central Lázaro Cárdenas passes just east of the park.

★**Palacio de Bellas Artes** ARTS CENTER

(Palace of Fine Arts; Map p76; ☎55-5512-2593; www.palacio.bellasartes.gob.mx; cnr Av Juárez & Eje Central Lázaro Cárdenas; museum admission M$43, Sun free; ⏲10am-6pm Tue-Sun; Ⓟ; Ⓜ Bellas Artes) Immense murals by world-famous Mexican artists dominate the top floors of this splendid white-marble palace, a concert hall and arts center commissioned by President Porfirio Díaz. Construction on the iconic building began in 1905 under Italian architect Adamo Boari, who favored neoclassical and art nouveau styles. Complications arose as the heavy marble shell sank into the spongy subsoil, and then the Mexican Revolution intervened. Architect Federico Mariscal eventually finished the interior in the 1930s, utilizing the more modern art-deco style.

On the 2nd floor are two early-1950s works by Rufino Tamayo: *México de hoy* (Mexico Today) and *Nacimiento de la nacionalidad* (Birth of Nationality), a symbolic depiction of the creation of the mestizo (mixed ancestry) identity.

At the west end of the 3rd floor is Diego Rivera's famous *El hombre en el cruce de caminos* (Man at the Crossroads), originally commissioned for New York's Rockefeller

Alameda Central, Plaza de la República & Around

Top Sights

1 Monumento a la Revolución ... A2
2 Palacio de Bellas Artes ... F2

Sights

3 Alameda Central ... E2
4 Biblioteca de México José Vasconcelos ... C4
5 Centro de la Imagen ... C5
6 El Caballito ... C2
7 La Ciudadela ... C5
8 Laboratorio de Arte Alameda ... D2
Monumento a la Revolución Observation Deck ... (see 1)
9 Museo de Arte Popular ... D3
10 Museo Franz Mayer ... E1
11 Museo Memoria y Tolerancia ... D3
12 Museo Mural Diego Rivera ... D2
Museo Nacional de Arquitectura ... (see 2)
13 Museo Nacional de la Estampa ... E2
Museo Nacional de la Revolución ... (see 1)
14 Museo Nacional de San Carlos ... B1
Paseo Cimentación ... (see 1)
15 Plaza de Santa Veracruz ... E2
16 Plaza Juárez ... E3

Sleeping

17 Boutique Hotel de Cortés ... D1
18 Casa de los Amigos ... A1
19 Hostel Suites DF ... B2
20 Hotel Edison ... A1
21 Hotel Marlowe ... E3
22 Palace Hotel ... A2
23 Plaza Revolución Hotel ... B2
24 Ramada Reforma ... C1

Eating

25 Churrería El Moro ... F4
26 El Cuadrilátero ... D4
27 El Huequito ... E4
28 Gotan Restaurante ... B2
29 Mi Fonda ... E4

Drinking & Nightlife

30 Bósforo ... D3
31 Café La Habana ... B3
32 Crisanta ... A2

Entertainment

Ballet Folklórico de México ... (see 2)
33 Cinemex Real ... D2
Palacio de Bellas Artes ... (see 2)

Shopping

34 Centro de Artesanías La Ciudadela ... C4
35 Gandhi ... F3
36 Mercado San Juan ... E4

Center. The Rockefellers had the original destroyed because of its anti-capitalist themes, but Rivera recreated it here in 1934.

On the north side are David Alfaro Siqueiros' three-part *La nueva democracia* (New Democracy) and Rivera's four-part *Carnaval de la vida mexicana* (Carnival of Mexican Life); to the east is José Clemente Orozco's *La katharsis* (Catharsis), depicting the conflict between humankind's 'social' and 'natural' aspects.

The 4th-floor **Museo Nacional de Arquitectura** (Map p76; ☎55-5512-1410; www.museonacionaldearquitectura.bellasartes.gob.mx; Avenida Juarez s/n; admission M$25, free Sun; ⏰10am-6pm Tue-Sun; Ⓜ Bellas Artes) features changing exhibits on contemporary architecture.

The recently renovated **Bellas Artes theater** (only available for viewing at performances) is itself a masterpiece, with a stained-glass curtain depicting the Valle de México. Based on a design by Mexican painter Gerardo Murillo (aka Dr Atl), it was assembled by New York jeweler Tiffany & Co from almost a million pieces of colored glass.

In addition, the palace stages outstanding temporary art exhibitions, seasonal opera and symphony performances, and the Ballet Folklórico de México (p124).

Alameda Central — PARK

(Map p76; Ⓜ Bellas Artes) Created in the late 1500s by mandate of then-viceroy Luis de Velasco, the Alameda took its name from the *álamos* (poplars) planted over its rectangular expanse. By the late 19th century the park was graced with European-style statuary and lit by gas lamps. It became the place to be seen for the city's elite.

Today the Alameda is a popular refuge, particularly on Sunday when families stroll its pathways. The park was spruced up recently with dancing fountains and well-manicured gardens rife with fragrant lavender plants.

Museo Mural Diego Rivera — MUSEUM

(Diego Rivera Mural Museum; Map p76; ☎55-5512-0754; www.museomuraldiegorivera.bellasartes.gob.mx; cnr Balderas & Colón; admission M$19, Sun free; ⏰10am-6pm Tue-Sun; Ⓜ Hidalgo) Home to one of Diego Rivera's most famous works, *Sueño de una tarde dominical en la Alameda Central* (Dream of a Sunday Afternoon in the Alameda Central), a 15m-long mural painted in 1947. Rivera imagined many of the figures who walked in the city from colonial times onward, among them Hernán Cortés, Benito Juárez, Porfirio Díaz and Francisco Madero.

All are grouped around a *Catrina* (skeleton in pre-revolutionary women's garb). Rivera himself, as a pug-faced child, and Frida Kahlo stand beside the skeleton. Charts identify all the characters. The museum was built in 1986 to house the mural, after its original location, the Hotel del Prado, was wrecked by the 1985 earthquake.

Laboratorio de Arte Alameda MUSEUM

(Alameda Art Laboratory; Map p76; ☎55-5510-2793; www.artealameda.bellasartes.gob.mx; Dr Mora 7; admission M$19, Sun free; ⏲9am-5pm Tue-Sun; Ⓜ Hidalgo) As is often the case with museums in the *centro,* the 17th-century former convent building that contains the Laboratorio de Arte Alameda is at least as interesting as its contents. Here you can catch installations by leading experimental artists from Mexico and abroad, with an emphasis on electronic and interactive media.

Plaza Juárez PLAZA

(Map p76; Ⓜ Bellas Artes) Representing the new face of the zone, the latest addition to the plaza is the **Museo Memoria y Tolerancia** (Memory & Tolerance Museum; Map p76; www.myt.org.mx; Plaza Juárez 12; admission M$65, audio guide M$70; ⏲9am-6pm Tue-Fri, 10am-7pm Sat & Sun; Ⓜ Bellas Artes), a mazelike museum of 55 halls dedicated to preserving the memory of genocide victims. The multimedia exhibit chronicles crimes committed against humanity in Cambodia, Guatemala, Sudan, Rwanda and former Yugoslavia, as well as those perpetrated during the Holocaust.

Behind the fully restored **Templo de Corpus Christi**, which now holds the DF's archives, the plaza's centerpiece is a pair of Tetris-block towers by leading Mexican architect Ricardo Legorreta: the 24-story **Foreign Relations Secretariat** and the 23-story **Tribunales** building front a set of 1034 reddish pyramids in a broad pool, a collaboration between Legorreta and Spanish artist Vicente Rojo.

Museo de Arte Popular MUSEUM

(Museum of Popular Art; Map p76; ☎55-5510-2201; www.map.df.gob.mx; cnr Independencia & Revillagigedo; admission adult/child under 13yr M$40/free, Sun free; ⏲10am-6pm Tue-Sun; Ⓜ Juárez) This museum is a major showcase for folk art. Contemporary crafts are thematically displayed from all over Mexico, including carnival masks from Chiapas, *alebrijes* (fanciful animal figures) from Oaxaca and trees of life from Puebla. The museum occupies the former fire department headquarters, itself an outstanding example of 1920s art deco by architect Vicente Mendiola. The ground-level shop sells quality handicrafts.

Museo Franz Mayer MUSEUM

(Map p76; ☎55-5518-2266; www.franzmayer.org.mx; Av Hidalgo 45; admission M$45, Tue free; ⏲10am-5pm Tue-Fri, 11am-6pm Sat & Sun; Ⓜ Bellas Artes) Occupies the old hospice of the San Juan de Dios order, which under the brief reign of Maximilian became a halfway house for prostitutes. The museum is the fruit of the efforts of German-born Franz Mayer. Prospering as a financier in his adopted Mexico, Mayer amassed the collection of Mexican silver, ceramics and furniture now on display. The exhibit halls open onto a sumptuous colonial patio, where you can grab a bite at the excellent Cloister Café.

Plaza de Santa Veracruz PLAZA

(Map p76; Ⓜ Bellas Artes) The sunken square north of the Alameda across Avenida Hidalgo is named for the slanting structure on the right, the **Iglesia de la Santa Veracruz**. Elaborately carved pillars flank the doorway of the 18th-century church.

Museo Nacional de la Estampa MUSEUM

(MUNAE; Map p76; ☎55-5521-2244; www.museonacionaldelaestampa.bellasartes.gob.mx; Av Hidalgo 39; admission M$12, Sun free; ⏲10am-6pm Tue-Sun; Ⓜ Bellas Artes) Devoted to the graphic arts, this museum has thematic exhibits from its collection of more than 12,000 prints. The museum also does interesting temporary expositions that showcase works from Mexico and abroad.

La Ciudadela PLAZA

(Map p76; Ⓜ Balderas) The formidable compound now known as 'The Citadel' started off as a tobacco factory in the late 18th century, though it's best known as the scene of the Decena Trágica (Tragic Ten Days), the coup that brought down the Madero government in 1913. Today it is home to the **Biblioteca de México José Vasconcelos** (National Library; Map p76; ☎55-4155-0836; www.bibliotecademexico.gob.mx; Plaza de la Ciudadela 4; ⏲8:30am-7:30pm; Ⓜ Balderas) FREE, which has holdings of more than 500,000 volumes and an extensive map collection. The central halls of the recently renovated building are given over to art exhibits.

Centro de la Imagen (Map p76; ☎55-4155-0850; http://centrodelaimagen.conaculta.gob.mx; Plaza de la Ciudadela 2; ⌚11am-6pm Tue-Sun; Ⓜ Balderas) FREE, the city's photography museum, is at the Calle Balderas entrance. This innovatively designed space stages compelling exhibitions, often focusing on documentary views of Mexican life.

Across the plaza, inside the Centro de Artesanías La Ciudadela (p127), vendors offer a wide array of crafts from around Mexico, including black pottery from Oaxaca, guitars from Michoacán and silver jewelry from Taxco. Prices are generally fair, even before you bargain.

Plaza de la República & Around

Dominated by the copper-domed Monumento a la Revolución, you'll find this recently revamped plaza west of the Alameda Central. The grand art deco building northeast of the plaza is the Frontón de México, a now-defunct jai-alai (a game like squash) arena.

★ **Monumento a la Revolución** MONUMENT
(Map p76; www.mrm.mx; Plaza de la República; 🚌 Plaza de la República) Originally meant to be a legislative chamber, construction of the Monumento a la Revolución was interrupted by the Revolution, and there was talk of demolishing the building, but instead it was modified and given a new role. Unveiled in 1938, it contains the tombs of the revolutionary and post-revolutionary heroes Pancho Villa, Francisco Madero, Venustiano Carranza, Plutarco Elías Calles and Lázaro Cárdenas.Both the monument and Plaza de la República on which it stands got a major makeover in 2010 to commemorate Mexico's centennial anniversary of the Revolution. Kids love frolicking in the plaza's geyserlike fountains, while at night the monument's renovated architectural features are highlighted by colorful lights.

The star attraction of the monument is the 65m-high **observation deck** (Map p76; www.mrm.mx; Plaza de la República; admission M$40, Wed free; ⌚noon to 8pm Mon, Tue & Thu, to 6pm Wed, to 10pm Fri & Sat, 10am-8pm Sun; 🚌 Plaza de la República), accessed by a glass elevator. The vertigo-inducing lift opens to a spiraling staircase that ascends to a wide terrace with a panoramic view of the city.

Underlying the plaza and monument, the new-look **Museo Nacional de la Revolución** (Map p76; National Museum of the Revolution; ☎55-5546-2115; www.facebook.com/museorevolucion; Plaza de la República; admission M$25, Sun free; ⌚9am-5pm Tue-Fri, to 6:30pm Sat & Sun) covers a 63-year period, from the implementation of the constitution guaranteeing human rights in 1857 to the installation of the post-revolutionary government in 1920. Explanatory text remains untranslated.

The monument also has an interesting new basement art gallery, the **Paseo Cimentación** (Map p76; admission M$20; ⌚noon to 8pm Mon, Tue & Thu, to 6pm Wed, to 10pm Fri & Sat, 10am-8pm Sun), where you can check out temporary art exhibits amid a labyrinth of gigantic steel beams that serve as the structure's foundation.

Museo Universitario del Chopo MUSEUM
(☎55-5546-5484; www.chopo.unam.mx; Enrique González Martínez 10; admission M$30, Tue free; ⌚10am-7pm Tue-Sun; 🚌 Revolución) You can't miss the prominent spires of this university-run museum. Parts of the old building, made of forged iron from Düsseldorf, were brought over in pieces and assembled in Mexico City around the turn of the 20th century. Chopo boast wide, open spaces – ramps serve as showroom floors and high ceilings permit larger-than-life exhibits for contemporary art works.

The museum also hosts modern dance performances and screens international and Mexican indie movies.

Museo Nacional de San Carlos MUSEUM
(Map p76; ☎55-5566-8342; www.mnsancarlos.com; Puente de Alvarado 50; admission M$31, Sun free; ⌚10am-6pm Tue-Sun; Ⓜ Revolución) Exhibits a formidable collection of European art from the 14th century to early 20th century, including works by Rubens and Goya. The unusual rotunda structure was designed by Manuel Tolsá in the late 18th century.

Paseo de la Reforma

Mexico City's grandest thoroughfare, known simply as 'Reforma,' traces a bold southwestern path from Tlatelolco to Bosque de Chapultepec, skirting the Alameda Central and Zona Rosa. Emperor Maximilian of Hapsburg laid out the boulevard to connect his castle on Chapultepec Hill with the old city center. After his execution, it was given its current name to commemorate the reform laws instituted by President Benito Juárez. Under the López Obrador administration, the avenue was smartly refurbished and its broad, statue-studded medians became a stage for book fairs and art exhibits. Currently new office towers and hotels springing up along its length.

Reforma links a series of monumental *glorietas* (traffic circles). A couple of blocks west of the Alameda Central is **El Caballito** (Map p76) a bright-yellow representation of a horse's head by the sculptor Sebastián. It commemorates another equestrian sculpture that stood here for 127 years and today fronts the Museo Nacional de Arte. A few blocks southwest is the **Monumento a Cristóbal Colón**, an 1877 statue of Columbus gesturing toward the horizon.

Reforma's intersection with Avenida Insurgentes is marked by the **Monumento a Cuauhtémoc** (Map p110), memorializing the last Aztec emperor. Two blocks northwest is the **Jardín del Arte**, site of a Sunday art market.

The **Centro Bursátil** (Map p110), an angular tower and mirror-ball ensemble housing the nation's *Bolsa* (stock exchange), marks the southern edge of the Colonia Cuauhtémoc. Continuing west you reach the symbol of Mexico City, the **Monumento a la Independencia** (Map p110; Paseo de la Reforma; ⏲lookout visits 10am-1pm Sat & Sun; Ⓜ Insurgentes) FREE. Known as 'El Ángel,' this gilded Winged Victory on a 45m pillar was sculpted for the independence centennial of 1910. Inside the monument are the remains of Miguel Hidalgo, José María Morelos, Ignacio Allende and nine other notables. Thousands of people descend on the monument for occasional free concerts and victory celebrations following important Mexican soccer matches.

At Reforma's intersection with Sevilla is the monument commonly known as **La Diana Cazadora** (Diana the Huntress; Map p110; Reforma & Sevilla) a 1942 bronze sculpture actually meant to represent the Archer of the North Star. The League of Decency under the Ávila Camacho administration had the sculptor add a loincloth to the buxom babe, and it wasn't removed until 1966.

A 2003 addition to the Mexico City skyline, the **Torre Mayor** (Map p110; ☎55-5283-8000; www.torremayor.com.mx; Paseo de la Reforma 505; Ⓜ Chapultepec) stands before the gate to Bosque de Chapultepec. The earthquake-resistant structure, which soars 225m above the capital, is anchored below by 98 seismic-shock absorbers. Unfortunately, the observation deck is permanently closed.

Across from the Torre Mayor, the 104m-high **Estela de Luz** (Pillar of Light; Map p110; Paseo de la Reforma s/n) was built to commemorate Mexico's bicentennial anniversary in 2010. But due to delays in construction and rampant overspending, the quartz-paneled light tower wasn't inaugurated until 2012. After eight former government officials were arrested in 2013 for misuse of public funds, it became known as the 'tower of corruption.' In the tower's basement you'll find the **Centro de Cultura Digital** (Map p110; www.centroculturadigital.mx; ⏲11am-7pm Tue-Sun; Ⓜ Chapultepec), a hit-and-miss cultural center with expositions on digital technology.

Metro Hidalgo accesses Paseo de la Reforma on the Alameda end, while the Insurgentes and Sevilla stations provide the best approach from the Zona Rosa. On the Insurgentes metrobús route, the 'Reforma' and 'Hamburgo' stops lie north and south of the avenue respectively. Along Reforma itself, any westbound 'Auditorio' bus goes through the Bosque de Chapultepec, while 'Chapultepec' buses terminate at the east end of the park. In the opposite direction, 'I Verdes' and 'La Villa' buses head up Reforma to the Alameda Central and beyond. 'Zocalo' buses also run along Reforma.

Zona Rosa

Wedged between Paseo de la Reforma and Avenida Chapultepec, the 'Pink Zone' was developed as a playground and shopping district during the 1950s, when it enjoyed a cosmopolitan panache. Since then, however, the Zona Rosa has been in gradual decline and has lost ground to more fashionable neighborhoods, such as Condesa and Roma, arriving at its current condition as a hodgepodge of touristy boutiques, strip clubs, discos and fast-food franchises. People-watching from its sidewalk cafes reveals a higher degree of diversity than elsewhere: it's one of the city's premier gay and lesbian districts and an expat magnet, with a significant Korean population. The city government renovated the Calle Génova corridor in an attempt to put the zone back in the pink.

Condesa

Colonia Condesa's striking architecture, palm-lined esplanades and joyful parks echo its origins as a haven for a newly emerging elite in the early 20th century. Today, mention 'La Condesa' and most people think of it as a trendy area of informal restaurants, hip boutiques and hot nightspots. Fortunately, much of the neighborhood's old flavor remains, especially for those willing to wander outside the valet-parking zones. Stroll the pedestrian medians along Ámsterdam, Avenida Tamaulipas or Avenida Mazatlán to admire art deco and California colonial-style buildings. The focus is the peaceful **Parque México**, the oval shape of which reflects its earlier use as a horse-racing track. Two blocks northwest is **Parque España**, which has a children's play area.

Roma

Northeast of Condesa, Roma is a bohemian enclave inhabited by artists and writers. This is where Beat writers William S Burroughs and Jack Kerouac naturally gravitated during their 1950s sojourn in Mexico City. Built at the turn of the 20th century, the neighborhood is a showcase for Parisian-influenced architecture, which was favored by the Porfirio Díaz regime. Some of the most outstanding examples stand along Colima and Tabasco. When in Roma, linger in the cafes and check out the art galleries and specialty shops along Colima. A stroll down Orizaba passes two lovely plazas – Río de Janeiro, with a statue of David, and Luis Cabrera, which has lovely fountains. On weekends inspect the **antique market** along Álvaro Obregón, the main thoroughfare.

Small, independent art galleries and museums are scattered around Roma. The website Arte Mexico (www.artemexico.org) has listings for the Roma and elsewhere.

Museo del Objeto del Objeto MUSEUM

(Museum of Objects; Map p84; www.elmodo.mx/en; Colima 145; admission adult/child under 12yr M$40/free; ⏲10am-6pm Wed-Sun; Durango) Packing a collection of nearly 100,000 pieces, some as old as the Mexican War of Independence (1810), this two-story design museum tells unique versions of Mexican history by compiling objects for thematic exhibits.

Centro de Cultura Casa Lamm CULTURAL BUILDING

(Map p84; ☎55-5511-0899; www.galeriacasalamm.com.mx; Álvaro Obregón 99; ⏲10am-6pm; Álvaro Obregón) FREE This cultural complex contains a gallery for contemporary Mexican painting and photography as well as an excellent art library.

MUCA Roma MUSEUM

(Map p84; ☎55-5511-0925; www.mucaroma.unam.mx; Tonalá 51; ⏲10am-6pm Tue-Sun; Durango) FREE Sponsored by Universidad Nacional Autónoma de México (UNAM), this university museum exhibits Mexican and international contemporary art with ties to science and new technology.

Bosque de Chapultepec

Chapultepec – Náhuatl for 'Hill of Grasshoppers' – served as a refuge for the wandering Aztecs before becoming a summer residence for their noble class. It was the nearest freshwater supply for Tenochtitlán; in the 15th century Nezahualcoyotl, ruler of nearby Texcoco, oversaw the construction of an aqueduct to channel its waters over Lago de Texcoco to the pre-Hispanic capital.

Today Mexico City's largest park, the Bosque de Chapultepec covers more than 4 sq km, with lakes, a zoo and several excellent museums. It also remains an abode of Mexico's high and mighty, containing the current presidential residence, **Los Pinos**, and a former imperial palace, the Castillo de Chapultepec.

Sunday is the park's big day, as vendors line the main paths and throngs of families come to picnic, navigate the lake on rowboats and crowd into the museums. Most of the major attractions are in or near the eastern **1a Sección** (1st Section; www.sma.df.gob.mx/bosquedechapultepec; Bosque de Chapultepec; ⏲5am-6pm Tue-Sun; Ⓜ Chapultepec), while a large amusement park and children's museum dominate the 2da Sección.

A pair of bronze lions overlooks the main gate at Paseo de la Reforma and Lieja. Other access points are opposite the Museo Tamayo, Museo Nacional de Antropología and by metro Chapultepec. The fence along Paseo de la Reforma serves as the **Galería Abierta de las Rejas de Chapultepec**, an outdoor photo gallery extending from the zoo entrance to the Museo Tamayo.

Chapultepec metro station is at the east end of the Bosque de Chapultepec, near the Monumento a los Niños Héroes and Castillo de Chapultepec. Auditorio metro station is on the north side of the park, 500m west of the Museo Nacional de Antropología. 'Auditorio' buses pass along the length of Paseo de la Reforma.

The 2nd Section of the Bosque de Chapultepec lies west of the Periférico. To get to the 2da Sección and La Feria amusement park, from metro Chapultepec find the 'Paradero' exit and catch a 'Feria' bus at the top of the stairs. These depart continuously and travel nonstop to the 2da Sección, dropping off riders at the Papalote Museo del Niño and La Feria. In addition to family attractions, there is a pair of upscale lakeview restaurants on the Lago Mayor and Lago Menor.

★Museo Nacional de Antropología MUSEUM

(National Museum of Anthropology; Map p90; ☎55-5553-6381; www.mna.inah.gob.mx; cnr Paseo de la Reforma & Calz Gandhi; admission adult/child under 14yr M$57/free, audio guides M$75; ⏰9am-7pm Tue-Sun; Ⓟ; Ⓜ Auditorio) This world-class museum stands in an extension of the Bosque de Chapultepec. Its long, rectangular courtyard is surrounded on three sides by two-level display halls. The 12 ground-floor *salas* (halls) are dedicated to pre-Hispanic Mexico, while upper-level *salas* show how Mexico's indigenous descendants live today, with the contemporary cultures located directly above their ancestral civilizations.

Everything is superbly displayed, with much explanatory text translated into English. Audio guides in English are available at the entrance. The vast museum offers more than most people can absorb in a single visit. Here's a brief guide to the ground-floor halls, proceeding counterclockwise around the courtyard.

Culturas Indígenas de México Currently serves as a space for temporary exhibitions.

Introducción a la Antropología Introduces visitors to the field of anthropology.

Poblamiento de América Demonstrates how the hemisphere's earliest settlers got here, and survived and prospered in their new environment.

Preclásico en el Altiplano Central Focuses on the pre-Classic period, treated here as running from approximately 2300 BC to AD 100, and the transition from a nomadic hunting life to a more settled farming life in Mexico's central highlands.

Teotihuacán Displays models and objects from the Americas' first great and powerful state.

Los Toltecas y su Época Covers cultures of central Mexico between about AD 650 and 1250; on display is one of the four basalt warrior columns from Tula's Temple of Tlahuizcalpantecuhtli.

Mexica Devoted to the Mexica, aka Aztecs. Come here to see the famous sun stone, unearthed beneath the Zócalo in 1790, and other magnificent sculptures from the pantheon of Aztec deities.

Culturas de Oaxaca Displays the fine legacy of Oaxaca's Zapotec and Mixtec civilizations.

Culturas de la Costa del Golfo Spotlights the important civilizations along the Gulf of Mexico including the Olmec, Totonac and Huastec. Stone carvings include two Olmec heads weighing in at almost 20 tons.

Maya Exhibits findings from southeast Mexico, Guatemala, Belize and Honduras. A full-scale replica of the tomb of King Pakal, discovered deep in the Templo de las Inscripciones at Palenque, is simply breathtaking.

Culturas del Occidente Profiles cultures of western Mexico.

Culturas del Norte Covers the Casas Grandes (Paquimé) site and other cultures from northern Mexico, and traces their links with indigenous groups of the US southwest.

In a clearing about 100m in front of the museum's entrance, indigenous Totonac people perform their spectacular *voladores* rite – 'flying' from a 20m-high pole – every 30 minutes.

Castillo de Chapultepec CASTLE

(Chapultepec Castle; Map p90; www.castillodechapultepec.inah.gob.mx; Bosque de Chapultepec; ⏰9am-5pm Tue-Sun; Ⓜ Chapultepec) A visible reminder of Mexico's bygone aristocracy, the 'castle' that stands atop Chapultepec Hill was begun in 1785 but not completed until after independence, when it became the national military academy. When Emperor Maximilian and Empress Carlota arrived in 1864, they refurbished it as their residence.

The castle sheltered Mexico's presidents until 1939 when President Lázaro Cárdenas converted it into the **Museo Nacional de Historia** (National History Museum; Map p90; ☎55-4040-5215; www.mnh.inah.gob.mx; adult/child under 13yr M$57/free; ⏰9am-5pm Tue-Sun).

Historical exhibits chronicle the period from the rise of colonial Nueva España to the Mexican Revolution. In addition to displaying such iconic objects as the sword wielded by José María Morelos in the Siege of Cuautla and the Virgin of Guadalupe banner borne by Miguel Hidalgo in his march for independence, the museum features a number of dramatic interpretations of

Roma & Condesa

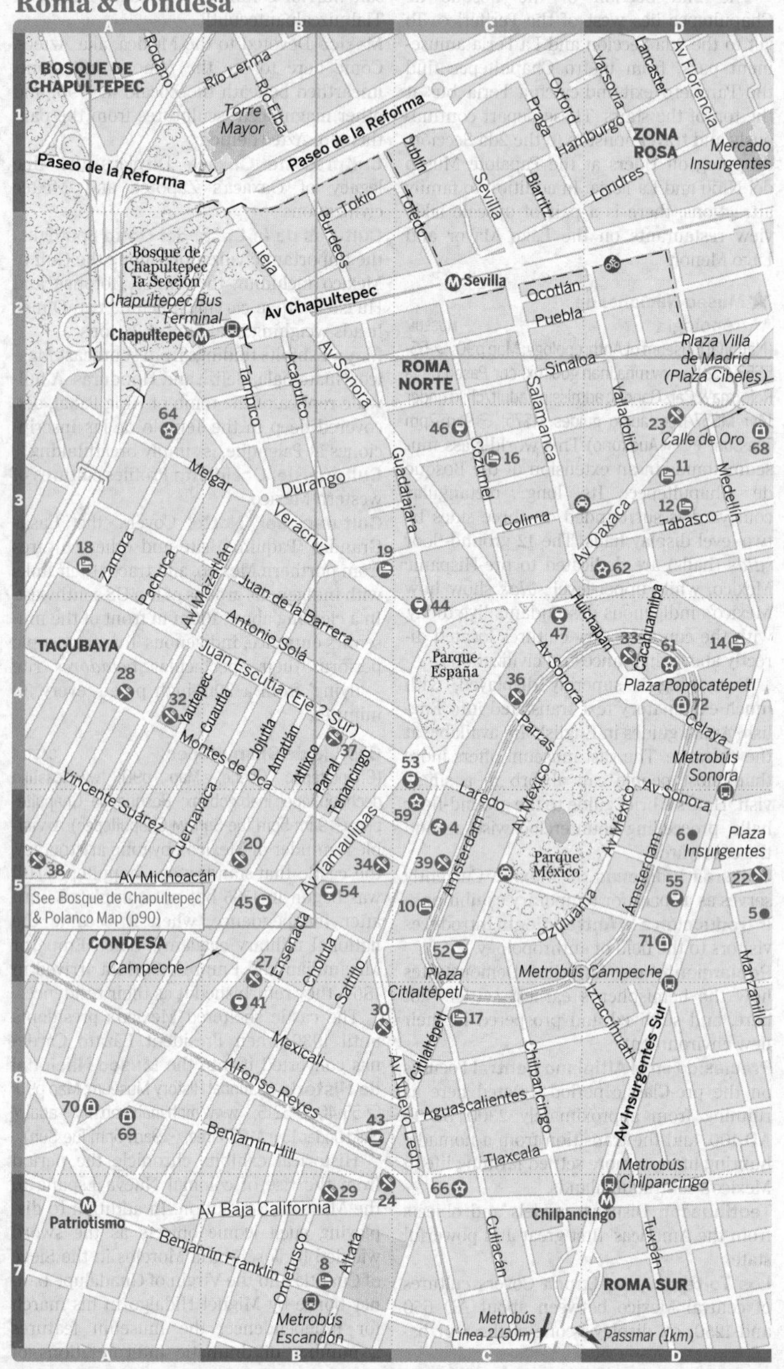

500 m
0.25 miles
JUÁREZ
ROMA
Cuauhtémoc
Insurgentes
Metrobús Insurgentes
Metrobús Cuauhtémoc
Metrobús Durango
Metrobús Jardín Pushkin
Metrobús Álvaro Obregón
Av Chapultepec
Av Insurgentes Sur
Av Oaxaca
Av Cuauhtémoc
Av Yucatán
Av Baja California
Viaducto Miguel Alemán
Plaza Romita
Plaza Río de Janeiro
Jardín Pushkin
Jardín Dr Chávez
Parque Juan Rulfo
Plaza Luis Cabrera
Mercado Medellín
Jardín Ramón López Vélarde
Hospital General
Centro Médico
Boletotal
See Zona Rosa Map (p110)
Museo del Juguete Antiguo México (750m)
Los Tolucos (1km)
MEXICO CITY

Roma & Condesa

Mexican history by leading muralists including Juan O'Gorman's panoramic *Retablo de la independencia* (Panel of Independence).

The east end of the castle preserves the palace occupied by Maximilian and Carlota, with sumptuously furnished salons opening onto an exterior deck that affords sweeping city views. On the upper floor, Porfirio Díaz' opulent rooms surround a patio where a tower marks the top of Chapultepec Hill, 45m above street level.

To reach the castle, follow the road that curves up the hill behind the Monumento a los Niños Héroes. Alternatively, a trainlike vehicle (M$13 round trip) runs up every 15 minutes while the castle is open.

Back at ground level, follow the south side of the hill's base to find the formidable **Tribuna Monumental de las Águilas**, dedicated to Mexico's WWII veterans. On the left side of the monument, enter the **Audiorama**, a pebbly garden with body-contoured benches where you can enjoy opera or classical music.

Museo de Arte Moderno MUSEUM
(Museum of Modern Art; Map p90; ☎55-5211-8331; www.mam.org.mx; cnr Paseo de la Reforma & Calz

Gandhi; admission M$25, Sun free; ⏲10:15am-5:30pm Tue-Sun; P; M Chapultepec) Exhibits work by noteworthy 20th-century and contemporary Mexican artists, including canvases by Dr Atl, Rivera, Siqueiros, Orozco, Tamayo, O'Gorman and Frida Kahlo's *Las dos Fridas,* possibly her best-known painting. It also has temporary expositions.

Museo Tamayo MUSEUM
(Map p90; www.museotamayo.org; Paseo de la Reforma 51; admission M$19, Sun free; ⏲10am-6pm Tue-Sun; P; M Auditorio) A multilevel structure built to house international modern art donated by Oaxaca-born painter Rufino Tamayo. The museum exhibits cutting-edge works from around the globe, which are thematically arranged with shows from the Tamayo collection. The Tamayo has a new rustic-chic restaurant, that makes an ideal breakfast stop, overlooking the park.

Zoológico de Chapultepec ZOO
(Map p90; www.chapultepec.df.gob.mx; Bosque de Chapultepec; ⏲9am-4:30pm Tue-Sun; 👪; M Auditorio) FREE Home to a wide range of the world's creatures in large open-air enclosures, the Chapultepec zoo was the first place outside China where pandas were born in captivity. The zoo has two of these rare bears, descendants of the original pair donated by the People's Republic in 1975. Endangered Mexican species include the Mexican grey wolf and the hairless xoloitzcuintle, the only surviving dog breed from pre-Hispanic times.

Jardín Botánico GARDENS
(Botanical Garden; Map p90; ☎55-5553-8114; Paseo de la Reforma s/n; ⏲10am-4pm Tue-Sun; M Chapultepec) FREE Highlighting Mexico's plant diversity, the 4-hectare complex is divided into sections that reflect the country's varied climatic zones. The garden also features a greenhouse full of rare orchids.

Monumento a Los Niños Héroes MONUMENT
(Map p90; Bosque de Chapultepec; M Chapultepec) The six marble columns marking the eastern entrance to the park commemorate the 'boy heroes,' six young cadets who perished in battle. On September 13, 1847, some 8000 US troops stormed Castillo de Chapultepec, which then housed the national military academy. Mexican General Santa Anna retreated before the onslaught, but the youths, aged 13 to 20, chose to defend the castle. Legend has it that one of them, Juan Escutia, wrapped himself in a Mexican flag and chose to leap to his death rather than surrender.

Papalote Museo del Niño MUSEUM
(Map p90; ☎55-5237-1773; www.papalote.org.mx; Bosque de Chapultepec; admission museum M$129, planetarium M$99, IMAX theater M$99; ⏲9am-6pm Tue-Fri, 10am-7pm Sat & Sun; P 👪; M Constituyentes) Your children won't want to leave this innovative, hands-on museum. Here kids can put together a radio program, channel their inner mad scientist, join an archaeological dig and try out all kinds of technological gadgets and games. Little ones also get a kick out of the planetarium and IMAX theater.

La Feria AMUSEMENT PARK
(Map p90; ☎55-5230-2121; www.feriachapultepec.com.mx; Bosque de Chapultepec; all-access admission M$190; ⏲8am-6pm Tue-Fri, 9:30am-8pm Sat & Sun; P 👪; M Constituyentes) An old-fashioned amusement park with some hair-raising rides. The all-access Platino pass is good for everything, including La Feria's best roller coasters.

Museo Jardín del Agua MURAL
(Map p90; Bosque de Chapultepec; admission M$22; ⏲10am-5pm Tue-Sun; M Constituyentes) Diego Rivera painted a series of murals for the inauguration of Cárcamo de Dolores, Chapultepec's waterworks facility built in the 1940s. Experimenting with waterproof paints, Rivera covered the collection tank, sluice gates and part of the pipeline with images of amphibious beings and workers involved in the project.

Outside the building, you can't miss another of Rivera's extraordinary works, **Fuente de Tláloc**, an oval pool inhabited by a huge mosaic-skinned sculpture of the Aztec god of water, rain and fertility. About 150m north is the beautiful **Fuente de Xochipilli**, dedicated to the Aztec 'flower prince,' with terraced fountains around a pyramid in the *talud-tablero* style typical of Teotihuacán.

Polanco

The affluent neighborhood of Polanco, north of Bosque de Chapultepec, arose in the 1940s as a residential alternative for a burgeoning middle class anxious to escape the overcrowded *centro*. Metro Polanco is in the center of the neighborhood while metro Auditorio lies on its southern edge.

Polanco is known as a Jewish enclave and also for its exclusive hotels, fine restaurants and designer stores along Avenida Presidente Masaryk. Some of the city's most prestigious museums and art galleries are here or in nearby Bosque de Chapultepec.

Museo Jumex MUSEUM

(www.fundacionjumex.org; Blvd Miguel de Cervantes Saavedra 303, Colonia Ampliación Granada; admission M$50, Fri free; 11am-8pm Tue-Sat, to 9pm Sun; P) Recently built to house one of Latin America's leading contemporary art collections. Temporary exhibits draw on 2600 pieces from renowned Mexican and international artists such as Gabriel Orozco, Francis Alys and Warhol. 'Ejército Defensa' buses departing from metro Chapultepec leave you one block south of the museum at Avenida Ejército Nacional and Avenida Ferrocarril de Cuernavaca.

The museum's other location, north of Mexico City in Ecatepec, remains open with a focus on more experimental art. It's a bit of a trek from the city, but one that many art lovers have been willing to make over the years. See website for directions.

Museo Soumaya Plaza Carso MUSEUM

(www.museosoumaya.org; Blvd Miguel de Cervantes Saavedra 303, Colonia Ampliación Granada; 10:30am-6:30pm) FREE Someone ought to tell Mexican billionaire Carlos Slim that bigger isn't always better. Named after his late wife, this six-story behemoth (plated with 16,000 aluminum hexagons) holds a large collection of sculptures by Frenchman Auguste Rodin and Catalan surrealist Salvador Dalí. The museum also contains worthy Rivera and Siqueiros murals and paintings by French impressionists, but there's too much filler.

To get here take an 'Ejército Defensa' bus from metro Chapultepec to the corner of Avenida Ejército Nacional and Avenida Ferrocarril de Cuernavaca, then walk one block north.

Galeria López Quiroga GALLERY

(Map p90; www.lopezquiroga.com; Aristóteles 169; 10am-7pm Mon-Fri, to 2pm Sat; M Polanco) FREE Specializes in sculptures, paintings and photography by contemporary Latin American and Mexican artists, including works by Francisco Toledo, Rufino Tamayo and José Luis Cuevas.

Xochimilco & Around

Almost at the southern edge of DF, a network of canals flanked by gardens is a vivid reminder of the city's pre-Hispanic legacy. Remnants of the *chinampas* (raised fertile land where indigenous inhabitants grew their food), these 'floating gardens' are still in use today. Gliding along the canals in a fancifully decorated *trajinera* (gondola) is an alternately tranquil and festive experience. On weekends a fiesta atmosphere takes over as the waterways become jammed with boats carrying groups of families and friends. Local vendors and musicians hover alongside the partygoers serving food and drink. Midweek, the mood is much calmer.

Though the canals are definitely the main attraction, Xochimilco has plenty to see. East of **Jardín Juárez** (Xochimilco Centro's main square) is the 16th-century **Parroquia de San Bernardino de Siena**, with elaborate gold-painted *retablos* (altarpieces) and a tree-studded atrium. South of the plaza, the bustling **Mercado de Xochimilco** covers two vast buildings: the one nearer the Jardín Juárez has fresh produce and an eating 'annex' for *tamales* and various prepared food; the other sells flowers, *chapulines* (grasshoppers), sweets and excellent *barbacoa* (savory barbecued mutton).

Xochimilco also boasts several visitor-friendly *pulquerías* (*pulque* bars), and about 2km east of Jardín Juárez is one of the city's best art museums.

To reach Xochimilco, take metro line 2 to the Tasqueña station. Then follow the signs inside the station to the transfer point for the *tren ligero*, a light-rail system that extends to neighborhoods not reachable by metro. Xochimilco is the last stop. Upon exiting the station, turn left (north) and follow Avenida Morelos to the market, Jardín Juárez and the church. If you don't feel like walking, bicycle taxis will shuttle you to the *embarcaderos* (boat landings) for M$30.

Canals HISTORIC SITE

(Xochimilco; boats per hour M$350, boat taxis one-way per person M$20; P; Xochimilco) Hundreds of colorful *trajineras* await passengers at the village's 10 *embarcaderos*. Nearest to the center are Belem, Salitre and San Cristóbal, about 400m east of the plaza, and Fernando Celada, 400m west of the plaza on Avenida Guadalupe Ramírez. On Saturdays and Sundays, 60-person *lanchas colectivas* (boat taxis) run between the Salitre and Nativitas *embarcaderos*.

Boats seat from 14 to 20 persons, making large group outings relatively cheap. Before boarding the *trajinera*, you can buy beer, soft drinks and food from vendors at the *embarcaderos* if you fancy an on-board picnic while cruising the canals.

Xochimilco, Náhuatl for 'Place where Flowers Grow,' was an early target of Aztec hegemony, probably due to its inhabitants' farming skills. The Xochimilcas piled up vegetation and mud in the shallow waters of Lake Xochimilco, a southern offshoot of Lago de Texcoco, to make the fertile gardens known as *chinampas*, which later became an economic base of the Aztec empire. As the *chinampas* proliferated, much of the lake was transformed into a series of canals. Approximately 180km of these waterways remain today. The *chinampas* are still under cultivation, mainly for garden plants and flowers such as poinsettias and marigolds. Owing to its cultural and historical significance, Xochimilco was designated a Unesco World Heritage site in 1987.

Museo Dolores Olmedo MUSEUM

(55-5555-1221; www.museodoloresolmedo.org.mx; Av México 5843; admission M$65, Tue free; 10am-6pm Tue-Sun; ; La Noria) Possibly the most important Diego Rivera collection of all belongs to this museum, ensconced in a peaceful 17th-century hacienda. Dolores Olmedo, a socialite and patron of Rivera, resided here until her death in 2002. The museum's 144 Rivera works – including oils, watercolors and lithographs from various periods – are displayed alongside pre-Hispanic figurines and folk art.

Another room is reserved for Frida Kahlo's paintings. In the estate's gardens, you'll see peacocks and xoloitzcuintles, a pre-Hispanic hairless dog breed.

To get here, from metro Tasqueña take the *tren ligero* (light rail) to La Noria station. Leaving the station, turn left at the top of the steps and descend to the street. Upon reaching an intersection with a footbridge, take a sharp left, almost doubling back on your path, onto Antiguo Camino a Xochimilco. The museum is 300m down this street.

San Ángel

Settled by the Dominican order soon after the Spanish conquest, San Ángel, 12km southwest of the center, maintains its colonial splendor despite being engulfed by the metropolis. It's often associated with the big Saturday crafts market held alongside the Plaza San Jacinto. Though the main approach via Avenida Insurgentes is typically chaotic, wander westward to experience the old village's cobblestoned soul; it's a tranquil enclave of colonial mansions with massive wooden doors, potted geraniums and bougainvillea spilling over stone walls.

La Bombilla station of the Avenida Insurgentes metrobús is about 500m east of the Plaza San Jacinto. Otherwise, catch a bus from metro Miguel Ángel de Quevedo, 1km east, or from metro Barranca del Muerto, 1.5km north along Avenida Revolución.

Plaza San Jacinto PLAZA

(Map p96; San Ángel Centro; La Bombilla) Every Saturday the Bazar Sábado brings masses of color and crowds of people to this square, 500m west of Avenida Insurgentes.

Museo Casa del Risco (Map p96; 55-5616-2711; www.isidrofabela.com; Plaza San Jacinto 15; 10am-5pm Tue-Sun; La Bombilla) FREE is midway along the plaza's north side. The elaborate fountain in the courtyard is a mad mosaic of Talavera tile and Chinese porcelain. Upstairs is a treasure trove of Mexican baroque and medieval European paintings.

About 50m west of the plaza is the 16th-century **Iglesia de San Jacinto** (Map p96) and its peaceful gardens.

Museo Casa Estudio Diego Rivera y Frida Kahlo MUSEUM

(Diego Rivera & Frida Kahlo Studio Museum; Map p96; 55-5550-1518; www.estudiodiegorivera.bellasartes.gob.mx; cnr Diego Rivera & Av Altavista; admission M$12, Sun free; 10am-6pm Tue-Sun; La Bombilla) If you saw the movie *Frida*, you'll recognize this museum, designed by Frida Kahlo and Diego Rivera's friend, architect and painter Juan O'Gorman. The artistic couple called this place home from 1934 to 1940 (Frida, Diego and O'Gorman each had their own separate house). Rivera's abode preserves his upstairs studio, while Frida's (the blue one) and O'Gorman's were cleared out for temporary exhibits.

Across the street is the San Ángel Inn. Now housing a prestigious restaurant, the former *pulque* hacienda is historically significant as the place where Pancho Villa and Emiliano Zapata agreed to divide control of the country in 1914.

It's a 2km walk or taxi ride from metrobús La Bombilla.

Bosque de Chapultepec & Polanco

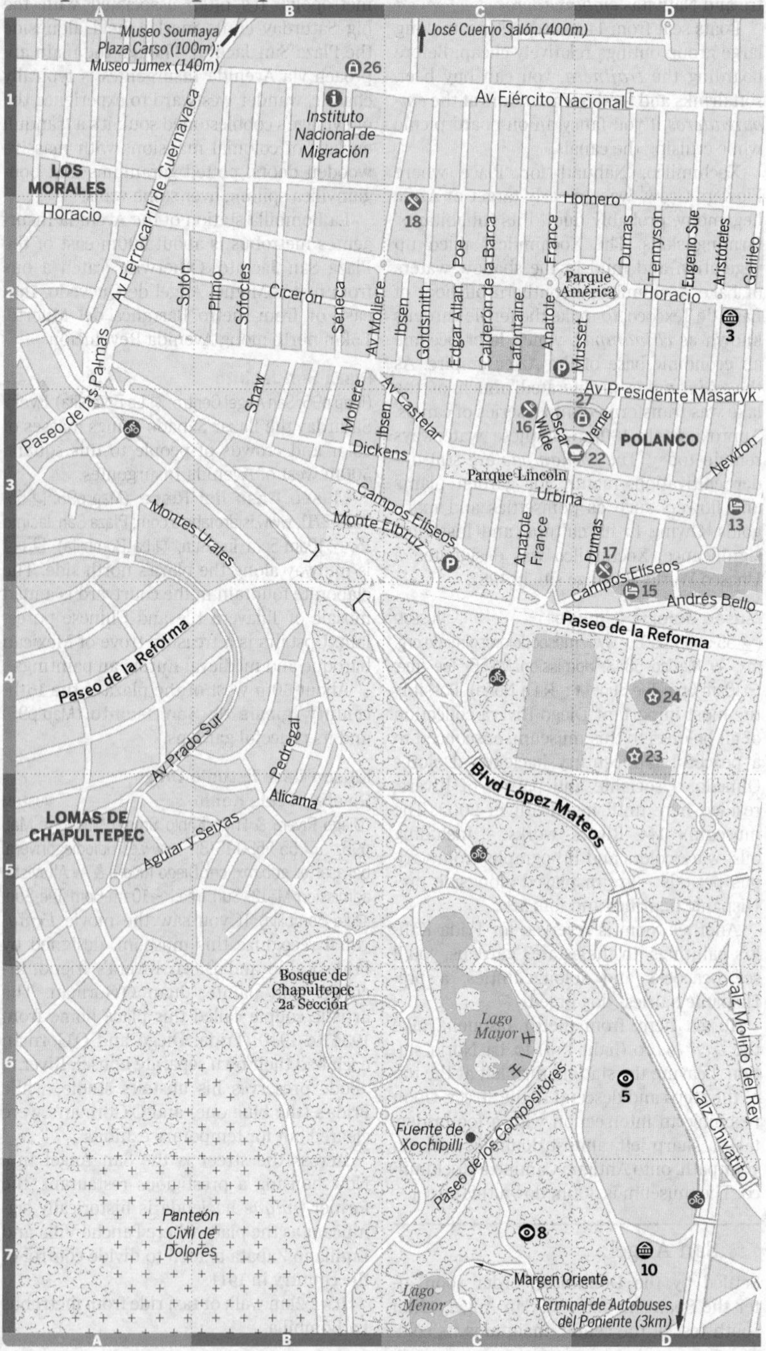

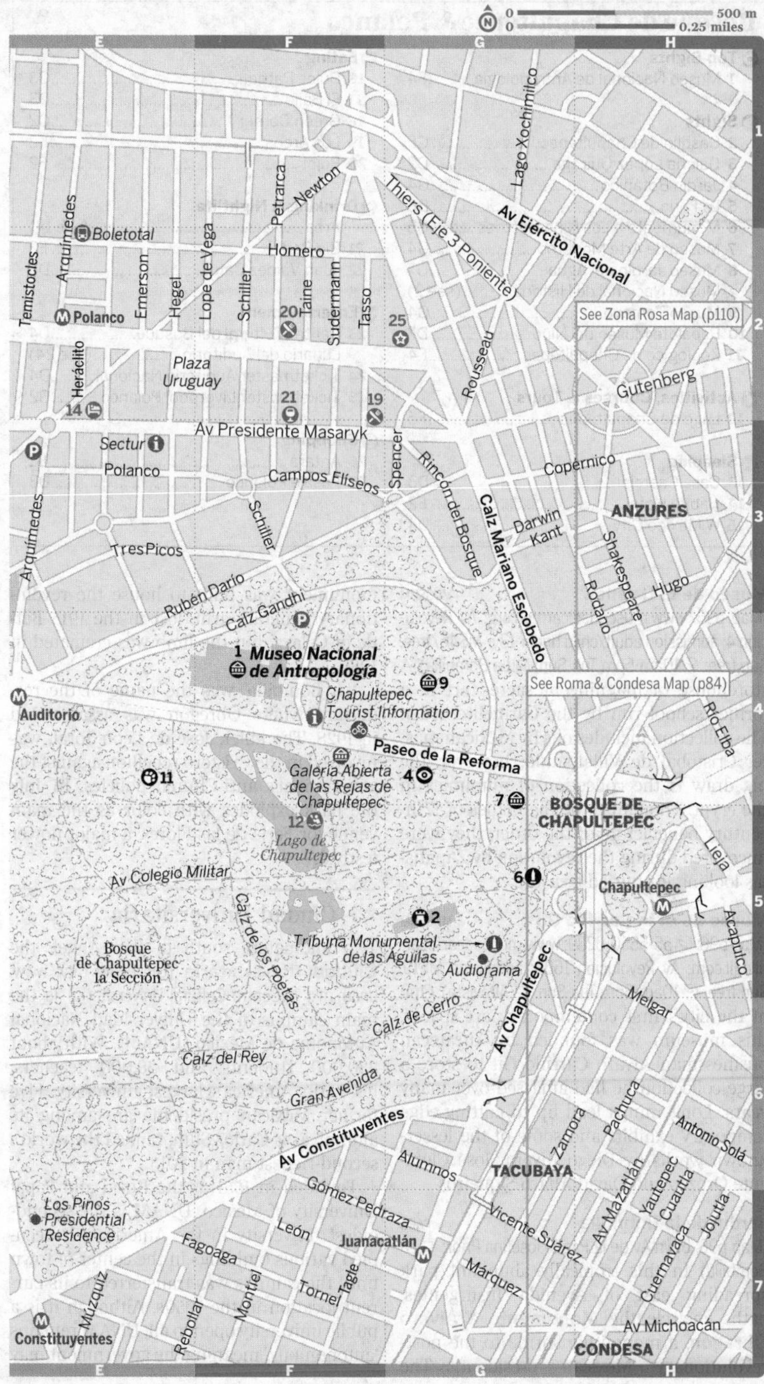
0 500 m
0 0.25 miles
Lago Xochimilco
Av Ejército Nacional
Thiers (Eje 3 Poniente)
Newton
Petrarca
Arquímedes
Boletotal
Homero
Temistocles
Polanco
Emerson
Hegel
Lope de Vega
Schiller
20
Taine
Sudermann
Tasso
25
See Zona Rosa Map (p110)
Rousseau
Heráclito
Plaza Uruguay
Gutenberg
14
21
19
Av Presidente Masaryk
Sectur
Polanco
Campos Elíseos
Spencer
Rincón del Bosque
Copérnico
Schiller
Arquímedes
Tres Picos
Calz Mariano Escobedo
Darwin
Kant
ANZURES
Shakespeare
Rodano
Hugo
Rubén Darío
Calz Gandhi
1 Museo Nacional de Antropología
9
Chapultepec Tourist Information
See Roma & Condesa Map (p84)
Auditorio
Río Elba
Paseo de la Reforma
11
Galería Abierta de las Rejas de Chapultepec
4
7
BOSQUE DE CHAPULTEPEC
12
Lago de Chapultepec
Lieja
Av Colegio Militar
6
Chapultepec
2
Calz de los Poetas
Tribuna Monumental de las Águilas
Audiorama
Acapulco
Bosque de Chapultepec 1a Sección
Av Chapultepec
Melgar
Calz de Cerro
Calz del Rey
Gran Avenida
Av Constituyentes
Zamora
Pachuca
Antonio Solá
Alumnos
TACUBAYA
Gómez Pedraza
Av Mazatlán
Yautepec
Cuautla
Los Pinos Presidential Residence
León
Juanacatlán
Vicente Suárez
Cuernavaca
Jojutla
Fagoaga
Tornel
Tagle
Márquez
Múzquiz
Montiel
Rebollar
Constituyentes
Av Michoacán
CONDESA

Bosque de Chapultepec & Polanco

Top Sights
1 Museo Nacional de Antropología F4

Sights
2 Castillo de Chapultepec G5
3 Galeria López Quiroga........ D2
4 Jardín Botánico G4
5 La Feria........ D6
6 Monumento a Los Niños Héroes G5
7 Museo de Arte Moderno G4
8 Museo Jardín del Agua........ C7
Museo Nacional de Historia ....(see 2)
9 Museo Tamayo........ G4
10 Papalote Museo del Niño D7
11 Zoológico de Chapultepec........E4

Activities, Courses & Tours
12 Lago de Chapultepec F5

Sleeping
13 Casa Castelar D3
14 Hábita Hotel........E2
15 W Mexico City D4

Eating
16 Dulce Patria........C3
17 El Bajío D3
18 Green Corner C2
19 Los Arcos........ F2
20 Pujol F2

Drinking & Nightlife
Área ....(see 14)
21 Big Red........ F2
22 Juan Valdez Café........D3

Entertainment
23 Centro Cultural del Bosque........D4
Lunario del Auditorio ....(see 24)
24 Ticketmaster Auditorio Nacional D4
25 Ticketmaster Liverpool Polanco G2

Shopping
26 Antara B1
27 Pasaje Polanco D3

Museo de El Carmen MUSEUM
(Map p96; www.museodeelcarmen.org; Av Revolución 4; admission adult/child under 13yr M$46/free, Sun free; 10am-5pm Tue-Sun; La Bombilla) A storehouse of magnificent sacred art in a former school run by the Carmelite order. The collection includes oils by Mexican master Cristóbal de Villalpando; however, the big draw is the collection of mummies in the crypt. Thought to be the bodies of 17th-century benefactors of the order, they were uncovered during the revolution by Zapatistas looking for buried treasure.

Museo de Arte Carrillo Gil MUSEUM
(Map p96; 55-5550-6289; www.museodeartecarrillogil.com; Av Revolución 1608; admission M$19, Sun free; 10am-6pm Tue-Sun; Altavista) One of the city's first contemporary art spaces, this museum was founded by Yucatecan businessman Álvaro Carrillo Gil to store a large collection he had amassed over many years. Long ramps lead up to cutting-edge temporary exhibits and some of the lesser-known works by Diego Rivera, José Clemente Orozco and David Alfaro Siqueiros.

Jardín de la Bombilla PARK
(Map p96; btwn Av de la Paz & Josefina Prior; La Bombilla) In this tropically abundant park spreading east of Avenida Insurgentes, paths encircle the **Monumento a Álvaro Obregón**, a monolithic shrine to the post-revolutionary Mexican president. The monument was built to house the revolutionary general's arm, lost in the 1915 Battle of Celaya, but the limb was cremated in 1989.

'La Bombilla' was the name of the restaurant where Obregón was assassinated in 1928. The killer, José de León Toral, was involved in the Cristero rebellion against the government's anti-Church policies. In July the park explodes with color as the main venue for Feria de las Flores, a major flower festival.

Ciudad Universitaria

Two kilometers south of San Ángel, the **Ciudad Universitaria** (University City; www.unam.mx; Centro Cultural Universitario) is the main campus of the Universidad Nacional Autónoma de México (UNAM). With about 330,000 students and 38,000 teachers, it's Latin America's largest university. Five former Mexican presidents are among its alumni, as is Carlos Slim, ranked the world's second-richest man in 2013.

Founded in 1551 as the Royal and Papal University of Mexico, UNAM is the second-oldest university in the Americas. It occupied various buildings in the center of town until the campus was transferred to its current location in the 1950s. Although it is a public university open to all, UNAM remains 'autonomous,' meaning the government may not interfere in its academic policies. It is Mexico's leading research institute and has long been a center of political dissent.

An architectural showpiece, UNAM was placed on Unesco's list of World Heritage sites in 2007. Most of the faculty buildings are scattered at the north end. As you enter from Avenida Insurgentes, it's easy to spot the **Biblioteca Central** (Central Library), 10 stories high and covered with mosaics by Juan O'Gorman. The south wall, with two prominent zodiac wheels, covers colonial times, while the north wall deals with Aztec culture. **La Rectoría**, the administration building at the west end of the vast central lawn, has a vivid, three-dimensional Siqueiros mosaic on its south wall, showing students urged on by the people.

Across Avenida Insurgentes stands the **Estadio Olímpico**, built of volcanic stone for the 1968 Olympics. With seating for over 72,000, it's home to UNAM's Pumas soccer club, which competes in the national league's Primera División. Over the main entrance is Diego Rivera's sculpted mural on the theme of sports in Mexican history.

East of the university's main esplanade, the **Facultad de Medicina** (Faculty of Medicine) features an intriguing mosaic mural by Francisco Eppens on the theme of Mexico's *mestizaje* (blending of indigenous and European races).

A second section of the campus, about 2km south, contains the **Centro Cultural Universitario**, a cultural center with five theaters, two cinemas, the delightful Azul y Oro restaurant and two excellent museums. To get to University City, take metrobús line 1 to the Centro Cultural Universitario (CCU) station. Or go to metro Universidad and hop on the 'Pumabús,' a free on-campus bus. The Pumabús has limited service on weekends and holidays.

Museo Universitario Arte Contemporáneo MUSEUM

(MUAC; ☎55-5622-6972; www.muac.unam.mx; Av Insurgentes Sur 3000, Centro Cultural Universitario; admission Thu-Sat M$40, Wed & Sun M$20; ⏲10am-6pm Wed, Fri & Sun, to 8pm Thu & Sat; P; Centro Cultural Universitario) Designed by veteran architect Teodoro González de León, the contemporary art museum's sloping, minimalist-style glass facade stands in stark contrast to the surrounding 1970s buildings. Inside you'll find cutting-edge temporary exhibitions occupying nine spacious halls with impressive lighting and high ceilings. The modern works here include paintings, audio installations, sculptures and multimedia art from Mexico and abroad.

Museo Universitario de Ciencias MUSEUM

(Universum; ☎55-5424-0694; www.universum.unam.mx; Circuito Cultural de Ciudad Universitaria s/n; adult/child M$69/59; ⏲9am-5pm Mon-Fri, 10am-5pm Sat & Sun; Centro Cultural Universitario) A huge science museum offering fun-filled attractions for kids, such as a planetarium and permanent exhibits that explore biodiversity, the human brain and much more. Nearby is the university sculpture garden, with a trail leading through volcanic fields past a dozen or so innovative pieces. The most formidable work is an enormous ring of concrete blocks by sculptor Mathias Goeritz.

Coyoacán

Coyoacán ('Place of Coyotes' in the Náhuatl language), about 10km south of downtown, was Cortés' base after the fall of Tenochtitlán. Only in recent decades has urban sprawl overtaken the outlying village. Coyoacán retains its restful identity, with narrow colonial-era streets, cafes and a lively atmosphere. Once home to Leon Trotsky and Frida Kahlo (whose houses are now fascinating museums), it has a decidedly countercultural vibe, most evident on weekends, when assorted musicians, mimes and crafts markets draw large but relaxed crowds to Coyoacán's central plazas.

The nearest metro stations to central Coyoacán, 1.5km to 2km away, are Viveros, Coyoacán and General Anaya. If you don't fancy a walk, get off at Viveros station, walk south to Avenida Progreso and catch an eastbound 'Metro Gral Anaya' pesero (Mexico City name for a *colectivo*) to the market. Returning, 'Metro Viveros' peseros go west on Malintzin; 'Metro Coyoacán' and 'Metro Gral Anaya' peseros depart from the west side of Plaza Hidalgo.

San Ángel–bound peseros and buses head west on Avenida Miguel Ángel de Quevedo, five blocks south of Plaza Hidalgo.

★**Museo Frida Kahlo** MUSEUM

(Map p114; ☎55-5554-5999; www.museofridakahlo.org.mx; Londres 247; admission M$80; ⏲10am-5:45pm Tue & Thu-Sun, 11am-5:45pm Wed; M Coyoacán) Renowned Mexican artist Frida Kahlo was born in, and lived and died in, Casa Azul (Blue House), now a museum. Almost

FRIDA & DIEGO

A century after Frida Kahlo's birth, and more than 50 years after Diego Rivera's death, the pair's fame and recognition are stronger than ever. In 2007 a retrospective of Kahlo's work at the Palacio de Bellas Artes attracted more than 440,000 visitors. Though attendance at the Rivera survey that followed was not so phenomenal, the show reminded visitors that the prolific muralist had been an international star in his own lifetime. The artists are inseparably linked in memory, and both artists were frequent subjects in each other's work.

Rivera first met Kahlo, 21 years his junior, while painting at the Escuela Nacional Preparatoria, where she was a student in the early 1920s. Rivera was already at the forefront of Mexican art; his commission at the school was the first of many semi-propaganda murals on public buildings that he was to execute over three decades. He had already fathered children by two Russian women in Europe, and in 1922 he married 'Lupe' Marín in Mexico. She bore him two more children before their marriage broke up in 1928.

Kahlo was born in Coyoacán in 1907 to a Hungarian-Jewish father and Oaxacan mother. She contracted polio at age six, leaving her right leg permanently thinner than her left. In 1925 she was horribly injured in a trolley accident that broke her right leg, collarbone, pelvis and ribs. She made a miraculous recovery but suffered much pain thereafter. It was during convalescence that she began painting. Pain – physical and emotional – was to be a dominating theme of her art.

Kahlo and Rivera both moved in left-wing artistic circles, and they met again in 1928; they married the following year. The liaison, described as 'a union between an elephant and a dove,' was always a passionate love-hate affair. Rivera wrote: 'If I ever loved a woman, the more I loved her, the more I wanted to hurt her. Frida was only the most obvious victim of this disgusting trait.'

In 1934, after a spell in the US, the pair moved into a new home in San Ángel, now the Museo Casa Estudio Diego Rivera y Frida Kahlo, with separate houses linked by an aerial walkway. After Kahlo discovered that Rivera had had an affair with her sister, Cristina, she divorced him in 1939, but they remarried the following year. She moved back into her childhood home, the Casa Azul (Blue House) in Coyoacán, and he stayed at San Ángel – a state of affairs that endured for the rest of their lives. Their relationship endured, too.

Despite the worldwide wave of Fridamania that followed the hit biopic *Frida* in 2002, Kahlo had only one exhibition in Mexico in her lifetime, in 1953. She arrived at the opening on a stretcher. Rivera said of the exhibition: 'Anyone who attended it could not but marvel at her great talent.' She died at the Blue House the following year. Rivera called it 'the most tragic day of my life... Too late I realized that the most wonderful part of my life had been my love for Frida.'

every visitor to Mexico City makes a pilgrimage here to gain a deeper understanding of the painter (and maybe to pick up a Frida handbag). Arrive early to avoid the crowds, especially on weekends.

Built by Frida's father Guillermo three years before her birth, the house is littered with mementos and personal belongings that evoke her long, often tempestuous relationship with husband Diego Rivera and the leftist intellectual circle they often entertained there. Kitchen implements, jewelry, outfits, photos and other objects from the artist's everyday life are interspersed with art, as well as a variety of pre-Hispanic pieces and Mexican crafts. The collection was greatly expanded in 2007 upon the discovery of a cache of previously unseen items that had been stashed in the attic.

Kahlo's art expresses the anguish of her existence as well as her flirtation with socialist icons: portraits of Lenin and Mao hang around her bed, and in another painting, *Retrato de la familia* (Family Portrait), the artist's Hungarian-Oaxacan roots are fancifully entangled.

Plaza Hidalgo & Jardín Centenario PLAZA

The focus of Coyoacán life, and the scene of most of the weekend fun, is its central plaza – actually two adjacent plazas: the **Jardín Centenario**, with the village's iconic coyotes frolicking in its central fountain; and the larger, cobblestoned **Plaza Hidalgo**, with a statue of the eponymous independence hero.

The **Casa de Cortés** (Map p114; ☎55-5484-4500; Jardín Hidalgo 1; ⏰9am-7pm; Ⓜ Coyoacán), on the north side of Plaza Hidalgo, is where conquistador Cortés established Mexico's first municipal seat during the siege of Tenochtitlán, and later had the defeated emperor Cuauhtémoc tortured to make him divulge the location of Aztec treasure (the scene is depicted on a mural inside the chapel). Contrary to popular thought, Cortés never actually resided here. The building now houses Coyoacán's delegation offices.

The **Parroquia de San Juan Bautista** (Map p114; Plaza Hidalgo) and its adjacent ex-monastery dominate the south side of Plaza Hidalgo. First erected in 1592 by the Franciscans, the single-nave church has a lavishly ornamented interior, with painted scenes all over the vaulted ceiling. Be sure to inspect the cloister, featuring Tuscan columns and a checkerboard of carved relief panels in the corner of the ceilings.

Half a block east, the **Museo Nacional de Culturas Populares** (Map p114; ☎55-4155-0920; www.culturaspopulareseindigenas.gob.mx; Av Hidalgo 289; admission M$12, Sun free; ⏰10am-6pm Tue-Thu, to 8pm Fri-Sun; Ⓜ Coyoacán) stages innovative exhibitions on folk traditions, indigenous crafts and celebrations in its various courtyards and galleries.

★Museo Casa de León Trotsky — MUSEUM

(Map p114; ☎55-5658-8732; www.museocasadeleontrotsky.blogspot.com; Av Río Churubusco 410; admission M$40; ⏰10am-5pm Tue-Sun; Ⓜ Coyoacán) The Trotsky home, now a museum, remains much as it was on the day when a Stalin agent, a Catalan named Ramón Mercader, caught up with the revolutionary and smashed an ice ax into his skull. Memorabilia and biographical notes are displayed in buildings off the patio, where a tomb engraved with a hammer and sickle contains Trotsky's ashes.

Having come second to Stalin in the power struggle in the Soviet Union, Trotsky was expelled in 1929 and condemned to death in absentia. In 1937 he found refuge in Mexico. At first Trotsky and his wife, Natalia, lived in Frida Kahlo's Blue House, but after falling out with Kahlo and Rivera they moved a few streets northeast.

Bullet holes remain in the bedroom, the markings of a failed assassination attempt. The entrance is at the rear of the old residence, facing Av Río Churubusco.

Anahuacalli — MUSEUM

(Diego Rivera Anahuacalli Museum; ☎55-5617-4310; www.museoanahuacalli.org.mx; Calle Museo 150; admission adult/child under 16yr M$35/15; ⏰11am-5pm Wed-Sun; Ⓟ; 🚊 Xotepingo) Designed by Diego Rivera to house his collection of pre-Hispanic art, this museum is a templelike structure of volcanic stone. The 'House of Anáhuac' (Aztec name for the Valle de México) also contains one of Rivera's studios and some of his work, including a study for *Man at the Crossroads*, the mural commissioned by the Rockefeller Center in 1934.

In November elaborate Day of the Dead offerings pay homage to the painter, and from April to early December the museum hosts free concerts on Sundays at 1pm, ranging from classical to regional folk music.

Anahuacalli is 3.5km south of Coyoacán. For M$100, you can visit both the Frida Kahlo Museum and Anahuacalli, with round-trip transport departing from the Casa Azul included.

Or take the *tren ligero* (light rail) from metro Tasqueña to the Xotepingo station. Exit on the west side and walk 200m to División del Norte; cross and continue 600m along Calle Museo.

Ex-Convento de Churubusco — HISTORIC BUILDING

(☎55-5604-0699; 20 de Agosto s/n, Colonia San Diego Churubusco; Ⓜ General Anaya) This was the scene of a historic military defeat, on August 20, 1847. Mexican troops defended the former convent against US forces advancing from Veracruz in a dispute over the US annexation of Texas. The US invasion was but one example in a long history of foreign intervention in Mexico, as compellingly demonstrated in Churubusco's **Museo Nacional de las Intervenciones** (National Interventions Museum; ☎55-5604-0699; www.museodelasintervenciones.com; 20 de Agosto s/n; admission M$46, Sun free; ⏰9am-6pm Tue-Sun; Ⓜ General Anaya).

The Mexicans fought off US forces until they ran out of ammunition and were beaten only after hand-to-hand fighting. Displays in the museum include an American map showing operations in 1847 and the plot by US ambassador Henry Lane Wilson to bring down the Madero government in 1913. Explanatory text is in Spanish.

San Ángel

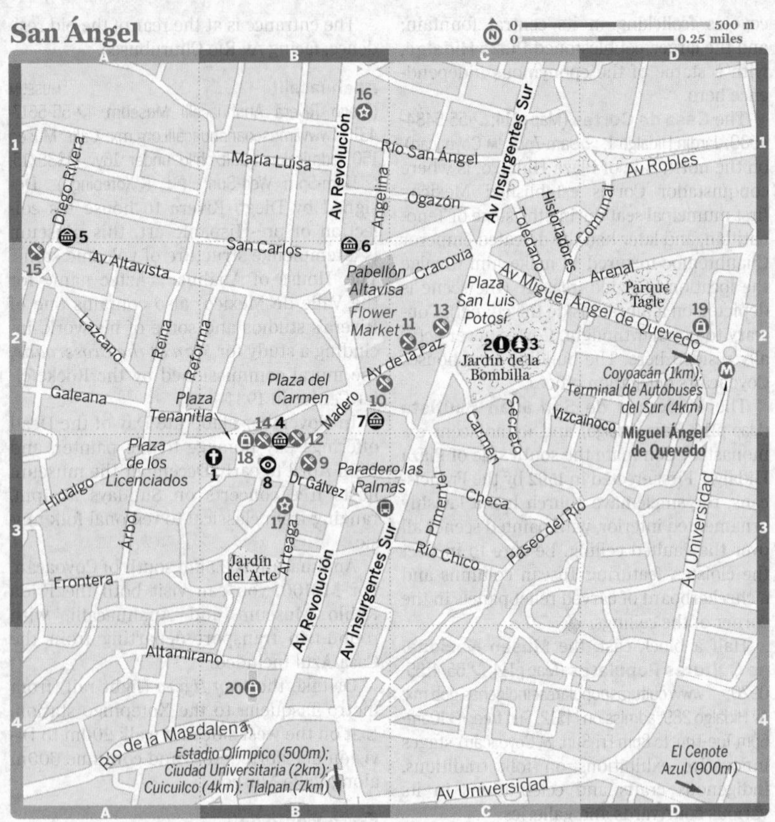

The superbly restored exhibit rooms, bordered by original frescoes, surround a small cloister where numbered stations provided instructions for meditating monks. Leaving the museum, wander amid the monastery's old orchard, now wonderful gardens.

The 17th-century former monastery stands within peaceful wooded grounds, 1.5km east of Plaza Hidalgo. To reach Churubusco from Coyoacán, catch an eastbound 'Metro General Anaya' bus from Carrillo Puerto, off Plaza Hidalgo. Otherwise, walk 500m west from the General Anaya metro station.

Viveros de Coyoacán PARK
(Map p114; ☎55-5484-3524; www.viveroscoyoacan.gob.mx; Av Progreso 1; ⏲6am-6pm; Ⓜ Viveros) A pleasant approach to Coyoacán's central plazas is via the Viveros de Coyoacán, the principal nurseries for Mexico City's parks and gardens. The 390-sq-km swath of greenery, 1km west of central Coyoacán, is popular with joggers and great for a stroll, but watch out for belligerent squirrels!

From metro Viveros, walk south (right, as you face the fence) along Avenida Universidad and take the first left, Avenida Progreso.

Plaza Santa Catarina PLAZA
(Map p114; Ⓜ Viveros) About a block south of Coyoacán's nursery is Plaza Santa Catarina, with the modest, mustard-colored church that gives the square its name. Across the street, the **Centro Cultural Jesús Reyes Heroles** (Map p114; ☎55-5554-5324; Francisco Sosa 202; ⏲9am-8pm; Ⓜ Viveros) is a colonial estate with a coffee shop and lovely grounds, where yuccas and jacarandas spring from carefully tended gardens.

Cuicuilco

One of the oldest significant remnants of pre-Hispanic settlement within the DF, Cuicuilco echoes a civilization that stood on the

San Ángel

Sights

1	Iglesia de San Jacinto	B3
2	Jardín de la Bombilla	C2
3	Monumento a Álvaro Obregón	C2
4	Museo Casa del Risco	B3
5	Museo Casa Estudio Diego Rivera y Frida Kahlo	A1
6	Museo de Arte Carrillo Gil	B2
7	Museo de El Carmen	B2
8	Plaza San Jacinto	B3

Eating

9	Barbacoa de Santiago	B3
10	Cluny	B2
11	El Cardenal San Ángel	C2
12	Fonda San Ángel	B3
13	Montejo	C2
14	Saks	B3
15	San Ángel Inn	A2
	Taberna del León	(see 20)

Drinking & Nightlife

	La Camelia	(see 12)

Entertainment

16	Centro Cultural Helénico	B1
17	El Breve Espacio Mezcalería	B3

Shopping

18	Bazar Sábado	B3
19	Gandhi	D2
20	Plaza Loreto	B4

shores of Lago de Xochimilco as far back as 800 BC. In its heyday in the 2nd century BC, the 'place of singing and dancing' counted as many as 40,000 inhabitants; at that time, the Teotihuacán civilization was only just beginning to rise to importance. The site was abandoned a couple of centuries later, however, after an eruption of the nearby Xitle volcano covered most of the community in lava.

Zona Arqueológica Cuicuilco ARCHAEOLOGICAL SITE
(www.inah.gob.mx; Av Insurgentes Sur s/n; 9am-5pm; P; Villa Olímpica) FREE The principal structure is a huge circular platform of four levels, faced with volcanic stone blocks, which probably functioned as a ceremonial center. Set amid a park with sweeping views of the area and studded with cacti and shade trees, it makes a nice picnic spot. The site has a small museum containing skulls and artifacts discovered during excavations.

Tlalpan

Tlalpan today is what Coyoacán used to be – an outlying village with a bohemian atmosphere coupled with some impressive colonial architecture. The municipal seat of Mexico City's largest *delegación,* Tlalpan sits at the foot of the southern Ajusco range and enjoys a cooler, moister climate. There are some fine restaurants along the arcades of the charismatic plaza. To get here take metrobús Línea 1 to Fuentes Brotantes and walk four blocks east to the main square.

La Jalisciense HISTORIC BUILDING
(Plaza de la Constitución 7; noon-11:30pm Mon-Sat; Fuentes Brotantes) This building opened its doors in 1870, making it arguably the oldest cantina in Mexico City – now that's a good reason to pop in and wet your whistle.

Museo de Historia de Tlalpán MUSEUM
(55-5485-9048; Plaza de la Constitución 10; 10am-6pm Tue-Sun; Fuentes Brotantes) FREE Hosts compelling contemporary art and historical exhibits in naturally lit galleries off the courtyard.

Casa Frisaac CULTURAL CENTER
(www.twitter.com/cfrissac; Plaza de la Constitución 1; 10am-6pm; Fuentes Brotantes) FREE This 19th-century estate, once the property of President Adolfo Lopez Mateos, now houses an art gallery with temporary exhibits, and a small auditorium for concerts and dance performances.

Capilla de las Capuchinas Sacramentarias CHAPEL
(55-5573-2395; Av Hidalgo 43; admission M$60; visiting hours 9:30-11:30am Mon-Fri; Fuentes Brotantes) There's a sublime simplicity about this chapel, located inside a convent for Capuchin nuns. Designed by modernist architect Luis Barragán in 1952, the austere altar, free of the usual iconography, consists only of a trio of gold panels. In the morning, light streams through a stained-glass window made by German-Mexican artist Mathias Goeritz. Visits by appointment only.

Tlatelolco & Guadalupe

Plaza de las Tres Culturas HISTORIC SITE
(Plaza of the Three Cultures; 55-5583-0295; www.tlatelolco.inah.gob.mx; cnr Eje Central Lázaro Cárdenas & Flores Magón; 8am-6pm; P; M Tlatelolco) FREE So named because it symbolizes the fusion of pre-Hispanic and Spanish roots

WORTH A TRIP

PARQUE NACIONAL DESIERTO DE LOS LEONES

Cool, fragrant pine and oak forests dominate this 20-sq-km **national park** (6am-5pm) in the hills surrounding the Valle de México. Some 23km southwest of Mexico City and 800m higher, it makes for a fine escape from the carbon monoxide and concrete.

The name derives from the **Ex-Convento del Santo Desierto de Nuestra Señora del Carmen** (55-5814-1172; Camino al Desierto de los Leones; admission M$11; 10am-5pm Tue-Sun), the 17th-century former Carmelite monastery within the park. The Carmelites called their isolated monasteries 'deserts' to commemorate Elijah, who lived as a recluse in the desert near Mt Carmel. The 'Leones' in the name may stem from the presence of wild cats in the area, but more likely it refers to José and Manuel de León, who once administered the monastery's finances.

The restored monastery has exhibition halls and a restaurant. Tours in Spanish are run by guides (garbed in cassock and sandals) who lead you through expansive gardens around the buildings and the patios within, as well as some underground passageways.

The rest of the park has extensive walking trails (robberies have been reported, so stick to the main paths). Next to El Leon Dorado restaurant, stairs lead down to a gorgeous picnic area with several small waterfalls and a duck pond.

Buses depart to the former *convento* from metro Viveros (in front of the 7-Eleven) at 7:30am Monday to Friday, or from Paradero las Palmas in San Ángel at 7:30am, noon and 3:30pm (also Monday to Friday). On Saturday and Sunday there are hourly departures from Paradero las Palmas and metro Viveros from 8am to 3:30pm. Be sure to ask the driver if the bus arrives as far as the *ex-convento* (some stop short in a mountain town called Santa Rosa).

into the Mexican *mestizo* identity, this plaza displays the architectural legacy of three cultural facets: the Aztec pyramids of Tlatelolco, the 17th-century Spanish Templo de Santiago and the modern tower that houses the Centro Cultural Universitario.

Recent archaeological finds have altered long-held views about Tlatelolco's history. According to the conventional version, Tlatelolco was founded by an Aztec faction in the 14th century on a separate island in Lago de Texcoco and later conquered by the Aztecs of Tenochtitlán. But a pyramid excavated on the site in late 2007 actually predates the establishment of Tenochtitlán by as much as 200 years. All agree, however, that Tlatelolco was the scene of the largest public market in the Valle de México, connected by a causeway to Tenochtitlán's ceremonial center.

During the siege of the Aztec capital, Cortés defeated Tlatelolco's defenders, led by Cuauhtémoc. An inscription about the battle in the plaza translates as 'This was neither victory nor defeat. It was the sad birth of the *mestizo* people that is Mexico today.'

You can view the remains of Tlatelolco's main pyramid-temple and other Aztec buildings from a walkway around them. Tlatelolco's main temple was constructed in stages, with each of seven temples superimposed atop its predecessors. The double pyramid on view, one of the earliest stages, has twin staircases that supposedly ascended to temples dedicated to Tláloc and Huitzilopochtli. Numerous calendar glyphs are carved into the outer walls.

Recognizing the significance of the site, the Spanish erected the **Templo de Santiago** here in 1609, using stones from the Aztec structures as building materials. Just inside the main doors of this church is the **baptismal font of Juan Diego**.

Tlatelolco is also a symbol of modern troubles. On October 2, 1968, hundreds of student protesters were massacred here by government troops on the eve of the Mexico City Olympic Games. The weeks before the Olympics had been marked by a wave of protests against political corruption and authoritarianism, and president Gustavo Díaz Ordaz, anxious to present an image of stability to the world, was employing heavy-handed tactics to stop the unrest.

On that October day, helicopters hovered over the Plaza de las Tres Culturas and a massive police contingent cordoned off the protest zone. Suddenly shots rang out, apparently from the balcony that served as a speakers' platform. Police then opened fire on the demonstrators and mayhem ensued. A government-authorized account reported

20 protesters killed, however, researchers and media reports estimate the real number is closer to 300.

The generally accepted theory, though there are many, is that the government staged the massacre, planting snipers on the balcony. To this day the incident still generates a massive protest march from Tlatelolco to the Zócalo on October 2.

Along Eje Central Lázaro Cárdenas, northbound trolleybuses pass right by the Plaza de las Tres Culturas.

Centro Cultural Universitario Tlatelolco MUSEUM
(☎55-5517-2818; www.tlatelolco.unam.mx; Flores Magón 1; admission M$30, Sun free; ⌚10am-6pm Tue-Sun; Ⓜ Tlatelolco) The events that occurred before, during and after the 1968 massacre on Plaza de las Tres Culturas are chronicled in Memorial del 68, a compelling multi media exhibit in the Centro Cultural Universitario Tlatelolco. The cultural center has two other outstanding permanent exhibits.

The shiny new Museo de Sitio houses more than 400 objects unearthed at the archaeological site, such as pre-Hispanic offerings and ceramic artifacts. The interactive museum continues on the 2nd floor in the tower building across the way, where you can learn about colonial-era Tlatelolco and the area's flora and fauna. The tower's 3rd floor is home to the Colección Stavenhagen, an extraordinary collection of more than 500 pre-Hispanic clay and stone sculptures, including amusing animal figures and phallic works.

Basílica de Guadalupe SHRINE
(www.virgendeguadalupe.org.mx; Plaza de las Américas 1; ⌚6am-9pm; Ⓜ La Villa-Basílica) FREE A cult developed around this site after a Christian convert named Juan Diego claimed in December 1531 that the Virgin Mary appeared before him on the Cerro del Tepeyac (Tepeyac Hill). After numerous sightings, as the story goes, the lady's image was miraculously emblazoned on Diego's cloak, causing a bishop to believe the story and build a shrine in her honor.

Over the centuries Nuestra Señora de Guadalupe came to receive credit for all manner of miracles, hugely aiding the acceptance of Catholicism by Mexicans. Despite the protests of some clergy, who saw the cult as a form of idolatry (with the Virgin as a Christianized version of the Aztec goddess Tonantzin), in 1737 the Virgin was officially declared the patron of Mexico. Two centuries later she was named celestial patron of Latin America and empress of the Americas, and in 2002 Juan Diego was canonized by Pope John Paul II. Today the Virgin's shrines around the Cerro del Tepeyac (formerly an Aztec shrine site) are the most revered in Mexico, attracting thousands of pilgrims daily and hundreds of thousands on the days leading up to her feast day, December 12. Some pilgrims travel the last meters to the shrine on their knees.

Around 1700, to accommodate the faithful flock, the four-towered Basílica de Guadalupe was erected at the site of an earlier shrine. But by the 1970s, the old yellow-domed building proved inadequate for the task, so the new Basílica de Nuestra Señora de Guadalupe was built next door. Designed by Pedro Ramírez Vázquez, it is a vast, round, open-plan structure with a capacity of more than 40,000 people. The image of the Virgin, dressed in a green mantle trimmed with gold, hangs above and behind the basilica's main altar, where moving walkways bring visitors as close as possible.

The rear of the Antigua Basílica is now the **Museo de la Basílica de Guadalupe** (☎55-5577-6022; admission M$5; ⌚10am-5:30pm Tue-Sun), which houses a fine collection of colonial art interpreting the miraculous vision.

Stairs behind the Antigua Basílica climb about 100m to the hilltop **Capilla del Cerrito** (Hill Chapel), where Juan Diego had his vision, then lead down the east side of the hill to the Parque de la Ofrenda, with gardens and waterfalls around a sculpted scene of the apparition. Continue on down to the baroque **Templo del Pocito**, a circular structure with a trio of tiled cupolas, built in 1787 to commemorate the miraculous appearance of a spring where the Virgen de Guadalupe had stood. From there the route leads back to the main plaza, re-entering it beside the 17th-century **Antigua Parroquia de Indios** (Parish of Indians).

To reach the Basílica de Guadalupe, take the metro to La Villa–Basílica station, then walk two blocks north along Calzada de Guadalupe. Or you can take any 'Metro Hidalgo–La Villa' bus heading northeast on Paseo de la Reforma. To return downtown, walk to Calzada de los Misterios, a block west of Calzada de Guadalupe, and catch a southbound 'Auditorio' or 'Zócalo' bus.

Activities

Bicycling

On Sunday mornings Paseo de la Reforma is closed to auto traffic from Bosque de Chapultepec to the Alameda Central, and you can join the legions of *chilangos* who happily skate or cycle down the avenue.

Bicitekas CYCLING

(Map p110; http://inigo.bicitekas.org; ⌚departure time 9:30pm Wed) For an ambitious trek, this urban cycling group organizes rides departing from the Monumento a la Independencia Wednesday evenings. Groups of up to 200 cyclists ride to destinations such as Coyoacán and the northwestern suburb of Ciudad Satélite. Participants must be sufficiently robust to handle excursions of up to 40km. Helmets and rear lights are recommended.

Kayaking

Michmani KAYAKING

(www.xochimilco.df.gob.mx/turismo/michmani_precios.html; Embarcadero Cuemanco, Xochimilco, off Anillo Periférico Sur; per hr M$50) Take in some of the quieter parts of the Xochimilco canals while kayaking, and do some birdwatching while you're at it. You'll spot ducks, egrets and herons, among many other migratory and endemic species, and you can also visit the many nurseries along the shores. To get here, go to metro General Anaya and exit the station on the east side of Calzada de Tlalpan, then walk 50m north to catch a 'Tláhuac Paradero' pesero. Get off at the Embarcadero Cuemanco entrance and walk about 1km to Michmani, just beyond the *embarcadero*.

Lago de Chapultepec KAYAKING

(Chapultepec Lake; Map p90; www.chapultepec.com.mx/visita.asp?Lugar=114; kayaks/paddleboats/rowboats per hr M$40/50/60; ⌚9am-4:30pm Tue-Sun; Ⓜ Auditorio) Take a kayak, paddleboat or rowboat out for a spin with the ducks on Chapultepec Lake.

Ice-Skating

As part of a government program to bring fun recreational activities to the city's poorer inhabitants, a huge ice-skating rink is installed in the Zócalo during the Christmas holiday season. Ice skates are loaned out free of charge, but you may have to wait up to an hour.

Courses

If you like to dance, learn a few great steps at the **Plaza de Danzón**, northwest of La Ciudadela, near metro Balderas. Couples crowd the plaza every Saturday afternoon to do the *danzón*, an elegant and complicated Cuban step that infiltrated Mexico in the 19th century. Lessons in *danzón* and other steps are given from 10am to 2:30pm and 4:30pm to 6pm; they cost M$30.

Centro de Enseñanza Para Extranjeros LANGUAGE COURSE

(Foreigners' Teaching Center; ☎55-5622-2470; www.cepe.unam.mx; Av Universidad 3002, Ciudad Universitaria; 6-week course US$477; 🚌Ciudad Universitaria) The national university offers six-week intensive classes, meeting for three hours daily from Monday through Friday. Students who already speak Spanish may take content courses on Mexican art and culture.

Escuela de Gastronomía Mexicana COOKING COURSE

(Map p90; ☎55-5264-2484; www.esgamex.com; Coahuila 207; 3hr course incl ingredients M$700-850; 🚌Campeche) Learn how to cook Mexican dishes from bilingual chefs. Popular classes include *pozole* (hominy soup), *mole poblano* (chicken in a chili and chocolate sauce) and *tamales* (corn-based snack with various fillings).

Tours

Turibús Circuito Turístico BUS TOUR

(Map p66; ☎55-5141-1360; www.turibus.com.mx; adult/child 4-12yr M$140/70, themed tours M$165-225; ⌚9am-9pm) Red double-decker buses run three *circuitos* (routes) across the city: Centro (downtown), Sur (south) and Basílica (north). Buses pass every hour or so and you can hop off and back on them at any designated stop. All routes stop on the west side of the cathedral. Fares are slightly higher on Saturdays and Sundays.

Turibús also offers themed tours, eg a cantina excursion. See the website for times.

Eat Mexico CULINARY EXPERIENCE

(☎US 917-930-7503, cell phone 55-43632896; www.eatmexico.com; tours US$85-145) Bilingual guides lead groups on three- to four-hour themed walking tours. Choose between street food, market fare, regional cuisine or a nocturnal tacos and mezcal crawl. Eat Mexico also does customized tours for specific culinary needs.

Mexico Soul & Essence CULINARY EXPERIENCE
(Map p84; ☎55-5564-8457, cell phone 55-29175408; www.mexicosoulandessence.com; tours US$95-175, cooking courses US$300) Customized culinary/cultural excursions by Ruth Alegría, one of the city's foremost food experts. She arranges dining outings, market tours and specialized trips. She also offers an entertaining Mexican cooking course.

Journeys Beyond the Surface TOUR
(☎cell phone 55-17452380; www.travelmexicocity.com.mx; group tours M$2275-2900) Personalized eight-hour walking tours on aspects of the DF experience, with an off-the-beaten-track attitude – for instance, you can do a murals, graffiti and street art excursion. The guides are well-versed in history and anthropology if you choose to visit pre-Hispanic and colonial-era sites.

Wayak TOUR
(☎55-5652-9331; www.wayak.mx; day trips per person M$460-660, balloon rides incl ground transportation M$2400) Want a breath of fresh air? This tour outfit does day trips to the colonial town of Taxco, the pyramids of Teotihuacán, or if you prefer, a balloon ride up above the pyramids. See website for details.

Festivals & Events

Mexico City celebrates some unique local events in addition to all the major nationwide festivals, which often take on a special flavor in the capital.

Festival de México CULTURAL
(www.festival.org.mx; ⌚Mar) The *centro histórico* hosts music, theater, dance and culinary events featuring talent from Mexico and abroad – it's the city's biggest cultural bash of the year.

Semana Santa RELIGIOUS
(⌚Mar or Apr) The most evocative events of Holy Week (late March or April) are in the Iztapalapa district, 9km southeast of the Zócalo, where a gruesomely realistic Passion Play is enacted on Good Friday.

Foundation of Tenochtitlán DANCE
(⌚Aug; Ⓜ Tlatelolco) Held on August 13 to celebrate the foundation of the Mexican capital, this is a major summit for Concheros (Aztec dancers) on Plaza de las Tres Culturas in Tlatelolco.

Grito de la Independencia FIREWORKS
(⌚Sep; Ⓜ Zócalo) On September 15, the eve of Independence Day, thousands gather in the Zócalo to hear the Mexican president's version of the *Grito de Dolores* (Cry of Dolores) – Hidalgo's famous call to rebellion against the Spanish in 1810 – from the central balcony of the Palacio Nacional at 11pm. Afterwards, there's a fireworks display.

Día de Muertos TRADITIONAL
(Day of the Dead; ⌚Nov) In the lead-up to Day of the Dead (November 1 and 2), elaborate *ofrendas* (altars) show up everywhere. Some of the best are at Anahuacalli (p95), Museo Dolores Olmedo (p89), the Zócalo (p69), and in the neighborhood of **San Andrés Mixquic** (www.mixquic.com.mx), in the extreme southeast of the Distrito Federal.

Fiesta de Santa Cecilia MUSIC
(⌚Nov; Ⓜ Garibaldi) The patron saint of musicians is honored with special fervor at Plaza Garibaldi on November 22.

Día de Nuestra Señora de Guadalupe RELIGIOUS
(⌚Dec; Ⓜ La Villa-Basílica) At the Basílica de Guadalupe, the Day of Our Lady of Guadalupe caps 10 days of festivities that honor Mexico's religious patron. The numbers of pilgrims reach millions by December 12, when groups of indigenous dancers perform nonstop on the basilica's broad plaza.

Sleeping

As a frequent destination for both Mexican and foreign visitors, the DF overflows with lodging options – everything from no-frills guesthouses to top-flight hotels. Some of the most reasonable places are in the *centro histórico*, while more luxurious accommodations, including branches of some major international chains, are concentrated in Polanco and the Zona Rosa. In the trendy Roma and Condesa neighborhoods, the offerings range from hostels to chic boutique hotels. Midrange lodgings abound in the Alameda and Plaza de la República areas, though they tend to trade character for neutral modern comfort. (Note that places with the word *garage* on the sign generally cater to short-term trysting guests.)

Centro Histórico

For nonbusiness travelers, the historic center is the obvious place to stay. Ongoing renovations of its infrastructure and preservation of its numerous historic edifices have boosted the zone's appeal, and it remains one of the more affordable areas.

★**Casa San Ildefonso** HOSTEL $
(Map p66; ☎55-5789-1999; www.casasanildefonso.com; San Ildefonso 38; dm M$220, d M$640, without bathroom M$540, all incl breakfast; ; Zócalo) A 19th-century building that most recently served as a storage facility for street vendors has been transformed into a cheerful hostel off a pedestrian thoroughfare. Unlike most downtown hostels, the high-ceiling dorms, private rooms and common areas here get wonderful sunlight. Guests have breakfast in a tranquil courtyard with a fountain, singing canaries and the gremlinesque mascot Delfina.

Hostal Regina HOSTEL $
(Map p66; ☎55-5709-4192; www.hostalcentrohistoricoregina.com; Calle 5 de Febrero 53; dm M$190, r without bathroom M$450, ste M$900, all incl breakfast; ; Isabel La Católica) Off the lively Regina corridor, this 18th-century historic building makes a great base to explore downtown. On offer are dorms with wood floors and high ceilings, private rooms with shared bathrooms and a two-story 'suite' that comfortably sleeps four. Guests socialize on the rooftop bar.

Mexico City Hostel HOSTEL $
(Map p66; ☎55-5512-3666; www.mexicocityhostel.com; República de Brasil 8; dm incl breakfast from M$170, d M$500, without bathroom M$400; ; Zócalo) Steps from the Zócalo, this colonial structure has been artfully restored, with original wood beams and stone walls as a backdrop for modern, energy-efficient facilities. Spacious dorms have four or six sturdy bunk beds on terracotta floors. Immaculate bathrooms trimmed with *azulejo* (painted ceramic tiles) amply serve around 100 occupants.

Hotel Isabel HOTEL $
(Map p66; ☎55-5518-1213; www.hotel-isabel.com.mx; Isabel La Católica 63; s/d M$330/450, without bathroom M$250/350; ; República del Salvador) A longtime budget-traveler's favorite, the Isabel offers large, well-scrubbed rooms with old but sturdy furniture, high ceilings and great balconies, plus a hostel-like social scene.

Hostel Mundo Joven Catedral HOSTEL $
(Map p66; ☎55-5518-1726; www.mundojovenhostels.com/hcatedral.php; República de Guatemala 4; dm/d from M$200/440, incl breakfast; ; Zócalo) Backpacker central, this HI affiliate is abuzz with a global rainbow of young travelers. Dorms are tidy and guests love the rooftop bar, but it's not the quietest of hostels.

Chillout Flat B&B $$
(Map p66; ☎55-6310-6497; www.chilloutflat.com.mx; Apt 102, Bolívar 8; s/d incl breakfast from M$850/950; ; Allende) Chill with other travelers in one of two downtown apartments that have been converted into colorful guesthouses with hardwood floors. Street-facing rooms in this lovely 1940s building recently got double-pane windows for noise reduction. Reservations a must.

Hotel Catedral HOTEL $$
(Map p66; ☎55-5518-5232; www.hotelcatedral.com; Donceles 95; s/d/ste from M$690/925/1010; ; Zócalo) This comfortable lodging clearly benefits from its prime location in the heart of the *centro histórico*. Rooms got a recent makeover with dark-wood furnishings and firm mattresses. For cityscape views, order a drink on the rooftop terrace.

Hotel Gillow HOTEL $$
(Map p66; ☎55-5510-0791; www.hotelgillow.com; Isabel La Católica 17; s/d/ste M$690/880/1100; ; Allende) In this historic building with friendly, old-fashioned service, remodeled rooms are done up with faux wood floors and flat-screen TVs. If available, request a double room with a private terrace.

Hampton Inn & Suites HOTEL $$$
(Map p66; ☎55-8000-5000; www.hamptonmexicocity.com; Calle 5 de Febrero 24; r/ste incl breakfast from M$1228/1747; ; Isabel La Católica) This well-preserved historic gem underwent an elaborate makeover to preserve its facade and Talavera-tiled walls. Well-appointed rooms with contemporary furnishings surround a six-story atrium with a stained-glass ceiling. A good seafood restaurant shares the property.

Gran Hotel Ciudad de México HOTEL $$$
(Map p66; ☎55-1083-7700; www.granhoteldelaciudaddemexico.com.mx; Av 16 de Septiembre 82; r/ste incl breakfast from M$3770/4420; ; Zócalo) The Gran Hotel flaunts the French art nouveau style of the pre-revolutionary era. Crowned by a stained-glass canopy crafted by Tiffany in 1908, the atrium is a fin de siècle fantasy of curved balconies, wrought-iron elevators and chirping birds in giant cages. Rooms do not disappoint in comparison. Weekend brunch (M$250) is served on a terrace overlooking the Zócalo.

NH Centro Histórico HOTEL $$$
(Map p66; 55-5130-1850; www.nh-hotels.com; Palma 42; r/ste from M$1890/2475; ; Zócalo) Riding the downtown development wave, Spanish chain NH planted a branch in the center. Lounges and rooms get a Euro-minimalist treatment, and spacious suites occupy the curved corners of the aerodynamically designed 1940s structure.

Alameda Central & Around

Like the *centro histórico,* this section is undergoing major renovations, though pockets of neglect are reminders of the 1985 earthquake that devastated the zone. By day the neighborhood bustles with shoppers, but after dark it quietens down considerably.

Hotel Marlowe HOTEL $$
(Map p76; 55-5521-9540; www.hotelmarlowe.com.mx; Independencia 17; s/d/ste M$670/810/870; ; San Juan de Letrán) The remodeled Marlowe stands across from Chinatown's pagoda gate. Grab a suite if available – they cost nearly the same as standard double rooms, plus they're brighter, more spacious and have small balconies. Fitness freaks will appreciate the gym with a view.

Boutique Hotel de Cortés BOUTIQUE HOTEL $$$
(Map p76; 55-5518-2181; www.boutiquehotel-decortes.com; Av Hidalgo 85; r/ste incl breakfast from M$2400/3480; ; Hidalgo) Formerly a hospice for Augustinian pilgrims, this boutique hotel offers tasteful rooms and suites encircling a lovely 17th-century baroque patio. Adding an artistic touch, the modern rooms feature floral-patterned hand-carved headboards and furnishings. The smart rooftop lounge bar overlooks the Alameda.

Plaza de la República & Around

Further away from the Zócalo, the area around the Monumento a la Revolución is awash with hotels, with a number of dives interspersed amid the business-class establishments. The semiresidential zone offers glimpses of neighborhood life.

Hostel Suites DF HOSTEL $
(Map p76; 55-5535-8117; www.facebook.com/hostelsuitesdf; Terán 38; dm/d incl breakfast from M$180/400; ; Plaza de la República) Near the Monumento a la Revolución, this small HI-affiliated hostel offers pleasant common areas, dorms with in-room bathrooms and a great central location t within walking distance of downtown.

Casa de los Amigos GUESTHOUSE $
(Map p76; 55-5705-0521; www.casadelosamigos.org; Mariscal 132; dm M$100, r without bathroom M$200; ; Revolución) The Quaker-run Casa is a guesthouse popular with NGO workers, activists and researchers, but it welcomes walk-in travelers. Vegetarian breakfast (M$30) is served and guests can take free weekly Spanish and yoga classes. You're not allowed to smoke or drink alcohol in the house. If you're interested in volunteer work, see the website for various options.

Hotel Edison HOTEL $
(Map p76; 55-5566-0933; Edison 106; s/d M$299/429; ; Revolución) Beyond the bunkerlike exterior, accommodations face a rectangular garden surrounded by pre-Hispanic motifs. Although they come with faded wallpaper and dated fixtures, some rooms are enormous, with large marble washbasins and closets.

Plaza Revolución Hotel HOTEL $$
(Map p76; 55-5234-1910; www.hotelplazarevolucion.com; Terán 35; s/d M$810/870; ; Plaza de la República) On a quiet street four blocks east of Plaza de la República, this shiny new establishment is a stylish option in an area where cut-rate hotels are the norm. Modern rooms with wood floors are done up in neutral colors and kept impeccably clean.

Ramada Reforma HOTEL $$
(Map p76; 55-5097-0277; www.ramadareforma.com; Puente de Alvarado 22; s/d incl breakfast from M$800/1150; ; Hidalgo) Choose from refurbished 'standard' digs in this hotel's older section or pricier 'superior' rooms in the new wing. A heated indoor pool awaits on the top floor. Just 1½ blocks from Reforma.

Palace Hotel HOTEL $$
(Map p76; 55-5566-2400; www.palace-hotel.com.mx; Ramírez 7; s/d/ste M$500/729/1044; ; Plaza de la República) Run by gregarious Asturians, the Palace has large, neatly maintained rooms, some with broad balconies giving terrific views down palm-lined Ramírez to the domed monument. Request a street-facing room if you want brighter digs. Cash-paying guests get substantial discounts.

QUIRKY MEXICO CITY

Anyone who's spent time in Mexico will understand why French poet André Breton called it 'the surrealist country par excellence.' Something strange lurks beneath the surface of everyday life.

Museo del Juguete Antiguo México (Antique Toy Museum; www.museodeljuguete.mx; Dr Olvera 15, cnr Eje Central Lázaro Cárdenas; admission M$50; ⏲9am-6pm Mon-Fri, to 4pm Sat, 10am-4pm Sun; P 👪; M Obrera) Mexican-born Japanese collector Roberto Shimizu has amassed more than a million toys in his lifetime, and this museum showcases about 60,000 pieces, ranging from life-sized robots to tiny action figures. Shimizu himself designed many of the unique display cases from recycled objects.

Several blocks west of the museum, at Dr Garciadiego 157, the same owners run a cultural center that houses dozens of works by local graffiti muralists and Belgian street artist ROA. The museum staff will gladly show you around the cultural center if it's closed.

Patrick Miller (Map p110; ☎55-5511-5406; www.patrickmiller.com.mx; Mérida 17; ⏲10:30pm-4am Fri; M Insurgentes) People-watching doesn't get any better than at this throbbing disco, founded by Mexico City DJ Patrick Miller. With a clientele ranging from black-clad '80s throwbacks to cross-dressers, the fun begins when dance circles open and regulars pull off moves that would make John Travolta proud.

La Faena (Map p66; ☎55-5510-4417; www.facebook.com/lafaenaoficial; Venustiano Carranza 49B; ⏲11am-11pm Mon-Thu, to 2am Fri & Sat, to 8pm Sun; 🚇 República del Salvador) This forgotten relic of a bar doubles as a bullfighting museum, with matadors in sequined outfits glaring intently from dusty cases, and bucolic canvases of grazing bulls.

Isla de las Muñecas (Embarcadero Cuemanco, Xochimilco; boat per hr M$350) For a truly surreal experience, head for Xochimilco and hire a gondola to the Island of the Dolls, where hundreds of creepy, decomposed dolls hang from trees. An island resident fished the playthings from the canals to mollify the spirit of a girl who had drowned nearby.

The best departure point for the four-hour round trip is Embarcadero Cuemanco. To get here, go to metro General Anaya and exit the station on the east side of Calzada de Tlalpan, then walk 50m north to catch a 'Tláhuac Paradero' pesero. Get off at the Embarcadero Cuemanco entrance.

Mercado de Sonora (cnr Fray Servando & Rosales, Colonia Merced Balbuena; ⏲10am-7pm; M Merced) This place has all the ingredients for Mexican witchcraft. Aisles are crammed with stalls hawking potions, amulets, voodoo dolls and other esoterica. This is also the place for a *limpia* (spiritual cleansing), a ritual involving clouds of incense and a herbal brushing. Sadly, some vendors at the market trade illegally in endangered animals. It's two blocks south of metro Merced.

Santa Muerte Altar (Alfarería, north of Mineros; M Tepito) Garbed in a sequined white gown, wearing a wig of dark tresses and clutching a scythe in her bony hand, the Saint Death figure bears an eerie resemblance to Mrs Bates from the film *Psycho*. The Santa Muerte is the object of a fast-growing cult in Mexico, particularly in crime-ridden Tepito, where many of her followers have lost faith in Catholicism. Enter the notoriously dangerous Tepito 'hood at your own risk. It's three blocks north of metro Tepito.

Zona Rosa & Around

Foreign businesspeople and tourists check in at the upscale hotels in this international commerce and nightlife area. Less-expensive establishments dot the quieter streets of Colonia Cuauhtémoc, north of Reforma, and Juárez, east of Insurgentes.

Casa González GUESTHOUSE **$$**
(Map p110; ☎55-5514-3302; www.hotelcasagonzalez.com; Río Sena 69; d/ste M$940/1200; P 🚭 ❄ @ 📶; M Insurgentes) A family-run operation for nearly a century, the Casa is a perennial hit with travelers seeking peace and quiet. Set around several flower-filled patios and semiprivate terraces, it's extraordinarily tranquil. Original portraits and

landscapes decorate some rooms, apparently done by a guest in lieu of payment.

Hotel María Cristina HOTEL $$
(Map p110; ☎55-5703-1212; www.hotelmariacristina.com.mx; Río Lerma 31; d/ste from M$860/1230; P ⊖ ❄ @ ☎; Reforma) Dating from the 1930s, this facsimile of an Andalucian estate makes an appealing retreat, particularly the adjacent bar with patio seating. Though lacking the lobby's colonial splendor, rooms are generally bright and comfortable.

Hotel Bristol HOTEL $$
(Map p110; ☎55-5533-6060; www.hotelbristol.com.mx; Plaza Necaxa 17; d M$930/1066; P ⊖ ❄ @ ☎; M Insurgentes) A good-value option in the Cuauhtémoc neighborhood, the Bristol caters primarily to business travelers, offering carpeted rooms with soothing colors and also an above-average restaurant.

Hotel Suites Amberes SUITES $$$
(Map p110; ☎55-5533-1306; www.suitesamberes.com.mx; Amberes 64; d/tr/q M$2000/2500/2900; P ⊖ ☎; M Insurgentes) Sure to please families and small groups, these spacious suites are basically large one- and two-bedroom apartments with a fully equipped kitchen, dining room and sofa bed. Street-facing rooms have the added plus of balconies. On the top floor is a sun deck, gym and sauna room.

Hotel Geneve HOTEL $$$
(Map p110; ☎55-5080-0800; www.hotelgeneve.com.mx; Londres 130; r incl breakfast M$2370, ste from M$3800; P ⊖ ❄ @ ☎; M Insurgentes) This Zona Rosa institution strives to maintain a belle époque ambience despite the globalized mishmash around it. The lobby exudes class, with dark wood paneling, oil canvases and high bookshelves. Rooms in the hotel's older rear section get a more pronounced colonial treatment, especially the 'vintage suites.'

Hotel Cityexpress BUSINESS HOTEL $$$
(Map p110; ☎55-1102-0280; www.cityexpress.com.mx; Havre 21; s/d incl breakfast M$1109/1192; P ⊖ ❄ @ ☎; Hamburgo) The Cityexpress emphasizes comfort and functionality, but decor outshines the neutral-modern look favored by most hotels in this price category.

St Regis Mexico City LUXURY HOTEL $$$
(Map p110; ☎55-5228-1818; www.stregis.com/mexicocity; Paseo de la Reforma 439; r/ste US$720/815; P ⊖ ❄ @ ☎ ≈; M Sevilla) The elegant St Regis occupies the lower 16 floors of a 31-story residential tower. The amenity-loaded rooms and suites perched high above afford sweeping views of the city, as do the gym and indoor infinity pool on the 15th floor. Rates drop by more than half for Friday and Saturday night stays.

Condesa

Thanks to the recent appearance of several attractive lodgings, this neighborhood south of Bosque de Chapultepec makes an excellent base with plenty of after-hours restaurants, bars and cafes.

★**Casa Comtesse** B&B $$
(Map p84; ☎55-5277-5418; www.casacomtesse.com; Benjamín Franklin 197; r incl breakfast from M$950; P ⊖ @ ☎; Escandón) Run by an amiable French owner, this 1940s building houses eight rooms adorned with tasteful art and furnishings, and a parquet-floored dining area. The Casa also has a graphic arts gallery with interesting works by Mexican artists, and can arrange affordable tours to the Teotihuacán ruins.

Stayinn Barefoot Hostel HOSTEL $$
(Map p84; ☎55-6286-3000; www.stayinnbarefoot.com; Juan Escutia 125; dm/d incl breakfast from M$180/650; ⊖ ☎; M Chapultepec) On the edge of Condesa, this artfully designed hostel is a breath of fresh air for a neighborhood lacking in mid-range accommodations. The cheerful lobby is done up in colorful mismatched tile floors and vintage furniture, while upstairs guests have use of a rooftop terrace. The Barefoot's welcoming mezcal bar seals the deal.

Hotel Roosevelt HOTEL $$
(Map p84; ☎55-5208-6813; www.hotelroosevelt.com.mx; Av Insurgentes Sur 287, cnr Av Yucatán; d from M$620, ste M$1000; P ⊖ ❄ ☎; Álvaro Obregón) On the eastern limits of Condesa and within easy reach of the Cuban club district, this friendly if functional hotel should appeal to nocturnally inclined travelers. Most of the suites have Jacuzzis and air-con.

★**Red Tree House** B&B $$$
(Map p84; ☎55-5584-3829; www.theredtreehouse.com; Culiacán 6; s/d/ste incl breakfast from US$113/137/274; ⊖ ☎; Campeche) The area's first B&B has all the comforts of home, if your home happens to be decorated with exquisite taste. Each of the 17 bedrooms and suites is uniquely furnished, and the roomy penthouse has a private patio. Downstairs, guests have the run of a cozy living

room and lovely rear garden, the domain of friendly pooch Abril.

The Red Tree has added five pleasant rooms in a house located a half-block away on Citlaltépetl.

★Villa Condesa BOUTIQUE HOTEL $$$

(Map p84; ☎55-5211-4892; www.villacondesa.com.mx; Colima 428; r incl breakfast from US$143; ; M Chapultepec) You can say *adiós* to hectic Mexico City from the moment you set foot in the Villa's leafy lobby. The 14 rooms in this striking historic building combine classic touches (each has a piece of antique furniture) with the modern trappings of a first-rate hotel. Reservations required and children under 12 not allowed. Guests have free use of bicycles.

Casa Stella B&B $$$

(Map p84; ☎55-6237-0102; www.casastella.com.mx; Ámsterdam 141; d incl breakfast from US$112; @; Campeche) Sitting pretty in a 1930s art deco building designed by famed architect Francisco Serrano, this house was recently converted into a B&B with seven rooms, some smaller than others, but all appealing in their own way. Ecofriendly Stella treats its own water, uses solar energy and collects rain water.

Roma

A slew of galleries, sidewalk cafes and bars lie within walking distance of most of the following places, and with party central Colonia Condesa conveniently nearby, you'll find more than enough late-night distractions.

Hostel Home HOSTEL $

(Map p84; ☎55-5511-1683; www.hostelhome.com.mx; Tabasco 303; dm incl breakfast M$150, r without bathroom M$450; @; Durango) Housed in a fine Porfiriato-era building and managed by easygoing staff, this 20-bed hostel is on the narrow tree-lined Calle Tabasco, a gateway to the Roma neighborhood.

Hostal 333 HOSTEL $

(Map p84; ☎55-5533-3609; www.hostal333.com; Colima 333; dm/d incl breakfast M$180/450; @; Durango) Guests revel in fiestas, barbecues and occasional gigs on a pleasant rooftop patio flanked by potted plants. Opt for standard-issue dorm rooms or private digs with your own bathroom.

Casa 180 GUESTHOUSE $$

(Map p84; ☎55-5533-9246, 55-55057777; www.180grados.mx; Colima 180; d M$1100; ; Durango) Stay in a master bedroom with antique furniture at this Roma guesthouse. You can't beat the location: Calle Colima is lined with restaurants, bars, interesting shops and art galleries. Your English-speaking host, who runs a clothing shop downstairs, is a great source of information.

Hotel Milán HOTEL $$

(Map p84; ☎55-5584-0222; www.hotelmilan.com.mx; Álvaro Obregón 94; s/d M$510/635; P@; Álvaro Obregón) Sitting on the main corridor of bohemian Roma, the Milán has gone modern with minimalist decor and contemporary art in its new-look lobby. In keeping with the makeover, upgraded rooms come with remodeled bathrooms.

Hotel Stanza HOTEL $$

(Map p84; ☎55-5208-0052; www.stanzahotel.com; Álvaro Obregón 13; r/ste M$820/1300; P@; Jardín Pushkin) A business travelers' hotel on the east end of Álvaro Obregón, the Stanza makes a cushy, relatively affordable base in the heart of the hopping Roma neighborhood.

Casa de la Condesa SUITES $$$

(Map p84; ☎55-5574-3186; www.extendedstaymexico.com; Plaza Luis Cabrera 16; ste incl breakfast from M$1209; ; Álvaro Obregón) Right on the delightful Plaza Luis Cabrera, the Casa makes a tranquil base for visitors on an extended stay, offering 'suites' that are more like studio apartments with kitchens. See the website for weekly rates.

La Casona BOUTIQUE HOTEL $$$

(Map p84; ☎55-5286-3001; www.hotellacasona.com.mx; Durango 280; r incl breakfast M$2200; ; M Sevilla) This stately mansion, restored to early-20th-century splendor, is one of the capital's most distinctive boutique hotels. Each of the 29 rooms is uniquely appointed to bring out its original charm.

Polanco

North of Bosque de Chapultepec, Polanco has excellent business and boutique hotel accommodations but very little to offer if you're pinching pesos.

Casa Castelar SUITES $$$

(Map p90; ☎55-5281-4990; www.casacastelar.com; Av Castelar 34; ste incl breakfast from US$137; @; M Auditorio) An affordable option by

Polanco standards, the large comfy suites here give you plenty of bang for your buck. The Castelar has no common areas, but breakfast is served at your door. Chapultepec Park's main sights are within walking distance.

Hábita Hotel BOUTIQUE HOTEL **$$$**
(Map p90; ☎55-5282-3100; www.hotelhabita.com; Av Presidente Masaryk 201; d incl breakfast from M$3406; P ⊖ ❄ ≋; M Polanco) Architect Enrique Norten turned a functional apartment building into a smart boutique hotel. Decor in the 36 rooms is boldly minimalist and the most economical digs measure 20 sq meters (call them cozy or just plain small). The rooftop bar, called Área, is a hot nightspot.

W Mexico City HOTEL **$$$**
(Map p90; ☎55-9138-1800; www.whotels.com; Campos Elíseos 252; r from US$189 Fri & Sat, US$389 Sun-Thu; P ⊖ ❄ @ ; M Auditorio) One of the four sentinels opposite the Auditorio Nacional, this 25-floor business hotel is determined to break away from the stodginess of its neighbors. Cherry and ebony colored rooms feature silken hammocks hanging in the shower area. Rates drop considerably on Fridays and Saturdays.

Xochimilco

There's no better way to appreciate the natural wonders of Xochimilco's canals than camping in the middle of it all.

Michmani CAMPGROUND **$**
(☎55-5489-7773; www.xochimilco.df.gob.mx/turismo/michmani_precios.html; Embarcadero Cuemanco, off Anillo Periférico Sur; campsites per person incl tent M$150, cabin M$650; P) Ecotourism center Michmani arranges stays at **La Llorona Cihuacoatl** (☎55-9147-4775, 55-5489-7773; lallorona_chillona@hotmail.com) campground, which sits on a peaceful off-grid *chinampa* (garden). The center rents tents, but you'll have to bring a sleeping bag, or you can stay in a tiny rustic cabin with two beds. Also available are barbecue grills and temascals (steam baths; M$250).

To get here, go to metro General Anaya and exit the station on the east side of Calzada de Tlalpan, then walk 50m north to catch a 'Tláhuac Paradero' pesero. Get off at the Embarcadero Cuemanco entrance and walk about 1km to Michmani, just beyond the *embarcadero*. From there a boat will take you to La Llorona.

Coyoacán & Ciudad Universitaria

The southern community has limited budget options and several appealing guesthouses. Check with the Coyoacán tourist office about short-term homestays.

Hostal Cuija Coyoacán HOSTEL **$**
(Map p114; ☎55-5659-9310; www.hostalcuijacoyoacan.com; Berlín 268; dm from M$210, r M$650; ⊖ @ ; M Coyoacán) This lizard-themed HI hostel offers a clean and affordable base to check out Coyoacán's sights. The house has pleasant common areas, but don't expect the smallish dorms and private rooms to wow you.

El Cenote Azul HOSTEL **$**
(☎55-5554-8730; www.elcenoteazul.com; Alfonso Pruneda 24, Colonia Copilco el Alto; dm M$150; ⊖ ; M Copilco) This laid-back hostel near the UNAM campus has six neatly kept four- or two-bed rooms sharing three Talavera-tiled bathrooms. The downstairs bar is a popular hangout for university students. See the website for directions.

★**Chalet del Carmen** GUESTHOUSE **$$**
(Map p114; ☎55-5554-9572; www.chaletdelcarmen.com; Guerrero 94; s/d/ste from M$677/977/1477; ⊖ ; M Coyoacán) Run by a friendly Coyoacán native and his Swiss wife, this ecofriendly house strikes a warm blend of Mexican and European aesthetics. The five rooms and two suites have antique furnishings and natural lighting. Guests have use of a kitchen and bicycles. Reservations a must.

Hostal Frida GUESTHOUSE **$$**
(Map p114; ☎55-5659-7005; www.hostalfridabyb.com; Mina 54; r M$750; ⊖ ; M Coyoacán) Don't let the 'hostal' tag fool you: this family-run place has well-appointed accommodations more along the lines of a guesthouse. Each of the six doubles occupies its own level in adjacent structures, and three come with kitchens.

Airport

Hotel Aeropuerto HOTEL **$$**
(☎55-5785-5318; www.hotelaeropuerto.com.mx; Blvd Puerto Aéreo 380; s/d M$590/750; P ⊖ ❄ ; M Terminal Aérea) Although there are several upscale hotels linked to the terminals, this affordable hotel across the street serves just fine for weary travelers. The only nonchain in the zone, it has helpful reception staff

and neutral modern rooms, some overlooking the airport runway through soundproof windows.

Turn left outside the domestic terminal; beyond the metro, take a left onto Blvd Puerto Aéreo and cross via the pedestrian bridge.

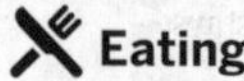

Eating

The capital offers eateries for all tastes and budgets, from soulful taco stalls to gourmet restaurants. In recent years, the city has emerged as a major destination for culinary travelers, as Mexican chefs win the sort of praise formerly reserved for their counterparts in New York and Paris. Most of the hottest venues for contemporary cuisine show up in Roma, Condesa and Polanco.

Budget eaters will find literally thousands of restaurants and holes-in-the-wall serving *comida corrida* (set lunch) for as little as M$50. Market buildings are good places to look for these, while *tianguis* (street markets) customarily have eating areas offering tacos and quesadillas.

Certain items can be found all over town. In the evening, vendors roam the streets on bicycles selling hot *tamales,* their arrival heralded by nasal-toned recordings through cheap speakers. You'll know the *camote* (sweet potato) man is coming by the shrill steam whistle emitted from his cart, heard for blocks around.

Centro Histórico

The historic center is a great place to enjoy traditional Mexican dishes in elegant surroundings.

★Los Cocuyos TAQUERÍA $
(Map p66; Bolívar 54; tacos M$8-15; ⏲10am-6am; Ⓜ San Juan de Letrán) *Suadero* (beef) tacos abound in the capital, but this place reigns supreme. Follow your nose to the bubbling vat of meats and go for the artery-choking *campechano,* a mixed beef and sausage taco. For the more adventurous eater, there are *ojo* (eye) or *lengua* (tongue) tacos.

EAT AROUND MEXICO IN A DAY

The big city has long attracted opportunity-seekers from all over the republic. Fortunately, these folks from Mérida, Chiapas, Jalisco and Guerrero strive to keep their traditions alive, first and foremost in the kitchen.

Con Sabor a Tixtla (Map p84; www.consaboratixtla.com; Chiapas 206, Colonia Roma; tacos M$21-25, mains M$80-125; ⏲1-6pm Mon & Tue, 10am-6pm Wed-Sun; 🖉; 🚌 Sonora) The home-cooked goodness of retired school teacher Enedina Bello González draws on two generations of family recipes from Tixtla, Guerrero. Specialties in this colorful Roma eatery include *pozole* (hominy soup) and *chiles rellenos tradicionales de Tixtla* (Tixtla-style stuffed chilies).

La Polar (☎55-5546-5066; www.lapolar.mx; Guillermo Prieto 129, Colonia San Rafael; birria M$112; ⏲7am-2am; Ⓟ; Ⓜ Normal) Run by a family from Ocotlán, Jalisco, this boisterous beer hall has essentially one item on the menu: *birria,* a spiced goat stew. Spirits are raised further by mariachis and *norteño* combos who work the half-dozen salons here.

Coox Hanal (Map p 66; ☎55-5709-3613; www.facebook.com/coox.hanal; 2nd fl, Isabel La Católica 83, Colonia Centro; mains M$48-120; ⏲10:30am-6:30pm; Ⓟ 📶; Ⓜ Isabel La Católica) Started in 1953 by boxer Raúl Salazar from Mérida, this establishment prepares top-notch Yucatecan fare such as *poc chuc* (grilled pork marinated in orange juice) and *cochinita pibil* (pit-cooked pork). And then there's the obligatory four-alarm *habanero* salsa.

Los Tolucos (Hernández y Dávalos 40, cnr Bolívar, Colonia Algarín; pozoles M$64-70; ⏲10am-9pm; Ⓟ; Ⓜ Lázaro Cárdenas) Voted the best *pozole* in a Mexico City radio station contest. The Guerrero-style green *pozole* here has been drawing people from far and wide for more than four decades. The restaurant is three blocks east of metro Lázaro Cárdenas.

Tamales Chiapanecos María Geraldine (Map p66; ☎55-5608-8993; Plaza Hidalgo, Coyoacán; tamales M$30-35; ⏲10am-10pm Sat & Sun; Ⓜ Coyoacán) At the passageway next to the San Juan Bautista church, look for these incredible *tamales* by Chiapas native doña María Geraldine. Wrapped in banana leaves, they're stuffed with ingredients such as olives, prunes and almonds, and laced with sublime salsas.

Taquería Los Paisas TAQUERÍA $
(Map p66; ☎55-5542-8139; Jesús María 131; tacos M$16-18; ⏰9am-midnight; Ⓜ Pino Suárez) This corner taco stand southeast of the Zócalo slings overstuffed steak, sausage, *pastor* (spit-roasted pork) and *campechano* (mixed) tacos. Help yourself from the heaping trays of garnishes.

La Casa del Pavo SANDWICHES $
(Map p66; ☎55-5518-4282; Motolinía 40; tortas M$30; ⏰9am-9pm; Ⓜ Allende) Tasty *tortas de pavo* (turkey sandwiches) with avocado are served hot off the griddle at this old-school greasy spoon.

Helus MIDDLE EASTERN $
(Map p66; ☎55-5522-2130; www.productoshelus.com.mx; República del Salvador 157; empanadas M$23, shawarmas M$40, pastries M$20-34; ⏰9am-7pm Mon-Fri, to 5pm Sat; ☑; Ⓑ Las Cruces) Lebanese pastries, empanadas, shawarmas and various vegetarian goodies are prepared by a distant relative of Mexican billionaire Carlos Slim.

Café El Popular CAFE $
(Map p66; ☎55-5518-6081; www.cafeelpopular.com.mx; Av 5 de Mayo 52; breakfast M$49-60; ⏰24hr; Ⓜ Allende) So popular was this tiny round-the-clock cafe that another more amply proportioned branch was opened next door. Fresh pastries, *café con leche* (coffee with milk) and good combination breakfasts are the main attractions.

Vegetariano Madero VEGETARIAN $
(Map p66; ☎55-5521-6880; Av Madero 56; set lunch M$75; ⏰8am-8pm; ☑; Ⓜ Zócalo) Despite its austere entrance, this is a lively upstairs restaurant where a pianist plinks out old favorites. The meatless menu includes a range of tasty variations on Mexican standards, and there are vegan options as well.

Mercado San Camilito MARKET $
(Map p66; Plaza Garibaldi; pozoles M$65-70; ⏰24hr; Ⓟ; Ⓜ Garibaldi) This block-long building contains more than 70 kitchens preparing, among other items, Jalisco-style *pozole*, a broth brimming with hominy kernels, and pork and served with garnishes such as radish and oregano. Specify *maciza* (meat) if pig noses and ears fail to excite you.

★ **Hostería de Santo Domingo** MEXICAN $$
(Map p66; ☎55-5526-5276; www.hosteriadesantodomingo.mx; Belisario Domínguez 72; chile en nogada M$205, mains M$60-210; ⏰9am-10:30pm Mon-Sat, to 9pm Sun; 📶; Ⓑ República de Chile) Whipping up classic Mexican fare since 1860, Mexico City's oldest restaurant has a festive atmosphere, enhanced by live piano music. The menu offers numerous dishes, but everyone comes here for the *chile en nogada* (an enormous *poblano* chili pepper stuffed with ground meat, dried fruit and bathed in a creamy walnut sauce). Beware: rumor has it the building is haunted.

Al Andalus MIDDLE EASTERN $$
(Map p66; ☎55-5522-2528; m_andalus171@yahoo.com.mx; Mesones 171; shawarma M$70, mains M$125-220; ⏰9am-6pm; Ⓜ Pino Suárez) In a superb colonial mansion in the Merced textile district, Al Andalus caters to the capital's substantial Lebanese community with old standbys such as shawarma, kebab and falafel.

Café de Tacuba MEXICAN $$
(Map p66; ☎55-5518-4950; www.cafedetacuba.com.mx; Tacuba 28; mains M$69-215, 4-course lunches M$220; ⏰8am-11:30pm; 📶; Ⓜ Allende) Before the band there was the restaurant. Way before. A fantasy of colored tiles, brass lamps and oil paintings, this mainstay has served *antojitos* (snacks such as tacos and *sopes* – corn tortillas layered with beans, cheese and other ingredients) since 1912. Lively *estudiantinas* (student musical groups) entertain the dinner crowd Wednesday through Sunday.

Restaurante Chon MEXICAN $$
(Map p66; ☎55-5542-0873; Regina 160; appetizers M$25-260, mains M$65-230; ⏰1-6:30pm Mon-Sat; 📶; Ⓜ Pino Suárez) Pre-Hispanic fare is the specialty of this cantina-style restaurant. Sample *maguey* (agave) worms, *chapulines* (grasshoppers) and *escamoles* (ant larvae). Wash it all down with flavored *pulque (a* fermented agave drink, aka 'the blood of the gods'). Menu items such as crocodile and gar are farm-raised.

Casino Español SPANISH $$
(Map p66; ☎55-5510-2967; www.casinoespanoldemexico.com; Isabel La Católica 29; 4-course lunches M$130; ⏰7am-noon & 1-6pm Mon-Fri; 📶; Ⓜ Zócalo) The old Spanish social center, housed in a fabulous Porfiriato-era building, has a popular cantina-style eatery downstairs, where the courses keep coming, and an elegant restaurant upstairs, which features classic Spanish fare such as *paella valenciana* (paella Valencia-style).

Zona Rosa

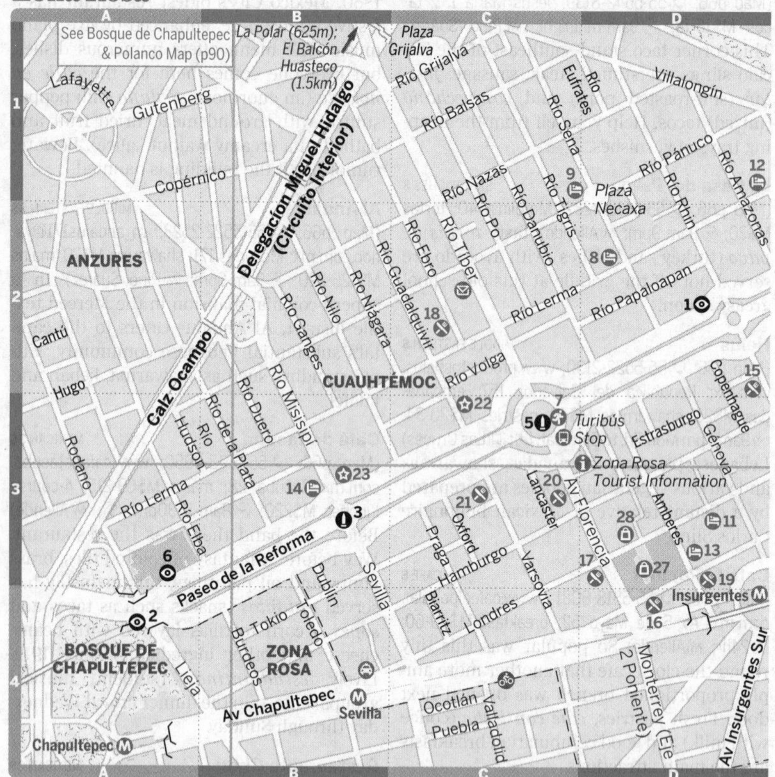

El Cardenal MEXICAN **$$$**
(Map p66; ☎55-5521-8815; www.restauranteelcardenal.com; Palma 23; breakfast M$62-82, lunch & dinner M$130-230; ⏰8am-6:30pm Mon-Sat, 9am-6:30pm Sun; 🅿📶; Ⓜ Zócalo) Possibly the finest place in town for a traditional meal, El Cardenal occupies three floors of a Parisian-style mansion and has a pianist playing sweetly in the background. Breakfast is a must, served with a tray of just-baked sweet rolls and a pitcher of frothy, semisweet chocolate. For lunch, the house specialty is the *pecho de ternera* (oven-roasted veal breast).

There's a new branch in the south, **El Cardenal San Ángel** (Map p96; Av de la Paz 32; ⏰8am-6:30pm; 🅿📶; 🚌 La Bombilla).

La Casa de las Sirenas MEXICAN **$$$**
(Map p66; www.lacasadelassirenas.com.mx; República de Guatemala 32; mains M$210-240; ⏰11am-11pm Mon-Sat, to 6pm Sun; 📶; Ⓜ Zócalo) Housed in a 17th-century relic, Sirenas has a top-floor terrace that looks toward the Zócalo via the Plaza del Templo Mayor. It's an ideal perch to enjoy regional dishes prepared with contemporary flair, such as chicken bathed in pumpkin seed *mole* (a type of chili sauce).

Los Girasoles MEXICAN **$$$**
(Map p66; ☎55-5510-0630; www.restaurantelosgirasoles.com; Plaza Tolsá; mains M$140-194; ⏰1-11:30pm Tue-Sat, to 9pm Sun & Mon; 🅿📶; Ⓜ Allende) This fine restaurant overlooking the grand Plaza Tolsá boasts an encyclopedic range of Mexican fare, from pre-Hispanic ant larvae and grasshoppers to contemporary dishes such as red snapper encrusted with *huanzontle* flowers.

Alameda Central & Around

Though places on the immediate perimeter of the Alameda cater to tourists, head down Luis Moya or along Ayuntamiento, south of

the Alameda, for pockets of the neighborhood's rustic heritage in the form of *torta* (sandwich) stands and chicken-soup vendors. Mexico City's modest *Barrio Chino* (Chinatown) covers a single paper-lantern-strung block of Calle Dolores, one block south of the park, but its mediocre restaurants are best avoided.

El Huequito TAQUERÍA $
(Map p76; www.elhuequito.com.mx; Ayuntamiento 21; tacos al pastor M$13; ⌚9:30am-10pm Mon-Sat, 10:30am-8:30pm Sun; Plaza San Juan) These old pros have been churning out delectable *tacos al pastor* (marinated pork roasted on a spit) since 1959. Several downtown Huequito branches offer the sit-down experience, but for some reason (the added touch of street grime perhaps?) the tacos are better here at the original location.

Zona Rosa

Sights
1 Centro Bursátil (Bolsa) D2
2 Centro de Cultura Digital A4
Estela de Luz .... (see 2)
3 La Diana Cazadora B3
4 Monumento a Cuauhtémoc F1
5 Monumento a la Independencia C3
6 Torre Mayor A3

Activities, Courses & Tours
7 Bicitekas C3

Sleeping
8 Casa González D2
9 Hotel Bristol C1
10 Hotel Cityexpress E2
11 Hotel Geneve D3
12 Hotel María Cristina D1
13 Hotel Suites Amberes D3
14 St Regis Mexico City B3

Eating
15 De Mar a Mar D2
16 Fonda El Refugio D4
17 King Falafel D3
18 Rokai C2
19 Tezka D3
20 Young Bin Kwan C3
21 Yug Vegetariano C3

Drinking & Nightlife
Nicho Bears & Bar .... (see 17)

Entertainment
22 Cinemex Casa de Arte C3
23 Cinépolis Diana B3
24 Patrick Miller F3

Shopping
25 Fonart F1
26 Jardín del Arte E1
27 Mercado Insurgentes D3
28 Plaza del Ángel D3
29 Reforma 222 .... E2

Churrería El Moro DESSERTS $
(Map p76; 55-5512-0896; www.elmoro.com.mx/Home/El_Moro.html; Eje Central Lázaro Cárdenas 42; hot chocolate with 4 churros M$60; ⌚24hr; M San Juan de Letrán) A respite from the Eje Central crowds, El Moro makes long, deep-fried *churros* (doughnut-like fritters), just made to be dipped in thick hot chocolate.

Mi Fonda SPANISH $
(Map p76; 55-5521-0002; López 101; paella M$70; ⌚11:30am-5pm Tue-Sun; Plaza San Juan) Working-class *chilangos* line up for their share of *paella valenciana,* made fresh daily and patiently ladled out by women in

white bonnets. Jesús from Cantabria oversees the proceedings.

El Cuadrilátero SANDWICHES $
(Map p76; ☎55-5521-3060; Luis Moya 73; tortas M$53-85; ⏰7am-8pm Mon-Sat; Ⓑ Plaza San Juan) Owned by wrestler Super Astro, this *torta* joint features a shrine to *lucha libre* (Mexican wrestling) masks. The mother of all *tortas,* the 1.3kg cholesterol-packed Torta Gladiador (egg, sausage, bacon, beef, chicken and hot dog) is free if you can gobble it in 15 minutes.

Plaza de la República & Around

Gotan Restaurante ARGENTINE $$
(Map p76; Baranda 17, Colonia Tabacalera; mains M$59-199; ⏰10am-8:30pm Mon-Fri; 📶; Ⓑ Plaza de la República) One of the best and most authentic Argentine restaurants in town, owned by a Buenos Aires native and her Mexican husband. It's all about the details: bread is baked daily and the meats and other key ingredients are imported from Argentina. Don't leave without trying the *postre de la nonna*, a delightful caramel custard.

Zona Rosa & Around

While the Zona Rosa is packed with places to eat and drink, with few exceptions the area is dominated by uninspiring 'international' fare and fast-food franchises. North of Paseo de la Reforma, many new restaurants and bars are cropping up in the Colonia Cuauhtémoc.

King Falafel MIDDLE EASTERN $
(Map p110; ☎55-5514-9030; Londres 178; falafel M$55, salads M$55-62; ⏰10am-7pm Mon-Sat; 📶🥕; Ⓜ Insurgentes) Run by an English-speaking Syrian Jew, this small eatery has a vegetarian-friendly menu of falafel in pita bread, mixed salads, tabouleh and fresh hummus.

Yug Vegetariano VEGETARIAN $$
(Map p110; ☎55-5333-3296; www.lovegetariano.com; Varsovia 3; buffet lunches M$85-95, mains M$54-98; ⏰7am-9pm Mon-Fri, 8:30am-8pm Sat & Sun; 📶🥕; Ⓜ Sevilla) The menu is gastro-heaven for vegetarians and vast enough for most carnivorous folk to find something they fancy. Choose from specialties such as squash-flower crepes, or go the lunch buffet route.

Rokai JAPANESE $$$
(Map p110; ☎55-5207-7543; www.facebook.com/rokaimexico?ref=stream; Río Ebro 87, Colonia Cuauhtémoc; tasting menu lunch/dinner M$290/420; ⏰2:30-5pm & 7-11pm Mon-Sat; 📶; Ⓜ Insurgentes) Rokai takes Japanese food to a new level in Mexico City. Tokyo-born, Los Angeles-raised chef Hiroshi Kawahito recommends the 'omakase,' a changing tasting menu consisting of meticulously prepared dishes such as sushi and sashimi. Each course (there are nine for dinner) leaves you wanting more. As a rule, Kawahito only works with fresh fish and seafood. Reserve ahead.

De Mar a Mar SEAFOOD $$$
(Map p110; ☎55-5207-5730; www.demaramar.mx; Niza 13; mains M$170-210; ⏰1-10pm Mon-Sat, to 6pm Sun; 📶; Ⓑ Hamburgo) One of the Zona Rosa's best new restaurants, the menu here was designed by chef Eduardo Garcia, a rising star on the Mexico City culinary scene. All dishes, especially the ceviches and *tostadas* (baked or fried tortillas), stand out for their fresh ingredients, and dessert is a slice of heaven.

Fonda El Refugio MEXICAN $$$
(Map p110; ☎55-5525-8128; www.fondaelrefugio.com; Liverpool 166; dishes M$150-220; ⏰1-11pm; 📶🥕; Ⓜ Insurgentes) Amid a collection of colorful pots and whimsical ceramic ornaments, since 1954 this family-run *fonda* (inn) serves Mexican favorites such as *mole poblano* (chicken in a chocolate-based sauce) and *chiles rellenos* (chilies stuffed with ground beef).

Tezka INTERNATIONAL $$$
(Map p110; ☎55-9149-3000; www.tezka.com.mx; Amberes 78; mains M$190-380, tasting menu M$520; ⏰1-5pm & 8-11pm Mon-Fri, 1-6pm Sat & Sun ; Ⓟ📶; Ⓜ Insurgentes) Specializing in contemporary Basque cuisine, Tezka ranks among Mexico City's finest restaurants. The regularly changing menu features elaborately prepared dishes such as rack of lamb, or dabble in the four-course tasting menu (two appetizers, a main dish and dessert).

Young Bin Kwan ASIAN $$$
(Map p110; ☎55-5208-9399; Av Florencia 15; bulgogi M$180; ⏰11am-10pm; 📶; Ⓜ Insurgentes) Enormous portions of *bulgogi* (marinated beef grilled at your table) are complemented by a fabulous array of side dishes (sesame leaves, bean sprouts and kimchi) at this large Korean dining hall.

Condesa

La Condesa has dozens upon dozens of informal bistros and cafes – many with sidewalk tables – competing for business along several key streets. The neighborhood's restaurant zone is at the convergence of Michoacán, Vicente Suárez and Tamaulipas; many good establishments ring Parque México.

Tacos Don Juan TAQUERÍA **$**
(Map p84; cnr Atlixco & Juan Escutia; tacos M$16-21; 10am-4pm Mon-Thu, to 3:30pm Fri, to 2pm Sat & Sun; Campeche) A seriously good taco joint that's usually swarming with locals. The offerings vary daily: on Friday and Saturday it's all about the *carnitas* (deep-fried pork) and on Sunday you can rely on an old standby – *bistec con longaniza* (beef with sausage) topped with whole beans. Open during breakfast and lunch hours only.

El Tizoncito TAQUERÍA **$**
(Map p84; 55-5286-7321; www.eltizoncito.com.mx; Av Tamaulipas 122; tacos from M$12.50; noon-3:30am Sun-Thu, to 5:30am Fri & Sat; ; M Patriotismo) Since this place claims to have invented *tacos al pastor,* half the fun is watching them deftly put it all together. If there are no seats, try the bigger location two blocks east on Campeche.

Taquería Hola TAQUERÍA **$**
(Map p84; 55-5286-4495; Ámsterdam 135, cnr Av Michoacán; tacos M$16; 9am-5pm Mon-Fri, to 2pm Sat & Sun; Campeche) Mid-morning, local snackers crowd this friendly hole-in-the-wall for a stand-up chomp. Choose from a remarkable array of taco fillings, all temptingly displayed in clay dishes.

El Califa TAQUERÍA **$**
(Map p84; 55-5271-7666; www.elcalifa.com.mx; Altata 22; tacos M$26-67; 1pm-4am; ; M Chilpancingo) This popular taco shop puts its own spin on the classic snack, grilling slices of beef and tossing them on handmade tortillas. Tables are set with a palette of savory salsas.

Nevería Roxy ICE CREAM **$**
(Map p84; 55-5286-1258; www.neveriaroxy.com.mx; cnr Mazatlán & Montes de Oca; scoops M$15-30; 11am-8pm; M Juanacatlán) The old-fashioned Roxy makes its own ice cream and sherbet on-site, including tropical flavors such as *zapote* (sapodilla) and guava. There's another branch at Avenida Tamaulipas 161, at Alfonso Reyes.

Orígenes Orgánicos ORGANIC **$$**
(Map p84; 55-5208-6678; www.origenesorganicos.com; Plaza Popocatépetl 41A; mains M$70-150; 8:30am-9:30pm Mon-Fri, 9am-6:30pm Sat & Sun; ; Sonora) More than just a place to buy soy milk and certified organic produce, this store-cafe facing one of Condesa's loveliest plazas prepares tasty meals with an emphasis on seasonal, organic ingredients.

Taj Mahal INDIAN **$$**
(Map p84; Francisco Márquez 134; mains M$120-199; 1-10pm Sun-Wed, to 11pm Thu-Sat; ; M Juancatlán) A hard-working Bangladeshi man who used to roam the Condesa selling clothes out of a suitcase now has his own restaurant specializing in Indian cuisine. Vegetarians will find many options here, including garlic naan, vegetable biryani and flavored yogurt drinks.

Café La Gloria FRENCH **$$**
(Map p84; 55-5211-4185; Vicente Suárez 41; mains M$95-180; 1pm-midnight Mon-Wed, to 1am Thu & Fri, 10am-midnight Sat & Sun; P; M Campeche) A hip bistro in the heart of the zone, La Gloria remains a popular meeting place thanks to the reliably good salads, zesty pastas and quirky art on display.

La Rambla STEAKHOUSE **$$**
(Map p84; Ometusco s/n, btwn Av Baja California & Benjamín Hill; mains M$65-150; 1:30-9:30pm Mon-Thu, to 11:30pm Fri & Sat, 1-6pm Sun; ; Escandón) Owned by a Montevideo native, this intimate Uruguayan steakhouse grills tender cuts such as *milanesa de res* (breaded steak) and does vegetarian pizzas for nonmeat eaters, all at reasonable prices.

Lampuga SEAFOOD **$$$**
(Map p84; 55-5286-1525; www.lampuga.com.mx; Ometusco 1, cnr Av Nuevo León; mains M$146-245; 1:30-11pm Mon-Sat, to 6pm Sun; ; M Chilpancingo) Fresh seafood is the focus of this appealing bistro. Tuna *tostadas* make great starters, as does the smoked marlin carpaccio; for a main course, have the catch of the day grilled over coals.

Pablo El Erizo SEAFOOD **$$$**
(Map p84; www.pabloelerizo.com; Montes de Oca 6; mains M$150-210, tacos & appetizers M$65-145; 1-9pm Mon & Tue, to 11pm Wed-Sat, to 6pm Sun; ; Campeche) Inspired by Baja California cuisine, this bistro has a knack for creating exceptional seafood dishes, such as seared tuna *tostadas* topped with crispy leeks and Ensenada-style shrimp tacos.

Coyoacán

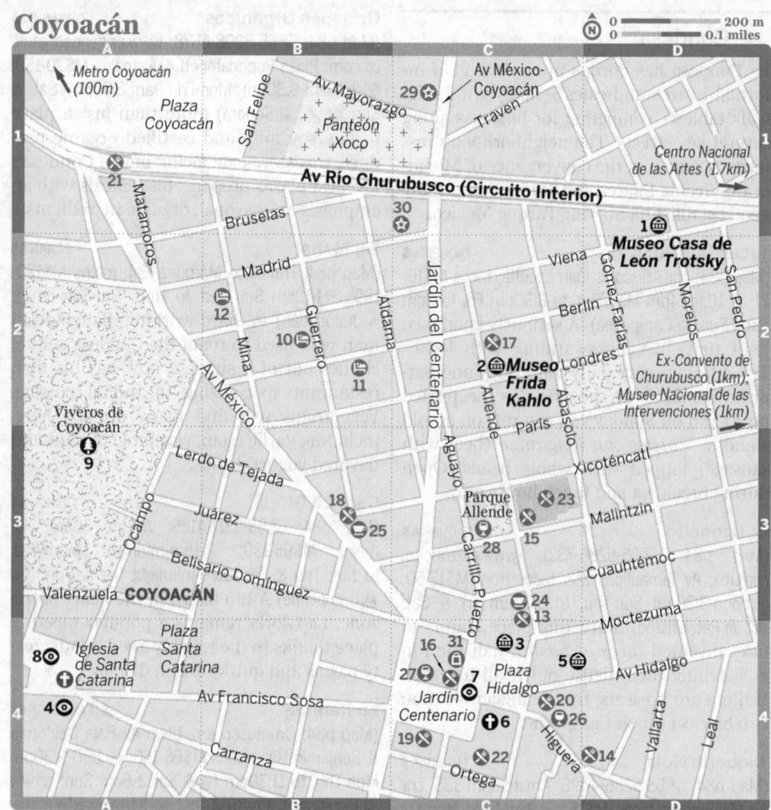

La Capital MEXICAN $$$

(Map p84; ☎55-5256-5159; www.restaurantelacapital.com; Av Nuevo León 137; mains M$105-195; ⏰1pm-1am Mon-Wed, to 2am Thu-Sat, to 7pm Sun; P 📶; M Chilpancingo) Riding the latest 'cantina chic' (oxymoron?) wave, the Capital does traditional Mexican fare with a gourmet twist. Try the chili-encrusted tuna or the duck enchiladas.

Rojo Bistrot FRENCH $$$

(Map p84; ☎55-5211-3705; www.rojobistrot.com; Ámsterdam 71; mains M$175-225; ⏰2-11pm Mon-Thu, to midnight Fri & Sat, to 5pm Sun; 📶; 🚌 Sonora) On a leafy corner near Parque México, this eatery is a hit as much for its vibrant social scene as for the French-inspired cuisine. Regulars praise the duck dishes – *confit de pato bistrot* and *magret de pato* in black cherry sauce.

Roma

★ El Hidalguense MEXICAN $

(Map p84; ☎55-5564-0538; Campeche 155; 3 tacos M$75; ⏰7am-6pm Fri-Sun; 📶; 🚌 Campeche) Slow-cooked over aged oak wood in an underground pit, the Hidalgo-style *barbacoa* at this family-run eatery is off-the-charts delectable. Get things started with a rich consommé or *queso asado* (grilled cheese with herbs), then move on to the tacos. Top it off by sampling the flavored *pulques*.

El Parnita MEXICAN $

(Map p84; ☎55-5264-7551; paulino@elparnita.com; Av Yucatán 84; tacos M$22-28, tortas M$39-59; ⏰1:30-6pm Tue-Sun; 📶; 🚌 Sonora) What began as a small street stall has morphed into a see-and-be-seen restaurant. This lunch-only establishment keeps it simple with a small menu of tried-and-true family recipes such as the *carmelita* (shrimp tacos with hand-

Coyoacán

Top Sights
1 Museo Casa de León Trotsky ... D1
2 Museo Frida Kahlo ... C2

Sights
3 Casa de Cortés ... C4
4 Centro Cultural Jesús Reyes Heroles ... A4
5 Museo Nacional de Culturas Populares ... C4
6 Parroquia de San Juan Bautista ... C4
7 Plaza Hidalgo & Jardín Centenario ... C4
8 Plaza Santa Catarina ... A4
9 Viveros de Coyoacán ... A3

Sleeping
10 Chalet del Carmen ... B2
11 Hostal Cuija Coyoacán ... B2
12 Hostal Frida ... B2

Eating
13 Churrería de Coyoacán ... C3
Corazón de Maguey ... (see 27)
14 El Caracol de Oro ... D4
15 El Jardín del Pulpo ... C3
16 El Kiosko de Coyoacán ... C4
17 El Mesón de los Leones ... C2
18 La Casa del Pan Papalotl ... B3
19 Los Danzantes ... C4
20 Mercado de Antojitos ... C4
21 Super Tacos Chupacabras ... A1
22 Tamales Chiapanecos María Geraldine ... C4
23 Tostadas Coyoacán ... C3

Drinking & Nightlife
24 Café El Jarocho ... C3
25 Café El Jarocho ... B3
26 Cantina La Coyoacana ... C4
27 El Hijo del Cuervo ... C4
28 La Bipo ... C3

Entertainment
29 Cineteca Nacional ... C1
30 Teatro Bar El Vicio ... C1

Shopping
31 Bazar Artesanal Mexicano ... C4

made tortillas) and the *viajero* taco (slow-cooked pork). Reserve ahead for Saturday and Sunday.

Panadería Rosetta BAKERY $
(Map p84; Colima 179; bread M$16-40, baguettes M$35-105; 8am-8pm Mon-Sat, to 5pm Sun; ; Durango) Sublime sweet bread and baguettes are made fresh daily at this small bakery owned by chef Elena Reygadas, sister of award-winning Mexican filmmaker Carlos Reygadas.

Ciénega COLOMBIAN $$
(Map p84; Coahuila 200; dishes M$100-130; 10am-7pm; ; Campeche) The background music of accordion-driven *vallenatos* (folk music) sets a feel-good mood at this popular Colombian comfort-food restaurant. Colombian expats go straight for the *sancocho* and *ajiaco* dishes, hearty stews just like *mamá* used to make.

★**Maximo Bistrot Local** FUSION $$$
(Map p84; 55-5264-4291; www.maximobistrot.com.mx; Tonalá 133; mains M$150-280; 1-11pm Tue-Sat, to 5pm Sun) If there's one place that best represents Mexico City's exciting new culinary scene, it's Maximo Bistrot. The constantly changing menu, which draws on European and Mexican recipes, features fresh, seasonal ingredients. Best of all – the place is totally unpretentious. Owner/chef Eduardo Garcia honed his cooking skills at Pujol under the tutelage of famed chef Enrique Olvera. Reservations a must.

Contramar SEAFOOD $$$
(Map p84; 55-5514-9217; www.contramar.com.mx; Durango 200; appetizers M$105-225, mains M$195-295; 12:30-6:30pm Sun-Thu, to 8pm Fri & Sat; P ; Durango) Seafood is the star at this stylish dining hall with a seaside feel. The specialty is tuna fillet – split, swabbed with red chili and parsley sauces, and grilled to perfection. Also a standout is the tuna *tostada*, topped with crispy onions. Reservations recommended.

Yuban MEXICAN $$$
(Map p84; www.yuban.mx; Colima 268; appetizers M$90-110, mains M$110-250; 1:30-11pm Tue-Thu, to 11:30pm Fri & Sat, to 6pm Sun; ; Durango) Savor the flavors of Oaxaca, such as exquisite *moles* and *tlayudas* (large tortillas folded over *chorizo* and cheese), plus some darn good mezcals. An adjoining venue stages plays and screens Mexican indie flicks.

Bosque de Chapultepec & Polanco

Polanco is home to the signature restaurants of several of Mexico City's internationally hot chefs. Other places listed here present excellent regional cuisine from the Mexican coast.

Green Corner SUPERMARKET $
(Map p84; 55-3093-8290; www.thegreencorner.org) A rare find in DF, this organic-food store purchases items from small producers throughout Mexico. Both this store and the **Polanco** branch (Map p90; Homero 1210; 8am-10pm; ; Polanco) sell organic fruit, vegetables and cheese; the Condesa store has a vegetarian-friendly restaurant.

El Bajío MEXICAN $$
(Map p90; 55-5281-8246; www.restauranteelbajio.com.mx; Dumas 7; mains M$54-186, tacos M$28-35; 8am-11pm Mon-Sat, 9am-10pm Sun; ; Auditorio) Owner Carmen 'Titita' Ramírez has built a reputation for producing down-home Veracruz-style food and regional dishes from all over Mexico. Meaty meals or tacos such as *barbacoa* and *carnitas* are El Bajío's signature fare.

★Pujol MEXICAN $$$
(Map p90; 55-5545-4111; www.pujol.com.mx; Petrarca 254; menú degustación M$695-995; 2-4pm & 6:30-11:30pm Mon-Sat; Polanco) Arguably Mexico's best gourmet restaurant, Pujol offers a contemporary take on classic Mexican dishes in a smartly minimalist setting. Famed chef Enrique Olvera regularly reinvents the menu, which is presented as a *menú degustación,* a multiple-course tasting extravaganza. It might take up to several weeks to get a table here, so reserve well ahead of time.

Dulce Patria MEXICAN $$$
(Map p90; 55-3300-3999; www.dulcepatriamexico.com; Anatole France 100; mains M$275-405; 1:30-11pm Mon-Sat, to 5pm Sun; ; Polanco) Cookbook author Martha Ortiz launched this restaurant several years ago after taking a brief sabbatical, and it certainly lives up to her high standards in spite of some unfortunate interior design choices. Reinvented traditional Mexican dishes such as *mole* enchiladas stuffed with plantain are deftly plated and delicious.

Los Arcos SEAFOOD $$$
(Map p90; 55-5531-9696; www.restaurantlosarcos.com; Tasso 330; mains M$128-268; 11am-10pm Mon-Wed, to 11pm Thu-Sat, to 8pm Sun; ; Polanco) Specializing in Pacific coast fare, this Mexican chain restaurant is definitely worth its salt. Try the *pescado a las brasas* (charbroiled whole fish sold by the kilo), and order a side dish of refried beans for good measure.

San Ángel

Barbacoa de Santiago MEXICAN $
(Map p96; Plaza San Jacinto 23; tacos & flautas M$18-26; 9am-7pm Sun-Fri, 8:30am-7:30pm Sat; La Bombilla) A quick and affordable *taquería* off the plaza, this place is known for its *barbacoa* and *flautas ahogadas* (fried rolled tacos dipped in a *chile pasilla* and *pulque* sauce).

Fonda San Ángel MEXICAN $$
(Map p96; 55-5550-1641; www.fondasanangel.com.mx; Plaza San Jacinto 3; mains M$115-240, breakfast buffet M$160; 8am-midnight Mon-Thu, to 1am Fri & Sat, 9am-7pm Sun; ; La Bombilla) On Saturday and Sunday, this attractive restaurant by the plaza does an abundant breakfast buffet with all kinds of egg dishes, pastries and freshly squeezed juices, plus great quesadillas.

Cluny FRENCH $$
(Map p96; 55-5550-7350; www.cluny.com.mx; Av de la Paz 57; salads M$75-115, mains M$98-220; 12:30pm-midnight Mon-Sat, to 11pm Sun; ; La Bombilla) For unpretentious French cuisine, this bistro located in an open-air shopping center hits the spot. Quiche, salads, crepes, decadently delicious desserts and generous portions are the order of the day.

Montejo YUCATECAN $$
(Map p96; 55-5550-1366; www.restaurantebarmontejo.com; Av de la Paz 16; mains M$115-190; 1-10:30pm Mon-Sat, to 7pm Sun; ; La Bombilla) Along a cobbled street lined with restaurants, this inconspicuous Yucatecan establishment whips up regional favorites such as *sopa de lima* (lime soup), *cochinita pibil* (marinated pork) and *papadzules* (tortillas stuffed with diced hard-boiled eggs and bathed in pumpkin-seed sauce).

Saks MEXICAN $$
(Map p96; 55-5616-1601; www.restaurantessaks.com.mx; Plaza San Jacinto 9; dishes M$125-202; 7:30am-6pm Mon, to midnight Tue-Fri, 8am-11pm Sat, to 8pm Sun; ; La Bombilla) Hang out on Saks' sunbathed terrace, which has live music, and choose from meatless specialties such as assorted crepes or *chile poblano envuelto en hojaldre* (chilies stuffed with trufflelike corn fungus and goat cheese).

Taberna del León MEXICAN $$$
(Map p96; ☎55-5616-2110; Plaza Loreto 173; dishes M$195-395; ⏰1:30-11pm Mon-Thu, to midnight Fri & Sat, to 6pm Sun; P 📶; 🚌Doctor Gálvez) Chef Monica Patiño is one of the new breed of female stars stirring up traditional cuisine in innovative ways. Seafood is the specialty here, with the likes of *robalo a los tres chiles* (bass in three-pepper chili sauce) and corn blini with Norwegian salmon.

San Ángel Inn MEXICAN $$$
(Map p96; ☎55-5616-1402; www.sanangelinn.com; Diego Rivera 50; breakfast M$70-120, lunch & dinner M$170-395; ⏰7am-1pm Mon-Fri, 8:30am-1pm Sat, to 10pm Sun; P 📶 👪; 🚌Altavista) Classic Mexican meals are served in the garden and various elegant dining rooms of this historic estate next to the Museo Casa Estudio Diego Rivera y Frida Kahlo. On Saturday and Sunday mornings, the Inn provides activities for kids in the rear garden, meaning it's margarita time for mom and dad.

Coyoacán

La Casa del Pan Papalotl VEGETARIAN $
(Map p114; www.casadelpan.com; Av México 25; breakfast M$59-90, lunch & dinner M$43-78; ⏰8am-10pm Mon-Fri, 9am-10pm Sat & Sun; 🌿; Ⓜ Coyoacán) This hugely popular vegetarian restaurant draws a loyal breakfast crowd thanks to its organic egg dishes, *chilaquiles* (tortilla strips drenched in salsa) and fresh-made *pan* (bread). For lunch, the lasagna with squash flower, mushrooms and *poblano* chili is a big hit.

Super Tacos Chupacabras TAQUERÍA $
(Map p114; www.tacoschupacabras.com; cnr Avs Río Churubusco & México; tacos M$10; ⏰24hr; Ⓜ Coyoacán) Named after Mexico's mythical 'goat sucker' (a vampire-like creature), this famous *taquería* under a freeway overpass slings wonderful beef and sausage tacos. The specialty here is the 'chupa,' a mixed-meat taco that contains 127 secret ingredients, or so they say. Avail yourself of the grilled onions, *nopales* (cactus paddles), whole beans and other tasty toppings.

Mercado de Antojitos MARKET $
(Map p114; Higuera 6; pozoles M$60; ⏰8am-11pm; Ⓜ Coyoacán) Near Coyoacán's main plaza, this busy spot has all kinds of snacks, including deep-fried quesadillas, *pozole* and *esquites* (boiled corn kernels served with a dollop of mayo). Look for the 'Pozole Estilo Michoacán' stall.

Tostadas Coyoacán MEXICAN $
(Map p114; ☎55-5659-8774; Allende 59; tostadas M$20-30; ⏰11am-6pm; Ⓜ Coyoacán) At this sprawling place inside Coyoacán's main market, between Malintzin and Xicoténcatl, the *tostadas* are piled high with things such as ceviche, marinated octopus and shredded chicken.

Churrería de Coyoacán DESSERTS $
(Map p114; Allende 38; bag of 4 churros M$20; ⏰8am-midnight Sun-Thu, 9am-1am Fri & Sat; Ⓜ Coyoacán) Here are Coyoacán's best deep-fried snacks. Get in line for a bag – chocolate-filled or straight up – then stroll over to Café El Jarocho (just next door) for coffee. Figure about three hours in the gym to work off these bad boys.

El Mesón de los Leones MEXICAN $
(Map p114; ☎55-5554-5916; Allende 161; mains M$55-90; ⏰11am-6pm Sun-Fri; Ⓜ Coyoacán) This long-time family-run restaurant satisfies diners with its unwaveringly authentic menu and genial atmosphere. Dig into specialties such as *carne asada estilo de León* – grilled beef accompanied with refried beans and tortillas in a dark *mole* sauce.

El Kiosko de Coyoacán ICE CREAM $
(Map p114; Plaza Hidalgo 6; per scoop M$25; ⏰9am-11pm Mon-Fri, to 12:30am Sat & Sun; Ⓜ Coyoacán) This obligatory weekend stop has homemade ice cream and popsicles in flavors ranging from mango with chili to *maracuya* (passion fruit).

El Caracol de Oro INTERNATIONAL $$
(Map p114; ☎55-5658-9489; Higuera 22B; dishes M$65-120; ⏰10am-11pm; Ⓜ Coyoacán) Coyoacán's alternative set occupies the jazzily painted tables here, munching on nouveau-natural fare such as chicken topped with apple curry and goat cheese, and cheese-stuffed chilies bathed in mango sauce.

Corazón de Maguey MEXICAN $$$
(Map p114; ☎55-5659-3165; www.corazondemaguey.com; Jardín Centenario 9A; mains M$149-289; ⏰1pm-1am; 📶; Ⓜ Coyoacán) Adorned with old glass jugs used for transporting booze, this attractive restaurant does traditional Mexican fare that's typically prepared in mezcal-producing regions, such as stuffed *chile ancho* peppers from Querétaro, Oaxacan *tlayudas* (large folded tortillas) and beef tongue in red *mole*, hailing from Puebla. It's also a prime spot to sample some of Mexico's finest mezcals.

Los Danzantes MEXICAN $$$

(Map p114; ☎55-5554-1213; www.losdanzantes.com; Jardín Centenario 12; mains M$170-360; ⏲1:30pm-midnight Mon-Fri, 9am-2am Sat, to 10:30pm Sun; 📶; Ⓜ Coyoacán) Los Danzantes puts a contemporary spin on traditional Mexican cuisine with dishes such as *huitlacoche* (trufflelike corn fungus) raviolis in *poblana* sauce, organic chicken in black *mole*, and *hoja santa* (Mexican pepperleaf) stuffed with cheese and *chipotle* chili. You'll also find mezcal from its own distillery.

El Jardín del Pulpo SEAFOOD $$$

(Map p114; cnr Allende & Malintzin; dishes M$170-220; ⏲11am-6pm; Ⓜ Coyoacán) Visitors descend on the communal tables at this market-corner place to devour shrimp tacos, fried whole fish, oyster cocktails and the namesake *pulpo* (octopus cooked in its own ink or in tequila).

Ciudad Universitaria

Azul y Oro MEXICAN $$

(☎55-5622-7135; www.azulrestaurantes.com; Centro Cultural Universitario; mains M$115-260; ⏲10am-6pm Mon & Tue, to 8pm Wed-Sat, 9am-7pm Sun; P 📶; 🚌 Centro Cultural Universitario) Chef Ricardo Muñoz searches high and low in Mexico for traditional recipes and reinvents them to perfection. Fruits of his labor include *buñuelos rellenos de pato* (fried snacks filled with shredded duck and topped with *mole negro*) and *pescado tikin xic* (an elaborate grouper dish with plantain and tortilla strips). Muñoz has a new downtown branch **Azul Histórico** (Map p66; ☎55-5510-1316; www.azulhistorico.com; Isabel La Católica 30; M$115-260; ⏲9am-11pm Mon-Thu, to 11:30pm Fri & Sat, to 10pm Sun; P 📶; Ⓜ Zócalo).

Tlalpan

La Voragine ITALIAN $$

(Madero 107, Colonia Tlalpan; mains M$80-120, pizzas M$125-230; ⏲1pm-2am Tue-Sat, to midnight Sun; 📶 🎤; 🚌 Fuentes Brotantes) Run by a fun-loving couple from New York and DF, this muraled pizzeria/bar prepares savory pizzas, exquisite manicotti and *fungi trifolati* (flambéed mushrooms in white-wine sauce). Or just drop in for a Mexican microbrew and enjoy the sunny patio upstairs. It's a half-block north of Tlalpan's main square.

Colonia del Valle & Around

Fonda Margarita MEXICAN $

(☎55-5559-6358; www.fondamargarita.com; Adolfo Prieto 1354, Colonia Tlacoquemécatl del Valle; mains M$42-65; ⏲5:30-11:30am Tue-Sun; 📶; 🚌 Parque Hundido) Possibly the capital's premier hangover-recovery spot, this humble eatery under a tin roof whips up batches of comfort food such as *longaniza en salsa verde* (sausage in green salsa) and *frijoles con huevo* (beans with egg). The *fonda* is beside Plaza Tlacoquemécatl, six blocks east of Avenida Insurgentes. There's usually a line to get in but it moves fast.

Drinking & Nightlife

Cafes, bars and cantinas are all key social venues on the capital's landscape. The traditional watering holes are, of course, cantinas – no-nonsense places with simple tables, long polished bars and old-school waiters. A humbler kind of drinking establishment rooted in ancient Mexican tradition, *pulquerías* serve *pulque* (a pre-Hispanic alcoholic beverage). These places are lately experiencing a resurgence, with young *chilangos* rediscovering the joys of sharing a pitcher of the milky quaff. Another drink being taken back by Mexican youth is mezcal, the rustic mother of tequila.

Mexico City has banned smoking inside bars, though many establishments provide open-air smoking areas.

The capital's thriving club scene has become an obligatory stop on the international DJ circuit. To find out what's going on, pick up flyers at Condesa's Malafama billiard hall.

The city's many dance aficionados have a circuit of clubs and *salones de baile* (dance halls) to choose from. At many clubs, it's customary to go in a group and share a bottle of rum or tequila (from around M$600, including mixers).

Centro Histórico

Hostería La Bota BAR

(Map p66; ☎55-5709-1117; San Jerónimo 40; ⏲1pm-midnight Sun-Wed, to 3am Thu-Sat; 📶; Ⓜ Isabel La Católica) 🌿 *Cerveza* (beer), mezcal and tapas are served amid a profusion of warped bullfighting bric-a-brac and recycled objects. A portion of your bar tab sponsors local art projects.

MEZCAL RENAISSANCE

In recent years the agave-based Mexican liquor mezcal, long thought of as just a poor rustic relative to tequila, has finally won the respect it deserves. Many bars around Mexico City now serve mezcal to the new breed of discerning aficionados.

La Clandestina (Map p84; Álvaro Obregón 298, Colonia Roma; 6pm-2am Tue-Sat; Álvaro Obregón) Fashioned after a rural mom-and-pop shop, the Clandestina provides a detailed menu describing the elaboration process of the mezcals dispensed from jugs on high shelves. In true clandestine fashion, there's no sign outside, so look for the 'Casa Rey' frameshop sign left behind by the previous tenants.

Bósforo (Map p76; http://es-la.facebook.com/bosfor0; Luis Moya 31, cnr Independencia, Colonia Centro; 6pm-2am Tue-Sat; M Juárez) Blink your eyes and you might walk right past the friendliest neighborhood *mezcalería* in town. Behind the Bósforo's nondescript curtain await top-notch mezcals, an eclectic mix of music and surprisingly good bar grub.

Al Andar (Map p66; Regina 27, Colonia Centro; noon-1am; ; M Isabel La Católica) Most of the late-night action at this tiny downtown bar spills out onto a convivial pedestrian thoroughfare. Choose from 25 varieties of quality mezcal while munching on *chapulines* (grasshoppers) and orange slices.

Alipús (Guadalupe Victoria 15, Colonia Tlalpan; 1:30pm-10pm Mon & Tue, to 11pm Wed, to midnight Thu, to 1am Fri & Sat, noon-8pm Sun; Fuentes Brotantes) From the makers of the popular Oaxaca-based mezcal brands Alipús and Los Danzantes, this quaint Tlalpan bar stocks some of the finest mezcal in all of Mexico (ie Danzantes Pechuga Roja), and the regional *antojitos* (snacks) are wonderful as well.

Mexicano (Map p66; Regina 27, Colonia Centro; 11am-11pm Mon-Thu, to 1:30am Fri-Sat; M Isabel La Católica) This rustic mezcal joint is a hangover waiting to happen. In addition to mezcal, Mexicano pours *pulque* and offers a good selection of microbrews. The 'puntas de madrecuixe' mezcal from Oaxaca, which packs 78.8% alcohol by volume, will strip the enamel off your teeth.

Salón Corona BAR

(Map p66; 55-5512-5725; www.saloncorona.com.mx; Bolívar 24; 10:30am-2pm; M Allende) Amiable staff serve up *tarros* (mugs) of light or dark *cerveza de barril* (draft beer) in this boisterous beer hall. It's a great place to get a taste of soccer-mad Mexico when a match is on TV, which is almost always.

Las Duelistas PULQUERÍA

(Map p66; www.facebook.com/PulqueriaLasDuelistas; Aranda 28; 10am-9pm Mon-Sat; Plaza San Juan) Now graffitied with pre-Hispanic psychedelia, this classic *pulquería* has been rediscovered by young artists and musicians. Despite the new look, the *pulque* is still dispensed straight from the barrel in a variety of flavors.

Bar La Ópera BAR

(Map p66; 55-5512-8959; www.barlaopera.com; Av 5 de Mayo 10; 1-11:30pm Mon-Sat, to 6pm Sun; M Allende) With booths of dark walnut and an ornate copper-colored ceiling (said to have been punctured by Pancho Villa's bullet), this late-19th-century watering hole remains a bastion of tradition.

La Risa PULQUERÍA

(Map p66; 55-5709-4963; www.facebook.com/pulquerialarisaoficial; Mesones 71; noon-10pm Mon-Sat, to 7pm Sun; M Isabel La Católica) University students squeeze into this intimate watering hole that has been pouring *pulque* since 1900. Be a sport and invite a struggling college kid to a mug.

Downtown Mexico BAR

(Map p66; www.downtownmexico.com; Isabel La Católica 30; 10am-11pm Sun-Thu, to 2am Fri & Sat; ; M Zócalo) The rooftop lounge bar at boutique hotel Downtown Mexico has become a popular spot to chill over drinks, and it's been known to host the occasional pool party with open bar and DJ sets.

Bar Mancera BAR

(Map p66; 55-5521-9755; www.facebook.com/barmancera; Venustiano Carranza 49; 2-10pm Mon-Thu, to 2am Fri & Sat; República del Salvador) More than a century old, this atmospheric gentlemen's salon seems preserved in amber, with ornate carved paneling and well-used domino tables.

Café Jekemir CAFE
(Map p66; 55-5709-7086; www.cafejekemir.com; Isabel La Católica 88; 8am-9pm Mon-Sat; ; Isabel La Católica) Run by a family of coffee traders from Orizaba, this old distribution outlet, now transformed into a popular cafe, prepares good Veracruz coffee and Lebanese snacks.

Zona Rosa & Around

The Pink Zone, an international party center, boasts a high concentration of bars and clubs, and prices reflect its tourist orientation. Amberes has become the hub of Zona Rosa's gay and lesbian bar scene.

Crisanta BAR
(Map p76; www.crisanta.mx; Av Plaza de la República 51; 9am-11pm Mon-Wed, to 2am Thu-Sat, to 10pm Sun; ; Plaza de la República) A welcome sight in a nation where two breweries control about 98% of the market, Crisanta makes its own porter and sells Mexican and foreign craft beers. Jazz groups play bimonthly on Friday and Saturday, and there's art on display in the back room. Antique furnishings and long wooden tables add character to the beer-hall atmosphere.

Café La Habana CAFE
(Map p76; 55-5535-2620; www.cafelahabana.blogspot.com; Av Morelos 62; 7am-1am Mon-Sat, 8am-11pm Sun; ; Expo Reforma) This grand coffeehouse is a traditional haunt for writers and journalists, who linger for hours over a *café americano*. Legend has it that Fidel and Che plotted strategy here prior to the Cuban revolution.

Condesa

Condesa's bar scene continues to thrive, and new places are popping up (and shutting down) all the time. The following are relatively well established and filled beyond capacity Thursday through Saturday evenings. The confluence of Avenidas Tamaulipas and Nuevo León has emerged as a major bar zone, earning it a reputation as a haven for *fresas* (literally 'strawberries'; a derogatory term for upper-class youth).

Pata Negra BAR
(Map p84; 55-5211-5563; www.patanegra.com.mx; Av Tamaulipas 30; 1:30pm-2am; ; Campeche) Nominally a tapas bar, this oblong salon draws a friendly mix of 20-something *chilangos* and expats. Live Veracruz-style *son jarocho* bands perform on Saturday, while the program during the week usually features jazz, salsa or funk music.

Black Horse PUB
(Map p84; 55-5211-8740; www.caballonegro.com; Mexicali 85; 6pm-2am Tue-Sat; ; Patriotismo) Besides its draw as a preferred spot to catch televised soccer matches, this British pub boasts an international social scene and has excellent funk, jazz and indie-rock bands playing the back room.

El Centenario CANTINA
(Map p84; 55-5553-5451; Vicente Suárez 42; noon-1am Mon-Wed, to 1:45am Thu-Sat; ; Campeche) Laden with bullfighting memorabilia, this cantina is an enclave of tradition amid the modish restaurant zone.

Chiquitito CAFE
(Map p84; www.chiquititocafe.com; Alfonso Reyes 232; 7:30am-7:30pm Mon-Sat; ; Chilpancingo) Small in size, huge on Veracruz flavor. Coffee shops are everywhere in the Condesa but few have the know-how to bring out the best in their beans. The baristas at this hole-in-the-wall have it all figured out.

Salón Malafama BAR
(Map p84; www.salonmalafama.com.mx; Av Michoacán 78; table per hr M$100; 10am-1am Mon-Thu, 11am-2:30am Fri & Sat, noon-midnight Sun; ; Campeche) This sleek billiard hall doubles as a bar and gallery for photo exhibits. The well-maintained tables are frequented by both pool sharks and novices.

Condesa df BAR
(Map p84; 55-5241-2600; www.condesadf.com; Veracruz 102; 2:30-11:30pm Sun-Wed, to midnight Thu, to 1am Fri & Sat; ; Chapultepec) The bar of the fashionable Condesa df hotel has become an essential stop on the Condesa circuit. Up on the roof, guests lounge on big-wheel wicker sofas and enjoy views of verdant Parque España across the way.

Pastelería Maque CAFE
(Map p84; 55-2454-4662; www.maque.com.mx; Ozuluama 4; 11am-10pm; Campeche) Condesa sophisticates gather in the mornings and evenings at this Parisian-style cafe-bakery near Parque México. Waiters bring around trays of freshly baked croissants and *conchas* (round pastries sprinkled liberally with sugar).

Roma

Cuban dance clubs abound in Roma, particularly near the intersection of Avenida Insurgentes and Medellín.

★Traspatio BAR
(Map p84; cnr Córdoba & Colima; ⏲1pm-midnight Tue & Wed, to 2am Thu-Sat, to 10pm Sun; 📶; 🚌Durango) For the urban backyard barbecue experience, you'll love this open-air beer garden. It's a great little hideaway for chatting over *cerveza* or mezcal and munching on a *choripán* (grilled sausage on a roll) or a portobello mushroom burger.

Los Insurgentes PULQUERÍA
(Map p84; www.facebook.com/pulqueriainsurgentes; Av Insurgentes Sur 226; ⏲2pm-1am Mon-Wed, 1pm-3am Thu-Sat; 🚌Durango) A testament to the city's booming *pulque* revival, this three-story Porfiriato-era house may not please the purists, but unlike a traditional *pulquería,* here you get live music, DJ sets and other alcoholic drinks not called *pulque.*

Mama Rumba DANCING
(Map p84; ☎55-5564-6920; www.mamarumba.com.mx; Querétaro 230; ⏲9pm-3am Wed & Thu, 8pm-4am Fri & Sat; 🚌Sonora) Managed by a Havana native, Mama Rumba features contemporary salsa, with music by the house big band. You can take a class on Wednesdays and Thursdays at 9pm and Fridays and Saturdays at 8pm. Mama Rumba has a larger branch in San Ángel at Plaza Loreto.

Cantina Covadonga CANTINA
(Map p84; www.banquetescovadonga.com.mx; Puebla 121; ⏲1pm-2am Mon-Wed, to 3am Thu & Fri; Ⓜ Insurgentes) Echoing with the sounds of clacking dominoes, the old Asturian social hall is a traditionally male enclave, though hipsters of both sexes have increasingly moved in on this hallowed ground.

La Bodeguita del Medio BAR
(Map p84; ☎55-5553-0246; www.labodeguitadelmedio.com.mx; Cozumel 37; ⏲1:30pm-2am Mon-Sat, to 12:30am Sun; Ⓜ Sevilla) The walls are tagged with verses and messages at this

GAY & LESBIAN MEXICO CITY

Now that the Distrito Federal (DF) assembly has approved a same-sex marriage law, Mexico City is seen as a bastion of tolerance in an otherwise conservative country. The long-time heart of gay life is the Zona Rosa – in particular Calle Amberes. Yet many night owls prefer the downtown scene along República de Cuba. **GayCities** (www.mexicocity.gaycities.com) has useful information on gay-friendly hotels, bars and clubs.

Marrakech Salón (Map p66; www.twitter.com/marrakechsalon; República de Cuba 18, Colonia Centro; ⏲7pm-2:30am Thu-Sat; Ⓜ Allende) Typical sights and sounds at this retro bar include bare-chested bartenders, bar-top dancing and festive music ranging from 1980s pop to hip-shaking *cumbias* (dance music from Colombia). It gets crowded and steamy, but no one seems to mind.

Nicho Bears & Bar (Map p110; www.bearmex.com; Londres 182, Zona Rosa; ⏲8pm-2:30am Thu-Sat; Ⓜ Insurgentes) Popular with thirty-somethings, this Zona Rosa bear den has a slightly more sophisticated air than many of the bars lining the raucous gay strip on nearby Amberes.

La Purísima (Map p66; www.twitter.com/la_purisima; República de Cuba 17, Colonia Centro; ⏲7pm-2:30am Thu-Sat; Ⓜ Allende) Esentially two bars in one: dance the night away in a rip-roaring, garish disco downstairs, or head upstairs for mezcal, *pulque* (milky, low-alcohol brew made from the *maguey* plant) and perhaps a karaoke session if the mood strikes.

Bar Oasis (Map p66; ☎55-5521-9740; República de Cuba 2G, Colonia Centro; ⏲5pm-2am; Ⓜ Allende) This packed disco cuts across class lines, with both cowboys and businessmen dancing against a Day-Glo cityscape. Stick around past midnight Friday to Sunday for shows featuring lip-synching trannies.

Tom's Leather Bar (Map p84; ☎55-5564-0728; www.toms-mexico.com; Av Insurgentes Sur 357, Colonia Condesa; ⏲9pm-3am Tue-Sun; 📶; 🚌Campeche) For those who dare to get medieval, Tom's provides the props, with heraldic shields, crossed swords and candelabras highlighting a decidedly decadent decor. When the fat lady sings, the show's about to begin.

animated branch of the famous Havana joint. Have a mojito (a Cuban drink of rum, lime juice and mint) and enjoy the excellent *son cubano* combos that perform here.

Los Bisquets Obregón CAFE
(Map p84; ☎55-5584-2802; www.lbbo.com.mx; Álvaro Obregón 60; 7am-midnight; ; Álvaro Obregón) *Chilangos* flock here for the *pan dulce* (sweet bread) and *café con leche*, dispensed from two pitchers, Veracruz-style.

Maison Francaise de Thé Caravanserai TEAHOUSE
(Map p84; ☎55-5511-2877; Orizaba 101; 10am-10pm Mon-Sat, noon-10pm Sun; ; Álvaro Obregón) This French-style tearoom has more than 170 blends categorized by their intended use or effects. Relax on comfortable sofas to enjoy your chosen brews ceremoniously served on silver trays.

Colonia del Valle

Java junkies will make a special trip to this neighborhood just for the coffee – it's that good!

Passmar CAFE
(www.cafepassmar.com.mx; cnr Adolfo Prieto & Av Coyoacán, Mercado Lázaro Cárdenas; 7:30am-8:30pm Mon-Fri, 8am-8pm Sat; ; La Piedad) You'll be hard-pressed to find a place that takes a cup o' Joe more seriously than Passmar, and the proof is in the artful presentation of the cappuccino. You'll find this award-winning coffee in Mercado Lázaro Cárdenas, six blocks east of La Piedad station on metrobús Línea 1.

Polanco

Though not as cutting-edge as Roma and Condesa, this well-heeled neighborhood gets quite lively after dark.

Área COCKTAIL BAR
(Map p90; ☎55-5282-3100; www.hotelhabita.com; Av Presidente Masaryk 201; 7pm-2am Mon-Sat; ; M Polanco) Atop the Hábita Hotel, this open-air roof lounge does a brisk trade in exotic martinis, with sweeping city views as a backdrop and videos projected on the wall of a nearby building.

Juan Valdez Café CAFE
(Map p90; www.facebook.com/cafe.juanvaldez.mexico; Oscar Wilde 9F; 8am-11pm Mon-Sat, to 9pm Sun; ; M Auditorio) Famed Colombian coffee chain Juan Valdez has set up shop in Polanco and, not surprisingly, it's all the rage. It's a good place to score some beans and enjoy a cup of some of Colombia's best premium coffee.

Big Red BAR
(Map p90; ☎55-5255-5277; Av Presidente Masaryk 101; noon-6pm Mon, to 8pm Tue, to 2am Wed-Sat; ; M Polanco) A volume dealer with drinks reasonably priced by the ounce, plus whatever mixer you choose. Thus the place attracts a broader cross-section of the populace than the usual Polanco *antro* (bar).

Xochimilco

Pulquería El Templo de Diana PULQUERÍA
(☎55-5653-4657; Madero 17, cnr Calle 5 de Mayo; 10am-9pm; Xochimilco) This classic *pulquería*, a block east of the main market, has a cheerful sawdust-on-the-floor vibe, with a mixed-age crowd enjoying giant mugs of the *maguey*-based beverage. Even a few females may pop in. Delivered daily from Hidalgo state, the *pulque* is expertly blended with flavorings like nescafe, *pistache* (pistachio), and *piñon* (pine nut).

Pulquería La Botijona PULQUERÍA
(Av Morelos 109; 10am-10pm; Xochimilco) Possibly the cleanest *pulque* dispenser in town, this institutional green hall near the train station is a friendly family-run establishment with big plastic pails of the traditional quaff lining the shelves.

San Ángel

La Camelia BAR
(Map p96; ☎55-5615-5643; www.facebook.com/lacameliasanangel; Madero 3; noon-9pm Sun-Thu, to 3am Fri & Sat; La Bombilla) This restaurant-cantina has been drawing Mexican celebrities since 1931, as evidenced by the stars' photos on the walls. Friday and Saturday are karaoke nights. Liquid courage comes in the form of tequila or *cerveza mexicana*.

Coyoacán

★**La Bipo** BAR
(Map p114; ☎55-5484-8230; www.facebook.com/labipo.coyoacan; Malintzin 155; 1pm-12:30am Mon-Wed, to 2am Thu-Sat, to 11pm Sun; ; M Coyoacán) Part-owned by Mexican heartthrob Diego Luna (of *Y Tu Mamá También* movie fame), this popular cantina plays up the kitschier elements of Mexican popular culture, with wall panels fashioned from plastic

crates and sliced tin buckets as light shades. The menu, consisting of Mexican snacks, is hit and miss. DJs spin assorted tunes upstairs from Wednesday to Saturday.

Cantina La Coyoacana CANTINA
(Map p114; Higuera 14; 1pm-2am; ; M Coyoacán) Enter through swinging saloon doors and head to the open-air patio, where wailing mariachis do their thing in this traditional drinking establishment.

Café El Jarocho CAFE
(Map p114; 55-5658-5029; www.cafeeljarocho.com.mx; Cuauhtémoc 134; 6am-1am Sun-Thu, to 2am Fri & Sat; M Coyoacán) This immensely popular joint churns out coffee for long lines of java hounds. As there's no seating inside, people have their drink standing in the street or sitting on curbside benches. A **branch** (Av México 25C) with seats is several blocks northwest of Jardín Centenario.

El Hijo del Cuervo BAR
(Map p114; 55-5658-7824; www.elhijodelcuervo.com.mx; Jardín Centenario 17; 4pm-midnight Mon-Wed, 1pm-1:30am Thu, to 2am Fri & Sat, to 11:30pm Sun; M Coyoacán) A Coyoacán institution, this stone-walled 'cultu-bar' on the Jardín Centenario is a longtime favorite on the local cultural scene. Jazz and rock groups perform on Tuesday, Wednesday and Thursday nights.

Tlatelolco & Around

Salón Los Ángeles DANCING
(55-5597-5181; www.salonlosangeles.mx; Lerdo 206, Colonia Guerrero; 6-11pm Tue & 5-11pm Sun; M Tlatelolco) Fans of dance hall music shouldn't miss the outstanding orchestras, nor the graceful dancers who fill the vast floor of this atmospheric ballroom. The live music, consisting of salsa and *cumbia* (dance music originating in Colombia) on Sunday and swing and *danzón* on Tuesday, draws a mostly older crowd. It's located in the rough Colonia Guerrero, so take a taxi.

Two-hour dance classes are offered on Mondays at 6pm and Tuesdays at 4pm.

☆ Entertainment

There's so much going on in Mexico City on any given evening, it's hard to keep track. **Tiempo Libre** (www.tiempolibre.com.mx), the city's comprehensive what's-on magazine, helps you sort it all out. It covers live music, theater, movies, dance, art and nightlife. Other useful publications with good websites are **La Semana de Frente** (www.frente.com.mx), **Donde Ir** (www.dondeir.com), **Chilango** (www.chilango.com) and Time Out Mexico (p130).

Ticketmaster sells tickets online for all the major venues, or visit any of its following branches: Auditorio Nacional (p125); **Liverpool Centro** (Map p66; Venustiano Carranza 92; 11am-7pm; M Zócalo); **Liverpool Polanco** (Map p90; Mariano Escobedo 425; 11am-8pm; M Polanco); **Mixup Centro** (Map p66; Av Madero 51; 10am-9pm Mon-Sat, 11am-8pm Sun; M Zócalo); **Mixup Zona Rosa** (Génova 76; M Insurgentes).

Cinemas

Ticket prices are around M$60 in commercial cinemas, with many places offering discounts on Wednesdays. Most movies are in original languages with Spanish subtitles, except for children's fare. *El Universal* and *La Jornada* have daily listings.

Cineteca Nacional CINEMA
(Map p114; 55-4155-1200; www.cinetecanacional.net; Av México-Coyoacán 389, Colonia Xoco; ; M Coyoacán) Mexican and foreign indie movies are shown on 10 screens at the recently renovated Cineteca. In November, the complex hosts the Muestra Internacional de Cine, an international film festival. From October to March you can catch free open-air screenings at dusk in the garden. A film museum was under construction at last visit.

Cine Tonalá CINEMA
(Map p84; www.cinetonala.com; Tonalá 261; ; Campeche) A pleasant multipurpose venue for independent cinema, plays and concerts.

Cinépolis Diana CINEMA
(Map p110; 55-5511-3236; www.cinepolis.com.mx; Paseo de la Reforma 423; M Sevilla) Commercial releases and international film-festival titles.

Cinemex Real CINEMA
(Map p76; 55-5257-6969; www.cinemex.com; Colón 17; M Hidalgo) Screens mostly Hollywood movies and the occasional Mexican hit.

Cinemex Casa de Arte CINEMA
(Cinemex Reforma; Map p110; 55-5257-6969; www.cinemex.com; Río Guadalquivir 104; M Insurgentes) Primarily art-house flicks.

Filmoteca de la UNAM CINEMA
(55-5704-6338; www.filmoteca.unam.mx; Av Insurgentes Sur 3000; Centro Cultural Universitario) Two cinemas at the Centro Cultural

Universitario screen films from a collection of more than 43,000 titles.

Dance, Classical Music & Theater

Orchestral music, opera, ballet, contemporary dance and theater are all abundantly represented in the capital's numerous theaters. Museums, too, serve as (often free) performance venues, including the Museo de la Secretaría de Hacienda y Crédito Público (p74) and the Museo de la Ciudad de México (p75). The national arts council (Conaculta) provides a rundown of events on its website (www.mexicoescultura.com).

If your Spanish is up to it, you might like to sample Mexico City's lively theater scene. **Mejor Teatro** (www.mejorteatro.com.mx) covers the major venues.

Palacio de Bellas Artes PERFORMING ARTS
(Map p76; www.bellasartes.gob.mx; Av Hidalgo 1; ⏲ box office 11am-7pm; Ⓜ Bellas Artes) The Orquesta Sinfónica Nacional and prestigious opera companies perform in Bellas Artes' ornate theater, while chamber groups appear in the recital halls. The venue is most famous, though, for the **Ballet Folklórico de México** (Map p76; www.balletamalia.com; ⏲ performances 8:30pm Wed, 9:30am & 8:30pm Sun; Ⓜ Bellas Artes), a two-hour festive blur of costumes, music and dance from all over Mexico. Tickets are usually available on the day of the show, or from Ticketmaster.

Centro Cultural Universitario PERFORMING ARTS
(☎ 55-5622-7003; www.cultura.unam.mx; Av Insurgentes Sur 3000; 🚌 Centro Cultural Universitario) Ensconced in the woodsy southern section of the national university campus, Centro Cultural Universitario comprises five theaters, including the Sala Nezahualcóyotl, home of the UNAM Philharmonic; the Teatro Alarcón, a drama stage; and the Sala Miguel Covarrubias, a contemporary dance venue.

Centro Nacional de las Artes PERFORMING ARTS
(CNA; ☎ 55-4155-0000; www.cenart.gob.mx; Av Río Churubusco 79, Colonia Country Club; 📶; Ⓜ General Anaya) A sprawling cultural institute near Coyoacán that has many free events across the artistic spectrum, including contemporary dance, theater, art shows and classical concerts. To get here, exit metro General Anaya (Línea 2) on the east side of Calzada de Tlalpan, then walk north to the corner and turn right.

Centro Cultural del Bosque PERFORMING ARTS
(Map p90; ☎ 55-5283-4600, ext 4408; www.ccb.bellasartes.gob.mx; cnr Paseo de la Reforma & Campo Marte, Colonia Chapultepec Polanco; ⏲ box office noon-3pm & 5-7pm Mon-Fri & prior to events; Ⓜ Auditorio) Behind the Auditorio Nacional, the Centro Cultural del Bosque features six theaters, including the Teatro de la Danza, dedicated to modern dance. On Saturday and Sunday afternoons, children's plays and puppet shows are often staged.

Foro Shakespeare THEATER
(Map p84; ☎ 55-5553-4642; www.foroshakespeare.com; Zamora 7, Colonia Condesa; Ⓜ Chapultepec) A small independent theater with an eclectic program. Jazz ensembles perform Thursday night in the theater's restaurant-bar.

Centro Cultural Helénico THEATER
(Map p96; ☎ 55-4155-0919; www.helenico.gob.mx; Av Revolución 1500, Colonia Guadalupe Inn; ⏲ box office 12:30-8:45pm Mon-Fri, 11:30am-8:45pm Sat, 11:30am-6:15pm Sun; 🚌 Altavista) This complex includes a 440-seat theater for major productions and a smaller cabaret-style venue for experimental plays.

Live Music

Mexico City's eclectic music offering rocks. On any given night, you can hear traditional Mexican, Cuban, jazz, electronica, garage punk and so on. Music sounds off everywhere: in concert halls, bars, museums – even on public transportation. Free gigs often take place at the Zócalo and at Monumento a la Revolución. The 'conciertos' sections of **Tiempo Libre** (www.tiempolibre.com.mx) and **Ticketmaster** (www.ticketmaster.com.mx) include show listings.

The thriving mariachi music scene at Plaza Garibaldi gets going by about 8pm and stays busy until 3am.

The street market Tianguis Cultural del Chopo (p129) has a stage at its north end every Saturday afternoon for young and hungry metal and punk bands.

★ **Centro Cultural de España** LIVE MUSIC
(Map p66; ☎ 55-5521-1925; www.ccemx.org; República de Guatemala 18; ⏲ 10pm-2am Wed-Sat; Ⓜ Zócalo) FREE Young hipsters pack the terrace of this place each weekend for its excellent DJ and live-music sessions. Located directly behind the cathedral, the rebuilt colonial structure is usually quaking by midnight.

El Plaza Condesa CONCERT VENUE
(Map p84; ☎55-5256-5381; www.elplaza.mx; Juan Escutia 4; Campeche) At the heart of the Condesa nightlife scene, this former movie theater now raises the curtain for pop and rock acts from Mexico and abroad.

Teatro de la Ciudad CONCERT VENUE
(Map p66; ☎55-5130-5740, ext 2006; www.cultura.df.gob.mx/index.php/recintos-menu/teatros/tcm; Donceles 36; box office 10am-3pm & 4-7pm; M Allende) Built in 1918 and modeled after Italy's La Scala opera house, this lavishly restored 1300-seat hall gets some of the more interesting touring acts in music, dance and theater.

José Cuervo Salón CONCERT VENUE
(☎55-5255-5322; www.ticketmaster.com.mx/jose-cuervo-salon-boletos-mexico/venue/163961; Lago Andrómaco 17, cnr Moliere, Colonia Ampliación Granada; box office 10am-6pm) A warehouse-sized venue for touring rock, world-music and salsa stars. With excellent sound, a wall-length bar and a dance floor for thousands, this is one of Mexico City's best concert halls. It's best reached by taxi.

Cafebrería El Péndulo LIVE MUSIC
(Map p84; www.forodeltejedor.com; Álvaro Obregón 86; ; Álvaro Obregón) Leading Mexican artists of varying musical genres play at this cafe-bookstore's rooftop venue. The adjoining open-air bar provides a nice atmosphere for hanging out after the show.

Ticketmaster Auditorio Nacional CONCERT VENUE
(Map p90; ☎55-9138-1350; Paseo de la Reforma 50, Bosque de Chapultepec; box office 10am-7pm Mon-Sat, 11am-6pm Sun; M Auditorio) Major gigs by Mexican and visiting rock and pop artists take the stage at the 10,000-seat Auditorio Nacional. The adjoining **Lunario del Auditorio** (Map p90; www.lunario.com.mx; M Auditorio) is a large club reserved mostly for jazz and folk acts.

★ **Salón Tenampa** MARIACHIS
(Map p66; ☎55-5526-6176; www.salontenampa.com; Plaza Garibaldi 12; 1pm-2am Sun-Thu, to 4am Fri & Sat; ; M Garibaldi) Graced with murals of the giants of Mexican song and enlivened by its own songsters, the Tenampa is a festive cantina on the north side of the plaza; a visit here is obligatory.

Multiforo Alicia CONCERT VENUE
(Map p84; ☎55-5511-2100; www.facebook.com/pages/Multiforo-Alicia/244833642369; Av Cuauhtémoc 91A; Jardín Pushkin) Behind the graffiti-scrawled facade is Mexico City's premier indie-rock club. A suitably dark, seatless space, the Alicia stages mostly up-and-coming punk, surf and ska bands, who hawk their music at the store downstairs. See Alicia's Facebook page for show times.

El Imperial Club CONCERT VENUE
(Map p84; ☎55-5525-1115; www.elimperial.tv; Álvaro Obregón 293, Colonia Roma; 10pm-2:30am Tue & Wed, to 4am Thu-Sat; M Sevilla) Mexican alternative rock bands and the occasional imported act perform in this ornate two-story house with antique furnishings and vintage touches throughout.

Caradura CONCERT VENUE
(Map p84; www.caradura.mx; 2nd fl, Nuevo León 73; 9pm-2:30am Tue-Sat; Campeche) One of the best spots in town to exorcise your demons while rockin' out to garage, rockabilly and postpunk sounds.

Pasagüero + La Bipo CONCERT VENUE
(Map p66; ☎55-5512-6624; www.facebook.com/pasaguero; Motolinía 33; 10pm-3:30am Thu-Sat; ; M Allende) Some visionary developers took a historic building and transformed its stonewalled ground level into a restaurant-bar for various cultural happenings, especially rock and electronica gigs.

El Under MUSIC
(Map p84; ☎55-5511-5475; www.facebook.com/realunder; Monterrey 80; 9pm-5am Fri & Sat; Durango) At this underground scene favorite, black-clad youth dance to the likes of Morrissey and Bauhaus on the old house's lower level, while upstairs local bands grind out everything from garage punk and rockabilly to death metal.

Zinco Jazz Club JAZZ
(Map p66; ☎55-5512-3369; www.zincojazz.com; Motolinía 20; 9pm-2am Wed-Sat; ; M Allende) A vital component in the *centro*'s rebirth, Zinco is a subterranean supper club featuring local jazz and funk outfits as well as touring artists. The intimate basement room fills up fast when big-name acts take the stage.

Ruta 61 BLUES
(Map p84; ☎55-5211-7602; www.ruta61.com.mx; Av Baja California 281; 7pm-1am Wed-Sat; M Chilpancingo) This split-level venue stages electric blues artists in the Buddy Guy/Howlin' Wolf mold. About once a month there's a direct-from-Chicago act, though you're more likely to see a local cover band.

El Balcón Huasteco LIVE MUSIC
(☎55-5341-6762; www.elbalconhuasteco.com; Sor Juana Inés de la Cruz 248, Colonia Agricultura; ⊙from 6:30pm Fri & Sat; Ⓜ Normal) This center for the preservation of the Huastec culture of Hidalgo and Veracruz stages performances by fiery trios and prepares snacks hailing from the region. Should you feel inspired, music and dance classes are offered here. It's two blocks north of metro Normal.

El Breve Espacio Mezcalería LIVE MUSIC
(Map p96; www.elbreveespacio.mx; Frontera 4; ⊙10am-5:30pm Mon-Wed, to 2am Thu-Sat; 📶; 🚌La Bombilla) Folk singers in the Silvio Rodríguez mold take the stage at this temple of *trova* (troubadour-type folk music) near San Ángel's Plaza San Jacinto.

Cabaret

La Perla CABARET
(Map p66; ☎55-1997-7695; www.facebook.com/cabaret.laperla; República de Cuba 44; ⊙showtimes 11pm & 1am Fri & Sat; 🚌República de Chile) Once a red-light venue, this cabaret has been reborn in the age of irony as a cradle of kitsch, with hilarious drag shows featuring traditional Mexican songstresses. Tickets go fast.

El Bataclán CABARET
(Map p84; ☎55-5511-7390; www.labodega.com.mx; Popocatépetl 25; ⊙9pm-1am Tue-Sat; 🚌Álvaro Obregón) A theater within a club (La Bodega), this classic cabaret venue showcases some of Mexico's more offbeat performers. Afterwards, catch top-notch Cuban *son* combos over a rum-based mojito.

Teatro Bar El Vicio CABARET
(Map p114; ☎55-5659-1139; www.lasreinaschulas.com; Madrid 13, Colonia del Carmen; ⊙9:30pm-2am Thu-Sun; Ⓜ Coyoacán) With liberal doses of politically and sexually irreverent comedy and a genre-bending musical program, this alternative cabaret is appropriately located in Frida Kahlo's old stomping grounds.

Sports

Most of the daily newspapers have a generous sports section where you can find out who is kicking which ball where. True enthusiasts should look for **La Afición** (www.laaficion.com), a daily devoted to sports.

Corridas de toros (bullfights) take place on Sunday around 4pm (check website for specific times) at the **Plaza México** (☎55-5133-1939; www.lamexico.com; Augusto Rodin 241, Colonia Noche Buena; 🚌Ciudad de los Deportes), one of the largest bullrings in the world, a few blocks west of Avenida Insurgentes. Bullfight season varies, but it usually runs from May to September and October to February.

The capital stages *fútbol* (soccer) matches in the national Primera División almost every weekend of the year. Mexico City has three teams: América, nicknamed Las Águilas (the Eagles); Las Pumas of UNAM; and Cruz Azul. There are two seasons: January to June and July to December, each ending in eight-team play offs and a two-leg final to decide the champion. The biggest match of all is El Clásico, between América and Guadalajara, which fills the Estadio Azteca with 100,000 flag-waving fans. Get tickets in advance for this one.

Tickets to soccer matches (M$90 to M$650 for regular season games) are usually available at the gate, or from Ticketmaster. There are several stadiums that host games.

Arena México MEXICAN WRESTLING
(Map p84; ☎55-5588-0266; www.arenamexico.com.mx; Dr Lavista 197, Colonia Doctores; ⊙7:30pm Tue & 8:30pm Fri; 🚌Cuauhtémoc) One of Mexico City's two wrestling venues, the 17,000-seat Arena México is taken over by a circus atmosphere each week, with flamboyant *luchadores* (wrestlers) such as Místico and Super Porky going at each other in tag teams or one-on-one. There are three or four bouts, building up to the headline match. Also check out the smaller **Arena Coliseo** (Map p66; ☎55-5526-1687; www.cmll.com/arena_coliseo.htm; República de Perú 77; ⊙5pm Sun, except 3rd Sun of the month; 🚌República de Chile).

Estadio Azteca STADIUM
(☎55-5487-3309; www.esmas.com/estadioazteca; Calz de Tlalpan 3665; 🚌Estadio Azteca) The country's biggest stadium (capacity 105,000) is home to the América soccer club. Games are played on weekend afternoons; check the website for kick-off times. Take the *tren ligero* (light rail) from metro Tasqueña to the Estadio Azteca station.

Estadio Olímpico STADIUM
(☎55-5325-9000; www.clubpumasunam.com; Av Insurgentes Sur 3000, Ciudad Universitaria; 🚌CU) Home of the Pumas soccer team. To get here, go right after exiting metrobús station CU and look for the bus stop for free university transportation (called the Pumabús). 'Ruta 6' goes to Estadio Olímpico.

Estadio Azul STADIUM
(☎55-5563-9040; www.cruz-azul.com.mx; Indiana 255, Colonia Nápoles; Ciudad de los Deportes) This soccer stadium is next door to the Plaza México bullring.

Diablos Rojos BASEBALL
(www.diablos.com.mx) Mexico City has one baseball team in the Liga Mexicana de Béisbol, the Diablos Rojos. During the regular season (April to July) they play every other week at **Foro Sol** (http://www.diablos.com.mx/forosol.php; cnr Av Río Churubusco & Av Viaducto Río de la Piedad, Colonia Granjas México; M Ciudad Deportiva). From the metro, it's a five-minute walk to the ballpark. See the Diablos website for game times.

Shopping

Shopping can be a real joy in Mexico City, with *artesanías* (handicrafts) vendors, quirky shops and street markets competing for your disposable income.

Chilangos increasingly shop in modern malls with designer-clothing stores and Starbucks franchises, and more of these shrines to consumerism are popping up all the time. Among the more pleasant are **Plaza Loreto** (Map p96; www.facebook.com/plazaloreto; cnr Av Revolución & Río de la Magdalena; 11am-8pm; ; Dr Gálvez) in San Ángel; the open-air **Antara** (Map p90; www.antara.com.mx; Av Ejército Nacional 843B; 11am-8pm; M Polanco) in Polanco; and **Reforma 222** (Map p110; www.codigoreforma222.com.mx; Paseo de la Reforma 222; 11am-9pm; M Insurgentes) at the east end of the Zona Rosa.

Rare-book aficionados can dig up some gems in the used bookstores along Donceles in the *centro*. Books in English can be found in top-end hotels, major museums and some bookstores.

Mexico City's markets are worth visiting, not just for their varied contents but also for a glimpse of the frenetic business conducted within. In most neighborhoods you'll find a *tianguis* (street market) at least once a week selling everything from fresh produce to clothing and antiques. *Tianguis* generally set up by 10am and finish around 5pm.

Centro Histórico & Around

Mexico City's smartest department-store chains, **El Palacio de Hierro** (Map p66; ☎55-5728-9905; www.palaciodehierro.com.mx; Av 20 de Noviembre 3; 11am-9pm; M Zócalo) and **Liverpool** (Map p66; ☎55-5262-9999; www.liverpool.com.mx; Venustiano Carranza 92; 11am-9pm; M Zócalo) both maintain their original 1930s stores downtown.

The streets around the Zócalo are lined with stores that specialize in everyday goods; you'll find plenty of shops selling similar items along the same street. To the west, used books show up on Donceles. Jewelry and gold outlets, as well as numismatics shops, are found along Palma, while opticians are east of the square on Avenida Madero. To the south, shoes are available on Avenida 20 de Noviembre, while along Bolívar, dozens of stores sell musical instruments. To the north, you'll find costume jewelry on República de Colombia and República de Venezuela.

Hundreds of computer stores huddle in the **Plaza de la Computación y Electrónica** (Map p66; www.plazadelatecnologia.com/mexico; Eje Central Lázaro Cárdenas 38; 10am-6pm; M San Juan de Letrán), south of Uruguay.

Centro de Artesanías La Ciudadela HANDICRAFTS
(Map p76; www.facebook.com/mercadodeartesaniaslaciudadela; cnr Balderas & Dondé; 10am-7pm Mon-Sat, to 6pm Sun; M Balderas) A favorite destination for good stuff from all over Mexico. Worth seeking out are Oaxaca *alebrijes* (whimsical painted animals), guitars from Paracho and Huichol beadwork. Prices are generally fair, even before you bargain.

Mumedi GIFTS
(Mexican Design Museum; Map p66; ☎55-5510-8609; www.mumedi.org; Av Madero 74; 11am-9pm Mon, 8am-9pm Tue-Sun; ; M Zócalo) This design-museum gift shop sells interesting pop-culture knick-knacks, handbags and jewelry crafted mostly by local artisans.

Mercado San Juan MARKET
(Map p76; www.mercadosanjuan.galeon.com; Pugibet 21; 8am-5pm Mon-Sat, to 4pm Sun; Plaza San Juan) Specializes in gourmet food items such as *huitlacoche* (trufflelike corn fungus) and rare fruit. Local chefs and foodies come here to score ingredients not available elsewhere in the city.

Plaza Downtown Mexico MALL
(Map p66; www.facebook.com/downtownmexico; Isabel La Católica 30; 11am-8pm Mon-Sat, to 6pm Sun; M Zócalo) Shops surrounding the central courtyard of a beautifully restored 18th-century colonial building sell crafts, ceramics, chocolate and clothes.

Casasola Fotografía SOUVENIRS
(Map p66; www.casasolafoto.com; Office 201, 2nd fl, Isabel La Católica 45; ⏲10am-7pm Mon-Fri, to 3pm Sat; República del Salvador) Odds are you've probably seen this studio's world-famous revolution-era sepia photos. Items on sale include framed pictures, calendars, T-shirts and postcards. Photo ID required to enter.

La Europea DRINK
(Map p66; ☎55-5512-6005; www.laeuropea.com.mx; Ayuntamiento 21; ⏲9am-8pm Mon-Sat, 11am-4pm Sun; Plaza San Juan) Get reasonably priced tequila, mezcal and wine at this well-stocked liquor store.

Dulcería de Celaya FOOD
(Map p66; ☎55-5521-1787; www.dulceriadecelaya.com; Av 5 de Mayo 39; ⏲10:30am-7:30pm; M Allende) Candy store operating since 1874, with candied fruits and coconut-stuffed lemons; worth a look just for the ornate building.

Galería Eugenio HANDICRAFTS
(Map p66; ☎55-5529-2849; Allende 84; ⏲11am-5:30pm Mon-Sat; M Garibaldi) Sells more than 4000 masks from all over the country; it's in the Lagunilla market area.

American Bookstore BOOKS
(Map p66; ☎55-5512-0306; Bolívar 23; ⏲10am-6:30pm Mon-Fri, to 5:30pm Sat; M Allende) Has novels and books on Mexico in English, plus Lonely Planet guides.

Gandhi BOOKS
(www.gandhi.com.mx) Citywide chain with a voluminous range of texts on Mexico and Mexico City. Branches at **Av Madero** (Map p66; Av Madero 32; ⏲10am-9pm Mon-Sat, 11am-8pm Sun; M Zócalo); **Bellas Artes** (Map p76; Juárez 4; ⏲10am-9pm Mon-Sat, 11am-9pm Sun; M Bellas Artes); **San Ángel** (Map p96; ☎55-2625-0606; Av Miguel Ángel de Quevedo 121; ⏲10am-10pm; M Miguel Ángel de Quevedo). There are two outlets on the same block in San Ángel.

Tianguis Dominical de la Lagunilla MARKET
(cnr Gónzalez Bocanegra & Paseo de la Reforma, Colonia Centro; ⏲10am-6pm Sun; M Garibaldi) At this collector's oasis you can hunt for antiques, old souvenirs and bric-a-brac; books and magazines are alongside La Lagunilla building.

La Lagunilla MARKET
(Map p66; cnr Rayón & Allende, Colonia Centro; ⏲9am-8pm Mon-Sat, 10am-7pm Sun; M Garibaldi) This enormous complex comprises three buildings: building No 1 contains clothes and fabrics, No 2 has food and No 3 sells furniture.

Tepito MARKET
(Map p66; Héroe de Granaditas, Colonia Tepito; ⏲10am-6pm Wed-Mon; M Lagunilla) The mother of all street markets: a maze of semipermanent stalls spreading east and north from La Lagunilla, with miles of clothes, pirated CDs, DVDs and electronics. Also known as a thieves' market for its smuggled goods and pickpockets. Enter crime-ridden Tepito at your own risk.

Zona Rosa & Around

★**Fonart** HANDICRAFTS
(www.fonart.gob.mx) This government-run crafts store sells quality wares, such as Olinalá-produced lacquered boxes and black pottery from Oaxaca. Branches at **Reforma** (Map p110; Paseo de la Reforma 116; ⏲10am-7pm Mon-Fri, to 4pm Sat & Sun; Reforma) and **Mixcoac** (Patriotismo 691; ⏲10am-8pm Mon-Fri, to 7pm Sat, 11am-5pm Sun; M Mixcoac). Prices are fixed.

Mercado Insurgentes ARTS & CRAFTS
(Map p110; Londres 154; ⏲10:30am-7:30pm Mon-Sat, to 4pm Sun; M Insurgentes) Packed with crafts – silver, pottery, leather, carved wooden figures – but you'll need to bargain to get sensible prices.

Plaza del Ángel ANTIQUES
(Map p110; www.antiguedadesmexico.com; Londres 161, btwn Amberes & Av Florencia; ⏲9am-4pm Sat & Sun; M Insurgentes) Flea market within a mall of high-end antique shops selling silver jewelry, paintings, ornaments and furniture.

Jardín del Arte ARTS & CRAFTS
(Map p110; btwn Sullivan & Villalongín, Colonia San Rafael; ⏲9am-5pm Sun; Reforma) Local artists line the pathways of a park to sell their paintings while vendors hawk art supplies.

Condesa & Roma

Condesa presents an enticing array of trendy boutiques, quirky shops and gourmet food stores. In Roma, much of the retail activity is along Álvaro Obregón and Colima.

Vértigo ARTS & CRAFTS
(Map p84; www.vertigogaleria.com; Colima 23; ⏲noon-8pm Mon-Fri, to 7pm Sat, to 6pm Sun; Jardín Pushkin) The store at this funky art gallery sells silkscreens, graphic T-shirts

and etchings made by popular Argentine illustrator Jorge Alderete. In addition to 'low brow' art shows, Vértigo stages acoustic music performances every so often.

La Naval DRINK
(Map p84; ☎55-5584-3500; www.lanaval.com.mx; Av Insurgentes Sur 373; ⏰9am-9pm Mon-Sat, 11am-7pm Sun; 🚌Campeche) This gourmet store stocks a tantalizing selection of mezcals and tequilas, as well as Cuban cigars.

Centro Cultural Bella Época BOOKS
(Map p84; ☎55-5276-7110; www.facebook.com/centroculturalbellaepoca; Av Tamaulipas 202, cnr Benjamín Hill, Colonia Condesa; 📶; Ⓜ Patriotismo) One of the largest bookstores in Latin America; shelves books, CDs and DVDs inside an impressive art deco cultural center.

Under the Volcano Books BOOKS
(Map p84; www.underthevolcanobooks.com; Celaya 25; ⏰11am-7pm Mon-Fri, to 5pm Sat & Sun; 🚌Sonora) Buys and sells used English-language titles; an excellent selection and very good prices.

Bazar de la Roma ANTIQUES
(Map p84; Jardín Dr Chávez, Colonia Doctores; ⏰10am-5pm Sat & Sun; 🚌Jardín Pushkin) East of Avenida Cuauhtémoc, this market has used and antique items, large and small: books, beer trays, posters and furniture. A similar antiques and art market runs along Álvaro Obregón on the same days.

Bazar del Oro MARKET
(Map p84; www.twitter.com/bazardeloro; Calle de Oro, Colonia Roma; ⏰11am-7pm Sat & Sun; 🚌Durango) This upscale street market between Avenida Insurgentes and Plaza Villa de Madrid has clothing, gifts and an excellent eating section.

El Hijo del Santo GIFTS
(Map p84; ☎55-5512-2186; www.elhijodelsanto.com.mx/coffeeshop; Av Tamaulipas 219; ⏰10am-9pm Mon-Sat; Ⓜ Patriotismo) Owned by wrestler El Hijo del Santo, this small specialty store sells (you guessed it) all things Santo. Among the offerings are kitschy portraits, hipster handbags and the ever-popular Santo mask.

Polanco

Polanco's Avenida Presidente Masaryk, aka the Rodeo Drive of Mexico, is lined with designer stores and other high-end establishments.

Pasaje Polanco SHOPPING CENTER
(Map p90; ☎55-5280-7976; Av Presidente Masaryk 360; ⏰11am-8pm Mon-Sat, to 7pm Sun; Ⓜ Polanco) A classy complex flanked by sophisticated boutiques, specialty stores and a large crafts shop selling handbags, wrestling masks and Day of the Dead folk art.

Coyoacán

Bazar Artesanal Mexicano HANDICRAFTS
(Map p114; www.facebook.com/bazarartesanalmexicanocoyoacan; Carrillo Puerto 25; ⏰11am-9pm Mon-Thu, 10am-11pm Fri-Sun; Ⓜ Coyoacán) Handmade jewelry, crafts and no shortage of touristy junk.

San Ángel

Bazar Sábado ARTS & CRAFTS
(Map p96; ☎55-5616-0082; www.elbazaarsabado.com; Plaza San Jacinto 11; ⏰10am-5:30pm Sat; 🚌La Bombilla) The Saturday bazaar showcases some of Mexico's best handcrafted jewelry, woodwork, ceramics and textiles. Artists and artisans also display their work in Plaza San Jacinto itself and in adjacent Plaza Tenanitla.

Other Neighborhoods

★ **Tianguis Cultural del Chopo** MUSIC
(www.tianguisculturaldelchopo.freeiz.com; Calle Aldama s/n, Colonia Guerrero; ⏰10am-5pm Sat; Ⓜ Buenavista) Gathering place for the city's various youth subcultures, with most of the vendor stalls selling clothes, DVDs and CDs. At the far end of the market is a concert stage for young-and-hungry bands. The main entrance is one block east of metro Buenavista.

Mercado de Jamaica MARKET
(cnr Guillermo Prieto & Congreso de la Unión, Colonia Jamaica; ⏰24hr; Ⓜ Jamaica) Huge, colorful flower market, featuring both baroque floral arrangements and exotic blooms. It's one block south of metro Jamaica.

Information

DANGERS & ANNOYANCES

Mexico City is generally portrayed as extremely crime-ridden, so first-time visitors are often surprised at how safe it feels. While crime rates remain significant – 38 muggings, two homicides and more than three shootings a day in 2012 – a few precautions greatly reduce any dangers.

Robberies happen most often in areas frequented by foreigners, including Plaza Garibaldi and the Zona Rosa. Be on your guard at the airport and bus stations. Crowded metro cars and buses are favorite haunts of pickpockets; keep a close eye on your wallet and avoid carrying ATM cards or large amounts of cash. In case of robbery, don't resist – hand over your valuables rather than risk injury or death.

Statistically, traffic takes more lives in the capital than street crime. Always look both ways when crossing streets, as some one-way streets have bus lanes running counter to the traffic flow, and traffic on some divided streets runs in just one direction. Never assume that a green light means it's safe to cross, as cars may turn into your path; cross with other pedestrians.

Although not as prevalent as in the 1990s, taxi assaults still occur. Many victims have hailed a cab on the street and been robbed by armed accomplices of the driver. Taxis parked in front of nightclubs or restaurants should be avoided unless authorized by the management. Rather than hailing cabs, find a *sitio* (taxi stand) or request a radio taxi.

EMERGENCY

The Agencia del Ministerio Público (city Attorney General's office) in the Zona Rosa has English-speaking staff to assist victims of crime.

Agencia del Ministerio Público (☎55-5345-5382; Amberes 54; ⏲24hr; Ⓜ Insurgentes) Report crimes and get legal assistance.

Cruz Roja (Red Cross; ☎065)

Fire (☎068)

Police (☎066)

IMMIGRATION

Instituto Nacional de Migración (National Migration Institute; ☎55-2581-0100; www.inm.gob.mx; Av Ejército Nacional 862; ⏲9am-1pm Mon-Fri) You'll need to come here if you want to extend a tourist permit, replace a lost one, or deal with other nonstandard immigration procedures. Catch the 'Ejercito' bus from metro Sevilla; it leaves you two blocks east of the office.

INTERNET ACCESS

Internet services are everywhere. Rates range from M$10 to M$30 per hour.

Plenty of cybercafes occupy the Insurgentes roundabout.

Centenario 4 (2nd fl, Jardín Centenario 4, Coyoacán; ⏲8am-6pm Mon-Fri; Ⓜ Viveros)

Conecte Café (2nd fl, Génova 71, cnr Londres, Zona Rosa; ⏲9:30am-3am Sun-Thu, to 6am Fri & Sat; Ⓜ Insurgentes)

Copy Land (Gante 12, Colonia Centro; ⏲9am-7pm Mon-Fri, 10am-2pm Sat; Ⓜ Allende)

Esperanto (☎55-5512-4123; Independencia 66, Colonia Centro; ⏲8am-10pm Mon-Sat; Ⓜ Juárez)

Tecno Informática (☎55-5211-6784; Vicente Suárez 25, Colonia Condesa; ⏲10am-10pm Mon-Sat; Ⓜ Patriotismo)

MAPS

Mexico City tourist modules hand out color maps with enlargements of the *centro histórico*, Coyoacán and San Ángel. If you need more detail, pick up a Guía Roji (www.guiaroji.com.mx) *Ciudad de México* map (M$260). Find them at Sanborns stores and larger newsstands.

Inegi (www.inegi.gob.mx) Centro (☎55-5130-7900; Balderas 71; ⏲9am-4pm Mon-Fri; Ⓜ Juárez); Colonia Mixcoac (Patriotismo 711, Colonia Mixcoac; ⏲9am-4pm Mon-Fri; Ⓜ Mixcoac) Mexico's national geographical institute publishes topographical maps covering the whole country (subject to availability). Headquarters are in Colonia Mixcoac.

MEDIA

English-language newspapers and magazines are sold at Sanborns stores and at **La Torre de Papel** (☎55-5512-9703; www.latorredepapel.com; Filomena Mata 6A, Colonia Centro; ⏲8am-6pm Mon-Fri, 9am-3pm Sat; Ⓜ Allende). Most of the following publications are sold at newsstands and all have helpful websites.

El Universal (www.eluniversal.com.mx) One of Mexico's oldest and biggest newspapers.

La Jornada (www.jornada.unam.mx) Newspaper known for its excellent cultural coverage and left-leaning news stories.

The News (www.thenews.com.mx) English-language daily with national and world news coverage.

Tiempo Libre (www.tiempolibre.com.mx) The city's Spanish-language what's-on weekly is sold at newsstands everywhere.

Time Out Mexico (www.timeoutmexico.mx) A great source for dining, cultural and entertainment listings; look for free copies in hotels, cafes, bars and nightclubs.

MEDICAL SERVICES

For recommendations for a doctor, dentist or hospital, call your embassy or Sectur, the tourism ministry. A list of area hospitals and English-speaking physicians (with their credentials) is on the **US embassy website** (mexico.usembassy.gov).

A private doctor's consultation generally costs between M$500 and M$1200.

The pharmacies in **Sanborns** (www.sanborns.com.mx) stores are among the most reliable, as are the following places.

Farmacia París (☎55-5709-3211; www.farmaciaparis.com; República de El Salvador 97, Colonia Centro; ⏰8am-11pm Mon-Sat, 9am-9pm Sun; 🚌Isabel La Católica)

Farmacia San Pablo (☎55-5354-9000; www.farmaciasanpablo.com.mx; cnr Av Insurgentes Sur & Chihuahua, Colonia Roma; ⏰24hr; 🚌Álavaro Obregón) Delivery service around the clock.

Hospital ABC (American British Cowdray Hospital; ☎55-5230-8000, emergency 55-5230-8161; www.abchospital.com; Sur 136 No 116, Colonia Las Américas; Ⓜ Observatorio) English-speaking staff provide quality care.

Hospital Ángeles Clínica Londres (☎55-5229-8400, emergency 55-5229-8445; www.hospitalangelesclinicalondres.com; Durango 50, Colonia Roma; Ⓜ Cuauhtémoc) Hospital and medical clinic.

Médicor (☎55-5512-0431; www.medicor.com.mx; Independencia 66, Colonia Centro; ⏰9am-9pm Mon-Sat, to 7pm Sun; Ⓜ Juárez) For homeopathic remedies.

MONEY

Most banks and *casas de cambio* (exchange offices) change cash and traveler's checks, but some handle only euros and US or Canadian dollars. Rates vary, so check a few places. The greatest concentration of ATMs, banks and *casas de cambio* is on Paseo de la Reforma between the Monumento a Cristóbal Colón and the Monumento a la Independencia.

CCSole (www.ccsole.com.mx; Niza 11, Zona Rosa; ⏰9:30am-5:30pm Mon-Fri; Ⓜ Insurgentes) Deals in a wide variety of currencies.

Centro de Cambios y Divisas (☎55-5705-5656; www.ccd.com.mx; Paseo de la Reforma 87F; ⏰8:30am-7:30pm Mon-Fri, 9am-5pm Sat, 9:30am-2:30pm Sun; 🚌Reforma)

POST

The Mexican postal service's website (www.correosdemexico.com.mx) lists branches throughout the city in addition to the ones mentioned below.

Palacio Postal (www.palaciopostal.gob.mx; Tacuba 1; ⏰8am-8pm Mon-Fri, to 4pm Sat & Sun; Ⓜ Bellas Artes) The stamp windows, marked *estampillas*, at the city's main post office stay open beyond normal hours. Even if you don't need stamps, check out the sumptuous interior.

Post Office Cuauhtémoc Branch (☎55-5207-7666; Río Tiber 87; ⏰8am-7pm Mon-Fri, 9am-3pm Sat; Ⓜ Insurgentes)

Post Office Plaza de la República Branch (Arriaga 11; ⏰8am-4pm Mon-Fri, 9am-1pm Sat; 🚌Plaza de la República)

TELEPHONE

There are thousands of Telmex card phones scattered around town. Pick up cards at shops or newsstands bearing the blue-and-yellow 'Ladatel' sign.

TOILETS

Use of the bathroom is free at some Sanborns stores. Most market buildings have public toilets; just look for the 'WC' signs. Hygiene standards vary at these latter facilities, and a fee of M$3 to M$5 is usually charged. Toilet paper is dispensed by an attendant on request.

TOURIST INFORMATION

The National Tourism Secretariat, **Sectur** (☎078, 55-5250-0151, US 800-482-9832; www.sectur.gob.mx), hands out brochures on the entire country, though you're better off at the tourism modules for up-to-date information about the capital.

The **Mexico City Tourism Secretariat** (☎800-008-90-90; www.mexicocity.gob.mx) has modules in key areas, including the airport and bus stations. Staff can answer your queries and distribute a map and practical guide. Staff members usually speak English. Most modules are open from 9am to 6pm daily.

Alameda Tourist Information (cnr Av Juárez & Dr Mora, Colonia Centro; Ⓜ Hidalgo)

Basilica Tourist Information (☎55-5748-2085; Plaza de las Américas 1, Basílica de Guadalupe; ⏰9am-3pm Mon & Tue, to 6pm Wed-Sun; Ⓜ La Villa-Basilica) On the plaza's south side.

Centro Tourist Information (☎55-5518-1003; Catedral; Ⓜ Zócalo) West of the Catedral Metropolitana.

Chapultepec Tourist Information (Paseo de la Reforma; Ⓜ Auditorio) Near the Museo Nacional de Antropología.

Coyoacán Tourist Information (☎55-5658-0221; Jardín Hidalgo 1, Coyoacán; ⏰10am-8pm; Ⓜ Coyoacán) Inside the Casa de Cortés.

Nativitas Tourist Information (☎55-5653-5209; Xochimilco; ⏰9am-4pm Mon-Fri, to 5pm Sat & Sun; 🚆Xochimilco) At the Nativitas boat landing.

Xochimilco Tourist Information (☎55-5676-0810; www.xochimilco.df.gob.mx/turismo; Pino 36; ⏰8am-7pm Mon-Fri, 9am-6pm Sat & Sun; Ⓜ Xochimilco) Just off the Jardín Juárez.

Zócalo Tourist Information (Templo Mayor; Ⓜ Zócalo) East of the Catedral Metropolitana.

Zona Rosa Tourist Information (☎55-5208-1030; cnr Paseo de la Reforma & Av Florencia; Ⓜ Insurgentes) On the Zona Rosa side of Monumento a la Independencia.

TRAVEL AGENCIES

A number of hostels and hotels have an *agencia de viajes* on-site or can recommend one nearby.

Mundo Joven (☎55-5482-8282; www.mundojoven.com) Airport (Sala E1, International Arrivals, Airport Terminal 1; ⊙9am-8pm Mon-Fri, 10am-5pm Sat, to 2pm Sun; Ⓜ Terminal Aérea); Polanco (Eugenio Sue 342, cnr Homero; ⊙10am-7pm Mon-Fri, to 2pm Sat; Ⓜ Polanco); Zócalo (República de Guatemala 4, Zócalo; ⊙9am-7pm Mon-Fri, 10am-2pm Sat; Ⓜ Zócalo) Specializes in travel for students and teachers, with reasonable airfares from Mexico City. Issues ISIC, ITIC, IYTC and HI cards.

Turismo Zócalo (☎55-8596-9649; www.turismozocalo.com; 2nd fl, Palma 34, Colonia Centro; ⊙10am-7pm Mon-Fri, to 1pm Sat; Ⓜ Zócalo) Inside the Gran Plaza Ciudad de México mall; also functions as a Boletotal outlet for bus bookings.

USEFUL WEBSITES

The following sites compile oodles of information on the capital.

Consejo Nacional Para la Cultura y las Artes (www.conaculta.gob.mx/cultura) Online arts and culture magazine that lists goings-on about town.

Secretaría de Cultura del Distrito Federal (www.cultura.df.gob.mx) Lists festivals, museums and cultural events.

Secretaría de Turismo (www.mexicocity.gob.mx) City tourism office's listings and practical information.

Sistema de Transporte Colectivo (www.metro.df.gob.mx) All about the Mexico City metro.

Getting There & Away

AIR

Aeropuerto Internacional Benito Juárez (☎55-2482-2424; www.aicm.com.mx; Capitán Carlos León s/n, Colonia Peñón de los Baños; 📶; Ⓜ Terminal Aérea) Mexico City's only passenger airport, and Latin America's largest, with an annual capacity of about 32 million passengers. The airport has two terminals, Terminal 1 (the main terminal) and Terminal 2 (located 3km from the main terminal). Carriers operating out of Terminal 2 include Aeromar, Aeroméxico, Copa Airlines, Delta and Lan. All other airlines depart from Terminal 1. Red buses (M$12.50) run between the two terminals, making stops at Puerta 7 in Terminal 1 and Puerta 3 in Terminal 2. The terminals also are connected by an *aerotrén*, a monorail service for ticketed passengers only.

Both terminals have *casas de cambio* (money exchange offices) and peso-dispensing ATMs. Car-rental agencies and luggage lockers are in Salas A and E2 of Terminal 1.

Direct buses to Cuernavaca, Querétaro, Toluca, Puebla and Córdoba depart from platforms adjacent to Sala E in Terminal 1 and from Sala D in Terminal 2. Ticket counters in Terminal 1 are on the upper level, off the food court. A pedestrian bridge off Sala B leads to an ADO bus terminal with service to Acapulco and Veracruz.

More than 20 airlines provide international service to Mexico City. You can fly direct from more than 30 cities in the USA and Canada, half a dozen each in Europe, South America and Central America/the Caribbean, as well as from Tokyo. Seven different airlines connect the capital to about 50 cities within Mexico.

BUS

Mexico City has four long-distance bus terminals serving the four compass points: Terminal Norte (north), Terminal Oriente (called TAPO; east), Terminal Poniente (Observatorio; west) and Terminal Sur (south). All terminals have baggage-check services or lockers, as well as tourist information modules, newsstands, card phones, internet, ATMs and snack bars.

There are also buses to nearby cities from the airport.

For trips of up to five hours, it usually suffices to go to the bus station, buy your ticket and go. For longer trips, many buses leave in the evening and may well sell out, so buy your ticket beforehand.

You can purchase advance tickets at **Oxxo** convenience stores throughout the city and **Boletotal** (☎55-5133-5133, 800-009-90-90; www.boletotal.mx), a booking agency for more than a dozen bus lines out of all four stations. (A 10% surcharge is added to the cost of the ticket up to a maximum of M$50.) Boletotal also offers purchase by phone with Visa or MasterCard. Boletotal branches:

Buenavista (Ticketbus; Buenavista 9, cnr Orozco y Berra; ⊙9am-2:30pm & 3:30-6:30pm Mon-Fri, to 2:30pm Sat; Ⓜ Revolución)

Polanco (Ticketbus; cnr Homero & Arquímedes; ⊙9am-3pm & 4-6:30pm Mon-Fri, 9am-12:30pm Sat; Ⓜ Polanco)

Roma Norte (Ticketbus; Mérida 156, cnr Zacatecas; ⊙9am-2:30pm & 3:30-6:45pm Mon-Fri, to 2:45pm Sat; Ⓜ Hospital General)

Zócalo (Turismo Zócalo; 2nd fl, Palma 34, Colonia Centro, inside Gran Plaza Ciudad de México; ⊙10am-7pm Mon-Fri, to 1pm Sat; Ⓜ Zócalo)

Lines

See the table on p134 for bus details and check schedules by visiting individual bus lines' websites.

ADO Group (☎800-702-80-00, 55-5133-2424; www.ado.com.mx) Includes ADO Platino (deluxe), ADO GL (executive), OCC (1st class), ADO (1st class) and AU (2nd class).

Autobuses Teotihuacán (55-5587-0501) Second class. No website.

Autovías (800-622-22-22; www.autovias.com.mx) First class.

Estrella Blanca Group (800-507-55-00, 55-5729-0807; www.estrellablanca.com.mx) Operates Futura, Costa Line and Elite (1st class).

Estrella de Oro (800-900-01-05, 55-5549-8520; www.estrelladeoro.com.mx) Executive and 1st class.

Estrella Roja (800-712-22-84, 55-5130-1800; www.estrellaroja.com.mx) First class.

ETN (800-800-03-86, 55-5089-9200; www.etn.com.mx) Includes ETN (deluxe) and Turistar (executive and deluxe).

Ómnibus de México (800-765-66-36, 55-5141-4300; www.odm.com.mx) First class.

Primera Plus (800-375-75-87; www.primeraplus.com.mx) Deluxe and 1st class.

Pullman de Morelos (800-624-03-60, 55-5549-3505; www.pullman.mx) Executive, deluxe and 1st class.

Terminals

Terminal de Autobuses del Norte (55-5587-1552; www.centraldelnorte.com.mx; Eje Central Lázaro Cárdenas 4907, Colonia Magdalena de las Salinas; M Autobuses del Norte) Largest of the four bus terminals. Serves points north, including cities on the US border, plus some points west (Guadalajara, Puerto Vallarta), east (Puebla) and south (Acapulco, Oaxaca). Deluxe and 1st-class counters are mostly in the southern half of the terminal. Luggage-storage services are at the far south end and in the central passageway.

Terminal de Autobuses de Pasajeros de Oriente (TAPO; 55-5522-9381; Calz Zaragoza 200, Colonia Diez de Mayo; M San Lázaro) For eastern and southeastern destinations, including Puebla, Veracruz, Yucatán, Oaxaca and Chiapas. Bus-line counters are arranged around a rotunda with a food court, internet terminals and ATMs. There's a left-luggage service in 'Túnel 1.'

Terminal de Autobuses del Poniente (Observatorio; 55-5271-0149; Av Sur 122, Colonia Real del Monte; M Observatorio) Also known as Observatorio, it's the point for buses heading to Michoacán and shuttle services running to nearby Toluca. In addition, ETN offers service to Guadalajara.

Terminal de Autobuses del Sur (Tasqueña; 55-5689-9745; Av Tasqueña 1320, Colonia Campestre Churubusco; M Tasqueña) Serves Tepoztlán, Cuernavaca, Taxco, Acapulco and other southern destinations, as well as Oaxaca, Huatulco and Ixtapa-Zihuatanejo. Estrella de Oro (Acapulco, Taxco) and Pullman de Morelos (Cuernavaca) counters are on the right side of the terminal, while OCC, Estrella Roja (Tepoztlán), ETN and Futura are on the left. In Sala 3, you'll find luggage-storage service and ATMs.

CAR & MOTORCYCLE

Rental

Rental car companies have offices at the airport, at bus stations and in the Zona Rosa area of the city. Rates generally start at about M$600 per day, but you can often do better by booking online. You can find a list of rental agencies online at the DF Tourism Secretariat website (www.mexicocity.gob.mx).

Avis (800-500-28-47, 55-5511-2228; www.avis.mx; Paseo de la Reforma 308; 7am-10:30pm Mon-Fri, 8am-4pm Sat & Sun; M Insurgentes)

Thrifty (55-5514-3404; www.thrifty.com; Paseo de la Reforma 322; M Insurgentes)

Roadside Assistance

If you leave the city, the *Ángeles Verdes* (Green Angels) can provide highway assistance between 8am and 6pm. Just phone 078 and tell them your location.

Routes In & Out of the City

Whichever way you come into the city, once you're past the last *caseta* (toll booth) you enter a no-man's-land of poorly marked lanes and chaotic traffic. These *casetas* are also the points from which 'Hoy No Circula' rules take effect (p137).

- If you're coming from Puebla (east), the highway eventually feeds traffic left into Calzada Zaragoza. Stay on Zaragoza for about 10km, then move left and follow signs for Río de la Piedad (aka Viaducto Miguel Alemán), exiting left after the metro crosses the highway. From the Viaducto, exits access all the key areas. Get off at Viaducto Tlalpan to reach the Zócalo, and Avenida Monterrey to Roma and the Zona Rosa.
- Coming out of the airport, keep left to head south along Blvd Puerto Aéreo. After you cross Zaragoza, watch for signs to Río de la Piedad and Viaducto Alemán.
- Heading for Puebla, Oaxaca or Veracruz, take the Viaducto Alemán east. This is most conveniently accessed off Avenida Cuauhtémoc (Eje 1 Poniente). Immediately after crossing over the Viaducto – by the Liverpool department store – turn left for the access ramp. Take the Viaducto to Calzada Zaragoza, then follow the signs for Oaxaca until you join the Puebla highway.
- From Querétaro (north of DF), the last toll booth as you approach the city is at Tepotzotlán. Continue south, following signs for Ciudad Satélite and Toreo. Move into the lateral road (running parallel to the main road) at the first signs indicating the 'Río San Joaquín' exit, which appears just north of the giant dome of the Toreo arena. Take this exit; the ramp curves left over the Periférico. Keep right as

BUSES FROM MEXICO CITY

DESTINATION	TERMINAL IN MEXICO CITY	BUS COMPANY	FARE (M$)	DURATION	FREQUENCY (DAILY)
Acapulco	Sur	Estrella de Oro	449-599	5hr	16
	Norte	Futura, Costa Line	455	5½-6hr	9
Bahías de Huatulco	Sur	OCC, Turistar	794-1020	15-15½hr	3
	Norte	OCC	794	16hr	4:45pm
Campeche	Oriente (TAPO)	ADO, ADO GL	1160-1396	16-18hr	6
	Norte	ADO	1174	17-18hr	2
Cancún	Oriente (TAPO)	ADO, ADO GL	1518-1788	24-27hr	5
Chetumal	Oriente (TAPO)	ADO	1252	19½-20hr	2
Chihuahua	Norte	Ómnibus de México	1355-1465	18-19hr	7
Cuernavaca	Sur	Pullman de Morelos	90-100	1¼hr	frequent
Guadalajara	Norte	ETN, Primera Plus	634-820	6-7hr	frequent
	Poniente	ETN	760-820	6¼hr	4
Guanajuato	Norte	ETN, Primera Plus	449-540	5-5½hr	14
Matamoros	Norte	ETN, Futura	1010-1310	12½-13½hr	3
Mazatlán	Norte	Elite	986	13-16hr	13
Mérida	Oriente (TAPO)	ADO, ADO GL	1310-1558	19-20½hr	6
Monterrey	Norte	ETN, Futura	931-1205	11-13hr	18
Morelia	Norte	Primera Plus	360	5hr	8
	Poniente	ETN	430	4-4¼hr	frequent
Nuevo Laredo	Norte	ETN, Futura, Turistar	1131-1465	15-15½hr	8
Oaxaca	Oriente (TAPO)	ADO, ADO GL, ADO Platino	474-808	6-6½hr	frequent
	Sur	ADO GL, OCC	500-582	6½hr	5
Palenque	Oriente (TAPO)	ADO	922	12¾hr	6:10pm
Papantla	Norte	ADO	286	5-6hr	7
Pátzcuaro	Norte	Autovías, Primera Plus	393-437	5hr	7
	Poniente	Autovías	437	5hr	11
Puebla	Airport	Estrella Roja	220	2hr	12
	Oriente (TAPO)	ADO, ADO GL, AU, Pullman de Morelos	120-162	2-2¼hr	frequent

DESTINATION	TERMINAL IN MEXICO CITY	BUS COMPANY	FARE (M$)	DURATION	FREQUENCY (DAILY)
Puerto Escondido	Sur	OCC, Turistar	804-1025	12-17½hr	2
Puerto Vallarta	Norte	ETN, Futura	948-1230	12-13½hr	5
Querétaro	Norte	ETN, Primera Plus	233-280	2¾-3hr	frequent
	Airport	Primera Plus	312	3hr	frequent
	Poniente	Primera Plus	233	3½-4hr	17
San Cristóbal de las Casas	Oriente (TAPO)	ADO GL, OCC	514-1052	13-14hr	7
	Norte	OCC	528	14-14½hr	4
San Luis Potosí	Norte	ETN, Primera Plus, Turistar	449-540	4½-5½hr	frequent
San Miguel de Allende	Norte	ETN, Primera Plus	337-405	3¼-4hr	7
Tapachula	Oriente (TAPO)	ADO GL, ADO Platino, OCC	1084-1570	16½-19½hr	11
Taxco	Sur	Estrella de Oro	175	2½hr	4
Teotihuacán	Norte	Autobuses Teotihuacán	40	1hr	hourly 6am-9pm
Tepoztlán	Sur	OCC	104	1hr	frequent
Tijuana	Norte	Elite	1900	41hr	12
Toluca	Airport	TMT Caminante	145	1¾hr	hourly
	Poniente	ETN	65	1hr	frequent
Tuxtla Gutiérrez	Oriente (TAPO)	ADO, ADO GL, ADO Platino, OCC	960-1430	11¾-12½hr	14
Uruapan	Poniente	Autovías, ETN	508-610	5¼-6hr	17
Veracruz	Oriente (TAPO)	ADO, ADO GL, ADO Platino, AU	334-494	5½-7¼hr	frequent
	Sur	ADO, ADO GL	414-494	5½-6¼hr	6
Villahermosa	Oriente (TAPO)	ADO, ADO GL, ADO Platino, AU	680-1370	10-12¼hr	24
Xalapa	Oriente (TAPO)	ADO, ADO GL, ADO Platino, AU	250-514	4½-5hr	frequent
Zacatecas	Norte	Ómnibus de México	645-695	8hr	14
Zihuatanejo	Sur	Costa Line, Futura	665	9hr	4
	Poniente	Autovías	661	9hr	3

you go over, then follow signs for 'Circuito Interior.' After passing the Corona factory, take the Thiers exit. Keep left, following signs for Reforma, and you'll end up on Río Misisipi, which intersects Reforma at the Diana roundabout. Turn left on Reforma to get to the *centro histórico,* or continue straight ahead for Roma.

➡ Leaving the city, the simplest option is to take Reforma to the west end of Bosque de Chapultepec, then a right exit to pick up the Periférico northbound.

➡ From Pachuca, Hidalgo and northern Veracruz, the highway feeds into Avenida Insurgentes. Follow the signs for the *centro histórico* and Zona Rosa. Leaving the city, take Insurgentes north (also the route to Teotihuacán).

➡ When coming from Cuernavaca (south), after the last toll booth on the autopista from Cuernavaca, continue straight, taking a right exit for Calzada Tlalpan (some signs are hidden behind trees). Calzada Tlalpan eventually feeds into Avenida 20 de Noviembre, which ends at the Zócalo. Leaving town, turn right (south) at the Zócalo onto Pino Suárez, which becomes Calzada Tlalpan. About 20km south, signs indicate a left exit for the *cuota* (toll highway) to Cuernavaca.

➡ From Toluca (west), about 4km past the high-rises of Santa Fe, keep left and follow signs for Paseo de la Reforma. Go straight down Reforma, past the Fuente de Petróleos and Bosque de Chapultepec to reach downtown. Heading west out of the city, take Paseo de la Reforma, which feeds right into the *cuota* to Toluca.

ℹ Getting Around

Mexico City has an inexpensive, easy-to-use metro and an equally cheap and practical bus system plying all the main routes. Taxis are plentiful, but some are potentially hazardous.

TO/FROM THE AIRPORT

The metro is a cheap option for getting to the airport, though hauling luggage amid rush-hour crowds can be a Herculean task. Authorized taxis provide a painless, relatively inexpensive alternative, as does the metrobús.

Metro

➡ The airport metro station is Terminal Aérea, on Línea 5 (yellow). It's 200m from Terminal 1: leave by the exit at the end of Sala A (domestic arrivals) and continue past the taxi stand to the station.

➡ To the city center, follow signs for 'Dirección Politécnico'; at La Raza (seven stops away) change for Línea 3 (green) toward 'Dirección Universidad.' Metro Hidalgo, at the west end of the Alameda, is three stops south; it's also a transfer point for Línea 2 (blue) to the Zócalo.

➡ To get to the Zona Rosa from the airport, take Línea 5 to 'Pantitlán,' the end of the line. Change for Línea 1 (pink) and get off at metro Insurgentes.

➡ There is no convenient metro link to Terminal 2, but red buses at the entrance of Terminal 2 go to metro Hangares (Línea 5).

Metrobús

➡ Línea 4 of the metrobús has luggage racks and on-board security cameras, making it a more comfortable option than the metro.

➡ Stops at Puerta 7 in Terminal 1 and Puerta 3 in Terminal 2. The ride costs M$30, plus you'll need to purchase a smart card for M$10 at machines inside the terminals. From Terminal 1, it's about 45 minutes to reach the Zócalo.

➡ The line runs five blocks north of the Zócalo, along República de Venezuela and Belisario Domínguez, then it heads west along Avenida Hidalgo past metro Hidalgo; to return to the airport, catch it along Ayuntamiento or República del Salvador. See www.metrobus.df.gob.mx for more information.

Taxi

➡ Safe and reliable taxis *autorizados* (authorized taxis) are controlled by a fixed-price ticket system.

➡ Purchase taxi tickets from booths located in Sala E1 (international arrivals) as you exit customs, and by the Sala A (domestic arrivals) exit.

➡ Fares are determined by zones. A ride to the Zócalo, Roma or Zona Rosa costs M$205, and to the Condesa it's M$235. One ticket is valid for up to four passengers. 'Sitio 300' taxis are the best.

➡ Porters may offer to take your ticket and luggage the few steps to the taxi, but hold on to the ticket and hand it to the driver. Drivers won't expect a tip for the ride, but will always welcome one.

TO/FROM THE BUS TERMINALS

The metro is the fastest and cheapest way to or from any bus terminal, but it's tricky to maneuver through crowded stations and cars. Taxis are an easier option: all terminals have ticket booths for secure *taxis autorizados,* with fares set by zone (M$20 surcharge is applied from 9pm to 6am). An agent at the exit will assign you a cab.

Terminal Norte Metro Línea 5 (yellow) stops at Autobuses del Norte, just outside the terminal. To the center, follow signs for 'Dirección Pantitlán,' then change at La Raza for Línea 3 (green) toward 'Dirección Universidad.' (The La Raza connection is a six-minute hike through a 'Tunnel of Science.'). The taxi kiosk is in the central passageway; a cab for up to four people to the Zócalo, Roma or Condesa costs about M$120.

Terminal Oriente (TAPO) This bus terminal is next door to metro San Lázaro. To the center or Zona Rosa, take Línea 1 (pink) toward 'Dirección Observatorio.' The authorized taxi booth is at the top (metro) end of the main passageway from the rotunda. The fare to the Zócalo is M$85; to the Zona Rosa, Roma and Condesa it's M$102.

Terminal Poniente Observatorio metro station, the western terminus of Línea 1 (pink), is a couple of minutes' walk across a busy street. A taxi ticket to Colonia Roma costs M$102, Colonia Condesa M$73 and the Zócalo M$135.

Terminal Sur It's a two-minute walk from metro Tasqueña, the southern terminus of Línea 2, which stops at the Zócalo. For the Zona Rosa, transfer at Pino Suárez and take Línea 1 to Insurgentes (Dirección Observatorio). Going to the terminal, take the 'Autobuses del Sur' exit, which leads upstairs to a footbridge. Descend the last staircase on the left, then walk through a street market to reach the building. Authorized taxis from Terminal Sur cost M$140 to the *centro histórico* and $152 to Condesa and Roma. Ticket booths are in sala 3.

BICYCLE

Bicycles can be a viable way to get around town and are often preferable to overcrowded, recklessly driven buses. Although careless drivers and potholes can make DF cycling an extreme sport, if you stay alert and keep off the major thoroughfares, it's manageable. The city government has encouraged bicycle use and it's definitely catching on.

Bikes are loaned free from a module on the west side of the Catedral Metropolitana. You'll also find booths at Plaza Villa de Madrid in Roma, at the intersection of Mazatlán and Michoacán in Condesa, and several along Paseo de la Reforma, near the Monumento a la Independencia and Auditorio Nacional. Leave a passport or driver's license for three hours of riding time. The modules operate from 10:30am to 6pm Monday to Saturday, and 9:30am to 4:30pm on Sunday.

The Mexico City government rents commuter bikes through **Ecobici** (Map p84; ☎55-5005-2424; www.ecobici.df.gob.mx; Av Nuevo León 78; rentals 1/3/7 days M$90/180/300; ⏲9am-6pm Mon-Fri, 10am-2pm Sat; 🚌Campeche) to visitors on a daily and weekly basis. You'll need a Visa or Mastercard credit card for the deposit and a passport or driver's license for ID. The bicycle share program works with smart cards and allows you to ride for up to 45 minutes between docking stations. To avoid paying a fine for exceeding 45 minutes, simply exchange the bike at a different station. Ecobici is a great option for exploring downtown, Roma and Condesa, neighborhoods with the greatest concentration of stations.

The *ciclovía* is an extensive bike trail that follows the old bed of the Cuernavaca railroad as far as the Morelos border. It extends from Avenida Ejército Nacional in Polanco through the Bosque de Chapultepec, skirting the Periférico freeway from La Feria to Avenida San Antonio, with several steep bridges over the freeways.

Another path follows Avenida Chapultepec along a protected median from Bosque de Chapultepec to the *centro histórico*, though a detour through the streets of Colonia Roma is ignored by motorists. A third route runs along Paseo de la Reforma from the Auditorio Nacional to downtown.

Every Sunday Paseo de la Reforma and several main downtown streets are closed off to traffic from 8am to 2pm and riders can enjoy a 26km '*ciclotón*' route that spans from Auditorio Nacional to the Basílica de Guadalupe.

CAR & MOTORCYCLE

Touring Mexico City by car is strongly discouraged, unless you have a healthy reserve of patience. Even more than elsewhere in the country, traffic rules are seen as suggested behavior. Red lights may be run at will, no-turn signs are ignored and signals are seldom used. On occasion you may be hit with a questionable traffic fine. Nevertheless, you may want to rent a car here for travel outside the city. Avoid parking on the street whenever possible; most midrange and top-end hotels have guest garages. If you do park on the street, keep in mind that some neighborhoods, such as Cuauhtémoc, Roma and Polanco, have *parquímetros* (green parking meters usually located at the middle of the block). Feed them or your vehicle will be booted.

To help combat pollution, Mexico City operates its 'Hoy No Circula' (Don't Drive Today) program, banning many vehicles from being driven in the city between 5am and 10pm on one day each week. Additionally, vehicles nine years and older are prohibited from operating one Saturday a month. Exempted from restrictions are rental cars and vehicles with a *calcomanía de verificación* (emissions verification sticker), obtained under the city's vehicle-pollution assessment system.For vehicles without the sticker (including foreign-registered ones), the last digit of the license-plate number determines the day when they cannot circulate. See the Locatel website (www.locatel.df.gob.mx, in Spanish) for more information.

DAY	PROHIBITED LAST DIGITS
Monday	5, 6
Tuesday	7, 8
Wednesday	3, 4
Thursday	1, 2
Friday	9, 0

METRO

The metro system (www.metro.df.gob.mx) offers the quickest way to get around Mexico City. Ridden by about 4.4 million passengers on an average weekday, it has 195 stations and more than 226km of track on 12 lines. Trains arrive every two to three minutes during rush hours. At M$5 a ride, it's one of the world's cheapest subways.

All lines operate from 5am to midnight weekdays, 6am to midnight Saturday and 7am to midnight Sunday and holidays. Platforms and cars can become alarmingly packed during rush hours (roughly 7:30am to 10am and 3pm to 8pm). At these times the forward cars are reserved for women and children, and men may not proceed beyond the 'Sólo Mujeres y Niños' gate.

With such crowded conditions, it's not surprising that pickpocketing occurs, so watch your belongings.

The metro is easy to use. Lines are color-coded and each station is identified by a unique logo. Signs reading 'Dirección Pantitlán,' 'Dirección Universidad' and so on name the stations at the end of the lines. Check a map for the direction you want. Buy a rechargeable smart card for M$10 at any station and then add credit (the card also works for all metrobús lines). Additionally, the metro sells *boletos* (tickets) at the *taquilla* (ticket window). Feed the ticket into the turnstile and you're on your way. When changing trains, look for 'Correspondencia' (Transfer) signs. Maps of the vicinity around each station are posted near the exits.

METROBÚS, PESERO & TROLLEYBÚS

Mexico City's thousands of buses and peseros operate from around 5am till 10pm daily, depending on the route; electric trolleybuses generally run until 11:30pm. Only a few routes run all night, notably those along Paseo de la Reforma. This means you'll get anywhere by bus and/or metro during the day but will probably have to take a few taxis after hours.

Metrobús

The metrobús is a wheelchair-accessible Volvo vehicle that stops at metro-style stations in the middle of the street, spaced at three- to four-block intervals. Access is by prepaid smart card, issued by machines for M$10 at the entrance to the platforms, and rides cost M$6. The rechargeable cards, which can also be used for the metro, are placed on a sensor device for entry. Most metrobús lines run from 5am to midnight. Línea (line) 1, the only metrobús route with 24-hour service, plies a dedicated lane along Avenida Insurgentes from metro Indios Verdes in northern DF down to the southern end of Tlalpan. Línea 2, which connects with Línea 1 at the Nuevo León station, runs west to east along Eje 4 Sur from metro Tacubaya to metro Tepalcates. Línea 3 operates on a north–south route from the Tenayuca station to Ethiopia, where you can transfer to Línea 2. Línea 4 runs from metro Buenavista and cuts through the *centro histórico* to metro San Lázaro. The line also has an 'aeropuerto' bus that goes to and from the airport for M$30.

Pesero

Peseros (also called microbúses or combis) are gray-and-green minibuses operated by private firms. They follow fixed routes, often starting or ending at metro stations, and will stop at virtually any street corner. Route information is randomly displayed on cards attached to the windshield. Fares are M$4 for trips of up to 5km, and M$4.50 for 5km to 12km. Add 20% to all fares between 11pm and 6am. Municipally operated trolleybuses and full-sized cream-and-orange buses (labeled 'RTP') only pick up at bus stops; fares are M$2 (M$4 for the express) regardless of distance traveled. Privately run green-and-yellow buses charge M$5.50 to M$6.

Trolleybús

Trolleybuses follow a number of the key *ejes* (priority roads) throughout the rest of the city.

Routes

Here are some more useful routes:

Autobuses del Sur & Autobuses del Norte (trolleybús) Eje Central Lázaro Cárdenas between north and south bus terminals (stops at Plaza de las Tres Culturas, Plaza Garibaldi, Bellas Artes/Alameda, metro Hidalgo).

Auditorio–La Villa (bus) Paseo de la Reforma between Auditorio Nacional and Basílica de Guadalupe (stops at Zona Rosa, Avenida Insurgentes, Alameda/metro Hidalgo, Plaza Garibaldi, Plaza de las Tres Culturas).

Metro Sevilla–P Masaryk (pesero) Between Colonia Roma and Polanco via Álvaro Obregón and Avenida Presidente Masaryk (stops at metro Niños Héroes, Avenida Insurgentes, metro Sevilla, Leibnitz).

Metro Tacubaya–Balderas–Escandón (pesero) Between *centro histórico* and Condesa, westbound via Puebla, eastbound via Durango (stops at Plaza San Juan, metro Balderas, metro Insurgentes, Parque España, Avenida Michoacán).

TAXI

Mexico City has several classes of taxi. Cheapest are the cruising red-and-gold street cabs, though they're not recommended due to the risk of assaults. If you must hail a cab off the street, check that it has actual taxi license plates: numbers are preceded with the letters A or B. Check that the number on them matches the number painted on the bodywork. Also look for the *carta de identificación* (called the *tarjetón*), a postcard-sized ID that should be displayed visibly inside the cab, and ensure that the driver matches the photo. If the cab you've hailed does not pass these tests, get another one.

In *libre* cabs (street cabs), fares are computed by *taxímetro* (meter), which should start at about M$9. The total cost of a 3km ride in moderate traffic – say, from the Zócalo to the Zona Rosa – should be M$30 to M$40. Between 11pm and 6am, add 20%.

Radio taxis, which come in many different colors, cost about three times as much as the others, but this extra cost adds an immeasurable degree of security. When you phone, the dispatcher will tell you the cab number and the type of car. If you have a mobile device, you can order a cab via the application Yaxi (www.yaxi.mx).

Some reliable radio-taxi firms, available 24 hours, are listed below. Maps in this chapter show the location of some key *sitios* (taxi stands) for radio taxis.

Radio Maxi Seguridad (☎55-5768-8557, 55-5552-1376)

Sitio Parque México (☎55-5286-7164, 55-5286-7129)

Taxi-Mex (☎55-9171-8888; www.taximex.com.mx)

Taxis Radio Unión (☎55-5514-8074, 55-5514-7861; www.taxisradiounion.com.mx)

Around Mexico City

Includes ➡

Best Places to Eat

- ➡ Las Ranas (p159)
- ➡ Restaurante y Cabañas San Diego (p154)
- ➡ La Sibarita (p179)

Best Places to Stay

- ➡ Pueblo Lindo (p193)
- ➡ Hotel Hacienda de Cortés (p185)
- ➡ Posada del Tepozteco (p178)

Why Go?

With its daunting size and seemingly endless sprawl, the megalopolis of Mexico City might seem like a challenge to escape from, but even if you're in Mexico's capital for only a week, the ancient ruins, *pueblos mágicos* (magical villages) and stunning mountain landscape of the surrounding area should not be missed. Mexico City – like many capitals – has little in common with even its closest neighbors.

While many visitors to the region take a day trip to the awe-inspiring archaeological complex at Teotihuacán, the area offers much more – from the captivating colonial cities of Taxco, Puebla and Cuernavaca, to the eccentric small towns of Valle de Bravo and Tepoztlán. For those eager to taste some crisp, particulate-free mountain air, there are *pueblitos* (small towns) like Cuetzalan and Real del Monte, the volcanic giants Popocatépetl and Iztaccíhuatl, and the lesser-known ruins of Xochicalco and Cantona to visit.

When to Go

Puebla City

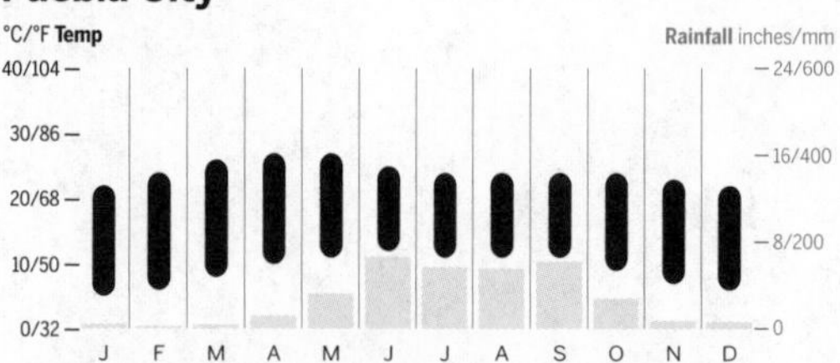

May–Oct During the rainy season showers bring wild mushrooms to the forests.

Sep It's nearly Independence Day and time to taste the seasonal specialty *chiles en nogada*.

Nov–Apr The drier months are cooler, making for pleasant daytime city exploration and casual hikes.

History

Long a cultural and economic crossroads, the region around present-day Mexico City has hosted a succession of important indigenous civilizations (notably the Teotihuacán, Toltec and Aztec societies). By the late 15th century, the Aztecs had managed to dominate all but one of central Mexico's states. Many archaeological sites and museums preserve remnants of pre-Hispanic history; Puebla's Museo Amparo provides an excellent overview of the region's history and cultures.

Postconquest, the Spanish transformed central Mexico, establishing ceramic industries at Puebla, mines at Taxco and Pachuca, and haciendas producing wheat, sugar and cattle throughout the region. The Catholic Church used the region as a base for its missionary activities, and left a series of imposing churches and fortified monasteries. Today, most towns retain a central plaza or *zócalo* surrounded by colonial buildings.

Getting There & Around

The cities, towns and (to a lesser extent) even the villages around Mexico City enjoy excellent, often first-class, bus links to both the capital and each other. Even the very smallest backwaters have comfortable daily services to Mexico City and to the closest transportation hub. While airports also serve Puebla, Toluca, Cuernavaca and Pachuca, it's nearly always cheaper and easier to fly to Mexico City and travel onward from there. For all but the most obscure sights, traveling by bus is the easiest and most affordable option.

NORTH OF MEXICO CITY

The biggest attraction north of Mexico City is the extraordinary complex at Teotihuacán, once the largest metropolis in the Americas and one of Mexico's most spectacular pre-Hispanic sights. Farther north, the well-preserved stone statues at Tula also draw visitors.

Far less visited but equally impressive are Parque Nacional El Chico and the mining village of Mineral del Chico – the perfect escape from the big city, with stunning views, wide open spaces and friendly locals.

Pachuca, the fast-growing capital of dynamic Hidalgo state, has brightly painted houses, an attractive colonial center and a great line in Cornish pasties. From Pachuca, well-paved routes snake east and north to the Gulf coast, through spectacular country such as the fringes of the Sierra Madre Oriental and the coastal plain.

Tepotzotlán

☎55 / POP 38,000 / ELEV 2300M

This *pueblo mágico* is an easy day trip from Mexico City, but feels far from the chaotic streets of the capital, despite the fact that urban sprawl creeps closer to Tepotzotlán's colonial center every year.

Sights

Museo Nacional del Virreinato MUSEUM

(National Museum of the Viceregal Period; ☎55-5876-0245; www.virreinato.inah.gob.mx; Plaza Hidalgo 99; admission M$55; ⏲9am-6pm Tue-Sun) There's a very simple reason to visit this wonderful museum comprising the restored Jesuit **Iglesia de San Francisco Javier** and an adjacent **monastery**. Much of the folk art and fine art on display – silver chalices, pictures created from inlaid wood, porcelain, furniture and religious paintings and statues – comes from Mexico City cathedral's large collection, and the standard is very high.

Once a Jesuit college of indigenous languages, the complex dates from 1606. Additions were made over the following 150 years, creating a showcase for the developing architectural styles of New Spain.

Don't miss the **Capilla Doméstica**, with a Churrigueresque main altarpiece that boasts more mirrors than a carnival funhouse. The facade is a phantasmagoric array of carved saints, angels, plants and people, while the interior walls and the Camarín del Virgen adjacent to the altar are swathed with gilded ornamentation.

Festivals & Events

Pastorelas (Nativity Plays) RELIGIOUS

Tepotzotlán's highly regarded *pastorelas* (nativity plays) are performed inside the former monastery in the weeks leading up to Christmas. Tickets, which include Christmas dinner and piñata smashing, can be purchased at La Hostería del Convento de Tepotzotlán after November 1, or via Ticketmaster (☎55-5325-9000; www.ticketmaster.com.mx).

Around Mexico City Highlights

1. Enjoy a sunset drink on **Cuetzalan's** tiny *zócalo* (p174) amid the dramatic scenery of the Sierra Madre Oriental
2. Be blown away by the spectacular pyramids at **Teotihuacán** (p146) or discover some of central Mexico's most magnificent, lesser-known ancient sites at **Xochicalco** (p186) and **Cantona** (p173)
3. Wander the steep cobblestone streets of **Taxco** (p189) and scope out the city's famed silver shops
4. Have a close encounter with Mexico's New Age culture in **Tepoztlán** (p176) and **Malinalco** (p200)
5. Feel the mountain mists sweep over you in tiny **Mineral del Chico** (p152)
6. Admire the impressive cathedral and many pretty, historic churches in **Puebla** (p154)
7. Climb volcanic peaks, like **La Malinche** (p172), **Nevado de Toluca** (p198) or **Iztaccíhuatl** (p165)

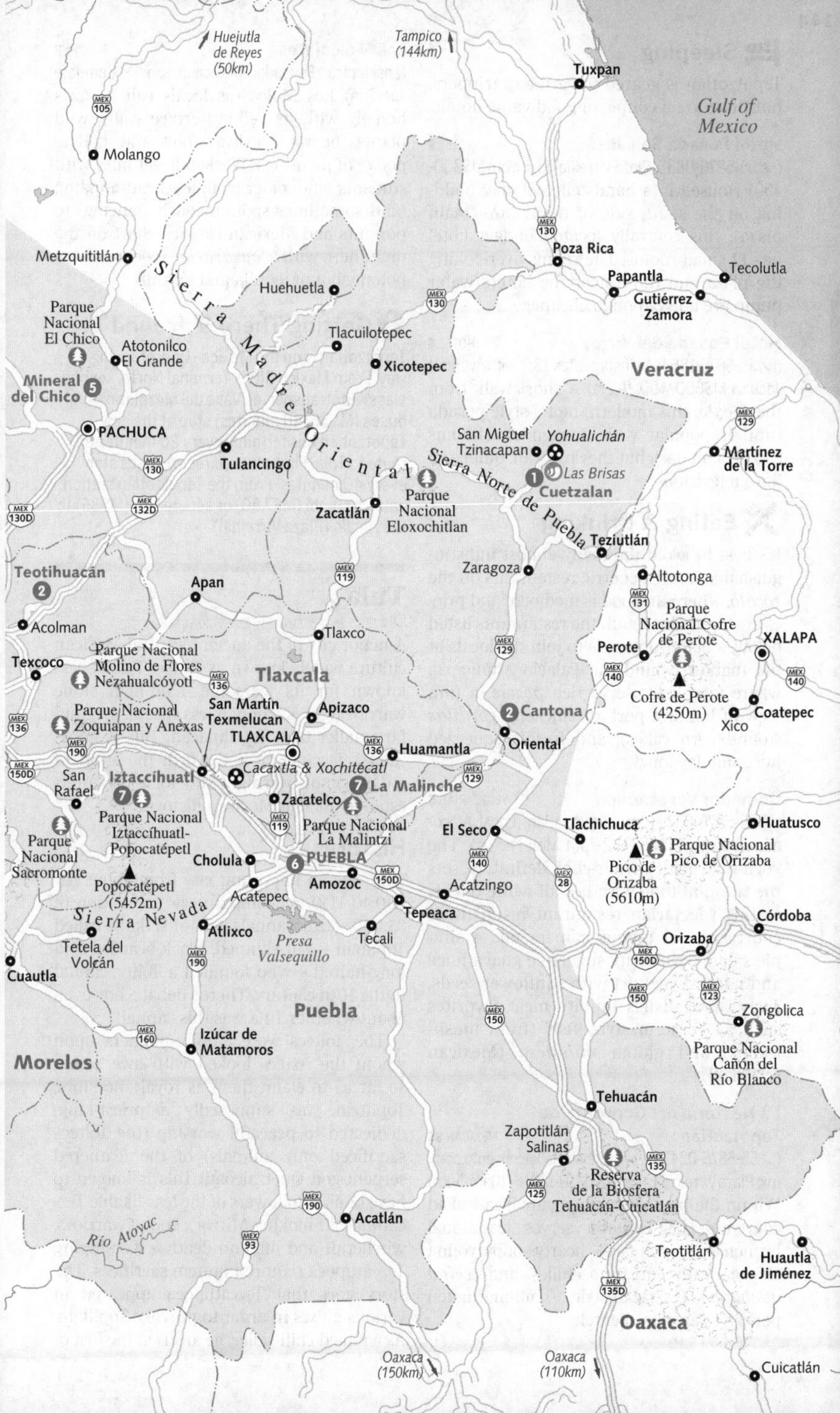

Huejutla de Reyes (50km)
Tampico (144km)
Tuxpan
Gulf of Mexico
Molango
Poza Rica
Metzquititlán
Sierra Madre Oriental
Huehuetla
Papantla
Tecolutla
Gutiérrez Zamora
Parque Nacional El Chico
Atotonilco El Grande
Tlacuilotepec
Xicotepec
Veracruz
Mineral del Chico
PACHUCA
Tulancingo
San Miguel Tzinacapan
Yohualichán
Las Brisas
Cuetzalan
Martínez de la Torre
Sierra Norte de Puebla
Parque Nacional Eloxochitlan
Zacatlán
Teziutlán
Zaragoza
Altotonga
Teotihuacán
Apan
Acolman
Tlaxco
Parque Nacional Cofre de Perote
Perote
XALAPA
Texcoco
Parque Nacional Molino de Flores Nezahualcóyotl
Tlaxcala
Cofre de Perote (4250m)
Coatepec
Xico
Parque Nacional Zoquiapan y Anexas
San Martín Texmelucan
Apizaco
Cantona
TLAXCALA
Oriental
Huamantla
San Rafael
Iztaccíhuatl
Cacaxtla & Xochitécatl
La Malinche
Zacatelco
Parque Nacional Iztaccíhuatl-Popocatépetl
Parque Nacional La Malintzi
Parque Nacional Sacromonte
Cholula
PUEBLA
El Seco
Tlachichuca
Huatusco
Parque Nacional Pico de Orizaba
Pico de Orizaba (5610m)
Popocatépetl (5452m)
Amozoc
Acatepec
Acatzingo
Tepeaca
Sierra Nevada
Atlixco
Tecali
Córdoba
Presa Valsequillo
Orizaba
Tetela del Volcán
Cuautla
Puebla
Zongolica
Parque Nacional Cañón del Río Blanco
Izúcar de Matamoros
Morelos
Tehuacán
Zapotitlán Salinas
Reserva de la Biosfera Tehuacán-Cuicatlán
Acatlán
Río Atoyac
Teotitlán
Huautla de Jiménez
Oaxaca
Oaxaca (150km)
Oaxaca (110km)
Cuicatlán

Sleeping

Tepotzotlán is geared toward day trippers, but there are a couple of good value hotels.

Hotel Posada San José HOTEL $
(☎55-5876-0835; Plaza Virreinal 13; r from M$300-450) Housed in a handsome colonial building on the south side of the *zócalo* (main plaza), this centrally located budget hotel has 12 small rooms. The rooms overlooking the plaza and those near the hotel's water pump are noisy, though cheaper.

Hotel Posada del Virrey HOTEL $
(☎55-5876-1864; Av Insurgentes 13; r with/without Jacuzzi M$600/400; P ᯤ) A short walk from the *zócalo*, this modern, motel-style posada (inn) is popular with weekenders. Rooms can be a bit dark but they're clean, quiet and have televisions.

Eating & Drinking

It's best to avoid the many almost indistinguishable, tourist-centric restaurants on the *zócalo*, where the food is mediocre and prices are high. Along with the restaurants listed below, a better option is to join the locals at the market behind the Palacio Municipal, where food stalls serve rich *pozole* (a thin stew of hominy, pork or chicken), *gorditas* (round corn cakes), and freshly squeezed juices all day long.

Comedor Vegetariano VEGETARIAN $
(☎55-5876-232; Plaza Tepotzotlán, Local A; comida corrida M$45; ⏲2-7pm Mon-Fri; ☑) The yoga-instructor-owner-chef definitely sets the tranquil tone with her all-white outfits at this vegetarian restaurant in an inner courtyard. Set menus can include a simple salad, corn soup, sugarfree guava juice and natural yoghurt with sunflower seeds. Tasty main dishes imitate meat favorites such as Veracruz-style 'fish' (from mushrooms) and gluten *milanesa* (Mexican schnitzel).

La Hostería del Convento de Tepotzotlán MEXICAN $$
(☎55-5876-0243; www.hosteriadelconvento.com.mx; Plaza Virreinal 1; mains M$110-180; ⏲10am-5pm) Within the monastery's bougainvillea-walled courtyard, La Hostería serves traditional brunch and lunch fare – hearty soups, young chicken with *manzano* chilies, and *cecina adobada* (Oaxacan-style chili-marinated pork) – to an elite clientele.

Los Molcajetes PUB
(Los Molca; Pensador Mexicano s/n; ⏲6pm-late Tue-Sun) Los Molca (as locals call it) feels homely with its yellow terrace walls, wild plants, hearty Mexican food and hodgepodge of paintings. Weekends get busy with students and older couples head-nodding (and sometimes spontaneously dancing) to pop hits and Mexican classics. Start off the night here with a '*cucaracha*' (cockroach), a potent shot of tequila and Kahlua.

Getting There & Around

Tepotzotlán is on the Mexico–Querétaro highway. From Mexico City's Terminal Norte, second-class Autotransportes Valle del Mezquital (AVM) buses (M$36, 40 minutes) stop at the new Tepotzotlán bus terminal every 20 minutes en route to Tula. First-class *(directo)* buses stop every 40 minutes. From the Tepotzotlán station, catch a combi (M$7.50) or secure taxi (M$35) to the *zócalo* (Plaza Virreinal).

Tula

☎773 / POP 27,000 / ELEV 2060M

A major city of the ancient, central-Mexican culture widely known as Toltec, Tula is best known for its fearsome 4.5m-high stone warrior figures. Though less spectacular and far smaller than Teotihuacán, Tula is nonetheless fascinating and worth the effort of a day trip or overnight stay for those interested in ancient Mexican history.

History

Tula was an important city from about AD 900 to 1150, reaching a peak population of 35,000. Aztec annals tell of a king called Topiltzin – fair-skinned, black-bearded and long-haired – who founded a Toltec capital in the 10th century. There's debate, however, about whether Tula was this capital.

The Toltecs were empire-builders upon whom the Aztecs looked with awe, going so far as to claim them as royal ancestors. Topiltzin was supposedly a priest-king, dedicated to peaceful worship (the Toltecs sacrificed only animals) of the feathered serpent-god Quetzalcóatl. Tula is known to have housed followers of the less-likable Tezcatlipoca (Smoking Mirror), god of warriors, witchcraft and life and death – worshiping Tezcatlipoca required human sacrifices. The story goes that Tezcatlipoca appeared in various guises in order to provoke Topiltzin. As a naked chili-seller, he aroused the lust of

Topiltzin's daughter and eventually married her. As an old man, he persuaded the teetotaling Topiltzin to get drunk.

The humiliated leader eventually left for the Gulf coast, where he set sail eastward on a raft of snakes, promising one day to return and reclaim his throne. (This myth caused the Aztec emperor Moctezuma much consternation when Hernán Cortés appeared on the Gulf coast in 1519.)

At Tula's height, its fertile land produced cacao and its artisans were famous for crafting volcanic glass obsidian. Then in 1170, the city was ransacked and went into decline. Neighboring tribes invaded and Tula was eventually destroyed by the Aztecs.

Sights

Zona Arqueológica ARCHAEOLOGICAL SITE
(admission M$46, video use M$46; 9am-5pm) Two kilometers north of Tula's center, ruins of the main ancient ceremonial site are perched on a hilltop, with views over rolling countryside (as well as the industrial sprawl nearby).

Throughout the site, explanatory signs are in English, Spanish and Náhuatl. Near the main museum and the entrance to the site, you'll find souvenir markets on the weekends. Both of the onsite museums are free with site admission.

The main **site museum** displaying ceramics, metalwork, jewelry and large sculptures is near the main entrance, at the far side of the *zona* from downtown.

➡ *Ball Court*

From the museum, the first large structure you'll reach is the **Juego de Pelota No 1** (Ball Court No 1). Archaeologists believe its walls were decorated with sculpted panels that were removed under Aztec rule.

➡ *Pirámide B*

At the top of **Pirámide B**, also known as the Temple of Quetzalcóatl or Tlahuizcalpantecuhtli (the Morning Star), the remains of three columnar roof supports – which once depicted feathered serpents with their heads on the ground and their tails in the air – remain standing. The four basalt warrior telamones (male figures used as supporting columns) at the top, and the four pillars behind, supported the temple's roof. Wearing headdresses, breastplates shaped like butterflies and short skirts held in place by sun disks, the warriors hold spear-throwers in their right hands and knives and incense bags in their left. The telamon on the left side is a replica of the original, now in Mexico City's Museo Nacional de Antropología. The columns behind the telamones depict crocodile heads (which symbolize the Earth), warriors, symbols of warrior orders, weapons and Quetzalcóatl's head.

On the pyramid's north wall are some of the carvings that once surrounded the structure. These show the symbols of the warrior orders: jaguars, coyotes, eagles eating hearts, and what may be a human head in Quetzalcóatl's mouth.

➡ *Gran Vestíbulo*

Now roofless, the **Gran Vestíbulo** (Great Vestibule) extends along the front of the pyramid, facing the plaza. The stone bench carved with warriors originally ran the length of the hall, possibly to seat priests and nobles observing ceremonies in the plaza.

➡ *Coatepantli*

Near the north side of Pirámide B is the **Coatepantli** (Serpent Wall), which is 40m long, 2.25m high and carved with geometric patterns and a row of snakes devouring human skeletons. Traces remain of the original bright colors with which most of Tula's structures were painted.

➡ *Palacio Quemado*

Immediately west of Pirámide B, the **Palacio Quemado** (Burned Palace) is a series of halls and courtyards with more low benches and relief carvings, one depicting a procession of nobles. It was probably used for ceremonies or reunion meetings.

➡ *Sala de Orientación Guadalupe Mastache*

On the far side of the plaza is a path leading to the **Sala de Orientación Guadalupe Mastache**, a small museum named after one of the archaeologists (a woman) who pioneered excavations here. It includes large items taken from the site, including the huge feet of caryatids (female figures used as supporting columns) and a visual representation of how the site might have looked in its prime.

Tula's fortress-like **cathedral**, just off the *zócalo*, was part of the 16th-century monastery of San José. Inside, its vault ribs are decorated in gold.

Sleeping

Hotel Casablanca HOTEL $
(773-732-11-86; www.casablancatula.com; Pasaje Hidalgo 11; s/d/tr M$350/400/450; P) This comfortable, practical business hotel is right

in the heart of Tula, located at the end of a narrow pedestrian street (look for the 'Milano' sign). Casablanca offers 36 rooms, all with cable TV, private bathroom and free wi-fi (the connection is best in the rooms closest to the lobby). Parking access is around back, via Avenida Zaragoza.

Hotel Real Catedral HOTEL **$$**
(☎773-732-08-13; www.tulaonline.com/hotelcatedral; Av Zaragoza 106; r M$822, ste M$1183-1420; P ❄ 📶) A street back from the plaza, the Real Catedral has some luxurious perks (a small gym, in-room coffeemakers, hair dryers and safes) for the price. Many of the inside rooms lack natural light, but the suites offer balconies and street views. There's also a great selection of black-and-white photos of Tula in the lobby. The room price includes an American breakfast.

Eating

Cocina Económica Las Cazuelas MEXICAN **$**
(Pasaje Hidalgo 129; menú del día M$40; ⏲7am-7pm Mon-Sat, to 6pm Sun) Come here for an excellent *menú del día* (menu of the day) that includes your choice of soup, main dishes such as *chiles rellenos* (cheese-filled chilis) and *milanesa* (a thin cut of fried, breaded meat) – and *agua* (water flavored with fresh fruit). The upstairs balcony, away from the kitchen, is cooler than the steamy, main dining room.

Mana VEGETARIAN **$**
(☎773 100-31-33; Pasaje Hidalgo 13; menu del día M$45; ⏲9am-5pm Sun-Fri; 🚭) This simple vegetarian restaurant serves a generous *menú del día* that includes wholewheat bread, vegetable soup and a pitcher of natural fruit juice. There's also a selection of veggie burgers, taquitos, quesadillas, soups and salads. Everything's fresh, hearty and homemade.

Getting There & Away

Tula's **bus depot** (Xicoténcatl 14) is a short walk from downtown. First-class **Ovnibus** (☎773-732-96-00; www.gvm.com.mx) buses travel to/from Mexico City's Terminal Norte (M$71, 1¾ hours, every 40 minutes) and direct to/from Pachuca (M$92, 1¼ hours, hourly). AVM runs 2nd-class buses to the same destinations every 15 minutes.

Getting Around

If you arrive in Tula by bus, the easiest way to get around is on foot. To reach the *zócalo* from the station, turn right on Xicoténcatl, then immediately left on Rojo del Río and walk two blocks to Hidalgo. Take a right on Hidalgo, which dead-ends at Plaza de la Constitución, Tula's main square.

To reach the Zona Arqueológica continue across the plaza to Quetzalcóatl, an attractive pedestrian street that leads to a footbridge over the Tula river. Take the stairs up the hillside to the right, and continue along Toltan-Del Tesoro to the site's secondary entrance.

Unfortunately, the town's bus station lacks an *empaque* (baggage check), which is problematic for daytrippers traveling with luggage.

Teotihuacán

☎594 / ELEV 2300M

This complex of awesome pyramids, set amid what was once Mesoamerica's greatest city, is among the region's most visited destinations. The sprawling site compares to the ruins of the Yucatán and Chiapas in terms of its significance, and anyone lucky enough to come here will be inspired by the astonishing technological might of the Teotihuacán (teh-oh-tee-wah-*kahn*) civilization.

Set 50km northeast of Mexico City, in a mountain-ringed offshoot of the Valle de México, Teotihuacán is known for its two massive pyramids, the Pirámide del Sol (Pyramid of the Sun) and the Pirámide de la Luna (Pyramid of the Moon), which dominate the remains of the metropolis. Teotihuacán was Mexico's biggest ancient city and the capital of what was probably Mexico's largest pre-Hispanic empire. Exploring the site is fascinating, although rebuffing the indefatigable hawkers is exhausting and crowds can be huge. The site is busiest in the middle of the day, so going early pays off.

The city's grid plan was plotted in the early part of the 1st century AD, and the Pirámide del Sol was completed – over an earlier cave shrine – by AD 150. The rest of the city was developed between about AD 250 and 600. Social, environmental and economic factors hastened its decline and eventual collapse in the 8th century.

The city was divided into quarters by two great avenues that met near La Ciudadela (the Citadel). One of them, running roughly north–south, is the famous Calzada de los Muertos (Avenue of the Dead) – so called because the later Aztecs believed the great buildings lining it were vast tombs, built by giants for Teotihuacán's first rulers. The major structures are typified by a *talud-tablero* style, in which the rising portions

Teotihuacán

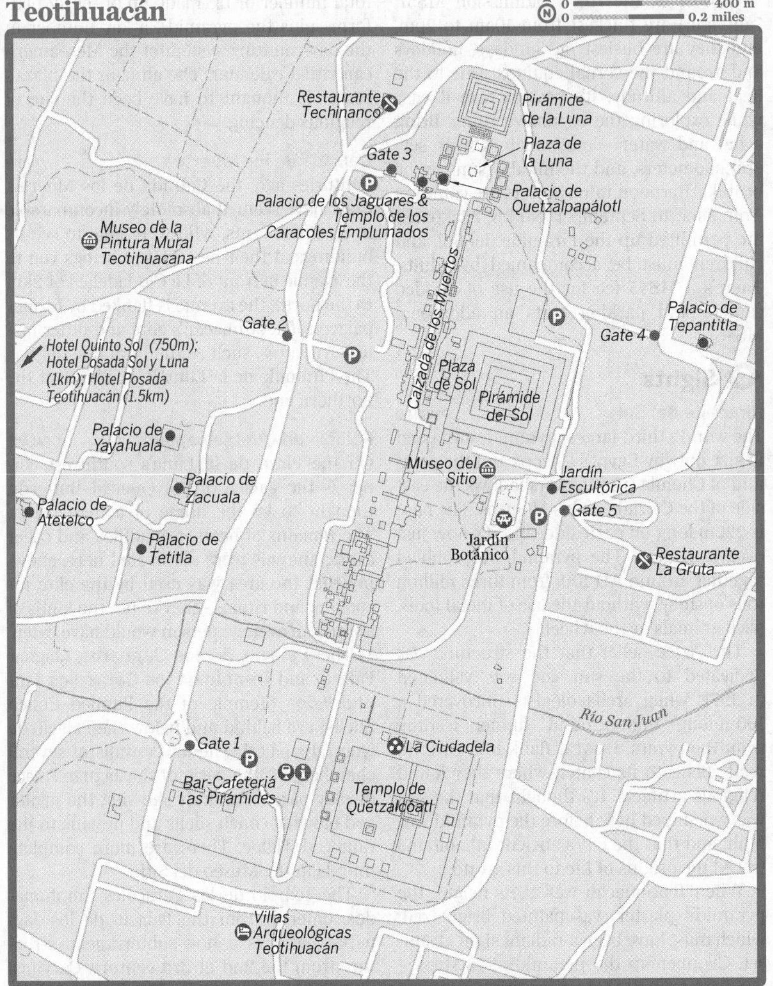

of stepped, pyramid-like buildings consist of both sloping *(talud)* and upright *(tablero)* sections. They were often covered in lime and colorfully painted. Most of the city was made up of residential compounds, some of which contained elegant frescoes.

Centuries after its fall, Teotihuacán remained a pilgrimage site for Aztec royalty, who believed that all of the gods had sacrificed themselves here to start the sun moving at the beginning of the 'fifth world,' inhabited by the Aztecs. It remains an important pilgrimage site: thousands of New Age devotees flock here each year to celebrate the vernal equinox (between March 19 and March 21) and to soak up the mystical energies believed to converge here.

Though ancient Teotihuacán covered more than 20 sq km, most of what can be seen today lies along nearly 2km of the Calzada de los Muertos. Buses arrive at a traffic circle by the southwest entrance (Gate 1); four other entrances are reached by the ring road around the site. There are parking lots and ticket booths at each entrance. Your ticket allows you to re-enter via any of them on the same day. The site museum is just inside the main east entrance (Gate 5).

Crowds at the **ruins** (admission M$51; 7am-5pm) are thickest from 10am to 2pm, and they are busiest on Sundays, holidays and around the vernal equinox. Due to the heat and altitude, it's best to take it easy while exploring the expansive ruins. Bring a hat and water – most visitors walk several kilometers, and the midday sun can be brutal. Afternoon rain showers are common from June to September. No big backpacks are permitted up the Pirámide del Sol, and children must be accompanied by adults. There's a M$45 fee for the use of a video camera and parking costs an additional M$45.

Sights

Pirámide del Sol PYRAMID

The world's third-largest pyramid, surpassed in size only by Egypt's Cheops and the pyramid of Cholula (p162), overshadows the east side of the Calzada de los Muertos. The base is 222m long on each side, and it's now just over 70m high. The pyramid was cobbled together around AD 100, from three million tons of stone, without the use of metal tools, pack animals or the wheel.

The Aztec belief that the structure was dedicated to the sun god was validated in 1971, when archaeologists uncovered a 100m-long underground tunnel leading from the pyramid's west flank to a cave directly beneath its center, where they found religious artifacts. It's thought that the sun was worshiped here before the pyramid was built, and that the city's ancient inhabitants traced the origins of life to this grotto.

When Teotihuacán was at its height, the pyramid's plaster was painted bright red, which must have been a radiant sight at sunset. Clamber up the pyramid's 248 steps – yes, we counted – for an inspiring overview of the ancient city.

Pirámide de la Luna PYRAMID

The Pyramid of the Moon, at the north end of the Calzada de los Muertos, is smaller than the Pirámide del Sol, but more gracefully proportioned. Completed around AD 300, its summit is nearly the same height as Pirámide del Sol because it's built on higher ground, and is worth scaling to put into perspective just how dominating the larger pyramid is.

The **Plaza de la Luna**, located just in front of the pyramid, is a handsome arrangement of 12 temple platforms. Some experts attribute astronomical symbolism to the total number of 13 (made up of the 12 platforms plus the pyramid), a key number in the day-counting system of the Mesoamerican ritual calendar. The altar in the plaza's center is thought to have been the site of religious dancing.

Calzada de los Muertos RUIN

Centuries ago, the Calzada de los Muertos must have seemed absolutely incomparable to its inhabitants, who were able to see its buildings at their best. Gate 1 brings you to the avenue in front of La Ciudadela. For 2km to the north, the avenue is flanked by former palaces of Teotihuacán's elite and other major structures, such as the Pirámide del Sol. The Pirámide de la Luna looms large at the northern end.

Palacio de Quetzalpapálotl PALACE

Off the Plaza de la Luna's southwest corner is the Palace of the Quetzal Butterfly, thought to be the home of a high priest. The remains of bears, armadillos and other exotic animals were discovered here, showing that the area was used by the elite for cooking and rituals - they're not the kinds of animal an average person would have eaten.

The **Palacio de los Jaguares** (Jaguar Palace) and **Templo de los Caracoles Emplumados** (Temple of the Plumed Conch Shells) are behind and below the Palacio de Quetzalpapálotl. The lower walls of several chambers off the patio of the Jaguar Palace display parts of murals showing the jaguar god blowing conch shells and praying to the rain god Tláloc. There are more complete murals in the Museo del Sitio.

The Templo de los Caracoles Emplumados, entered from the Palacio de los Jaguares' patio, is a now-subterranean structure from the 2nd or 3rd century. Carvings on what was its facade show large shells – possibly used as musical instruments.

La Ciudadela RUIN

The expansive, square complex called the Citadel is believed to have been the residence of the city's supreme ruler. Four wide walls topped by 15 pyramids enclose a huge open space, with a major pyramid to the east called the **Templo de Quetzalcóatl**, built around AD 250. The rooms here may have been the city's administrative center. Skeletal remains of 137 human victims have been found under and around this temple, showing that they were brought from diverse parts of Mesoamérica to be sacrificed.

The four surviving steps of the Templo de Quetzacóatl's facade (there were originally seven) are adorned with striking carvings. In the *tablero* panels, the feathered serpent deity alternates with a two-fanged creature identified as the fire serpent, bearer of the sun on its daily journey across the sky. Imagine their eye sockets laid with glistening obsidian glass and the pyramid painted blue, as it once was. On the *talud* (the pyramid's slope) panels are side views of the plumed serpent. Some experts think the carvings depict war, while others interpret them as showing the creation of time.

Museo del Sitio MUSEUM

(Museo de Teotihuacán; ☎594-958-20-81; ⏲9am-4:30pm) Further north along the Calzada de los Muertos, toward the pyramids and across the river, there is a path to the right leading to the site museum, just south of the Pirámide del Sol. It's a refreshing stop midway through a site visit, and admission is included in the ticket. Nearby are the **Jardín Escultórica** (a lovely sculpture garden with Teotihuacán artifacts), a botanic garden, public toilets, a snack bar, picnic tables and a bookstore with designer gifts.

The museum is divided thematically, with information provided in English and Spanish. There are excellent displays of artifacts, fresco panels and a confronting display of real skeletons buried in the ground, demonstrating ancient local beliefs on death and the afterlife.

Palacio de Tepantitla PALACE

This priest's residence, 500m northeast of the Pirámide del Sol, is home to Teotihuacán's most famous fresco, the worn **Paradise of Tláloc**. The rain god Tláloc is shown attended by priests, with people, animals and fish nearby. Above is the sinister portrait of the **Great Goddess of Teotihuacán**, thought to be a goddess of the darkness and war because she is often shown with jaguars, owls and spiders – underworld animals. Look for her fanged nosepiece and her shields adorned with spiderwebs.

Museo de la Pintura Mural Teotihuacana MUSEUM

(☎594-958-20-81; ⏲9am-4:30pm) This impressive museum showcases murals from Teotihuacán, as well as reconstructions of murals you'll see at the ruins. Admission is included in the site ticket.

Palacio de Tetitla & Palacio de Atetelco PALACE

A group of palaces lies west of Teotihuacán's main area, several hundred meters northwest of Gate 1. Many of the murals, discovered in the 1940s, are well preserved or restored, and perfectly intelligible. Inside the sprawling **Palacio de Tetitla**, no fewer than 120 walls are graced with murals of Tláloc, jaguars, serpents and eagles. Some 400m west is the **Palacio de Atetelco**, whose vivid jaguar or coyote murals – a mixture of originals and restorations – are in the Patio Blanco (White Patio) in the northwest corner.

About 100m further northeast are **Palacio de Zacuala** and **Palacio de Yayahuala**, a pair of enormous walled compounds that probably served as communal living quarters. Separated by the original alleyways, the two structures are made up of numerous rooms and patios but few entranceways.

Sleeping

The town of San Juan Teotihuacán, 2km from the archaeological zone, has a few good overnight options, which make sense if you want to start early at the site before the crowds arrive.

Hotel Posada Teotihuacán HOTEL $

(☎594-956-04-60; Canteroco 5, San Juan Teotihuacán; s/d/tr M$180/250/330; P) The rooms at this centrally located, family-run, budget posada are smallish but clean and all have a TV and private bathroom. There is only one individual and one triple room, so book ahead for these.

Hotel Posada Sol y Luna HOTEL $$

(☎594-956-23-68, 594-956-23-71; www.posadasolyluna.com; Cantú 13, San Juan Teotihuacán; r M$450-596, ste 730-785; P 📶) At the east end of town, en route to the pyramids, this well-run hotel has 16 fine but unexciting rooms, all with TV and bathroom. Junior suites have rather ancient Jacuzzis in them – not worth paying extra for.

Hotel Quinto Sol HOTEL $$$

(☎594-956-18-81; www.hotelquintosol.com.mx; Av Hidalgo 26, San Juan Teotihuacán; s/d/tr/q M$970/1200/1400/1550; P @ 📶 🏊) There's a reason the Quinto Sol is where most tourist groups stay when visiting the ruins at Teotihuacán. With its fine facilities – including a decent-size pool, large, well-appointed rooms, in-room security boxes and room service – this is one of the best-equipped hotels in town.

Villas Arqueológicas Teotihuacán HOTEL **$$$**
(☎55-5836-9020; www.villasarqueologicas.com.mx; Periférico Sur s/n, Zona Arqueológica; r M$1132-1554; P @ ≋) Just south of the Zona Arqueológica, this elegant hotel has a small gym, heated outdoor pool, a well-lit tennis court, playground and a spa with temascal (a traditional Mexican steam bath). There's also a refined Mexican restaurant. Wi-fi signal is only accessible in the lobby.

Eating

Eating near the ruins is usually a pricey and disappointing experience. Touts can offer to drive you to and from their restaurant, only for you to find that their deals are not so great and that you're stuck without other nearby options. You're much better off bringing a picnic, though there are a couple of adequate restaurants worth seeking out. The most convenient is on the 3rd floor of the old museum building near Gate 1, where the busy **Bar-Cafetería Las Pirámides** offers panoramic views of La Ciudadela.

★**Restaurante Techinanco** MEXICAN **$$**
(☎594-958-23-06; Zona Arqueológica ring road; mains M$75-120; ⏰9am-6pm) A short walk from Gate 3, behind the Pirámide de la Luna, this homey restaurant serves excellent home cooking at comparatively reasonable prices. The small menu takes in local favorites from enchiladas to authentic homemade *moles* (chili-sauce dishes). Ask about the curative massages (from M$600) or call in advance for a temascal.

Restaurante La Gruta MEXICAN **$$$**
(☎594-956-01-27; www.lagruta.com.mx; Zona Arqueológica ring road; mains M$182-269; ⏰10am-6pm) Set in a vast, cool cave a short distance from Gate 5, this tourist-centric restaurant is unapologetically gimmicky. Yet the food, while pricey, is surprisingly good and there's a 40-minute folkloric dance show on Saturdays at 3:30pm and Sundays 3:30pm and 5:30pm. Reservations are a good idea.

Information

There's an **information booth** (☎594-956-02-76; www.inah.gob.mx; ⏰7am-6pm) near the southwest entrance (Gate 1). Free Spanish-only site tours by authorized guides are available, with **reservations** (☎594-958-20-81).

Head to **Lonely Planet** (www.lonelyplanet.com/mexico/north-of-mexico-city/teotihuacan) for planning advice, author recommendations, traveler reviews and insider tips.

Getting There & Away

During daylight hours, Autobuses México–San Juan Teotihuacán runs buses from Mexico City's Terminal Norte (outside metro Autobuses del Norte) to the ruins (M$40, one hour) every hour from 7am to 6pm. When entering the Terminal Norte, turn left and walk to the second-to-last desk on the concourse. Make sure your bus is headed for 'Los Pirámides,' not the nearby town of San Juan Teotihuacán (unless you are heading to accommodations there). There have been reports from readers of armed robberies on these buses. Check with the **US State Department** (www.travel.state.gov) for current warnings.

At the ruins, buses arrive and depart from near Gate 1, also making stops at Gates 2 and 3. Return buses are more frequent after 1pm. The last bus back to Mexico City leaves at 6pm; some terminate at Indios Verdes metro station, but most continue to Terminal Norte.

Getting Around

To reach the pyramids from San Juan Teotihuacán, take a taxi (M$35) or any combi (M$12) labeled 'San Martín' departing from Avenida Hidalgo, beside the central plaza. Combis returning to San Juan stop on the main road outside Gates 1, 2 and 3.

Pachuca

☎771 / POP POP 267,000 / ELEV 2425M

The unassuming capital of Hidalgo state is scattered over steep, wide hills and crowned with a massive Mexican flag and a towering statue of Christ. Its charming, brightly painted town center is visible for miles around, although far-from-lovely urban sprawl has developed beyond the candy-box houses of the old town.

Even so, Pachuca is an underappreciated provincial capital, an excellent staging post for trips north and east into the dramatic Sierra Madre Oriental, or just to the nearby Mineral del Chico, and an appealing place to spend a couple of days away from the tourist bustle.

Silver was unearthed nearby as early as 1534, and Real del Monte's mines still produce quite a respectable amount of ore. Pachuca was also the gateway through which *fútbol* (soccer) entered Mexico, introduced in the 19th century by miners from

Cornwall, England. The Cornish population also gave the town its signature dish, meat pastries known as *pastes* (pasties; and recognizable to any Brit as a Cornish pasty, albeit with some typically Mexican fillings).

Sights

The 40m-high **Reloj Monumental** (Clock Tower), built between 1904 and 1910 to commemorate the independence centennial, overshadows the north end of Pachuca's *zócalo,* Plaza de la Independencia, which is flanked by Avenida Matamoros on the east and Avenida Allende on the west. Guerrero runs parallel to Avenida Allende, 100m to the west. Some 700m to the south, Guerrero and Avenida Matamoros converge at the modern Plaza Juárez.

Cuartel del Arte CULTURAL BUILDING
(cnr Hidalgo & Arista; 10am-6pm Tue-Sun) FREE This gorgeous, sprawling cultural center is an oasis of calm at Pachuca's bustling heart. Formerly the Convento de San Francisco, the complex includes three excellent museums, an art gallery, a theater, a library and several lovely plazas. It's worth looking into the impressive (and still functioning) Parroquia de San Francisco church as well. From Plaza de la Independencia, walk two blocks east to Hidalgo and about 650m south to the corner of Hidalgo and Arista.

One highlight is the excellent **Museo Nacional de la Fotografía**, which displays early imaging technology and stunning selections from the 1.5 million photos in the National Institute of Anthropology and History (INAH) archives. The images – some by Europeans and Americans, many more by pioneering Mexican photojournalists such as Nacho López and Agustín Victor Casasola – provide a fascinating glimpse of Mexico from 1873 to the present.

Museo de Minería MUSEUM
(771-715-09-76; www.distritominero.com.mx; Mina 110; adult/student M$25/20; 10am-6pm Tue-Sun) Two blocks south and half a block east of the *zócalo,* Pachuca's mining museum provides a good overview of the industry that shaped the region. Headlamps, miners' shrines and old mining maps are on display, and photos depict conditions in the shafts from the early years to the present. There's a M$20 charge to use a camera and a M$50 charge for the use of a video camera. The museum also coordinates a *ruta de turismo cultural minero* (mining culture tourism route) in English, Spanish or French which visits several mining sites in the region.

Tours

Tranvía Turístico TRAM
(771-718-71-20; www.tranviaturisticopachuca.com; adult/child M$60/50; 11am-6pm Wed-Fri, 10:30am-6:30pm Sat & Sun) Motor trolley tours depart hourly from the plaza's west side, traveling to 24 sites around the city, including the hilltop statue of Christ. The entire trip takes just over an hour.

Sleeping

Hotel Noriega HOTEL $
(771-715-01-50; Av Matamoros 305; s M$300, d M$320-350;) The Noriega looks like a greenhouse with hundreds of plants in ornate pots, and thriving trees that push up to the glass ceiling. Rooms are potluck, though, so see a few before checking in. Some are claustrophobic, while others are large and airy. Wi-fi is sketchy away from the lobby. An in-room TV costs extra, or you can watch *lucha libre* (Mexican wrestling) in the lobby with the staff.

Hotel de los Baños HOTEL $$
(771-713-07-00; Av Matamoros 205; s M$380, d M$480, t/q M$550/600;) With its beautifully tiled old-world lobby, the Baños is one of Pachuca's most charming midrange hotels. Some of the 56 rooms have been renovated and others have antique fittings and lack natural light. Those with a preference should ask to see a couple of different room styles. Parking is an extra M$40. The hotel is located a block south of the clock tower.

Hotel Emily BUSINESS HOTEL $$$
(771-715-08-28, 800-501-63-39; www.hotelemily.com.mx; Plaza Independencia; r M$1300, ste M$1600;) On the south side of the *zócalo,* Emily has an excellent location, with balconies overlooking the Reloj Monumental. Rooms are modern and stylish, with flat-screen televisions, laundry service and gym access. The hotel restaurant has generic but surprisingly tasty food in a sterile setting.

Eating & Drinking

Pachuca's famous regional specialty *pastes* (pasties) are available all over town, including at the bus station. Baked in pizza ovens, they contain a variety of fillings – such

DON'T MISS

REAL DEL MONTE

This gorgeous mountain town is a tangle of houses, restaurants and pasty shops scattered across a pine tree-carpeted hillside. The air is thin here, so don't be surprised if you find yourself with a mild case of altitude sickness, but it's also clean and so crisp it seems colder than it likely is (bring a sweater, if not a coat).

Two kilometers past the Hwy 105 turnoff for Parque Nacional El Chico, Real del Monte (officially known as Mineral del Monte) was the scene of a miners' strike in 1776 (commemorated as the first strike in the Americas). Most of the town was settled in the 19th century, after a British company commandeered the mines. Cornish-style cottages line many of the steep, cobbled streets.

★ **Hotel Paraíso Real Hospedaje-Cafetería** (☎771-797-02-20; www.hotelparaisoreal.com; s/d Sun-Thu M$500/600, Fri & Sat M$800/1000; P 📶) has a friendly, family-run vibe and clean, modern rooms with tiled floors, cable TV and room service. There's an eclectic mix of rooms; some have low ceilings, while others have Jacuzzis (an additional M$100), balconies and views over town. Another good option, just next door, is **Hotel Real del Monte** (☎771-715-56-54; www.hotelesecoturisticos.com.mx; r Sun-Thu M$600, Fri & Sat M$700; 📶), a 15-room hotel run by the same high-standards company that operates the two main hotels in the nearby town of Mineral del Chico.

Second-class buses depart Pachuca's terminal for Real del Monte (M$9, 30 minutes, hourly). Combis (M$8, 30 minutes, every 30 minutes) leave from the northwest corner of Plaza de la Constitución, north of the *zócalo*.

as beans, pineapple and rice pudding – probably never imagined by the Cornish miners who brought this English culinary tradition to Mexico.

Mina La Blanca Restaurant Bar MEXICAN **$$**
(☎771-715-18-96; www.restaurantlablanca.com.mx; Av Matamoros 201; mains M$56-145; ⏰8am-10pm) Pachuca's most famous restaurant, La Blanca has been serving traditional *hidalguense* food – including *pastes* and a mean *caldo de hongo* (mushroom soup) – since 1953. The walls, adorned with black-and-white photos and stained glass windows depicting industrial mining scenes, speak of Pachuca's history. This is also a great place to come for a low-key drink in the evening.

Euro Bistro INTERNATIONAL **$$$**
(fb.com/eurobistro.mx; Av Revolución 805; mains M$100-215; ⏰2-11pm Mon-Sat, 2-8pm Sun; 📶) For something international, this upscale European-style bistro serves dishes ranging from fried calamari and Cobb salads to fish and chips and *medallón de res* (beef medallions) in mustard sauce. There's a decent wine list (though only two wines by the glass), jazz playing quietly in the background and an exciting dessert list, including a mean lemon-meringue parfait.

Espresso Central LOUNGE
(Av Revolución 1008; snacks M$33-55; ⏰8am-midnight Mon-Sat; 📶) In a stylish, two-story building constructed from converted shipping containers, Espresso Central has quality espressos, domestic microbrews, decent wine, chai, crepes and bagels. At night, the cafe becomes a hip night spot, where Pachuca's cool kids and suit-wearers hang out most nights of the week.

Shopping

Artesanos de Pachuca HANDICRAFTS
(Jardín de los Niños Héroes; ⏰11am-6pm Sat & Sun & holidays) This cute market, set on the crossroads of Allende and Matamoros, is a curious mix of trinkets and handmade crafts that you won't see anywhere else. There is a sense of hunting for treasure as you pass screenprinted T-shirts, lead soldiers, Mexican sweets, paintings, jewelry, ornate picture frames and other crafts made by this local collective of artists.

Information

ATMs are numerous around the Plaza de la Independencia.

Internet (Technopolis; Allende 502; M$5 per hr; ⏰9am-9pm Mon-Fri, 10am-9pm Sat & Sun)

Tourist Module (☎771-715-14-11; www.pachuca.gob.mx; Plaza de la Independencia; ⏰8:30am-4:30pm) Behind the clock tower; offers advice and colorful pamphlets to surrounding towns.

Getting There & Away

Pachuca's **bus station** (☎771-713-34-47; Cam Cueso) is 20 minutes from downtown. There's an ADO 1st-class bus service to/from Mexico City's TAPO terminal (M$78, 1 hour 40 min, every half or one hour), Terminal Norte in Mexico City (M$78, 1½ hours, every 10 minutes), Poza Rica (M$184, 4½ hours, two daily) and Puebla (M$164, two hours, three daily). Some routes have GL elite service with wi-fi. Buses also go frequently to and from Tula and Querétaro.

Three scenic roads (Hwys 85, 105 and 130/132D) climb into the forested, often foggy, Sierra Madre Oriental.

Getting Around

From the bus station, green-and-white *colectivos* marked 'Centro' deposit passengers at the Plaza de la Constitución (M$6.50), a short walk from the *zócalo;* in the reverse direction, hop on along Avenida Allende. By taxi the trip costs M$35.

Around Pachuca

Mineral del Chico

☎771

You can take an easy and very lovely day trip or weekend retreat from Pachuca to the nearly 3000-hectare **El Chico National Park** (www.parqueelchico.gob.mx), which was established in 1898, and the charming old mining village **Mineral del Chico**, which is among the newest *pueblos mágicos* and outshines the much larger Pachuca. The views are wonderful, the air is fresh and the mountains have some great hiking among spectacular rock formations and beautiful waterfalls. Most Mexicans who visit on the weekend hardly leave El Chico's cute main street. Not surprising when the locals are this friendly, proving their motto '*pueblo chico, gente grande*' (small town, great people).

Sights & Activities

Colectivos marked 'Carboneras' (M$6) will drop you at the trailhead to the *mirador* (lookout) at **Peña del Cuervo**. From there, it's about a 25-minute walk.

Ask at the local hotels or the park's **visitors center** (Centro de Visitantes; Carretera Pachuca–Mineral del Chico Km 7.5), a 10-minute drive from the village, for details about possible guided outdoor activities.

You can take an easy 1.5km self-guided walk to **Río del Milagro**, a small river dotted with abandoned mines and surrounded by trees. From the left of the church, walk downhill till the end, continue left along the pathway till you reach the road and signs for the river. Walk carefully along the road and you will come to a path on your right down to the river with a valley vista. Bring warm clothes as the temperature can change in a snap in the afternoon.

A street back from the main street Corona del Rosal in most directions will reveal views of the valley. A good spot is the maze of walkways behind the **Capilla del Calvario**, a rustic 19th-century chapel on Calvario, uphill from the church.

Sleeping & Eating

Mineral del Chico is an established weekend getaway, but it can feel like a ghost town during the week, when visitors may be hard pressed to find an open place to eat after dark and even some hotels shutter their doors. However, the available hotels often lower their prices, and you'll have the trails and peaks almost entirely to yourself.

There are several **campgrounds** (campsites M$150, cabins M$400) with rudimentary facilities between Km 7 and Km 10 on Carretera Pachuca en route to Mineral del Chico.

Hospedaje El Chico GUESTHOUSE $
(☎771-715-47-41; Corona del Rosal 1; r M$350-550; wi-fi) This small, 10-room homestay is a decent budget option, with clean if unexciting rooms. You'll have to ring the buzzer to get in. If El Chico appears to be closed mid-week, ask next door at Casa Biseña. The same family owns both businesses.

Hotel El Paraíso LODGE $$
(☎771-715-56-54; www.hotelesecoturisticos.com.mx; Carretera Pachuca s/n; r Sun-Thu M$850, Fri & Sat from M$950; P wi-fi) Nestled inside large, well-maintained grounds at the base of the mountain, with a fast-flowing stream running nearby, El Paraíso certainly has a location worthy of its name. The large, modern rooms lack individuality or charm, but they're very comfortable. A full-board option is available.

Fonda el Fresno MEXICAN $
(☎771-715-32-57; Corona del Rosal 10; set menu M$45; ⏲9am-9pm) This little bakery is more than a sweet place for a coffee. Out back, the grandparents make *sopa de papa* (potato soup) that zings with fresh parsley,

vegetarian enchiladas (on request) with generous slices of avocado, and fresh *agua de melón* (cantaloupe-juice drink). Streams of people come just for a tastebud tweaking *cocol* (M$3.5, brown sugar and caraway-seed bread triangle).

★Restaurante y Cabañas San Diego CABAÑAS **$$**
(☎771-125-6173; Carretera Pachuca s/n; mains M$80-120) Off the highway beside a rushing creek on the way into town (look for signs at the turnoff to El Paraíso), San Diego is a true mountain escape. Head down to the wood fish shack, where you can watch trout being caught and prepared. The *a la mexicana* style, stuffed with Oaxacan cheese, tomatoes, chilies and thick chunks of garlic, is excellent.

There are also two comfortable but rustic cabins available for rent, one smaller (up to four people, M$700) than the other (up to 10 people, M$1800).

Hotel Posada del Amanecer HOTEL **$$**
(☎771-715-56-54; www.hotelesecoturisticos.com.mx; Morelos 3; r Sun-Thu from M$700, Fri & Sat M$950; P 📶) This 11-room adobe complex has spacious modern rooms with colonial touches on two levels beside a lovely patio. With no phones or TVs, it's a peaceful getaway. Children under 12 stay free. Massage, spa treatments and adventure activities such as rock climbing are offered for an extra fee.

ℹ Getting There & Away

From Pachuca, blue-and-white *colectivos* climb the windy roads up to Mineral del Chico (M$12, 40 minutes) every 20 minutes from 8am to 6pm from Calle Hidalgo, outside the Mercado Juárez on the corner of Avenida de la Raza. The last service back to Pachuca is at 7pm.

There's no direct transit service from Real del Monte, but those wanting to avoid a trip back to Pachuca to transfer *colectivos* can hire a taxi for about M$150.

EAST OF MEXICO CITY

The views get seriously dramatic as you head east from the capital, the landscape peppered with the snow-capped, volcanic peaks of Popocatépetl, Iztaccíhuatl, La Malinche and Pico Orizaba – the country's highest summit. The rugged Cordillera Neovolcánica offers anything from invigorating alpine strolls to demanding technical climbs. Unpredictable Popocatépetl, however, remains off-limits due to volcanic activity.

The gorgeous colonial city of Puebla – Mexico's fifth-largest city – is the dominant regional center, a local transportation hub and a big tourist draw with its cathedral, rich culinary traditions, intriguing history and excellent museums. The surrounding state of Puebla is predominantly rural and home to approximately half a million indigenous people. This enduring presence provides the region with a rich handicraft legacy, with products including pottery, carved onyx and fine hand-woven and embroidered textiles.

Tlaxcala, the capital of the tiny state of the same name, has emerged as an attractive destination in its own right, with an exciting array of new restaurants, museums and boutique hotels. Far-flung Cuetzalan, meanwhile, is surrounded by lush, dramatic scenery and is one of Mexico's most time-forgotten villages.

Puebla

☎222 / POP 1.5 MILLION / ELEV 2160M

Once a bastion of conservatism, Catholicism and tradition, Puebla has come out of its colonial-era shell. The city retains a fantastically well-preserved center, a stunning cathedral and a wealth of beautiful churches, while younger *poblanos* (people from Puebla) are embracing the city's increasingly thriving art and nightlife scenes.

The city is well worth a visit, with 70 churches in the historic center alone, more than a thousand colonial buildings adorned with the *azulejos* (painted ceramic tiles) for which the city is famous, and a long culinary history that can be explored in any restaurant or food stall. For a city of its size, Puebla is far more relaxed and less gridlocked than you might expect.

History

Founded by Spanish settlers in 1531 as Ciudad de los Ángeles, with the aim of surpassing the nearby pre-Hispanic religious center of Cholula, the city became known as Puebla de los Ángeles ('La Angelópolis') eight years later, and quickly grew into an important Catholic center. Fine pottery had long been crafted from the local clay, and after the colonists introduced new materials and techniques Puebla pottery evolved as both an art and an industry. By the late 18th century, the city had emerged as a major producer of glass and textiles. With 50,000 residents by 1811, Puebla remained Mexico's second-biggest city until Guadalajara overtook it in the late 19th century.

In 1862 General Ignacio de Zaragoza fortified the Cerro de Guadalupe against the French invaders, and on May 5 that year his 2000 men defeated a frontal attack by 6000, many of whom were handicapped by diarrhea. This rare Mexican military success is the reason for annual (and increasingly corporate-sponsored and drunken) celebrations in the USA, where the holiday is far more significant than in Mexico and hundreds of streets are named Cinco de Mayo. Few seem to remember that the following year the reinforced French took Puebla and occupied the city until 1867. *Touché!*

Modern Puebla is still centered around the city's Old Town, with the large, leafy *zócalo* and Mexico's tallest cathedral at its heart. The *centro histórico* is home to most of the attractions, hotels and restaurants of interest to international travelers, most of which are within a few blocks of the main plaza.

The Zona Esmeralda, 2km west of the *zócalo,* is a stretch of Avenida Juárez with chi-chi boutiques, upscale restaurants and trendy nightclubs.

Sights

Zócalo PLAZA
Puebla's central plaza was originally a marketplace where bullfights, theater and hangings occurred, before assuming its current arboretum-like appearance in 1854. The surrounding arcades date from the 16th century. The plaza fills with an entertaining mix of clowns, balloon hawkers, food vendors and people enjoying the free wi-fi on weekend evenings.

Catedral CATHEDRAL
(cnr Avs 3 Oriente & 16 de Septiembre) Puebla's impressive cathedral, which appears on Mexico's M$500 bill, occupies the entire block south of the *zócalo*. Its architecture is a blend of severe Herreresque-Renaissance and early baroque styles. Construction began in 1550, but most of it took place under Bishop Juan de Palafox in the 1640s. At 69m, the towers are Mexico's tallest. The dazzling interior, the frescoes and the elaborately decorated side chapels are awe-inspiring, and most have bilingual signs explaining their history and significance.

Museo Amparo MUSEUM
(☎222-229-38-50; www.museoamparo.com; Calle 2 Sur 708; adult/student M$35/25, Mon free; ⏰10am-6pm Wed-Mon) This superb private museum, housed in two linked 16th- and 17th-century colonial buildings, is loaded with pre-Hispanic artifacts. Displayed with explanatory information sheets in English and Spanish, the collection is staggering.

Notice the thematic continuity in Mexican design – the same motifs appear again and again on dozens of pieces. An example: the collection of pre-Hispanic cult skeleton heads are eerily similar to the candy skulls sold for Día de los Muertos.

Templo de Santo Domingo CHURCH
(cnr Avs 5 de Mayo & 4 Poniente) This fine Dominican church features a stunning **Capilla del Rosario** (Rosary Chapel), south of the main altar, which is the main reason to come here. Built between 1650 and 1690, it's heavy on gilded plaster and carved stone, with angels and cherubim seemingly materializing from behind every leaf. See if you can spot the heavenly orchestra. Outside the entrance in the **Zona de Monumentos**, you'll often find sculpture exhibitions.

Casa de la Cultura CULTURAL BUILDING
(☎222-232-12-27; Av 5 Oriente 5; ⏰10am-8pm) Occupying the entire block facing the south side of the cathedral, the former bishop's palace is a classic 17th-century brick-and-tile edifice, which now houses government offices, the Casa de la Cultura and the State Tourist Office. Inside are art galleries, a bookstore and cinema, and a congenial cafe out back in the courtyard.

Upstairs is the 1646 **Biblioteca Palafoxiana** (☎222-777-25-81; admission M$25, Sun free; ⏰10am-5pm Tues-Sun), the first public library in the Americas. The library's gorgeous shelves – carved cedar and white pine – house thousands of rare books, including the 1493 *Nuremberg Chronicle* and one of the earliest New World dictionaries.

Iglesia de la Compañía CHURCH
(cnr Av Palafox y Mendoza & Calle 4 Sur) This Jesuit church with a 1767 Churrigueresque facade is also called Espíritu Santo. Beneath the altar is a tomb said to be that of a 17th-century Asian princess who was sold into slavery in Mexico and later freed.

She was supposedly responsible for the colorful china poblana costume – a shawl, frilled blouse, embroidered skirt, and gold and silver adornments. This costume

Puebla

became a kind of 'peasant chic' in the 19th century. But *china* (*chee*-nah) also meant 'maidservant,' and the style may have evolved from Spanish peasant costumes.

Next door is the 16th-century **Edificio Carolino** (cnr Av Palafox y Mendoza & Calle 4 Sur), now the main building of the Universidad Autónoma de Puebla.

Museo del Ferrocarril MUSEUM
(www.museoferrocarriles.org.mx; Calle 11 Norte 1005; admission M$12, Sun free; 9am-5pm Tue-Sun;) This excellent railway museum is housed in Puebla's former train station and the spacious grounds surrounding it, and has activities for kids. There are ancient steam-powered monsters through to relatively recent passenger carriages, and you can enter many of them. One carriage contains an excellent collection of photos of various derailments and other disasters that occurred during the 1920s and '30s.

Templo de San Francisco CHURCH
(Av 14 Oriente; 8am-8pm) The north doorway of this church is a good example of 16th-century plateresque; the tower and fine brick-and-tile facade were added in the 18th century. In the north chapel is the mummified body of San Sebastián de Aparicio, a Spaniard who migrated to Mexico in 1533 and planned many of the country's roads before becoming a monk. Since he's now the patron saint of drivers, merchants and farm workers, his canonized corpse attracts a stream of worshipers.

Museo de la Revolución MUSEUM
(222-242-10-76; Av 6 Oriente 206; adult/student M$25/20, Sun free; 10am-5pm Tue-Sun) This pockmarked 19th-century house was the scene of the first battle of the 1910 Revolution. Betrayed only two days before a planned uprising against the dictatorship of Porfirio Díaz, the Serdán family (Aquiles, Máximo, Carmen and Natalia) and 17 others

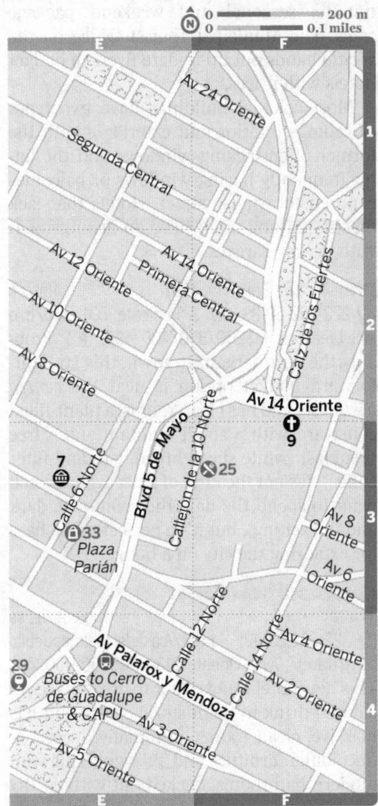

Puebla

Sights

	Biblioteca Palafoxiana	(see 1)
1	Casa de la Cultura	C3
2	Catedral	C3
3	Edificio Carolino	D3
4	Iglesia de la Compañía	D3
5	Museo Amparo	C4
6	Museo Bello	C3
7	Museo Casa del Alfeñique	E3
8	Museo de la Revolución	D2
9	Templo de San Francisco	F3
10	Templo de Santo Domingo	C2
11	Zócalo	C3

Activities, Courses & Tours

12	Turibus	C3

Sleeping

13	Casona de la China Poblana	D3
14	El Sueño Hotel & Spa	C4
15	Gran Hotel San Agustín	B2
16	Hotel Casa de la Palma Travel	D3
17	Hotel Colonial	D3
18	Hotel Mesón de San Sebastián	C4
19	Hotel Provincia Express	C3
20	Mesón Sacristía de la Compañía	D4
21	NH Puebla	B2

Eating

22	Amalfi Pizzeria	D3
23	El Mural de los Poblanos	C3
24	El Patio de las Ranas	C2
25	La Purificadora	F3
26	La Zanahoria	D4
27	Las Ranas	C2
28	Mercado de Sabores Poblanos	A1
	Restaurante Sacristía	(see 20)

Drinking & Nightlife

29	A Go Go	E4
30	All Day Café	D4
31	Café Milagros	D4

Entertainment

32	Celia's Cafe	D4

Shopping

33	El Parián Crafts Market	E3
34	Talavera Uriarte	A1

fought 500 soldiers until only Aquiles, their leader, and Carmen were left alive. Aquiles, hidden under the floorboards, might have survived if the damp hadn't provoked a cough that gave him away. Both were subsequently killed. The house retains its bullet holes and some revolutionary memorabilia, including a room dedicated to female insurgents.

Museo Casa del Alfeñique MUSEUM

(☎222 232-42-96; Av 4 Oriente 416; adult/student M$25/20, Sun free; ⏲10am-5pm Tue-Sun) This renovated colonial house is an outstanding example of the over-the-top 18th-century decorative style *alfeñique,* characterized by elaborate stucco ornamentation and named after a candy made from sugar and egg whites. The 1st floor details the Spanish conquest, including indigenous accounts in the form of drawings and murals. The 2nd floor houses a large collection of historic and religious paintings, local furniture and household paraphernalia, although all labeling is in Spanish only.

Museo Bello MUSEUM

(☎222-232-94-75; www.museobello.org; Av 3 Poniente 302; adult/student M$25/20, Sun free; ⏲10am-4pm Tue-Sun) This house is filled with the diverse art and crafts collection of the 19th-century industrialist Bello family. The new entrance fee is worth it for the exquisite French, English, Japanese and Chinese porcelain and a large collection of Puebla Talavera. The museum closes every January for maintenance.

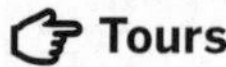

Tours

Turibus BUS TOUR
(☎771-226-72-89; www.turibus.com.mx; adult/child M$160/90; ⏲departs 11:45am) Operated by ADO bus lines, this four-hour, double-decker bus tour gives an overview of Puebla's *centro histórico* and the nearby town of Cholula. Leaves from the west side of the *zócalo*.

Festivals & Events

Feria de Puebla MUSIC
Starting in late April and ending in late May, this fair honors the state's achievements with cultural and music events.

Cinco de Mayo PARADE
The city's May 5 celebrations mark the day, 150 years ago, when the Mexican army defeated the French. There's typically a parade.

Festival del Mole Poblano FOOD
In early June the city celebrates its most famous contribution to the culinary arts: *mole poblano,* a thick sauce of chilis, fruits, nuts, spices and chocolate.

Festival del Chile en Nogada FOOD
Leaving no culinary stone unturned, in August the city's savvy restaurateurs promote the country's 'patriotic recipe' – a chili stuffed with picadillo and topped in a luscious walnut cream sauce.

Día de Muertos TRADITIONAL
Puebla has jumped on the bandwagon, with a four-day citywide cultural program starting in late October devoted to the Day of the Dead.

Sleeping

Puebla's hotel scene is crowded and competitive, with a huge range of accommodations options and new arrivals constantly stirring things up. Quite a few boutique three- and four-star hotels aimed at discerning travelers have kept standards high.

Many hotels in the city can be spotted some way off with illuminated 'H' signs over their entrance, although some of the newer generation don't advertise quite so directly. It's worth searching online for special last-minute, seasonal and weekend package rates. The Municipal Tourist Office on the *zócalo* hands out up-to-date flyers of budget hotels with prices.

Most colonial buildings have two types of room – interior and exterior – with the former often lacking windows and the latter frequently having windows or balconies exposed to a noisy street. Hotels that lack on-site parking often have an arrangement with nearby garages.

Gran Hotel San Agustín HOTEL $
(☎222-232-50-89; Av 3 Poniente 531; s/d/tr/q incl breakfast M$260/350/400/460; P) Probably the best bargain in town, this straightforward budget option is near the *centro histórico*, and has clean rooms, a plant-filled courtyard with a small fountain and a free breakfast (white sliced bread, jam and filter coffee). It's not the kind of place where you'll want to spend the day (the rooms are dark and unexciting), but it's a perfectly fine base for exploring the city on a budget.

Hotel Casa de la Palma Travel BOUTIQUE HOTEL $$
(☎222-232-23-42; http://casadelapalmapuebla.com/travel/; Av 3 Oriente 213; r M$650-900; wi-fi) This new hotel is next door to great places to eat and drink in the historic centre and has massive, clean rooms, minimally decorated in colonial furniture and Talavera. This with modern bathrooms, decked out with earthy marble floors, make Palma Travel extremely good value. Upstairs rooms come with king-sized beds. The helpful staff speak English and French.

Hotel Provincia Express BUSINESS HOTEL $$
(☎222-246-35-57; Av Reforma 141; s incl breakfast (except Mon) M$400, d incl breakfast (except Mon) M$500-600; P @ wi-fi) This wonderful place has one of the most stunning tiled interiors in Puebla and rooms come at knock-down prices. Refitted in 2007 the rooms themselves are simple but modern and spotlessly clean, while the corridors and facade are visually exciting. Provincia Express's popularity, coupled with thin doors, means it can be noisy at night. The included breakfast is not available on Mondays.

Hotel Colonial HOTEL $$
(☎800-013-00-00, 222-246-46-12; www.colonial.com.mx; Calle 4 Sur 105; s/d/tr M$710/810/910; @ wi-fi) Once part of a 17th-century Jesuit monastery and existing as a hotel in various forms since the mid-19th century, the

Colonial exudes heritage from its many gorgeously furnished rooms (half with colonial decor, half modern). There's a good restaurant, lobby wi-fi and a fantastic gilt elevator. An unbeatable vibe and location despite occasional street- and live-music noise.

NH Puebla BUSINESS HOTEL **$$**
(☎222-309-19-19, 800-726-0528; www.nh-hotels.com; Calle 5 Sur 105; r US$87-US$111; P ❄ 📶 🏊) Attracting both business travelers and pleasure seekers, the NH has had a modern makeover and offers good service without being stuffy. The rooms are large and contemporary, with extremely comfortable beds, good views and access to the rooftop bar and a small pool and gym.

Hotel Mesón de San Sebastián BOUTIQUE HOTEL **$$$**
(☎222-242-65-23; www.mesonsansebastian.com; Av 9 Oriente 6; r incl breakfast M$1300-1700; 📶) This elegant boutique hotel has a colorful courtyard, accommodating staff who speak English, and garners praise for being family-friendly. Each of the 17 rooms are individually decorated and named after a saint. All rooms have TV, phone, minibar and antique furnishings. During quiet periods the hotel offers discounts of up to 40%.

El Sueño Hotel & Spa BOUTIQUE HOTEL **$$$**
(☎800-690-84-66, 222-232-64-89, 222-232-64-23; www.elsueno-hotel.com; Av 9 Oriente 12; ste incl breakfast M$1550-2900; P ❄ 📶) An oasis of minimalist chic amid the colonial bustle of Puebla's old town, El Sueño's 11 rooms are sleek, high-ceilinged and thematically decorated. Each is inspired by a different female Mexican artist. There's a hot tub and sauna, plasma TVs in the rooms and a martini bar in the lobby. Rooms are discounted on Sundays.

Mesón Sacristía de la Compañía BOUTIQUE HOTEL **$$$**
(☎222-242-45-13; www.mexicoboutiquhotels.com/mesonsacristia; Calle 6 Sur 304; ste incl breakfast M$1600-2000; P 📶) With eight rooms set around a bright, kitschy, pink courtyard, this small inn feels like the home of an eccentric grandmother. The junior suites are actually just standard rooms, while the two master suites are bigger and worthy of the title. The downstairs restaurant, which serves aromatic US-style breakfasts and refined *poblano* cuisine, gets rave reviews from guests.

Casona de la China Poblana LUXURY HOTEL **$$$**
(☎222-242-56-21; www.casonadelachinapoblana.com; cnr Calle 4 Norte & Av Palafox y Mendoza; ste M$2242-3776; P) This elegant boutique hotel is stunning and knows it. Shamelessly dubbing itself Puebla's 'most exclusive hotel,' the China Poblana has massive, gorgeous suites decorated in a mixture of styles, a lovely courtyard and La Cocina de la China Poblana (its restaurant).

Eating

Puebla's culinary heritage, of which *poblanos* are rightly proud, can be explored in a range of eateries throughout the city, from humble street-side food stalls to elegant colonial-style restaurants. However, given the city's renown as a culinary center, it's surprising how few truly excellent high-end restaurants there are.

Mercado de Sabores Poblanos MARKET **$**
(Av 4 Poniente btw Calles 11 & 13 Norte) The 6570-sq-m Mercado de Sabores Poblanos is a thrilling addition to Puebla's food scene. A sparkling food court serves local specialties like *cemitas* (a style of sandwich/burger unique to Puebla), *pipián verde* (green pumpkin-seed sauce), and *tacos árabes* (Arabic taco) from 130-odd vendors.

★**Las Ranas** TAQUERÍA **$**
(☎222-242-47-34; Av 2 Poniente 102; tacos & tortas M$8-20; ⏰noon-9:15pm) A true local institution, this is *the* place to try one of Puebla's great dishes: the *taco árabe*. At Las Ranas, you'll find unbelievably moist *al pastor* (shepherd-style) pork. Marinated and spit-grilled, then rolled in fresh, slightly charred Middle Eastern–style flat bread, these tacos are as simple as they are unforgettable. Both the main restaurant and its annex across the street **El Patio de las Ranas** (Av 2 Poniente 205) are perpetually full but the food – especially at this price – is worth the wait.

La Zanahoria VEGETARIAN **$**
(☎222-232-48-13; Av 5 Oriente 206; mains M$20-60, set meals M$60; ⏰7am-9pm; 🖉) This (entirely meat-free) godsend for vegetarians is an excellent place for lunch, and is just moments from the *zócalo*. The drawcard is the popular daily buffet (adult/child M$73/40 Monday to Thursday, M$94/49 Friday to Sunday) from 1-6pm in the spacious interior colonial courtyard, which features over 20 dishes and salads, such as corn croquettes, *chilaquiles* and Middle Eastern tabbouleh.

The extensive a la carte menu includes everything from veggie *hamburguesas* to *nopales rellenos* (stuffed cactus paddles). In the front of the restaurant is the express service area (including a juice bar and a healthfood snack shop).

El Mural de los Poblanos MEXICAN **$$**
(☎222-242-05-03; www.elmuraldelospoblanos.com; Av 16 de Septiembre 506; mains M$75-195; ⏲1-10pm Sun-Wed, noon-11pm Thu-Sat) Set back from the street in a gorgeous, plant-filled colonial courtyard, El Mural de los Poblanos serves excellent, traditional *poblano* dishes in an elegant setting. The house speciality is five kinds of *mole*. Other favorites include the smoky goat-cheese-stuffed *chile ancho relleno* (dried *poblano* chili) and the trilogy of *cemitas*. Reservations are a good idea on busy Friday and Saturday nights and holidays.

Amalfi Pizzeria PIZZERIA **$$**
(☎222-403-77-97; Av 3 Oriente 207B; pizzas M$100-160) It's easy to see why this excellent wood-oven pizzeria – with dim lighting, terracotta walls and beamed ceilings – is a popular date spot. In addition to a wide selection of fine, thin-crust pies, there's decent wine and traditional Italian accompaniments, like caprese salads. Because the dining room is small, a reservation wouldn't hurt.

Restaurante Sacristía MEXICAN **$$**
(☎222-242-45-13; Calle 6 Sur 304; mains M$95-142; ⏲8am-11:30pm Mon-Sat, 8am-7pm Sun) Set in the delightful colonial patio of the boutique hotel Mesón Sacristía de la Compañía, this is an elegant place for a meal of authentic *mole* and creative twists on rich *poblano* cuisine, or a cocktail or coffee in the intimate Confesionario bar. Live piano and violin soloists (and flower petals by request) lend a romantic ambience most nights from around 9pm.

If you like what you taste, inquire about the small-group cooking classes.

La Purificadora INTERNATIONAL **$$$**
(www.lapurificadora.com; Callejón de la 10 Norte 802, Paseo San Francisco, Barrio El Alto; mains M$115-235; Ⓟ) The restaurant at La Purificadora, one of Puebla's newest and chicest boutique hotels, is set in a spare, loft-like space with unfinished walls and long, narrow wood-plank tables. The menu, meanwhile, tends toward the indulgent and elaborate, with dishes such as jumbo shrimp with *chipotle* hollandaise or a cassoulet of Mennonite *asadero* cheese, dehydrated tomato and confit of onion.

Drinking & Nightlife

During the day students pack the sidewalk tables along the pedestrian-only block of Avenida 3 Oriente, near the university. At night, mariachis lurk around Callejón de los Sapos – Calle 6 Sur between Avenidas 3 and 7 Oriente – but they're being crowded out by the bars on the nearby Plazuela de los Sapos. These rowdy watering holes are packed on weekend nights, when many of them become live-music venues.

All Day Café CAFE
(☎222-242-44-54; Ave 7 Oriente; sandwiches M$40-55, sushi M$60) This cafe-bar, a student hangout just off the Plazuela de los Sapos,

PUEBLA'S SEASONAL TREATS

Justly famous for its incredible cuisine, Puebla also offers an array of seasonal, local delicacies that adventurous eaters should not miss.

Escamoles (March to June) – Ant larvae, look like rice and usually sautéed in butter.

Gusanos de maguey (April to May) – Worms that inhabit the maguey plant, typically fried in a drunken chili and *pulque* (a low alcohol brew made from the maguey plant) sauce.

Huitlacoche (June to October) – Inky-black corn fungus with an enchanting, earthy flavor. Sometimes spelt *cuitlacoche*.

Chiles en nogada (July to September) – Green chilies stuffed with *picadillo* (a mix of ground meat and dried fruit), covered with a creamy walnut sauce and sprinkled with red pomegranate seeds.

Chapulines (October to November) – Grasshoppers purged of digestive matter, then dried, smoked or fried in lime and chili powder.

is housed in a bright courtyard and turns into a club in the evenings. It serves a range of sandwiches, sushi, pastries, coffees and cocktails all day long (as the name suggests).

A Go Go LOUNGE
(Av 3 Oriente 603; [wi-fi]) A young crowd hang out at this arty venue, decorated with graffiti murals and '50s wallpaper. Live bands and DJs play in the cavernous bar, while the spacious courtyard has a summery buzz that is fuelled by the cheap, creative cocktails and good-sized bar food late into the evening.

Café Milagros CAFE
(cnr 3 Av Oriente & Calle 6 Sur; frappé M$35, pizzas M$90; ⏲10am-9pm Mon-Fri, 11am-9pm Sat & Sun) This is what a Mexican cafe would look like in a cartoon. Think shrines to Frida Kahlo, day of the dead trinkets, *lucha libre* (Mexican wrestling) paintings, devil masks, and colorful wood tables. It's a popular backdrop for sharing a passable pizza with a friend or sipping a frappé solo with your electronic gadget.

Celia's Cafe LIVE MUSIC
(5 Oriente 608; mains M$60-145; ⏲8pm-midnight Wed-Sat) Try before you buy at this sprawling bar/restaurant. Every *mole poblano* (Mexico's most famous dish), coffee and tequila shot is served up in (purchasable) Talavera-ware whipped up in Celia's own studio. From 8pm, musicians add old-world romance to the poblano decor with live piano, *trova* (troubadour-type folk music) or *bohemia* (more love songs).

Shopping

Puebla has plenty of shops selling the colorful, hand-painted ceramics known as Talavera. There are several good stores on the Plazuela de los Sapos and the streets around it. Designs reveal Asian, Spanish-Arabic and Mexican indigenous influences. Bigger pieces are expensive, delicate and difficult to transport.

A number of shops along Avenida 6 Oriente, to the east of Avenida 5 de Mayo, sell traditional handmade Puebla sweets such as *camotes* (candied sweet potato sticks) and *jamoncillos* (bars of pumpkin-seed paste).

For quirky antique stores, head to Callejón de los Sapos, around the corner of Avenida 5 Oriente and Calle 6 Sur. Most shops open from 10am through to 7pm. On Sunday, there is a lively outdoor antiques market here and at the Plazuela de los Sapos.

Talavera Uriarte CERAMICS
(☎222-232-15-98; www.uriartetalavera.com.mx; Av 4 Poniente 911; ⏲9am-7pm Mon-Fri, 10am-5pm Sat, 10am-4pm Sun) Unlike most of Puebla's Talavera shops, Uriarte still makes its pottery onsite. The showroom displays a gorgeous selection of high-quality, intricately painted pieces. Founded in 1824, the company is now owned by a Canadian expat. Factory tours are offered 10am to 1pm Monday through Friday.

El Parián Crafts Market HANDICRAFTS
(Plaza Parián) Browse local Talavera, onyx and trees of life, as well as the types of leather, jewelry and textiles that you'll find in other cities. Some of the work is shoddy, but there's also some quality handiwork and prices are reasonable.

Information

EMERGENCY

Cruz Roja (Red Cross; ☎222-235-86-31)
Tourist Police (☎800-903-92-00)

INTERNET ACCESS

There are several places to get online along Calle 2 Sur; most charge M$5 to M$10 per hour.

MEDICAL SERVICES

Hospital UPAEP (☎222-229-81-34; Av 5 Poniente 715)

MONEY

ATMs are plentiful throughout the city. Banks on the *zócalo* and Avenida Reforma have exchange and traveler's check facilities.

POST

Main Post Office (☎222-232-64-48; Av 16 de Septiembre s/n)

TOURIST INFORMATION

Municipal Tourist Office (☎222-404-50-08, 222-404-50-47; Portal Hidalgo 14; ⏲9am-8pm Mon-Fri, to 3pm Sun) English- and French-speaking office with free maps and excellent information on what's on in town.

State Tourist Office (☎222-246-20-44; Av 5 Oriente 3; ⏲8am-8pm Mon-Sat, 9am-2pm Sun) Information for destinations outside of Puebla. In the Casa de Cultura building, facing the cathedral yard.

Getting There & Away

AIR

Puebla's international airport **Aeropuerto Hermanos Serdán** (☎222-232-00-32; www.aeropuerto-puebla.es.tl) has patchy service, and until management improves and airlines offer additional routes, the Toluca airport is likely a better option. There are, however, several domestic Volaris flights. The airport is 22km west of Puebla, off Hwy 190.

BUS

Puebla's full-service **Central de Autobuses de Puebla** (CAPU; ☎222-249-72-11; www.capu.com.mx; Blvd Norte 4222) is 4km north of the *zócalo* and 1.5km off the autopista.

From Mexico City and towns to the west, most buses to and from Puebla use the capital's TAPO station, though some travel to Terminal Norte. The trip takes about two hours.

Both **ADO** (www.ado.com.mx) and **Estrella Roja** (ER; ☎800-712-22-84; www.estrellaroja.com.mx) travel frequently between the two cities, operating both 1st-class and deluxe buses with wi-fi internet.

From CAPU, there are buses at least once a day to almost everywhere to the south and east.

Frequent 'Cholula' *colectivos* (M$7.50, 30 minutes) leave from Avenida 6 Poniente near the corner with Calle 13 Norte.

CAR & MOTORCYCLE

Puebla is 123km east of Mexico City by Hwy 150D. Traveling east of Puebla, 150D continues to Orizaba (negotiating a cloudy, winding 22km descent from the 2385m-high Cumbres de Maltrata en route), Córdoba and Veracruz.

Getting Around

Most hotels and places of interest are within walking distance of Puebla's *zócalo*. At the CAPU bus station, buy a ticket at the kiosk for an **authorized taxi** (www.taxisautorizadoscapu.com; M$55) to the city center. Alternatively, follow signs for 'Autobuses Urbanos' and catch combi 40 (M$6) to Avenida 16 de Septiembre, four blocks south of the *zócalo*. The ride takes 15 to 20 minutes.

From the city center to the bus station, catch any northbound 'CAPU' *colectivo* from Blvd 5 de Mayo at Avenida Palafox y Mendoza, three blocks east of the *zócalo*, or from the corner of Calle 9 Sur and Avenida Reforma. All city buses and *colectivos* cost M$6.

Call **Radio Taxi** (☎222-243-70-59) for secure taxi service within the city – a good idea if you're traveling alone or going out at night.

Cholula

☎222 / POP 120,000 / ELEV 2170M

Though it's almost a suburb of Puebla these days, Cholula is far different in its history and relaxed daytime ambience. Owing to its large student population, the town has a surprisingly vibrant nightlife and some decent restaurants and accommodations options within a short walk of the huge *zócalo*.

Cholula is also home to the widest pyramid ever built – the Pirámide Tepanapa. Despite this claim to fame, the town's ruins are largely ignored because, unlike those of Teotihuacán or Tula, the pyramid has been so badly neglected over the centuries that it's virtually unrecognizable as a manmade structure.

History

Between around AD 1 and 600, Cholula grew into an important religious center, while powerful Teotihuacán flourished 100km to the northwest. Around AD 600, Cholula fell to the Olmeca-Xicallanca, who built nearby Cacaxtla. Some time between AD 900 and 1300 the Toltecs and/or Chichimecs took over and it later fell under Aztec dominance. There was also artistic influence from the Mixtecs to the south.

By 1519 Cholula's population had reached 100,000 and the Great Pyramid was unused and overgrown. Cortés, having befriended the neighboring Tlaxcalans, traveled here at the request of the Aztec ruler Moctezuma, but it was a trap and Aztec warriors had set an ambush. The Tlaxcalans tipped off Cortés about the plot and the Spanish struck first. Within a day they killed 6000 Cholulans before the city was looted by the Tlaxcalans. Cortés vowed to build a church here for every day of the year, or one on top of every pagan temple, depending on which legend

BUSES FROM PUEBLA

DESTINATION	FARE (M$)	DURATION	FREQUENCY (DAILY)
Cuetzalan	161	3½hr	4
Mexico City (TAPO or Tasqueña)	120-154	2-2½hr	50
Oaxaca	358-422	4-4½hr	6
Veracruz	288	3½hr	28

you prefer. Today there are 39 churches – far from 365 but still plenty for a small town.

The Spanish developed nearby Puebla to overshadow the old pagan center and Cholula never regained its importance, especially after a severe plague in the 1540s decimated its indigenous population.

Sights

Zona Arqueológica PYRAMID

(☎222-235-97-20; admission M$41; ⏲9am-6pm Tue-Sun) The **Pirámide Tepanapa**, located two blocks to the southeast of Cholula's central plaza, looks more like a hill than a pyramid and has a domed church on top so it's tough to miss. The town's big drawcard is no letdown with miles of tunnels veining the inside of the structure. The Zona Arqueológica comprises the excavated areas around the pyramid and the tunnels underneath.

Visitors enter via the tunnel on the north side, which takes you on a spooky route through the center of the pyramid. Several pyramids were built on top of each other during various reconstructions, and over 8km of tunnels have been dug beneath the pyramid by archaeologists to penetrate each stage, with 800m accessible to visitors. You can see earlier layers of the building from the access tunnel, which is a few hundred meters long.

The access tunnel emerges on the east side of the pyramid, from where you can follow a path around to the **Patio de los Altares** on the south side. Ringed by platforms and unique diagonal stairways, this plaza was the main approach to the pyramid. Three large stone slabs on its east, north and west sides are carved in the Veracruz interlocking scroll design. At its south end is an Aztec-style altar in a pit, dating from shortly before the Spanish conquest. On the mound's west side is a reconstructed section of the latest pyramid, with two earlier exposed layers.

The Pirámide Tepanapa is topped by the brightly decorated **Santuario de Nuestra Señora de los Remedios**. It's a classic symbol of conquest, though possibly an inadvertent one as the church may have been built before the Spanish realized the mound contained a pagan temple. You can climb to the church for free via a path starting near the northwest corner of the pyramid.

The small **Museo de Sitio de Cholula** (Calz San Andrés), across the road from the ticket office and down some steps, provides the best introduction to the site with a cutaway model of the pyramid mound showing the various superimposed structures. Admission is included in the site ticket.

Zócalo PLAZA

The **Ex-Convento de San Gabriel** (Plaza de la Concordia), facing the east side of Cholula's huge *zócalo* (also known as the Plaza de la Concordia), includes a tiny but interesting **Franciscan library** and three fine churches, all of which will appeal to travelers interested in antique books and early religious and Franciscan history. On the left, as you face the ex-convent from the *zócalo,* is the Arabic-style **Capilla Real**, which has 49 domes and dates from 1540. In the middle is the 19th-century **Capilla de la Tercera Orden**, and on the right is the **Templo de San Gabriel** founded in 1530 on the site of a pyramid.

Museo de la Ciudad de Cholula MUSEUM

(Casa del Caballero Águila; ☎222-261-90-53; cnr Av 5 de Mayo & Calle 4 Oriente; admission M$20, Sun free; ⏲9am-3pm Thu-Tue) The excellent Museo de la Ciudad de Cholula is housed in a fantastically restored colonial building on the *zócalo*. The small but strong collection includes ceramics and jewelry from the Pirámide Tepanapa, as well as later colonial paintings and sculptures. Most interestingly, you can watch through a glass wall as museum employees painstakingly restore smashed ceramics and repair jewelry.

Festivals & Events

Festival de la Virgen de los Remedios DANCE

Perhaps the most important Cholulan holiday of the year, this festival is celebrated the week of September 1. There are traditional dances daily atop the Great Pyramid. Cholula's regional feria is held during the following weeks.

Quetzalcóatl Ritual CULTURAL

On both the spring (late March) and fall (late September) equinoxes, this pre-Hispanic ritual is re-enacted with poetry, sacrificial dances, firework displays and music performed on traditional instruments at the pyramids.

Shrove Tuesday HISTORICAL

Masked Carnaval dancers re-enact a battle between French and Mexican forces in Huejotzingo, 14km northwest of Cholula off Hwy 190.

Cholula

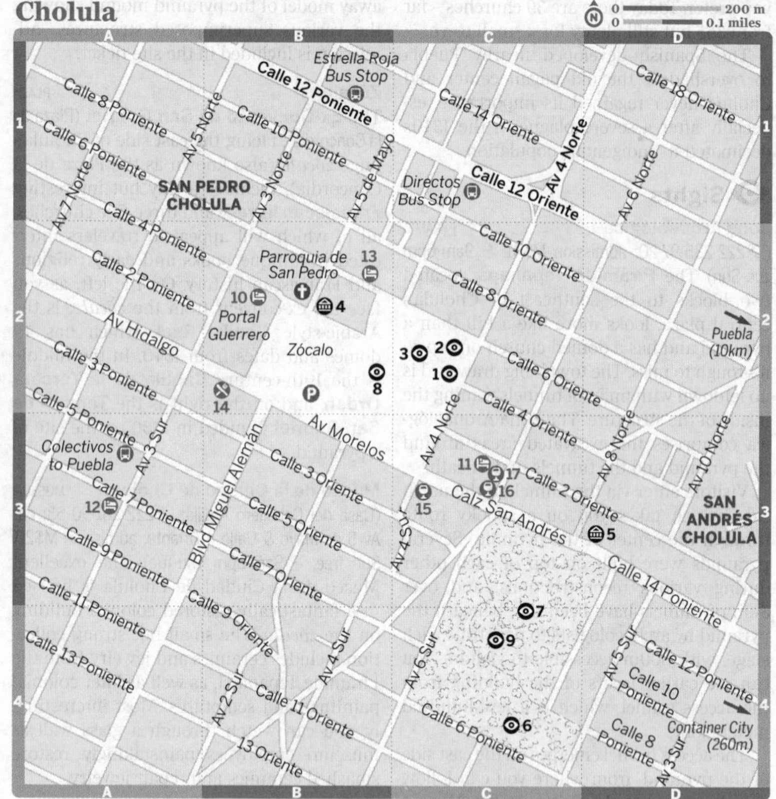

Sleeping

With a clutch of good-value hotels and a couple of boutique favorites, Cholula makes an attractive alternative to staying in Puebla for those who prefer a laid-back pace.

Hotel Real de Naturales BUSINESS HOTEL **$$**
(222-247-60-70; www.hotelrealdenaturales.com; Calle 6 Oriente 7; s/tr/q M$550/650/750, ste M$950-1000; P) This new 45-room hotel was built in the colonial style to blend into the surrounding architectural landscape and it succeeds with its shady courtyards, tile baths, tasteful black and white photography and elegant archways. Its central location and many considered details make it an excellent bargain for the price.

Casa Calli BOUTIQUE HOTEL **$$**
(222-261-56-07; www.hotelcasacalli.com; Portal Guerrero 11; r from M$490; P) Right on the *zócalo*, the hotel contains 40 stylishly minimalist rooms, an attractive pool and an Italian restaurant-bar in the lobby. Prices are reasonable and weekend spa packages are available (from M$1980).

★ **Estrella de Belem** LUXURY HOTEL **$$$**
(222-261-19-25; www.estrelladebelem.com.mx; Calle 2 Oriente 410; r incl breakfast M$1888-2478; P) This beautiful hotel has just six rooms, each with gorgeous, thoughtful touches like radiant-heat floors, noise-blocking windows, bathtubs and LCD TVs. The master suites are especially luxurious, with fireplaces and Jacuzzis. Common areas include a lovely, grassy courtyard and a small, rooftop swimming pool that has views over the town. No children under 12.

Hotel La Quinta Luna LUXURY HOTEL **$$$**
(222-247-89-15; www.laquintaluna.com; Av 3 Sur 702; r incl breakfast M$1650, ste M$1942-3965; P) This rarefied hotel is popular with a wealthy weekender crowd. The six stylish

Cholula

Sights

1 Capilla de la Tercera Orden C2
2 Capilla Real C2
3 Ex-Convento de San Gabriel C2
4 Museo de la Ciudad de Cholula B2
5 Museo de Sitio de Cholula D3
6 Patio de los Altares C4
7 Santuario de Nuestra Señora de los Remedios C4
8 Templo de San Gabriel B2
9 Zona Arqueológica C4

Sleeping

10 Casa Calli B2
11 Estrella de Belem C3
12 Hotel La Quinta Luna A3
13 Hotel Real de Naturales B2

Eating

14 Güero's B2

Drinking & Nightlife

15 Bar Reforma C3
16 La Lunita C3
17 Maaema C3

rooms occupy a thick-walled 17th-century mansion set around a charming garden and are a gorgeous mix of colonial antiques, plush bedding, flatscreen TVs, and contemporary art. Meetings with the featured artists are happily arranged. There's a great library and the excellent restaurant is open to nonguests who reserve ahead.

Eating & Drinking

Güero's MEXICAN $$

(222 247-11-04; Av Hidalgo 101; mains M$42-106; 9am-11pm;) Decorated with antique photos of Cholula, this lively, family-friendly hangout has been a Cholula institution since 1955. Besides pizza, pasta and burgers, hearty Mexican choices include *pozole, cemitas* and quesadillas, all served with a delicious *salsa roja* (red sauce).

Maaema CLUB

(maaema.mx; Av 6 Norte 1; 2pm-midnight Sun-Thurs, to 3am Fri & Sat) It's easy to strike up a conversation with the casual, young crowd at this busy new restaurant-club, where all the furniture is recycled. Chat about the bicycle stools, sewing-machine tables or sawn-in-half bathtub sofas. Then admire the roofgarden view of the church atop Pirámide Tepanapa, lit up like a golden beacon, while the electro plays. Their veggie burgers and bar food isn't bad either.

Container City BAR

(www.containercity.com.mx; cnr Calle 12 Oriente & Av 2 Sur) This collection of trendy bars, restaurants, clubs and shops is hopping at night. Set in revamped and stacked former-shipping containers, it's the hangout of choice for Cholula's fashionistas and hipsters.

Bar Reforma CANTINA

(cnr Avs 4 Norte & Morelos; 6pm-12:30am Mon-Sat) Attached to Hotel Reforma, Cholula's oldest drinking spot is a classic, corner abode with swinging doors and plastic flowers, specializing in iceless margaritas and freshly prepared sangrias. After 9pm it's popular with the university pre-clubbing crowd.

La Lunita CANTINA

(222-247-00-11; www.lalunita.com; cnr Avs Morelos & 6 Norte 419; mains M$52-162) In the shadow of the pyramid, this raucous, family-run bar has been in business since 1939. Painted in bright colors and decorated with an assortment of old advertising posters and other knickknacks, La Lunita looks a lot like the movie version of a Mexican cantina. It's popular with locals who come for its broad-ranging menu, live music, football on TV and plentiful drinks.

Getting There & Away

Frequent *colectivos* to Puebla (M$7.50, every 20 minutes) leave from the corner of Calles 5 Poniente and 3 Sur, while larger *directos*, or buses (M$8, every 30 minutes), leave from the corner of Calles 2 Norte and 12 Oriente. Buses and *colectivos* stop two or three blocks north of the *zócalo*.

Popocatépetl & Iztaccíhuatl

Mexico's second- and third-highest peaks, volcanoes Popocatépetl (po-po-ka-*te*-pet-l; 5452m) and Iztaccíhuatl (is-ta-*see*-wat-l; 5220m) form the eastern rim of the Valle de México, about 40km west of Puebla and 70km southeast of Mexico City. While the craterless Iztaccíhuatl is dormant, Popocatépetl (Náhuatl for 'Smoking Mountain,' also called 'Don Goyo' and 'Popo') is very active, and its summit has been off-limits for the last decade. Legend has it that Iztaccíhuatl resembles a sleeping woman who laid down and died with grief for Popocatépetl, who returned from war to find her gone, and is still now explosively angry for his loss. Between 1994 and 2001, Popo's major bursts of activity triggered evacuations of 16 villages and warnings to the 30 million people who live within striking distance of the crater. In 2013, explosions catapulted ash 3km into the sky, forcing six US airlines to cancel flights to and from airports in Mexico City and Toluca.

Mexico's **Centro Nacional de Prevención de Desastres** (National Disaster Prevention Center; ☎24hr hotline 55-5205-1036; www.cenapred.gob.mx) monitors volcanic activity via variations in gas emissions and seismic intensity. Though almost entirely in Spanish, the website posts daily webcam photo captures and updates on conditions.

Historically, Popo has been relatively tranquil, with most activity occurring in the cooler winter months when ice expands and cracks the solidified lava around the crater rim. The last really big blast occurred over a thousand years ago, and volcanologists estimate that there's a 10% chance of one in the near future. In recent years, the only danger to visitors has been the air quality. The air can feel heavily polluted when there is volcanic activity, so asthmatics and people with breathing difficulties should check pollution levels before they head outdoors, and drink plenty of water. The good news is that the fetching Iztaccíhuatl (White Woman), 20km north of Popo from summit to summit, remains open to climbers.

Hiking & Climbing

Izta's highest peak is **El Pecho** (5220m). All routes require a night on the mountain and there's a shelter hut between the staging point at La Joya, the main southern trailhead, and Las Rodillas, one of Itza's lesser peaks, that can be used during an ascent of El Pecho. On average, it takes at least five hours to reach the hut from La Joya, then another six hours from the hut to El Pecho, and six hours back to the base.

Before making the ascent, climbers must contact the **Parque Nacional Iztaccíhuatl-Popocatépetl** (☎597-978-38-29; http://iztapopo.conanp.gob.mx; Plaza de la Constitución 9B, Amecameca; ⏲9am-6pm Mon-Fri, to 3pm Sat), located on the southeast side of Amecameca's *zócalo*, to register. All visitors must pay the M$27 per day park entrance fee. The park's website also offers excellent maps and a handy downloadable English-language climbing guide.

About 24km up from Amecameca, there are lower-altitude trails through pine forests and grassy meadows near the Paso de Cortés, the trailhead which leads to breathtaking glimpses of nearby peaks. La Joya is another 4km from there. *Colectivos* departing from Amecameca's plaza for Paso de Cortés cost M$40. From the national park office, taxis will take groups to La Joya (40 minutes) for a negotiable M$350.

Basic shelter is available at the **Altzomoni Lodge** (beds per person M$27), roughly halfway between the Paso de Cortés and La Joya. You must reserve in advance at the park office and bring bedding, warm clothes and drinking water.

Climate & Conditions

It can be windy and well below freezing any time of year on Izta's upper slopes, and it's nearly always below freezing near the summit at night. Ice and snow are fixtures here; the average snow line is 4200m. The ideal months for ascents are November to February, when there is hard snowpack for crampons. The rainy season (April to October) brings with it the threat of whiteouts, thunderstorms and avalanches.

Anyone can be affected by altitude problems, including life-threatening altitude sickness. Even the Paso de Cortés is at a level where you should be aware of the symptoms.

Guides

Iztaccíhuatl should be attempted *only* by experienced climbers. Because of hidden crevices on the ice-covered upper slopes, a guide is advisable. Besides the following reader recommendations, the national park office may have suggestions.

Livingston Monteverde (www.tierradentro.com), who is based in Tlaxcala, is a founding member of the Mexican Mountain Guide Association, with 25 years of climbing experience. He speaks fluent English, basic French and some Hebrew and Italian.

Mario Andrade (☎55-1826-2146; mountainup@hotmail.com) is an authorized, English-speaking guide, based in Mexico City, who has led many Izta climbs. His fee is US$350 for one person, less per person for groups. The cost includes round-trip transportation from Mexico City, lodging, mountain meals and rope usage.

Tlaxcala

☎246 / POP 90,000 / ELEV 2250M

The capital of Mexico's smallest state is unhurried and unself-conscious, with a compact colonial downtown defined by grand government buildings, imposing churches and one of the country's more stunning central plazas. Despite its small stature, Tlaxcala is neither timid nor parochial. With a large student population, good restaurants and bars, and a handful of excellent museums, the city has a surprisingly vibrant cultural life. Because there's no single attraction that puts Tlaxcala on tourist itineraries it remains largely undiscovered – despite its location less than two hours from Mexico City.

Two large central plazas converge at the corner of Avenidas Independencia and Muñoz. The northern one, which is surrounded by colonial buildings, is the *zócalo* called Plaza de la Constitución. The southern square is Plaza Xicohténcatl. Traveling by bus you'll arrive a 10-minute walk from the *zócalo* at the city's hilltop station.

History

In the last centuries before the Spanish conquest, numerous small warrior kingdoms *(señoríos)* arose in and around Tlaxcala. Some of them formed a loose federation that remained independent of the Aztec empire as it spread from the Valle de México in the 15th century. The most important kingdom seems to have been Tizatlán, now in ruins on the northeast edge of Tlaxcala.

When the Spanish arrived in 1519, the Tlaxcalans fought fiercely at first but ultimately became Cortés' staunchest allies against the Aztecs (with the exception of one chief, Xicohténcatl the Younger, who tried to rouse his people against the Spanish and is now a Mexican hero). In 1527 Tlaxcala became the seat of the first bishopric in New Spain but a plague in the 1540s devastated the population and the town has played only a supporting role ever since.

Sights

Museo de Arte de Tlaxcala MUSEUM
(☎246-462-15-10; Plaza de la Constitución 21; adult/student/under 12 M$20/10/free, Sun free; ⏲10am-6pm Tue-Sun) This fantastic contemporary art museum houses an excellent cache of early Frida Kahlo paintings which were returned to the museum after several years on loan to other museums around the world. Both the museum's main building on the *zócalo* and the smaller **branch** (Guerrero 15) FREE hold interesting temporary exhibits and a good permanent collection of modern Mexican art.

Plaza de la Constitución PLAZA
It's easy to pass an afternoon reading or just people-watching in Tlaxcala's shady, spacious *zócalo* – especially now that the plaza offers free wi-fi access.

The 16th-century **Palacio Municipal**, a former grain storehouse, and the **Palacio de Gobierno** occupy most of its north side. Inside the latter there are vivid murals of Tlaxcala's history by Desiderio Hernández Xochitiotzin. The 16th-century building on the plaza's northwest side is the **Palacio de Justicia**, the former Capilla Real de Indios, built for the use of indigenous nobles. The handsome mortar bas-reliefs around its doorway include the seal of Castilla y León and a two-headed eagle, symbol of the Hapsburg monarchs who ruled Spain in the 16th and 17th centuries.

Off the northwest corner of the *zócalo* is the orange stucco and blue-tile **Parroquia de San José**. As elsewhere in the *centro histórico,* bilingual signs explain the significance of the church and its many fountains.

Museo Vivo de Artes y Tradiciones Populares MUSEUM
(☎246-462-23-37; Blvd Sánchez 1; adult/student M$15/8; ⏲10am-6pm Tue-Sun) This popular arts museum has displays on Tlaxcalan village life, weaving and *pulque*-making, sometimes with demonstrations. Artisans serve as guides to the over 3000 artifacts on display. The cafe and handicrafts next door at the **Casa de Artesanías** are also worth a look.

Museo de la Memoria MUSEUM
(☎246-466-07-92; Av Independencia 3; adult/student M$15/free; ⏲10am-5pm) This modern history museum looks at folklore through a multimedia lens, and has well-presented exhibits on indigenous government, agriculture and contemporary festivals. Explanations are only in Spanish.

Santuario de la Virgen de Ocotlán CHURCH
(M$6) One of Mexico's most spectacular churches is an important pilgrimage site for those who believe the Virgin appeared here in 1541 – her image stands on the main altar

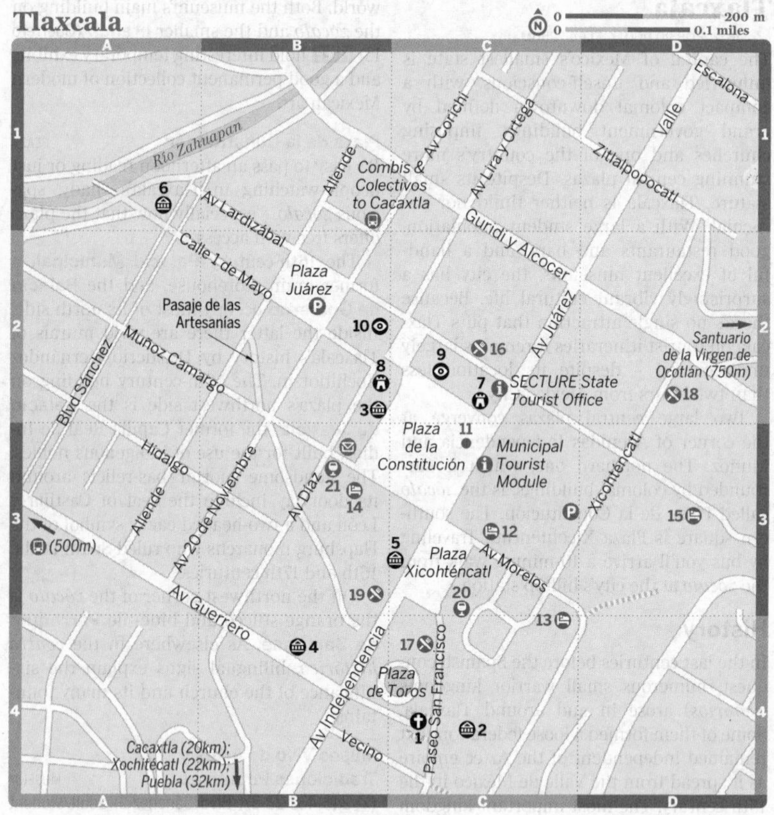

Tlaxcala

Sights

1 Capilla Abierta....C4
Casa de Artesanías....(see 6)
2 Ex-Convento Franciscano de la Asunción....C4
3 Museo de Arte de Tlaxcala....B2
4 Museo de Arte de Tlaxcala Museum....B4
5 Museo de la Memoria....C3
Museo Regional de Tlaxcala....(see 2)
6 Museo Vivo de Artes y Tradiciones Populares....A1
7 Palacio de Gobierno....C2
8 Palacio de Justicia....B2
9 Palacio Municipal....C2
10 Parroquia de San José....B2

Activities, Courses & Tours

11 Tranvía El Tlaxcalteca....C3

Sleeping

12 Hostería de Xicohténcatl....C3
13 Hotel Alifer....C4
14 Hotel Posada San Francisco....B3
15 Posada La Casona de Cortés....D3

Eating

16 Antiokía....C2
17 Fonda del Convento....C4
18 La Zana-Hora....D2
19 Tirol....B3

Drinking & Nightlife

20 Pulquería Tía Yola....C3
21 Vinos y Piedra....B3

in memory of the apparition. The classic Churrigueresque facade features white stucco 'wedding cake' decorations contrasting with plain red tiles. During the 18th century, indigenous artisan Francisco Miguel spent 25 years decorating the altarpieces and the chapel beside the main altar.

Visible from most of the town, the hilltop church is 1km northeast of the *zócalo*. Walk north from the *zócalo* on Avenida Juárez/Avenida Independencía for three blocks, then turn right onto Zitlalpopocatl. Alternatively, 'Ocotlán' *colectivos* travel along this same route.

Ex-Convento Franciscano de la Asunción HISTORIC BUILDING

This former monastery is up along a shaded path from the southeast corner of Plaza Xicohténcatl. Built between 1537 and 1540, it was one of Mexico's earliest monasteries and its church – which is the city's cathedral – has a beautiful Moorish-style wooden ceiling.

Just below the monastery, beside the 19th-century Plaza de Toros (bullring), is a **capilla abierta** (open chapel) with three unique Moorish-style arches. One of the entrances is locked, but you can access the *capilla* from other entry points.

Museo Regional de Tlaxcala (☎246-462-02-62; adult M$41, under 13 & over 60 free; ⊙10am-6pm), housed within the monastery building, has a large collection of religious paintings and sculpture and some pre-Hispanic artifacts from nearby archaeological sites.

Courses

Estela Silva's Mexican Home Cooking School COOKING COURSE

(☎246-468-09-78; www.mexicanhomecooking.com) Learn to cook *poblano* cuisine with Señora Estela Silva and her sous-chef husband Jon Jarvis, in the couple's Talavera-tiled kitchen in Tlacochcalco, 10km south of Tlaxcala. The English-Spanish bilingual course includes all meals plus lodging in private rooms with fireplaces (transportation to/from the school can be arranged). An all-inclusive, six-night/five-day course is US$1798 but shorter stays can also be arranged.

Tours

Tranvía El Tlaxcalteca BUS TOUR

(☎246-458-53-24; Plaza de la Constitución, Portal Hidalgo 6; adult/child M$50/35; ⊙every 2hr 10am-7pm) This motorized streetcar visits 33 downtown sights with Spanish narration. No reservations necessary.

Festivals & Events

Virgen de Ocotlán RELIGIOUS

On the third Monday in May, the figure of the Virgen de Ocotlán is carried from its hilltop perch at the Santuario de La Virgen de Ocotlán to neighboring churches, attracting equal numbers of onlookers and believers. Throughout the month, processions commemorating the miracle attract pilgrims from around the country.

Nacional de Danza Folklórica DANCE

This vibrant celebration brings dancers from around the country to Tlaxcala's Teatro Xicohténcatl during the last week of September.

Fiesta de Todos los Santos TRADITIONAL

Tlaxcala's Fiesta de Todos los Santos draws people from around the state between late October and mid-November, when *charrería* (horsemanship), bullfights and other rodeo-inspired pageantry take center stage. The festival kicks off with a *pamplonada* (running of the bulls) and includes Día de Muertos activities.

Sleeping

★Posada La Casona de Cortés BOUTIQUE HOTEL $$

(☎246-462-20-42; lacasonadecortes.com.mx; Av Lardizábal 6; r from M$795, ste $M1015; P 📶) Set around a lush courtyard with fruit trees and a fountain, this affordable boutique hotel seems almost too good to be true. The rooms, which have firm beds, tiled floors and high-pressure showers, are decorated with Mexican *artesanías* (handicrafts). The bar has a working 1950s jukebox and a roof deck with views of church steeples and volcanic peaks.

Hotel Alifer BUSINESS HOTEL $$

(☎246-462-30-62; www.hotelalifer.com.mx; Av Morelos No 11; r M$450-650; P 📶) The motel-style Hotel Alifer is up a small hill from the *zócalo* and while some rooms are a bit dingy and dark (avoid bottom-floor rooms that face the echoing hallways and lack exterior windows), upstairs rooms are clean and spacious with TV and phone. There's free wi-fi in the lobby.

Hostería de Xicohténcatl GUESTHOUSE $$
(☎246-466-33-22; Portal Hildalgo 10; s/d/tr M$400/450/600, ste M$650-1200; P 📶) Half of the 16 rooms at this straightforward budget *hostería* are large, multiroom suites with kitchens, making it a bargain for families, groups or those in town for an extended stay. The *hostería* is clean, if a bit sterile, and the location – right on Plaza Xicohténcatl – is excellent. Wi-fi only reaches rooms closest to the lobby.

Hotel Posada San Francisco LUXURY HOTEL $$$
(☎246-462-60-22; www.posadasanfrancisco.com; Plaza de la Constitución 17; r M$1400, ste M$1900-2800; P ❄ 📶 🏊) The bull fighter themed bar at this hotel is the kind of place you'd expect to find a famous author swilling fine tequila – check out the stained-glass ceiling in the lobby, the pool and the airy patio restaurant. While the building evokes 17th-century grandeur, the rooms are modern. All have bathtubs – a rarity in Mexican hotels – and air-conditioning.

Eating & Drinking

For a small city, Tlaxcala has an impressive number – and diversity – of good restaurants. The eastern side of the *zócalo* is overrun by underwhelming sidewalk cafes but there are better options on the south side and on the nearby Plaza Xicohténcatl. Tlaxcala's market is one of the most pleasant around.

La Zana-Hora VEGETARIAN $
(☎246-462-27-03; Calle Xicohténcatl #21B; comida corrida $48; ⊙1-5:30pm Mon-Fri lunch, closed Sat & Sun; 🌱) All your pesos pay for the tasty vegetarian dishes here, not the basic decor. The menu includes a self-service salad bar, while the potato and *nopal* (cactus) burgers are smothered in a *mole verde* (a type of chili sauce) so nutty that it's almost satay.

Antiokía CAFE $
(☎246-144-13-32; Av Lardizábal 35C; ⊙6-10:30pm Mon-Sat) There's no sign outside this romantic, hole-in-the-wall hangout but you'll know it by the smell – an irresistible mix of chocolate, freshly ground coffee and exotic teas. Mostly a cafe and dessert shop, Antiokía also serves savory fondues and paninis.

Pulquería Tía Yola PULQUE BAR
(☎246-462-73-09; Plaza Xicohténcatl 7; ⊙10am-9pm) Sip one of a dozen or so flavors of house-made *pulque* in a stone courtyard decorated with Día de los Muertos figurines and mosaics of Aztec gods. The sidewalk tables along the plaza are a prime location for weekend people-watching.

Vinos y Piedra WINE BAR
(☎246 466-21-57; Plaza de la Constitución 19; tapas M$35-160; ⊙9am-midnight Mon-Sat, to 9pm Sun) This wine bar is complete with spittoons at each table, a basement wine cellar (visible through a section of see-through floor) and domestic and imported *vinos*. This hangout for Tlaxcala's elite serves elegant tapas-style small plates with an emphasis on high-falutin dishes such as grapes rolled in blue cheese. The sidewalk tables are great for an evening drink.

Fonda del Convento REGIONAL CUISINE $$
(☎246-462-07-65; Paseo de San Francisco 1; mains M$79-141; ⊙8am-8pm) This unassuming home-style restaurant has been a local favorite for four decades. The menu focuses on traditional Tlaxcalteco cuisine, including *gusanos* (maguey worms), *escamoles* (ant larvae), *mole poblano*, rabbit in *pulque* and a family-recipe *pipián* (green pumpkin-seed sauce).

Tirol MEXICAN $$
(☎246-462-37-54; Av Independencia 7A; mains M$50-250, Sat & Sun buffet lunch/dinner M$110/180; ⊙8am-9pm Tue-Sun) Modern with stark white decor and attentive service, this excellent, upscale restaurant is popular for its weekend buffet and swanky ambience after dark. The 'Platón Moctezuma' (M$450) – insect tasting-plate – is grand enough for an Aztec emperor, piled with *escamoles* (ant larvae), *chinocuiles* (red grubs that feed on maguey) and regular white *gusanos* (grubs).

Information

Several banks on Avenida Juárez, near the tourist office, exchange dollars and have ATMs. Internet cafes are plentiful, but there's also free wi-fi in and around the *zócalo*.

Farmacia Cristo Rey (Av Lardizábal 15; ⊙24hr) Around-the-clock pharmacy.

Hospital General (☎246-462-35-55; Corregidora s/n)

Police (☎246-464-52-57)

Post Office (cnr Avs Muñoz & Díaz)

SECTURE State Tourist Office (☎246-465-09-60; www.tlaxcala.gob.mx/turismo; cnr Avs Juárez & Lardizábal; ⊙9am-6pm Mon-Fri, 10am-6pm Sat) The English-speaking staff are eager to sing Tlaxcala's praises and equip travelers with good maps and a handful of brochures. They're also found at the tourist module on the east side of the *zócalo*, beside a useful bird's-eye view wall map of the town.

Getting There & Away

Tlaxcala's bus terminal sits on a hill 1km west of the central plaza. For Mexico City's TAPO terminal, **ATAH** (246-466-00-87) runs 1st-class buses (M$134, two hours) every 15 minutes. Frequent 2nd-class Verde buses go to Puebla (M$20). Taxis between the station and downtown cost M$35.

Getting Around

Most *colectivos* (M$5) passing the bus terminal are heading into town, although it takes just ten minutes to walk. Exit the terminal, turn right down the hill till you hit Avenida Guerrero, then turn right past the towering steps of **Escalinata de Héroes**. To reach the terminal from the center, catch a blue-and-white *colectivo* on the east side of Blvd Sánchez. Taxis between the terminal and the *zócalo* cost M$35.

Cacaxtla & Xochitécatl

These sister sites, about 20km southwest of Tlaxcala and 32km northwest of Puebla, are among Mexico's most intriguing.

Cacaxtla (ca-*casht*-la) is one of Mexico's most impressive ancient ruins with its many high-quality, vividly painted depictions of daily life. Rather than being relegated to a museum collection, these works – including frescoes of a nearly life-size jaguar and eagle warriors engaged in battle – are on display within the site itself. Located atop a scrubby hill with wide views of the surrounding countryside, the ruins were discovered in 1975 when men from the nearby village of San Miguel del Milagro, looking for a reputedly valuable cache of relics, dug a tunnel and uncovered a mural.

The much older ruins at Xochitécatl (so-chi-*te*-catl), 2km away and accessible from Cacaxtla on foot, include an exceptionally wide pyramid as well as a circular one. A German archaeologist led the first systematic exploration of the site in 1969, but it wasn't until 1994 that it was opened to the public.

History

Cacaxtla was the capital of a group of Olmeca-Xicallanca, or Putún Maya, who arrived in central Mexico as early as AD 450. After the decline of Cholula (which they probably helped bring about) in around AD 600, they became the chief power in southern Tlaxcala and the Puebla valley. Cacaxtla peaked from AD 650 to 950 and was abandoned by AD 1000 in the face of possibly Chichimec newcomers.

Two kilometers west of Cacaxtla and atop a higher hill, the ruins of Xochitécatl predate Christ by a millennium. Just who first occupied the spot is a matter of dispute, but experts agree that where Cacaxtla primarily served as living quarters for the ruling class Xochitécatl was chiefly used for gory Quecholli ceremonies honoring Mixcoatl, god of the hunt. That isn't to say Cacaxtla didn't hold similar ceremonies – the discovery of the skeletal remains of hundreds of mutilated children attest to Cacaxtla's bloody past.

Sights

Cacaxtla ARCHAEOLOGICAL SITE

From the parking lot opposite the site entrance it's a 200m walk to the ticket office, museum and restaurant.

From the ticket office it's another 600m downhill to the main attraction – a natural platform, 200m long and 25m high, called the **Gran Basamento** (Great Base), now sheltered under an expansive metal roof. Here stood Cacaxtla's main civic and religious buildings and the residences of its ruling priestly classes. At the top of the entry stairs is the **Plaza Norte**. From here, the path winds clockwise around the ruins until you reach the **murals**, many of which clearly show Maya influence among the symbols from the Mexican highlands. This combination of styles in a mural is unique to Cacaxtla.

Before reaching the first mural you'll come to a small patio, of which the main feature is an **altar** fronted by a small square pit, in which numerous human remains were discovered. Just beyond the altar you'll find the **Templo de Venus** which contains two anthropomorphic sculptures – a man and a woman – in blue, wearing jaguar-skin skirts. The temple's name is attributed to the appearance of numerous half-stars around the female figure which are associated with Earth's sister planet, Venus.

On the opposite side of the path, away from the Plaza Norte, the **Templo Rojo** contains four murals, only one of which is visible. Its vivid imagery is dominated by a row of corn and cacao crops whose husks contain human heads.

Facing the north side of Plaza Norte is the long **Mural de la Batalla** (Battle Mural), dating from before AD 700. It shows two warrior groups, one wearing jaguar skins and the other bird feathers, engaged in ferocious battle. The Olmeca-Xicallanca (the jaguar warriors with round shields) are clearly repelling invading Huastecs (the bird warriors with jade ornaments and deformed skulls).

Beyond the Mural de la Batalla, turn left and climb the steps to see the second major **mural group**, behind a fence to your right. The two main murals (c AD 750) show a figure in a jaguar costume and a black-painted figure in a bird costume (believed to be the Olmeca-Xicallanca priest-governor) standing atop a plumed serpent.

Xochitécatl ARCHAEOLOGICAL SITE

Because of its outline and the materials used, archaeologists believe the circular **Pirámide de la Espiral** was built between 1000 and 800 BC. Its form and hilltop location suggest it may have been used as an astronomical observation post or as a temple to Ehécatl, the wind god. From here the path passes three other pyramids.

The **Basamento de los Volcanes**, which is all that remains of the first pyramid, is the base of the Pirámide de los Volcanoes and made of materials from two periods. Cut square stones were placed over the original stones, visible in some areas, and then stuccoed over. In an interesting twist, the colored stones used to build Tlaxcala's municipal palace appear to have come from this site.

The **Pirámide de la Serpiente** gets its name from a large piece of carved stone with a snake head at one end. Its most impressive feature is the huge pot found at its center, carved from a single boulder, which was hauled from another region. Researchers surmise it was used to hold water.

Experts speculate that rituals honoring the fertility god were held at the **Pirámide de las Flores**, due to the discovery of several sculptures and the remains of 30 sacrificed infants. Near the pyramid's base – Latin America's fourth widest – is a pool carved from a massive rock, where the infants were believed to have been washed before being killed.

Tours

México Viejo TOUR

(246-466-85-83; mexicoviejotours.com; Interior 2, Guridi y Alcocer 50, Tlaxcala; adult/child M$570/390; depart 10am, return 2:30pm) A guided tour of the history of the site, this is a good option for travelers with more money than time.

Getting There & Away

Considering how close the archeological zone is to Mexico City, Tlaxcala and Puebla – it's roughly smack in the middle of the three cities – getting to and from Cacaxtla-Xochitécatl via public transit is inconvenient and time-consuming.

Cacaxtla is 1.5km uphill from a back road between San Martín Texmelucan (near Hwy 150D) and Hwy 119, the secondary road between Tlaxcala and Puebla. To reach the site from Tlaxcala, catch a 'San Miguel del Milagro' *colectivo* from the corner of Escalona and Sánchez Piedras, which will drop you off about 500m from Cacaxtla.

From Puebla, Flecha Azul buses go direct from the CAPU terminal to the town of Nativitas, about 3km east of Cacaxtla; from there, catch a 'Zona Arqueológica' *colectivo* to the site.

Between Cacaxtla and Xochitécatl, taxis (M$50) are available on weekends, or walk the 2km (about 25 minutes).

La Malinche

The long, sweeping slopes of this dormant 4460m volcano, named after Cortés' indigenous interpreter and lover, dominate the skyline northeast of Puebla.

The main route to the volcano is via Hwy 136; turn southwest at the 'Centro Vacacional Malintzi' sign. Before you reach the center, you must register at the entrance of the **Parque Nacional La Malintzi**. La Malinche, Mexico's fifth-tallest peak, is snowcapped only a few weeks each year, typically in May.

Centro Vacacional IMSS Malintzi (55-5238-2701; centrosvacacionales.imss.gob.mx; campsites M$50, cabins up to 6 people M$790-1170, up to 9 people M$1240; P), operated by the Mexican Social Security Institute, has 50 cabins, including rustic and 'luxury' options, at a frosty 3333m. This family-oriented resort has woodsy grounds and fine views of the peak. The remodeled cabins are basic but include TV, fireplace, hot water and kitchen with refrigerator. It gets crowded from Friday to Sunday but is quiet midweek. Those not staying can park here for M$35. Prices are about M$100 higher on weekends and holidays.

Beyond the vacation center, the road becomes impassable by car. It's about 1km by footpath to a ridge, from where it's an arduous five-hour round-trip hike to the top. Hikers should take precautions against altitude sickness.

Huamantla

☎247 / POP 52,000 / ELEV 2500M

Huamantla has invested greatly in its downtown area, gussying up its colonial city center and renovating its charming *zócalo*. With La Malinche looming over town, this is a pleasant base camp for exploring the surrounding countryside, once you get past its sprawling suburbs.

Huamantla sees a few sleepless nights during its annual **feria** in August. The day before the Feast of the Assumption (August 15), locals blanket the town's streets with elaborate carpets of flowers and colored sawdust. The following Saturday, there's a Pamplona-esque running of the bulls, similar to that in Spain – but more dangerous since the uncastrated males charge from two directions. During the feria, rates double and rooms are reserved well in advance. If everything is full, seek out a room in Puebla or Tlaxcala.

Sights

Museo de Títere MUSEUM
(☎247 472-10-33; Parque Juárez 15; adult/student & senior/child M$20/10/5, Sun free; ⏰10am-5pm Tue-Sat, 10am-3pm Sun) The national puppet museum displays dolls and marionettes from all around the world in a fantastic new building on the *zócalo*. It's a fun stop for the young and young at heart.

Sleeping & Eating

★**Hacienda Soltepec** HISTORIC HOTEL $$
(☎247-472-14-66; Carretera Huamantla–Puebla Km 3; r from M$670, ste from M$790; P) Just outside of town, this gorgeous renovated hacienda is a former movie set (María Félix stayed here for months while filming one of her classics), with views of La Malinche, horse stables, tennis courts and a fantastic in-house restaurant. The hacienda's owner leads a fun *pulque* tour (no more than four people, M$400).

Hotel Centenario HOTEL $$
(☎247-472-05-87; Juárez Norte 209; r M$300-600, ste M$700; P@) Just a short walk from the *zócalo*, Hotel Centenario has 33 bright pink rooms which are spacious, with new bathrooms and wi-fi access. The staff are helpful, and there's a good coffee shop in the lobby.

La Casa de los Magueyes MEXICAN $$
(Reforma Sur 202; mains M$90-154) A wonderful home-style restaurant that serves regional dishes made with seasonal ingredients such as *maguey* buds and wild mushrooms.

Getting There & Away

Oro and Suriano have frequent services from Puebla. ATAH runs buses here from Tlaxcala's main station every seven minutes (M$24). The bus doesn't always stop at a station, so be sure to tell the driver that you're going to Huamantla Centro to avoid missing the town entirely.

Cantona

Given its isolation, a good distance from any town of significance, the vast and incredibly well-preserved Mesoamerican city of **Cantona** (admission M$41; ⏰9am-7pm) is virtually unknown to travelers. With 24 ball courts discovered, this is now believed to be the biggest single urban center in Mesoamerica, stretched over 12 sq km in an ethereal lava-bed landscape dotted with cacti and yucca and enjoying incredible views of the Pico de Orizaba to the south.

The site was inhabited from AD 600 to 1000 and is of interest for two main reasons: unlike most other Mesoamerican cities, no mortar was used to build it, meaning all the stones are simply held in place by their weight. It's also unique in its design sophistication – all parts of the city are linked by an extensive network of raised roads connecting some 3000 residences. There are several small pyramids and an elaborate **acropolis** at the city's center. With good information panels in English and an access road, Cantona is now being promoted as a tourist attraction. The new **Museo de Sitio de Cantona** (☎276-596-53-07; adults/students M$45/free, Sun free; ⏰9am-6pm) is a modern, well organized onsite museum displaying 598 pre-Hispanic objects from the inhabitants of Cantona, with a large showcase of volcanic obsidian, including a 2000-year-old obsidian dagger used for human sacrifice. The focus is on how the people of the region once lived, really bringing it to life with cooking implements and the reconstruction of a thatched hut. The information panels are unfortunately only in Spanish for now.

From Oriental, which is the nearest decent-sized town, Grupo Salazar covered pickup-truck *colectivos* leave every 20 minutes from the corner of Carretera Federal

Puebla–Teziutlan and 8 Poniente for Cantona. The trucks have 'Tepeyahualco' (M$35, 45 minutes) on their windshield. Tell the driver your destination when you board.

Otherwise, taxis to the site are M$150 or more for a round-trip. If you have your own transportation, visiting Cantona makes for a good side trip en route to Cuetzalan.

Cuetzalan

233 / POP 6000 / ELEV 980M

One of the most exhilarating trips in the region, the gorgeous drive to Cuetzalan is an adventure in itself. Beyond the Zaragoza turnoff, the road becomes dramatic, snaking up hills and around hairpin bends, and offering breathtaking views. At the end of it all is the remote, humid town of Cuetzalan (Place of the Quetzals). A striking village built on a precipitous slope, Cuetzalan is famed for its vibrant festivals and Sunday *tianguis* (a weekly street market) that attract scores of indigenous people in traditional dress. On the clearest days you can see all the way from the hilltops to the Gulf coast, 70km away, as the quetzal flies.

Three structures rise above Cuetzalan's skyline: the plaza's freestanding **clock tower**, the Gothic spire of the **Parroquia de San Francisco** and, to the west, the tower of the French Gothic **Santuario de Guadalupe**, with its highly unusual decorative rows of *jarritos* (clay vases).

Sights

Las Brisas & Cascada del Salto WATERFALL

About 5km northeast of town, there's a pair of lovely waterfalls. The natural swimming pools beneath the falls are enticing – bring your bathing kit. Rickshaw mototaxis will deposit you at the trailhead and await your return.

Festivals & Events

Feria del Café y del Huipil TRADITIONAL

For several lively days around October 4, Cuetzalan celebrates both its patron saint, St Francis of Assisi, and the start of the coffee harvest with the Festival of Coffee and Huipiles, featuring hearty drinking, traditional quetzal dancing and airborne *voladores* (literally 'fliers'), the Totonac ritual in which men, suspended by their ankles, whirl around a tall pole.

The *voladores,* whose tradition was recognized as an Intangible Cultural Heritage by Unesco in 2009, perform for tourists (and tips) several times a day on weekends. It's a remarkable, not-to-be-missed performance.

Sleeping

Posada Jaqueline GUESTHOUSE $

(233-331-03-54; Calle 2 de Abril 2; s/d M$100/150) Jaqueline's 20 basic but clean rooms, overlooking the uphill side of the *zócalo,* are one of Cuetzalan's best-value-in-town options. Some upstairs rooms share a balcony and have views over the town.

Taselotzin LODGE $

(233-331-04-80; www.taselotzin.mex.tl; Yoloxóchitl, Barrio Zacatipan; dm/s/d/tr/q M$150/340/565/748/943, cabins for up to 4 people M$1100; P wi-fi) Just outside Cuetzalan, this hostel is run by an association of Nahua craftswomen who campaign for fair trade. The 10-room hotel offers traditional massages and a restaurant that serves local dishes. Follow the right-hand fork past the turnoff to the Puebla road; watch for an inconspicuous sign on the right-hand side, about 300m downhill.

Tosepan Kali LODGE $$

(233-331-09-25; www.tosepankali.com; Carretera Cuetzalan, Km 1.5, San Miguel Tzinacapan; s/d/tr/q incl breakfast M$350/700/1050/1400; pool) High on a hill midway between Cuetzalan and the nearby town of San Miguel Tzinacapan, Tosepan Kali looks like a treehouse nestled into the dense foliage. Constructed largely of bamboo and stone, this beautiful ecohotel – its name means 'our house' in Náhuatl – is the work of a local indigenous cooperative, and includes a large pool with valley views.

Hotel Posada Cuetzalan HOTEL $$

(233-331-01-54; www.posadacuetzalan.com; Zaragoza 12; s/d/tr/q M$655/913/1085/1220; P wi-fi pool) This handsome hotel, 100m uphill from the *zócalo,* has three large courtyards full of chirping birds, a swimming pool, a good restaurant featuring local fruit liqueurs and 36 well-kept rooms with tropical colors, tiled floors, lots of lightly stained wood and cable TV. There's wi-fi in the front rooms near the office.

Hotel La Casa de la Piedra BOUTIQUE HOTEL $$$

(233-331-00-30; www.lacasadepiedra.com; García 11; r M$810-1200, ste M$1530-1970; P pool) All 16 rooms in this renovated-yet-rustic former coffee-processing warehouse have picture windows and refinished wood floors.

Upstairs, the two-level suites accommodate up to four people and offer expansive views of the valley; downstairs rooms have tiled bathrooms, rough stone walls, and one or two beds.

Eating & Drinking

Regional specialties, sold at many roadside stands, include fruit wines, smoked meats and herbal liqueurs.

Restaurante Yoloxóchitl MEXICAN $
(233-331-03-35; Calle 2 de Abril No 1; mains M$35-60;) Beautifully decorated with plants, antiques, and ancient jukeboxes, Yoloxóchitl has views over the cathedral and a selection of salads, *antojitos* (tortilla-based snacks) and meat dishes, as well as wild mushrooms pickled in *chipotle* chili.

La Terraza SEAFOOD $$
(233-331-02-62; Hidalgo 33; mains M$80-150; 9am-9pm) This family-run restaurant – decorated with photos of the town's annual festivities – is extremely popular with locals for its large selection of breakfasts, *mariscos* (seafood), quesadillas, *platillos de la región,* and crawfish (in season).

Bar El Calate BAR
(233-331-05-66; Morelos 9B; shots from M$8) On the west side of the *zócalo,* this is *the* place to sip homemade hooch. There are 36 flavors, including liquors infused with coffee, limes, berries – you name it. Try the all-curing *yolixpán,* which is a local herbal liquor with an anis flavor.

Shopping

Centro de Desarrollo Artesanal Matachiuj ARTS & CRAFTS
(Hidalgo 917; 9am-7pm Wed-Mon) This new fair-trade market has a range of quality weavings and other crafts that come with the benefit of meeting the producer, as many wares are made onsite by local artisans.

Information

On the east side of the *zócalo,* there's a semi-helpful **tourist office** (233-331-00-15; 8am-4pm) with much-needed (although very unclear) town maps. Next door, Santander has an ATM.

Getting There & Away

From 6am to 6pm, Vía runs four buses a day between Puebla and Cuetzalan (M$161, 3½ hours). It pays to check road conditions and buy your return bus tickets in advance during the rainy season. Primera Plus runs six buses a day, starting at 4am, between Cuetzalan and Mexico City's TAPO bus station (M$350, six hours). The last bus to TAPO leaves at 3:50pm. There are additional services on Sundays.

Getting Around

On the town's steep streets, three-wheeled mototaxis (from M$25 or about M$100 an hour) offer rides with a thrill. Covered pickup trucks provide transportation (M$7) to nearby *pueblitos*.

Yohualichán

About 8km northeast of Cuetzalan, the last 2km via a steep cobblestone road, this ceremonial **pre-Hispanic site** (admission M$35; 9am-5:30pm) has niche pyramids similar to El Tajín's that are in varying states of ruin. The site is impressive and well worth a visit, not least for the great views from this side of the valley. The entrance is adjacent to Yohualichán's church and town plaza. To get here, ask at the tourist office for a *camión* (truck) passing by the pyramids.

SOUTH OF MEXICO CITY

A host of great destinations sit south of the Mexican capital, including mystical Tepoztlán, breathtaking Taxco and the superb caves at Grutas de Cacahuamilpa. The main road south from Mexico City, Hwy 95D, climbs from the smog-choked Valle de México into refreshing pine forests above 3000m and then descends to Cuernavaca, 'the city of eternal spring,' a long-time popular escape from Mexico City and a home-away-from-home for many North Americans and Chilangos who own second houses here.

The state of Morelos, which encompasses Cuernavaca and Tepoztlán, is one of Mexico's smallest and most densely populated. Valleys at different elevations have a variety of microclimates, and many fruits, grains and vegetables have been cultivated here since pre-Hispanic times. The archaeological sites at Tepoztlán and Xochicalco show signs of the agricultural Tlahuica civilization and the Aztecs who subjugated them. During the colonial era, most of the region was controlled by a few families, including descendants of Cortés. You can visit their palaces and haciendas, along with 16th-century churches and monasteries. Unsurprisingly, the *campesinos* of Morelos were fervent supporters of the Mexican Revolution, and local lad Emiliano Zapata is the state's hero. Those with an interest in the peasant revolutionary leader should head to Cuautla, the first city that Zapata conquered, and 6km further south to Anenecuilco, where he was born.

The mountainous state of Guerrero boasts utter gems such as the silver-mining tourist mecca Taxco, one of the best-preserved colonial towns in Mexico.

Tepoztlán

739 / POP 14,000 / ELEV 1700M

A weekend trip from the capital to Tepoztlán rarely disappoints. This beautifully situated small town with a well-preserved historic center surrounded by soaring jagged cliffs is just 80km south of Mexico City. As the birthplace of Quetzalcóatl, the omnipotent serpent god of the Aztecs over 1200 years ago (according to Mesoamerican legend), Tepoztlán is a major Náhuatl center and a mecca for New Agers who believe the area has a creative energy.

This *pueblo mágico* boasts an impressive pyramid, a great crafts market and a host of charming restaurants and hotels. It also retains indigenous traditions, with some elders still speaking Náhuatl and younger generations learning it in school, making it a rarity among the towns ringing the Mexican capital.

Everything in Tepoztlán is easily accessible on foot, except the cliff-top Pirámide Tepozteco, a 2.5km strenuous hike away. Street names change in the center of town; for example Avenida 5 de Mayo becomes Avenida Tepozteco north of the *zócalo*.

Sights

Pirámide Tepozteco PYRAMID

(admission M$42, Sun free; 9am-5pm) The uncontested main sight in town is this 10m-high pyramid, although it's actually some 400m *above* the town, perched atop a sheer cliff at the end of a very steep paved path that begins at the end of Avenida Tepozteco. Built in honor of Tepoztécatl, the Aztec god of the harvest, fertility and *pulque*, the pyramid is more impressive for its location than for its actual size. Be warned that the path is tough, so head off early to beat the heat and wear decent shoes. The 2km walk is not recommended to anyone not physically fit. At the top, depending on haze levels, the serenity and panorama of the valley make the effort worthwhile. Spotting the odd coati (raccoon-like animal) there is also a bonus. A store at the peak sells refreshments, but climbers should bring water with them anyway. Video camera use is M$45. The hike itself is free but to get close to the pyramid you must pay the admission fee.

Ex-Convento Domínico de la Natividad CHURCH

This monastery, situated east of the *zócalo*, and the attached church were built by Dominican priests between 1560 and 1588. The plateresque church facade has Dominican seals interspersed with indigenous symbols, floral designs and various figures, including the sun, moon and stars, animals, angels and the Virgin Mary. Upstairs, various cells house a bookstore, galleries and a **regional history museum**.

The monastery's arched entryway is adorned with an elaborate **seed mural** of pre-Hispanic history and symbolism. Every year during the first week of September local artists sow a new mural from 60 varieties of seeds.

Museo de Arte Prehispánico Carlos Pellicer MUSEUM

(739-395-10-98; Pablo González 2; admission M$10; 10am-6pm Tue-Sun) Behind the Dominican church, this archaeology museum has a small but interesting collection of pieces from around the country, donated by Tabascan poet Carlos Pellicer Cámara. The objects on display, a mix of human and animal figures, are lively and vibrant. The stone fragments depicting a pair of rabbits – the symbol for Ometochtli, the leader of the 400 rabbit gods of drunkenness – were discovered at the Tepozteco pyramid site.

Courses

La Villa Bonita COOKING COURSE

(777-169-72-32; www.lavillabonita.com; Aniceto Villamar 150, Colonia Tierra Blanca; 3-4 day courses incl 7 nights accommodations US$950-1950) On a hillside above town, this cooking school is the project of Ana García, one of Mexico's most celebrated chefs. García's course earns rave reviews from students. The six guest rooms have French doors opening onto a gorgeous patio overlooking the Tepoztlán valley, with a swimming pool carved out of

Tepoztlán

Sights

1 Ex-Convento Domínico de la Natividad B3
2 Museo de Arte Prehispánico Carlos Pellicer B3

Sleeping

3 Hotel Posada Ali B1
4 Posada del Tepozteco A3
5 Posada Nican Mo Calli B1

Eating

6 El Brujo A2
7 El Ciruelo B2
8 El Mango Biergarten-Restaurante B3
La Sibarita .... (see 4)
9 Los Buenos Tiempos A3
10 Los Colorines A2
11 Tepoznieves A3

volcanic rock. Check the website for other packages.

Festivals & Events

Tepoztlán is a hyper-festive place, with many Christian feasts superimposed on pagan celebrations. With eight *barrios* (neighborhoods) and an equal number of patron saints, there always seems to be some excuse for fireworks.

Carnaval DANCE

During the five days preceding Ash Wednesday (46 days before Easter Sunday), Carnaval features the colorful dances of the Huehuenches and Chinelos with feather headdresses and beautifully embroidered costumes.

Fiesta del Templo RELIGIOUS

On September 7, an all-night celebration goes off on Tepozteco hill near the pyramid, with copious consumption of *pulque* in honor of Tepoztécatl. The following day is the Fiesta del Templo, a Catholic celebration featuring theater performances in Náhuatl. The holiday was first intended to coincide with – and perhaps supplant – the pagan festival, but the *pulque*-drinkers get a jump on it by starting the night before.

Sleeping

Tepoztlán has a range of good accommodation options, but as a small town with lots of visitors, it can sometimes be hard to find a room during festivals and on weekends. If you can't find a room, keep your eyes peeled for private homes offering weekend rooms, marked with *hospedaje económico* signs.

Posada Nican Mo Calli HOTEL $$

(☎739-395-31-52; www.hotelnican.com; Netzahualcóyotl 4A; r M$1150, ste M$1250-2100; P 🛜 ≋) With brightly painted public areas, a heated pool, stylish rooms (some with balconies and great mountain views) and plenty of animals hanging around, Nican Mo Calli is just right for a romantic weekend away and one of the best options in town. Rates discounted during the week.

Hotel Posada Ali GUESTHOUSE $$

(☎739-395-19-71; posadaali.com; Netzahualcóyotl 2C; r M$550-900; P 🛜 ≋) Ali is a friendly hotel with a mix of 20 comfortable rooms, from the small, darker and more affordable rooms on the lower floors to the larger upstairs. There's a *frontón* (jai alai) ballcourt and a small pool. The roof garden has lounge chairs for calming mountain views. Light sleepers may not like the nearby church bells throughout the night.

Posada del Valle RESORT **$$**

(☎739-395-05-21; www.posadadelvalle.com.mx; Camino a Mextitla 5; r M$950 Sun-Thurs, M$1450 Fri & Sat, spa package M$3240; P ≋) Located east of town, this hotel-spa has quiet, romantic rooms (no children under 16) and a good Argentine restaurant. Spa packages, which cost extra, include two nights' accommodations, breakfast, massages and a visit to the temascal (indigenous Mexican steam bath). It's 2km down Avenida Revolución 1910 – just follow the signs for the final 100m to the hotel.

★**Posada del Tepozteco** LUXURY HOTEL **$$$**

(☎739-395-00-10; www.posadadeltepozteco.com; Paraíso 3; r US$208-245, ste US$290-430; P @ ≋) This refined hotel was built as a hillside mansion in the 1930s. The 20 rooms are airy and individually decorated, most boasting magnificent views over town, and share a wonderful garden and pool. The guest book contains famous names, including Angelina Jolie, who stayed in room 5 when she dropped by. Rates are discounted up to 30% during the week.

Eating & Drinking

This small town is hopping on weekends, when cafes and bars fill up with enthusiastic visitors. Unfortunately for those visiting midweek, many of the best spots are only open Friday to Sunday.

El Brujo BAKERY **$**

(Av 5 de Mayo; breakfasts M$65-75; ⏲9am-9pm; ☑) This wonderful bakery-restaurant on the town's main drag is the best bet for a full breakfast (with excellent omelettes and Mexican standards like *chilaquiles* – strips of fried corn tortillas, bathed in sauce). It also has great coffee and fantastic desserts. Just looking at the cake case is likely to start you salivating.

Los Buenos Tiempos BAKERY **$**

(☎739-395-05-19; Av Revolución 1910 No 14B; pastries M$7-35) Head here for the best pastries around – the smell drifting over the *zócalo* alone will probably bring you on autopilot. There's also good coffee and a lively social scene, and it's a great place to buy a pastry breakfast to take up to the pyramid with you.

Tepoznieves ICE CREAM **$**

(Av Revolución 1910 s/n; scoops M$10-25) A homegrown ice-cream emporium, Tepoznieves serves some 100 heavenly flavors, including exotic scoops such as cactus and pineapple-chili. There are several branches across town.

La Sombra del Sabino CAFE **$$**

(☎739-395-03-69; www.lasombradelsabino.com.mx; Av Revolución 1910 No 45; mains M$95-105; ⏲10am-7pm Wed-Sun; ☎) This 'literary cafe' and bookstore serves coffee, tea, wine or beer and simple fare – pastries, sandwiches and salads – in a contemplative garden setting. La Sombra del Sabino also hosts readings and events, and sells a small selection of English-language books.

El Mango Biergarten-Restaurante GERMAN **$$**

(☎739-395-22-53; www.elmango.org; Campesinos 7; mains M$60-145; ⏲2-9pm Fri-Sun) Craving goulash, spaetzle, bratwurst and hearty, freshly baked bread? This German-run beer garden, just down the hill from the *zócalo*, serves genuine German food. To wash it down, Mango's beer list includes both imported European beers and domestic, artisanal *cerveza*. There's live jazz and blues on weekends. See the website for event calendar.

Axitla MEXICAN **$$**

(☎739-395-05-19; Av Tepozteco; breakfast M$40-110, mains M$80-150; ⏲10am-7pm Wed-Fri, from 9am Sat & Sun) This Swiss Family Robinson–style sprawling treehouse, just off the pathway to the archaeological site, is set amid thick forest. There's a good selection of breakfasts available (M$40 to M$100) and a wide-ranging Mexican and international menu, including chicken breast stuffed with *huitlacoche* in *chipotle* sauce, sweet and sour ribs, and quail.

Los Colorines MEXICAN **$$**

(☎739-395-01-98; Av Tepozteco 13; M$52-146; ⏲9am-9pm; ☑ ☺) Inside the pink exterior of this buzzing restaurant, the hearty Mexican fare bubbles away in *cazuelas* (clay pots) and tastes fresh and traditional – try the regional *chiles rellenos* (stuffed chilies) or *huauzontle* (broccoli-like flower buds smothered in cheese). Eating here is a joy for the piñatas, spaciousness and the sense of being at a fiesta at grandma's colourful ranch. Cash only.

★La Sibarita MEXICAN $$$

(☎739-395-00-10; www.posadadeltepozteco.com; Posada del Tepozteco; mains M$200-300; ⏰8am-10pm Sun-Thu, 8am-11pm Fri & Sat) High on a hill above town, the restaurant at Posada del Tepozteco has gorgeous views of the valley below. With surreal cliffs and a pyramid overhead, the restaurant's setting is striking. The menu features dishes such as chicken breast stuffed with goat cheese, *róbalo* (snook) carpaccio in vinaigrette and rose-petal *nieve* (frozen dessert) – all paired with imported wines.

El Ciruelo INTERNATIONAL $$$

(☎739 395-12-03; www.elciruelo.com.mx; Zaragoza 17; mains M$145-235; ⏰1-7pm Mon-Thu & Sun, to 11pm Fri & Sat; 👪) Set in a courtyard with views of the cliffs and pyramid, this long-standing favorite serves an impressive upscale menu of dishes from *camarones al curry* (curried shrimp) and *salmón chileno a la mantequilla* (Chilean salmon in butter sauce) to good pizzas, salads and international dishes, though prices seem a bit inflated. Saturdays and Sundays have special play areas for kids.

Shopping

Tepoz has a fantastic, atmospheric daily **market** that convenes on the *zócalo*. It's at its fullest on Wednesday and Sunday. As well as the daily fruit, vegetable, clothing and crafts on sale, on Saturday and Sunday stalls around the *zócalo* sell a wide selection of handicrafts.

Information

On the west side of the plaza, Bancomer and HSBC have ATMs. There are several internet cafes scattered around town.

Getting There & Around

Don't confuse Tepoztlán with Tepotzotlán to the north of Mexico City.

Pullman de Morelos/OCC (www.pullman.com.mx; Av 5 de Mayo 35) runs 1st-class buses to/from Mexico City's Terminal Sur (M$104, 1 hour, hourly 5am to 8pm) and direct buses to/from Mexico City's airport ($145, 1½ hours, three daily).

Ometochtli direct buses run to Cuernavaca (M$20, 45 minutes) every 20 minutes, 6am to 9pm. They leave from Ometochtli station, on the hill leading out of town on the Cuernavaca–Tepotzlán road (at the west end of Av 5 de Mayo). Unfortunately this route has become notorious lately for robberies on the bus, sometimes armed and violent. It is safer to take a secure taxi (M$100-150) or go via Mexico City's Terminal Sur.

ADO buses to Cuautla (M$20, 45 minutes) depart frequently from the Hwy 115D tollbooth just outside town.

Cuautla

☎735 / POP 154,000 / ELEV 1300M

Cuautla (*kwout*-la) has none of Tepoztlán's scenic beauty nor any of the architectural merit of Cuernavaca, but it does have sulfur springs that have attracted people for centuries, as well as serious revolutionary credentials.

Cuautla was a base for one of Mexico's first leaders in the independence struggle, José María Morelos y Pavón, until he was forced to leave when the royalist army besieged the town in 1812. A century later it became a center of support for Emiliano Zapata's revolutionary army. However, if Mexican history and *balnearios* (thermal bathing places) aren't your thing, there's not much for you here – modern Cuautla is a perfectly pleasant town, but there's little to see and do aside from the above.

The two main plazas are the Plaza Fuerte de Galeana, better known as the Alameda (a favorite haunt of mariachis-for-hire at weekends), and the *zócalo*.

Sights

Ex-Convento de San Diego HISTORIC BUILDING

In 1911 presidential candidate Francisco Madero embraced Emiliano Zapata at Cuautla's old **train station** (in the Ex-Convento de San Diego). Steam enthusiasts will want to come on Saturday, when Mexico's only steam-powered train fires up for short rides from 4pm to 9pm. The Ex-Convento is now home to Cuautla's **tourist office** (☎735-352-52-21; ⏰9am-8pm).

Museo Histórico del Oriente MUSEUM

(☎735-352-83-31; Callejón del Castigo 3; admission M$31, Sun free; ⏰9am-5pm Tue-Sun) The former residence of José María Morelos houses the Museo Histórico del Oriente. Each room here covers a different historical period with displays of pre-Hispanic pottery, good maps and early photos of Cuautla and Emiliano Zapata. The Mexican War of Independence rebel leader's remains lie beneath the imposing **Zapata monument** in the middle of the Plazuela Revolución del Sur.

Activities

Balnearios (thermal baths)

Cuautla's best-known *balneario* (thermal bath) is the riverside **Agua Hedionda** (Stinky Water; ☎735-352-00-44; www.aguahedionda.mx; end of Av Progreso; Mon-Fri adult/child M$50/30, Sat & Sun & Holidays adult/child M$75/40; ⏲6:30am-5:30pm). Waterfalls replenish two lake-sized pools with sulfur-scented tepid water. Take an 'Agua Hedionda' bus (M$6) from the Plazuela Revolución del Sur. There's a two-for-the-price-of-one deal on Thursdays.

Other *balnearios* worth visiting include **El Almeal** (Hernández; adult/child M$50/30, campsites per person M$60; ⏲9am-6pm) and the nicer **Los Limones** (Gabriel Teppa 14; adult/child M$65/45; ⏲8:30am-6pm). Both places are served by the same spring (no sulfur) and have extensive shaded picnic grounds. Prices are reduced by M$10 Monday to Friday. Children under 3 free.

Sleeping & Eating

Hotel Defensa del Agua HOTEL $
(☎735-352-16-79; Defensa del Agua 34; s/tr/q M$200/370/450, d M$300; P 🌀) This modern, clean hotel is set out in a motel style with a small pool and spacious rooms with TV, phone and fan. There's a very handy Italian Coffee Company branch in the building for breakfast. Avoid rooms with windows facing the noisy street.

Hotel & Spa Villasor RESORT $$
(☎735-303-55-03; www.hotelvillasor.com.mx; Av Progreso; s/d M$473/614, ste M$1050; P ❄ 📶 🌀) Out of town and located opposite the Agua Hedionda baths, this modern place has a large pool and comfortable rooms equipped

¡QUE VIVA ZAPATA!

A peasant leader from Morelos state, Emiliano Zapata (1879–1919) was among the most radical of Mexico's revolutionaries, fighting for the return of hacienda land to the peasants with the cry '*¡Tierra y libertad!*' (Land and freedom!). The Zapatista movement was at odds with both the conservative supporters of the old regime and their liberal opponents. In November 1911, Zapata disseminated his *Plan de Ayala*, calling for restoration of all land to the peasants. After winning numerous battles against government troops in central Mexico (some in association with Pancho Villa), he was ambushed and killed in 1919. The following route traces some of Zapata's defining moments.

Ruta de Zapata

In Anenecuilco, 6km south of Cuautla, what's left of the adobe cottage where Zapata was born (on August 8, 1879) is now the **Museo de la Lucha para la Tierra** (Casa Museo Emiliano Zapata; Av Zapata; admission M$35; ⏲10am-5pm).

About 20km south is the **Ex-Hacienda de San Juan Chinameca** (Cárdenas; ⏲9:30am-5pm) in Chinameca, where in 1919 Zapata was lured into a fatal trap by Colonel Jesús Guajardo, following the orders of President Venustiano Carranza, who was eager to dispose of the rebel leader and consolidate the post-revolutionary government. Pretending to defect to the revolutionary forces, Guajardo set up a meeting with Zapata, who arrived at Chinameca accompanied by a guerrilla escort. Guajardo's men gunned down the general before he crossed the abandoned hacienda's threshold, before taking his corpse to Cuautla to claim the bounty placed on his head.

The hacienda has a small and, unfortunately, horribly maintained museum with a meager collection of photos and newspaper reproductions. But there's a statue of Zapata astride a rearing horse at the entrance, where you can still see the bullet holes where the revolutionary died and where old men gather to celebrate their fallen hero.

From Chinameca head 20km northwest to Tlaltizapán, the site of the excellent **Cuartel General de Zapata** (Guerrero 2; ⏲10am-6pm Tue-Sun), the main barracks of the revolutionary forces. Here you can see Zapata's rifle (the trigger retains his fingerprints), the bed where he slept and the outfit he was wearing at the time of his death (riddled with bullet holes and stained with blood).

Though it's possible to do this route via *colectivo* (yellow 'Chinameca' combis traveling to Anenecuilco and Chinameca leave from the corner of Garduño and Matamoros in Cuautla every 10 minutes), it can be an all-day ordeal. The Morelos state tourism office in Cuernavaca arranges tours of the route.

with phone, fan and cable TV. With its own spa treatments, Villasor is the best option for relaxation, but it's not convenient for those without transportation.

Alameda SANDWICHES $
(Los Bravos & Ferrara; breakfasts M$50-85; ⏲7:30am-7:30pm; ✎) Situated between the *zócalo* and Plaza Alameda, this bright, tropical-hued fast-food diner serves excellent breakfasts, including large, tasty omelets and a dazzling array of freshly squeezed fruit juices. For lunch, it has a full range of hamburgers, *tortas* and sandwiches, including many vegetarian options.

Las Golondrinas MEXICAN $$
(☎735-354-13-50; www.lasgolondrinas.com.mx; Catalán 19A; mains M$75-125; ⏲8am-11:30pm) Set in a 17th-century building filled with plants and koi ponds, Las Golondrinas offers an attractive atmosphere and excellent service. House specialities include a range of *molcajetes* (spicy stews cooked in a large stone mortar).

Getting There & Away

OCC (☎800-702-80-00; www.ado.com.mx) has 1st-class buses to Mexico City's Terminal Sur (M$116, 2 hours, every 15 minutes). Across the street, **Pullman de Morelos** (☎735-352-73-71; www.pullman.com.mx) travels to Tepoztlán (M$20, 45 minutes, every 20 minutes).

Cuernavaca

☎777 / POP 339,000 / ELEV 1480M

There's always been a formidable glamour surrounding Cuernavaca (kwer-na-*va*-ka), the capital of Morelos state. With its vast, gated haciendas and sprawling estates, it has traditionally attracted high-society visitors year-round for its warmth, clean air and attractive architecture.

Today this tradition continues, even though urban sprawl has put a decisive end to the clean air, and you're more likely to see vacationing North Americans and college students studying Spanish on month-long courses than meet international royalty or great artists in the street.

History

The first settlers to the valleys of modern Morelos are believed to have arrived in 1500 BC. In the centuries between 200 and 900 AD they organized a highly productive agricultural society and developed Xochicalco and other large constructions throughout the region. Later, the dominant Mexica (Aztecs) called them Tlahuica, which means 'people who work the land.' In 1379 a Mexica warlord conquered Cuauhnáhuac, subdued the Tlahuica and exacted an annual tribute that included 16,000 pieces of *papal amate* (bark paper) and 20,000 bushels of corn. The tributes payable by the subject states were set out in a register the Spanish later called the Códice Mendocino, in which Cuauhnáhuac was represented by a three-branch tree; this symbol now graces Cuernavaca's coat of arms.

The Mexica lord's successor married the daughter of the Cuauhnáhuac leader, and from this marriage was born Moctezuma I Ilhuicamina, the 15th-century Aztec king who was a predecessor to Moctezuma II Xocoyotzin, encountered by Cortés. Under the Aztecs, the Tlahuica traded extensively and prospered. Their city was a learning and religious center, and archaeological remains suggest they had a considerable knowledge of astronomy.

When the Spanish arrived the Tlahuica were fiercely loyal to the Aztecs. In April 1521 they were finally overcome and Cortés torched the city. Soon the city became known as Cuernavaca, a more Spanish-friendly version of its original appellation.

In 1529 Cortés received his belated reward from the Spanish crown when he was named Marqués del Valle de Oaxaca, with an estate that covered 22 towns, including Cuernavaca, and 23,000 indigenous Mexicans. After he introduced sugar cane and new farming methods, Cuernavaca became a Spanish agricultural center, as it had been for the Aztecs. Cortés' descendants dominated the area for nearly 300 years.

With its salubrious climate, rural surroundings and colonial elite, Cuernavaca became a refuge for the rich and powerful in the 1700s and 1800s, including José de la Borda, the 18th-century Taxco silver magnate. Borda's lavish home was later a retreat for Emperor Maximilian and Empress Carlota. Cuernavaca has also attracted many artists and achieved literary fame as the setting for Malcolm Lowry's 1947 novel *Under the Volcano*.

Sights & Activities

Jardín Juárez GARDENS
(Guerrero, NW cnr of Plaza de Armas) Adjoining the northwest corner of the Plaza de Armas

Cuernavaca

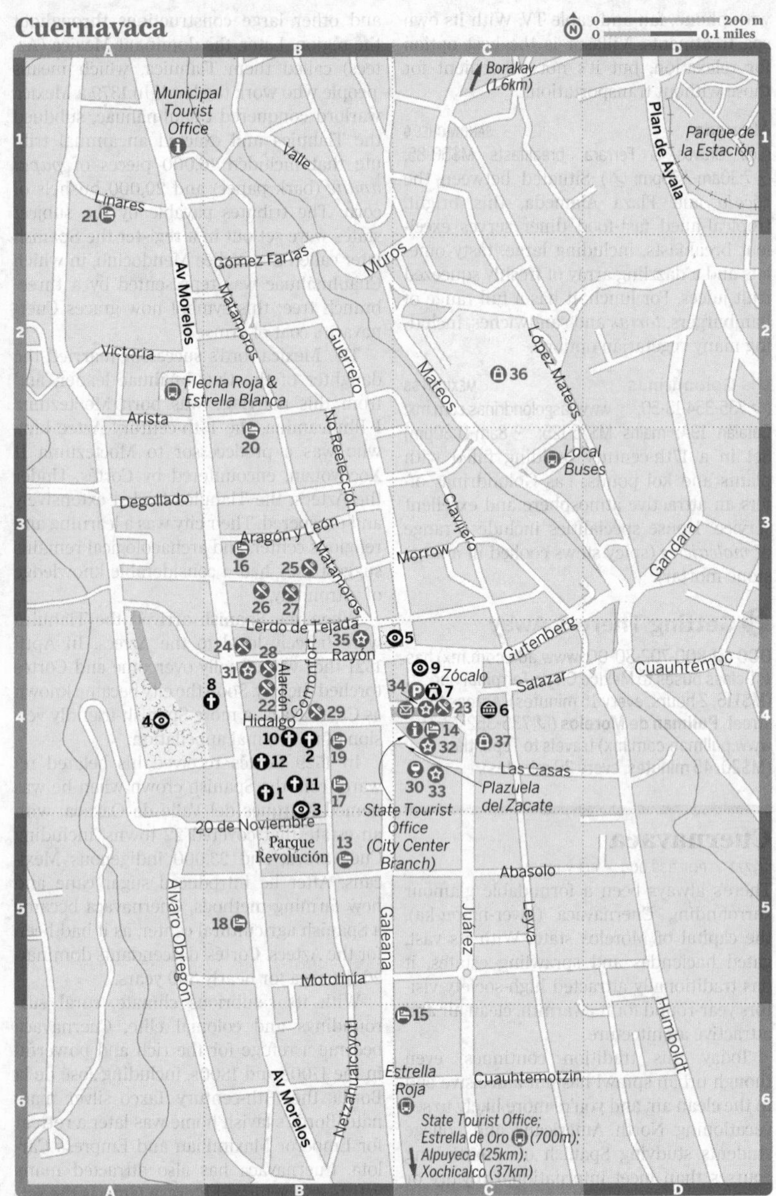

is the Jardín Juárez, where the central gazebo (designed by tower specialist Gustave Eiffel) houses juice and sandwich stands. Live band concerts on Thursday and Sunday evenings start at 6pm. Roving vendors sell balloons, ice cream and corn on the cob under the trees, which fill up with legions of cacophonous grackles at dusk.

Even more entertaining are the guitar trios who warm up their voices and instruments before heading to the cafés across the

Cuernavaca

Sights

1	Capilla Abierta de San José	B4
2	Capilla del Carmen	B4
3	Casa de la Torre	B4
4	Jardín Borda	A4
5	Jardín Juárez	C4
	Museo Regional Cuauhnáhuac	(see 6)
	Museo Robert Brady	(see 3)
6	Palacio de Cortés	C4
7	Palacio de Gobierno	C4
8	Parroquia de Guadalupe	B4
9	Plaza de Armas	C4
10	Recinto de la Catedral	B4
11	Templo de la Asunción de María	B4
12	Templo de la Tercera Orden de San Francisco	B4

Sleeping

13	Casa Colonial	B5
14	Hostería del Sol	C4
15	Hotel Antigua Posada	C6
16	Hotel Colonial	B3
17	Hotel Juárez	B4
18	Hotel Laam	B5
19	Hotel Las Hortensas	B4
20	La Casa Azul	B3
21	Las Mañanitas	A1

Eating

22	Café del Gringo	B4
23	Casa Hidalgo	C4
24	Iguana Green's	B4
25	La Comuna	B3
26	La India Bonita	B3
27	La Maga Café	B3
28	L'arrosoir d'Arthur	B4
	Restaurant Las Mañanitas	(see 21)
29	Trattoria Marco Polo	B4

Drinking & Nightlife

30	El Romántico	C4

Entertainment

31	Cine Teatro Morelos	B4
32	Face to Face	C4
33	La Plazuela	C4
34	Los Arcos	C4
35	Teatro Ocampo	B4

Shopping

36	Mercado Adolfo López Mateos	C2
37	Mercado de Artesanías y Plata	C4

street to serenade willing patrons. You can request a ballad or two for around M$75.

Plaza de Armas SQUARE, PLAZA

(Zócalo; Gutenberg) Cuernavaca's *zócalo,* the Plaza de Armas, is flanked on the east by the Palacio de Cortés, on the west by the **Palacio de Gobierno** and on the northeast and south by restaurants and roving bands of mariachis. It's the only main plaza in Mexico without a church, chapel, convent or cathedral overlooking it.

Although you can't enter the Palacio de Gobierno, it is a nice spot to contemplate some attractive architecture and enjoy the music.

Palacio de Cortés HISTORIC BUILDING

Cortés' imposing medieval-style fortress stands opposite the southeast end of the Plaza de Armas. Construction of this two-story, stone, fortress-style palace was accomplished between 1522 and 1532 and was built on the base of the pyramid that Cortés destroyed after taking Cuauhnáhuac. The base is still visible from various points on the ground floor. Cortés resided here until he turned tail for Spain in 1541. The palace remained with Cortés' family for most of the next century but by the 18th century it was being used as a prison. During the Porfirio Díaz era it became government offices.

Since 1974 the palace has housed the excellent **Museo Regional Cuauhnáhuac** (admission M$41; ⏲9am-6pm Tue-Sun), which has two floors of exhibits highlighting Mexican cultures and history. The last ticket is sold at 5:30pm. On the ground floor exhibits focus on pre-Hispanic cultures, including the local Tlahuica and their relationship with the Aztec empire. Most labeling is in Spanish only, with a few well-translated exceptions.

Upstairs covers events from the Spanish conquest to the present. On the balcony is a fascinating mural by Diego Rivera, commissioned in the mid-1920s by Dwight Morrow, then US ambassador to Mexico. Flowing from right to left, scenes from the Conquest through to the 1910 Revolution emphasize the cruelty, oppression and violence that have characterized Mexican history.

Recinto de la Catedral CHURCH

Cuernavaca's cathedral stands in a large high-walled *recinto* (compound) – the entrance gate is on Hidalgo. Like the Palacio de Cortés, the cathedral was built in a grand fortress-like style, in an effort to impress, intimidate and defend against the natives. Franciscans started work on what was one of Mexico's earliest Christian missions in

1526, using indigenous labor and stones from the rubble of Cuauhnáhuac. The first structure was the **Capilla Abierta de San José**, an open chapel on the cathedral's west side.

The cathedral itself, the **Templo de la Asunción de María**, is plain and solid, with an unembellished facade. The side door, which faces north to the compound's entrance, shows a mixture of indigenous and European features – the skull and crossbones above it is a symbol of the Franciscan order. Inside are frescoes rediscovered early in the 20th century. Cuernavaca was a center for Franciscan missionary activities in Asia and the frescoes – said to show the persecution of Christian missionaries in Japan – were supposedly painted in the 17th century by a Japanese convert to Christianity.

The cathedral compound also holds two smaller churches. On the right as you enter is the **Templo de la Tercera Orden de San Francisco**. Its exterior was carved in 18th-century baroque style by indigenous artisans and its interior has ornate, gilded decorations. On the left as you enter is the 19th-century **Capilla del Carmen** where believers seek cures for illness.

Museo Robert Brady MUSEUM

(☎777-316-85-54; www.bradymuseum.org; Netzahualcóyotl 4; admission M$35; ⏲10am-6pm Tue-Sun) Let's face it, who wouldn't want to be independently wealthy and spend their life traveling around the world collecting art for their lavish Mexican mansion? If that option isn't open to you, visit this museum – easily Cuernavaca's best – and live vicariously. The one-time home of American artist and collector Robert Brady (1928–86), this museum, which is housed in the **Casa de la Torre**, is a wonderful place to spend time appreciating the exquisite taste of one man. Brady lived in Cuernavaca for 24 years after a spell in Venice, but his collections range from Papua New Guinea and India to Haiti and South America.

Originally part of the monastery within the Recinto de la Catedral, the house is a stunning testament to a man who knew what he liked. Every room, including the two gorgeous bathrooms and kitchen, is bedecked in paintings, carvings, textiles, antiques and folk arts from all corners of the earth. Among the treasures are works by well-known Mexican artists including Rivera, Tamayo, Kahlo and Covarrubias, as well as Brady's own paintings (check out his spot-on portrait of his friend Peggy Guggenheim). The gardens are lovely too, with a very tempting (but off-limits) swimming pool in one of them and a little cafe in the other.

Classic and contemporary films are shown in the museum's courtyard every Thursday at 5pm for a M$25 donation. Movies are in their original language with Spanish subtitles.

Jardín Borda GARDEN

(☎777-318-82-50; Av Morelos 271; adult/child M$30/15, Sun free; ⏲10am-5:30pm Tue-Sun) Beside the 1784 **Parroquia de Guadalupe**, this extravagant property, inspired by Versailles, was designed in 1783 for Manuel de la Borda as an addition to the stately residence built by his father José de la Borda. From 1866 Emperor Maximilian and Empress Carlota entertained their courtiers here and used the house as a summer residence.

The gardens are formally laid out on a series of terraces with paths, steps and fountains, and they originally featured a botanical collection with hundreds of varieties of ornamental plants and fruit trees. Because of a water shortage, the baroque-style fountains operate only on weekends.

Duck into the house to get an idea of how Mexico's 19th-century aristocracy lived. In typical colonial style, the buildings are arranged around courtyards. In one wing, the **Museo de Sitio** has exhibits on daily life during the empire period and original documents with the signatures of Morelos, Juárez and Maximilian.

Several romantic paintings in the **Sala Manuel M Ponce**, a recital hall near the entrance of the house, show scenes of the garden in Maximilian's time. One of the most famous paintings depicts Maximilian in the garden with La India Bonita, the 'pretty Indian' who later became his lover.

Papalote Museo del Niño MUSEUM

(Av Vicente Guerrero 205; admission M$120; ⏲10am-8pm Fri-Wed, to 11pm Thu) Built as part of a land deal with the city, this excellent children's museum has an odd location in a shopping center beside a Costco, about 4km north of downtown, but for travelers with children it's well worth seeking out. Geared towards education, technology and play, the museum includes a large Lego exhibit, musical elements and lots of bright colors. There's an IMAX in the same complex and discounts for families and groups.

Courses

Cuernavaca is a well-established center for studying Spanish at all levels and has dozens of language schools. As such, standards are high, teaching is usually very thorough and prices competitive (generally M$2500 to M$5000 per week, plus fees and housing). The best schools offer small-group or individual instruction at all levels, with four to five hours per day of intensive instruction plus a couple of hours' conversation practice. Classes begin each Monday, and most schools recommend a minimum enrollment of four weeks.

With so many teaching styles and options, prospective students should research the choices carefully. Contact the tourist office for an extensive list of schools.

Festivals & Events

Carnaval CARNIVAL

Over the five days leading up to Ash Wednesday (falling on late February or early March), Cuernavaca's colorful Carnaval celebrations feature parades and art exhibits, plus street performances by Tepoztlán's Chinelo dancers.

Feria de la Primavera CULTURAL

From late March to early April, the city's Spring Fair includes cultural and artistic events plus concerts and a beautiful exhibit of the city's spring flowers.

Sleeping

Some of the best boutique hotels in the country are here, aimed squarely at weekend refugees from the capital. Budget hotels tend to be simple and spare, while midrange hotels are few and far between. The town fills up with visitors from Mexico City at weekends and holidays, when prices rise significantly at many hotels.

Hotel Colonial HOTEL $

(777-318-64-14; Aragón y León 19; s/d/tr/q M$285/350/450/500;) While basic, this relaxed budget hotel is excellent value. There's a garden at its center, cable TV, a free water cooler and decorative floors. The upstairs rooms with balconies and tall ceilings are best.

Hotel Juárez HOTEL $

(777-314-02-19; Netzahualcóyotl 19; r M$350;) The rooms at this basic and well-located hotel are large and airy but lack natural light. To compensate, a breezy terrace overlooks a large grassy backyard, an attractive swimming pool and Cuernavaca's clay-tiled rooftops. It's nothing fancy but it's a good budget option, especially for a dip in the clean pool.

Hotel Las Hortensas HOTEL $

(777-318-52-65; www.hotelhortensias.com; Hidalgo 13; s M$300, d M$350-400) Cheap and central, Las Hortensas has small, sparse rooms, a lush garden and staff that seem to constantly be cleaning. Street-side rooms are noisy, so bring earplugs or ask for one of the darker interior rooms.

Hostería del Sol GUESTHOUSE $$

(777-318-32-41; Callejón de la Bolsa del Diablo; r M$450-750;) This well-located charmer has reasonable prices and is spotlessly clean. Half of the hotel's six rooms share bathrooms, while all rooms are beautifully decorated in traditional blue and yellow tones. It's best to ring ahead, although staff don't speak English. Rooms with windows facing the Plazuela del Zacate can be noisy on weekends.

Hotel Antigua Posada HOTEL $$

(777-310-21-79; www.hotelantiguaposada.com.mx; Galeana 69; r incl breakfast M$935-1100, ste incl breakfast M$1100-1200;) This exclusive little hideaway is a short walk from the center of town and boasts just 11 rooms behind its unpromising exterior. Once inside there's a lovely courtyard and great service. The rooms are gorgeous, complete with wooden beams and rustic touches.

Hotel Laam BUSINESS HOTEL $$

(777-314-44-11; www.laamhotel.com.mx; Av Morelos 239; ste M$850-1520;) With a slick, motel feel and comfortable, if sterile, rooms (some with huge terraces), this newish hotel is good value. Set back from the road, giving it distance from street noise, Hotel Laam comes with a tiled swimming pool and well-tended grounds.

★ **Hotel Hacienda de Cortés** HISTORIC HOTEL $$$

(800-220-76-97, 777-315-88-44; www.hotelhaciendadecortes.com; Plaza Kennedy 90; r from M$2350, ste $2937-6000;) Built in the 16th century by Martín Cortés (successor to Hernán Cortés as Marqués del Valle de Oaxaca), this former sugar mill was renovated in 1980 and boasts 23 rooms of various levels of luxury, each with its own private garden and terrace. There's a swimming pool too, built

WORTH A TRIP

XOCHICALCO

Atop a desolate plateau with views for miles around, **Xochicalco** (☎777-379-74-16; admission M$59; ⊙9am-6pm, last ticket 5pm) is a relatively easy day trip from Cuernavaca that shouldn't be missed. Large enough to make the journey worthwhile, but not so well known as to be overrun with tourists, this exceptional site is one of the most impressive in the region.

A Unesco World Heritage site and one of central Mexico's most important archaeological sites, Xochicalco (so-chee-*cal*-co) is Náhuatl for 'place of the house of flowers.' The collection of white stone ruins, many still to be excavated, covers approximately 10 sq km. They represent the various cultures – Tlahuica, Toltec, Olmec, Zapotec, Mixtec and Aztec – for which Xochicalco was a commercial, cultural and religious center. When Teotihuacán began to weaken around AD 650 to 700, Xochicalco began to rise in importance, achieving its peak between AD 650 and 900, with far-reaching cultural and commercial relations. Around AD 650 Zapotec, Maya and Gulf coast spiritual leaders convened here to correlate their respective calendars. Xochicalco remained an important center until around 1200, when its excessive growth precipitated a demise similar to that of Teotihuacán.

The site's most famous monument is the **Pirámide de Quetzalcóatl**. Archaeologists have surmised from its well-preserved bas-reliefs that astronomer-priests met here at the beginning and end of each 52-year cycle of the pre-Hispanic calendar. Site signs are in English and Spanish, but information at the excellent, ecologically sensitive **museum**, situated 200m from the ruins, is in Spanish only.

From October through May, the site sometimes offers a nighttime **light show** (☎for reservations 737-374-30-90; xochicalco.mor@inah.gob.mx) (M$7) on Friday and Saturday nights. It's quite a spectacle, but call ahead because the shows are not regular.

From Cuernavaca's market, buses with 'Xochi' on their windshield (M$14) depart every 30 minutes for the site entrance. On arrival, you'll need to walk to the museum to buy tickets. The last return bus leaves around 6pm. Alternatively, take a taxi (M$25) from the site to the nearby town of Alpuyeca, where there are frequent buses back to Cuernavaca.

around old stone columns, and an excellent restaurant. It's approximately 4km southeast of the center of town.

La Casa Azul BOUTIQUE HOTEL **$$$**
(☎777-314-21-41, 777-314-36-34; www.hotelcasaazul.com.mx; Arista 17; r M$1550, ste M$2050-2550; P 📶 🏊) This 24-room boutique hotel is a short walk from the town center and has lots of charm. Originally part of the Guadalupe Convent, the hotel has soothing fountains, two pools and a great selection of local arts and crafts throughout. Prices go up at the weekend.

Las Mañanitas LUXURY HOTEL **$$$**
(☎777-362-00-00; www.lasmananitas.com.mx; Linares 107; ste incl breakfast Sun-Thu M$2351-4828; P ❄ 📶 🏊) If you're really out to impress someone, book a room at this stunning place. It's a destination hotel – you may not want to leave for the whole weekend – so the fact that it's not in the center of town isn't too important. The large rooms are beautifully understated, many with terraces overlooking the gardens, full of peacocks and a heated pool. Prices rise on weekends.

Casa Colonial BOUTIQUE HOTEL **$$$**
(☎777-312-70-33, 800-623-08-43; www.casacolonial.com; Netzahualcóyotl 37; r M$1365, ste $1705-2050; P 📶 🏊) Set in a charming garden around a large pool, this 16-room, 19th-century mansion with beautifully furnished rooms has been lovingly restored and cleverly updated. Staff speak good English.

Eating

Cuernavaca is a great food town which has a few excellent high-end restaurants and plenty of good cafes. There are, however, surprisingly few enticing midrange options.

La Comuna CAFE **$**
(☎777 318-27-57; Morrow 6; mains M$30-55, comida corrida M$40; ⊙9am-9pm Mon-Sat; 📶) Decorated with fair-trade handicrafts and serving 'slow food' set meals – as well as excellent organic coffee and cheap beer – Comuna is

the home of Cuerna's political left. There's a book exchange, art on the walls and regular lectures.

Iguana Green's MEXICAN $
(Rayón 24; mains M$33-80; 7am-11pm) With food this good and this cheap it would easy for Iguana Greem's to be just another anonymous *pozole* shop and still draw crowds, but the family that runs this friendly little restaurant takes obvious pride in creating a festive space – with brightly colored chairs and tables and a mural along the wall.

Café del Gringo CAFE $
(Juan Ruiz de Alarcón 9; coffee M$35-50, burger meals $50-77; 8am-11pm;) Beyond the bags of coffee beans and industrial grinder at the entrance hides a leafy courtyard with a fountain, couples sipping cappuccinos, and students devouring chicken fajitas. The many veggie options include a spicy Rastaburger, and spaghetti bolognese. And yes, a gringo owns the place and grinds his own beans.

La India Bonita MEXICAN $$
(777-318-69-67; www.laindiabonita.com; Morrow 115; mains M$75-190; 8am-9:30pm) Set in a lush courtyard, Cuernavaca's oldest restaurant also has some of its best traditional Mexican food – from *brocheta al mezcal* (skewered meats marinated in *mezcal*) to *chile en nogada* (*poblano* pepper in walnut sauce) – with the occasional enticing twist. India Bonita operates a tasty bakery next door.

L'arrosoir d'Arthur FRENCH $$
(http://larrosoir.com.mx; Calle Juan Ruiz de Alarcón 13; menú del día M$85-135; 9am-midnight) As much a hangout and nightspot as a restaurant, this French-owned restaurant in a loft space downtown has excellent, affordable French dishes (crepes, cassolette, chicken in mustard sauce), good cocktails and wines. On the weekends, the chilled, European vibe gets more energetic with live music, theater, dance and poetry events.

La Maga Café MEXICAN $$
(Morrow 9; Buffet M$91; 1-5pm Mon-Sat;) The colourful buffet at La Maga features multitudes of glazed pots filled with salads, pastas, fruit, vegetables, and specials of the day, such as glistening *pollo en adobo* (chicken marinated in chili and herbs) and *tortas de elote* (cheesy corn croquettes). There are also great vegetarian options and a community vibe with music. Arrive early to nab a window seat.

Trattoria Marco Polo PIZZERIA $$
(777-318-40-32; Hidalgo 30; pizzas M$66-142; 1-10:30pm Mon-Thurs, to midnight Sat, to 10pm Sun; P) Italian dishes, including a broad range of excellent, thin-crust pizza, and an attractive setting just across from the cathedral make this a decent option for reasonably priced international fare.

★ **Restaurante Hacienda de Cortés** INTERNATIONAL $$$
(777-315-88-44, 800-220-76-97; www.hotelhaciendadecortes.com.mx; Plaza Kennedy 90; mains M$95-320; 7am-12:30pm, 1:30-5pm, 7-11pm) Situated within the Hotel Hacienda de Cortés, this elegant but unpretentious hotel restaurant serves an excellent selection of salads and delicious international dishes, including a fantastic vegetarian lasagne, tuna in almond sauce with risotto, and well-prepared Angus steaks. The dining room is spectacular, with massive vines climbing the walls and wrought-iron chandeliers overhead.

Restaurant Las Mañanitas FRENCH $$$
(www.lasmananitas.com.mx; Linares 107; breakfasts M$105-285, mains M$265-500; 8am-noon & 1-11pm) The restaurant and bar of Cuernavaca's most famous hotel Las Mañanitas is a luxurious splurge, open to all. The expansive menu has a heavy French accent, with dishes such as entrecôte Bourguignon, and sumptuous desserts. Reserve a table inside the mansion or on the terrace where you can watch wildlife wander among modern garden sculptures.

Casa Hidalgo MEXICAN $$$
(777-312-27-49; Jardín de los Héroes 6; mains M$155-225) Directly opposite the Palacio de Cortés, with a great terrace and upstairs balcony, this is popular restaurant attracts a well-heeled crowd of local socialites and wealthy visitors. The menu is eclectic – try cold mango–agave soup with jicama or *tlaxcalteca* chicken breast stuffed with cheese and roasted *poblano* pepper with three salsas: squash blossom, spinach and *chipotle*.

Drinking & Nightlife

There's a buzzing nightlife in Cuernavaca, supported by a year-round student population that keeps nightspots busy every night of the week. The Plazuela del Zacate and the adjacent alley Las Casas have a good mix of rowdy and laid-back bars – all open around sunset and staying open until the last patron leaves. There are no cover charges and almost every downtown bar offers two-for-one drink specials most nights of the week.

The more upmarket clubs impose a modest cover charge but women are usually let in for free. Some clubs enforce dress codes and trendier places post style police at the door. Things really get going after 11pm.

El Romántico BAR

(Plazuela del Zacate) This small bar has very functional stainless-steel tables and isn't especially romantic. The real attraction is cheap drinks and a jubilant crowd.

Borakay CLUB

(777-316-49-02; Av Teopanzolco 503; 10pm-late Wed-Sat) Borakay is an upscale, indoor-outdoor club for Cuerna's hipster elite. Dress to impress.

Face to Face GAY

(Plazuela del Zacate) The crowd at this gay club is a mix of students and older locals. It's quiet during the week, but picks up pace from Thursday through the weekend when drag acts such as Frida Ciccone perform and the venue is showered in frenetic laser lights. The entrance, opposite neighbouring bar El Romántico, is nondescript and easy to miss – look out for the doorperson on a stool.

La Plazuela DJ

(Las Casas) This is the home of pumping house and techno clubs with that tell-tale accordion of Mexican *norteño* thrown into the mix.

Entertainment

Hanging around the central plazas is a popular activity, especially on Sunday evenings, when open-air concerts are often staged. There are often recitals at Jardín Borda (p184) on Thursday nights, too.

If your *español* is up to it, sample Cuernavaca's theater scene.

Cine Teatro Morelos CINEMA

(777-318-10-50; Av Morelos 188; tickets from M$25;) Morelos' state theater hosts quality film series, plays and dance performances. There's a full schedule posted out front and a bookstore and cafe inside.

Teatro Ocampo THEATER

(777-318-63-85; Jardín Juárez 2) Near Jardín Juárez (p181), this theater stages contemporary plays. A calendar of cultural events is posted at its entrance.

Los Arcos SALSA

(Jardín de los Héroes 4; minimum consumption M$60; salsa 9-11:30pm Tues, Thurs, Fri & Sun) Come here to dance salsa, not on a stage but around the tables of families having dinner on the terrace, with crowds of appreciative onlookers. The live band's carnival beats can be heard from the other side of the plaza and have a magnetic effect on your swivelling hips.

Shopping

There are some good quality *guayaberas* (men's appliqued shirt), *huipiles* (long, sleeveless tunics) and upmarket souvenirs in the plaza opposite the cathedral and along the same street.

Mercado de Artesanías y Plata ARTESANÍAS

(Handicrafts and Silver Market; 10am-8pm daily) This relaxed market has handicrafts such as the coconut lamps and handpainted ceramics that can be found all over Mexico. It's a shady place to browse and prices are reasonable. Look out for handmade *chinelo* dolls with upturned beards – a specialty of Morelos. To find the market, look for the huge statue of Mr Morelos at the entrance.

Mercado Adolfo López Mateos MARKET

(Adolfo López Mateos; 8am-6pm daily) A sprawling, semi-covered market, selling fresh produce and other wares, Mercado Adolfo López Mateos bursts with the smells of fruit, meats, flowers and smoked chilies.

Information

EMERGENCY

Ambulance (777-311-85-02)

Cruz Roja (Red Cross; 777-315-35-05)

Tourist Police (800-903-92-00)

INTERNET ACCESS

There's internet access at the Futura and Estrella Blanca bus station.

Cyber Gasso (Miguel Hidalgo 22; M$7 per hr; 7:30am-9:30pm Mon-Sat, 9:30am-9:30pm Sun) Hidalgo (Hidalgo 40); Gutenberg (Gutenberg 198).

LAUNDRY

Nueva Tintorería Francesa (Juárez 2; per kg M$15; 9am-7pm Mon-Fri, to 2:30pm Sat)

MEDICAL SERVICES

Hospital Inovamed (☎777-311-24-82; Cuauhtémoc 305) In Colonia Lomas de la Selva, 1km north of town.

POST

Main Post Office (Plaza de Armas; ⏰8am-6pm Mon-Fri)

TOURIST INFORMATION

There's an information booth in the cathedral, at the north end of the *zócalo* (9am-6pm daily) and other kiosks around town, including at most bus stations. Ask for maps.

Municipal Tourist Office (☎777-329-44-04; www.cuernavaca.gob.mx/turismo; Av Morelos 278; ⏰9am-6pm) Also has a tourist police office.

State Tourist Office (☎800-987-82-24, 777-314-38-72, 777-314-38-81; www.morelosturistico.com; Av Morelos Sur 187) This excellent tourist office has a wealth of brochures, maps and information. Also has a City Center (☎777-314-39-20; www.morelosturistico.com; City Center, Hidalgo 5) branch.

Getting There & Away

Hwy 95D (the Mexico City–Acapulco toll road) skirts the city's east side. If you're driving from the north take the Cuernavaca exit and cross to Hwy 95 (where you'll see a statue of Zapata on horseback). Hwy 95 becomes Blvd Zapata, then Avenida Morelos as you descend south into town. From Avenida Matamoros (still traveling south) the Avenida Morelos is one way, north-bound only. To reach the center, veer left down Avenida Matamoros.

BUS

Cuernavaca's main-line bus companies operate the following separate long-distance terminals.

See the table below for daily 1st-class and deluxe services from Cuernavaca. All are available from the Estrella Roja depot except for Mexico City Airport, which leaves from the Pullman de Morelos depot. A bus to Toluca leaves from the Estrella Blanca depot at 6:45pm (3hrs, M$185).

Estrella de Oro (EDO; ☎777-312-30-55; www.estrelladeoro.com.mx; Av Morelos Sur 812)

Estrella Roja (ER; ☎777-318-59-34; www.estrellaroja.com.mx; cnr Galeana & Cuauhtemotzin)

Flecha Roja & Estrella Blanca (FR & EB; ☎777-312-26-26; www.estrellablanca.com.mx; Av Morelos 503, btwn Arista & Victoria) Futura and ETN services leave from here as well.

Pullman de Morelos (PDM; ☎777-318-09-07; www.pullman.com.mx; cnr Abasolo & Netzahualcóyotl)

CAR & MOTORCYCLE

Cuernavaca is 89km south of Mexico City, a 2hr drive on Hwy 95 or a one-hour trip via Hwy 95D. Both roads continue south to Acapulco – Hwy 95 detours through Taxco, Hwy 95D is more direct and much faster.

Getting Around

You can walk to most places of interest in central Cuernavaca. Local buses (M$6) advertise their destinations on their windshields. Many local buses, and those to nearby towns, leave from the southern corner of the city's labyrinthine market, Mercado Adolfo López Mateos. Taxis to most places in town cost M$35. There have been reports of robberies on local buses in Cuernavaca, so exercise caution if you must use them.

The bus depots are in walking distance of the *zócalo* except the Estrella de Oro bus terminal, 1km south (downhill) of the center, which is reachable on the Ruta 20 bus down Galeana; in the other direction, catch any bus heading up Avenida Morelos. Ruta 17 buses head up Avenida Morelos and stop within one block of the Pullman de Morelos terminal at Casino de la Selva.

Taxco

☎762 / POP 53,000 / ELEV 1800M

The first sight of Taxco (*tass*-ko) across the steep valley as you approach it from the north is enough to take your breath away. Scattered down a precipitous hillside surrounded by dramatic mountains and cliffs, its perfectly preserved colonial architecture and the twin belfries of its baroque masterpiece, the Templo de Santa Prisca, make for

BUSES FROM CUERNAVACA

DESTINATION	FARE (M$)	DURATION	FREQUENCY (DAILY)
Cuautla	50	1½hr	28
Mexico City	82-110	1½hr	40
Mexico City International Airport	150	2hr	24
Taxco	75	1½hr	14
Tepoztlán	18	½hr	28

Taxco

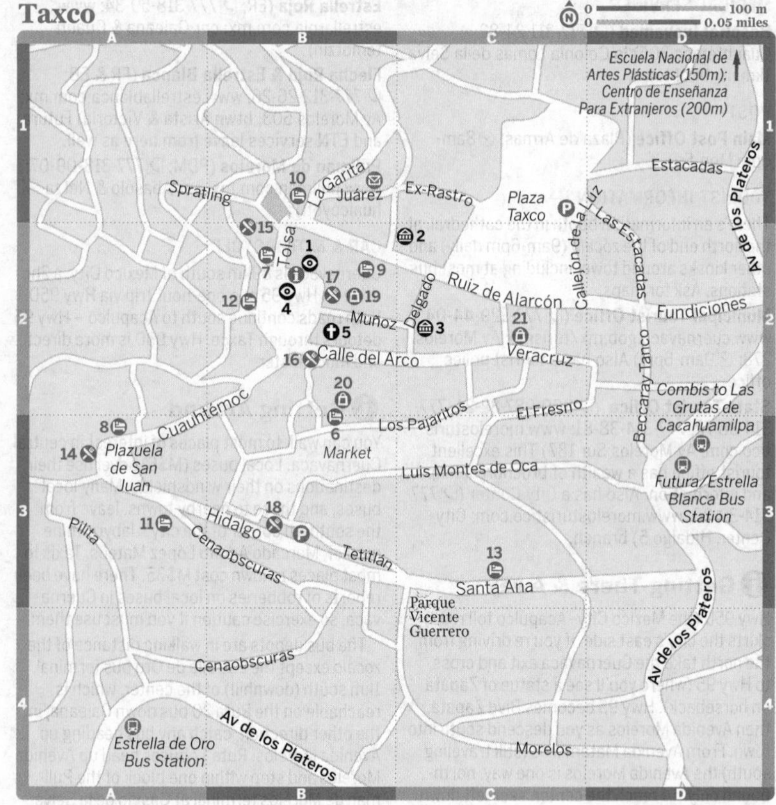

one of the most beguiling views anywhere in the central highlands.

Taxco, 160km southwest of Mexico City, has ridden the waves of boom and bust associated with the fantastically wealthy silver deposits discovered here in the 16th century and right up until the early 20th century. With its silver now almost depleted, the town has fallen back on tourism to sustain it. As such, it's a rare example of preservation-centric development in Mexico. Unlike many colonial-era towns, Taxco has not been engulfed by industrial suburbs, and its status as a national historical monument means that even new buildings must conform to the old in scale, style and materials.

The downside of this embrace of the past is that the town sometimes feels like a museum piece that's given itself over to visitors, who flood Taxco during the weekend and during festivals. Despite this, Taxco is a striking small city and one of the best weekend trips from the capital.

History

Taxco was called Tlachco (Ball-Playing Place) by the Aztecs, who dominated the region from 1440 until the Spanish arrived. The colonial city was founded by Rodrigo de Castañeda in 1529, with a mandate from Hernán Cortés. Among the town's first Spanish residents were three miners – Juan de Cabra, Juan Salcedo and Diego de Nava – and the carpenter Pedro Muriel. In 1531, they established the first Spanish mine in North America.

The Spaniards came searching for tin, which they found in small quantities, but by 1534 they had discovered tremendous lodes of silver. That year the Hacienda El Chorrillo was built, complete with water wheel, smelter and aqueduct – the remains of the

Taxco

Sights

1 Casa Borda B2
2 Museo de Arte Virreinal C2
3 Museo Guillermo Spratling C2
4 Plaza Borda (Zócalo) B2
5 Templo de Santa Prisca B2

Sleeping

6 Casa de Huespedes Arellano B3
7 Hotel Agua Escondida B2
8 Hotel Casa Grande A3
9 Hotel Emilia B2
10 Hotel Mi Casita B1
11 Hotel Santa Prisca A3
12 Posada Los Balcones B2
13 Pueblo Lindo C3

Eating

14 Hostería Bar El Adobe A3
15 La Hacienda de Taxco B2
La Sushería ..... (see 9)
16 Pizza Pazza B2
17 Pozolería Tía Calla B2
18 Restaurante Santa Fe B3

Shopping

19 EBA Elena Ballesteros B2
20 Mercado de Artesanías Plata B2
21 Nuestro México Artesanias C2
Patio de las Artesanías ..... (see 17)

latter form the old arches (Los Arcos) over Hwy 95 at the north end of town.

The prospectors quickly depleted the first silver veins and fled Taxco. Further quantities of ore were not discovered until 1743. Don José de la Borda, who had arrived in 1716 from France at the age of 16 to work with his miner brother, accidentally unearthed one of the region's richest veins. According to the legend, Borda was riding near where the Templo de Santa Prisca now stands when his horse stumbled, dislodged a stone and exposed the precious metal.

Borda went on to introduce new techniques of draining and repairing mines, and he reportedly treated his indigenous workers better than most colonial mine owners. The Templo de Santa Prisca was the devout de la Borda's gift to Taxco. His success attracted more prospectors, and new silver veins were found and played out. With most of the silver gone, Taxco became a quiet town with a dwindling population and economy.

In 1929 a US architect and professor named William (Guillermo) Spratling arrived and, at the suggestion of the then US ambassador Dwight Morrow, set up a silver workshop as a way to rejuvenate the town. (Another version has it that Spratling was writing a book and resorted to the silver business because his publisher went bust. A third has it that Spratling had a notion to create jewelry that synthesized pre-Hispanic motifs with art deco modernism.) The workshop evolved into a factory, and Spratling's apprentices began establishing their own shops. Today, Taxco is home to hundreds of silver shops, many producing for export.

While one of the joys of Taxco is getting lost while aimlessly wandering the pretty streets, it's actually a very easy place to find your way around. The twin belfries of Santa Prisca make the best landmark, situated as they are on the *zócalo,* **Plaza Borda**. Nearly all of the town's streets are one way, with the main road Avenida de los Plateros being the only major two-way street. This is where both bus stations are located and is the road for entering and leaving the town. The basic *colectivo* route is a counterclockwise loop going north on Avenida de los Plateros and south through the center of town.

Sights & Activities

Templo de Santa Prisca — CHURCH

The icon of Taxco, Santa Prisca was a labor of love for town hero José de la Borda. The local Catholic hierarchy allowed the silver magnate to donate this church to Taxco on the condition that he mortgage his mansion and other assets to guarantee its completion. The project nearly bankrupted him but the risk was well worth it – the resulting building is one of Mexico's most beautiful and striking pieces of baroque architecture. It was designed by Spanish architects Juan Caballero and Diego Durán, and was constructed between 1751 and 1758.

Perhaps Santa Prisca's most striking feature (best viewed side-on) is the contrast between its belfries, with their elaborate Churrigueresque facade overlooking the Plaza Borda, and the far more simple, constrained and elegant nave. The rose-colored stone used on the facade is extraordinarily beautiful in the sunlight – look out for the oval bas-relief depiction of Christ's baptism above the doorway. Inside, the intricately sculpted, gold-covered altarpieces are equally fine Churrigueresque specimens.

Museo Guillermo Spratling MUSEUM
(☎762-622-16-60; Delgado 1; admission M$31; ⊙9am-5pm Tue-Sat, to 3pm Sun) This very well laid-out three-story history and archaeology museum is off an alley behind Templo de Santa Prisca. It contains a small but excellent collection of pre-Hispanic jewelry, art, pottery and sculpture from US silversmith William Spratling's private collection. The phallic cult pieces are a particular eye-opener. On the basement floor there are examples of Spratling's designs using pre-Hispanic motifs. The top floor hosts occasional temporary exhibits.

Museo de Arte Virreinal MUSEUM
(☎762-622-55-01; Ruiz de Alarcón 12; adult/student M$20/15; ⊙10am-6pm Tue-Sun) This charming, rather rag-tag religious art museum is housed in a wonderful old house that is often referred to as Casa Humboldt, even though the famous German explorer and naturalist Friedrich Heinrich Alexander von Humboldt slept here for only one night in 1803. The museum hosts a small but well-displayed collection of art, which is labeled in English and Spanish. The most interesting exhibit describes restoration work on Santa Prisca, during which some fabulous material (including tapestries, woodwork altarpieces and rich decorative fabrics) was discovered in the basement of the house, and there is also an interesting display on the Manila Galleons, which pioneered trade between the Americas and the Far East.

Casa Borda CULTURAL BUILDING
(☎762-622-66-34; Centro Cultural Taxco, Plaza Borda; ⊙10am-6pm Tue-Sun) FREE Built by José de la Borda in 1759, the Casa Borda serves as a cultural center hosting experimental theater and exhibiting contemporary sculpture, painting and photography by Guerrero artists. The building, however, is the main attraction. Due to the unevenness of the terrain, the rear window looks out on a precipitous four-story drop, even though the entrance is on the ground floor.

Teleférico CABLE CAR
(one-way/round-trip adult M$65/85, child M$50/65; ⊙8am-7pm) From the north end of Taxco, near Los Arcos, a Swiss-made gondola ascends 173m to the Hotel Monte Taxco resort affording fantastic views of Taxco and the surrounding mountains. To find the entrance, walk uphill from the south side of Los Arcos and turn right through the Escuela Nacional de Artes Plásticas gate.

Courses

Taxco's cozy mountain atmosphere and relative safety makes it a popular place for foreigners, especially Americans, to study Spanish and silverwork.

Centro de Enseñanza Para Extranjeros LANGUAGE
(CEPE; ☎762-622-34-10; www.cepe.unam.mx; Ex Hacienda El Chorrillo s/n; courses from M$2942 per month) This branch of Mexico City's Universidad Nacional Autónoma de México offers intensive Spanish-language courses in the atmospheric Ex-Hacienda El Chorrillo. The art school next door (enap.unam.mx) offers workshops in painting and jewelry from US$1200.

Festivals & Events

Be sure to reserve your hotel in advance if your visit coincides with one of Taxco's annual festivals. Check exact dates of moveable feasts with the tourist office.

Fiestas de Santa Prisca & San Sebastián RELIGIOUS
Taxco's patron saints are honored on January 18 (Santa Prisca) and January 20 (San Sebastián), when locals parade by the Templo de Santa Prisca for an annual blessing, with their pets and farm animals in tow.

Jornadas Alarconianas ARTS
This summertime cultural festival, honoring Taxco-born playwright Juan Ruiz de Alarcón, presents concerts and dance performances by internationally renowned performing artists.

Día del Jumil FOOD
The Monday after the Day of the Dead (November 2), locals celebrate the *jumil* – the edible beetle said to represent the giving of life and energy to Taxco residents for another year. Many families camp on the Cerro de Huixteco (above town) over the preceding weekend, and townsfolk climb the hill to collect *jumiles* and share food and camaraderie.

Feria de la Plata CRAFTS
The week-long national silver fair convenes in late November or early December. Craft competitions are held and some of Mexico's best silverwork is on display. Other festivities include rodeos, concerts, dances and *burro* (donkey) races.

Las Posadas CULTURAL
From December 16 to 24, nightly candlelit processions fill Taxco's streets with door-to-door singing. Children are dressed up to resemble biblical characters. At the end of the night, they attack piñatas.

Sleeping

Taxco has a wealth of hotels, from large four- and five-star resorts to charming family-run posadas. During holiday weekends, when the hordes arrive from Mexico City, it's a good idea to reserve ahead.

Earplugs are also a good idea. Owing to the innumerable Volkswagen taxis that serve as transportation in this, the steepest of hill towns, street noise is a problem nearly everywhere.

Hotel Casa Grande HOTEL $
(☎762-622-09-69; www.hotelcasagrande.com.mx; Plazuela de San Juan 7; s with/without bathroom M$250/170, d M$390/250, tr M$450/300;) Its excellent location and hypnotic terrace views over the Plazuela makes Casa Grande the most attractive budget option in town. But bring your earplugs as the music from the restaurant-bar La Concha Nostra goes late into the night, especially on weekends.

Casa de Huespedes Arellano GUESTHOUSE $
(☎762-622-02-15; Los Pajaritos 23; dm M$120, s with/without bathroom M$220/180, d M$340/280) Taxco's backpacker-friendly guesthouse has basic, clean rooms and three well-tended balconies of flowers, caged birds, and a variety of rooms and ample terraces for relaxing. Rooms can sleep up to five people (M$720).

Hotel Agua Escondida BUSINESS HOTEL $$
(☎762-622-07-36, 800-504-03-11; www.aguaescondida.com; Plaza Borda 4; s/d/ste M$570/850/1500; P@) Facing the *zócalo*, Hotel Agua Escondida has two swimming pools and a cafe-bar on a high terrace with unmatchable views of Santa Prisca. The 60 comfortable rooms, popular with visiting silver importers, have colonial furnishings and are sometimes discounted during the week, depending on the surly staff. Rooms with balconies overlooking the street suffer from traffic noise.

★ **Hotel Mi Casita** INN $$
(☎762-627-17-77; www.hotelmicasita.com; Altos de Redondo 1; s/tr/ste from M$550/750/850, d M$650-750 incl breakfast; @) This elegant colonial home run by a family of jewelry designers boasts 12 beautifully and individually decorated rooms just moments from the *zócalo*, with wraparound balconies with views over the cathedral. The comfortable rooms feature original hand-painted bathroom tiles, three with Talavera bathtubs, some with private terraces and all with fans.

Posada Los Balcones HOTEL $$
(☎762-622-02-50; Plazuela de los Gallos 5; s/d M$500/650;) As its name suggests, many of the 15 rooms at this straightforward hotel have small balconies overlooking the boisterous narrow street below. Just moments from Santa Prisca, Los Balcones is centrally located. Every spacious room has its own bathroom and TV.

Hotel Santa Prisca HOTEL $$
(☎762-622-00-80; Cenaobscuras 1; s M$430, d M$550-650, tr M$600-700, ste M$750-870; P) The 31-room Santa Prisca has traditional Mexican decor and a welcoming courtyard garden. It has a great location, too, right in the thick of things. Rooms are smallish, but most have breezy private balconies. All have two beds, and newer, sunnier rooms cost a bit more. The parking lot is reached via a tunnel at the hotel's uphill end.

Hotel Emilia HOTEL $$
(☎762-622-67-17; www.hotelemiliacastillo.com; Ruiz de Alarcón 7; s/d/tr M$600/650/750) All 14 rooms are spotlessly clean and have beautiful tiled bathrooms. Owned by a family of famous silver workers, this intimate hotel has colonial charm and reasonable prices. Sadly, it's in an especially noisy location – ask for a room at the back but don't miss the views from the rooftop terrace.

Pueblo Lindo HOTEL $$$
(☎762-622-34-81; www.pueblolindo.com.mx; Hidalgo 30; r & ste incl breakfast from M$1150-1450; P@) This luxurious hotel manages to balance style and substance, embracing a modern Mexican-inspired aesthetic with bright colors and wooden furnishings. There's a bar-lounge and excellent service. The rooftop pool has fantastic views over Taxco, as do many of the rooms. Discounts are available when booking 30 days in advance.

Eating

Many of the best spots in town to grab a bite are also a good place for a drink.

Pozolería Tía Calla MEXICAN $
(762-622-56-02; Plaza Borda 1; mains M$44-64; 1-10pm Wed-Mon) No fine vistas or breezy *terrazas* (terraces) here – just authentic *pozole*, served up in Auntie Calla's basement. Pick your poison: chicken or pork. Pork comes loaded with *chicharrón* (fried pork skin), avocado and all the fixings. No matter your choice, the broth is always pork-based. The beer steins are chilled and there's *fútbol* on the *tele*. What more could you ask for?

La Sushería JAPANESE $
(Ruiz de Alarcón 7; sushi M$50-85, cocktails M$30-60; 1-11pm;) This new sushi restaurant in the lobby of Hotel Emilia is a great addition to Taxco, with its designer furniture but casual vibe. The sushi is fresh and finished nicely with the green-tea ice cream – heaven in a cocktail glass. If you're here on a date or a business lunch, the slick booths are the perfect place to impress.

Restaurante Santa Fe MEXICAN $
(762-622-11-70; Hidalgo 2; mains M$60-95; 8am-9pm) In business for over 50 years, Santa Fe is a favorite among locals for its fairly priced traditional fare like *conejo en chile ajo* (rabbit in garlic and chili). The walls are plastered with patron photos and some excellent black-and-white shots of ye olde Taxco. The three-course *menú del día* is a bargain at M$75.

Pizza Pazza PIZZA $$
(Calle del Arco 1; pizzas M$95-110; midday-1am) This is a perfect place to take in the town's scenery – the buzzing *zócalo*, Santa Prisca, twinkling white mountain homes in the background and Taxco's statue of Jesus are all visible from the roof terrace. These features make the thin-crust pizzas at Pizza Pazza seem closer to heaven than they probably are, but we don't mind.

La Hacienda de Taxco MEXICAN $$
(762-622-11-66; Plaza Borda 4; mains M$55-130; 7:30am-10:30pm;) Offering an extensive menu of traditional Mexican dishes (including house-made jam in the morning and a 20-ingredient, house-made *mole* in the afternoon), La Hacienda also has considerate touches, like the option of egg-white-only breakfasts, vegetarian dishes and child-sized portions.

Hostería Bar El Adobe MEXICAN $$
(762-622-14-16; Plazuela de San Juan 13; mains M$55-150) This place doesn't have the *zócalo* views, but the interior is charmingly decorated with black-and-white photos of everyone from Pancho Villa to Elvis. Plus the cute balcony tables are more private. On weekends, there's *pozole* (M$65), live *trova* music on Saturday night and a buffet on Sunday (M$115).

Shopping

Patio de las Artesanías JEWELRY
(Plaza Borda) If you are looking for silver, there are several shops to wander through in the Patio de las Artesanías building.

EBA Elena Ballesteros JEWELRY
(762-622-37-67; www.ebaplata.com; Muñoz 4) EBA Elena Ballesteros has creative, well-crafted silver designs.

Mercado de Artesanías Plata JEWELRY
(11am-8pm) For quantity rather than quality, trawl the vast, haphazardly displayed masses of rings, chains and pendants at the Mercado de Artesanías Plata. You can haggle for good prices here, even if you have to search hard for something unique.

Nuestro México Artesanias HANDICRAFTS
(762-622-09-76; Veracruz 8; 10am-6pm) Treasure hunters will love fossicking in this storehouse of handicrafts from across Mexico. Most of the favourite souvenirs are here – coconut masks, papier-mâché devils, flying

BUSES FROM TAXCO

DESTINATION	FARE (M$)	DURATION	FREQUENCY (DAILY)
Acapulco	230	4-5hr	7 EDO
Cuernavaca	75	1½hr	5 EDO
	71	1½hr	4 from Futura terminal
Mexico City (Terminal Sur)	175	3hr	4 EDO
	173	3hr	5 from Futura terminal

cherubs, fish windchimes, and, yes, silver. Here though, the prices are marked and close to what you pay on the street outside.

Information

Several banks around the main plazas and bus stations have ATMs. There are card phones near Plaza Borda, and quieter ones in nicer hotel lobbies.

Cruz Roja (Red Cross; ☎065)

Hospital General (☎762-622-93-00)

Police (☎762-622-10-17)

Post Office (Palacio Municipal, Juárez 10)

Tourist Module (Plaza Borda) There's a tourism kiosk in the main plaza that mostly exists to hand out brochures and push tours.

Getting There & Away

The shared Futura/Estrella Blanca terminal on Avenida de los Plateros offers luggage storage. The Estrella de Oro (EDO) terminal is at the south end of town.

For more frequent bus services to the coast, take a shared taxi ($24) from in front of the bus station to the nearby town of Iguala, about 30 minutes away.

Getting Around

Apart from walking, combis (white Volkswagen minibuses) and taxis are the best way to navigate Taxco's steep and narrow cobbled streets.

Combis (M$4.50) are frequent and operate from 7am to 8pm. 'Zócalo' combis depart from Plaza Borda, travel down Cuauhtémoc to Plazuela de San Juan, then head down the hill on Hidalgo. They turn right at Morelos, left at Avenida de los Plateros, and go north until La Garita, where they turn left and return to the *zócalo*. 'Arcos/Zócalo' combis follow the same route except that they continue past La Garita to Los Arcos, where they do a U-turn and head back to La Garita. Combis marked 'PM' (for Pedro Martín) go to the southern end of town from Plaza Borda, past the Estrella de Oro bus station. Taxis cost M$20 to M$35 for trips around town.

Parque Nacional Grutas de Cacahuamilpa

One of central Mexico's most stunning natural sights, the **Cacahuamilpa caverns** (http://cacahuamilpa.conanp.gob.mx; admission with guide adult/child M$70/46; ⏲10am-7pm) is a must-see for anyone visiting Taxco or Cuernavaca. The scale of the caves is hard to imagine, with vast chambers up to 82m high leading 1.2km beneath the mountainside, inside of which are mind-blowing stalactites and stalagmites.

Unfortunately, individual access to the (perfectly safe) pathway through the caves is not allowed. Instead, visitors are allocated free guides who lead large group tours (departures each hour on the hour), with constant stops to point out shapes (Santa Claus, a kneeling child, a gorilla) in the rock. At the end of the one-hour tour, you can wander back to the entrance – with the lights now off – at your own pace. Most guides do not speak English.

From the cave exit it's possible to follow a steep path 15 minutes to the fast-flowing **Río Dos Bocas**. There are spectacular views year-round and tranquil pools for swimming during the dry season. Bring bug spray.

Weekends are often very crowded, with long lines and large group tours – making mid-week a more pleasant time for a visit. There are restaurants, snacks and souvenir shops near the entrance. Between the entrance and the caves, it's possible to take a short zipline (M$70) across the treetops, or you can just walk the 150 metres around. The last ticket for the caverns is sold at 5pm.

Getting There & Away

To reach the caverns, take an Estrella Blanca 'Grutas' bus from the main Avenida de los Plateros bus terminal in Taxco (M$28, 40 minutes, every 30 minutes) or taxi (M$180). Buses deposit you at the crossroad where the road splits off to Cuernavaca. From there, walk 350m downhill to the park's visitor center. Return buses leave from the same crossroad (every 30 minutes, last bus 8pm).

WEST OF MEXICO CITY

The area to the west of Mexico City is dominated by the large industrial and administrative city of Toluca, the capital of the state of Mexico. While pleasant, Toluca has little to recommend it to travelers and most bypass it en route to the area's two wonderful small-town, colonial gems. Malinalco is a sleepy and remote village with some fascinating pre-Hispanic ruins perched above it, and Valle de Bravo, a cosmopolitan getaway favored by Mexico's elite is located on the shores of a large, artificial reservoir that's a dramatic two-hour drive west of Toluca. The countryside surrounding Toluca itself is scenic with pine forests, rivers and a huge extinct volcano, the Nevado de Toluca.

Toluca

722 / POP 490,000 / ELEV 2660M

Like many colonial Mexican cities, Toluca's development has created a ring of urban sprawl around what remains a very picturesque old town. The traffic problems alone can be enough to dampen the city's appeal, however those who make time to visit will find Toluca a pleasant, if bustling, small city. It's an enjoyable place to spend a day exploring attractive plazas, lively shopping arcades, art galleries and museums.

Toluca was an indigenous settlement from at least the 13th century. The Spanish founded the modern city in the 16th century after defeating the resident Aztecs and Matlazincas, and it became part of Hernán Cortés' expansive domain, the Marquesado del Valle de Oaxaca. Since 1830 it's been the capital of Mexico state, which surrounds the Distrito Federal on three sides, like an upside-down U.

The main road from Mexico City becomes Paseo Tollocan on Toluca's eastern edge, before bearing southwest and becoming a ring road around the city center's southern edge. Toluca's bus station and the huge Mercado Juárez are 2km southeast of the center, off Paseo Tollocan.

The vast Plaza de los Mártires, with the cathedral and Palacio de Gobierno, marks the town center. Most of the action, however, is concentrated a block south in the pedestrian precinct. Shady Parque Alameda is three blocks west along Hidalgo.

Sights

The 19th-century **Portal Madero**, running 250m along Avenida Hidalgo, is lively, as is the commercial arcade along the pedestrian street to the east, which attracts mariachis after 9pm. A block north, the large, open expanse of **Plaza de los Mártires** is surrounded by fine old government buildings; the 19th-century **cathedral** and the 18th-century **Templo de la Santa Veracruz** are on its south side. On Plaza Garibay's north side is the 18th-century **Templo del Carmen.**

★Cosmovitral Jardín Botánico GARDENS
(Cosmo Stained-Glass Window Botanical Garden; 722-214-67-85; cnr Juárez & Lerdo de Tejada; adult/child M$10/5; 9am-6pm Tue-Sun) At the northeast end of Plaza Garibay, the stunning and unique Cosmovitral Jardín Botánico was built in 1909 as a market. The building now houses 3500 sq meters of lovely gardens, lit through 48 stained-glass panels by the Tolucan artist Leopoldo Flores.

Centro Cultural Mexiquense MUSEUM
(State of Mexico Cultural Center; 722-274-12-00; Blvd Reyes Heroles 302; admission M$10, Sun free; 10am-3pm Tue-Fri, 10am-6pm Sat, 10am-3pm Sun) This large cultural center, 4.5km west of the city center, houses three good museums (which all keep the same hours). It's no must-see but still a worthwhile diversion for visitors interested in local arts and crafts, local archaeology and modern art.

To get here it's easiest to take one of the plentiful *colectivos* from outside the Mercado Juárez – just look for 'Centro Cultural' on its destination board. The circuitous ride takes 20 minutes. Get off by the large grass roundabout near the Monterrey University Toluca Campus, cross to the opposite side and the museum complex is through the gate and down the road. From downtown you can take a cab (M$40).

Museo de Antropología e História MUSEUM
(722-274-12-00; Blvd Reyes Heroles 302; admission M$10, Sun free; 10am-3pm Tue-Fri, 10am-6pm Sat, 10am-3pm Sun) The standout museum, Museo de Antropología e História presents exhibits on the state's history from prehistoric times to the 20th century, with a good collection of pre-Hispanic artifacts. It also traces pre-Hispanic cultural influences up to the modern day in tools, clothing, textiles and religion. Nearly all the labels are only in Spanish.

Museo de Culturas Populares MUSEUM
(722-274-12-00; Blvd Reyes Heroles 302; admission M$10, Sun free; 10am-3pm Tue-Fri, 10am-6pm Sat, 10am-3pm Sun) This museum has a wonderfully varied collection of Mexico's traditional arts and crafts, with some astounding 'trees of life' from Metepec, whimsical Day of the Dead figures and a fine display of *charro* (cowboy) gear. There are also mosaics, traditional rugs, a loft and a gift shop.

Museo de Arte Moderno MUSEUM
(722-274-12-00; Blvd Reyes Heroles 302; admission M$10, Sun free; 10am-3pm Tue-Fri, 10am-6pm Sat, 10am-3pm Sun) Traces the development of Mexican art from the late-19th-century Academia de San Carlos to the Nueva Plástica and includes paintings by Tamayo, Orozco and many others. There's an impressive spherical mural of people fight-

ing against slavery, which makes up part of the building itself, as well as exhibits of challenging pieces of contemporary art.

Museo Modelo de Ciencias e Industria MUSEUM
(MUMCI; www.mumci.org; Av Hidalgo Oriente No 201; admission M$50; ⏲10am-6pm Tue-Fri, to 8pm Sat & Sun) The Museo Modelo de Ciencias e Industria is one of the odder museums you're likely to encounter in Mexico. Devoted to the corporate history of the Modelo beer company, the museum is a propaganda machine extolling the virtues of one of Mexico's most famous conglomerates. It is, however, good for a laugh. The best thing going for the complex, besides the attractive facade, is its **IMAX** (admission M$70, combined museum ticket $110; ⏲last show 4:30pm) theater, which is incredibly well-priced and shows mostly English movies with Spanish subtitles.

Museo de Bellas Artes MUSEUM
(☎722-215-53-29; Degollado 102; adult/child M$10/5; ⏲10am-6pm Tue-Sat, to 3pm Sun) The ex-convent buildings adjacent to the Templo del Carmen, on the north side of Plaza Garibay, house Toluca's Museo de Bellas Artes, which exhibits paintings from the colonial period to the early 20th century.

Tours

Tranvía TRAM
(☎722-330-50-54; www.tranviatoluca.com; adult/child M$40/30; ⏲departs hourly 11am-5pm) This motorized tram leaves from the cathedral and visits two dozen sites in the city in 50 minutes.

Sleeping

Hotel Colonial INN $
(☎722-215-97-00; Hidalgo Oriente 103; s/d/tr M$350/400/500; P 📶) The rooms overlooking the busy main road are the best, but also the loudest, at this well-run and excellent-value hotel. The impressive lobby and friendly staff are other good reasons to come here. Rates include free parking nearby in a lot on Juárez.

Hotel Don Simon BUSINESS HOTEL $$
(☎722-213-26-96; Matamoros 202; r M$700; P @ 📶) The rooms at Don Simon are immaculately clean and bright, if a little heavy on the brown furnishings of yesteryear, which continue into the attached restaurant. It's a definite winner for good value in central Toluca – the staff are friendly, the street is quiet and it's just a short walk to the Cosmovitral.

Fiesta Inn Toluca Centro BUSINESS HOTEL $$$
(☎722-167-89-00; www.fiestainn.com; Allende Sur 124; r/ste M$2370/2850; P @ 📶) This modern, sleek, 85-room Fiesta Inn (formerly the Gran Hotel) has airy, comfortable rooms, a small gym and a cafe-bar-restaurant in the lobby. There's a second Fiesta Inn near the airport.

Eating & Drinking

Toluqueños take snacking and sweets very seriously and you can join them in the arcades around Plaza Fray Andrés de Castro. Other stalls sell candied fruit and *jamoncillos* (pumpkin-seed pastes), and *mostachones* (sweets made of burned milk). Most eateries in the center are open from around 8am to 9pm.

★La Gloria Chocolatería y Pan 1876 CAFE $
(Quintana Roo; snacks M$10-35; ⏲11am-11pm) You feel lucky just to be here, and you'll almost certainly be the only foreign visitor when you come. This wonderful, friendly, family-run cafe serves a tempting menu of local cuisine, from *tacos al pastor* (spicy pork tacos) and delicious *sermones* (sandwiches) stuffed with oven-baked pork or shredded chicken bathed in *mole poblano*.

Arte Café Libros ETC CAFE $
(☎722-213-87-32; fb.com/arte.cafe.libros.etc; Independencia #101, upstairs; coffee M$15-30, baguettes M$35-80; ⏲9am-6pm Mon-Fri; 📶) The name sums it up nicely – art by local artists, fresh coffee and baguettes on the terrace, and plenty of books to browse or buy. The ETC would be the live music, film festivals and odds and ends for sale such as t-shirts, healing herbs and jewelry. Closed weekends unless there is an event on.

Hostería Las Ramblas MEXICAN $$
(☎722-215-54-88; Calle 20 de Noviembre 107D; mains M$90-150; ⏲9am-8pm) Located on a pedestrian mall, this atmospheric restaurant feels like a throwback to the 1950s, with white tablecloths and retro decor. Attentive waiters serve full breakfasts, including some excellent vegetarian options like the *omelette campesino* – *panela* cheese, *rajas* (*poblano* chili) and zucchini – and a variety of lunch and dinner entrees like *mole verde* and *conejo al ajillo* (liberally garlicked rabbit).

Shopping

Casart ARTS & CRAFTS

(Casa de Artesanía; Aldama 102; ⏲10am-6pm Tue-Sun) This new downtown location of Casart – the state organization promoting local crafts – is fantastic both for its beautiful home, set around a courtyard, and its wonderful selection of quality arts and crafts. Prices are fixed and therefore higher than you might be able to get haggling in markets for an inferior product (for the cheapest prices, go directly to the source).

Information

There are banks with ATMs near Portal Madero.

Cruz Roja (Red Cross; ☎722-217-33-33)

City Tourist Office (☎ext 104 722-384-11-00; www.toluca.gob.mx/turismo; Plaza Fray Andrés de Castro, Edificio B, Local 6, Planta Baja)

State Tourist Office (☎722-212-59-98; www.edomexico.gob.mx; cnr Urawa & Paseo Tollocan) Inconveniently located 2km southeast of the center, but with English-speaking staff and good maps.

Tourist Information Kiosk (Palacio Municipal) Helpful kiosk with free city map.

Getting There & Away

The modern, efficient and low-stress **Aeropuerto Internacional de Toluca** (☎722-279-28-00; www.vuelatoluca.com) is an excellent alternative to Mexico City's massive and intimidating airport. Conveniently located off Hwy 15, about 10km from downtown, the airport is adjacent to the industrial zone and a group of business-friendly chain hotels.

Toluca is the hub for budget airline **Interjet** (www.interjet.com.mx), which offers flights to Las Vegas and all over Mexico.

Spirit Airlines (☎800-772-7117; www.spirit.com) and **Volaris** (☎800-122-80-00; www.volaris.com.mx) also offer international service. They fly travelers between Toluca and several cities in the United States, including Los Angeles, Chicago, Las Vegas, Houston, San Francisco, Seattle, Newark, Miami, New York and Atlanta.

Europcar (www.europcar.com), **Dollar** (www.dollar.com) and **Alamo** (www.alamo.com) all have rental-car offices at Toluca International Airport.

There are frequent buses from the airport to both Mexico City (M$90 Interjet Shuttlebus to Polanco, Reforma or WTC) and the capital's Aeropuerto Internacional (M$130 Caminante Shuttlebus), which take an hour or two, depending on traffic. An authorized taxi from the airport to downtown Toluca costs about M$20 and takes 20-30 minutes.

Toluca's **bus station** (Berriozábal 101) is 2km southeast of the center. Ticket offices for many destinations are on the platforms or at the gate entrances, and it's fair to say it can be a confusing place.

Getting Around

Large 'Centro' buses go from outside Toluca's bus station to the town center (M$8, 20 minutes) along Lerdo de Tejada. From Juárez in the center, 'Terminal' buses go to the bus station. Taxis from the bus station to the city center cost around M$40.

Nevado de Toluca

Among the highest peaks in the region, the long-extinct volcano Nevado de Toluca (also known as Xinantécatl) is Mexico's fourth-tallest peak. The Nevado has two summits on the crater rim. The lower summit, Pico del Águila (4620m), is closer to the parking area and is the more common day-hike. The main or highest summit is called Pico del Fraile (4704m) and requires an additional three to four hours of hiking time.

The earlier you reach the summit, the better the chance of clear views. The crater contains two lakes, El Sol and La Luna. The summit area can be snowy from November to March, and is sometimes good for cross-country skiing but the **Parque Nacional Nevado de Toluca** is closed during the heaviest snowfalls. On 1 October 2013, the

BUSES FROM TOLUCA

DESTINATION	FARE (M$)	DURATION	FREQUENCY (DAILY)
Cuernavaca	67	2hr	24
Mexico City (Poniente)	42-65	1 hr	40
Morelia	245	2hr	14
Taxco	91	3hr	7
Valle de Bravo	67	2¼hr	10
Zihuatanejo	486	9 hr	3

Mexican government redesignated the national park as a *zona protegida* (protected area), legalizing and legitimizing the unregulated mining activity that had been going on there. Most people still continue to call it a national park.

From the park entrance a road winds 3.5km up to the **main gate** (entrance per vehicle M$20, per pickup truck M$40; ⏲10am-5pm); last entry is at 3pm. From there it's a 17km drive along an unsurfaced road up to the crater. Dress warmly – it gets chilly up top.

Just beyond the gate, **Posada Familiar** (campsite/dm M$75/150) offers basic lodging at a heavily used refuge with shared hot showers, a kitchen (without utensils) and a common area with a fireplace. Bring extra blankets. On Saturday and Sunday, food is served at stalls around Parque de los Venados and at the gate near the summit. Midweek, bring your own food and water.

From Toluca, taxis will take you to the trailhead for upwards of M$250, or there and back (including time for a look around) for a negotiable M$500. Be sure to hire a newer taxi; the road up is very rough and dusty. Most international car rental companies also have offices in Toluca.

Mario Andrade leads one-day **climbs** (☎55-1826-2146; mountainup@hotmail.com; US$200 incl transportation, 1 meal & park entrance) and also guides climbers on Izta ascents.

Valle de Bravo

☎726 / POP 28,000 / ELEV 1800M

With one of the loveliest colonial centers in central Mexico, the *pueblo mágico* of Valle de Bravo is an utter charmer and a wonderful spot for an escape from Mexico City. A long, winding and occasionally stunning mountain road runs the 85km west from Toluca, taking you to the shores of Lake Avandaro – this is an artificial lake, the result of the construction of a hydroelectric station.

The setting here is reminiscent of the northern Italian lakes, with thickly wooded, mist-clad hills and red terracotta roofing used throughout the town. Valle, as it's known, is famous for being the weekend retreat of choice for the capital's well-connected upper classes. The views at the lakeside are stunning but the beguiling and largely intact colonial center is arguably the real draw here. Boating on the lake is very popular as well, as are hiking and camping in the hills around the town. Valle is set up well for visitors. There's a tourist-info kiosk on the wharf and essential services, including ATMs and internet cafes, are found around the main plaza, which is a 10-minute walk uphill from the waterfront.

In late October or early November, the week-long **Festival de las Almas**, an international arts and culture extravaganza, brings in music and dance troupes from all over Europe and Latin America.

Activities

Kosawi YOGA

(☎726-262-07-63; fb.com/espacio.kosawi; Vergel 2; yoga classes M$100; 👪) Streams of families escape business-minded Mexico City for leisurely Valle de Bravo every weekend. So no wonder Kosawi has drop-in classes for prenatal yoga, acrobatics for kids, or 'danzayoga', which rolls contemporary dance and yoga into one. The converted courtyard is clean and minimalist, and despite being only one block north of the cathedral, feels a world away.

Sleeping

For a small town, this popular weekend escape from Mexico City has a good selection of budget posadas and midrange hotels. The most affordable options are within two blocks of the bus station.

Posada Familiar Los Girasoles GUESTHOUSE $

(☎726-262-29-67; Plaza Independencia 1; s/d M$400, tr M$500, q M$600-750) This nine-room posada has an enviable location on the *zócalo*. It has spacious and spotlessly clean rooms, complete with rustic touches and a warm, family-run feeling. Expect to be asked where you're from and shown photos of former guests (all 'friends') who have stayed here.

Hotel Casanueva BOUTIQUE HOTEL $$$

(☎726-262-17-66; Villagrán 100; s/d/ste M$780/980/1200) Set on the west side of the *zócalo*, the Casanueva has individually designed rooms decorated with tasteful arts and crafts. The most stylish option downtown, the hotel's suite, which sleeps four, is especially lovely. Some rooms have private balconies over the square.

Rodavento RESORT $$$

(☎726-251-41-82; www.rodavento.com; Carretera Valle de Bravo–Los Saucos Km 3.5; ste from M$2500; P❄🏊) Set on a sprawling property outside of Valle, this rustic-luxe hotel distinguishes itself with its natural design – using earth tones, traditional wood stoves, and sliding glass doors opening onto the forest, gardens and a private lake.

El Santuario RESORT **$$$**
(726-262-91-00; www.elsantuario.com; Carretera Colorines, San Gaspar; r from M$4095; P) Twenty minutes outside town, this gorgeous hillside hotel has an infinity pool, fountains, an in-house spa and rooms with magnificent lake views. There's also a golf course, horse stables and a marina with sailboat rentals.

Eating

There are scores of restaurants and cafes along the wharf and around the *zócalo*; many are only open from Friday to Sunday. If there ever was a time to try *esquites* (lime and chili-flavoured corn in a cup) from street stalls, this is it. Villagrán on the west of the *zócalo* has very clean food stands.

★**Ciento Once** INTERNATIONAL **$$**
(http://cientooncevalle.blogspot.com; Calzada de Santa María 111; tapas M$35-100) Visit the plant-filled back deck of this modern restaurant for house-made bread, a wide range of authentic tapas, a small selection of excellent mains – including tuna steaks and *arrachera* (grilled beef) – and some quality wine, all made by a former anthropologist who relocated from Mexico City.

Restaurante Paraíso FISH **$$**
(726-262-47-31; Fray Gregorio Jiménez de la Cuenca s/n; mains M$75-160; 8am-11pm) With fantastic lake views and a sprawling menu of seafood specialties, plus excellent and imaginatively prepared local trout, come early and watch the sunset from the rooftop patio.

Los Churros y Las Alcachofas de Valle FUSION **$$**
(cnr 16 de Septiembre & El Vergel; mains M$85-124; 1-11pm) Late into the evening, the children are bright eyed and high on the fresh hot *churros* (doughnut-like fritters) at this family-friendly restaurant, a block north of the cathedral. The casual vibe isn't just for families – couples come for the sharp vinaigrette *alcachofas* (artichokes), which play nicely with the creamy salmon.

Information

Tourist Information Stand (zócalo east side; 9am-5pm) Staff speak a bit of English, give directions and have free maps and tour brochures.

Getting There & Away

Considering the hordes of tourists who descend on Valle each weekend, transportation options are relatively few. Most visitors are affluent Mexicans, who come by car.

Autobuses company México-Toluca-Zinacantepec y Ramales runs hourly 2nd-class *directos* from early morning to late afternoon between Mexico City's Terminal Poniente (M$113, three hours) and Valle de Bravo's small bus terminal on Calle 16 de Septiembre. For a scenic ride ask for the southern, 'Los Saucos' route, which travels along Hwy 134 and through a national park. If driving that's the route to take as well.

There is no direct bus between Malinalco and Valle de Bravo. You have to travel via Toluca or Mexico City.

Malinalco

714 / POP 7000 / ELEV 1740M

Set in a valley of dramatic cliffs and ancient ruins, this *pueblo mágico* is rapidly becoming the next Tepoztlán. Weekends now see crowds, but still far fewer than those that descend on more easily accessible weekend escapes. The drive to Malinalco is one of the most enjoyable to be had in the area, with dramatic scenery lining the road south of Toluca.

There are already a clutch of hippie stores, a handful of international restaurants and, it seems, a surprising number of boutique hotels. The town is far from fully developed though – and it's almost unnervingly quiet mid-week, when it can still be a challenge to find a decent place to eat outside of the *zócalo*.

The village itself has a charming colonial core set around a well-preserved convent and two central plazas which sit side by side. In the larger plaza, the **tourist module** (www.malinalco.net; 9am -6pm) offers limited help and there's an ATM on Hidalgo, on the convent's north side. **Cyber Malinalco** (Hidalgo 104; per hr M$10) offers reasonably priced internet access.

Sights

Aztec Temples ARCHAEOLOGICAL SITE
(admission M$46; 9am-6pm Tue-Sun) An invigorating 358-step hike up the mountainside above Malinalco takes you to one of the country's few reasonably well-preserved **temples**, from where there are stunning

views of the valley and beyond. From the main square follow signs to the *zona arqueológica,* which take you up the hillside on a well-maintained footpath with signs in Spanish, English and Náhuatl; the last ticket is sold at 5pm. The site itself is fascinating and includes El Paraíso de los Guerreros (a mural that once covered an entire wall) depicting fallen warriors becoming deities and living in paradise.

The Aztecs conquered the region in 1476 and were busy building a ritual center here when they were conquered by the Spanish. **El Cuauhcalli** (the Temple of the Eagle and Jaguar Knight, where sons of Aztec nobles were initiated into warrior orders) survived because it was hewn from the mountainside itself. The entrance is carved in the form of a fanged serpent.

Temple IV (located on the far side of the site) continues to baffle archaeologists. As the room is positioned to allow the first rays of sunlight to hit it at dawn, there has been speculation that this place was part of a Mexica sun cult, a solar calendar or a meeting place for nobles – or some combination of these.

Situated near the site entrance, the **Museo Universitario Dr Luis Mario Schneider** (714-147-12-88; admission M$10; 10am-4pm Tue-Sun) explores the region's history and archaeology in a beautiful modern museum space.

Augustinian Convent CHURCH

FREE A well-restored 16th-century **convent**, fronted by a tranquil tree-lined yard, faces the central plaza. Impressive frescoes fashioned from herb- and flower-based paint adorn its cloister.

Courses

ReciclArte Malinalco CRAFTS

(fb.com/reciclarte.malinalco; cnr Juárez & Galeana; drop-in classes M$15; 10am-2pm Sat & Sun;) This craft workshop, just downhill from the market, teaches kids how to reuse materials such as newspapers and bike innertubes, transforming them into picture frames, earrings and other giftables with a Mexican artesan twist. The teachers at these community classes mainly speak Spanish, but activities are mostly show and copy, and open to all who drop by (even for a sticky beak).

Tours

Tour Gastronómico Prehispánico CULINARY EXPERIENCE

(55-5509-1411; aplegaspi@prodigy.net.mx) This pre-Hispanic food tour includes a visit to the market, a cooking class using traditional utensils and methods, and a three-course meal.

Sleeping

This small town has an inordinate number of hotel rooms, but reservations remain a good idea. Because Malinalco is geared toward weekend visitors, you'll have no trouble finding a room Sunday to Thursday nights – though some of the nicer hotels aren't open for walk-ins (or at all) mid-week.

Hotel Santa Mónica GUESTHOUSE $

(714-147-00-31; Hidalgo 109; r M$350;) Just a few steps from the *zócalo* and en route to the archaeological zone, this is one of the better budget options, with clean, if shabby, rooms (all with private bathroom and TV) scattered around a simple courtyard. Prices are even lower midweek.

El Asoleadero HOTEL $$

(714-147-01-84; cnr Aldama & Comercio; r M$450-500, with kitchen M$600-650;) Just uphill from Malinalco's main drag, El Asoleadero offers spacious, modern and airy rooms with stunning views of the *pueblito* (village) and surrounding cliffs. You can enjoy the million-peso vista from the courtyard's small pool with a cold beer from the lobby.

Casa Mora BOUTIQUE HOTEL $$$

(714-147-05-72; www.casamora.net; Calle de la Cruz 18; ste incl breakfast M$2500-2700;) You'll feel more like a houseguest than a tourist at this beautifully appointed oasis. It's the pet project of a local artist who maintains five beautiful rooms, all of which enjoy an intimate and romantic atmosphere. Unfortunately, Mora's location makes getting to and fro without your own transportation fairly inconvenient. Prices are lower mid-week.

Casa Navacoyan BOUTIQUE HOTEL $$$

(714-147-04-11; www.casanavacoyan.com; Prolongación Calle Pirul 62; ste incl breakfast from M$1800-2000;) This gorgeous, hotel on the outskirts of town has just six rooms – each decorated in a sort of upscale, homestyle aesthetic, like staying at your wealthy aunt's house in the country. The immaculately groomed yard is the real attraction, with palm trees, a gorgeous pool and views of Malinalco's famed hills and cliffs.

Eating

Perhaps surprisingly for such a small town, Malinalco has a few very good restaurants. Unfortunately for those visiting midweek though, most of the better options are only open Friday through Sunday.

★ **Los Placeres** INTERNATIONAL **$$**
(☎714-147-03-90; Principal s/n; mains M$75-190; ⏱2-10pm Fri, 9am-11pm Sat, 9am-6pm Sun;) This artsy restaurant on Malinalco's *zócalo* serves international fare (Niçoise salad or chicken curry), alongside creative takes on traditional Mexican dishes, like omelets with *poblano* sauce, trout with *ancho* chilies or fondue *al tequila*. There are elaborate murals, tile-mosaic tabletops and the likes of Robert Johnson on the sound system.

El Puente de Má-Li INTERNATIONAL **$$**
(☎714-147-17-43; Hidalgo 22; mains M$80-130; ⏱1pm-6pm Tue-Thu, to 11pm Fri & Sat, 9am-6pm Sun) After the tiny bridge as you leave the *zócalo* for the ruins, this atmospheric restaurant is set around a colonial dining room and a great back garden where you can try a selection of *antojitos*, pastas, soups and steaks.

Koi ASIAN **$$**
(☎714-147-16-21; Morelos 18; mains M$55-150; ⏱2pm-midnight Fri & Sat, to 8pm Sun & Mon) With its artful, Asian-inspired touches and creative menu, Koi is an unexpected pleasure. Offerings include Pad Thai, fish tempura and asparagus teriyaki – all of which are tasty but scarcely resemble their Asian namesakes.

Getting There & Away

Most public transportation to Malinalco goes via Tenancingo. **Águila** (☎800-224-84-52; www.autobusesaguila.com.mx), however, runs two buses each afternoon (4:20pm and 6:20pm) from Mexico City's Terminal Poniente (M$85, 2 hours) to Malinalco. If you can't wait, Águila also run twice an hour between Terminal Poniente and Tenancingo (M$75, 2 hours).

From Tenancingo, take the *colectivo* (M$12, 30 minutes) or taxi (M$65) to Malinalco. Águila buses do not have toilets on board. The weekend-only direct bus from Malinalco to Terminal Poniente runs at 3:50pm and 5:10pm from outside the Santander bank on Hidalgo.

From Toluca, take an Águila bus to Tenancingo (M$19, one hour, every 10 to 20 minutes) and ask the driver to let you off at the *colectivo* to Malinalco (M$12, 30 minutes).

Though the distances are short, traveling from Malinalco to Cuernavaca can take hours. It is, however, possible to hire a taxi (M$165, about one hour) and travel between the two towns via the incredibly scenic trip through Puente Caporal-Palpan-Miacatlán, to the town of Alpuyeca, near the Xochicalco ruins. From there, it's easy to flag one of the frequent buses traveling along Hwy 95, and continue either north (to Cuernavaca and Mexico City) or south (to Taxco and the coast).

Ixtapan de la Sal

☎721 / POP 18,000 / ELEV 1880M

Ixtapan is known throughout Mexico for its curative waters. They have attracted visitors since the town was founded centuries ago by indigenous travelers from the Pacific coast, who were amazed to discover salt water inland while on their way to Tenochtitlán. Despite its long history, there's not much to see here and the only reason to stop is to visit **Ixtapan Parque Acuático** (☎800-493-27-26; www.parqueixtapan.com; adult/child M$180/free; ⏱spa 8am-7pm, aquatic park 9am-6pm), a sprawling water park mixing curative thermal water pools with waterfalls, water slides, a wave pool and a miniature railway. There's a range of hotels in town.

Águila buses run from Toluca (M$41, one hour, every 20 minutes) and Taxco (M$51, 1¼ hours; every 45 minutes).

Veracruz

Includes ➡

Best Places to Eat

- ➡ El Brou (p222)
- ➡ Las Delicias Marinas (p217)
- ➡ Restaurante Mesón Xiqueño (p227)
- ➡ Los Canarios (p212)
- ➡ Ulúa Fish (p212)

Best Places to Stay

- ➡ Posada del Emperador (p232)
- ➡ Mesón del Alférez Xalapa (p220)
- ➡ Hotel Azúcar (p243)
- ➡ Hotel Posada Doña Lala (p246)

Why Go?

Taking up much of Mexico's Caribbean coastline, the long and diverse state of Veracruz is where the Spanish conquest of the Aztecs began. It was also the cradle of the aptly named Veracruz Mesoamerican culture at El Tajín and is home to Mexico's highest peak, soaring, snow-capped Orizaba.

As a destination it's routinely overlooked by travelers, and while it's true that the beaches are better in the Yucatán and the colonial towns more impressive in Mexico's central and western highlands, Veracruz has a steady supply of charms in both categories. It also lays claim to the World Heritage site of colonial Tlacotalpan, the impressive Biosphere Reserve of Los Tuxtlas and some gorgeous *pueblos mágicos* (magical villages) including hilly Papantla, cobbled Coscomatepec and the coffee-growing center of Xico.

Its biggest attraction, however, is its quietness. Wherever you go here, you'll find yourself well off the beaten path, with discoveries just waiting to be made.

When to Go

Veracruz City

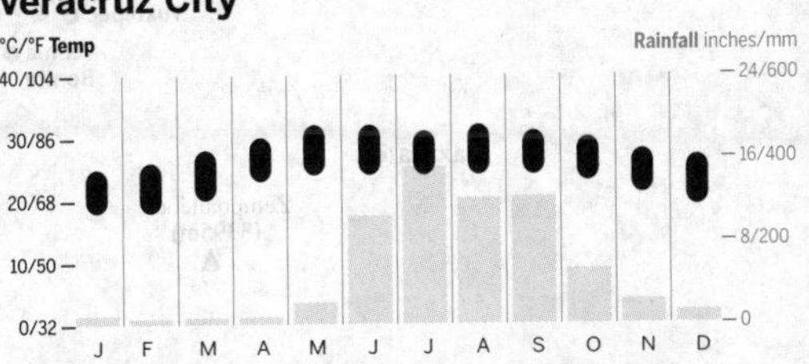

Oct Cheap prices, bearable temperatures and barely another tourist in sight.

Feb–Mar The Veracruz Carnaval kicks off the biggest party on Mexico's eastern coast.

Nov–Feb Peak tourist season for non-Mexicans with less rain and balmy temperatures.

Veracruz Highlights

1 Decipher a triumvirate of Mesoamerican cultures in Xalapa's architecturally magnificent **Museo de Antropología** (p218)

2 Marvel at the many colors of colonial **Tlacotalpan** (p245), perhaps Mexico's least known World Heritage site

3 Imagine past glories at the extensive ruins of **El Tajín** (p241)

4 Take a boat across Laguna de Sontecomapan for fresh fish on the beach at **La Barra** (p254)

5 Sip gourmet coffee in the cloud forest–encased towns of **Coatepec** (p224) or **Xico** (p226)

6 Climb (or at least take the cable car) up Mexico's highest mountain, magnificent **Pico de Orizaba** (p235)

7 Watch grown men fly at a one-of-a-kind *voladores* ceremony in **Papantla** (p237)

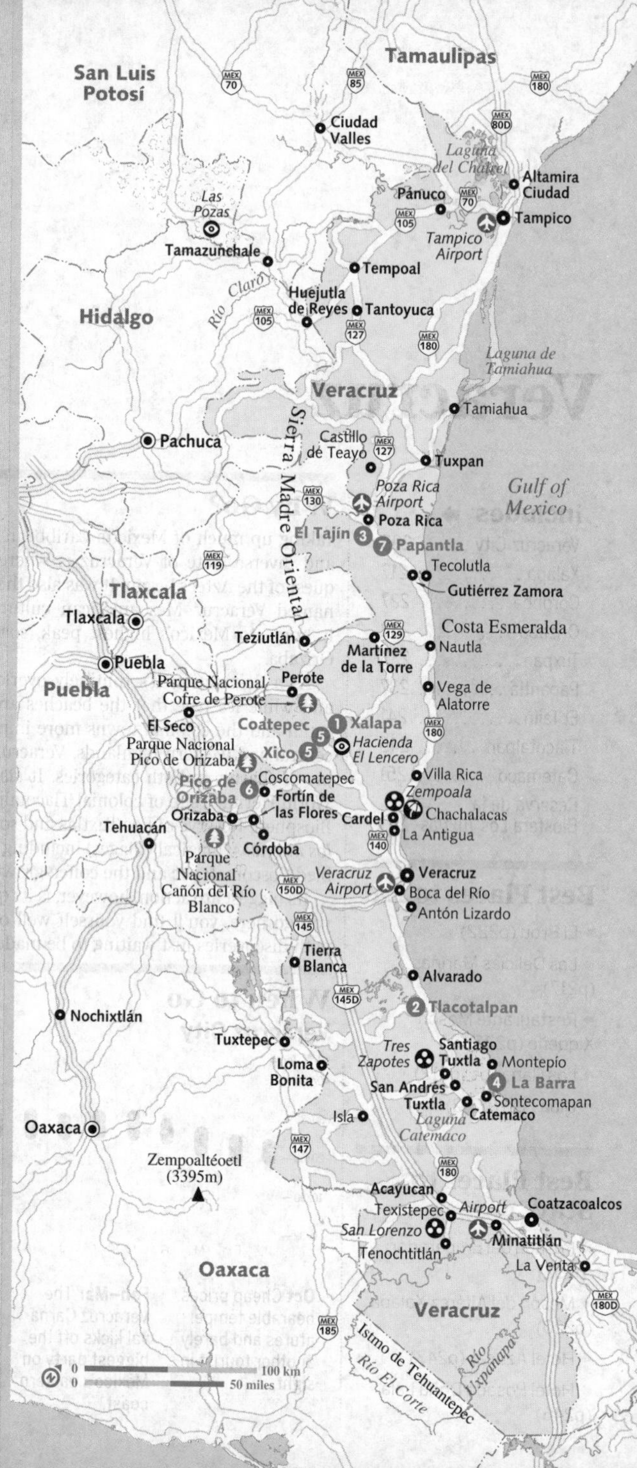

History

The Olmecs, Mesoamerica's earliest known civilization, built their first great center around 1200 BC at San Lorenzo in southern Veracruz state. In 900 BC the city was violently destroyed, but Olmec culture lingered for several centuries at Tres Zapotes. During the Classic period (AD 250–900) the Gulf coast developed another distinctive culture, known as the Classic Veracruz civilization. Its most important center was El Tajín, which was at its peak between AD 600 and 900. In the post-Classic period the Totonacs established themselves in the region south of Tuxpan. North of Tuxpan, the Huastec civilization flourished from AD 800 to 1200. During this time, the warlike Toltecs also moved into the Gulf coast area. In the mid-15th century, the Aztecs took over most of the Totonac and Huastec areas, exacting tributes of goods and sacrificial victims, and subduing revolts.

When Hernán Cortés arrived in April 1519, he made Zempoala's Totonacs his first allies against the Aztecs by vowing to protect them against reprisals. Cortés set up his first settlement, Villa Rica de la Vera Cruz (Rich Town of the True Cross), and by 1523 all the Gulf coast was in Spanish hands. Forced slavery, newly introduced diseases and the ravages of war severely reduced indigenous populations.

Veracruz harbor became an essential trade and communications link with Spain and was vital for anyone trying to rule Mexico, but the climate, tropical diseases and pirate threats inhibited the growth of Spanish settlements.

Under dictator Porfirio Díaz, Mexico's first railway linked Veracruz to Mexico City in 1872, stimulating industrial development. In 1901 oil was discovered in the Tampico area, and by the 1920s the region was producing a quarter of the world's oil. In the 1980s the Gulf coast still held well over half of Mexico's reserves and refining capacity. Today, the region is not as large a player as it used to be, but is still a significant contributor to Mexico's oil economy.

Dangers & Annoyances

Mexico's infamous drug war migrated to Veracruz in early 2011 with nasty gang wars claiming lives in Veracruz City, Boca del Río and Xalapa. At its peak, 35 victims of drug violence were unceremoniously dumped on the street in Veracruz City. This resulted in the dismissal of the entire city police force by the central government, on the basis that it had become so infiltrated by the Zetas drug cartel that it was no longer fit for purpose. Things have quietened down a little since then and, despite some understandably bad press, the state remains relatively safe for travelers. At the time of writing, no foreign tourists and few innocent Mexican bystanders had been directly affected by the violence.

The biggest risk to most travelers is petty theft in cheap hotel rooms and pickpocketing in crowded market areas, especially in big cities. Hurricanes threaten between June and November; check out the **US National Hurricane Center website** (www.nhc.noaa.gov) for the latest. Mosquitoes in coastal regions can carry dengue fever, especially in central and southeastern Veracruz.

Veracruz City

229 / POP 552,000

Veracruz, like all great port cities, is an unholy mélange of grime, romance and melted-down cultures. Conceived in 1519, this is Mexico's oldest European-founded settlement, but, usurped by subsequent inland cities, it's neither its most historic, nor its most visually striking. Countless sackings by the French, Spanish and North Americans have siphoned off the prettiest buildings, leaving a motley patchwork of working docks and questionable hybrid architecture, punctuated by the odd stray colonial masterpiece. But Veracruz' beauty is in its grit rather than its grandiosity. A carefree spirit reigns in the *zócalo* (main square) most evenings, where the primary preoccupation is who to cajole into a *danzón* (traditional couples dance).

History

Hernán Cortés arrived at the site of present-day Veracruz on Good Friday, April 21, 1519, and began his siege of Mexico. By 1521 he had crushed the Aztec empire.

Veracruz provided Mexico's main gateway to the outside world for 400 years. Invaders and pirates, incoming and outgoing rulers, settlers, silver and slaves – all came and went, making Veracruz a linchpin in Mexico's history. In 1569 English sailor Francis Drake survived a massive Spanish sea attack here. In 1683 vicious Frenchman Laurent de Gaff and his 600 men held Veracruz' 5000 inhabitants captive, killing escapees,

Veracruz

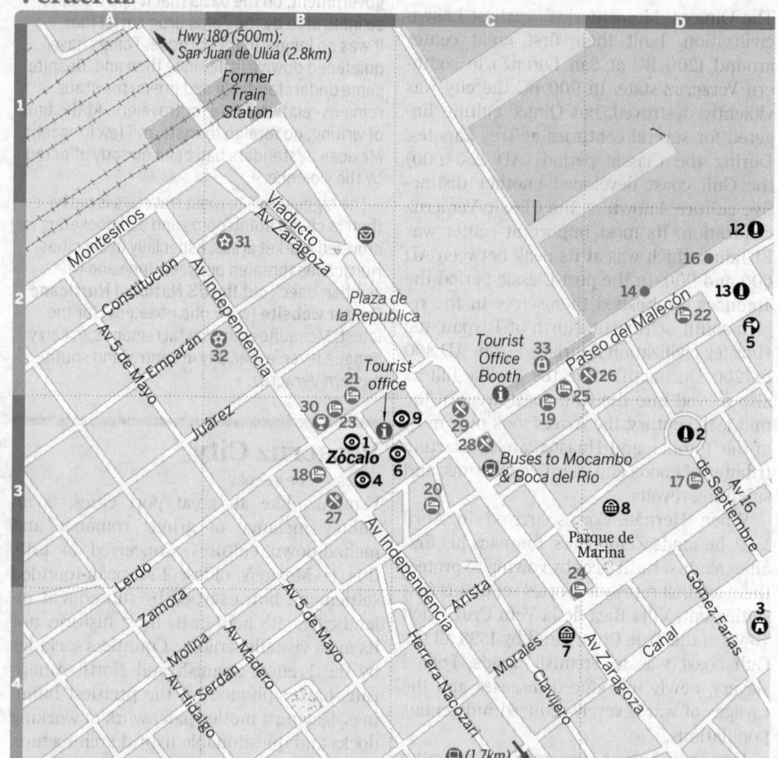

looting, drinking and raping. Soon after, they left much richer.

Under bombardment from a French fleet in the Pastry War, General Antonio López de Santa Anna was forced to flee Veracruz in 1838, wearing nothing but his underwear. But the general managed to respond heroically, expelling the invaders. When Winfield Scott's army attacked Veracruz during the Mexican-American War, more than 1000 Mexicans died before the city surrendered.

In 1861 Benito Juárez announced that Mexico couldn't pay its debts to Spain, France and Britain. The British and Spanish planned only to take over Veracruz' customhouse, but retreated on seeing that Frenchman Napoleon III sought to conquer Mexico. After Napoleon III's five-year intervention ended, Veracruz experienced revitalization. Mexico's first railway was built between Veracruz and Mexico City in 1872, and foreign investment poured into the city.

US troops occupied Veracruz in 1914, halting a delivery of German arms to dictator Victoriano Huerta. Later in the Revolution, Veracruz was briefly the capital of the reformist Constitutionalist faction led by Venustiano Carranza.

Today Veracruz is an important deepwater port, handling exports, manufacturing and petrochemical industries. Tourism, particularly from the domestic sector, is another large income earner.

Sights

★Zócalo PLAZA

Any exploration of Veracruz has to begin in its *zócalo* (also called the Plaza de Armas and Plaza Lerdo), the city's unofficial outdoor 'stage' where inspired organized events overlap with the day-to-day improvisation of Mexican life. The handsome public space is framed on three sides by *portales* (arcades), the 17th-century **Palacio Municipal** and an

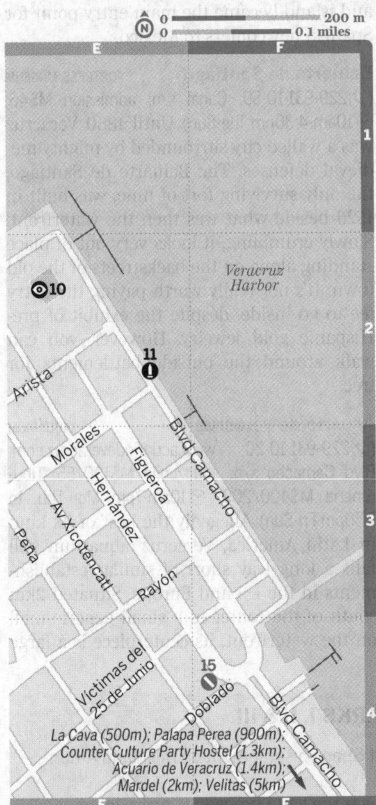

Veracruz

Top Sights

1 Zócalo....B3

Sights

2 Altar a la Patria....D3
3 Baluarte de Santiago....D4
4 Cathedral....B3
5 Faro Carranza....D2
6 Fototeca....C3
7 Museo de la Ciudad de Veracruz....C4
8 Museo Histórico Naval....D3
9 Palacio Municipal....C3
10 Pemex Building....E2
11 Statue of Alexander Von Humboldt....E2
12 Statue of the Spanish Emigrant....D2
13 Statue Venustiano Carranza....D2

Activities, Courses & Tours

Amphibian....(see 21)
14 Harbor Tours....D2
15 Scubaver....F4
16 Tranvías Bus....D2

Sleeping

17 El Faro....D3
18 Gran Hotel Diligencias....B3
19 Hawaii Hotel....C3
20 Hotel Casa Blanca....C3
21 Hotel Colonial....B2
22 Hotel Emporio....D2
23 Hotel Imperial....B3
24 Mesón del Mar....C3
25 Ruíz Milán Hotel....C2

Eating

26 Gran Café de la Parroquia....D2
27 Gran Café del Portal....B3
Los Canarios....(see 22)
28 Mariscos Tano....C3
29 Nieves de Malecón....C3

Drinking & Nightlife

Bar El Estribo....(see 18)
30 Bar Prendes....B3

Entertainment

31 Las Barricas....B2
32 Teatro Principal Francisco Javier Clavijero....B2

Shopping

Libros y Arte Fototeca....(see 6)
33 Mercado de Artesanías....C2

18th-century **cathedral**. The level of activity accelerates throughout the day until the evening, when the *zócalo* becomes thick with music, entertainers, merrymakers and bystanders.

Museo de la Ciudad de Veracruz MUSEUM
(Veracruz City Museum; ☎229-931-63-55; Av Zaragoza 39; ⏲10am-6pm Mon-Sat, to 3pm Sun) FREE Worth a visit for the charming colonial-era building alone, the Museo de la Ciudad de Veracruz does a good job of recounting the city's history from the pre-Hispanic era, and also gives a feel for the essence of this proud and lively city through explanations of its music, diverse ethnic roots, and politics. There are some labels in English, and models and dioramas to boot.

Museo Histórico Naval MUSEUM
(☎229-931-40-78; Arista 418; ⏲9am-5pm Tue-Sun) FREE Occupying a former naval academy, the Museo Histórico Naval offers gratis tuition in Mexico's maritime heritage, with rooms full of weapons and model ships to explore. There are also exhibits focusing on

the US attacks on Veracruz in 1847 and 1914. It was being renovated at the time of writing, but should reopen in 2014.

San Juan de Ulúa FORTRESS, MUSEUM

(☎229-938-51-51; www.sanjuandeulua.com.mx; admission M$57; ⏲9am-4:30pm Tue-Sun) The city's colonial fortress has been almost swallowed up by the modern port, and you have to squint to pick it out amid the container ships and cranes across the harbor. The central part of the fortress was a prison, and a notoriously inhumane one, during the Porfirio Díaz regime. Today, San Juan de Ulúa is an empty ruin of passageways, battlements, bridges and stairways undergoing lengthy renovations. Guided tours are available in Spanish and, sometimes, English. To get there, you can take a taxi (M$50) or, weather permitting, a *lancha* (boat taxi; M$30) from the *malecón* (beach promenade).

The fort was originally built on an island that's since been connected to the mainland by a causeway. The earliest fortifications date from 1565 and a young Francis Drake got his comeuppance here in a violent battle in 1569. During the colonial period the fort and island became the main entry point for Spanish newcomers to Mexico.

Baluarte de Santiago FORTRESS, MUSEUM

(☎229-931-10-59; Canal s/n; admission M$46; ⏲10am-4:30pm Tue-Sun) Until 1880 Veracruz was a walled city surrounded by mighty medieval defenses. The Baluarte de Santiago, the only surviving fort of nine, was built in 1526 beside what was then the waterfront. Slowly crumbling, it looks very out of place standing alone on the backstreets of the old town. It's not really worth paying the entry fee to go inside, despite the exhibit of pre-Hispanic gold jewelry. However, you can walk around the outside battlements for free.

Acuario de Veracruz AQUARIUM

(☎229-931-10-20; www.acuariodeveracruz.com; Blvd Camacho s/n; adult/child M$100/55, Tiburonería M$400/200; ⏲10am-7pm Mon-Thu, to 7:30pm Fri-Sun) Allegedly the best of its kind in Latin America, Veracruz' aquarium still falls a long way short of similar establishments in the US and Europe. Situated 2km south of the center in a small generic mall on the waterfront, its centerpiece is a large

THE FOUNDING OF VERACRUZ – MARKS I, II & III

There is an intriguing murkiness about the first Spanish settlement on mainland America north of Panama.

Popular myth suggests that Hernán Cortés was the first European to arrive in the Veracruz area, but, in truth, fellow Spaniard Juan de Grijalva beat him to it by about six months. Grijalva docked on the Isla de Sacrificios in late 1518, where he found evidence of human sacrifice and spent 10 days trading with Mesoamerican natives.

Cortés' more famous flotilla arrived via the Yucatán coast in 1519, and quickly set up a temporary camp on a beach opposite the island of San Juan de Ulúa on the site of present-day Veracruz. However, a real city wasn't established here for another 80 years. Instead, Cortés and his men quickly abandoned their malaria-ridden camp and trekked 40km north to the Totonac settlement of Zempoala where they were courted by the corpulent chief, Xicomecoatl, with whom they made a cynical alliance against the Aztecs. Xicomecoatl sent Cortés' entourage 30km further north to the city of Quiahuiztlán with 400 Zempoala-hired porters, where they were met by a population of 15,000 curious citizens. With their ships already docked on the adjacent coast, Cortés was determined to cut legal ties with Diego Velázquez, his overseer in Cuba, and decided to found a town near Quiahuiztlán, declaring himself the legal *adelantado* (governor). Christened Villa Rica de la Vera Cruz (Veracruz Mk I), it consisted of little more than a fort, a chapel and some barracks but, small as it was, it was the first recorded European-founded settlement in North America. Around 1524, due to its limitations as a port, the town was moved south to La Antigua (Veracruz Mk II) and sited several kilometers inland on the banks of the Río Antigua, where small ships could be docked. But as the Spanish empire grew, Antigua's river location made it less practical for larger ships, meaning supplies had to be hauled overland to San Juan de Ulúa, where they often fell prey to smugglers. As a result, around 1599, Veracruz was moved for a third time back to the site of the original encampment on the coast opposite San Juan de Ulúa.

doughnut-shaped tank filled with sharks, rays and turtles that glide around visitors. For a really dramatic encounter, though, climb into the *Tiburonería,* a transparent safety cage that is lowered into a pool of feeding sharks.

Fototeca ARTS CENTER
(☎229-932-87-67; Callejón El Portal de Miranda 9; ⏲9am-1pm & 2-7pm Tue-Sun) FREE On the southeast side of the *zócalo,* this small arts center has rotating photographic and video exhibitions. It's spread over three floors of a restored colonial building, though sometimes only the ground floor is operating.

Faro Carranza LIGHTHOUSE
(Paseo del Malecón) Facing the waterfront on the *malecón,* Faro Carranza holds a lighthouse and navy offices guarded by a large **statue of Venustiano Carranza**. It was here that the 1917 Mexican Constitution was drafted. Every Monday morning the Mexican navy goes through an elaborate parade in front of the building.

Museo Agustín Lara MUSEUM
(☎229-937-02-09; Ruiz Cortines s/n, Boca del Río; adult/student M$20/10; ⏲10am-2:30pm & 4-6pm Tue-Fri, 10am-2:30pm Sat & Sun) A monument to one of Veracruz' most famous musical icons, this museum displays a range of Agustín Lara's personal belongings, furniture and memorabilia in the musician's old city residence. It is situated just off Blvd Camacho, 4km south of the city center.

Activities

Diving & Snorkeling

You wouldn't expect lucid diving right near such an oil-rigged city, but Veracruz has some good options (including at least one accessible wreck) on the reefs near the offshore islands. Visibility is best in May.

Scubaver DIVING
(☎229-932-39-94; www.scubaver.net; Hernández y Hernández 563; 2 dives M$880) This friendly and centrally located outfit is used to dealing with foreigners.

Veracruz Adventures DIVING, SNORKELING
(☎229-931-53-58; www.veracruzadventures.com; Blvd Camacho 681A; 1/2 dives M$550/750) Dive school offering quality equipment, and diving and snorkeling excursions from the Veracruz area. Guides speak English.

Mundosubmarino DIVING
(☎229-980-63-74; www.mundosubmarino.com.mx; Blvd Camacho 3549) Recommended operator offering day and night dives, plus a range of courses and excursions.

Courses

Language Immersion School LANGUAGE
(☎229-931-47-16; www.veracruzspanish.com; Alacio Pérez 61; 1st week per person incl homestay, classes & food US$675, 2nd week onwards US$600) This laid-back, North American–owned school offers Spanish courses which focus on learning about the city and its culture. Class size is limited to two people, so you'll get extremely high levels of personal attention, and there's far more than usual included in weekly packages, from immersive trips into the city, to ecotourism and scuba diving options.

Tours

Amphibian ADVENTURE
(☎229-931-09-97; www.amphibianveracruz.com; Hotel Colonial lobby, Lerdo 117; per person from M$450) In addition to offering activity-based tours, Amphibian also conducts diving and snorkeling trips, rafting trips to nearby rivers, rappelling, and sightseeing excursions.

Aventura Extrema ADVENTURE
(☎229-202-65-57; www.aventuraextrema.com) Offers rappelling, horseback riding, rafting and hiking around Veracruz.

Harbor Tours BOAT
(☎229-935-94-17; www.asdic.com.mx; adult/child from M$90/50; ⏲8am-9pm) Boats from the *malecón* offer 45-minute tours of the harbor, plus a variety of other excursions.

Tranvías Bus BUS
(tours M$30-45) This open-air bus with trolley-like wooden trimmings gives one-hour city tours to the beat of tropical tunes. It's better at night when it's merrily lit up with colored lights. Departs from Paseo del Malecón.

Festivals & Events

Carnaval CARNIVAL
Veracruz erupts into a nine-day party before Ash Wednesday in February or March. Flamboyant parades wind through the city daily, beginning with one devoted to the 'burning of bad humor' and ending with the 'funeral of Juan Carnaval.' Throw in fireworks, dances, salsa and samba music, handicrafts,

folklore shows and children's parades, and it adds up to be one of Mexico's greatest fiestas. See the tourist office for a program of events.

Sleeping

Hotel prices vary greatly according to demand and can shift from day to day at busy times (mid-July to mid-September, Carnaval, Semana Santa, Christmas and New Year). Book in advance for these times and be aware that prices may increase by 10% to 40%. Out of season there are big savings to be made. When choosing where to stay, bear in mind that while it's entertaining, the *zócalo* can be loud at night.

Hotel Casa Blanca HOTEL $
(229-200-46-25/24; Trigueros 49; r M$300-470;) Veracruz' best budget option doesn't pretend to be posh: yesterday's bed sheets are hung up on the 1st-floor balconies to dry, and sometimes it feels all but deserted. But the old colonial frontage gives way to spacious and charming public areas and simple rooms with large beds and a desk in each. Try for a room upstairs where there's more light.

Counter Culture Party Hostel HOSTEL $
(229-260-25-73, 299-242-60-31; www.counterculture-partyhostels.com; Xicoténcatl 1835 btwn Enríquez & Pérez; dm/r M$175/M$330;) This party hostel is *the* place to come if you want a raucous time in Veracruz. With no curfew, no rules against bringing your own drinks, and cheap beer available from the bar, it's all about boozy fun here. There are bus excursions to nightspots every Thursday, Friday and Saturday night, while communal dinners ensure you'll make friends very quickly.

El Faro HOTEL $
(229-931-65-38; www.hotelelfaro.com.mx; Av 16 de Septiembre 223; r M$350-400, q M$550;) This no-frills place is a central budget option, just a short wander from the seafront. Room prices go up depending on the size and number of beds, and the cheaper ones can be very dark, with no natural daylight. That said, it's clean, safe and in the heart of the city.

★ **Mesón del Mar** BOUTIQUE HOTEL $$
(229-932-50-43; www.mesondelmar.com.mx; Morales 543; s/d/tr M$500/750/900;) This colonial charmer boasts friendly staff, well cared for rooms with tall ceilings (many have mezzanines with extra sleeping spaces) and buckets of local atmosphere. Balconies, beautifully tiled bathrooms, ceiling fans and wooden furniture all add to the mix, and while calling it a boutique hotel may be slightly overstating the case, this is certainly Veracruz' best midrange option.

Hotel Imperial HISTORIC HOTEL $$
(229-931-34-70, 229-932-12-04; www.hotelimperialveracruz.com; Lerdo 153; r/ste from M$850/950;) Claiming to be the oldest hotel in the Americas, the Imperial certainly has heritage; it's been open nonstop since 1793. Indeed, its splendid public areas (check out the elevator!) and superb location are its main draws; many of the rooms are actually disappointingly modern and consequently rather characterless. Go for the far more atmospheric ones at the front of the building.

Hawaii Hotel HOTEL $$
(229-989-88-88; hawaii@infosel.net.mx; Paseo del Malecón 458; s/d/tr M$700/800/1000; P) Who knows why it's called the Hawaii Hotel? The 30-room hotel looks more like the prow of a boat, with a marble and white decor inside. However, it's the best value on the *malecón*, and some of the spacious rooms have marvelous views of it. Extras such as hairdryers and fridges make for a comfortable stay.

Hotel Colonial HOTEL $$
(229-932-01-93; www.hcolonial.com.mx; Lerdo 117; r M$595-960; P@) Dated and confusingly sprawling, the Colonial continues to rest on its main laurel – a central *zócalo* location. With a curious blend of colonial and 1970s styles, the Artex-wallpapered rooms are somewhat musty, but have all the basic comforts you need, and some have great views.

Not surprisingly given the location, the rooms can be noisy, but the hotel has so many nooks and crannies that it's easy to secure a more tranquil escape at the back.

Ruíz Milán Hotel HOTEL $$
(229-932-37-77; www.ruizmilan.com; cnr Paseo del Malecón & Gómez Farías; r/ste from M$580/M$850; P) This smartened up property on the *malecón* offers decent value, comfortable rooms and friendly staff who work hard to make guests feel welcome. Rooms are spacious and have been gradually improved by management, and yet deals (as

low as M$500 per night) can still be had in low season.

Nu Hotel HOTEL $$
(☎229-937-09-17; www.nuhotel.com.mx; Av La Fragua 1066; s/d M$450/500; P⊖❄🛜) The Nu has pitched itself amid the scruffy next-to-bus-station hovels and declared war. It's no contest really, especially at these prices. Savor the clean, minimalist-chic rooms and the cool downstairs cafe. The staff is young and casual. The only real drawback is the location, 3km south of the *zócalo,* which isn't really handy for anything – except the buses, of course.

Gran Hotel Diligencias LUXURY HOTEL $$$
(☎229-923-02-80, 800-505-55-95; www.granhoteldiligencias.com; Av Independencia 1115; r M$2000, ste M$2500-3500; P⊖❄@🛜≋) The fanciest option on the *zócalo* has a very smart lobby full of fresh flowers and abuzz with livery-clad bellhops. Upstairs the huge rooms deliver elegance, if not personality, though touches such as coffeemakers and remodeled bathrooms sweeten the deal. You'll find more atmosphere downstairs in the adjoining El Estribo Bar and Villa Rica restaurant.

★ **Hotel Emporio** LUXURY HOTEL $$$
(☎229-932-00-20; www.hotelesemporio.com/veracruz; Paseo del Malecón 244; r incl breakfast from M$2366, ste from M$3000; P⊖❄🛜≋) Veracruz' best hotel is well worth splashing out on, especially if it's running special deals (as little as M$990 in low season). As if the lavish interior (three pools, a gym, a cocktail bar and huge light-filled rooms) wasn't enough, there's also its dynamite location on the liveliest stretch of the *malecón,* with the historic Gran Café de la Parroquia next door.

The whole place is shot through with arty touches and the rooms are spacious, each with their own large balcony and beautifully appointed bathroom.

Eating

Two main factors strongly influence Veracruz cooking: its location by the ocean and its role as a port. The first factor means there's an abundance of seafood. The second has made it a melting pot for various foreign cultures and dishes.

Using seafood and the pre-Hispanic diet of beans, corn and squash as a base, the local cuisine has absorbed Spanish and Afro-Caribbean influences over the last five centuries to create such genre-blending dishes as *huachinango a la veracruzana* (red snapper in a spicy tomato sauce), *arroz a la tumbada* (a kind of paella-like soup) and *pollo encacahuatado* (chicken in a peanut sauce). Excellent seafood can be procured anywhere, but the condensed strip of *palapas* (thatched-roof shelters) on the *malecón* just south of the aquarium has made it their (sometimes expensive) specialty.

The *zócalo* cafes under the ever-lively, music-filled *portales* are popular spots for drinks and food. They all offer the same

GRAN CAFÉ DE LA PARROQUIA

To say that Veracruz' greatest 'sight' is a cafe might seem like a slur on this grizzled port city's reputation. But walk into the **Gran Café de la Parroquia** (☎229 932-25-84; www.laparroquia.com; Gómez Farías 34; mains M$40-180; ⏲6am-midnight) – over two centuries old – and the penny will quickly drop. With its immense but un-showy interior, the Parroquia pulls in anything from 2000 to 4000 customers a day, and every facet of Veracruz' diverse personality is on show here. Patrons hold court, make noise and, more significantly, tap their spoons on their coffee glasses. The spoon-tapping – a Parroquia tradition dating from the 1890s – is to attract the attention of the ultra-professional waiters. Gliding like ballet dancers between the tables, they carry two huge steaming jugs, one filled with coffee and the other with hot milk. The de rigueur drink in the Parroquia is *lechero*, a milky coffee brought to your table as an espresso measure in the bottom of a glass. Tap your spoon on the glass rim and – hey presto – a white-jacketed waiter quickly appears, extends his jug high in the air, and fills your glass with scientific precision.

The Parroquia has inspired some spin-offs in recent years, but none come close to matching the atmosphere and spirit of the original on Veracruz' Paseo del Malecón. Recommended items on the menu include quesadillas, fruit plates, spicy soups and possibly the best *tres leches* cake you'll ever taste.

tasty, price-hiked varieties. Cheaper and better alternatives nearby include an array of late-night restaurants with outdoor seating on Molina and Av Zaragoza (mains M$40 to M$60) – try La Marina Dorada, La Gaviota or Bar El Girasol for their own takes on *comida veracruzana*. You can also join *jarochos* (inhabitants of Veracruz) in the mazes of Mercado Hidalgo, where you can find nooks that serve cheap, delectable local favorites like *cocteles de mariscos* (seafood cocktails), *mondongo* (prepared cow stomach) and delicious *moles*.

Mariscos Tano SEAFOOD **$**
(Molina 20; meals M$35-100; ⏲8am-10pm) A de facto rehearsal room for a trio of local *jarocho* musicians, Tano is an unintentionally retro seafood joint crammed with faded photos of the owner posing with Vegas girls and mustachioed *hombres* in kipper ties c 1975. The food is economical and tasty, and the atmosphere kind of salt-of-the-sea Veracruz with a *son* (folk music) soundtrack.

Nieves de Malecón ICE CREAM **$**
(☎229-931-70-99; Av Zaragoza 286; scoops from M$20; ⏲8am-midnight) *Jarochos* prefer sorbets *(nieves)* over ice cream and this is one of the town's sorbet favorites, sandwiched between the *malecón* and the *zócalo*. Loquacious 'callers' stand outside drumming up business, competing with a rival place (with its own 'callers') directly across the street. Try the delicious mamey flavor, or opt for the Veracruz staple, vanilla.

★ **Los Canarios** SPANISH, MEXICAN **$$**
(Paseo del Malecón 224; meals M$75-270; ⏲1-11pm; 👪) With large windows overlooking the *malecón*, it's hard to resist this fancy place in the super-smart Hotel Emporio. Slink inside and reacquaint yourself with à la mode Spanish cooking, mixed, of course, with a few Mexican inflections. The paella's excellent, the breaded chicken is unusually succulent, and the service doesn't miss a beat.

Look out for the superb seafood brunch (M$230) served all day Friday to Sunday.

Gran Café del Portal CAFE, INTERNATIONAL **$$**
(☎229-931-27-59; Av Independencia 1187; mains M$60-245; ⏲7am-midnight; 📶) This smart and impressively decorated place just off the *zócalo* is actually quite relaxed despite its surface formality. Indeed, service can be positively laid-back, though the deft aim of the coffee/milk-pouring waiters is as precise as any you'll find in Veracruz. Full meals are available, as well as the mainstays of milky coffee and pastries.

Ulúa Fish SEAFOOD **$$$**
(☎229-922-76-64; Ruíz Cortines 2; mains M$100-300; ⏲7am-noon & 2-11pm Tue-Sun) This upscale cafe was opened by famous chef José Burela Picazzo, who founded a cooking school in the city and wrote a cookbook about the local specialties of Veracruz state. If you are in the mood to slam your credit card for excellent seafood, this is the place.

To get here, head 4km south from the city center on Blvd Camacho before turning right at the major junction with Ruíz Cortines. The restaurant is 300m along on the left.

Villa Rica Mocambo SEAFOOD **$$$**
(www.villaricamocambo.com.mx; Calz Mocambo 527, Boca del Río; mains M$160-350; ⏲noon-10pm Sun-Wed, to midnight Thu-Sat) For those on short itineraries, there aren't many reasons to make the pilgrimage to Boca del Río. But food – and this restaurant in particular – could swing it. Fish is the all-encompassing ingredient, from charcoal-grilled octopus to stuffed sea bass, and the beachside service is attentive.

Mardel ARGENTINE **$$$**
(☎229-937-56-42; www.mardel.com.mx; Blvd Camacho 2632; mains M$75-250; ⏲7am-11pm Mon-Sat, to 7pm Sun; 📶) Owned by a retired Argentine football player, this upscale restaurant has a great seafront position and specializes in rib-eye steaks. There are also Mexican and Spanish influences on the extensive menu, but regulars advise sticking to the staple: a perfectly cooked slab of cow. The TVs showing sports can be a distraction or a delight, depending on your point of view.

Palapa Perea SEAFOOD **$$$**
(cnr Av 16 de Septiembre & Azueta; mains M$100-250; ⏲9am-8pm) This place may not look like much, but it has an excellent reputation for serving some of the best seafood dishes in Veracruz (quite an accolade!). Its location, a few blocks back from the seafront, means that it's locals rather than visitors who come here, and while the jukebox is on the loud side, the food is sublime.

BEACHES & LAGOONS

Inseparable from the *jarocho* (Veracruz) identity is the beach. You'll find pleasant stretches of them all the way down through Boca del Río. As a rule of thumb, the further from the oil rigs the better, but locals can be seen enjoying them all.

Alternatively, you can find *lanchas* (boat taxis; M$120) by the aquarium that will take you to **Cancuncito**, a sandbar off the coast touted as the best beach in Veracruz, with light sand and clear water. Another part of the *lancha* beat is the **Isla de Sacrificios**, an island once used for Totonac human sacrifice and later as a leprosy colony. It's now part of a protected nature and marine reserve called **Parque Marino Nacional Sistema Arrecifal Veracruzano**. Sometimes, when tourism is low, *lanchas* aren't to be found, but harbor-tour boats stop there on some tours.

Some 11km from the center, the gritty, off-shoot town of **Boca del Río** has a smattering of brightly colored seafood restaurants overlooking the mouth of the river on Blvd Camacho. Also, *lanchas* offering **boat tours** to mangrove forests leave from here. Over the bridge, the coastal road continues about 8km further down the coast from Boca del Río to **Mandinga**, known for its seafood (especially *langostinos bicolores* – two-colored prawns), where you can hire a boat (from the *zona de restaurantes*) to take you around mangrove lagoons rich with wildlife.

Drinking & Nightlife

The *portales* cafes are drinking strongholds. But head south some distance on the *malecón* and you'll find the majority of the city's fast-paced and ever-changing nightlife.

Bar El Estribo — BAR

(☎229-923-02-80; Av Independencia 1115; ⏲9am-late) Because Gran Hotel Diligencia's bar is raised up above sidewalk level and fenced off, it's the only place on the *zócalo* where one can eat and drink outside without hawkers in your face selling their stock every 10 minutes. The Pepito sandwich is good, as are the drink and wine selections.

Bar Prendes — BAR

(Lerdo; ⏲9am-late) For a front-row seat for whatever's happening in the *zócalo* on any given night, look no further than Prendes; its trendy modern furniture occupies a prize slice of real estate under the *portales*. Beers come in long tubes with taps at the bottom for groups.

La Cava — BAR

(Blvd Camacho btwn Uribe & Barragán; ⏲5pm-close) Definitely a neighborhood favorite, this tiny bar illuminated by black lights seems to host lots of laughter and cocktail-induced intimacy.

Velitas — BAR

(cnr Blvd Camacho & Militar; ⏲5pm-close) With its romantic, tiki-torch ambience, this popular little seaside *palapa* is a laid-back place to grab a cocktail while checking out the ocean and the people strolling past on the boulevard. On weekends there's live music.

☆ Entertainment

Of course, there are always marimbas and mariachis on the *zócalo*. And the coastline boulevard is known as *la barra más grande del mundo* (the biggest bar in the world), *barra* referring both to the sandbar and the drinks bar. During holiday times, it's an outdoor party with live music and dancing in the streets. Many venues line Blvd Camacho.

Teatro Principal Francisco Javier Clavijero — THEATER

(Emparán 166) This theater has a long history and has had many incarnations. It moved here in 1819 and adopted its current architectural style (French neoclassical with some tremendous mosaics) in 1902. The latest refurb was in 2011. Plays, musicals and classical concerts are performed here.

Las Barricas — LIVE MUSIC, CLUB

(☎229-100-37-76; www.lasbarricascentro.com; Constitución 72; cover Fri & Sat & for live music M$50-120; ⏲6pm-2am Mon-Sat) This *jarocho*-recommended live-music venue and club plays a variety of music: reggaeton, salsa, pop, rock etc. It's on the small side, so expect to be packed in with the raucous, jovial crowd, especially on weekends.

PASEO DEL MALECÓN & BOULEVARD

Veracruz' harbor is a busy oil port with rigs off the coast, but that somehow adds to the gritty romanticism of the **waterfront walk** on the *malecón* (harbor boardwalk). Start at the rows of vendor stalls at the Mercado de Artesanías, which sell a kaleidoscope of souvenirs. Here you'll pass the high-rise **Pemex building**, which is an early example of modern Mexican architecture and has some interesting murals.

Heading south, the *malecón* becomes a wide pedestrian walkway called the *bulevar* (pronounced 'boo-ley-bar'). Following the coast, it continues south roughly 8km, passing lighthouse piers, statues of famous government figures, and monuments to the city's defenders and sailors who died at sea. Two notable recent additions are the **statue of the Spanish emigrant**, celebrating Veracruz' role as a disembarkation point for immigrants, and the **statue of Alexander Von Humboldt**, the German naturalist/explorer who visited the area in 1803–04 and collected important information about the flora and indigenous cultures.

Two blocks inland from the *malecón* is the 1998 **Altar a la Patria**, an obelisk marking the buried remains of those who defended Veracruz during its numerous conflicts.

La Casona de la Condesa CLUB
(☎229-130-12-82; www.casonadelacondesa.com; Blvd Camacho 1520; cover Fri & Sat M$30-60; ⏲10pm-5am Tue-Sun) La Casona attracts an older (ie not teenage) crowd and offers solid live music at night. It is situated close to the seafront, 5km south from the city center on Blvd Camacho.

Shopping

Avenida Independencia is the city's main shopping thoroughfare. Souvenirs are best procured at the Mercado de Artesanías on the *malecón*. You can buy cheap bottles of vanilla here and good-quality coffee. Jewelry – especially silver – is also economical and sometimes engraved with interesting Aztec/Maya motifs.

Mercado de Artesanías MARKET, SOUVENIRS
(Paseo del Malecón) Souvenir city populates 30-plus tiny adjacent booths that line the stretch of the *malecón* closest to the *zócalo*, selling everything from T-shirts to vanilla.

Libros y Arte Fototeca BOOKS
(☎229-934-22-33; Callejón El Portal de Miranda 9; ⏲10am-1pm & 2-7pm Tue-Sun) Inside the Fototeca building on the corner of the *zócalo*, this place has good regional and international selections.

Information

EMERGENCY

Ambulance, Fire & Police (☎066)

LEFT LUGGAGE

There's a 24-hour facility in the 2nd-class terminal of the bus station.

MEDICAL SERVICES

Beneficencia Española (☎229-262-23-00; www.benever.com.mx; Av 16 de Septiembre 955) A hospital that can offer general medical services to visitors to Mexico.

Hospital Regional (☎229-931-31-20; Av 20 de Noviembre 1074)

MONEY

There's a cluster of banks with ATMs a block north of the *zócalo*, and a generally wide availability throughout the city. Most banks change US dollars, some change euros as well.

POST

Post Office (Plaza de la República 213) A five-minute walk north of the *zócalo*.

TELEPHONE

Card phones proliferate around the *zócalo*.

TOURIST INFORMATION

Tourist Office (☎229-922-95-33; www.veratur.gob.mx; Palacio Municipal; ⏲8am-3pm) Has helpful staff and plenty of maps and brochures. There's another small booth (cnr Paseo del Malecón & Arista; ⏲9am-9pm) at the far western end of the Mercado de Artesanías.

Getting There & Away

AIR

Veracruz International Airport (VER; www.asur.com.mx) is 18km southwest of the center, near Hwy 140. Frequent flights to Monterrey, Villahermosa, Mérida, Cancún and Mexico City are offered by **Aeroméxico** (www.aeromexico.com),

Aeromar (www.aeromar.com.mx) and **MAYair** (www.mayair.com.mx) in addition to a handful of other national airlines. Direct flights to/from Houston are offered by **United Airlines** (www.united.com).

BUS

Veracruz is a major hub, with good services up and down the coast and inland along the Córdoba–Puebla–Mexico City corridor. Buses to and from Mexico City can be heavily booked at holiday times.

Bus Station (Av Díaz Mirón btwn Tuero Molina & Orizaba) The bus station is located 3km south of the *zócalo* and has ATMs. The 1st-class/deluxe area is in the part of the station closest to Calle Orizaba. For more frequent and slightly cheaper and slower 2nd-class services, enter on the other side from Avenida Lafragua. There's a 24-hour luggage room here.

CAR & MOTORCYCLE

Local and international car-rental agencies have desks at Veracruz airport. There are also some other agencies scattered around town. Rates start at M$300 per day.

Getting Around

Veracruz airport is small, modern and well organized, with a cafe and several shops. There's no bus service to or from town; official taxis cost M$220 to the *zócalo*. You must buy a ticket upfront from a booth in the arrivals hall, which helps to avoid being ripped off. Going the other way, just M$100 is the going rate, but agree on a price before you get in.

To get downtown from the 1st-class bus station, take a bus marked 'Díaz Mirón y Madero' (M$8). It will head to Parque Zamora then up Avenida Madero. For the *zócalo*, get off on the corner of Avenida Madero and Lerdo and turn right. Returning to the bus stations, pick up the same bus going south on Avenida 5 de Mayo. Booths in the 1st- and 2nd-class stations sell taxi tickets to the center (*zócalo* area; M$35). In the tourist office, you can get a summary sheet of official taxi-ride costs, which is helpful for guarding against tourist price inflation.

Buses marked 'Mocambo-Boca del Río' (M$8 to Boca del Río) leave regularly from the corner of Avenida Zaragoza and Serdán, near the *zócalo;* they go via Parque Zamora and Blvd Camacho to Playa Mocambo (20 minutes) and on to Boca del Río (30 minutes). AU buses also go there from the 2nd-class station.

CENTRAL VERACRUZ

Curvy Hwy 180 follows the coast past dark-sand beaches to Cardel, where Hwy 140 branches west to Xalapa, the state capital. Charming mountain towns sprinkle the inland volcanic ranges, which are laced with dramatic river gorges. From Veracruz, Hwy 150D heads southwest to Córdoba, Fortín de las Flores and Orizaba, on the edge of the Sierra Madre.

BUSES FROM VERACRUZ

DESTINATION	FARE (M$)	DURATION	FREQUENCY (DAILY)
Catemaco	144	3½hr	hourly
Córdoba	122	1½hr	2
Mexico City (TAPO)	414	5½hr	frequent
Oaxaca	466	7½hr	4
Orizaba	140	2½hr	frequent
Papantla	210	4hr	6
Puebla	288	3½hr	12
San Andrés Tuxtla	138	3hr	12
Santiago Tuxtla	130	2½hr	12
Tampico	488	9½hr	5
Tuxpan	276	6hr	frequent
Villahermosa	450	7½hr	frequent
Xalapa	104	2hr	frequent

Selection of daily 1st-class ADO departures from Veracruz.

Buses also go to Campeche, Cancún, Chetumal, Matamoros, Mérida, Nuevo Laredo and Salina Cruz.

Central Coast

The beaches north of the city of Veracruz are a popular Mexican vacation spot, and the area also boasts the impressive Zempoala ruins.

Zempoala

☎296 / POP 9200

The pre-Hispanic Totonac town of Zempoala (or Cempoala) stands 42km north of Veracruz and 4km west of Hwy 180 in modern Zempoala. The turnoff is by a Pemex station 7km north of Cardel. There's a *voladores* pole and performances are enacted sporadically – normally during Semana Santa and holidays. Zempoala is most easily reached through Cardel – take a bus marked 'Zempoala' (M$12) from beside Hotel Cardel, or a taxi (M$70).

History

Zempoala became a major Totonac center after about AD 1200 and fell to the Aztecs in the mid-15th century. The 30,000-person town had defensive walls, underground water and drainage pipes. As Hernán Cortés approached the town, one of his scouts reported that the buildings were made of silver – but it was only white paint shining in the sun.

Zempoala's chief – a corpulent fellow nicknamed *el cacique gordo* (the fat chief) by the Spanish – struck an alliance with Cortés for protection against the Aztecs. But his hospitality didn't stop the Spanish from smashing statues of his gods and lecturing his people on the virtues of Christianity. It was at Zempoala in 1520 that Cortés defeated the expedition sent by Cuba's Spanish governor to arrest him.

A smallpox epidemic between 1575 and 1577 decimated Zempoala and most of the survivors moved to Xalapa. By the 17th century the town was abandoned. The present town dates from 1832. Townsfolk fled from here in 1955 during category 5 Hurricane Janet, which caused further damage to the ruins.

Sights

Zempoala Archaeological Site ARCHAEOLOGICAL SITE

(admission M$42; 9am-6pm) Though not as monumental as El Tajín, the Zempoala Archaeological Site is still astounding, with a lovely mountain backdrop. There are four Spanish-speaking guides at the site who give explanations for free (tips recommended). Roberto del Moral Moreno is the only one who knows some English. He charges approximately M$100 per tour. The small site museum has some interesting clay figurines, polychrome plates and obsidian flints; it's best to check it out first.

Most of the buildings are faced with smooth, rounded, riverbed stones, but many were originally plastered and painted. A typical feature is battlement-like 'teeth' called *almenas*. The **Templo Mayor** (Main Temple), uncovered in 1972, is an 11m-high pyramid with a wide staircase ascending to the remains of a shrine. When they first encountered Zempoala, Cortés and his men lodged in **Las Chimeneas**, whose hollow

DANZÓN DAYS

It's hard to wander far in Veracruz without stumbling into a plaza-full of romantic *jarochos* indulging in the city's favorite pastime, the *danzón*. An elegant tropical dance, it melds influences of the French contra dance with the rhythms of African slaves.

As with most Latin American dances, the *danzón* has its roots in Cuba. It was purportedly 'invented' in 1879 by popular band leader Miguel Failde, who showcased his catchy dance composition *Las Alturas de Simpson* in the port city of Matanzas. Elegant and purely instrumental in its early days, the *danźon* required dancers to circulate in couples rather than groups, a move which scandalized white polite society of the era. By the time the dance arrived in Mexico, brought by Cuban immigrants in the 1890s, it had become more complex, expanding on its peculiar syncopated rhythm, and adding other instruments such as the conga to form an *orquesta típica*.

Though the *danzón* faded in popularity in Cuba in the 1940s and '50s with the arrival of the *mambo* and the *chachachá*, in Mexico it continued to flourish. Indeed, since the 1990s the *danzón* has undergone a huge revival in Veracruz, particularly among mature citizens. The bastion of the dance is the *zócalo* on Friday and Saturday evenings.

columns were thought to be chimneys – hence the name.

The circle of stones in the middle of the site is the **Circulo de los Guerreros**, where lone captured soldiers battled against groups of local warriors. Few won.

There are two main structures on the west side. One is known as the **Templo del Sol** and has two stairways climbing its front side in typical Toltec-Aztec style. The sun god was called Tonatiun and sacrifices were offered to him here on the **Piedra de Sacrificios**. The 'fat chief,' officially known as Xicomecoatl, sat facing the macabre spectacle on the appropriately large **altar**.

To its north, the second structure is the **Templo de la Luna**, with a structure similar to Aztec temples to the wind god, Ehecatl.

East of Las Chimeneas is **Las Caritas** (Little Heads), named for niches that once held several small pottery heads.

Another large temple to the wind god, known as the **Templo Dios del Aire**, is in the town itself – go back south on the site entrance road, cross the main road in town and then go around the corner to the right. The ancient temple, with its characteristic circular shape, is beside an intersection.

Getting There & Away

The bus from Cardel (M$12) drops you right outside the entrance to the archaeological site.

La Antigua

296 / POP 990

The city of Veracruz' second incarnation (1525–99) reveals little of its past identity with its languid grid of sleepy, cobbled streets and moss-covered ruins. People still live here, but it's a backwater these days, albeit a pleasant one, and worth a detour for its historical significance and well-known fish restaurant, Las Delicias Marinas.

A Spanish settlement was established here in 1525, and it's rumored that this is where conquistador Cortés moored his boats to a **ceiba tree**. The tree – gnarly and gigantic – is still standing. The eye-catching ruined building, half-strangled by tree roots and vines, is a 16th-century **custom house**, sometimes erroneously called the 'Casa de Cortés.' The tiny walled **Ermita del Rosario church**, probably dating from 1523, is considered to be the oldest in the Americas.

Lanchas will motor you along the pleasant Río Antigua for around M$50 to M$100 per person, depending on numbers.

Along the river there's a cluster of seafood restaurants. At the end of the row, adjacent to a pedestrian-only suspension bridge, the celebrated **Las Delicias Marinas** (Río Huitzilapan waterfront; mains M$90-200) serves exquisite fresh and saltwater fish that could emulate anything in Veracruz. There's music and dance entertainment here at weekends.

Colectivo taxis charge M$6 to M$10 from the village to the highway 1km away, where buses to Veracruz and Cardel pass every 15 minutes or so. Flag down the driver just north of the toll booth.

Xalapa

228 / POP 458,000 / ELEV 1427M

Familiar to the world primarily due to the super hot, green chili that was named after it, Xalapa (also spelled Jalapa, but always pronounced ha-*la*-pa) is actually about as different to the fiery jalapeño pepper as can be – unlike sweaty coastal Veracruz City, Xalapa's highland location makes it temperate and often quite cloudy. Coolness defines the city in other ways too: this is Mexico in an Afghan coat with a heavy literary tome under its arm, thanks to a large student population. The city is lively at night and has a thriving cultural scene (the city has its own branch of the Hay Festival of Literature & the Arts, for example).

The state capital of Veracruz, Xalapa is a traffic-asphyxiated place, whose unattractive urban sprawl gives way to a far more alluring center, full of well-kept parks, bustling pedestrian streets and colonial architecture. The superb anthropological museum is the main pull for visitors here, but the gargantuan pre-Hispanic relics are supplemented by hip bars, weighty bookstores and a superb array of quality coffee joints, making this one of Mexico's most enjoyable state capitals.

History

Founded by Totonacs in the early 1200s, Xalapa was part of the Aztec empire when Hernán Cortés and his men passed through in 1519. Because of its appealing climate and location, Spain strategically placed a monastery here to proselytize to the indigenous population. By the 17th century it had evolved into a commercial axis and meeting hub. Today Xalapa is still a commercial center for coffee, tobacco and flowers.

Xalapa

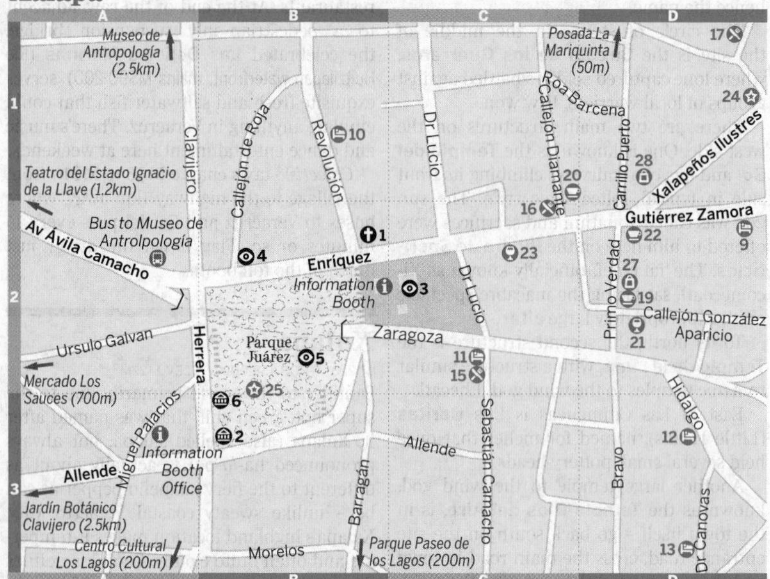

Sights

★Museo de Antropología — MUSEUM

(☎228-815-09-20; Av Xalapa s/n; adult/student M$50/25, audioguide M$23; ⊙9am-5pm Tue-Sun) Set in spacious gardens on the west side of Avenida Xalapa, 4km northwest of the center, the building that encases this remarkable museum (containing Mexico's second-finest archaeological collection) is a work of art in its own right – a series of interconnecting galleries that fall like a regal staircase down the side of a lush hill. Viewing archaeological treasures has rarely been this pleasurable. As there's so much to see, allow yourself plenty of time to visit.

The exhibits' scale and breadth rival the museum's intricate layout. Three key Gulf coast pre-Hispanic civilizations are represented – namely the Olmecs, the Totonacs and the Huastecs – and the exhibits are presented chronologically within their sections with clearly labeled explanations in Spanish. Laminated English information sheets are attached to the wall at the entrance to each new room, but a good audioguide in English (bring ID to leave as collateral) explains the most important items in detail. Several spaces concentrate on the Olmec culture from southern Veracruz, from which comes the most celebrated piece, the sculpture **El Señor de Las Limas**. There's also an array of fine work associated with the pre-Hispanic ball game.

There's a small cafe on the upper floor and a truly excellent bookstore, while the walk back up the hill through the beautifully kept garden is a delight.

To get there, take a 'Camacho-Tesorería' bus (M$8) from the corner of Enríquez and Parque Juárez. To return, take a bus marked 'Centro.' A taxi costs M$30.

Parque Juárez — PLAZA

Xalapa's centrally located main square feels like a terrace, with its south side overlooking the valley below and the snowcapped cone of Pico de Orizaba beckoning in the distance. Greener and better kept than most other plazas in Mexico, you'll find monkey puzzle trees and manicured hedges among the shoe-shiners, balloon sellers and wandering minstrels.

On the plaza's north side is the neoclassical **Palacio Municipal** (1855) and on the east side is the **Palacio de Gobierno**, the seat of Veracruz' state government. The Palacio de Gobierno has a fine mural by Mario Orozco Rivera depicting the history of justice above the stairway near the eastern entrance on Enríquez.

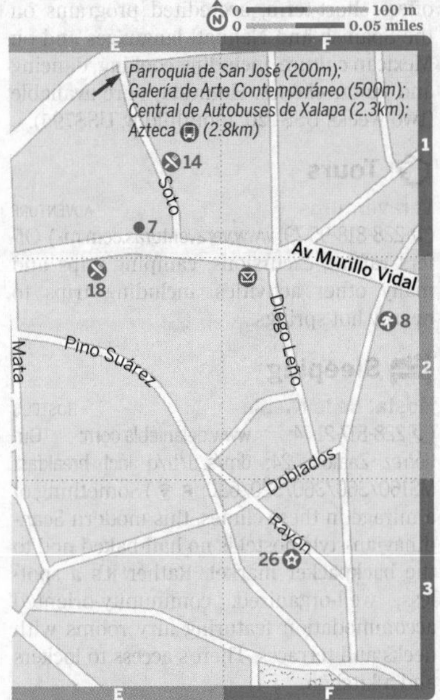

Xalapa

Catedral Metropolitana CATHEDRAL
(cnr Enríquez & Revolución) An unfinished masterpiece, Xalapa's cathedral lacks a second tower but still impresses with its scale and grandiosity. Moreover, rather than compensating for its steep hillside position, the architecture makes full use of it to inspire awe as you enter, forcing you to raise your head to see the alter and giant crucifix centerpiece. A mélange of neo-Gothic and baroque, the church contains the remains of St Rafael Guízar y Valencia, beatified by Pope John Paul II in 1995.

Parque Paseo de los Lagos PARK
(Zona Universitaria) Xalapans escape the monstrous traffic just south of Parque Juárez in this serendipitous park, which has 3km of delightful lakeside paths, most commonly used for jogging (and making out). At its northern end is the **Centro Cultural Los Lagos** (☎228-812-12-99; Paseo los Lagos s/n), a lovely cultural center; check out the bulletin board to find out about cultural events and drop-in dance or yoga classes.

Pinacoteca Diego Rivera GALLERY
(☎228-818-18-19; Herrera 5; ⏲10am-7pm Tue-Sat) FREE Tucked beneath the west side of the plaza, this small gallery houses a modest collection of Rivera's works, as well as pieces from other Mexican artists. There's excellent coffee to be had at the Jarochostyle Café outside.

Parque Ecológico Macuiltépetl PARK
(⏲5am-7pm) Atop a hill north of the city, this 40-hectare park is actually the heavily wooded cap of an extinct volcano called Nevado de Toluca. Spiraling to the top, the park's paths are a treasure for the city's surprisingly robust fraternity of joggers, and provide expansive views of Xalapa and the surrounding area.

Museo Casa de Xalapa MUSEUM
(Herrera 7; ⏲9am-7pm) FREE For a quick exposé of Xalapan history, head to this

museum in an old colonial house close to Parque Juárez. It's small, but lovingly put together.

Galería de Arte Contemporáneo GALLERY
(☎info 228-818-04-12; Xalapeños Ilustres 135; ⊙10am-7pm Tue-Sun) FREE The town's contemporary art gallery is in a renovated colonial building 1km east of the center. Showing an interesting range of temporary exhibitions and some ceramics, there's also a small movie theater that screens art house films, mostly for free.

Parroquia de San José CHURCH
(cnr Xalapeños Ilustres & Arieta) In the learned San José quarter, this church dates from 1770 and confirms Xalapa's penchant for asymmetrical one-towered religious edifices. Architecturally, it displays an unusual blend of baroque and Mudejar styles, including some horseshoe arches. Directly behind is the **Mercado Alcalde y García**, a covered market recently spiced up with some cool new cafe-restaurants in the lower levels.

Jardín Botánico Clavijero PARK
(☎228-842-18-27; Antigua Carretera a Coatepec Km 2.5; ⊙9am-5pm) Southwest of the town center, this attractive park has an expansive collection of subtropical and cloud-forest plants. The pines are particularly prolific.

Activities

Local tour operators offer cultural trips to outlying towns and archaeological sites, and also provide easygoing sports-oriented outdoor excursions such as hiking, rafting and rappelling.

Bird-Watching BIRD-WATCHING
(☎228-818-18-94; straub_robert@yahoo.com; US$25-100) Local bird-watching guide Robert Straub, a member of COAX (a conservation-minded bird-watching club), offers tours in the area, or can hook up birders with experienced local guides if he is busy. Straub authored a bird-watching guide to Veracruz, *Guía de Sitios* – proceeds go to Pronatura, a conservation nonprofit.

Courses

Escuela para Estudiantes Extranjeros LANGUAGE
(School for Foreign Students; ☎228-817-86-87; www.uv.mx/eee; Gutiérrez Zamora 25; courses per hr from US$20, for 2 weeks US$250 plus registration fee US$100) The Universidad Veracruzana's Escuela para Estudiantes Extranjeros offers short-term, accredited programs on the Spanish and Náhuatl languages and on Mexican culture, including cooking, dancing and guitar classes. Homestays are available (two weeks US$420, month-long US$795).

Tours

Veraventuras ADVENTURE
(☎228-818-95-79; www.veraventuras.com.mx) Offers rafting excursions, camping trips and many other activities, including trips to nearby hot springs.

Sleeping

Hostal de la Niebla HOSTEL $
(☎228-817-21-74; www.delaniebla.com; Gutiérrez Zamora 24; dm/s/d/tr/q incl breakfast M$160/360/360/520/680; P 📶) Something of a mirage in these climes, this modern Scandinavian-style hostel is no half-baked nod to the backpacker market. Rather it's a spotless, well-organized, community-oriented accommodation featuring airy rooms with decks and terraces. There's access to lockers and a kitchen.

Posada Casa Regia HOTEL $
(☎228-812-05-91; www.posadacasaregia.com; Hidalgo 12; s/d M$380/430; P 📶) Pleasant and colorful, this small hotel lures you in with its fancy plant- and tile-filled lobby, though the inward-facing rooms are rather less exciting. Parking costs M$90 per night, and there's no breakfast.

Hotel Limón HOTEL $
(☎228-817-22-04; Revolución 8; s/d/tr M$180/240/330; 📶) The term 'dusty jewel' could have been invented with the Hotel Limón in mind. The 'dusty' part refers to the rooms, which are perfectly adequate but crying out for a refurb. The 'jewel' is the blue-tiled courtyard, seemingly inherited from richer past owners. A good economical option for the unfussy, it's also very central (just steps from the cathedral).

★**Mesón del Alférez Xalapa** HISTORIC HOTEL $$
(☎228-818-01-13; www.pradodelrio.com; Sebastián Camacho 2; r incl breakfast M$750, ste incl breakfast from M$930; ❄ 📶) This gorgeous place right in the center of town manages to get it all just right. It's a quiet oasis from the roaring traffic outside, with beautiful split-level rooms (beds upstairs, living room below), flower-filled greenery and the best breakfast

VERACRUZ' MESOAMERICAN CULTURES

Several pre-Hispanic cultures inhabited the central Gulf coast if Mexico. Here's a brief who's who.

Olmec Often referred to as the 'mother culture' of the civilizations that followed, the Olmecs invented many of Mesoamerica's cultural hallmarks, including colossal stone heads carved from basalt boulders, the legendary Mesoamerican ball game and the macabre practice of human sacrifice. As early agriculturists, they emerged in southern Veracruz and Tabasco in the regional centers of San Lorenzo (35km southeast of Acayucan), La Venta (in present-day Tabasco) and, later, Tres Zapotes. Their culture flourished from around 1200 to 900 BC in San Lorenzo and from about 800 to 400 BC in La Venta.

Classic Veracruz The Classic period (AD 250 to 900) saw the rise of a number of statelets with a shared culture, together known as the Classic Veracruz civilization. The artistic hallmark of Classic Veracruz is a style of abstract carving featuring pairs of curved and interwoven parallel lines. This civilization was particularly obsessed with the ball game; its most important center, El Tajín, which flourished from about AD 600 to 900, contains 17 ball courts.

Totonac The Gulf coast's most colorful culture flowered between AD 800 and 1200 on the thin coastal strip between Zempoala and Papantla. Calling their land Totonacapan, the Totonacs built great cities such as Zempoala and Quiahuiztlán where they practiced weaving and embroidery, and farmed the land for maize, squash, cotton and vanilla. Though big proponents of the Mesoamerican ball game, the Totonacs also concocted more lasting legacies such as the *voladores* rite, which still survives today. Despite aiding the Spanish in their quest to defeat the Aztecs, Totonacapan quickly fell to smallpox and Spanish treachery after the 1520s. Currently there are still around 244,000 native Totonac speakers, mainly in northern Veracruz and the Sierra Norte de Puebla.

Huastec Native to the far north of Veracruz state, the ancient Huastecs spoke a language related to Maya. Historical evidence suggests that they migrated north from the Yucatán Peninsula around 1000 BC. Industrious cotton farmers and painters of elaborate pottery, the Huastecs were also known for their musical prowess; *huapango*, played by a trio of two guitars and a violin, has made notable contributions to mariachi music. Huastec culture reached its zenith between AD 800 and 1200. The language has survived into modern times and still has approximately 145,000 speakers.

in town in its refined La Candela restaurant. A sublime bargain.

Posada del Cafeto HISTORIC HOTEL **$$**
(☎228-817-00-23; www.pradodelrio.com; Dr Canovas 8; r incl breakfast from M$540; @📶) Centrally located on a quiet side street, the Cafeto hides the noisy city behind its thick colonial walls. The dual inner patios with their finely sculpted stairways and arches create a kind of 'secret garden' feel. Rooms are spacious, individually decorated and very comfortable. Breakfast in a cute onsite cafe is included.

Posada La Mariquinta GUESTHOUSE **$$**
(☎228-818-11-58; www.lamariquinta.xalapa.net; Alfaro 12; s/d from M$580/720, ste M$720-1150; P🚭📶) This homey, plant-filled guesthouse is set in an 18th-century colonial residence with rooms arranged around a lovely garden. The rooms feel a little on the stale side for these prices, but it's a quiet refuge from the city and popular with longer term guests. Whatever you do, don't miss the fabulous library-cum-reception room, stuffed with old books and furniture.

Eating

Stylish cafes and restaurants abound in Xalapa, many offering interesting regional menus and vegetarian choices. Callejón González Aparicio, between Primo Verdad and Mata, is an alley loaded with hip international eateries and even hipper crowds. One local specialty worth trying is *chiles rellenos* (stuffed peppers).

La Fonda MEXICAN **$**
(☎228-818-72-82; Callejón Diamante 1; dishes M$50-100; ⏲8am-5:30pm) A microcosm of the Xalapa eating experience, La Fonda

invites you to squeeze past the tortilla-making señorita at the door and climb upstairs, where the mural-festooned interior gives onto a narrow plant-adorned balcony overlooking the main street. The menu juxtaposes formidable *mole* with *chileatole de pollo* (chicken soup with little floating cobs of corn).

The daily all-you-can-eat buffet (8am to 1pm) is a steal at M$70 per person.

Plazoleta MEXICAN $

(228-165-56-00; Gutiérrez Zamora 46; dishes M$40-110; 8am-10pm Mon-Sat, to 6pm Sun;) This popular cafeteria has street-view seating as well as tables placed around trees and vines in a courtyard. There's a climbing frame out back to keep kids happy, while its excellent value all-you-can-eat buffet (M$48 per person) will please all comers. As well as traditional Mexican food, there's an extensive coffee menu and fresh fruit juices on tap.

Mercado de la Rotonda MARKET $

(Revolución s/n; 7am-6pm) Located at the north end of Revolución, this untouristed market has numerous orderly eateries offering delicious regional food on the cheap.

★**El Brou** MEDITERRANEAN $$

(Soto 13; mains M$60-150; 9am-6pm;) *El brou* is Catalan for 'cauldron,' and this reflects the pan-Mediterranean background of the people involved in this superb place. Housed in a delightful high-ceilinged colonial lounge, El Brou gets it right on all counts. Modern touches to its traditional decor manage to look chic rather than tacky, while the varied menu offers a delicious take on Mediterranean cuisine.

★**La Candela** MEXICAN $$

(Sebastián Camacho 2; mains M$70-160; 8am-3:30pm;) You have to know about this spot to find it (it's hidden downstairs in the Mesón del Alférez Xalapa), but you'll be glad you did once you've joined the crowd of loyal regulars here. Inventive Mexican cuisine, a suite of steaks (we highly recommend the Tampiqueña) and various other local specialties make this place a winner.

Breakfasts here are accepted by nearly all Xalapeños as being the best in town.

Piacevole Bistro PIZZERIA $$

(228-186-59-23; Insurgentes 3; mains M$70-150; 2-11pm;) You may have to fight to get a seat at this excellent pizzeria and wine bar (there are only four tables), but it's well worth the effort. The formula is winningly simple: handmade pasta and pizza, some excellent Mexican wines (yes, these exist), cool decor and an animated clientele. There are plans to expand, and delivery is available.

Drinking

Xalapa has two branches of Veracruz' Gran Café de la Parroquia (p211): one on Enríquez opposite Parque Juárez and the other on Zaragoza. Unfortunately neither can match the original for size and atmosphere. Elsewhere, indie cafes abound.

★**Café Cali** CAFE

(Callejón Diamante 23A; 9am-11pm) A real diamond in Diamond Alley, Café Cali sits next to its eponymous roasting room, which causes delicious coffee smells to permeate the whole block. The interior is classic bohemia, but it's the superb cakes (light, buttery and worth writing home about) that are the main draw.

Espresso 58 CAFE

(Primo Verdad 7; coffee M$13-25; 8am-11pm;) A sleek modern joint that attracts an equal smattering of wi-fi geeks and loquacious student debaters. The in-house Café Mahal coffee (locally grown, of course) is *muy rico* and the baristas are charming.

Jugos California JUICE BAR

(228-817-22-71; Enríquez 26; juices M$20-40; 7am-9:30pm) Besides *antojitos* (typical Mexican snacks), this place serves fantastic volcano-like fruit salads, delicious juice combos, smoothies and even chocolate soy shakes.

Angelo Casa de Té CAFE

(228-841-08-39; Primo Verdad 21A; 8am-9pm) Linger over a pot of rose tea – one of many tea choices here – while savoring homemade cookies.

Cubanías BAR

(Callejón González Aparicio; 5pm-1:30am;) Veracruz' Cuban influences rise to the surface in this boisterous bar, with mojitos, beer and – should you be peckish – large Cuban sandwiches on offer. It guards the entrance to Callejón González Aparicio and live music rocks up later on.

Entertainment

Being a university town, Xalapa has a vivacious nightlife. The loudest buzz can be found in jam-packed Callejón González Aparicio, the covered alley off Primo Verdad filled with trendy bars.

★Tierra Luna PERFORMING ARTS
(228-812-13-01; Rayón 18; 9am-10pm Mon-Thu, 9am-2am Fri & Sat;) A sanctuary for arty types, Tierra Luna provides a changing roster of poetry readings and music in its historic high-ceilinged theatre space. It also serves tasty cafe fare (mains M$50 to M$90), including a breakfast menu and a range of alcoholic drinks. Do not miss the eponymous *tierra y luna* cake (half chocolate cake, half cheesecake). There's a small bookstore and a craft store too.

Centro Recreativo Xalapeño ARTS CENTER
(Xalapeños Ilustres 31; 9am-8pm) On bookish Xalapeños Ilustres, this cultural center is the font of pretty much everything that passes for 'art' in Xalapa. Jam sessions, tango classes, art expos, sculpture competitions and Cine Francés all kick off here; keep your eye on the poster board. The building is an attractive 19th-century colonial gem with a courtyard and small cafe (Luna Negra).

El Ágora ARTS CENTER
(228-818-57-30; Parque Juárez; 10am-10pm Tue-Sun, 9am-6pm Mon;) A busy and sleekly modern arts center with a cinema, theater, gallery, bookstore and cafe.

Teatro del Estado Ignacio de la Llave THEATER
(228-818-08-34; cnr Llave & Av Ávila Camacho; from 8pm) The impressive state theatre hosts both the Orquesta Sinfónica de Xalapa and the Ballet Folklórico of the Universidad Veracruzana. It is situated 1.5km northwest of Parque Juárez, up Avenida Ávila Camacho.

Shopping

An epicenter of Xalapa's alternative culture is Callejón Diamante, an alley lined with boutiques and street vendors selling cheap jewelry, incense and paraphernalia. Bookstores line Xalapeños Ilustres. This is *the* place to get your hair braided or your back tattooed.

Popularte HANDICRAFTS
(228-841-12-02; Xalapeños Ilustres 3; 9am-6pm Mon-Sat) High-quality local handicrafts made by, and supporting, Veracruz' indigenous communities.

Café Colón COFFEE
(Primo Verdad 15) Old-school coffee roasters will grind Coatepec's best in front of your eyes in this aromatic store. It sells for around M$140 per kilo.

Information

MEDICAL SERVICES

Centro de Especialidades Médicas (228-814-45-00; www.cemev.gob.mx; Ruíz Cortines 2903; 8am-6pm) Excellent medical care.

MONEY

There are banks with 24-hour ATMs along Enríquez and Gutiérrez Zamora.

POST

Post Office (cnr Gutiérrez Zamora & Diego Leño)

TOURIST INFORMATION

An **information booth** (www.xalapa.gob.mx; Palacio Municipal; 9am-3pm & 4-7pm Mon-Fri) in the Palacio Municipal has helpful info and maps. There's another larger **office** (Palacios 9; 9am-3pm & 4-7pm Mon-Fri) nearby.

JALCOMULCO – RAFTING ADVENTURES

Surrounded by lush ravines and just 30km southeast of Xalapa, this town hugs the Río Antigua (known as the Río Pescados) and is very picturesque. The area is rich with caves and luscious swimming spots, but it's most famous for its rapids, which accommodate white-water enthusiasts from the beginner through to the more advanced.

There are a number of tour operators offering local activities. Those recommended include **Aventuras Sin Límites** (800-837-43-30; www.raftingsinlimite.com; Zaragoza 58), **Huitzilapan Expediciones** (279-832-36-10; www.huitzilapanexpediciones.com.mx; Juárez 52) and **México Verde** (800-362-88-00; www.mexicoverde.com; Carretera Tuzamapan-Jalcomulco Km 4; trips from M$660), which has its own resort on the road coming into town from the northwest.

There are buses (M$30) to Jalcomulco from Xalapa at the Azteca bus terminal, as well as buses from Cardel.

USEFUL WEBSITES

Xalapa Mio (www.xalapamio.com)
Xalapa Tourist Network (www.xalapa.net)

Getting There & Away

Xalapa is a transportation hub with excellent connections throughout the state and beyond.

BUS

Xalapa's modern and well-organized bus station, the **Central de Autobuses de Xalapa** (CAXA; Av 20 de Noviembre), is 2km east of the center and has an ATM, cafes and telephones. Second-class buses for Xico and Coatepec regularly leave from Mercado Los Sauces, about 1km west of the center on Circuito Presidentes. First-class services are offered by ADO and good 2nd-class services by AU.

Buses to Jalcomulco leave from the **Azteca bus station** (Niños Heroes 85).

CAR & MOTORCYCLE

Xalapa is famous for its traffic choked streets, and driving here can be a challenging prospect; just negotiating the sprawling suburbs to find the center can be difficult as signage is poor.

Hwy 140 to Puebla is narrow and winding until Perote; the Xalapa–Veracruz highway is very fast and smooth. Going to the northern Gulf coast, it's quickest to go to Cardel, then north on Hwy 180.

Getting Around

For buses from CAXA to the center, follow signs to the taxi stand, then continue downhill to the main Avenida 20 de Noviembre. The bus stop is to the right. Any bus marked 'Centro' will pass within a block or two of Parque Juárez (M$8). For a taxi to the center, you have to buy a ticket in the bus station (M$35). To return to the bus station, take the 'Camacho-CAXA-SEC' bus from Avenida Ávila Camacho or Hidalgo.

Around Xalapa

The dramatic landscapes around Xalapa cradle some charming mountain towns and worthwhile places.

Hacienda El Lencero

Almost as old as New Spain itself, this former posada *(inn)* was initiated in 1525 by Juan Lencero, a soldier loyal to Hernán Cortés, and served as a resting place for tired travelers toiling between a newly Europeanized Mexico City and the coast. Today it is the **Museo Ex-Hacienda El Lencero** (Carretera Xalapa-Veracruz Km 10; adult/child M$40/30; ⌚10am-5pm), incorporating a superbly restored house furnished with antiques, along with some delightful gardens embellished with a lake and a 500-year-old fig tree.

To get to the estate travel 12km southeast of Xalapa on the Veracruz highway, and then turn down a signposted road branching off to the right for a few kilometers. From Xalapa, catch one of the regular 'Miradores' buses (M$11) from the Plaza Cristal shopping center.

Coatepec

☎228 / POP 53,600 / ELEV 1200M

Waking up and smelling the coffee has rarely been this epiphanic. Cradled in the Sierra Madre foothills, Coatepec's coffee production has long been its raison d'être, a fact that will become instantly clear as soon as

BUSES FROM XALAPA

DESTINATION	FARE (M$)	DURATION	FREQUENCY (DAILY)
Cardel	64	1hr	18
Mexico City (TAPO)	278	4½hr	6
Papantla	218	4hr	14
Puebla	172	2½hr	15
Tampico	470	9½hr	2
Veracruz	98	2hr	frequent
Veracruz airport	268	1½hr	5
Villahermosa	492	8½hr	7

The daily ADO services listed in the table leave from CAXA.

Destinations also served by ADO include Acayucan, Campeche, Cancún, Catemaco, Córdoba, Mérida, Orizaba and Poza Rica..

you step off the bus and inhale. The settlement dates from 1701 and coffee has been grown in the surrounding cloud forests for almost as long. The crop has brought wealth to the town; Coatepec – which lies a mere 15km south of Xalapa – is adorned with rich colonial buildings. In 2006, it was nominated a *pueblo mágico* by the Mexican government for its cultural, historical and natural relevance. In late September, Coatepec vivaciously celebrates its patron saint, San Jerónimo, making it an excellent time to visit.

Sights

Parque Miguel Hidalgo PLAZA

Coatepec's main square is green and bereft of the worst of the town's traffic. In its center stands a glorious *glorieta* (traffic circle) that doubles up as a cafe. Set back from the road on the eastern side is the unashamedly baroque **Parroquia de San Jerónimo**, named after the city's patron saint.

Cerro de las Culebras LOOKOUT

Cerro de las Culebras (Snake Hill; Coatepec in the Náhuatl language) is easily accessible from the town center. The walk takes you up cobbled steps to a lookout tower with a white statue of Christ on top. From here there are magnificent city and mountain views. To get there, walk three blocks west from the main plaza on Lerdo, then north all the way up Independencia.

Museo y Jardin de Orquideas MUSEUM, GARDEN

(Aldama 20; 10am-5pm Wed-Sun) FREE Coatepec's humid cloud forests support numerous species of orchid and an amiable local *señora* has collected many of them for this museum/garden a few blocks from the main square. Displays highlight both cultivation and conservation techniques. Reserve 30 minutes to see the full gamut. A guided tour costs M$30 per person.

Museo El Cafétal Apan MUSEUM

(www.elcafe-tal.com; Carretera Coatepec-Las Trancas Km 4; admission M$40; 9am-5pm) If you want to learn a bit more about the history of coffee in the region, visit this museum that displays antique coffee-making tools. There are hands-on demonstrations showing how coffee is produced, and also coffee tastings. It's a bit out of town; a taxi will cost M$40.

Cascada Bola de Oro WATERFALL

The nearest waterfall to town is in the environs of a well-known Coatepec coffee *finca* (estate), which also has various trails and a natural swimming pool. To get there follow Calle 5 de Mayo north to a bridge, continue north on Calle Prieto and then turn left into Calle Altamirano. After passing the last shop, hang a right, cross a bridge and turn left onto a path. The tourist office dispenses useful maps.

Sleeping

Ashram Coatepec HOSTEL $

(228-816-10-55; www.ashramdecoatepec.org; Mina 100; dm/campsite M$100; P) On the outskirts of town, this ashram has yoga, meditation and walking trails through its lush grounds. The immaculate treatment of the gorgeous meditation and yoga spaces isn't replicated in the dormitories, but it's a decent place to hang your hat and extremely good value. All food here is vegetarian.

★ **Casa Real del Café** HISTORIC HOTEL $$

(228-816-63-17; www.casarealdelcafe.com.mx; Gutiérrez Zamora 58; d/ste incl breakfast M$900/1100; P) This colonial-style hotel is owned by local coffee farmers whose aromatic products fortuitously find their way into the onsite Antiguo Beneficio cafe. Split-level rooms offer historic luxury with dark wood and gorgeously tiled bathrooms, while the communal courtyard sports reclining chairs, a spa and a reading room with a full set of the Encyclopedia Britannica.

Posada de Coatepec HISTORIC HOTEL $$$

(228-816-05-44; www.posadacoatepec.com.mx; Hidalgo 9; r/ste incl breakfast from M$1300/2000; P) Coatepec's hallmark hotel is in a resplendent colonial-era building; the central courtyard is overflowing with plants and features a gurgling fountain. It boasts a pool, exhibits from local artists, tranquil gardens and a full-sized antique coach parked in the lobby. The rooms are large, but rather on the dark and musty side, as is typical with colonial mansions.

Given this, it's a little overpriced, but its impressive public areas can't be beaten for atmosphere.

Eating

Casa Coffino CAFE, INTERNATIONAL $

(www.coffino.com.mx; Jiménez del Campillo 17; snacks M$50-110; 8am-10pm;) An interesting cafe encased in a head-turning art nouveau-style building a block from the plaza. Coffino's specialty is its own rich coffee (called *Café de Altura*), but it also serves light food, cakes and smoothies in a beautiful flower-filled courtyard.

El Caporal SEAFOOD, INTERNATIONAL **$$**
(Luís de San José 3B; mains M$60-200; 8am-midnight) Set in an impressive colonial mansion on Coatepec's main square, El Caporal has hefty paella, large prawns and well-seasoned fish fillets. There's also a long wine list – Chilean and Spanish vintages dominate. Next door in the same blue house is the lighter **La Vereda Cafeteria**.

Drinking & Entertainment

★ **El Café de Avelino** CAFE
(Aldama 6; noon-5pm) The best coffee in Coatepec (no mean feat!) comes from a cafe with one table and two chairs occupying the lobby of the magnificent Mansión de los Azulejos (House of Tiles). Owner Avelino Hernández – known locally as the *Poeta del Café* (coffee poet) – brews minor miracles from his Coatepec, Cosailton, Xico and Teocelo brands. You can buy the beans for M$200 per kilo.

Casú CAFE
(La Casa del Café; 5 de Mayo; 9am-7pm) A charming cafe run by a friendly team of coffee roasters, who serve up their delicious wares (think fantastic coffee and mouthwatering cakes) in a lovely back garden space a short distance from the main square.

El Kiosko CAFE
(Parque Hidalgo; 8am-7pm) Small alfresco cafe selling java out of the old *glorieta* (traffic circle) in the center of the plaza.

Shopping

La Misión SOUVENIRS, ACCESSORIES
(228-816-41-32; Aldama 6; 9am-7pm) In this shop you'll find carefully selected local items such as organic coffee, essential oils, *maguey* honey and soy milk.

Information

There's a helpful **tourist office** (9am-2pm & 4-7pm Mon-Fri, 9:30am-6:30pm Sat & Sun) in the Palacio Municipal on Parque Hidalgo. Check out the excellent www.somoscoatepec.com website for lots of information in English.

Getting There & Away

Regular buses (M$9.50) arrive from Xalapa's CAXA and Los Sauces terminals, or a taxi is M$80. Buses for Xico (M$8) leave from Constitución between Aldama and Juárez. The ADO **bus station** (5 de Mayo s/n) serves Puebla and Mexico City.

Xico

228 / POP 18,600 / ELEV 1300M

Slowly emerging from Coatepec's shadow, quieter and hillier Xico is, arguably, a far more beguiling place, and in 2011 joined the ranks of Mexico's government-sanctioned *pueblos mágicos* (magical towns). Just 8km away from Coatepec, Xico attracts devotees of *mole* and handicrafts rather than coffee, while its cobbled streets and varied colonial architecture make it an increasingly popular weekend retreat. Within Mexico the town is best known for its annual Fiesta de Santa Magdalena, held each July and famous for a running of the bulls à la Pamplona in Spain.

Sights

Café Gourmet Pepe COFFEE PLANTATION
(228-846-74-71; Carretera Xico-Coatepec Km 1; tour M$60) This is an almost-organic, shade-grown coffee plantation that offers tours and sells delicious coffee and liquors. Get off at the first bus stop in Xico and walk back 150m to where you'll see signs on the right.

Cascada de Texolo WATERFALL
It's a pleasant, signposted 3km walk from Xico and past an ex-hacienda to the plunging 80m **Cascada de Texolo** and the **Cascada de la Monja** (Waterfall of the Nun). It's a luxurious place to take a dip, and eighties' movie fans should look out: the former cascade featured in *Romancing the Stone* (1984); the said 'stone' was hidden behind it.

Museo del Vestido MUSEUM
(Parroquia, cnr Av Hidalgo & Juárez; admission M$10; 3-7:30pm Tue-Sun) An esoteric, niche museum displaying a revolving collection of St María Magdalena's past festival dresses dating from 1910.

Casa-Museo Totomoxtle MUSEUM
(cnr Aldama & Juárez; 10am-4pm) FREE A small museum highlighting the town's peculiar artisanal pastime of making intricate and detailed figures from *hojas de maiz* (maize leaves). Only in Xico!

Festivals & Events

Fiesta de Santa Magdalena RELIGIOUS

The mother of all festivals takes place in Xico between July 15 and 24. Gigantic floral arches are raised, and streets are artistically decorated with carpets of colored sawdust in preparation for the saint's procession. The Magdalena statue in the Parroquia de Santa María Magdalena (located at the end of Avenida Hidalgo) is clothed in a different elaborate dress each day for 30 days around the fiesta. A running of the bulls takes place through the streets on July 22.

Sleeping & Eating

Posada los Naranjos HOTEL $

(228-153-54-54; Av Hidalgo 193; r from M$350; P) With just nine rooms and right in the center of town, this no-frills place is a decent budget option, but not much more. Rooms are clean and simple, and there's a pleasant cafe here too. It's a short amble down Xico's main street from the church.

Hotel Paraje Coyopolan HOTEL $$

(228-813-12-66; www.coyopolan.com; Venustiano Carranza Sur s/n; s/d incl breakfast M$450/585; P) It's all about bright colours and lively Mexican design at this super place right on the river just outside the town. The hotel arranges hiking, canyoning and rappelling in the surrounding mountains and canyons, making it a great base for outdoor activities. The onsite restaurant also serves superb regional food.

★ **Las Magdalenas** BOUTIQUE HOTEL $$$

(228-813-03-14; www.lasmagdalenas.com.mx; Hidalgo 123; r M$1280-1590) Opened in 2013 and indicative of Xico's rising star status, this gorgeous colonial house has been impressively transformed into a boutique hotel. It boasts a fabulous garden full of flowers, four split-level rooms (with three more to come) and generous discounts during the week. Rooms are surprisingly modern for such an old world setting, but all round this place is a winner.

Los Portales Texolo MEXICAN $

(Hidalgo 109; mains M$50-100; 8am-8pm Tue-Sun) Some way down Av Hidalgo from the church, you'll arrive at a small square that is popular with ecstatic birds at sunset. Here you'll find this friendly local place, where delicious *xiqueño* specialties such as *chiles en nogada* and *mole* are served outside, amid Xico's colonial splendour.

★ **Restaurante Mesón Xiqueño** MEXICAN $$

(Av Hidalgo 148; meals M$50-150; 9am-9pm) Near the corner with Calle Carranza is Mesón Xiqueño, Xico's best known restaurant. Here you can try the famous local *mole,* served in a number of different ways, while dining at one of the tables spread out over the lovely courtyard.

Shopping

Derivados Acamalin Productos Xiquenial Artesanías FOOD

(Av Hidalgo 150; 9am-7pm) Xico's trademark *mole* (a complex mix of chocolate, banana, apple, chili, sucrose and numerous secret ingredients) can be procured at Derivados Acamalin Productos Xiquenial Artesanías. Also sells organic coffee for M$100 per kilo.

Information

Tourist Office (228-813-16-18; Av Hidalgo 76; 9am-6pm) The small tourist office is encased in the Casa de la Cultura and is a friendly source of information for the town and its surroundings.

Getting There & Away

From Xalapa, take a bus to Xico (M$18) from Los Sauces terminal. From Coatepec, Xico buses (M$8) frequently leave from Constitución, one block southeast of the main plaza.

Córdoba

271 / POP 140,000 / ELEV 924M

Mention you're going to Córdoba to a coastal dweller and you may well get a sarcastic eye roll. *Cordobeses* are often seen as haughtier and less modest than their more down-to-earth *jarocho* brethren, though 'urbane' would be a kinder description.

Not to be confused with its famous namesakes in Spain and Argentina, Córdoba, Veracruz, has an illustrious history and a justifiable sense of civic pride; the contract that sealed Mexico's independence was signed here in 1821. The city itself was originally founded in 1618 as a staging post between Mexico City and the coast, with the purpose of protecting the Spanish crown's interests from the local slave rebellion, led by Gaspar Yanga, that was strong in the area.

As an overnight stop, Córdoba trumps other central Veracruz cities such as Orizaba and Fortín de las Flores on the strength of its main plaza. It's a 24-hour live 'show,' where theater-goers in high heels dodge hungry pigeons and grandpas moonlight as marimba players. Watching over it all is an impressive baroque cathedral, easily the most resplendent in the state.

Be aware that Córdoba has a complicated system of street numbering – a map from your hotel or the tourist office will be a big help.

Sights

Most of Córdoba's sights ring its main plaza, Parque de 21 de Mayo, which is a sight in itself.

★Parque de 21 de Mayo PLAZA

Not overly endowed with sights per se, Córdoba's main plaza vies with Veracruz City's as the region's most entertaining. It's far larger than the port city's plaza, though a seemingly unending line of musicians makes up for any lack of intimacy. Opposite the cathedral on the square's west side is the splendiferous **Palacio Municipal**, replete with an interior mural that Diego Rivera would have been hard-pressed to emulate.

Ex-Hotel Zevallos HISTORIC BUILDING

(Parque de 21 de Mayo) Built in 1687, this is the former home of the *condes* (counts) of Zevallos. It's on the northeast side of Parque de 21 de Mayo, behind the *portales* (arcades). Plaques in the courtyard record that Juan O'Donojú and Agustín de Iturbide met here on August 24, 1821, and agreed on the terms for Mexico's independence. They also concurred that a Mexican, not a European, should be head of state. The building is now full of restaurants and cafes.

Catedral de la Inmaculada Concepción CATHEDRAL

(Parque de 21 de Mayo) Dating from 1688, this blue baroque cathedral has an elaborate facade flanked by twin bell towers. The showy interior is surprisingly ornate for Mexico, with gold-leaf detailing and marble floors. The chapel features candlelit statues with altars, such as a gruesome Jesus on the cross and an eerily despairing Virgen de la Soledad. The mixture of glitz and gore is a visual metaphor for a disturbing historical dichotomy: the richness of the conquistadors and the misery that the indigenous people subsequently endured.

Museo de Antropología MUSEUM

(Calle 3 btwn Av 3 & 5; ⏲10am-6pm) FREE This museum has a modest but interesting collection of artifacts including a fine Aztec ball-court marker and some Olmec figurines. There's also a replica of the magnificent statue of El Señor de Las Limas that resides in Xalapa's Museo de Antropología. You'll find it just off the main square, opposite the Centro Cultural Municipal.

Parque Ecológico Paso Coyol PARK

(☎271-714-20-84; cnr Calle 6 & Av 19, Bella Vista; admission M$2) This park is a jewel in the urban rough. Formerly a 4-hectare abandoned lot overrun by 'delinquents,' this eco-conscious park is now patronized by *cordobeses,* who run and walk trails that snake around gardens punctuated with exercise stations. Your meager entrance fee pays for both *campesinos* (country people) and biologists alike to maintain the place. Follow Calle 3 south from the plaza for 1.5km. The street changes name, weaves through a suburb and bottoms out at the park.

Festivals & Events

Good Friday RELIGIOUS

On the evening of Good Friday, Córdoba marks Jesus' crucifixion with a procession of silence, in which thousands of residents walk through the streets behind an altar of the Virgin. Everyone holds a lit candle, no one utters a word and the church bells are strangely quiet.

Sleeping

Hotel Palacio HOTEL $

(☎271-712-21-88; www.hotelpalaciocordoba.com.mx; cnr Calle 2 & Av 3; r M$440; P ❄ ᯤ) The best budget option in Córdoba is this large place with a smart, bright lobby and rather less impressive, characterless rooms, only some of which have air-con. However, it's just a block from the plaza and has its own underground car park, so it's fine for an overnight stay.

Hotel Mansur HOTEL $$

(☎271-712-60-00; www.hotelmansur.com.mx; Av 1 No 301, cnr Calle 3; s/d M$520/535, ste M$735-1000; P ❄ ᯤ) Claiming five stories of prime viewing space above Córdoba's main plaza, the Mansur, with its vast balconies equipped with thick wooden chairs, makes you feel as if you're part of the 'show' going on below. The old world lobby has lots of wood and silver-framed mirrors, but the rooms themselves, while perfectly decent, are somewhat on the characterless side.

There's no price hike for rooms at the front, so request one of these unless it's peace and quiet you're after.

Hotel Layfer HOTEL $$
(☎271-714-05-05; www.hoteleslayfer.com; Av 5 No 908, btwn Calle 9 & 11; s/d/tr M$735/895/1055; P❄📶🏊) Definitely Córdoba's fanciest hotel (if not necessarily its best), the Layfer has sleek modern rooms arranged around a central swimming pool. Bamboo decor gives the place a refined air, even if the rooms are nothing special. Mileage is added with a wide array of extras including complimentary body-care products, a bar, gym, restaurant and games room.

Hotel Bello HOTEL $$
(☎271-712-81-22; www.hotelbello.com/cordoba; cnr Av 2 & Calle 5; s/d/tr M$550/650/690; P❄@📶) Brightly painted in yellow and thus hard to miss, this modern hotel is spotless and well located just moments from the main square. The rooms are fresh, some with great views towards Pico de Orizaba, and the staff are affable. Go for the top-floor balcony rooms.

Eating

Córdoba has a lively eating scene with plenty of choice. For a cheap meal, try the little eateries on Avenida 5 in between Calles 1 and 2.

★Calufe Café CAFE, SANDWICHES $
(Calle 3 No 212 btwn Av 4 & 2; ⏱8am-8pm Sun-Wed, until midnight Thu-Sat; 📶) If only all cafes could be like this. Calufe occupies the interior of an agreeably peeling colonial mansion with eclectic nooks arranged around a dimly lit plant-filled courtyard. Guitar and vocal duos provide a melancholy musical backdrop in the evenings. Calufe sells its own blend of coffee, along with melt-in-the-mouth coffee cake and other interesting organic snacks.

Crepas y Carnes Los 30s MEXICAN $$
(Av 9 between Calle 20 & 22; crepes M$100, mains M$90-250; ⏱12:30pm-midnight Sun-Wed, 12:30pm-1am Thu-Sat; 📶) A sprawling and hugely popular place amid a long stretch of restaurants along Av 9. Terming itself *'cocina del barrio'* (cookery of the quarter), it has a colonial feel, and its walls are decked with art and old photographs. The crepes are excellent, and range from the savory to the very sweet. There's also pizza, fish, pasta and various grills on the extensive menu.

Mulata INTERNATIONAL $$
(Av 1 No 721, btwn Calle 7 & 9; dishes M$50-150; ⏱8am-midnight; 📶) Mulata was named after a beautiful African slave who, according to legend, escaped from prison through the picture she drew in her cell. Appropriately, you'll find a gorgeous mural here, as well as creative, internationally influenced food and bakery items. The breakfast is good, as are the salads, soups and steaks.

Tabachín MEXICAN $$
(Av 1 No 101, cnr Calle 1; mains M$55-160; ⏱8am-1am) Eating downstairs at the Zevallos puts you in among the marimba players and wandering salesmen, but mixing in the street-level melee brings down the prices seen upstairs by a good 20%. Tabachín's specialty dish is the giant *Plato Cordobés*, a raft of meats easily divided between two, unless you're exceptionally hungry.

El Balcón del Zevallos PARRILLA, MEXICAN $$$
(Av 1 No 101, cnr Calle 1; mains M$100-200; ⏱5pm-midnight Mon-Thu, from 1pm Fri-Sun) The upper floor of the eerily beautiful former Hotel Zevallos claims the prize for Córdoba's best fine-dining restaurant, with a refined inner sanctum and a balcony overlooking the plaza. There's an extensive wine list here (the usual Spanish and Chilean suspects),

BUSES FROM CÓRDOBA

DESTINATION	FARE (M$)	DURATION	FREQUENCY (DAILY)
Fortín	10	25min	hourly
Mexico City (TAPO)	318	5hr	frequent
Oaxaca	360	6½hr	7
Orizaba	30	40min	frequent
Puebla	194	3hr	frequent
Veracruz	122	1½hr	frequent
Xalapa	182	3hr	hourly

Selection of Deluxe and 1st-class buses from Córdoba.

and good meat dishes cooked *a la parrilla* (on the barbecue). Service is sharp but not overly officious.

Information

Banks around the Plaza de Armas have 24-hour ATMs.

Hospital Covadonga (☎271-714-55-20; www.corporativodehospitales.com.mx; Av 7 No 1610; ⌚24hr) Urgent medical care at all hours.

Tourist Office (☎271-712-43-44; Centro Cultural Municipal, Av 3 cnr Calle 3; ⌚8:30am-4pm & 6-7:30pm Mon-Fri, 10am-2pm Sat & Sun) Helpful staff offer maps and information. Volunteers sometimes give tours of the city.

Getting There & Around

BUS

Córdoba's **bus station** (Av Privada 4), which has deluxe, 1st-class and 2nd-class services, is 2.5km southeast of the plaza. To get to the town center from the station, take a local bus marked 'Centro' or buy a taxi ticket (M$30). To Fortín de las Flores and Orizaba, it's more convenient to take a local bus from the corner of Avenida 11 and Calle 3 than to go out to the Córdoba bus station.

CAR & MOTORCYCLE

Córdoba, Fortín de las Flores and Orizaba are linked by toll Hwy 150D, the route that most buses take, and by the much slower Hwy 150. A scenic back road goes through the hills from Fortín, via Huatusco, to Xalapa.

Fortín de las Flores

☎271 / POP 21,000 / ELEV 970M

The mid-point on the Córdoba–Orizaba urban axis, Fortín de las Flores is where you can briefly come up for air in a tranquil cut-flower cultivation center with nurseries and private gardens. Though it's a peaceful weekend retreat for Mexico City's middle class, those from further afield might find it better day-trip fodder from bases in Córdoba or Orizaba. Fortín's annual **flower festival** runs for a week in late April or early May.

Activities

Barranca de Metlac HIKING

Fortín's most striking feature is this deep bio-diverse ravine, carved out by the Río Metlac. Spanning it is the **Puente de Metlac**, the highest rail bridge in North America, measuring 131m high by 90m long. Alongside it sits a slightly older and marginally lower road bridge. The original rail bridge, the **Puente de San Miguel**, sits a couple of kilometers to the north. Built in 1873, it sweeps across the canyon in an unusual curve. The Barranca hides some excellent hikes.

For the quickest access, head west from the center of Fortín down Avenida 1 which turns into the Fortín Viejo road. This quiet road bends steeply downhill for about 2km to join another busier road. Pass over the river here, turn immediately right and follow a dirt forest road north alongside the river to **El Corazón** (admission M$15), a basic facility with a weathered swimming pool and a snack-shack. Past the pool and to the left-hand side of an electricity plant, a pathway leads you to a huge staircase (440 steps) up to the Metlac road bridge for vertiginous and verdant views. To get back to Fortín, cross the bridge and cut back along the path that forks to the right at its eastern side.

A 6km stretch of old railway line to the north of the Puente de Metlac has been converted into a **Vía Verde** for walkers and cyclists. This beautiful juxtaposition of nature and 19th-century engineering includes seven tunnels, two stations, a bridge house ruin and the original 1873 bridge.

Cecila Rábago CULTURAL TOUR

(☎cell phone 271-120-20-30; cecirabago@hotmail.com; 1-4 people per day M$1000-1200) A well-established, bilingual tour guide in the area, Cecila's an expert on history and sites in the Fortín–Córdoba–Orizaba area. A firecracker of a lady, she can offer tours of the city and organic coffee plantations, take you on all-day hiking excursions off the tourist track, and many other things in between.

Sleeping

★**Hotel Posada Loma** HOTEL $$

(☎271-713-06-58; www.posadaloma.com; Carretera Córdoba-Fortín Km 333; s/d incl breakfast M$750/885, bungalows sleeping 4 incl breakfast M$1770; P ⊖ ❄ 📶 ≈) Its location (on the busy main road to Córdoba, 1km outside the center of Fortín) may not initially suggest a garden oasis, but once you drive up the hill and leave the traffic behind, that's exactly what you get here. The rooms are spacious, with private terraces, tasteful wooden furniture and big fireplaces for the winter months.

The real reason to come here is the grounds; a marvel of greenhouses, orchid collections, flower-filled gardens, terraces and a pool. The renowned breakfast in its restaurant – with exotic fresh-juice blends and spectacular views of Pico de Orizaba – is unbeatable, as is the flora tour by its friendly and knowledgeable owner, Lolis Álvarez.

Hotel Fortín de las Flores HOTEL $$
(☎271-713-00-55; Av 2 btwn Calles 5 & 7; s/d M$450/595; P ❄ 📶 🏊) Charming gardens and a good pool offset the austerity in evidence elsewhere at this long-established central option. Rooms are attractively tiled, have antique air-con units and good bathrooms, while the pool has super views towards Pico de Orizaba. The whole place has a not-unpleasant faded-glory-hacienda feel about it. Skip the breakfast.

Eating

A number of cafes and restaurants surround the main plaza.

Kiosko Café MEXICAN $
(Av 3 btwn Calles 1 & 3; mains M$45-80; ⏲7:30am-11:30pm; 📶) Smack in the middle of the main plaza, this cafe enjoys unmatched real estate. Formerly the library, it now serves coffee, fresh juices and simple meals in the sunshine. The *sopa azteca* (spicy tortilla soup) is excellent.

El Parián MEXICAN $
(☎271-713-11-67; Av 1 btwn Calles Norte 1 & Norte 2; mains M$35-100; ⏲8am-10pm) Just off the central plaza, El Parián offers good service and a pleasant atmosphere, even if it is a little dark inside. The M$49 set lunch is a great deal, and there's a good selection of other dishes available, from breakfasts and *antojitos* (Mexican snacks) to steak.

Information

Tourist Office (☎271-713-01-02; Palacio Municipal; ⏲8am-4pm Mon-Fri) You'll find the small but helpful tourist office in the Palacio Municipal, upstairs on the right-hand side. Town maps are available here.

Getting There & Away

In Fortín, local bus services arrive and depart from Calle 1 Oriente, on the northeast corner of the plaza. Frequent 2nd-class buses go to Córdoba and Coscomatepec. The ADO **bus station** (cnr Av 2 & Calle 6) has 1st-class bus departures. The 2nd-class bus to Orizaba goes through the gorgeous countryside but is more crowded and slower.

Coscomatepec

☎272 / POP 15,000 / ELEV 1588M

Easily one of Veracruz state's most enchanting towns, tongue-twister Coscomatepec (simply Cosco to anyone living there) is likely to work its magic on you quickly and irreversibly. Set amid the foothills of Pico de Orizaba, which towers in the distance when the clouds part, the steep, cobbled colonial streets and the charming main square all look like a film set for old Mexico. Shops selling intricate handmade saddles, leather goods, quality cigars and delicious bread all draw visitors, while a clutch of good hotels highlight the town's growing reputation as a weekend getaway from Veracruz, Xalapa and Mexico City.

Sights & Activities

You can take tours through the famous bakery, cigar factory and saddle shops. These are arranged through the **tourist office** (☎272 737-04-80; cnr Amez & Argüelles s/n; ⏲9am-4pm Mon-Fri) in the **Plaza Municipal**. There's also info on a variety of activities, such as hiking, rappelling, horseback riding, zip-lining and rock climbing in the area, which is rich with caves, rivers, old bridges and waterfalls.

If you're a climber (with your own equipment) or a hiker, and want someone to show you cool places, call experienced, bilingual local climbing and hiking guide **Edson Escamilla** (☎273-105-13-43, cell phone 273-737-04-81; x_on56@hotmail.com; per person per day

BUSES FROM FORTÍN DE LAS FLORES

DESTINATION	FARE (M$)	DURATION	FREQUENCY (DAILY)
Córdoba	10	25min	8
Mexico City (TAPO)	283	4½hr	3
Orizaba	28	25min	10
Veracruz	114	2hr	6
Xalapa	172	3½hr	4

1st-class bus departures from the ADO bus station.

plus tip M$300-600). He's awfully nice and shows people around locally, as well leading climbs to Pico de Orizaba.

A superb and famous **tack store** (☎272 737-00-68; Victoria 8) displays incredibly ornate, artisanal saddles and horse tack. More leather gear can be admired in **Proyecciones Artesanales** (Av Guadalupe Victoria 8). For Cosco's famous bread head to **La Fama** (Guerrero 6); it's been baking it since 1924.

Sleeping & Eating

Plaza Real HOTEL $
(☎273-737-00-96; Av Bravo cnr López Rayón; d/tw/tr M$390/$490/690; 📶) One block to the east of the main square, this new and currently rather poorly signed hotel has plenty of quirks; one of the rooms is a dental surgery, and the owner drives his SUV into the lobby to park it overnight. But it's a solid and good value choice, with spacious, pleasantly painted rooms and sunflower tiled basins.

It can be somewhat noisy in the evenings here, as the rooms surround an atrium where sound travels impressively. Do try to get a room at the front of the building, as these are the only ones with natural light.

Hotel Virrey HOTEL $
(☎271-711-14-94; Jimenez (Calle 4) cnr Juárez; r from M$400; 📶) This impressive 17-room hotel in the middle of town is a welcome addition to Cosco's accommodation offerings. It offers sparkling clean, brightly painted, floor-tiled rooms, and the owners promised that wireless internet would be available when it opened.

Hotel San Antonio HOTEL $
(☎272-737-03-20; Bravo (Av 1) 35; r M$250-370) Cosco's bargain-basement option has a fine location right on the plaza, though the unexciting rooms are on the musty side. There's a popular local restaurant on the ground floor.

★ **Posada del Emperador** HISTORIC HOTEL, HOSTEL $$
(☎272-737-15-20; www.laposadadelemperador.com; cnr Av Juárez (Calle 2) & Domínguez (Av 3); dm M$150, r from M$588, ste M$1056; ❄📶🏊) Competing with a handful of others for the title of Best Hotel in the State, the Emperador wins over all but the most unromantic with its beautiful historical decor, antique furniture, four-poster beds, exquisite views and its plant-filled interior. In addition to the private rooms, an onsite hostel offers a couple of spotless 12-berth separate-sex dorms, plus a shared kitchen and bathrooms.

Fated Habsburg emperor Maximilian apparently stopped here in the 1860s (hence the name) before his date with destiny and a firing squad. The hotel also boasts an extensive spa with massage, hot tubs, pool and temascal (a pre-Hispanic steam bath), as well as wonderful valley views from the restaurant and terrace. There's even a small chapel.

La Carreta MEXICAN $$
(cnr Av Juárez & Domínguez; meals M$60-110; ⌚8am-8pm) Easily the best place to eat in town (for the valley view alone), the perfectly poised La Carreta sits inside the equally exquisite Posada del Emperador. Despite its fancy setting, food here is reasonably priced and there's even a M$50 *menú del día*. Try the excellent *bistec de res a la mexicana*.

Getting There & Away

From Fortín, Coscomatepec is a one-hour bus ride (M$17); a taxi costs M$60 to M$70. Regular buses also connect to Córdoba. The **bus terminal** (Miguel Lerdo de Tejada btwn Reforma & Gutiérrez Zamora) is five minutes' walk northeast of the main plaza.

Orizaba

☎272 / POP 121,000 / ELEV 1219M

Orizaba manages to surprise you. At first sight it's a workaday medium-sized Mexican town, but it actually has several idiosyncratic sights, a pleasant old colonial center, some lovely parks and a gorgeous riverside walk. It's also within easy reach of Mexico's highest mountain, the magnificent Pico de Orizaba, and a new cable car (opening in 2014) will make accessing this dormant volcano easier than ever before. The most striking sight in town is Gustave Eiffel's unique art nouveau Palacio de Hierro (Iron Palace), while the most revealing is the excellent art museum, home to the second-largest Diego Rivera collection in Mexico.

Orizaba was founded by the Spanish to guard the Veracruz–Mexico City road. An industrial center in the late 19th century, its factories were early centers of the unrest that led to the unseating of dictator Porfirio

Díaz. In 1898, a Scotsman running a local steel factory founded Mexico's first soccer team, called Orizaba Athletic Club. Today the city has a big brewery and is home to cement, textile and chemical industries.

Sights

★Palacio de Hierro MUSEUM, LANDMARK

(Parque Castillo; museums admission free; 9am-7pm) The so-called 'Iron Palace' is Orizaba's fanciful art nouveau landmark, built entirely from iron and steel. The palace's interior has been recently converted into half a dozen small **museums**. Most notable are the **Museo de la Cerveza**, tracking Orizaba's famous beer industry; the **Museo de Fútbol** (soccer); the **Museo de Presidentes** with pics and info of *every* Mexican president, and the **Museo Interactivo** with a small planetarium and some science exhibits, including a bed of nails you can lie on.

Also on site are the **Museo de Banderas** (flags) and **Museo de las Raíces de Orizaba** (archaeological artifacts).

Alexandre Gustave Eiffel, a master of metallurgy who gave his name to the Eiffel Tower and engineered the Statue of Liberty's framework, designed this pavilion, which was built in Paris. Orizaba's mayor, eager to acquire an impressive European-style Palacio Municipal, bought it in 1892. Piece by piece it was shipped, then reassembled in Orizaba.

★Museo de Arte del Estado MUSEUM

(State Art Museum; 272-724-32-00; cnr Av Oriente 4 & Sur 25; admission M$15; 10am-5pm Tue-Sun) Orizaba's wonderful Museo de Arte del Estado is housed in a gorgeously restored colonial building dating from 1776. The museum is divided into rooms that include Mexico's second-most-important permanent Diego Rivera collection, with 33 of his original works. There are also contemporary works by regional artists. Guides give complimentary tours in Spanish. The museum is frustratingly situated a good 2km east of Parque Castillo.

Teleférico de Orizaba CABLE CAR

(Sur 4 btwn Calles Poniente 3 & Poniente 5) Still under construction at the time of writing, this ambitious project is due to open in 2014. It will whiz visitors from its riverside site across from the Palacio Municipal right up to the side of Pico de Orizaba for incredible views and easy access to hiking routes.

Parque Castillo PLAZA

Smaller than your average Mexican city plaza, Parque Castillo is bereft of the normally standard Palacio Municipal (town hall), which sits several blocks away on Av Colón Poniente. Instead, it is watched over by the eclectic Palacio de Hierro and a 17th-century parish church, the **Catedral de San Miguel Arcángel**. On the south side is the neoclassical and still-functioning **Teatro Ignacio de la Llave** (1875), which is a veritable font of opera, ballet and classical music concerts.

Parque Alameda PARK

(Av Poniente 2 & Sur 10;) About 1km west of the center, Parque Alameda is either a very large plaza or a very small park depending on your expectations. What it doesn't lack is activity. Aside from the obligatory statues of dead heroes, you'll find an outdoor gym, a bandstand, food carts, shoe-shiners and a kids playground, including a huge jungle of bouncy castles and air-filled slides. Practically the whole city rolls in at weekends after Sunday Mass.

Activities

Río Orizaba WALKING, OUTDOORS

Unusually for a Mexican city, Orizaba has an unbroken collection of pleasant paths bordering its clean eponymous river. There are 13 bridges along the way including a suspension bridge and the arched Puente La Borda, dating from 1776. A good starting point is off Poniente 8, about 600m northwest of the Palacio de Hierro. From here you can head north to the Puente Tlachichilico or south to Puente La Borda.

Adventure Tours ADVENTURE TOUR

A number of adventure tour operators are based in Orizaba. They can arrange various outdoor activities in nearby hills, mountains and canyons, including climbs partway up Pico de Orizaba. Highlights of the area include the gorgeous Cañón de la Carbonera near Nogales and the Cascada de Popócatl near Tequila. Recommended operators include **Alberto Gochicoa** (cell phone 272-103-73-44) and **Erick Carrera** (cell phone 272-134-55-71).

Sleeping

Higher-end options are on the Avenida Oriente 6 traffic strip. Low-end choices are near the center.

Gran Hotel de France HISTORIC HOTEL $
(☎272-725-23-11; Av Oriente 6 No 186 btwn Calles Sur 5 & Sur 6; s/d M$345/445; P ⊖ ❄ ☎) This historic late-19th-century building has a splendid, high-ceilinged patio with *azulejos* tiles, hanging plants and a fountain, although the colonial atmosphere suffers somewhat from the *telenovelas* blaring from various TV sets in the lobby. The rooms are pleasantly simple, if a little on the dark side.

Hotel del Río HOTEL $
(☎272-726-66-25; Av Poniente 8 No 315 btwn Calles Norte 5 & Norte 7; r from M$450; P ❄ ☎) A very pleasant place in an attractive location right by the Orizaba River. This hotel has simple modern rooms in an old building, and a congenial, bilingual owner.

Hotel Plaza Palacio HOTEL $
(☎272-725-99-23; Poniente 2 2-Bis; s/d/tr M$335/400/460; ☎) You can't get more central than this place; the windows look directly onto the Palacio de Hierro. It's nothing special architecturally and the rooms are clean but not particularly characterful. But you do get cable TV and a fan, as well as the town right on your doorstep.

Hotel Posada del Viajero HOTEL $
(☎272-726-33-20; Madero Norte 242; s/d M$180/260; P) This narrow, central hotel doesn't look overly appealing from the outside, but it's clean, safe, cheap and run by an exceptionally helpful and friendly family.

Casa Real Hotel HOTEL $$$
(www.casarealorizaba.com; Oriente 6, 64 btwn Calles Sur 9 & Sur 11; r/ste from M$1132/1450; P ⊖ ❄ ☎ ☒) One of Orizaba's finest properties combines modern luxuries (flat-screen TVs and high water pressure) with traditional Mexican elements (tiled floors to keep the rooms cool and smart dark wooden furniture). The staff are courteous and eager to please, there's a good onsite restaurant and the location is very central, with the 1st-class bus terminal across the street.

Eating & Drinking

In sedate Orizaba many restaurants close early. Head to the plaza for noteworthy Orizaban snacks including *garnachas* (open tortillas with chicken, onion and tomato salsa) and filled *pambazos* (soft white bread rolls dipped in pepper sauce).

El Interior CAFE $
(Av 4 cnr Calle Sur 9; snacks M$30-70) A small literary cafe connected to a book and craft store, the Interior is handily sandwiched between Parque Castillo and the Museo de Arte del Estado.

La Pergola MEXICAN $
(cnr Av Oriente 8 & Sur 7; mains M$40-100; ⏰7am-10pm) There are actually two Pergolas, both near the main drive-by of Avenida Oriente 6. Which you choose is a toss-up; both offer no-nonsense Mexican food and receive a communal 'thumbs up' from local opinion.

Mariscos Boca del Río SEAFOOD $$
(☎272-726-52-99; Av Poniente 7 btwn Calles Sur 10 & Sur 8; seafood M$80-170; ⏰9am-8pm Tue-Sun; ☎ 👪) This wildly popular place is generally accepted to be the best seafood restaurant in town. Serving big portions, it's a favorite with family groups, and there's a welcome childrens play area, as well as valet parking.

★**Gran Café de Orizaba** CAFE, INTERNATIONAL
(☎272-724-44-75; Palacio de Hierro, cnr Av Poniente 2 & Madero; snacks M$35-70; ⏰8am-8pm; ☎) How often in Mexico can you sit back

BUSES FROM ORIZABA

DESTINATION	FARE (M$)	DURATION	FREQUENCY (DAILY)
Córdoba	30	40min	every 30min
Fortín de las Flores	28	25min	hourly
Mexico City (TAPO)	279	4hr	frequent
Mexico City (Terminal Norte)	288	4hr	8
Oaxaca	338	5hr	3
Puebla	180	2hr	frequent
Veracruz	140	2½hr	frequent
Xalapa	194	4hr	hourly

Daily 1st-class bus departures.

and enjoy a coffee and cake on the balcony of a regal cafe, inside an iron palace designed by Gustave Eiffel? Exactly – but this is your chance. The delightful decor, smart staff and selection of sandwiches, crepes and cakes make this an obvious place to break up your exploration of Orizaba.

Information

Banks with ATMs are on Avenida Oriente 2, a block south of the plaza.

Hospital Orizaba (272-725-50-19; www.corporativodehospitales.com.mx; Sur 5 No 398)

Tourist Office (272-728-91-36; www.orizaba.travel; Palacio de Hierro; 9am-7pm) Has enthusiastic staff and plenty of brochures. City maps cost M$10.

Getting There & Around

BUS

Local buses from Fortín and Córdoba stop four blocks north and six blocks east of the town center, around Avenida Oriente 9 and Norte 14. The AU 2nd-class bus station is at Zaragoza Poniente 425, northwest of the center.

The modern 1st-class **bus station** (cnr Av Oriente 6 & Sur 13) handles all ADO, ADO GL and deluxe UNO services.

CAR & MOTORCYCLE

Toll Hwy 150D, which bypasses central Orizaba, goes east to Córdoba and west, via a spectacular ascent, to Puebla (160km). Toll-free Hwy 150 runs east to Córdoba and Veracruz (150km) and southwest to Tehuacán, 65km away over the hair-raising Cumbres de Acultzingo.

Pico de Orizaba

Mexico's tallest mountain (5611m), called Citlaltépetl (Star Mountain) in the Náhuatl language, is 25km northwest of Orizaba. From the summit of this dormant volcano, one can see the mountains Popocatépetl, Iztaccíhuatl and La Malinche to the west and the Gulf of Mexico to the east. The only higher peaks in North America are Mt McKinley in Alaska and Mt Logan in Canada.

Unless you're an experienced climber with mountaineering equipment, you'll need a guide in addition to a good level of fitness. There are a number of recommendable guide companies from the US, but the only local one is **Servimont** (245-451-50-19; www.servimont.com.mx; Ortega 1A, Tlachichuca; packages from M$5000), a climber-owned outfit passed down through the Reyes family. As the longest-running operation in the area, it also acts as a Red Cross rescue facility. It's based in the small town of Tlachichuca (2600m), which is a common starting point for expeditions. Book your expedition with Servimont two to four months in advance and allow four to seven days to acclimatize, summit and return.

Mexico's Volcanoes by RJ Secor offers some good info, and topographical maps can be mail-ordered way ahead of time or bought in person from **Inegi** (www.inegi.gob.mx) offices in Veracruz or Xalapa. The best climbing period is October to March; the most popular is December and January.

Hostel accommodations at Servimont's base camp (which is a former soap factory adorned with interesting mountaineering antiques) are included in your package. Those not traveling with Servimont can stay at the friendly, family-run **Hotel Citlaltepetl** (245-451-51-69; makina_tropikal@hotmail.com; Morelos 102; s/d/tr M$150/280/390) in Tlachichuca. To get here from Orizaba, catch a bus from the 1st-class terminal to Ciudad Serdán (M$48, two hours), then another to Tlachichuca (M$16, one hour).

NORTHERN VERACRUZ

The northern half of Veracruz state, between the coast and southern fringes of the Sierra Madre Oriental, mainly consists of lush rolling pastureland. Laguna de Tamiahua is the region's largest wetland, while the Gulf has some fine, isolated (though sometimes polluted) beaches. The major archaeological attraction is El Tajín.

At the regular army checkpoints along this coast, the soldiers are usually very respectful toward tourists.

Tuxpan

783 / POP 85,000

Tuxpan (sometimes spelled Túxpam), 300km north of Veracruz and 190km south of Tampico, is a steamy fishing town and minor oil port. If you pass through, you can enjoy excellent seafood, take a trip across the broad Río Tuxpan to visit a little museum devoted to Cuban-Mexican friendship, or join vacationing Mexicans on Playa Norte, the beach 12km to the east. The town itself is no great beauty, but it is quite well set up for overnighting travelers who happen to be passing through.

Sights & Activities

Museo de la Amistad México-Cuba MUSEUM
(Mexican-Cuban Friendship Museum; Obregón s/n; 9am-7pm) FREE The Mexican-Cuban Friendship Museum has a room filled with displays on José Martí, pictures of Che Guevara and Castro, and other memorabilia. To get to the museum, take a boat (M$4) across the river from the quay near the ADO bus station, walk several blocks south to Obregón, then turn right. The museum is at the western end of Obregón, on the river. Cuban-themed cultural events happen here on Friday nights.

On November 25, 1956, the errant lawyer-turned-revolutionary, Fidel Castro, set sail from the Río Tuxpan with 82 poorly equipped soldiers to start an uprising in Cuba. The sailing was made possible thanks to an encounter in Mexico City between Castro and Antonio del Conde Pontones (aka 'El Cuate'). On meeting Castro for the first time, Pontones, a legal arms dealer, was immediately taken by the Cuban's strong personality and agreed to help him obtain guns and a boat. To smooth the process he bought a house on the south side of the Río Tuxpan where he moored the boat and allowed Fidel to meet in secret. Today that house is the Museo de la Amistad México-Cuba.

Playa Norte BEACH
Tuxpan's beach, 12km east of town, is a wide strip stretching 20km north from the Río Tuxpan's mouth. *Palapa* restaurants make it a chilled-out place to eat cheap seafood and take a break from the city. Flag down the local buses marked 'Playa' (M$14, 25 minutes); they leave regularly from the south side of Blvd Reyes Heroles by the river quay and drop you at the south end of the beach.

Paseos Turísticos Negretti BOAT TRIPS, DIVING
(783-835-45-64; www.turismonegretti.mx; Recrea s/n) A local tour operator that organizes diving (M$2000 per 8-person group, not including equipment), fishing (M$400 per boat per hour), boat trips to nearby mangroves (M$550 for two hours), kayaking (M$100 per person) and water-skiing (M$300 for 30 minutes). It has an office on the south side of the Río Tuxpan where the cross-river ferry docks.

Aqua Sports DIVING, FISHING
(783-837-02-59; Carretera Tuxpan-La Barra Km 8.5; 2 dives M$1200) Aqua runs diving and fishing trips out to nearby reefs or the Isla de Lobos. Visibility for diving is best between May and August, and from January to March you can fish for giant tarpon. Its office is around 8km from the center going toward the beach.

Sleeping

As a popular holiday spot for Mexico, there's a wide range of hotels in Tuxpan, though they fill up quickly during holiday periods.

Hotel Florida HOTEL $$
(783-834-02-22; www.hotel-florida.com.mx; Av Juárez 23 btwn Morelos & Garizurieta; s/d incl breakfast M$600/775; P) The centrally located Florida, opposite the Palacio Municipal, has friendly staff, a continental breakfast included, spacious rooms with big windows, and communal decks that look over bustling (read noisy) Avenida Juárez. Check out your room before, though: the

BUSES FROM TUXPAN

DESTINATION	FARE (M$)	DURATION	FREQUENCY (DAILY)
Matamoros	672	11hr	2
Mexico City (Terminal Norte)	282	6hr	hourly
Papantla	64	2hr	hourly
Poza Rica	37	1hr	hourly
Tampico	209	4hr	hourly
Veracruz	276	6hr	hourly
Villahermosa	598	14hr	4
Xalapa	283	6hr	8

1st-class bus departures from the ADO station.

inner rooms have no windows looking outside. Higher category rooms with a few extra comforts aren't really worth the price hike.

Hotel Reforma HOTEL $$
(☎783-834-11-46; hotelreforma@prodigy.net; Av Juárez 25 btwn Garizurieta & Ortega; s/d M$620/700; P ❄ ☜) Similar to the Florida next door, the Reforma offers a smart atrium lobby with a small waterfall and some 99 comfortable if rather functional rooms. They include flat-screen TVs and relentless brown carpeting. There's a smart restaurant downstairs.

Eating

Parque Reforma (the town's main plaza) is a block back from the *malecón* on Juárez, and is flanked by restaurants and cheap eateries. For the best seafood, locals will direct you downriver to a strip of *palapas* in the fishing community of La Mata; it's 6km east of the center, at the mouth of the Laguna de Tampamachoco. There are more *palapas* at Playa Norte.

El Mejicano MEXICAN $
(Parque Reforma, cnr Morelos & Corregidora; mains M$45-100; ⊙7am-midnight; ☜) This friendly, popular place has a cafeteria feel and gets busy mid-afternoon with local office workers coming for a cheap and delicious lunch. Try the excellent chicken tacos and wash them down with a cool *agua de jamaica* (hibiscus iced tea). Service comes with good intentions but can be on the slow side.

Los Quijotes CAFE $$
(Av Juárez 23; mains M$60-150; ⊙6am-midnight) A full restaurant inside the Hotel Florida, Los Quijotes serves up the normal roster of Mexican dishes, including steaks and enchiladas. There's also a killer *crepa con cajeta* (dulce de leche pancake).

ℹ Information

Tuxpan's simple **tourist booth** (www.forotuxpan.com; Palacio Municipal; ⊙9am-7pm Mon-Fri, 10am-2pm Sat) has no English-speaking employees, but they make up for a lack of language skills with vast reserves of enthusiasm: you'll go away overloaded with maps and brochures. Plenty of ATMs can be found on Avenida Juárez.

ℹ Getting There & Around

Most 1st-class buses leaving Tuxpan are *de paso* (passing through). Booking a seat in advance might be a good idea. There are several bus terminals, but the 1st-class ADO **bus station** (cnr Rodríguez & Av Juárez) is the most convenient from the center.

There is a M$4 ferry service across the river at various points between Guerrero and Parque Reforma.

Papantla

☎784 / POP 53,500 / ELEV 196M

Getting off the bus in Papantla, it's easy to feel as if you've decamped to the Andean altiplano. Spread across a succession of wooded hills, this is a solidly indigenous city whose geography belongs in La Paz, but whose history, look and feel is distinctly pre-Hispanic or, more precisely, Totonac. Predating the Spanish conquest, the city was founded around AD 1230. Traditionally a launching pad for people visiting the nearby ruins of El Tajín, Papantla has carved its own niche in recent years, stressing its indigenous heritage and promoting its central position in the world's best vanilla-growing region. You'll see Totonacs wearing traditional clothing here – the men in loose white shirts and trousers, the women in embroidered blouses and *quechquémitls* (traditional capes). Meanwhile *voladores* 'fly' and local artisans peddle handicrafts in the attractive main square.

Sights

Zócalo PLAZA
Officially called Parque Téllez, Papantla's *zócalo* is terraced into the hillside below the Iglesia de la Asunción. Wedged beneath the cathedral and facing the square is a symbolic 50m-long relief **mural**. Depicting Totonac and Veracruz history, it was designed by Papantla artist Teodoro Cano in 1979. A serpent stretches along the mural, bizarrely linking a pre-Hispanic stone carver, El Tajín's Pirámide de los Nichos, and an oil rig.

Iglesia de Nuestra Señora de la Asunción CHURCH
(Zócalo) Overlooking the *zócalo* from its high platform, this church is notable for its large cedar doors and quartet of indoor canvases by a Jalisco artist. Begun in 1570 by the Franciscans, it was added to in stages over the subsequent centuries; the bell tower wasn't completed until 1875.

Outside stands a 30m-high *voladores* (fliers) pole. Ritualistic performances normally take place every two hours between 11am and 7pm Monday to Saturday. During low

PAPANTLA'S VOLADORES: BUNGEE-JUMPING PIONEERS

The idea of launching yourself head first from a great height with only a rope tied around your ankles for support is popularly thought to have been conceived by bungee-jumping New Zealanders in the 1980s. But in truth, Papantla's Totonac *voladores* (fliers) have been flinging themselves off 30m-high wooden poles (with zero safety equipment) for centuries. Indeed, so old is this rather bizarre yet mystic tradition, no one is quite sure how or when it started.

The rite begins with five men in elaborate ceremonial clothing climbing to the top of the pole. Four of them sit on the edges of a small frame at the top and rotate the frame to twist the ropes around the pole. The fifth man dances on the platform above them while playing a *chirimía*, a small drum with a flute attached. When he stops playing, the others fall backward. Arms outstretched, they revolve gracefully around the pole and descend to the ground, upside down, as their ropes unwind.

One interpretation of the ceremony is that it's a fertility rite and the fliers make invocations to the four corners of the universe. It's also noted that each flier circles the pole 13 times, giving a total of 52 revolutions. The number 52 is not only the number of weeks in the modern year but also was an important number in pre-Hispanic Mexico, which had two calendars, one corresponding to the 365-day solar year, the other to a ritual year of 260 days. The calendars coincided every 52 solar years.

Voladores ceremonies are best observed at El Tajín, outside Papantla's cathedral, and occasionally at Zempoala.

season (October to April), performances can be seen at 9am, noon, 4pm and 7pm Friday to Sunday.

Museo de la Ciudad Teodoro Cano MUSEUM

(Curti s/n; admission M$40; ⏲10am-7pm Tue-Sun) Legendary Paplantla artist Teodoro Cano (b 1932) was once a student of Mexican art giant Diego Rivera. This small museum displays a handful of Cano's fine paintings, which are an alluring combination of both dark and ebullient scenes that are drawn almost exclusively from Totonac culture. The Totonac theme extends to the museum's other artifacts, including photos and traditional clothing displays. It may be small but it's immensely satisfying. A modern onsite auditorium hosts regular cultural events.

Volador Monument MONUMENT

(Callejón Centenario s/n) At the top of the hill towers Papantla's *volador* monument, a 1988 statue by Teodoro Cano, portraying a musician playing his pipe and preparing for the four fliers to launch. To reach the monument, take Calle Centenario heading uphill from the southwest corner of the cathedral yard, before turning left into steep Callejón Centenario.

Casa de la Cultura ARTS CENTER

(Pino Suárez s/n; ⏲10am-2pm Mon-Sat) The Casa de la Cultura hosts art classes and a display of local artwork on the top floor.

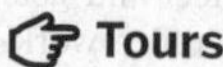

Tours

Gaudencio Simbrón WALKING

(☎783-842-01-21; per day M$400) Guide Gaudencio Simbrón is more commonly known as *el de la ropa típica* (the guy who wears traditional clothes), because he sports Totonac costume. He works through Hotel Tajín and can guide you through El Tajín, Papantla and its environs.

Festivals & Events

Feria de Corpus Christi CULTURAL

The fantastic Feria de Corpus Christi, in late May and early June, is the big annual event in Papantla. As well as the bullfights, parades and *charreadas* (Mexican rodeos) that are usual in Mexico, Papantla celebrates its Totonac cultural heritage with spectacular indigenous dances. The main procession is on the first Sunday when *voladores* fly in elaborate ceremonies several times a day.

Festival de Vainilla FOOD

A major celebration in Papantla, the Vanilla Festival on June 18 features indigenous dancers, gastronomic delights sold in street stalls, and all manner of different vanilla products.

Sleeping

Hotel Familiar La Pasadita HOTEL $

(784-842-43-53; Obispo de las Casas 102; r M$350-650; P) It's worth paying extra for rooms with windows here; they're less damp and have more space than the truly uninviting cheapest options. The location is good though, a couple of blocks downhill from the *zócalo* – follow the direction of traffic through the main square and down the hill, then take a right at the Super Che Supermarket.

Hotel Tajín HOTEL $$

(784-842-01-21; www.hoteltajin.com.mx; cnr Núñez & Domínguez 104; s/d/tr M$449/597/697, ste M$839-1139; P) So what if the interior is a little dated; the Tajín is an intrinsic part of the Papantla experience with a prime edge-of-*zócalo* location and an Italianate pool and onsite Parroquia cafe. The whole place oozes character, even if its 62 rooms range from the cozy to the ho-hum.

It's just off the *zócalo*; if you're facing the church, follow the road beneath it to the left.

Hotel Provincia Express HOTEL $$

(784-842-16-45; provinciaexpress_papantla@hotmail.com; Enríquez 103; r incl breakfast from M$580;) This welcome addition to Papantla's hotel scene is annoyingly unsigned, but it's easy to find as it's on the *zócalo*, facing the church across the square. There are 20 rooms in two categories – the spacious, bright and pleasant ones facing the main square (an extra M$70 each) or the rather cell-like, dark ones with smelly toilets elsewhere.

LAS POZAS

Take a wealthy English eccentric, an idyllic tract of Mexican jungle and an extremely hyperactive imagination, and you'd still struggle to come up with the audacious, bizarre and – frankly – madcap experiment that is **Las Pozas** (The Pools; www.xilitla.org; adult/child M$50/25; 9am-6pm).

Situated on the sweeping slopes of the Sierra Madre Oriental, near the mountain town of Xilitla (he-*leet*-la), Las Pozas is a monumental sculpture garden built in thick jungle that links a series of concrete temples, pagodas, bridges, pavilions and spiral stairways with a necklace of natural waterfalls. The surreal creation stands as a memorial to the imagination and excessive wealth of Edward James (1907–84). A drop-out English aristocrat and poet, he became a patron of Salvador Dalí in the late 1930s and subsequently went on to amass the largest private collection of surrealist art in the world.

In 1945 James' adventures took him to Xilitla where he met Plutarco Gastelum, who helped build Las Pozas. It began with 40 local workers crafting giant, colored concrete flowers beside an idyllic jungle stream. Then, for 17 years, James and Gastelum created ever larger and stranger structures – many of which were never finished – at an estimated cost of US$5 million.

James died in 1984, leaving no provision to maintain his creation which, since 2008, has been in the hands of a Mexican-run nonprofit foundation. The extravagant labyrinth of surreal sculptures and edifices with stairways leading nowhere (to heaven?) covers 36 hectares and is worth a significant diversion for anyone with the vaguest creative inclinations. If you're in fairly good shape, you could spend the whole day contemplating the lovely swimming holes and mazelike trails.

Las Pozas has a good onsite **restaurant** (10am-6pm) and there are several small campsites and posadas nearby. For the true Las Pozas experience, you should stay at **Posada El Castillo** (489-365-00-38; www.junglegossip.com; Ocampo 105; r incl breakfast M$890;), the surrealist-inspired former Gastelum home (and also James' lodgings), now transformed into a verdant Pozas-esque guesthouse run by the Gestelum family in the heart of Xilitla.

To get to Las Pozas you'll need to connect through Tuxpan to Tampico. From here regular connections travel to Xilitla. There are also buses from Xilitla to San Luis Potosí (M$360). A taxi from Xilitla to the Las Pozas site is M$65, or it's an easy 2km walk. Guided tours are available from M$200 (Spanish) and M$250 (English).

Needless to say, it's well worth paying the extra M$70 for the rooms facing the square; ask for rooms one to six. Skip the breakfast.

Eating

Papantla's *zócalo* is home to a good selection of local restaurants and cafes. **Mercado Juárez**, at the southwest corner of the plaza opposite the cathedral, has stalls that sell cheap, fresh regional food.

Café Catedral BAKERY, CAFE **$**
(cnr Domínguez & Curato; 8am-10pm) The town's best coffeehouse (ask any local) doubles as a bakery. Grab a cake, muffin or *pan dulce* (sweet bread) from one of the display cases, sit at a cheap cafe table, and wait for the chief *señora* to come round with an old-fashioned tin jug to fill up your cup.

Everyone seems to know everyone else here, and local gossip bounces off the walls.

Caffe Gourmet Voladorini CAFE, DESSERTS **$**
(Calle Centenario; 9am-10pm;) The Voladorini is new, cool and minimalist, and the coffee and cakes are very tempting. It's perched like a theater box above the *zócalo* action, next to La Hacienda.

★**Plaza Pardo** MEXICAN **$$**
(784-842-00-59; 1st fl, Enríquez 105; mains M$75-130; 7:30am-11:30pm;) There's no place better to absorb the atmosphere of Papantla than the Plaza Pardo's delightful balcony overlooking the *zócalo*, so be sure to get a table there. While the interior is perfectly pleasant, it's a big step down in romance and views. The menu offers a large range of *antojitos*, fish and meats all cooked in inventive ways.

Restaurante La Hacienda MEXICAN **$$**
(Calle Centenario; mains M$70-120; 7:30am-10:30pm) While perhaps La Hacienda has the most charming balcony in town, the view isn't quite as good as can be had elsewhere on the *zócalo*. That aside, it has good service, great steaks and full breakfasts (M$40 to M$65). The menu also encompasses fish, seafood, burgers and *antojitos mexicanos*.

Restaurante Totonaco INTERNATIONAL **$$**
(Hotel Tajín, Núñez 104; mains M$75-140; 8am-10pm;) This air-conditioned hotel bar-restaurant has an extensive international menu. There's also a short wine list (M$80 to M$140), and it serves cocktails made with locally produced vanilla extract. There's a breakfast menu (M$30 to M$95) but for better coffee head out past the hotel pool to the onsite Parroquia Cafe.

Shopping

Here in Mexico's leading vanilla-growing center, you'll find quality vanilla extract, vanilla pods and *figuras* (pods woven into the shapes of flowers, insects or crucifixes). There's a good artisan store on the southwest corner of the *zócalo*. You'll also encounter traditional Totonac clothing and handmade baskets.

Information

The helpful **tourist office** (784-842-38-37; 8am-6pm Mon-Fri) is inside the Palacio Municipal on the *zócalo*. It's a bit hidden; enter by the main door and ask the security guard for directions. There's a small kiosk outside the Palacio Municipal that's staffed at weekends too, which has helpful maps of the town center and the surrounding region.

You'll find two banks with ATMs on Enríquez just east of the *zócalo*. The post office is four blocks northwest of the plaza.

Getting There & Away

A few long-distance buses leave from Papantla's quaint ADO **bus station** (cnr Juárez & Venustiano Carranza), a short, steep walk from the center. Taxis from the ADO to the center

BUSES FROM PAPANTLA

DESTINATION	FARE (M$)	DURATION	FREQUENCY (DAILY)
Mexico City (Terminal Norte)	200	5hr	6
Poza Rica	30	40min	hourly
Tampico	304	5½hr	3
Tuxpan	64	2hr	hourly
Veracruz	210	4hr	10
Xalapa	230	4hr	8

1st-class bus departures from the ADO station.

are M$15 to M$20. You can make bus reservations online or at the ticket counter just east of the plaza. At the 2nd-class **bus station** (cnr 20 de Noviembre & Olivo), just off the plaza by the Pemex station, Transportes Papantla (TP) serves the coastal towns to the south and has slightly less expensive buses to Poza Rica and Tuxpan.

El Tajín

For an ancient city 'rediscovered' accidentally by an officious Spaniard looking for illegal tobacco plantations in 1785, El Tajín paints a bold contemporary picture. Situated on a plain surrounded by low, verdant hills 6km west of Papantla, the extensive ruins are the most impressive reminder of Classic Veracruz civilization and the state's most visited tourist site.

Probably founded in AD 100, El Tajín (the name is Totonac for 'thunder,' 'lightning' or 'hurricane') reached its zenith as a city and ceremonial center between AD 600 and 900. Around 1230 the site was abandoned, possibly after a fire and attacks by Chichimecs. Quickly engulfed by the jungle, it lay unknown to the Spanish until 1785.

Among El Tajín's special features are rows of square niches on the sides of buildings, numerous ball courts and sculptures depicting human sacrifice connected with the ball game. Archaeologist José García Payón believed that El Tajín's niches and stone mosaics symbolized day and night, light and dark, and life and death in a universe composed of dualities, though many are skeptical of this interpretation.

Sights

The **El Tajín site** (admission M$57; 9am-5pm) covers an area of about 10 sq km. To see everything, you'll walk a few kilometers over a couple of hours. There's little shade and it can get blazingly hot, so an early start is a good idea. Most buildings and carvings have some sort of labeling in English and Spanish, but many of the information boards are weathered and hard to read, meaning that if you want to understand the site in detail, a guided tour will be a great help. A multilingual guide service is available for M$250 per hour for one to six people. Do drop in to the onsite museum at the entrance (included in your ticket price) to see an excellent model of the site and some impressive relics and handicrafts discovered here.

Bordering the parking lot are stalls selling food and handicrafts. The visitor center has a restaurant, a left-luggage room, an information desk and souvenir shops. Those seeking more information should look for the book *Tajín: Mystery and Beauty,* by Leonardo Zaleta, sometimes available in several languages in the souvenir shops.

Plaza Menor — PLAZA

Beyond the Plaza del Arroyo in the south of the site flanked by pyramids on four sides, is the Plaza Menor (Lesser Plaza), which is part of El Tajín's main ceremonial center and its possible marketplace, with a low platform in the middle. All of the structures located around this plaza were probably topped by small temples, some decorated with red or blue paint, traces of which remain.

Juego de Pelota Sur — BALL COURT

Some 17 ball courts have been found at El Tajín. The Juego de Pelota Sur (Southern Ball Court) dates back to around 1150 and is the most famous of the courts, due mainly to the six relief carvings on its walls, which depict the various aspects of the ball game ritual.

The panel on the northeast corner is the easiest to make out: in the center, three ballplayers perform a ritual post-game sacrifice with one player ready to plunge a knife into the chest of another, whose arms are held by the third player. Death gods and a presiding figure look on. The other panels depict various scenes of ceremonial drinking of *pulque* (a milky, low-alcohol brew made from the *maguey* plant).

The Juego de Pelota de las Pinturas (Ball Court of the Paintings), to one side of the Pirámide de los Nichos, is so called as it has two very impressively preserved red and blue geometric friezes on its north-facing side.

Pirámide de los Nichos — PYRAMID

El Tajín's most emblematic structure, the beautifully proportioned Pyramid of the Niches, is just off the Plaza Menor. The six lower levels, each surrounded by rows of small square niches, climb to 18m. Archaeologists believe that there were originally 365 niches, suggesting that the building may have been used as a kind of calendar.

El Tajín Chico — STRUCTURES

The path north toward Plaza El Tajín Chico passes the **Juego de Pelota Norte**

(Northern Ball Court), which is smaller and older than the southern court and bears fainter carvings on its sides.

El Tajín Chico was the government area of the ancient city and would have been home to the ruling classes. Many of the buildings at El Tajín Chico have geometric stone mosaic patterns known as 'Greco' (Greek).

Edificio I, probably once a palace, has some terrific carvings. **Estructura C**, on the east side, with three levels and a staircase facing the plaza, was initially painted blue. **Estructura A**, on the plaza's north side, has an arch construction known as a corbeled arch, with two sides jutting closer to each other until they are joined at the top by a single slab, which is typical of Maya architecture. Its presence here is yet another oddity in the jigsaw puzzle of pre-Hispanic cultures.

Northwest of Plaza El Tajín Chico is the unreconstructed **Plaza de las Columnas** (Plaza of the Columns), one of the site's most important structures. It originally housed a large open patio and adjoining buildings stretching over the hillside. Some wonderful reassembled carved columns are displayed in the museum.

★ Voladores Performances INDIGENOUS CULTURE

A 30m-high *voladores* pole stands outside the entrance to the ruins. Totonacs perform the *voladores* rite (which was traditionally carried out only once a year) three times per day beside the visitor center. Before they start, a performer in Totonac regalia requests donations (M$20) from the audience.

Getting There & Away

Frequent buses come from Poza Rica. From Papantla, buses (M$15) marked 'Pirámides Tajín' leave every 20 minutes or so from Calle 16 de Septiembre directly behind Hotel Tajín. The site is 300m from the highway – buses drop you off near the market, before the entrance to Tajín. Taxis to/from from Papantla cost M$50. There are usually one or two waiting outside the ruins.

South of Papantla

Hwy 180 runs near the coast for most of the 230km between Papantla and Veracruz. Highlights include a turtle conservation project, the sparkling Costa Esmeralda and Quiahuiztlán, a stunning, out-of-the-way Totonac site. The area is bereft of tourists during low season.

Tecolutla

☎766 / POP 4600

This lazy seaside town, with a pleasant enough strip of sand and a slew of seafood restaurants and cheap hotels nearby, passes for one of Veracruz' more pleasant beachfronts. Cancún this most definitely isn't. Instead, the place is as dead as a doornail midweek when it's not a holiday, though in high summer and during Semana Santa it's a different story. There are banks and ATMs on the plaza.

Activities

★ Grupo Ecologista Vida Milenaria VOLUNTEERING

(☎766-846-04-67; www.vidamilenaria.org.mx; Niños Heros 1; donation required) This small turtle conservation center (a short walk from the center where Niños Héroes hits the ocean) is run by Fernando Manzano Cervantes, known locally as 'Papá Tortuga.' In addition to educating the public, he has been effectively protecting and releasing green and Kemp's ridley turtles here for over

35 years. Visitors are welcome to look at the hatchlings.

If you stop by, think about buying a trinket souvenir because this is a privately funded show. Volunteers are especially needed here in April and May, when patrolling the beaches (35km worth) and collecting the turtle eggs is imperative. Most of the patrolling is done at night between 10pm and 6am. Camping and the use of kitchen and bathroom facilities is free to volunteers.

The highest number of turtles are released in June, but in late October you can join hundreds of locals in celebrating the release of the baby turtles in the Festival de Las Tortugas.

Boat Trips BOAT TRIPS
(per group M$350-450) Walk toward the Río Tecolutla on Emilio Carranza and you'll hit the *embarcadero* (pier), where boats will take you fishing or through dense mangrove forests rich with wildlife, including pelicans.

Sleeping

Hotels abound in this tourist-reliant town. Smarter options are outside the town itself, but there are plenty of cheap hotels near the plaza, and nicer ones toward the ocean.

Real del Mar HOTEL $$
(766-846-03-80; www.hotelrealdelmar.com; cnr Aldama & Galeana; r from M$950; P ❄ ≋) As posh as Tecolutla gets, this aspiring 'resort' has light, colorful rooms, some with oceanview balconies. Rooms surround an indoor pool and a three-story, sea-themed mural. It's comfortable, if a little bland, but the welcome is sincere and prices plummet outside the high season.

Aqua Inn Hotel HOTEL $$
(766-846-03-58; www.tecolutla.com.mx/aquainn; cnr Aldama & Av Obregón; r from M$1000; P ❄ ≋) This modern place in the middle of town and a short walk from the water has clean, functional rooms, all with cable TV. There's a small rooftop pool, and a cool cafe and restaurant. Prices drop steeply outside high season, making it a bargain during off-peak times.

★**Hotel Azúcar** BOUTIQUE HOTEL $$$
(232-321-06-78; www.hotelazucar.com; Carretera Federal Nautla-Poza Rica Km 83.5; r from M$3700; P ❄ ≋) Not in Tecolutla itself, this impressive, newly designed hotel has nevertheless raised the bar by several feet for local hoteliers. The Azúcar offers luxurious accommodation right on the beach, with rustic chic decor, gorgeous whitewashed public areas topped in thatch, a sumptuous pool, impressive spa and sublimely laid-back restaurant.

Eating

Unless you hate fresh, inexpensive seafood, you'll enjoy the high-quality fare on offer in Tecolutla. On the beach, all the *palapa* places sell cold beer, while vendors hawk seafood cocktails. There are numerous eateries along the walk from the plaza to the beach on Avenida Obregón.

El Cotarro SEAFOOD $
(766-845-16-71; Av Obregón s/n; mains M$40-90) It may not keep up with its neighbors' kitschy sea-themed decor, but El Cotarro's food is delicious, fresh and inexpensive. The *mojarra al ajo* is a freshly caught tilapia drenched in garlic.

Porteño Café CAFE, SANDWICHES $
(cnr Aldama & Av Obregón; 8am-8pm) The cafe downstairs at the Aqua Inn serves *antojitos* and panini as well as good coffee.

Getting There & Away

Tecolutla is 41km east of Papantla. There are regular 2nd-class Transportes Papantla buses between Tecolutla and Papantla (M$35) that arrive and depart from outside the church in Avenida Obregón, one block west of the main plaza. There is also a small but swanky 1st-class ADO **bus station** (cnr Abasolo & Ahumada) a few blocks from the main plaza. Many buses to and from Tecolutla have to transfer through Gutiérrez Zamora. ADO offers services to some major cities including Mexico City's Terminal Norte (M$258), as well as frequent services to Poza Rica (M$52) and Papantla (M$42).

Costa Esmeralda & Around

The Emerald Coast stretches roughly between La Guadalupe and Nautla, and its waters, more accurately described as semiprecious, lap the grayish-blond sands, which are a huge draw for Mexican holidaymakers. It's a spot that will probably have limited appeal to travelers for whom Cancún is also a possible destination, not least as the main coastal road runs directly behind the beaches for much of their length, and development has been as haphazard as it ever is in Mexico.

That said, it's a raging summer spot where waves crash on 20km of beaches, and Mexican families descend en masse to enjoy fresh fish, cold beer and swimming. The rest of the year, especially midweek, it's tranquil and a good match for beach lovers and crowd haters. You can throw down cash for upscale digs, or do it on the cheap. Advertised and unadvertised campgrounds proliferate.

At the mouth of the Río Filobobos (known as Río Bobos and famous for its rapids), head southwest of Nautla on Hwy 131 and you'll hit **Tlapacoyan**, where a handful of rafting companies are based, and where the waterfall Cascada de Encanto provides a gorgeous swimming spot. **Aventura Extrema** (229-202-65-57; www.aventuraextrema.com.mx; rafting packages from M$750) has facilities near Tlapacoyan and offers one- to three-day packages including food, accommodations or camping, and various other adventure activities. A highlight of Bobos rafting is the two riverside archaeological sites, **Caujilote** and **Vega de la Peña**, which most companies stop to visit.

Five kilometers south of Nautla is **Hotel Istirinchá** (235-317-42-01; www.istirincha.com.mx; Hwy 180 Km 102; r from M$1200, ste M$1800; P), a hard-to-classify resort/eco-hotel with some genuine green credentials. Once a tract of deforested land used for cattle grazing, the 70-hectare site has been transformed since it was bought in 1999 by a private owner intent on returning it to its natural jungle-like habitat. There's a lagoon for kayaking, an isolated driftwood-covered beach, trails through pines and palm trees, and a collection of caged animals such as toucans and crocodiles. The organized activities, including horseback riding and cycling, are a little tame, but it's a lovely place to wander. Rooms are bright and comfortable, if a little overpriced. There's also a restaurant and pool. Turtles nest on the beach from June to August. You'll see signs at the entrance on the highway and it's about a 20-minute walk to the hotel from where the bus leaves you.

To get to any coastal location on Costa Esmeralda, take a nondirect bus on Hwy 180 and tell the driver where you want to stop.

Punta Villa Rica & Around

Between Nautla and Veracruz, the coast is remarkably wild and unexplored, despite its weighty historical significance. The only blemish is Mexico's sole nuclear power station, on **Laguna Verde**, about 80km north of Veracruz port on Hwy 180. It's been in operation since 1989.

Sights & Activities

Villa Rica VILLAGE

Standing in this tiny, dusty fishing village 69km north of modern-day Veracruz, it's hard to believe you're gazing at the site of the first European-founded settlement north of Panama in mainland America. These days the historic settlement doesn't even merit a label on Google Maps, though there's a smattering of houses here, along with a small hotel, a couple of rustic restaurants and the weed-covered foundations of some buildings constructed by Cortés and his men soon after their arrival.

Never properly consolidated, the 'Veracruz that once was,' founded as Villa Rica de la Vera Cruz in 1519, lasted only until 1524 when it was moved to present-day La Antigua. There's a small and attractive curved beach, and you can trace it around past some dunes and across an isthmus to the **Cerro de la Cantera**, a rocky outcrop famed for its plunging *quebraditas* (ravines).

Villa Rica is about 1km east of the main Hwy 180. Ask any bus driver on the Cardel–Nautla run to stop at the entrance road to the Quiahuiztlán ruins. From here it's an easy walk to the village.

★Quiahuiztlán ARCHAEOLOGICAL SITE

(admission M$35, free Sun; 9am-5pm) Perched like a mini–Machu Picchu on a plateau beneath a horn-shaped mountain (the Cerro de Metates), Quiahuiztlán (place of the rains) is a pre-Hispanic Totonac town and necropolis. Counting 15,000 inhabitants at the time of Cortés' arrival in 1519, its history before that is sketchy, although there was certainly a settlement here by AD 800. Enjoying a commanding view of the Gulf coast, the now-deserted site has two pyramids, more than 70 tombs (each resembling a small temple) and some carved monuments.

Rock climbers revere the precipitous Cerro de Metates (with routes graded 5.6 to 5.8) that rises behind. It's a pleasant 3km walk up a winding paved road to the part of the site that overlooks the ocean. From here you can experience the sacred Totonac ruins in solitude and amid nature, unlike more touristed ruins. The first question most of the sporadic visitors to these amazing Totonac ruins ask is: why, given its historic importance and stunning setting, is there no one else here? Alas, there's no logical answer.

Rather it's best just to relish the tranquility and keep mum. If you want to arrive by a Hwy 180 bus, have the driver drop you at the Quiahuiztlán turnoff.

★EcoGuías La Mancha ECOTOURISM
(☎296-100-11-63; www.ecoturismolamancha.com; La Mancha-Actopan, Carretera Federal Cardel-Nautla Km 31; campsites own/borrowed tent M$60/100, cabañas per person/entire M$150/1200) All hail this progressive association of locals that has developed a homespun, grass-roots environment education center. The facilities, located 1km from the beach, offer interpretive walks, bird-watching excursions, apiary tours, horseback riding and kayak tours where you can see mangroves and wildlife. Accommodations are rustic (eight-person cabins or rent-a-tents), but it's a great off-the-beaten-path choice that supports the local community. From the La Mancha eastbound turnoff on Hwy 180, it's 1km down the road. Bring repellent.

Sleeping & Eating

Rustic accommodations are available at EcoGuías La Mancha. All the eating options can be found on Villa Rica's compact main drag, which leads from the main coastal road to the beach.

Villas Arcon HOTEL $$
(☎229-272-70-30; www.villasarcon.com; Villa Rica; s/d M$700/850; P ❄ 📶 🏊) At the entrance to Villa Rica, this attractively set low-rise resort hotel might be a little overpriced, but it does allow you to live in some comfort while getting in touch with Mexico's gritty essence. Comfortable rooms surround a pool and it's a short walk through the village to the beach.

Restaurante Totonacapan SEAFOOD $
(Villa Rica; mains M$60-120; ⏲noon-8pm) The jovial proprietor often calls innocent bystanders over to this alfresco thatched-roof affair, the last structure on the town's main road and just where the beach begins. The food is ocean-fresh fish and shrimp.

Restaurant Miriam SEAFOOD $
(Villa Rica; mains M$50-120; ⏲10am-7pm) Friendly Miriam and her extended family serve up delicious seafood dishes to order, in what is essentially an extension of their living room. Be warned, when she offers you her *picantísimo* (spiciest) dish, she's not kidding!

SOUTHEAST VERACRUZ

Southeast Veracruz is arguably the most beautiful part of the state, and yet tourism is still on a very modest scale. Here you'll find languorous wetlands, volcano-dappled rainforest, breathtaking lakes and the superb **Reserva de la Biosfera Los Tuxtlas**, a well-run Biosphere Reserve that will appeal to anyone wanting to get off the beaten track. As part of the former heartland of ancient Olmec culture, the area is laden with archaeological sites, not to mention the area's sleeper hit, Tlacotalpan, a Unesco World Heritage site that will enchant anyone lucky enough to head this way.

Tlacotalpan

☎288 / POP 7600

Possibly the finest Unesco World Heritage town that no one's ever heard of, Tlacotalpan is a near-perfect identikit of early-19th-century colonial architecture, completely unblemished by modern interferences, save for a light (by Mexican standards) smattering of traffic. The color palette is extraordinary here; the lucid sunsets over the adjacent Río Papaloapan add subtle oranges and yellows to the rainbow of colonial houses, bringing to mind a Havana where the houses haven't been allowed to decay.

Once an important river port, Tlacotalpan has changed little since the 1820s. The town, Unesco-listed in 1998, was hit by devastating floods in September 2010 which inundated 500 historic buildings and prompted the evacuation of 8500 people. The recovery has been remarkable, with only a high watermark drawn onto a wall on Calle Alegre to show how disastrous the flooding was.

Sights & Activities

Tlacotalpan's two plazas, Hidalgo and Zaragoza, are directly adjacent to each other. Together they harbor equally magnificent churches; the light blue **Capilla o Santuario de la Candelaria** dating from 1779 and furnished with local coral stone, and the neoclassical **Iglesia San Cristobal**, begun in 1812 and gorgeously painted in blue and white.

Be sure to take a stroll by the riverside and down Cházaro, which starts from the Palacio Municipal and has wall-to-wall, whacky-colored, colonial-style houses and buildings with columns, tiles and high arches.

Museo Salvador Ferrando MUSEUM
(Alegre 6; admission M$20; 11am-6pm Tue-Sat, 12:30-7pm Sun) The Ferrando, named for a Tlacotalpan artist, is the best of Tlacotalpan's handful of mini-museums. It displays assorted artifacts, furniture, paintings and other knickknacks within a charming old colonial mansion.

Casa Museo Agustín Lara MUSEUM
(Beltrán 6; admission M$20; 10am-6pm Mon-Sat) This museum features memorabilia of *tlacotalpeño* Agustín Lara (1900–70), a legendary musician, composer and Casanova.

Villin Montalio HANDICRAFTS
(5 de Mayo 53; 9am-6pm Mon-Sat) Tlacotalpan is well known for its locally made cedar furniture, and such skills were in demand after the 2010 floods. Drop by this office/workshop to see it being made, and to see some of the finished products on display as well.

Mini-Zoológico Museo MUSEUM
(Av Carranza 25; donation M$15; 10am-5pm Mon-Sat) Lovers of the utterly bizarre should hotfoot it to the home of Don Pío Barrán. He keeps several enormous crocodiles and a range of artifacts, including a locally excavated mastodon tooth and a sword that supposedly belonged to Porfirio Díaz.

Boat Rides BOAT TOUR
(hour-long ride M$300) If you walk the *malecón* near the restaurants, you're bound to run into a *lanchero* offering to whisk you down the scenic river for an hour-long boat ride to see a nearby lagoon. It's not the Amazon, but it's a lovely way to spend a late afternoon.

Festivals & Events

Día de la Candelaria RELIGIOUS
In late January and early February, Tlacotalpan's huge Candelaria festival features bull-running in the streets. An image of the Virgin is also floated down the river, followed by a flotilla of small boats.

Sleeping

Prices triple or quadruple during the Candelaria holiday, during which reservations, made weeks ahead of time, are essential.

Hotel Reforma HOTEL $
(288-884-20-22; tlacoreforma@hotmail.com; Av Carranza 2; r with fan/air-con M$250/400;) This simple place, right on the town's main square, is the cheapest bed in town. While it can be noisy here at weekends, it's still a pretty decent deal. The rooms are clean but, admittedly, the mattresses are aged.

★**Hotel Posada Doña Lala** HISTORIC HOTEL $$
(288-884-25-80; www.hoteldonalala.com; Av Carranza 11; s/d M$850/950;) With its smart pink facade looking towards the river, Doña Lala is a marker for the center of town, but it's also a friendly and comfortable hotel, with spacious, spotless rooms, high ceilings and great views if you're lucky enough to score a room on the square. There's an excellent restaurant downstairs and even an indoor pool to enjoy.

Casa de la Luz GUESTHOUSE $$
(288-884-23-31; www.casadelaluz-mexico.com; Aguirre 15; r/ste M$550/800;) Once the home of the town's midwife, this gorgeous old house has been beautifully looked after by its friendly ex-pat owner, Bill. He welcomes guests into his home and goes to extraordinary lengths to ensure they're happy and well looked after during their stay. There are two rooms available: one standard double, and one suite with two double beds.

There's also an apartment, which can be rented for longer stays.

Hotel Casa del Río HOTEL $$
(288-884-29-47; www.casadelrio.com.mx; Cházaro 39; r/ste M$750/1100;) Creating modern, stylish, minimalist rooms in a colonial mansion is definitely a challenge, but the Hotel Casa del Río gets it right with nine spacious offerings. Its best feature is definitely the terrace overlooking the river.

Eating

The riverside is lined by fish restaurants that operate from lunchtime to sunset each day, serving up the catch of the day. Try **Restaurant Tlacotalpan** or **La Ribera del Papaloapan**, both of which are opposite the Hotel Posada Doña Lala.

El K-Fecito CAFE $
(Plaza Zaragoza; snacks $30-70; 5pm-1am) On the joining point of the two main plazas and serving great coffee, cakes and various simple snacks, El K-Fecito seems to have it all, and becomes packed in the late evening. The staff sometimes provides mosquito coils but, if you're planning on sitting alfresco, do bring repellent.

★Rokala MEXICAN $$
(Plaza Zaragoza; mains M$80-155; ⏱6pm-1am; 📶) With its unbeatable position under the colonial arches on the Plaza Zaragoza, this friendly place with alfresco dining buzzes year-round. Mains range from fresh fish and prawns plucked from the river to meat grills and typical *antojitos*. For atmosphere alone it's a clear winner, and it serves as the town meeting point come sundown.

Now if only it weren't for those damn mosquitoes!

Restaurant Doña Lala MEXICAN $$
(Av Carranza 11; mains M$75-160; ⏱7am-7pm; 📶) Easily the smartest eating option in town, this place inside the hotel of the same name has a friendly staff and is patronised by a crowd of local eccentrics who vie for the best seats on its terrace. The wide-ranging selection of Mexican dishes won't disappoint; the only annoyance is that it's not open in the evenings.

☆ Entertainment

Tlacotalpan is surprisingly lively at night for such a small town. Indeed, at weekends, you may need ear plugs to sleep. Bars around Plaza Zaragoza and along Av Carranza spill out into the streets, music is loud and the party goes on into the wee hours. More formal gatherings convene in the gorgeous French-style **Teatro Netzahualcoyotl** (Av Carranza).

ℹ Information

There's an ATM in one side of Hotel Posada Doña Lala, near the plaza.

Tourist Office (Alegre & Lerdo de Tejada; ⏱9am-3pm Mon-Fri) Right off Plaza Hidalgo. The office has helpful maps.

ℹ Getting There & Around

Hwy 175 runs from Tlacotalpan up the Papaloapan valley to Tuxtepec, then twists and turns over the mountains to Oaxaca (320km). ADO, whose riverside station is situated outside the Mercado Municipal, three blocks east of the center, offers services to Mexico City (M$506), Puebla (M$386), Xalapa (M$196), San Andrés Tuxtla (M$70) and Veracruz (M$99). Frequent 2nd-class buses that stop along the riverside strip go to and from Veracruz.

Wonderfully flat, Tlacotalpan is a perfect spot for bike riding. You can arrange bike hire through **Bici Cletando** (☎288-100-46-86; per hour M$30), who rent bikes from a stand outside the Iglesia La Candelaria on Plaza Zaragoza. They'll deliver them to your hotel if you call them.

Santiago Tuxtla

☎294 / POP 15,000 / ELEV 180M

Santiago centers on a lovely, verdant main plaza – one of the state's prettiest – and is surrounded by the rolling green foothills of the volcanic Sierra de los Tuxtlas. It's far more laid-back and a touch more charming than its built-up neighbor San Andrés, with its plaza strewn with ladies arm-in-arm, couples lip-to-lip and shoes getting vigorously shined. It's not on the tourist track per se, but the intriguing little museum, the close proximity (23km) to Tres Zapotes, and the possibility of a tranquil stay at Mesón de Santiago all make it worth a visit.

All buses arrive and depart near the junction of Morelos and the highway. To

BUSES FROM SANTIAGO TUXTLA

DESTINATION	FARE (M$)	DURATION	FREQUENCY (DAILY)
Catemaco	32	50min	hourly
Córdoba	232	3½hr	1 Fri-Mon
Mexico City	514-540	8hr	3
Puebla	422	5½hr	2
San Andrés Tuxtla	26	20min	frequent
Tlacotalpan	56	1 hr	5
Veracruz	130	2½hr	frequent
Villahermosa	288	4hr	1 Fri, Sun, Mon
Xalapa	218	4½hr	4

1st-class bus departures.

get to the center, continue down Morelos, then turn right into Ayuntamiento, which leads to the main plaza, a few blocks away.

Sights

Olmec Head MONUMENT

(Plaza Olmeca) Dominating the main plaza, this stone monolith is known as the 'Cobata head,' after the estate where it was found. Thought to be a very late Olmec production, it's the biggest known Olmec head, weighing in at 40 tons, and is unique in that its eyes are closed.

Museo Tuxteco MUSEUM

(☎294-947-10-76; Ayuntamiento; admission M$42; ⏲9am-5pm Tue-Sun) This museum on the main plaza exhibits artifacts such as Olmec stone carvings, including a colossal head, a monkey-faced *hacha* (axe) with obsidian eyes, and a Tres Zapotes altar replica. There's also an interesting Spanish colonial room, with impressive suits of armour and a bust of poor Cuauhtémoc, the last Aztec emperor. Sadly there's no labeling in English.

Festivals & Events

Santiago celebrates the festivals of San Juan (June 24) and Santiago Apóstol (June 25) with processions and dances, including the *Liseres*, in which the participants wear jaguar costumes.

The week before Christmas is also a time of huge festivity.

Sleeping & Eating

★Mesón de Santiago HOTEL $$

(☎294-947-16-70; www.mesonsantiago.com.mx; 5 de Mayo 202; s/d M$550/600; P❄📶🏊) With a freshly renovated interior and a well preserved colonial exterior, this fantastic place right on the main plaza is an unexpected gem in such a quiet and little-visited place. The peaceful courtyard is immaculate and has a small pool. Rooms are tastefully decorated, with deeply burnished wood furniture, beautifully tiled bathrooms and domed staircases.

Restaurant Colonial MEXICAN $

(Hwy 180; mains M$50-120; ⏲8am-8pm) This is the smartest place in town (OK, that's not saying a huge amount), where you'll find *cocina típica* with a focus on seafood and grilled meat. It's just a little up the hill from the ADO bus station (in the direction of Veracruz) on the main road through the town.

La Joya MEXICAN $

(☎294-947-01-77; cnr Juárez & 2 de Abril; mains M$30-60; ⏲7am-11pm) The crummy plastic tablecloths, alfresco-only chairs and rustic, open-to-view kitchen scream 'Montezuma's revenge,' but fear not: La Joya delivers where it matters – good, tasty Mexican food. It's on a corner of the main plaza, to one side of the Olmec head.

Getting There & Around

All local and regional buses and *colectivo* taxis to San Andrés Tuxtla are frequent and stop at the junction of Morales and Hwy 180. A private taxi between the towns is M$60. Frequent 2nd-class buses also go to Catemaco, Veracruz, Acayucan and Tlacotalpan.

While the TLT and AU stops are just down Morelos, there's an ADO bus station on the highway itself, at the corner with Morelos.

Tres Zapotes

☎294 / POP 3500

The important late-Olmec center of Tres Zapotes is now just a series of mounds in cornfields. However, interesting artifacts are displayed at the museum in the town of Tres Zapotes, 23km west of Santiago Tuxtla. The trip to this tiny town is not convenient, but might be worth it if archaeology floats your boat.

Tres Zapotes was occupied for over 2000 years, from around 1200 BC to AD 1000. It was probably first inhabited while the great Olmec center of La Venta (Tabasco) still flourished. After the destruction of La Venta (about 400 BC), the city carried on in what archaeologists call an 'epi-Olmec' phase – the period during which the Olmec culture dwindled, as other civilizations (notably Izapa and Maya) came to the fore. Most finds are from this later period.

The small **Museo de Tres Zapotes** (admission M$30; ⏲9am-5pm) notably has the 1.5m Tres Zapotes head, an Olmec head dating from about 100 BC. The biggest piece, Stela A, depicts three human figures in the mouth of a jaguar. Other pieces include a sculpture of what may have been a captive with hands tied behind his back, and the upturned face of a woman carved into a throne or altar. The museum attendant is happy to answer questions in Spanish or give a tour (tipping is appreciated).

The road to Tres Zapotes goes southwest from Santiago Tuxtla; a 'Zona Arqueológica' sign points the way from Hwy 180. Eight kilometers down this road, you fork right onto a paved stretch for the last 15km to Tres Zapotes. It comes out at a T-junction, from where you go left then left again to reach the museum. From Santiago Tuxtla there are 2nd-class buses (M$26) and taxis (M$25/90 *colectivo*/private). Taxis leave from the Sitio Puente Real, on the far side of the pedestrian bridge at the foot of Zaragoza (the street going downhill beside the Santiago Tuxtla museum).

San Andrés Tuxtla

☎294 / POP 62,000 / ELEV 300M

Like a lot of modern towns, San Andrés puts function before beauty. The busy service center of the Los Tuxtlas region is best used for bus connections and link-ups to its more enticing peripheral sights, including a volcano and a giant waterfall. Cigar aficionados will definitely want to visit, as San Andrés is Mexico's cigar capital. The center of town is orderly and attractive, with a soaring orange and yellow tiled church on the main plaza.

Sights & Activities

★Salto de Eyipantla WATERFALL
(admission M$10) Twelve kilometers southeast of San Andrés, a 244-step staircase leads down to the spectacular Salto de Eyipantla, a 50m-high, 40m-wide waterfall. To avoid the steps (and a soaking), you can also enjoy it from a *mirador* (lookout). Part of Mel Gibson's movie *Apocalypto* was filmed here.

Follow Hwy 180 east for 4km to Sihuapan, then turn right to Eyipantla. Frequent TLT buses (M$12) make the trip from San Andrés, leaving from the corner of Cabada and 5 de Mayo, near the market.

Santa Clara Cigar Factory CIGAR FACTORY
(☎294-947-99-00; Blvd 5 de Febrero 10; ⏲9am-9pm Mon-Sat, 8am-9pm Sun) FREE Watch and inhale as the *puros* are speedily rolled by hand at this cigar factory, on the highway, a block or so from the bus station. Cigars of assorted shapes and sizes, including the monstrous Magnum, are available at factory prices, and the 50 *torcedores* employed here (together rolling 10,000 *puros* a day) are happy to demonstrate their technique.

Laguna Encantada LAKE
The 'Enchanted Lagoon' occupies a small volcanic crater 3.5km northeast of San Andrés in jungle-like terrain. A dirt road goes there, but no buses do. Some locals advise not walking by the lake alone, so check with the guides at the nearby Yambigapan homestay for updates.

Cerro de Venado NATURE RESERVE
(admission M$5) This new 23-hectare reserve, created in 2009 with the planting of thousands of trees, is 2.5km from Laguna Encantada on the road to Ruíz Cortines. There are 500 steps up to a 650m hill with fabulous views of the town, lake and mountains, plus some caged animals.

Ruíz Cortines HIKING
(☎cell phone 294-1005035; Ejido Ruíz Cortines; campsites/cabañas M$50/400) Tucked at the base of a volcano, an hour north of San Andrés Tuxtla, this little village has installed very rustic *cabañas* and offers horseback

BUSES FROM SAN ANDRÉS TUXTLA

DESTINATION	FARE (M$)	DURATION	FREQUENCY (DAILY)
Catemaco	26	25min	hourly
Córdoba	260	3½hr	1
Mexico City	582	8hr	3
Puebla	438	6½hr	2
Santiago Tuxtla	28	20min	hourly
Tlactotalpan	76	1½hr	5
Veracruz	148	3hr	hourly
Villahermosa	298	5hr	4
Xalapa	248	5hr	7

1st-class bus departures from the ADO.

riding, and hikes to caves. Its highlight is the breathtaking all-day hike up Volcán San Martín (1748m). A taxi from San Andrés Tuxtla costs M$100, while a *pirata* (pickup truck) costs M$25.

Sleeping

San Andrés doesn't have a lot of choice, but you'll be comfortable.

Yambigapan CABINS, CAMPING **$**
(☎294-104-46-39, (English) 294-103-84-10; www.yambigapan.com; campsites/s/d M$25/300/400; P) Three kilometers or so from San Andrés, this family-run rural homestay has two very rustic *cabañas* with spectacular views. Not to be missed are the **cooking classes** from the *doña* of the house, Amelia, who will teach you traditional Mexican cooking and its history (in Spanish) in her homely kitchen for M$200.

There's swimming in the nearby river, Arroyo Seco, and guided hikes. An all-day summit of Volcán San Martín can also be arranged. Taxi (M$35 to M$40) is the easiest way to arrive. Or ask a *pirata* going to Ruíz Cortines to leave you at the turnoff and follow the signs for Yambigapan that eventually lead you up a long dirt driveway. It should cost about M$10.

Hotel Posada San Martín HOTEL **$$**
(☎294-942-10-36; www.hotelposada-sanmartin.com; Av Juárez 304; s/d/tr M$488/575/660; P ❄ 📶 🏊) Midway between the main road and the main plaza, this hacienda-style posada is a fabulous deal and a very unexpected find. It has a pool set in a peaceful garden and antiques scattered about its public areas. The rooms are spacious, clean and all have charmingly tiled sinks.

Hotel del Parque HOTEL **$$**
(☎294-942-01-98; reservaciones@hoteldelparque.com; Madero 5; s/d M$472/597; P ❄ 📶) San Andrés' main central option is clean, modern and has a busy cafe on the ground floor where locals love to drink coffee and gossip. Some rooms have lovely views of the cathedral and, although bathrooms are rather pokey and on the old side, this is a good choice.

Eating

Yambigapan MEXICAN **$**
(Hotel Posada San Martín, Av Juárez 304; mains M$30-50; ⏱7:30am-8pm; 📶) Inside Hotel Posada San Martín, the town's nicest hotel, you'll find this small, cozy restaurant, run by the same management who run the Yambigapan homestay 3km out of town. Here you'll find lots of cheap local dishes that came originally from the kitchen of *doña* Amelia, all served in a cute spot by the hotel pool.

Restaurante Winni's BAKERY, INTERNATIONAL **$**
(☎294-942-01-10; Madero 10; mains M$30-100; ⏱7am-1am; 📶) Join the rest of San Andrés on the corner of the main plaza and sip an espresso while munching a pastry or a well-priced meal. You may have to fight to get served during the lunchtime rush.

Information

The tiny **tourist office** (Madero 1; ⏱8:30am-3:30pm) inside the Palacio Municipal is on the west side of the main plaza. A Banamex (with ATM) is on the south side; the market is three blocks west.

THE WITCHING HOUR

On the first Friday in March each year, hundreds of *brujos* (shamans), witches and healers from all over Mexico descend on Catemaco to perform a mass cleansing ceremony. The event is designed to rid them of the previous year's negative energies, though in recent years the whole occasion has become more commercial than supernatural. Floods of Mexicans also head into town at this time to grab a shamanic consultation or *limpia* (cleansing), and eat, drink and be merry in a bizarre mix of otherworldly fervor and hedonistic indulgence.

Witchcraft traditions in this part of Veracruz go back centuries, mixing ancient indigenous beliefs, Spanish medieval traditions and voodoo practices from West Africa. Many of these *brujos* multitask as medicine men or women (using both traditional herbs and modern pharmaceuticals), shrinks and black magicians, casting evil spells on enemies of their clients. If you want to arrange a consultation, contact a tour agency, or ask along the *malecón*.

Getting There & Around

San Andrés is the transportation center for Los Tuxtlas, with fairly good bus services in every direction. First-class buses with ADO and 2nd-class with AU depart from their respective stations on Juárez just off the Santiago Tuxtla–Catemaco highway, and about a 10-minute walk from the center. Rickety but regular 2nd-class TLT buses are often the quickest way of getting to local destinations. They leave from a block north of the market and skirt the north side of town on 5 de Febrero (Hwy 180). Frequent *colectivo* taxis to Catemaco and Santiago also leave from the market – they're speedier than the bus but cost a fraction more.

Catemaco

294 / POP 28,000 / ELEV 340M

Sleepy Catemaco is an unlikely traveler hotspot, and yet it's the obvious base for exploring Reserva de la Biosfera Los Tuxtlas. Small and not a little scruffy, it's reminiscent of a dusty backpacker destination from the 1980s, but without a significant number of backpackers. With a long tradition of shamans who will exorcise your nasty spirits, a gorgeous lakeside setting and alluring natural sights branching out in all directions, Catemaco is somewhere anyone getting to know the region will want to pass through.

Sights & Activities

Laguna Catemaco LAKE

Catemaco sits on the shore of the 16km-long Laguna Catemaco, which is ringed by volcanic hills and is actually a lake and not a lagoon. East of town are a few modest gray-sand beaches where you can take a dip in cloudy water.

Basílica del Carmen CHURCH

Catemaco's main church was named a basilica (ie a church with special ceremonial rights) in 1961, due primarily to its position as a pilgrimage site for the Virgen del Carmen. It's said she appeared to a fisherman in a cave by Laguna Catemaco in 1664, in conjunction with a volcanic eruption. A statue of the virgin resides in the church and is venerated on her feast day every July 16.

The intricate interior and haunting stained glass of the church belie its modernity; the current building only dates from 1953, though it looks at least a century older.

Catemaco

Sights
1 Basílica del Carmen ... C2

Activities, Courses & Tours
2 Catemacoturs ... C2

Sleeping
3 Hotel Acuario ... B1
4 Hotel Los Arcos ... B2

Eating
5 Il Fiorentino ... C2
6 La Ola ... B2

Drinking & Nightlife
7 La Panga ... A2

Shopping
8 Fractal Naturaleza ... A2

Catemaco

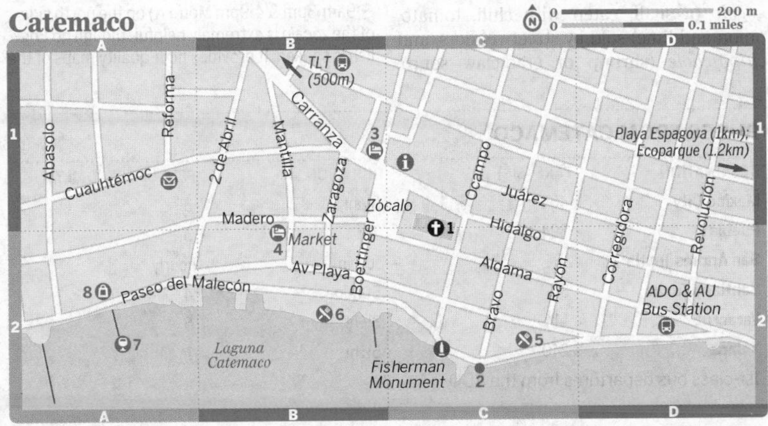

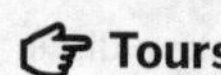

Tours

Catemacoturs ADVENTURE
(☎294-941-58-49; Paseo del Malecón s/n) Based in a *palapa* hut on the *malecón*, these guys rent beat-down adventure gear and offer tours around the lake and to the coast.

Sleeping

Hotel Acuario HOTEL $
(☎294-943-04-18; www.hotelacuariocatemaco.com; cnr Boettinger & Carranza; r M$350-650;) This friendly budget option has 25 clean rooms just off the *zócalo*. It's well kept, though plain and fan-cooled. Some rooms have balconies and views – try for one of these, as those at the back lack natural daylight. Cable TV is a bonus.

Hotel Los Arcos HOTEL $$
(☎294-943-00-03; www.arcoshotel.com.mx; Madero 7; r from M$750;) This is the smartest option in the town itself. Centrally located, it's a friendly, well-run place with spacious and airy rooms, each with its own semi-private outdoor space and seating area. There's cable TV and even a pool.

Hotel La Finca RESORT $$$
(☎294-947-97-00; www.lafinca.mx; Hwy 180 Km 47; r from M$1500;) This friendly resort on the lake shore, some 2km west of the town, is rather pricey, but it's easily the most comfortable place to stay in Catemaco. Rooms have large, lake-view balconies, and a pool with slides and a hot tub. It's a deal outside peak seasons. It provides *lancha* and spa services.

Eating

The lake provides the specialties here: *tegogolo* (a snail, eaten with chili, tomato, onion and lime) sold by street vendors, and *chipalchole* (shrimp or crab-claw soup). Many similar-standard restaurants serving fresh fish line the *malecón*.

Il Fiorentino ITALIAN $$
(Paseo del Malecón 11; mains M$85-120; ⏰6:30-10:30pm Tue-Fri, 3-11:30pm Sat, 1:30-11pm Sun;) Smarter than your average Italian-abroad restaurant, Il Fiorentino serves handmade pasta, Piedmontese wine, cappuccinos and great cake. It's on the *malecón* and run by an Italian – of course.

La Ola SEAFOOD, MEXICAN $$
(Paseo del Malecón s/n; dishes M$65-140; ⏰11am-9pm;) A vast waterfront restaurant on the *malecón*, serving seafood including *pargo* (red snapper), *a la veracruzana* (spicy sauce) or *empanizado* (in breadcrumbs).

Drinking

La Panga BAR
(Paseo del Malecón s/n; mains M$85-160; ⏰9am-2am, restaurant until 7pm) This bar-restaurant, floating on the lake with its own boardwalk, is an idyllic place to lean back, sip *cerveza* and grab a bite to eat while the sun disappears beyond the lake and the rolling hills.

Shopping

Fractal Naturaleza HANDICRAFTS
(☎294-103-16-84; Paseo del Malecón s/n; ⏰10am-9pm Mon-Fri, 9am-10pm Sat & Sun) An excellent place to check out souvenirs made by local Los Tuxtlas artisans, this store does its best to support local art and textiles. It also brews coffee.

Information

Catemaco slopes gently down toward the lake. A **tourist office** (☎434-943-00-16; Municipalidad; ⏰9am-3pm & 4-9pm Mon-Fri) on the north side of the *zócalo* is extremely helpful, though no English is spoken. It provides high-quality maps of the

BUSES FROM CATEMACO

DESTINATION	FARE (M$)	DURATION	FREQUENCY (DAILY)
Mexico City	460	9½hr	3
Puebla	394	7hr	3
San Andrés Tuxtla	26	30min	hourly
Santiago Tuxtla	32	50min	4
Veracruz	144	3½hr	5
Xalapa	240	5½hr	1

1st-class bus departures from the ADO.

surrounding region. The **post office** (Cuauhtémoc s/n) is four blocks west of the central plaza.

Getting There & Away

ADO and AU buses operate from a lakeside **bus terminal** (cnr Paseo del Malecón & Revolución). Local 2nd-class TLT buses run from a bus station 700m west of the plaza by the highway junction and are a bit cheaper and more frequent than the 1st-class buses. *Colectivo* taxis arrive and depart from El Cerrito, a small hill about 400m to the west of the plaza on Carranza.

To arrive at communities surrounding the lake and toward the coast, take inexpensive *piratas*. They leave from a corner five blocks north of the bus station.

Reserva de la Biosfera Los Tuxtlas

The various nature reserves around Catemaco were conglomerated in 2006 into this Biosphere Reserve under Unesco protection. This unique volcanic region, rising 1680m above the coastal plains of southern Veracruz, lies 160km east of the Cordillera Neovolcánica, making it something of an ecological anomaly. Its complex vegetation is considered the northernmost limit of rainforest in the Americas. Being severely economically depressed, the region has little tourism infrastructure. Nevertheless, what it does have is worthwhile.

Laguna Catemaco

To explore Laguna Catemaco, there are *lancheros* along the *malecón* who offer boat trips. Boats can be paid for *colectivo* (ie per place) or can be hired for up to six people. Expect to pay M$100 *colectivo* or M$500 for a private *lancha* for an hour's boat trip. You can visit several islands on the lake; on the largest, **Isla Tenaspi**, Olmec sculptures have been discovered. **Isla de los Changos** (Monkey Island) shelters red-cheeked monkeys, originally from Thailand. They belong to the Universidad Veracruzana, which acquired them for research.

On the northeast shore of the lake, the **Reserva Ecológica de Nanciyaga** (294-943-01-99; www.nanciyaga.com; Carretera Catemaco-Coyame; 9am-2pm & 4-6pm; P) is a kind of reserve within a reserve and pushes an indigenous theme in a small tract of rainforest. The grounds are replete with a temascal, an ancient planetarium and Olmec-themed decorations and replicas. Day visitors are welcome. One night's lodging (M$1654 for two people) in solar-powered rustic cabins includes a mineral mud bath, a massage, a guided walk and the use of

Los Tuxtlas

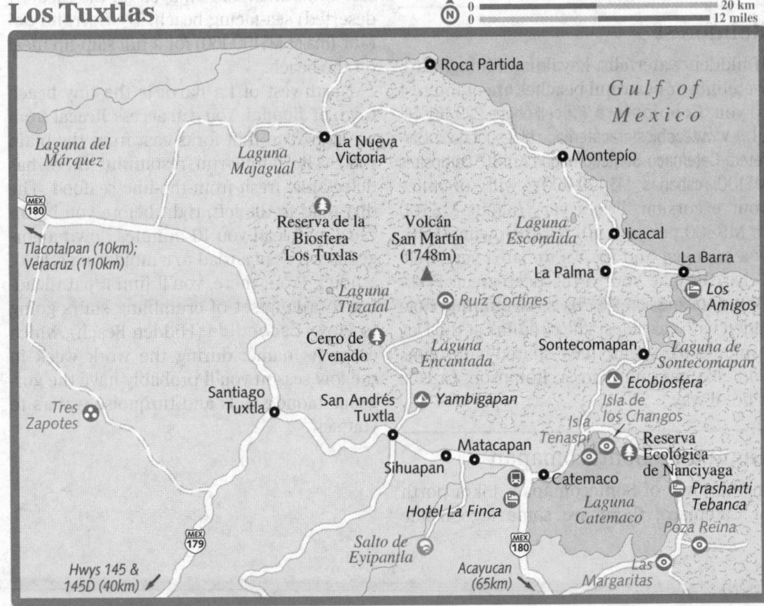

kayaks. You have to walk to the bathrooms (torches provided), so it's not for everyone, but it provides an incredible experience for those who want to be very close to nature. Arrive by *pirata* (M$10), taxi (M$80) or boat (M$50 per person; hire in Catemaco).

Follow the lake's eastern shore along the dirt road another 8km and you can earn a bit more luxury at the meditative **Prashanti Tebanca** (294-107-79-98; www.prashanti.com.mx; 2-/4-/6-person units M$1000/1200/1400; P). It's a rather more comfortable version of Nanciyaga with a *nuevo*-Buddhist vibe, although one that's rather overpriced for what it offers. They organize boat and jeep tours.

To get a truly local vibe, seek out basic but gorgeously located **Las Margaritas** (294-945-52-51, 294-945-52-71; dm M$150, cabaña for 2 M$750), a little village with a guesthouse on the south shore of the lake. No *colectivo* boats go here, so arrive by private *lancha* from Catemaco's *malecón* (M$400) or by bumpy *pirata* (M$20). The rural setting by the lake is stunning, and village life goes on all around you. The six-people dorms are extremely basic though, so only come if you're happy to rough it. A M$700 per person per night charge includes full board and a bed in a dorm, as well as guided tours to the El Chininal archaeological site and to waterfalls.

Rainforest

If hidden waterfalls, kayaking, hiking, birdwatching or beautiful beaches are of interest to you, **Ecobiosfera** (cell phone 229-161-44-91; www.ecobiosferacatemaco.blogspot.de; Carretera Catemaco-Sontecomapan Km 10; campsites M$100, cabañas M$400-800) will organize your excursion. Prices vary (about M$400 to M$800 per person), but the owner, Felix, is a biologist and knows the area very well. Felix can take you to the deep-green **Poza Reina** (admission M$25), a swimming hole laden with cascades. The *cabañas* at the Dos Amantes base camp have shared bathrooms and are charming in a Robinson Crusoe kind of way.

Laguna de Sontecomapan

In the town of Sontecomapan, 15km north of Catemaco, there are some lagoon-side restaurants and the idyllic **Pozo de los Enanos** (Well of the Dwarves) swimming hole, where local youths launch, Tarzanlike, from ropes into the water. You can catch a *lancha* from Sontecomapan to anywhere else on the lake. Taxis from Catemaco cost M$50, or a *pirata* M$15. The new **Hotel Imperial** (294-947-42-03; r M$550) in the middle of town offers clean, spacious rooms and rocking chairs on the communal balcony.

Los Amigos (294-943-01-01; www.losamigos.com.mx; dm incl breakfast M$210, cabañas 2 people M$590, 6 people M$1690) is a well-run, peaceful retreat close to where the *laguna* enters the ocean. The fantastic *cabañas* tucked into the verdant hillside have lovely balconies sporting hammocks and spectacular views of the bay. There are nature trails to a beautiful lookout, kayak rentals and a restaurant. The boat ride there from Sontecomapan is about 15 to 30 minutes.

The Coast

The small fishing village of **La Barra**, with its pleasant beaches and seafood restaurants, can be reached by a *lancha* from Sontecomapan (M$450 including a tour of the mangroves on the way), or via a side road going east from La Palma, 8km north of Sontecomapan. Do not miss a lunch of *sierra* fish cooked simply in soy sauce, garlic, salt and butter, and enjoyed on the (usually deserted) sea-facing beach. Try **Estrella del Mar** (mains M$100-160) for a full slap-up meal on the beach.

Northwest of La Barra is the tiny beach town of **Jicacal**. You can access Jicacal from a rough road that forks east from the main road. The family-run restaurant there has delectable, fresh-from-the-line seafood. The dirt road to the left, right before you hit Jicacal, will lead you 10 minutes down a gorgeous wreck of a road to a moldering relic of a hotel. From there, you'll find a path leading to a long set of crumbling stairs going to **Playa Escondida** (Hidden Beach), which earns its name; during the work week in the low season you'll probably have the gorgeous blond sands and turquoise waters to yourself.

Yucatán Peninsula

Includes ➡

Best Places to Eat

- ➡ Kinich (p321)
- ➡ El Camello (p290)
- ➡ Olivia (p270)
- ➡ La Chaya Maya (p308)
- ➡ Eladio's (p320)
- ➡ A lo Natural (p298)

Best Swimming Spots

- ➡ Playa Norte (p268)
- ➡ Banco Chinchorro (p295)
- ➡ Laguna Bacalar (p297)
- ➡ Cenote Xlacah (p319)

Why Go?

With charming colonial cities (both heavily touristed and virtually unheard of), world-famous Maya ruins, thumping nightlife centers, sleepy country villages, talcum-powder beaches facing crystal turquoise waters, and more dive sites than you could ever cram into a single vacation, the Yucatán is one sweet destination.

Despite patches of overzealous development, the natural beauty of the Yucatán abides. The coo of the motmot still reverberates overhead, while below the creepy-crawlies continue to writhe. Further down, subterranean rivers gurgle through massive limestone caverns.

Around here, the past is the present and the present is the past: the two intertwine like brawling brothers. You'll witness it in the towering temples of the Maya, Toltecs and Itzáes, in the cobblestone streets of colonial centers, and in the culture of the Maya themselves, quietly maintaining their traditions as the centuries tick by.

When to Go

Playa del Carmen

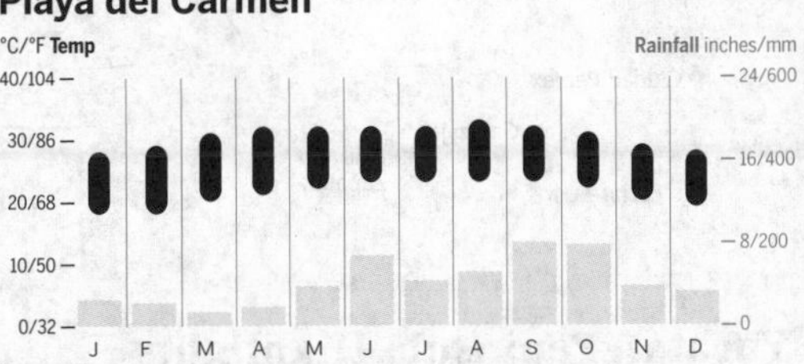

Jun–Aug The summer is hot – the ocean heats up and occasional afternoon rains are very welcome.

Sep & Oct Hurricane season means frequent rain, although temperatures are still warm.

Nov–May It's cooler and rains less. The ocean gets warmer and clearer around February.

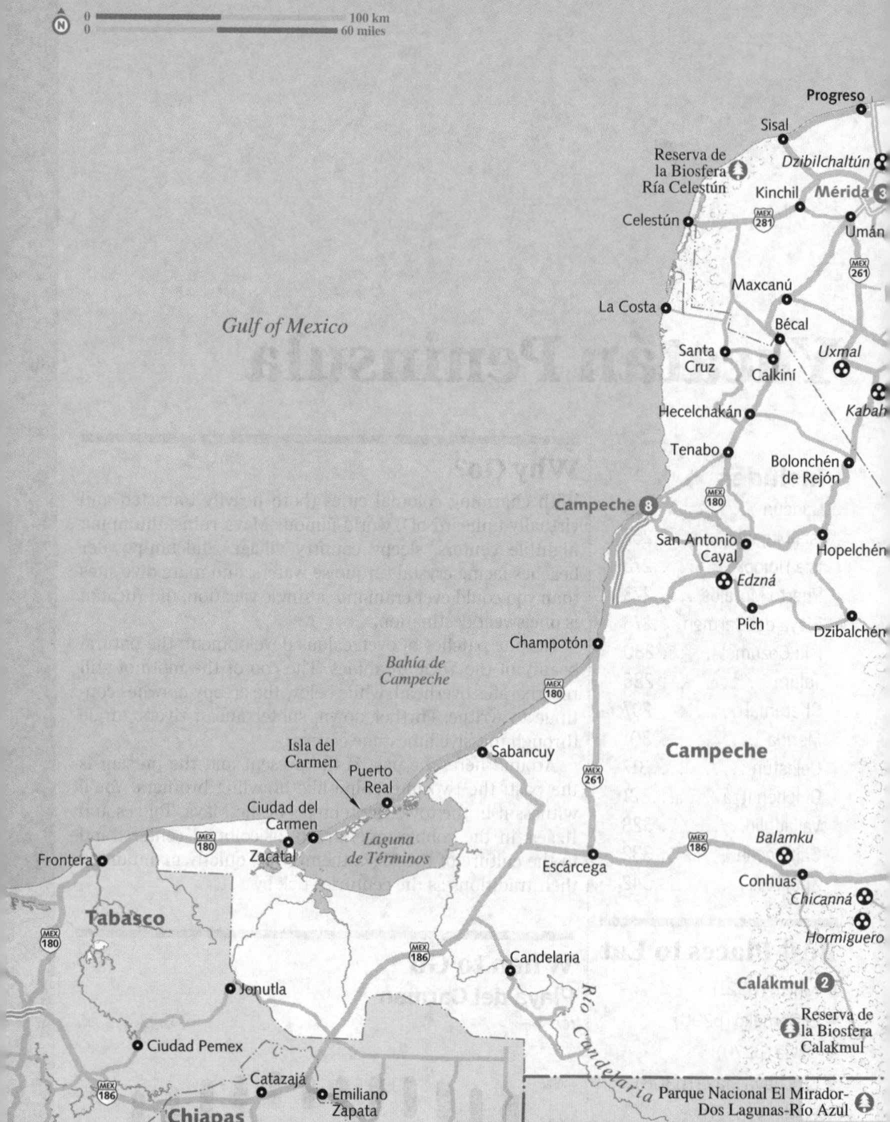

0 100 km
0 60 miles

Progreso
Sisal
Reserva de la Biosfera Ría Celestún
Dzibilchaltún
Kinchil
Mérida
Celestún
MEX 281
Umán
MEX 261
Maxcanú
La Costa
Gulf of Mexico
Bécal
Santa Cruz
Calkiní
Uxmal
Kabah
Hecelchakán
Tenabo
Bolonchén de Rejón
Campeche 8
MEX 180
San Antonio Cayal
Hopelchén
Edzná
Pich
Dzibalchén
Champotón
Bahía de Campeche
MEX 180
Isla del Carmen
Sabancuy
Campeche
MEX 261
Puerto Real
Ciudad del Carmen
MEX 180
MEX 186
Balamku
Frontera
Zacatal
Laguna de Términos
Escárcega
Conhuas
Chicanná
Hormiguero
Tabasco
MEX 180
MEX 186
Candelaria
Calakmul 2
Jonutla
Río Candelaria
Reserva de la Biosfera Calakmul
Ciudad Pemex
Catazajá
MEX 186
Emiliano Zapata
Parque Nacional El Mirador-Dos Lagunas-Río Azul
Chiapas
GUATEMALA

Yucatán Peninsula Highlights

1. Start in **Xcalak** (p296), for a morning of bird-watching, then head out for a dive at **Banco Chinchorro** (p295)
2. Haul yourself up the massive pyramid of **Calakmul** (p341), watching as toucans soar past toward their jungle hideaways
3. Marvel at the colonial architecture or attend a free concert in **Mérida** (p301)
4. Find out why they named **Chichén Itzá** (p321) the 'seventh modern wonder of the world,' or why **Ek' Balam** (p331) should have made the list

5 See two of the Yucatán's top draws in **Tulum** (p286), with Maya ruins overlooking a perfect Caribbean beach

6 Stay out until dawn in one of the beachfront clubs in **Playa del Carmen** (p276), before taking the ferry across to **Isla Cozumel** (p280) the next day to snorkel and swim

7 Get up close and personal with the whale sharks off **Isla Mujeres** (p267)

8 Head away from the crowds to the beautiful colonial cities of **Campeche** (p332) and **Valladolid** (p328)

History

The Maya – accomplished astronomers and mathematicians, and architects of some of the grandest monuments ever known – created their first settlements in what is now Guatemala as early as 2400 BC. Over the centuries, Maya civilization expanded steadily northward, and by AD 550 great Maya city-states were established in southern Yucatán. In the 10th century the great cities of southern Yucatán slowly dissolved, as attention shifted northward to new power centers such as Chichén Itzá.

The last of the great Maya capitals, Mayapán, started to collapse around 1440, when the Xiu Maya and the Cocom Maya began a violent and protracted struggle for power. In 1540, Spanish conquistador Francisco de Montejo the Younger (son of legendary conquistador Francisco de Montejo the Elder) utilized the tensions between the still-feuding Maya sects to conquer the area. The Spaniards allied themselves with the Xiu against the Cocom, finally defeating the Cocom and gaining the Xiu as reluctant converts to Christianity.

Francisco de Montejo the Younger, along with his father and cousin (named…you guessed it, Francisco de Montejo), founded Mérida in 1542 and within four years brought most of the Yucatán Peninsula under Spanish rule. The Spaniards divided the Maya lands into large estates where the natives were put to work as indentured servants.

When Mexico won its independence from Spain in 1821, the new Mexican government used the Yucatecan territory to create huge plantations for the cultivation of tobacco, sugarcane and *henequén* (agave rope fiber). The Maya, though legally free, were enslaved in debt peonage to the rich landowners.

In 1847 the Maya rose up in a massive revolt against the Spanish. This was the beginning of the War of the Castes. Finally, in 1901, after more than 50 years of sporadic, but often intense, violence, a tentative peace was reached. However, it would be another 30 years before the territory of Quintana Roo came under official government control. To this day some Maya do not recognize that sovereignty.

The commercial success of Cancún in the early 1970s led to hundreds of kilometers of beachfront property along the Caribbean coast being sold off to commercial developers, displacing many small fishing communities. While many indigenous people still eke out a living by subsistence agriculture or fishing, large numbers now work in the construction and service industries. Some individuals and communities, often with outside encouragement, are having a go at ecotourism, opening their lands to tourists and/or working as guides.

QUINTANA ROO

You'd think that solitude would be in short supply in Quintana Roo (pronounced 'kin-tah-nah *roh*'), one of Mexico's most visited states. But beyond the open-bar excesses of Cancún and dubiously credentialed 'eco-parks' of the Riviera Maya, you might just find your own quiet slice of paradise.

There are glaring-white beaches stretching all the way from Cancún to the Belizean border, unassuming Caribbean islands protected by the barrier reef, and impressive Maya sites throughout this long-arching sliver of limestone, salt and sea.

The high season for Quintana Roo is basically December to April. Prices (and crowds) peak from mid-December to mid-January, late February to early March (the US spring break) and a week on either side of Easter.

Cancún

☎998 / POP 630,000

Like Las Vegas, Ibiza or Rio de Janeiro, Cancún is a party city that just won't give up. Top that off with a pretty good beach and you have one of Central America's biggest tourist draws, bringing in as many as four million visitors (mostly from the US) each year.

Hurricanes Wilma and Emily whipped into town in 2005, destroying hotels and carrying off tons of Cancún's precious beach sand. The hotels have been rebuilt, and the government has invested nearly US$100 million on beach nourishment – an environmentally questionable practice where sand is dredged from the ocean floor and pumped onto the beachfront.

Sights & Activities

Museo Maya de Cancún MUSEUM
(Maya Museum; Map p260; www.inah.gob.mx; Blvd Kukulcán, Km 17.5; admission incl San Miguelito M$57; ⌚9am-6pm Tue-Sun; 🚌R-1) Housing one of the most important collections of Maya

artifacts in all of Mexico, this modern, new museum is a welcome sight in a city known more for its party scene than cultural attractions. On display are some 350 pieces found at key sites in and around the peninsula, ranging from jewelry to ceramics and sculptures.

The museum is situated at the northern end of the San Miguelito archaeological site, which is believed to have been connected to the El Rey site further south by a series of low buildings that were demolished in the 1970s during the construction of the Zona Hotelera. There are around 40 structures here, including an 8m pyramid, and the lush, jungly grounds make for a pleasant stroll even in the midday heat.

Museo Subacuático de Arte DIVING
(MUSA Underwater Museum; ☎998-848-83-12; www.musacancun.com) Work began on Cancún's underwater art museum in late 2009. The aquatic 'museum' will eventually feature some 400 sculptures by Jason de Caires Taylor submerged at various depths in the shallow waters between here and Isla Mujeres. Tour and dive operators offer diving, snorkeling and submarine tours of the site.

Zona Arqueológica El Rey ARCHAEOLOGICAL SITE
(Map p260; Blvd Kukulcán, Km 17.5; admission M$42; 8am-5pm; R-1) In the Zona Arqueológica El Rey, on the west side of Blvd Kukulcán between Km 17 and Km 18, there's a small temple and several ceremonial platforms. The site gets its name from a sculpture excavated here of a dignitary, possibly a *rey* (king), wearing an elaborate headdress.

Beaches

Under Mexican law, you have the right to walk and swim on every beach in the country, except those within military compounds. In practice, it is difficult to approach many stretches of beach without walking through the lobby of a hotel, particularly in the Zona Hotelera. However, unless you look suspicious or like a local (hotels tend to discriminate against locals, particularly the Maya), you'll usually be able to cross the lobby without problems and proceed to the beach.

Starting from Ciudad Cancún in the northwest, all of the Zona Hotelera's beaches are on the left-hand side of Blvd Kukulcán (the lagoon is on your right). The following are listed north to south, with their respective Km markers on Blvd Kukulcán:

Playa Las Perlas BEACH
(Map p260; Km 2.5) A small beach with a great kids' playground, bathrooms and free palm-thatch-covered tables. Free parking. Access from north side of the Holiday Inn.

Playa Langosta BEACH
(Map p260; Km 5) In the middle of the north end of Zona Hotelera, Playa Langosta is a gem of a place for swimming. Facing Bahía de Mujeres, the beach is coated with Cancún's signature powdered coral sand and the waters are quite shallow, making it good for snorkeling. If you've had enough of the water there are lots of beach restaurants and bars.

Playa Pez Volador BEACH
(Map p260; Km 5.5) Popular with families for its calm, shallow foreshore. There's free parking (but tip the guys 'minding' your car). Access is from the huge flagpole flying the Mexican flag.

Playa Tortugas BEACH
(Map p260; Km 6.3) One of the busiest beaches around, with loud music, cheap restaurants, deck chair and umbrella hire and a bungee jump (US$35). Access from the ferry terminal, where there is free parking, if you can find a spot.

Playa Caracol BEACH
(Map p260; Km 8.7) Next to the Isla Mujeres ferry dock, this tiny stretch of sand is probably the least inviting, but you can head left when you hit the water to get to the lovely beach 'belonging' to the Hotel Riu. No parking.

Playa Gaviota Azul BEACH
(Map p260; Km 8.8) A beautiful little curve at the end of the bay, mostly monopolized by beach clubs. Access is from the north side of Cocobongo's where there is extremely limited free parking.

Playa Chac-Mool BEACH
(Map p260; Km 9.5) With no parking, this is one of the quieter beaches. Lifeguard on duty and parasailing available. No food but there are stores and restaurants near the access, opposite the Señor Frogs bar.

Playa Marlin BEACH
(Map p260; Km 12.5) A long, lovely stretch of sand with lifeguards on duty and deck chairs, umbrellas and tables for rent. There's no food, but there is an Oxxo convenience

Cancún

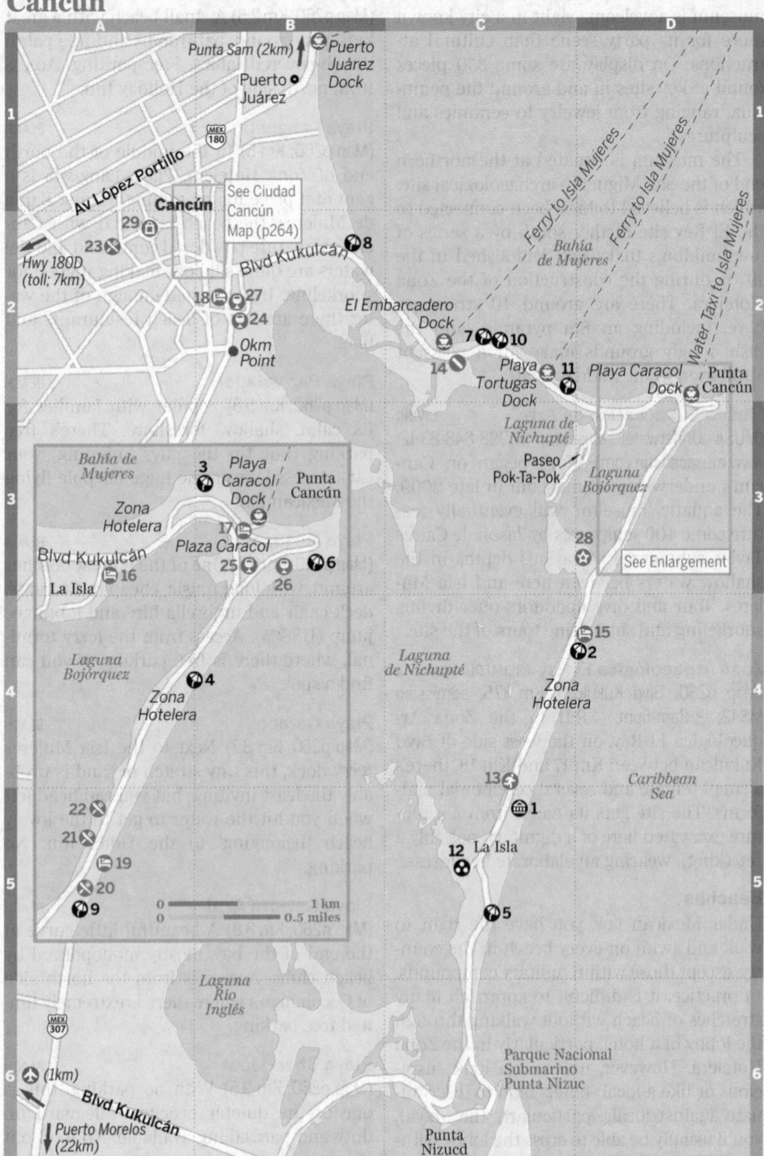

store nearby on Blvd Kukulcán, north of the beach access at Kukulcán Plaza.

Playa Ballenas BEACH

(Map p260; Km 14.2) A long, quiet stretch of beach squeezed between luxury hotels. Wave runners (M$70, 30 minutes), bodyboards and parasailing (M$700, 12 minutes) available. Free parking. Access from the dirt road on the south side of Golden Parnassus hotel.

Cancún

Playa Delfines BEACH
(Map p260; Km 17.5) Delfines is about the only beach with a public car park; unfortunately, its sand is coarser and darker than the exquisite fine sand of the more northerly beaches. On the upside, the beach has great views, there are some nearby Maya ruins to check out and, as the last beach along the boulevard, it is rarely crowded.

Water Sports

Specialized operators and hotels offer nearly every water-based activity you could imagine, including PADI open-water certification (M$5521), parasailing (M$656), snorkeling trips (M$512), submarine tours (M$532), speedboat tours (M$864), swimming with dolphins (from M$1310) and wave runner hire (M$1178 per hour).

Aqua World WATER SPORTS
(Map p260; ☎998-848-83-00; www.aquaworld.com.mx; Blvd Kukulcán, Km 15.2) Aqua World has a little bit of everything to keep kids entertained for hours on end. It offers bodyboard rentals, submarine and boat tours and many other fun-filled water activities.

Scuba Cancún DIVING
(Map p260; ☎998-849-75-08; www.scubacancun.com.mx; Blvd Kukulcán, Km 5.2; 1-/2-tank dives M$656/788, equipment rental extra) A family-owned and PADI-certified dive operation with many years of experience, Scuba Cancún was the first dive shop in Cancún. It offers a variety of snorkeling, fishing and diving options (including cenote and night dives). It also does snorkeling and diving trips to the underwater sculpture museum, aka MUSA.

Koko Dog'z WATER SPORTS
(Map p264; ☎998-887-36-35; www.kokodogz.com; Av Náder 42-1; ⏲noon-8pm Mon-Fri, to 6pm Sat; 🚌R-1) Sells all sorts of boards – surf, kite, boogie, skim, skate and paddle.

Tours

Most hotels and travel agencies work with companies that offer tours to surrounding attractions.

Turimex BOAT, ARCHAEOLOGICAL TOURS
(Map p264; ☎998-887-40-90; www.turimexcun.com; Av Cobá 5) Offers a variety of reasonably priced packages to popular destinations such as Tulum, Chichén Itzá and the Riviera Maya fun parks. Options include boat and archaeology tours, ecotours and water sports.

Sleeping

Cancún is actually made up of two very distinct areas: the downtown area, Ciudad Cancún, which is on the mainland, and Isla Cancún, a sandy spit of an island, which is usually referred to as the Zona Hotelera (Hotel Zone).

Downtown

The downtown area has numerous hostels, budget digs (mostly around Parque Las Palapas) and some charming small hotels. The main north–south thoroughfare is Avenida Tulum, a 1km-long tree-shaded boulevard lined with banks, shopping centers and restaurants. Though the hotels here aren't near the water, the beach is just a taxi or bus ride away.

Hostel Ka'beh HOSTEL $

(Map p264; ☎998-892-79-02; www.cancunhostel.hostel.com; Alcatraces 45; dm incl breakfast from M$190, r M$550; ; R-1) A very well set-up little hostel, with good indoor and outdoor hangout areas, an ample kitchen, reasonably spacious dorms and probably the fanciest hostel bathroom you're ever likely to see.

★ **Hotel El Rey del Caribe** HOTEL $$

(Map p264; ☎998-884-20-28; www.elreydelcaribe.com; cnr Avs Uxmal & Náder; s/d M$852/983; ; R-1) El Rey is a true eco-hotel that recycles, employs solar collectors and cisterns, uses gray water on the gardens, and has some rooms with composting toilets. This is a beautiful spot with a swimming pool and Jacuzzi in a jungly courtyard that's home to a small family of *tlacuaches* (opossums). All rooms have fully equipped kitchenettes, comfortable beds and fridges.

Hotel Bonampak HOTEL $$

(Map p260; ☎998-884-02-80; www.hotelbonampak.com; Av Bonampak 225 ; r M$850; P; R-27) Good value by Cancún standards, rooms at this business-style hotel boast comfy new mattresses, dark wood furnishings and LCD TVs. Ask for a room overlooking the sunny pool area.

Colonial Cancún HOTEL $$

(Map p264; ☎998-884-15-35; www.economyclasshotels.com; Tulipanes 22; d incl breakfast M$850; ; R-1) Rooms are anything but colonial – still they're pleasant enough and they overlook a leafy central courtyard with a tinkling fountain. Get a room toward the back to distance yourself from the street noise in this party zone.

Hotel Plaza Caribe HOTEL $$

(Map p264; ☎998-884-13-77; www.hotelplazacaribe.com; Pino; r/ste M$1000/1400; P; R-1) Directly across from the bus terminal between Avenidas Tulum and Uxmal, this business-class hotel offers 140 comfortable rooms with full amenities, including a pool, a restaurant and gardens with peacocks roaming about. Rooms have white-tile floors, good beds and clean bathrooms.

Zona Hotelera

Blvd Kukulcán, a four-lane divided avenue, leaves Ciudad Cancún and goes eastward out onto the narrow island almost universally referred to as the Zona Hotelera, home to many restaurants, bars and hotels. Big chain hotels dominate the strip, but there are a few boutique gems.

Hotels here rarely have numbered addresses. Instead, because the vast majority are on Blvd Kukulcán, their location is described in relation to the 0km marker at the north end of Blvd Kukulcán.

Hostal Mayapan HOSTEL $

(Map p260; ☎998-883-32-27; www.hostalmayapan.com; Blvd Kukulcán, Km 8.5; dm incl breakfast from M$260, r from M$390; ; R-1) Located in an abandoned mall, this is the only budget spot in the Zona Hotelera. Thanks to its location just 30m from the beach, it's one of our favorite hostels in town. The rooms are super-clean and there's a little hangout spot in an atrium (the old food court?).

Grand Royal Lagoon HOTEL $$

(Map p260; ☎998-883-12-70; www.grandroyallagoon.jimdo.com; Quetzal 8A; r/ste M$1000/1100; P; R-1) A breezy place and relatively affordable for the hotel zone, the Grand Royal offers cable TV, safes and a small pool. Most rooms have two double beds, while some have kings, lagoon views and balconies. The hotel is 100m off Blvd Kukulcán near Km 7.7.

Casa Turquesa BOUTIQUE HOTEL $$$

(Map p260; ☎cell phone 998-1932260; www.casaturquesa.com; Blvd Kukulcán, Km 13.5; r M$2867-33,387; ; R-1) With over 600

NAVIGATING CANCÚN

Addresses on Blvd Kukulcán, the road that runs southeast from Ciudad Cancún through the Zona Hotelera, are given in kilometers, measured from the boulevard's northern terminus. This point is identified by a roadside 'Km 0' marker and each subsequent kilometer is similarly marked.

works of art distributed through the lobbies, hallways and 35 rooms here, this place is more art gallery than hotel. And there's even more art in the attached gallery. All the luxe amenities are here, including an infinity pool overlooking the ocean, a tennis court, a gourmet restaurant, a hushed, intimate atmosphere and quietly luxurious rooms.

Me by Melia LUXURY HOTEL **$$$**
(Map p260; ☎998-881-25-00; www.mebymelia.com; Blvd Kukulcán, Km 12; s/d all-inclusive M$4500/6800; P ⊖ ❄ @ ☎ ≋; 🚌R-1) Distancing itself as much as possible from Cancún's workaday package tour scene, the Me is all about sleek modern lines and contemporary art, with a good dash of attitude thrown in. All rooms have 'essential luxuries' such as rain showers, designer furniture, huge beds and massive TVs. The rooms with ocean views are a pretty good deal for the price – those without, less so.

Eating

Many people eat at their hotels, but Mercados 23 and 28 have a number of tiny eateries, and Parque Las Palapas has food stalls. Most of the best budget restaurants are found in the downtown area.

For groceries, try **Comercial Mexicana** (Map p264; cnr Avs Tulum & Uxmal; ⏲7am-11pm), a central supermarket close to the bus station.

Tacos Rigo TAQUERÍA **$**
(Map p260; Av Playa 50; tacos from M$15; ⏲11am-11:30pm) There's a taco joint on nearly every block in Cancún, but locals drive all the way across town to come to this one. One bite and you'll understand why.

Fish Fritanga SEAFOOD **$$**
(Map p260; Blvd Kukulcán, Km 12.5; mains M$120-300; ⏲11am-11pm; ☎; 🚌R-1) With plastic tables set under little *palapa* (palm-thatch) huts on a sandy floor, this is one of the Zona Hotelera's back-to-basics places. Good-value seafood, killer 1L mojitos, and a great place for sunset drinks overlooking the lagoon. If you need to go even further back to basics, it runs a cut-price taco stand out front.

Pescaditos SEAFOOD **$$**
(Map p264; Av Yaxchilán 69; snacks M$40, mains M$80-250; ⏲11:30am-midnight; ☎) The namesake *pescaditos* (fried fish sticks served with a mayo-chipotle sauce) are the star attraction here, but the other fresh fish and seafood dishes are well worth trying.

Perico's MEXICAN **$$$**
(Map p264; Av Yaxchilán 61; mains M$100-250; ⏲noon-1am; ☎) With a lively atmosphere and an attentive staff, Perico's, probably one of the city's longest-running restaurants, sticks to the family recipes, putting out some of the tastiest seafood, steak and Yucatecan food in town. Dinner is accompanied by a show – live marimba, comedy skits and the occasional conga line. Lunch service is much mellower – plan accordingly.

La Destilería MEXICAN **$$$**
(Map p260; Blvd Kukulcán, Km 12.75; mains M$180-250; ⏲1pm-midnight; ☎; 🚌R-1) Serious Mexican food can be hard to come by in the Zona Hotelera, but this place gets the thumbs-up from locals and visitors alike. It's all good, but the chicken dishes – with goat cheese sauce, or *mole poblano* (in a sauce of chilies, fruits, nuts, spices and chocolate) – are the standouts.

La Habichuela Sunset FUSION **$$$**
(Map p260; ☎998-840-62-80; Blvd Kukulcán, Km 12.6; mains M$250-400; ⏲noon-midnight; ☎; 🚌R-1) Putting a Caribbean twist on Mexican classics with some Italian thrown in may sound like a recipe for disaster, but this regularly recommended restaurant does it in style. Floor-to-ceiling windows with lagoon views and some great Maya artwork and decorations seal the deal.

Lorenzillo's SEAFOOD **$$$**
(Map p260; ☎998-883-12-54; www.lorenzillos.com.mx; Blvd Kukulcán, Km 10.5; mains M$295-460, lobster M$620-780; ⏲1pm-12:30am; P ❄ ☎; 🚌R-1) Reputed by locals to be Cancún's best seafood restaurant, Lorenzillo's gives you 20 separate choices for your lobster supper, including a taste bud–popping chipotle, plum and tamarind sauce. Facing the lagoon, it's a wonderful sunset joint.

Drinking & Nightlife

For a very local night out in the downtown area, check out the bars around the base of the **Plaza de Toros** (Map p260; Bullring, cnr Avs Bonampak & Sayil). Names and tastes change quickly here; go for a wander and see where the action is. Don't worry about eating first – the all-night *taquerías* (taco stalls) here are some of the best in town.

The Zona Hotelera's dance clubs are clustered around Km 9, just south of Punta Cancún. There's not a whole lot to tell them apart – grinding dance music, shouting DJs,

Ciudad Cancún

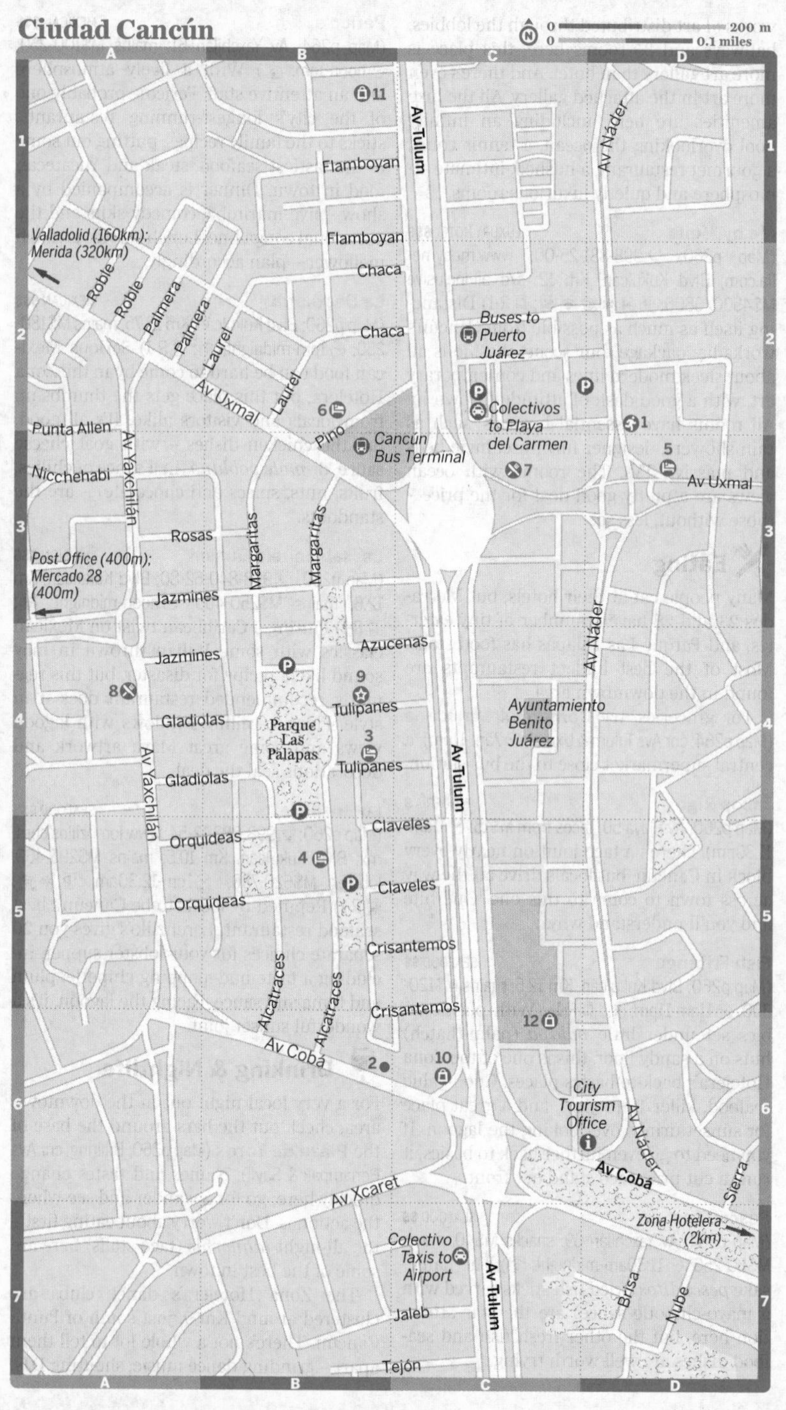

YUCATÁN PENINSULA CANCÚN

Ciudad Cancún

Activities, Courses & Tours
1 Koko Dog'z D2
2 Turimex B6

Sleeping
3 Colonial Cancún B4
4 Hostel Ka'beh B5
5 Hotel El Rey del Caribe D3
6 Hotel Plaza Caribe B2

Eating
7 Comercial Mexicana C3
Perico's .... (see 8)
8 Pescaditos A4

Entertainment
9 Roots B4

Shopping
10 Chedraui Supermarket C6
11 Mercado 23 .... B1
12 Mercado Municipal Ki-Huic C6

people doing things they probably won't be telling their mother about. The cover charge is around M$180, or you can opt for an all-you-can-drink bracelet which may cost as much as M$780. Most people get the bracelet. Some of these places don't open before 10pm, and most don't close until dawn.

La Chopería BAR
(Map p260; Bullring, cnr Avs Bonampak & Sayil; ⏲4pm-3am) This rough and ready bar at Plaza de Toros draws a crowd, as much for the icy air-con as the draft beer.

Black Pub PUB
(Map p260; cnr Avs Bonampak & Sayil; ⏲1pm-4am Mon-Sat) If Plaza de Toros is a bit raw for you, head across Av Sayil to the Malecón Las Américas. The Black Pub has live music Wednesdays and Saturdays and there are some other stylish little bars up on the roof terrace.

Dady'O CLUB
(Map p260; ☎998-883-33-33; Blvd Kukulcán, Km 9.5; ⏲10pm-4am; 🚌R-1) One of Cancún's classic dance clubs. The setting is a five-level, black-walled faux cave with a two-level dance floor and what seems like zillions of laser beams and strobes. The predominant beats are Latin, house, techno and pop, and the crowd is mainly 20-something.

Mandala DANCING
(Map p260; ☎998-848-83-80; Blvd Kukulcán, Km 9; ⏲10pm-4:30am; 🚌R-1) At least tries to be a little upscale, with vaguely interesting decor and not-too-mainstream music.

☆ Entertainment

Cinemark CINEMA
(Map p260; ☎998-883-56-04; www.cinemark.com.mx; La Isla Shopping Village, Blvd Kukulcán, Km 12.5; tickets from M$90; 🚌R-1) Hollywood movies in English with Spanish subtitles.

Roots JAZZ
(Map p264; ☎998-884-24-37; www.rootsjazzclub.com; Tulipanes 26; cover M$60; ⏲7pm-2am Thu-Sat; 🚌R-1) Pretty much the coolest nightspot in Ciudad Cancún, Roots features mostly jazz bands and the occasional international act. It's also a pretty decent restaurant, serving pasta, salads, seafood and meat dishes, with main dishes running from M$120 to M$190.

Shopping

Locals head to either **Mercado 28** (Mercado Veintiocho; Map p260; cnr Xel-Há & Sunyaxchén; ⏲6am-7pm) or **Mercado 23** (Map p264; Av Tulum s/n; ⏲6am-7pm; 🚌R-1) for clothes, shoes, inexpensive food stalls, hardware items and so on. Of the two, Mercado 23 is the least frequented by tourists. If you're looking for a place *without* corny T-shirts, this is where to go.

Mercado Municipal Ki-Huic MARKET
(Map p264; Av Tulum; ⏲6am-10pm; 🚌R-1) This warren of stalls and shops carries a wide variety of souvenirs and handicrafts.

Chedraui Supermarket DEPARTMENT STORE
(Map p264; cnr Avs Tulum & Cobá; ⏲7am-11pm) The upstairs clothing department here sometimes has souvenir-grade items at very affordable prices.

ℹ Information

EMERGENCY

Cruz Roja (Red Cross; ☎998-884-16-16) Ambulance service.
Fire (☎998-884-12-02)
Police (☎998-884-19-13; Blvd Kukulcán, Km 13.5; 🚌R-1)
Tourist Police (☎998-885-22-77)

IMMIGRATION

Instituto Nacional de Migración (INM, National Migration Institute; ☎998-881-35-60; www.inm.gob.mx; cnr Avs Náder & Uxmal; ⏲9am-1pm Mon-Fri)

MEDICAL SERVICES

Hospital Americano (☎998-884-61-33; Viento 15) This medical center, off Av Tulum, offers 24-hour emergency service and has English-speaking staff. Handy to know, if things don't go according to plan.

MONEY

There are several banks with ATMs on Avenida Tulum, between Avenidas Cobá and Uxmal.

POST

Main Post Office (cnr Avs Xel-Há & Sunyaxchén; ⏲8am-4pm Mon-Fri, 9am-12:30pm Sat) Downtown at the edge of Mercado 28. You can also post mail in the red postal boxes sprinkled around town.

TELEPHONE

Phoning by Voice Over Internet Protocol (VOIP), such as Skype, can be done at most internet cafes.

Call Center (Av Cobá 5) At Soberanis Hostal. Offers good rates on international calls and calls to other parts of Mexico.

TOURIST INFORMATION

Cancún Visitors Bureau (www.cancun.travel) An informative website, but no tourist office.

City Tourism Office (Map p264; ☎998-887-33-79; www.cancun.gob.mx; cnr Avs Cobá & Náder; ⏲8am-4pm Mon-Fri, 9am-12:30pm Sat) The only city tourist office in town; has ample supplies of printed material.

Getting There & Away

AIR

About 8km south of the city center, **Aeropuerto Internacional de Cancún** (☎998-848-72-00; www.asur.com.mx; Carretera Cancún-Chetumal, Km 22) is the busiest airport in southeast Mexico.

Cancún is served by many direct international flights and by connecting flights from Mexico City; the airport website has a list of airlines. Low-cost carriers **Viva Aerobus** (☎Mexico City 55-4777-5050, US 888-935-9848; www.vivaaerobus.com), **Interjet** (☎800-011-23-45; www.interjet.com) and **Volaris** (☎800-122-80-00; www.volaris.com) all have services from Mexico City. **MayAir** (www.mayair.com.mx) flies to Isla Cozumel.

BOAT

Ferries from Cancún to Isla Mujeres leave from several docks around Cancún (p271).

BUS & TAXI

Public and luxury buses leave from the **bus terminal** (Map p264; cnr Avs Uxmal & Tulum) in Ciudad Cancún. *Colectivos* (set-route minibuses) for Playa del Carmen (M$34) leave every half hour (or when full) from the parking lot north of Comercial Mexicana, across Avenida Tulum from the bus terminal.

BUSES FROM CANCÚN

DESTINATION	FARE (M$)	DURATION	FREQUENCY (DAILY)
Chetumal	205-305	5½-6½hr	frequent
Chichén Itzá	122	3-4hr	hourly 7am-1pm
Chiquilá (for Isla Holbox)	95	3½-4hr	6 buses
Felipe Carrillo Puerto	140-190	3½-4hr	frequent
Mérida	88-354	4-6hr	15 ADO, hourly Oriente
Mexico City (Terminal Norte)	1536-1788	24hr	3 buses
Mexico City (TAPO)	1518-1788	22-24hr	2 buses
Palenque	490-816	12-13hr	4 buses
Playa del Carmen	32-48	1-1¼hr	every 15min
Puerto Morelos	22-26	40min	use Playa del Carmen buses
Ticul	237-324	6hr	11 buses
Tizimín	92	3-4hr	5 Noreste & Mayab
Tulum	80-104	2¼-3hr	frequent ADO & Mayab
Valladolid	95-150	2-3hr	frequent
Villahermosa	748-1260	12hr	frequent

Boletotal (www.boletotal.mx) is an excellent online source of up-to-date bus schedules.

CAR

Rental-car agencies **Avis** (☎800-288-88-88, 998-176-80-39; www.avis.com.mx; Blvd Kukulkán Km 12.5, Centro Comercial La Isla) and **Hertz** (☎800-709-50-00; www.hertz.com) have facilities at the airport and La Isla Shopping Village in the Zona Hotelera. It's worth inquiring about promotions and added costs – the daily rate can vary by as much as M$400 between companies. Hwy 180D, the 238km toll road *(cuota)* running much of the way between Cancún and Mérida, costs M$398 for the distance and has only two exits before the end. The first, at Valladolid, costs M$251 to reach from Cancún, and the second, at Pisté (for Chichén Itzá), is an additional M$61.

Getting Around

TO/FROM THE AIRPORT

ADO buses (M$52 to downtown, M$124 to Playa del Carmen) and airport shuttles (M$150 per person to downtown) wait outside the departures area of Terminals 2 and 3.

Taxis into town or to the Zona Hotelera will cost around M$600 (up to four people) if you catch them right outside the airport. If you follow the access road out of the airport, however, and past the traffic-monitoring booth (a total trip of about 300m), you can often flag down an empty taxi that is leaving the airport and it will take you into town for much less (you can try for M$200).

Colectivos head to the airport from a stand in front of the Hotel Cancún Handall on Avenida Tulum about a block south of Avenida Cobá. They charge M$30 per person and leave when full. The official rate for private taxis is M$185.

BUS

To reach the Zona Hotelera from downtown, catch any bus with 'R1,' 'Hoteles' or 'Zona Hotelera' displayed on the windshield. These buses travel along Avenida Tulum toward Avenida Cobá, then eastward on Avenida Cobá. The one-way fare is M$8.50, but since change is often unavailable this varies between M$8 and M$9.

To reach Puerto Juárez and the Isla Mujeres ferries, catch a Ruta 13 ('Pto Juárez' or 'Punta Sam'; M$8.50) bus heading north on Avenida Tulum. Some R1 buses make this trip as well.

TAXI

Cancún's taxis don't have meters. Fares are set for given journeys, but always agree on a price before getting in. From downtown, you'll pay around M$150 to Punta Cancún, and M$80 to Puerto Juárez. Hourly and daily rates should run to about M$240 and M$2400 respectively.

COSTA VS RIVIERA

Traveling through the coastal region of Quintana Roo you're likely to see two phrases bandied about by the tourist industry – the Costa Maya and the Riviera Maya. While they're occasionally used interchangeably, they are in fact two distinct regions. The Costa Maya is about 100km of beachfront stretching from Xcalak in the south to Reserva de la Biosfera Sian Ka'an in the north. The Riviera Maya begins at the northern boundary of the Costa Maya and stretches north to Cancún (or further, depending on which real estate brochure you're reading).

Isla Mujeres

☎998 / POP 16,000

If you are going to visit just one of Quintana Roo's islands, then Isla Mujeres (Island of Women) is the place for you. It's not as crowded as Cozumel, yet offers more to do and see than uber laid-back Holbox. Sure, there are quite a few tacky tourist shops, but folks still get around by golf cart and the crushed-coral beaches are better than those of Cozumel or Holbox. There's not much here, but that's the whole point: come to bask in the shallows or stretch out on the sand, to snorkel or scuba dive, or just to chill.

Sights & Activities

Museo Capitán Dulché MUSEUM

(www.capitandulche.com; Carretera a Garrafón, Km 4.5; admission M$65; 10am-6pm) And you thought Isla Mujeres had no culture! Here you get not only a maritime museum detailing the island's naval history but also a sculpture garden dotted with dozens of grinding stones. Also here is one of the best beach clubs – and we're not just saying that because of the cool boat bar.

Other facilities include a decent little restaurant (mains M$140 to M$200), plus scuba, snorkeling and massage.

Isla Mujeres Turtle Farm FARM

(Isla Mujeres Tortugranja; ☎998-888-07-05; Carretera Sac Bajo, Km 5; admission M$30; 9am-5pm) In the 1980s, efforts by a local fisherman led to the founding of the Isla

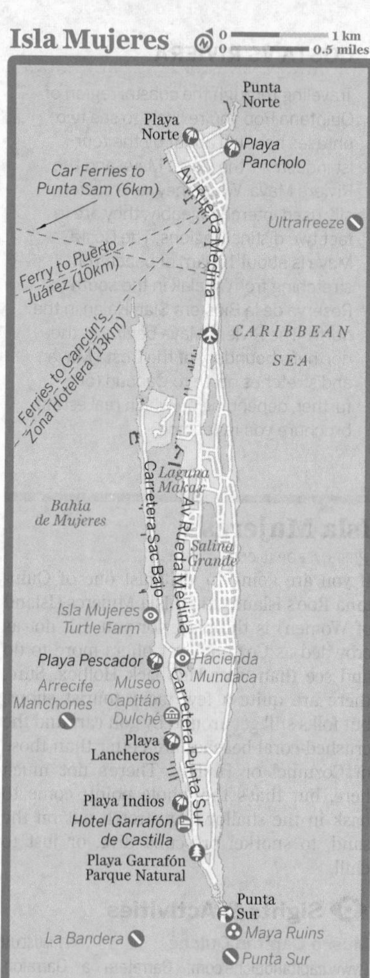

Mujeres *tortugranja* (turtle farm), 5km south of town, which protects the turtles' breeding grounds. During the nesting season, you can see turtle hatchlings at various stages of development, and other examples of local marine life.

Beaches

Playa Norte BEACH

(Map p270) FREE Once you reach Playa Norte, the island's main beach, you won't want to leave. Its warm shallow waters are the color of blue-raspberry syrup and the beach is crushed coral. Unlike the exposed beaches on the east coast, Playa Norte is safe and the water is only ever chest-deep.

Playa Garrafón Reef Park BEACH, PARK

(☎cell phone 998-1933360; www.garrafon.com; Camino Sac Bajo Km 6; admission M$745; ⏰10am-5pm) In the south of the island is Playa Garrafón Reef Park, where the steep admission fee gets you snorkeling, a beach, a buffet, an open bar, and the use of kayaks. The star attraction – an over-the-water zip-line – costs an additional M$250 a pop. There's more sand 1.5km north at Playa Lancheros.

Punta Sur LOOKOUT, GARDENS

(ruins admission M$30) At the southern point you'll find a lighthouse, sculpture garden and the worn remains of a temple dedicated to Ixchel, Maya goddess of the moon and fertility. Various hurricanes have pummeled the ruins over time and there's now little to see other than the sculpture garden, the sea and Cancún in the distance. Taxis from town cost about M$88.

Diving, Snorkeling & Bird-Watching

Within a short boat ride of the island are a handful of lovely dives, such as **Barracuda**, **La Bandera**, **El Jigueo**, **Ultrafreeze** and **Arrecife Manchones**. You can expect to see sea turtles, rays and barracuda, along with a wide array of hard and soft corals. At all of the reputable dive centers you need to show your certification card.

Snorkeling with whale sharks (around M$1620) just off Isla Contoy is the latest craze. The season runs from July through September. Folks at local dive shops can arrange your trip. To protect and preserve the reefs, an M$38 fee is charged for all diving and swimming. Also popular are bird-watching tours of Isla Contoy (p272).

Fisherman's Cooperative Booth TOUR

(Map p270; ☎998-134-61-03; Av Rueda Medina, cnr Madero; snorkeling incl lunch M$285-430, Contoy island tours M$900; ⏰8am-8pm) This local cooperative offers snorkeling tours of various sites including the reef off Playa Garrafón, whale-shark tours and day trips to Isla Contoy. Book through the small office at the entrance to the dock.

Aqua Adventures DIVING

(Map p270; ☎998-236-43-16; www.diveislamujeres.com; Juárez, cnr Morelos; 2-tank dives M$882-1025, whale-shark tour M$1620; ⏰9am-

7pm) Great option for snorkeling with whale sharks and reef dives.

Sea Hawk Divers DIVING
(Map p270; ☎998-877-12-33; seahawkdivers@hotmail.com; Carlos Lazo; 1-/2-tank dives M$908/1100, resort course M$1230, PADI M$4540 ;) Offers resort courses and PADI Open Water certification and has some very comfortable rooms (single M$400, double M$600).

Sleeping

★Poc-Na Hostel HOSTEL $
(Map p270; ☎998-877-00-90; www.pocna.com; Matamoros 15; dm M$115-175, r M$300/400;) This hostel is only moments away from lovely Playa Pancholo and is tastefully decorated with shells and hibiscus flowers. The *palapa*-roofed common area has picnic benches, hammocks and good tunes for chilling out. The property extends through 100m of sand and coconut palms to the edge of the Caribbean. You'll never be bored with all the activities offered here.

Apartments Trinchan GUESTHOUSE, APARTMENT $
(Map p270; ☎cell phone 998-1666967; atrinchan@prodigy.net.mx; Carlos Lazo 46; r with fan/air-con M$350/400, apt M$450-500;) Since it has no website, you'll have to take our word for it when we say this is one of the best budget deals in town – and the beach is right around the corner. If available, opt for one of the spacious apartments.

Cabañas María del Mar HOTEL $$
(Map p270; ☎998-877-01-79; www.cabanasdelmar.com; Carlos Lazo 1; r M$750-950;) One of the better deals in this price range. Rooms are nothing special, but the jungly grounds, good-sized pool and killer location (just steps away from Playa Norte) make it great.

Hotel Belmar HOTEL $$
(Map p270; ☎998-877-04-30; www.hotelbelmarisla.com; Hidalgo 110; s/d M$576/800;) Above Rolandi's pizzeria and run by the same friendly family. All rooms are comfy and well kept, with tiled floors, and some have balconies. Prices vary with the season.

Hotel Sueño Maya HOTEL $$
(Map p270; ☎998-877-16-95; www.hotelsuenomaya.com; Av Madero; r without/with kitchenette M$500/600;) Large, modern rooms a few steps from the beach. Windows all face internal corridors, making it a bit stuffy, but a good deal otherwise.

Hotel Na Balam HOTEL $$$
(Map p270; ☎998-881-47-70; www.nabalam.com; Calle Zazil-Ha 118; r/ste incl breakfast M$1978/3124;) Butterflies flit around the beautiful hibiscus and palm garden, and many rooms face Playa Norte. All rooms are decorated with simple elegance and have safes, hammocks, private balconies or patios...and no TVs. The hotel offers yoga and meditation classes as well as massage services, and has a pool and restaurant.

Hotel Playa la Media Luna HOTEL $$$
(Map p270; ☎998-887-07-59; www.playamedialuna.com; Sección Rocas, Lotes 9 & 10, Punta Norte; r from M$1250;) This big beachfront hotel maintains an intimate feel through clever design, driftwood decorations and wooden walkways connecting the rooms. Standard rooms are fine – upgrade to the presidential for ocean views from the Jacuzzi on your balcony.

Eating

For cheap eats, check the **Mercado Municipal** (Map p270; Guerrero; mains M$35-80; ⏲6am-4pm) during the day and the food stalls on the plaza outside the Iglesia de la Inmaculada Concepción at night.

PASSENGER FERRIES FROM CANCÚN TO ISLA MUJERES

DEPARTS FROM	FARE (M$)	DURATION	DAILY
El Embarcadero	145	25min	6 between 9am and 4:30pm
Zona Hotelera dock	145	25min	4 between 10:10am and 4:50pm
Playa Tortugas	145	25min	hourly 9am-5pm
Puerto Juárez	70	25min	every 30min 5am-8:30pm, then hourly until 11:30pm

Isla Mujeres (Town)

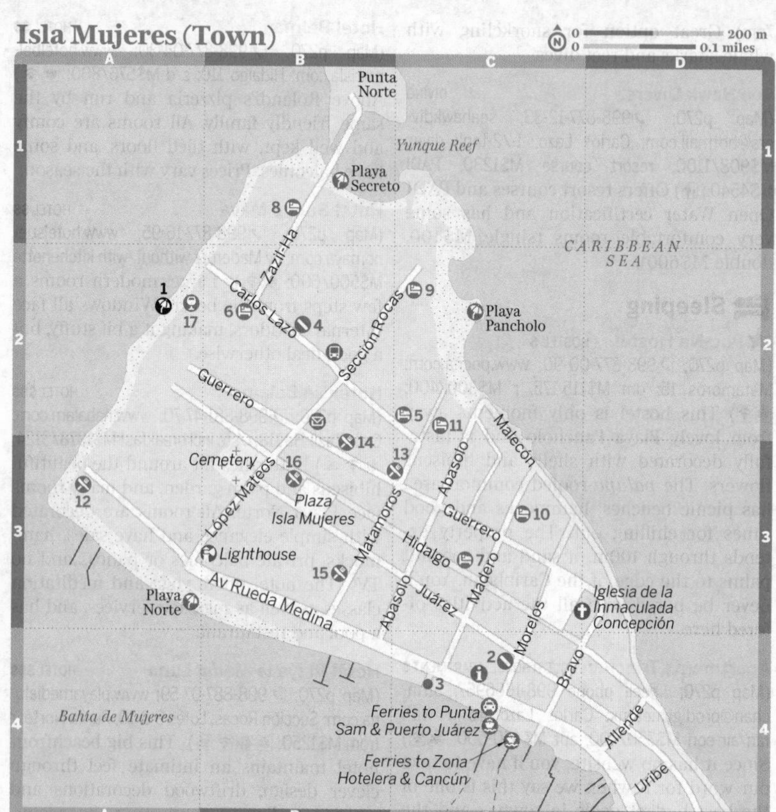

★ **Mañana** CAFE $

(Map p270; ☎998-877-05-55; cnr Matamoros & Guerrero; dishes M$45-90; ⏰8am-4pm; 📶🌱) A good-vibe place with colorful hand-painted tables, super-friendly service and some excellent veggie options. The hummus-and-veggie baguette is the restaurant's signature dish. Mañana is perhaps the best lunch spot on the island and it also has coffee, *licuados* (blends of fruit or juice with water or milk, and sugar) and some Middle Eastern dishes. There's a book exchange, too.

Rooster CAFE $

(Map p270; Hidalgo s/n; breakfasts M$50-80; ⏰7am-3pm; ❄📶) The undeniable king of the breakfast providers on the island, this cute little cafe has a couple of tables out front and blasting air-con inside. The menu covers the classics and throws in a couple of inventive twists, all served up with excellent coffee and attentive service.

★ **Olivia** MEDITERRANEAN $$

(Map p270; ☎998-877-17-65; www.olivia-islamujeres.com; Matamoros; mains M$88-180; ⏰5-9:30pm Tue-Sat) This delightful, Israeli-run restaurant makes everything from scratch, from Moroccan-style fish (served on a bed of couscous) to chicken shawarmas rolled in fresh-baked pita bread. Arrive early if you want a candlelit table out back in the garden.

Café del Mar INTERNATIONAL $$$

(Map p270; Av Rueda Medina; mains M$150-300; ⏰10am-midnight) The loungiest and beach-clubbiest place on the island also has some of the best food, with a small but inventive fusion menu focusing on salads, seafood and pastas. The deck chairs and beach beds are a great place to finish off that daiquiri (and maybe order another).

Isla Mujeres (Town)

Sights
1 Playa Norte A2

Activities, Courses & Tours
2 Aqua Adventures C4
3 Fisherman's Cooperative Booth C4
4 Sea Hawk Divers B2

Sleeping
5 Apartments Trinchan C2
6 Cabañas María del Mar B2
7 Hotel Belmar C3
8 Hotel Na Balam B1
9 Hotel Playa la Media Luna C2
10 Hotel Sueño Maya C3
11 Poc-Na Hostel C2

Eating
12 Café del Mar A3
13 Mañana C3
14 Mercado Municipal B3
15 Olivia B3
16 Rooster B3

Drinking & Nightlife
17 Buho's A2
Poc-Na Hostel .... (see 11)

Drinking & Entertainment

Isla Mujeres' highest concentration of nightlife is along Hidalgo, and hot spots on or near the beach form an arc around the northern edge of town.

Buho's BAR
(Map p270; Playa Norte; 10am-midnight) The quintessential swing-bar experience right on the beach.

Poc-Na Hostel BAR
(Map p270; www.pocna.com; Matamoros 15; 11pm-3am Mon-Sat;) A beachfront joint with bonfires and more hippies than all the magic buses in the world. It's a scene, and an entertaining one at that.

Information

Hospital Integral Isla Mujeres (998-877-17-92; Guerrero, btwn Madero & Morelos) Doctors available 24/7.

HSBC (Av Rueda Medina)

Police (998-877-04-58)

Post Office (Map p270; cnr Guerrero & López Mateos; 9am-4pm Mon-Fri)

Tourist Information Office (Map p270; 998-877-03-07; Av Rueda Medina; 9am-4pm Mon-Fri) Between Madero and Morelos; offers a number of brochures and some members of the staff speak English.

Getting There & Away

There are several points of embarkation to reach Isla Mujeres. **Ultramar** (www.granpuerto.com.mx) runs passenger ferries to Isla Mujeres from docks at Playa Tortugas, El Embarcadero and Playa Caracol in the Zona Hotelera in Cancún. There are also services from Puerto Juárez (4km north of Cancún).

If you have a vehicle, head to Punta Sam, about 8km north of Cancún center. Walk-ons and vehicle passengers pay M$38; drivers are included in the fare for cars (M$256), as are riders in the fare for motorcycles (M$87) and bicycles (M$82). The crossing takes about an hour.

To get to Punta Sam or Puerto Juárez from Cancún, catch any northbound bus (M$8.50) displaying those destinations and/or 'Ruta 13' on Avenida Tulum. Some R1 (Zona Hotelera; M$9.50) buses make the trip as well; ask before boarding.

Getting Around

BICYCLE

Cycling is a great way to get around the island. A number of shops rent bikes for about M$30 per hour or M$150 per day. Some places ask for a deposit of about M$100. **David** (cell phone 998-2231365; cnr Matamoros & Guerrero) has a decent selection.

BUS & TAXI

Local buses depart about every 25 minutes from a bus stop next to the Centro de Convenciones (near the back of the market) or from the ferry dock and head along Avenida Rueda Medina. However, services can be erratic. You can get to the entrance of Hacienda Mundaca, a 300m walk from the Isla Mujeres Turtle Farm (ask for the *tortugranja*), and as far south as Playa Lancheros (1.5km north of Playa Garrafón). Get taxis from the stand near the Puerto Juárez ferry dock, near the junction of Av Rueda Medina and Morelos, or flag one down. Rates are set by the municipal government and posted at the taxi stand. As always, agree on a price before getting in.

SCOOTER & GOLF CART

Many people find golf carts a good way to get around the island, and convoys of them can be seen tooling down the roads. They

A GAME OF DOMINOES – SWIM WITH THE WHALE SHARKS

Between mid-May and mid-September, massive whale sharks congregate off the coast of Isla Contoy to feed on plankton. Locals call them dominoes because of their speckled skin.

The best time to swim with these gentle giants is in July. A trip will cost you between M$900 and M$1200, depending on who you go with. When swimming with the whale sharks you are not allowed to touch the fish, and are required to wear either a life jacket or wetsuit to ensure you do not dive below the shark.

Anybody vaguely related to tourism on Isla Mujeres can set you up with a trip, but for local knowledge, the best equipment and guaranteed departures, it's best to go with one of the dive operators. Most outfits include a quick snorkel and a spot of fishing in the trip, along with lunch, drinks and snacks.

average M$180 per hour and M$600 all day (9am to 5pm). **Gomar** (☎998-877-16-86; Av Rueda Medina, cnr Bravo; golf carts per hr/day M$180/600, scooter per day M$250) has a good selection in varying sizes.

Scooters are also available but inspect them carefully before renting. Costs vary, and are sometimes jacked up in high season, but generally start at about M$100 per hour, with a two-hour minimum, and M$400 all day (9am to 5pm).

Parque Nacional Isla Contoy

Spectacular Isla Contoy is a bird-lover's delight: a national park and sanctuary that is an easy day trip from Isla Mujeres. About 800m at its widest point and more than 7km long, it has dense foliage that provides shelter for more than 100 species of birds, including brown pelicans, olive cormorants, turkeys, brown boobies and frigates. This is also a good place to see red flamingos, snowy egrets and white herons.

Most of the trips stop for snorkeling en route to Contoy, which sees about 1500 visitors a month. Bring binoculars, mosquito repellent and sunscreen.

For M$140 per person, a park biologist will take you on a tour of **Laguna Puerto Viejo**, a prime nesting site; funds go toward park upkeep and research projects. **Amigos de Isla Contoy** (☎998-884-74-83; www.islacontoy.org; Plaza Bonita Mall) has an office in Mercado 28 in downtown Cancún, and its website has good information on the island's ecology.

Getting There & Away

Daily visits to Contoy are offered by the Fisherman's Cooperative Booth (p268) on Isla Mujeres. The trip (M$900 per person) lasts from 9am to 5pm and includes a light breakfast, lunch (with fish caught en route), snorkeling (gear provided), park admission, scientific information on the island, and your choice of purified water, soft drinks or beer.

Isla Holbox

☎984 / POP 1500

Isn't life great when it's low-fi and low-rise? That's the attitude on friendly Isla Holbox (pronounced 'hol-bosh'), with its sand streets, colorful Caribbean buildings and lazing, sun-drunk dogs. The water is not the translucent turquoise common to Quintana Roo beaches, because here the Caribbean mingles with the darker Gulf of Mexico.

The island is about 30km long and from 500m to 2km wide, with seemingly endless beaches, tranquil waters and a galaxy of shells in various shapes and colors. Lying within the 1541-sq-km Yum Balam reserve, Holbox is home to more than 150 species of birds, including roseate spoonbills, pelicans, herons, ibis and flamingos.

Holbox gained fame for the number of whale sharks that used to congregate here, but the sharks now tend to be found closer to Isla Mujeres, meaning that tours leaving from Holbox spend a lot longer on the boat ride out and back. Any of the hotels can arrange tours and snorkeling.

Sleeping

Budget hotels are clustered around the plaza in Holbox town. Upscale accommodations are scattered along the beachfront on the island's northern shore in what locals call the Zona Hotelera.

Hostel Tribu HOSTEL $

(984-875-25-07; www.tribuhostel.com; Av Pedro Joaquín Coldwell; dm/r from M$125/450;) With so many activities available here (from salsa lessons to yoga and kayaking), it doesn't take long to settle in with the tribe. Six-room dorms and private rooms are clean, colorful and cheerful. Tribu also has a book exchange and a bar that stages Sunday jam sessions. From the plaza, it's one block north and two blocks west.

Casa Lupita HOTEL $$

(984-875-20-17; www.casalupitaholbox.com; Calle Palomino; r M$500-1100, ste M$900-1400;) A great midrange option on the east side of the plaza. The spacious rooms here catch good breezes and the suites have private balconies overlooking the action on the town square.

★ **Casa Takywara** HOTEL $$$

(984-875-22-55; www.takywara.com; r incl breakfast from M$1590;) Out at the quiet western end of town, on the beach, this beautiful hotel stands out for its striking architecture and stylishly decorated rooms with kitchenettes and sea-view balconies. It's built next to a patch of protected wetland, which is home to a pet crocodile. Rates drop considerably in low season.

Eating

Ky Waa BAKERY $$

(Tiburón Ballena, Plaza El Pueblito; sandwiches M$90-130; 8am-10pm) For a good range of breakfasts, fresh-from-the-oven baked goods and yummy sandwiches, grab a table on the breezy deck outside this Brazilian-run bakery/cafe.

Raices SEAFOOD $$

(Beachfront; mains M$100-280; 1-9pm) Don't let the humble surrounds of this beachfront eatery put you off – this is some of the best seafood in town. The coconut lobster is definitely worth a look, but the traditional Maya Tikin Xic fish is the star of the show.

Edelyn Pizzería & Restaurant PIZZERIA $$

(Plaza Principal; pizzas M$80-280, mains M$90-190; noon-11pm) You'll see other places on the island trying to cash in on the lobster pizza craze, but these guys claim to be the originals. There are many other items on the menu if you're not sold on the cholesterol-heavy pairing of cheese and shellfish. It's on the east end of the plaza.

Information

Bancomer has an ATM on the 2nd story of the Alcaldía on the plaza. There's another one in the Hotel Palapa. Sometimes they both run out of money (particularly on weekends), so it's a good idea to bring enough cash to float your trip.

Emergency (066) Police, fire or medical assistance.

Getting There & Around

A *barco* (boat) ferries passengers (M$80, 25 minutes) to Holbox from the port village of Chiquilá, northwest of Cancún. Ferries leave 11 times daily during the week with a couple of extra services on weekends. The last boat leaves Chiquilá at 8pm. Smaller, faster and wetter *lanchas* (motorboats) make the crossing whenever anyone's willing to pay M$350 to M$400 for the entire boat (up to about six people with gear; the fare is higher after dark).

Buses (all 2nd class) leave Chiquilá for Cancún (M$90, 3½ hours) at 5:30am and 1:30pm; Tizimín (M$80, 2½ to four hours) at 5:30am and 7:30am; and Valladolid (M$90, 2½ hours) at 5:30am. Drivers usually wait for boats to arrive before departing. If you're driving, you can either park your vehicle in the Chiquilá parking lot for M$50 per day (8am to 6pm or any fraction thereof) or take your chances parking it on the pier (which is crowded in high season).

Rentadora El Brother (984-875-20-18; Av Tiburón Ballena, north of plaza; cart per hr/day M$120/700) See the Brother if you need to rent a golf cart.

Puerto Morelos

998 / POP 9200

Halfway between Cancún and Playa del Carmen, Puerto Morelos retains its quiet, small-town feel despite the building boom north and south of town. While the village offers enough restaurants and bars to keep you entertained by night, it's really the shallow Caribbean waters that draw visitors here. Another reason to come is to hit the artisans' market, one block south of the plaza's west corner. To fund your purchases, there's an HSBC ATM on the plaza.

Sights & Activities

Jardín Botánico Yaax Che GARDENS

(998-206-99-23; www.ecosur.mx/jb/Yaax-Che; Carretera Chetumal-Cancún, Km 320; adult/child M$120/60; 8am-4pm Mon-Sat;) Two kilometers south of the Puerto Morelos turnoff is this 60-hectare nature reserve with nearly 3km of trails. The garden has sections dedicated to epiphytes (orchids and bromeliads), palms, ferns, succulents (cacti and their relatives) and plants used in traditional Maya medicine.

The preserve also holds a small Maya altar, an ethnological museum and a large animal population, including the only coastal troops of spider monkeys left in the region.

Boca del Puma SWIMMING
(998-241-28-55; www.bocadelpuma.com; Ruta de los Cenotes, Km 16; adult/child 5-14yr from M$1588/795; 9am-5pm;) Slip into the refreshingly chilly waters of the Boca del Puma cenote, 16km west of Puerto Morelos. Also on offer are horseback riding, bicycling and zip-lining.

Dive In Puerto Morelos DIVING
(998-206-90-84, USA 801-443-4879; www.diveinpuertomorelos.com; Av Rojo Gómez; 1-tank/2-tank/cenote M$795/992/1985; 7:30am-6pm Mon-Sat) Offers both reef and cenote dives, as well as PADI Open Water certification for M$5290. It's just past the plaza's northwest end.

Courses

Little Mexican Cooking School COOKING
(998-251-80-60; www.thelittlemexicancookingschool.com; Av Rojo Gómez 768, cnr Lázaro Cárdenas; per class M$1613; 10am-3:30pm Tue-Fri) Ever wonder how to cook some of that delicious regional Mexican cuisine that you've been trying? Here's your chance. During this six-hour course you'll learn about ingredients used in Mexican cooking and how to prepare at least seven dishes. See website for available courses.

Puerto Morelos Language Center LANGUAGE COURSE
(998-871-01-62; www.puertomorelosspanishcenter.com; Av Niños Héroes 46) Offers group and private Spanish classes.

> **BEACH SAFETY**
>
> A system of colored pennants warns beachgoers of potential dangers:
>
> **Blue** Normal, safe conditions.
>
> **Yellow** Use caution; changeable conditions.
>
> **Red** Unsafe conditions; use a swimming pool instead.

Sleeping

Posada Amor HOTEL $$
(998-871-00-33; www.posada-amor.wix.com/puertom; Av Rojo Gómez; s with fan/air-con M$492/550, d with air-con M$660;) About 100m southwest of the plaza, Posada Amor has been in operation for many years. The simple white-walled rooms have some creative touches. There's a shady back area with tables and plenty of plants, the restaurant offers good meals, and there's a friendly expat bar. Prices drop by 15% from May to October.

Posada El Moro HOTEL $$
(998-206-90-05; www.posadaelmoro.com; Av Rojo Gómez; r incl continental breakfast with fan/air-con M$760/875; P) This property has cheery geraniums in the halls and courtyard, and white walls with red trim. Some rooms have kitchenettes, all have couches that fold out into futons, and there's a small pool. Prices drop substantially in low season. It's northwest of the plaza.

Casa Caribe HOTEL $$$
(998-251-80-60; www.casacaribepuertomorelos.com; Av Rojo Goméz Lt 8; r M$1610;) Simply and elegantly decorated, the spacious rooms here have sweeping beach views from private balconies. The hotel sits on lovely, lush grounds with plenty of shady sitting areas. Only one room has air-conditioning, but all receive fantastic sea breezes. There's a three-night minimum stay.

Eating

There are a number of attractive little beachside eateries – go for a wander along the attractive *malecón* (esplanade) and see which one grabs your fancy.

Le Café d'Amancia CAFE $
(Av Rojo Goméz; sandwiches M$40-60; 7am-2pm & 5-10pm;) This is a spotlessly clean place with a pleasing ambience. It serves bagels, sandwiches, pies, good strong coffee, and fruit and veggie *licuados*. It's on the southwest corner of the plaza.

Al Chile CAFE $
(Av Rojo Goméz; set lunches M$60 ; 9am-10pm Thu-Tue;) A couple of blocks south of the plaza, this little cafe-bar serves good-value set lunches and a wide range of fresh juices.

THE RIVIERA FUN PARKS

In an area bursting with natural attractions, it may seem odd that 'ecoparks' are such huge business. Or considering the scale of tourism in the region, it may not. The road from Cancún to Tulum is dotted with these places, and while they're a little too Disney for some, the mix of adventure, activities and low-risk interaction with nature make them a pretty fun day out, particularly if you've got the kids along. Following is a list of some of the best.

Selvática (998-898-43-12; www.selvatica.com.mx; Ruta de los Cenotes, Km 19; canopy tour incl transfer from Puerto Morelos and Cancún hotels adult/child 5-12yr M$1283/635; tours 9am-1:30pm Mon-Sat;) An award-winning zip-line park about 16km west of Puerto Morelos that takes you through the jungle on a circuit of 12 lines, the longest being 350m, the highest 20m. Then cool off in a private cenote.

Hidden Worlds (984-877-85-35; www.hiddenworlds.com; Carretera 307, Km 116; basic admission adult/child 5-11yr M$777/388; 9am-5pm) Zip lines, sky cycles, rappelling, snorkel tours and various other innovative, cenote-focused options. Good for older kids. It's located 25km south of Playa del Carmen.

Xplor (998-251-65-60; www.xplor.travel; all-inclusive adult/child 5-12yr M$1412/712; 9am-5pm;) Six kilometers south of Playa del Carmen, this park features seven circuits that take you zip-lining, rafting, driving amphibious jeeps and swimming in an underground river.

Río Secreto (984-877-23-77; www.riosecreto.com; Carretera 307, Km 283.5; basic admission adult/child 6-11yr M$895/453; 9am-6pm) Hike and swim through a 600m-long underground cavern 5km south of Playa del Carmen.

Aktun Chen (998-881-94-00; www.indiana-joes.com; Hwy 307, Km 107; full tour incl hotel pick-up adult/child M$1257/751; 9am-5pm Mon-Sat;) Forty kilometers south of Playa del Carmen, this small park features a 600m-long cave, a 12m-deep cenote, 10 zip-lines and a small zoo.

Xcaret (984-147-65-60; www.xcaret.com; Hwy Chetumal-Puerto Juárez, Km 282; adult/child 5-12yr M$1157/578; 8:30am-9:30pm;) One of the originals in the area, with loads of nature-based activities and stuff for the grown-ups like the Mexican wine cellar and day spa. It's located 6km south of Playa del Carmen.

Xel-Há (998-251-65-60, USA & Canada 888-922-7381; www.xelha.com; Hwy Chetumal-Puerto Juárez, Km 240; adult/child 5-11yr M$1027/514; 8:30am-6pm;) Billing itself as the world's largest outdoor aquarium, built around a natural inlet 13km north of Tulum. There are lots of water-based activities on offer.

Pangea INTERNATIONAL $$
(Beachfront; mains M$80-150; 10am-6pm Mon-Thu, until midnight Fri & Sat;) Laid-back but with attentive service, this is probably the best of the beachfront restaurants. The menu ranges through healthy eats, seafood and Mexican classics and features a decent cocktail list.

Shopping

Alma Libre BOOKS
(www.almalibrebooks.com; Av Tulum; 10:30am-1:30pm & 3-8pm, closed Jun–mid-Nov) Has more than 20,000 new and used books. The friendly owners are a great resource for information about the area, as is the website, which has vacation rental listings, a monthly newsletter and other interesting info. The store also sells gifts and local gourmet food products.

Getting There & Away

Most Playa Express and Riviera buses between Cancún and Playa del Carmen will drop you on the highway, from where it's about 2km to the central plaza. The Riviera bus running between Cancún airport and Playa del Carmen will sometimes enter the town on request, and some Mayab buses also come into town. The 2nd-class bus fare from Cancún is M$22.

Taxis are usually waiting at the turnoff to shuttle people into town (M$25), or you can wait for a *colectivo* (M$5) to happen past. In town, taxis and *colectivos* hang around the west side of the plaza.

Playa del Carmen

☎984 / POP 150,000

Playa del Carmen is the hippest city in all of the Yucatán Peninsula. Sitting coolly on the lee side of Cozumel, the town's beaches are the place to see and be seen by vacationing Europeans and the occasional American. The waters aren't as clear as those of Cancún or Cozumel, and the beach sands aren't quite as champagne-powder perfect as they are further north, but still Playa (as it's locally known) grows and grows.

With daily cruise-ship visitors, Playa is starting to feel like a mass-tourism destination, but it retains its European chic, and you only need to head two blocks west of the haughty pedestrian strip on Quinta Avenida to catch glimpses of the non-touristy side of things.

Playa del Carmen

Activities, Courses & Tours

1 Dive Mike ... C5
2 International House ... B4
3 Phantom Divers ... C4
4 Playa Lingua del Caribe ... B2

Sleeping

5 Casa de las Flores ... A6
6 Fusion ... C5
7 Grand Hostel ... A6
8 Hotel Villa del Mar ... B6
9 Las Palapas ... C1
10 Posada Papagayo ... B6

Eating

11 Chez Céline ... B1
12 Club Náutico Tarraya ... C6
13 Yaxché ... B2

Drinking & Nightlife

14 Blue Parrot Bar ... C4
15 Caiman ... B2
16 La Santanera ... B4
17 Playa 69 ... B6

Sights & Activities

Beaches

Beachgoers will agree that it's pretty darn nice here. **Mamita's Beach**, north of Calle 28, is considered the best. If crowds aren't your thing, go north of Calle 38, where a few scrawny palms serve for shade. Many go topless in Playa, though it's not a common practice in most of Mexico, and generally frowned upon by locals – except the young bucks, of course. If you fancy a break from the sand, an **art walk** takes place every Thursday from 6pm to 11pm on Quinta Avenida.

Diving & Snorkeling

Prices are similar at most outfits: options include resort dives (M$1110), one-tank dives (M$800), two-tank dives (M$932), cenote dives (M$1460), snorkeling (M$400), whale-shark tours (M$2200) and open-water certification (M$3730).

Dive Mike DIVING
(☎984-803-12-28; www.divemike.com; Calle 8) Dive Mike, between Quinta Avenida and the beach, offers snorkeling tours by boat to reefs and a secluded beach including refreshments and all gear. English, German, French, Italian and Spanish are spoken.

Phantom Divers DIVING
(☎984-879-39-88; cnr 1 Av & Calle 14) A well-regarded, often recommended setup offering all the usuals, plus diving with bull sharks from November to March (M$930 to M$1860 depending on experience and proximity to sharks).

Courses

International House LANGUAGE COURSE
(☎984-803-33-88; www.ihrivieramaya.com; Calle 14; per week M$2930) Offers homestays, a small residence hall and 20 hours per week of Spanish class. Prices listed are for group classes. One-on-one instruction costs M$400 per hour.

Playa Lingua del Caribe LANGUAGE COURSE
(☎984-873-38-76; www.playalingua.com; Calle 20; 1 week without/with homestay M$3000/6330) Offers Spanish courses of 20 hours per week as well as homestays. It also has occasional classes in Maya language, cooking and even salsa dancing. It charges an additional M$1200 registration fee for all new enrollments.

Tours

Alltournative ADVENTURE TOUR
(☎984-803-99-99; www.alltournative.com; Hwy Chetumal-Puerto Juárez, Km 287; ⏰9am-7pm) Alltournative's packages include zip-lining, rappelling and kayaking, as well as custom-designed trips. It also takes you to nearby Maya villages for an 'authentic' experience that could easily be had on your own. The

Playa del Carmen

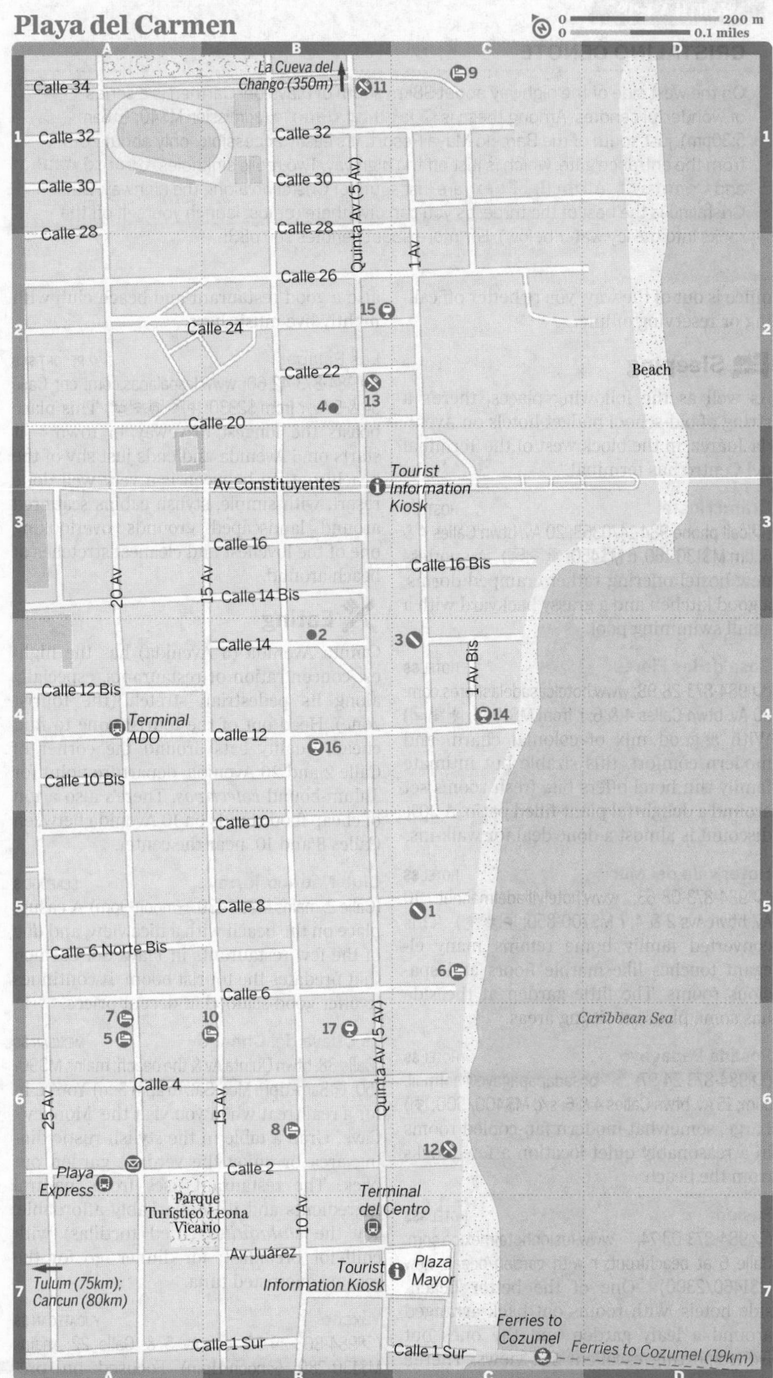

WORTH A TRIP

CRISTALINO CENOTE

On the west side of the highway about 38km south of Playa del Carmen is a series of wonderful cenotes. Among these is **Cristalino Cenote** (admission M$40; ⏲6am-5:30pm), just south of the Barceló Maya Resort. It's easily accessible, only about 70m from the entrance gate, which is just off the highway. Two more sinkholes, **Cenote Azul** and **Cenote El Jardín del Edén**, are just south of Cristalino along the highway. But Cristalino is the best of the three, as you can dive there (or just launch yourself off the rocks into the icy water below). For more about cenotes see p835.

office is out of the way; you're better off calling or reserving online.

Sleeping

As well as the following places, there's a string of old-school budget hotels on Avenida Juárez, in the block west of the Terminal del Centro bus terminal.

Grand Hostel HOSTEL **$**

(☎cell phone 984-1470363; 20 Av, btwn Calles 4 & 6; dm M$130-160, d M$450; ❄📶🏊) A spotless new hostel offering rather cramped dorms, a good kitchen and a grassy backyard with a small swimming pool.

Casa de las Flores HOTEL **$$**

(☎984-873-28-98; www.hotelcasadelasflores.com; 20 Av, btwn Calles 4 & 6; r from M$1065; ❄📶🏊) With a good mix of colonial charm and modern comfort, this sizable but intimate family-run hotel offers big, fresh rooms set around a delightful plant-filled patio. A 20% discount is almost a done deal for walk-ins.

Hotel Villa del Mar HOTEL **$$**

(☎984-873-08-63; www.hotelvilladelmar.net; 10 Av, btwn Avs 2 & 4; r M$700-850; P❄📶) This converted family home retains many elegant touches like marble floors and spacious rooms. The little garden at the side has some pleasant sitting areas.

Posada Papagayo HOTEL **$$**

(☎984-873-24-97; posadapapagayo@hotmail.com; 15 Av, btwn Calles 4 & 6; s/d M$400/500; 📶) Large, somewhat modern fan-cooled rooms in a reasonably quiet location a few blocks from the beach.

Fusion HOTEL **$$$**

(☎984-873-03-74; www.fusionhotelmexico.com; Calle 6 at beachfront; r with garden/ocean view M$1460/2300) One of the better beachside hotels, with rooms out back arranged around a leafy garden and the ones out front sporting excellent sea views. There's also a good restaurant and beach club with nightly live music here.

Las Palapas RESORT **$$$**

(☎984-873-42-60; www.laspalapas.com; cnr Calle 34 & 5 Av; r from $2330; P❄@📶🏊) This place boasts the longest driveway in town – it starts on 5 Avenida and ends just shy of the beachfront. In between is a very well done resort, with simple, stylish cabins scattered around landscaped grounds overlooking one of the loveliest and cleanest stretches of beach around.

Eating

Quinta Avenida (5 Avenida) has the highest concentration of restaurants, especially along its pedestrian stretch (the tourist zone). Head out of the tourist zone to find cheap, quality eats around the corner of Calle 2 and 20 Avenida, departure point for Tulum-bound *colectivos*. There's also a ton of cheap food stands on 10 Avenida between Calles 8 and 10, near the center.

Club Náutico Tarraya SEAFOOD **$**

(Calle 2; mains M$50-130; ⏲noon-9pm) A casual place on the beach with a nice view, and one of the few restaurants in Playa del Carmen that predates the tourist boom. It continues to offer good seafood at decent prices.

La Cueva del Chango MEXICAN **$$**

(Calle 38, btwn Quinta Av & the beach; mains M$90-150; ⏲8am-11pm Mon-Sat, to 2pm Sun) You're in for a real treat when you visit the 'Monkey's Cave.' Grab a table in the stylish rustic dining area or enjoy the verdant garden out back. The restaurant uses fresh, natural ingredients and it's remarkably affordable. Try the *chilaquiles* (fried tortillas) with chili for breakfast; for dinner, go for the sesame-encrusted tuna.

Yaxché YUCATECAN **$$**

(☎984-803-29-36; cnr Av 5 & Calle 22; mains M$130-280; ⏲noon-11pm) Focused on preserving Maya culinary culture, this large but atmospheric restaurant is probably the most original in town. Food isn't exactly out there, but there are some surprising combinations and little-known ingredients in use.

Chez Céline BREAKFAST **$$**
(cnr 5 Av & Calle 34; breakfast from $80; ⏲7am-11pm; ❄📶) Good, healthy breakfasts and a range of yummy baked goods are what keeps this French-run bakery-cafe busy.

Drinking & Nightlife

The party generally starts on Quinta Avenida (5 Avenida) then heads down to the beach clubs. Walk along the beach between Calles 6 and 16 to see where the action is.

La Santanera CLUB
(Calle 12, btwn 5 & 10 Avs; entry around M$100; ⏲10am -late) Probably the best of the downtown dance clubs, with international DJs doing their thing downstairs and an atmospheric chill-out lounge upstairs.

Caiman BAR
(24 Calle, btwn 1 & 5 Avs; ⏲11am-2pm) A hard thing to find in Playa – a bar with cool music where you can just go for a few relaxed drinks. No cover, no dance floor, no rah rah rah. Just a sweet little bar.

Playa 69 GAY
(www.rivieramayagay.com; Callejón, off Quinta Av btwn Calles 4 & 6; ⏲8pm-2am Tue, to 6am Wed-Sun) This gay dance club proudly features guest strippers from such far-flung places as Australia and Brazil.

Blue Parrot Bar BAR
(☎984-873-00-83; www.blueparrot.com/beachclub; Calle 12; ⏲10am-4am) This is the Blue Parrot Suites' immensely popular open-sided *palapa* beachfront bar with swing chairs, a giant outdoor dance stage and lots of sand. The bar also has a nightly fire-dancers' show on the beach.

Information

Banamex (cnr Calle 12 & 10 Av)
Post Office (cnr 20 Av & Calle 2; ⏲9am-3pm Mon-Fri, to 12:45pm Sat)
Tourist Information Kiosk (cnr Constituyentes & 5 Av) Tons of brochures, and the occasional useful answer. There's a second kiosk (Plaza Major) on the main square.

Getting There & Away

BOAT

México Waterjets (www.mexicowaterjets.com) has ferries to Cozumel (M$155 one way) leaving hourly between 6am and 11pm from a jetty at the end of Calle 1 Sur; buy tickets at the booth. The air-conditioned catamaran takes about a half hour, depending on weather. A slower open-air boat (same price but running less regularly) operates mostly in the summer season.

Car ferries also operate on this route (p284).

BUS

Playa has two bus terminals, but each sells tickets and provides information for at least some of the other's departures. Most 1st-class bus lines arrive and depart from the newer one, **Terminal ADO** (cnr 20 Av & Calle 12). A taxi from Terminal ADO to the main plaza will cost about M$25.

All 2nd-class bus lines (including Mayab) are serviced at the old bus station, **Terminal del**

BUSES FROM PLAYA DEL CARMEN

DESTINATION	FARE (M$)	DURATION	FREQUENCY (DAILY)
Cancún	48-72	1hr	frequent
Cancún airport	120	1hr	frequent ADO
Chetumal	250-302	5-5½hr	frequent ADO & Mayab
Chichén Itzá	270	3-4hr	ADO 8am
Cobá	66-92	1-1¾hr	2 ADO
Mérida	220-550	5hr	frequent ADO & ADO GL
Palenque	626-756	12-13hr	3 ADO & ADO GL
San Cristóbal de las Casas	792-948	16-18hr	3 ADO & ADO GL
Tulum	66	1hr	frequent Riviera & Mayab
Valladolid	100-155	2½-3½hr	frequent ADO & Mayab

Centro (cnr Av Juárez & Quinta Av). Riviera's buses (which don't entirely deserve the designation '1st class' anyhow) also use the old terminal. Riviera buses to Cancún and its airport have a separate ticket counter on the Avenida Juárez side of the terminal. Fast buses to downtown Cancún (M$30, one hour) are run by **Playa Express** (Calle 2 Norte).

COLECTIVO

Colectivos are a great option for cheap travel southward to Tulum (M$40, 45 minutes). They depart from Calle 2 near 20 Avenida as soon as they fill (about every 10 or 15 minutes) from 5am to 10pm. They will stop anywhere along the highway between Playa and Tulum, charging a minimum of M$20. Luggage space is somewhat limited, but they're great for day trips. From the same spot, you can grab a *colectivo* to Cancún (M$30, one hour) or Akumal (M$30, 30 minutes).

Isla Cozumel

987 / POP 79,000

Around 71km south of Cancún, Cozumel has been a popular diving spot since 1961, when Jacques Cousteau, led by local guides, showed its spectacular reefs to the world. Today, the island is one of Mexico's top cruise-ship and diving destinations. Called Ah-Cuzamil-Peten (Island of Swallows) by its earliest inhabitants, this is Mexico's third-largest island, measuring 53km by 14km, but the only built-up area is San Miguel on the northwest coast. While diving and snorkeling are the main draws, there are decent beaches, and San Miguel offers lots of shopping 'deals' (often not very cheap) and a pleasant town square in which to spend the afternoon. There are also some small Maya ruins and a few eco-themed parks.

For nearly everything you need to know about Cozumel, visit www.everythingcozumel.com.

History

Maya settlement on Cozumel dates from AD 300. During the post-Classic period, Cozumel flourished as a trade center and, more importantly, a ceremonial site. Every Maya woman living on the Yucatán Peninsula and beyond was expected to make at least one pilgrimage here to pay tribute to Ixchel (the goddess of fertility and the moon) at a temple erected in her honor. Archaeologists believe this temple was at San Gervasio, a bit north of the island's geographical center.

Sights

After checking out the Museo de la Isla de Cozumel in San Miguel, rent a vehicle or take a taxi to see the rest of the island; cyclists will need to brave the regular strong winds on the island. If you're really pinching pesos, local buses head to the island's east side (going as far as Playa Chen Río then turning back again), leaving from the **El Caracol** roundabout at the corner of Benito Juárez and Avenida 65 in San Miguel.

Museo de la Isla de Cozumel — MUSEUM

(987-872-14-34; www.cozumelparks.gob.mx; Av Melgar; admission M$52; 9am-4pm Mon-Sat) The Museo de la Isla de Cozumel presents a clear and detailed picture of the island's flora, fauna, geography, geology and ancient Maya history. Thoughtful and detailed signs in English and Spanish accompany the exhibits. It's a good place to learn about coral before hitting the water, and it's one not to miss before you leave the island.

Parque Chankanaab — AMUSEMENT PARK

(987-872-40-14; www.cozumelparks.gob.mx; Carretera Costera Sur, Km 9; adult/child 3-11yr M$273/182; 8am-4pm Mon-Sat; P) The price of admission here includes access to a sea lion show, a nice beach and pool, a botanical garden with 400 tropical plant species, a limestone lagoon inhabited by turtles, a crocodile exhibit and a pre-Hispanic tour. Other activities, including snorkeling, diving, snuba (diving with an air supply from the surface) and temascal steam baths, will cost you extra.

The park has a restaurant and snack shops. A taxi from town costs M$130.

El Cedral — ARCHAEOLOGICAL SITE

(24hr) FREE About 15km south of San Miguel, this Maya ruin is the oldest on the island. It's the size of a small house and has no ornamentation. El Cedral is thought to have been an important ceremonial site; the small church standing next to the tiny ruin today is evidence that the site still has religious significance for locals.

Parque Punta Sur — WILDLIFE RESERVE

(987-872-40-14; www.cozumelparks.gob.mx; Carretera Costera Sur, Km 27; adult/child 3-11yr M$156/104; 9am-4pm Mon-Sat) At this ecotouristic park, you can visit a lighthouse and a small nautical museum. About 10 minutes away by car is an observation tower where you can see migratory birds and possibly crocodiles. This park area offers a beach, a

Isla Cozumel

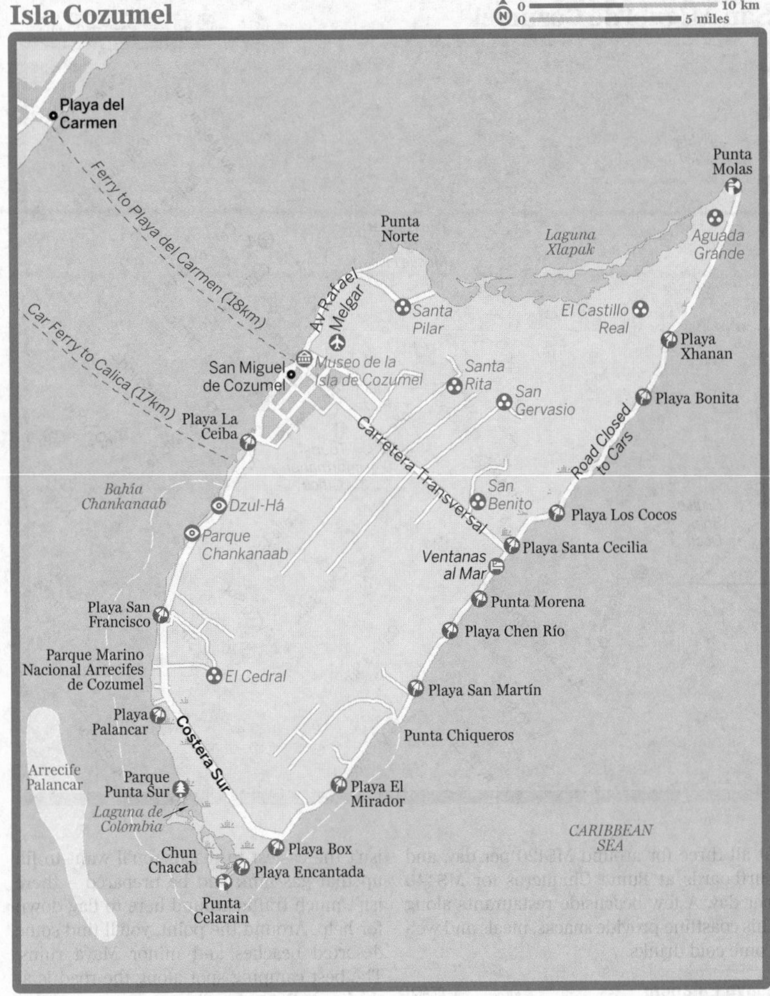

restaurant and three midday boat tours of **Laguna Colombia**. You'll need a vehicle or taxi (M$300 one-way) to get here.

San Gervasio ARCHAEOLOGICAL SITE

(www.cozumelparks.com; Carretera Traversal, Km 7.5; admission M$98; ⌚8am-4pm) This overpriced Maya complex is Cozumel's only preserved ruins, but the entry fees are hardly justified by the limited structures on display. San Gervasio is thought to have been the site of the sanctuary of Ixchel, goddess of fertility, and thus an important pilgrimage site at which Maya women – in particular prospective mothers – worshipped.

Beaches

The best beaches are on the southwest coast, facing the lagoon, but most have been snapped up by big resorts and are hard to access.

The eastern shoreline is the wildest part of the island and presents some beautiful seascapes and many small blowholes (check out the shoreline around Km 30.5). Swimming is dangerous on most of the east coast because of riptides and undertows, but with a bit of care you can sometimes swim at **Punta Chiqueros**, **Playa Chen Río** and **Punta Morena**. You can rent bodyboards

San Miguel de Cozumel

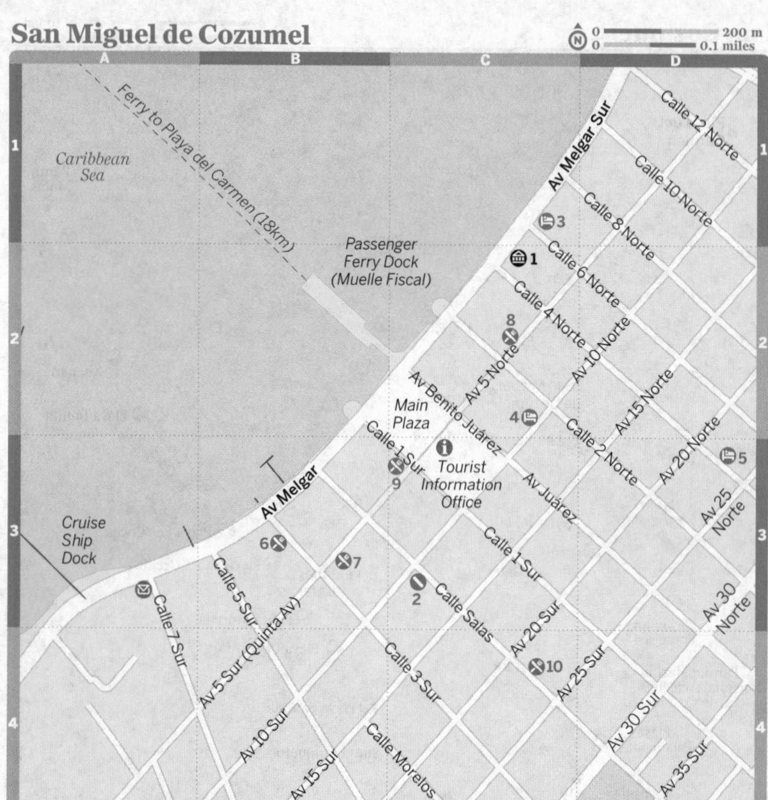

at all three for around M$120 per day, and surfboards at Punta Chiqueros for M$440 per day. A few beachside restaurants along this coastline provide snacks, meals and welcome cold drinks.

Playa Palancar BEACH

FREE About 17km south of San Miguel, Palancar is one of the best beaches. It has a beach club renting hydro bikes, kayaks, snorkel gear and sailboats, plus a restaurant and a dive operation. Near the beach, **Arrecife Palancar** (Palancar Reef) has some very good diving (it's known as Palancar Gardens), as well as fine snorkeling (Palancar Shallows).

Punta Molas RUIN

FREE Head northeast, fellow traveler, and you'll find yourself at the isolated lighthouse of Punta Molas. But take a 4WD (and exercise caution if you want to preserve the insurance on your rental vehicle), as this point isn't the easiest to reach. You'll want to fill up that gas tank and be prepared – there isn't much traffic around here to flag down for help. Around the point, you'll find some deserted beaches and minor Maya ruins. The best camping spot along the road is at the lovely **Playa Bonita**.

Activities

Diving

Despite the massive impact of Hurricane Wilma in 2005, Cozumel, with its 65 surrounding reefs, remains one of the most popular diving destinations in the world, famous for drift dives on pristine coral walls.

The top dives in the area include **Santa Rosa Wall**, **Punta Sur Reef**, **Colombia Shallows** and **Palancar Gardens**. Prices vary, but in general expect to pay about M$1271 for a two-tank dive and M$5619 for PADI open-water certification.

San Miguel de Cozumel

Deep Blue DIVING
(☎987-872-56-53; www.deepbluecozumel.com; Calle Salas 200) Has very good gear and fast boats. Offers nitrox tanks (M$130 extra) and can provide the practical component of e-learning PADI certification.

Snorkeling

Good snorkeling can be found at **Casitas Beach Club**, just north of San Miguel de Cozumel, and **Dzul-Há** to the south. Snorkelers are required to pay M$20 for park admission. The best snorkeling sites are reached by boat. A half-day boat tour will cost from M$650 to M$780.

Sleeping

Hostelito HOSTEL $
(☎987-869-81-57; www.hostelcozumel.com; Av 10 Norte, btwn Av Benito Juárez & Calle 2 Norte; dm M$150, d/q with air-con from M$450/650; ❄📶) The hostel's tagline says it all: affordable *and* clean. There's one shared dorm room downstairs for guys and gals, giant lockers and amazingly clean showers. (How's that for truth in advertising?) Upstairs you'll find a great terrace, kitchen and common area, as well as private double rooms or group rooms that sleep four to nine people.

Tamarindos B&B $$
(☎987-872-61-90; www.tamarindobedandbreakfast.com; Calle 4, btwn Avs 20 & 25; r M$467-787, apt M$934-1067; ❄📶) Delightfully and individually decorated by the French owner, these rooms are set around a leafy garden a few blocks from the central plaza. The owners also rent out extremely comfortable apartments with fully equipped kitchens in a separate complex with a big swimming pool.

Guido's Boutique Hotel BOUTIQUE HOTEL $$$
(☎987-872-09-46; www.guidosboutiquehotel.com; Av Melgar 23, btwn Calles 6 & 8 Norte; ste M$1468-1735; ❄📶) Right on the main strip with an ocean view, Guido's has four chic suites that can accommodate four to eight guests. With full kitchens, large common areas and private balconies, the spacious suites are ideal for families and groups. The same owners run a great Italian restaurant downstairs.

Ventanas al Mar HOTEL $$$
(www.ventanasalmarcozumel.com; Carretera Costera Oriente, Km 43.5; r/ste incl breakfast M$1430/2400; P📶) Notable as it's the only windward hotel on the island, Ventanas al Mar might be right for you if you are looking to get away from it all (way away from it all). Rooms are large, somewhat basic and fresh – there's no air-con, but with these whipping sea breezes that shouldn't be a problem. After dark if you don't want to eat at the hotel's restaurant you'll need to go into town as the windward-side restaurants close at night. There's no telephone.

Eating

Cheapest of all eating places are the little market *loncherías* (lunch stalls) next to the **Mercado Municipal** (Calle Salas, btwn Avs 20 & 25 Sur; ⏲7am-4pm).

El Coffee Cozumel CAFE $
(cnr Calle 3 Sur & Av Melgar; sandwiches & breakfasts from M$55; ⏲7am-11pm; 📶) A tempting array of baked goods, good-value set lunches and the best coffee on the island make this place popular with locals and visitors alike.

El Foco TAQUERÍA $
(Av 5 Sur, btwn Salas & 3 Sur; mains M$50-100; ⏲5pm-1am) Looking for a late-night taco fix? These folks have got your back, in a very tasty way.

Kinta MEXICAN $$
(☎987-869-05-44; www.kintacozumel.com; Av 5 Norte; mains M$120-195; ⏲5:30-11pm Tue-Sun) Putting a gourmet twist on Mexican classics, this chic bistro is one of the best restaurants on the island. The grilled scallops and shrimp with tomato-corn salsa and cilantro pesto is delightful, even more so when served in the garden.

Los Dorados de Villa MEXICAN $$
(☎987-872-01-96; Calle 1 Sur; mains M$80-150; ⏲8am-11pm; ✎) Near the edge of the plaza, this place specializes in food from the Distrito Federal (Mexico City and surroundings), but has a wide variety of Mexican dishes, including seafood and cuts of meat. There's a vegetarian menu as well. The spinach crepes are great, as are the complimentary chips.

Information

There are ATMs, banks and internet joints on the plaza.

Clínica Médica Hiperbárica (Hyperbaric Chamber; ☎987-872-14-30; Calle 5 Sur, btwn Avs Melgar & 5 Sur)

Post Office (cnr Calle 7 Sur & Av Melgar Sur; ⏲9am-4:30pm Mon-Sat)

Tourist Information Office (☎987-869-02-11; Plaza del Sol, 2nd fl; ⏲8am-3pm Mon-Fri) Pick up maps and travel brochures here.

Getting There & Away

AIR

The airport is 2km northeast of San Miguel – follow the signs along Avenida Melgar. Some airlines fly direct from the USA; European flights are usually routed via the USA or Mexico City. Interjet (p266) services Mexico City; MayAir (p266) serves Cancún, Mérida, Villahermosa and Veracruz.

BOAT

Passenger ferries run to Cozumel from central Playa del Carmen. The passenger ferries offered by México Waterjets (p279) or **Ultramar** (www.granpuerto.com.mx) both cost M$155 one way. There's normally a passenger ferry every hour to and from Cozumel, depending on the season, and services run from 6am to midnight.

Transbordadores del Caribe (☎987-872-76-88; www.transcaribe.net) Car ferries to Cozumel leave from the port at Calica (officially known as the Terminal Marítima Punta Venado) just south of Playa del Carmen. Schedules are not set in stone, but currently there are four car ferries between Cozumel and Calica between 6:00am and 8:30pm Monday to Saturday and two daily on Sundays. Fares are M$781 for cars and M$1245 for a van-sized vehicle (both fares include the driver's passage).

You need to line up at least one hour before departure (earlier is better, they say).

Getting Around

TO/FROM THE AIRPORT

The airport is about 2km northeast of town. You can take a *colectivo* from the airport into town for about M$95 (slightly more to the hotels south of town), but you'll have to take a taxi (M$180 from town, up to M$300 from southern hotels) to return to the airport.

BICYCLE

A full day bicycle rental typically costs around M$120 (depending on season) and can be a

EXPLORE MORE SOUTH OF PLAYA DEL CARMEN

South of Playa del Carmen are several worthwhile coastal villages. These areas tend toward upscale tourism, and offer spectacular diving, snorkeling and some amazing beaches. Here are a few of our faves:

Rancho Punta Venado (☎998-887-11-91; www.puntavenado.com; horseback riding from M$1200; ⏲8am-5pm) Five kilometers south of Xcaret, this is a great spot for horseback riding.

Paamul Seventeen kilometers south of Playa del Carmen. The secluded beach makes this area popular with visiting RV travelers, sea turtles and divers alike. **Paamul Hotel** (☎984-875-10-50; www.paamul.com; Carretera Cancún-Tulum, Km 85; campsites/cabañas M$600/1300, r from M$1600; P ❄ ≋) offers lodgings and diving services.

Xpu-Há This is a sugar-sweet beach area 38km south of Playa del Carmen.

Tankah A few kilometers south of the Hwy 307 turnoff for Punta Solimán you'll find this cozy beach community. Visit www.tankah.com for info.

Xcacel-Xcacelito Just 3km north of Xel-Há, this is the state's most important turtle-nesting beach. Volunteer with turtles through **Fauna y Cultura de México** (☎984-871-52-44; www.florafaunaycultura.org) or just check out the lovely cenote and snorkeling found here.

Bahías de Punta Solimán These beautiful bays have stylish private houses for rent – www.locogringo.com has a good offering.

great way to get to the northern and southern beaches on the west side of flat Cozumel. **Sol y Mar** (987-869-05-45; 2 Calle Norte btwn Avs 5 & 10) has a decent selection. The completely separate bicycle/scooter lane on the Carretera a Chankanaab sees a good deal of car traffic from confused tourists and impatient cab drivers, so be careful.

CAR & MOTORCYCLE

There are plenty of agencies around the main plaza in San Miguel, but prices drop about 50% if you book at agencies located between the dock and the fringes of the tourist zone. Rates start at around M$500 all-inclusive, though you'll pay more during late December and January. All rental contracts should automatically include third-party insurance *(daños a terceros)*, which runs about M$150 per day. Collision insurance is usually about M$150 extra with a M$5000 deductible for the cheapest vehicles.

Nobody seems to be renting motorbikes these days, but **Shark Rider** (Av 5 Norte, btwn Av Benito Juárez & Calle 2 Norte; mountain/racing bikes/scooters per day M$130/195/250; 8am-7pm) offers scooters, as do many other places in town. There is a helmet law, and it is enforced.

Rentadora Isis (987-872-33-67; rentadoraisis@prodigy.net.mx; Av 5 Norte, btwn Calles 2 Norte & 4 Norte; 8am-6:30pm) A fairly no-nonsense place with cars in good shape, Rentadora Isis rents VW Beetles for around M$400 per day, with little seasonal variation in prices.

TAXI

Fares in and around town are M$45 per ride; to the hotel area costs M$90 and day trips around the island are M$800 to M$1200; luggage may cost extra.

Akumal

984

Famous for its beautiful beach and large, swimmable lagoon, Akumal (Place of the Turtles) does indeed see sea turtles come ashore to lay their eggs every summer, although fewer and fewer arrive each year, thanks to development along the coast. Akumal is one of the Yucatán Peninsula's oldest resort areas and consists primarily of pricey hotels, condominiums and residential developments (occupied mostly by North Americans and Canadians) on nearly 5km of wide beach bordering four consecutive bays. All sights and facilities are reached by taking the first turnoff, Playa Akumal, as you come south on the highway.

Sights & Activities

Although increasing population is taking its toll on the reefs that parallel Akumal, diving remains the area's primary attraction.

Centro Ecológico Akumal MUSEUM
(984-875-90-95; www.ceakumal.org; 9am-1pm & 2-6pm Mon-Fri; P) FREE To learn more about the area's ecology, check out the Centro Ecológico Akumal. The center, on the east side of the road at the town's entrance, has a few exhibits on reef and turtle ecology, and, for those aged over 21, it offers six- to 12-week volunteer programs that cost M$3000 to M$20,500 per month, including lodging.

Laguna Yal-Kú SWIMMING
(adult/child 4-12yr M$153/115; 9am-5pm;) Laguna Yal-Kú is a beautiful lagoon 2km north of the Playa Akumal entrance. The rocky lagoon, without a doubt one of the region's highlights, runs about 500m from its beginning to the sea. It is home to large schools of brightly colored fish, and the occasional visiting turtle. There is a tasteful sculpture garden along the shore.

Showers, parking and bathrooms are included in the admission price, lockers are an extra M$39, and snorkel gear and life jackets cost M$64 each to rent. Taxis from the Playa Akumal entrance charge about M$90 to the lagoon.

Akumal Dive Shop DIVING
(984-875-90-32; www.akumaldiveshop.com; 1-/2-tank dive M$700/1160, fishing per boat M$2000-2670) Dive trips and deep-sea fishing excursions are offered by Akumal Dive Shop, at the town entrance. It also does snorkeling trips to the reef and beaches unreachable by car for M$534.

Sleeping & Eating

You'll find a bunch of holiday houses for rent on www.akumalvacations.com.

Just outside the entrance to Playa Akumal are two minimarkets that stock a good selection of inexpensive food. **Turtle Bay Café** (8am-11:30pm), inside and just north of the entrance, has a great range of expat-pleasing dishes. Across the road, **Lonchería Akumalito** (sandwiches & mains M$50-110; 7am-9pm) is good for cheap Mexican eats.

Hotel Maria José HOTEL $
(984-802-72-02; r with fan/air-con M$250/400;) There's not much joy for budget travelers

in Akumal, but across the highway in Akumal Pueblo (about a 10-minute walk or M$35 taxi ride from the beach), this family-run place offers rather sparse but clean rooms.

Vista del Mar HOTEL **$$$**
(984-875-90-60; www.akumalinfo.com; r from M$1376, apt M$2900; P) Akumal accommodations tend to be expensive, but this hotel has compact but pleasant rooms with beach-view balconies and patios for a reasonable price. More spacious two-bedroom condos are good for families and small groups. You can also rent bikes here for M$20 per hour.

Getting There & Away

Most 2nd-class buses and *colectivos* traveling between Tulum and Playa del Carmen will drop you on the highway, from where it's about 800m to the entrance to town. In either direction, the fare is M$20 by bus, or M$25 by *colectivo*.

Tulum

984 / POP 28,000

With its sugar-like sands, jade-green water, balmy breezes and glorious sunshine, Tulum is one of the top beaches in Mexico. And where else can you get all that *and* a dramatically situated Maya ruin? There are also fun cenotes, excellent diving, great snorkeling, and a variety of lodgings and restaurants to fit every budget.

There is one big drawback: the town center, where the really cheap eats and sleeps are found, sits right on the highway, making it feel more like a truck stop than a tropical paradise. The Zona Hotelera on the shore is a more appealing place to stay. Wherever you stay, Cobá to the west and the massive Reserva de la Biosfera Sian Ka'an to the south make doable day trips.

History

Most archaeologists believe that Tulum was occupied during the late post-Classic period (AD 1200–1521) and that it was an important port town during its heyday. The Maya sailed up and down this coast, maintaining trading routes all the way down into Belize. When Juan de Grijalva sailed past in 1518, he was amazed by the sight of the walled city, its buildings painted a gleaming red, blue and yellow and a ceremonial fire flaming atop its seaside watchtower.

The ramparts that surround three sides of Tulum (the fourth side being the sea) leave little question as to its strategic function as a fortress. Several meters thick and 3m to 5m high, the walls protected the city during a period of considerable strife between Maya city-states. Not all of Tulum was situated within the walls. The vast majority of the city's residents lived outside them; the civic-ceremonial buildings and palaces likely housed Tulum's ruling class.

The city was abandoned about 75 years after the Spanish conquest. It was one of the last of the ancient cities to be abandoned; most others had been given back to nature long before the arrival of the Spanish. But Maya pilgrims continued to visit over the years, and indigenous refugees from the Caste War took shelter here from time to time.

'Tulum' is Maya for 'wall,' though its residents called it Zama (Dawn). The name Tulum was apparently applied by explorers during the early 20th century.

Sights

Tulum Ruins RUIN
(admission M$57; 8am-5pm; P) The ruins of Tulum preside over a rugged coastline, a strip of brilliant beach and green-and-turquoise waters that'll leave you floored. It's true the extents and structures are of a modest scale and the late post-Classic design is inferior to those of earlier, more grandiose projects – but wow, those Maya occupants must have felt pretty smug each sunrise. Present-day Tulum is growing fast: since 2006 the population has more than doubled and there are no signs of it slowing down.

Tulum is a prime destination for large tour groups. To best enjoy the ruins without feeling like part of the herd, you should visit them either early in the morning or late in the afternoon. Parking costs M$60 for cars and M$120 for vans and pickups. A M$20 train takes you to the ticket booth from the entrance, or just hoof the 300m. Taxi cabs from town charge M$50 and can drop you off at the old entrance road, about an 800m walk from the ticket booth. There's a less-used southern foot entrance from the beach road.

Exploring the Ruins

Visitors are required to follow a prescribed route around the ruins. From the ticket booth, head north along nearly half the length of Tulum's enormous **wall**, which measures approximately 380m south to

Tulum Ruins

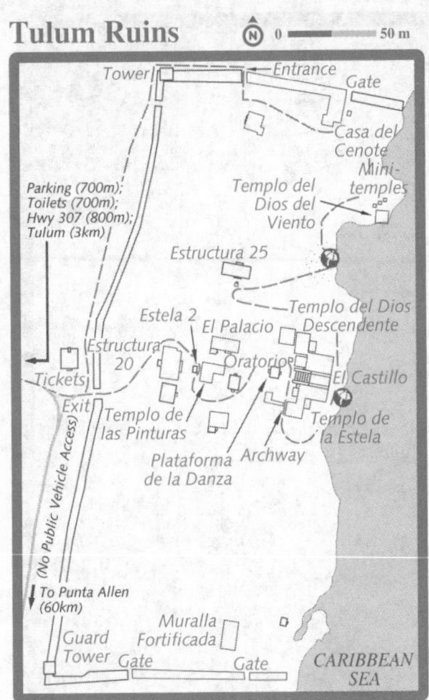

north and 170m along its sides. The **tower** at the corner, once thought to be a guard post, is now believed by some to have been a type of shrine. Rounding the corner, you enter the site through a breach in the north wall.

Once inside, head east toward the **Casa del Cenote**, named for the small pool at its southern base, where you can sometimes see the glitter of little silvery fish as they turn sideways in the murky water. A small tomb was found in the casa. Walk south toward the bluff holding the **Templo del Dios del Viento** (Temple of the Wind God) – roped off at the time of research – which provides the best views of El Castillo juxtaposed with the sea below.

Below the Wind God's hangout is a lovely little stretch of **beach** (also roped off at last visit). Next, head west to **Estructura 25**, which has some interesting columns on its raised platform and, above the main doorway (on the south side), a beautiful stucco frieze of the Descending God. Also known as the Diving God, this upside-down, part-human figure appears elsewhere at Tulum, as well as at several other east-coast sites and Cobá. It may be related to the Maya's reverence for bees (and honey), perhaps a stylized representation of a bee sipping nectar from a flower.

South of Estructura 25 is **El Palacio**, notable for its ornamentation, with X-shaped figures lined up above the eaves. From here, head east back toward the water and skirt the outside edge of the central temple complex (keeping it to your right). Along the back are some good views of the sea. Heading inland again on the south side, you can enter the complex through a corbeled archway past the restored **Templo de la Estela** (Temple of the Stela), also known as the Temple of the Initial Series. Stela 1, now in the British Museum, was found here. It was inscribed with the Maya date corresponding to AD 564 (the 'initial series' of Maya hieroglyphs in an inscription gives its date). At first this confused archaeologists, who believed Tulum had been settled several hundred years later than this date. It's now thought that Stela 1 was brought to Tulum from Tankah, a settlement 4km to the north dating from the Classic period.

At the heart of the complex you can admire Tulum's tallest building, a watchtower appropriately named **El Castillo** (The Castle) by the Spaniards. Note the Descending God in the middle of its facade, and the Toltec-style 'Kukulcánes' (plumed serpents) at the corners, echoing those at Chichén Itzá. To the Castillo's north is the small, lopsided **Templo del Dios Descendente**, named for the relief figure above the door. South of the Castillo you'll find steps leading down to a (usually very crowded) beach, where you can go for a swim.

After some beach time, heading west toward the exit will take you to the two-story **Templo de las Pinturas**, constructed in several stages around AD 1400 to 1450. Its decoration was among the most elaborate at Tulum and included relief masks and colored murals on an inner wall. The murals have been partially restored, but are nearly impossible to make out. This monument might have been the last built by the Maya before the Spanish conquest and, with its columns, carvings and two-story construction, it's probably the most interesting structure at the site.

Activities

Snorkeling or swimming right from the beach is possible and fun, but be extra careful of boat traffic (a dive flag is a good idea), as the strip between the beach and reef offshore is traveled both by dive boats and fishermen.

Tulum

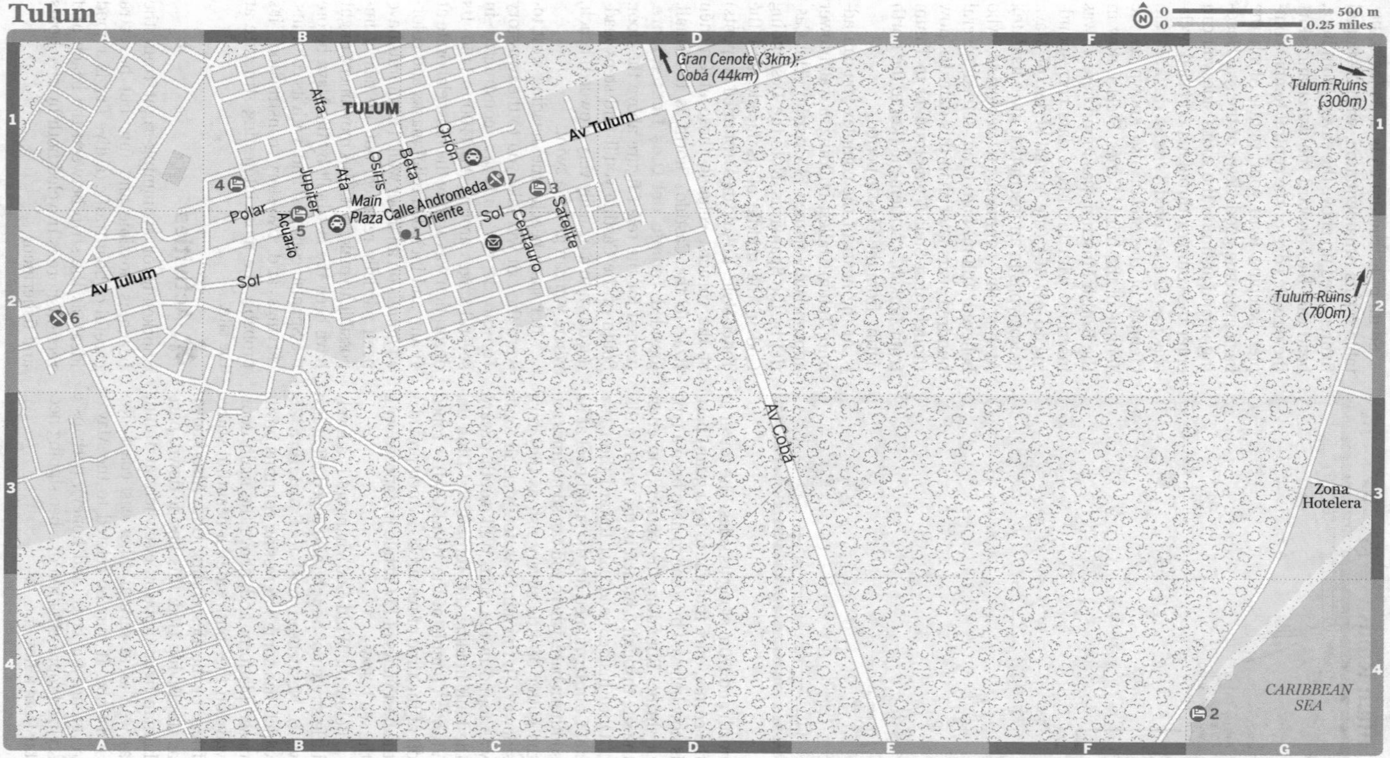

0 500 m
0 0.25 miles

Gran Cenote (3km); Cobá (44km)
Tulum Ruins (300m)
Tulum Ruins (700m)
TULUM
Av Tulum
Av Cobá
Alfa
Afa
Osiris
Beta
Orión
Jupiter
Polar
Acuario
Main Plaza
Calle Andromeda Oriente
Sol
Centauro
Satelite
Zona Hotelera
CARIBBEAN SEA
1
2
3
4
5
6
7

Tulum

Activities, Courses & Tours

Sleeping

Eating

Dive Tulum DIVING
(☎984-876-23-67; www.divetulum.com; Carretera Tulum-Boca Paila, Km 8.5) Offers cenote and reef diving and regular snorkeling trips (M$325).

Courses

Yoga Shala Tulum YOGA
(☎cell phone 984-1418116; www.yogashalatulum.com; Carretera Tulum–Punta Allen, Km 8.4) About 8km south of the T-junction in the Zona Hotelera, Shala Tulum offers daily yoga classes (M$200). The weekly pass (M$670) is a good deal for serious stretchers – you can attend any or all of the 17 classes per week.

Tours

Community Tours Sian Ka'an ECOTOUR
(Map p288; ☎984-871-22-02; www.siankaantours.org; cnr Osiris & Sol; ⏲office 7am-8pm) Community Tours Sian Ka'an runs tours to the magnificent Reserva de la Biosfera Sian Ka'an, stopping at various ancient Maya sites, including the Muyil archaeological site south of Tulum. Community Tours is a sustainable tourism project run by locals from Maya communities.

Sleeping

Tulum Pueblo

The town center, sometimes referred to as Tulum Pueblo, straddles the highway (called Avenida Tulum through town) southwest of the Cobá junction. It's at least 3km to the beach from here, but transportation options are plentiful. Still, if you want sand and surf at your doorstep, head for the Zona Hotelera.

Weary Traveler HOSTEL $
(Map p288; ☎984-871-23-90; www.wearytravelerhostel.com; Av Tulum, Tulum Pueblo; dm/r incl breakfast from M$150/350;) A great place to meet friends, the Weary Traveler is known for a full breakfast and a great central courtyard with hammocks and picnic benches. It even has its own bar. The hostel also has a shuttle to the beach for M$15. Don't worry about the odd electronic check-in…normally somebody is around to help you get settled in.

Secret Garden HOTEL $$
(Map p288; ☎cell phone 984-1578001; www.secretgardentulum.com; cnr Acuario & Sagitario; r M$670-936;) Set back from the main drag in a quiet residential area, this one offers rustic, fan-cooled rooms with stylish thatched roofs, and more comfortable air-con units. The garden is indeed a draw – shady and lush and filled with birdsong – and about as tranquil as you could hope to get downtown.

Hotel Posada 06 BOUTIQUE HOTEL $$$
(Map p288; ☎cell phone 984-1166757; www.posada06tulum.com; Calle Andromeda Oriente 17; r/ste M$1471/1740;) All polished concrete and designer furniture, this is probably the hippest hotel in the pueblo. Rooms are set around a charming little courtyard featuring a curvy swimming pool constructed around a big tree.

Zona Hotelera

From the highway at the Cobá junction, a road leads about 3km to the coastal road servicing the Zona Hotelera. This string of waterfront lodgings extends more than 10km south of the ruins, and the road eventually enters the Reserva de la Biosfera Sian Ka'an, continuing some 50km past Boca Paila to Punta Allen. The best options are on the beach side of the coastal road.

Chavez Camping CABAÑAS $
(Carretera Tulum-Boca Paila, Km 9; campsite/tent per person M$90/130, cabins M$300-400) Pretty much the last bastion of the hippies on the beach at Tulum is this simple, somewhat funky setup. There's a shared kitchen, beachfront access, plenty of traveling vibe (aka drum circles) and the two creaky old wooden cabins are a reminder of how things used to be here, not so long ago.

Diamante K CABAÑAS **$$**
(Map p288; ☎984-876-21-15; www.diamantek.com; Carretera Tulum-Boca Paila, Km 2.5; cabin with/without bathroom from M$1100/400;) A great midrange option on the beach, cabins here range from budget-rustic to rustic-chic. Those with bathrooms vary hugely in size and design – check out a few if you can.

Ahau Tulum CABAÑAS **$$**
(☎984-144-33-48; www.ahautulum.com; Carretera Tulum-Boca Paila, Km 7.5; s/d without bathroom M$521/909, ste M$3344-5485;) A fantastic range of rooms here. The singles are no big deal, but everything above has a smooth, rustic atmosphere. The suites have fantastic beachfront locations, excellent attention to detail (ceiling fan *inside* your mosquito net, anyone?) and sweet balconies out over the sand. Huts with shared bathroom are set back from the beach.

Zulum HOTEL **$$$**
(☎cell phone 984-1576633; www.zulumhotels.com; Carretera Tulum-Boca Paila, Km 6.5; r M$1690-2860;) This is what Tulum does best – a blend of laid-back rustic charm and hip styling. The beachfront rooms are the obvious winners, but all are good, and made even better by the bar/restaurant built out over the sand.

Eating

Most restaurants are located in Tulum Pueblo. In the Zona Hotelera, head to one of the hotels for good eats.

★**El Camello** SEAFOOD **$$**
(Map p288; Av Tulum, cnr Av Kukulcán; mains M$90-150; 10:30am-9pm Mon, Tue & Thu-Sat, to 6pm Sun) Founded by a local fishermen's cooperative, this immensely popular roadside eatery guarantees fresh fish and seafood. Locals don't even need to look at the menu – it's all about the fish and mixed seafood ceviche (seafood marinated in lemon or lime juice, garlic and seasonings).

Le Bistro FRENCH **$$**
(Map p288; Centauro, btwn Av Tulum & Calle Andromeda Oriente; mains M$90-140; 8am-11:30pm Sun-Fri) Simple, elegantly prepared French food at excellent prices. Seafood features heavily on the menu but there are steaks, chicken and tasty baguettes to choose from too.

Hartwood FUSION **$$$**
(www.hartwoodtulum.com; Carretera Tulum-Boca Paila, Km 7.6; mains M$280; 6-10pm Wed-Sun) This sweet 'n' simple nouveau cuisine eatery is tucked down on the beach road. Ingredients are fresh and local, flavors and techniques are international. The menu is small and changes daily, and the open kitchen and simple decor serve to accentuate the delicious dishes. It's 3.5km south of the T-junction on the coast road.

Information

Tulum Pueblo has Telmex pay phones, internet cafes, numerous currency-exchange booths, a couple of ATMs, two **HSBC banks** (Av Tulum btwn Afa & Osiris; 8am-5pm Mon-Sat) and a **post office** (Map p288; cnr Orión & Venus; 9am-3:30pm Mon-Fri).

Getting There & Away

The **bus terminal** (Map p288; Av Tulum) is toward the southern end of Tulum Pueblo. When leaving Tulum, you can also wait at Crucero

BUSES FROM TULUM

DESTINATION	FARE (M$)	DURATION	FREQUENCY (DAILY)
Cancún	88-104	2hr	frequent ADO
Chetumal	204-248	3½-4hr	frequent ADO & Mayab
Chichén Itzá	148-158	3½hr	2 ADO, 2nd class at 3:30pm
Cobá	48-60	45min	2 ADO & 2 Mayab
Felipe Carrillo Puerto	62-90	1½hr	frequent ADO & Mayab
Mérida	182-290	4hr (2nd-class takes much longer)	frequent ADO & Mayab
Playa del Carmen	35-72	1hr	frequent ADO & Mayab
Valladolid	83-90	2hr	frequent ADO & Mayab

Ruinas (on the northern approach to Tulum on Hwy 307) for intercity buses and the *colectivos* to Playa del Carmen.

If you're headed for Valladolid, be sure your bus is traveling the short route through Chemax, not via Cancún. *Colectivos* leave from Avenida Tulum for Playa del Carmen (M$40, 45 minutes) and Punta Allen (at 2pm; M$220, four hours). *Colectivos* for Felipe Carrillo Puerto (M$55, one hour) leave from just south of the Weary Traveler hostel.

Getting Around

Except for the shuttles operated from the youth hostels, there are no *colectivos* out to the beach. You'll need to hire a taxi, rent a bike or walk. And it can be a long, hot walk.

Bicycles can be a good way to get around. Some hotels have them free for guests. **Cabañas Punta Piedra** (Carretera Tulum–Punta Allen, Km 5.2) rents bikes (M$120 per day) and scooters (M$450 per day).

There are two taxi stands in Tulum Pueblo, one south of the bus terminal and the other four blocks north on the opposite side of the street. Taxi fares are fixed and pretty cheap; from either stand to the ruins is M$45. Fares to most *cabañas* mentioned here are M$60 to M$80.

Around Tulum

Gran Cenote

A little over 3km from Tulum on the road to Cobá is **Gran Cenote** (Hwy 109; snorkeling M$120; 8am-6pm), a worthwhile stop on your way between Tulum and the Cobá ruins, especially if it's a hot day. You can snorkel among small fish and see underwater formations in the caverns here if you bring your own gear. A cab from downtown Tulum costs around M$50 one way, or it's an easy bike ride.

Cobá

984 / POP 1300

Imagine a mix between an Amsterdam bike path and a set from *Raiders of the Lost Ark* and you've pretty much got Cobá. It's set deep in the jungle and many of the ruins have yet to be excavated. Walk (or ride) along ancient *sacbé* pathways (stone-paved avenues; *sacbeob* is the plural in Maya), climb up vine-covered mounds, and ascend to the top of Nohoch Mul for a spectacular view of the surrounding jungle. A small town has grown up around the lake to the west of the ruins.

History

Cobá was settled much earlier than nearby Chichén Itzá and Tulum, and construction reached its peak between AD 800 and 1100. Archaeologists believe that this city once covered an area of 50 sq km and held a population of 40,000 Maya.

Cobá's architecture is a curiosity: its towering pyramids and stelae resemble the architecture of Tikal, which is several hundred kilometers away, rather than the much nearer sites of Chichén Itzá and the northern Yucatán Peninsula.

Some archaeologists theorize that an alliance with Tikal was made through marriage, to facilitate trade between the Guatemalan and Yucatecan Maya. Stelae appear to depict female rulers from Tikal holding ceremonial bars and flaunting their power by standing on captives. These Tikal royal females, when married to Cobá's royalty, may have brought architects and artisans with them.

Archaeologists are also baffled by the extensive network of *sacbeob* in this region, with Cobá as the hub. The longest runs nearly 100km, from the base of Cobá's great pyramid Nohoch Mul to the Maya settlement of Yaxuna. In all, some 40 *sacbeob* passed through Cobá, parts of the huge astronomical 'time machine' that was evident in every Maya city.

Sights

Cobá Ruins ARCHAEOLOGICAL SITE

(www.inah.gob.mx; admission M$57, guides M$500-750; 8am-5pm; P) This site at the end of the road on the southeast corner of Laguna Cobá, has a parking lot that charges M$40 per car. Be prepared to walk several kilometers on paths, depending on how much you want to see. If you arrive after 11am you might feel a bit like a sheep in a flock.

A short distance inside, at the Grupo Cobá, there is a concession renting bicycles at M$35 per day. These can only be ridden within the site, and are useful if you really want to get around the further reaches; also they're a great way to catch a breeze and cool off. If the site is crowded, however, it's probably best to walk. Pedicabs (two people and driver cost M$170 for two hours) are another popular option for those who are tired or have limited mobility.

Bring insect repellent and water (although the shop next to the ticket booth sells both at reasonable prices). There is a drink stand within the site near the Nohoch Mul pyramid.

Grupo Cobá ARCHAEOLOGICAL SITE

Walk just under 100m along the main path from the entrance and turn right to get to **La Iglesia** (The Church), the most prominent structure in the Grupo Cobá. It's an enormous pyramid; if you were allowed to climb it, you could see the surrounding lakes (which look lovely from above on a clear day) and the Nohoch Mul pyramid.

Take the time to explore Grupo Cobá; it has a couple of corbeled-vault passages you can walk through. Near its northern edge, on the way back to the main path and the bicycle concession, is a very well-restored **juego de pelota** (ball court).

Grupo de las Pinturas ARCHAEOLOGICAL SITE

The Grupo de las Pinturas (Paintings Group) lies east of the Grupo Cobá. If you're on a bike, you'll have to park it here and return to it (this is the case at a few other spots as well). The temple here bears traces of glyphs and frescoes above its door and remnants of richly colored plaster inside.

You approach the temple from the southeast. Leave by the trail at the northwest (opposite the temple steps) to see two stelae. The first of these is 20m along, beneath a *palapa*. Here, a regal figure stands over two others, one of them kneeling with his hands bound behind him. Sacrificial captives lie beneath the feet of a ruler at the base. You'll need to use your imagination, as this and most of the other stelae here are quite worn. Continue along the path past another badly weathered stela and a small temple to rejoin the Nohoch Mul path and turn right (or, if you rented a bike, turn around or go left to retrieve it).

Grupo Macanxoc ARCHAEOLOGICAL SITE

About 200m beyond the *juego de pelota*, the path forks. Going straight gets you to the Grupo Macanxoc, a group of recently restored stelae that bore reliefs of royal women who are thought to have come from Tikal. It's a 1km walk, but the flora along the way is interesting.

Nohoch Mul ARCHAEOLOGICAL SITE

Northeast of the Grupo Macanxoc you will reach another **juego de pelota** on the right side of the path. Look at the ground in the center of the court to spot a carved stone skull (the winner or the loser of the ball game?) and the carved relief of a jaguar. More weathered stelae lie at the north end. After the ball court, the track bends between piles of stones – a ruined temple – and you reach a junction of sorts. Turn right (east) and head to the structure called **Xaibé**. This is a tidy, semicircular stepped building, almost fully restored. Its name means 'the Crossroads,' as it marks the juncture of four separate *sacbeob*.

Going north from here takes you past **Templo 10** and **Stela 20**. The exquisitely carved stela – worn, but not nearly so badly as the others – bears the date AD 730 and a familiar theme: a ruler standing imperiously over two captives. In front of it is a modern line drawing depicting the original details.

By this time you will have noticed **Nohoch Mul** (Big Mound) just to the north. Also known as the Great Pyramid, which sounds a lot better than Big Mound, Nohoch Mul reaches a height of 42m, making it the second-tallest Maya structure on the Yucatán Peninsula. Calakmul's Estructura II, at 45m, is the tallest. Climbing the old steps can be scary for some.

Two diving gods are carved over the doorway of the temple at the top (built in the post-Classic period, AD 1100–1450), similar to the sculptures at Tulum. The view from up top is over many square kilometers of flat scrubby forest, with peeks of lake, and Xaibé as the sole visible Maya structure. Still, it's inspiring.

After descending, walk past Templo 10 and turn right to make a loop back to the ruined-temple junction. In all it's a 1.4km (or half-hour) walk back to the site entrance.

Activities

A 40m-high, 500m-long **zip-line** across the lagoon starts from a tower in the car park and costs M$130 per zip.

About 6km south of Cobá on the road to Chan Chen you'll find a series of three locally administered **cenotes** that are good for swimming: Choo-Ha, Tamcach-Ha and Multún-Ha. Prices are M$45 (one cenote), M$70 (two cenotes) and M$100 (all three cenotes).

OFF THE BEATEN TRACK

THE TALKING CROSS

In the small town of Felipe Carrillo Puerto you'll find what must be one of the oddest tourist attractions in the region: the Shrine to the Talking Cross. The story goes like this: in 1849, when the War of the Castes turned against them, the Maya of the northern Yucatán Peninsula made their way to Carrillo Puerto seeking refuge. Regrouping, they were ready to sally forth again in 1850 when a 'miracle' occurred. A wooden cross erected at a cenote on the western edge of the town began to 'talk,' exhorting the Maya to continue the struggle against the Spanish and promising victory. The talking was actually done by a ventriloquist, but the people looked upon it as the authentic voice of their aspirations.

The oracle guided the Maya in battle for more than eight years, until their great victory, conquering the fortress at Bacalar. Carrillo Puerto today remains a center of Maya pride. The talking cross has been returned to its shrine, the **Santuario de la Cruz Parlante** (⌚4am-8pm), and Maya from around the region still come to visit it, more for what it represents in the Maya people's struggle against inequality and injustice than for any supposed miraculous properties. Crowds gather here especially on May 3, the Day of the Holy Cross.

Felipe Carrillo Puerto is just off the main highway and has frequent bus connections with Cancún (M$57 to M$94, three to four hours), Tulum (M$57 to M$90, 1½ hours) and Chetumal (M$74 to M$128, two to three hours). Should you choose to stay, there are good hotels and restaurants around the plaza.

Sleeping & Eating

There's no organized campsite, but you can try finding a place along the shore of the lake. The lake is inhabited by crocodiles, but safe swimming is possible in several local cenotes.

Hotel Sac-bé HOTEL **$**
(☎984-144-30-06; r with fan/air-con M$350/450; ❄) The best digs in town. Clean and friendly, the Sac-bé is on the main strip heading into Cobá. The chickens are a bit noisy in the morning, but it has a restaurant, nice hot showers and so-so beds.

Hostel Cob-ja CABAÑAS **$**
(☎984-876-57-82; cabin without bathroom M$130) Serious budget-watchers should be happy in these somewhat cramped wood and flywire cabins at the entrance to town. There's a kitchen for guest use and bikes for hire.

Restaurant Ki-Jamal MEXICAN **$$**
(mains M$70-160; ⌚8am-5pm; Ⓟ) Owned by the local Maya community, Ki-Jamal (which means tasty food in Maya) actually does some tasty traditional dishes. Head upstairs for a lake view and possibly a quiet meal – that is if no tour groups drop in. It's right off the ruins' parking lot.

Getting There & Away

Most buses serving Cobá swing down almost to the lake to drop off passengers before turning around, but Restaurant El Bocadito serves as the de facto bus station. Buses run six to eight times daily between Tulum and Cobá (M$36 to M$48, 45 minutes); four of these also serve Playa del Carmen (M$72 to M$94, one to 1¾ hours). Buses also run to Valladolid (M$33 to M$66, 45 minutes) and Chichén Itzá (M$62 to M$102, 1½ hours).

Day-trippers from Tulum can reach Cobá by forming a group to split the cost of a taxi, which costs about M$750 round-trip, including two hours at the site.

The road from Cobá to Chemax is arrow-straight and in good shape. If you're driving to Valladolid or Chichén Itzá, this is the way to go.

Tulum to Punta Allen

Punta Allen sits at the end of a narrow spit of land that stretches south nearly 40km from its start below Tulum. There are some charming beaches along this coast, with plenty of privacy, and most of the spit is within the protected, wildlife-rich Reserva de la Biosfera Sian Ka'an. Hurricane Dean whipped the region in 2007, but the mangrove forest was not substantially damaged.

At the time of research, one *colectivo* made the three-hour trip between Tulum and Punta Allen daily, leaving Tulum center at 2pm and arriving in Punta Allen about 5pm and charging foreigners the somewhat painful price of M$240. It returns to Tulum (departing Punta Allen at 5am) the next day. You can also come by boat – talk to Community Tours Sian Ka'an (p289) in Tulum.

RESERVA DE LA BIOSFERA SIAN KA'AN

Over 5000 sq km of tropical jungle, marsh, mangroves and islands on Quintana Roo's coast have been set aside by the Mexican government for this large biosphere reserve. In 1987 the UN classified it as a World Heritage site – an irreplaceable natural treasure. Sian Ka'an (Where the Sky Begins) is home to howler monkeys, anteaters, foxes, ocelots, pumas, crocodiles, eagles, raccoons, tapirs, peccaries, giant land crabs, jaguars and hundreds of bird species, including *chocolateras* (roseate spoonbills) and some flamingos.

The entrance gate to the reserve – where you pay the M$23 entry fee – is about 10km south of Tulum. At the gate, there's a short nature trail taking you to the rather nondescript **Ben Ha** cenote. The trail is short, so go ahead and have a gander. There are no hiking trails deeper inside the reserve, so it's best explored with a professional guide. Community Tours Sian Ka'an (p289) runs tours of the reserve out of Tulum that include pickup in Tulum's Zona Hotelera. If you can get to Punta Allen, the tourism cooperatives there offer a range of tours.

Boca Paila Camps (Cesiak; ☎984-871-24-99; www.cesiak.org; Carretera Tulum-Boca Paila; r from M$934; P) Entering the reserve by the road to Punta Allen, you'll pass Boca Paila Camps. Stay the night in the hotel's pimped-out wall tents or just stop by to see what they do at the turtle rescue operation on site (M$350) or rent a kayak (M$450). If you'd prefer a guided tour, you can do that, too. Activities on offer include kayaking (M$650), boating (M$1050), bird-watching (M$1050) and fly-fishing.

Sol Caribe (☎cell phone 984-1393839; www.solcaribe-mexico.com; Carretera Tulum-Punta Allen, Km 50; r from M$2200; wifi) Deep in the reserve, Sol Caribe features almost comically large rooms that all face the sea and get wonderful breezes (no need for air-con). The style is rustic-chic: polished concrete floors with *palapa* roofs. It sits on its own perfect crescent-shaped bay.

Punta Allen

☎984 / POP 470

The town of Javier Rojo Gómez is more commonly referred to as Punta Allen, the name of the point 2km south. This is truly the end of the road. The 400 or so residents mostly work as fishermen, though a few work in restaurants popular with day-trippers. There's also a healthy reef 400m from shore that offers snorkelers and divers wonderful sights.

The area is known primarily for its catch-and-release bonefishing; tarpon and snook are very popular sport fish as well. The tourism cooperatives in town (inquire at Galletanes, Xo-ken or Vigía Grande eateries), do fishing trips for about M$3200 for a half day, or M$4500 for a full day.

A three-hour tour of the lagoon, including turtles, bird-watching and a quick snorkel, costs M$1700 per boat. You'll be offered trips by one of the three co-ops. Encourage your captain not to get so close to birdlife that he scares it away. Though very rare, manatee spottings are possible.

There are no ATMs or internet cafes in town. Electricity generally works between 11am and 2pm, and 6:30pm and 11:30pm.

Sleeping & Eating

The best places to eat in town are the beachfront restaurants.

Casa de la Sirena HOTEL **$$**
(☎cell phone 984-1391241; www.casasirena.com; r M$508-1010) The funkiest rooms in town are owned by a US expat (ask for the shipwreck stories). Rooms are charming, spacious and quirky.

Hotel Costa del Sol BUNGALOW **$$**
(☎cell phone 984-1132639; www.bungaloscostadelsol.com; campsites M$200, r M$600-700) At the entrance to town, this beachfront spot has quaint fan-cooled bungalows and a laid-back feel. The restaurant is pretty decent, and it has karaoke on weekend nights. Offers significant low-season discounts.

Getting There & Away

The best way to reach Punta Allen by public transportation is by *colectivo* (M$240) out of

Tulum: one leaves daily from Tulum center at 2pm and arrives about three hours later. The return service to Tulum leaves Punta Allen at 5am. Driving in a rental car is another option, but prepare for 5km/h to 10km/h speeds and more than a few transmission-grinding bumps.

Mahahual

983

The arrival of the cruise ships hasn't been as life-altering for Mahahual as many feared – it retains much of its small-town charm, with a pleasant *malecón* (beach-front walkway) packed with tourist services and surrounded by what is still a very laid-back Caribbean village. There's an ATM in the Centro Comercial Maj-Ah-Ual, halfway along the *malecón*.

Sights & Activities

Mahahual Beach BEACH

FREE The beach right off Mahahual's beautiful *malecón* has great sand, plus water so shallow you can wade out a good 100m.

Banco Chinchorro DIVE SITE

Divers won't want to miss the reefs and underwater fantasy worlds of the Banco Chinchorro, the largest coral atoll in the northern hemisphere. Some 45km long and up to 14km wide, Chinchorro's western edge lies about 30km off the coast, and dozens of ships have fallen victim to its barely submerged ring of coral. There are plenty of shipwreck sites worth exploring. Along the way you'll also spot coral walls and canyons, rays, turtles, giant sponges, grouper, tangs, eels and, in some spots, reef, tiger and hammerhead sharks.

There's good snorkeling as well, including **40 Cannons**, a wooden ship in 5m to 6m of water. Looters have taken all but about 25 of the cannons, and it can only be visited in ideal conditions. The atoll and its surrounding waters were made a biosphere reserve (Reserva de la Biosfera Banco Chinchorro) to protect them from depredation, but the reserve lacks the personnel and equipment needed to patrol such a large area, and many abuses go undetected.

Local tour operators arrange fishing trips (M$800 per hour for up to four people) and 2½-hour snorkeling tours (M$267 per person). Look for them beachside along the *malecón*.

Gypsea Divers DIVING

(cell phone 983-1303714; www.gypseadivers.com) Offers diving (two tanks M$1070), snorkeling and fishing trips. Find it on the *malecón*.

Sleeping & Eating

Addresses are given as distances from the military checkpoint at the north entrance to town. There are about a dozen restaurants along the *malecón*, each offering a standard assortment of seafood, Mexican favorites and pub grub.

Quieter, more upscale accommodations are 2km south of the town center – see www.mahahual-southbeach.com for details.

Hotel Jardin HOTEL $

(983-700-59-46; hostal.jardin.mahahual@gmail.com; dm/d M$130/400;) For the price, a surprisingly stylish little three-room hotel, set back from the beach in the center of town. Rooms are spacious and spotless and the dorms are the best in town by far.

Hotel Maya Luna CABAÑAS $$

(983-836-09-05; www.hotelmayaluna.com; Km 5.2; cabañas from M$1100;) Four sweet little bungalows on a lovely stretch of beach south of town. Kayaks are available and there's a good restaurant onsite (try the stuffed pineapple, a Mexican/Euro/Indonesian extravaganza; M$150).

Hotel Matan Ka'an HOTEL $$

(983-834-56-79; www.matankaan.com; Calle Huachinango; r/ste from M$960/1440; P) On the south side of the soccer field, this large whitewashed hotel has a relaxed resort feel, plenty of common areas and large, clean rooms. We only wish 'the gift from the heavens' – that's what Matan Ka'an means in Maya – included beach access, but hey, the ocean is only 100m away.

100% Agave MEXICAN $

(mains M$60-100; 11am-late) Good cheap Mexican food, with the ramshackle ambience adding to the flavor. La Bodeguita across the road is a fun, authentic local drinking spot.

Getting There & Around

Mahahual is 127km south of Felipe Carrillo Puerto, and approximately 100km east of Bacalar. There are buses for Chetumal (M$115, 2½ hours, 6:30pm), Cancún (M$260, five hours, 5:30pm) and Laguna Bacalar (M$80, two hours, 6:30pm).

Xcalak

☎983

The rickety wooden houses, beached fishing launches and lazy gliding pelicans make this tiny town plopped in the middle of nowhere a perfect escape. Blessed by virtue of its remoteness and the Chinchorro atoll (preventing the creation of a cruise-ship port), Xcalak may yet escape the development boom.

Today, there are no signs of Xcalak getting a bank, grocery store or gas station anytime soon, so stock up before you come.

Sights & Activities

The mangrove swamps stretching inland from the coastal road hide some large lagoons and form tunnels that invite kayakers to explore. There's a remote Maya ruin on the western side of the lagoon. Your hotelier can tell you how to get there.

XTC Dive Center DIVING
(www.xtcdivecenter.com; coast road, Km 0.3; 2-tank dives to Banco Chinchorro M$2580, snorkeling trips M$325) About 300m north of town on the coast road, this center offers dive and snorkel trips (from M$300) to the wondrous barrier reef just offshore, and two-tank dives at Banco Chinchorro. It also offers PADI open-water certificates for M$5655, as well as fishing and bird-watching tours and guided kayaking expeditions, either in the ocean or the network of mangroves behind town. To visit Chinchorro, you can get your M$50 biosphere reserve wristband here or at the park office in town.

Be aware that this is the only dive operator licensed to take boats out to Chinchorro.

Sleeping

With the exception of the 'downtown' Caracol Caribe, most hotels are found on the old coastal road leading north from town. Addresses are expressed in kilometers north along the coast from town.

Caracol Caribe HOTEL $
(☎983-839-83-81; Centro; r M$350) Basic, reasonably comfortable rooms a block from the beach. And that's about as 'budget' as this town gets, sorry.

Costa de Cocos RESORT $$
(www.costadecocos.com; coast road, Km 1; r incl breakfast M$900; P) Most guests stay here for the fly-fishing and scuba-diving tours available. It doesn't have a very good beach for swimming, but the *palapa* rooms are a good deal. There's no telephone.

Hotel Tierra Maya HOTEL $$$
(☎983-839-80-12; www.tierramaya.net; coast road, Km 2; r M$1368-2280) A modern beachfront hotel with six lovely rooms (three quite large), each tastefully appointed and with many architectural details. Each of the rooms has mahogany furniture and a balcony facing the sea; the bigger rooms even have small refrigerators.

Eating

The most reliable eats in town (in terms of opening hours) can be found at the Coral Bar & Grill, attached to XTC Dive Center.

Toby's SEAFOOD $
(Leona Vicario s/n; mains M$70-160; 11am-8pm) On the main drag in town, the friendly chit-chat and well-prepared fish and seafood dishes here make this a popular expat spot. Try the coconut shrimp and you'll know why.

Leaky Palapa INTERNATIONAL $$
(www.leakypalaparestaurant.com; mains M$95-210; 5-10pm Thu-Sun Nov-May, Fri & Sat only Jun-Oct) Chef Marla and owner Linda have turned an old standby into a new sensation, serving wonderful meals, such as lobster in caramel ginger sauce. Opinion is unanimous that this is the best place to go to treat your taste buds. From the lighthouse, walk two blocks north and one block inland. Online reservations required.

Getting There & Around

Cabs from Limones, on Hwy 307, cost about M$650 (including to the northern hotels). Buses to Chetumal (and Limones) leave at 5am and 2pm and cost M$75. The bus stops by the lighthouse.

Driving from Limones, turn right (south) after 55km and follow the signs to Xcalak (another 60km). Keep an eye out for the diverse wildlife that frequents the forest and mangroves; a lot of it runs out into the road. The coastal road between Mahahual and Xcalak is closed.

You can hire a boat at the XTC Dive Center for M$600 per person (minimum five people) to take you to San Pedro, Belize.

Laguna Bacalar

☎983

A large, clear, turquoise freshwater lake with a bottom of gleaming white sand, Laguna Bacalar comes as a surprise in this region of tortured limestone and scrubby jungle.

The small, sleepy town of Bacalar, just east of the highway, 125km south of Felipe Carrillo Puerto, is the only settlement of any size on the lake. It's noted mostly for its old Spanish fortress and its popular *balnearios* (bathing places).

There's a small **tourist kiosk** (Central Plaza; 9am-8pm Mon-Fri, 10am-6pm Sat) inside the real estate office on the plaza.

Sights & Activities

Fortress FORTRESS

(admission M$62; 9am-7pm Tue-Thu & Sun, to 8pm Fri & Sat) The fortress above the lagoon was built to protect citizens from raids by pirates and the local indigenous population. It also served as an important outpost for the Spanish in the Caste War. In 1859 it was seized by Maya rebels, who held the fort until Quintana Roo was finally conquered by Mexican troops in 1901.

Today, with formidable cannons still on its ramparts, the fortress remains an imposing sight. It houses a museum exhibiting colonial armaments and uniforms from the 17th and 18th centuries.

Balneario SWIMMING

(admission M$10; 7am-7pm) This swimming spot lies a few hundred meters north along the *costera* (waterfront avenue) below the fort. There are some small restaurants along the avenue and near the *balneario*, which is very busy on weekends.

Cenote Azul SWIMMING

(Hwy 307; life vests M$35; 8am-6pm) FREE Just shy of the south end of the *costera* is this cenote, a 90m-deep natural pool with an onsite bar and restaurant (mains M$80 to M$250). It's 200m east of Hwy 307, so many buses will drop you nearby.

Sleeping & Eating

Yaxche Centro HOSTEL $

(☎983-834-20-81; www.ecoaventurabacalar.com.mx; 9 Av, btwn Calles 22 & 24; dm M$170; P 📶) The hostelling scene in Bacalar picked up about 1000% when this place opened up – dorms are spacious enough, the garden is huge and jungly and it has a decent central location, a few blocks west of the plaza and a 10-minute walk to the water.

Amigos B&B Laguna Bacalar B&B $$

(☎983-834-20-93; www.bacalar.net; d M$800; P ❄ @ 📶) Right on the lake and about 500m south of the fort, this ideally located property has five spacious guest rooms with hammocks, terraces and a comfy shared common area. Breakfast will cost you an additional M$100.

Casita Carolina GUESTHOUSE $$

(☎983-834-23-34; www.casitacarolina.com; d from M$600, campsites M$200; P 📶) A delightful place about 1½ blocks south of the fort, the Casita has a large lawn leading down to the lake, five fan-cooled rooms and a deluxe *palapa* that sleeps up to four. Kayaks are available for guest use.

Orizaba MEXICAN $

(Av 7, btwn Calles 24 & 26; mains M$60-100; 8am-4:30pm) Highly recommended by locals and expats alike, this place prepares home-style Mexican favorites in a casual setting.

Getting There & Away

Southbound 2nd-class buses go through Bacalar town on Calle 7, passing a block uphill from the central square *(el parque)*, which is just above the fortress and has a taxi stand. Northbound 2nd-class buses run along Calle 5, a block downhill from Calle 7. Most 1st-class buses don't enter town, but many will drop you along Hwy 307 at the turnoffs to Hotel Laguna and Cenote Azul; check before you buy your ticket.

If you're driving from the north and want to reach the town and fortress, take the first Bacalar exit and continue several blocks before turning left (east) down the hill. From Chetumal, head west to catch Hwy 307 heading north; after 25km on the highway you'll reach the signed right turn for Cenote Azul and the *costera*.

Chetumal

☎983 / POP 150,000

The capital city of Quintana Roo, Chetumal has stylish, friendly people, some decent restaurants and a lively music scene. The bayside esplanade hosts carnivals and events (Carnaval is late February or early March), and the modern Maya museum is impressive (though a bit short on artifacts). Extensive Maya ruins, amazing jungle and the border to neighboring Belize are all close by.

History

Before the Spanish conquest, Chetumal was a Maya port, but the town was not officially 'settled' until 1898, when Spanish troops moved in to put a stop to the illegal trade in arms and lumber by descendants of War of the Castes rebels. Dubbed Payo Obispo, the town changed its name to Chetumal in 1936. In 1955, Hurricane Janet virtually obliterated downtown, but the city was rebuilt to a grand plan with a grid of wide boulevards along which traffic speeds (be careful at stop signs).

Sights

Museo de la Cultura Maya MUSEUM

(983-832-68-38; Av de los Héroes 68, cnr Av Gandhi; admission M$62; 9am-7pm Tue-Sun) The Museo de la Cultura Maya is the city's claim to cultural fame – a bold showpiece beautifully conceived and executed. It's organized into three levels, mirroring Maya cosmology. The main floor represents this world; the upper floor the heavens; and the lower floor Xibalbá, the underworld. The various exhibits cover all of the Mayab (lands of the Maya).

Scale models show the great Maya buildings as they may have appeared, including a temple complex set below Plexiglas you can walk over. Though artifacts are in short supply, there are replicas of stelae and a burial chamber from Honduras' Copán, reproductions of the murals found in Room 1 at Bonampak, and much more. Ingenious mechanical and computer displays illustrate the Maya's complex calendrical, numerical and writing systems.

Museo de la Ciudad MUSEUM

(Local History Museum; Héroes de Chapultepec, cnr Av de los Héroes; admission M$15; 9am-7pm Tue-Sat, to 2pm Sun) The Museo de la Ciudad is small but neatly done, displaying historic photos, military artifacts and old-time household items (even some vintage telephones and a TV). All labels are in Spanish, but even if you don't read the language, it's worth visiting for 15 minutes of entertainment.

Sleeping

Hotel Ucum HOTEL $

(983-832-07-11, 983-832-61-86; www.hotelucumchetumal.com; Av Gandhi 167, btwn Avs de los Héroes & 16 de Septiembre; d with fan/air-con M$220/380;) Despite its rather unfortunate name (a town in Campeche), it offers decent rooms as far as dirt-cheap budget accommodations go, plus a (slightly murky) swimming pool and a restaurant serving good, inexpensive food.

Hotel Platas HOTEL $$

(983-832-03-54; http://hotelplatas.com; Elías Calles 205; r M$500;) In a relatively quiet spot just off the main drag, this one gets the thumbs up for big, airy rooms featuring two super-comfy king-size beds.

Hotel Los Cocos HOTEL $$

(983-835-04-30; www.hotelloscocos.com.mx; Av de los Héroes 134, cnr Héroes de Chapultepec; d/ste with air-con from M$912/1824;) Has a great location and a seriously mirrored lobby that gets your inner disco dancer rising. There's also a nice swimming pool, a Jacuzzi, a gym and a popular sidewalk restaurant.

Eating & Drinking

Near the ADO 2nd-Class Terminal, you'll find a row of small, simple eateries serving cheap meals at the **Mercado Ignacio Manuel Altamirano**. If you're wondering where everybody is on the weekend, head down to the *malecón,* the 3km strip of seafront restaurants and bars that serves as the city's playground.

★ A lo Natural MEXICAN $

(Elias Calles, btwn Avs de los Héroes & 5 de Mayo; mains around M$25; 11am-11:30pm) Excellent, freshly prepared *tortas* (sandwiches), quesadillas, *gringas* (tacos with a quesadilla base), *dobladas* (stuffed folded tortillas) and other street-style snacks are to be found at this friendly and spotless open-air eatery just off the main street.

La Pantoja YUCATECAN $

(cnr Avs Gandhi & 16 de Septiembre; mains M$50-100; 7am-7pm) A sweet little family-run place serving up regional and Mexican standards, daily lunch specials and meal-sized *tortas*.

Café-Restaurant Los Milagros CAFE $

(983-832-44-33; Zaragoza, cnr Av 5 de Mayo; mains M$25-65; 7:30am-9pm Mon-Sat, to 1pm Sun) Serves great espresso and food outdoors. A favorite with Chetumal's student and intellectual set, it's a good spot to chat it up with locals or while away the time with a game of dominoes.

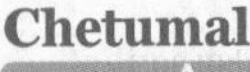

Chetumal

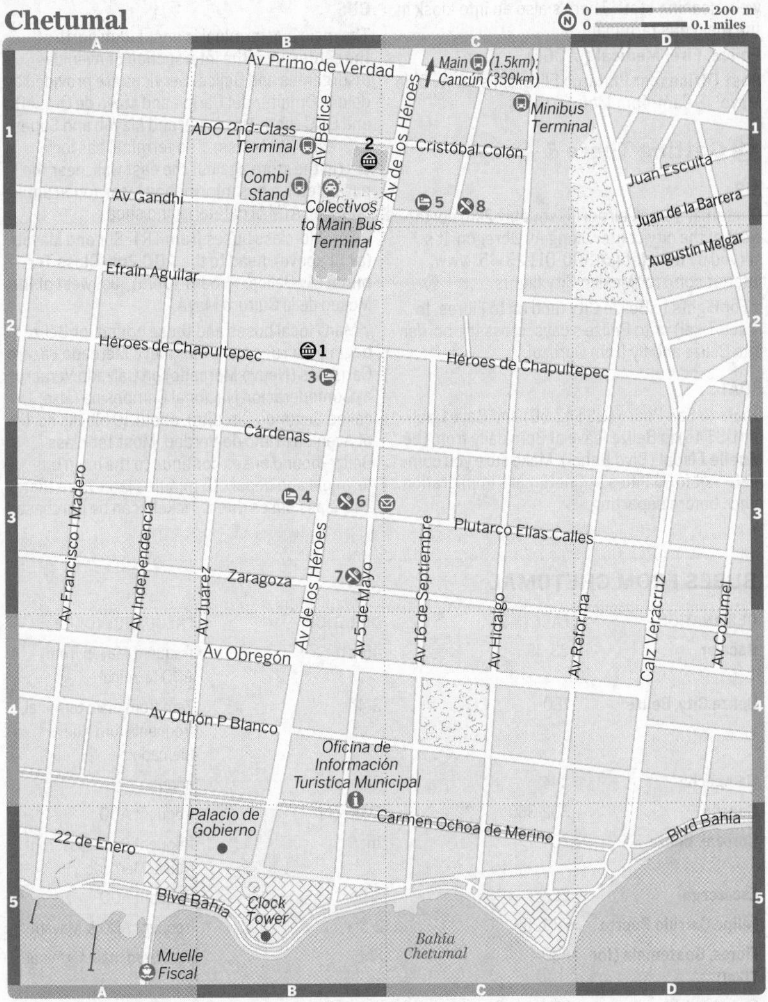

Information

There are several banks and ATMs around town, including an ATM inside the bus terminal.

Cruz Roja (Red Cross; ☎983-832-05-71; cnr Avs Independencia & Héroes de Chapultepec; ⏲24hr) For medical emergencies.

Immigration Office (☎983-832-63-26; ⏲9am-1pm Mon-Fri) Located about 800m north of the *glorieta* (roundabout); ask for the *oficina de inmigración*.

Oficina de Información Turistíca Municipal (Municipal Tourist Office; ☎983-833-24-65; cnr Carmen Ochoa de Merino & Av 5 de Mayo; ⏲8am-4pm Mon-Fri) Has brochures and

Chetumal

Sights

1 Museo de la Ciudad B2
2 Museo de la Cultura Maya B1

Sleeping

3 Hotel Los Cocos B2
4 Hotel Platas B3
5 Hotel Ucum C1

Eating

6 A lo Natural B3
7 Café-Restaurant Los Milagros B3
8 La Pantoja C1

well-meaning staff. There's also an info kiosk in the main bus terminal.

Police, Fire, Medical (☎066)

Post Office (cnr Plutarco Elías Calles & Av 5 de Mayo; ⌚9am-4pm Mon-Fri)

Getting There & Away

AIR

Chetumal's small airport is roughly 2km northwest of the city center along Av Obregón. It's served by **Interjet** (☎800-011-23-45; www.interjet.com) for Mexico City flights.

For flights to Belize City (and on to Flores, to reach Tikal) or to Belize's cays, cross the border into Belize and fly from Corozal.

BOAT

Boats to San Pedro (US$42.50) and Caye Caulker (US$45) in Belize leave at 3pm daily from the **Muelle Fiscal** (Blvd Bahai). Make sure you complete exit formalities at Chetumal's immigration office before departing.

BUS

The main bus terminal is about 2km north of the center, near the intersection of Avenidas Insurgentes and Belice. Services are provided by deluxe Omnitur del Caribe and Maya de Oro; ADO and OCC (both 1st class); and Mayab and Super Expresso (2nd class). The terminal has lockers (in the store against the east wall, near the pay toilets), a bus information kiosk (open until 3pm), an ATM, a cafeteria and shops.

For 2nd-class buses from TRT, Sur and Mayab (a cut above), head to the **ADO 2nd-Class Terminal** (Av Belice; ⌚6am-10pm), just west of the Museo de la Cultura Maya.

Many local buses and those bound for Belize begin their runs from the Nuevo Mercado Lázaro Cárdenas (Neuvo Mercado) on Calzada Veracruz at Confederación Nacional Campesina (also called Segundo Circuito), about 10 blocks north of Avenida Primo de Verdad. Most 1st-class Belize-bound buses continue to the main bus terminal and depart 15 minutes later from there; 2nd-class buses don't. Tickets can be purchased

BUSES FROM CHETUMAL

DESTINATION	FARE (M$)	DURATION	FREQUENCY (DAILY)
Bacalar	28-35	45min	frequent Mayab from ADO terminal
Belize City, Belize	180	3-4hr	7am from main terminal, frequent from Nuevo Mercado
Campeche	344	6hr	noon
Cancún	302-360	5½-6½hr	frequent ADO
Corozal, Belize	30	1hr	frequent 2nd-class from Nuevo Mercado
Escárcega	222	4-6hr	frequent ADO
Felipe Carrillo Puerto	78-128	2-3hr	frequent ADO & Mayab
Flores, Guatemala (for Tikal)	430	8hr	7am from main terminal
Mahahual	100	4hr	2 ADO
Mérida	246-366	6-8hr	frequent 1st & 2nd class
Orange Walk, Belize	35-50	2¼hr	frequent 1st- & 2nd-class Novelos & Northern from Nuevo Mercado
Palenque	394-468	7-8hr	3 daily
Tulum	150-204	3½-4hr	frequent
Valladolid	182	6hr	2 Mayab from main terminal
Villahermosa	458	7-9hr	5 ADO
Xcalak	95	5hr	2 Mayab from ADO terminal
Xpujil	106	2-3hr	10 ADO

on board the buses or (1st class only) at the main terminal.

The **minibus terminal** (cnr Avs Primo de Verdad & Hidalgo) has infrequent services to Bacalar (M$30) – you're probably better off getting a shared taxi (see below).

Check your bus details before departure because buses leave from multiple locations, and schedules and departure points are subject to rapid change.

TAXI

Gibson's Tours & Transfers (☎ in Belize 501-623-86-28; www.gibsonstoursandtransfers.com; Santa Elena–Corozal border) has taxis to the border (M$380) and Corozal (M$760).

If you're heading for Bacalar and want to go by taxi, look for the cabs with 'Bacalar' written on the door (they hang out around the Cruz Roja on Independencía). These vehicles have come from Balacar and drivers will be looking for a fare back again, so the price is typically lower (sometimes as low as M$35) than offered by Chetumal-based taxis.

ℹ Getting Around

For journeys in town taxis charge a flat fare of M$25. From the traffic circle at Avenida de los Héroes, you can also get a shared combi (van) for M$3 to the town center on the Santa María or Calderitas lines. To reach the main bus terminal from the center, catch a *colectivo* from Avenida Belice behind the Museo de la Cultura Maya. Ask to be left at the *glorieta* at Avenida Insurgentes. Head west to reach the terminal.

YUCATÁN STATE

A vast expanse of largely undeveloped Gulf coastline, some fantastic nature reserves, a couple of cosmopolitan cities and some world-famous archaeological sites have made Yucatán state a favorite with travelers for decades.

The depth of experience here is almost incomparable – for city lovers, Mérida is big and bustling but wonderfully preserved, with gloriously crumbling, stately buildings on every downtown block. Smaller cities like Valladolid shift down a couple of gears and the pace of life in places like Izamal is downright dreamy.

Archaeology fans are in for various treats, too, from the international-superstar attraction of Chichén Itzá to the lesser-known but equally worthy Uxmal. If you can arrange the transportation, a trip along the Ruta Puuc can take you to four or five ruins in just one day.

Bird-watchers are well catered for, too – the nature reserves protecting the estuaries around Celestún and Río Lagartos are home to eye-popping populations of waterfowl, most notably flamingos.

Mérida

☎999 / ELEV 22M / POP 830,000

Since the Spanish conquest, Mérida has been the cultural capital of the entire peninsula. At times provincial, at others *'muy cosmopolitano,'* it is a town steeped in colonial history, with narrow streets, broad central plazas and the region's best museums. It's also a perfect hub city to kick off your adventure into the rest of Yucatán state. There are cheap eats, good hostels and hotels, thriving markets, and goings-on just about every night somewhere in the downtown area.

Long popular with European travelers looking to go beyond the hubbub of Quintana Roo's resort towns, Mérida is not an 'undiscovered Mexican gem' like some of the tourist brochures claim. Simply put, it's a tourist town, but a tourist town too big to feel like a tourist trap. And as the capital of Yucatán state, Mérida is also the cultural crossroads of the region.

Note that odd-numbered streets run east-west; even-numbered streets run north-south. Intersections are more useful for orientation than house numbers; addresses in Mérida are usually given in this form: 'Calle 57 No 481 x 56 y 58' (between streets 56 and 58).

History

Francisco de Montejo the Younger founded a Spanish colony at Campeche, about 160km to the southwest, in 1540. From this base he took advantage of political dissension among the Maya people, conquering T'ho (now Mérida) in 1542. By the decade's end, Yucatán was mostly under Spanish colonial rule.

When Montejo's conquistadors entered T'ho, they found a major Maya settlement of lime-mortared stone that reminded them of the Roman architecture in Mérida, Spain. They promptly renamed the city and proceeded to build it into the regional capital, dismantling the Maya structures and using the materials to construct a cathedral and other stately buildings. Mérida took its

Mérida

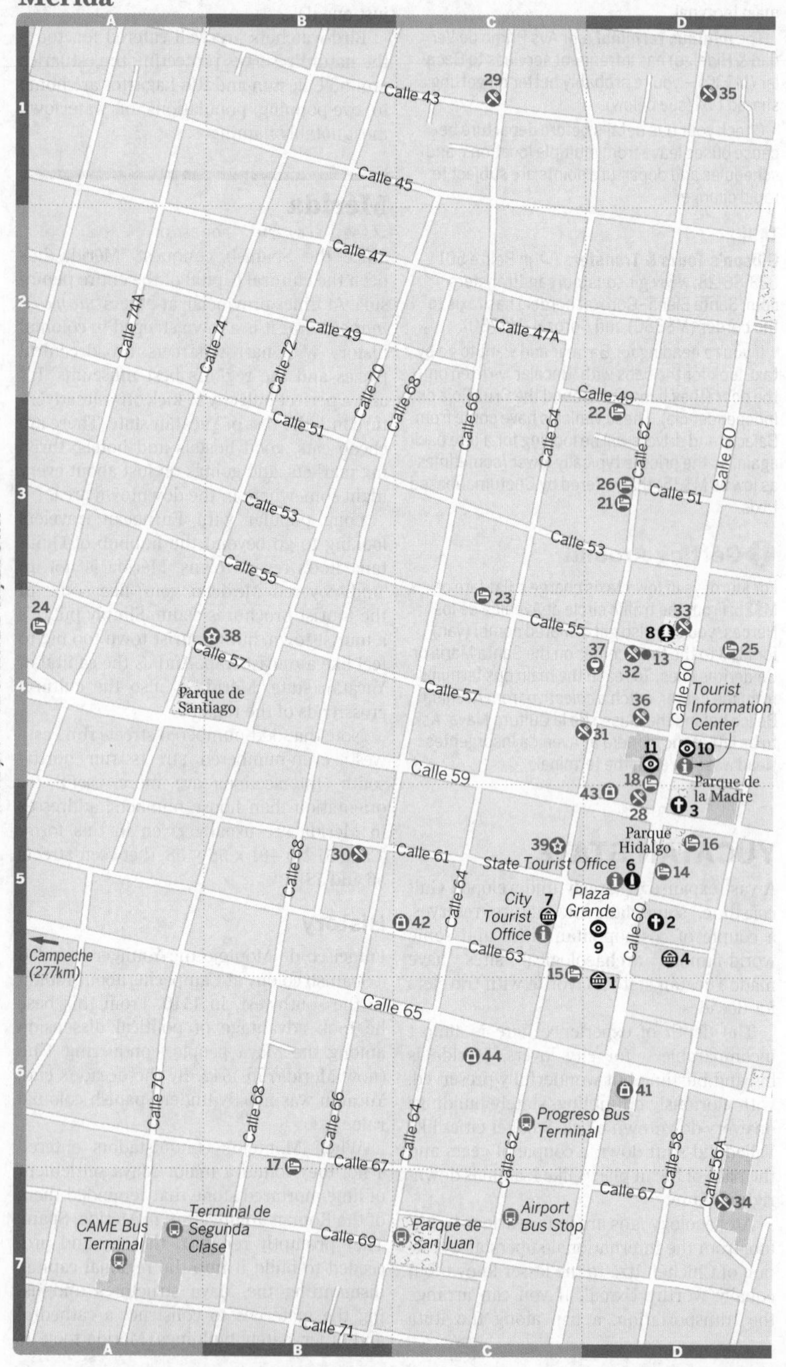
A
B
C
D
1
2
3
4
5
6
7
Calle 43
Calle 45
Calle 47
Calle 47A
Calle 49
Calle 51
Calle 53
Calle 55
Calle 57
Calle 59
Calle 61
Calle 63
Calle 65
Calle 67
Calle 69
Calle 71
Calle 74A
Calle 74
Calle 72
Calle 70
Calle 68
Calle 66
Calle 64
Calle 62
Calle 60
Calle 58
Calle 56A
Parque de Santiago
Tourist Information Center
Parque de la Madre
Parque Hidalgo
State Tourist Office
City Tourist Office
Plaza Grande
Campeche (277km)
Progreso Bus Terminal
Airport Bus Stop
CAME Bus Terminal
Terminal de Segunda Clase
Parque de San Juan
1
2
3
4
6
7
8
9
10
11
13
14
15
16
17
18
21
22
23
24
25
26
28
29
30
31
32
33
34
35
36
37
38
39
41
42
43
44

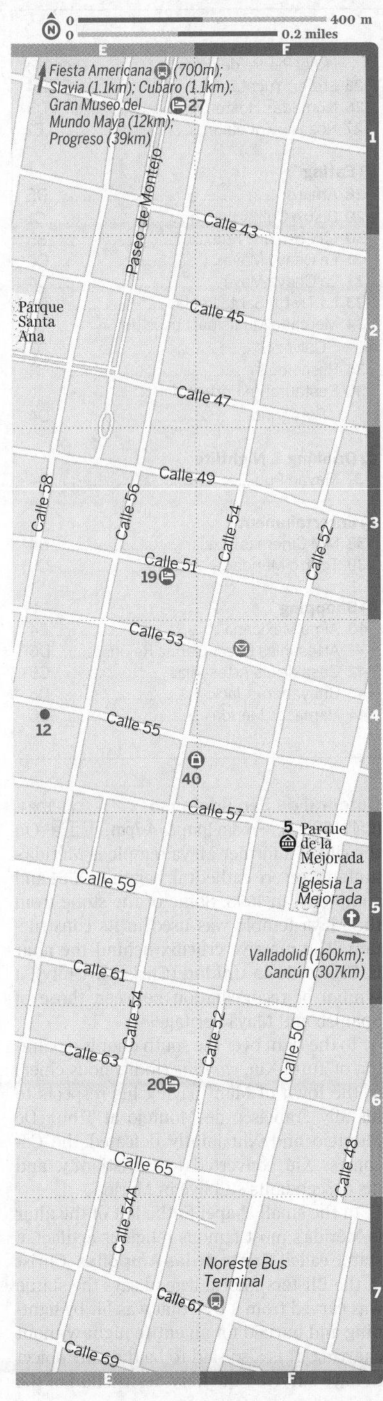

colonial orders directly from Spain, not from Mexico City, and Yucatán has had a distinct cultural and political identity ever since.

During the War of the Castes, only Mérida and Campeche were able to hold out against the rebel forces. On the brink of surrender, the ruling class in Mérida was saved by reinforcements sent from central Mexico in exchange for Mérida's agreement to take orders from Mexico City.

Mérida today is the peninsula's center of commerce, a bustling city that has benefited greatly from the *maquiladoras* (assembly plants) that opened in the 1980s and '90s and the tourism industry that picked up during those decades.

Sights

On Sundays the extremely popular Biciruta sees Calle 60 and part of the Paseo de Montejo closed off to traffic as people take to the streets biking, skating and dog walking. Bikes can be hired (M$20 per hour) at the Plaza Grande or the southern end of the Paseo Montejo.

Plaza Grande — PLAZA

FREE One of the prettiest plazas in Mexico, with huge laurel trees shading the park's benches and wide sidewalks. This was the religious and social center of ancient T'ho; under the Spanish it was the Plaza de Armas, the parade ground, laid out by Francisco de Montejo (the Younger). There's a crafts market Sunday and dance or live music nearly every night.

Casa de Montejo — MUSEUM

(Museo Casa Montejo; www.casasdeculturabanamex.com/museocasamontejo; Calle 63 No 506, Palacio de Montejo; 10am-7pm Tue-Sat, to 2pm Sun) FREE Casa de Montejo is on the south side of the Plaza Grande and dates from 1549. It originally housed soldiers but was soon converted into a mansion that served members of the Montejo family until 1970. Today it houses a bank and a museum with a permanent exhibition of renovated Victorian, neo-Rococo and neo-Renaissance furnishings of the historic building.

Outside, take a close look at the facade, where triumphant conquistadors with halberds hold their feet on the necks of generic barbarians (though they're not Maya, the association is inescapable). Typical of the symbolism in colonial statuary, the vanquished are rendered much smaller than the victors; works on various churches throughout the

Mérida

Sights

1 Casa de Montejo ... D6
2 Catedral de San Ildefonso ... D5
3 Iglesia de Jesús ... D5
4 Museo de Arte Contemporáneo ... D5
5 Museo de Arte Popular de Yucatán ... F5
6 Palacio de Gobierno ... D5
7 Palacio Municipal ... C5
8 Parque Santa Lucía ... D4
9 Plaza Grande ... D5
10 Teatro Peón Contreras ... D4
11 Universidad Autónoma de Yucatán ... D4

Activities, Courses & Tours

12 Calle 55 Spanish School ... E4
Historic Centre Tours ... (see 7)
13 Turitransmérida ... D4

Sleeping

14 Gran Hotel ... D5
15 Hostel Zocalo ... C5
16 Hotel Caribe ... D5
17 Hotel Casa Becil ... B6
18 Hotel del Parque ... D4
19 Hotel del Peregrino ... E3
20 Hotel Dolores Alba ... E6
21 Hotel Hacienda Mérida ... D3
22 Hotel Marionetas ... D3
23 Hotel Medio Mundo ... C4
24 Hotel Mérida Santiago ... A4
Hotel Piedra de Agua ... (see 14)
25 Luz en Yucatán ... D4
26 Nómadas Hostel ... D3
27 Rosas y Xocolate ... E1

Eating

28 Amaro ... D5
29 Bistro Cultural ... C1
30 La Casa de Frida ... B5
31 La Chaya Maya ... C4
32 La Chaya Maya ... D4
33 La Tratto Santa Lucía ... D4
34 Mercado Municipal Lucas de Gálvez ... D7
35 Rescoldo's ... D1
36 Restaurante Pórtico del Peregrino ... D4

Drinking & Nightlife

37 Mayan Pub ... D4

Entertainment

38 MM Cinemas ... B4
39 Teatro Mérida ... C5

Shopping

40 Alma Mexicana ... E4
41 Artesanías Bazar García Rejón ... D6
42 Casa de las Artesanías ... C5
43 Guayaberas Jack ... D5
44 Hamacas Mérida ... C6

region feature big priests towering over or in front of small indigenous people. Also gazing across the plaza from the facade are busts of Montejo the Elder, his wife and his daughter.

Gran Museo del Mundo Maya MUSEUM
(www.granmuseodelmundomaya.com; Calle 60 Nte No 299E; adult/child under 12yr M$150/50; 8am-5pm Wed-Mon) Considered an important addition to Mérida's rich cultural tradition, this new Maya-themed museum showcases a permanent exhibit of 500 artifacts ranging from stone sculptures and jewelry to ceramics and etchings. Opened in 2012, the museum is divided into six sections: ancient Maya, modern Maya, culture and nature, art and science, society, and world view.

You'll find the museum about 12km north of downtown along the road to Progreso. Public transport departing from Calle 58, between Calles 57 and 59, heads to the Gran Plaza mall, which is a short walk away from the museum.

Catedral de San Ildefonso CATHEDRAL
(Calle 60 s/n; 6am-1pm & 4-7pm) FREE On the site of a former Maya temple is Mérida's hulking, severe cathedral, begun in 1561 and completed in 1598. Some of the stone from the Maya temple was used in its construction. The massive crucifix behind the altar is **Cristo de la Unidad** (Christ of Unity), a symbol of reconciliation between those of Spanish and Maya heritage.

To the right over the south door is a painting of Tutul Xiu, *cacique* (indigenous chief) of the town of Maní paying his respects to his ally Francisco de Montejo at T'ho. (De Montejo and Xiu jointly defeated the Cocomes; Xiu converted to Christianity, and his descendants still live in Mérida.)

In the small chapel to the left of the altar is Mérida's most famous religious artifact, a statue called **Cristo de las Ampollas** (Christ of the Blisters). Local legend says the statue was carved from a tree that was hit by lightning and burned for an entire night without charring. It is also said to be the only object to have survived the fiery destruction of the church in the town of Ichmul (though it was blackened and blistered from the heat). The statue was moved to the Mérida cathedral in 1645.

Other than these items, the cathedral's interior is largely plain, its rich decoration having been stripped away by angry peasants at the height of anticlerical fervor during the Mexican Revolution.

Museo de Arte Contemporáneo MUSEUM

(Macay; ☎999-928-32-36; www.macay.org; Pasaje de la Revolución, btwn Calles 58 & 60; ⏲10am-6pm) FREE Housed in the former archbishop's palace, the attractive Museo de Arte Contemporáneo holds permanent exhibitions of Yucatán's most famous painters and sculptors, as well as revolving exhibitions by local craftspeople.

Palacio Municipal HISTORIC BUILDING

(City Hall; Calle 62) FREE Originally built in 1542, Mérida's Palacio Municipal was twice refurbished, in the 1730s and the 1850s. It's worth having a poke around inside for the collection of baroque furnishings, impressive murals and the elevated rear patio, constructed on the base of the Maya pyramid located here in pre-colonial times.

Palacio de Gobierno PUBLIC ART

(Calle 61; ⏲8am-9.30pm) FREE Built in 1892, the Palacio de Gobierno houses the state of Yucatán's executive government offices (and a tourist office). Have a look inside at the murals painted by local artist Fernando Castro Pacheco. Completed in 1978, they were 25 years in the making and portray a symbolic history of the Maya and their interaction with the Spaniards.

Museo de Arte Popular de Yucatán MUSEUM

(Yucatecan Museum of Popular Art; Calle 50A No 487; ⏲10am-5pm Tue-Sat, to 3pm Sun) FREE In a building built in 1906, the Museo de Arte Popular de Yucatán has a small rotating exhibition downstairs that features pop art from around Mexico. The upstairs exhibitions give you an idea of how locals embroider *huipiles* (long, woven, white sleeveless tunics with intricate, colorful embroidery), carve ceremonial masks and weave hammocks.

Calle 60

Calle 60 is one of Mérida's most historic streets. The 17th-century **Iglesia de Jesús** (Calle 60), also called Iglesia de la Tercera Orden, rises a block north of the Plaza Grande, beyond shady Parque Hidalgo. Built by the Jesuits in 1618, it is the sole surviving edifice from a complex of buildings that once filled the entire city block.

North of the church is the enormous bulk of the **Teatro Peón Contreras** (cnr Calles 60 & 57; ⏲9am-6pm Tue-Sat), built between 1900 and 1908, during Mérida's *henequén* (agave plant fibres) heyday. It boasts a main staircase of Carrara marble, a dome with faded frescoes by Italian artists, and various paintings and murals throughout the building.

Across Calle 60 from the theater is the main building of the **Universidad Autónoma de Yucatán** (Calle 60). The modern university was established in the 19th century by Governor Felipe Carrillo Puerto and General Manuel Cepeda Peraza.

A block north of the university is pretty little **Parque Santa Lucía** (cnr Calles 60 & 55), with arcades on the north and west sides. When Mérida was a lot smaller, this was where travelers would get on or off the stagecoaches that linked towns and villages with the provincial capital. The **Bazar de Artesanías**, the local handicrafts market, is held here at 10am on Sunday.

The downtown portion of Calle 60 is closed off to traffic Thursday through Sunday nights, making for a nice stroll.

Courses

You can often find a private language tutor through your hostel. Alternatively, **Benjamin Franklin Academy** (☎999-928-00-97; www.benjaminfranklin.com.mx; cnr Calles 57 & 54) and **Calle 55 Spanish School** (☎999-274-31-30; www.calle-55.com; Calle 55 btwn Calles 56 & 58) offer Spanish courses.

Tours

Many hotels will book tours, as will Nómadas Hostel, which also arranges a variety of other tours.

Historic Centre Tours WALKING TOUR

(☎999-942-00-00, ext 80119; www.merida.gob.mx/turismo; Calle 62, Plaza Grande; ⏲8am-8pm) FREE The city tourist office offers free guided walking tours of the historic center departing daily from the Palacio Municipal at 9:30am. You can also rent audio guides here for M$80 if you prefer to go it alone.

Turibus GUIDED TOUR

(☎999-946-24-24; www.turibus.com.mx; adult/child M$120/50) Offers hop-on, hop-off tours of Mérida in English and Spanish on its double-decker Circuito Turístico bus, passing by Plaza Grande, Paseo de Montejo and Parque de las Américas among other places. Buy tickets on board.

Turitransmérida TOUR
(☎999-924-11-99; www.turitransmerida.com.mx; Calle 55, btwn Calles 60 & 62) Turitransmérida is one of the largest of the many agencies offering group tours to sites around Mérida, including Celestún, Chichén Itzá, the Ruta Puuc and Izamal.

Festivals & Events

Anniversary of the Universidad de Yucatán CULTURAL
For most of February the Universidad de Yucatán celebrates its anniversary with free performances by the Ballet Folklórico, concerts of Afro-Cuban music and *son* (Mexican folk music that blends elements of indigenous, Spanish and African musical styles), and other manifestations of Yucatán's cultural roots.

Carnaval RELIGIOUS
Prior to Lent, in February or March, Carnaval features colorful costumes and nonstop festivities. It's celebrated with greater vigor in Mérida than anywhere else in Yucatán state.

Festival de Trova Yucateca MUSIC
Performances of *trova yucateca* (traditional ballads) are held in March.

Semana Santa RELIGIOUS
(Holy Week) A major celebration in Mérida over Easter week, with processions and performances of passion plays.

Cristo de las Ampollas Processions Religious PARADE
Between September 22 and October 14, *gremios* (guilds or unions) venerate the Cristo de las Ampollas (Christ of the Blisters) statue in the Catedral de San Ildefonso with processions.

Exposición de Altares de los Muertos RELIGIOUS
On October 31, families prepare shrines to welcome the spirits of loved ones back to earth for Day of the Dead. Many Maya prepare elaborate dinners outside their homes, and Mérida observes the occasion with festivities and displays in the town center from 11am on November 1 until 11am the next day.

Sleeping

Nómadas Hostel HOSTEL $
(☎999-924-52-23; www.nomadastravel.com; Calle 62 No 433; dm from M$140, d with/without bathroom M$440/340; P @ ☜ ≈) This is hands down Mérida's best hostel. There are mixed and women's dorms, as well as private rooms. Guests have use of a fully equipped kitchen with fridge, laundry facilities and an amazing pool out back.

Hostel Zocalo HOSTEL $
(☎999-930-95-62; www.hostalzocalo.com; Calle 63 No 508; dm M$140, r with/without bathroom from M$450/300; @ ☜) A great location in a beautiful old colonial building make this hostel unique. It has firm beds and a big buffet breakfast. The service can be a bit gruff, though, and you may have problems getting hot water.

Hotel Casa Becil HOTEL $
(☎999-924-67-64; hotelcasabecil@yahoo.com.mx; Calle 67 No 550C, btwn Calles 66 & 68; s/d with fan M$290-340, d with air-con M$400; ❄) Almost a hostel but not quite, the Casa Becil's friendly owner calls it a 'BBC' for breakfast, bed and coffee. It offers very inexpensive, clean rooms with a fully equipped kitchen downstairs, an intimate courtyard, a sun deck, beautiful tiled floors, a left-luggage service, a book exchange, tours and more. The rooms are breezy, without a hint of stuffiness, and the owner speaks excellent English.

★ **Luz en Yucatán** BOUTIQUE HOTEL $$
(☎999-924-00-35; www.luzenyucatan.com; Calle 55 No 499; r M$736-1004, apt M$790-1190; P ❄ ☜ ≈) While many much blander hotels are loudly claiming to be 'boutique', this one is quietly ticking all the boxes – individually decorated rooms, fabulous common areas and a wonderful pool/patio area out back. The house it offers for rent across the road, which sleeps seven people and has a hot tub, is just as good, if not better.

Hotel Marionetas HOTEL $$
(☎999-928-33-77; www.hotelmarionetas.com; Calle 49 No 516, btwn Calles 62 & 64; r from M$850; ❄ @ ☜ ≈) Another beautiful colonial hotel set around an inviting patio. The rustic-chic breakfast area overlooking the pool is a nice touch and there are plenty of tastefully selected handicrafts and furnishings serving for decoration. Rooms are everything they should be, but get one upstairs for more ventilation.

Hotel Caribe HOTEL $$

(999-924-90-22; www.hotelcaribe.com.mx; Calle 59 No 500, btwn Calles 58 & 60; s/d from M$740/820;) With the setting – surrounded by church spires, with a charming fountain tinkling in the courtyard and a fantastic rooftop pool – you can forgive the rooms for being plain here, but they're spacious and clean enough. They could be fancier, but then they could be pricier, too.

Hotel del Peregrino HOTEL $$

(999-924-30-07; www.hoteldelperegrino.com; Calle 51 No 488, btwn Calles 54 & 56; r M$790-890;) A tranquil little place, offering medium-sized, oddly shaped rooms around a small but pretty patio. The open-air Jacuzzi on the upstairs terrace is a bonus.

Hotel Medio Mundo HOTEL $$

(999-924-54-72; www.hotelmediomundo.com; Calle 55 No 533; d incl breakfast M$910-1105;) This former private residence has been completely remodeled and painted in lovely colors. Its ample, simply furnished rooms have super-comfortable beds, beautiful tiled sinks and plenty of natural light. One of the two courtyards has a small swimming pool, the other a fountain. The well-traveled, charming hosts make their guests feel at home.

Gran Hotel HOTEL $$

(999-923-69-63; www.granhoteldemerida.com; Calle 60 No 496; s/d M$800/900; P) This was indeed a grand hotel when built in 1901. Some rooms in this old-timer have received a modern makeover; others have the same old period furnishings and faded carpets. Despite the wear, they retain many elegant and delightful decorative flourishes.

Hotel Dolores Alba HOTEL $$

(999-928-56-50; www.doloresalba.com; Calle 63, btwn Calles 52 & 54; s M$550-650, d M$650-750; P) Rooms here are on three floors (with an elevator) around two large courtyards. Those in the pricier, modern wing have shiny new tile floors and flat-screen TVs, and they face the lovely pool. The hotel has secure parking and is quiet, well managed and friendly.

Hotel del Parque HOTEL $$

(999-924-78-44; www.hoteldelparque.com.mx; Calle 60, btwn Calles 57 & 59; s/d M$450/550; P) Rooms here, while generously-sized, are nothing special, but this is probably the best deal in this price range in the immediate downtown area.

Hotel Mérida Santiago HOTEL $$$

(cell phone 999-2854447; www.hotelmeridasantiago.com; Calle 74a No 499, btwn Calles 57 & 59a; r M$1200-1500; P) With just six rooms, it's a good idea to book ahead here. Rooms are spacious (and bathrooms huge) and stylishly decorated with hand-picked, locally made items. The Dutch/Mexican couple who run it are full of info and tips.

Hotel Piedra de Agua BOUTIQUE HOTEL $$$

(999-924-23-00; www.piedradeagua.com; Calle 60 No 498, btwn Calles 59 & 61; r M$1600-2400; P) Once a grand old house and now a grand new hotel, this one does it right, with stylish furnishings, good beds, sharp service and a good mix of colonial and modern ambience. The backyard bar is a bonus as is the small gym. Off-season and walk-in discounts go as high as 40%.

Rosas y Xocolate BOUTIQUE HOTEL $$$

(999-924-29-92; www.rosasandxocolate.com; Paseo de Montejo No 480; r M$2880-3550, ste M$4690-8700; P) Built from the remains of two mansions and reusing many of the original materials, this medium-sized boutique hotel goes all-out, with custom-made furniture, Bose sound systems in every room and open-air baths. The requisite air-conditioned gym, full-day spa and gourmet restaurant are all onsite.

Hotel Hacienda Mérida BOUTIQUE HOTEL $$$

(999-924-43-63; www.hotelhaciendamerida.com; Calle 62, btwn Calles 51 & 53; r/ste from M$2062/2852; P) Leading the way in the upscale boutique category, the Hacienda is lovely by night, with illuminated columns leading you past the pool to your classically styled chambers. For all-out luxury consider upgrading to a 'VIP' room, but it'll cost you a pretty peso.

PASEO DE MONTEJO

Paseo de Montejo, which runs parallel to Calles 56 and 58, was an attempt by Mérida's 19th-century city planners to create a wide boulevard similar to the Paseo de la Reforma in Mexico City or the Champs-Élysées in Paris. Europe's architectural and social influence can be seen along the Paseo in the fine mansions built by wealthy families around the end of the 19th century.

Eating & Drinking

The best combination of drinking and people-watching is to be had at the tables belonging to the restaurants on Calle 60, in front of Parque Hidalgo. Snacks and more serious meals are available at reasonable prices.

Bistro Cultural FRENCH $
(cnr Calles 43 & 66; set meals M$60; ⏲9am-5pm Mon-Fri) Drop into this cute little French-run cafe to choose from one of the two rotating dishes of the day – the food is excellent and prices very reasonable.

Mercado Municipal Lucas de Gálvez MARKET $
(cnr Calles 56a & 67; mains & ceviche M$60; ⏲6am-5pm) This market has Mérida's least expensive eateries. Upstairs joints have tables and chairs and more diverse menus offering main courses of beef, fish or chicken. Look for *recados* (spice pastes). Downstairs at the north end are some cheap *taquerías* (taco stalls), while near the south end are *cotelerías* – seafood shacks specializing in shellfish cocktails as well as ceviche.

★La Chaya Maya MEXICAN $$
(Calle 55 No 510; mains M$57-175; ⏲7am-11pm) Popular with locals and tourists alike, this restaurant occupies a lovely downtown colonial building. Consider La Chaya Maya your introduction to classic Yucatean fare like *relleno negro* (black turkey stew) or *cochinita pibil* (slow-cooked pork). The original branch is at the corner of Calles 62 and 57.

La Tratto Santa Lucía ITALIAN $$
(Calle 60, btwn Calles 53 & 55; mains M$100-200; ⏲11am-midnight) With five popular restaurants scattered around the city, these guys must be doing something right. And that something is high-quality Italian food at reasonable prices. This outlet features a great downtown location, with tables set out on the lovely Parque Santa Lucía.

Rescoldo's MEDITERRANEAN $$
(Calle 62 No 366, btwn Calles 41 & 43; mains M$90-160; ⏲6-10pm Tue-Thu, to 11pm Fri & Sat) Offering up wood-fired pizzas, calzones and yummy pastas and rounding it off with homemade gelato, this highly recommended Mediterranean restaurant is a great place to get a little variety in your diet.

La Casa de Frida MEXICAN $$
(www.lacasadefrida.com.mx; Calle 61 No 526; mains M$120-175; ⏲6-10pm Mon-Sat) Go here for delicious duck in *mole* sauce or another well-prepared Mexican classic, *chile en nogada* (stuffed poblano chili). Don't be surprised if pet bunny Coco hops into the dining area to greet you – there's no rabbit on the menu here!

Slavia FUSION $$
(cnr Paseo de Montejo & Calle 29; mains M$120-250; ⏲7pm-2am) In front of the *Monumento a la Patria* (Monument to the Fatherland), this incongruous little place is jam-packed with Asian knickknacks and serves up some good fusion food, with an emphasis on carpaccios and fondues. It doubles as a popular bar – the crowd is a bit older and the atmosphere more relaxed than at many places downtown.

Cubaro CAFE $$
(cnr Paseo de Montejo & Calle 29; mains M$115-240; ⏲5pm-2am) Sister restaurant to the popular Slavia, this is a relaxed spot and has some great outdoor areas, including a terrace with a close-up view of the *Monumento a la Patria* (Monument to the Fatherland). The menu is fairly conventional, but everything is carefully prepared and the service is very crisp.

Amaro INTERNATIONAL $$
(☎999-928-24-51; www.restauranteamaro.com; Calle 59 No 507; mains M$80-220; ⏲11am-2am; 🌶) This romantic dining spot is in the courtyard of the house where Andrés Quintana Roo – poet, statesman and drafter of Mexico's Declaration of Independence – was born in 1787. The menu includes Yucatecan dishes and a variety of vegetarian plates, as well as some continental dishes. Best visited at night when singers perform *trova* ballads.

Restaurante Pórtico del Peregrino MEXICAN $$
(☎999-928-61-63; Calle 57, btwn Calles 60 & 62; mains M$80-150; ⏲noon-midnight) There are several pleasant, traditional-style dining rooms surrounding a small courtyard in this upscale eatery. Yucatean dishes such as *pollo pibil* (chicken flavored with *achiote* – annatto spice – and wrapped in banana leaves) are its forte, but you'll find many international dishes and a broad range of seafood and steaks too. *Mole poblano,* a chocolate and chili sauce, is a house specialty.

Mayan Pub BAR
(www.mayanpub.com; Calle 62, btwn Calles 55 & 57; 7pm-3am Wed-Sun) Popular with backpackers and *meridiano* (local) would-be backpackers, this place keeps it real with a pool table, a big beer garden out back and live music acts.

Entertainment

Mérida offers many cultural and musical events in parks and historic buildings, put on by local performers of considerable skill, and admission is usually free. Check with one of the tourist information offices for news of upcoming events. The website www.yucatantoday.com offers monthly news and often highlights seasonal events.

Mérida has several cinemas, most of which show first-run Hollywood fare in English, with Spanish subtitles (ask *'¿inglés?'* if you need to be sure), as well as other foreign films and Mexican offerings. Cinema tickets cost about M$45 for evening shows, M$25 for matinees. Try **MM Cinemas** (www.cinemex.com; Calle 57, btwn Calles 70 & 72) or **Teatro Mérida** (Calle 62, btwn Calles 59 & 61).

Shopping

Mérida is a fine place for buying Yucatecan handicrafts. Purchases to consider include hammocks and traditional Maya clothing such as the colorful, embroidered *huipiles* (indigenous woman's sleeveless tunic), panama hats and, of course, the wonderfully comfortable *guayaberas* (thin-fabric shirts with pockets and appliquéd designs worn by Yucatecan men).

During the last days of February or the beginning of March, handicraft artisans from all over Mexico fill the Plaza Grande for the **Ki-Huic** market.

Casa de las Artesanías HANDICRAFTS
(999-928-66-76; Calle 63, btwn Calles 64 & 66; 9:30am-10pm Mon-Sat) A good place to start looking for handicrafts, this government-supported market for local artisans sells just about everything. Prices are fixed.

Artesanías Bazar García Rejón HANDICRAFTS
(cnr Calles 60 & 65) A wide variety of products concentrated into one area of shops.

Guayaberas Jack CLOTHING
(www.guayaberasjack.com.mx; Calle 59 No 507A; 10am-8:30pm Mon-Sat, to 2:30pm Sun) The *guayabera* is the classic Mérida shirt, but in buying the wrong one you run the risk of looking like a waiter. Drop into this famous shop to avoid getting asked for the bill.

Hamacas Mérida HANDICRAFTS
(999-924-04-40; www.hamacasmerida.com.mx; Calle 65, btwn Calles 62 & 64; 9am-7pm Mon-Fri, to 2pm Sat) Has a large catalog with hammocks in all kinds of sizes, shapes and colors, plus it ships worldwide.

Alma Mexicana ARTS & CRAFTS
(www.casaesperanza.com; Calle 54, btwn Calles 55 & 57; 9:30am-6pm Mon-Sat, 11am-3pm Sun) Sells Mexican folk art and crafts as well as other interesting gift items.

Information

EMERGENCY

Cruz Roja (Red Cross; 999-924-98-13)
Emergency (066)
Police (999-942-00-70)

MEDICAL SERVICES

Clínica Mérida (999-924-18-00; Av de los Itzáes 242)

MONEY

Banks and ATMs are scattered throughout the city.

POST

Post Office (999-928-54-04; Calle 53 No 469, btwn Calles 52 & 54; 9am-4pm Mon-Fri, for stamps only 9am-1pm Sat)

TOURIST INFORMATION

The free Spanish/English magazine *Yucatán Today* (www.yucatantoday.com) has excellent tips on things to do in Mérida and around Yucatán.

City Tourist Office (999-942-00-00; Calle 62, Plaza Grande; 8am-8pm Mon-Sat, to 2pm Sun) Just south of the main entrance to the Palacio Municipal, this office is staffed with helpful English speakers. It offers free walking tours of the city at 9:30am, as well as audio guides for M$80.

State Tourist Office (999-930-31-01; Calle 61, Plaza Grande; 8am-9pm Mon-Sat, to 8pm Sun) In the entrance to the Palacio de Gobierno. There's usually an English speaker on hand.

Tourist Information Center (999-924-92-90; cnr Calles 60 & 57a; 8am-9pm Mon-Sat, to 8pm Sun) On the southwest edge of the Teatro Peón Contreras, this office always has an English speaker on hand.

Getting There & Away

AIR

Mérida's tiny but modern airport is a 10km, 20-minute ride southwest of the Plaza Grande off Hwy 180 (Avenida de los Itzáes). It has car-rental desks, an ATM and a currency-exchange booth.

Most international flights to Mérida are connections through Mexico City or Cancún. Nonstop international services are provided by **United Airlines** (999-926-31-00, in USA 800-900-5000; www.united.com; Paseo Montejo No 437, at Calle 29) from Houston, several times weekly. Low-cost airlines Interjet (p266), Volaris (p266) and VivaAerobus (p266) serve Mexico City. MayAir (p266) runs prop planes to Cancún and Isla Cozumel.

BUS

Mérida is the bus transportation hub of the Yucatán Peninsula. Take the usual precautions with your gear on night buses and those serving popular tourist destinations (especially 2nd-class buses) at any time.

BUSES FROM MÉRIDA

DESTINATION	FARE (M$)	DURATION	FREQUENCY (DAILY)
Campeche (short route)	128-202	2½-3½hr	hourly ADO, 3 ADO GL (from CAME, Terminal de Segunda Clase)
Cancún	185-490	4-6hr	2 Oriente, frequent ADO, OCC & ADO GL (from CAME, Terminal de Segunda Clase, Noreste terminal)
Celestún	52	2hr	6 daily Oriente from Noreste terminal
Chetumal	246-392	6-8hr	4 ADO, 5 Mayab from CAME
Chichén Itzá	72	1¾-2½hr	frequent ADO from CAME, Terminal de Segunda Clase
Escárcega	105-284	5-5½hr	5 Sur, 3 ADO (from CAME, Terminal de Segunda Clase)
Izamal	26	1½hr	frequent Oriente from Noreste terminal
Mayapán Ruinas	22	1½hr	hourly Sur from Noreste terminal, continuing to Oxkutzcab
Mexico City (Terminal Norte)	1404	21hr	2pm
Palenque	448	8-9hr	4 daily ADO, OCC (from CAME, Terminal de Segunda Clase)
Playa del Carmen	200-556	4½-8hr	frequent Mayab, OCC & ADO (from CAME, Terminal de Segunda Clase)
Río Lagartos	130-170	3-4hr	1st-class Noreste 5:30pm from Noreste terminal
Ticul	45	1¾hr	3 Mayab from Terminal de Segunda Clase; frequent combis from Parque de San Juan
Tizimín	93-128	2½-4hr	frequent from Noreste terminal
Tulum	159-240	4hr	frequent Mayab & ADO (from CAME, Terminal de Segunda Clase)
Uxmal	55	1-1½hr	5 Oriente from Terminal de Segunda Clase

There are a number of bus terminals, and some lines operate from (and stop at) more than one terminal. Tickets for departure from one terminal can often be bought at another, and destinations overlap greatly among bus lines. Some lines offer round-trip tickets to nearby towns that reduce the fare quite a bit. Check out www.ticketbus.com.mx.

CAME Bus Terminal (999-920-44-44; Calle 70, btwn Calles 69 & 71) Sometimes referred to as the 'Terminal de Primera Clase,' Mérida's main bus terminal has mostly 1st-class buses – including ADO, Platino and ADO GL – to points around the Yucatán Peninsula and faraway places such as Mexico City.

Fiesta Americana Bus Terminal (999-924-83-91; cnr Calle 60 & Av Colón) A small 1st-class terminal on the west side of the hotel complex servicing guests of the luxury hotels on Avenida Colón, north of the city center. Departures for Cancún, Villahermosa and Playa del Carmen.

Noreste Bus Terminal (cnr Calles 67 & 50) Noreste, Sur and Oriente bus lines use this terminal. Destinations served from here include many small towns in the northeast part of the peninsula, including Tizimín and Río Lagartos; Cancún and points along the way; and small towns south and west of Mérida, including Celestún (served by Occidente), Ticul, Ruinas de Mayapán and Oxkutzcab.

Some Oriente buses depart from Terminal de Segunda Clase and stop here; others depart from here (eg those to Izamal and Tizimín).

Parque de San Juan (Calle 69, btwn Calles 62 & 64) From all around the Parque de San Juan, vans and combis (vans or minibuses) depart for Dzibilchaltún, Muna, Oxkutzcab, Tekax, Ticul and other points.

Progreso Bus Terminal (999-928-39-65; Calle 62 No 524) Serves Progreso and Dzibilchaltún.

Terminal de Segunda Clase (Calle 69) Also known as Terminal 69 (Sesenta y Nueve) or simply Terminal de Autobuses, this terminal is just around the corner from the CAME bus terminal. ADO, Mayab, Oriente and Sur run mostly 2nd-class buses to points in the state and around the peninsula.

CAR

The most flexible way to tour the many archaeological sites around Mérida is by rental car, especially if you have two or more people to share costs. Assume you will pay a total of M$600 to M$650 per day (tax, insurance and gas included) for short-term rental of a cheap car, although shopping around you might luck onto one for half that. Getting around Mérida's sprawling tangle of one-way streets and careening buses is better done on foot or on a careening bus.

Several agencies have branches at the airport as well as on Calle 60 between Calles 55 and 57, including **National** (999-923-24-93; www.nationalcar.com; Calle 60 No 486F; 7am-10pm), **Veloz** (999-928-03-73; Calle 60 No.486) and **Payless** (999-924-14-78; Calle 60 No 486). All rent for about M$350 to M$500 a day. You'll get the best deal by booking ahead of time over the internet.

Getting Around

TO/FROM THE AIRPORT

Bus 69 (Aviación) travels between the airport and the city center every 15 to 30 minutes until 9pm, with occasional service until 11pm. The half-hour trip (M$10) is via a roundabout route; the best place to catch it is on Calle 62, between Calles 67 and 69.

A taxi from the city center to the airport should cost about M$110 (but it's hard to get this price *from* the airport, so walk out to the main street and flag one down or else be prepared to pay M$250).

BUS

Most parts of Mérida that you'll want to visit are within five or six blocks of the Plaza Grande and are easily accessible on foot. Given the slow speed of city traffic, particularly in the market areas, travel on foot is also the fastest way to get around.

City buses are cheap at M$10, but routes can be confusing. Most start in suburban neighborhoods, skirt the city center and terminate in another distant suburban neighborhood. To travel between the Plaza Grande and the upscale neighborhoods to the north along Paseo de Montejo, catch the Ruta 164 on the corner of Calles 59 and 58, north of the Parque Hidalgo. To return to the city center, catch any bus heading south on Paseo de Montejo displaying the same sign and/or 'Centro.'

TAXI

There are more and more *taxímetros* (metered taxis) in town. For regular taxi service, rates should generally be fixed, with a M$30 minimum fare, which will get you from the bus terminals to all downtown hotels. Be sure to agree on a price beforehand if there's no meter. Most rides within city limits do not exceed M$60. Taxi stands can be found at most of the *barrio* (neighborhood) parks, or dial 999-928-31-00 or 999-923-40-96; service is available 24 hours (dispatch fees cost an extra M$10 to M$20).

South of Mérida

There's a lot to do and see south of Mérida. The major draws are the old *henequén* plantations, some still used for cultivating leaves, and the well-preserved Maya ruins like Uxmal and the lesser-known sites along the Ruta Puuc.

Uxmal

Pronounced 'oosh-mahl,' **Uxmal** (Hwy 261, Km 78; admission M$234, parking M$22, guides M$550; ⏲8am-5pm; 👪) is one impressive set of ruins, easily ranking among the top Maya archaeological sites. The ruins cover a huge area, and many structures are in good condition, bearing a riot of ornamentation. Adding to Uxmal's appeal is its setting in the hilly Puuc region, which lent its name to the architectural patterns in this area. *Puuc* means 'hills,' and these, rising up to about 100m, are the first relief from the flatness of the northern and western portions of the peninsula.

You now need to pay extra if you want to see the 45-minute **sound-and-light show** (M$72; ⏲8pm summer, 7pm winter). It's in Spanish, but recorded translations are available (M$45).

History

Uxmal was an important city, and its dominance extended to the nearby towns of Sayil, Kabah, Xlapak and Labná. Although Uxmal means 'Thrice Built' in Maya, it was actually constructed five times.

That a sizable population flourished in this dry area is yet more testament to the engineering skills of the Maya, who built a series of reservoirs and *chultunes* (cisterns) lined with lime mortar to catch and hold water during the dry season. First settled in about AD 600, Uxmal was influenced by highland Mexico in its architecture, most likely through contact fostered by trade. This influence is reflected in the town's serpent imagery, phallic symbols and columns. The well-proportioned Puuc architecture, with its intricate, geometric mosaics sweeping across the upper parts of elongated facades, was also strongly influenced by the slightly earlier Río Bec and Chenes styles.

The scarcity of water in the region meant that Chac, the rain god or sky serpent, was supreme in importance. His image is ubiquitous at the site, in the form of stucco masks protruding from facades and cornices. There is much speculation as to why Uxmal was largely abandoned in about AD 900; one theory is that drought conditions may have reached such proportions that the inhabitants had to relocate. Later, the Xiu dynasty, which had controlled Uxmal for several hundred years, moved their seat of power to near present-day Maní, launching a rebellion against the kingdom of Mayapán, which had usurped much of the power in the region.

Rediscovered by archaeologists in the 19th century, Uxmal was first excavated in 1929 by Frans Blom. Although the site has been restored, much is yet to be discovered.

Sights

Casa del Adivino ARCHAEOLOGICAL SITE

As you climb the slope to the ruins, the Casa del Adivino comes into view. This tall temple (the name translates as 'Magician's House'), 39m high, was built in an unusual oval shape. Consisting of round stones held rudely together with lots of cement, it seems crude compared to other structures at Uxmal, but what you see is a restored version of the temple's fifth incarnation. Four earlier temples were completely covered by the final rebuilding by the Maya, except for the high doorway on the west side, which remains from the fourth temple. Decorated in elaborate Chenes style (a style that originated further south), the doorway proper forms the mouth of a gigantic Chac mask.

Cuadrángulo de las Monjas ARCHAEOLOGICAL SITE

The 74-room, sprawling Nuns' Quadrangle is directly west of the Casa del Adivino. Archaeologists are divided over whether this was a military academy, royal school or palace complex. The long-nosed face of Chac appears everywhere on the facades of the four separate temples that form the quadrangle. The northern temple, the grandest of the four, was built first, followed by the southern, then the eastern and finally the western.

Several decorative elements on the exuberant facades show signs of Mexican, perhaps Totonac, influence. The feathered-serpent (Quetzalcóatl, or in Maya, Kukulcán) motif along the top of the west temple's facade is one of these. Note also the stylized depictions of the *na* (traditional Maya thatched hut) over some of the doorways in the northern and southern buildings.

South of Mérida

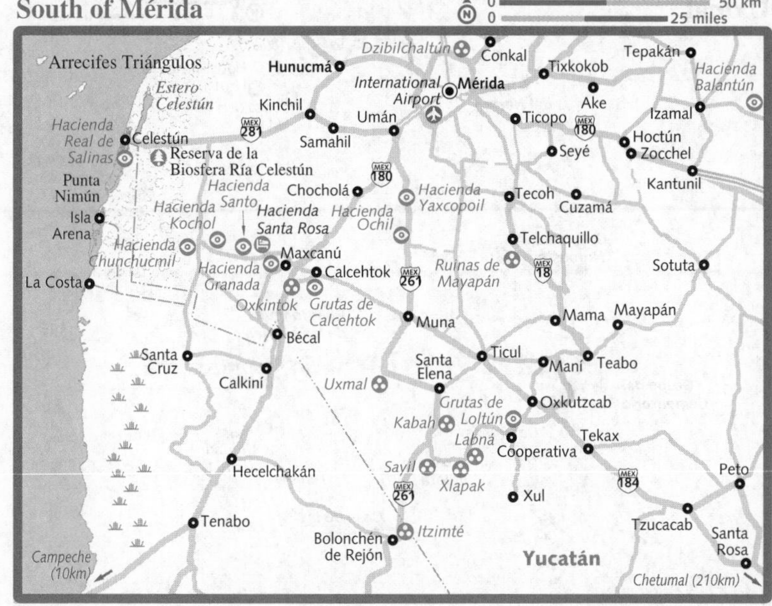

Passing through the corbeled arch in the middle of the south building of the quadrangle and continuing down the slope takes you through the **Juego de Pelota** (Ball Court). From here you can turn left and head up the steep slope and stairs to the large terrace. If you've got time, you could instead turn right to explore the western **Grupo del Cementerio** (which, though largely unrestored, holds some interesting square blocks carved with skulls in the center of its plaza), then head for the stairs and terrace.

Casa de las Tortugas ARCHAEOLOGICAL SITE

To the right at the top of the stairs is the House of the Turtles, which takes its name from the turtles carved on the cornice. The Maya associated turtles with the rain god, Chac. According to Maya myth, when the people suffered from drought, so did the turtles, and both prayed to Chac to send rain.

The frieze of short columns, or 'rolled mats,' that runs around the temple below the turtles is characteristic of the Puuc style. On the west side of the building a vault has collapsed, affording a good view of the corbeled arch that supported it.

Palacio del Gobernador ARCHAEOLOGICAL SITE

The Governor's Palace, with its magnificent facade nearly 100m long, has been called 'the finest structure at Uxmal and the culmination of the Puuc style' by Mayanist Michael D Coe. The buildings have walls filled with rubble, faced with cement and then covered in a thin veneer of limestone squares; the lower part of the facade is plain, the upper part festooned with stylized Chac faces and geometric designs, often lattice-like or fretted.

Other elements of Puuc style are the decorated cornices, rows of half-columns (as in the House of the Turtles) and round columns in doorways (as in the palace at Sayil).

Gran Pirámide ARCHAEOLOGICAL SITE

The 32m-high pyramid has been restored only on its northern side. Archaeologists theorize that the quadrangle at its summit was largely destroyed in order to construct another pyramid above it. That work, for reasons unknown, was never completed. At the top are some stucco carvings of Chac, birds and flowers.

El Palomar ARCHAEOLOGICAL SITE

West of the Gran Pirámide sits a structure whose roofcomb is latticed with a pattern reminiscent of the Moorish pigeon houses built into walls in Spain and northern Africa – hence the building's name, which means the Dovecote or Pigeon House. The

Uxmal

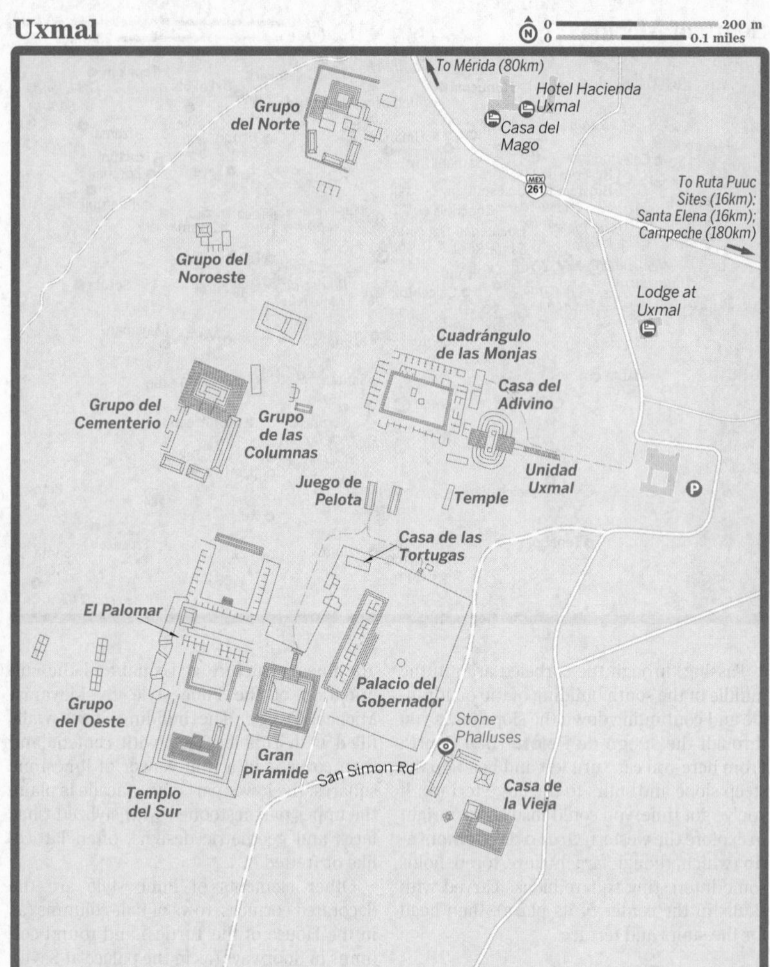

nine honeycombed triangular 'belfries' sit on top of a building that was once part of a quadrangle.

Casa de la Vieja ARCHAEOLOGICAL SITE
Off the southeast corner of the Palacio del Gobernador's platform is a small complex, now largely rubble, known as the Casa de la Vieja (Old Woman's House). In front of it is a small *palapa* (thatch-roof shelter) that covers several large phalluses carved from stone.

Sleeping & Eating

There is no town at Uxmal, just a cluster of hotels. More services can be found in Santa Elena, 16km away, or in Ticul, 30km to the east.

Casa del Mago HOTEL $$
(☎997-976-20-32; www.casadelmago.com; Hwy 261, Km 78; r incl breakfast M$555; P 📶 🏊) The only midrange option in Uxmal, Casa del Mago consists of four basic rooms with red-tile floors and ceiling fans. Guests have use of the adjoining, sister property's pool. These are the cheapest rooms in town so book ahead.

Lodge at Uxmal LUXURY HOTEL **$$$**
(☎998-887-24-95, in USA 877-240-5864; www.mayaland.com; Hwy 261, Km 78; r from M$2040; P ❄ 🛜 🏊) Uxmal's newest luxury hotel's rooms could be nicer for the price, but you can't beat the easy access to the ruins and the pool certainly adds value. Some of the more expensive rooms have Jacuzzis. We doubt that Stephens and Catherwood enjoyed such luxury when they passed through the area in the late 1830s!

Hotel Hacienda Uxmal HISTORIC HOTEL **$$$**
(☎997-976-20-12, in USA 877-240-5864; www.mayaland.com; Hwy 261, Km 78; r from M$2348; P ❄ 🛜 🏊) This Mayaland Resort is 500m from the ruins. It housed the archaeologists who explored and restored Uxmal. Wide, tiled verandas, high ceilings, great bathrooms and a beautiful swimming pool make this a very comfortable place to stay. There are even rocking chairs to help you kick back after a hard day of exploring.

ℹ Getting There & Away

Uxmal is 80km from Mérida. Most buses plying the inland route between Mérida and Campeche can drop you off at Uxmal, Santa Elena, Kabah or the Ruta Puuc turnoff. When leaving Uxmal, passing buses may be full (especially on Saturday and Monday). Some people avoid the hassle and rent a car or book a tour in Mérida. If you do get stuck, a taxi to nearby Santa Elena shouldn't cost more than M$180.

Santa Elena

The nearest town to Uxmal is Santa Elena, 16km east of Uxmal and 8km north of Kabah on the inland Mérida–Campeche bus route. There's a small **museum** (admission M$10; ⏲9am-6:30pm Mon-Fri, to 7pm Sat & Sun) dedicated to a gruesome find – the 18th-century child mummies that were found buried beneath the adjoining cathedral – and some *henequén*-related exhibits.

The **Pickled Onion** (☎cell phone 997-1117922; www.thepickledonionyucatan.com; cabins incl breakfast from M$528; P 🛜 🏊) hotel and eatery offers the chance to stay in an adobe-walled Maya hut. The primitive rooms keep you cool with a *palapa* roof. We love the pool and its surrounding gardens, and the restaurant (mains M$70 to M$100), which features sizzling fajitas and yummy cold gazpacho and avocado soups, is said to be the best in town.

There's a pleasant garden at **Bungalows Sacbé** (☎997-978-51-58; www.sacbebungalows.com.mx; bungalows with fan/air-con from M$310/350; P ❄ 🏊), and all the rooms have fans, good screens and decent beds. To get here, ask the bus driver to drop you off at the *campo de béisbol* (baseball field) *de Santa Elena*. It's about 200m south of the town's southern entrance.

On Hwy 261 at the southern entrance to Santa Elena, **Restaurante El Chac-Mool** (☎997-978-51-17; www.facebook.com/chacmooluxmal; mains M$60-110; ⏲9am-10pm) is a friendly place serving Yucatecan food that includes a hearty vegetarian plate of rice, beans and fried bananas. It has basic rooms and a little store, too.

Kabah

After Uxmal, Kabah (AD 750 to 950) was the most important city in the region. The **ruins** (admission M$42; ⏲8am-5pm) straddle Hwy 261. The guard-shack-cum-souvenir-shop (selling snacks and cold drinks) and the bulk of the restored ruins are on the east side of the highway.

The facade of **El Palacio de los Mascarones** (Palace of Masks) is an amazing sight, covered in nearly 300 masks of Chac, the rain god or sky serpent. Most of their huge curling noses are broken off; the best intact beak is at the building's south end. These curled-up noses may have given the palace its modern Maya name, Codz Poop (Rolled Mat).

Once you're up to your ears in noses, head around the back to check out the two restored **atlantes** (an *atlas* – plural *atlantes* – is a male figure used as a supporting column). These are especially interesting, as they're among the very few 3D human figures you'll see at a Maya site. One is headless and the other wears a jaguar mask atop his head.

From here be sure to check out **El Palacio** (The Palace), with its groups of decorative *columnillas* (little columns) on the upper part of the facade; these are a distinctive characteristic of Puuc architectural style. A couple of hundred meters through the jungle from here is **Templo de las Columnas**. This building has more rows of impressive decorative columns.

Across the highway from El Palacio, a path leads to the **Gran Pirámide** (Great

Pyramid). From here, the path ends at the impressive, restored **El Arco**. It's said that the *sacbé* leading from here goes through the jungle all the way to Uxmal, terminating at a smaller arch; in the other direction it goes to Labná. Once, much of the Yucatán Peninsula was connected by these marvelous 'white roads' of rough limestone.

Kabah is 104km from Mérida, a ride of about two hours. Heading away from the site, buses will usually stop if you flag them down at the entrance to the ruins.

Ruta Puuc

Just 5km south of Kabah on Hwy 261, a road branches off to the east and winds past the ruins of Sayil, Xlapak and Labná, ending at the Grutas de Loltún. This is the Ruta Puuc, and its sites offer some marvelous architectural detail and a deeper acquaintance with the Puuc Maya civilization, which flourished between about AD 750 and 950.

The Ruta Puuc circuit bus (based in Mérida) is not currently running; until this is reinstated, the most convenient way to visit the Ruta Puuc sites is by car.

Sights

Sayil ARCHAEOLOGICAL SITE

(admission M$42; 8am-5pm) Sayil is best known for El Palacio, a huge three-tiered building that has an 85m-long facade and is reminiscent of the Minoan palace on Crete. The distinctive columns of Puuc architecture are used here often, either as supports for the lintels, as decoration between doorways or as a frieze above them, alternating with stylized Chac masks and 'descending gods.'

Taking the path south from the palace for about 400m and bearing left, you come to the temple named **El Mirador**, whose rooster-like roofcomb was once painted a bright red. About 100m beyond El Mirador, beneath a protective *palapa*, is a stela bearing the relief of a fertility god with an enormous phallus, now sadly weathered.

A bit further along, the Grupo Sur offers beautiful jungle-covered ruins with tree roots twisting through the walls.

The ruins of Sayil are 4.5km from the junction of the Ruta Puuc with Hwy 261.

Xlapak ARCHAEOLOGICAL SITE

(8am-5pm) FREE The ornate *palacio* at Xlapak (*shla-pak*) is quite a bit smaller than those at nearby Kabah and Sayil, measuring only about 20m in length. It's decorated with the inevitable Chac masks, columns and colonnettes and fretted geometric latticework of the Puuc style. The building is interesting and on a bit of a lean.

Plenty of motmots brighten up the surrounding forests. From the entrance gate at Sayil, it's 6km east to the entrance gate at Xlapak. The name means 'Old Walls' in Maya and was a general term among local people for ancient ruins.

Museo de Cacao MUSEUM

(www.ecomuseodelcacao.com; adult/child M$90/60; 9am-6pm) Just off the highway between Xlapak and Labná, this fascinating new museum focuses on the history and use of cacao, a sacred drink of the Maya. Five thematically organized huts take on different aspects of cacao's cultivation and preparation, as well as traditional Maya architecture, burial rites and clothing. The cafe here makes for a good lunch stop, too.

Labná ARCHAEOLOGICAL SITE

(admission M$42; 8am-5pm) This is *the* site not to miss on the Ruta Puuc. Archaeologists believe that, at one point in the 9th century, some 3000 Maya lived at Labná. To support such numbers in these arid hills, water was collected in *chultunes* (cisterns). At Labná's peak there were some 60 *chultunes* in and around the city; several are still visible among the temples.

El Palacio, the first building you come to at Labná, is one of the longest in the Puuc region, and much of its interesting decorative carving is in good shape, thanks in part to a massive renovation project completed in 2006. On the west corner of the main structure's facade, straight in from the big tree near the center of the complex, is a serpent's head with a human face peering out from between its jaws, the symbol of the planet Venus. Toward the hill from this is an impressive Chac mask, and nearby is the lower half of a human figure (possibly a ballplayer) in loincloth and leggings.

The lower level has several more well-preserved Chac masks, and the upper level contains a large *chultún* that still holds water. The view of the site and the hills beyond from there is impressive.

Labná is best known for **El Arco**, a magnificent arch once part of a building that separated two quadrangular courtyards. It now appears to be a gate joining two small plazas. The corbeled structure, 3m wide and 6m high, is well preserved, and the reliefs decorating its upper facade are exuberantly Puuc in style.

Flanking the west side of the arch are carved *na* (thatched Maya huts) with multi-tiered roofs. Also on these walls, the remains of the building that adjoined the arch, are lattice patterns atop a serpentine design. Archaeologists believe a high roofcomb once sat over the fine arch and its flanking rooms.

Standing on the opposite side of the arch and separated from it by the *sacbé* is a pyramid known as **El Mirador**, topped by a temple. The pyramid itself is largely stone rubble but the crowning temple, with its 5m-high roofcomb, is well positioned to be a lookout, hence the name.

From the entrance gate at Xlapak, it's 3.5km east to the gate at Labná.

Grutas de Loltún

Fifteen kilometers northeast of Labná, a sign points out the left turn to the **Grutas de Loltún** (Loltún Caverns; adult/child under 13yr M$105/6, parking M$22; ⏲9am-4pm; 👪), 5km further northeast. The road passes through lush orchards and some banana and palm groves, a refreshing sight in this dry region.

These caverns are the largest, most interesting cave system on the Yucatán Peninsula, and a treasure trove of data for archaeologists. Carbon dating of artifacts found here reveals that humans used the caves 2200 years ago. Chest-high murals of hands, faces, animals and geometric motifs were apparent as recently as 20 years ago, but so many people have touched them that barely a trace remains. Now, visitors to the illuminated caves see mostly natural limestone formations, some of which are quite lovely.

To explore the labyrinth, you must take a scheduled guided tour at 9:30am, 11am, 12:30pm, 2pm, 3pm or 4pm. The service of the guides is included in the admission price, but since they receive little of that, an additional tip (M$20 to M$50 per person) is appreciated.

ℹ Getting There & Away

Renting a car is the best option for reaching the Grutas, and once you're out of Mérida it's easy going on pretty good roads.

There is a bus service to Oxkutzcab (*osh-kootz-kahb*; M$43, 1½ hours), with departures at 8:30am and 4pm, from the Noreste bus terminal in Mérida. Loltún is 7km southwest of Oxkutzcab, and there is usually some transportation along the road. *Camionetas* (pickups) charge about M$15 for a ride.

A taxi from Oxkutzcab will cost M$140 or so one-way.

Ruinas de Mayapán

These **ruins** (admission M$35; ⏲8am-5pm) are some 50km southeast of Mérida, off Hwy 18. Though far less impressive than many Maya sites, Mayapán is historically significant – it was one of the last major dynasties in the region. The site's main attractions are clustered in a compact core, and visitors usually have the place to themselves.

Among the structures that have been restored is the **Castillo de Kukulcán**, a climbable pyramid with fresco fragments around its base and, at its rear side, friezes depicting decapitated warriors. The reddish color from the original paint job is still faintly visible. The **Templo Redondo** (Round Temple) is vaguely reminiscent of El Caracol at Chichén Itzá. Also notable are the **Sala de los Mascarones**, with well-preserved carvings of Chac and quetzal birds on its south side, and the **Templo del Cenote**, built precariously close to a roped-off entrance to a cave system underneath the site.

ℹ Getting There & Away

The Ruinas de Mayapán are just off Hwy 18, a few kilometers southwest of the town of Telchaquillo. Sur runs hourly 2nd-class buses between 5:30am and 8pm from the Noreste bus terminal in Mérida to Oxkutzcab that will let you off near the entrance to the ruins (M$19, 1½ hours) and pick you up on your way back. You may want to consider renting a car to get here.

Celestún

☎988 / POP 6800

West of Mérida, Celestún is a sleepy sun-scorched fishing village that moves at a turtle's pace – and that's the way locals like it. There's a pretty little square in the center of this town and you'll encounter some nice beaches (though the water is a bit turbid), but the real draw here is the Reserva de la Biosfera Ría Celestún, a wildlife sanctuary abounding in waterfowl, with flamingos as the star attraction.

DIY: EXPLORE THE BACK ROADS SOUTH OF MÉRIDA

There are numerous attractions worth seeing as you travel south from Mérida. Here are a few of our favorites.

Hacienda Yaxcopoil (999-900-11-93; www.yaxcopoil.com; Hwy 261, Km 186; admission M$75, r M$1040; 8am-6pm Mon-Sat, 9am-5pm Sun; P) A vast estate that grew and processed *henequén*. Many of its numerous French Renaissance–style buildings have undergone picturesque restorations.

Hacienda Ochil (999-924-74-65; www.haciendaochil.com; Hwy 261, Km 176; admission M$30, mains M$92-125; 10am-6pm; P) Provides a fascinating, though basic, look at how *henequén* was grown and processed.

Grutas de Calcehtok (999-276-81-22; Hwy 184; 1hr 4-person tour M$200; 9:30am-3:30pm Mon-Fri, 8am-5pm Sat & Sun;) These caves are said by some to compose the longest dry-cave system on the Yucatán Peninsula.

Oxkintok (adult/child under 13yr M$42/free, guides M$400; 8am-5pm; P) Inscriptions found at this site contain some of the oldest known dates in the Yucatán, and indicate that the city was inhabited from the pre-Classic to the post-Classic period (300 BC to AD 1500), reaching its greatest importance between AD 475 and 860.

Ruined hacienda route A fascinating alternative return route if you're driving out of Celestún is to turn south off Hwy 281 where a sign points to Chunchucmil. En route, you'll pass a series of old haciendas.

Ruta de los Conventos (Route of the Convents) The section of Highway 18 between the Mérida ring road and Oxkutzcab passes a string of tiny villages, each with a historic cathedral or church, many in beautiful disrepair.

Cuzamá Three kilometers east of the town of Cuzamá, accessed from the small village of Chunkanan, are the Cenotes de Cuzamá, three amazing limestone sinkholes, accessed by horse-drawn rail cart, in the grounds of an old *henequén* hacienda.

Sights & Activities

Reserva de la Biosfera Ría Celestún WILDLIFE RESERVE

Best visited on a boat tour from Celestún, the 591-sq-km Reserva de la Biosfera Ría Celestún is home to a huge variety of animals and birdlife, including a large flamingo colony. The best months to see the flamingos are from March or April to about September, outside the season of the *nortes* (northerly winds).

Morning is the best time of day, though from 4pm onward the birds tend to concentrate in one area after the day's feeding, which can make for good viewing.

Bird-Watching

Flamingos, white pelicans, cormorants, anhingas and many other species frequent the shores and waters of the *ría* (estuary). Inland from the stretches of beach north of town lies a large section of scrub stretching east to the estuary that provides good **birding** opportunities. South and east of town, toward the abandoned Hacienda Real de Salinas, is another good area for nature observation.

Tours

In Celestún, you can hire a motorboat for bird-watching, either from the bridge on the highway into town (about 1.5km inland) or from the beach itself (boats depart from outside Restaurant Celestún, at the foot of Calle 11). Tours from the bridge are mainly set up for tour groups, but if you arrive with a group of four or more it works out OK. The cost per boat is M$1200 for an hour or M$1500 for two hours; tours take you to see the flamingos, mangrove tunnels and a spring. The longer tour also takes in a 'petrified forest' and the spot where the sea and mangroves meet. There's a M$27 park entrance fee for each passenger. It's not hard to strike a better deal beachside, where the 'long' tour goes for M$200 per person or M$1600 per boat (negotiable).

Also offering tours in town is **Manglares de Dzinitún** (999-232-59-15; www.

manglaresdedzinitun.com.mx; tours M$300), an ecotour outfit that does kayak, canoe and mountain-bike tours. The canoe tour runs through a mangrove tunnel to some good birding spots, made all the better by the lack of engine noise. To get here from the beach, turn right on the street after the second transmission tower. It's about 300m ahead.

An alternative is to arrange a flamingo tour from Mérida with Turitransmérida (p306).

Sleeping

The hotels are all on the beach road. More upscale accommodations are found heading north out of town.

Hotel María del Carmen HOTEL **$**
(988-916-21-70; hotelmariadelcarmen@hotmail.com; cnr Calles 12 & 15; d with fan/air-con M$300/450; P ❄ ᯤ) This place has 14 barebones beachfront rooms; ones on the upper floors have balconies facing the sea. Prices drop when business is slow.

★**Hotel Celeste Vida** HOTEL **$$**
(988-916-25-36; www.hotelcelestevida.com; Calle 12; r/apt M$1100/1500; P ᯤ) This friendly little Canadian-run place offers comfortably decked-out rooms with full kitchen, and an apartment that sleeps four. All have water views and the beach at your doorstep. Kayak and bike use are free for guests and you can pay an extra M$120 to have a breakfast basket delivered to your room each morning. The hotel is 1.5km north of Calle 11.

Ecoparaíso Xixim RESORT **$$$**
(988-916-21-00; ste M$3863-4615; P ᯤ) Quietly luxurious beachfront cabins facing onto the foredune. The 'eco' philosophy means no air-con, but the design keeps the cross-breezes flowing. Cabins are strung out along a signed nature trail showing over 40 indigenous plants.

The restaurant serves reasonably priced meals (which is good because Celestún is 11km away) and the open-air upstairs bar is a good place to while away the hours.

Eating

Beachfront restaurants close at around 6pm (or earlier) on weeknights – if you're hungry, head for the plaza where there are snack stalls and a decent fast-food place.

Restaurant Los Pampanos SEAFOOD **$$**
(Calle 12; mains M$60-140; 11am-7pm) A tranquil joint on the beach, north of Calle 11, this is a great spot for afternoon drinks on the sand. Try the octopus ceviche or a fish fillet stuffed to the brim with shellfish.

La Palapa SEAFOOD **$$**
(Calle 12; mains M$80-150; 11am-7pm) A cut above the other seaside joints, La Palapa has an expansive dining area looking down to the sea, attentive staff and savory seafood dishes, including coconut-coated shrimp served in a coconut shell.

Information

Don't plan on using high-speed internet here. There's an ATM in the Super Willy's supermarket on the plaza, but bring some cash anyway – it's been known to dry up.

Getting There & Away

From the Noreste bus terminal in Mérida, buses head for Celestún (M$52, two hours) six times daily between 5:15am and noon. The route terminates at Celestún's plaza, a block inland from Calle 12. Buses back to Mérida run from 5am to 8pm.

By car from Mérida, the best route to Celestún is via the new road out of Umán.

Dzibilchaltún

Lying about 17km northeast of central Mérida, **Dzibilchaltún** (Place of Inscribed Flat Stones; adult/child under 13yr M$170/56, parking M$22; 9am-6pm Tue-Sun; P) was the longest continuously utilized Maya administrative and ceremonial city, serving the Maya from around 1500 BC until the European conquest in the 1540s. At the height of its greatness, Dzibilchaltún covered 15 sq km. Some 8400 structures were mapped by archaeologists in the 1960s, but only a few of these have been excavated and restored.

The **Templo de las Siete Muñecas** (Temple of the Seven Dolls), which got its name from seven grotesque dolls discovered here during excavations, is a 1km walk from the central plaza. It would be most unimpressive but for its precise astronomical orientation: the rising and setting sun of the equinoxes lights up the temple's windows and doors, making them blaze like beacons, signaling the year's important turning points.

The **Cenote Xlacah**, now an eminently swimmable public swimming hole (don't forget your swimsuit), is more than 40m deep. The water is clean and crystal clear and provides welcome respite from the midday heat. In 1958 a National Geographic Society diving expedition recovered more than 30,000 Maya artifacts, many of ritual significance, from the cenote. The most interesting of these are now on display in the site's museum. South of the cenote is **Estructura 44**, which at 130m is one of the longest Maya structures in existence.

Minibuses and *colectivos* depart frequently from Mérida's Parque de San Juan for the village of Dzibilchaltún Ruinas (M$14, 30 minutes), a little over 1km from the ruins. Taxis cost around M$250 roundtrip.

Progreso

☎969 / POP 54,000

If Mérida's heat has you dying for a quick beach fix, head to Progreso (also known as Puerto Progreso). The sand is brilliant white but the water is murky; visibility even on calm days rarely exceeds 5m. Winds can hit here full force off the Gulf in the afternoon and can blow well into the night, which means good kiteboarding and windsurfing (check with www.marinasilcer.com to see if it can arrange rentals).

From the plaza on Calle 80, it is six short blocks to the waterfront *malecón* (Calle 19) and *muelle* (wharf); along the way are two Banamex banks, one with an ATM. Even-numbered streets here run east–west; odd ones north–south.

Just east of Progreso, **Laguna Rosada** is a good spot for flamingo sightings, and you can head on to **Telchac Puerto**, home to many summer houses for Mérida's well-to-do. Along the way, take time to stop at an observation tower in **Uaymitún** and the **Xcambó** Maya ruins.

Sleeping & Eating

El Boarding House HOSTEL $

(☎cell phone 969-1030294; www.hostelprogreso.com; cnr Calles 21 & 54; dm/d M$120/320; @📶) Progreso's only hostel is set in an awesome mansion a block back from the beach. When the current renovations are complete, this place should be one sweet deal.

Playa Linda Hotel HOTEL $$

(☎985-858-05-19, 999-220-83-18; Calle 76, btwn Calles 19 & 21; r/ste from M$500/800; ❄📶) The best deal on the beachfront, offering a good range of rooms (more expensive ones have kitchenette and sea-facing balconies). The suites work well for families or groups. The only drawback? No pool.

★**Eladio's** SEAFOOD $$

(www.eladios.com.mx; cnr Calles 19 & 80; mains M$75-155; ⏲10am-9pm; 📶) The local's choice is this casual beachfront eatery under the *palapa* roof. Five complimentary sampler plates of seafood and salads come to your table before your main dish arrives, so you better be good and hungry.

Getting There & Away

Progreso is 33km north of Mérida along a fast four-lane highway that's basically a continuation of the Paseo de Montejo. The **bus station** (Calle 29, btwn Calles 80 & 82) has numerous Mérida-bound buses from 5:20am to 10pm.

Izamal

☎988 / POP 26,000

Just under 70km east of Mérida, Izamal is a quiet, colonial gem of a town, nicknamed La Ciudad Amarilla (the Yellow City) for the yellow paint that brightens the walls of practically every building. It is easily explored on foot and makes a great day trip from Mérida.

In ancient times, Izamal was a center for the worship of the supreme Maya god, Itzamná, and the local sun god, Kinich-Kakmó. A dozen temple pyramids were devoted to these or other gods. It was probably these bold expressions of Maya religiosity that provoked the Spaniards to build the enormous Franciscan monastery that stands today at the heart of this town.

Sights

Convento de San Antonio de Padua MONASTERY

(Calle 31; admission free, sound-and-light show M$90, museum M$5; ⏲6am-8pm, sound-and-light show 8.30pm Tue, Thu & Sat, museum 10am-1pm & 3-6pm Mon-Sat, 9am-5pm Sun) When the Spaniards conquered Izamal, they destroyed the major Maya temple, the Ppapp-Hol-Chac pyramid, and in 1533 began to build from its stones one of the first monasteries in the western hemisphere. Work on Convento de San Antonio de Padua was finished in 1561. Under the monastery's arcades, look for building stones with an unmistakable mazelike design; these were clearly taken from the earlier Maya temple.

The monastery's principal church is the **Santuario de la Virgen de Izamal**, approached by a ramp from the main square. The ramp leads into the **Atrium**, a huge arcaded courtyard in which the **fiesta of the Virgin of Izamal** takes place each August 15. There's a **sound-and-light show** here three nights a week.

At some point the 16th-century **frescoes** beside the entrance of the sanctuary were completely painted over. For years they lay concealed under a thin layer of whitewash until a maintenance worker who was cleaning the walls discovered them.

The church's original altarpiece was destroyed by a fire believed to have been started by a fallen candle. Its replacement, impressively gilded, was built in the 1940s. In the niches at the stations of the cross are some superb small figures.

In the small courtyard to the left of the church, look up and toward the Atrium to see the original sundial projecting from the roof's edge. A small **museum** at the back commemorates Pope John Paul II's 1993 visit to the monastery. He brought with him a silver crown for the statue of the patron saint of Yucatán, the Virgin of Izamal.

The monastery's front entrance faces west. The best time to visit is in the morning, as the church is occasionally closed during the afternoon siesta.

Kinich-Kakmó ARCHAEOLOGICAL SITE

(8am-5pm) FREE Three of the town's original 12 Maya pyramids have been partially restored. The largest (and the third largest in Yucatán) is the enormous Kinich-Kakmó, three blocks north of the monastery. You can climb it for free.

Sleeping & Eating

Several *loncherías* (snack bars) occupy spaces in the market on the convent's southwest side.

Posada Zamná HOTEL $

(Calle 30 btwn Calles 31 & 31a; r with fan/air-con M$280/350;) A simple posada offering probably the best budget rooms in town in a great location, right on the Parque Zamná and a few steps away from the convent. There's no telephone.

Hotel Macan ché HOTEL $$

(988-954-02-87; www.macanche.com; Calle 22 No 305; r with fan/air-con incl breakfast from M$600/720, casita M$1750;) Pebbled pathways wind through a lush garden setting to fan-cooled bungalows and out to the neocolonial styled building housing the air-conditioned rooms. The casita (a self-contained house) sleeps six and features a full kitchen and balcony overlooking the lovely pool area.

★**Kinich** MEXICAN $$

(www.kinichizamal.com; Calle 27 No 299, btwn Calles 28 & 30; mains M$100-150; noon-9pm) This is fresh, handmade Yucatecan cuisine at its best. The *papadzules kinich* – rolled tortillas stuffed with diced egg and topped with pumpkin-seed sauce and smoky sausage – is a delightful house specialty.

Getting There & Away

Izamal's bus terminal is two short blocks west of the monastery. Coming from Mérida, buses to Izamal (M$22, 1½ hours) leave from the Noreste bus terminal. Buses run on from Izamal to Valladolid (M$48, two hours). Coming from Chichén Itzá you must change buses at Hoctún.

Chichén Itzá

985

The most famous and best restored of the Yucatán Maya sites, **Chichén Itzá** (Mouth of the Well of the Itzáes; http://chichenitza.inah.gob.mx/; off Hwy 180, Pisté; admission M$234, sound & light show M$72 ; 8am-5pm Tue-Sun), while tremendously overcrowded – every gawker and

THE OTHER BIG BANG

In the small town of Chicxulub, just outside Progreso, is an even smaller plaque dedicated to arguably the biggest event in planet earth's history. It's widely believed that around here, 65-odd million years ago, the Chicxulub meteor smashed into the planet. Many scientists believe this event led to a catastrophic change in the climate, leading to the extinction of the dinosaurs and drastically altering the course of evolution of life on earth.

There's not much to see here apart from the plaque, but if you're into visiting sites of historical importance, you could hardly find a bigger one than this.

his or her grandmother is trying to check off the new Seven Wonders of the World – will still impress even the most jaded visitor. Many mysteries of the Maya astronomical calendar are made clear when one understands the design of the 'time temples' here.

At the vernal (spring) and autumnal equinoxes (March 20 to 21 and September 21 to 22), the morning and afternoon sun produces a light-and-shadow illusion of the serpent ascending or descending the side of El Castillo's staircase. Chichén is mobbed on these dates, however, making it difficult to get close enough to see. The illusion is almost as good in the week preceding and following each equinox, and is recreated nightly in the sound-and-light show year-round.

The western entrance has a large parking lot and a big visitors center with parking for M$22. As at most sites, filming with a video camera costs M$45 extra, and tripods require a special permit from Mexico City. Explanatory plaques around the site are in Spanish, English and Maya. You can hire a guide for M$600.

The 45-minute sound-and-light show in Spanish begins at 8pm each evening in summer and 7pm in winter. Devices for listening to English, French, German or Italian translations (beamed via infrared) rent for M$45. Specify the language you need or it may not be broadcast.

Other than a few minor passageways, climbing on the structures is not allowed.

History

Most archaeologists agree that the first major settlement at Chichén Itzá, during the late Classic period, was pure Maya. In about the 9th century the city was largely abandoned, for reasons unknown. It was resettled around the late 10th century, and some Mayanists believe that shortly thereafter it was invaded by the Toltecs.

Toltec culture was fused with that of the Maya, incorporating the Toltec cult of Quetzalcóatl (Kukulcán, in Maya). Throughout the city, you will see images of both Chac, the Maya rain god, and Quetzalcóatl, the plumed serpent.

The substantial fusion of highland central Mexican and Puuc architectural styles makes Chichén unique among the Yucatán Peninsula's ruins. The fabulous El Castillo and the Plataforma de Venus are outstanding architectural works, built during the height of Toltec cultural input.

The warlike Toltecs contributed more than their architectural skills to the Maya. They elevated human sacrifice to a near obsession, and there are numerous carvings of the bloody ritual in Chichén demonstrating this. After a Maya leader moved his political capital to Mayapán, while keeping Chichén as his religious capital, Chichén Itzá fell into decline. The city was finally abandoned – this time for good – in the 14th century, but the once-great city remained the site of Maya pilgrimages for many years.

Sights

El Castillo ARCHAEOLOGICAL SITE

Entering the grounds, El Castillo (aka the Pyramid of Kukulcán) rises before you in all its grandeur. The structure is actually a massive Maya calendar formed in stone. The first temple here was pre-Toltec, built around AD 800, but the present 25m-high structure, built over the old one, has the plumed serpent sculpted along the stairways and Toltec warriors represented in the doorway carvings at the top of the temple.

Each of El Castillo's nine levels is divided in two by a staircase, making 18 separate terraces that commemorate the 18 20-day months of the Maya Vague Year. The four stairways have 91 steps each; add the top platform and the total is 365, the number of days in the year. On each facade of the pyramid are 52 flat panels, which are reminders of the 52 years in the Maya calendar round.

To top it off, during the spring and autumn equinoxes, light and shadow form a series of triangles on the side of the north staircase that mimic the creep of a serpent (note the carved serpent's heads flanking the bottom of the staircase). You won't get to see the carvings atop the temple, however, as ascending the pyramid is not allowed.

The older pyramid inside El Castillo has a red jaguar throne with inlaid eyes and spots of jade; also lying behind the screen is a *chacmool* (Maya sacrificial stone sculpture). The entrance to **El Túnel**, the passage up to the throne, is at the base of El Castillo's north side. You can't go in, though.

Gran Juego de Pelota ARCHAEOLOGICAL SITE

The great ball court, the largest and most impressive in Mexico, is only one of the city's eight courts, indicative of the importance the games held here. The court, to the left of the visitors center, is flanked by temples at either end and is bounded by towering parallel walls set with stone rings.

Along the walls of the ball court are stone reliefs, including scenes of decapitations of players. The court exhibits some interesting acoustics: a conversation at one end can be heard 135m away at the other, and a clap produces multiple loud echoes.

Templo del Barbado & Templo de los Jaguares y Escudos TEMPLE

The structure at the northern end of the ball court, called the Temple of the Bearded Man after a carving inside, has some finely sculpted pillars and reliefs of flowers, birds and trees. The Temple of the Jaguars and Shields, built atop the southeast corner of the ball court's wall, has columns with carved rattlesnakes and tablets with etched jaguars.

Inside are faded mural fragments depicting a battle.

Plataforma de los Cráneos ARCHAEOLOGICAL SITE

The Platform of Skulls (Tzompantli in Náhuatl, a Maya dialect) is between the Templo de los Jaguares and El Castillo. You can't mistake it, because the T-shaped platform is festooned with carved skulls and eagles tearing open the chests of men to eat their hearts. In ancient days this platform was used to display the heads of sacrificial victims.

Plataforma de las Águilas y los Jaguares TEMPLE

Adjacent to the Tzompantli, the Platform of the Eagles and Jaguars has carvings of both animals gruesomely grabbing human hearts in their claws. It is thought that this platform was part of a temple dedicated to the military legions responsible for capturing sacrificial victims.

Cenote Sagrado ARCHAEOLOGICAL SITE

From the Tzompantli, a 300m rough stone *sacbé* runs north (a five-minute walk) to the huge sunken well that gave this city its name – *chi chen* translates to 'mouth of the well'. The Sacred Cenote is an awesome natural sinkhole, some 60m in diameter and 35m deep. The walls between the summit and the water's surface are ensnared in tangled vines and other vegetation. There are ruins of a small steam bath next to the cenote, as well as a concession stand with toilets.

Plaza de las Mil Columnas RUIN

Comprising the Templo de los Guerreros (Temple of the Warriors), the Templo de Chac-Mool (Temple of Chac-Mool) and the Baño de Vapor (Sweat House or Steam Bath), this group, behind El Castillo, takes its name (Group of the Thousand Columns) from the forest of pillars stretching south and east.

El Osario ARCHAEOLOGICAL SITE

The Ossuary, otherwise known as the Bonehouse or the **Tumba del Gran Sacerdote** (High Priest's Grave), is a ruined pyramid to the southwest of El Castillo. As with most of the buildings in this southern section, the architecture is more Puuc than Toltec. It's notable for the beautiful serpent heads at the base of its staircases.

A square shaft at the top of the structure leads into a cave beneath that was used as a burial chamber; seven tombs with human remains were discovered inside. A snack bar with telephone and toilets stands nearby.

El Caracol ARCHAEOLOGICAL SITE

Called El Caracol (The Snail) by the Spaniards for its interior spiral staircase, this **observatory**, to the south of the Ossuary, is one of the most fascinating and important of all Chichén Itzá's buildings (but, alas, you can't enter). Its circular design resembles some central highlands structures, although, surprisingly, not those of Toltec Tula.

In a fusion of architectural styles and religious imagery, there are Maya Chac raingod masks over four external doors facing the cardinal points. The windows in the observatory's dome are aligned with the appearance of certain stars at specific dates. From the dome the priests decreed the times for rituals, celebrations, corn planting and harvests.

Edificio de las Monjas & La Iglesia PALACE

Thought by archaeologists to have been a palace for Maya royalty, the so-called Edificio de las Monjas (Nunnery), with its myriad rooms, resembled a European convent to the conquistadors, hence their name for the building. The building's dimensions are imposing: its base is 60m long, 30m wide and 20m high.

The construction is Maya rather than Toltec, although a Toltec sacrificial stone stands in front. A smaller adjoining building to the east, known as La Iglesia (The Church), is covered almost entirely with carvings. On the far side at the back there are some passageways that are still open, leading a short way into the labyrinth inside. They are dank and slippery, they smell of bat

Chichén Itzá

It doesn't take long to realize why the Maya site of Chichén Itzá is one of Mexico's most popular tourist draws. Approaching the grounds from the main entrance, the striking castle pyramid **El Castillo** 1 jumps right out at you – and the wow factor never lets up.

It's easy to tackle Chichén Itzá in one day. Within a stone's throw of the castle, you'll find the Maya world's largest **ball court** 2 alongside eerie carvings of skulls and heart-devouring eagles at the Temple of Jaguars and the Platform of Skulls. On the other (eastern) side are the highly adorned **Group of a Thousand Columns** 3 and the **Temple of Warriors** 4. A short walk north of the castle leads to the gaping **Sacred Cenote** 5, an important pilgrimage site. On the other side of El Castillo, you'll find giant stone serpents watching over the High Priest's Grave, aka El Osario. Further south, marvel at the spiral-domed **Observatory** 6, the imposing Nunnery and Akab-Dzib, one of the oldest ruins.

Roaming the 47-hectare site, it's fun to consider that at its height Chichén Itzá was home to an estimated 90,000 inhabitants and spanned approximately 30 sq km. So essentially you're looking at just a small part of a once-great city.

THE LOWDOWN

» **Arrive** at 8am and you'll have a good three hours or so before the tour-bus madness begins. Early birds escape the merchants, too.

» **Remember** that Chichén Itzá is the name of the site; the actual town where it's located is called Pisté.

ADINA TOVY/GETTY IMAGES ©

El Caracol

Observatory

Today they'd probably just use a website, but back in the day priests would stand from the dome of the circular observatory to announce the latest rituals and celebrations.

Grupo de las Mil Columnas

Group of a Thousand Columns

Not unlike a hall of fame exhibit, the pillars surrounding the temple reveal carvings of gods, dignitaries and celebrated warriors.

ROSS BARNETT/GETTY IMAGES ©

LOLA L. FALANTES/GETTY IMAGES ©

El Castillo

The Castle

Even this mighty pyramid can't bear the stress of a million visitors ascending its stairs each year. No climbing allowed, but the ground-level view doesn't disappoint.

ROSS BARNETT/GETTY IMAGES ©

Gran Juego de Pelota

Great Ball Court

How is it possible to hear someone talk from one end of this long, open-air court to the other? To this day, the acoustics remain a mystery.

Entrance

Parking Lot

Visitors Center

Tumba del Gran Sacerdote (High Priest's Grave)

Templo de los Jaguares (Temple of Jaguars)

Plataforma de los Cráneos (Platform of Skulls)

1 2 3 4 5

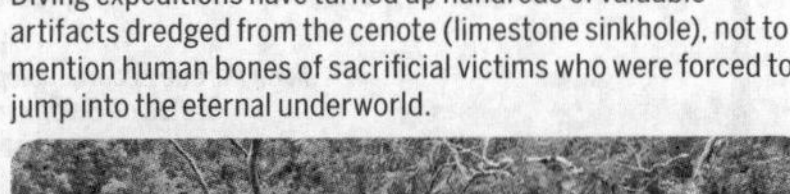

Cenote Sagrado

Sacred Cenote

Diving expeditions have turned up hundreds of valuable artifacts dredged from the cenote (limestone sinkhole), not to mention human bones of sacrificial victims who were forced to jump into the eternal underworld.

Templo de los Guerreros

Temple of Warriors

The Maya associated warriors with eagles and jaguars, as depicted in the temple's friezes. The revered jaguar, in particular, was a symbol of strength and agility.

EDUCATION IMAGES/UIG/GETTY IMAGES ©

JUAN CARLOS MUNOZ/GETTY IMAGES ©

Chichén Itzá

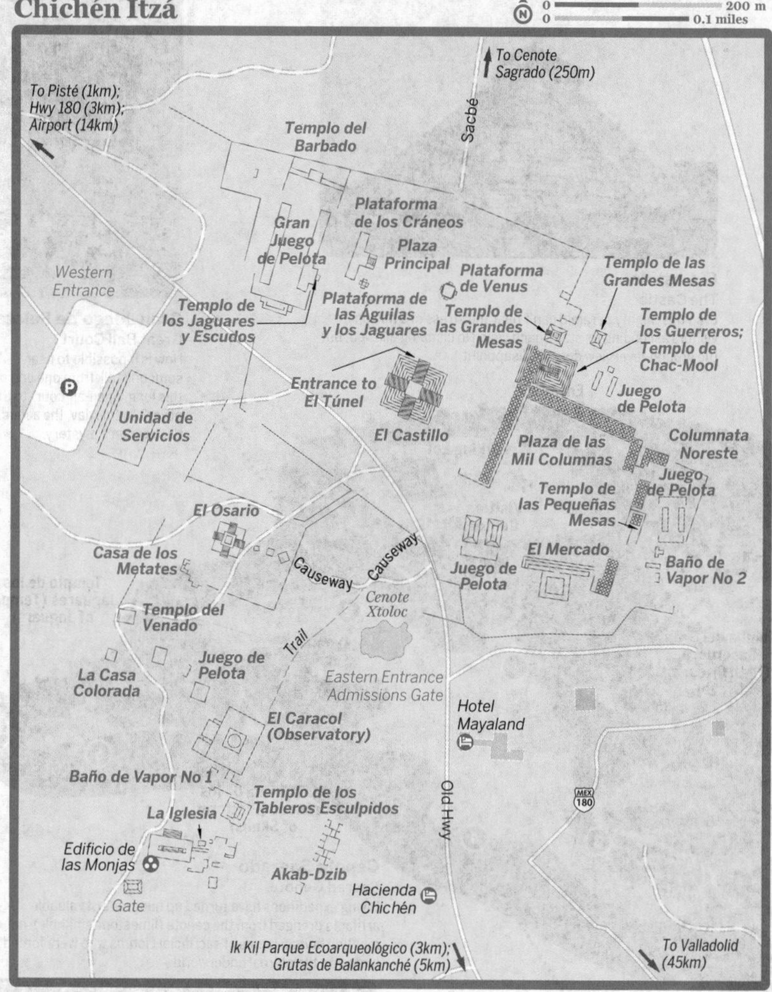

urine, and it's easy to twist an ankle as you go, but Indiana Jones wannabes will find the experience totally cool.

Akab-Dzib ARCHAEOLOGICAL SITE

East of the Nunnery, the Puuc-style Akab-Dzib is thought by some archaeologists to be the most ancient structure excavated here. The central chambers date from the 2nd century. The name means 'Obscure Writing' in Maya and refers to the south-side annex door, whose lintel depicts a priest with a vase etched with hieroglyphics that have yet to be successfully translated.

Ik Kil Parque Ecoarqueológico SWIMMING

(adult/child M$70/35; ⌚8am-6pm) A little over 3km southeast of the eastern entrance to the ruins, a dramatic natural cenote has been developed into a divine swimming spot. Small cascades of water plunge from the high limestone roof, which is ringed by greenery. It has a good buffet and nice *cabañas* (M$1250) onsite. Get your swim in by no later than 1pm to beat the tour groups.

Grutas de Balankanché CAVE

(Hwy 180; adult/child 7-12yr M$105/6; ⌚9am-4pm) In 1959 a guide to the Chichén ruins was exploring a cave on his day off when he came upon a narrow passageway. He followed the passageway for 300m, meandering through a series of caverns. In each, perched on mounds amid scores of glistening stalactites, were hundreds of ceremonial treasures the Maya had placed there 800 years earlier.

Among the discovered objects were ritual *metates* and *manos* (grinding stones), incense burners and pots. In the years following the discovery, the ancient ceremonial objects were removed and studied. Eventually most of them were returned to the caves, and placed exactly where they were found.

Outside the caves, you'll find a good **botanical garden** (displaying native flora with information on the medicinal and other uses of the trees and plants) and a small **museum**. The museum features photographs taken during the exploration of the caves, and descriptions (in English, Spanish and French) of the Maya religion and the offerings found in the caves. Also on display are photographs of modern-day Maya ceremonies called Ch'a Chaac, which continue to be held in all the villages on the Yucatán Peninsula during times of drought and consist mostly of praying and making numerous offerings of food to Chac.

Compulsory 45-minute tours (minimum six people, maximum 30) have melodramatic, not-very-informative recorded narration that is nearly impossible to make out. If you'd like it in a particular language, English is at 11am, 1pm and 3pm; Spanish is at 9am, noon, 2pm and 4pm; and French is at 10am.

Be warned that the cave is unusually hot, and ventilation is poor in its further reaches. The lack of oxygen (especially after a few groups have already passed through) makes it difficult to draw a full breath until you're outside again.

The turnoff for the caverns is 6km east of Chichén Itzá on the highway to Valladolid (Hwy 180). Second-class buses heading east from Pisté toward Valladolid will drop you at the Balankanché road. The entrance to the caves is 350m north of the highway junction.

Sleeping

Most of Chichén's lodgings, restaurants and services are ranged along 1km of highway in the village of Pisté, to the western side of the ruins. It's 1.5km from the ruins' main entrance to the first hotel in Pisté. Hwy 180 is known as Calle 15a as it passes through Pisté.

Posada Olalde HOTEL $

(985-851-00-86; cnr Calles 6 & 17; s/d M$250/300;) Two blocks south of the highway by Artesanías Guayacán, this is the best of Pisté's several posadas. It has clean, quiet rooms, a few tame parakeets and four decent-sized bungalows. Some toilets are missing seats. All accommodations are fan-cooled, and the friendly manager speaks Spanish and English, as well as some Maya.

Hotel Chichén Itzá HOTEL $$

(Best Western; 985-851-00-22, in USA 800-235-4079; www.mayaland.com; Calle 15 No 45; r/ste M$940/1445; P) On the west side of Pisté, this hotel has 42 pleasant rooms with tiled floors and old-style brick-tiled ceilings. Rooms in the upper range face the pool and the landscaped grounds, and all have firm beds and minibars. Parents may bring two kids under 13 years for free.

Hacienda Chichén RESORT $$$

(999-920-84-07, in USA 877-631-4005; www.haciendachichen.com; Zona Hotelera, Km 120; d from M$2630; P) About 300m from the ruins' entrance, this resort is on the grounds of a 16th-century estate. The hacienda's elegant main house and ruined walls make a great setting, and huge ceiba trees offer welcome shade. The archaeologists who excavated Chichén during the 1920s lived here in bungalows, which have been refurbished and augmented with new ones.

Hotel Mayaland HOTEL $$$

(985-851-01-00, in USA 800-235-4079; www.mayaland.com; d/ste M$3029/4485; P) The Mayaland is less than 100m from the site's eastern entrance: from the lobby and front rooms you can look out at El Caracol. The rooms, pools and garden bungalows are nice and all, but when you're at El Caracol you'll wish the hotel hadn't cut an ugly swath through the jungle just so patrons could have a better view.

Eating

The highway through Pisté is lined with more than 20 eateries, large and small.

Lonchería Fabiola's MEXICAN $

(Calle 15a s/n; mains M$50-100; 7am-7pm) For a good, honest, cheap feed it's hard to go past this humble little place at the end of the strip of eateries opposite the church. The *pollo yucateco* (Yucatecan chicken) comes highly recommended.

Las Mestizas MEXICAN $$
(Calle 15 s/n; mains M$40-100; ⏲8am-10pm) The place to go in town if you're craving decent Yucatecan fare. There's indoor and outdoor seating – though an outdoor table may mean you'll be getting some tour-bus fumes to go along with that *cochito* (roasted pork).

Getting There & Away

Oriente has ticket offices at the east and west end of Pisté, and 2nd-class buses passing through town stop almost anywhere along the highway. Many 1st-class buses only stop at the ruins and the west end of town, close to the toll highway.

First-class buses serve Mérida (M$120, 1¾ hours, 5:15pm), Cancún (M$202, 2½ hours, 4:30pm) and Tulum (M$148, 2½ hours, 2 daily).

Oriente's 2nd-class buses bound for Mérida (M$72, 2½ hours) pass through hourly between 8:15am and 4:15pm. Hourly Oriente buses to Valladolid (M$24, 50 minutes) and Cancún (M$122, 4½ hours) pass between 7am and 5:30pm. There's also 2nd-class service to Tulum (M$90, three hours) and Playa del Carmen (M$130, four hours).

Shared vans to Valladolid (M$25, 40 minutes) pass through town regularly.

Getting Around

During Chichén Itzá's opening hours, many 1st- and 2nd-class buses run to the ruins (check with the driver), and they will take passengers from town for about M$10, providing they have room. For a bit more, 2nd-class buses will also take you to the Cenote Ik Kil and the Grutas de Balankanché (be sure to specify your destination when buying your ticket). If you plan to see the ruins and then head directly to another city by 1st-class bus, buy your bus ticket at the visitors center before hitting the ruins, for a better chance of getting a seat.

There is a taxi stand near the west end of town; the price to the ruins is around M$30. There are usually taxis loitering at Chichén's parking lot.

Valladolid

☎985 / POP 74,000

Known locally as the Sultaness of the East, Yucatán's third-largest city is known for its quiet streets and sun-splashed pastel walls. It's worth staying here for a few days or even a week, as the provincial town makes a great hub for visits to Río Lagartos, Chichén Itzá, Ek' Balam and a number of nearby cenotes. The city resides at that magic point where there's plenty to do, yet it still feels small, manageable and affordable.

There's a helpful **tourist office** (cnr Calles 40 & 41; ⏲9am-9pm Mon-Sat, 9am-2pm Sun) in the town hall building on the plaza.

History

Valladolid has seen its fair share of turmoil and revolt over the years. The first Spanish settlement was founded in 1543 near the Chouac-Ha lagoon, some 50km from the coast, but it was too hot and there were way too many mosquitoes for Francisco de Montejo, nephew of Montejo the Elder, and his merry band of conquerors. So they upped and moved their city to the Maya ceremonial center of Zací (sah-*see*), where they faced heavy resistance from the local Maya. Eventually the Elder's son, Montejo the Younger, took the town. The Spanish conquerors, in typical fashion, ripped down the town and laid out a new city following the classic colonial plan.

During much of the colonial era, Valladolid's physical isolation from Mérida kept it relatively autonomous from royal rule, and the Maya of the area suffered brutal exploitation, which continued after Mexican independence. Barred from entering many areas of the city, the Maya made Valladolid one of their first points of attack following the outbreak of the War of the Castes in 1847 in Tepich, not far south on the border with Quintana Roo. After a two-month siege, the city's defenders were finally overcome.

Sights

★Casa de los Venados GALLERY
(☎985-856-22-89; www.casadelosvenados.com; Calle 40, btwn Calles 41 & 43; entry by donation; ⏲tours 10am daily or by appointment) Featuring over 3000 pieces of museum-quality Mexican folk art, this private collection is unique in that objects are presented in a house, in the context that they were originally designed for, instead of being roped off in glass cases. The tour (English and Spanish) lasts for about an hour and touches on the origins of some of the more important pieces and the story of the award-winning restored colonial home that houses them.

Templo de San Bernardino & Convento de Sisal CHURCH
(Church of San Bernardino; cnr Calles 49 & 51; convent admission M$30; ⏲9am-6pm Mon-Fri, to 3pm Sat) The Templo de San Bernardino and the Convento de Sisal are about 700m southwest

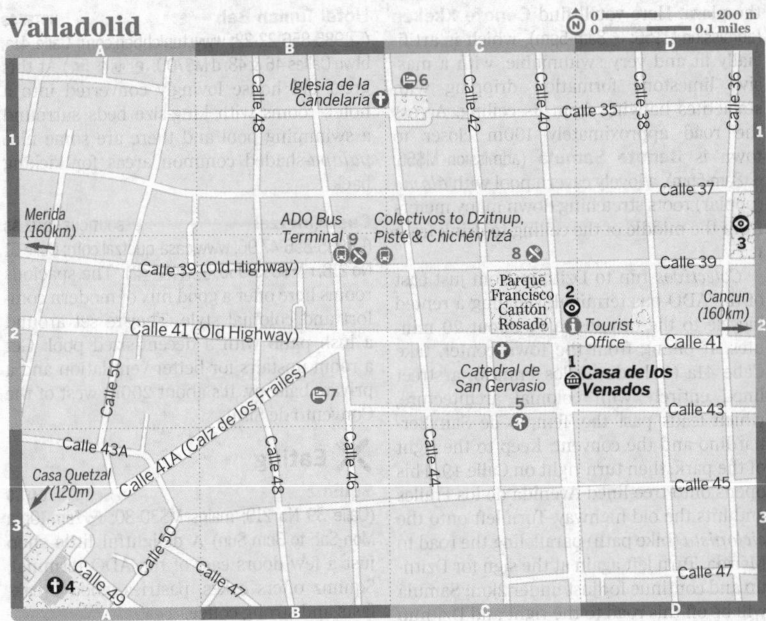

Valladolid

Top Sights
1 Casa de los Venados C2

Sights
2 Ayuntamiento C2
3 Cenote Zací D1
4 Templo de San Bernardino & Convento de Sisal A3

Activities, Courses & Tours
5 Mexigo C2

Sleeping
6 Hostel La Candelaria C1
7 Hotel Tunich-Beh B2

Eating
8 Hostería del Marqués C2
9 Squimz B2

of the plaza. They were constructed between 1552 and 1560 to serve the dual functions of fortress and church. The church's charming decoration includes beautiful rose-colored walls, arches, some recently uncovered 16th-century frescoes, and a small image of the Virgin on the altar.

These are about the only original items remaining; the grand wooden *retablo* (altarpiece) dates from the 19th century. The adjacent convent's walled grounds hold a cenote with a vaulted dome built over it and a system of channels that once irrigated the large garden.

Ayuntamiento NOTABLE BUILDING
(Town Hall; Calle 40, btwn Calles 39 & 41; ⏲8am-8pm Mon-Sat) Go upstairs in the Ayuntamiento to see a series of murals painted by Yucatecan artist Manuel Salazar depicting the arrival of the Spanish, the Maya resistance and the eventual colonization of Valladolid and the Yucatán.

Activities

There are several underground cenotes around Valladolid, including **Cenote Zací** (www.cenotezaci.com.mx; Calle 36; admission M$15; ⏲7am-6pm), set in a park that also holds traditional stone-walled thatched houses and a small zoo. People swim in Zací, but being mostly open, it is prone to dust and algae build-up and water-table contamination. Entry is from Calle 39.

A bit more enticing but less accessible are the cenotes at **Dzitnup**, 7km west of the plaza. Here you'll find **Cenote Xkekén** (admission M$56; ⏲8am-5pm), which is artificially lit and very swimmable, with a massive limestone formation dripping with stalactites hanging from its ceiling. Across the road approximately 100m closer to town is **Cenote Samulá** (admission M$56; ⏲8am-5pm), a lovely cavern pool with *álamo* (poplar) roots stretching down many meters from the middle of the ceiling to drink from it.

Colectivos run to Dzitnup from just east of the ADO bus terminal. Pedaling a rented bicycle to the cenotes takes about 20 minutes. If biking from the town center, take Calle 41a (Calzada de los Frailes), a street lined entirely with colonial architecture, which leads past the Templo de San Bernardino and the convent. Keep to the right of the park, then turn right on Calle 49. This opens onto tree-lined Avenida de los Frailes and hits the old highway. Turn left onto the *ciclopista* (bike path) paralleling the road to Mérida. Turn left again at the sign for Dzitnup and continue for just under 2km; Samulá will be off this road to the right and Dzitnup a little further along on the left.

Sleeping

Hostel La Candelaria HOSTEL $
(☎985-856-22-67; www.hostelvalladolidyucatan.com; Calle 35 No 201F; dm/r incl breakfast M$120/280; @ 📶) A friendly place right on a quiet little square, this hostel can get a little cramped and hot, but there are two kitchens, a cozy garden area complete with hammocks, a gals-only dorm, and plenty of hangout space, making it the best budget option in town. The hostel also rents bikes for M$15 per hour.

Hotel Tunich-Beh HOTEL $$
(☎985-856-22-22; www.tunichbeh.com; Calle 41a, btwn Calles 46 & 48; d M$700; P ❄ 📶 🏊) At this great old house lovingly converted into a hotel, rooms with king-size beds surround a swimming pool and there are some nice *palapa*-shaded common areas for kicking back.

Casa Quetzal BOUTIQUE HOTEL $$
(☎985-856-47-96; www.casa-quetzal.com; Calle 51 No 218; r M$895-950; P ❄ 📶 🏊) The spacious rooms here offer a good mix of modern comfort and colonial style. They're set around a lush patio with a decent-sized pool. Get a room upstairs for better ventilation and a private balcony. It's about 200m west of the Convento de Sisal.

Eating

Squimz CAFE $
(Calle 39 No 219; mains M$30-80; ⏲7am-10pm Mon-Sat, to 3pm Sun) A delightful little shop just a few doors east of the ADO terminal, Squimz offers cakes, pastries, good breakfasts and strong coffee.

Hostería del Marqués MEXICAN $$
(☎985-856-20-73; www.mesondelmarques.com; El Mesón del Marqués, Calle 39 No 203; mains M$70-220; ⏲7am-11pm; P ❄) Dine in a tranquil colonial courtyard with a bubbling fountain, or the air-con salon looking onto it. The restaurant specializes in Yucatecan fare – ie *longaniza* Valladolid (Valladolid-style sausage), *cochinita pibil* (marinated pork) – and there are also international dishes such as Angus beef cuts.

BUSES FROM VALLADOLID

DESTINATION	FARE (M$)	DURATION	FREQUENCY (DAILY)
Cancún	95-150	2-3hr	frequent
Chichén Itzá (Pisté)	24-62	45min	frequent Oriente & ADO
Chiquilá (for Isla Holbox)	90	2½hr	Oriente 2:45am
Cobá	35-38	45min	frequent Mayab
Izamal	53	2hr	2 Oriente
Mérida	95-180	2½-3½hr	hourly ADO & 2nd-class Oriente
Playa del Carmen	106-150	2½-3½hr	frequent ADO & Oriente
Tizimín	25	1hr	20 Mayab & Oriente
Tulum	72-90	2hr	10 ADO, 7am Mayab

Getting There & Away

BUS

Valladolid's main bus terminal is the convenient **ADO bus terminal** (cnr Calles 39 & 46). The main operators are Oriente, Mayab and Expresso (2nd class), and ADO and Super Expresso (1st class).

COLECTIVO

Faster, more reliable and more comfortable than 2nd-class buses are the *colectivos* that leave for various points as soon as their seats are filled. Most operate from 7am or 8am to about 7pm. Direct services to Mérida (M$105, 2½ hours) depart from the ADO bus terminal. Direct *colectivos* to Cancún (M$140, 2½ hours) leave from Calle 38 between Calles 39 and 41. Confirm they're nonstop before you board.

Colectivos for Pisté and Chichén Itzá (M$25, 40 minutes) leave from a lot just east of the ADO bus terminal, and those bound for Tizimín (M$35, 40 minutes) leave from a lot north of the plaza on Calle 40 between Calles 35 and 37. To reach Ek' Balam (M$40, 30 minutes), take a *colectivo* bound for Santa Rita from the corner of Calles 44 and 37.

Getting Around

Bicycles are a great way to see the town and get out to the cenotes. You can hire them from Hostel La Candelaria or **Mexigo** (www.mexigotours.com; Calle 43 btwn Calles 40 & 42; bike hire per hour/day M$15/90; 8am-8pm), which also offers a range of guided bike tours of the area.

Ek' Balam

The fascinating ruined city of **Ek' Balam** (admission M$130, guide M$500-600; 8am-5pm) reached its peak in the 8th century, before being suddenly abandoned. Vegetation still covers much of the archaeological site, but excavations and restoration continue to add to the sights, including an interesting ziggurat-like structure near the entrance, as well as a fine arch and a ball court.

Most impressive is the gargantuan **Acrópolis**, whose well-restored base is 160m long and holds a 'gallery' – actually a series of separate chambers. Built atop the base is Ek' Balam's massive main pyramid, reaching a height of 32m and sporting a huge jaguar mouth with 360-degree dentition. Below the mouth are stucco skulls, while above and to the right sits an amazingly expressive figure. On the right side stand unusual winged human figures (some call them Maya angels, although a much more likely explanation is that they are shaman or medicine men).

The turnoff for the archaeological site is 17km north of Valladolid, and the ruins are another 6km east from the turnoff. Nearby is the **X-Canché Cenote** (cell phone 985-1009915; www.ekbalam.com.mx/cenote-xcanche; admission M$30; 8am-5pm), which offers swimming, adventure activities, camping (M$70) and comfortable cabins (M$450); it's a 1.5km walk from the Ek' Balam parking lot – or get a pedicab for M$60 round-trip.

Sleeping & Eating

★ **Genesis Eco-Retreat** GUESTHOUSE **$$**
(cell phone 985-1004805; www.genesisretreat.com; Ek' Balam pueblo; d without/with bathroom from M$570/705; @) The Genesis Eco-Retreat offers B&B intimacy in a quiet, eco-friendly setting. This is a true eco-hotel: gray water is used for landscaping and some rooms are naturally cooled. The place is postcard-beautiful – there's a chilling dip pool and a temascal (steam bath) onsite – and the owners offer delicious veggie meals.

The hotel is sometimes closed between September and early October.

Getting There & Away

From Valladolid, *colectivos* leave from Calle 44 between Calles 35 and 37 bound for Ek' Balam (M$40, 30 minutes). A round-trip taxi ride from Valladolid with an hour's wait at the ruins will cost around M$450.

Río Lagartos

986 / POP 3400

With the largest and most spectacular flamingo colony in Mexico, Río Lagartos definitely warrants a trip. Situated 103km north of Valladolid and 52km north of Tizimín, this fishing village lies within the **Reserva de la Biosfera Ría Lagartos**. The mangrove-lined estuary is also home to snowy egrets, red egrets, tiger herons, snowy white ibis, hundreds of other bird species and a small number of the crocodiles that gave the town its name (Alligator River) – Spanish explorers mistook the inlet for a river and the crocs for alligators, and the rest is history.

The Maya knew the place as Holkobén and used it as a rest stop on their way to the nearby lagoons (Las Coloradas), from which they extracted salt. (Salt continues to be extracted today, on a much vaster scale.) Intrepid travelers can head east of town past

Las Coloradas on a coastal dirt road all the way to the small township of **El Cuyo**.

Most residents aren't sure of the town's street names, and signs are few. The road into town is the north–south Calle 10, which ends at the waterfront Calle 13. There's no bank or ATM in town, so bring lots of cash.

Tours

Flamingo Tours BIRD-WATCHING
The brilliant orange-red flamingos can turn the horizon fiery when they take wing. Depending on your luck, you'll see either hundreds or thousands of them. The best months for viewing are June to August. The four primary haunts, in increasing distance from town, are Punta Garza, Yoluk, Necopal and Nahochín (all flamingo feeding spots named for nearby mangrove patches).

To see the flamingos, you'll need to rent a boat and driver. Prices vary by boat, group size and destination, but bank on around M$900 per boat (maximum six people). You'll see more bird life if you head out at sunrise or around 4pm. Plan on packing something to eat the night before, as most restaurants open long after you'll be on the water. Croc spotting, fishing and photography trips can also be arranged.

You can negotiate a trip with one of the eager agents in the waterfront kiosks near the entrance to town; it's nearly impossible to get through town without being approached. They speak English and will connect you with a captain (who usually doesn't). The best guides are to be found at **Restaurante-Bar Isla Contoy** (☎986-862-00-00; www.riolagartosecotours.net16.net; Calle 19 No 134) and Restaurante La Torreja.

Sleeping & Eating

Posada Las Gaviotas HOTEL $
(☎986-862-05-07; cnr Calle 12 & riverfront; d M$350) This simple budget option right on the riverfront offers clean fan-cooled rooms bathed in avocado green. Little luxuries like toilet seats may be absent.

Hotel Villas de Pescadores HOTEL $$
(☎986-862-00-20; www.hotelriolagartos.com.mx; cnr Calles 14 & 9; d M$500-800; P Wi-Fi) Near the water's edge, this attractive hotel offers nine very clean rooms, each with good cross-ventilation (all face the estuary), two beds and a fan. Upstairs rooms have balconies, and there's a rooftop lookout tower where guests can watch the sun set or sip a relaxing beverage.

Restaurante La Torreja SEAFOOD $
(Calle 9, btwn Calles 12 & 14; mains M$60-150; ⏲8am-9pm) Offers good meals down on the waterfront near the lighthouse. This is a good place to meet other travelers and form groups for the boat tours.

Getting There & Away

Several Noreste buses run daily to Río Lagartos from Tizimín (M$30, one hour) and Mérida (M$130-176, three to four hours). Noreste and Mayab also serve Cancún (M$160, three to four hours) three times daily.

CAMPECHE STATE

Campeche state is home to vast stretches of tangled jungle, some of the region's least visited and most imposing Maya ruins, forgotten pastoral villages, bird-choked coastal lagoons and an inspiring colonial-era capital city. It's the least touristed of the Yucatán states, and it exudes a laid-back, provincial charm. The massive restored Edzná archaeological site is probably the best-known sight, but this is also the wildest corner of the peninsula, and the Reserva de la Biosfera Calakmul is Mexico's largest. Beyond the cacophonous roar of the howlers and hiccupping frogs rise more massive ruined Maya cities, such as Calakmul and Becán. Along the coast, the Laguna de Términos is a prime location for bird-watching expeditions.

Campeche

☎981 / POP 820,000

Campeche is like a colonial fairyland. The walled city center is a tight enclave of perfectly restored pastel-colored buildings, narrow cobblestone streets, fortified ramparts and well-preserved mansions from the 18th and 19th centuries. Added to Unesco's list of World Heritage sites in 1999, the state capital has been so painstakingly restored you'll wonder if it's real. Nearly 2000 historic buildings have been renovated, but beyond the walls lies a typical Mexican provincial capital, complete with a frenetic market, a quiet *malecón* and old fishing docks.

Besides the numerous mansions built by wealthy Spanish families during Campeche's heyday, two segments of the city's famous wall have also survived, as have seven of the *baluartes* (bastions or bulwarks) that were built into it.

History

The Spanish first set their sights on Campeche – then a Maya trading village called Ah Kim Pech (Lord Sun Sheep-Tick) – in 1517, but resistance by the local Maya prevented the Spaniards from fully conquering the region for nearly a quarter of a century. A Spanish outpost was founded in 1531 but quickly abandoned due to Maya hostility. By 1540, however, the conquistadors had gained sufficient control, under the leadership of Francisco de Montejo the Younger, to found a permanent settlement, which they named Villa de San Francisco de Campeche.

The city emerged as the major port for the Yucatán Peninsula, but it faced regular pirate attacks. After a particularly appalling assault in 1663 left the city in ruins, the king of Spain ordered construction of Campeche's famous walls, putting an end to the periodic carnage. Today the economy of the city is largely driven by fishing and, increasingly, tourism, which to some extent has funded the downtown area's renovation.

Sights & Activities

Plaza Principal PLAZA

Shaded by spreading carob trees, and ringed by tiled benches with broad footpaths radiating from a belle epoque kiosk, Campeche's appealingly modest central square started life in 1531 as a military camp. Over the years it became the focus of the town's civic, political and religious activities, and it remains the core of public life. The plaza is seen at its best on weekend evenings, when it's closed to traffic and concerts are staged.

Catedral de Nuestra Señora de la Purísima Concepción CATHEDRAL

(Calle 55; 6:30am-9pm) FREE Dominating Plaza Principal's east side is the two-towered cathedral. The limestone structure has stood on this spot for more than three centuries, and it still fills beyond capacity most Sundays. Statues of Sts Peter and Paul occupy niches in the baroque facade; the sober, single-nave interior is lined with colonial-era paintings.

Centro Cultural Casa Número 6 HISTORIC BUILDING

(Calle 57 No 6; admission M$10, audio guide M$15; 9am-9pm) During the pre-revolutionary era, when this mansion was occupied by an upper-class *campechano* family, Número 6 was a prestigious plaza address. Wandering the premises, you'll get an idea of how the city's high society lived back then. The front sitting room is furnished with Cuban-style furniture and inside are exhibition spaces, a pleasant back patio and a gift shop.

Forts & Bastions

After a particularly blistering pirate attack in 1663, the remaining inhabitants of Campeche set about erecting protective walls around their city. Built largely by indigenous labor with limestone extracted from nearby caves, the barrier took more than 50 years to complete. Stretching over 2km around the urban core and rising to a height of 8m, the hexagonal wall was linked by eight bastions. The seven that remain display a treasure trove of historical paraphernalia. You can climb atop the bulwarks and stroll sections of the wall for sweeping views of the port.

Puerta del Mar GATE

(Sea Gate; cnr Calles 8 & 59) FREE The Puerta del Mar provided access from the sea, opening onto a wharf where small craft delivered goods from ships anchored further out. The shallow waters were later reclaimed so the gate is now several blocks from the waterfront.

★ **Museo de la Arquitectura Maya** MUSEUM

(Calle 8; admission M$35; 9am-5:30pm Tue-Sun) Set in the **Baluarte de Nuestra Señora de la Soledad**, designed to protect the Puerta del Mar, this is the one must-see museum in Campeche. It provides an excellent overview of the many Maya sites around Campeche state and the key architectural styles associated with them.

Museo de la Ciudad MUSEUM

(Calle 8; admission M$15; 9am-8pm) Named after Spain's King Carlos II, the **Baluarte de San Carlos** houses a small but worthwhile museum chronologically illustrating the city's tempestuous history via well-displayed objects: specimens of dyewood, muskets, a figurehead from a ship's prow and the like. The dungeon downstairs alludes to the building's use as a military prison during the 1700s.

Campeche

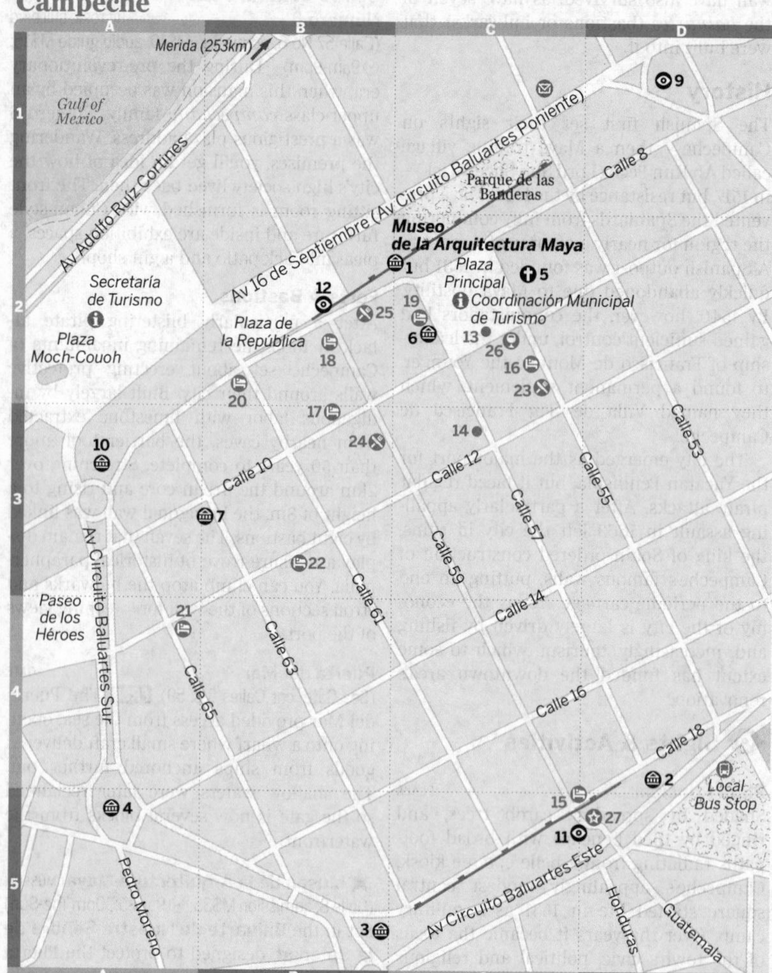

Baluarte de Santa Rosa HISTORIC BUILDING
(cnr Calle 14 & Av Circuito Baluartes Sur; 9am-3pm) FREE The Baluarte de Santa Rosa has some pirate-themed woodcuts and information on the city's forts.

Baluarte de San Juan HISTORIC BUILDING
(Calle 18; 8am-7:30pm Tue-Sun) FREE The smallest of the seven bulwarks, the Baluarte de San Juan is also the only one still attached to the original city wall.

Puerta de Tierra GATE
(Land Gate; Calle 18; admission M$10; 9am-6pm) The Puerta de Tierra, on the eastern side of the town wall, was opened in 1732 as the principal ingress from the suburbs. It is now the venue for a sound-and-light show (M$50; 8pm Thursday to Sunday).

Baluarte de San Francisco HISTORIC BUILDING
(Calle 18) FREE Once the primary defensive bastion for the adjacent Puerta de Tierra, the Baluarte de San Francisco houses a small arms museum.

Galería y Museo de Arte Popular MUSEUM
(Museum & Gallery of Folk Art; cnr Avs Circuito Baluartes Este & Circuito Baluartes Norte; 9am-9pm) FREE Directly behind Iglesia de San Juan de

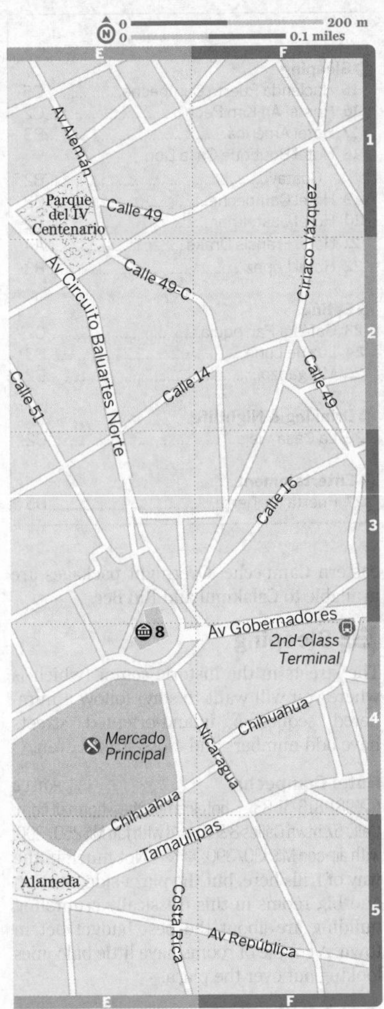

Dios, the **Baluarte de San Pedro** served a post-piracy defensive function when it repelled a punitive raid from Mérida in 1824. Carved in stone above the entry is the symbol of San Pedro: two keys to heaven and the papal tiara. Inside is a museum displaying beautiful indigenous handicrafts. Climb the steep ramp to the roof and look between the battlements to see San Juan's cupola.

Jardín Botánico Xmuch Haltún GARDENS
(cnr Calles 8 & 49; adult/child 3-12yr M$10/5; ⏲8am-9pm) Completed in 1704 – the last of the bulwarks to be built – the **Baluarte de Santiago** houses this appealing botanical garden with numerous endemic and some non-native plants. It's not a huge place, but provides a green and peaceful spot to rest up for a bit.

Fuerte Museo San José del Alto FORT
(Calle Francisco Morazán; admission M$35; ⏲9:30am-5pm Tue-Sun; P) Built in the late 18th century, this neatly restored fort sits atop the Cerro de Bellavista. Cross a drawbridge over a moat to enter the museum, which illustrates the port's maritime history through ship models, weaponry and other paraphernalia, including a beautiful ebony rudder carved in the shape of a hound. From the parapets you can see where the town ends and the mangroves begin.

To get here, catch a 'Bellavista Josefa' or 'Morelos' bus from the market; some might also be marked 'San Jose del Alto'. You might have to walk a few hundred meters from where the bus lets you off. Taxis cost around M$50.

Museo Arqueológico de Campeche & Fuerte de San Miguel MUSEUM, FORT
(Campeche Archaeological Museum; Av Escénica s/n; admission M$42; ⏲8:30am-5pm; P) Campeche's largest colonial fort faces the Gulf of Mexico some 4km southwest of the city center. Inside is the excellent Museo Arqueológico de Campeche, where you can admire treasures from the Maya sites of Calakmul and Edzná, and from Isla de Jaina, an island north of the city once used as a burial site for Maya aristocracy.

Stunning jade jewelry and exquisite vases, masks and plates are thematically arranged in 10 exhibit halls. The star attractions are the jade burial masks from Calakmul. Also displayed are stelae, seashell necklaces and clay figurines. Equipped with a dry moat and working drawbridge, the fort itself is a thing of beauty. The roof deck, ringed by 20 cannons, affords wonderful harbor views.

To get here take a bus or combi (marked 'Lerma') from the market. Ask the driver to let you off at the access road (just say 'Fuerte de San Miguel), then hike 300m up the hill. Taxis charge M$50 from the center.

Other Sights

A popular path for joggers, cyclists, strolling friends and cooing sweethearts, the *malecón*, Campeche's waterfront promenade, makes for a breezy sunrise ramble or sunset bike ride.

Campeche

Top Sights
1 Museo de la Arquitectura Maya........... C2

Sights
2 Baluarte de San Francisco D4
3 Baluarte de San Juan B5
4 Baluarte de Santa Rosa......................... A5
5 Catedral de Nuestra Señora de la Purísima Concepción........................ C2
6 Centro Cultural Casa Número 6........... C2
7 Ex-Templo de San José B3
8 Galería y Museo de Arte Popular........... E4
9 Jardín Botánico Xmuch Haltún.............. D1
10 Museo de la Ciudad A3
11 Puerta de Tierra C5
12 Puerta del Mar.. B2

Activities, Courses & Tours
13 Tranvía de la Ciudad............................. C2
14 Xtampak Tours C3

Sleeping
15 Hacienda Puerta Campeche.................C5
16 Hostel Ah Kim Pech C2
17 Hotel América B3
18 Hotel Boutique Casa Don Gustavo..B2
19 Hotel Campeche....................................C2
20 Hotel Castelmar.....................................B2
21 Hotel Francis Drake A4
22 Hotel López B3

Eating
23 Café La Parroquia..................................C2
24 Luz de Luna B3
25 Marganzo..B2

Drinking & Nightlife
26 La Casa Vieja..C2

Entertainment
27 Puerta de Tierra.....................................D5

Ex-Templo de San José HISTORIC BUILDING
(former San José Church; cnr Calles 10 & 63) Faced with blue-and-yellow tiles, the Ex-Templo de San José is a wonder to behold; note the lighthouse, complete with weather vane, atop the right spire. Now an exhibition space, the church was built in the early 18th century by Jesuits who ran it as an institute of higher learning until they were booted out of Spanish domains in 1767.

Tours

Tranvía de la Ciudad TOUR
(tours adult/child 11yr & under M$100/20; hourly 9am-noon & 5-8pm) Daily bilingual tours by motorized *tranvía* (trolley) depart from the Plaza Principal and last 45 minutes. They cover Campeche's historical center, some traditional neighborhoods and part of the *malecón*. Occasionally, another trolley called *El Guapo* goes to the Fuerte de San Miguel and Fuerte de San José (though these tours don't leave enough time to visit the forts' museums).

Check schedules at the ticket kiosk in the Plaza Principal.

Xtampak Tours TOUR
(981-811-64-73; www.toursencampeche.com; Calle 57 No 14; 8am-8pm Mon-Sat, to 2pm Sun) Offers comprehensive city tours at 9am and 2pm daily (per person M$300, four hours), as well as archaeological tours to Edzná (M$250), the Chenes sites (M$950) and eastern Campeche. Overnight packages are available to Calakmul and Río Bec.

Sleeping

The streets in the historic center (which is where you will want to stay) follow a numbered sequence: inland-oriented streets have odd numbers and cross-streets even.

Hotel Campeche HOTEL $
(981-816-51-83; hotelcampeche@hotmail.com; Calle 57, btwn Calles 8 & 10; s/d with fan M$250/290, with air-con M$330/390;) Not much in the way of frills here, but the plaza-side location and big rooms in this classically crumbling building are about the best budget bet in town. A couple of rooms have little balconies looking out over the plaza.

Hostel Ah Kim Pech HOSTEL $
(981-816-25-30; Calle 55, btwn Calles 10 & 12; dm M$100;) Undergoing serious renovations at the time of research, this one promises to be the best hostel in town, with OK dorms, a great location and a swimming pool and games room.

★**Hotel López** HOTEL $$
(981-816-33-44; www.hotellopezcampeche.com.mx; Calle 12 No 189; d/tr/q/ste M$620/670/720/900;) This elegant hotel is one of Campeche's best midrange options. Small but modern and comfortably appointed rooms open onto curvy art-deco balconies around oval courtyards full of

pleasant greenery. Bring your swimsuit for the lovely pool out back.

Hotel América HOTEL $$
(☎981-816-45-76; www.hotelamericacampeche.com; Calle 10 No 252; s/d M$500/620; P ❄ @ ≈) A large central hotel, the América is a good midrange choice. The highlight here is a pretty courtyard restaurant with tables and umbrellas – don't worry, the music dies down at night. Nearly 50 large, clean rooms are located in the surrounding arcaded corridors – they can vary, so check out a few if you can.

Hotel Francis Drake HOTEL $$
(☎981-811-56-26; www.hotelfrancisdrake.com; Calle 12 No 207; s/d/ste M$820/900/1060; ❄ ≈) A somewhat baroque lobby leads on to cool, fresh rooms with a sprinkling of tasteful decoration. Bathrooms and balconies are tiny, but the rooms are huge, with king-sized beds and separate sitting areas.

Hotel Castelmar HOTEL $$
(☎981-811-12-04; www.castelmarhotel.com; Calle 61 No 2; s/d M$800/1000; ❄ ≈ ≋) Once an army barracks, the Castelmar has been operating as a hotel for 100 years now. Oversized crucifixes and other colonial-era-inspired ornaments add to the charm, as do the amazingly thick walls. Feel free to sing in the shower – nobody will hear you.

Hotel Boutique Casa Don Gustavo BOUTIQUE HOTEL $$$
(☎981-816-80-90; www.casadongustavo.com; Calle 59 No 4; r/ste from M$3000/3500; P ❄ ≈ ≋) This beautiful boutique hotel offers 10 rooms decorated with antique furniture, though everything is so perfectly museum-like it's almost hard to relax. Give it a shot at the small pool with hammocks nearby, or try the rooftop Jacuzzi. Rooms have huge modern bathrooms, colorful tiled hallways line an outdoor courtyard, and there's a restaurant. Check the website for promotions.

Hacienda Puerta Campeche BOUTIQUE HOTEL $$$
(☎981-816-75-08; www.luxurycollection.com; Calle 59 No 71; r M$7039-9331; P ❄ @ ≈ ≋) This beautiful boutique hotel has 15 suites with high ceilings and separate lounges – just right for that afternoon massage. Perfectly manicured gardens and grassy lawns offer peace, while the partly covered pool has nearby hammocks that are fit for a Maya king.

It also runs a restored luxury hacienda 26km outside the city, on the way to the Edzná ruins.

Eating & Drinking

The emblematic *campechano* dish is *pan de cazón* – a tortilla sandwich filled with minced shark meat and beans and smothered in tomato sauce. Wash one down with an *horchata de coco* (rice and coconut drink) and you'll be livin' *la vida local.*

Calle 59 is partly closed off to traffic, and a little dining precinct is blossoming, with outdoor seating and wandering musicians, making it a lovely place to eat or get a few drinks once the sun goes down.

Café La Parroquia MEXICAN $
(☎981-816-25-30; Calle 55 No 8; mains M$45-150, lunch specials M$70-80; ⊙24hr) Open 24 hours, this casual restaurant appeals to both locals and foreigners with its wide-ranging menu and attentive staff. Order everything from fried chicken to grilled pork to turkey soup, plus regional specialties and seafood dishes such as ceviche. Tons of drinks make it all go down easy, and don't miss the creamy flan for dessert.

★**Luz de Luna** INTERNATIONAL $$
(☎981-811-06-24; Calle 59 No 6; mains M$90-150; ⊙8am-10pm Mon-Sat) Carved, painted tables and folksy decor add atmosphere to this popular restaurant on a pedestrian street. The menu choices are equally interesting – try the shrimp salad, chicken fajitas, flank steak or vegetarian burritos. There are plenty of breakfast options as well, especially omelets.

Marganzo MEXICAN $$
(☎981-811-38-98; Calle 8 No 267; mains M$100-180; ⊙7am-11pm) Marganzo is popular with tourists, for good reason – the food is great, the portions large and the complimentary appetizers numerous. An extensive menu covers everything from international fare to regional treats like *cochinita pibil* (suckling pig cooked in banana leaves). Service is attentive, and wandering musicians provide entertainment.

La Casa Vieja BAR, RESTAURANT
(Calle 10 No 319A; ⊙8:30am-12:30am) There's no better setting for an evening cocktail than La Casa Vieja's colonnaded balcony overlooking the Plaza Principal.

☆ Entertainment

There's invariably someone performing on the Plaza Principal every Saturday and Sunday evening from around 6:30pm. For Campeche's hottest dance bars and clubs, head 1km south from the city center along the *malecón* past the Torres del Cristal skyscraper.

Incidents from Campeche's pirate past are re-enacted several nights a week in the **Puerta de Tierra** (adult/child 4-10yr M$50/25; ⏲8pm Thu-Sun), in a Disney-esque extravaganza with lots of cannon blasts and flashing lights.

ℹ Information

MEDICAL SERVICES

Cruz Roja (Red Cross; ☎981-815-24-11; cnr Av Las Palmas & Ah Kim Pech) Medical services; some 3km northeast of downtown.

Hospital Dr Manuel Campos (☎981-811-17-09; Av Circuito Baluartes Norte, btwn Calles 14 & 16)

MONEY

Campeche has numerous banks with ATMs, open 8am to 4pm Monday to Friday, 9am to 2pm Saturday.

POST

Central Post Office (cnr Av 16 de Septiembre & Calle 53; ⏲8:30am-4pm Mon-Fri, 8-11:30am Sat)

TOURIST INFORMATION

Coordinación Municipal de Turismo (☎981-811-39-89; Plaza Principal; ⏲9am-9pm) Maintains a booth in the central kiosk of the main plaza.

Secretaría de Turismo (☎981-127-33-00; www.campeche.travel; Plaza Moch-Couoh; ⏲8am-9pm Mon-Fri, to 8pm Sat & Sun) Good information on the city and Campeche state.

ℹ Getting There & Away

AIR

The airport is 6km southeast of the center.

Aeroméxico (☎800-021-40-00; www.aeromexico.com) flies to Mexico City at least twice daily. Regular flights are also offered by low-cost carriers VivaAerobus (p266) and Interjet (p266).

BUS

Campeche's **main bus terminal** (☎981-811-99-10; Av Patricio Trueba 237), usually called the ADO or 1st-class terminal, is about 2.5km south of Plaza Principal via Avenida Central. Buses provide 1st-class and deluxe services to major cities as well as 2nd-class services to Sabancuy (M$102), Hecelchakán (M$58), Candelaria (M$168) and points in Tabasco. To get to the new terminal, catch any 'Las Flores,' 'Solidaridad' or 'Casa de Justicia' bus by the post office.

The **2nd-class terminal** (☎981-811-99-10; Av Gobernadores 289), often referred to as the 'old

BUSES FROM CAMPECHE

DESTINATION	FARE (M$)	DURATION	FREQUENCY (DAILY)
Bolonchén de Rejón	76	3hr	6 from 2nd-class terminal
Cancún	460-548	7hr	7 buses
Chetumal	240-344	6hr	ADO noon, 2 from 2nd-class terminal
Hopelchén	58	1½hr	hourly from 2nd-class terminal
Mérida (via Bécal)	172-202	2½hr	half-hourly ADO & ADO GL
Mérida (via Uxmal)	102	4½hr	half-hourly from 2nd-class terminal
Mexico City	1176-1394	17hr	4 buses
Palenque	300	6hr	4 buses
San Cristóbal de Las Casas	434	9hr	9:45pm ADO
Villahermosa	336-444	6hr	frequent
Xpujil	168-244	5hr	ADO 2pm, 3 Sur from 2nd-class terminal

The destinations in the table are from the 1st-class terminal unless otherwise noted.

ADO' station, is east of the Mercado Principal. Second-class buses to Hopelchén (M$58), Bolonchén, Xpujil and Bécal (M$53) depart from here. To reach the 2nd-class terminal, catch a 'Terminal Sur' or 'Ex-ADO' bus from the post office.

To get to Edzná (M$35, one hour), catch a Valle Edzná *colectivo* from Calle Chihuahua near the corner of Calle Nicaragua, by the Mercado Principal. They leave every half hour from 7am to 7pm.

The destinations in the table are from the 1st-class terminal unless otherwise noted.

CAR

If you're heading for Edzná or taking the long route to Mérida or the fast toll road going south, take Calle 61 to Avenida Central and follow signs for the airport and either Edzná or the *cuota* (toll road). For the non-toll route south, just head down the *malecón*. For the short route to Mérida go north on the *malecón*.

Arriving in Campeche from the south via the *cuota*, just turn left at the roundabout signed for the *universidad*, then turn right up the *malecón* when you hit the coast, and you will arrive instantly oriented.

In addition to some outlets at the airport, several car-rental agencies can be found downtown. Rates are generally higher than in Mérida or Cancún.

Pirata Rent a Car (cell phone 981-1271457; Calle 8 No 2, Hotel Castelmar)

Getting Around

Local buses leave from the Mercado Principal or across Avenida Circuito Baluartes from the market. Most go at least partway around the Circuito before heading to their final destinations. The flat fare is M$5.50.

Taxis charge between M$25 and M$45 for rides within the city – prices go up at night. Tickets for authorized taxis from the airport to the center (M$120) are sold from a booth in the terminal.

Consider renting a bicycle for a ride along the *malecón* or through the streets of the Centro Histórico. **Buenaventura** (981-144-33-88; www.viajesbuenaventura.com.mx; Av 16 de Septiembre 122 Local 3; 9am-3pm & 5-8pm Mon-Sat) has a good selection of bikes; rates are M$30 for the first hour, then M$20 per hour thereafter, or M$150 per day (including helmet and lock).

Drivers should note that even-numbered streets in the Centro Histórico take priority, as indicated by the red (stop) or black (go) arrows at every intersection.

Around Campeche

Edzná

The closest major ruins to Campeche are about 53km to the southeast. **Edzná** (admission M$46; 8am-5pm) once covered more than 17 sq km and was inhabited from approximately 600 BC to the 15th century AD. Most of the visible carvings date from AD 550 to 810. Though it's a long way from such Puuc Hills sites as Uxmal and Kabah, some of the architecture here has elements of the Puuc style. What led to Edzná's decline and gradual abandonment remains a mystery.

Beyond the entrance is a *palapa* protecting carvings and stelae from the elements. A path from here leads about 400m through vegetation to the zone's big draw, the **Plaza Principal** (follow the signs for the Gran Acrópolis), which is 160m long, 100m wide and surrounded by temples. On your right as you enter from the north is the **Nohochná** (Big House), a massive, elongated structure that was topped by four long halls probably used for administrative tasks, such as the collection of tributes and the dispensing of justice. The built-in benches facing the main plaza were designed for spectators to view theatrical and ritual events.

Across the plaza is the **Gran Acrópolis**, a raised platform holding several structures, including Edzná's major temple, the 31m-high **Edificio de los Cinco Pisos** (Five-Story Building). It rises five levels from its vast base to the roofcomb and contains many vaulted rooms. A great central staircase of 65 steps goes right to the top. Some of the weathered carvings of masks, serpents and jaguar heads that formerly adorned each level are now in the *palapa* near the ticket office.

The current structure is the last of four remodels, and was done primarily in the Puuc architectural style. Scholars generally agree that this temple is a hybrid of a pyramid and a palace. The impressive roofcomb is a clear reference to the sacred buildings at Tikal in Guatemala.

In the Pequeña Acrópolis, to the south of the main plaza, is the *palapa*-protected **Templo de Mascarones** (Temple of Masks), which features carved portrayals of the sun god, Kinich-Ahau. The central motif is the head of a Maya man whose face has been modified to give him the appearance of a jaguar.

DIY: EXPLORE MORE OF CAMPECHE

Leave the beaten track and head out into the less-explored corners of Campeche. Here are some ideas to get you started.

Chenes sites Northeastern Campeche state is dotted with more than 30 sites in the distinct Chenes style, recognizable by the monster motifs around doorways in the center of long, low buildings of three sections, and by temples atop pyramidal bases.

Laguna de Términos The largest lagoon in the Gulf of Mexico area, the Laguna de Términos comprises a network of estuaries, dunes, swamps and ponds that together form a uniquely important coastal habitat.

Bécal While on the surface Bécal may look like a somnolent *campechano* town, underneath a multitude is laboring away at the traditional craft of hat making.

Getting There & Away

From Campeche, minibuses (M$35, one hour) leave from Calle Chihuahua every half hour from 7am to 7pm.

Xtampak Tours (p336) in Campeche provides a shuttle service from Campeche to Edzná (M$300, minimum two passengers) as well as guided tours of the site for an additional M$800.

Leaving the site by car, you can either go north on Hwy 120 to pick up Hwy 261 east to Hopelchén, or alternatively head toward Dzibalchén and the Chenes site of Hochob by going south to Pich, then east to Chencoh, 54km from Edzná over a decent but little-used road.

Bolonchén de Rejón & Xtacumbilxunaan

Heading east from Campeche, you'll reach San Antonio Cayal, then Hopelchén (with a Pemex gas station), where Hwy 261 turns north. After 34km, the town of Bolonchén de Rejón appears out of the lush countryside. This small outpost is famous for its Festival of Santa Cruz, held each year on May 3.

Bolonchén de Rejón is close to the **Grutas de Xtacumbilxunaan** (admission M$50; 10am-5pm Tue-Sun;), pronounced 'grutas de *shtaa*-koom-beel-shoo-*nahn*' (go on, give it a shot), about 3km south of town. Lighted steps lead down to a barely visible cenote, beyond which a passage leads 100m deeper into the bedrock, bedecked with stalactites and stalagmites. Be aware that the wooden ladder is for demonstration purposes only, to show how the Maya used to descend to the cave floor. Doing so yourself would be very foolish. Sur buses traveling between Hopelchén and Mérida will drop you at the cave entrance. In addition, *colectivos* depart for Bolonchén from the north side of Hopelchén's plaza, passing near the caves. Check with the driver for return times.

Hwy 261 continues north into Yucatán state to Uxmal, with a side road leading to the ruins along the Ruta Puuc.

South of Campeche

The southern part of the peninsular region – now bordering modern-day Guatemala – was the earliest established, longest inhabited and most densely populated territory in the Maya world. Here you will find the most ancient and most architecturally elaborate archaeological sites on the peninsula. Heading south from Campeche, you'll reach Escárcega, where Hwy 186 cuts due east across southern-central Campeche state and on to Chetumal in Quintana Roo – a 273km ride. This route passes several fascinating Maya sites and goes through the ecologically diverse Reserva de la Biosfera Calakmul.

The largest settlement between Escárcega and Chetumal is Xpujil. Situated on Hwy 186 about 2km west of the Campeche-Quintana Roo border, Xpujil is a great place from which to stage your exploration of the region. The only gas station in the same stretch is about 5km east of Xpujil.

The predominant architectural styles of the region's archaeological sites are Río Bec and Chenes. The former is characterized by long, low buildings that look like they're divided into sections, each with a huge serpent or monster-mouth door. The facades are decorated with smaller masks, geometric designs (with many X forms) and columns. At the corners of the buildings are tall, solid towers with extremely small, steep, nonfunctional steps, topped by small false temples. Many of these towers have roofcombs. The Chenes architectural style shares most of these characteristics, except for the towers.

Balamkú

Discovered in 1990, **Balamkú** (Temple of the Jaguar; admission M$35; ⌚8am-5pm) is 60km west of Xpujil (88km east of Escárcega). This small site's attractions are its frescoes and an exquisite, ornate stucco frieze. Amazingly, much original color is still visible on both the frescoes and the frieze. You'll notice toads dominate the designs at Balamkú. These amphibians, not only at home on land and in water, were considered to move easily between this world and the next. The toad was a revered spirit guide who helped humans navigate between earth and the underworld.

The frescoes are open to public viewing, but the frieze is housed in a locked building. The caretaker will open the door – a tip is appreciated.

A taxi from Xpujil to Balamkú costs M$900 (round trip including a two hour wait).

Calakmul

In 1931, US botanist Cyrus Lundell became the first outsider to 'discover' **Calakmul** (admission M$46, park fee M$54; ⌚8am-5pm), which means 'Adjacent Mounds.' Mayanists consider Calakmul to be a site of vital archaeological significance. The site bears comparison in size and historical significance to Tikal in Guatemala, its chief rival for hegemony over the southern lowlands during the Classic era.

From about AD 250 to 695, Calakmul was the leading city in a vast region known as the Kingdom of the Serpent's Head. Its perpetual rival was Tikal, and its decline began with the power struggles and internal conflicts that followed the defeat of Calakmul's king Garra de Jaguar (Jaguar Paw).

As at Tikal, there are indications that construction occurred over a period of more than a millennium. Beneath Edificio VII, archaeologists discovered a burial crypt with some 2000 pieces of jade, and tombs continue to yield spectacular jade burial masks; many of these objects are on display in Campeche city's Museo Arqueológico (p335). Dotted around the site are at least 120 carved stelae, though many are eroded.

So far, only a fraction of Calakmul's 100-sq-km expanse has been cleared, and few of its 6500 buildings have been consolidated, let alone restored; however, exploration and restoration are ongoing.

Lying at the heart of the vast **Reserva de la Biosfera Calakmul**, the ruins are surrounded by rainforest, which is best viewed from the top of one of the several pyramids. There are over 250 bird species living in the reserve, and you are likely to see ocellated turkeys, parrots and toucans. Other wildlife protected by the reserve includes jaguars, spider monkeys, pumas, ocelots and white-lipped peccaries.

Twenty kilometers down the access road is the ultramodern **Museo del Centro de Comunicación y Cultura** (⌚7am-3pm) FREE which showcases fossil finds from the region and some ceramics from Calakmul, and has a small botanical garden featuring plants traditionally used by the Maya for food and medicine.

Sleeping & Eating

Campamento Yaax'che CAMPGROUND $
(☎cell phone 983-1011921; www.ecoturismocalakmul.com; campsites per person M$70, with tent from M$200) More than just a campground, Yaax'che, 7km along the access road from Hwy 186 to Calakmul, is the base for tours by Servidores Turísticos Calakmul, a training center for local guides and an experiment in sustainable ecotourism. You can rent a pre-pitched tent or set up your own under a thatched shelter. There's no electricity and facilities are primitive – douse-yourself showers and lime decomposition latrines. Regional fare (meals M$65 to M$75) is prepared over wood fires with variable results.

VISITING CALAKMUL

Calakmul is *big* – you could easily spend a few hours wandering around the site and if you stop to look at details, take photos and climb temples, this could stretch to a couple more. If all that activity is likely to get you peckish, pack some snacks and water – the nearest eats are 40km away.

Hotel Puerta Calakmul HOTEL $$$
(☎998-892-26-24; www.puertacalakmul.com.mx; Hwy 186, Km 98; cabañas from M$2100; P ✦ ≋) This upscale jungle lodge is 700m from the highway turnoff. The 15 spacious bungalows are quite nice though not luxurious, and all come with mosquito nets and overhead fans. There's a decent, screened-in restaurant where you can dine from 7am to 9:30pm (mains M$100 to M$270), plus a small pool.

Getting There & Away

Xtampak Tours (p336) in Campeche and Río Bec Dreams (p342) near Chicanná run tours to Calakmul.

If you are driving, the turnoff to Calakmul is 56km west of Xpujil, and the site is 60km south of the highway at the end of a decent paved road. A toll of M$56 per car (more for heavier vehicles) and M$28 per person is levied by the *municipio* (township) of Calakmul at the turnoff from Hwy 186. A cab to Calakmul from Xpujil costs M$900 including a couple of hours waiting time.

Chicanná

Aptly named 'House of the Snake's Jaws,' this **archaeological site** (admission M$42; ⊙8am-5pm) is best known for the remarkably well-preserved doorway on Estructura 11, featuring a hideous fanged visage. Buried in the jungle 11km west of Xpujil and 400m south of Hwy 186, Chicanná is a mixture of Chenes and Río Bec architectural styles. The city attained its peak during the late Classic period, from AD 550 to 700, as a sort of elite suburb of Becán.

★ **Río Bec Dreams** (www.riobecdreams.com; Hwy 186, Km 142; cabañas for two M$550-1150; extra person M$150; P ✦) provides unquestionably the best accommodations in the area. This Canadian-run jungle lodge has thatched-roof 'jungalows' sharing a bathhouse, and *cabañas* with private bathrooms in the woods. Environmentally sound facilities include composting toilets, rainwater collection devices and solar electricity.

A taxi from Xpujil to Chicanná costs around M$350 (round trip including one-hour waiting time).

Becán

Eight kilometers west of Xpujil, this archaeological site is perched atop a rock outcrop, encircled by a 2km moat that snakes its way around the entire city to protect it from attack. Becán (literally 'path of the snake') is also the Maya word for 'canyon' or 'moat.' Seven causeways crossed the moat, providing access to the city. Becán was occupied from 550 BC until AD 1000.

This is among the largest and most elaborate sites in the area. The first thing you'll come to is a plaza. If you walk while keeping it to your left, you'll pass through a rock-walled passageway and beneath a corbeled arch. You will soon reach a huge twin-towered temple with cylindrical columns at the top of a flight of stairs. This is **Estructura VIII**, dating from about AD 600 to 730. The view from the top of this temple has become partially obscured by the trees, but on a clear day you can still see structures at the Xpuhil ruins to the east.

Northwest of Estructura VIII is Plaza Central, ringed by 30m-high **Estructura IX** (the tallest building at the site) and the more interesting **Estructura X**. In early 2001, at X's far south side, a stucco mask still bearing some red paint was uncovered. It is enclosed in a wooden shelter with a window for viewing.

In the jungle to the west are more ruins, including the Plaza Oeste, which is surrounded by low buildings and a ball court. Much of this area is still being excavated and restored, so it's only intermittently open to the public.

Loop back east, through the passageway again, to the plaza; cross it diagonally to the right, climbing a stone staircase to the Plaza Sureste. Around this plaza are Estructuras I through IV; a **circular altar** (Estructura IIIA) lies on the east side. **Estructura I** has the two towers typical of the Río Bec style. To exit, you can go around the plaza counterclockwise and descend the stone staircase on the southeast side, or go down the southwest side and head left.

A taxi from Xpujil to Becán costs around M$350 (round trip including one hour waiting time).

Xpujil

☎983 / POP 4000

The hamlet of Xpujil (pronounced 'shpu-*heel*') lies at the junction of Hwy 186 (which runs east to Chetumal and west to Chiapas) and Hwy 269, which runs north to meet Hwy 261 at Hopelchén, a short hop from Campeche. A good base from which to explore the area's sites, Xpujil is growing rapidly in the anticipation of a tourist boom. However, it still has no bank or laundry, and the nearest gas station is 5km east of town. Several restaurants, a couple of hotels and a taxi stand are near the bus depot.

From the junction, the ruins of Xpuhil are less than 1km west, Becán is 8km west, Chicanná is 11.5km west, Balamkú is 60km west and the Calakmul ruins are 120km southwest.

Sights

Xpuhil ARCHAEOLOGICAL SITE
(admission M$42; 8am-5pm) About 1km west of the main junction in Xpujil, these ruins are a striking example of the Río Bec style. The three towers (rather than the usual two) of **Estructura I** rise above a dozen vaulted rooms. The central tower, soaring 53m, is the best preserved. With its banded tiers and impractically steep stairways leading up to a temple that displays traces of a zoomorphic mask, it gives a good idea of what the other two must have looked like back in Xpujil's 8th-century heyday.

Go around back to see a fierce jaguar mask embedded in the wall below the temple.

Tours

Servidores Turísticos Calakmul ECOTOUR
(983-871-60-64; www.ecoturismocalakmul.com; Carretera Escárcega-Chetumal, Km 153; 9am-2pm & 3-7pm Mon-Sat) Around 200m east of the Xpujil junction, this operator provides interesting nature-themed ecotours led by trained guides from nearby communities.

Sleeping

There are rustic hotels in town, and more accommodations in Zoh-Laguna, 10km north of Xpujil.

Hotel Calakmul HOTEL $
(983-871-60-29; www.hotelcalakmul.com.mx; Av Calakmul No 70; cabañas M$350, r from M$590; P) At the west end of town, about 350m west of the stoplight, is this large hotel offering the most comfortable rooms in town. The six so-called *'cabañas'*, near the parking lot, are tiny shacks set too close together and sharing outside bathrooms – a very odd combination with the more modern hotel.

Hotel Victoria HOTEL $
(983-871-60-27; Hwy 186; r with fan/air-con M$200/300; P@) The best of a clutch of fairly nondescript hotels around the main intersection, this one has large, clean rooms and a reasonable on-site restaurant.

Cabañas Mercedes CABIN $
(cell phone 983-1149769; Calle Zapote s/n; cabañas s/d M$200/250) Fifteen very basic bungalows with mosquito nets, ceiling fans and open-shower bathrooms can be found at this rustic place. Decent meals are served in the thatched-roof restaurant (mains M$70 to M$80). Your well-informed host, Don Antonio, knows about the area's ruins.

Eating

Aside from the hotel restaurants, there are various greasy spoons clustered around the bus station and roadside *taquerías* toward the Xpuhil ruins.

Concha del Caribe MEXICAN $
(Hwy 186; mains M$60-120; 7am-10pm) Opposite the bus terminal, this is a good choice for seafood, meat and snacks, washed down with an ice-cold *agua de jamaica* (hibiscus tea).

Getting There & Around

No buses originate in Xpujil, so you just have to hope there's a vacant seat on one passing through. The **bus terminal** (983-871-60-27; Hwy 186) is just east of the Xpujil junction, on the north side of the highway. You can hire a taxi in town to take you to Zoh-Laguna for around M$60.

There are also taxi *colectivos* to Chetumal (M$100 per person, 1½ hours).

To reach Becán, Hormiguero, Calakmul or other sites you will need to book a tour or hire a cab. The taxi stand is on the north side of the junction.

South of Xpujil

Río Bec

Southeast of Xpujil, you can explore a series of remote Maya sites at Río Bec. You're best off hiring a guide with a 4WD truck; it's possible to arrange this in Xpujil or at the Ejido 20 de Noviembre (a collective farm located roughly 28km southeast of Xpujil). The going rate is M$650 to M$800. A taxi from Xpujil would be the other option, although depending on road conditions, drivers may be reluctant to go. Alternatively, check with Río Bec Dreams (p342) near Chicanná.

Hormiguero

Spanish for 'anthill,' **Hormiguero** (8am-5pm) FREE is an ancient site, with some buildings dating as far back as AD 50; however, the city flourished during the late Classic period. It has one of the most impressive buildings in the region. Entering the site, you will see the 50m-long **Estructura II**, which has a giant Chenes-style monster-mouth doorway with much of its decoration in good condition. Also check out **Estructura V**, 60m to the north.

Hormiguero is reached by heading 14km south from Xpujil junction, then turning right and heading another 8km west on a shoddily paved road. A cab from Xpujil to Hormiguero will cost you around M$250.

East of Xpujil

Continuing east from Xpujil brings you to the archaeological sites of Dzibanché, Kinichná and Kohunlich. There is also growing interest in the pre-Classic site of Ichkabal, 20km northeast of Dzibanché, but the ruins have yet to be opened to the public. Ask around for the latest. The following sights are in Quintana Roo and can also be accessed from Chetumal.

Sights

Dzibanché & Kinichná ARCHAEOLOGICAL SITE
(combined admission M$46; 8am-5pm) Though a chore to get to, these twin sites are definitely worth a visit for their secluded, semi-wild nature. Dzibanché (meaning 'writing on wood') was a major city extending more than 40 sq km. Several buildings have been excavated, but the road to the ruins is lined with huge mounds covered in trees, hiding further palaces and pyramids.

A little further down the road, Kinichná is a hilltop site whose partially excavated acropolis affords panoramic views of the countryside. The road between the two is poorly signposted. If you're driving, keep veering left; once you see the hill, keep moving toward it.

Kohunlich ARCHAEOLOGICAL SITE
(admission M$55, guide M$250; 8am-5pm) This archaeological site sits on a carpet of green. The ruins, dating from both the late pre-Classic (AD 100 to 200) and the early Classic (AD 300 to 600) periods, are famous for the great **Templo de los Mascarones** (Temple of the Masks), a pyramid-like structure with a central stairway flanked by huge, 3m-high stucco masks of the sun god.

A few hundred meters southwest of Plaza Merwin are the **27 Escalones** (27 Steps), the remains of an extensive residential area.

The hydraulic engineering used at Kohunlich was a great achievement; most of the platforms, plazas and pyramids were laid out to channel rainwater into Kohunlich's once enormous reservoir.

Sleeping

Explorean LUXURY HOTEL $$$
(800-504-50-00; www.explorean.com; Km 5.65; s/d all-inclusive from M$6883/8259;) Along the entrance road to Kohunlich is the super-deluxe Explorean, which ticks all the boxes – infinity pool, hushed, sophisticated ambience, staff in flowing white uniforms etc. Cabins (more like small houses) are cool and comfortably furnished. Activities such as tours of the ruins and night kayaking are included in the price.

Check the website for seasonal discounts and promotions.

Getting There & Away

Dzibanché and Kohunlich lie just off Hwy 186, but there is no public transportation to either site. The best way to visit is by car, or on a tour from Xpujil – local tour operators run trips to both sites for around M$850.

If you are driving, the turnoff for Dzibanché is about 44km west of Chetumal and 63km east of Xpujil (look out for the Zona Arqueológica sign). The ruins are 24km north and east along a nicely paved road (turn right after the town of Morocoy to reach the site).

The turnoff to Kohunlich is 3km west of the Dzibanché turnoff along Hwy 186; from the junction, a paved road runs for 8.5km to the ruins.

Kohunlich could conceivably be reached by taking an early bus to the village of Francisco Villa near the turnoff, then either walking the 8.5km to the site. Flag down a bus from the main highway to get back to Chetumal or Xpujil.

Chiapas & Tabasco

Includes ➡

Best Hidden Waterfalls

- ➡ Las Nubes (p396)
- ➡ Cascada de las Golondrinas (p389)
- ➡ El Aguacero (p354)
- ➡ Tapijulapa (p414)
- ➡ El Chiflón (p400)

Best Places to Stay

- ➡ Casa Mexicana (p407)
- ➡ Boutique Hotel Quinta Chanabnal (p386)
- ➡ Madre Sal (p405)
- ➡ La Joya Hotel (p365)
- ➡ Hotel Casa Delina (p399)

Why Go?

Chilly pine-forest highlands, sultry rainforest jungles and attractive colonial cities exist side by side within Mexico's southernmost states, a region awash with the legacy of Spanish rule and the remnants of ancient Maya civilization. Palenque and Yaxchilán are evocative vestiges of powerful Maya kingdoms, and the presence of modern Maya is a constant reminder of the region's rich and uninterrupted history. The colonial hubs of San Cristóbal de las Casas and Chiapa de Corzo give way to sandbar beaches and fertile plots of coffee and cacao in the Soconusco, and for outdoor adventurers, excursions to Laguna Miramar and the Cañón del Sumidero are unmissable.

Nature lovers willing to venture off the beaten track will swoon over the frothy cascades and exotic animals of the Lacandón Jungle and the El Triunfo reserve.

When to Go

San Cristóbal de las Casas

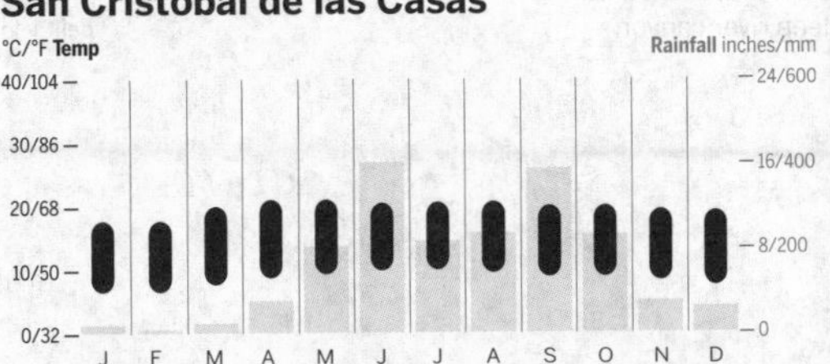

Jan Fiesta Grande de Enero in Chiapa de Corzo.

Jun–Nov Nesting season for sea turtles along the beaches of the Pacific coast.

Nov–Apr Driest months, though evenings in San Cristóbal are chilly November to February.

Chiapas & Tabasco Highlights

1. Scale the jungly hills and soaring Maya temples of **Palenque** (p377)
2. Stroll the high-altitude cobblestone streets of **San Cristóbal de las Casas** (p356)
3. Cruise through the waterway and sheer high rock cliffs of the spectacular **Cañón del Sumidero** (p353)
4. Spend a few splendid days hiking and relaxing at pristine mountain-ringed **Laguna Miramar** (p396)
5. Explore the towering mangroves and watch for nesting turtles at **Madre Sal** (p405)
6. Flit between the sapphire and emerald lakes of **Lagos de Montebello** (p402)
7. Wander amid the roar of howler monkeys at the riverside Maya ruins of **Yaxchilán** (p394)
8. Play under the spray of **El Aguacero** (p354) and cool off in a deep river canyon

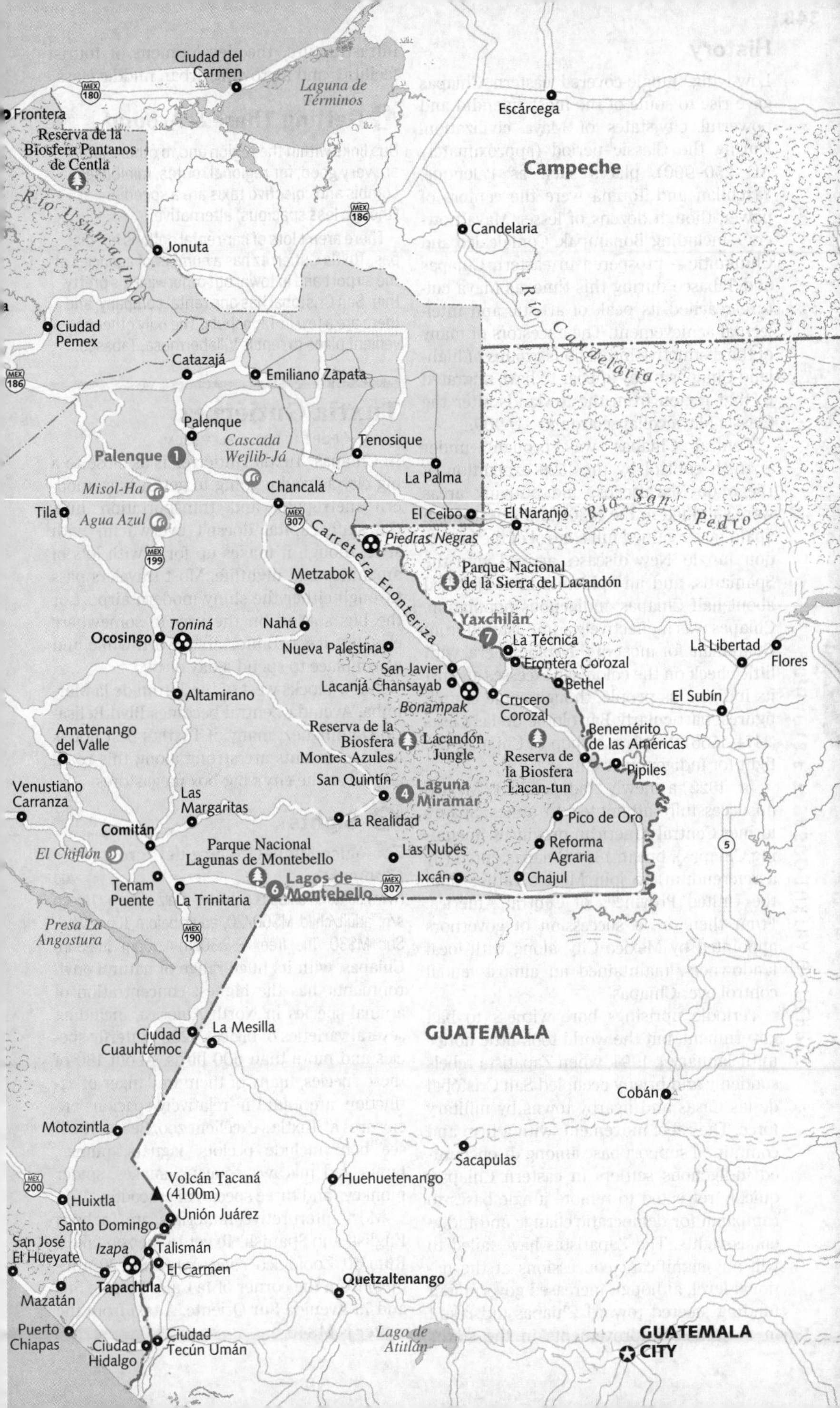

Ciudad del Carmen
Laguna de Términos
Frontera
Escárcega
Reserva de la Biosfera Pantanos de Centla
Campeche
Río Usumacinta
Candelaria
Jonuta
Río Candelaria
Ciudad Pemex
Catazajá
Emiliano Zapata
Palenque
Cascada Wejlib-Já
Tenosique
Palenque
La Palma
Misol-Ha
Chancalá
Tila
Agua Azul
El Ceibo
El Naranjo
Río San Pedro
Carretera Fronteriza
Piedras Negras
Metzabok
Parque Nacional de la Sierra del Lacandón
Yaxchilán
Ocosingo
Toniná
Nahá
La Técnica
La Libertad
Flores
Nueva Palestina
Frontera Corozal
San Javier
Bethel
Lacanjá Chansayab
Crucero Corozal
El Subín
Altamirano
Bonampak
Amatenango del Valle
Reserva de la Biosfera Montes Azules
Lacandón Jungle
Benemérito de las Américas
Reserva de la Biosfera Lacan-tun
Pipiles
San Quintín
Laguna Miramar
Venustiano Carranza
Las Margaritas
La Realidad
Pico de Oro
Comitán
Parque Nacional Lagunas de Montebello
Reforma Agraria
El Chiflón
Las Nubes
Tenam Puente
La Trinitaria
Lagos de Montebello
Ixcán
Chajul
Presa La Angostura
GUATEMALA
Ciudad Cuauhtémoc
La Mesilla
Cobán
Motozintla
Sacapulas
Volcán Tacaná (4100m)
Huehuetenango
Huixtla
Unión Juárez
Santo Domingo
San José El Hueyate
Izapa
Talismán
El Carmen
Tapachula
Quetzaltenango
Mazatán
Puerto Chiapas
Ciudad Hidalgo
Ciudad Tecún Umán
Lago de Atitlán
GUATEMALA CITY
MEX 180
MEX 186
MEX 307
MEX 199
MEX 190
MEX 200
5

History

Low-lying, jungle-covered eastern Chiapas gave rise to some of the most splendid and powerful city-states of Maya civilization. During the Classic period (approximately AD 250–900), places such as Palenque, Yaxchilán and Toniná were the centers of power, though dozens of lesser Maya powers – including Bonampak, Comalcalco and Chinkultic – prospered in eastern Chiapas and Tabasco during this time, as Maya culture reached its peak of artistic and intellectual achievement. The ancestors of many of the distinctive indigenous groups of highland Chiapas today appear to have migrated to that region from the lowlands after the Classic Maya collapse around AD 900.

Central Chiapas was brought under Spanish control by the 1528 expedition of Diego de Mazariegos, and outlying areas were subdued in the 1530s and '40s, though Spain never gained full control of the Lacandón Jungle. New diseases arrived with the Spaniards, and an epidemic in 1544 killed about half Chiapas' indigenous population. Chiapas was ineffectively administered from Guatemala for most of the colonial era, with little check on the colonists' excesses against its indigenous people, though some church figures, particularly Bartolomé de las Casas (1474–1566), the first bishop of Chiapas, did fight for indigenous rights.

In 1822 a newly independent Mexico unsuccessfully attempted to annex Spain's former Central American provinces (including Chiapas), but in 1824 Chiapas opted (by a referendum) to join Mexico rather than the United Provinces of Central America. From then on, a succession of governors appointed by Mexico City, along with local landowners, maintained an almost feudal control over Chiapas.

Periodic uprisings bore witness to bad government, but the world took little notice until January 1, 1994, when Zapatista rebels suddenly and briefly occupied San Cristóbal de las Casas and nearby towns by military force. The rebel movement, with a firm and committed support base among disenchanted indigenous settlers in eastern Chiapas, quickly retreated to remote jungle bases to campaign for democratic change and indigenous rights. The Zapatistas have failed to win any significant concessions at the national level, although increased government funding steered toward Chiapas did result in noticeable improvements in the state's infrastructure, the development of tourist facilities and a growing urban middle class.

Getting There & Around

Bus links within the region and to other states are very good; for regional routes, minibuses, combis and *colectivo* taxis are a speedier (though less spacious) alternative.

There aren't lots of car-rental options in Chiapas. Tuxtla Gutiérrez has a number of agencies at the airport and in town, but otherwise it's pretty thin. San Cristóbal has one rental company, and there are a few in Tapachula. The only other convenient place to rent is Villahermosa, Tabasco.

Tuxtla Gutiérrez

961 / POP 540,000 / ELEV 530M

In Chiapas, Tuxtla Gutiérrez is as close to a big city as you're going to get. A busy modern metropolis and transportation hub, the state capital doesn't overwhelm with style, though it makes up for it with lots of amenities and nightlife. Most travelers pass through either the shiny modern airport or the bus station on the way to somewhere else, but it's a comfortable, worthwhile and warm place to spend a day or two.

A few blocks west of the Jardín de la Marimba, Avenida Central becomes Blvd Belisario Domínguez; many of Tuxtla's best hotels and restaurants are strung along this road, as well as the city's big-box megastores.

Sights

Zoológico Miguel Álvarez del Toro (Zoomat) ZOO

(www.semahn.chiapas.gob.mx; Calz Cerro Hueco s/n; adult/child M$60/20, adult before 10am Wed-Sun M$30, Tue free; 8:30am-4:30pm Tue-Sun) Chiapas, with its huge range of natural environments, has the highest concentration of animal species in North America, including several varieties of big cat, 1200 butterfly species and more than 600 birds. About 180 of these species, many of them in danger of extinction, are found in relatively spacious enclosures at Tuxtla's excellent zoo. Beasts you'll see here include ocelots, jaguars, pumas, tapirs, red macaws, toucans, snakes, spider monkeys and three species of crocodile.

Most interpretive materials are in both English and Spanish. To get to the zoo take a Ruta 60 'Zoológico' *colectivo* (M$6, 20 minutes) from the corner of 1a Calle Oriente Sur and 7a Avenida Sur Oriente. A taxi from the center is M$40.

Museo de la Marimba MUSEUM
(9a Calle Poniente Norte; admission M$30; ⏲10am-9pm Tue-Sun) On the Jardín de la Marimba, this small museum showcases 100 years of this ubiquitous instrument, with both antique and modern models on display and a photo exhibition of the most revered marimba performers.

Plaza Cívica PLAZA
Bustling and broad, Tuxtla's main plaza occupies two blocks flanked by an untidy array of concrete government and commercial structures. At its southern end, across Avenida Central, you'll find nice hill views in front of the whitewashed modern **Catedral de San Marcos**. The cathedral's clock tower tinkles out a tune on the hour to accompany a kitsch merry-go-round of apostles' images, which emerges from its upper levels.

Museo del Café MUSEUM
(www.museodelcafe.chiapas.gob.mx; 2a Calle Oriente Norte 236; admission M$10; ⏲9am-5pm Mon-Sat) Operated by the state government, this small museum contains exhibits (in Spanish only) on the cultivation and processing of everyone's favorite bean. The rooms are pleasantly air-conditioned and tantalized visitors receive a cup of brew to savor in the building's pretty courtyard.

Parque Madero PARK
The park's **Museo Regional de Chiapas** (☎961-613-43-75; Calz de los Hombres Ilustres; admission M$46; ⏲9am-6pm Tue-Sun), an imposing modern building, has a sampling of lesser archaeological pieces from Chiapas' many sites, and a slightly more interesting history section, running from the Spanish conquest to the revolution, all in Spanish only.

Parque Madero also contains the lush oasis of the **Jardín Botánico** (admission free) and a low-key children's theme park.

Take a Ruta 3 or 20 *colectivo* from 6a Av Norte Poniente.

Tours

Transporte Panorámico Cañón del Sumidero TOUR
(☎cell phone 961-1663740) Daily bus tours leave from Tuxtla's Jardín de la Marimba at 9:30am and 1pm if a minimum of five people show up. Three tours are available: viewing the canyon from above at five *miradores* (lookout points; M$150, 2½ hours), a *lancha* (motorboat) trip with return transportation (M$350, 4½ hours) and an all-day *miradores* and *lancha* trip (M$400, morning departure only). Call to reserve a day beforehand to confirm departures.

Private regional tours also available.

DON'T MISS

JARDÍN DE LA MARIMBA

To take your *paseo* with the locals, stop by this leafy plaza in the evening. It's located eight blocks west of Plaza Cívica, and the whole city seems to turn out here for the free nightly marimba concerts (6pm to 9pm), especially at weekends. Couples of all ages dance around the central bandstand, and the scores of sidewalk cafes – which stay open until at least 10pm or 11pm – serve some of the best coffee in town.

Sleeping

Good budget hotels cluster in the city center, while most midrange and luxury hotels – primarily big international chains – are strung out along Avenida Central Poniente and Blvd Belisario Domínguez west of the center. The larger hotels offer sizable online and weekend discounts.

★**Hostal Tres Central** HOSTEL $
(☎961-611-36-74; www.facebook.com/TresCentral; Calle Central Norte 393; dm M$150, r with/without bathroom M$500/350; P⊖❄@📶) This brand-new hostel – and Tuxtla's one and only – is a stylish Ikea-esque respite with uber-comfortable beds in either four-person dorms or spacious two-bed privates (those with shared bathroom have a shower and sink in the room). The rooftop terrace views of the surrounding hills can't be beat. No kitchen facilities, though a cafe-bar is in the works.

Hotel Casablanca HOTEL $
(☎961-611-03-05, 800-560-44-22; hotelcasablank@hotmail.com; 2a Av Norte Oriente 251; s M$179, d M$248-300, d/tr/q with air-con M$466/542/638; ⊖❄📶) A tranquil open courtyard blooms with palms, and funky-fabulous abstract murals in brilliant lime green, hot pink and electric blue give the rooms a dash of unexpected pizzazz. The upstairs rooms have air-con and more light.

Tuxtla Gutiérrez

Tuxtla Gutiérrez

Sights
1 Catedral de San Marcos ... C3
2 Jardín Botánico ... F1
3 Jardín de la Marimba ... A2
4 Museo de la Marimba ... A2
5 Museo del Café ... D2
6 Museo Regional de Chiapas ... F1
7 Parque Madero ... F1
8 Plaza Cívica ... C2

Sleeping
9 Hostal Tres Central ... C2
10 Hotel Casablanca ... C2
11 Hotel Catedral ... D2
12 Hotel María Eugenia ... D3
13 Hotel Santa María ... A2

Eating
14 Horno Mágico ... D3
15 La Macarena ... B2
16 Las Pichanchas ... E3
17 Restaurante La Casona ... C3

Hotel Catedral HOTEL $
(961-613-08-24; www.hotel-catedral.net; 1a Av Norte Oriente 367; s/d/tr M$350/400/450, with air-con M$450/500/550; P) A friendly family-run place, this excellent budget option has neat, super-clean rooms with dark wood furniture and ceiling fans. It also has comfortable hall couches. Pass on the noisier downstairs rooms off the lobby. Free drinking water and morning coffee.

Hotel Santa María HOTEL $$
(961-614-65-77; hotelsantamariatuxtla@hotmail.com; 8a Calle Poniente Norte 160; r M$450-600, tr M$700; P) Situated on the pretty Jardín de la Marimba and near a number of good coffeehouses, this small hotel has rooms featuring folksy decorations and nice bathrooms with mosaic tiling.

Hotel María Eugenia HOTEL $$
(800-716-01-49, 961-613-37-67; www.mariaeugenia.com.mx; Av Central Oriente 507; s/d

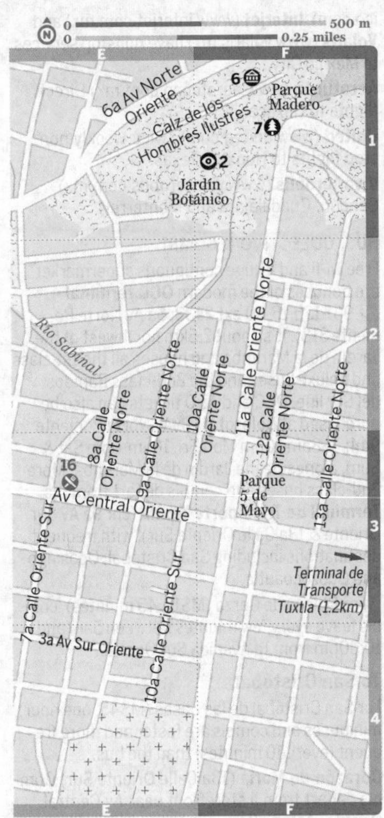

M$900/1000, d Fri & Sat M$650 ; P ⊖ ❄ @ ≈ ≋) A good full-service option in the center, its 83 airy, bright and spacious rooms have either a king-sized or two double beds, and many have great views.

Hilton Garden Inn HOTEL $$$
(☎961-617-18-00; www.tuxtlagutierrez.hgi.com; cnr Blvd Belisario Domínguez & Blvd Los Castillos; r Sun-Thu M$1770, Fri & Sat M$1300, ste $2360; P ⊖ ❄ @ ≈ ≋) The luxurious 167-room Hilton sits in a commercial area 2.5km west of the Jardín de la Marimba. Gadget-lovers will appreciate the mp3 player/alarm clock, adjustable pillowtop mattresses and internet-ready televisions, and style fans will groove on the rainforest showerheads and Herman Miller chairs.

Eating

Lots of upscale and international chain options are west of the center, along Blvd Belisario Domínguez, and a number of enjoyable cafes cluster in the center around the Jardín de la Marimba.

Horno Mágico BAKERY, CAFE $
(2a Calle Oriente Norte 116; pastries M$25; ⊙8am-10pm Mon-Fri, 2-10pm Sat) A new outpost of the San Cristóbal fave, with tasty fresh croissants and pastries and an air-conditioned upstairs for sipping espresso. Live jazz on Wednesday nights.

Restaurante La Casona MEXICAN $
(1a Av Sur Poniente 134; breakfast M$33-60, mains M$50-82; ⊙7am-11pm; P) Beyond the stately carved wooden doors is a dramatic tableclothed dining room with high ceilings and interior arches in a century-old building. Dine on regional dishes such as *pollo juchi* (fried chicken with pickled vegetables and potatoes) or *tasajo en salsa de chirmol* (sliced beef in tomato sauce) and listen to marimba performances from 2pm to 6pm.

La Macarena SPANISH $$
(2a Av Norte Poniente 369; mains M$70-190; ⊙2pm-midnight Tue-Sat, 2-6pm Sun) An Osborne bull presides over a dramatically lit back patio, an excellent setting for authentic tapas, *bocadillos* (sandwiches), paella and *fidegua* (paella made with noodles).

Las Pichanchas CHIAPANECO $$
(www.laspichanchas.com.mx; Av Central Oriente 837; mains M$100-155; ⊙noon-11pm; 👪) This courtyard restaurant specializes in Chiapas food with live marimba music and, from 8:30pm to 10pm every night, a show of colorful traditional Chiapas dances that whips up quite a party atmosphere. Try the tasty *tamales* or *pechuga jacuané* (chicken breast stuffed with beans in a *hoja santa* sauce), and leave room for *chimbos*, a dessert made from egg yolks and cinnamon.

Ring the bell over the table to order its signature Pumpo drink.

Shopping

Casa Chiapas HANDICRAFTS
(www.casachiapas.gob.mx; Blvd Belisario Domínguez 2035 at Calle 22a Poniente Sur; ⊙9am-8pm Mon-Fri, 10am-8pm Sat & Sun) The Chiapas state crafts shop, 2km west of Plaza Cívica, sells a great range of the state's *artesanías* (handicrafts), from Amatenango 'tigers' and funky Cintalapa ceramic suns to colorful highland textiles.

Information

INTERNET ACCESS

Conect@-2 (Av Central Oriente 214; per hr M$5; ⏲8am-9:30pm)

Quality Shop (Av Central Poniente 853; per hr M$5; ⏲8:30am-9:40pm)

MONEY

There's an ATM at the departure level of the airport.

Banorte (Av Central Oriente, btwn 2a & 3a Calle Oriente Sur; ⏲9am-5pm Mon-Fri, to 2pm Sat) Changes dollars.

Scotiabank (cnr Ave Central Oriente & 4a Calle Oriente; ⏲8:30am-4pm Mon-Fri)

POST

Post Office (1a Av Norte Poniente) In the Palacio Federal.

TOURIST INFORMATION

Information Kiosk (⏲9am-2pm & 4-8pm) At the Plaza Cívica.

Municipal Tourism Office (9a Calle Poniente Norte; ⏲9am-2pm & 4-8pm) Inside the Museo de la Marimba.

Secretaría de Turismo (☎800-280-35-00, 961-617-05-50; www.turismochiapas.gob.mx; ⏲8am-4pm Mon-Fri) The main state tourism office has a toll-free phone number for Chiapas information; English speakers rarely available.

Getting There & Away

AIR

Tuxtla's small and gleaming **Aeropuerto Ángel Albino Corzo** (☎961-153-60-68) is 35km southeast of the city center and 18km south of Chiapa de Corzo. **Aeroméxico** (www.aeromexico.com), **Interjet** (www.interjet.com.mx) and **Volaris** (www.volaris.mx) have nonstop services to Mexico City.

Aerotucán (www.aerotucan.com.mx) Direct flights to Oaxaca.

United (www.united.com) Twice-weekly nonstop flights to Houston,Texas.

VivaAerobus (www.vivaaerobus.com.mx) Cancún, Guadalajara and Monterrey.

BUS, COLECTIVO & COMBI

Free wi-fi and a huge contiguous supermarket are bonuses of the modern **OCC terminal** (☎961-125-15-80 ext 2433; 5a Av Norte Poniente 318). It's about 2.5km northwest of the Jardín de la Marimba and houses all the 1st-class and deluxe buses and the 2nd-class Rápidos del Sur line. OCC and ADO tickets can also be purchased at **Boletotal** (1a Av Norte Poniente 944; ⏲8am-10pm Mon-Fri, 10am-6pm Sat & Sun), alongside the Jardín de la Marimba. More 2nd-class buses and combis depart from the **Terminal de Transporte Tuxtla** (cnr 9a Av Sur Oriente & 13a Calle Oriente Sur), with frequent destinations including San Cristóbal, Ocosingo and Ocozocoautla.

For Chiapa de Corzo (M$11, 45 minutes), combis leave every few minutes between 5am and 10:30pm from 1a Avenida Sur Oriente.

To San Cristóbal

For San Cristóbal de las Casas (M$45, one hour), minibuses and combis are faster and more frequent (every 10 minutes) than the bus.

Corazón de María (13a Calle Oriente Sur) Combis depart from a storefront near Av Central Oriente; 4am to 9pm.

Ómnibus de Chiapas (cnr 15a Calle Oriente Sur & 4a Av Sur Oriente) Comfortable minibuses (called 'sprinters'); 5am to 10pm.

BUSES FROM TUXTLA GUTIÉRREZ

DESTINATION	FARE (M$)	DURATION	FREQUENCY (DAILY)
Cancún	900-1558	17-20hr	6
Comitán	76-90	3hr	17
Mérida	680-1178	13-14hr	5
Mexico City (TAPO & Norte)	480-1470	11½-12hr	25
Oaxaca	424-510	10hr	4
Palenque	210-272	6-6½hr	5
Puerto Escondido	454	11-12hr	2
San Cristóbal de las Casas	40-50	1¼hr	27
Tapachula	316-572	4½-6hr	18
Tonalá	122-170	2-2½hr	21
Villahermosa	286-346	4-5hr	16

DON'T MISS

CAÑÓN DEL SUMIDERO

The Sumidero Canyon is a spectacular fissure in the earth, found north of Tuxtla Gutiérrez. In 1981 the Chicoasén hydroelectric dam was completed at its northern end, damming the Río Grijalva, which flows through the canyon, and creating a 25km-long reservoir. Traveling between Tuxtla and Chiapa de Corzo, the road crosses the Grijalva just south of the canyon mouth.

The most impressive way to see the canyon is from a **lancha** (motorboat; return trip M$160; ⏲8am-4pm) that speeds between the canyon's towering rock walls. It's about a two-hour return trip, starting at either Chiapa de Corzo or the Embarcadero Cahuaré, 5km north of Chiapa along the road to Tuxtla. You'll rarely have to wait more than half an hour for a boat to fill up. Bring a drink, something to shield you from the sun and, if there's any chance of bad weather, some warm clothing or a waterproof jacket.

It's about 35km from Chiapa de Corzo to the dam. Soon after you pass under Hwy 190, the canyon walls tower an amazing 800m above you. Along the way you'll see a variety of birds – herons, cormorants, vultures, kingfishers – plus probably a crocodile or two. The boat operators will point out a few odd formations of rock and vegetation, including one cliff face covered in thick hanging moss, resembling a giant Christmas tree. *Lanchas* sometimes have to plow through a sheen of floating plastic garbage when wet-season rains wash in trash from Tuxtla Gutiérrez.

CAR & MOTORCYCLE

In addition to companies at the airport, in-town rental agencies include an **Alamo** (www.alamo.com; 5a Av Norte Poniente 2260) near the OCC bus station and **Europcar** (www.europcar.com; Blvd Belisario Domínguez 2075).

Getting Around

A biodiesel bus service called **ConejoBus** (M$6; ⏲5am-11pm) plies Blvd Belisario Domínguez–Avenida Central. For other areas, consult www.tuxmapa.com.mx for local combi routes. Taxi rides within the city cost M$30 to M$35.

TO/FROM THE AIRPORT

From the airport, pre-pay taxis (one to three passengers) meet all flights and go to central Tuxtla (M$210, 40 minutes), Chiapa de Corzo (M$240, 30 minutes) and San Cristóbal (M$600 private or M$200 shared, one hour). OCC runs minibuses directly from the terminal to San Cristóbal (M$160) at 9am, 1pm, 4pm and 8:30pm, though the schedule is subject to change.

Monarca Viajes (cell phone 961-1328191; monarcaviajes@hotmail.com) Does door-to-door transfers between town and the airport for M$250 (one to three passengers); reserve in advance.

West of Tuxtla Gutiérrez

Consider renting a car in Tuxtla to hit both the Sima de las Cotorras and El Aguacero, though tour agencies in both Tuxtla and San Cristóbal can organize day trips here. To get there independently you'll need to travel via Ocozocoautla (also called Coita) – from Tuxtla's Terminal de Transporte Tuxtla, take the minibus with a pineapple on its side (M$15, 30 minutes). A number of tour agencies in San Cristóbal offer rafting, climbing and hiking expeditions into the incredible **Río La Venta canyon**, one of the most beautiful and least-visited natural attractions of Chiapas.

Sima de las Cotorras

The **Sima de las Cotorras** (Abyss of the Parrots; adult/child over 9yr M$20/10) is a dramatic 160m-wide sinkhole that punches 140m down into the earth. At sunrise, a green cloud of screeching parrots spirals out for the day, trickling back before dusk. With binoculars you can see a series of red pre-Hispanic rock paintings that decorate one side of the cliff face, and you can also hike or rappel down inside this intriguing subterranean hole.

Lodging (cell phone 968-1178081; www.simaecoturismo.com; campsite M$100, tent & sleeping bag rental M$250-300, d/q/6-person cabaña M$400/600/700; P) is available (the spacious six-person, two-room *cabañas* are well worth the extra cost), as well as a good **restaurant** (mains M$60-70; ⏲8am-6pm) serving scrumptious *tamales* and handmade tortillas.

From the last stop in Ocozocoautla (Coita), located on Hwy 190 right at the signed turnoff for the Sima, take a taxi (M$200 to M$250, 50 minutes) or call the lodging number to arrange a pickup (M$250 per vanload). Three daily Piedra Parada *colectivos* (M$10) also leave from this stop, but let you off 4km before the Sima.

Driving from Tuxtla, it's reasonably well signed all the way. Go all the way through Ocozocoautla, turning right at the minibus terminal (there's a blue turn-off sign here, but it's not visible coming from this direction), go 3.5km north, then 12km on a good dirt road.

El Aguacero

Forget the gym – the 724 well-built steps to El Aguacero (cell phone, no reception during business hrs 968-1069019; www.facebook.com/ElAguaceroOficial; admission M$27; 7am-5pm) will suffice as your workout du jour. Plunging into the sheer Río La Venta canyon, El Aguacero is a gorgeous series of frothy stair-steps that tumble and spray. In drier months (usually December through May), you can stroll along sandy riverbed beaches to the waterfall. When the water's high, it's a half-hour hike from the staircase along a shady jungle trail.

Unless the bridge has been repaired along the jungle route, there's a narrow cliff ledge bypass that isn't recommended for children. From December through May, you can also explore an underground river running through the 200m **El Encanto cave**. An hour-long tour (M$150) includes all equipment (helmet, headlamp etc).

Camping (campsite per person M$50, campsite & equipment for 4 people M$250) and hammock space (with showers) are available, and a small *comedor* usually serves quesadillas (M$15).

From Ocozocoautla (Coita), *colectivos* to El Gavilán/Las Cruces (M$10) can drop you off at the highway turnoff, from where it's a 3km walk down to the entrance. If the stairs up from the river leave you in a heap, management charges M$60 per vanload to drive you back up or M$150 for a ride to or from Ocozocoautla. Drivers should look for the turnoff sign about 15km west of Ocozocoautla.

Chiapa de Corzo

961 / POP 45,000 / ELEV 450M

An overlooked jewel set 12km east of Tuxtla Gutiérrez on the way to San Cristóbal, Chiapa de Corzo is a small and attractive colonial town with an easygoing, provincial air. Set on the north bank of the broad Río Grijalva, it's the main starting point for trips into the Cañón del Sumidero.

Chiapa de Corzo has been occupied almost continuously since about 1200 BC. Before the Spaniards arrived, the warlike Chiapa tribe had their capital, Nandalumí, a couple of kilometers downstream, on the opposite bank of the Grijalva. When Diego de Mazariegos invaded the area in 1528, the Chiapa hurled themselves by the hundreds to their death in the canyon rather than surrender.

Mazariegos founded a settlement called Chiapa de Los Indios here, but quickly shifted his base to San Cristóbal de las Casas, where he found the climate and natives more manageable.

Sights

The *embarcadero* (jetty) for Cañón del Sumidero boat trips is two blocks south of the plaza down 5 de Febrero. Look for the road lined with vendors.

Plaza — PLAZA

Impressive arcades frame three sides of the plaza, and a beefy tree called **La Pochota** buckles the sidewalk with its centuries-old roots. Venerated by the indigenous people who founded the town, it's the oldest ceiba tree along the Río Grijalva. But the focal point of the plaza is **La Pila** (also called the Fuente Colonial), a handsome brick fountain completed in 1562 in Mudejar-Gothic style. It's said to resemble the Spanish crown.

Templo de Santo Domingo de Guzmán — CHURCH

(Mexicanidad Chiapaneca 10) The large Templo de Santo Domingo de Guzmán, one block south of the main plaza, was built in the late 16th century by the Dominican order. Its adjoining convent is now the **Centro Cultural** (997-616-00-55; Mexicanidad Chiapaneca 10; 10am-5pm Tue-Sun) FREE, home to an exposition of the wood and lino prints of talented Chiapa-born Franco Lázaro Gómez (1922–49), as well as the **Museo de la Laca**, which is dedicated to the local craft specialty: lacquered gourds. The museum holds pieces dating back to 1606.

Chiapa de Corzo Archaeological Site ARCHAEOLOGICAL SITE
(Av Hidalgo, Barrio Benito Juárez; 8am-4:30pm) FREE On a trade route between the Pacific and the Gulf, the sprawling Chiapa de Corzo settlement had close ties to neighboring Maya and Olmec cultures. At its peak, it counted about 200 structures, but was abandoned around 500 AD. After years of excavation, three Zoque pyramid structures are now on view here, 1.5km east of the main plaza. These visible structures were built between 1600 and 1800 years ago, but sit on mounds dating back as far as 750 BC.

Though the guarded ruins receive few visitors, it's worth an hour to climb around the deserted temples and marvel at the big-sky countryside. Recent excavation of one nearby mound (not open to the public) unearthed the oldest known pyramid tomb in Mesoamerica and new evidence linking it to Olmec centers such as La Venta.

The site entrance is near the Nestlé plant and the old highway (on the road that goes to La Topada de la Flor), but the site isn't signed from the road. Taxis charge about M$100 round-trip from the plaza with an hour of wait time.

Festivals & Events

Fiesta Grande de Enero TRADITIONAL
Held for a week in mid-January, this is one of Mexico's liveliest and most extraordinary festivals, including nightly dances involving cross-dressing young men, known as Las Chuntá. Women don the highly colorful, beautifully embroidered *chiapaneca* dress, and blond-wigged, mask-toting *Parachicos* (impersonating conquistadors) parade on a number of days. A canoe battle and fireworks extravaganza follow on the final evening.

Sleeping

Hotel Los Ángeles HOTEL $
(961-616-00-48; www.hotel-chiapas.com; Grajales 2; r M$410-450, tr/q M$500/550; P) This hotel at the southeast corner of the main plaza has spotless rooms with hot-water bathrooms, cable TV, fans and older air-con units. Upstairs rooms are bigger and catch more breeze.

Hotel La Ceiba HOTEL $$
(961-616-03-89; www.laceibahotel.com; Av Domingo Ruíz 300; r/tr/q M$780/850/1020; P) The most upscale place in town (though the rooms are quite simple), La Ceiba has a full-service spa and restaurant, an inviting pool, a lush garden and 87 well-kept air-conditioned rooms with cable TV. It's two blocks west of the main plaza.

Eating

Restaurants on the *embarcadero* have near identical, and equally overpriced, menus. The river views are nice, though battling marimba players tend to amp up the noise level. The market (southeast of the plaza) is your best bet for an inexpensive meal. *Tascalate* (see the boxed text p402) can be found on most menus, and many shops sell the drink powder.

Restaurant Los Corredores CHIAPANECO $
(Madero 35; mains M$70-130; 8am-6:30pm) Facing the southwest corner of the main plaza, Los Corredores does a bit of everything: good breakfasts, reasonably priced fish plates and a few local specialties including *pepita con tasajo* (beef with a spicy pumpkin-seed sauce). It displays a fascinating collection of historical town photos.

Restaurant Jardines de Chiapa CHIAPANECO $$
(www.restaurantesjardines.com.mx; Madero 395; mains M$89-155; 9am-7pm Apr-Oct, 8am-6pm Nov-Mar) Not too far from the main plaza, this large place is set around a garden patio with atmospheric brick columns. The long menu includes tasty *cochinito al horno* (oven-baked pork).

Information

The **state tourism office** (961-616-10-13; Calz Grajales 1947; 8am-4pm Mon-Fri) is on the road between the highway and the main plaza, across from the Súper Che supermarket; there's also a **tourism information kiosk** (8am-8pm Mon-Fri, to 4pm Sat & Sun) on the plaza. ATMs are available facing the plaza.

Getting There & Away

Combis from Tuxtla Gutiérrez (M$11, 45 minutes) leave frequently from 1a Avenida Sur Oriente (between Calles 5a and 7a Oriente Sur) between 5am and 10:30pm. They arrive at and return to Tuxtla from the north side of the main plaza.

There's no direct transportation between San Cristóbal and the center of Chiapa de Corzo. From San Cristóbal, catch a Tuxtla-bound combi and ask to be let off at the Chiapa de Corzo stop on the highway (M$35, 30 minutes). From there, cross the highway and flag down a combi (M$6) to the plaza. From Chiapa de Corzo to San Cristóbal, catch a combi from the plaza back to the highway and then flag down a combi heading to San Cristóbal. You'll rarely wait more than a few minutes for a connecting combi in either direction.

San Cristóbal de las Casas

☎967 / POP 160,000 / ELEV 1940M

Set in a gorgeous highland valley surrounded by pine forest, the colonial city of San Cristóbal (cris-*toh*-bal) has been a popular travelers' destination for decades. It's a pleasure to explore San Cristóbal's cobbled streets and markets, soaking up the unique ambience and the wonderfully clear highland light. This medium-sized city also boasts a comfortable blend of city and countryside, with restored century-old houses giving way to grazing animals and fields of corn.

Surrounded by dozens of traditional Tzotzil and Tzeltal villages, San Cristóbal is at the heart of one of the most deeply rooted indigenous areas in Mexico. A great base for local and regional exploration, it's a place where ancient customs coexist with modern luxuries.

The city is a hot spot for sympathizers (and some opponents) of the Zapatista rebels, and a central location for organizations working with Chiapas' indigenous people. In addition to a solid tourist infrastructure and a dynamic population of artsy and politically progressive foreigners and Mexicans, San Cristóbal also has a great selection of accommodations and a cosmopolitan array of cafes, bars and restaurants.

History

Diego de Mazariegos founded San Cristóbal as the Spanish regional base in 1528. Its Spanish citizens made fortunes from wheat, while the indigenous people lost their lands and suffered diseases, taxes and forced labor. The church afforded some protection against colonist excesses. Dominican monks reached Chiapas in 1545, and made San Cristóbal their main base. The town is now named after one of them, Bartolomé de las Casas, who was appointed bishop of Chiapas and became the most prominent Spanish defender of indigenous people in colonial times. In modern times Bishop Samuel Ruiz, who passed away in 2011, followed in Las Casas' footsteps, defending the oppressed indigenous people and earning the hostility of the Chiapas establishment.

San Cristóbal was the state capital of Chiapas from 1824 to 1892, but remained relatively isolated until the 1970s, when tourism began to influence its economy. Recent decades have seen an influx of indigenous villagers into the 'Cinturón de Miseria' (Belt of Misery), a series of impoverished,

SAN CRISTÓBAL IN...

Two Days

Start the day inhaling the rich aroma of a locally roasted cup of **Chiapan coffee** and then limber up with a **yoga class**. Put on some comfortable walking shoes and explore the colonial churches of **Templo de Santo Domingo** and the **cathedral**, and then get lofty, climbing the twin hills of **Cerro de San Cristóbal** and **Cerro de Guadalupe** to survey the city.

Spend the second day visiting the traditional indigenous villages of **San Lorenzo Zinacantán** and **San Juan Chamula** by horseback or bicycle, and in the evening drop by a **cinema** to catch a movie on local history or current events.

Four Days

With more time, build on the itinerary above and refresh your sagging Spanish with a few days of **language classes**. Dig deeper into the local culture with visits to the **Museo de la Medicina Maya** and the ethno-history landmark of **Na Bolom**.

Browse for the best of local *artesanías* at **women's weaving cooperatives** and the paper- and book-making workshop of **Taller Leñateros**. Jaunt out of town to gawk at the trippy cave formations at the **Grutas de San Cristóbal**. Linger over cocktails and snacks at a convivial bar and groove to the music at **Café Bar Revolución**.

violence-ridden, makeshift colonies around San Cristóbal's *periférico* (ring road). Many of these people are here because they have been expelled from Chamula and other communities as a result of internal politico-religious conflicts. Most of the craft sellers around Santo Domingo church and the underage hawkers around town come from the Cinturón de Miseria.

San Cristóbal was catapulted into the international limelight on January 1, 1994, when the Zapatista rebels selected it as one of four places from which to launch their revolution, seizing and sacking government offices in the town before being driven out within a few days by the Mexican army. Political and social tensions remain, but San Cristóbal continues to attract travelers, real estate investment and a growing middle class.

San Cristóbal and Los Altos de Chiapas – the state's central highlands, mostly 2000m to 3000m high – have a temperate climate. Daytime temperatures are usually warm, but evenings can get very cold between November and February, when you'll want a good jacket to ward off chills.

Sights

San Cristóbal is very walkable, with straight streets rambling up and down several gentle hills. Heading east from Plaza 31 de Marzo, Real de Guadalupe has a pedestrian-only section with a concentration of places to stay and eat. Another pedestrian mall, the Andador Turístico, runs up Hidalgo and Avenida 20 de Noviembre.

Plaza 31 de Marzo PLAZA

The leafy main plaza is a fine place to take in San Cristóbal's unhurried highland atmosphere. Shoe-shiners, newspaper sellers and *ambulantes* (mobile street vendors) gather around the elaborate iron bandstand.

The **Hotel Santa Clara**, on the plaza's southeast corner, was built by Diego de Mazariegos, the Spanish conqueror of Chiapas. His coat of arms is engraved above the main portal. The building is a rare secular example of plateresque style in Mexico.

Catedral CATHEDRAL

(Plaza 31 de Marzo) On the north side of the plaza, the cathedral was begun in 1528 but wasn't completed until 1815 because of several natural disasters. Sure enough, new earthquakes struck in 1816 and also 1847, causing considerable damage, but it was restored again from 1920 to 1922. The gold-leaf interior has five gilded altarpieces featuring 18th-century paintings by Miguel Cabrera.

DON'T MISS

CENTRO DE TEXTILES DEL MUNDO MAYA

Centro de Textiles del Mundo Maya (Calz Lázaro Cárdenas; M$46; 9am-6pm Tue-Sun) Upstairs inside the Ex-Convento de Santo Domingo, this excellent new museum showcases over 500 examples of handwoven textiles from throughout Mexico and Central America. Two permanent exhibition rooms display *huipiles* (long sleeveless tunics) – including a 1000-year-old relic fashioned from tree bark. Videos show how materials and clothes are created, and there are some explanations in English. Admission is bundled with the Museo de los Altos de Chiapas.

Museo de los Altos de Chiapas MUSEUM

(Calz Lázaro Cárdenas s/n; admission M$46; 9am-6pm Tue-Sun) One of two museums inside the Ex-Convento de Santo Domingo, which is located on the western side of the Templo de Santo Domingo, this museum has several impressive archaeological relics – including stelae from Chincultik – as well as exhibits on the Spanish conquest and evangelization of the region.

Templo & Ex-Convento de Santo Domingo de Guzmán CHURCH

(Utrilla; 6:30am-2pm & 4-8pm) FREE Located just north of the center of town, the 16th-century Templo de Santo Domingo is San Cristóbal's most beautiful church, especially when its facade catches the late-afternoon sun. This baroque frontage, with outstanding filigree stucco work, was added in the 17th century and includes the double-headed Hapsburg eagle, then the symbol of the Spanish monarchy. The interior is lavishly gilded, especially the ornate pulpit.

On the western side, the attached former monastery contains a regional museum and an excellent Maya textile museum. Around Santo Domingo and the neighboring **Templo de la Caridad** (built in 1712), Chamulan women and bohemian types from around Mexico conduct a colorful daily crafts

San Cristóbal de las Casas

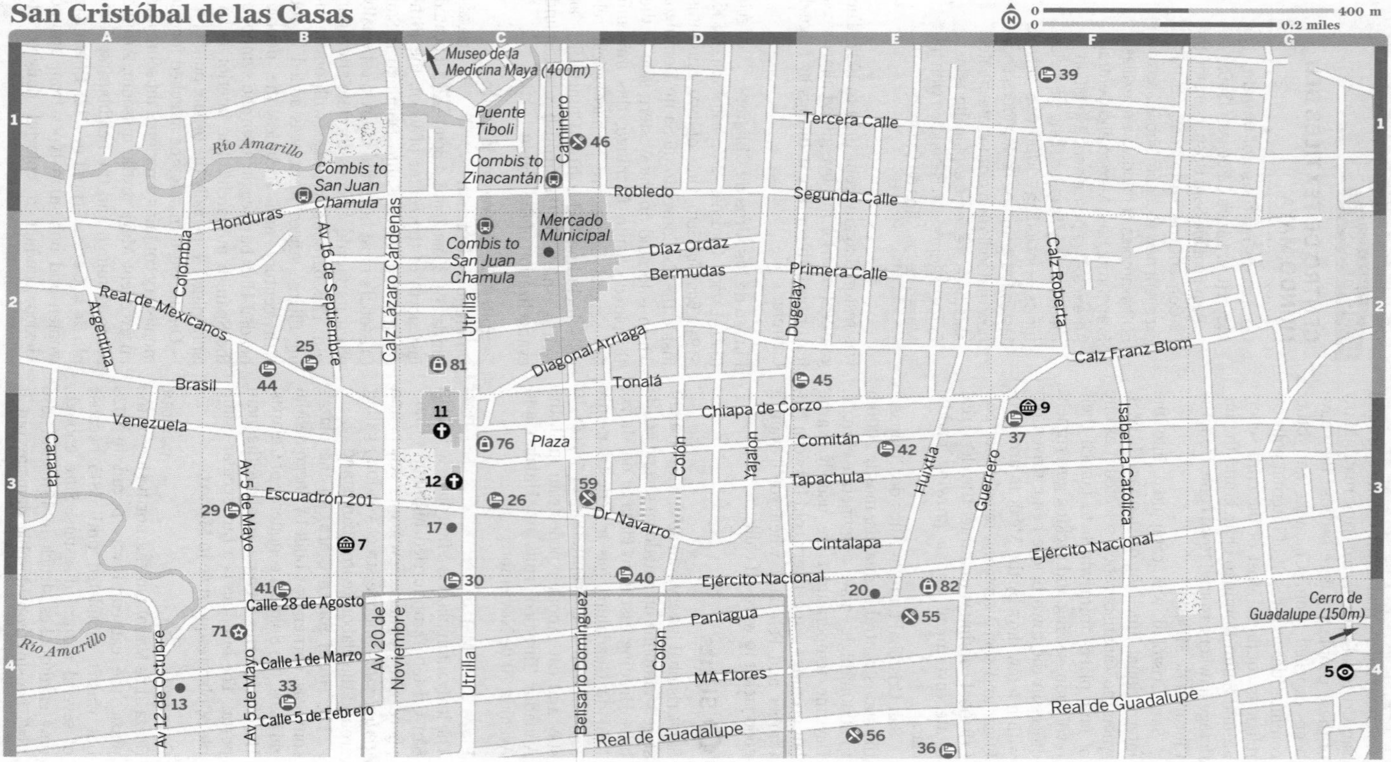

0 — 400 m
0 — 0.2 miles

Museo de la Medicina Maya (400m)
Puente Tiboli
Caminero
46
Río Amarillo
Combis to San Juan Chamula
Combis to Zinacantán
Robledo
Tercera Calle
Segunda Calle
39
Honduras
Mercado Municipal
Combis to San Juan Chamula
Díaz Ordaz
Bermudas
Primera Calle
Calz Roberta
Colombia
Av 16 de Septiembre
Calz Lázaro Cárdenas
Utrilla
Dugelay
Real de Mexicanos
Argentina
25
44
81
Diagonal Arriaga
Calz Franz Blom
Brasil
Tonalá
45
11
9
37
Venezuela
Chiapa de Corzo
76
Plaza
Comitán
42
Canada
12
Colón
Yajalon
Huixtla
Guerrero
Isabel La Católica
Tapachula
59
Escuadrón 201
26
29
Av 5 de Mayo
Dr Navarro
17
7
Cintalapa
Ejército Nacional
30
40
Ejército Nacional
20
82
41
Calle 28 de Agosto
Cerro de Guadalupe (150m)
Paniagua
55
71
Río Amarillo
Av 20 de Noviembre
Belisario Domínguez
Colón
Calle 1 de Marzo
MA Flores
5
13
Av 12 de Octubre
33
Av 5 de Mayo
Calle 5 de Febrero
Real de Guadalupe
Real de Guadalupe
56
36

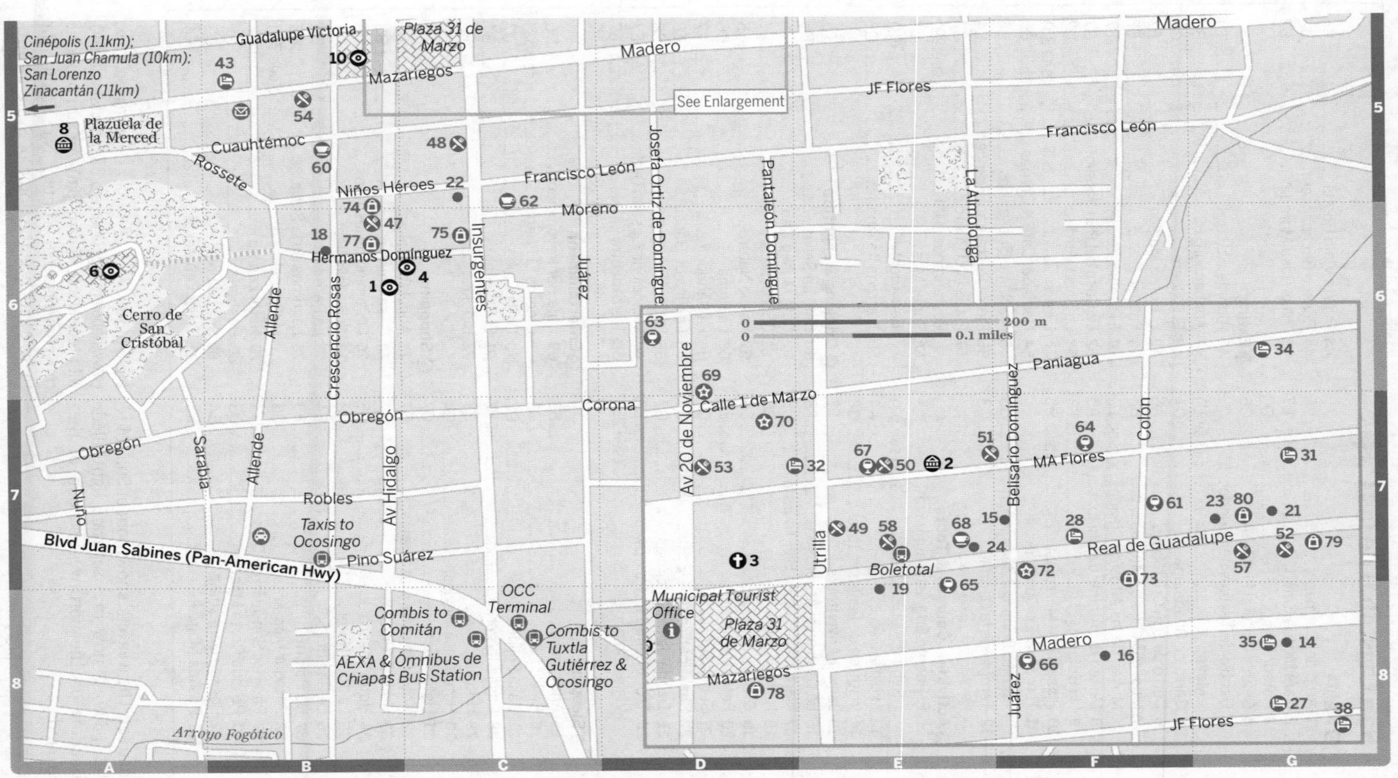

Cinépolis (1.1km);
San Juan Chamula (10km);
San Lorenzo
Zinacantán (11km)
Plazuela de la Merced
Guadalupe Victoria
Plaza 31 de Marzo
Mazariegos
Madero
JF Flores
See Enlargement
Francisco León
Cuauhtémoc
Rossete
Niños Héroes
Hermanos Domínguez
Moreno
Insurgentes
Juárez
Josefa Ortiz de Domíngue
Pantaleón Domíngue
La Almolonga
Cerro de San Cristóbal
Allende
Crescencio Rosas
Av Hidalgo
Obregón
Corona
Sarabia
Nuño
Robles
Taxis to Ocosingo
Pino Suárez
Blvd Juan Sabines (Pan-American Hwy)
OCC Terminal
Combis to Comitán
Combis to Tuxtla Gutiérrez & Ocosingo
AEXA & Ómnibus de Chiapas Bus Station
Arroyo Fogótico
0 200 m
0 0.1 miles
Av 20 de Noviembre
Calle 1 de Marzo
Paniagua
Utrilla
Belisario Domínguez
Colón
MA Flores
Real de Guadalupe
Boletotal
Municipal Tourist Office
Plaza 31 de Marzo
Mazariegos
Madero
Juárez
JF Flores
A
B
C
D
E
F
G
5
6
7
8

San Cristóbal de las Casas

Sights

1 Arco del Carmen ... B6
2 Café Museo Café ... E7
3 Catedral ... D7
4 Centro Cultural El Carmen ... C6
Centro de Textiles del Mundo Maya ... (see 11)
5 Cerro de Guadalupe ... G4
6 Cerro de San Cristóbal ... A6
7 Museo Bichos e Insectos ... B3
Museo de los Altos de Chiapas ... (see 11)
8 Museo del Ámbar de Chiapas ... A5
9 Na Bolom ... F3
10 Plaza 31 de Marzo ... B5
11 Templo & Ex-Convento de Santo Domingo de Guzmán ... C3
12 Templo de la Caridad ... C3

Activities, Courses & Tours

El Puente Spanish Language School ... (see 52)
13 Explora ... A4
14 Instituto de Lenguas Jovel ... G8
15 Jaguar Adventours ... F7
16 La Casa en el Árbol ... F8
17 Marcosapata o En Bici Tours ... C3
18 Nichim Tours ... B6
19 Otisa ... E8
20 Petra Vertical ... E4
21 SendaSur ... G7
22 Shaktipat Yoga ... C5
23 Tienda de Experiencias ... G7
24 Trotamundos ... E7
Viajes Chincultik ... (see 28)

Sleeping

25 Anthara Hotel ... B2
26 Bela's B&B ... C3
27 Casa Felipe Flores ... G8
28 Casa Margarita ... F7
29 Hotel b'o ... B3
30 Hotel Casa Mexicana ... C4
31 Hotel Casavieja ... G7
32 Hotel Diego de Mazariegos ... D7
33 Hotel El Paraíso ... B4
34 Hotel Posada Jovel ... G6
35 La Joya Hotel ... G8
36 Le Gite del Sol ... E4
37 Na Bolom ... F3
38 Parador Margarita ... G8
39 Parador San Juan de Dios ... F1
40 Posada Corto Maltese ... D3
41 Posada Ganesha ... B4
42 Posada Moguel ... E3
43 Puerta Vieja Hostel ... B5
44 Rossco Backpackers ... B2
45 Villas Casa Morada ... E2

Eating

46 Alebrije ... C1
47 Anabanana ... B6
48 El Caldero ... C5
49 El Horno Mágico ... E7
50 Falafel ... E7
51 Il Piccolo ... E7
52 La Casa del Pan Papalotl ... G7
53 La Salsa Verde ... D7
L'Eden ... (see 33)
54 Namandí Café & Crepas ... B5
55 No Name Quesadillas ... E4
56 Pierre Restaurant Francés ... E4
57 Pizzería El Punto ... G7
Restaurante LUM ... (see 29)
58 Super Más ... E7
TierrAdentro ... (see 68)
59 Trattoria Italiana ... C3

Drinking & Nightlife

60 Café La Selva ... B5
Café Museo Café ... (see 2)
61 Cocoliche ... F7
62 Kakao Natura ... C5
63 La Ruina ... D6
64 La Sandunga ... F7
65 La Viña de Bacco ... E8
66 Latino's ... F8
67 Mezcalería Gusana Grela ... E7
68 TierrAdentro ... E7

Entertainment

69 Cafe Bar Revolución ... D6
Cinema El Puente ... (see 52)
70 Dada Club ... D7
71 El Paliacate ... B4
72 Kinoki ... F7

Shopping

73 Abuelita Books ... F7
74 Casa Chiapas ... B5
75 El Camino de los Altos ... C6
76 J'pas Joloviletik ... C3
77 La Pared ... B6
78 Lágrimas de la Selva ... D8
Meltzanel ... (see 30)
79 Nemi Zapata ... G7
80 Poshería ... G7
81 Sna Jolobil ... C2
82 Taller Leñateros ... E4

market. The weavers' showroom of Sna Jolobil (p369) is now in a separate light-filled building on the northwest section of the grounds.

Na Bolom HISTORIC BUILDING
(www.nabolom.org; Guerrero 33; admission M$40, with tour M$50; 7am-7pm) An atmospheric museum/research center, Na Bolom for many years was the home of Swiss anthro-

pologist and photographer Gertrude Duby-Blom (Trudy Blom; 1901–93) and her Danish archaeologist husband Frans Blom (1893–1963). Na Bolom means 'Jaguar House' in the Tzotzil language (as well as being a play on its former owners' name). It's full of photographs, archaeological and anthropological relics and books.

The house tour provides a revealing insight into the lives of the Bloms and the Chiapas of half a century and more ago – though the picture presented of the Lacandones does dwell more on their past than their present. The Bloms bought the 19th-century house in 1950, and while Frans explored and surveyed ancient Maya sites all over Chiapas (including Palenque, Toniná and Chinkultic), Trudy studied, photographed and fought to protect the scattered Lacandón people of eastern Chiapas and their jungle environment.

Since Trudy's death, Na Bolom has continued the thrust of the Bloms' work, with the house operating as a museum and research center for the study and support of Chiapas' indigenous cultures and natural environment, and as a center for community and environmental programs in indigenous areas. The library of more than 9000 books and documents here is a major resource on the Maya. Na Bolom also offers guest rooms and meals made with organic vegetables grown in its garden.

Museo de la Medicina Maya MUSEUM

(Av Salomón González Blanco 10; admission M$20; ⌚9am-5pm Mon-Fri, to 4pm Sat & Sun) This award-winning museum on the northern edge of town introduces the system of traditional medicine used by many indigenous people in the Chiapas highlands. Exhibits include displays of a ritual scene inside a church and a midwife assisting at a birth, a dated video about the work of traditional midwives and a new display about the issue of native plants and corporate biopiracy.

The museum is run by Organización de Médicos Indígenas del Estado de Chíapas (Omiech), a group of 600 indigenous healers, midwives, herbalists and prayer specialists. Traditional Maya medicine is a matter of praying to the spirit of the earth, listening to the voice of the blood and expelling bad spirits from the soul, with the aid of candles, bones, pine needles, herbs and the occasional chicken sacrifice. Information is available in English, Spanish, French and German. Also on site is a medicinal plant garden, a herbal pharmacy and a *casa de curación*, where treatments are done. It's a 20-minute walk north from Real de Guadalupe or M$25 by taxi.

TWO VIEWPOINTS

Want to take in the best views in town? Well, you'll have to work for them, because at this altitude the stairs up these hills can be punishing. The **Cerro de San Cristóbal** (off Hermanos Dominguez) and **Cerro de Guadalupe** (off Real de Guadalupe) lord over the town from the west and east, respectively, and churches crown both lookouts. The Iglesia de Guadalupe becomes a hot spot for religious devotees around the Día de la Virgen de Guadalupe. These areas are not considered safe at night.

Museo del Ámbar de Chiapas MUSEUM

(www.museodelambar.com.mx; Plazuela de la Merced; admission M$20; ⌚10am-2pm & 4-8pm Tue-Sun) Chiapas amber – fossilized pine resin, around 30 million years old – is known for its clarity and diverse colors. Most is mined around Simojovel, north of San Cristóbal. This museum explains all things amber (with information sheets in English, French, German, Japanese and Italian), and displays and sells some exquisitely carved items and insect-embedded pieces. Note that a number of nearby jewelry shops have appropriated the museum's name.

Arco del Carmen GATE

The Arco del Carmen, at the southern end of the Andador Turístico on Hidalgo, dates from the late 17th century and was once the city's gateway.

Centro Cultural El Carmen CULTURAL BUILDING

(Hermanos Domínguez s/n; ⌚9am-6pm Tue-Sun) FREE The ex-convent just east of the Arco del Carmen is a wonderful colonial building, with a large peaceful garden. It's now the Centro Cultural El Carmen, hosting art and photography exhibitions and the occasional musical event.

Café Museo Café MUSEUM

(MA Flores 10; admission M$30; ⌚7am-10:30pm) This combined cafe and coffee museum is a venture of Coopcafé, a grouping of more than 17,000 small-scale, mainly indigenous, Chiapas coffee growers. The museum covers the history of coffee and its cultivation in Chiapas, from highly exploitative beginnings to the community-based indigenous coffee production that's increasingly well marketed today. The information is translated into English. You can taste some of that flavorful organic coffee in the cafe.

Museo Bichos e Insectos MUSEUM
(16 de Septiembre 23; admission M$25; ⏲10am-2pm & 4-8pm Mon-Sat, 11am-6pm Sun; 👪) A small museum but still home to over 2000 insects (only a few of them live, and very few of the mounted ones are labeled). Check out old wasp nests, huge beetles, leaf insects, spiders, crickets, butterflies and dragonflies. Live insects and other creepy crawlies include scorpions, beetles and centipedes; you can hold a tarantula too.

Courses

Several good language schools offer instruction in Spanish, with flexibility to meet most level and schedule requirements. Weekly rates given following are for three hours' tuition five days a week, but many variations (classes only, hourly instruction, homestays etc) are available.

La Casa en el Árbol LANGUAGE COURSE
(☎967-674-52-72; www.lacasaenelarbol.org; Madero 29; individual/group classes per week US$195/120, homestay & meals per week US$135) The 'Tree House' is an enthusiastic, socially committed school that teaches Tzeltal and Tzotzil as well as Spanish. It offers lots of out-of-school activities and is also a base for volunteer programs. Mexican cooking classes and a medical-Spanish program are also available.

Instituto de Lenguas Jovel LANGUAGE COURSE
(☎967-678-40-69; www.institutojovel.com; Madero 45; individual/group classes per week US$195/120, homestay & meals per week US$140-161) Instituto Jovel is professional and friendly, and has a top-class reputation among students. Most tuition is one-to-one, and it has a beautiful location. Classes in Mexican cooking and salsa dancing are offered too.

THE ZAPATISTAS

On January 1, 1994, the day the North American Free Trade Agreement (Nafta) was implemented, a previously unknown leftist guerrilla army emerged from the forests to occupy San Cristóbal de las Casas and other towns in Chiapas. The Ejército Zapatista de Liberación Nacional (EZLN, Zapatista National Liberation Army) linked antiglobalization rhetoric with Mexican revolutionary slogans, declaring that they aimed to both overturn the oligarchy's centuries-old hold on land, resources and power, and improve the wretched living standards of Mexico's indigenous people.

The Mexican army evicted the Zapatistas within days, and the rebels retreated to the fringes of the Lacandón Jungle to wage a propaganda war, mainly fought via the internet. The Zapatistas' balaclava-clad, pipe-puffing Subcomandante Marcos (a former university professor named Rafael Guillén) rapidly became a cult figure. High-profile conventions against neoliberalism were held, international supporters flocked to Zapatista headquarters at La Realidad, and Zapatista-aligned peasants took over hundreds of farms and ranches in Chiapas.

A set of accords on indigenous rights and autonomy was negotiated between the Zapatistas and the Mexican government but never ratified, and tension and killings escalated in Chiapas through the 1990s. According to Amnesty International, the paramilitary groups responsible for a massacre in Acteal in 1997 were armed by the authorities. By 1999 an estimated 21,000 villagers had fled their homes after a campaign of intimidation.

After a high-profile Zapatista media campaign, La Otra Campaña (The Other Campaign), during Mexico's 2006 presidential election, the EZLN has mostly remained dormant, with only the occasional conference and mobilization, its political influence slight outside its own enclaves. The movement still maintains five regional 'Juntas de Buen Gobierno' (Committees of Good Government) and many autonomous communities, though some former supporters have grown disillusioned and many have left the movement.

Further background is available in *The Zapatista Reader*, an anthology of writers from Octavio Paz and Gabriel García Márquez to Marcos himself, and Bill Weinberg's *Homage to Chiapas: The New Indigenous Struggles in Mexico*.

El Puente Spanish Language School LANGUAGE COURSE
(967-678-37-23; www.elpuenteweb.com; Real de Guadalupe 55; individual/group classes per week $US160/140, with homestay & meals US$250/230) Housed in the Centro Cultural El Puente, which also has a vegetarian cafe, a cinema and gallery. Classes are offered for any period, starting from one day.

Shaktipat Yoga YOGA
(cell phone 967-1303366; shaktipat.yoga@gmail.com; Niños Héroes 2; class M$50) A studio in the healing arts complex of Casa Luz with multilingual vinyasa, ashtanga and hatha yoga classes. Multi-class discounts.

Tours

Agencies in San Cristóbal (open approximately 8am to 9pm) offer a variety of tours, often with guides who speak English, French or Italian, though many offer transportation only. The following are typical day-trip prices per person (usually with a minimum of four people):

- Chiapa de Corzo & Cañón del Sumidero (M$250 to M$300, six to seven hours)
- Lagos de Montebello & El Chiflón waterfalls (M$300, nine to 10 hours)
- Palenque, Agua Azul & Misol-Ha (M$400, 14 hours)

Nichim Tours ADVENTURE TOUR
(967-678-35-20; www.chiapastoursyexpediciones.com; Hermanos Domínguez 5A) Full-service agency offering adventurous tours to the Selva El Ocote, as well as regional day trips to amber mines and workshops, and indigenous markets. Multilingual guides.

SendaSur ECOTOUR
(967-678-39-09; infosendasur@prodigy.net.mx; Real de Guadalupe 46B; 9am-2pm & 4-7pm Mon-Fri, 9am-noon Sat) A partner-based ecotourism network in Chiapas, SendaSur can help with independent travel and reservations in the Lacandón and El Ocote jungle regions.

Petra Vertical ADVENTURE TOUR
(967-631-53-76; www.petravertical.com; Paniagua 48A) Regional climbing, rappelling and rafting excursions, with destinations including the Sima de las Cotorras, El Aguacero, the Cañon de la Venta, and the Chorreadero waterfall and cave system near Chiapa de Corzo. Also organizes walking trips from San Cristóbal to the Arcotete river cave and the Huitepec reserve.

Explora ADVENTURE TOUR
(967-631-74-98; www.ecochiapas.com; Calle 1 de Marzo 30; 9:30am-2pm & 4-8pm Mon-Fri, 9:30am-2pm Sat) Adventure trips to the Lacandón Jungle, including multiday river kayaking and rafting.

Viajes Chincultik TOUR
(967-678-09-57; www.tourshotel.com.mx; Casa Margarita, Real de Guadalupe 34) Regional tours and transfers at good prices.

Tienda de Experiencias TOUR, BUS TOUR
(967-631-57-32; www.experienceshop.mx; Real de Guadalupe 40A) A new agency with small group tours to artisan cooperatives, scuba/snuba diving in cenotes and other eclectic 'experiences.' Its Jungle Connection hop-on/hop-off bus route circles the Lacandón.

Jaguar Adventours CYCLING
(967-631-50-62; www.adventours.mx; Belisario Domínguez 8A; bicycle rentals per hr/day M$40/M$200; 9am-2:30pm & 3:30-8pm Mon-Sat, 9am-2:30pm Sun) Does bicycle tours to Chamula and Zincantán (M$600), plus longer expeditions. Prices start at M$400 per person. Also rents quality mountain bikes with helmet and lock.

Marcosapata o En Bici Tours CYCLING, HIKING
(967-104-73-09; tonodmar@hotmail.com) Offers tailored hiking tours (M$220) and bike tours visiting San Lorenzo Zinacantán, San Juan Chamula and Rancho Nuevo (M$340 to M$380) or the Cañon del Sumidero (M$570). Ask for Marco Antonio Morales at the clothing store at Utrilla 18; Marco speaks English and French.

Otisa TOUR
(967-678-19-33; www.otisatravel.com; Real de Guadalupe 3C) Major operator that does all the standard tours.

Trotamundos TOUR
(967-678-70-21; www.turismotrotamundos.com; Real de Guadalupe 26C) Regional transportation, Tuxtla airport transfers and trips to Laguna Miramar.

Festivals & Events

Semana Santa RELIGIOUS
The crucifixion is acted out on Good Friday in the Barrio de Mexicanos, northwest of town.

Feria de la Primavera y de la Paz CULTURAL
(Spring & Peace Fair) Easter Sunday is the start of the weeklong town fair, with parades, musical events and bullfights.

Festival Internacional Cervantino Barroco ARTS

In late October, this free weeklong cultural program keeps things hopping with world-class music, dance and theater. See www.conecultachiapas.gob.mx for more information.

Sleeping

San Cristóbal has a wealth of budget accommodations, but also a number of appealing and atmospheric midrange hotels, often set in colonial or 19th-century mansions, along with a smattering of top-end luxury. The high seasons here are during Semana Santa and the following week, and the months of July and August, plus the Día de Muertos and Christmas–New Year holidays. Most prices dip at least 20% outside high season.

Posada Corto Maltese GUESTHOUSE $

(967-674-08-48; www.posadacortomaltese.com; Ejército Nacional 12; dm M$120, r/tr without bathroom M$300/350;) A simple place, its enormous fruit-tree garden buzzes with hummingbirds and roaming chickens (buy eggs and cook in the guest kitchen) and includes a kids' treehouse and a brick oven. It's a respite for folks who treasure green space in the city.

Le Gite del Sol HOTEL $

(967-631-60-12; www.legitedelsol.com; Madero 82; s/d/tr/q with shared bathroom M$180/220/330/340, s/d/tr/q M$250/320/420/520;) A bountiful breakfast complements simple rooms with floors of radiant sunflower yellow and bathrooms that look a bit like oversized shower stalls, or pleasant rooms with shared facilities in a newer location across the street. French and English spoken, and kitchen facilities available.

Puerta Vieja Hostel HOSTEL $

(967-631-43-35; www.puertaviejahostel.com; Mazariegos 23; dm M$120, r/tr/q without bathroom M$370/540/680, r/tr/q M$500/660/800, all incl breakfast;) A spacious new hostel in a high-ceilinged colonial building with a large garden, kitchen, temascal and sheltered interior courtyard, its dorms (one for women only) are good-sized, and the rooftop ones have fab views. Private rooms have one queen and a bunk bed. Room and board exchanges are available for a minimum one-month volunteer commitment.

Rossco Backpackers HOSTEL $

(967-674-05-25; www.backpackershostel.com.mx; Real de Mexicanos 16; dm M$140-165, d/tr/q M$500/700/800, all incl breakfast;) Backpackers is a friendly, sociable and well-run hostel with good dorm rooms (one for women only), a guest kitchen, a movie-watching loft and a grassy garden. Private upstairs rooms have nice skylights. A free night's stay if you arrive by bicycle or motorcycle!

Posada Ganesha GUESTHOUSE $

(967-678-02-12; Calle 28 de Agosto 23; dm/s/d/tr without bathroom incl breakfast M$120/180/280/400;) An incense-infused posada trimmed in Indian fabrics, this is a friendly and vibrant place to rest your head, with a simple guest kitchen and a pleasant lounge area. The free-standing *cabaña* room is especially nice. Yoga sessions (M$35) twice daily Monday to Friday.

Bela's B&B B&B $$

(967-678-92-92; www.belasbandb.com; Dr Navarro 2; s incl breakfast without bathroom US$50, s/d incl breakfast US$80/95;) A dreamy oasis in the center of town, this tranquil dog-friendly B&B will seduce you with its lush garden, electric blankets, towel dryers and on-site massages. The five comfortable rooms are trimmed in traditional local fabrics and some have lovely mountain views. Discounts available for longer stays.

Hotel Posada Jovel HOTEL $$

(967-678-17-34; www.hoteljovel.com; Paniagua 28; posada per person without bathroom M$100, posada d/tr/q M$500/550/650, hotel d/tr/q M$800/1000/1200;) Most rooms in the economical 'posada' building are basic and OK; those below can be musty and some share bathrooms. For more comfort, head to the 'hotel' section across the street. Here, rooms surrounding a pretty garden are larger and more brightly decorated, come with cable TV and access a wonderful terrace with views. Restaurant available.

Casa Margarita HOTEL $$

(967-678-09-57; www.tourshotel.com.mx; Real de Guadalupe 34; s/d/tr/q incl full breakfast M$600/700/850/950;) This popular and well-run travelers' haunt offers tastefully presented, impeccably clean rooms with reading lights.

Anthara Hotel HOTEL $$
(967-674-77-32; www.antharahotel.com; Real de Mexicanos 7; d M$700-900;) Solar-heated hot water and heated floors distinguish this three-floor hotel centered around a small garden courtyard. Rooms have dark wood furniture and large closets, though bathrooms aren't particularly ample. Snag 301 for choice mountain views.

Na Bolom HOTEL $$
(967-678-14-18; www.nabolom.org; Guerrero 33; s/d/tr/ste incl breakfast M$830/1110/1320/1520; P) This famous museum/research institute, about 1km from Plaza 31 de Marzo, has 16 stylish (though not necessarily luxurious) guest rooms, all loaded with character and all but two with log fires. Meals are served in the house's stately dining room. Room rates include a house tour.

★**La Joya Hotel** B&B $$$
(967-631-48-32; www.lajoyahotelsancristobal.com; Madero 43A; r incl breakfast US$145-175; P@) A visual feast, San Cristóbal's new boutique hotel offers five rooms ripped from a luxury shelter magazine, with exquisite cabinetry, enormous bathrooms and antiques curated from the owners' world travels. Fireplace sitting areas and heaters grace each room, and a rooftop terrace beckons with hill views. Attentive service includes afternoon snacks, bedtime tea, and a specially prepared light dinner for late international arrivals.

★**Villas Casa Morada** APARTMENT $$$
(967-678-44-40; www.casamorada.com.mx; Dugelay 45; r & apt M$1600, 2-bedroom villa M$2250; P@) Beautiful murals and tilework adorn these tasteful, modern apartments with kitchen, phone, cable TV, heaters, fireplaces and daily cleaning. Rooms face a tranquil fruit-tree-filled garden, and there's a small restaurant and bar. Note that its two 'deluxe superior' units are just standard rooms without kitchens and not good value.

Casa Felipe Flores B&B $$$
(967-678-39-96; www.felipeflores.com; JF Flores 36; r incl breakfast USD$99-145;) A dreamy colonial guesthouse decorated with outstanding Mexican and Guatemalan art, crafts and furnishings, this 200-year-old building contains five fireplace rooms set off two flowery courtyards. The lounge is a wonderful place to have a glass of wine and leaf through the library. A cozy rooftop room with a private terrace looks out over tiled rooftops and clusters of bougainvillea.

Hotel Bo BOUTIQUE HOTEL $$$
(967-678-15-15; www.hotelbo.mx; Av 5 de Mayo 38; r US$246-315, ste US$472-577; P@) San Crístobal meets Miami Beach in a boutique hotel that breaks the traditional colonial-architecture barrier with super-modern, trendy lines and unique, artsy touches. The large rooms and suites are very elegant and boast glass-tile bathrooms with ceiling showers, while the flowery gardens host fine water features.

Hotel Diego de Mazariegos HOTEL $$$
(967-678-08-33; www.diegodemazariegos.com; Calle 5 de Febrero 1; r M$1200, ste M$1600-1800; P) This classy, long-established hotel occupies two 18th-century mansions built around beautiful, wide courtyards. The 76 rooms are large and decked out with traditional fabrics and fittings, but also have modern comforts including cable TV. Some have fireplaces, and the suites have spa tubs.

Hotel El Paraíso HOTEL $$$
(967-678-00-85; www.hotelposadaparaiso.com; Calle 5 de Febrero 19; s/d/tr M$950/1210/1470;) Combining colonial style with a boutique-hotel feel, El Paraíso has a bright wood-pillared patio, a stunning garden sitting area and loads of character. The high-ceilinged rooms are not huge, but all have natural light, and several are bi-level with an extra bed upstairs. The in-house restaurant, L'Eden, is excellent.

Parador Margarita HOTEL $$$
(967-116-01-64; www.tourshotel.com.mx; JF Flores 39; s/d/tr/q incl breakfast M$980/1300/1500/1700; P) Rooms along a pretty courtyard here sport one king- or two queen-sized beds, and some include details like fireplaces, stained-glass windows and bathroom skylights. Other pluses include in-room heaters and a pleasant back patio overlooking a large lawn.

Hotel Casavieja HOTEL $$$
(967-678-68-68; www.casavieja.com.mx; MA Flores 27; r/tr/ste M$1400/1550/2000; P@) A beautifully renovated 18th-century house with lots of wooden pillars, balustrades and an old-world atmosphere, Casavieja boasts large comfortable rooms with modern amenities arranged around flowery courtyards.

Parador San Juan de Dios BOUTIQUE HOTEL $$$
(967-678-11-67; www.sanjuandios.com; Calz Roberta 16; r M$1800, ste M$3400-6000;) A stunning boutique hotel on the northern edge of town, the Parador San Juan de Dios offers voluminous and luxurious suites furnished with fascinating antiques and modern art.

Hotel Casa Mexicana HOTEL $$$
(967-678-06-98; www.hotelcasamexicana.com; Calle 28 de Agosto 1; d/tr M$1500/1600, ste M$1800-2200;) A gallery as well as a charming colonial hotel, the stylish and inviting Casa Mexicana displays modern art alongside traditional fabrics and solid-wood pillars and furnishings. The main patio is filled with a lush tropical garden, the 54 attractive rooms are equipped with cable TV, and you'll find a restaurant, bar and sauna.

Posada Moguel APARTMENT $$$
(967-116-09-57; posadamoguel@hotmail.com; Comitán 41B; apt M$1200-2000;) Seven somewhat austere apartments sleep two to six people at this family-run complex set around a tiled patio with potted plants. All have kitchen, fireplace, and living and dining rooms, and some have up to three bedrooms and two floors. Weekly and monthly discounts.

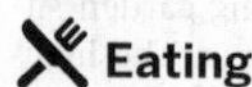

The foodie jackpot of Chiapas, San Cristóbal has more tantalizing food options than any other place in the state. If you can verbalize a culinary craving, chances are some restaurant exists here to fulfill it. Vegetarians are embarrassingly spoiled for choice. *¡Provecho!*

Real de Guadalupe Area

Self-caterers can stock up at the centrally located **Super Más** (Real de Guadalupe 22; 8am-10pm) market, and there are a number of fruit and vegetable shops on Dugelay where the pedestrianized section of Real de Guadalupe ends.

★**TierrAdentro** MEXICAN $
(Real de Guadalupe 24; set menu M$45-110; 7:30am-11pm;) A popular gathering center for political progressives and coffee-swigging, laptop-toting locals (not that they're mutually exclusive), this large indoor courtyard restaurant, cafe and pizzeria is a comfortable place to while away the hours. It's run by Zapatista supporters, who hold frequent cultural events and conferences on local issues.

El Horno Mágico BAKERY $
(Utrilla 7; bread & pastries M$15-30; 8:30am-9pm) For picnic fixings or a tasty snack, scoop up some crusty French breads (the pecan is divine), chocolate croissants or a savory pastry.

La Casa del Pan Papalotl VEGETARIAN $
(Real de Guadalupe 55; mains M$50-107; 8am-10:30pm Mon-Sat, 9am-4:30pm Sun;) This courtyard vegetarian restaurant does a particularly filling buffet lunch from 1pm to 5pm (M$80 to M$110). Fresh bread and locally grown organic ingredients are staples here, and its shop sells excellent house-made tofu.

Pizzería El Punto PIZZERIA $$
(Real de Guadalupe 47; pizzas M$85-135; noon-10pm;) Forget the cardboard crap that passes for pizza in some parts; these crispy pies are the best in town, bar none. The central branch of this excellent pizzeria has a full bar, swanky black and red decor and a lovely balcony overlooking Real de Guadalupe.

Pierre Restaurant Francés FRENCH $$
(Real de Guadalupe 73; mains M$85-350; 1:30-10pm;) Everything – including pasta, butter, cheese and bread – is made from scratch at this scrumptious French restaurant with a seasonal menu. A few favorites include duck ravioli with wild mushrooms, *verduras salteadas en hojaldra* (vegetable pastry) and the dessert tarts. Vegetarian mains as well.

West of Plaza 31 de Marzo

Namandí Café & Crepas CREPERIE, CAFE $
(Mazariegos 16C; crepes M$71-99; 8:30am-10:30pm;) Nattily attired staff serve baguette sandwiches, pastas and good coffee at this large modern cafe and restaurant, but the fresh-off-the-griddle crepes are the main draw. Try a savory *crepa azteca* with chicken, corn and peppers drizzled with *salsa poblana*. Kids love the glassed-in modern play space, and frazzled parents can take advantage of free childcare while they're on site (paid babysitting also available).

L'Eden MEXICAN, EUROPEAN $$
(Hotel El Paraíso, Calle 5 de Febrero 19; mains M$64-168; 7am-11pm;) This quality restaurant's tempting European and Mexican menu includes *fondue suiza, sopa azteca* and suc-

culent meat dishes. There's a good-sized wine list too, including French and Spanish vintages.

Restaurante LUM MEXICAN $$
(Hotel Bo, Av 5 de Mayo 38; mains M$95-170; 7am-11pm) This swanky indoor-outdoor restaurant that serves up the regional cuisines of Chiapas, Veracruz and the Yucatán is in San Cristóbal's first designer hotel. Custom-made lamps, reflecting pools and walls of geometrically stacked firewood create a funky contemporary ambience.

South of Plaza 31 de Marzo

Anabanana MEXICAN, BREAKFAST $
(Hidalgo 9; mains M$25-77; 10am-6pm Mon-Sat) This long-time *tortas* (sandwiches) and juice joint on a pedestrian street is a cute and good-value choice for typical Mexican food and no-frills international options. Great for people-watching, plus good breakfasts.

El Caldero MEXICAN $
(Insurgentes 5; soups M$59; 9am-10pm) Simple, friendly little El Caldero specializes in delicious, filling Mexican soups – *pozole* (shredded pork in broth), *mondongo* (tripe), *caldo* (broth) – with avocados, tortillas and various salsas. One vegetarian option too.

North of Plaza 31 de Marzo

★ **No Name Quesadillas** MEXICAN $
(Paniagua 49B; quesadilla M$30; 8-10:30pm Thu-Tue;) A sweet couple sells gourmet quesadillas and flavored *atoles* (sweet, corn-based hot drinks) at this signless storefront with romantic courtyard seating. The menu changes daily: vegetarian Sunday through Tuesday, seafood Thursday, meat on Friday – pretty cheeky in this mostly Catholic country – and a mixed bag on Saturday.

Get a gander at ingredients like wild mushrooms, crunchy seasonal ants, squash flowers and spicy chorizo, and line up early before the food sells out.

Alebrije MEXICAN $
(Caminero 4; mains M$25-50; 8:30am-6pm Mon-Sat) A fun, economical and busy *cocina popular* across from the Mercado Municipal, Alebrije serves freshly prepared food like *enfrijoladas con pollo* (tortillas with bean sauce, cheese and chicken), *chilaquiles* and *pollo con verduras* (chicken and vegetables) to a dedicated local clientele.

Falafel FELAFEL $
(MA Flores 4; mains M$45-90; 1-9pm Mon-Sat;) A small place with a brilliant mural of a mustachioed sun; its filling namesake meal comes wrapped in freshly baked pitas. Hebrew readers should browse the book exchange.

La Salsa Verde TAQUERÍA $
(Av 20 de Noviembre 7; 5 tacos M$50-95; 8am-midnight;) Meat sizzles on the open-air grill and TVs blare at this taco institution (more than 30 years in business), with tables of families and club-goers packed into its two large dining rooms.

Il Piccolo ITALIAN $$
(MA Flores 12; mains M$120-180, pizzas M$80-160; 1-11pm Tue-Sun;) Piccolo's large new space has a wood-fired oven and kids' trampoline in a huge back garden with dynamite views. The menu features steaks and pizzas as well as delectable fresh pasta. For a laugh, ask the owner about the women's restroom.

Trattoria Italiana ITALIAN $$
(Dr Navarro 10; mains M$120-145; 2-10pm Mon & Thu-Sat, 2-5:30pm Sun) This mother-and-daughter-run Italian eatery specializes in ravioli, handmade fresh every day. Depending on what's in season, expect fillings of sea bass with eggplant, four cheese with walnut and arugula, or rabbit with rosemary and green olive. The sauces are divine – don't miss the mango, chipotle and gorgonzola if it's around.

Drinking & Nightlife

The aroma of roasted highland-grown coffee beans wafts through the streets of San Cristóbal, and a strong dose is never far away. Along with the Café Museo Café (p361), try **Café La Selva** (Crescencio Rosas 9; 8:30am-11pm;) or **TierrAdentro** (Real de Guadalupe 24; 7:30am-1am;) for the good stuff – organic, indigenous-grown and delicious.

La Sandunga COCKTAIL BAR
(MA Flores 16; 7pm-3am Thu-Sat, plus Tue & Wed high season) Small and stylish, the walls at La Sandunga sport pop art, and the fresh fruit cocktails are divine, made sweeter by the gourmet *botanas* (free snacks) accompanying them. Rock bands play Friday and Saturday at 11:30pm.

Cocoliche COCKTAIL BAR
(Colón 3; noon-midnight;) By day a bohemian international restaurant (mains M$50 to M$95), in the evening Cocoliche's mismatched Chinese lanterns and wall of funky posters set the scene for hanging out with friends over boozy *licuados* (milkshakes). Jostle for a sofa near the fireplace on chilly nights, and check out the nightly Latin jazz and salsa, and occasional theater events at 9pm.

La Viña de Bacco WINE BAR
(967-119-19-85; Real de Guadalupe 7; 2pm-midnight Mon-Sat) At San Cristóbal's first wine bar, chatty patrons spill out onto the street, a pedestrian block of the main drag. It's a convivial place, pouring a large selection of Mexican options (among others), starting at a reasonable M$20 per glass. A free tapa with every glass of wine.

Mezcalería Gusana Grela MEZCALERÍA
(MA Flores 2; 7pm-3am Mon-Sat) Wedge yourself in at one of a handful of tables and try some of the dozen or so artisanal mezcals (M$30 to M$40) from Oaxaca, many of which are fruit-infused.

Kakao Natura CAFE
(Moreno 2A; 8am-10pm) For something different, melt into a hot chocolate at this *chocolatería*. The dozen or so varieties of artisanal chocolates (M$7 each) make fine gifts – if you can resist eating them yourself.

La Ruina CLUB
(Calle 28 de Agosto 13; 10pm-late Wed-Sat) Everyone drifts here after hours to dance the rest of the night away in a diminutive wooden building with full bar and cheap beer. Work it to a fun mix of *cumbia*, hip hop, dub step, reggae and salsa.

Latino's CLUB
(967-678-99-27; Madero 23; admission Fri & Sat M$40; 8pm-3am Mon-Sat) A bright restaurant and dance spot where the city's *salseros* gather to groove. A salsa/*merengue/cumbia/bachata* band plays at 11pm Thursday through Saturday.

Entertainment

Most live-music venues are free, and clubs generally enforce the no-smoking law.

★Cafe Bar Revolución LIVE MUSIC
(www.elrevo.com; Calle 1 de Marzo 11; 1pm-1am) There's always something fun at Revolución, with two live bands nightly (at 8:30pm and 10:30pm) and an eclectic lineup of salsa, rock, blues, jazz and reggae. Dance downstairs or order a mojito or caipirinha and chat in the quieter upstairs *tapanco* (attic).

El Paliacate ARTS CENTER
(Av 5 de Mayo 20; 6-11pm Tue-Sat) An alternative cultural space with a small restaurant and a bar serving wine, beer and artisan mezcal, El Paliacate's main stage hosts music events including rock en Tzotzil, *son jarocho* (folk music) and experimental bands, plus the occasional documentary film or theater presentation. There's bike parking inside and chill-out rooms upstairs.

Dada Club JAZZ
(967-631-75-61; www.dadaclubjazz.net; Calle 1 de Marzo 6A; 9am-1am Tue-Sun;) Deep red walls and flickering flame lamps set the backdrop for the best jazz and blues in town. An intimate balcony hovers beside the stage, where live music runs from 9:30pm to midnight. A garden area expands the space and serves organic breakfasts.

Cinema

San Cristóbal is a fine place to immerse yourself in Mexican and Latin American cinema, political documentaries and art-house movies. West of the center, the **Cinépolis** (www.cinepolis.com; adjacent to the Chedraui) multiplex plays first-run flicks for M$54; the cinemas listed below charge M$30.

Kinoki CINEMA
(967-678-50-46; www.facebook.com/KinokiForoCulturalIndependiente; Belisario Domínguez 5A; noon-midnight;) With a beautiful upstairs space and terrace, this art gallery and tea salon screens two films nightly at 6:30pm and 8:30pm. Private cinema rooms available with over 3500 movies on hand.

Cinema El Puente CINEMA
(967-678-37-23; Centro Cultural El Puente, Real de Guadalupe 55; Mon-Sat) Screenings at 6pm and 8pm.

Shopping

Real de Guadalupe and the Andador Turístico have some upscale craft shops, but the busy daily crafts market around Santo Domingo and La Caridad churches is also a good place to check out. In addition to textiles, another Chiapas specialty is amber, sold in numerous jewelry shops. When buying amber, beware of plastic imitations: the real thing is never cold and never heavy, and when rubbed should produce static electricity and a resiny smell.

Taller Leñateros ARTS & CRAFTS
(www.tallerlenateros.com; Paniagua 54; 8:30am-5pm Mon-Fri, to noon Sat) A society of Maya artists, the 'Woodlanders' Workshop' crafts exquisite handmade books, posters and fine art prints from recycled paper infused with local plants, using images inspired by traditional folk art. It's an open workshop, so you can watch the art in progress.

Poshería DRINK
(Real de Guadalupe 46A; 10am-9pm) Pick up a bottle of artisanal *pox* infused with honey, chocolate or fruits like *nanche*. Definitely not what the common folk are drinking, since bottles sell for M$50 to M$200 and the alcohol content averages only about 14%.

Meltzanel CLOTHING
(Calle 28 de Agosto 3; 9am-2pm & 4-8pm Mon-Fri, 10am-8pm Sat) Modern designs fashioned from traditional Maya textiles.

Abuelita Books BOOKS
(Colón 2; noon-6pm, closed Wed & Sun;) A great place for a leisurely browse over homemade brownies, hot coffee or a steamy tea; come here to replenish your reading material from an excellent selection of new and used books in English (other languages also available). Free English movies on Thursday nights.

Nemi Zapata HANDICRAFTS, COFFEE
(Real de Guadalupe 57A; 9:30am-6pm Mon-Sat) A fair-trade store that sells products made by Zapatista communities: weavings, embroidery, coffee and honey, as well as EZLN cards, posters and books.

Lágrimas de la Selva JEWELRY
(Plaza 31 de Marzo; 10am-9pm) A lovely jewelry store where you can watch jewelers work with amber.

Casa Chiapas HANDICRAFTS
(www.casachiapas.gob.mx; cnr Niños Héroes & Hidalgo; 9am-9pm Mon-Fri, 9am-8pm Sat, 10am-2pm Sun) Sells a good range of Chiapas crafts.

La Pared BOOKS
(Hidalgo 13B; 10:30am-8:30pm Tue-Sun) New and used books in English and other languages.

Information

IMMIGRATION

Instituto Nacional de Migración (967-678-02-92; Diagonal Hermanos Paniagua; 9am-1pm Mon-Fri) On a corner with the Pan-American Hwy, 1.2km west of the OCC bus station.

INTERNET ACCESS

San Cristóbal de las Casas has dozens of inexpensive internet cafes. In addition to the Plaza 31 de Marzo, most cafes have free wi-fi.

Fast-Net Cyber Café (Real de Guadalupe 15D; per hr M$10)

INDIGENOUS WOMEN'S WEAVING COOPERATIVES

The outstanding indigenous *artesanías* of the Chiapas highlands are textiles such as *huipiles* (sleeveless tunics), blouses and blankets, and Tzotzil weavers are some of the most skilled and inventive in Mexico.

J'pas Joloviletik (Utrilla 43; 9am-2pm & 4-7pm Mon-Fri, plus some Sat & Sun) A 30-year-old cooperative, J'pas Joloviletik – the name means 'those that weave' in Tzotzil – is comprised of 184 women from 12 communities, and they have a spacious shop on the east side of the Templo de Santo Domingo.

Sna Jolobil (snajolobil@prodigy.net.mx; Calz Lázaro Cárdenas s/n; 9am-2pm & 4-7pm Mon-Sat) Next to the Templo de Santo Domingo, Sna Jolobil – Tzotzil for 'The Weaver's House' – exhibits and sells some of the very best *huipiles*, blouses, skirts, rugs and other woven items, with prices ranging from a few dollars for small items to thousands for the best *huipiles* (the fruit of many months' work).

A cooperative of 800 weavers from the Chiapas highlands, it was founded in the 1970s to foster the important indigenous art of backstrap-loom weaving, and has revived many half-forgotten techniques and designs.

El Camino de los Altos (Insurgentes 19; 10am-3pm & 4-8pm Mon-Sat) Creators of the exquisite furnishings inside the Hotel Bo, El Camino de los Altos is a collaboration of French textile designers and 130 Maya weavers.

Los Faroles (Real de Guadalupe 33; per hr $8)

MEDICAL SERVICES

Dr Luis José Sevilla (967-678-16-26, cell phone 967-1061028; Calle del Sol 12; 6am-10pm) Speaks English and Italian; can make house calls. Located west of the center near the Periférico.

Hospital de la Mujer (967-678-07-70; Insurgentes 24) General hospital with emergency facilities.

MONEY

Most banks require your passport if you want to change cash, though they only change money Monday through Friday. There are also handy ATMs at the OCC bus station and on the southern side of the Plaza 31 de Marzo.

Banamex (Insurgentes btwn Niños Héroes & Cuauhtémoc; 9am-4pm Mon-Sat) Has an ATM; exchanges dollars.

Banco Azteca (Plaza 31 de Marzo; 9am-8pm) Hidden in the back of the Elektra furniture store; exchanges dollars and euros. Dollar exchange limited to US$300 daily per person.

Lacantún Money Exchange (Real de Guadalupe 12A; 9am-9pm Mon-Sat, 9am-2pm & 4-7pm Sun) Open outside bank hours but rates are worse.

POST

Main Post Office (Allende 3; 8am-4pm Mon-Fri, 8am-2pm Sat)

TELEPHONE

Lada Ahorro (Av 20 de Noviembre btwn Calle 28 de Agosto & Escuadrón 201; 9am-9pm) Inexpensive international calls.

TOURIST INFORMATION

Municipal Tourist Office (967-678-06-65; Palacio Municipal, Plaza 31 de Marzo; 9am-9pm) Staff are generally knowledgeable about the San Cristóbal area; English spoken.

Getting There & Away

A fast toll *autopista* (M$45 for cars) zips to San Cristóbal from Chiapa de Corzo. Follow the highway signs that say '*cuota*' (toll). It's best to travel the winding stretch of road between San Cristóbal and Palenque during daylight, as highway holdups – though by no means common – do occasionally occur. When taking a bus along this route, consider stowing valuables in the checked luggage compartment.

AIR

San Cristóbal's airport has no regular passenger flights; the main airport serving town is at Tux-

BUSES FROM SAN CRISTÓBAL DE LAS CASAS

DESTINATION	FARE (M$)	DURATION	FREQUENCY (DAILY)
Campeche	434	10hr	1
Cancún	350-994	18-19hr	3 OCC, 1 AEXA
Ciudad Cuauhtémoc (Guatemalan border)	100	3¼hr	3
Comitán	45-56	1¾hr	Frequent OCC & *colectivos*
Mérida	618	12¾hr	1
Mexico City (TAPO & Norte)	514-1232	13-14hr	12
Oaxaca	474-762	11-12hr	4
Ocosingo	40-68	2hr	7 OCC, 4 AEXA, frequent *colectivos*
Palenque	110-196	5hr	6 OCC, 4 AEXA
Pochutla	462	11-12hr	2
Puerto Escondido	518	12½-13hr	2
Tuxtla Gutiérrez	35-50	1-1¼hr	Frequent OCC; 4 AEXA; frequent Ómnibus de Chiapas sprinters; frequent *colectivos;* 24hr Taxis Jovel *colectivos* taxis
Tuxtla Gutiérrez airport (Ángel Albino Corzo)	178	1½hr	5
Villahermosa	274-326	5½-7hr	2

tla Gutiérrez. Five daily direct OCC minibuses (M$178) run to the Tuxtla airport from San Cristóbal's main bus terminal (four in the other direction); book airport-bound tickets in advance, and consult www.ado.com.mx for schedules to/from 'Ángel Albino Corzo Aeropuerto.'

A number of tour agencies run shuttles to the Tuxtla airport for around M$250 per person.

Taxis Jovel (☎967-678-23-53; Pan-American Hwy at Allende) Taxis Jovel picks up passengers for the airport, charging M$450 per carload (M$53 *colectivo*); reserve a day beforehand.

BUS & COLECTIVO

The Pan-American Hwy (Hwy 190, Blvd Juan Sabines, 'El Bulevar') runs through the southern part of town, and nearly all transportation terminals are on it or nearby. From the OCC bus terminal, it's six blocks north up Insurgentes to the central square, Plaza 31 de Marzo.

The main 1st-class **OCC terminal** (☎967-678-02-91; cnr Pan-American Hwy & Insurgentes) is also used by ADO and UNO 1st-class and deluxe buses, plus some 2nd-class buses. Tickets can also be purchased at **Boletotal** (☎967-678-85-03; www.boletotal.mx; Real de Guadalupe 16; ⏰7:30am-10pm) in the center of town. AEXA buses and Ómnibus de Chiapas minibuses share a terminal across the street from the OCC terminal.

All *colectivo* vans (combis) and taxis have depots on the Pan-American Hwy a block or so from the OCC terminal. They generally run from 5am until 9pm and leave when full. *Colectivo* taxis to Tuxtla, Comitán and Ocosingo are available 24 hours; if you don't want to wait for it to fill, you must pay for the empty seats.

For Tuxtla Gutiérrez, comfortable Ómnibus de Chiapas 'sprinter' minibuses (M$45) are the best bet; they leave every 10 minutes.

For Guatemala, most agencies offer a daily van service to Quetzaltenango (M$350, eight hours), Panajachel (M$350, 10 hours) and Antigua (M$450, 12 hours); Viajes Chincultik is slightly cheaper, and also has van service to Guatemala City and Chichicastenango. Otherwise, go to Ciudad Cuauhtémoc and pick up onward transportation from the Guatemala side.

CAR & MOTORCYCLE

Optima (☎967-674-54-09; optimacar1@hotmail.com; Mazariegos 39) San Cristóbal's only car-rental company, Optima rents manual transmission cars for M$600 per day and M$3600 per week, including unlimited kilometers, insurance and taxes. Sizable discounts are given for payment in cash. Drivers must be 25 or older and have a credit card.

AMATENANGO DEL VALLE

The women of this Tzeltal village by the Pan-American Hwy, 37km southeast of San Cristóbal, are renowned potters. Pottery here is still fired by a pre-Hispanic method, building a wood fire around the pieces rather than putting them in a kiln. Amatenango children find a ready tourist market with *animalitos* – little pottery animal figures that are inexpensive but fragile. If you visit the village, expect to be surrounded within minutes by young *animalito* sellers. From San Cristóbal, take a Comitán-bound bus or combi.

Getting Around

Combis (M$6) go up Crescencio Rosas from the Pan-American Hwy to the town center. Taxis cost M$25 within town and M$30 at night.

To self-propel, Jaguar Adventours (p363) rents good-quality mountain bikes.

Croozy Scooters (☎cell phone 967-6832223; Belisario Domínguez 7; scooters per 3hr/day M$250/400, motorcycles per 3hr/day M$350/500; ⏰10am-6pm) Croozy Scooters rents well-maintained Italika CS 125cc scooters and 150cc motorcycles. The price includes a free tank of fuel, maps, locks and helmets; passport and M$500 deposit required.

Around San Cristóbal

The inhabitants of the beautiful Chiapas highlands are descended from the ancient Maya and maintain some unique customs, costumes and beliefs.

Markets and festivals often give the most interesting insight into indigenous life, and there are lots of them. Weekly markets at the villages are nearly always on Sunday. Proceedings start as early as dawn, and wind down by lunchtime. Occasions like **Carnaval** (late February/early March), for which San Juan Chamula is particularly famous, **Semana Santa**, and **Día de Muertos** (November 2) are celebrated almost everywhere.

During the day, walking or riding by horse or bicycle along the main roads to San Juan Chamula and San Lorenzo Zinacantán should not be risky; however, it's not wise to wander into unfrequented areas or down isolated tracks.

Tours

Exploring the region with a good guide can open up doors and give you a feel for indigenous life and customs you could never gain alone. All San Cristóbal agencies offer four- or five-hour trips to local villages, usually San Juan Chamula and San Lorenzo Zinacantán, for about M$200, or four- or five-hour guided horseback rides to San Juan Chamula for the same price. Don't take anything too valuable with you; thefts have occurred in the past.

Alex & Raúl Tours CULTURAL
(☎967-678-91-41; www.alexyraultours.wordpress.com; per person M$200) Enjoyable and informative minibus tours in English, French or Spanish. Raúl and/or a colleague wait at the wooden cross in front of San Cristóbal's cathedral from 8:45am to 9:30am daily, going to San Juan Chamula and Zinacantán. Trips to Tenejapa, San Andrés Larraínzar or Amatenango del Valle (M$225) can also be arranged for a minimum of four people.

Getting There & Away

Transportation to most villages goes from points around the Mercado Municipal in San Cristóbal. Combis to San Juan Chamula (M$12) leave from spots on Calle Honduras and Utrilla frequently; for Zinacantán, combis (M$14) and *colectivo* taxis (M$16) go at least hourly, from a yard off Robledo. Transportation runs from before daybreak to around dusk.

San Juan Chamula

POP 3300 / ELEV 2200M

The Chamulans are a fiercely independent Tzotzil group. Their main village, San Juan Chamula, 10km northwest of San Cristóbal, is the center for some unique religious practices – although conflicts between adherents of traditional Chamulan Catholicism and converts to evangelical, Pentecostal

Around San Cristóbal de las Casas

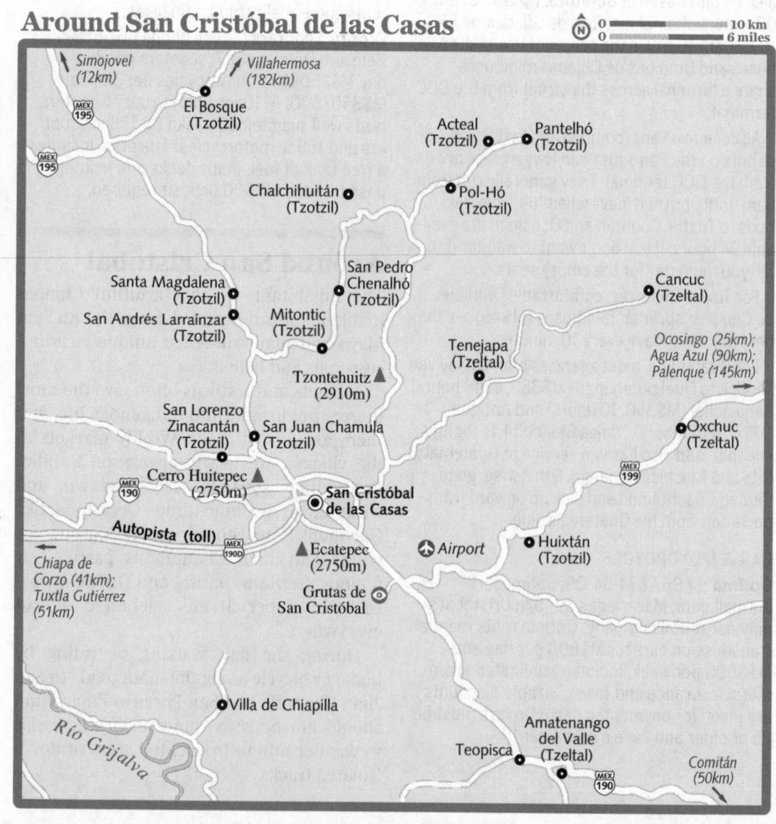

and other branches of Christianity have resulted in the expulsion of many thousands of Chamulans from their villages in the past couple of decades. Here, as in other places in Mexico and Central America, rejection of Catholicism was also in part a political rejection of the longstanding supremacy of the Catholic mestizo majority. In San Juan Chamula, evangelicalism is associated with the Zapatista movement. Most of the evangelical exiles now inhabit the shantytowns around San Cristóbal.

Chamulan men wear loose homespun tunics of white wool (sometimes, in cool weather, thicker black wool), but *cargo*-holders – those with important religious and ceremonial duties – wear a sleeveless black tunic and a white scarf on the head. Chamulan women wear fairly plain white or blue blouses and/or shawls and woolen skirts.

Outsiders can visit San Juan Chamula, but a big sign at the entrance to the village strictly forbids photography inside the village church or at rituals. Do *not* ignore these restrictions; the community takes them very seriously. Nearby, around the shell of an older church, is the village **graveyard**. Though it's no longer practiced, traditionally black crosses were for people who died old, white for the young, and blue for others.

Sunday is the weekly **market**, when people from the hills stream into the village to shop, trade and visit the main church. A corresponding number of tourist buses also streams in, so you might prefer to come another day (though due to local superstitions, there are fewer worshippers on Wednesdays).

Festivals & Events

Carnaval CARNIVAL

During Carnaval, groups of minstrels stroll the roads in tall, pointed hats with long, colored tassels, strumming guitars and chanting. Much *pox* (pronounced 'posh'), an alcoholic drink made from sugarcane, is drunk. Festivities also mark the five 'lost' days of the ancient Long Count calendar, which divided time into 20-day periods (18 of these make 360 days, leaving five to complete a year).

Fiesta de San Juan Bautista RELIGIOUS

Up to 20,000 people gather to dance and drink on June 24.

DON'T MISS

TEMPLO DE SAN JUAN

Standing beside the main plaza, Chamula's main church is a ghostly white, with a vividly painted arch of green and blue. Inside the darkened sanctuary, hundreds of flickering candles, clouds of copal incense, and worshippers kneeling with their faces to the pine-needle-carpeted floor make a powerful impression. Chamulans revere San Juan Bautista (St John the Baptist) above Christ, and his image occupies a more important place in the church.

You must obtain tickets (M$20) at the **tourist office** (7am-6pm) beside the plaza before entering.

Chanting *curanderos* (literally 'curers'; medicine men or women) may be rubbing patients' bodies with eggs or bones, and worshippers often drink soft drinks (burps are believed to expel evil spirits) or copious amounts of *pox*. Images of saints are surrounded with mirrors and dressed in holy garments.

Change of Cargo-Holders TRADITIONAL

The annual rotation of the honored (but expensive) community leadership positions known as *cargos;* December 30 to January 1.

San Lorenzo Zinacantán

POP 3900 / ELEV 2558M

The orderly village of San Lorenzo Zinacantán, about 11km northwest of San Cristóbal, is the main village of the Zinacantán municipality (population 36,000). Zinacantán people, like Chamulans, are Tzotzil. The men wear distinctive pink tunics embroidered with flower motifs and may sport flat, round, ribboned palm hats. Women wear pink or purple shawls over richly embroidered blouses.

A small **market** is held on Sundays until noon, and during fiesta times. The most important celebrations are for **La Virgen de La Candelaria** (Aug 7-11) and **San Sebastián** (Jan 19-22).

The people of Zinacantán are great flower growers. They have a particular love for the geranium, which – along with pine branches – is offered in rituals for a wide range of benefits.

The huge central **Iglesia de San Lorenzo** (admission M$15) was rebuilt following a

> **TAKING PHOTOS**
>
> It's important to be respectful of local customs in this part of Mexico. Indigenous villages are often extremely close-knit, and their people can be suspicious of outsiders and particularly sensitive about having their photos taken. In some villages cameras are, at best, tolerated – and sometimes not even that. You may put yourself in physical danger by taking photos without permission. If in any doubt, ask first.

fire in 1975. Photography is banned in the church and churchyard.

Grutas de San Cristóbal

To get here, take a Teopisca-bound combi (M$20) from the Pan-American Hwy, about 150m southeast of the OCC bus station in San Cristóbal, and ask for 'Las Grutas.'

Grutas de San Cristóbal CAVE
(admission M$20, parking M$10; ⏲8am-4:30pm) The entrance to this long cavern is situated in pine woods 9km southeast of San Cristóbal, a five-minute walk south of the Pan-American Hwy. The first 350m or so of the cave is lit and open for viewing, with a concrete walkway threading through a dazzling chasm of stalagmites and stalactites. An extensive army base buffers the caves, but visitors are still welcome. Horseback riding is available from the parking area, where you'll also find *comedores*.

Ocosingo

☎919 / POP 42,000 / ELEV 900M

A respite from both the steamy lowland jungle and the chilly highlands, the bustling regional market town of Ocosingo sits in a gorgeous and broad temperate valley midway between San Cristóbal and Palenque. The impressive Maya ruins of Toniná are just a few kilometers away.

The market area along Avenida 2 Sur Oriente, three to five blocks east (downhill) from the central plaza, is the busiest part of town. The **Tianguis Campesino** (Peasants' Market; cnr Av 2 Sur Oriente & Calle 5 Sur Oriente; ⏲6am-5pm) is for the area's small-scale food producers to sell their goods direct; only women are allowed to trade here, and it's a colorful sight, with most of the traders in traditional dress.

The valleys known as Las Cañadas de Ocosingo, between Ocosingo and the Reserva de la Biosfera Montes Azules to the southeast, form one of the strongest bastions of support for the Zapatistas, and Ocosingo saw the bloodiest fighting during the 1994 uprising, with about 50 rebels killed here by the Mexican army.

Ocosingo spreads east (downhill) from Hwy 199. Avenida Central runs down from the highway to the broad central plaza, overlooked from its east end by the Templo de San Jacinto. Some hotels, restaurants and services are along Calle Central Norte, running off the north side of the plaza.

Sleeping

Hotel Central HOTEL $
(☎919-673-00-24; cnr Av Central & Calle Central; s/d/tr/q M$300/350/450/550, air-con extra M$100; P⊖❄☕) Fronting the plaza, the comfortable Hotel Central has ample rooms with cable TV and fan, and a great terrace. Ask for one of the upstairs rooms; corner room 12 is especially bright and breezy.

Hospedaje Esmeralda GUESTHOUSE $
(☎919-673-00-14; rosi_esmeralda@hotmail.com; Calle Central Norte 14; s/d/tr/q without bathroom M$180/200/300/400; P☕) This small guesthouse has five adequate rooms, all with bright indigenous bedcovers and fans. There's a restaurant (mains M$62 to M$85), and the owners – who know the area inside out – are happy to give information to non-guests if you buy a drink or meal. It also offers horseback-riding excursions (M$300, two hours) in the countryside outside Ocosingo.

Eating

Restaurant Los Rosales MEXICAN, BREAKFAST $
(Hotel Margarita, Calle Central Norte 19; breakfast M$40-70, mains M$70-110; ⏲7am-11pm; ☕) With a wall of windows looking out over the rooftops to views of never-ending green mountains, this upstairs eatery makes a pleasant place to plot your day.

Las Delicias MEXICAN, BREAKFAST $$
(Av Central 5; mains M$78-120; ⏲7am-11pm; ☕) On the plaza-facing veranda of the Hotel Central, this restaurant has big portions and good breakfasts (M$41 to M$82).

Shopping

Fábrica de Quesos Santa Rosa FOOD
(☎919-673-00-09; 1a Calle Oriente Norte 11; cheese per kg M$80; ⏰8am-2pm & 4-8pm Mon-Sat, 8am-2pm Sun) Ocosingo is known for its *queso amarillo* (yellow cheese). There are nine main types sold by this cheesemaker, including '*de bola*,' which comes in 1kg balls with an edible wax coating and a crumbly, whole-fat center. Free factory tours available during business hours.

Information

Santander (cnr Calle Central Norte & Av 1a Norte; ⏰9am-4pm Mon-Fri, 10am-2pm Sat) and the plaza-side **Banamex** (Av Central; ⏰9am-4pm Mon-Fri) both exchange dollars and have ATMs. Santander changes euros too. The plaza's a free wi-fi hotspot, and internet cafes there charge M$8 per hour.

The **Municipal Tourism Office** (⏰8am-4pm Mon-Fri), with a kiosk on the plaza and a ground-floor office in the plaza-front Palacio Municipal, has regional and city maps, though you're better off getting actual information at Hospedaje Esmeralda.

Getting There & Away

Ocosingo's **OCC bus terminal** (☎919-673-04-31) is on Hwy 199, 600m west of the plaza; the 1st-class **AEXA bus terminal** (☎cell phone 919-1140679; www.autobusesaexa.com.mx) is across the road. In addition to San Cristóbal,

INDIGENOUS PEOPLES OF CHIAPAS

Of the 4.8 million people of Chiapas, approximately a quarter are indigenous, with language being the key ethnic identifier. Each of the eight principal groups has its own language, beliefs and customs, a cultural variety that makes Chiapas one of the most fascinating states in Mexico.

Travelers to the area around San Cristóbal are most likely to encounter the Tzotziles and the Tzeltales. Their traditional religious life is nominally Catholic, but integrates pre-Hispanic elements. Most people live in the hills outside the villages, which are primarily market and ceremonial centers.

Tzotzil and Tzeltal clothing is among the most varied, colorful and elaborately worked in Mexico. It not only identifies wearers' villages but also continues ancient Maya traditions. Many of the seemingly abstract designs on these costumes are in fact stylized snakes, frogs, butterflies, birds, saints and other beings. Some motifs have religious-magical functions: scorpions, for example, can be a symbolic request for rain, since they are believed to attract lightning.

The Lacandones dwelled deep in the Lacandón Jungle and largely avoided contact with the outside world until the 1950s. They now number less than 1000 and mostly live in three main settlements in that same region (Lacanjá Chansayab, Metzabok and Nahá), with low-key tourism being one of their major means of support. Lacandones are readily recognizable in their white tunics and long black hair cut in a fringe. Most Lacandones have now abandoned their traditional animist religion in favor of Presbyterian or evangelical forms of Christianity.

Traditionally treated as second-class citizens, indigenous groups mostly live on the least productive land in the state, with the least amount of government services or infrastructure. Many indigenous communities rely on subsistence farming and have no running water or electricity, and it was frustration over lack of political power and their historical mistreatment that fueled the Zapatista rebellion, putting a spotlight on the region's distinct inequities.

Today, longstanding indigenous ways of life are challenged both by evangelical Christianity – opposed to many traditional animist-Catholic practices and the abuse of alcohol in religious rituals – and by the Zapatista movement, which rejects traditional leadership hierarchies and is raising the rights and profile of women. Many highland indigenous people have emigrated to the Lacandón Jungle to clear new land, or to Mexican and US cities in search of work.

Despite all obstacles, indigenous identities and self-respect survive. Indigenous people may be suspicious of outsiders, and may resent interference in their religious observances or other aspects of their life, but if treated with due respect they are likely to respond in kind.

BUSES FROM OCOSINGO

DESTINATION	FARE (M$)	DURATION	FREQUENCY (DAILY)
Palenque	50-128	2½hr	6 OCC, 3 AEXA; very frequent *colectivos*
San Cristóbal de las Casas	40-68	2¼hr	4 OCC, 4 AEXA; very frequent *colectivos*
Tuxtla Gutiérrez	95-168	3½hr	4 OCC, 4 AEXA

Tuxtla Gutiérrez and Palenque, buses from the OCC terminal also go to Campeche, Cancún, Mérida and Villahermosa. The main *colectivo* terminal is across the street from AEXA.

A walled lot behind the market is the terminus for trucks to Nahá (M$50, 2½ hours, 11am and noon) and Laguna Miramar.

Toniná

The towering ceremonial core of **Toniná** (☎919-108-22-39; admission M$46; ⊙8am-5pm), overlooking a pastoral valley 14km east of Ocosingo, comprises one of the Maya world's most imposing temple complexes. This was the city that brought mighty Palenque to its knees.

The year AD 688 saw the inauguration of the Snake Skull–Jaguar Claw dynasty, with ambitious new rulers bent on controlling the region. Palenque was their rival state, and when Toniná captured the Palenque ruler K'an Joy Chitam II in 711, it's likely that he had his head lopped off here.

Toniná became known as the Place of the Celestial Captives, because its chambers held the captured rulers of Palenque and other Maya cities, who were destined to be ransomed for large sums or decapitated. A recurring image in Toniná sculpture is of captives before decapitation, thrown to the ground with their hands tied.

To enter the site, follow the road from the entrance and **site museum** (⊙closed Mon), which details Toniná's history (in Spanish) and contains most of the best artifacts. The road turns into a footpath, crosses a stream and climbs to the broad, flat Gran Plaza. At the south end of the Gran Plaza is the **Templo de la Guerra Cósmica** (Temple of Cosmic War), with five altars in front of it. Off one side of the plaza is a **ball court**, inaugurated around AD 780 under the rule of the female regent Smoking Mirror. A decapitation altar stands cheerfully beside it. In 2011, archaeologists discovered two life-size stone sculptures of captive warriors inscribed as being from Copán (in Honduras), confirming that Maya kingdom's wartime alliance with Palenque.

To the north rises the ceremonial core of Toniná, a hillside terraced into a number of platforms, rising 80m above the Gran Plaza. At the right-hand end of the steps, rising from the first to the second platform, is the entry to a **ritual labyrinth** of passages.

Higher up on the right-hand side is the **Palacio de las Grecas y de la Guerra** (Palace of the Grecas and War). The grecas are a band of geometrical decoration forming a zigzag x-shape, possibly representing Quetzalcóatl. To its right is a rambling series of chambers, passages and stairways, believed to have been Toniná's administrative headquarters.

Higher again is Toniná's most remarkable sculpture, the **Mural de las Cuatro Eras** (Mural of the Four Eras). Created between AD 790 and 840, this stucco relief of four panels – the first, from the left end, has been lost – represents the four suns, or four eras of human history. The people of Toniná believed themselves to be living in the fourth sun – that of winter, mirrors, the direction north and the end of human life. At the center of each panel is the upside-down head of a decapitated prisoner. Blood spurting from the prisoner's neck forms a ring of feathers and, at the same time, a sun. In one panel, a dancing skeleton holds a decapitated head. To the left of the head is a lord of the underworld, resembling an enormous rodent.

Up the next set of steps is the seventh level, with remains of four temples. Behind the second temple from the left, more steps descend into the very narrow **Tumba de Treinta Metros** (Thirty-Meter Tomb), an impossibly slim passageway that's definitely not for the claustrophobic!

Above here is the acropolis, the abode of Toniná's rulers and site of its eight most important temples – four on each of the two levels. The right-hand temple on the lower level, the **Templo del Monstruo de la Tierra** (Temple of the Earth Monster), has Toniná's best-preserved roofcomb, built around AD 713.

On the topmost level, the tallest temple, the **Templo del Espejo Humeante** (Temple of the Smoking Mirror), was built by Zots-Choj, who took the throne in AD 842. In that era of the fourth sun and the direction north, Zots-Choj had to raise this, Toniná's northernmost temple, highest of all, which necessitated a large, artificial northeast extension of the hill.

Getting There & Away

Combis to Toniná (M$12) leave from a roofed depot just behind Ocosingo's Tianguis Campesino every 30 minutes. The last one returns around 5:30pm. A taxi costs M$100.

Agua Azul & Misol-Ha

These spectacular water attractions – the thundering cascades of Agua Azul and the 35m jungle waterfall of Misol-Ha – are both short detours off the Ocosingo–Palenque road. During the rainy season, they lose part of their beauty as the water gets murky, though the power of the waterfalls is magnified.

Both are most easily visited on an organized day tour from Palenque, though it's possible, for about the same price, to go independently. One reason to visit on your own is to spend more time at Misol-Ha, which is usually a shorter tour stop. Agua Azul is especially built-up and crowded with vendors.

Agua Azul WATERFALL

(admission M$38) Agua Azul is a breathtaking sight, with its powerful and dazzling white waterfalls thundering into turquoise (outside rainy season) pools surrounded by verdant jungle. On holidays and weekends the place is thronged; at other times you'll have few companions. The temptation to swim is great, but take extreme care, as people do drown here. The current is deceptively fast, the power of the falls obvious, and there are many submerged hazards like rocks and dead trees.

The turnoff for Agua Azul is halfway between Ocosingo and Palenque, some 60km from each. A paved road leads 4.5km down to Agua Azul from Hwy 199. A well-made stone and concrete path with steps runs 700m up beside the falls from the parking area, which is packed with food and souvenir stalls. Basic lodging is also available.

Unfortunately, theft isn't uncommon, so don't bring valuables, keep an eye on your belongings and stick to the main paved trail.

Misol-Ha WATERFALL

(total admission M$30) Just 20km south of Palenque, spectacular Misol-Ha cascades approximately 35m into a wonderful wide pool surrounded by lush tropical vegetation. It's a sublime place for a dip when the fall is not excessively pumped up by wet-season rains. A path behind the main fall leads into a cave, which allows you to experience the power of the water close up. Misol-Ha is 1.5km off Hwy 199 and the turnoff is signposted; two separate *ejidos* (communal landholdings) charge admission.

Sleeping & Eating

Centro Turístico Ejidal Cascada de Misol-Ha CABANAS $

(☎ in Mexico City 55-5551-3377; www.misol-ha.com; d/tr M$290/400, f with kitchen M$520-630, restaurant mains M$70-130; ⏲ restaurant 7am-7pm, to 10pm high season; P ⊖) Has great wooden cabins among the trees near the waterfall, with fans, hot-water bathrooms and mosquito netting, plus a good open-air restaurant. Nighttime swims are dreamy.

Getting There & Away

Most Palenque travel agencies offer daily Misol-Ha and Agua Azul trips. Trips cost around M$300 including admission fees, and last six or seven hours, spending 30 to 60 minutes at Misol-Ha and two to three hours at Agua Azul. Trips can also be organized to deposit you in San Cristóbal afterward for an additional M$100.

To visit the sites independently from Palenque, negotiate a taxi or take an Ocosingo-bound combi from 5a Poniente Sur to the *cruceros* (turnoffs). At Agua Azul (M$35), *camionetas* run down to the entrance. There's no regular transportation in from the Misol-Ha highway junction (M$25), but it's a pretty 1.5km pastoral walk.

Palenque

☎916 / POP 43,000 / ELEV 80M

Deservedly one of the top destinations of Chiapas, the soaring jungle-swathed temples of Palenque are a national treasure and one of the best examples of Maya architecture in Mexico. Modern Palenque town, a few kilometers to the east, is a sweaty, humdrum place without much appeal except as a jumping-off point for the ruins and a place to find internet access. Many prefer to

Palenque

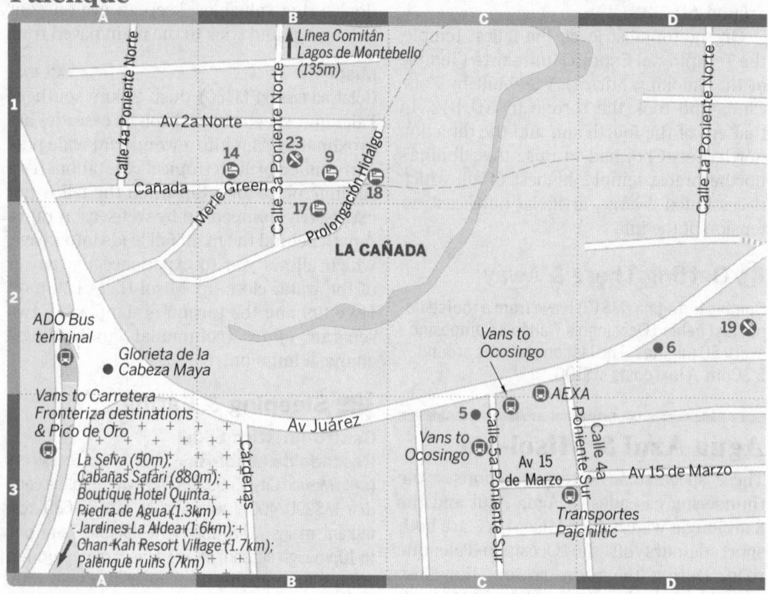

base themselves at one of the forest hideouts along the road between the town and the ruins, including the funky travelers' hangout of El Panchán.

History

The name Palenque (Palisade) is Spanish and has no relation to the city's ancient name, which may have been Lakamha (Big Water). Palenque was first occupied around 100 BC, and flourished from around AD 630 to around 740. The city rose to prominence under the ruler Pakal, who reigned from AD 615 to 683. Archaeologists have determined that Pakal is represented by hieroglyphics of sun and shield, and he is also referred to as Escudo Solar (Sun Shield). He lived to the then-incredible age of 80.

During Pakal's reign, many plazas and buildings, including the superlative Templo de las Inscripciones (Pakal's own mausoleum), were constructed in Palenque. The structures were characterized by mansard roofs and very fine stucco bas-reliefs.

Pakal's son Kan B'alam II (684–702), who is represented in hieroglyphics by the jaguar and the serpent (and is also called Jaguar Serpent II), continued Palenque's expansion and artistic development. He presided over the construction of the Grupo de las Cruces temples, placing sizable narrative stone steles within each.

During Kan B'alam II's reign, Palenque extended its zone of control to the Río Usumacinta, but was challenged by the rival Maya city of Toniná, 65km south. Kan B'alam's brother and successor, K'an Joy Chitam II (Precious Peccary), was captured by forces from Toniná in 711, and probably executed there. Palenque enjoyed a resurgence between 722 and 736, however, under Ahkal Mo' Nahb' III (Turtle Macaw Lake), who added many substantial buildings.

After AD 900, Palenque was largely abandoned. In an area that receives the heaviest rainfall in Mexico, the ruins were soon overgrown, and the city remained unknown to the Western world until 1746, when Maya hunters revealed the existence of a jungle palace to a Spanish priest named Antonio de Solís. Later explorers claimed Palenque was capital of an Atlantis-like civilization. The eccentric Count de Waldeck, who in his 60s lived atop one of the pyramids for two years (1831–33), even published a book with fanciful neoclassical drawings that made the city resemble a great Mediterranean civilization.

It was not until 1837, when John L Stephens, an amateur archaeology enthusiast from New York, reached Palenque with

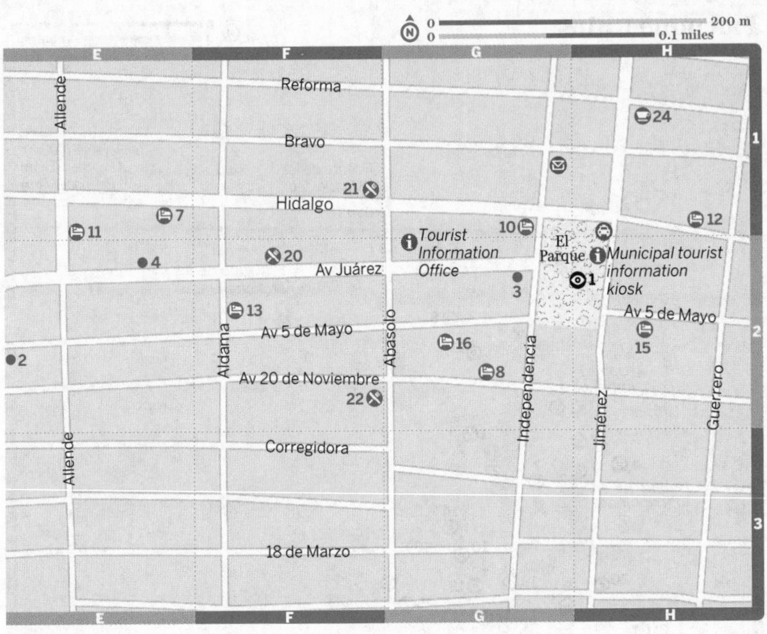

Palenque

Sights
1 El Parque H2

Activities, Courses & Tours
2 Servicios Turísticos de Palenque E2
3 Transportador Turística Scherrer & Barb G2
4 Turística Maya Chiapas E2
5 Viajes Kukulcán C3
6 Viajes Misol-Ha D2

Sleeping
7 Hostal San Miguel E1
8 Hotel Canek G2
9 Hotel Chablis B1
10 Hotel Chan-Kah Centro G1
11 Hotel Lacandonia E1
12 Hotel Lacroix H1
13 Hotel Maya Rue F2
14 Hotel Maya Tulipanes B1
15 Hotel Palenque H2
16 Hotel Posada Tucán G2
17 Hotel Xibalba B2
18 Yaxkin B1

Eating
19 Abarrotes Monterrey D2
20 Aluxes F2
21 Café de Yara F1
Café Jade .... (see 18)
22 Restaurant Las Tinajas F2
23 Restaurant Maya Cañada B1

Drinking & Nightlife
24 Italian Coffee Company H1

artist Frederick Catherwood, that the site was insightfully investigated. Another century passed before Alberto Ruz Lhuillier, the tireless Mexican archaeologist, uncovered Pakal's hidden crypt in 1952. Today it continues to yield fascinating and beautiful secrets – most recently, a succession of sculptures and frescoes in the Acrópolis del Sur area, which have vastly expanded our knowledge of Palenque's history.

Frans Blom, the mid-20th-century investigator, remarked: 'The first visit to Palenque is immensely impressive. When one has lived there for some time this ruined city becomes an obsession.' It is certainly not hard to understand why.

Sights

Hwy 199 meets Palenque's main street, Avenida Juárez, at the **Glorieta de la Cabeza**

Palenque Ruins

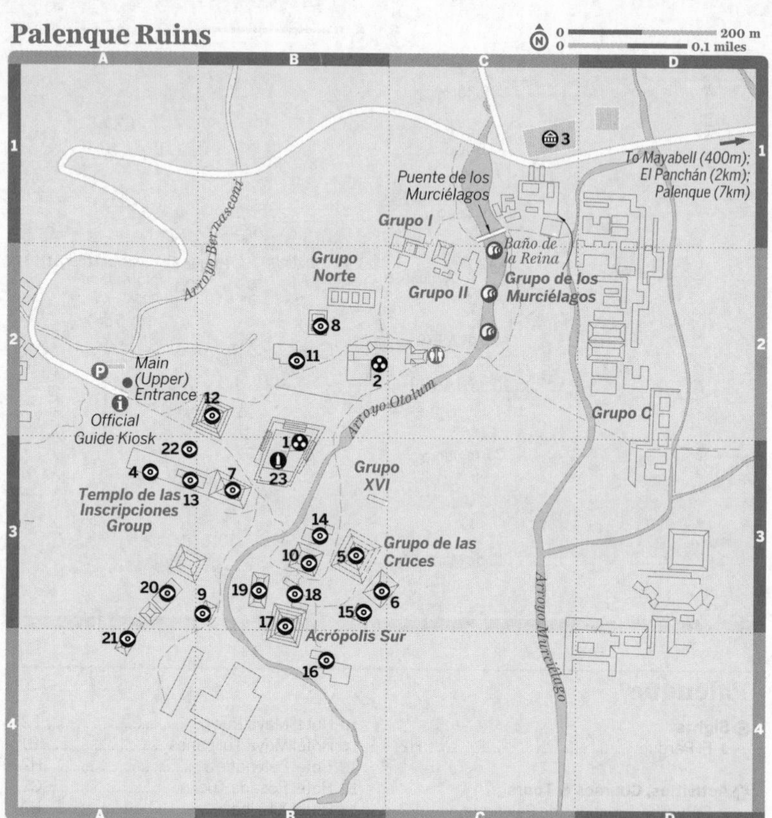

Maya (Maya Head Statue; Map p378), a roundabout with a large statue of a Maya chieftain's head, at the west end of the town. The new main ADO bus station is here, and Juárez heads 1km east from this intersection to the central square, **El Parque** (Map p378).

A few hundred meters south from the Maya head, the paved road to the Palenque ruins, 7.5km away, diverges west off Hwy 199. This road passes the site museum after about 6.5km, then winds on about 1km further uphill to the **main entrance to the ruins**.

Palenque Ruins ARCHAEOLOGICAL SITE
(admission M$57; 8am-5pm, last entry 4:30pm)
Ancient Palenque stands at the precise point where the first hills rise out of the Gulf coast plain, and the dense jungle covering these hills forms an evocative backdrop to Palenque's exquisite Maya architecture. Hundreds of ruined buildings are spread over 15 sq km, but only a fairly compact central area has been excavated. Everything you see here was built without metal tools, pack animals or the wheel.

As you explore the ruins, try to picture the gray stone edifices as they would have been at the peak of Palenque's power: painted blood-red with elaborate blue and yellow stucco details. The forest around these temples is still home to howler monkeys, toucans and ocelots. The ruins and surrounding forests form a national park, the **Parque Nacional Palenque**, for which you must pay a separate M$27 admission fee at Km 4.5 on the road to the ruins.

Palenque sees more than 1000 visitors on an average day, and visitation spikes in the summer holiday season. Opening time is a good time to visit, when it's cooler and not too crowded, and morning mist may still be wrapping the temples in a picturesque haze. Refreshments, hats and souvenirs are avail-

Palenque Ruins

Sights

1	El Palacio	B3
2	Juego de Pelota	B2
3	Museo de Sitio	C1
4	Templo de la Calavera	A3
5	Templo de la Cruz	B3
6	Templo de la Cruz Foliada	B3
7	Templo de las Inscripciones	B3
8	Templo del Conde	B2
9	Templo del Jaguar	B3
10	Templo del Sol	B3
11	Templo X	B2
12	Templo XI	B2
13	Templo XIII	A3
14	Templo XIV	B3
15	Templo XIX	B4
16	Templo XVII	B3
17	Templo XX	B3
18	Templo XXI	B3
19	Templo XXII	B3
20	Templo XXIV	A3
21	Templo XXV	A4
22	Tomb of Alberto Ruz Lhuillier	A3
23	Tower	B3

able outside the main entrance. Vendors line many of the paths through the ruins.

Official site **guides** are available by the entrance. Two Maya guide associations offer informative two-hour tours for up to seven people, which cost M$800 in Spanish or M$980 in English, French, German or Italian. French, German and Italian speakers may have to wait a bit longer as there are fewer guides available.

Most visitors take a combi or taxi to the ruins' main (upper) entrance, see the major structures and then walk downhill to the museum, visiting minor ruins along the way.

Combis to the ruins (M$20 each way) run about every 10 minutes during daylight hours. In town, look for 'Ruinas' combis anywhere on Juárez west of Allende. They will also pick you up or drop you off anywhere along the town-to-ruins road.

Be aware that the mushrooms sold by locals along the road to the ruins from about May to November are of the hallucinogenic variety.

➡ Templo de las Inscripciones Group

(Map p380) As you walk in from the entrance, passing to the south of the overgrown **Templo XI** (Map p380), the vegetation suddenly peels away to reveal many of Palenque's most magnificent buildings in one sublime vista. A line of temples rises in front of the jungle on your right, culminating in the Templo de las Inscripciones about 100m ahead; El Palacio, with its trademark tower, stands to the left of the Templo de las Inscripciones; and the Grupo de las Cruces rises in the distance beneath a thick jungle backdrop.

The first temple on your right is Templo XII, called the **Templo de la Calavera** (Temple of the Skull; Map p380) for the relief sculpture of a rabbit or deer skull at the foot of one of its pillars. The second temple has little interest. Third is **Templo XIII** (Map p380), containing a tomb of a female dignitary, whose remains were found colored red (as a result of treatment with cinnabar) when unearthed in 1994. You can look into this **Tumba de la Reina Roja** (Tomb of the Red Queen) and see her sarcophagus. With the skeleton were found a malachite mask and about 1000 pieces of jade. Based on DNA tests and resemblances to Pakal's tomb next door, the theory is that the 'queen' buried here was his wife Tz'ak-b'u Ajaw. The **tomb of Alberto Ruz Lhuillier** (Map p380), who discovered Pakal's tomb in 1952, lies under the trees in front of Templo XIII.

The **Templo de las Inscripciones** (Temple of the Inscriptions; Map p380), perhaps the most celebrated burial monument in the Americas, is the tallest and most stately of Palenque's buildings. Constructed on eight levels, the Templo de las Inscripciones has a central front staircase rising 25m to a series of small rooms. The tall roofcomb that once crowned it is long gone, but between the front doorways are stucco panels with reliefs of noble figures. On the interior rear wall are three panels with the long Maya inscription, recounting the history of Palenque and this building, for which Mexican archaeologist Alberto Ruz Lhuillier named the temple. From the top, interior stairs lead down into the tomb of Pakal (now closed to visitors indefinitely, to avoid further damage to its murals from the humidity inevitably exuded by visitors). Pakal's jewel-bedecked skeleton and jade mosaic death mask were removed from the tomb to Mexico City, and the tomb was recreated in the Museo Nacional de Antropología. The priceless death mask was stolen in an elaborate heist in 1985 (though recovered a few years afterwards), but the carved stone sarcophagus lid remains in the closed tomb – you can see a replica in the site museum.

➡ El Palacio

(Map p380) Diagonally opposite the Templo de las Inscripciones is El Palacio, a large

DIGGING DEEPER

Maya Exploration Center (www.mayaexploration.org) A group of archaeologists, academics and artists who work on Maya sciences such as astronomy and math and offer specialized tours.

Group of the Cross Project (www.mesoweb.com/palenque) A Palenque archaeologists' site with detailed findings from its landmark 1997–2002 dig.

INAH (www.inah.gob.mx) The Mexican national antiquities department posts recent news and discoveries, sometimes in English.

structure divided into four main courtyards, with a maze of corridors and rooms. Built and modified piecemeal over 400 years from the 5th century on, it was probably the residence of Palenque's rulers.

Its **tower** (Map p380), built in the 8th century by Ahkal Mo' Nahb' III and restored in 1955, has remnants of fine stucco reliefs on the walls, but you're not allowed to climb up inside it. Archaeologists believe the tower was constructed so that Maya royalty and priests could observe the sun falling directly into the Templo de las Inscripciones during the winter solstice.

The northeastern courtyard, the **Patio de los Cautivos** (Patio of the Captives), contains a collection of relief sculptures that seem disproportionately large for their setting; the theory is that they represent conquered rulers and were brought from elsewhere.

In the southern part of the complex, the extensive subterranean bathrooms included six toilets and a couple of sweat baths.

➡ Grupo de las Cruces

Pakal's son, Kan B'alam II, was a prolific builder, and soon after the death of his father started designing the temples of the Grupo de las Cruces (Group of the Crosses). All three main pyramid-shaped structures surround a plaza southeast of the Templo de las Inscripciones. They were all dedicated in AD 692 as a spiritual focal point for Palenque's triad of patron deities. The 'cross' carvings in some buildings here symbolize the ceiba tree, which in Maya belief held up the universe.

The **Templo del Sol** (Temple of the Sun; Map p380), on the west side of the plaza, has the best-preserved roofcomb at Palenque. Carvings inside, commemorating Kan B'alam's birth in AD 635 and accession in 684, show him facing his father. Some view this beautiful building as sure proof that Palenque's ancient architects were inspired by the local hallucinogenic mushrooms. Make up your own mind!

Steep steps climb to the **Templo de la Cruz** (Temple of the Cross; Map p380), the largest and most elegantly proportioned in this group. The stone tablet in the central sanctuary shows the lord of the underworld smoking tobacco on the right and Kan B'alam in full royal attire on the left. Behind is a reproduction of a panel depicting Kan B'alam's accession.

On the **Templo de la Cruz Foliada** (Temple of the Foliated Cross; Map p380), the corbel arches are fully exposed, revealing how Palenque's architects designed these buildings. A well-preserved inscribed tablet shows a king (probably Pakal) with a sun shield emblazoned on his chest, corn growing from his shoulder blades, and the sacred quetzal bird on his head.

➡ Acrópolis Sur

In the jungle south of the Grupo de las Cruces is the **Southern Acropolis**, where archaeologists have made some terrific finds in recent excavations. You may find part of the area roped off. The Acrópolis Sur appears to have been constructed as an extension of the Grupo de las Cruces, with both groups set around what was probably a single long open space.

Templo XVII (Map p380), between the Cruces group and the Acrópolis Sur, contains a reproduction carved panel depicting Kan B'alam, standing with a spear, with a bound captive kneeling before him (the original is in the site museum).

In 1999, in **Templo XIX** (Map p380), archaeologists made the most important Palenque find for decades: an 8th-century limestone platform with stunning carvings of seated figures and lengthy hieroglyphic texts that detail Palenque's origins. A reproduction has been placed inside Templo XIX. The central figure on the long south side of the platform is the ruler Ahkal Mo' Nahb' III, who was responsible for several of the buildings of the Acrópolis Sur, just as the Grupo de las Cruces was created by Kan B'alam II. Also on view is a wonderful reproduction of a tall stucco relief of U Pakal, the son of Ahkal Mo' Nahb'.

Also discovered in 1999, **Templo XX** (Map p380) contains a red frescoed tomb built in 540 that is currently Palenque's most active dig. Archaeologists began restoration work inside the tomb in 2012, and now believe that it might be the final resting place of K'uk B'alam I, an ancestor of Pakal.

In 2002 archaeologists found in **Templo XXI** (Map p380) a throne with very fine carvings depicting Ahkal Mo' Nahb', his ancestor the great Pakal, and his son U Pakal.

➡ Grupo Norte

North of El Palacio is a **Juego de Pelota** (Ball Court; Map p380) and the handsome buildings of the Northern Group. Crazy Count de Waldeck lived in the so-called **Templo del Conde** (Temple of the Count; Map p380), constructed in AD 647.

➡ Palenque Northeastern Groups

East of the Grupo Norte, the main path crosses Arroyo Otolum. Some 70m beyond the stream, a right fork will take you to **Grupo C**, a set of jungle-covered buildings and plazas thought to have been lived in from about AD 750 to 800.

If you stay on the main path, you'll descend some steep steps to a group of low, elongated buildings, probably occupied residentially from around AD 770 to 850. The path goes alongside the Arroyo Otolum, which here tumbles down a series of small falls forming natural bathing pools known as the **Baño de la Reina** (Queen's Bath). Unfortunately, one can't bathe here anymore.

The path then continues to another residential quarter, the **Grupo de los Murciélagos** (Bat Group), and then crosses the **Puente de los Murciélagos**, a footbridge across Arroyo Otolum.

Across the bridge and a bit further downstream, a path goes west to **Grupo 1** and **Grupo 2**, a short walk uphill. These ruins, only partly uncovered, are in a beautiful jungle setting. The main path continues downriver to the road, where the museum is a short distance along to the right.

Museo de Sitio MUSEUM

(Map p380; Carretera Palenque-Ruinas Km 7; admission free with ruins ticket; ⏲9am-4:30pm Tue-Sun) Palenque's site museum is worth a wander, displaying finds from the site and interpreting, in English and Spanish, Palenque's history. Highlights include a blissfully air-conditioned room displaying a copy of the lid of Pakal's sarcophagus (depicting his rebirth as the maize god, encircled by serpents, mythical monsters and glyphs recounting his reign) and finds from Templo XXI. Entry to the sarcophagus room permitted every half hour.

El Panchán NEIGHBORHOOD

(www.elpanchan.com; Carretera Palenque-Ruinas Km 4.5) Just off the road to the ruins, El Panchán is a legendary travelers' hangout, set in a patch of dense rainforest. It's the epicenter of Palenque's alternative scene and home to a bohemian bunch of Mexican and foreign residents and wanderers. Once ranchland, the area has been reforested by the remarkable Morales family, some of whom are among the leading archaeological experts on Palenque. El Panchán has several (mostly rustic) places to stay, a couple of restaurants, a set of sinuous streams rippling their way through every part of the property, nightly entertainment (and daily drumming practice), a meditation temple, a temascal (pre-Hispanic steam bath) and a constant stream of interesting visitors from all over the world.

☞ Tours

Numerous travel agencies in Palenque offer transportation packages to Agua Azul and Misol-Ha, to Bonampak, Yaxchilán and Lacanjá Chansayab, and to Flores, Guatemala. Agencies, mostly open from around 8am to 9pm daily, include: **Servicios Turísticos de Palenque** (Map p378; ☎916-345-13-40; www.stpalenque.com; Av 5 de Mayo), **Turística Maya Chiapas** (Map p378; ☎916-345-07-98; Av Juárez 123), **Viajes Kukulcán** (Map p378; ☎916-345-15-06; www.kukulcantravel.com; Av Juárez) and **Viajes Misol-Ha** (Map p378; ☎916-345-22-71; Av Juárez 148).

★Transportador Turística Scherrer & Barb TOUR

(Map p378; ☎cell phone 916-1033649; fermerida_69@hotmail.com; Av Juárez 1) Offers the most eclectic tours in town, including the remote Lacandón communities of Metzabok and Nahá (day trip M$1300, two days M$2300), Guatemala's Piedras Negras archaeological site (M$2300), and cool day trips off the Carretera Fronteriza like the Cascada de las Golondrinas, Cascada Welib-já and various bird-watching and kayaking destinations. All with a minimum of four people; English and Italian spoken.

Sleeping

The first choice to make is whether you want to stay in or out of Palenque town. Most out-of-town places, including El Panchán, are along the road to the ruins. Except for the leafy La Cañada area in the west, Palenque town is not particularly attractive, but if you stay here you'll have plenty of restaurants and services nearby.

Prices given here are for the high season, which is mid-July to mid-August and mid-December to early January, and Semana Santa. Rates drop by up to 35% at other times.

In Town

Yaxkin HOSTEL $
(Map p378; 916-345-01-02; www.hostalyaxkin.com; Prolongación Hidalgo 1; dm M$150, d without/with bathroom M$250/350, r with air-con & bathroom M$500;) Channeling laid-back El Panchán from pretty La Cañada, this former disco has been revamped into a modern hostel with a guest kitchen, ping-pong table, multiple lounges and a swank restaurant-bar and cafe. Rooms without air-con are monastic but funky. The fan-cooled dorms (one for women only) and private rooms with air-con feel more pleasant and comfortable.

Hotel Posada Tucán HOTEL $
(Map p378; 916-345-18-59; ismahpt@hotmail.com; Av 5 de Mayo 3; r M$200, r/tr/q with air-con M$300/350/450;) Textured walls sponged in crazy color combos (hot pink with purple! Superman blue and red!) spice up the fair-sized, basic and spotless rooms with TV and well-tiled bathrooms. Super-nice staff.

Hostal San Miguel HOTEL $
(Map p378; 916-345-01-52; hostalmiguel1@hotmail.com; Hidalgo 43; dm M$120, r/tr with fan M$400/450, r/tr with air-con M$500/550;) Who doesn't love a hotel with towel animals? A quiet and clean economical choice; rooms have good light and views from the upper floors. Dark two- and four-bed dorms don't have hot water or air-con, and all air-con rooms have two queen beds.

Hotel Lacandonia HOTEL $$
(Map p378; 916-345-00-57; Allende 77; s/d/tr/q M$500/600/700/750;) A modern hotel with a subtle splash of style. Tasteful airy rooms all have wrought-iron beds, reading lights and cable TV, and there's a good restaurant. The upstairs rooms facing the street have cute balconies and the best light.

Hotel Chan-Kah Centro HOTEL $$
(Map p378; 916-345-03-18; Av Juárez 2; s/d/tr/q M$450/600/750/800;) In the center and right on the park, this classy place has 17 air-conditioned and stone-adorned rooms with terraces and a park-view restaurant. The corner rooms are best. Wi-fi in the restaurant only.

Hotel Lacroix HOTEL $$
(Map p378; 916-345-15-35; www.lacroixhotel.wordpress.com; Hidalgo 10; r M$700-800;) This well-tended 16-room hotel near El Parque sports tasteful sponge-painted peach rooms – upper ones with small balconies – and attractive murals. There's a large pool with a tinted translucent roof, a casual restaurant and super-friendly service.

Hotel Maya Rue HOTEL $$
(Map p378; 916-345-07-43; maya_rue@hotmail.com; Aldama; r/tr M$700/800;) Tree-trunk beams and dramatic lighting add unexpected style to this 12-room offering combining traditional materials and industrial chic. Some rooms have shaded private balconies, but all are spacious and come with cable TV. Cafe on premises.

Hotel Xibalba HOTEL $$
(Map p378; 916-345-04-11; www.hotelxibalba.com; Merle Green 9, La Cañada; d/tr/q M$750/850/950;) Located in the tranquil neighborhood of La Cañada, this midrange hotel offers 35 pleasant, clean and tiled rooms with cable TV. Definite Maya theme here, with rock-accented architectural details, pastel colors and a replica of the lid from Pakal's sarcophagus on display. Restaurant on premises.

Hotel Palenque HOTEL $$
(Map p378; 916-345-01-03; www.hotelpalenque.com.mx; Av 5 de Mayo 15; d/q incl breakfast M$850/950;) All 28 rooms here are plain but very clean, and most have two queen beds. The upstairs rooms – off a breezy wide walkway – have gorgeous hill views. The fruit-tree garden, pretty terrace bar with pool and restaurant are all pleasant spots to relax.

Hotel Canek HOTEL $$
(Map p378; 916-345-01-50; www.hotelcanek.com; Av 20 de Noviembre 43; r/tr/f M$550/650/1500;) A good, well-maintained choice

with simple, good-sized rooms, though some are dark – get an upper one facing the street if you can. Fabulous rooftop terrace with *palapa* and hammocks.

Hotel Chablis HOTEL **$$$**
(Map p378; ☎916-345-08-70; www.hotelchablis.com; Merle Green 7, La Cañada; r/tr/q M$1250/1340/1490; P ⊕ ❄ @ ⇧ ≋) A new wing and sophisticated new restaurant have upped the offerings (and the prices) of this well-presented hotel. Each spacious room has one king- or two queen-sized beds and a balcony.

Hotel Maya Tulipanes HOTEL **$$$**
(Map p378; ☎800-714-47-10, 916-345-02-01; www.mayatulipanes.com.mx; Cañada 6, La Cañada; r/tr M$1450/1600; P ⊕ ❄ @ ⇧ ≋) Entered through a muraled foyer, this La Cañada hotel has large, comfortable, air-conditioned rooms with two wrought-iron double beds and minimalist decor. It's designed around a pretty garden with a small pool and restaurant. Contact for discounts.

Outside Town

While Palenque town hosts traffic and commerce, the surrounding area, especially between town and the ruins, offers some magical spots where howler monkeys romp in the tree canopy and unseen animals chirp after dark. The compound of El Panchán is a travelers' favorite, with low-key budget *cabañas* nestled in the stream-crossed jungle. Frequent daytime combis between town and the ruins will drop you off and pick you up anywhere along this road.

Margarita & Ed Cabañas GUESTHOUSE **$**
(☎cell phone 916-3486990; Carreterra Palenque-Ruinas Km 4.5, El Panchán; cabaña M$260, r with fan M$270-370, d/tr/q with air-con M$450/550/650; P ❄) With the most spotless digs in the jungle, Margarita has welcomed travelers to her exceptionally homey place for decades. Bright, clean and cheerful rooms have good mosquito netting, and the more rustic screened *cabañas* are well kept too, with reading lights and private bathrooms. There's free drinking water, a book exchange, and a lovely newer building with super-spacious rooms.

El Jaguar CABAÑAS **$**
(☎cell phone 916-1192829; www.elpanchan.com; El Panchán; campsite per person M$30, dm/s/d/tr M$80/150/250/300; P) Formerly known as Rakshita's, the no-frills Jaguar is a psychedelic fantasy of colorful murals and DIY construction. Dorm mosquito netting and ground-level room security are iffy; the two-story units are pretty groovy. All have hot water and fans.

Jungle Palace CABAÑAS **$**
(☎cell phone 916-1147420; www.elpanchan.com; El Panchán; s/d/tr M$200/250/300, without bathroom M$100/150/200) A basic option in El Panchán, the Jungle Palace offers rudimentary though well-screened and secure cabins with fans and hot water; some units back onto a stream. The best are freestanding, while others share walls and have less privacy.

Chato's Cabañas CABAÑAS **$**
(☎cell phone 916-1092829; www.elpanchan.com; El Panchán; s/d/tr/q M$220/300/400/450; P) Dotted around the Panchán jungle, Chato's wood and concrete cabins have sponge-painted walls, decorative window bars, fans and well-screened windows, and some include nice little porches.

Jardines La Aldea HOTEL **$$**
(☎916-345-16-93; www.hotellaaldea.net; Carretera Palenque-Ruinas Km 2.8; r M$1100-1200; P ❄ ⇧ ≋) The four-star Aldea has 33 large, beautiful and bright *palapa*-roofed rooms set amidst lovely grounds. Each room has an outside terrace with hammock. It's a stylish place, with a peaceful hilltop restaurant and a wonderful pool area. There are no TVs, making it an ideal place to get away from it all.

Mayabell HOTEL, CAMPGROUND **$$**
(☎cell phone 916-3416977; www.mayabell.com.mx; Carretera Palenque-Ruinas Km 6; campsites per person M$60, vehicle site with hookups M$180, cabaña without bathroom M$300, r with fan/air-con M$750/950; P ❄ ⇧ ≋) With a sprawling jungle-side pool frequented by monkeys, this spacious grassy campground has tons of clean and comfortable sleeping options, plus an enjoyable restaurant. Rooms with air-con are very homey and comfortable; those with fan are more basic, as are the shared bathrooms. It's just 400m from Palenque's site museum.

Cabañas Safari CABAÑAS **$$**
(☎916-345-00-26; www.cabanasafari.com.mx; Carretera Palenque-Ruinas Km 1; camping per person without/with gear M$100/150, d bungalow without bathroom M$250, r/tr M$950/1070; P ❄ ⇧ ≋) Comfort and connectivity aren't sacrificed

at these jungly *palapa*-roofed cabañas with air-con, private porches, flat-screen TV and in-room wi-fi. Rocks, tree branches and wall murals give personality to the spacious (including some two-level) air-con rooms; three circular fan-cooled bungalows are teeny tiny. There's a plunge pool, temascal and full restaurant, plus a paintball course in the works.

★Boutique Hotel Quinta Chanabnal BOUTIQUE HOTEL **$$$**
(☎916-345-53-20; www.quintachanabnal.com; Carretera Palenque-Ruinas Km 2.2; r US$177, ste US$295-413; P❄🛜🏊) The Maya-inspired architecture and impeccable service at this decadent boutique hotel will leave you swooning. Enter through heavy wood doors carved by local artisans into spacious stone-floor suites that contain majestically draped four-poster beds and cavernous bathrooms. Water features on the premises include a creek, a small lagoon and a multitiered swimming pool.

Massages, a temascal and a fine restaurant are available. The Italian owner, a Maya expert, also speaks German, French, English and Spanish.

Piedra de Agua BOUTIQUE HOTEL **$$$**
(☎916-345-08-42; www.palenque.piedradeagua.com; Carretera Palenque-Ruinas Km 2.5; r US$150; P⊖🛜🏊) Spare off-white-and-wood minimalism marks this new designer *cabaña* compound that pampers guests with oodles of bath products, plush robes, private terrace tubs and hammocks outside every room, but no air-con. Breakfast, a bar and massages are available, though the lap pool and Jacuzzi are the most popular amenities.

Chan-Kah Resort Village RESORT **$$$**
(☎916-345-11-00; www.chan-kah.com.mx;Carretera Palenque-Ruinas Km 3; r/tr/q M$1770/1890/2010, ste M$2340-4330; P⊖❄@🛜🏊) Swimmers will go woozy contemplating the Chan-Kah's stupendous 70m stone-lined swimming pool in lush jungle gardens. A large quality resort on the road to the ruins, it has handsome well-spaced wood-and-stone cottages with generous bathrooms, ceiling fans, terrace and air-con. It's rarely busy, except when tour groups block-book the place.

Eating

Palenque is definitely not the gastronomic capital of Mexico. There's a decent variety of restaurants, though some are laughably overpriced. A number of inexpensive stands and sit-down spots can be found near the AEXA bus terminal and on the east side of El Parque in front of the church.

★Don Mucho's MEXICAN, INTERNATIONAL **$**
(Carretera Palenque-Ruinas Km 4.5, El Panchán; mains M$40-130; ⏲7am-11pm) The hot spot of El Panchán, popular Don Mucho's provides great-value meals in a jungly setting, with a candlelit ambience at night. Busy waiters bring pasta, fish, meat, plenty of *antojitos,* and pizzas (cooked in a purpose-built Italian-designed wood-fired oven) that are some of the finest this side of Naples.

Live music – usually *andina, cumbia* or Cuban – starts around 8pm Friday through Sunday (at 9:30pm other nights), plus there's a rousing fire-dancing show most nights at 11pm.

Café de Yara CAFE **$**
(Map p378; Hidalgo 66; breakfasts M$45-85, mains M$65-125; ⏲7am-11pm; 🛜) A sunny start to the day, this modern and beautiful corner cafe has great breakfasts and excellent organic Chiapan coffee. On Friday and Saturday evenings in high season, the lights get intimate and diners are serenaded with salsa, *trova* and other live music.

Café Jade MEXICAN, CHIAPANECO **$**
(Map p378; Prolongación Hidalgo 1; breakfast M$38-57, mains M$45-79; ⏲7am-11pm; 🛜) A chill indoor/outdoor spot on the ground floor of the Yaxkin hostel, with long sofa seating at tree plank tables. Good for breakfast, Chiapan specialties and chicken dishes.

Abarrotes Monterrey SUPERMARKET **$**
(Map p378; Av 5 de Mayo; ⏲7am-9pm) The largest supermarket in the center, but no fresh produce.

Restaurant Las Tinajas MEXICAN **$$**
(Map p378; cnr Av 20 de Noviembre & Abasolo; mains M$80-110; ⏲7am-11pm) It doesn't take long to figure out why this place is always busy. It slings enormous portions of excellent home-style food – enough to keep you (and possibly another person) fueled up for hours. *Pollo a la veracruzana* (chicken in a tomato/olives/onion sauce) and *camarones al guajillo* (shrimp with a not-too-hot type of chili) are both delicious, as is the house salsa.

La Selva MEXICAN **$$**
(☎916-345-03-63; Hwy 199; mains M$70-195; ⏲11:30am-11:30pm) Palenque's most upscale

restaurant serves up well-prepared steaks, seafood, salads and *antojitos* under an enormous *palapa* roof, with jungle-themed stained-glass panels brightening one wall. Try the *pigua* (freshwater lobster) when it's available in the fall. Reserve ahead in high season.

Restaurant Maya Cañada MEXICAN $$
(Map p378; Merle Green s/n; breakfast M$75-105, mains M$70-188; ⏲7am-11pm; 📶) This relatively upmarket and professionally run restaurant in the shady La Cañada area serves fine steaks, regional specialties and terrific seafood kebabs. It's open to the air and has a cool upstairs terrace.

Drinking & Nightlife

Palenque doesn't have much of a nightlife scene. In the evenings, you'll often spot more travelers waiting for a night bus than out on the town. Along the ruins road, you can listen to live music at Mayabell, and Don Mucho's has hip-swinging live ensembles plus fire dancers performing nightly. In town, the **Aluxes** (Map p378; Av Juárez 49; mains M$80-125; ⏲3pm-midnight) restaurant serves interesting cocktails and has live *trova* music Friday through Sunday from 9pm on; some options can also be found by poking around La Cañada. Bars in the center tend toward the unsavory.

Italian Coffee Company CAFE
(Map p378; cnr Jiménez & Reforma; ⏲8am-11pm; 📶) Weary traveler, welcome to air-conditioned nirvana.

Information

EMERGENCIES

The **Fiscalía** (☎916-345-15-40; cnr Corregidora & Jiménez; ⏲9am-3pm & 6-9pm Mon-Fri, 10am-2pm & 6-9pm Sat & Sun, 24hr next door for emergencies) is the place to report crimes against tourists. Translators available.

IMMIGRATION

Instituto Nacional de Migración (⏲24hr) About 1.5km north of town on Hwy 199; hail a *colectivo* taxi (M$7) that's headed in that direction.

INTERNET ACCESS

There are loads of internet cafes in town (nothing is available at El Panchán); rates run M$8 to M$10 per hour. The main plaza, El Parque, is a free wi-fi hot spot.

Ciber Encuentro (Hidalgo btwn Abasolo & Independencia; ⏲8am-10pm)

Ciber Vlos (Av Juárez 133; ⏲8am-10pm)

MEDICAL SERVICES

Clínica Palenque (Velasco Suárez 33; ⏲8:30am-1:30pm & 5-9pm) Dr Alfonso Martínez speaks English.

MONEY

Both of these banks change dollars and euros (bring a copy of your passport).

Banco Azteca (Av Juárez, btwn Allende & Aldama; ⏲9am-9pm daily)

Bancomer (Av Juárez 96; ⏲8:30am-4pm Mon-Fri) Also has an ATM.

POST

Post Office (Map p378; Independencia; ⏲8am-8:30pm Mon-Fri, to noon Sat)

TELEPHONE

There are numerous *casetas* (phone centers) charging M$2 per minute to the US and M$5 per minute for other international calls.

TOURIST INFORMATION

Municipal tourist information kiosk (Map p378; El Parque; ⏲9am-2pm & 6-9pm Mon-Fri)

Tourist Information Office (Map p378; cnr Av Juárez & Abasolo; ⏲9am-9pm Mon-Sat, 9am-1pm Sun) The state tourism office's help center has the most reliable town, regional and transportation information, as well as maps. Its regional office (☎916-345-03-56; ⏲8am-4pm Mon-Fri), outside the center, can answer questions by phone.

Getting There & Away

AIR

In 2014, Palenque's long-deserted airport finally opened to commercial flights. Interjet kicked off a twice-weekly service to Mexico City, though frequency could increase and other routes may be added if there's sufficient demand. Otherwise, the closest major airport is Villahermosa; ADO runs a direct airport service in comfortable minibuses.

PALENQUE BUS WARNING

It's best to travel the winding stretch of road between Palenque and San Cristóbal during daylight, as highway holdups – though by no means common – do occasionally occur. There have also been recent reports of thefts on the night bus from Mérida. When taking buses along these routes, consider stowing valuables in the checked luggage compartment.

BUSES FROM PALENQUE

DESTINATION	FARE (M$)	DURATION	FREQUENCY (DAILY)
Campeche	300	5-5½hr	4 ADO
Cancún	250-684	12-13½hr	4 ADO, 2 AEXA
Mérida	448	8hr	4 ADO
Mexico City (1 TAPO & 1 Norte)	922-934	13½hr	2 ADO
Oaxaca	672	15hr	1 ADO
Ocosingo	65-128	2½hr	4 ADO, 5 AEXA, very frequent vans
San Cristóbal de las Casas	110-312	5hr	5 ADO, 5 AEXA
Tulum	584-694	10-11hr	4 ADO
Tuxtla Gutiérrez	150-272	6½hr	5 ADO, 5 AEXA
Villahermosa	65-134	2½hr	17 ADO, 16 AEXA
Villahermosa airport	236	2¼hr	12 ADO

BUS

In a new spacious new location behind the Maya head statue, **ADO** (Map p378; ☎916-345-13-44) has the main bus terminal, with deluxe and 1st-class services, an ATM and left-luggage facilities; it's also used by OCC (1st class). It's a good idea to buy your outward bus ticket a day in advance.

AEXA (Map p378; ☎916-345-26-30; www.autobusesaexa.com.mx; Av Juárez 159), with 1st-class buses, and Cardesa (2nd class) is about 300m east on Avenida Juárez.

COLECTIVOS

Vans to Ocosingo (M$50) wait on Calle 5a Poniente Sur and leave when full.

Many combis for destinations along the Carretera Fronteriza (including Lacanjá Chansayab, Bonampak, Yaxchilán and Benemérito de las Américas) and for Pico de Oro leave from an outdoor *colectivo* terminal (Map p378) just south of the new ADO bus station. See Getting There & Away (p389) and individual destinations for specific information.

Getting Around

Taxis charge M$50 (up to M$60 at night) to El Panchán or Mayabell, and M$60 to the ruins. Combis (M$20) from the center ply the ruins road til dark. **Radio Taxis Santo Domingo** (☎916-345-01-26) has on-call service.

Bonampak, Yaxchilán & the Carretera Fronteriza

The ancient Maya cities of Bonampak and Yaxchilán, southeast of Palenque, are easily accessible thanks to the Carretera Fronteriza (Hwy 307), a good paved road running parallel to the Mexico–Guatemala border, all the way from Palenque to the Lagos de Montebello, around the fringe of the Lacandón Jungle. Nights here are wonderfully quiet, the sky screaming with stars and the ground twinkling with fireflies. Bonampak, famous for its frescoes, is 152km by road from Palenque; the bigger and more important Yaxchilán, with a peerless jungle setting beside the broad and swift Río Usumacinta, is 173km by road, then about 22km by boat.

The Carretera Fronteriza is the main thoroughfare connecting a number of excellent ecotourism projects, dreamy waterfalls, Lacandón villages and lesser-known archaeological ruins. It's also the main route from Chiapas to Guatemala's northern Petén region (home of several major Maya sites, including mighty Tikal) via the town of Frontera Corozal. Phones in this region usually have satellite service or Guatemala-based numbers.

Tours

Organized tours can be helpful in this region if you have limited time and aren't driving. Always check package inclusions and exclusions, so you can plan your meals and park fees. The standard tours (including entry fees and some meals) per person offered by Palenque travel agencies:

- Bonampak and Yaxchilán day trips (M$650 to M$700) usually include two meals and transportation in an air-conditioned van – a good deal since independent transportation to both is time-consuming and tours include the Bonampak transportation fee; two-day trips (M$1300 to M$1400) include an overnight stay at Lacanjá Chansayab

➡ Transportation to Flores, Guatemala (M$350 to M$450, 10 to 11 hours) by van to Frontera Corozal, river launch up the Usumacinta to Bethel in Guatemala, and public bus on to Flores

➡ Flores via Bonampak and Yaxchilán (M$1200 to M$1400, two days) with an overnight in Lacanjá Chansayab

In Palenque, Transportador Turística Scherrer & Barb (p383) organizes more off-the-beaten-path trips to the region, including the Lacandón villages of Nahá and Metzabok and waterfalls in the area; San Cristóbal-based SendaSur (p363) can help with reservations for independent travelers.

Information

DANGERS & ANNOYANCES

Drug and human trafficking are facts of life in this border region, and the Carretera Fronteriza more or less encircles the main area of Zapatista rebel activity and support, so expect numerous military checkpoints along the road and from this area to Palenque and Comitán. These checkpoints generally increase security for travelers, but don't tempt easy theft by leaving money or valuables unattended during stops. For your own security, it's best to be off the Carretera Fronteriza before dusk. For similar reasons all border crossings with Guatemala are places you should aim to get through early in the day.

In the rainy months of September and October, rivers are usually too swollen for safe swimming.

Don't forget insect repellent.

Getting There & Away

From Palenque, Autotransporte Chamoán runs vans to Frontera Corozal (M$100, 2½ to three hours, every 40 minutes from 4am to 5pm), leaving from the outdoor *colectivo* terminal nearby the Maya head statue and south of the bus station. Use it for visits to Bonampak and Lancanjá Chansayab, because upon request the drivers will stop at the junction closest to the ruins, known as Crucero Bonampak (M$80, two hours), instead of the San Javier stop on the highway.

Línea Comitán Lagos de Montebello (☎916-345-12-60; Velasco Suárez btwn Calles Calles 6a & 7a Poniente Norte), west of Palenque market, runs hourly vans to Benemérito de las Américas (M$100) 10 times daily (3:30am to 2:45pm), with most continuing around the Carretera Fronteriza to the Lagos de Montebello (M$260, seven hours to Tziscao) and Comitán (M$275, eight hours).

> **HORA DE DIOS**
>
> This part of Mexico tends to ignore daylight saving time, as do *colectivo* companies that originate in cities like Comitán and Palenque that service the region. From April through October, check your watch against the company's to double-check transportation schedules. If they're using 'God's time,' you'll be departing an hour later than the official 'government time.'

Both companies stop at San Javier (M$60, two hours), the turnoff for Lacanjá Chansayab and Bonampak, 140km from Palenque, and at Crucero Corozal (M$90, 2½ hours), the intersection for Frontera Corozal. For Cascada Wejlib-Já and Nueva Palestina, take any Carretera Fronteriza-bound combi from Palenque.

Gas stations along the Carretera Fronteriza are limited. From Palenque to Comitán (via the Chajul cutoff road) you'll find them in Chancalá and Benemérito only, but plenty of entrepreneurial locals sell reasonably priced gasoline from large plastic containers. Look for homemade '*Se vende gasolina*' signs.

Palenque to Bonampak

Cascada Wejlib-Já WATERFALL

(admission M$20; ⏲7:30am-7pm) Thirty kilometers from Palenque, these 25m-high curtains of water aren't the most dramatic water features in the area, but the turquoise river pools make excellent swimming spots. Amenities include a cross-river zip-line (M$40) and a simple restaurant. From Palenque, take a combi to the well-signed highway entrance (M$30, 30 minutes); it's a 700m walk in.

Cascada de las Golondrinas WATERFALL

(Nueva Palestina; admission M$20, campsite M$50; ⏲restaurant 9am-4pm) A lovely water feature tucked 10km off the highway, two rivers cascade dramatically from a high point of 35m and you can swim in clear blue water during the dry season. A wooden boardwalk crosses the outflow, and at dusk hundreds of swallows duck in to bed down in a cave beneath the falls, streaming out at dawn.

From Palenque, take a combi to the turnoff for Nueva Palestina (M$50, two hours), where taxis charge M$100 one-way to the falls. Arrange a return pickup. Drivers should go 9km toward Nueva Palestina to the signed turnoff; the falls are another 1km in.

Plan de Ayutla ARCHAEOLOGICAL SITE

(near Nueva Palestina) The remote Maya ruins of Plan de Ayutla sit on an evocatively overgrown 24 hectare site, with buildings in various states of excavation and abandonment. From the dirt lot under dense tree canopy, follow a winding path up the rise to the **North Acropolis**, one of three constructed on natural hills. Visitors can explore a maze of interconnected rooms over four levels of the former residential palace complex.

The most significant building in this acropolis is **Structure 13**, a dramatically vaulted structure with an exterior decorated with unique stepped apron moldings. It was here that archaeologists recently discovered an astronomical observatory with two upper rooms containing window channels aligned to view the winter solstice and the solar zenith.

Plan de Ayutla was inhabited between 150 BC and AD 1000 and is believed to have been a regional seat of power between 250 BC and AD 700. Based on its size and features, including its ball court – at 65m long the largest in the upper Usumacinta River region – archaeologists have two theories about the site's history. One hypothesis is that it was the city of Sak T'zi' (White Dog), which battled Toniná, Yaxchilán and Piedras Negras – and whose bloody defeat by Bonampak may be depicted in that site's famed murals, or perhaps it is the ancient city of Ak'e' (Turtle), where the royalty of Bonampak originated.

By car, drive 11km into Nueva Palestina from the highway; when the paved road turns left next to a clutch of lodgings signs, continue straight onto a gravel road. At about 4.5km, follow the signed left at the junction (the right turn goes to the village of Plan de Ayutla, not the ruins) and then travel another 3km to the clearly visible site. *Ejido* representatives, if present, may charge a small fee. Arriving by combi at the Nueva

OFF THE BEATEN TRACK

METZABOK & NAHÁ

Situated in the Lacandón Jungle between Ocosingo and the Carretera Fronteriza town of Chancalá, the small and isolated Lacandón villages of Metzabok and Nahá straddle a network of underground rivers in a protected biodiversity zone that's home to wildlife including jaguars, tapirs, howler monkeys and ocelots. Inhabitants here still follow many Lacandón traditions and customs.

The main Lacandón settlement of Nahá contains the lodgings of **Centro Ecoturístico Nahá** (☎55-5150-5953; www.nahaecoturismo.com; r without bathroom M$350, 1-/2-bedroom cabaña M$750/950), with simple well-screened rooms or startlingly luxurious *cabañas* with hot-water bathrooms. A creekside village **restaurant** (breakfast M$55, lunch or dinner M$90) serves Mexican and traditional Lacandón dishes. With a guide (one/two hours M$350/650), you can travel on foot or by canoe to various lagoons and learn about the area's flora and fauna.

In Metzabok, villagers offer *lancha* trips (up to M$650 per boat) along forest-ringed Laguna Tzibana, where you can see a moss-framed limestone wall painted with vivid red prehistoric pictograms, and hike to a lookout point above the tree canopy. Unless you want to camp (M$50 per person) and have your own transportation, Metzabok is best for a day trip, as its *cabaña* accommodations aren't well-tended, public transportation is iffy and food can be scarce.

From Palenque, **Transportes Pajchiltic** (Map p136; Av 15 de Marzo) vans leave for Metzabok (M$40, three hours) and Nahá (M$50, four hours) at 9am, 11am (sometimes) and 2pm. The solitary departure back leaves Nahá at 1am and Metzabok at 3am (ouch!). Schedules don't use daylight saving time in either direction. Note that service to Metzabok is unreliable in both directions; it will stop at the junction (6km away) if the driver decides there aren't enough passengers to bother with the detour.

From Ocosingo, trucks to Nahá (M$50, 2½ hour, 11am and noon) leave from a walled lot behind the market.

Palestina highway turnoff, you can negotiate a taxi fare with waiting time.

Bonampak

Bonampak's setting in dense jungle hid it from the outside world until 1946. Stories of how it was revealed are full of mystery and innuendo, but it seems that Charles Frey, a young WWII conscientious objector from the US, and John Bourne, heir to the Singer sewing-machine fortune, were the first outsiders to visit the site when Chan Bor, a Lacandón, took them there in February 1946. Later in 1946 a photographer from the US, Giles Healey, was also led to the site by Chan Bor and found the Templo de las Pinturas, with its famous murals.

The site of **Bonampak** (admission M$46; ⊙8am-4:30pm) spreads over 2.4 sq km, but all the main ruins stand around the rectangular Gran Plaza. Never a major city, Bonampak spent most of the Classic period in Yaxchilán's sphere of influence. The most impressive surviving monuments were built under Chan Muwan II, a nephew of Yaxchilán's Itzamnaaj B'alam II, who acceded to Bonampak's throne in AD 776. The 6m-high **Stele 1** in the Gran Plaza depicts Chan Muwan II holding a ceremonial staff at the height of his reign. He also features in **Stele 2** and **Stele 3** on the Acrópolis, which rises from the south end of the plaza.

However, it's the vivid frescoes inside the modest-looking **Templo de las Pinturas** (Edificio 1) that have given Bonampak its fame – and its name, which means 'Painted Walls' in Yucatecan Maya. Some archaeologists theorize that the murals depict a battle between Bonampak and the city of Sak T'zi', which is believed to be Plan de Ayutla.

Diagrams outside the temple help interpret these murals, which are the finest known from pre-Hispanic America, but which have weathered badly since their discovery. (Early visitors even chucked kerosene over the walls in an attempt to bring out the colors!) Room 1, on the left as you face the temple, shows the consecration of Chan Muwan II's infant son, who is seen held in arms toward the top of the right end of the room's south wall (facing you as you enter). Witnessing the ceremony are 14 jade-toting noblemen. The central Room 2 shows tumultuous battle scenes on its east and south walls and vault, while on the north wall Chan Muwan II, in jaguar-skin battle dress, presides over the torture (by finger-

Bonampak

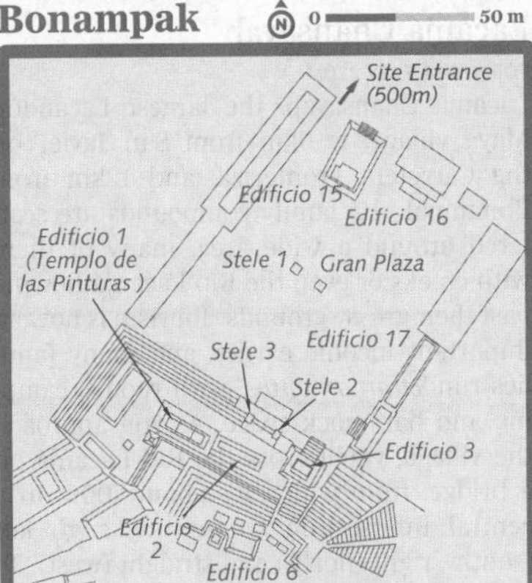

nail removal) and sacrifice of prisoners. A severed head lies below him, beside the foot of a sprawling captive. Recently restored and now blazing with vivid color, Room 3 shows a celebratory dance on the Acrópolis steps by lords wearing huge headdresses, and on its east wall three white-robed women puncture their tongues in a ritual bloodletting. The sacrifices, the bloodletting and the dance may all have been part of the ceremonies surrounding the new heir.

In reality, the infant prince probably never got to rule Bonampak; the place was abandoned before the murals were finished, as Classic Maya civilization evaporated.

Don't forget to look up at the intricately carved lintels when entering Edificios 1 and 6.

The Bonampak site abuts the Reserva de la Biosfera Montes Azules, and is rich in wildlife. Drinks and snacks are sold at the entrance to the Monumento Natural Bonampak protected zone, 8km before the ruins, and by the archaeological site entrance.

Getting There & Away

Bonampak is 12km from San Javier, the turnoff town on the Carretera Fronteriza. If you get dropped off at San Javier instead of Crucero Bonampak (8km further in) taxis from San Javier charge M$20.

Get ready to open your wallet: the community charges M$20 per person to enter the town of Lacanjá, and private vehicles are prohibited beyond the Crucero Bonampak, where van drivers charge an exorbitant M$150 round-trip per van to the ruins and back.

Lacanjá Chansayab

POP 380 / ELEV 320M

Lacanjá Chansayab, the largest Lacandón Maya village, is 6km from San Javier on the Carretera Fronteriza, and 12km from Bonampak. Its family compounds are scattered around a wide area, many of them with creeks or even the Río Lacanjá flowing past their grassy grounds. Tourism is now an important income earner, and many families run '*campamentos*' with rooms, camping and hammock space. As you approach the village, you'll cross the Río Lacanjá on a bridge, from which it's about 700m to a central intersection where tracks go left (south), right (north) and straight (west). To the west, there's an air-conditioned **internet café** (per hour M$15; ⏲8am-9pm) in the compound of Campamento Vicente Paniagua.

The *campamentos* all offer guided walks through the surrounding forests to the 8m-high, 30m-wide **Cascada Ya Toch Kusam** waterfall, some partially unearthed ancient Maya **Lacanjá ruins**, and the 2.5km-long **Laguna Lacanjá**. The waterfall can actually be reached by a self-guided trail, the 2.5km **Sendero Ya Toch Kusam** (admission M$35), which starts 200m west from the central intersection. To continue from the falls to the ruins (a further 2km or so), you do need a guide. A typical three-hour guided walk to the falls and ruins costs M$250 to M$500 per group, plus the admission fee for the trail.

The Lacandón people are amiable and welcoming, but you'll need to dig deeper to see evidence of their old way of life: the villagers here are now predominantly Presbyterian and attuned to the modern world, and only some wear the traditional long white Lacandón tunic.

Sleeping & Eating

Rates dip at least 10% outside high season.

Cabañas Los Tulipanes CABAÑAS $

(☎community phone 55-5151-2253; d/q M$350/750) This new place just right at the central town intersection has a cute garden, a large porch and three sunny two-queen rooms with garishly colored mosquito nets and shower curtains for bathroom doors.

THE LACANDÓN JUNGLE

Chiapas contains swathes of wild green landscape that have nourished its inhabitants for centuries. But this rich trove of natural resources also makes it a contentious prize in the struggle for its water, lumber and oil and gas reserves.

The Selva Lacandona (Lacandón Jungle), in eastern Chiapas, occupies just 0.25% of Mexico. Yet it contains more than 4300 plant species (about 17% of the Mexican total), 450 butterfly species (42% of the national total), at least 340 bird species (32% of the total) and 163 mammal species (30% of the Mexican total). Among these are such emblematic creatures as the jaguar, red macaw, white turtle, tapir and harpy eagle.

This great fund of natural resources and genetic diversity is the southwest end of the Selva Maya, a 30,000-sq-km corridor of tropical rainforest stretching from Chiapas across northern Guatemala into Belize and the southern Yucatán. But the Lacandón Jungle is shrinking fast, under pressure from ranchers, loggers, oil prospectors, and farmers desperate for land. From around 15,000 sq km in the 1950s, an estimated 3000 to 4500 sq km of jungle remains today. Waves of land-hungry settlers deforested the northern third of the Lacandón Jungle by about 1960. Also badly deforested are the far eastern Marqués de Comillas area (settled since the 1970s) and Las Cañadas, between Ocosingo and Montes Azules. Most of what's left is in the Reserva de la Biosfera Montes Azules and the neighboring Reserva de la Biosfera Lacan-tun.

The Mexican government deeded a large section of the land to a small number of Lacandón families in the 1970s, creating tensions with other indigenous communities whose claims were put aside. Land within the region remains incredibly contested. Lacandones and their advocates consider themselves to be an environmentally sensitive indigenous group defending their property against invasive settlers. Other communities within the reserve, who provide some of the Zapatista rebels' strongest support, view it as an obfuscated land grab and pretext for eviction under the guise of environmental protection. Zapatista supporters also argue that the settlers are using the forests in sustainable ways, and claim that the government seeks to exploit the forests for bioprospecting (patenting) traditional plants.

Campamento Río Lacanjá CABAÑAS $$
(www.ecochiapas.com/lacanja; dm M$162, r/tr/q without bathroom M$550/650/750, Ya'ax Can r/tr/q M$750/850/950, restaurant mains M$60-75; P) About 2km south of the central intersection, these rustic semi-open-air wood-framed cabins with mosquito nets stand close to the jungle-shrouded Río Lacanjá and are open to the sights and sounds of the forest and river. A separate group of large rooms with fans, called Cabañas Ya'ax Can, have two solid wooden double beds, tile floors and a hot-water bathroom.

As well as guided walks, **rafting trips** on the Río Lacanjá – which has waterfalls up to 2.5m high but no rapids – are offered for a minimum of four people. A half-day outing including Lacanjá ruins and Cascada Ya Toch Kusam (both reached on foot from the river) costs M$500 per group (up to 10 people), and overnight rafting and camping trips also visiting the Bonampak ruins are around M$1250 per person. Rafting trips and tours based at Campamento Río Lacanjá can be reserved through Explora (p363) in San Cristóbal.

Campamento Topche CABAÑAS $$
(campamento-topche@hotmail.com; r/tr without bathroom M$400/500, r/tr M$600/900, cabañas M$1000; P ⊖ ᯤ) About 550m west of the central intersection, this *campamento* has a few options: comfortable rooms with terracotta tile floors and a vaulted and mosquito-proofed *palapa* roof; wood-cabin rooms with shared bathroom, mosquito nets and walls that don't reach the ceiling; and detached jungly *cabañas* next to the river. All have hot water. Satellite wi-fi is available for M$20 per hour.

Signs to here also say 'Campamento Enrique Paniagua.' His daughter runs a good garden **restaurant** (meals M$80; ⏲7am-9pm) next door.

Getting There & Away

For transportation from Palenque, see Getting There & Away (p389). The community collects M$20 per person at the town entrance. If you're traveling from Yaxchilán, combis charge M$40 between Crucero Corozal and San Javier.

Frontera Corozal

POP 5200 / ELEV 200M

This riverside frontier town (formerly Frontera Echeverría) is the stepping-stone to the beautiful ruins of Yaxchilán, and is on the main route between Chiapas and Guatemala's Petén region. Inhabited mainly by Chol Maya, who settled here in the 1970s, Frontera Corozal is 16km by paved road from Crucero Corozal junction on the Carretera Fronteriza. The broad Río Usumacinta, flowing swiftly between jungle-covered banks, forms the Mexico–Guatemala border here.

Long, fast, outboard-powered *lanchas* come and go from the river *embarcadero*. Almost everything you'll need is on the paved street leading back from the river here – including the **immigration office** (⏲8am-6pm), 400m from the *embarcadero*, where you should hand in/obtain a tourist permit if you're leaving for/arriving from Guatemala.

Museo de la Cuenca del Usumacinta MUSEUM
(Museum of the Usumacinta Basin; admission M$20; ⏲8am-3pm) The Museo de la Cuenca del Usumacinta, opposite the immigration office, has good examples of Chol Maya dress, and some information in Spanish on the area's postconquest history, but pride of place goes to two fine and intricately carved steles retrieved from the nearby site of Dos Caobas. If it's not open, inquire at the Restaurante Imperio Maya next door.

Sleeping & Eating

Escudo Jaguar CABAÑAS $$
(☎in Guatemala 502-5353-5637; www.escudojaguarhotel.com; campsite per person M$100, d cabaña without bathroom M$280-345, d cabaña M$579-870, tr cabaña M$1059, restaurant mains M$42-95, breakfasts M$31-64; P) Often used by tour groups, Escudo Jaguar overlooks the river 300m from the *embarcadero*. Its solidly built thatched *cabañas* are all kept spotless, and come equipped with fan and mosquito netting. The best are very spacious and have hot showers and terraces strung with hammocks. The restaurant serves straightforward, but well-prepared Mexican dishes.

Nueva Alianza CABAÑAS $$
(☎in Guatemala 502-4638-2447; www.hotelnuevaalianza.com; campsite per person M$50, s/d without bathroom M$150/300, r M$600-700, f M$800; P ᯤ) Friendly Nueva Alianza, among trees 150m along a side road from the museum, has small, plain but cheerful budget rooms with wooden walls that don't reach the ceiling, and newer stand-alone rooms with bathrooms. All have fans, good wooden

furniture and hot water. There's a good on-site **restaurant** (mains M$80, breakfast M$70) and the only internet access in town (M$15 per hour or M$50 per day).

Getting There & Away

If you can't get a bus or combi direct to Frontera Corozal, get one to Crucero Corozal, 16km southeast of San Javier on the Carretera Fronteriza, where taxis (M$30 per person *colectivo*) run to Frontera Corozal. The *ejido* hits up visitors entering or leaving Frontera Corozal for a M$15 per person toll; keep your ticket for exiting unless you're continuing on to Guatemala.

Autotransporte Chamoán vans run hourly from Frontera Corozal *embarcadero* to Palenque (M$100, 2½ to three hours), with the last departure at 4pm or when full.

Lancha organizations have desks in a thatched building near the *embarcadero*, and all charge about the same prices for service to Bethel, Guatemala (boat for 1-3/4/5-7/8-10 people M$400/500/600/750), which is 40 minutes upstream. From Bethel, hourly buses depart to Flores (4½ hours) from 8am to 4pm. Make sure the driver stops at the Bethel immigration office.

Yaxchilán

Jungle-shrouded **Yaxchilán** (admission M$55; 8am-4:30pm, last entry 3:30pm) has a terrific setting above a horseshoe loop in the Río Usumacinta. The location gave it control over river commerce, and along with a series of successful alliances and conquests, made Yaxchilán one of the most important Classic Maya cities in the Usumacinta region. Archaeologically, Yaxchilán is famed for its ornamented facades and roofcombs, and its impressive stone lintels carved with conquest and ceremonial scenes. A flashlight is helpful for exploring parts of the site.

Howler monkeys *(saraguates)* inhabit the tall trees here, and are an evocative highlight. You'll almost certainly hear their visceral roars, and you stand a good chance of seeing some. Spider monkeys, and occasionally red macaws, can also be spotted here at times.

Yaxchilán peaked in power and splendor between AD 681 and 800 under the rulers Itzamnaaj B'alam II (Shield Jaguar II, 681–742), Pájaro Jaguar IV (Bird Jaguar IV, 752–68) and Itzamnaaj B'alam III (Shield Jaguar III, 769–800). The city was abandoned around AD 810. Inscriptions here tell more about its 'Jaguar' dynasty than is known of almost any other Maya ruling clan. The shield-and-jaguar symbol appears on many Yaxchilán buildings and steles; Pájaro Jaguar IV's hieroglyph is a small jungle cat with feathers on its back and a bird superimposed on its head.

Yaxchilán

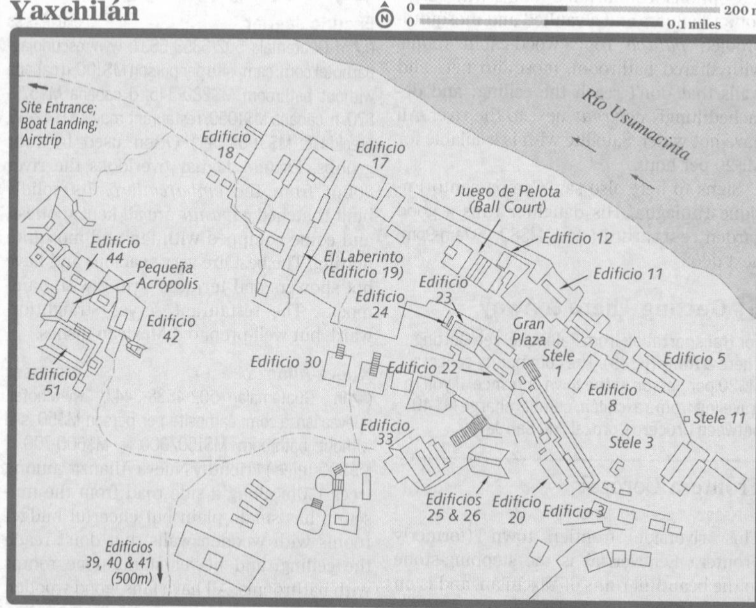

At the site, drinks are sold at a shack near the river landing. Most of the main monuments have information boards in three languages, including English.

Sights

As you walk toward the ruins, a signed path to the right leads up to the **Pequeña Acrópolis**, a group of ruins on a small hilltop – you can visit this later. Staying on the main path, you soon reach the mazelike passages of **El Laberinto** (Edificio 19), built between AD 742 and 752, during the interregnum between Itzamnaaj B'alam II and Pájaro Jaguar IV. Dozens of bats shelter under the structure's roof today. From this complicated two-level building you emerge at the northwest end of the extensive **Gran Plaza**.

Though it's difficult to imagine anyone here ever wanting to be any hotter than they already were, **Edificio 17** was apparently a sweat house. About halfway along the plaza, **Stele 1**, flanked by weathered sculptures of a crocodile and a jaguar, shows Pájaro Jaguar IV in a ceremony that took place in AD 761. **Edificio 20**, from the time of Itzamnaaj B'alam III, was the last significant structure built at Yaxchilán; its lintels are now in Mexico City. **Stele 11**, at the northeast corner of the Gran Plaza, was originally found in front of Edificio 40. The bigger of the two figures visible on it is Pájaro Jaguar IV.

An imposing stairway climbs from Stele 1 to **Edificio 33**, the best-preserved temple at Yaxchilán, with about half of its roofcomb intact. The final step in front of the building is carved with ball-game scenes, and splendid relief carvings embellish the undersides of the lintels. Inside is a statue of Pájaro Jaguar IV, minus his head, which he lost to treasure-seeking 19th-century timber cutters.

From the clearing behind Edificio 33, a path leads into the trees. About 20m along this, fork left uphill; go left at another fork after about 80m, and in some 10 minutes, mostly going uphill, you'll reach three buildings on a hilltop: **Edificio 39**, **Edificio 40** and **Edificio 41**.

Getting There & Away

Lanchas take 40 minutes running downstream from Frontera Corozal, and one hour to return. The boat companies are in a thatched building near the Frontera Corozal *embarcadero*, all charging about the same prices for trips (return journey with 2½ hours at the ruins for 1-3/4/5-7/8-10 people M$800/950/1300/1600). *Lanchas* normally leave frequently until 1:30pm or so; try to hook up with other travelers or a tour group to share costs.

Benemérito de las Américas to Las Nubes

South of Frontera Corozal is the far eastern corner of Chiapas, known as Marqués de Comillas (for its Spanish former landowner). After oil explorers opened tracks into this jungle region in the 1970s, settlers poured in from all over Mexico. Ranching and logging have made some rich, while others profit from smuggling drugs or immigrants. Rough-and-ready Benemérito de las Américas is the region's main town. Destinations in this area are often reached via Comitán.

REFORMA AGRARIA

Las Guacamayas LODGE **$$$**

(☎ in Guatemala 502-5157-9610; www.lasguacamayas.mx; Ejido Reforma Agraria; dm M$300, cabaña M$1350-1650, ste M$1950; P ⊖ @) This beautiful and welcoming ecolodge is right on the bank of the broad Río Lacantún, one of the Usumacinta's major tributaries, with the Reserva de la Biosfera Montes Azules on the opposite bank. Large, superbly comfortable thatch-roofed *cabañas*, with full mosquito screens, verandas and ample bathrooms with hot showers, are spread around the extensive grounds, linked by wooden walkways. Dorms are shared two-bed rooms with common bathrooms.

Las Guacamayas is the heart of an impressive community program to protect scarlet macaws (guacamayas). This spectacular and endangered member of the parrot family once ranged as far north as Veracruz, but its only Mexican home today is far eastern Chiapas. Numbers at Reforma Agraria have increased to more than 110 pairs since 1991, when the 14.5-sq-km macaw reserve was founded. The birds move in and out of the reserve in seasonal pursuit of food; the best months for observing them are December to June, when they are nesting. Ask to see the chick aviary on site and about the possibility of accompanying staff when they monitor nests.

There's a good restaurant overlooking the river, serving Mexican meals (breakfast M$60 to M$80, mains M$75 to M$150). From March through May, the river level drops and you can swim and take advantage of a sandy beach area.

Two-hour guided macaw-spotting walks cost M$900; they're best in the early morning or at dusk. Boat trips into the Montes Azules reserve cost M$1750/1950 for two/three hours. (All activities are per tour with an eight-person maximum.) You should spot crocodiles and howler monkeys, and with luck toucans and white-tailed deer. Villagers in Reforma Agraria also rent out horses for about M$100 per hour, and charge about M$50 per person to camp and M$100 to rent gear. In low season, all prices drop around 20%, and include breakfast in September and October.

Getting There & Away

The road to Reforma Agraria turns west off the Carretera Fronteriza 8km south of Benemérito. It's paved all the way through, rejoining the Carretera Fronteriza 5km south of Chajul, though large (but navigable) potholes, messy rainy-season mudslides and the occasional crumbling of the shoulder pavement will keep your eyes on the road.

From the *colectivo* lot near the bus terminal in Palenque, combis run to Pico de Oro (M$120, four hours) at 8am, 10am, noon and 2pm. Occasional *camionetas* also run between Benemérito and Pico de Oro (M$40, 30 minutes), though you'll often have to hire a taxi (M$40 per person *colectivo* or M$150 private) if it's past early morning. *Camionetas* run from Pico de Oro to Reforma Agraria (M$25, 30 minutes), and vice versa, about hourly from 6am until early afternoon. You can also take a taxi to Reforma Agraria from Frontera Corozal (M$600), Benemérito (M$300) or Pico de Oro (M$150); prices are per carload.

From Comitán, 18 vans a day run to Reforma Agraria (M$145 to M$155, 4½ hours), passing through the Lagos de Montebello en route, though only those from Transportes Tzoyol will drop you off directly in front of Las Guacamayas. Otherwise it's a 1km walk in from the road.

LAS NUBES & AROUND

Las Nubes is 12km off the Carretera Fronteriza, 55km from Tziscao. From Transportes Tzoyol (p400) in Comitán, there are five daily combis (M$68, 3½ to four hours) between 7:30am and 4:30pm, and five daily returns.

Activities

Ecoturismo Xbulanjá RAFTING

(in Guatemala 502-3137-5691; www.xbulanja.com; admission M$15, campsite M$30-50, cabañas M$700, restaurant mains M$50-100) From Embarcadero Jerusalén, just east of the Las Nubes highway turnoff, this Tseltal cooperative offers Class III rafting to Las Nubes (M$2200 two to six passengers, 2½ hours), and its lodging and restaurant are a cheaper alternative to Las Nubes. Rafting trip prices include return.

Sleeping

Las Nubes LODGE $$

(in Guatemala 502-4972-0204; www.causasverdeslasnubes.com; campsites per person M$50, cabaña M$950) A bit of a trek but well worth it, Las Nubes is a heavenly retreat among scores of cascades and rapids on the turquoise Río Santo Domingo. Some of the river pools are great swimming spots – it's M$20 per person to swim here if you're not staying the night. A swinging bridge straddles a fierce section of water-carved canyon, making an excellent vantage point from which to swoon over the grandest waterfalls.

A 15-minute hike up to a mirador rewards you with jungle views. There's an adrenaline-pumping zip-line (M$100), and you can spelunk and rappel from February through June.

Fifteen well-built *cabañas* have hot water and nice porches, and a waterside restaurant serves meals (breakfast M$60, lunch and dinner M$85), but no alcohol (you can bring your own). Rates drop 25% in low season.

Laguna Miramar

ELEV 400M

Ringed by rainforest, pristine Laguna Miramar, 140km southeast of Ocosingo in the **Reserva de la Biosfera Montes Azules** (Montes Azules Biosphere Reserve), is one of Mexico's most remote and exquisite lakes. Frequently echoing with the roars of howler monkeys, the 16-sq-km lake is bathtub-warm and virtually unpolluted. Rock ledges extending from small islands make blissful wading spots, and petroglyphs and a turtle cave are reachable by canoe.

LAS NUBES–LAGUNA MIRAMAR SHORTCUT

If you're visiting both places via public transit, you can avoid the east-west backtracks to the highway by walking between Las Nubes and Loma Bonita, a town about halfway in along the road to the *lanchas* for Laguna Miramar. It's approximately a 5km hike (40 minutes, with some hills) from the swinging bridge at Las Nubes to Loma Bonita, where you can catch onward combis.

The lake is accessible thanks to a successful ecotourism project in the small Maya community of **Emiliano Zapata** (community phone 200-124-88-80- 81- 82; www.lagunamiramar.com), near its western shore. If you arrive independently, ask for the Comité de Turismo. Through this representative you must arrange and pay for the services you need – a guide costs M$150 per day (maximum three people), a day-use fee is M$40, and rental of a *cayuco* (traditional canoe) for exploring the lake is M$150. Sleeping bags, hammocks and tents are available to rent (M$150 per person) and, for groups, local women can be hired to purchase and cook your food at the lake. Bring cash to cover your expenses.

The 7km walk from Emiliano Zapata to the lake, through *milpas* (cornfields) and forest that includes *caoba* (mahogany) and *matapalo* (strangler fig) trees, takes about 1½ hours and can be very muddy – good closed shoes are highly recommended. At the lake, you will hear howler monkeys. Other wildlife includes spider monkeys, tapirs, macaws and toucans; butterflies are prolific. Locals fish for *mojarra* (perch), and will assure you that the lake's few crocodiles are not dangerous.

Sleeping & Eating

At the lakeshore, you can sling a hammock or camp (per person M$40) under a *palapa* shelter. If you arrive after noon, you'll need to stay in Emiliano Zapata, as the guides want to make it home before dark. The village has a handful of simple **cabañas** (per person M$120) with river views, all with one queen and one twin bed, a fan and shared bathrooms. A number of *comedores* make meals for about M$30. You can also rent a hammock and mosquito net (M$50) and string them up in a roofed area next to the *cabañas*.

Getting There & Away

Try to visit outside the rainy season (late-August to November), when land access is very difficult, and walking the muddy foot trail feels like an aerobics class in quicksand. If you're determined to go then, you can rent a pair of tall rubber boots (M$20) or a hard-working horse (M$300 return). Some agencies in San Cristóbal de las Casas run three- or four-day trips to Miramar from San Cristóbal via the river route, with prices from M$4500 per person.

AIR

Servicios Aéreos San Cristóbal (p400) has small-plane charter flights (up to four passengers) to San Quintín from Comitán (M$4500 per plane one-way).

After you land, follow the dirt road opposite a military complex beside San Quintín's airstrip. It leads to Emiliano Zapata, about a 15- to 20-minute walk; the ecotourism project is at the far end of the village.

BOAT

Take a combi from Comitán to La Democracia (across the bridge from Amatitlán) or Plan de Río Azul (see p399 for information) and hire a *lancha* (M$925 one-way, maximum eight passengers, two hours) to Emiliano Zapata via the Río Jatate. In La Democracia (by prior arrangement), **Hipólito Vásquez** (community phone 55-1454-5788-89-90) is the only area *lanchero* who carries life vests. Most other boats depart from 4km on in Plan de Río Azul, where *lanchas* (M$1200 to M$2000 per boat) leave on demand until about 3pm. La Democracia and Plan de Río Azul are a rough 16km and 20km respectively from the Carretera Fronteriza highway; the first half is paved.

BUS & COLECTIVO

Transportation from Comitán and Ocosingo services San Quintín and Emiliano Zapata. The Comitán route is slightly shorter (the road is paved to Guadalupe Tepeyec, just before La Realidad; the Ocosingo road is paved to La Garrucha) and uses combis instead of trucks. Though San Quintín is technically the last stop, drivers will drop you off five minutes further in Emiliano Zapata if requested. The ecotourism project can usually organize in-town pickups for the return. Schedules are subject to change, and daylight saving time isn't used. Unpaved sections of road can be challenging in the rainy season.

From Comitán

Transportes Las Margaritas (6a Calle Sur Oriente 51, btwn 4a & 5a Av Oriente Sur) combis service Las Margaritas (M$16, 25 minutes) frequently. From Las Margaritas, **Grupo Monteflor** (cnr Av Central Sur & 1a Calle Sur Poniente, near the plaza) and **Transportes Río Euseba** (3a Av Oriente Sur btwn Calle Central & 1a Calle Oriente Sur, near the market) have daily departures to San Quintín (M$85, 4½ to six hours) from 5am to noon. The companies each depart about every two hours, but the schedules are staggered; they mostly alternate every hour. Combis return from San Quintín from 2am until noon.

From Ocosingo

Trucks leave for San Quintín (M$80, five to six hours in dry season) from a large walled lot at the back of the market. Departures are at 9am, 10:30am, noon, 2pm and 3:30pm, or when crammed full. Return trucks at midnight, 2am, 5am, 8am and noon.

Comitán

963 / POP 98,000 / ELEV 1560M

With a pretty **plaza** of modern sculpture pieces and mature flat-topped trees where birds flock and chirp in the evening, the colonial town of Comitán has a pleasant, artsy atmosphere. Set on a high plain 90km southeast of San Cristóbal, Comitán contains some good places to stay and eat, a few interesting museums, and there are several natural and archaeological attractions less than an hour away in the verdant countryside.

Sights

Iglesia de Santo Domingo CHURCH

(8am-2pm & 4:30-8pm) On the plaza, the Iglesia de Santo Domingo dates back to the 16th and 17th centuries, and sports unusual and handsome blind arcading on its tower. Its former monastic buildings next door are now the **Centro Cultural Rosario Castellanos** (1a Av Oriente; 9am-9pm) FREE, which has a pretty wood-pillared patio featuring a mural on local history.

Casa Museo Dr Belisario Domínguez MUSEUM

(Av Central Sur 35; adult/child M$5/2.50; 10am-6:45pm Tue-Sat, 9am-12:45pm Sun) Just south of the main plaza is the Casa Museo Dr Belisario Domínguez, the family home of Comitán's biggest hero and the site of his medical practice. It provides (in Spanish) fascinating insights into the state of medicine and the life of the professional classes in early-20th-century Chiapas (with a reconstruction of the on site pharmacy), as well as the heroic tale of Domínguez' political career, ending in his assassination.

Museo Arqueológico de Comitán MUSEUM

(1a Calle Sur Oriente; 9am-6pm Tue-Sun) FREE This museum, just east of the plaza, displays artifacts from the area's many archaeological sites (Spanish interpretation only). The misshapen pre-Hispanic skulls on display were deliberately 'beautified' by squeezing infants' heads between boards.

Sleeping

Hotel del Virrey HOTEL $

(963-632-18-11; hotel_delvirrey@hotmail.com; Av Central Norte 13; d M$380-480, tr M$500-700; P) Resident turtles splash in a fountain at the Virrey, a 19th-century house with rooms of varying sizes radiating from a flower-draped courtyard. All have cable TV, and smaller upstairs rooms enjoy a nice view of nearby El Calvario church.

Comitán

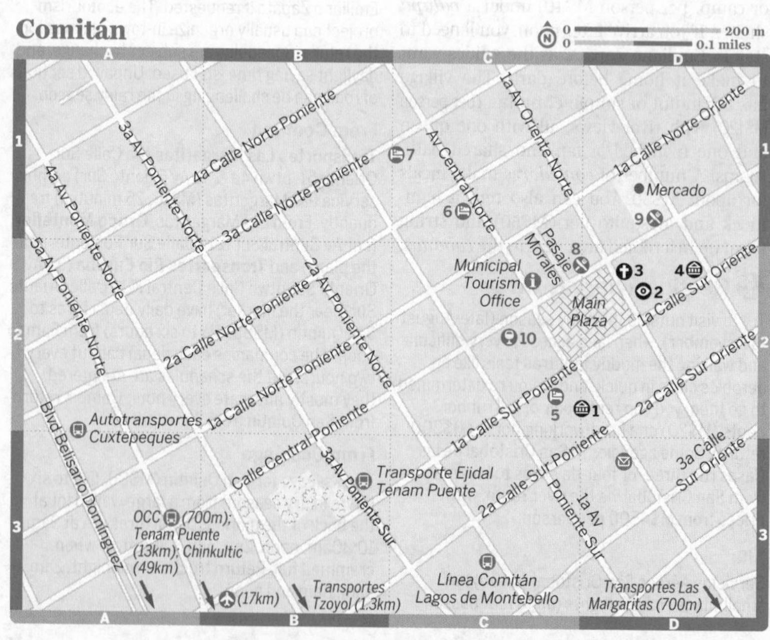

Hotel Posada El Castellano HOTEL **$$**
(☎963-632-33-47; www.posadaelcastellano.com.mx; 3a Calle Norte Poniente 12; s/d/tr M$490/530/570; P ⊖ @ ≋) This excellent hotel is colonial in style but modern in build and amenities. Comfy rooms, equipped with fan, cable TV, solid wood furniture and firm beds, are on two floors around wood-pillared patios. The staff are amiable and there's a nice restaurant.

★**Hotel Casa Delina** BOUTIQUE HOTEL **$$$**
(☎963-101-47-93; www.hotelcasadelina.com; 1a Calle Sur Poniente 6; r M$1200-1300; P ⊖ ≋) Attentive restoration and the work of contemporary Mexican and international artists have transformed this 250-year-old mansion into one of the most stylish hotels in Chiapas. Set along a courtyard with original wood-pillared arches and tiling and a gorgeous garden, the eight luxurious rooms blend colonial grandeur and playful industrial chic. An on-site cafe serves excellent organic Chiapan coffees.

Eating & Drinking

A handful of good typical restaurants lines the west side of the plaza.

Yuli Moni Comedor MEXICAN **$**
(Mercado; quesadillas M$17-25; ⊙8am-5pm; ✓) Come here for an inexpensive meal or snack. This mercado *comedor* has tasty and filling quesadillas, and the *nopales* (cactus) and mushrooms are also good options for vegetarians.

Comitán

Sights
1 Casa Museo Dr Belisario Domínguez ... D2
2 Centro Cultural Rosario Castellanos ... D2
3 Iglesia de Santo Domingo ... D2
4 Museo Arqueológico de Comitán ... D2

Sleeping
5 Hotel Casa Delina ... C2
6 Hotel del Virrey ... C1
7 Hotel Posada El Castellano ... C1

Eating
8 500 Noches ... C2
9 Yuli Moni Comedor ... D1

Drinking & Nightlife
10 Shangri La ... C2

500 Noches SPANISH **$$**
(Calle Central, Plaza; mains M$90-165; ⊙1pm-1am; ≋) Soaring ceilings and romantic nooks populate this cavernous restaurant specializing in fondues, tapas and 80-plus wines. The big draw is the live *trova* (starting at 7pm nightly), so it's worth coming by for drinks or dessert even if small plates aren't your thing. Plaza seating too.

Shangri La BAR, CAFE
(Calle Central Poniente 6; ⊙5pm-1am Mon-Sat) Colorful bottles line the entrance, and low lights and an open fireplace make this an inviting place for coffee, cocktails and the free snacks that come with them. Cozy up in a futon or beanbag in the toasty attic or inspect the walls plastered with photos of its happy patrons.

Information

BBVA Bancomer (cnr 1a Av Oriente Sur & 1a Calle Sur Oriente; ⊙8:30am-4pm Mon-Fri, 9:30am-4pm Sat) Changes euros (but not dollars) Monday through Friday; ATM.

Ciber@dictos (Pasaje Morales; per hr M$8; ⊙9:15am-9:15pm) Internet.

Instituto Nacional de Migración (☎963-632-22-00; Carretera Panamericana; ⊙9am-1pm Mon-Fri) The immigration office is on the Pan-American Hwy, just past the turnoff for Tzimol, 5km south of the town center.

Municipal Tourism Office (Av Central Norte; ⊙8am-8pm, to 9pm Thu & Sun)

Post Office (Av Central Sur 45; ⊙8:30am-4:30pm Mon-Fri, 8:30am-noon Sat)

Getting There & Around

The Pan-American Hwy (Hwy 190), named Blvd Belisario Domínguez here but usually just called 'El Bulevar,' passes through the west of town.

Comitán's **OCC bus terminal** (☎963-632-09-80; Blvd Belisario Domínguez Sur 43) is on the Pan-American Hwy. Besides the destinations following, it also serves Mexico City, Villahermosa, Playa del Carmen and Cancún. Across the road from the OCC terminal, 'centro' combis (M$6) run to the main plaza; a taxi is M$25.

Numerous *colectivos* have terminals on Hwy 190 between 1a and 2a Calles Sur Poniente, about 500m north of the OCC terminal; they depart when full. For San Cristóbal, vans (M$45) and *colectivo* taxis (M$50) are available until 9pm. Vans for Ciudad Cuauhtémoc (M$40, until 8pm), which usually say 'Comalapa,' and Tuxtla Gutiérrez (M$82, until 6pm) are also available.

Linea Comitán Lagos de Montebello (2a Av Poniente Sur 23) Runs vans to the Lagos de Montebello and along the Carretera Fronteriza,

BUSES FROM COMITÁN

DESTINATION	FARE (M$)	DURATION	FREQUENCY (DAILY)
Ciudad Cuauhtémoc	78	1½hr	3
Oaxaca	558	14½hr	1
Palenque	250	7hr	2
San Cristóbal de las Casas	48-56	1¾hr	19
Tapachula	206	6hr (via Motozintla)	5
Tuxtla Gutiérrez	76-90	3hr	18

with departures to Laguna Bosque Azul (M$40, one hour) and Tziscao (M$45, 1¼ hours) every 20 minutes from 3am to 5pm; to Reforma Agraria (M$155, 4½ hours) 10 times from 3am until 2pm; and to Palenque (M$275, eight hours) eight times daily, 3:30am to 11am. Schedules don't use daylight saving time.

Servicios Aéreos San Cristóbal (☎963-632-46-62; www.chiapasdesdeelcielo.com; Carretera Panamericana Km 1262) Runs day trips to Bonampak and Yaxchilán with overflights of Las Nubes and Laguna Miramar (M$13,500 round trip, including site fees), plus a new service that adds on a Palenque flight and overnight and a return overflight of Agua Azul (M$19,500, not including lodging or Palenque site fees). Prices are per four-passenger plane, not per person.

Transportes Tzoyol (☎963-632-77-39; 4a Av Poniente Sur 1039, at 13a Calle Sur Poniente) Runs vans to Reforma Agraria (M$145) eight times daily, 2:30am to 3pm, as well as to Plan de Río Azul (M$80, 3½ hours), the connection for boats to Laguna Miramar, four times a day between 4:30am and 2pm. It doesn't use daylight saving time.

Around Comitán

El Chiflón

These mighty waterfalls tumble off the edge of an escarpment 41km southwest of Comitán. For an up-close experience of sheer awesome power, El Chiflón is hard to beat.

One of two local *ejido* projects along the banks of the Río San Vicente, **Centro Ecoturístico Cadena de Cascadas El Chiflón** (☎963-596-97-09; www.chiflon.com.mx; admission M$20, cabañas d/q M$450/800, campsites per person M$25; ⏲8am-5pm; ⊜) has set up a number of attractive amenities on the approach to the falls, including a dozen comfortable, well-built *cabañas*, all with river view, bathroom and tight window netting, and a good open-air **restaurant** (mains M$70 to M$110). A small interpretive center provides information (in Spanish) on the river and wildlife in the area.

A 1km approach road heads up from Hwy 226 to the parking area, from which a well-made path leads 1.3km up alongside the forest-lined river (which has nice swimming spots) to a series of increasingly dramatic and picturesque waterfalls. Reaching the 120m **Velo de Novia** fall, prepare to be drenched by flying spray. You can also fly across the river on a zip-line (M$150).

In the dry season, from roughly February through July, the falls form a foamy line and the blue river water is safe enough to swim in. But during the rainy season, rapid currents turn the river a muddy brown, the falls gush with abandon and swimming is a death wish.

From Comitán, **Autotransportes Cuxtepeques** (Blvd Belisario Domínguez Sur btwn 1a & 2a Calles Norte Poniente) runs hourly vans and buses to the El Chiflón turnoff on Hwy 226 (M$25, 45 minutes) from 4am to 8pm. **Mototaxis** (per person M$5) wait there to ferry passengers up the road. Drivers should take the Tzimol turnoff from the Pan-American Hwy, 5km south of central Comitán.

Tenam Puente

These **Maya ruins** (admission M$35; ⏲9am-4pm) feature three ball courts, a 20m tiered pyramid and other structures rising from a terraced, wooded hillside. Like Chinkultic, Tenam Puente was one of a set of fringe Classic Maya settlements in this part of Chiapas that (unlike more famed lowland sites such as Palenque and Yaxchilán) seem to have survived in the post-Classic period, possibly as late as AD 1200. It has a pleasant rural setting and good long-distance views.

A 5km-long paved road leads west to the site from Hwy 190, 9km south of Comitán. **Transporte Ejidal Tenam Puente** (3a Av

Poniente Sur 8) runs combis (M$15) every 45 minutes, 8am to 6pm. The last combi from the ruins returns at 4pm. A taxi costs about M$250 return (with an hour at the ruins).

Parador-Museo Santa María

Evocative of a past era, the beautiful hotel-museum **Parador-Museo Santa María** (963-632-51-16; www.paradorsantamaria.com.mx; Carretera La Trinitaria-Lagos de Montebello Km 22; r M$1760, 6-8 person tent M$6000;), 1.5km off the road to the Lagos de Montebello, is the most luxurious and atmospheric place to stay in the Comitán area. The restored 19th-century hacienda is decorated throughout with period furniture and art; some of the eight rooms have tiled bathtubs and fireplaces, and all look out over expansive grassy lawns to the countryside beyond.

An odd but opulent newer lodging addition is an enormous Arabian-style tent, furnished with Oriental rugs, a bathroom with a Jacuzzi tub and animal-mouth faucets, and lavish room-dividing curtains. Gaze out over green hills from the solar-heated pool.

The chapel here is a **religious art museum** (admission M$25; 9am-6pm) with an interesting array of colonial-era work from Europe and the Philippines as well as Mexico and Guatemala. The excellent **Restaurant Los Geranios** (mains M$130-250; 8am-9pm) serves Chiapan and international dishes prepared with organic ingredients (including coffee) grown on site.

Look for the 22km marker from La Trinitaria on the Montebello road. Prices drop 30% in the low season, but book in advance for high season.

Chinkultic

Chinkultic (admission M$42; 8am-5pm) was a minor Maya power during the late Classic period and, like Tenam Puente, may have survived into post-Classic times. Of 200 mounds scattered over a wide area of dramatically situated ruins, only a few have been cleared, but the site is worth a visit. Note that the site is closed periodically; it's best to check whether it is open with the Comitán tourist office before heading out there.

The ruins are in two groups. From the entrance, first take the path to the left, which curves around to the right below one of Chinkultic's biggest structures, E23, covered in vegetation. The path reaches a grassy plaza with several weathered steles, some carved with human figures, and a ball court on the right.

Return to the entrance, from which another path heads to the **Plaza Hundida** (Sunken Plaza), crosses a stream, then climbs steeply up to the **Acrópolis**, a partly restored temple atop a rocky escarpment, with remarkable views over the surrounding lakes and forests and down into a cenote 50m below – into which the Maya used to toss offerings of pottery, beads, bones and obsidian knives.

Chinkultic is situated about 48km from Comitán, on the road to Lagos de

TO/FROM GUATEMALA: CIUDAD CUAUHTÉMOC

Very frequent *colectivos* (M$40) and intermittent buses (M$50) run between Ciudad Cuauhtémoc and Comitán (1½ hours). From Ciudad Cuauhtémoc, three daily OCC buses run to San Cristóbal de las Casas (M$100, 3½ hours) and beyond from 11am to 10pm, but it's usually quicker to get to Comitán and pick up onward transportation there. Other (infrequent) destinations include Palenque, Cancún and Tapachula.

Mexican immigration (8am-10pm) is across the street from the OCC terminal; *colectivos* generally assume that travelers need to be dropped off there. The Guatemalan border post is 4km south at La Mesilla, and 'Línea' combis (M$8) and taxis (M$10 *colectivo*, M$40 private) ferry people between the two sides. There are banks and moneychangers on both sides of the border, which closes to car traffic from 9pm to 6am.

From La Mesilla, mototaxis (M$5/Q3) can drop you at the 2nd-class bus depot. Second-class buses leave very frequently from 6am to 6pm for Huehuetenango (Q20, two hours) and Quetzaltenango (Q40, four hours), where you can find onward connections to Guatemala City. About 1km inside the border (just past the curve in the highway), first-class **Línea Dorada** (www.lineadorada.info) has direct daily departures to Guatemala City (Q170, eight hours) at 11am and 8pm.

DRINKS OF CHIAPAS

Comiteco A unique variant of mezcal made with a mix of *maguey* (agave) and *piloncillo* (cooked sugarcane). It's smoother and more syrupy than tequila, with a clear appearance or a greenish tint. Traditionally made in Comitán.

Tascalate A cold sweet concoction prepared from ground cacao, pine nuts, toasted corn, cinnamon and *achiote* (annatto). Very interesting and super delicious!

Pox Inexpensive grain alcohol made from sugarcane, it's pronounced (and sometimes spelled) 'posh.' The undisputed choice for those who want to pass out cold on the street, but not so deadly when mixed with lots of fruit juice.

Pozol A thick, heavy mixture of *masa* (cornmeal dough) in water, it's often mixed with sugar and sometimes has chili or chocolate added. It's the equivalent of an energy drink, and you can see indigenous people everywhere carrying it around in reused plastic 1L bottles. Travelers often take a ball of the *masa* and make some up when there's water available.

Montebello. Combis for the lakes can drop you at the intersection (M$40 from Comitán); the site is 2km north via a paved access road.

Lagos de Montebello

The temperate pine and oak forest along the Guatemalan border east of Chinkultic is dotted with more than 50 small lakes of varied hues, known as the Lagos (or Lagunas) de Montebello. The area is very picturesque, refreshing and peaceful. The paved road to Montebello turns east off Hwy 190 just north of La Trinitaria, 16km south of Comitán. It passes Chinkultic after 32km, and enters the Parque Nacional Lagunas de Montebello 5km beyond. A further 800m along is a ticket booth, where you must pay a M$27 park admission fee. Here the road forks – north to the Lagunas de Colores (2km to 3km) and east to the village of Tziscao (9km), beyond which it becomes the Carretera Fronteriza, continuing east to Ixcán and ultimately circling back up to Palenque.

Sights & Activities

From the park ticket booth, the northward road leads to the Lagunas de Colores, five lakes with vivid hues that range from turquoise to deep green: **Laguna Agua Tinta**, **Laguna Esmeralda**, **Laguna Encantada**, **Laguna Ensueño** and, the biggest, **Laguna Bosque Azul**, on the left where the paved road ends.

There's a nice 15-minute walk from here to the **Grutas San Rafael del Arco**, a group of caves. There's no signage, but you can hire guides for a small fee. There's an area where a river rushes through a natural rock arch, a riverside cave downstream, and a more extensive cave that turns out to be the bottom of a sinkhole.

In the Laguna Ensueño (and sometimes Bosque Azul) parking lot, *camiones* (trucks) do shared three- to five-hour lake tours for about M$500 per vehicle, though it can be harder to get a group together on weekdays. Local boys offer multi-lake horseback excursions that include **Dos Cenotes** (M$150, two to three hours), a pair of sinkholes in the forest, or to the Laguna de Montebello (about one hour away).

Along the eastward road from the park ticket booth, after 3km a track leads 200m north to the **Laguna de Montebello**, one of the area's larger lakes, with a flat open area along its shore, and more boys offering horseback rides to Dos Cenotes. The local *ejido* charges a M$20 entrance fee to access the lake areas along the Tziscao road; pay once and keep your receipt for the other lakes. About 3km further along the Tziscao road, another track leads left to the **Cinco Lagunas** (Five Lakes). Only four are visible from the road, but the second, **La Cañada**, on the right after about 1.5km, is one of the most beautiful Montebello lakes, nearly cut in half by two rocky outcrops.

About 1km nearer to Tziscao, another track leads 1km north to cobalt-blue **Laguna Pojoj**, which has an island in the middle that you can visit on simple rafts. **Laguna Tziscao**, on the Guatemalan border, comes into view 1km past the Pojoj junction. The turnoff to the Chuj-speaking village of Tziscao, a pretty and spread-out place stretching down to the lakeside, is a little further on.

Sleeping & Eating

The Laguna Ensueño and Laguna Bosque Azul parking lot have basic *comedores* that serve drinks and simple meals, and food options exist at most other lakes as well.

Villa Tziscao CABAÑAS, CAMPGROUND $

(in Guatemala 502-5780-2775; www.centroecoturisticotziscao.com.mx; campsites per person M$50, 1-/2-/3-bed r or cabaña M$400/750/950;) By the lake in Tziscao village (2km from the highway turnoff), this medium-sized lakeside complex is run by an *ejido* cooperative. Extensive, grassy grounds include a sandy beach with terrific views across the lake to the foothills of the Cuchumatanes in Guatemala. Comfortable rooms in the main hotel building have new beds and bathroom tiling, plus flat-screen TVs.

More rustic wooden *cabañas* are also available, but skip the shoreside units, as they're partially submerged for weeks during the rainy season. All accommodations have a private bathroom with hot water, and campers can use the kitchen. The hotel also has a restaurant (breakfast M$70, mains M$90).

You can rent two-person kayaks (M$50 per hour), or **bicycles** (M$150 for four hours) to go exploring.

La Esmeralda CHALET $

(cell phone 963-1094329; cabin M$400-500) Like a cute little summer camp, these well-built two-story wood chalets have hot water, two channels of TV and a **restaurant** (mains M$50-60). It's located 500m east off the road between Laguna Ensueño and Laguna Encantada.

Getting There & Away

Public transportation from Comitán is a snap, making it an easy day trip. Vans go to the end of the road at Laguna Bosque Azul and to Tziscao, and will drop you at the turnoffs for Parador Museo Santa María, Chinkultic and the other lakes. The last vehicles back to Comitán leave Tziscao and Laguna Bosque Azul in the early evening.

From San Cristóbal, a number of agencies offer tours that take in the lakes, throw in a visit to El Chiflón and get you back by dinnertime.

El Soconusco & Beaches

Chiapas' fertile coastal plain, 15km to 35km wide, is called the Soconusco, and is named for the Aztecs' most distant 15th-century province, called Xoconochco. It's hot and humid year-round, with serious rainfall from mid-May to mid-October. The lushly vegetated Sierra Madre de Chiapas, rising steeply from the plain, provides an excellent environment for coffee, bananas and other crops. Olive ridley and green sea turtles and the occasional leatherback nest along the coastline from June through November, and **turtle preservation projects** exist in Puerto Arista, Boca del Cielo, La Encrucijada and Chocohuital/Costa Azul.

The endless beach and ocean are wonderfully clean and warm here, but take care where you go in – the surf is often rough, and riptides (known as *canales*) can quickly sweep you out a long way. Bring bug repellent for overnights, as sandflies can be fierce from May through October.

Lagos de Montebello

Tonalá

☎966 / POP 35,000

This sweaty, bustling town on Hwy 200 is the jumping-off point for the northern beaches. You can check your email on the corner facing the plaza at **Cyber Cristy** (Av Rayon; per hr M$10; ⊙8am-10pm) and use the ATM at **Banamex** (Hidalgo 137), a block east of the plaza on the main drag. Get cash if you're heading for nearby beaches, as there aren't ATMs there.

A fine central choice fronting the east side of the plaza, the **Hotel Galilea** (☎966-663-02-39; Hidalgo 138; s/d/tr M$320/420/450; P❄📶) has a convenient restaurant and clean medium-sized rooms with dark wooden furniture that give it an old-world feel. **Hotel Grajandra** (☎966-663-01-44; Hidalgo 204; s/d/tr M$490/590/900; P⊖❄📶✖) is a friendly place next to the OCC bus terminal, with bright, large rooms with 1970s-era decor and a breezy upstairs restaurant. One block east from the plaza (behind the Hotel Galilea), **Restaurant Nora** (Independencia 10; mains M$73-155; ⊙8am-6pm Mon-Fri, 8am-4pm Sat) has served ample portions in its wood-beamed dining room since 1964.

Colectivo taxis for Puerto Arista (M$20, 20 minutes), Boca del Cielo (M$30, 35 minutes) and Madre Sal (M$40) run from Matamoros between 20 de Marzo and Belisario Domínguez, four blocks east of the plaza and one block downhill. Puerto Arista combis (M$17) leave from Juárez between 20 de Marzo and 5 de Mayo, one block further downhill. Combis to Madre Sal (M$30) depart from near the market on 5 de Mayo between Juárez and Allende; a private taxi costs M$200. *Colectivo* taxis for Pijijiapan (M$40) can be found on Hidalgo between 5 de Mayo and 20 de Mayo. Taxis and combis run until about 7pm.

From the central plaza, the **OCC bus terminal** (☎966-633-05-40; Hidalgo) is 600m west and the 2nd-class **Rápidos del Sur** (RS; Hidalgo btwn Belisario Domínguez & Iturbide) is 250m east. Both lines have frequent services to Tapachula (M$116 to M$186, three to four hours), Pijijiapan (M$36 to M$72, one hour) and Tuxtla Gutiérrez (M$94 to M$144, 2½ to three hours).

Puerto Arista

☎994

The state's most developed beach town is 18km southwest of Tonalá, though unless you visit during weekends, summer or holidays, when hotel prices rise and vacationing *chiapanecos* jam the place and its beachfront *palapa* seafood eateries, it's a small, ultrasleepy fishing town. There are no ATMs.

During the nesting season, a state government **turtle conservation project**

OFF THE BEATEN TRACK

IGLESIA VIEJA

Believed to be the regional capital of the Zoque during the Classic period, these newly opened **ruins** (⊙8am-5pm) FREE were inhabited between AD 250 and 400, and adventurous visitors can visit two restored groupings. The site's most prominent characteristics are its use of megalithic granite architecture, and its most impressive structure, the namesake 'Old Church,' is a 95m by 65m pyramid utilizing stone blocks weighing over a ton each. Instead of steps, the apex is reached via a ramp – look for the petroglyph cross at the south side of its base.

The other distinctive feature here is the presence of many carved anthropomorphic and zoomorphic monuments scattered throughout the site. The most well-known are the **Sapodrilo** (it appears to be a cross between a toad and a crocodile), and the **Altar de las Cuatras Caras** (Altar of the Four Faces).

An exuberant authority on regional archaeological sites, the distinguished **Ricardo López Vassallo** (☎966-663-01-05, cell phone 966-1042394; rilova36@hotmail.com) lives in Tonalá and can organize transportation and his services as a guide (and possibly his son for English speakers). He is paid by the government, so visitors only pay for transportation. It's worth consulting him on road conditions if you want to drive independently.

From the signed turnoff at Km 10 of the Tonalá-Arriaga highway, it's about 9km (30 minutes) east off the main road; a high-clearance vehicle is required mid-May through November because the last 2km up can be washed out, but walking a section may still be required.

(10am-5pm) FREE collects thousands of newly laid olive ridley turtle eggs from 40km of beach, incubating them and releasing the hatchlings when they emerge seven weeks later. You can stop in to see the turtle nursery, located about 3km northwest along the single street from the lighthouse (taxis charge M$25), or volunteer with beach patrols and hatchling releases by contacting San Cristóbal-based **Natató** (www.natate.org).

Sleeping & Eating

José's Camping Cabañas CABAÑAS **$**
(994-600-90-48; campsites per person M$50, RV sites M$150-170, dm M$100, s/d/tr M$300/350/400, without bathroom M$170/200/250; P) Run by a longtime Canadian expat, this laid-back fruit-tree compound has simple *cabañas* with mosquito nets, fans and screens, shaded sitting areas and powerful showers. Meals (M$40 to M$120) are available and the small pool is open in season. Go 800m southeast from the lighthouse, then turn left (inland).

Garden Beach Hotel HOTEL **$$**
(994-600-90-42; www.gardenbeach.mx; Matamoros 800; r M$900-1100, tr M$1400; P) Across the street from the beach and 800m southeast of the lighthouse, this hotel's comfortable, pastel-shaded, air-conditioned rooms have flat-screen TVs and up to three double beds. The upper floors have great ocean views. It has a beachfront open-air **restaurant** (mains M$100-160) and big double pool (nonguests pay M$50 unless they eat at the restaurant).

Madre Sal

Drift to sleep pondering the ocean waves at **Madre Sal** (cell phone 966-1007296, cell phone 966-6666147; www.elmadresal.com; Manuel Ávila Camacho; hammock site M$100, q campsite with gear M$250, cabaña M$600; P), a cooperative ecotourism project 25km south of Puerto Arista. Named for a mangrove species, its **restaurant** (meals M$60-120) and almost 20 thatched two-bed en suite *cabañas* (with mosquito nets) sit astride a skinny bar of pristine land between a lagoon and the Pacific that's reached via *lancha* (M$15 round-trip) through dense mangrove forest.

Guests use candles after the 11pm power shut-off, and crabs skitter along the sand when stars fill the night sky. In season, sea turtles come ashore to lay eggs, and the night watchman can wake you if you want to watch or help collect the eggs for the Boca del Cielo hatchery.

Though the water can be rough, the beach is spotless, and there's excellent bird-watching in the mangroves, including 13 species of herons. Three-hour *lancha* trips are available (M$650 per boat, maximum 12 people), including one for bird- and crocodile-spotting.

From Tonalá, take a taxi (M$40 shared, M$200 private) or combi (M$30) to Manuel Ávila Camacho; combis charge an extra M$5 to the *embarcadero*, or you can walk five minutes.

Reserva de la Biosfera La Encrucijada

This large biosphere reserve protects a 1448-sq-km strip of coastal lagoons, sandbars, wetlands, seasonally flooded tropical forest and the country's tallest mangroves (some above 30m). The ecosystem is a vital wintering and breeding ground for migratory birds, and harbors one of Mexico's biggest populations of jaguars, plus spider monkeys, turtles, crocodiles, caimans, boa constrictors, fishing eagles and lots of waterfowl – many in danger of extinction. Bird-watching is good any time of year, but best during the November-to-March nesting season. The reserve can be visited via access points from Pijijiapan and Escuintla, and *lancha* rides take you through towering mangroves.

RIBERA COSTA AZUL

A laid-back coastal jewel, the beautiful black sandbar of Ribera Costa Azul (also called Playa Azul) is a thin strip of palm-fringed land between ocean and lagoon accessed from the Chocohuital *embarcadero*, 20km southwest of Pijijiapan. Camping is generally free, though restaurants ask that you eat your meals (seafood M$110) there to do so. Outside of the busy high season, **Palapa Sinai** is usually the one place open year-round for meals and simple rooms. *Lanchas* (M$10 one way) ferry passengers to the sandbar, and birding and mangrove trips (M$250 per boat per hour) can also be organized.

If you don't want to camp, head 300m north of the Chocohuital dock and pull up a pool chair at the **Refugio del Sol** (cell phone 962-6252780; www.refugiodelsol.com.mx; r Mon-Thu/Fri-Sun M$1200/1500, nonguest pool day use adult/child M$350/250; P) hotel. Spacious modern rooms feature rainforest showers, plasma TVs and great beds with duvets. Request a room with a patio or terrace. There's a M$100 pool-fee discount if you eat in the **restaurant** (mains M$165-190, snacks M$50-120).

From Pijijiapan, combis for Chocohuital (M$20, 40 minutes, 5am to 6pm) leave hourly from 1a Av Norte Poniente 27 between 2a and 3a Poniente Norte; the last one returns at 8pm.

EMBARCADERO LAS GARZAS

The **Red de Ecoturismo La Encrucijada** (www.ecoturismolaencrucijada.com), a network of community cooperatives, is a clearinghouse for information on tours and lodging. Private *lancha* tours (M$800 to M$1500, up to 10 passengers) can also be organized to local beaches and bird-watching spots. *Lanchas* also serve a number of small communities where you can overnight or camp in simple *cabañas*. At the settlement of **Barra de Zacapulco** – which also has a sea-turtle breeding center – you can usually camp or sling a hammock for free if you eat your meals at one of its simple **comedores** (seafood plates M$80). A community cooperative there offers a half dozen basic solar-powered **cabañas** (☎cell phone 918-5962500; r M$450) with fans, screened windows and cold-water bathrooms.

To get here, take a bus along Hwy 200 to Escuintla, then a *colectivo* taxi to Acapetahua (M$6, 10 minutes). Beside the abandoned railway in Acapetahua, take a combi 18km to Embarcadero Las Garzas (M$20, 20 minutes, every 30 minutes until 5pm). From Embarcadero Las Garzas, *colectivo lanchas* go to communities including Barra de Zacapulco (M$45, 25 minutes). The last boat back from Barra de Zacapulco may be as early as 4pm, and the last combi from Embarcadero Las Garzas to Acapetahua goes at about 5pm.

Tapachula

☎962 / POP 200,000 / ELEV 100M

Mexico's bustling southernmost city, 'the 'Pearl of the Soconusco,' doesn't quite live up to its nickname, though it does have an interesting combination of urban sophistication and tropical tempo. The city is an important commercial center, not only for the Soconusco but also for cross-border trade with Guatemala.

A hot, humid and busy place year-round, Tapachula's heart is the large, lively **Parque Hidalgo**, with vistas of the towering 4100m cone of Volcán Tacaná to the north on clear days. Most travelers simply pass through here on their way to or from Guatemala, but it makes a good base for a number of interesting nearby attractions.

Sights

★Museo Arqueológico del Soconusco MUSEUM

(Av 8a Norte 20; admission M$35; ⊙9am-6pm Tue-Sun) The modern, well-displayed Museo

OFF THE BEATEN TRACK

RESERVA DE LA BIOSFERA EL TRIUNFO

The luxuriant cloud forests, high in the remote El Triunfo Biosphere Reserve in the Sierra Madre de Chiapas, are a bird-lover's paradise and a remarkable world of trees and shrubs festooned with epiphytes, ferns, bromeliads, mosses and vines.

The Sierra Madre de Chiapas is home to almost 400 bird species, of which more than 30 are nonexistent or rare elsewhere in Mexico. This is the one place in the country where chances are good of seeing the resplendent quetzal. Visitors see hundreds of butterfly species and, often, jaguar and tapir tracks.

Visits are limited and controlled. Most visitors go in the driest months, January to May; avoid the wettest months, September and October. Make arrangements about six months in advance by contacting **Claudia Virgen** (☎961-125-11-22; www.ecobiosfera.org.mx), the visitor program coordinator. A normal five-day visit from Tuxtla (US$630 to US$795 per person, minimum eight people, maximum 12) starts with one night in a hotel in the nearest town, Jaltenango (also called Ángel Albino Corzo), followed by three nights at the basic Campamento El Triunfo, 1850m high in the reserve. The price includes meals, bilingual guides who are expert bird-spotters, transportation between Jaltenango and the coffee-growing village of Finca Prusia, and mules to carry your baggage on the 14km hike between Finca Prusia and Campamento El Triunfo (three to four hours uphill on the way in). The **Mesoamerican Ecotourism Alliance** (www.travelwithmea.org) also organizes private trips.

Arqueológico del Soconusco faces Parque Hidalgo. Steles and ceramics from Izapa are prominent. On these steles the top fringe represents the sky and gods, the middle depicts earthly life and the bottom fringe shows the underworld. There are also 5000-year-old stone heads and figurines from the coastal marshes, a collection of pre-Hispanic musical instruments (including scrapers made from human bones), and other items displaying Olmec, Teotihuacán, Maya and Aztec influences. Goths will adore the turquoise-encrusted skull.

Activities

Misión México VOLUNTEERING
(www.lovelifehope.com) A refuge for abused and orphaned street children, this small nonprofit was founded by an Australian couple who incorporated their love of surfing. There's a family-style environment, and volunteers pitch in with all aspects of the kids' day-to-day lives. A unique component here is its surf school, which helps foster confidence and healing, and volunteers who can surf are highly encouraged. Some Spanish proficiency is helpful and a one-month minimum commitment and background check are required.

Sleeping

Hotel Diamante HOTEL $
(962-628-50-32; Calle 7a Poniente 43; r/q M$285/395, with air-con M$500/600;) A good-value hotel with modern air-conditioning, clean rooms and cable TV. Rooms 12 through 16 have dynamite views of Volcán Tacaná.

★ **Casa Mexicana** BOUTIQUE HOTEL $$
(962-626-66-05; www.casamexicanachiapas.com; Av 8a Sur 19; r M$792-1089, tr/q M$1185/1285, incl full breakfast;) An exquisite boutique hotel paying homage to Mexican women in history. Guests can choose from sumptuous rooms named for heroines such as human rights lawyer Digna Ochoa or Zapatista commander Ramona. Antiques, lush plants and all kinds of interesting art create a soothing, creative feel. The 10 rooms on two floors surround a tropical garden-patio that even has a small pool.

With a small bar and a restaurant serving excellent homemade meals, this is a fabulous place to stay.

Galerías Hotel y Arts HOTEL $$
(962-642-75-90; www.galeriashotel.com.mx; Av 4a Norte 21; s M$445-520, d/tr M$645/775;) Stylish, contemporary and boutique-on-a-budget, Galerías is an excellent small hotel with jazzy art prints and large, comfortable air-conditioned rooms. Double rooms are spacious. Two cozy but comfy singles are a good deal for those going solo.

Hotel Mo Sak HOTEL $$
(962-626-67-87; www.hotelmosak.com; Av 4a Norte 97; d M$490-550;) Helpful, attentive staff round out this modern hotel with minimalist furniture and free morning coffee. King-bed rooms have kitchenettes.

Eating

Scores of clean and popular *comedores* are hidden upstairs at the **Mercado Sebastián Escobar** (Av 10a Norte; mains M$50-65; 6am-5pm), dishing out mammoth plates of cooked-to-order Chinese food. Snag a bench seat at the plastic-tablecloth-covered picnic tables and come hungry!

Gramlich Café Terraza CAFE $
(Calle 1a Poniente 14; coffees & snacks M$12-35, mains M$50-70; 9am-9:30pm Mon-Sat, 3-9:30pm Sun) The Gramlich Café serves its delectable brew along with an extended menu of breakfasts, sandwiches and Thai salads. Seat yourself on the shaded sidewalk patio or inside with the turbo-charged air conditioning.

Long-Yin CHINESE $
(962-626-24-67; Av 2a Norte 36; mains $65-120; 9am-8pm;) Just one portion easily feeds two ravenous diners at this excellent red-lantern-festooned place run by a fourth-generation immigrant family. Vegetarians should beeline here for the fabulous tofu dishes. Delivery available, but it's worth seeing the building across the street.

Los Comales Grill MEXICAN $$
(Av 8a Norte 4; mains M$70-150; 24hr) To feel like you're in the thick of things, dine in this open-air Parque Hidalgo restaurant – it's been here for over half a century. The menu includes good *caldo tlalpeño* (hearty chicken, vegetable and chili soup) and decent steaks. There's marimba music Thursday, Saturday and Sunday evenings from 8pm to 11pm.

Tapachula

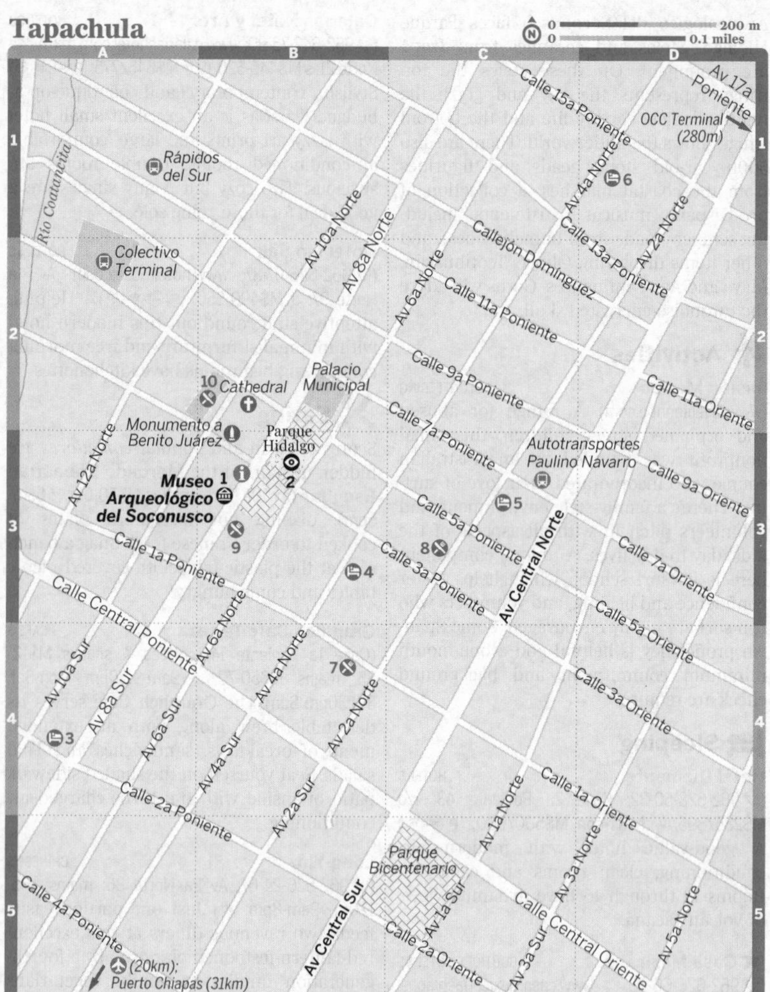

Information

Banorte (cnr Av 2a Norte & Calle Central Poniente; ⊙9am-5pm Mon-Fri, 9am-2pm Sat) Changes dollars Monday through Friday; ATM.

Chiapas Divisas (Av 4a Norte 17; ⊙8:30am-8:30pm Mon-Fri, 8:30am-6:30pm Sat, 8:30am-2:30pm Sun) Currency exchange.

Cyber Amigos (Av 4a Norte 44; internet per hr M$8; ⊙8am-10pm)

Instituto Nacional de Migración (☎962-625-05-59; Vialidad 435, Fracc Las Vegas; ⊙9am-1pm) Immigration office.

Sanatorio Soconusco (☎962-626-50-74; Av 4a Norte 68, at Calle 11 Poniente) A clinic with 24-hour emergency service.

Tourist Office (www.turismochiapas.gob.mx/sectur/tapachula; Av 8a Norte; ⊙8am-4pm Mon-Fri) A helpful office in the Antiguo Palacio Municipal.

Getting There & Away

AIR

Tapachula's modern **airport** (Carretera Tapachula-Puerto Madero Km 18.5;) is 20km southwest of the city. It's a drowsy place, with

Tapachula

Top Sights
1 Museo Arqueológico del Soconusco....B3

Sights
2 Parque Hidalgo....B3

Sleeping
3 Casa Mexicana....A4
4 Galerías Hotel y Arts....B3
5 Hotel Diamante....C3
6 Hotel Mo Sak....D1

Eating
7 Gramlich Café Terraza....B4
8 Long-Yin....C3
9 Los Comales Grill....B3
10 Mercado Sebastián Escobar....B2

just three daily flights to/from Mexico City on **Aeroméxico** (☎962-626-39-21; Calle Central Oriente 4).

BUS

Deluxe and 1st-class buses go from the **OCC terminal** (☎962-626-28-81; Calle 17a Ote, btwn Avs 3a & 5a Norte), 1km northeast of Parque Hidalgo. The main 2nd-class services are by **Rápidos del Sur** (RS; Calle 9a Poniente 62). For info on daily departures (from OCC unless otherwise stated), see the table below.

Other buses from the OCC station go to Palenque, Puerto Escondido and Villahermosa. There are also five daily buses from here to Guatemala City (five to six hours), with tickets sold at the main counter: **Trans Galgos Inter** (www.transgalgosinter.com.gt) at 6am, noon and 11:45pm (M$305), **Línea Dorada** (www.lineadorada.com.gt) at 3pm (M$220) and **Tica Bus** (www.ticabus.com) at 7am (M$247).

Galgos also runs a 6am bus to San Salvador, El Salvador (M$400, nine hours), via Escuintla in Guatemala. Tica Bus continues all the way to Panama City (M$1720), with several long overnight stops en route.

For destinations in western Guatemala, including Quetzaltenango, it's best to get a bus from the border.

COLECTIVO

A large **colectivo terminal** (Calle 5a Poniente) houses most of the regional taxi and combi companies.

Getting Around

CAR & MOTORCYCLE

Tapachula's two rental agencies carry both automatic and manual transmission cars.

AVC Rente un Auto (☎962-626-23-16, cell phone 962-6225444; per day from M$750) In-town pick-up service available.

Europcar (☎962-120-80-10; www.europcar.com; Airport) Best rates online.

TAXI

Taxis within the central area (including the OCC terminal) cost M$25.

Sociedades Transportes 149 (☎962-625-12-87) has a booth in the airport arrivals hall, charging M$80 per person for a *colectivo* from the airport to the center; it's M$180 for a private taxi (up to three people) in either direction.

Around Tapachula

Izapa

The pre-Hispanic ruins at Izapa are important to archaeologists, and of real interest to archaeology buffs. Izapa flourished from approximately 200 BC to AD 200, and its carving style (mostly seen on tall slabs known as steles, fronted by round altars) shows descendants of Olmec deities with their upper lips unnaturally lengthened. Some Maya monuments in Guatemala are similar, and

BUSES FROM TAPACHULA

DESTINATION	FARE (M$)	DURATION	FREQUENCY (DAILY)
Comitán	206	6hr (via Motozintla)	6
Escuintla	30-74	1½hr	7 OCC, very frequent RS
Mexico City	1084-1570	17-18hr	10
Oaxaca	424-552	13hr	3
Pijijiapan	80-144	2½hr	very frequent RS
San Cristóbal de las Casas	278-358	7½-8hr (via Motozintla)	7
Tonalá	116-220	3-4hr	very frequent OCC & RS
Tuxtla Gutiérrez	200-572	4½-6hr	very frequent OCC & RS

Izapa is considered an important 'bridge' between the Olmecs and the Maya. Izapa had 91 known stele-and-altar pairings, and you can see some well-preserved examples in the Tapachula museum.

Izapa is around 11km east of Tapachula on the Talismán road. There are three groups of **ruins** (Grupo A & B admission by donation, northern group free; ⊙8am-5pm Wed-Sun). The northern group is on the left side of the road if you're arriving from Tapachula – watch for the low pyramid mounds; you'll also see a ball court and several carved steles and altars. For the other groups, go back 700m toward Tapachula and take a signposted road to the left. After 800m you'll reach a fork with signs to Izapa Grupo A and Izapa Grupo B, each about 250m further on and looked after by caretaking families that will request a small donation. Grupo A has 10 very weathered stele-and-altar pairings around a field. Grupo B is a couple of grass-covered mounds and more stone sculptures, including three curious ball-on-pillar affairs.

To get there from Tapachula, take a combi (M$12) from the *colectivo* terminal or any Talismán-bound bus.

Santo Domingo, Unión Juárez & Volcán Tacaná

☎962

At 4100m, Volcán Tacaná's dormant cone towers over the countryside north of Tapachula. Even if you're not interested in climbing to its summit, two villages on its gorgeously verdant lower slopes make an attractive day trip, their cooler climate offering welcome relief from the Tapachula steam bath. The scenic road up is winding but well paved.

Santo Domingo lies 34km northeast of Tapachula, amid coffee plantations. The village's gorgeous three-story wooden 1920s *casa grande* has been restored. It belonged to the German immigrants who formerly owned the coffee plantation here, but it's now the **Centro Ecoturístico Santo Domingo** (☎962-627-00-60; www.centroecoturisticosantodomingo.com; ⊙8am-8pm) and has a **restaurant** (mains M$50-90), a small creaky-floored coffee museum (M$5) and a well-tended tropical garden and pool (M$10; free with a meal).

About 9km beyond Santo Domingo, passing some gorgeous waterfalls tucked in around tight turns, Unión Juárez (population 2600, elevation 1300m) is the starting point for ascents of Tacaná and other, less demanding walks. Tapachula folk like to come up here on weekends and holidays to cool off and feast on *parrillada,* a cholesterol-challenging plate of grilled meat and a few vegetables.

Another local place to head for is **Pico del Loro**, a parrot-beak-shaped overhanging rock that offers fine panoramas. The rock is 5km up a drivable track that leaves the Santo Domingo–Unión Juárez road about halfway between the two villages. Ask directions to some of the various lookouts over the valley of the Río Suchiate (the international border), or to the **Cascadas Muxbal**, a natural toboggan slope, about one hour's walk from Unión Juárez.

SUMMITING TACANÁ

The best months to climb Tacaná are late November to March. There are two routes up the mountain from Unión Juárez. Neither requires any technical climbing, but you need to allow two or three days for either, preferably plus time to acclimatize. Be prepared for extreme cold at the top. The less steep route is via Chiquihuites, 12km from Unión Juárez and reachable by vehicle. From there it's a three-hour walk to Papales, where you can sleep in huts for a small donation. The ascent from Papales to the summit takes about five hours. The other route is via Talquián (about two hours' walk from Unión Juárez) and Trigales (five hours from Talquián). It takes about six hours to climb from Trigales to the summit. The two routes meet a couple of hours below the summit, and on both you have access to camping areas.

Combis from Unión Juárez will carry you to the small town of Córdoba, about halfway to Talquián, also passing the turnoff for Chiquihuites (about 1½ hours' walk away). It's a good idea to get a guide for Tacaná in Unión Juárez or organize one to meet you. The **Hotel Colonial Campestre** (☎962-647-20-15; fernandao772@hotmail.com) can find guides (about M$300 per day) with three days' notice.

Sleeping & Eating

There are plenty of *comedores* and restaurants around the plaza in Unión Juárez, though lodging is nothing extraordinary.

Hotel Colonial Campestre HOTEL $
(962-647-20-15; Unión Juárez; r M$350-500; P) Rambling and Escher-esque, this hotel has spacious rooms with bathroom, TV and good views (especially from room 26). It also has a **restaurant** (mains M$60-100; parrillada for two M$200). Look for the arch a couple of blocks below the plaza, and ask to see the tunnel and antique movie theater.

Hotel Aljoad HOTEL $
(962-647-21-06; Unión Juárez; d/tr M$200/250; P) Just north of the plaza, the super-basic Aljoad has tidy rooms around a cluttered patio, all with hot-water bathrooms.

Getting There & Away

From Tapachula, first take a combi from the *colectivo* terminal to Cacahoatán (M$15, 30 minutes), 20km north. From where these terminate in Cacahoatán, Transportes Tacaná combis travel to Santo Domingo (M$14, 30 minutes) and Unión Juárez (M$17, 45 minutes).

Coffee Fincas

The hills north of Tapachula are home to numerous coffee *fincas* (ranches), many of them set up by German immigrants more than a century ago. *Fincas* with tours, restaurants and overnight accommodations include the luxurious **Finca Argovia** (962-626-29-66 ext 105; www.argovia.com.mx; d M$1600-1800, f M$2100-2300, ste M$2500;) and **Finca Hamburgo** (962-626-64-04; www.fincahamburgo.com; f/ste from M$1350/2100; P) and the more rustic organic and biodynamic farm of **Finca Irlanda** (962-625-92-03 ext 107; www.fincairlanda.grupopeters.com; r per person M$600;).

Border Towns

If you're not taking a direct bus to Guatemala from the OCC station, you can go to the border for connections. It's 20km from Tapachula to the international border at **Talismán**, opposite El Carmen in Guatemala. The border crossing between **Ciudad Hidalgo**, 37km from Tapachula, opposite Ciudad Tecún Umán in Guatemala, is busier and has more onward connections. Both border points have money-changing facilities and are open 24 hours – though you should get through by early afternoon for greater security and to guarantee onward transportation. Watch out for moneychangers passing counterfeit bills at both crossings.

Getting There & Away

From Tapachula, **Autotransportes Paulino Navarro** (962-626-11-52; Calle 7a Poniente 5) combis head to Ciudad Hidalgo (M$24, 50 minutes) every 10 minutes, 4:30am to 10pm. Across the border in Ciudad Tecún Umán, frequent buses leave until about 6pm for Guatemala City (five hours) by the Pacific slope route, through Retalhuleu and Escuintla. Buses to Quetzaltenango (three hours) depart hourly from 5am to 6pm.

Combis for Talismán (M$15, 30 minutes) leave from the Tapachula *colectivo* terminal every 10 minutes, 5am to 9pm. The majority of bus services from El Carmen, which include around 20 a day to Guatemala City (seven hours), go via Ciudad Tecún Umán, and then head along the Pacific slope route. For Quetzaltenango, you can take one of these and change at Coatepeque or Retalhuleu, but it's easier to get a *colectivo* taxi to Malacatán, on a more direct road to Quetzaltenango via San Marcos, and then look for onward transportation from there.

For Lake Atitlán or Chichicastenango, you need to get to Quetzaltenango first.

Tabasco

They say that the state of Tabasco has more water than land, and looking at all the lagoons, rivers and wetlands on the map you can certainly see why, especially during the rainy season. It's always hot and sweaty here, but marginally less so when you catch a breeze along the Gulf of Mexico or venture into the southern hills. Travelers to Villahermosa and coastal Tabasco should note the region is subject to seasonal floods, though few travelers linger in Tabasco longer than it takes to see the outstanding Olmec stone sculpture in Villahermosa's Parque-Museo La Venta. Located north of Chiapas and abutting the Gulf of Mexico, Tabasco is the site of extensive onshore and offshore oil exploration by Mexico's state oil company (Pemex).

HIGHLIGHTS OF TABASCO

Tabasco has hosted as rich a procession of cultures as anywhere in Mexico. In pre-Hispanic times, Tabasco was the prosperous nexus of a far-reaching trade network extending around the Yucatán coast to Honduras, up the rivers to the jungles and mountains of Guatemala, and westward to highland central Mexico. Olmec religion, art, astronomy and architecture deeply influenced all of Mexico's later civilizations.

La Venta

Though most monuments from La Venta are at Villahermosa's Parque-Museo La Venta, this ancient **Olmec ceremonial site** (☎923-232-04-23; admission M$42; ⊙10am-4:30pm) still fascinates as the largest and most important 'capital' of Mexico's mother culture. La Venta flourished between about 800 and 400 BC on a natural plateau rising about 20m above an area of fertile, seasonally flooded lowlands. Matthew Stirling is credited with discovering, in the early 1940s, four huge Olmec heads sculpted from basalt, the largest more than 2m high.

The museum at the site entrance holds three badly weathered Olmec heads, plus replicas of some of the finest sculptures that are no longer here. The heart of the site is the 30m-high Edificio C-1, a rounded pyramid constructed out of clay and sand. Ceremonial areas and more structures stretch to the north and south.

Comalcalco

The impressive Maya ruins of ancient **Comalcalco** (admission M$46; ⊙8am-4pm), 50km northwest of Villahermosa, are unique because many of their buildings are constructed of bricks and/or mortar made from oyster shells. Comalcalco was at its peak between AD 600 and 1000, when it was ruled by the Chontals. It remained an important center of commerce for several more centuries, trading in a cornucopia of pre-Hispanic luxury goods.

A **museum** at the entrance has a fine array of sculptures and engravings of human heads, deities, glyphs and animals such as crocodiles and pelicans.

The first building you encounter is the great brick tiered pyramid, **Templo 1**. At its base are the remains of large stucco sculptures, including the feet of a giant winged toad. Further temples line Plaza Norte, in front of Templo I. In the far (southeast) corner of the site rises the **Gran Acrópolis**, which has views from its summit over a canopy of palms to the Gulf of Mexico. The Acrópolis is fronted by **Templo V**, a burial pyramid that was once decorated on all sides with stucco sculptures of people, reptiles, birds and aquatic life. At Templo V's western foot is **Templo IX**, which has a tomb lined by nine stucco sculptures showing a Comalcalco lord with his priests and courtiers. Above Templo V is the crumbling profile of **El Palacio**, with its parallel 80m-long corbel-arched galleries, probably once Comalcalco's royal residence. Information is in both Spanish and English.

Hacienda La Luz (☎933-337-11-22; www.haciendalaluz.mx; Blvd Rovirosa 232; 1hr tour per person M$80; ⊙tours 9am, 11am, 1pm & 3pm Tue-Sun), one of several local plantations making chocolate from home-grown cacao, is just 300m from Comalcalco's central Parque Juárez: walk 250m west along Calle Bosada to its end at Blvd Rovirosa, turn right and you'll see the hacienda's gateposts across the road. The tour takes you round the beautiful house,

Villahermosa

☎993 / POP 640,000

This sprawling, flat, hot and humid city, with more than a quarter of Tabasco's population, was never the 'beautiful town' its name implies. It's settled on the winding Río Grijalva, but Villahermosa's most attractive attribute became its worst enemy when the river burst its banks and engulfed the city in 2007.

Oil money has pumped modernity and commerce into some of the outer districts, where you'll find glitzy malls, imposing public buildings and luxury hotels.

Sights

The central area of this expansive city is known as the Zona Luz, and extends north–south from Parque Juárez to the Plaza de Armas, and east–west from the Río Grijalva to roughly Calle 5 de Mayo. The main bus

gardens and cacao plantation, shows traditional methods of turning cacao beans into chocolate, and concludes with a chocolate drink. English is spoken.

Tapijulapa

The prettiest village in Tabasco, riverside Tapijulapa sits among the lushly forested hills of far southern Tabasco, 36km from Teapa. It boasts a 17th-century church presiding over beautiful white houses with red-tiled roofs and potted flowers. **Mesón de la Sierra** (932-322-40-27; mesondelasierra@hotmail.com; r M$500;), located two blocks north of the plaza on the staircase to the church, is a comfortable five-room inn with a light-drenched Mediterranean feel and a prime location for appreciating the spectacular forested hills beyond town. Locals also rent a variety of well-appointed rooms through the town's **Hotel Communitario** (932-322-41-50, cell phone 932-1060684; La Casa de la Turista, main plaza; r M$200-500;) network.

The beautiful jungle park **Villa Luz** (9am-5pm) is a five-minute boat ride along the Río Oxolotán from the village *embarcadero*. From the landing, it's a 1km walk to the park's **Casa Museo**, the former country villa of Tomás Garrido Canabal, the rabidly anticlerical governor of Tabasco in the 1920s and '30s (he demolished Villahermosa's 18th-century baroque cathedral, banned alcohol and gave women the vote). From here other paths lead 600m to the beautiful **cascadas** (waterfalls) tumbling into a river, with pools for a refreshing dip, and 900m to the **Cueva de las Sardinas Ciegas** (Cave of the Blind Sardines), named for the sightless fish that inhabit the sulfurous river inside the cave.

To reach Tapijulapa from Villahermosa, take a CAT bus to Tacotalpa and change.

Reserva de la Biosfera Pantanos de Centla

This 3030-sq-km biosphere reserve protects a good part of the wetlands around the lower reaches of two of Mexico's biggest rivers, the Usumacinta and the Grijalva. These lakes, marshes, rivers, mangroves, savannas and forests are an irreplaceable sanctuary for countless creatures, including the West Indian manatee and Morelet's crocodile (both endangered), six kinds of tortoise, tapir, ocelots, jaguars, howler monkeys, 60 fish species and 255 bird species.

The **Centro de Interpretación Uyotot-Ja** (913-106-83-90; www.casadelagua.org.mx; Carretera Frontera-Jonuta Km 12.5; admission M$25, reserve fee M$25; 9am-5pm Tue-Sun) visitor center, or 'Casa de Agua,' is 13km along the Jonuta road from Frontera, beside the broad, winding Río Grijalva. A 20m-high observation tower overlooks the awesome confluence of the Grijalva, the Usumacinta and a third large river, the San Pedrito – a spot known as Tres Brazos (Three Arms). Boat trips are available into the mangroves, where you should see crocodiles, iguanas, birds and, with luck, howler monkeys. March to May is the best birding season.

From Villahermosa, ADO, CAT and Cardesa buses service Frontera (near the site of conquistador Hernán Cortés' 1519 first battle against native Mexicans), where *colectivos* run the 15-minute trip to the reserve.

stations are between 750m and 1km north of the center.

Parque-Museo La Venta PARK, MUSEUM

(Av Ruíz Cortines; admission M$40; 8am-4pm;) This fascinating outdoor park, zoo and museum was created in 1958, when petroleum exploration threatened the highly important ancient Olmec settlement of La Venta in western Tabasco. Archaeologists moved the site's most significant finds, including three colossal stone heads, to Villahermosa.

Plan two to three hours for your visit, and take mosquito repellent (the park is set in humid tropical woodland). Parque-Museo La Venta lies 2km northwest of the Zona Luz, beside Avenida Ruíz Cortines, the main east–west highway crossing the city. It's M$25 via *colectivo*.

Inside, you first come to a **zoo** devoted to animals from Tabasco and nearby regions:

cats include jaguars, ocelots and jaguarundi, and there are white-tailed deer, spider monkeys, crocodiles, boa constrictors, peccaries and plenty of colorful birds, including scarlet macaws and keel-billed toucans.

There's an informative display in English and Spanish on Olmec archaeology as you pass through to the **sculpture trail**, the start of which is marked by a giant ceiba (the sacred tree of the Olmec and Maya). This 1km walk is lined with finds from La Venta. Among the most impressive, in the order you come to them, are **Stele 3**, which depicts a bearded man with a headdress; **Altar 5**, depicting a figure carrying a child; **Monument 77**, 'El Gobernante,' a very sour-looking seated ruler; the monkey-faced **Monument 56**; **Monument 1**, the colossal head of a helmet-wearing warrior; and **Stele 1**, showing a young goddess (a rare Olmec representation of anything female). Animals that pose no danger (such as coatis, squirrels and black agoutis) roam freely around the park.

Museo de Historia Natural MUSEUM
(Av Ruíz Cortines; admission M$20; 8am-5pm Tue-Sun, last admission 4pm; P) Just outside the Parque-Museo La Venta entrance, the small Museo de Historia Natural has good displays on dinosaurs, space, early humanity and Tabascan ecosystems (all in Spanish).

Museo Regional de Antropología MUSEUM
(http://iec.tabasco.gob.mx; Periférico Carlos Pellicer; admission M$50; 9am-4:30pm Tue-Sun; P) Villahermosa's shiny, newly rebuilt regional anthropology museum holds some excellent exhibits on Olmec, Maya, Nahua and Zoque cultures in Tabasco – including Tortuguero number 6, the infamous tablet *solely* responsible for the dire 'end of world' predictions forecast for December 21, 2012. It's in the CICOM complex, a 15-minute walk from Zona Luz and just south of the Paseo Tabasco bridge.

Sleeping

An oil town, Villahermosa has scores of comfortable midrange and top-end chain hotels, most of which offer heavily discounted online and weekend rates. Inviting budget options are scarcer.

Hotel Oriente HOTEL $
(993-312-01-21; hotel-oriente@hotmail.com; Madero 425; d with fan M$250-330, d with air-con M$350-440, tr with fan/air-con M$420/540;) The Oriente is a friendly and well-run downtown hotel sporting simple budget rooms, all with TV. Rooms overlooking the main street are bright, but bring earplugs for noise. It's small, so reserve two days in advance.

Hotel Provincia Express HOTEL $$
(993-314-53-78; www.hotelesprovinciaexpress.infored.mx; Lerdo de Tejada 303; r incl breakfast M$500-600; P) Excellent value in a central location, this hotel has small but tidy and pleasant rooms and a homey yellow color scheme. It's on a pedestrian street, so get a window if possible; avoid the windowless rooms. There's a cafe in the lobby.

Hotel Olmeca Plaza HOTEL $$$
(800-201-09-09, 993-358-01-02; www.hotelolmecaplaza.com; Madero 418; r Mon-Thu M$1573, Fri-Sun M$886; P) The classiest downtown hotel also has an open-air pool and a well-equipped gym. Rooms are modern and comfortable, with ample desks and good large bathrooms, and there's a quality on-site restaurant.

Eating & Drinking

A large city, Villahermosa has an eclectic collection of hotel restaurants, chain restaurants and eateries specializing in seafood and international cuisines.

Café Punta del Cielo CAFE $
(Plaza de Armas; coffee M$23-39; 7am-10pm;) A respite from the raging heat and humidity, this small air-conditioned glass box next to the Torre del Caballero footbridge is a dream come true. Primarily a cafe, it serves premium hot and cold coffee drinks (some organic), as well as *panini* and light snacks. Go for brain freeze with an arctic frappé.

★**La Dantesca** ITALIAN, PIZZERIA $$
(Hidalgo 406, near Parque Los Pajaritos; mains M$60-97, pizza M$145; 1-10pm) Locals flock to this lively trattoria for its fantastic brick-oven pizzas, house-made pastas and scrumptious desserts. Most folks come for the pizza, but the ravioli verde with *requesón* and *jamaica* (a ricotta-like cheese and hibiscus flowers) and other pastas are superb.

Restaurante Madan MEXICAN $$
(Madero 408; mains M$50-140; 7am-11pm;) It's not glamorous, but this very reliable and popular hotel restaurant two blocks west of the river has good Mexican dishes and efficient, friendly service.

Rock & Roll Cocktelería SEAFOOD $$
(Reforma 307; mains M$120-180; ⌚10am-10pm) A maelstrom of heat, swirling fans and blaring TVs. Everyone's here for the seafood cocktails (though it also has good *ceviche* and seafood stew) and cheap beer. It's on a pedestrian street across from the Miraflores Hotel, and has 60 years under its belt.

Information

There are plentiful internet cafes charging about M$10 to M$12 per hour. Most banks have ATMs and exchange dollars.

Funny Zone (Mina; ⌚8am-9pm Mon-Sat) Internet cafe across from the ADO bus station.

HSBC (cnr Juárez & Lerdo de Tejada; ⌚9am-5pm Mon-Fri) Bank on pedestrianized street.

Oficina de Convenciones y Visitantes de Tabasco (OCV; ☎800-216-08-42; www.visitetabasco.com) Statewide information.

Tourism Information Kiosk (⌚9am-6pm Mon-Sat) At the ADO bus terminal; has maps and can book hotels.

Getting There & Away

AIR

Villahermosa's **Aeropuerto Rovirosa** (☎993-356-01-57) is 13km east of the center, off Hwy 186. Aeroméxico is the major airline, and daily nonstop flights to/from Villahermosa include the following:

Aeroméxico (www.aeromexico.com) Flys to Mérida, Mexico City and Veracruz; lots of international connections via Mexico City.

Interjet (www.interjet.com.mx) To Mexico City.

MAYAir (www.mayair.com.mx) To Mérida and Veracruz.

United (www.united.com) To Houston.

VivaAerobus (☎993-356-02-07; www.vivaaerobus.com.mx) To Mexico City, Cancún, Monterrey and Guadalajara.

AIRPORT BUS TO PALENQUE

The Villahermosa airport has a handy counter for **ADO** (www.ado.com.mx), with almost hourly minibuses departing daily to Palenque (M$236, 2¼ hours) between 7:30am and 9:30pm. Check the website for schedules to/from 'Aeropuerto Villahermosa.'

BUS & COLECTIVO

Deluxe and 1st-class buses depart from the **ADO bus station** (ADO; ☎993-312-84-22; Mina 297), which has wi-fi, 24-hour left luggage and is located 750m north of the Zona Luz.

Transportation to most destinations within Tabasco leaves from other terminals within walking distance north of ADO, including the 2nd-class **Cardesa bus station** (Cardesa; cnr Hermanos Bastar Zozaya & Castillo) and the main 2nd-

BUSES FROM VILLAHERMOSA

DESTINATION	FARE (M$)	DURATION	FREQUENCY (DAILY)
Campeche	280-554	5½-7hr	22 ADO
Cancún	435-1260	12½-14½hr	20 ADO
Comalcalco	20-24	1-1½hr	very frequent Cardesa
Frontera	47-58	1-1½hr	very frequent ADO, CAT & Cardesa
Mérida	430-960	8-9½hr	28 ADO
Mexico City (TAPO)	680-1370	10-12hr	21 ADO
Oaxaca	584	13½hr	4 ADO
Palenque	65-134	2½hr	22 ADO, very frequent Cardesa
San Cristóbal de las Casas	326	7½hr	1 ADO
Tacotalpa	38	1½hr	very frequent CAT
Tenosique	110-174	3½hr	11 ADO, very frequent CAT
Tuxtla Gutiérrez	286-416	4-5hr	18 ADO
Veracruz	450-690	6-8½hr	23 ADO
Villahermosa airport	174	30min	16 ADO

class bus station, the **Central de Autobuses de Tabasco** (CAT; ☎993-312-29-77; cnr Av Ruíz Cortines & Castillo) on the north side of Avenida Ruíz Cortines (use the pedestrian overpass).

Getting Around

Comfortable ADO minibuses ferry passengers between the airport and the ADO bus terminal (M$174); they run hourly between 6am and 9pm. Taxis to the center cost M$200. Alternatively, walk 500m past the airport parking lot for a *colectivo* (M$20) from the Dos Montes taxi stand. These terminate in the market on Carranza, about 1km north of the Zona Luz.

A system of *colectivo* taxis (M$20) provides the backbone of the center's public transit. Flag one down to ask if they're going your way, or join a queue at a stand outside a large store or transportation terminal, where proficient handlers ask for your destination and quickly assign you a shared taxi. There's no fee for the match-up, and no haggling necessary. Private taxis charge M$45 within the center.

Oaxaca

Includes ➡

Best Off the Beaten Track

- Concepción Bamba (p486)
- Lachatao (p452)
- Playa Escobilla (p468)
- Chacahua (p465)
- Santiago Apoala (p452)

Best Places to Stay

- Casa Oaxaca (p433)
- Punta Placer (p473)
- Oceanomar (p476)
- Hotel Las Golondrinas (p431)
- El Diablo y la Sandía (p431)

Why Go?

The state of Oaxaca (wah-*hah*-kah) has a special magic felt by Mexicans and foreigners alike. A redoubt of indigenous culture, it's home to the country's most vibrant crafts and art scene, some outstandingly colorful and extroverted festivities, a uniquely savory cuisine and varied natural riches.

At the center of the state in every way stands beautiful, colonial Oaxaca city, an elegant and fascinating cultural hub. Nearby, the forested Sierra Norte is home to successful community-tourism ventures enabling visitors to hike, bike and ride horses amid delicious green landscapes.

To the south, across rugged, remote mountains, is Oaxaca's fabulous coast, with its endless sandy beaches, pumping Pacific surf, seas full of dolphins, turtles and fish, and a string of beach towns and villages that will make any traveler happy: lively Puerto Escondido; planned but relaxed Bahías de Huatulco; and the mellow delights of Zipolite, San Agustinillo and Mazunte.

When to Go

Oaxaca City

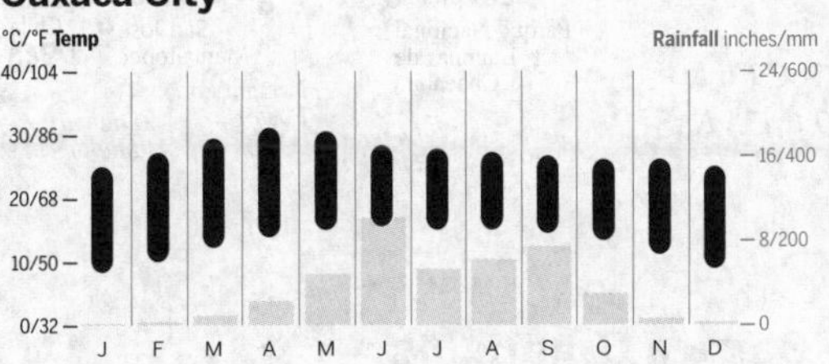

Jan–Mar Driest months: a lively coastal winter-escapee scene, best hiking in the Sierra Norte.

Jul & Aug Guelaguetza festival in Oaxaca city; summer-vacation fun time on the coast.

Late Oct & Nov Día de Muertos celebrations; Fiestas de Noviembre in Puerto Escondido.

Oaxaca Highlights

1. Indulge in the culture, color, crafts, cuisine – and mezcal – of festive, colonial **Oaxaca city** (p420)

2. Chill out for longer than you planned at the travelers' hangouts of **Zipolite** (p469), **San Agustinillo** (p472) or **Mazunte** (p474)

3. Ride the surf on the gorgeous beaches of **Puerto Escondido** (p454)

4. Hike through otherworldly cloud forests between the

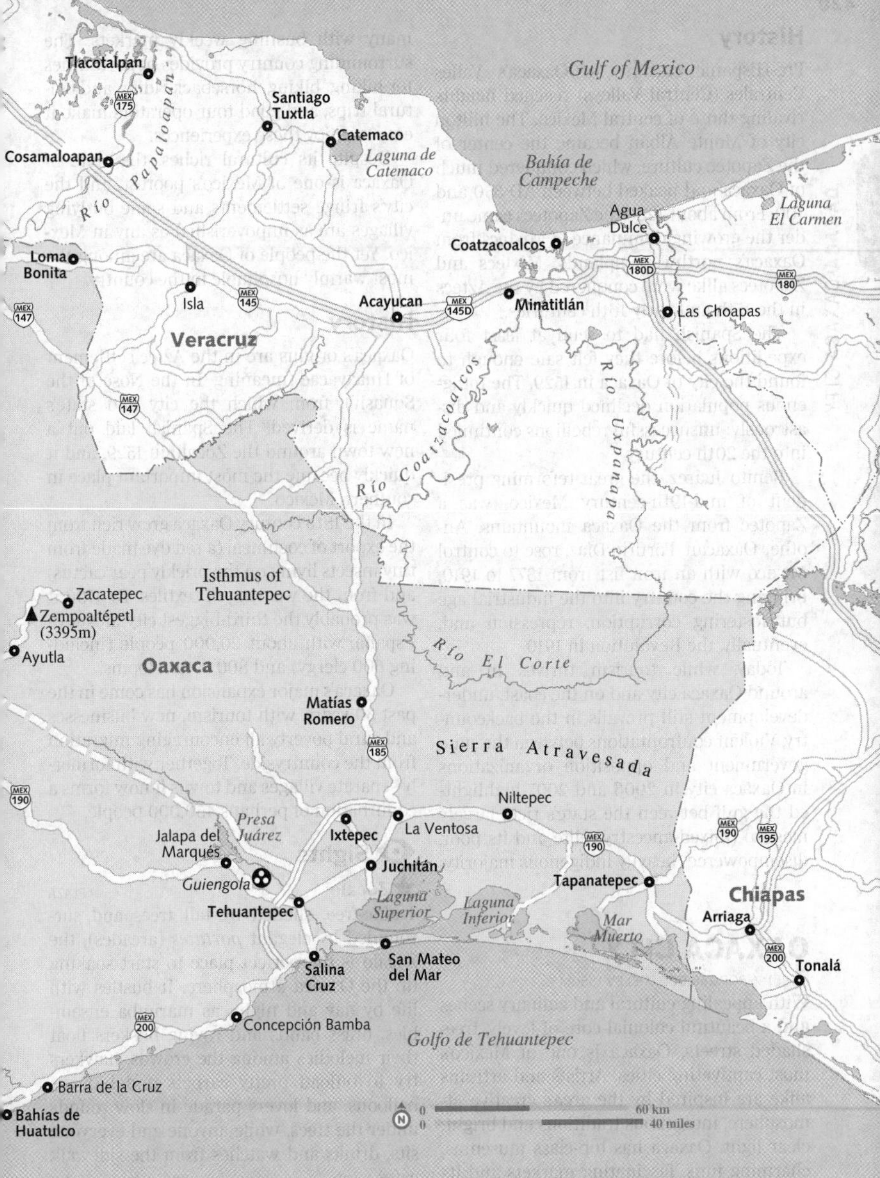

villages of the **Pueblos Mancomunados** (p451)

5 Enjoy the majestic setting and mysterious architecture of **Monte Albán** (p442)

6 Get a feel for indigenous village life at the markets and fiestas of the **Valles Centrales** (p442)

History

Pre-Hispanic cultures in Oaxaca's Valles Centrales (Central Valleys) reached heights rivaling those of central Mexico. The hilltop city of Monte Albán became the center of the Zapotec culture, which conquered much of Oaxaca and peaked between AD 350 and 700. From about 1200 the Zapotecs came under the growing dominance of Mixtecs from Oaxaca's northwest uplands. Mixtecs and Zapotecs alike were conquered by the Aztecs in the 15th and early 16th centuries.

The Spanish had to send at least four expeditions before they felt safe enough to found the city of Oaxaca in 1529. The indigenous population declined quickly and disastrously: unsuccessful rebellions continued into the 20th century.

Benito Juárez, the great reforming president of mid-19th-century Mexico, was a Zapotec from the Oaxaca mountains. Another Oaxacan, Porfirio Díaz, rose to control Mexico with an iron fist from 1877 to 1910, bringing the country into the industrial age but fostering corruption, repression and, eventually, the Revolution in 1910.

Today, while tourism thrives in and around Oaxaca city and on the coast, underdevelopment still prevails in the backcountry. Violent confrontations between the state government and opposition organizations in Oaxaca city in 2006 and 2007 highlighted the gulf between the state's rich, largely mestizo (mixed-ancestry) elite and its poor, disempowered, heavily indigenous majority.

OAXACA CITY

951 / POP 260,000 / ELEV 1550M

With appealing cultural and culinary scenes and a beautiful colonial core of lovely, tree-shaded streets, Oaxaca is one of Mexico's most captivating cities. Artists and artisans alike are inspired by the area's creative atmosphere, indigenous traditions and bright, clear light. Oaxaca has top-class museums, charming inns, fascinating markets and its own subtle version of Mexican cuisine. The easygoing pace frequently breaks out into the fireworks of a fiesta, and there's some brightly colored event unfolding in the streets or the Zócalo (Oaxaca's lovely central square) almost every day.

Set at the nexus of three mountain-flanked valleys, the city is surrounded by fascinating archaeological sites and villages, many with bustling weekly markets. The surrounding country provides opportunities for hiking, biking, horseback riding and cultural trips, and good tour operators make it easy to enjoy these experiences.

Despite its cultural riches, the state of Oaxaca is one of Mexico's poorest, and the city's fringe settlements and some outlying villages are as impoverished as any in Mexico. Yet the people of Oaxaca are among the most warmly hospitable in the country.

History

Oaxaca's origins are in the Aztec settlement of Huaxyácac (meaning 'In the Nose of the Squash'), from which the city and state's name is derived. The Spanish laid out a new town around the Zócalo in 1529, and it quickly became the most important place in southern Mexico.

In the 18th century Oaxaca grew rich from the export of cochineal (a red dye made from tiny insects living on the prickly pear cactus) and from the weaving of textiles. By 1796 it was probably the third-biggest city in Nueva España, with about 20,000 people (including 600 clergy) and 800 cotton looms.

Oaxaca's major expansion has come in the past 30 years, with tourism, new businesses and rural poverty all encouraging migration from the countryside. Together with formerly separate villages and towns it now forms a conurbation of perhaps 450,000 people.

Sights

★Zócalo — PLAZA

Traffic-free, shaded by tall trees and surrounded by elegant *portales* (arcades), the Zócalo is the perfect place to start soaking up the Oaxaca atmosphere. It bustles with life by day and night, as marimba ensembles, brass bands and roving buskers float their melodies among the crowds, hawkers try to offload pretty carpets and hideous balloons, and lovers parade in slow rounds under the trees, while anyone and everyone sits, drinks and watches from the sidewalk cafes.

The adjoining **Alameda** plaza is also traffic-free but without the cafes, and is ripe for people-watching with its trinket-toting vendors, gawking tourists and informal clothes market.

Palacio de Gobierno

A 19th-century wonder of marble and murals, the State Government Palace occupies the Zócalo's southern flank. The large-scale stairway **mural** (1980) by Arturo García Bustos depicts famous Oaxacans and Oaxacan history, including Benito Juárez and his wife Margarita Maza, and José María Morelos, Porfirio Díaz, Vicente Guerrero (being shot at Cuilapan) and 17th-century nun and love poet Juana Inés de la Cruz.

The building also houses the interactive **Museo del Palacio** (admission M$25, Sun free; ⏲9:30am-6pm, to 5pm Mon, to 4pm Sun), whose main displays, with a primarily educational purpose and in Spanish only, range over evolution, the pre-Hispanic ball game, geology, biodiversity and more, with a Oaxacan handle on universal themes. Also here is what is very probably the world's largest tortilla – a 300kg *tlayuda*, decorated with the history of Mexico by Enrique Ramos.

➡ Catedral

Oaxaca's cathedral, begun in 1553 and finished (after several earthquakes) in the 18th century, stands just north of the Zócalo. Its main facade, facing the Alameda, features fine baroque carving.

Calle Alcalá STREET

Alcalá is the dignified, mainly traffic-free street that runs from the Catedral to the Templo de Santo Domingo, lined by colonial-era stone buildings that are now home to alluring shops, galleries, museums, cafes and bars, making for an always-interesting stroll and a lively nocturnal scene.

★Templo de Santo Domingo CHURCH

(cnr Alcalá & Gurrión; ⏲7am-1pm & 4-8pm, except during Mass) Gorgeous Santo Domingo is the most splendid of Oaxaca's churches, with a finely carved baroque facade and nearly every square inch inside decorated in 3-D relief with intricately colored and gilt designs swirling around a profusion of painted figures. Most elaborate of all is the 18th-century **Capilla de la Virgen del Rosario** (Rosary Chapel) on the south side of the nave. The whole church takes on a magically warm glow during candlelit evening Masses.

Santo Domingo was built mainly between 1570 and 1608 as part of the city's Dominican monastery, with the finest artisans from Puebla and elsewhere helping in its construction. Like other big buildings in this earthquake-prone region, it has immensely thick stone walls.

Santo Domingo de Guzmán (1172–1221), the Spanish monk who founded the Dominican order, appears as the right-hand one of the two figures holding a church in the center of the facade, and his elaborate family tree adorns the ceiling immediately inside the main entrance. The Dominicans observed strict vows of poverty, chastity and obedience, and in Mexico they protected the indigenous people from other colonists' excesses.

★Museo de las Culturas de Oaxaca MUSEUM

(☎951-516-29-91; Alcalá; admission $57, video M$45; ⏲10am-6:15pm Tue-Sun) The Museum of Oaxacan Cultures, housed in the beautiful monastery buildings adjoining the Templo de Santo Domingo, is one of Mexico's best regional museums. The rich displays take you right through the history and cultures of Oaxaca state up to the present day, and emphasize the direct lineage from Oaxaca's pre-Hispanic to contemporary cultures in areas such as crafts, medicine and food.

A gorgeous stone cloister serves as antechamber to the museum proper. The greatest treasure is the Mixtec hoard from Tomb 7 at Monte Albán, in Room III. It dates from the 14th century, when Mixtecs reused an old Zapotec tomb to bury one of their kings and his sacrificed servants, along with a stash of beautifully worked silver, turquoise, coral, jade, amber and pearls, finely carved bone, crystal goblets, a skull covered in turquoise, and a lot of gold. The treasure was discovered in 1932 by Alfonso Caso.

Halls I to IV are devoted to the pre-Hispanic period, halls V to VIII to the colonial period, halls IX to XIII to Oaxaca in the independence era and after, and the final room (XIV) to Santo Domingo Monastery itself. At the end of the long corridor past hall IX, glass doors give a view into the beautifully ornate choir of the Templo de Santo Domingo.

The museum's explanatory material is in Spanish only, but you can rent an English-language audio guide for M$50. Also here is a good book and souvenir shop.

Jardín Etnobotánico GARDENS

(Ethnobotanical Garden; ☎951-516-79-15; www.jardinoaxaca.org.mx; cnr Constitución & Reforma; 2hr tours in English or French M$100, 1hr tours in Spanish M$50; ⏲English tours 11am Tue, Thu & Sat, Spanish tours 10am, noon & 5pm Mon-Sat, French tours 5pm Tue) In former monastic grounds behind the Templo de Santo Domingo, this garden features plants from around Oaxaca state, including a staggering variety of cacti. Though it has been growing only since the

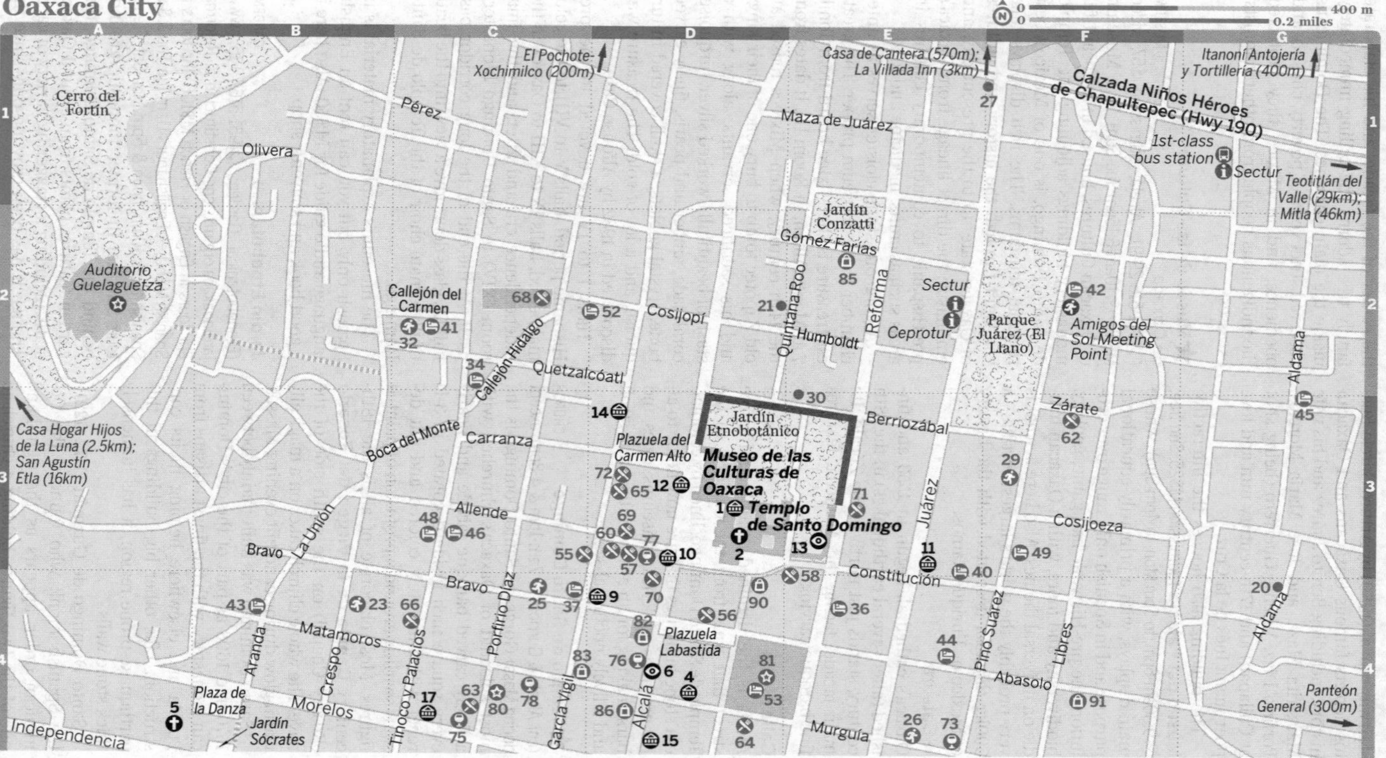
Oaxaca City
400 m
0.2 miles
El Pochote-Xochimilco (200m)
Casa de Cantera (570m); La Villada Inn (3km)
Itanoní Antojería y Tortillería (400m)
Calzada Niños Héroes de Chapultepec (Hwy 190)
1st-class bus station
Sectur
Teotitlán del Valle (29km); Mitla (46km)
Cerro del Fortín
Pérez
Maza de Juárez
Olivera
Jardín Conzatti
Gómez Farías
Auditorio Guelaguetza
Callejón del Carmen
Cosijopí
Quintana Roo
Humboldt
Reforma
Sectur
Ceprotur
Parque Juárez (El Llano)
Amigos del Sol Meeting Point
Aldama
Callejón Hidalgo
Quetzalcóatl
Jardín Etnobotánico
Berriozábal
Zárate
Casa Hogar Hijos de la Luna (2.5km); San Agustín Etla (16km)
Boca del Monte
Carranza
Plazuela del Carmen Alto
Museo de las Culturas de Oaxaca
Templo de Santo Domingo
Juárez
Allende
Cosijoeza
Bravo
La Unión
Constitución
Bravo
Porfirio Díaz
Matamoros
Plazuela Labastida
Aranda
Crespo
Tinoco y Palacios
García Vigil
Alcalá
Pino Suárez
Libres
Aldama
Abasolo
Plaza de la Danza
Jardín Sócrates
Morelos
Murguía
Independencia
Panteón General (300m)

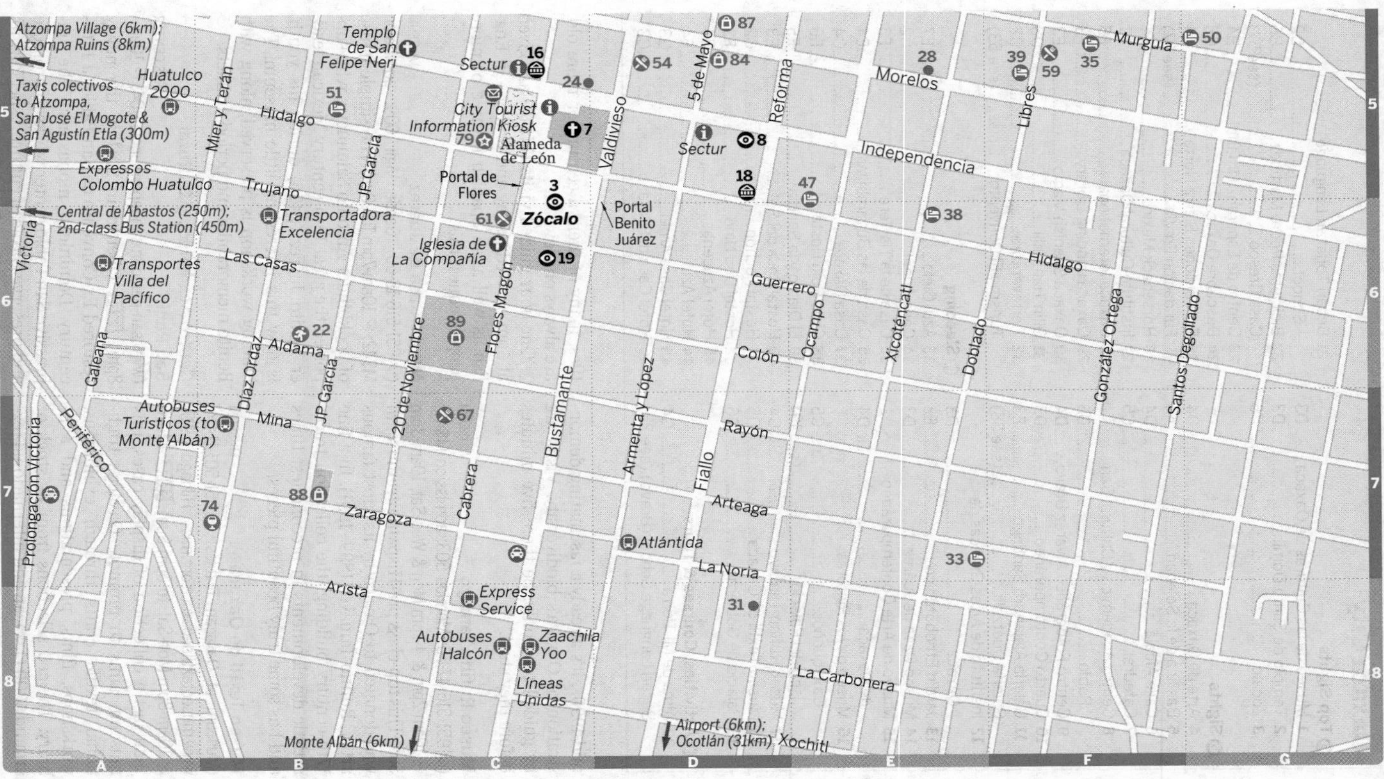

Atzompa Village (6km); Atzompa Ruins (8km)
Templo de San Felipe Neri
Sectur
Murguía
Morelos
Libres
Huatulco 2000
Taxis colectivos to Atzompa, San José El Mogote & San Agustín Etla (300m)
Mier y Terán
Hidalgo
JP García
City Tourist Information Kiosk
Alameda de León
Valdivieso
5 de Mayo
Reforma
Independencia
Expressos Colombo Huatulco
Trujano
Portal de Flores
Zócalo
Portal Benito Juárez
Central de Abastos (250m); 2nd-class Bus Station (450m)
Transportadora Excelencia
Victoria
Iglesia de La Compañía
Las Casas
Transportes Villa del Pacífico
Hidalgo
Guerrero
Ocampo
Xicoténcatl
Doblado
González Ortega
Santos Degollado
Aldama
Díaz Ordaz
Galeana
JP García
20 de Noviembre
Flores Magón
Colón
Autobuses Turísticos (to Monte Albán)
Mina
Bustamante
Armenta y López
Rayón
Periférico
Prolongación Victoria
Cabrera
Fiallo
Arteaga
Zaragoza
Atlántida
La Noria
Arista
Express Service
Autobuses Halcón
Zaachila
Yoo
Líneas Unidas
La Carbonera
Monte Albán (6km)
Airport (6km); Ocotlán (31km)
Xochitl

Oaxaca City

Top Sights

1 Museo de las Culturas de Oaxaca D3
2 Templo de Santo Domingo D3
3 Zócalo C5

Sights

4 Arte de Oaxaca D4
5 Basílica de la Soledad A4
6 Calle Alcalá D4
7 Catedral C5
8 Centro Académico y Cultural San Pablo D5
9 Centro Fotográfico Álvarez Bravo D4
10 Cuarto Contemporáneo D3
11 Galería Alejandro Santiago E3
Galería Quetzalli .... (see 58)
12 Instituto de Artes Gráficas de Oaxaca D3
13 Jardín Etnobotánico E3
14 Museo Casa de Juárez D3
15 Museo de Arte Contemporáneo de Oaxaca D4
16 Museo de los Pintores Oaxaqueños C5
Museo del Palacio .... (see 19)
17 Museo Rufino Tamayo C4
18 Museo Textil de Oaxaca D5
19 Palacio de Gobierno C6

Activities, Courses & Tours

20 Alma de Mi Tierra G4
Becari Language School (Bravo) .(see 25)
21 Becari Tonatzin Language School D2
22 Bicicletas Pedro Martínez B6
Casa Crespo .... (see 57)
23 Centro de Esperanza Infantil B4
24 Descubre Oaxaca C5
25 Expediciones Sierra Norte C4
Fundación En Vía .... (see 27)
26 Horseback Mexico E4
27 Instituto Cultural Oaxaca F1
28 Oaxaca International E5
29 Oaxaca Lending Library F3
30 Oaxaca Spanish Magic E3
31 Ollin Tlahtoalli D8
32 Tierraventura C2
Turismo El Convento .... (see 53)

Sleeping

33 Azul Cielo E7
34 Casa Ángel C2
35 Casa de la Tía Tere F5
36 Casa de las Bugambilias E4
37 Casa Oaxaca C4
38 Cielo Rojo Hostal E6
39 El Diablo y la Sandía F5
40 Hostal Casa del Sol E3
41 Hostal Pochón C2
42 Hostel Don Nino F2
43 Hotel Azucenas B4
44 Hotel Azul E4
45 Hotel Casa Arnel G3
46 Hotel Casa del Sótano C3

mid-1990s, it's already a fascinating demonstration of Oaxaca's biodiversity. Visits are by guided tour only: be there five minutes before they start.

Museo Rufino Tamayo MUSEUM
(☎951-516-47-50; Morelos 503; admission M$40; ⏲10am-2pm & 4-7pm Mon & Wed-Sat, 10am-3pm Sun) This top-class pre-Hispanic art museum was donated to Oaxaca by its most famous artist, Rufino Tamayo (1899–1991). In a fine 17th-century building, the collection traces artistic developments in preconquest times and has some truly beautiful pieces.

Museo Textil de Oaxaca MUSEUM
(Museum of Oaxacan Textiles; ☎951-501-11-04; www.museotextildeoaxaca.org.mx; Hildago 917; ⏲10am-8pm Mon-Sat, to 6pm Sun) FREE More than just a collection of display cases, this museum aims to promote Oaxaca's traditional textile crafts through exhibitions, workshops, films, presentations and a library. Themed selections from its stock of around 5000 Oaxacan and international textiles, many of them a century or more old, are always on view.

One-hour guided visits (M$10) are given at 5pm on Wednesday and Friday – in English as well as in Spanish if three or more people request this.

Museo Casa de Juárez MUSEUM
(☎951-516-18-60; García Vigil 609; admission M$42; ⏲10am-7pm Tue-Sun) The simple house of bookbinder Antonio Salanueva, who supported the great 19th-century Mexican leader Benito Juárez (p426) during his youth, is now this interesting little museum. The binding workshop is preserved, along with Benito memorabilia and period artifacts.

Centro Académico y Cultural San Pablo ARTS CENTER
(www.san-pablo.mx; Independencia 904; ⏲10am-8pm) FREE Opened in 2011 in the newly restored Ex-Convento de San Pablo (a 16th-century Dominican monastery), the impressive San Pablo center works to promote and preserve Oaxacan culture, especially its

47 Hotel Dainzú E5
48 Hotel Las Golondrinas C3
49 La Casa de Mis Recuerdos F3
50 Learning Center G5
51 Parador San Andrés B5
52 Posada Don Mario D2
53 Quinta Real Oaxaca D4

Eating
54 Café Brújula D5
55 Café Brújula C3
Cafe El Ágora .... (see 45)
56 Café Los Cuiles D4
57 Casa Crespo D3
58 Casa Oaxaca E4
59 Cenaduría Tlayudas Libres F5
60 Comala D3
61 El Asador Vasco C6
62 El Típico F3
63 El Trompo C4
64 Jaguar Yuú D4
65 La Biznaga D3
La Olla .... (see 36)
66 Manantial Vegetariano C4
67 Mercado 20 de Noviembre C7
68 Mercado Sánchez Pascuas C2
69 Pitiona D3
70 Restaurante Los Danzantes D4
71 Vieja Lira E3
72 Zandunga D3

Drinking & Nightlife
Café del Jardín .... (see 61)
73 Candela E4
74 Cuish B7
75 In Situ C4
76 La Cantinita D4
77 Los Amantes D3
78 Txalaparta C4

Entertainment
79 Hotel Monte Albán C5
80 La Nueva Babel C4
81 Quinta Real Oaxaca D4

Shopping
82 Amate Books D4
83 Casa de las Artesanías de Oaxaca C4
84 La Casa del Rebozo D5
85 La Cava E2
86 La Mano Mágica D4
87 MARO D5
88 Mercado de Artesanías B7
89 Mercado Juárez C6
90 Shkáala D4
91 Unión de Palenqueros de Oaxaca F4

indigenous aspects, through temporary exhibitions (of which there are always a couple), classes, seminars, presentations and conferences.

It has a print library with valuable anthropological archives and a sound library with recordings of indigenous music.

Basílica de la Soledad CHURCH
(Independencia) The image of Oaxaca's patron saint, the Virgen de la Soledad (Virgin of Solitude), stands above the altar in the 17th-century Basílica de la Soledad. The church, with a richly carved baroque facade, stands where the image is said to have miraculously appeared in a donkey's pack in 1543.

Activities

If you're interested in doing some volunteering while here, it's worth noting that most of Oaxaca's Spanish-language schools offer opportunities for their students, and in some cases for nonstudents too.

Tierraventura OUTDOORS
(951-516-46-44; www.tierraventura.com; Callejón del Carmen 108; 10am-2pm & 4-6pm Mon-Fri) Well-organized Tierraventura, run by a multilingual European and Mexican team, offers a big variety of trips and activities focused on hiking, cycling, nature, meeting locals and supporting local tourism projects. Local guides accompany travelers wherever possible. Per-person prices range from M$900 to M$1200 on day trips, and M$1200 to M$2000 per day on longer trips.

Options include one-day cycling trips in the Valle de Tlacolula and hiking from one to six days in the Pueblos Mancomunados. Tierraventura also offers rare opportunities to learn about and experience traditional medicine through a partnership with Ceciproc, an NGO working to improve health in indigenous communities. You can take a traditional herbal cleansing and temascal (steam bath) at its Oaxaca premises, or a mountain walk focusing on medicinal plants.

Expediciones Sierra Norte OUTDOORS
(951-514-82-71; www.sierranorte.org.mx; Bravo 210; 9:30am-7pm Mon-Fri, to 2pm Sat) Some of Oaxaca's most exhilarating outdoor adventures are to be had among the mountain

BENITO JUÁREZ

One of the few Mexican national heroes with a truly unsullied reputation, the great reforming president Benito Juárez (1806–72) was born a humble Zapotec villager in Guelatao, 60km northeast of Oaxaca. His parents died when he was three. At the age of 12, young Benito walked to Oaxaca and found work at the house of Antonio Salanueva, a bookbinder. Salanueva saw the boy's potential and helped pay for an education he otherwise might not have received.

Juárez later started training for the priesthood, but abandoned this to work as a lawyer for poor villagers. He rose to become Oaxaca's state governor from 1848 to 1852, opening schools and cutting bureaucracy, and was made justice minister in Mexico's new liberal government of 1855. His Ley Juárez (Juárez Law), which transferred the trials of soldiers and priests charged with civil crimes to ordinary civil courts, was the first of the Reform Laws, which sought to break the power of the Catholic Church. These laws provoked the War of the Reform of 1858 to 1861, in which the liberals eventually defeated the conservatives.

Juárez was elected Mexico's president in 1861 but had been in office only a few months when France invaded Mexico, forcing him into exile. In 1866–67, with US support, Juárez ousted the French and their puppet emperor, Maximilian. One of Juárez' main political achievements was to make primary education free and compulsory. He died in 1872, a year after being elected to his fourth presidential term. Oaxacans are fiercely proud of him and today countless streets, statues, schools, villages and cities all around Mexico preserve his name and memory. If the world followed his famous maxim '*Entre los individuos, como entre las naciones, el respeto al derecho ajeno es la paz*' ('Between individuals as between nations, respect for the rights of others is peace'), it would be a much better place.

villages of the Pueblos Mancomunados (p451), where community-run Expediciones Sierra Norte maintains a network of good trails, comfortable *cabañas* (cabins), and horses and bikes for rent. This city office has copious information (including a useful guide-map for M$50) and some English-speaking staff, and can make reservations for *cabañas* and other services.

Bicicletas Pedro Martínez CYCLING, HIKING
(951-514-59-35; www.bicicletaspedromartinez.com; Aldama 418; 9am-8pm Mon-Sat, 10am-3pm Sun) This friendly team headed by Mexican Olympic cyclist Pedro Martínez offers a variety of exciting, mostly off-road rides (as well as some great day walks) amid some of Oaxaca state's best scenery. Van support cuts out the less interesting bits and hardest climbs. The shortest options are half-day or full-day rides in the Valle de Tlacolula: the full-day option costs M$1350 per person for two people or M$1150 with four.

The two-day 'Cascadas y Mangos' jaunt (M$2550 to M$2900 per person) runs from Nochixtlán to spectacular Santiago Apoala (p452), then across the scenic Tehuacán-Cuicatlán biosphere reserve. The three- or four-day Ruta Los Coatlanes takes you right down to Puerto Escondido on the Pacific coast, crossing the Sierra Madre del Sur, for M$5610 to M$5900 per person.

Horseback Mexico HORSEBACK RIDING
(cell phone 951-1997026; www.horsebackmexico.com; Murguía 403; 11am-6pm Sun-Fri) This experienced, enthusiastic Canadian- and American-run outfit offers a variety of equestrian adventures for all levels from beginners up. Two-hour rides on Arabian and Mexican Criollo horses in the local valleys and hills cost M$850 per person including round-trip transportation from Oaxaca.

Other options include a 'Ride, Cook & Eat' half-day, overnight rides and one-week riding vacations, which might be based at its Rojas de Cuauhtémoc ranch, 15km east of the city (which has comfortable guest accommodations), or riding village to village in the picturesque Sierra Norte.

Centro de Esperanza Infantil VOLUNTEERING
(951-501-10-69; www.oaxacastreetchildrengrassroots.org; Crespo 308; 9am-5pm Mon-Fri, to 2pm Sat) This is a nonpolitical, nonreligious center that sponsors and cares for about 600 children from poor families who, without assistance, could not get an education.

The staff welcomes donations, sponsors and visitors, and volunteers can help with tutoring (especially in mathematics, Spanish and English), administrative work or projects with the children. Even a half-day of assistance can be helpful.

Some knowledge of Spanish is useful for volunteers, but not essential. Volunteers offering workshops, for example in art, handicrafts or photography, are especially welcome. About 10 kids from here go on to graduate from university each year.

Oaxaca Lending Library LIBRARY
(☎951-518-70-77; http://oaxlibrary.org; Pino Suárez 519; ⏲10am-2pm & 4-7pm Mon-Fri, 10am-1pm Sat) A hub for foreign residents and language learners, the library boasts a sizable collection of books and magazines on Oaxaca and Mexico in English and Spanish. Visitor membership (per one/two months M$180/250) allows you to borrow books and DVDs. English-Spanish *intercambio* (language exchange) sessions happen on Saturday mornings, and further *intercambio* and volunteer opportunities are posted on the busy notice board.

Courses

Oaxaca is a very popular place for visitors to learn some Spanish or take a course in Mexican cooking.

Language Courses

Oaxaca has a clutch of reputable language schools, all offering small-group instruction at varied levels and most emphasizing spoken language. At most schools you can start any Monday (at some you can start any day). Most offer individual tuition if wanted, plus volunteer opportunities and optional activities like dance or cooking classes, trips and *intercambios*. Enrollment/registration fees, textbooks and materials are sometimes hidden costs.

Schools can arrange accommodations with families or in hotels, apartments and in some cases their own student houses. Family accommodations with a private room typically cost around US$18/23/26 a day with one/two/three meals.

Becari Language School LANGUAGE COURSE
(15/20/30hr per week US$150/200/300) Bravo (☎951-514-60-76; www.becari.com.mx; Bravo 210); Tonatzin (☎951-516-46-34; http://becariqr.com; Quintana Roo 209) This highly rated, medium-sized school has two separate branches: you can study at either or both. Maximum class size is five and optional extras include salsa dance, weaving and cooking. It also offers special courses such as medical Spanish, Zapotec language and Spanish for volunteers and children. The Tonatzin branch has a temascal, too.

Amigos del Sol LANGUAGE COURSE
(☎951-133-60-52, cell phone 951-1968039; www.oaxacanews.com/amigosdelsol.htm; Calzada San Felipe del Agua 322; 15/20/25hr per week US$158/200/238) Professional, good-value, flexible school popular with travelers. Maximum class size is three and you can start any weekday – usually the same day if you like. Contact the school by email or call 8am to 9:30am, 12:30pm to 1:30pm or after 8pm. There's no minimum duration and no registration charge.

The school is in a residential area in the north of the city, with free transportation for the short drive from its meeting point at Pino Suárez 802, facing Parque Juárez (El Llano).

Instituto Cultural Oaxaca LANGUAGE COURSE
(ICO; ☎951-515-34-04; www.icomexico.com; Juárez 909; 15/20/32hr per week US$140/157/178) A larger, long-established school with a professional approach and ample gardens where some of the learning takes place. The 32-hour-a-week main program includes eight hours of cultural workshops (dance, cooking, arts, crafts and more) and four hours' *intercambio*. You can study for any period from one week up; four weeks is typical.

Oaxaca International LANGUAGE COURSE
(☎951-503-42-28; www.oaxacainternational.com; Morelos 1107; 10/15/20/30hr per week US$80/120/160/240) Has classes limited to four students and also offers special programs for professionals in several fields. Two weekly cultural excursions are included in the fees.

Ollin Tlahtoalli LANGUAGE COURSE
(☎951-514-55-62; www.ollinoaxaca.org.mx; Ocampo 710; 15/20hr per week US$120/140) This operation has earned a reputation for pragmatic language learning and good volunteer opportunities in indigenous empowerment programs such as art workshops, filmmaking projects and English teaching. Email in advance to discuss your needs. For volunteers, a three-week commitment is needed.

CONTEMPORARY ART IN OAXACA

Of Mexico's major art hubs, Mexico City may have the most and the fanciest galleries, and Monterrey the most impressive presentations, but only in Oaxaca will you find such a concentration of talent, innovation and galleries within a small, accessible area.

A delight in color and light, a dreamlike feeling and references to indigenous mythology have long been trademarks of Oaxacan art. Two artists laid the basis for today's flourishing scene: the great muralist Rufino Tamayo (1899–1991) and European-influenced Francisco Gutiérrez (1906–45).

The next generation was led by three artists. The colorful art of Rodolfo Morales (1925–2001) from Ocotlán, with its childlike angel figures, has deep roots in local myths. Rodolfo Nieto (1936–85) populated his work with fantasy animals and dream figures. Francisco Toledo (b 1940), from Juchitán, works in many media, often focusing on grotesque beasts.

Workshops for young artists organized by Tamayo in the 1970s encouraged talents such as Abelardo López, Ariel Mendoza and Alejandro Santiago. Their work is highly varied, but indigenous roots and a dreamlike quality run through a lot of it. More or less contemporary is Sergio Hernández, whose limitless imagination melds the figurative with the abstract and fantastic. Artists who came to the fore around the turn of the 21st century, such as Demián Flores and Soid Pastrana, often reject representation and the 'folklorism' of earlier Oaxacan art in favor of postmodernism, video works and graphic compositions loaded with symbols designed to make us ponder. A wave of political and social unrest in Oaxaca in 2006 saw a burgeoning of street art, some of which can still be seen around the city.

Top Galleries & Museums

Museo de Arte Contemporáneo de Oaxaca (MACO; 951-514-22-28; www.museomaco.com; Alcalá 202; admission M$20, Sun free; 10:30am-8pm Wed-Mon) First-rate contemporary Mexican and international art, in a beautifully revamped colonial house.

Museo de los Pintores Oaxaqueños (Museum of Oaxacan Painters, MUPO; 951-516-56-45; http://museodelospintores.blogspot.co.uk; Independencia 607; admission M$20, Sun free; 10am-8pm Tue-Sat, 10am-6pm Sun) Changing exhibitions by artists from Oaxaca and elsewhere – often provocative contemporary work.

Cuarto Contemporáneo (cuartocontemporaneo.plaztika.com; Interior 3, Plaza Santo Domingo, Alcalá 407; noon-8pm Mon-Sat, to 7pm Sun) FREE Innovative space where you might catch installations, performances or experimental-media art by young Oaxacan artists. The gallery also involves poor communities around Oaxaca's periphery through a roving 'art bus.'

Galería Alejandro Santiago (Juárez 500; 11am-7.30pm Mon-Sat) FREE Dedicated to Alejandro Santiago (1965–2013), creator of the most celebrated work of recent Oaxacan art – his installation *2501 Migrantes*, comprising 2501 different human figures sculpted in clay, representing all the people who had migrated for economic reasons from his home village of Teococuilco in Oaxaca's northern mountains.

Arte de Oaxaca (951-514-15-32; www.artedeoaxaca.com; Murguía 105; 11am-3pm & 5-8pm Mon-Sat) FREE This commercial gallery presents a wide range of quality art, and includes a room devoted to Rodolfo Morales.

Centro Fotográfico Álvarez Bravo (951-516-98-00; www.cfmab.blogspot.com; Bravo 116; 9:30am-8pm Wed-Mon) FREE With a taste for provocative social commentary, this contemporary gallery displays quality work by international photographers.

Galería Quetzalli (951-514-26-06; Constitución 104; 10am-2pm & 5-8pm Mon-Sat) FREE A leading serious commercial gallery, handling some of the biggest names, such as Francisco Toledo and Sergio Hernández.

Instituto de Artes Gráficas de Oaxaca (Oaxaca Graphic Arts Institute, IAGO; 951-516-69-80; www.institutodeartesgraficasdeoaxaca.blogspot.com; Alcalá 507; 9:30am-8pm Mon-Sat) FREE Offers changing exhibitions of graphic art as well as a superb arts library.

Oaxaca Spanish Magic LANGUAGE COURSE
(☎951-516-73-16; www.oaxacaspanishmagic.com; Berriozábal 200; 15/20hr per week US$120/140) This small, well-priced school gets good reports for friendliness, effectiveness and making learning fun.

Cooking Classes

Oaxaca has its own spicy take on Mexican cuisine, based on its famous seven *moles* (sauces based on nuts, chilies and spices), pre-Hispanic culinary traditions and unforgettable flavor combinations. Several expert cooks regularly impart their secrets to visitors: the following recommended classes are (or can be) held in English, and generally include market visits to buy ingredients, plus a good mezcal with your meal.

La Casa de los Sabores COOKING
(☎951-516-66-68; www.casadelossabores.com; La Olla, Reforma 402; per person US$75) Pilar Cabrera, owner of La Olla (p435), gives classes most Wednesday and Friday mornings. Participants (minimum four, maximum 10) prepare and eat one of 16 Mexican or Oaxacan lunch menus. Make inquiries and reservations at La Olla: participants meet there at 9:30am and are delivered back there around 2:30pm after a market visit and the class and lunch, which take place at a house in Colonia Reforma, north of the center.

Alma de Mi Tierra COOKING
(☎951-513-92-11; www.almademitierra.net; Aldama 205, Barrio Jalatlaco; per person US$75) Nora Valencia, from a family of celebrated Oaxacan cooks, conducts five-hour classes for four to 10 people at her home in quaint Barrio Jalatlaco; 48 hours' notice is needed.

Seasons of My Heart COOKING
(☎cell phone 951-5080469; www.seasonsofmyheart.com; group day class incl transportation per person US$85, longer courses & tours from US$1500) This well-known cooking school at a ranch near San Lorenzo Cacaotepec in the Valle de Etla is run by food writer and Oaxacan food expert Susana Trilling. It offers half-day or one-day group classes (most Wednesdays), weeklong courses, and culinary tours around Oaxaca state and other Mexican regions.

Casa Crespo COOKING
(☎951-516-09-18; www.casacrespo.com; Allende 107; per person US$65) Amiable Óscar Carrizosa gives four-hour classes in Oaxacan cuisine at 10am daily except Monday, at his restaurant near the Templo de Santo Domingo. No minimum class size.

Tours

Guided trips can save hassles, be fun and tell you more than you might otherwise learn. A typical small-group day trip to El Tule, Teotitlán del Valle, Mitla, Hierve El Agua and a mezcal factory costs M$180 to M$300 per person; guided trips to Monte Albán are M$140 to M$180. Admission fees and meals are usually extra. You can book these tours at many accommodations, or direct with agencies such as **Descubre Oaxaca** (☎951-514-58-06; www.descubreoaxaca.com; Independencia 709; ⏲8:30am-8:30pm), at the lower end of the price range, or **Turismo El Convento** (☎951-516-18-06; www.oaxacatours.mx; Quinta Real, 5 de Mayo 300; ⏲8:30am-7pm Mon-Sat, 9am-2pm Sun), at the higher.

Fundación En Vía VILLAGE LIFE
(☎951-515-24-24; www.envia.org; Instituto Cultural Oaxaca, Juárez 909; tour per person US$50; ⏲tours 1pm Thu & 9am Sat) Nonprofit organization En Vía, staffed largely by volunteers, provides interest-free microfinance loans to small groups of women in several villages outside Oaxaca, to help them develop small businesses. The program is funded by En Vía's unique six-hour tours, which take you into the women's houses for lunch and explanations of local crafts and the village economy.

Traditions Mexico CULTURAL, CRAFTS
(www.traditionsmexico.com) Indefatigable traveler Eric Mindling has been exploring southern Mexico for more than 20 years, and his trips yield insights into Oaxacan artisanry, festivals, history and culture that few tours match. The tours get well off the beaten track to little-visited corners of Oaxaca state and emphasize contact with artisans and village life.

Personalized one-day tours start at US$300 for up to four people. Scheduled trips of six to eight nights cost between US$1600 and US$1900 per person.

Festivals & Events

All the major national festivals are celebrated here, and local festivals seems to happen every week somewhere in the city. The biggest and most spectacular of Oaxacan festivals is the Guelaguetza (see boxed text, p430).

GUELAGUETZAS LARGE & SMALL

The Guelaguetza is a brilliant feast of Oaxacan folk dance staged on the first two Mondays after July 16 in the large, semi-open-air Auditorio Guelaguetza on Cerro del Fortín. (The dates vary only when July 18, the anniversary of Benito Juárez' death, falls on a Monday. Guelaguetza then happens on July 25 and August 1.) The event takes place at 10am and 5pm on each of the Mondays, lasting about three hours. Magnificently costumed dancers from the seven regions of Oaxaca state perform a succession of dignified, lively or comical traditional dances, tossing offerings of produce to the crowd as they finish. Excitement climaxes with the incredibly colorful pineapple dance by women of the Papaloapan region, and the stately Zapotec Danza de las Plumas (Feather Dance), which symbolically re-enacts the Spanish conquest. The auditorium holds about 11,000 people: tickets for the front sections of seating (A and B, together holding about 3500 people) for each show go on sale about two months ahead through the state tourism office, Sectur (p440), and www.ticketmaster.com.mx, for M$800 to M$1000. The remaining seats (sections C and D) are free and first come, first served.

The Guelaguetza period also sees many other colorful celebrations in Oaxaca, including a mezcal fair and fantastically festive Saturday-afternoon parades along Calle Alcalá. Thousands of people flock into the city for the festivities (including visiting pickpockets, so stay alert).

Smaller Guelaguetzas are held in outlying towns and villages, such as Zaachila, Cuilapan, Tlacolula, Atzompa, Tlacochahuaya, Mitla and San Agustín Etla, usually on the same days, and can make a refreshing change from what might seem the over-commercialized hubbub of Oaxaca.

The Guelaguetza celebrations have their origins in a colonial-era fusion of indigenous festivities with Christian celebrations for the Virgen del Carmen. The current format dates back to 1932.

Día de Muertos TRADITIONAL

Oaxaca's Muertos (Day of the Dead) celebrations are among the most vibrant in Mexico, with concerts, exhibitions and other special goings-on starting days beforehand. Homes, cemeteries and some public buildings are decorated with fantastically crafted *altares de muertos* (altars of the dead), streets and plazas are decked with *tapetes de arena* (colored sand patterns and sculptures), and *comparsas* (satirical fancy-dress groups) parade through the streets.

Oaxaca's main cemetery, the Panteón General, 1km east of downtown, is the scene of concerts in the evenings of October 31 and November 1. Many villages, too, stage special events, with some Oaxaca accommodations and agencies arranging visits: the candlelit graveyard vigil through the October 31–November 1 night in Santa Cruz Xoxocotlán, a few kilometers south of the city, is particularly beautiful.

Oaxaca FilmFest FILM

(http://oaxacafilmfest.mx) A great weeklong program of independent films from around the world, at several city venues. All showings are free and all are in their original language with subtitles in Spanish, English or both. Dates vary: the 2014 event will be held in early October.

Noche de los Rábanos TRADITIONAL

Amazing figures carved from specially grown giant radishes are displayed in the Zócalo on December 23, the Night of the Radishes.

Sleeping

Accommodations range from bargain-priced hostels to luxury hotels in historic colonial buildings. There are plenty of charming midrange B&Bs and hotels. Some places (mostly midrange and top-end) raise rates for four peak seasons: Semana Santa, Guelaguetza, Día de Muertos and Christmas to New Year's.

Azul Cielo HOSTEL $

(951-205-35-64; http://azulcielohostel.mex.tl; Arteaga 608; dm/d incl breakfast M$130/460; @) A sunny, grassy garden is at the heart of this attractive hostel with the comfy atmosphere of a private home. A semi-open lounge area sits at one end, along with the two dorms and clean, modern kitchen. The six brightly decorated private rooms at the other end boast murals, good fans and wooden furniture. Free bikes (two hours a day) and a cooked breakfast add to the appeal.

Casa Ángel HOSTEL $
(☎951-514-22-24; www.casaangelhostel.com; Tinoco y Palacios 610; dm M$150-170, s/d M$500/600, without bathroom M$300/400, all incl breakfast; ⊖@☏) An excellent hostel, run by a friendly and helpful young team and kept scrupulously clean. Rooms are thoughtfully designed and the bright common areas include a good kitchen, a plasma screen with Netflix, and a great roof terrace with a BBQ every Sunday.

Four of the five attractive en suite private rooms have their own little terraces, and the dorms – most holding just three or four people – have good solid bunks with private reading lights.

Hostal Casa del Sol HOSTEL $
(☎951-514-41-10; www.hostalcasadelsol.com.mx; Constitución 301; dm/d/tr incl breakfast M$160/450/550; ⊖☏) This well-run, friendly spot is as much budget hotel as hostel, and offers exceptionally good value. There are five large, clean and attractive private rooms with touches of art and crafts, and one spacious eight-person dorm, all set around a leafy courtyard. Beds and bunks are solid and comfortable and the shared bathrooms are clean. The guest kitchen is open 8:30am to 6pm.

Hostal Pochón HOSTEL $
(☎951-516-13-22; http://pochonhostal.wix.com/hostalpochonofficial; Callejón del Carmen 102; dm M$135-140, d without bathroom M$325-370, incl breakfast; ⊖@☏) Popular Pochón, on a quiet street, provides five dorms for up to six people each (one for women only) and four private rooms with comfortable beds. Well kept and well run, it has a full kitchen and good common areas, and the included breakfast is worthwhile. It also offers free drinking water, bike rentals, cooking classes and cheap phone calls.

Cielo Rojo Hostal HOSTEL $
(☎951-514-17-68; www.cielorojohostel.com; Xicoténcatl; dm M$140-160, d M$360, incl breakfast; @☏) This hostel gives guests that bit extra with free two-hour city tours, themed trips to some offbeat destinations outside the city, and occasional live-music nights. The four dorms are clean and reasonably sized and all except one have their own bathroom, and there's a pleasant-enough white-tiled patio downstairs. The hostel supports social projects and is run on environmentally sound lines.

★Hotel Las Golondrinas HOTEL $$
(☎951-514-32-98; www.hotellasgolondrinas.com.mx; Tinoco y Palacios 411; s M$600, d M$650-730; ⊖@☏) Lovingly tended by friendly owners and staff, this lovely small hotel has about 30 rooms around three beautiful, leafy patios. Rooms are tastefully decorated and immaculately clean, and good breakfasts (dishes M$35 to M$70) are served on one of the patios. It's very well run and very good value.

★El Diablo y la Sandía B&B $$
(☎951-514-40-95; http://eldiabloylasandia.com; Libres 205; s M$800-900, d M$900-1200, incl breakfast; ⊖☏) This B&B is as quaintly stylish as its name ('The Devil and the Watermelon') and has a welcoming atmosphere. A tasty Oaxacan breakfast emerges daily from the big kitchen range, and the five rooms are spotlessly clean with comfy beds and pretty, very original Oaxacan *artesanías* (handicrafts). Four are set around a light-filled courtyard, the other is beside the roof terrace.

There's a cozy sitting room with drinks and snacks available, and the kitchen is available for guests to use after breakfast.

Hotel Azucenas HOTEL $$
(☎951-514-79-18, 800-717-25-40, in the USA & Canada 800-882-6089; www.hotelazucenas.com; Aranda 203; s/d M$725/775; ⊖@☏) The Azucenas is a small, friendly, very-well-run Canadian-owned hotel in a beautifully restored century-old house. The 10 attractive, cool, tile-floored rooms have ample bathrooms, and a continental buffet breakfast (M$50) is served on the lovely roof terrace. There's a three-night minimum stay at some peak periods. No children under six.

Posada Don Mario GUESTHOUSE $$
(☎951-514-20-12; www.posadadonmario.com; Cosijopí 219; s/d M$450/550, without bathroom M$320/450, incl breakfast; ⊖@☏) Cute, cheerful and friendly, this courtyard guesthouse has an intimate feel and is well priced for what it offers. The neat, brightly decorated rooms are well kept, the five up on the roof terrace being particularly appealing. Helpful traveler services include bookings for cooking classes, tours and transportation to the coast.

Hostel Don Nino HOSTEL $$
(☎951-518-59-85; www.hosteldonnino.com; Pino Suárez 804; dm M$150-180, s M$500-700, d M$600-800, all incl breakfast;) Part hostel, part hotel, friendly Don Nino offers modern and immaculately clean amenities (spacious common areas with leather couches, cable TV on plasma screens, quality mattresses and bedding, good kitchen, plenty of good clean bathrooms). The freebies (wi-fi, filtered water, internet terminals, shampoo, hairdryers, lockers) help make it one of Oaxaca's best-value lodgings.

There are women's, men's and mixed dorms, all reasonably spacious with solid wooden bunks and reading lights, and also an in-house **restaurant-bar** (mains M$50-100; 8am-6pm).

Hotel Casa del Sótano HOTEL $$
(☎951-516-24-94; www.facebook.com/hotelcasadelsotano; Tinoco y Palacios 404; s/d/tr/q/ste M$700/850/950/1050/1300;) Offering a stunning terrace view of Oaxaca's rooftops and church towers, this elegant hotel is excellent value. The attractive, very clean rooms sport great beds, traditional-style furniture and a spot of antique art.

Hotel Casa Arnel HOTEL $$
(☎951-515-28-56; www.casaarnel.com.mx; Aldama 404, Barrio Jalatlaco; s US$40-65, d US$45-75;) A longtime travelers' haunt, this family-run budget hotel is five minutes' walk from the 1st-class bus station. Clean, smallish, well-kept rooms, with attractive color schemes, surround a big, leafy courtyard, and the upstairs terrace has great views.

Plenty of helpful traveler services are offered and the bright little **Cafe El Ágora** (dishes M$25-75; 7am-10pm), next door and under the same ownership, does a fine range of breakfasts, light meals, teas and coffees.

Hotel Dainzú HOTEL $$
(☎951-516-18-21; www.hoteldainzuoaxaca.com; Hidalgo 1013; s/d incl breakfast M$515/645;) A neat little downtown hotel, with spick-and-span, medium-size rooms sporting curly wrought-iron bedheads, along with a pretty patio with a fountain.

Casa de la Tía Tere HOTEL $$
(☎951-501-18-45; www.casadelatiatere.com; Murguía 612; s M$770-890, d M$890-1670, bungalow M$1300-2100, all incl breakfast;) One of the few midrange accommodations with a swimming pool. The 20 rooms are large and mostly bright, all boasting good showers. The three 'bungalow' rooms around the well-maintained pool have their own kitchens, and one is two-bedroom with sitting and dining areas. Tía Tere also offers a large, clean kitchen and dining room, plus free coffee.

Casa Adobe B&B $$
(☎951-517-72-68; www.casaadobe-bandb.com; Independencia 11, Tlalixtac de Cabrera; s/d incl breakfast US$49/59, apt US$50-55;) Eight kilometers east of the city on a quiet lane in the village of Tlalixtac de Cabrera, Casa Adobe is a charming rural retreat full of lovely art and crafts, and a good base for both visits to the city and exploring outlying areas. The three rooms are set round a verdant little patio where breakfast is served, and there's a nice roof terrace and cozy sitting room.

The owners will pick you up on arrival in Oaxaca and offer a free ride to town on your first day (otherwise an M$80 taxi ride or M$10 by *taxi colectivo*). They'll also tell you about good restaurants nearby. There's a two-day minimum stay.

Parador San Andrés HOTEL $$
(☎051-514-10-11; www.hotelesdeoaxaca.com/hotelParadorSanAndres.html; Hidalgo 405; s/d M$500/550;) This friendly little hotel has nice clean, reasonable-sized rooms with bright bedspreads, and is just 2½ blocks from the Zócalo. All six rooms have two double beds and there's a pleasant little roof patio.

Learning Center B&B $$
(Centro de Aprendizaje; ☎951-515-01-22; www.tolc.org.mx; Murguía 703; s/d incl breakfast US$35/45, apt US$60;) The Learning Center is a successful, free, nonprofit tutoring center for young Oaxacans and villagers who need help in continuing their education or developing careers. What guests pay for the two neat B&B rooms and the attractive apartment here makes a contribution to running costs. All accommodations have fans, good bathrooms and wi-fi. Big discounts for monthly stays.

La Villada Inn HOSTEL $$
(☎951-518-62-17; www.lavillada.com; Felipe Ángeles 204 , Ejido Guadalupe Victoria; dm US$13, s/d/tr/q US$28/38/45/56, s/tr without bathroom US$18/42;) Though set on the city's far northern edge, La Villada is worth considering for its good facilities, helpful

English-speaking staff and spacious premises. The mostly adobe-built rooms boast good wooden furniture, though they lack fans or mosquito screens. The hostel owners will send a taxi to the bus station if you call on arrival. Once you're here, they'll tell you about buses to/from downtown.

There's no guest kitchen but there is a **restaurant** (M$35-65; 8am-7pm) with breakfasts and light dishes, plus an excellent swimming pool, a bar, a nice yoga room and a temascal (M$350 per person).

★Casa Oaxaca BOUTIQUE HOTEL **$$$**

(951-514-41-73; www.casaoaxaca.com.mx; García Vigil 407; s M$2150, d M$2850-3890, incl breakfast;) The seven large rooms and suites in this converted 18th-century house are in stunning contemporary Oaxacan style with original art and *artesanías* (handicrafts). It has a lovely pool in the rear patio, art exhibits in the beautiful main courtyard, and a small restaurant (open to nonguests only by reservation). Mezcal tastings and cooking classes with the chef are on offer, too. No kids under 12.

Casa de las Bugambilias B&B **$$$**

(951-516-11-65, in the USA & Canada 866-829-6778; http://lasbugambilias.com; Reforma 402; s US$70-115, d US$80-125, incl breakfast;) Delightful Bugambilias has nine rooms decorated with inspired combinations of antiques and folk and contemporary art. Some have air-con and/or a balcony; all have fans. The gourmet two-course Oaxacan breakfast is a big treat.

The family also runs two smaller, similarly attractive B&Bs not far away, as well as the adjoining La Olla (p435) restaurant and the Casa de los Sabores (p429) cooking school.

La Casa de Mis Recuerdos B&B **$$$**

(951-515-56-45, in the USA & Canada 877-234-4706; www.misrecuerdos.net; Pino Suárez 508; s US$60-80, d US$90-100, incl breakfast;) A marvelous decorative aesthetic prevails throughout this welcoming guesthouse. Old-style tiles, mirrors, masks and all sorts of other Mexican crafts, plus traditional and modern art, adorn the rooms and halls, and the comfy beds boast wrought-iron bedheads. The best rooms overlook a fragrant central patio, and the Oaxacan breakfast, a highlight, is served in a beautiful dining room. There's a minimum stay of three nights.

The owners also offer B&B at similar prices in two pretty smaller houses not much further from the center. Family member Nora Valencia does cooking classes at her school Alma de Mi Tierra.

Hotel Azul BOUTIQUE HOTEL **$$$**

(951-501-00-16; www.hotelazuloaxaca.com; Abasolo 313; r incl breakfast US$167-212, ste incl breakfast US$238-643;) The classy, contemporary Azul has a Francisco Toledo–designed fountain in the cactus-walled rear patio, and suites adorned with work by other renowned Oaxacan artists and sculptors. The very comfy standard rooms are in minimalist black, white and red with plenty of quality touches.

The courtyard **restaurant** (mains M$96-258) serves a mix of traditional Oaxacan and fusion dishes, and the hotel also boasts an in-house gallery and a roof terrace with bar in the evenings.

Quinta Real Oaxaca HISTORIC HOTEL **$$$**

(951-501-61-00; www.quintareal.com/oaxaca; 5 de Mayo 300; r from M$4175;) This 16th-century convent was converted into a very classy hotel in the 1970s. The old chapel is a banquet hall, and one of the five attractive courtyards contains a swimming pool; beautiful thick stone walls help keep the place cool. The 91 rooms are nicely done in colonial styles. Call or check online for special rates, which can cut costs considerably.

Eating

From swish restaurants dealing in French-styled fusion to street vendors doling out spicy *tamales* (steamed corn dough with fillings), Oaxaca's food is among Mexico's most inventive and memorable. Do get a good sampling of *mole* sauces, which come in seven colors and are served over all manner of meats and vegetable-based mains. But the *moles* are just the beginning of Oaxaca's flavors. Other specialties include *tasajo* (slices of pounded beef), *tlayudas* (big crisp tortillas with varied toppings that usually include a spread of *asiento*, pork lard, which vegetarians can ask to be omitted), *memelas* (thick, smallish tortillas topped with cheese, beans, chili sauce and sometimes more), *tostadas* (small, crisped corn tortillas with assorted toppings), *quesillo* (stringy cheese), *chapulines* (grasshoppers! – usually fried with chili powder and garlic) and steaming hot chocolate, often spiced with cinnamon.

HOLY MOLE

Oaxaca's multicolored *moles* (nut-, chili- and spice-based sauces) have become the region's culinary signature. To Mexicans, the meat the *mole* is served over is secondary in importance to the flavor of the *mole* itself. Oaxaca's most famous variety, *mole negro*, is a smoky, savory delight bearing a hint of chocolate. It is the most complex and labor-intensive to create, though its popularity ensures that it's easy to find. While in Oaxaca, seek out the other colors of the *mole* family:

Mole amarillo A savory *mole* using a base of tomatillo (a small, husked tomatolike fruit). It's spiced with cumin, clove, cilantro and the herb *hoja santa*, and often served over beef.

Mole verde A lovely, delicate sauce thickened with corn dough and including tomatillos, pumpkin seeds, the herbs *epazote* and *hoja santa*, and different nuts such as walnuts and almonds. Often served with chicken.

Mole colorado A forceful *mole* based on the flavors of *ancho, pasilla* and *cascabel* chilies, black pepper and cinnamon.

Mole coloradito (or mole rojo) This sharp, tangy, tomato-based blend might remind gringos of their neighborhood Mexican joint back home; it is exported in dumbed-down form as enchilada sauce.

Mancha manteles The brick-red 'tablecloth stainer' has a deep, woody flavor, often used to complement tropical fruit.

Chíchilo negro A rare *mole* whose defining ingredients include *chilguacle negro, mulato* and *pasilla* chilies, avocado leaves (which give it a touch of anise flavor), tomatoes and corn dough.

Café Los Cuiles CAFE $

(www.cuiles.com; Plazuela Labastida 115; salads, soups & snacks M$35-75; ⌚8am-10pm; 📶✍) Los Cuiles is a nice spot for breakfast, mango lassi, organic coffee and good light eats (including organic salads), with a handy central location and a spacious lounge-gallery feel.

Jaguar Yuú CAFE $

(Murguía 202; breakfasts & light dishes M$40-65; ⌚8am-10pm Mon-Sat, 10am-10pm Sun) Good for crepes, salads, baguettes and manifold coffee and tea options, Jaguar Yuú offers a lounge-gallery area as well as regular cafe tables. It's a popular stop for a young, arty, mainly local crowd.

Mercado Sánchez Pascuas OAXACAN $

(cnr Porfirio Díaz & Callejón Hidalgo; dishes M$13-22; ⌚8am-4pm) This excellent indoor food market has a great local feel, and its *comedores* (food stalls) provide a delicious, down-to-earth eating experience. Head to the ones toward the west end of the main building (where you eat at counters right in front of the cooks), ask for a *tamal*, *memela* or empanada, and practice your Spanish in deciding what you want on or in it.

Cenaduría Tlayudas Libres OAXACAN $

(Libres 212; tlayudas M$30-50; ⌚9pm-6am) Drivers double-park along the entire block to eat at this after-dark streetside institution. The filling, tasty *tlayudas* are large, light and crisp, and half the fun is taking in the late-night scene as motherly cooks fan the charcoal grills, raising showers of sparks.

Mercado 20 de Noviembre MARKET $

(cnr Flores Magón & Aldama; dishes M$30-45; ⌚7am-10pm) Dozens of *comedores* inside this large market serve up Oaxacan and Mexican staples like *tlayudas*, *chiles rellenos* (stuffed chilies) and *moles* - but the treat is the hugely popular *carne asada* (grilled meat) hall on the east side, filled with the aroma of meat grilling over hot coals.

A half-kilogram of *tasajo* or *cecina enchilada* (slices of chili-coated pork) for M$35, with a couple of M$12 sides of grilled onions, guacamole or *nopal* (strips of prickly-pear cactus pad, without the prickles) should more than satisfy two people.

Itanoní Antojería y Tortillería OAXACAN $

(www.itanoni.com; Belisario Domínguez 513, Colonia Reforma; mains M$45-70; ⌚7am-4pm Mon-Sat, 8am-2pm Sun; ✍) This semi-rustic eatery is dedicated to exploring the unique tastes of native Mexican corn varieties, and takes the craft of tortillas and *antojitos* (light tortilla-based dishes) to rare heights. There are plenty of options for vegetarian *tetelas* (a pre-Hispanic tortilla wrap) and a divine 'spiritual egg' dish, which deep-fries a whole egg encased in *hoja santa* leaves. It's about 1km north of the 1st-class bus station.

Manantial Vegetariano VEGETARIAN $

(Tinoco y Palacios 303; breakfasts M$45-50, mains M$40-75; ⏲9am-9pm Mon-Sat; ☑) In a colorfully decorated courtyard, the Manantial serves up well-prepared veggie versions of Mexican staples such as enchiladas and *chiles rellenos*, as well as fresh salads, crepes and a few meat dishes. There's a daily set lunch for M$85.

El Trompo TAQUERÍA $

(Porfirio Díaz 211; items M$8-26; ⏲4pm-4am) Unassuming El Trompo is the perfect solution to late-night hunger pangs with its satisfying *antojitos* including tacos, quesadillas, *sincronizadas* (cheese and ham between two tortillas) and *gringas* (quesadillas with cheese and pork).

★La Biznaga OAXACAN, FUSION $$

(☎951-516-18-00; www.labiznaga.com.mx; García Vigil 512; mains M$90-220; ⏲1-10pm Mon-Thu, 1-11pm Fri & Sat) Locals and visitors alike jam the atmospheric courtyard for delicious nouveau-Oaxacan fusion dishes. The choices are chalked on blackboards – you might start with a turkey *tamal* in *mole negro*, follow up with a beef fillet in mezcal with dried plums and *pasilla* chilies, and finish with the guava with chocolate mousse.

For lighter appetites and budgets, there are quesadillas, soups and quiches for under M$90. There's a great bar too, including draft microbrew beer.

★La Olla OAXACAN $$

(☎951-516-66-68; www.laolla.com.mx; Reforma 402; breakfasts M$75-95, mains M$100-185; ⏲8am-10pm Mon-Sat; 📶☑) This superb little restaurant and cafe produces a spectrum of marvelous Mexican (mainly Oaxacan) specialties from pumpkin-flower soup and fish quesadillas to beef in *mole chíchilo*, as well as good rye-bread tortas, juices and salads, all with an emphasis on organic and local ingredients. And it does terrific breakfasts and a great four-course set lunch (M$115) too!

Comala OAXACAN, INTERNATIONAL $$

(Allende 109; dishes M$65-115; ⏲9am-midnight Mon-Sat; 📶) A neat and gently arty cafe-bar with a black-and-red theme and lively evening atmosphere, Comala serves up a successful mix of Oaxacan specialties – including a great *botana oaxaqueña* (plate of assorted Oaxacan snacks such as meats, cheeses and, of course, grasshoppers) – and more international fare including what are probably the best burgers in town. Good breakfasts too.

El Típico OAXACAN $$

(Zárate 100; mains M$75-90; ⏲8:30am-6pm) This bright lunch spot serves up hearty helpings of home-style Oaxacan favourites to an appreciative, mostly local clientele. Daily specials usually include one of four different Oaxacan *moles* served on chicken or beef, and another good bet is the *guías con tasajo* – a thick vegetable soup accompanied by a large *tlayuda* with melted cheese and a slab of *tasajo*.

Friendly service, bright check tablecloths and fresh flowers contribute to the warm ambience.

Zandunga OAXACAN $$

(García Vigil 512E; mains M$130-160; ⏲2-11pm Mon-Sat; 📶) The Isthmus of Tehuantepec has its own take on Oaxacan cuisine based on local ingredients including tropical fruits and seafood, with many dishes cooked in banana leaves. Festive Zandunga brings those flavors to Oaxaca and the M$325 *botana* (a sampler of dishes that easily serves two) is perfect for whiling away a couple of hours with some of the restaurant's many mezcals (M$35 to M$160 a glass).

★Casa Oaxaca FUSION $$$

(☎951-516-85-31; www.casaoaxacaelrestaurante.com; Constitución 104-4; mains M$170-320; ⏲1-11pm Mon-Sat, 1-9pm Sun) Casa Oaxaca restaurant works magic combining Oaxacan and European ingredients and flavors: witness the crispy duck tacos with red *mole*, or the Isthmus-style venison in yellow *mole*. Presentation is outstanding, and all is enhanced by the choice of courtyard or roof-terrace dining areas, the bar for pre-dinner drinks and a good wine selection.

Restaurante Los Danzantes FUSION $$$

(☎951-501-11-84; www.losdanzantes.com; Alcalá 403; mains M$135-245; ⏲1-11pm) Excellent Mexican fusion food in a spectacular architect-designed patio makes Los Danzantes one of Oaxaca's special dining spots. You might start with the hierba santa leaves rolled round two cheeses in a tomatillo-and-chili sauce, follow up with the beef fillet and grasshopper sauce, and top it off with the crème brûlée and walnut crumble! There's quality house mezcal too.

Danzantes fare on a budget is available via the M$115 set lunch, served 1pm to 4pm Wednesday and Friday.

Pitiona OAXACAN **$$$**
(☎951-514-06-90; www.pitiona.com; Allende 108; mains M$180-320, tasting menus from M$580; ⌚1-11pm) Oaxacan chef José Manuel Baños, who has worked at the renowned El Bulli in Spain, takes the ingredients and flavors of his homeland to new creative heights here at Pitiona. The delicious *sopa de fideos* (noodle soup) comes with floating capsules of liquid cheese, and the beef tongue is done in a chili marinade and topped with potato foam.

Some dishes are so artistically presented it's a shame to eat them – but the restaurant's atmosphere is refreshingly relaxed. Fine mezcals too.

El Asador Vasco OAXACAN, SPANISH **$$$**
(☎951-514-47-55; www.asadorvasco.com; Portal de Flores 10A; mains M$140-260; ⌚1:30-11:30pm) For a meal, rather than a drink or snack, overlooking the Zócalo, the prime choice is the Asador Vasco's upstairs terrace, which provides good Oaxacan, Basque and international food. It's strong on meat, seafood and Oaxacan specialties, and has a pretty good international wine list. For a table with a plaza view on a warm evening, reserve earlier in the day.

Vieja Lira ITALIAN **$$$**
(www.viejalira.com; Reforma 502; mains M$130-240; ⌚noon-11pm) Vieja Lira tops the list of Oaxaca's Italian restaurants with its tasty food, atmospheric setting in a stone-arched courtyard and good service. Choose from 11 types of pasta and 16 sauces, or go for the good lasagna or a pizza. International wines available.

Casa Crespo OAXACAN **$$$**
(www.casacrespo.com; Allende 107; mains M$140-190; ⌚1-11pm Tue-Sun; wi-fi) Casa Crespo offers up delicious dishes from Oaxaca state's seven regions, with market-fresh ingredients. Try its *caldo de piedra* (a shrimp-and-fish soup cooked at your table by a pre-Hispanic method using hot stones inside the bowl). Or go for the seven-dish tasting menu (M$550). Great views from the roof terrace, by the way.

Drinking & Nightlife

Oaxaca's drinking opportunities come in large number and great variety. Alcalá, García Vigil and nearby streets are quite a party zone on Friday and Saturday nights. Several Oaxacan eateries are also fine places for a drink, including Comala (p435), which fills up with a convivial mixed crowd in the evenings, and La Biznaga (p435), where you can snack over draft microbrews or quality mezcal.

★**Los Amantes** MEZCALERÍA
(http://mezcalerialosamantes.blogspot.com; Allende 107; ⌚4-10pm Tue-Sun) Squeeze into this quirky little tasting room near Santo Domingo church for the perfect mezcal primer. Friendly bar staff will explain all about the three different artisanal mezcals, made by small-scale producers, that they give you to taste for M$150.

In Situ MEZCALERÍA
(http://insitumezcaleria.wix.com/inicio; Morelos 511; ⌚3-11pm Mon-Sat; wi-fi) A don't-miss stop on any mezcal trail, In Situ is run by Ulíses Torrentera, author of several books on mezcal. It stocks a vast variety of artisanal mezcals and a three-type tasting is M$150.

Café del Jardín CAFE
(☎951-514-76-16; Portal de Flores 10; ⌚8am-11:30pm) The Jardín has a peerless position beneath the arches at the Zócalo's southwest corner. In the evening you're likely to be serenaded by one of Mexico's funkiest marimba ensembles.

Café Brújula CAFE
(www.cafebrujula.com; baked goods, sandwiches & salads M$18-68; wi-fi) Alcalá (Alcalá 104; ⌚8am-9pm Mon-Sat, 9am-9pm Sun; wi-fi) García Vigil (García Vigil 409D; ⌚8am-9pm Mon-Sat; wi-fi) Brújula's two branches are pleasantly tranquil spots to hook into the wi-fi over some of the best coffee in town (a strong, flavorsome, organic bean from cooperative growers near the Oaxacan coast), a fruit smoothie or home-baked banana bread.

Cuish MEZCALERÍA, LIVE MUSIC
(http://mezcalcuish.blogspot.com; Díaz Ordaz 712; ⌚10am-10pm) Cuish is an *expendio* (drink retailer) rather than a bar, but it has a quaint, narrow bar anyway and will happily let you

MEZCAL

When Oaxacans tell you mezcal is a *bebida espirituosa* (spirit) they're not just saying it's a distilled liquor; they're hinting at an almost-spiritual reverence for the agave-based king of Oaxacan drinks. When you sip mezcal, you're imbibing the essence of a plant that has taken at least seven, sometimes 70 years to reach maturity. Mezcal is a drink for special occasions, a drink to share with friends, a drink that can put people into a kind of trance – a drink to be respected while being enjoyed. *'Para todo mal, mezcal,'* they say, *'Para todo bien, también.'* (When things are bad, mezcal; when things are good, mezcal too.)

It's strong stuff (usually 40% to 50% alcohol content, sometimes over 60%): sip it slowly and savor it. A glass of reasonable mezcal in a bar is unlikely to cost less than M$15 and a top-class one can be M$100.

Mezcal-type drinks are produced in many parts of Mexico but only those that meet established criteria from certain specific areas can be marketed as 'mezcal'. Around 60% of this (and most of the best) is produced in and around Oaxaca's Central Valleys.

Mezcal can be made from around 20 different species of agave (or *maguey* – the words are synonymous). The process begins when the mature agave sprouts its *quiote*, the long, once-in-a-lifetime flower-bearing spike. The plant's *piña* (heart), with the leaves removed, is then cooked for several days over a wood fire, typically in an oven in the ground. This sweetens the *piña*, which is then crushed to fibers and fermented with water for several weeks. The resulting liquid is distilled to produce mezcal.

You can observe this process and sample the product any day at dozens of mezcal factories and *palenques* (small-scale producers) in the Oaxaca area, especially around Mitla and along the road to it, and above all at the village of Santiago Matatlán, about 7km past the Mitla turnoff on Hwy 90, which produces about half of all Oaxaca's mezcal.

Beginner's Guide

Agave silvestre Wild, uncultivated agave; mezcals made from these are prized for their organic nature, special tastes and usually small-scale production methods.

Añejo Mezcal that has been aged for over a year; can have a particularly smooth taste

Arroqueño An agave variety that produces a sweet mezcal

Espadín The agave species from which nearly all non-*silvestre* mezcal is produced. It has a high sugar content and matures quickly.

Joven Young (unaged) mezcal

Minero Mezcal from Santa Catarina Minas, 6km east of Ocotlán, which known for particularly high-quality mezcals distilled in clay pots. To ensure you're drinking the real thing, look for the top-class Real Minero brand (www.realminero.com.mx).

Tobalá The best-known mezcal-producing wild agave, found chiefly in mountainous areas; many top *tobalás* come from around the town of Sola de Vega

Pechuga Mezcal with flavors obtained from a chicken or turkey breast *(pechuga)*, or fruits or spices, hung in the distillation vessel; confusingly, some mezcals to which a simple strip of sweetening agave leaf has been added after distillation may also be called *pechuga*. Genuine *pechuga* has its extra flavor imparted during distillation.

Reposado 'Rested' mezcal, which has been aged for between two months and one year before drinking; a halfway house between *joven* and *añejo*

The famous *gusano* (worm) is actually a moth caterpillar that feeds on the agave and is found mostly in bottles of cheaper mezcal. While no harm will come from swallowing it, there is definitely no obligation! Mezcal is, however, often served with a little plate of orangey powder that is a mix of salt, chili and ground-up *gusanos*. Along with slices of orange or lime, this nicely counterpoints the mezcal taste.

Much hot air is talked about the best types of mezcal, and how and when to drink them. The best way to judge a mezcal is by how much you like it!

OAXACA'S FAVORITE HOT DRINK

Chocolate is an ancient Mexican treat and a Oaxacan favorite. A bowl of steaming hot chocolate, with porous sweet bread to dunk, is the perfect warmer when winter sets in 1500m above sea level. The basic mix, to which hot milk or water is added, typically contains cinnamon, almonds and sugar, as well as ground-up cocoa beans. The area around Oaxaca's Mercado 20 de Noviembre has several shops specializing in this time-honored treat, as well as chocolate for *moles* (dishes with chili-based sauces). You can sample many varieties of chocolate at any of these places, and most have vats where you can watch the mixing. If you're feeling adventurous try *champurrado* or *tejate*, traditional drinks combining chocolate with corn.

sample a mezcal before you buy (M$150 to M$320 for a 0.75L bottle). It's an outlet for small organic producers making mezcal from wild agaves.

The upstairs gallery hosts live music from around 9pm several nights a week – the Wednesday night jazz has a good party scene.

Txalaparta DANCING
(http://facebook.com/txalapartabar; Matamoros 206; admission M$30-50; ⏲2pm-3am) By day Txalaparta is a colorful three-room bar with hookahs; around midnight it becomes a place to dance to assorted rhythms from Latin to jazz, world music, trip hop, reggae and more (sometimes with live bands or guest DJs). It gets a good party atmosphere going on Friday and Saturday nights, with a 20-to-35 crowd.

Candela DANCING
(☎951-514-20-10; Murguía 413; admission M$50; ⏲from 10pm Thu-Sat) Candela's writhing salsa, *cumbia* (dance music from Columbia) and merengue band and beautiful colonial-house setting have kept it high on the Oaxaca nightlife lists for years. The band starts at 11pm: arrive earlier for a good table. Salsa classes are held on Thursday evenings.

La Cantinita BAR, DANCING
(Alcalá 303; admission free; ⏲10pm-4am) This bright and loud party bar, with a live pop/rock band from 11pm, is a place to go if you're in spring-break mode.

☆ Entertainment

Oaxaca has a vibrant cultural life. You'll find what's-on listings (including concerts and plenty of art-house movie showings) at **Qué Pasa Oaxaca** (www.quepasaoaxaca.com), **El Jolgorio Cultural** (www.eljolgoriocultural.org.mx), which is also distributed as a free magazine) and **Oaxaca Calendar** (www.oaxacacalendar.com).

Look out for gigs by local bands La China Sonidera (pop *cumbia*) and Los Molcajete (*son jarocho*) who always whip up a great atmosphere.

La Nueva Babel LIVE MUSIC
(Porfirio Díaz 224; admission free to M$30; ⏲9am-2am) There's live music of some sort at 10pm almost every night at this squeezy little bar – it could be *son*, *trova*, jazz, folk, *cumbia*... The atmosphere varies from buzzing to grave-like depending who's on and on who's there, but it's popular with travelers.

Guelaguetza Shows

If you're not in Oaxaca for the Guelaguetza dance festival itself, it's well worth attending one of the regular imitations.

Quinta Real Oaxaca DANCE
(☎951-501-61-00; 5 de Mayo 300; incl buffet dinner M$393; ⏲7pm Fri) This highly colorful three-hour event at one of Oaxaca's top hotels is the best of the regular Guelaguetza shows.

Casa de Cantera DANCE
(☎951-514-75-85; www.casadecantera.com; Ortiz Armengol 104, Colonia Reforma; admission M$185; ⏲8:30pm) A lively mini-Guelaguetza with live music is staged here nightly if at least 20 people reserve by the same afternoon. It's not very conveniently located, about 2km north of the center. Food and drinks are available during the show.

Hotel Monte Albán DANCE
(☎951-516-27-77; Alameda de León 1; admission M$90; ⏲8:30pm) This hotel presents a 1½-hour Guelaguetza show nightly if enough people (sometimes 10 is sufficient) reserve by 6:30pm. It's usually with recorded music, but worth 90 minutes of your time if you can't get to one of the others.

Shopping

The state of Oaxaca has the richest, most inventive folk-art scene in Mexico, and the city is its chief marketplace. You'll find the highest-quality crafts mostly in smart stores, but prices are lower in the markets. Some artisans have grouped together to market their products directly in their own stores.

Oaxacan artisans' techniques remain fairly traditional – back-strap and pedal looms, hand-turning of pottery – but new products frequently appear in response to the big demand for Oaxacan crafts. The ubiquitous wooden fantasy animals known as *alebrijes* were developed within the last couple of decades from toys that Oaxacans had been carving for centuries.

Other special products to look for include the distinctive black pottery from San Bartolo Coyotepec; blankets, tapestries and rugs from Teotitlán del Valle; creative pottery figures made in Ocotlán and Atzompa; *huipiles* (indigenous women's sleeveless tunics) and other colorful textiles; assorted jewelry; and stamped and colored tin from Oaxaca city itself. Many shops can mail things home for you.

Oaxaca's crowded commercial area, stretching over several blocks southwest of the Zócalo, can be just as fascinating as its craft markets. Oaxacans flock here, and to the big Central de Abastos market, for all their everyday needs.

★El Pochote-Xochimilco FOOD, HANDICRAFTS
(Xochimilco Churchyard, Juárez, Barrio de Xochimilco; 8:30am-3:30pm Fri & Sat) A small and very relaxed open-air market dealing in natural products, especially crafts and food, nearly all sold by their makers. Look for the amazing Yukee pine-needle baskets, and stop for some blue-corn tortillas with fabulous toppings at Guadalupe's food stall.

Mercado Juárez MARKET
(cnr Flores Magón & Las Casas; 6am-9pm) This daily indoor market, a block south of the Zócalo, peddles a fascinating mix of flowers, hats, shoes, cheap clothes and jewelry, baskets, leather belts and bags, fancy knives, mezcal, herbs, spices, meat, fruit, vegetables and almost every other food a Oaxacan could need. Women hawk mounds of grasshoppers outside the Flores Magón entrance.

Mercado de Artesanías HANDICRAFTS
(Crafts Market; cnr JP García & Zaragoza; 9am-9pm) This indoor crafts market is almost entirely devoted to woven and embroidered textiles – tablecloths, bags, blouses, *huipiles*, shawls and more.

Central de Abastos MARKET
(Periférico; 6am-8pm) The enormous main market, nearly 1km west of the Zócalo, is a hive of activity all week, with Saturday the biggest day. You can find almost anything here, and it's easy to get lost among the household goods, *artesanías* and overwhelming quantities of fruit, vegetables, sugarcane, maize and other produce grown from the coast to the mountaintops. Each type of product has its own section.

La Mano Mágica HANDICRAFTS
(951-516-42-75; Alcalá 203; 10:30am-3pm & 4-8pm Mon-Sat) You'll find some wonderfully original and sophisticated craft products at this shop and gallery, including extraordinarily fine weavings by one of its owners, Arnulfo Mendoza of Teotitlán del Valle. Some Mendoza creations go for tens of thousands of dollars.

La Casa del Rebozo HANDICRAFTS
(5 de Mayo 114; 9am-9pm Mon-Sat, 10am-6pm Sun) A cooperative of 84 artisans from around Oaxaca state, La Casa del Rebozo stocks quality pottery, textiles, baskets, bags, *alebrijes* and tinware.

Shkáala HANDICRAFTS
(5 de Mayo 412-1; 10am-2pm & 4-8pm Mon-Sat) This craft store has some very original and attractive earrings, embroidered blouses, necklaces and mini-*alebrijes*, with many items made by its owner.

Casa de las Artesanías de Oaxaca HANDICRAFTS
(951-516-50-62; Matamoros 105; 9am-9pm Mon-Sat, 10am-6pm Sun) A large store selling the work of 80 family workshops and craft organizations from around Oaxaca state.

MARO HANDICRAFTS
(951-516-06-70; 5 de Mayo 204; 9am-8pm) A rabbit warren of a store offering a big range of appealing work at good prices, nearly all made by members of the MARO women artisans' cooperative.

Amate Books BOOKS
(Alcalá 307; 10:30am-7:30pm Mon-Sat) Probably the best English-language bookstore in Mexico, stocking almost every in-print English-language title related to Mexico.

PEOPLES OF OAXACA

Much of Oaxaca's distinctive atmosphere derives from its indigenous population, who officially comprise almost half the state's 3.8 million people – unofficial estimates put the figure higher (up to 80%). Indigenous peoples are generally at the bottom of the economic and social scale here, as they are throughout Mexico, but they are rich in culture, and are the driving force behind Oaxaca's fine *artesanías* (handicrafts) and unique festivities, and a key inspiration for its booming art scene and amazing cuisine.

Each of Oaxaca's 15 indigenous groups has its own language, customs and colorful costume (though some members now speak only Spanish and many now wear mainstream clothing). You will probably have most contact with the Zapotecs, possibly 800,000 strong, who live mainly in and around the Valles Centrales and on the Isthmus of Tehuantepec. Many of the artisans and market traders in and around Oaxaca city are Zapotec. Up to 750,000 Mixtecs are spread around the mountainous borders of Oaxaca, Guerrero and Puebla states. The state's other large indigenous groups include 300,000 or so Mazatecs and 200,000 Chinantecs in the far north, and some 170,000 Mixes in the mountains northeast of the Valles Centrales.

In Oaxaca city you may well see Triquis; the women wear long, bright-red *huipiles* (sleeveless tunics). The Triquis are only about 30,000 strong and have a long history of conflict with mestizos and Mixtecs over land rights in their remote home region of western Oaxaca.

La Cava DRINK

(951-515-23-35; Gómez Farías 212B; 10am-3pm & 5-8pm Mon-Sat) Particularly high-quality mezcal from Santa Catarina Minas as well as elsewhere (over M$1200 for the best bottles), plus a top range of Mexican wines.

Unión de Palenqueros de Oaxaca DRINK

(951-513-04-85; Abasolo 510; 9am-9pm) This hole-in-the-wall place is the outlet for a group of small-scale mezcal producers from Santiago Matatlán. It has excellent and very well priced (between M$60 to M$400 per liter) smoky *añejo* and fruit-infused varieties.

Information

EMERGENCY

Ambulance, Fire & Police (066, 060)

Ceprotur (Centro de Protección al Turista; 951-502-12-00 ext 1525; Juárez 703; 8am-8pm) Helps tourists with legal problems, complaints, lost documents and the like.

INTERNET ACCESS

Internet shops are plentiful in Oaxaca City, and most charge around M$10 per hour. There is free wi-fi in some public spaces, including Parque Juárez.

MEDICAL SERVICES

Hospital Reforma (951-516-09-89; www.hospitalreforma.com.mx; Reforma 613) Central private hospital, which is generally considered to have the best doctors in the city.

MONEY

There are plenty of ATMs around the center, and several banks and *casas de cambio* (exchange houses) will change cash US dollars.

Banamex (cnr Porfirio Díaz & Morelos; 10am-5pm Mon-Fri) Often has the best dollar exchange rates.

CI Banco (Armenta y López 203; 8:30am-6pm Mon-Fri, 9am-2pm Sat) Exchanges cash US and Canadian dollars, euros, pounds sterling, yen and Swiss francs, and US dollar and euro traveler's checks.

POST

Main Post Office (Alameda de León; 8am-7pm Mon-Fri, 8am-3pm Sat)

TOURIST INFORMATION

City Tourist Information Kiosk (Alameda de León; 10am-6pm) English-speaking and keen to help.

Sectur (951-502-12-00, 951-516-01-23; www.oaxaca.travel; Juárez 703; 9am-8pm) The Oaxaca state tourism department has a helpful, English-speaking information office, plus further desks (also English-speaking) at the Museo de los Pintores Oaxaqueños (10am-8pm Tue-Sun), 1st-class bus station (8am-8pm) and Teatro Macedonio Alcalá (Independencia 900; 9am-8pm).

TRAVEL AGENCIES

Conav (Portal de Flores 1, Zócalo; ⌚8:30am-8pm Mon-Fri, 8:30am-7pm Sat) A useful downtown air-ticket agency.

USEFUL WEBSITES

Lonely Planet (www.lonelyplanet.com/mexico/oaxaca-state/oaxaca) Planning advice, author recommendations, articles, images and video.

Oaxaca Tu México (www.oaxaca.travel) The official state tourism site.

Oaxaca Wiki (oaxaca.wikispaces.com) A goldmine of information and photos on what's happening in and around Oaxaca. Dig around.

Planeta.com (www.planeta.com) This conscientious travel site has tons of good info on Oaxaca.

Getting There & Away

AIR

Oaxaca Airport (☎951-511-50-88; www.asur.com.mx) Six kilometers south of the city, 500m west off Hwy 175.

Aeroméxico (☎951-516-10-66; www.aeromexico.com; Hidalgo 513; ⌚9am-6pm Mon-Fri, 9am-4pm Sat) To/from Mexico City several times daily.

Aerotucán (☎951-502-08-40; www.aerotucan.com.mx; Emilio Carranza 303, Colonia Reforma; ⌚8am-8pm Mon-Fri, 8am-6pm Sat) Thirteen-seat Cessnas make spectacular half-hour hops to Puerto Escondido (M$1940) and Bahías de Huatulco (M$1970), on the Oaxaca coast, both daily. Also flies to Tuxtla Gutiérrez three times weekly.

Interjet (☎951-502-57-23; www.interjet.com.mx; Plaza Mazari, Calzada Porfirio Díaz 256, Colonia Reforma; ⌚9am-7pm Mon-Fri, 9am-5pm Sat, 10am-2pm Sun) Mexico City once or twice daily.

United (☎800-900-50-00; www.united.com) Houston, Texas at least five times weekly.

Vivaaerobus (☎554-000-01-80; www.vivaaerobus.com) Budget airline flying to/from Cancún and Monterrey twice weekly.

Volaris (☎800-122-80-00; www.volaris.com) Flights to Tijuana.

BUS & VAN

The **1st-class bus station** (Terminal ADO; ☎951-515-12-14; Calz Niños Héroes de Chapultepec 1036) is 2km northeast of the Zócalo. It's used by ADO Platino and ADO GL (deluxe service), ADO and OCC (1st class) and Cuenca (2nd class). You can buy tickets for these bus lines downtown at **Boletotal** (www.boletotal.mx), **Valdivieso** (Valdivieso 2; ⌚7:30am-9:30pm) and **20 de Noviembre** (20 de Noviembre 103; ⌚8am-10pm Mon-Sat, 8am-9pm Sun).

The **2nd-class bus station** (Central de Autobuses de Segunda Clase; Las Casas), 1km west of the Zócalo, is mainly useful for buses to villages around Oaxaca. More convenient transportation to many of these villages, as well as the archaeological site Monte Albán, is provided by minibus, van and *taxi colectivo* services leaving from various points around the city.

For destinations on the Oaxaca coast such as Puerto Escondido, Bahías de Huatulco and Pochutla, buses from the 1st-class bus station take a long and expensive route via Salina Cruz. Unless you're prone to travel sickness on winding mountain roads, it's much better, cheaper and quicker to use one of the van services that go directly to the coast by Hwy 131 (to Puerto Escondido) or Hwy 175 (to Pochutla and Huatulco):

Atlántida (☎951-514-13-46; cnr Armenta y López & La Noria) To Pochutla.

BUSES & VANS FROM OAXACA CITY

DESTINATION	FARE (M$)	DURATION	FREQUENCY (DAILY)
Bahías de Huatulco	180-358	7-8hr	11 Expressos Colombo, 8 Huatulco 2000, 4 from 1st-class terminal
Mexico City (TAPO)	474-808	6-6½hr	23 from 1st-class terminal
Pochutla	150-312	6-9hr	11 Atlántida, 25 Líneas Unidas, 4 from 1st-class terminal
Puebla	292-588	5hr	10 from 1st-class terminal
Puerto Escondido	170-318	7-10hr	14 Express Service, 18 Villa del Pacífico, 4 from 1st-class terminal
San Cristóbal de las Casas	474-762	10-11hr	4 from 1st-class terminal
Tapachula	422-552	11-12½hr	2 from 1st-class terminal
Tehuantepec	204	4½hr	14 from 1st-class terminal
Veracruz	466-560	6-7½hr	3 from 1st-class terminal

Express Service (☎951-516-40-59; Arista 116) To Puerto Escondido.

Expressos Colombo Huatulco (Trujano 600) To Bahías de Huatulco.

Huatulco 2000 (Hidalgo 208) To Bahías de Huatulco.

Líneas Unidas (☎951-187-55-11; Bustamante 601) To Pochutla.

Transportes Villa del Pacífico (Galeana 322A) To Puerto Escondido.

CAR & MOTORCYCLE

Hwy 135D branches off the Mexico City–Veracruz highway (150D) to make a spectacular traverse of Oaxaca's northern mountains to Oaxaca city. Automobile tolls from Mexico City to Oaxaca total M$430; the trip takes five to six hours. Toll-free alternative Hwy 190, via Huajuapan de León, takes several hours longer.

The roads of Oaxaca state are mostly poorly maintained but away from congested Oaxaca city, traffic is light and the scenery is fantastic to drive through. Walk-in rental prices in Oaxaca start around M$600 a day with unlimited kilometers.

Alamo (http://alamomexico.com.mx) Airport (☎951-511-62-20; ⊙9am-7pm); Center (☎951-514-85-34; 5 de Mayo 203; ⊙9am-7pm)

Europcar (www.europcar.com.mx) Airport (☎951-143-83-40; ⊙6am-11pm); Center (☎951-516-93-05; Matamoros 101; ⊙8am-2pm & 3-8pm Mon-Sat, 8am-5pm Sun)

Only Rent-A-Car (www.onlyrentacar.com; 5 de Mayo 215A; ⊙8am-8pm)

ℹ Getting Around

TO/FROM THE AIRPORT

The Transporte Terrestre ticket-taxi desk in the airport charges M$60 per person anywhere downtown in a van, or M$250 for a whole cab. Taxis from downtown to the airport generally cost M$140.

BICYCLE

Two full-service shops, **Bicicletas Pedro Martínez** (www.bicicletaspedromartinez.com; Aldama 418; per 4hr/day M$200/250; ⊙9am-8pm Mon-Sat, 10am-3pm Sun) and **Zona Bici** (www.zonabici.com.mx; García Vigil 406; per 4hr/day M$150/200; ⊙10am-8pm Mon-Sat), rent out good mountain bikes and sell bikes and equipment.

BUS

City buses cost M$5.50 or M$6. From outside the 1st-class bus station, westbound 'Juárez' buses will take you down Juárez and Ocampo, three blocks east of the Zócalo; 'Tinoco y Palacios' and 'T Y Palacios' buses go down Tinoco y Palacios, two blocks west of the Zócalo. To return to the bus station, take an 'ADO' bus north up Pino Suárez or Crespo.

TAXI

Taxis anywhere within the central area, including the bus stations, cost M$40.

VALLES CENTRALES

The countryside and villages around Oaxaca are a big part of its appeal. The city stands at the meeting point of three valleys that have been a center of civilization since pre-Hispanic times: the Valle de Tlacolula, stretching 50km east from the city; the Valle de Zimatlán, reaching about 100km south; and the Valle de Etla, stretching about 40km north. These Valles Centrales (Central Valleys) have a population that's mostly indigenous Zapotec. They're full of fascinating archaeological sites and traditional villages and towns that stage bustling weekly markets, produce fine specialty *artesanías*, and celebrate their own colorful local fiestas. All are within easy day-trip distance of Oaxaca city.

Monte Albán

Monte Albán (☎951-516-12-15; admission M$57; ⊙8am-5pm; 🅿) stands on a flattened hilltop 400m above the valley floor, just a few kilometers west of Oaxaca. The city from which the ancient Zapotecs ruled Oaxaca's Valles Centrales is one of Mexico's most spectacular pre-Hispanic sites, with temples, palaces, tall stepped platforms, an observatory and a ball court all arranged in orderly fashion with wonderful 360-degree views over the city, surrounding valleys and distant mountain ranges.

At the entrance to the site are a good museum (explanations in Spanish only), a cafe and a bookstore. Official guides offer their services outside the ticket office for tours in Spanish, English, French or Italian (around M$250 for a small group). The heart of the site, the Gran Plaza, is wheelchair accessible via an elevator and special walkways (ask at the ticket booth for the elevator to be activated). Explanatory signs are in Spanish, English and Zapotec.

History

Monte Albán was first occupied around 500 BC, probably by Zapotecs moving from the previous main settlement in the Valles Centrales, the less defensible San José El Mogote in the Valle de Etla. Monte Albán had early cultural connections with the Olmecs to the northeast.

The years up to about 200 BC (known as phase Monte Albán I) saw the leveling of the hilltop, the building of temples and probably palaces, and the growth of a town of 10,000 or more people on the hillsides. Hieroglyphs and dates in a dot-and-bar system carved during this era may mean that the elite of Monte Albán were the first people in Mexico to use a developed writing system and written calendar. Between 200 BC and AD 350 (phase Monte Albán II) the city came to dominate more and more of the Oaxaca region.

The city was at its peak from about 350 to 700 (Monte Albán III), when the main and surrounding hills were terraced for dwellings, and the population reached about 25,000. Monte Albán was the center of a highly organized, priest-dominated society, controlling the extensively irrigated Valles Centrales, which held at least 200 other settlements and ceremonial centers (several of which, like nearby Atzompa, can be visited). Many buildings here were plastered and painted red. Nearly 170 underground tombs from this period have been found, some of them elaborate and decorated with frescoes, though none are open to visitors.

Between about 700 and 950 (Monte Albán IV) the place was abandoned and fell into ruin. Phase Monte Albán V (950–1521) saw minimal activity, although Mixtecs arriving from northwestern Oaxaca reused some old tombs here to bury their own dignitaries.

Sights

Gran Plaza PLAZA

About 300m long and 200m wide, the Gran Plaza is the center of Monte Albán. Some of its structures were temples, others were elite residential quarters. Many of them are now

Monte Albán

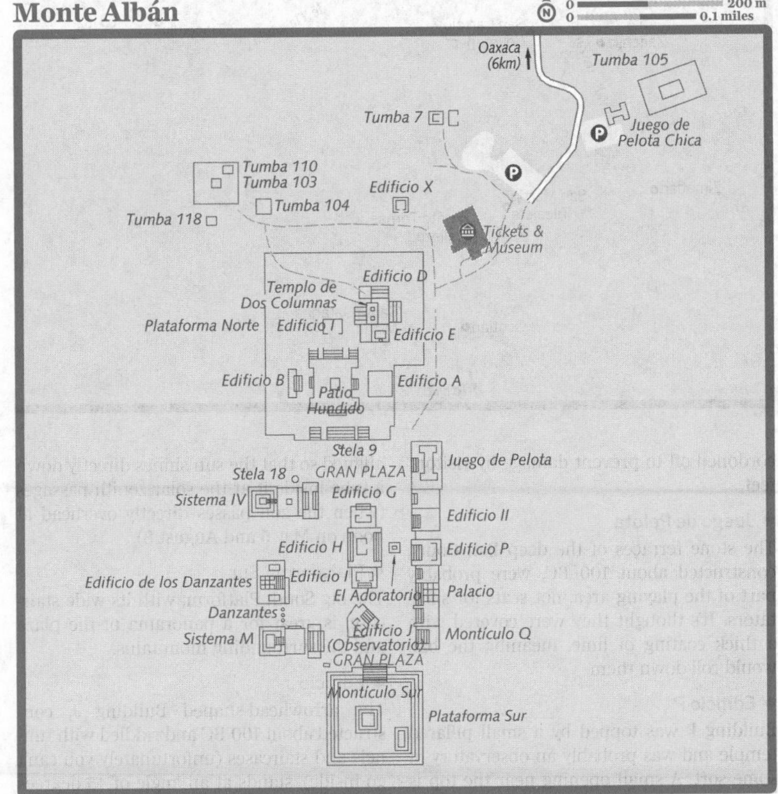

Valles Centrales

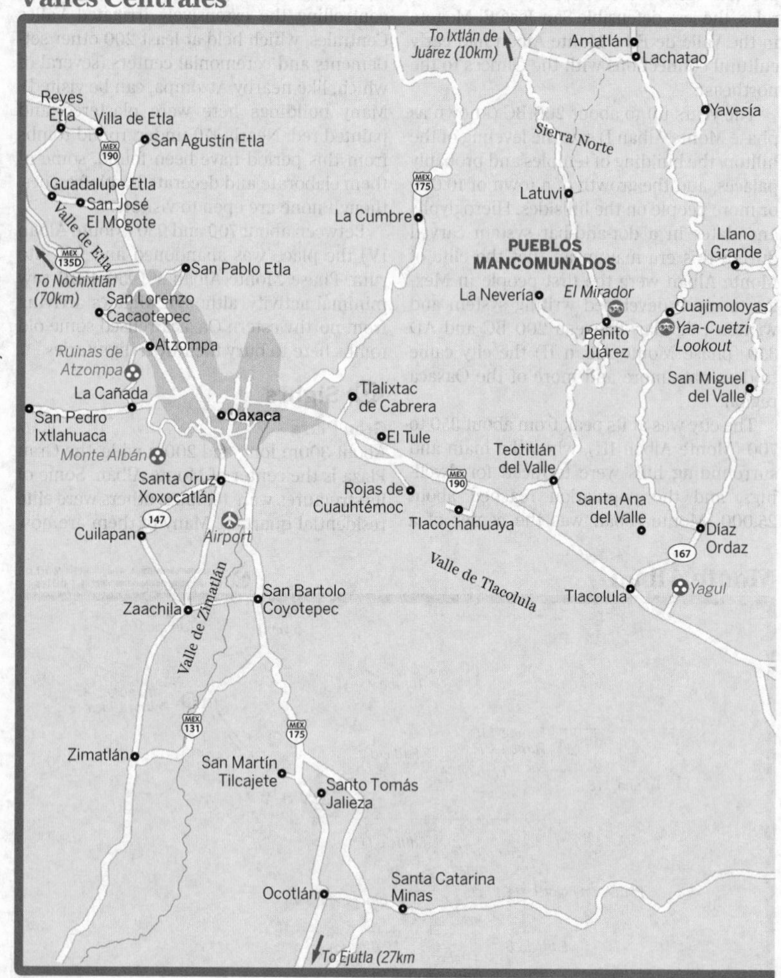

cordoned off to prevent damage by visitors' feet.

➡ Juego de Pelota

The stone terraces of the deep Ball Court, constructed about 100 BC, were probably part of the playing area, not seats for spectators. It's thought they were covered with a thick coating of lime, meaning the ball would roll down them.

➡ Edificio P

Building P was topped by a small pillared temple and was probably an observatory of some sort. A small opening near the top is aligned so that the sun shines directly down a tube inside it at the solar zenith passages (when the sun passes directly overhead at noon on May 5 and August 8).

➡ Plataforma Sur

The big South Platform, with its wide staircase, is great for a panorama of the plaza and the surrounding mountains.

➡ Edificio J

The arrowhead-shaped Building J, constructed about 100 BC and riddled with tunnels and staircases (unfortunately you can't go inside), stands at an angle of 45 degrees

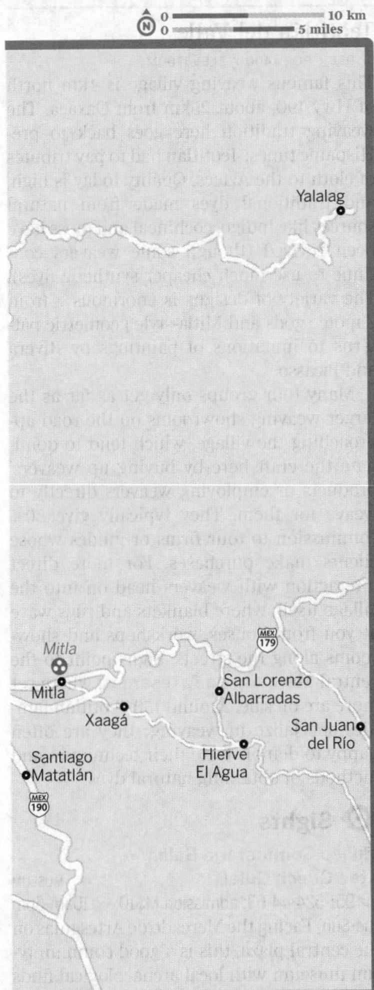

to the other Gran Plaza structures and was an observatory. Figures and hieroglyphs carved on its walls record Monte Albán's military conquests.

➡ Edificio de los Danzantes

This structure combines an early (Monte Albán I) building that contained famous carvings known as Danzantes and a later structure, which was built over it. The Danzantes (Dancers), copies of some of which are seen around the lower part of the building, depict naked men, thought to be sacrificed leaders of conquered neighboring towns. Carved between 500 and 100 BC, they generally have thick-lipped open mouths (sometimes down-turned in Olmec style) and closed eyes. Some have blood flowing where they have been disemboweled. Hieroglyphs accompanying them are the earliest known examples of true writing in Mexico.

Plataforma Norte PLATFORM

The North Platform, on top of a rock outcrop, is almost as big as the Gran Plaza, and offers the best views overall. It was rebuilt several times over the centuries. The 12 column bases at the top of the stairs were part of a roofed hall. On top of the platform is a ceremonial complex created between AD 500 and 800.

The complex includes the **Patio Hundido** (Sunken Patio), which has an altar at its center; **Edificios D**, **VG E** and **E**, which were topped with adobe temples; and the **Templo de Dos Columnas**.

ℹ Getting There & Away

A few companies run buses to Monte Albán from Oaxaca for M$50 round-trip. **Autobuses Turísticos** (Mina 501, Oaxaca) has departures hourly (half-hourly on Saturday and Sunday) from 8:30am to 3:30pm, starting back from the site between noon and 5pm.

Valle de Tlacolula

The Valle de Tlacolula, east of Oaxaca, is home to the pre-Hispanic sites of Mitla and Yagul as well as what's claimed to be the world's biggest tree and many of the best weavings you'll see in the Oaxaca area.

ℹ Getting There & Away

The following places, except Hierve El Agua, are all within walking distance of the Oaxaca–Mitla road, Hwy 190. Fletes y Pasajes (Fypsa) buses to Mitla (M$16, 1¼ hours), about every half-hour from Oaxaca's 2nd-class bus station, will drop you anywhere along this road. You can catch *taxis colectivos* direct to El Tule (M$12, 15 minutes), Teotitlán del Valle (M$16, 30 minutes), Tlacolula (M$18, 40 minutes) or Mitla (M$20, one hour) from the corner of Hwy 190 and Derechos Humanos, 500m east of Oaxaca's 1st-class bus station, immediately past the baseball stadium. For Teotitlán, there are also Valle del Norte buses (M$10, 45 minutes, about hourly, 7am to 7pm) from the 2nd-class bus station.

MARKET DAYS

Weekly markets in the Valles Centrales towns offer all manner of foodstuffs and produce, as well as handicrafts and domestic goods. The scene is not to be missed; markets draw buyers and sellers from near and far, and bombard the senses with colors, sounds, smells and the voices of indigenous languages, in a ritual that has been taking place for hundreds, if not thousands, of years. Markets are at their busiest in the morning, and most of them start to wind down in the early afternoon.

Sunday Tlacolula

Tuesday Atzompa

Wednesday Zimatlán; Villa de Etla

Thursday Zaachila; Ejutla

Friday Ocotlán; San Bartolo Coyotepec; Santo Tomás Jalieza

El Tule

POP 7600 / ELEV 1550M

The village of El Tule, 10km east of Oaxaca along Hwy 190, draws crowds of visitors for one very good reason: **El Árbol del Tule** (Tree of El Tule; admission M$10; ⌚8am-8pm), which is claimed to be the largest tree in the world. Most reckonings actually put California's General Sherman ahead in total volume, but at about 11m in diameter, El Árbol del Tule is certainly the world's widest. This vast *ahuehuete* (Montezuma cypress), 42m high, dwarfs the pretty 17th-century village church in whose churchyard it towers. The tree is at least 1500 years old, which means it was already growing when the ancient city of Monte Albán was at its peak. Long revered by Oaxacans, the Árbol del Tule is under threat from local urban growth and irrigated agriculture, which tap its water sources. Local campaigners say its aquifers must be protected if it is to survive.

The popular, family-run **El Milenario** (Guerrero 4A; mains M$60-80; ⌚9am-8pm), one block south of the tree (past the Mercado de Artesanías), is a fine place to stop for lunch, serving up classic Oaxacan dishes such as *tlayudas*, *tasajo* and *moles* with chicken, in a cheerful atmosphere.

Teotitlán del Valle

☎951 / POP 4400 / ELEV 1700M

This famous weaving village is 4km north of Hwy 190, about 25km from Oaxaca. The weaving tradition here goes back to pre-Hispanic times: Teotitlán had to pay tributes of cloth to the Aztecs. Quality today is high, and traditional dyes made from natural sources like indigo, cochineal and moss have been revived (though some weavers continue to use much cheaper synthetic dyes). The variety of designs is enormous – from Zapotec gods and Mitla-style geometric patterns to imitations of paintings by Rivera and Picasso.

Many tour groups only get as far as the larger weaving showrooms on the road approaching the village, which tend to dominate the craft here by buying up weavers' products or employing weavers directly to weave for them. They typically give 30% commission to tour firms or guides whose clients make purchases. For more direct interaction with weavers head on into the village itself, where blankets and rugs wave at you from houses, workshops and showrooms along the streets. Signs point to the central **Mercado de Artesanías**, where yet more are on sale. Around 150 Teotitlán families specialize in weaving; they are often happy to demonstrate their techniques and methods of obtaining natural dyes.

Sights

Museo Comunitario Balaa Xtee Guech Gulal MUSEUM

(☎951-524-44-63; admission M$10; ⌚10am-6pm Tue-Sun) Facing the Mercado de Artesanías on the central plaza, this is a good community-run museum with local archaeological finds and displays on local crafts and traditions (in English as well as Spanish and Zapotec). Contact the museum one day ahead to organize an interesting two- to three-hour guided walk up **Cerro de Picacho**, a sacred hill with pre-Hispanic remnants just outside the village, costing M$75/100/200 for two/four/10 people.

Templo de la Virgen de la Natividad CHURCH

(⌚6am-6pm) From the plaza, steps rise to this handsome 17th-century church with a fine broad churchyard and colorful 18th-century frescoes inside. It was built atop a Zapotec ceremonial site, many of whose carved stones can be seen in the church walls; look especially in the inner patio.

Tlacolula

POP 14,000 / ELEV 1650M

Tlacolula, 31km from Oaxaca, holds one of the Valles Centrales' major **markets** every Sunday, with the area around the church becoming a packed throng. Crafts, foods and plenty of everyday goods are on sale. It's a treat for lovers of market atmosphere. Inside the church, the 16th-century **Capilla del Santo Cristo** chapel is a riot of golden, indigenous-influenced decoration that's comparable to the Capilla de la Virgen del Rosario in Oaxaca's Santo Domingo. Among the ceiling ornamentation, spot the plaster martyrs holding their severed heads in their own hands.

Yagul

The **Yagul ruins** (admission M$42; ⏲8am-5pm; 🅿) are finely sited on a cactus-covered hill, 1.5km north of the Oaxaca–Mitla road. The signposted turnoff is 34km from Oaxaca. If you don't have a vehicle you'll have to walk the 1.5km: caution is advised on this isolated road.

Yagul was a leading Valles Centrales settlement after the decline of Monte Albán, and most of what's visible was built between AD 750 and 950. **Patio 4**, down to the left as you enter the main part of the site from the ticket office, was surrounded

WORTH A TRIP

ATZOMPA

The recently opened archaeological site of Atzompa, 6km northwest of central Oaxaca, is a fascinating complement to the larger, more famous Monte Albán. Together with Atzompa village's museum and crafts market it provides fascinating proof of the continuity of Atzompa's pottery-making expertise from pre-Hispanic times to the present day. The pleasant village center has several straightforward *comedores* if you fancy stopping for a bite.

Still partly under excavation, the **Atzompa ruins** (⏲8am-5pm; 🅿) sit on top of Cerro El Bonete hill 2km above Atzompa village. The site flourished from AD 650 to 850 and provides spectacular views of its contemporary (and probably parent city) Monte Albán, 4km south, as well as of Oaxaca and of the Valle de Etla stretching away to the north. Three ceremonial plazas, one ball court and the remains of two large residences have been exposed to view. An especially intriguing feature is the reconstructed pottery-firing oven on the north side – identical to ovens still used by the potters of modern Atzompa. At research time access to the ruins was free, but a charge may be introduced, possibly through a combined ticket with Monte Albán.

Halfway down the road from the ruins to Atzompa village, the **Museo Comunitario** (Community Museum; admission M$10; ⏲10am-5pm) exhibits some very fine pieces of pottery found at the ruins, including detailed effigies of nobility or deities and huge pots used for storing water, grain or seeds. The work of over 100 contemporary Atzompa potters is on sale in the village's **Mercado de Artesanías** (Crafts Market; Av Libertad 303; ⏲9am-7pm). Items range from animal figures and lampshades to pots, plates, cups and more – some bearing Atzompa's characteristic green glaze, introduced in colonial times, others in more colorful, innovative styles. Prices are reasonable but much of the best work goes to shops in Oaxaca and elsewhere.

Getting There & Away

Access to the ruins is by paved road, either 2km up from Atzompa village, or 3km up from La Cañada village on the road from Oaxaca to San Pedro Ixtlahuaca. From Monte Albán, vehicles can drive direct to La Cañada and the ruins without returning to Oaxaca. However, the section from La Cañada up to the ruins is one-way only, meaning you cannot descend from the ruins to La Cañada. There's no public transportation to the site except taxis (M$150 round-trip from Oaxaca, less from Atzompa village).

Taxis colectivos to Atzompa village (M$6.50, 20 minutes) leave from Trujano on the north side of Oaxaca's 2nd-class bus station.

by four temples. On its east side is a carved-stone animal, probably a jaguar. Next to the central platform is the entrance to one of several multichambered **underground tombs**.

The beautiful **Juego de Pelota** (Ball Court) is the second biggest in Mesoamerica (after one at Chichén Itzá on the Yucatán Peninsula). The labyrinthine **Palacio de los Seis Patios** (Palace of the Six Patios), above the ball court, was probably the leader's residence. Its now creamy-yellow walls were originally plastered and painted red.

It's well worth climbing the **Fortaleza** (Fortress), the rocky hill towering above Yagul. It's topped by several ruins, and the views are marvelous.

Approaching Yagul from the main road, you can make out a large white rock painting of a person/deity/tree/sun on a cliff-face on the **Caballito Blanco** rock outcrop to your right. This is the most obvious feature of a recently declared Unesco World Heritage site, the **Prehistoric Caves of Yagul and Mitla**, which extends about 6km east from here. Caves here have yielded evidence of the earliest plant domestication in North America, about 10,000 years ago, and other valuable details about the transition from hunting and gathering to agriculture over a period of several thousand years. Unfortunately the site has been closed to the public to prevent further vandalism after some of the ancient paintings were covered in aerosol paint.

Mitla

951 / POP 8200 / ELEV 1700M

A modern Zapotec town surrounds the unique ruins of Mitla, 46km southeast of Oaxaca. The ruins date from the final two or three centuries before the Spanish conquest in the 1520s, and comprise what was probably the most important Zapotec religious center at the time – a cult center dominated by high priests who performed literally heart-wrenching human sacrifices. The geometric stone 'mosaics' of ancient Mitla have no peers in ancient Mexico: the 14 different designs are thought to symbolize the sky and earth, a feathered serpent and other important beings, in sophisticated stylized forms. Each little piece of stone was cut to fit the design, then set in mortar on the walls and painted. Many Mitla buildings were also adorned with painted friezes.

Sights

Ancient Mitla ARCHAEOLOGICAL SITE

(admission Grupo de las Columnas M$42, other groups free; 8am-5pm; P) Mitla's ancient buildings are thought to have been reserved for specific occupants – one group for the high priest, one for the king and so forth. Visitors usually just see the two main groups in the town, the Grupo de las Columnas and the adjacent Grupo del Norte, though the remains of other structures are scattered for many kilometers around.

If you're using public transport, ask to disembark at the fork known as La Cuchilla as you enter Mitla. From here it's 1.2km north to the ruins' ticket office: go north along Av Morelos, through the plaza and along Calles 5 de Febrero and Reforma toward the three-domed Iglesia de San Pablo. The ticket office is normally behind this church, but was temporarily relocated in front of it at the time of writing. A three-wheeler moto-taxi from La Cuchilla costs M$10.

Sleeping & Eating

Hotel Don Cenobio HOTEL $$

(951-568-03-30; www.hoteldoncenobio.com; Av Juárez 3; r M$699-925, mains M$70-120; P) Set on the central plaza, this is easily Mitla's best hotel. The 23 comfortable rooms are decorated with attractively multicolored carved headboards and furniture from Guadalajara. In and around the grassy central garden are a swimming pool, bar and the hotel's restaurant, serving Oaxacan fare.

Restaurante Doña Chica OAXACAN $$

(951-568-02-25; Av Morelos 41; mains M$70-90; 11am-8pm) Less than 100m from La Cuchilla, spotless, bright Doña Chica serves delicious Oaxacan dishes like *moles,* enchiladas and *tasajo* from an open kitchen. Good soups, *antojitos* and salads round out the careful menu.

Shopping

Mitla's streets are sprinkled with shops selling local mezcal. Many of them will invite you to taste a couple of varieties – as will many of the small-scale mezcal distilleries along the road toward Oaxaca. Many other shops, and the large **Mercado de Artesanías** near the ruins, sell local textiles including lots of hammocks. Some of the tablecloths are attractive buys.

Hierve El Agua

At Hierve El Agua, 14km southeast of Mitla, bubbling **mineral springs** (admission M$20; 8am-7pm; P) run into bathing pools with a spectacular cliff-top location and expansive panoramas. Water dribbling over the cliff edge for millennia has created mineral formations that look like huge frozen waterfalls. Hierve El Agua means 'the water boils,' but the mineral-laden water is actually cold, though just about swimmable. Altogether the pools here make for a unique bathing experience; there are changing rooms just above the pools.

Hierve El Agua is a popular outing for Oaxacans on their days off. Above the pools and cliffs are a number of **comedores** (antojitos M$20-35; 8am-7pm), plus **cabañas** (per person M$100) providing simple rooms with one bathroom per two rooms.

Hierve El Agua is on the itinerary of some day tours from Oaxaca, but the only public transportation is by the *camionetas* (pickup trucks) of Transportes Zapotecos del Valle Oriente (M$40 one-way) from La Cuchilla in Mitla. They leave when they have enough passengers. If you're driving, take the 'Hierve El Agua' exit from the highway that bypasses Mitla to the south. This passes through the village of Xaagá, from which an unpaved, very scenic road leads 11km to the site.

Valle de Zimatlán

South from Oaxaca, Hwy 175 goes through San Bartolo Coyotepec, famed for its black pottery, and Ocotlán, which has one of the Valles Centrales' busiest weekly markets. Hwy 147 goes to Cuilapan and Zaachila.

San Bartolo Coyotepec

951 / POP 4000 / ELEV 1550M

Barro negro, the polished, surprisingly light black pottery that you find in hundreds of forms around Oaxaca comes from San Bartolo Coyotepec, 11km south of the city. To head to the original source, look for the signs to the **Alfarería Doña Rosa** (951-551-00-11; Juárez 24; 9am-7pm; P), a short walk east off the highway. It was Rosa Real Mateo (1900–80) who invented the method of burnishing the *barro negro* with quartz stones for the distinctive shine. Her family *alfarería* (potters' workshop) is now the biggest in the village, and they will demonstrate the process to anyone who asks. The pieces are hand-molded by an age-old technique using two saucers as a rudimentary potter's wheel. They are then fired in pit kilns and turn black from smoke and the iron oxide in the clay.

The **Museo Estatal de Arte Popular de Oaxaca** (951-551-00-36; www.facebook.com/meapo.oaxaca; admission M$20; 10am-6pm Tue-Sun), on the south side of the main plaza, features a collection of fine *barro negro* plus changing exhibitions of quality folk art from around Oaxaca state.

Autobuses Halcón (Bustamante 606A, Oaxaca) runs buses from Oaxaca city to San Bartolo (M$7, 20 minutes) every few minutes.

San Martín Tilcajete

San Martín Tilcajete, 1km west of Hwy 175, 24km south of Oaxaca, is the source of many of the bright copal-wood *alebrijes* seen in Oaxaca. You can see and buy them in makers' houses, many of which have 'Alebrijes' or 'Artesanías de Madera' (Wooden Handicrafts) signs outside. **Jacobo & María Ángeles Ojeda** (www.tilcajete.org; Olvido 9) make particularly wonderful *alebrijes*. Good pieces are also displayed at **Azucena Zapoteca** (mains M$60-130; 8am-6pm), a popular lunch stop serving Oaxacan specialties, beside Hwy 175 opposite the Tilcajete turnoff.

Ocotlán-bound buses from Oaxaca will drop you at the turnoff to San Martín (M$15, 35 minutes). *Taxis colectivos* run from Ocotlán itself.

Ocotlán

POP 15,000 / ELEV 1500M

Ocotlán, 31km south of Oaxaca, was the hometown of the artist Rodolfo Morales (1925–2001), who turned his international success to the area's benefit by setting up the **Fundación Cultural Rodolfo Morales** (www.fcrom.org.mx), which has done marvelous restoration work on local churches and promotes the area's arts, heritage, environment and social welfare. One major restoration was the handsome 16th-century **Templo de Santo Domingo** just off Ocotlán's main plaza, which now sports beautiful, colorful paintwork inside and out. The foundation also turned the adjoining **Ex-Convento de Santo Domingo** (admission M$15; 9am-6pm), previously a dilapidated jail, into a first-class art museum, which includes several of Morales' own canvases and a room of folk art dominated by Ocotlán's most renowned artisans, the Aguilar sisters. Morales' ashes are here, too.

The four Aguilar sisters and their families create whimsical, colorful pottery figures of women with all sorts of unusual motifs. Their houses are together on the west side of the main road entering Ocotlán from the north – spot them by the pottery women on the wall, almost opposite the Hotel Real de Ocotlán. Most renowned is **Guillermina Aguilar** (Morelos 430), who turns out, among other things, miniature 3-D re-creations of Frida Kahlo works.

Most visitors come to Ocotlán on Friday, when its big **weekly market** sprawls around the central plaza. The covered **Mercado Morelos** (⏲6:30am-8pm), on the plaza's west side, is worth a look any day, and contains several *comedores* serving bargain Oaxacan food for M$20 to M$35 per dish. One, **La Cocina de Frida**, is presided over by a local woman who resembles Frida Kahlo – and dresses for the part.

Automorsa (Bustamante 601, Oaxaca) runs buses from Oaxaca to Ocotlán (M$15, 45 minutes) about every 10 minutes, 6am to 9pm. *Taxis colectivos* to Ocotlán from Prolongación Victoria in Oaxaca cost M$20.

Cuilapan

POP 12,000 / ELEV 1560M

Cuilapan (Cuilápam), 9km southwest of Oaxaca, is one of the few Mixtec towns in the Valles Centrales. It's the site of a beautiful, historic Dominican monastery, the **Ex-Convento Dominicano** (admission to cloister M$35; ⏲9am-5pm; P), whose pale stone seems almost to grow out of the land.

In 1831 Mexican independence hero Vicente Guerrero was executed here by soldiers supporting the rebel conservative Anastasio Bustamante, who had ousted the liberal Guerrero from the presidency. Guerrero had fled by ship from Acapulco, but the ship's captain put in at Huatulco and betrayed him to the rebels, who transported him to Cuilapan to die.

A long, low unfinished **church** in front of the monastery has stood roofless since work on it stopped in 1560. It has stately arches and some detailed stone carving. Behind is the church that succeeded it, which contains the **tomb of Juana Donají** (daughter of Cosijoeza, the last Zapotec king of Zaachila) and is open only for Mass (usually 7am to 8am and 5pm to 6pm). Around the church's right-hand end is a two-story Renaissance-style **cloister**: a painting of Guerrero hangs in the small room where he was held. Outside, a **monument** marks the spot where he was shot.

Zaachila Yoo (Bustamante 601, Oaxaca) runs buses from Oaxaca to Cuilapan (M$7, 30 minutes) about every 15 minutes. *Taxis colectivos* from Prolongación Victoria in Oaxaca cost M$11 (20 minutes).

Zaachila

☎951 / POP 14,000 / ELEV 1520M

This part-Mixtec, part-Zapotec town, 6km southeast of Cuilapan, has a big, busy Thursday market. It was a Zapotec capital from AD 1400 until the Spanish conquest. Behind the village church overlooking the main plaza, a sign indicates the entrance to Zaachila's **Zona Arqueológica** (Archaeological Zone; admission M$35; ⏲9am-5pm), a small assortment of mounds where you can enter two small ancient Mixtec tombs. Tumba 1 has sculptures of owls, a turtle-man figure and various long-nosed skull-like masks. Tumba 2 has no decoration, but was home to a Mixtec treasure hoard that's now in the Museo Nacional de Antropología in Mexico City. When Mexican archaeologists first tried to excavate these tombs in the 1940s and 1950s, they were run off by irate Zaachilans. The tombs were finally excavated under armed guard in 1962. You can see photos of some of the objects that were carted off.

Zaachila Yoo (p450) runs buses between Oaxaca and Zaachila (M$7, 40 minutes) about every 15 minutes. *Taxis colectivos* (M$12, 20 minutes) leave from the corner of Bustamante and Zaragoza in Oaxaca.

San Agustín Etla

☎951 / POP 3700 / ELEV 1800M

Pretty San Agustín sits on the Valle de Etla's eastern slopes, 18km northwest of Oaxaca. Its large, early-20th-century textile mill has been superbly restored as the **Centro de las Artes de San Agustín** (☎951-521-30-42; www.casa.oaxaca.gob.mx; Independencia s/n , Barrio Vistahermosa; admission free; ⏲9am-6pm), an arts center with two long, large halls used for concerts, conferences and often-wonderful craft or art exhibitions. The center also hosts many courses and workshops.

Balneario Vista Hermosa (951-521-20-49; Hidalgo 16; adult/child M$80/70; 10am-6pm;) makes a fun day out if you are in Oaxaca with kids. Its six swimming pools, in hillside gardens, include two that are heated, one that's big and shallow, and a couple with waterslides. It has a modest **restaurant** (dishes M$30-75) and a bar.

The turnoff for San Agustín from Hwy 190 is on the east side of the road, 13.5km from central Oaxaca, marked by a tiny 'San Sebastián Etla' sign beside the large-ish Instituto Euro-Americano. It's 4km up to the village. *Taxis colectivos* to San Agustín (M$12, 30 minutes) go from Trujano on the north side of Oaxaca's 2nd-class bus station.

SIERRA NORTE

The mountains separating the Valles Centrales from low-lying far northern Oaxaca are called the Sierra Juárez, and the more southerly parts of this range, closest to Oaxaca, have become known as the Sierra Norte. These beautiful, forested highlands are home to several successful community ecotourism ventures providing comfortable accommodations and a wonderful opportunity to get out on foot, mountain bike or horseback into some of Mexico's loveliest landscapes. Over 400 bird species, 350 butterflies, all six Mexican wild cats and nearly 4000 plants have been recorded in the Sierra Norte. Be prepared for cool temperatures: in the higher, southern villages it can snow in winter. The wettest season is from late May to September; there's little rain from January to April.

Pueblos Mancomunados

The Pueblos Mancomunados (Commonwealth of Villages) are eight remote villages (Amatlán, Benito Juárez, Cuajimoloyas, La Nevería, Lachatao, Latuvi, Llano Grande and Yavesía) in the thickly forested highlands north of the Valle de Tlacolula. They offer highly recommended wilderness escapes and an up-close communion with Zapotec village life. More than 100km of scenic tracks and trails run between the villages and to local beauty spots and places of interest, and you can easily enjoy several days exploring. Elevations in these hills range from 2200m to over 3200m, and the landscapes, with canyons, caves, waterfalls and panoramic lookouts, are spectacular.

For centuries, these villages have pooled the natural resources of their 290-sq-km territory, sharing the profits from forestry and other enterprises. In recent years they have also turned to ecotourism to help stave off economic difficulties and population decline. All offer a friendly welcome, comfortable, good-value *cabañas* (mostly with hot-water bathrooms and fireplaces), meals, guides, and horses and mountain bikes for rent.

Several Oaxaca agencies offer trips to the Pueblos Mancomunados, but it's not difficult to visit independently. Six of the villages (the exceptions are Lachatao and Yavesía) cooperate in an excellent combined ecotourism program, Expediciones Sierra Norte (p425), which has a helpful office in Oaxaca city. Each participating village also has an ecotourism office open from about 9am to 9pm daily, where it's possible just to roll up and organize what you need on the spot, but reservations are a good idea at vacation times and weekends. Horses must be reserved at least one day ahead.

Local guides, knowledgeable about the wildlife, ecology, folklore and history of these sierras, are available for excursions. You don't generally need one to follow the main routes between villages, but for smaller trails a guide is recommended. English-speaking guides cost a little extra and should be requested two or three days ahead.

Each village has at least one *comedor* serving good local meals (with vegetarian options available) from 8am to 8pm. Prices in the Expediciones Sierra Norte villages are as follows:

- private *cabaña:* M$540 for two people including firewood
- shared *cabaña:* M$180 per person
- meals: M$60 to M$65 each
- camping: M$55 per person
- tent rental: M$60 per night
- bicycle: M$120/175 per three hours/day
- horse: M$235/350/465 per three/four/five hours
- guide for up to six people: hiking M$175 to M$350, biking M$300 to M$410, horse M$410 to M$700, depending on route
- one-time access fee: adult/child M$60/35

Lachatao village runs its own separate, particularly dynamic ecotourism program,

Lachatao Expediciones (☎951-514-00-55, cell phone 951-1597194; www.lachataoexpediciones.com.mx) , with similar services and prices. One of the most attractive and interesting villages, with exceptionally good *cabañas*, Lachatao lies on routes between Expediciones Sierra Norte villages, but any reservations here have to be made separately.

Sights & Activities

The easiest-to-reach villages are **Cuajimoloyas**, **Llano Grande** and **Benito Juárez**, all at the Sierra Norte's higher, southern end, nearest to Oaxaca. It's possible to base yourself in one village and take local walks or rides from there. Some superb lookout points are easily accessible from the southern villages, such as **El Mirador**, a 2.5km walk from Benito Juárez, or the 3200m-high **Yaa-Cuetzi** lookout, on the edge of Cuajimoloyas. Yaa-Cuetzi is the starting point of a spectacular 900m-long **zip-line** (M$235), which carries you over the Cuajimoloyas rooftops at speeds reaching 65km/hr. Cuajimoloyas also hosts the gastronomic **Feria de Hongos Silvestres** (Wild Mushroom Festival) over a weekend in July, August or September each year.

Tiny **La Nevería** is less visited but very welcoming and pretty, and additional routes from here take you through the forests to La Cumbre on Hwy 175, or right down to Tlalixtac de Cabrera in the Valle de Tlacolula.

One special highlight walk is the beautiful **Latuvi-Lachatao canyon trail**, part of a pre-Hispanic track from the Valles Centrales to the Gulf of Mexico that passes through cloud forests festooned with bromeliads and hanging mosses (keep your eyes peeled for trogons, too).

Lachatao is one of the most atmospheric villages, with a huge 17th-century church containing an extraordinary wealth of sculpture, an excellent community museum, and the spectacular, cliff-top, pre-Hispanic site **Cerro del Rayo** (Xia-Yetza) 2km west. From Lachatao or nearby **Amatlán** you can visit the remains of a colonial textile hacienda and old gold mines, and do a spot of rappelling in the mines. Lachatao hosts some interesting arts festivals, one of which includes pre-Hispanic ceremonies on Cerro del Rayo around the spring equinox (March 21 to 23).

Getting There & Away

It's a good idea to check with Expediciones Sierra Norte in Oaxaca for current public transportation details.

THE SOUTHERN VILLAGES

Cuajimoloyas and Llano Grande have the best public services: four daily Flecha del Zempoaltépetl buses from Oaxaca's 2nd-class station (to Cuajimoloyas M$42, two hours; to Llano Grande M$45, 2½ hours). Expediciones Sierra Norte will transport up to five people to any of its villages for M$1700 round-trip in a double-cabin Nissan pickup; reserve at least one day before.

OFF THE BEATEN TRACK

SANTIAGO APOALA

This small, remote village, lying in a green, Shangri La–like valley flanked by cliffs, is a great spot for hiking, biking and climbing. In traditional Mixtec belief, this valley was the birthplace of humanity, and the scenery around Apoala is appropriately spectacular, with the 60m waterfall **Cascada Cola de la Serpiente**, the 400m-deep **Cañón Morelos** and a number of caves among the highlights.

It's easiest to come with an agency from Oaxaca, but cheaper to arrange things independently through the village's community-tourism unit, the **Unidad Ecoturística** (Ecotourism Unit; ☎555-151-91-54; cnr Pino Suárez & Independencia; 8am-8pm) , which runs cozy **cabañas** (d/q M$400/600, meals M$40-50) and offers mountain-bike rental (per three hours/day M$30/150) and guides (per person M$10 to M$30, depending on route). It's not normally necessary to book ahead (and the phone often doesn't work anyway) as it has plenty of *cabañas*.

Santiago Apoala is 40km north of the town of Nochixtlán, along a rough, unpaved road that takes two hours to drive. Nochixtlán is served by nine daily buses from Oaxaca's 1st-class bus station (M$98, one to 1½ hours). Between Nochixtlán and Apoala you might be lucky enough to find an occasional *camioneta* or bus, but normally you'll need a taxi (M$250 one-way).

For Benito Juárez get out at the Benito Juárez turnoff ('desviación de Benito Juárez'), 3km before Cuajimoloyas, and walk 3.5km west along the unpaved road to Benito Juárez. From Benito Juárez, La Nevería is a 9km walk west, and Latuvi 10km north.

AMATLÁN & LACHATAO

You can reach the northern villages of Amatlán and Lachatao by heading to Ixtlán de Juárez on Hwy 175 (M$46 to M$64, 1½ hours, 14 daily buses from Oaxaca's 1st-class station), then taking a *camioneta* to Amatlán (M$30, 45 minutes) or Lachatao (M$30, one hour) from beside the *escuela primaria* (primary school) in central Ixtlán at 7am, noon and 3pm, Monday to Saturday only. They start back from Lachatao at 6am, 9am and 1pm, Monday to Saturday. In both directions, the *camionetas* run one hour later during daylight saving from April to October. A taxi from Ixtlán to Lachatao costs around M$200.

There is also a bus to Amatlán and Lachatao (both M$50, 2½ to three hours) at 4pm Monday, Tuesday, Friday and Saturday and 7pm Sunday from beside the Ixcotel *gasolinera* (gas station) on Calle Niño Perdido, just off Hwy 190, 1.5km east of the 1st-class bus station in Oaxaca. It starts back for Oaxaca from Lachatao at 5:30am the same days (3pm on Sunday). In all cases departures are one hour later during daylight saving.

WESTERN OAXACA

Western Oaxaca is dramatic and mountainous, with a fairly sparse population and some thick forests as well as overfarmed and deforested areas. Along with adjoining parts of Puebla and Guerrero states, it is known as the Mixteca, for its Mixtec indigenous inhabitants. The region offers a chance to get well off the beaten track, enjoy hiking, biking or climbing in remote areas and see some outstanding colonial architecture. Guided trips are available from Oaxaca with operators such as Tierraventura (p425) and Bicicletas Pedro Martínez (p426).

Yanhuitlán, Coixtlahuaca & Teposcolula

The beautiful 16th-century **Dominican monasteries** in the villages of Yanhuitlán, Coixtlahuaca and San Pedro Teposcolula rank among Mexico's finest architectural treasures. Their scale – especially the enormous *capilla abierta* (open chapel) spaces used for mass conversions – testifies to the size of indigenous populations when the Spanish arrived. The monasteries' restrained stonework fuses medieval, plateresque, Renaissance and indigenous styles, and all three have ornate interior decoration, including enormous gilded wooden *retablos* (altarpieces). Recent works have restored their grandeur and added interesting **museums**, which are all open from 10am to 5pm daily except Monday, with admission of M$35 at Yanhuitlán and Teposcolula and by donation at Coixtlahuaca. The monastery churches are usually open from about 9am to 2pm and 4pm to 6pm, though you may have to ask at the museums for the key-keeper to be found. Should you want to stay overnight, Coixtlahuaca and San Pedro Teposcolula have a few acceptable, basic hotels and inns.

The **Templo y Ex-Convento de San Juan Bautista** in Coixtlahuaca is 4km east of the Coixtlahuaca tollbooth on Hwy 135D, about 30km north of Nochixtlán. The church's Renaissance-style, white-stone main facade is magnificent, and the graceful, ruined *capilla abierta* bears Mixtec religious symbols, most notably serpents and eagles.

The **Templo y Ex-Convento de Santo Domingo** at Yanhuitlán towers above Hwy 190, some 14km northwest of Nochixtlán. Built atop an old Mixtec religious site, it has beautiful carving on its north and west facades, and a fine Mudejar ceiling suspended beneath the choir loft, which contains an impressive pipe organ.

The **Templo y Ex-Convento de San Pedro y San Pablo** dominates San Pedro Teposcolula on Hwy 125 about 30km west of Yanhuitlán. The monastery has a particularly stately *capilla abierta* with beautifully carved arches; the museum in the adjacent monastic buildings contains a sizable collection of early colonial art.

Getting There & Away

All three villages can be seen in a longish but not difficult day trip by car from Oaxaca. Public transportation options include **Transportadora Excelencia** (Díaz Ordaz 314, Oaxaca), which runs comfortable vans every half-hour to Yanhuitlán (M$60, one hour) and Teposcolula (M$80, 1¾ hours). **Fletes y Pasajes** (Fypsa) runs 2nd-class buses (M$90, 1½ hours, 12 daily) from Oaxaca's 2nd-class bus station to the Caseta Coixtlahuaca tollbooth on Hwy 135D, from which it's a 3km walk or *taxi colectivo* ride east to Coixtlahuaca village.

OAXACA COAST

Oaxaca's spectacular Pacific coast has everything you need for a great time by the ocean. With several varied, relaxed beach destinations, and the near-empty shoreline between them strung with long golden beaches and lagoons full of wildlife, it's hard to go wrong. Offshore are dolphins, turtles and whales, plus diving, snorkeling and sportfishing – alongside some of North America's best surfing swells.

In this tropical climate, the pace is never too hectic and the people are welcoming. In the center of the coast, three beach villages – Zipolite, San Agustinillo and Mazunte, are perfect for just taking it easy, with a laid-back traveler vibe. Further west is Puerto Escondido, a larger fishing, market and vacation town with a string of great beaches (including Playa Zicatela, home to the pumping surf of the Mexican Pipeline). Toward the coast's eastern end is Bahías de Huatulco, a modern, planned resort along a string of beautiful bays with a pleasantly low-key atmosphere.

This coast is one of the world's most important sea-turtle nesting areas, and the bird and aquatic life of the many lagoons along it will delight nature lovers. The coastal plain is backed everywhere by dramatic, forested mountains, and the trip down here from Oaxaca city is a spectacular experience in itself, whether you go by bus, car or light plane. There are airports at Huatulco and Puerto Escondido, both with daily flights from Oaxaca and Mexico City. Huatulco is the more convenient for the Zipolite-to-Mazunte area and also has some direct flights from the USA and Canada.

Most of the year's rain here falls between June and September, turning everything green. From October the landscape starts to dry out, though conditions can remain humid. May is the hottest month.

Puerto Escondido

954 / POP 40,000

Loved by surf bums, water-sports junkies and perma-tan international travelers, this 'Hidden Port' is one of the most enjoyable spots on Mexico's Pacific coast. By day, you can surf, snorkel, dive, swim, go sportfishing or look for turtles, dolphins and whales. By night, a busy cafe, restaurant and bar scene brings live music and a freewheeling, unpretentious nightlife. Development has happened gradually over several decades and remained on a human scale, and part of Puerto's charm is that it remains a fishing port and market town as well as a tourist destination.

The heart of town rises above the small Bahía Principal. The Carretera Costera (Hwy 200) runs across the hill above the bay, dividing the upper town – where buses arrive and most locals live and work – from the lower, more touristic part. The lower town's main strip is traffic-free Avenida Pérez Gasga, known as El Adoquín (*adoquín* is Spanish for paving stone). The hub of the surf and traveler scene is Playa Zicatela, stretching 3km southeast from the east end of Bahía Principal. Rinconada, a quiet residential area above Playa Carrizalillo, west of the center, has further places to stay, restaurants and services.

Sights

★Playa Zicatela BEACH

(Map p460; P) Long, straight Zicatela is Puerto Escondido's happening beach, with enticing cafes, restaurants and accommodations, as well as the waves of the legendary **Mexican Pipeline**. Most of the action, including the Pipeline, is at Zicatela's northern end (nearest town). Nonsurfers beware: the waters here have a lethal undertow and are not safe for the boardless. Lifeguards rescue several careless people most months. The Punta Zicatela area at Zicatela's far southern end also has decent surf, and a mellower vibe.

Bahía Principal BEACH

Puerto Escondido's central bay is long enough to accommodate restaurants at its west end, a small fishing fleet in its center (Playa Principal), and sun worshippers and young bodyboarders at its east end (Playa Marinero), where the waters are a little cleaner. Pelicans wing in inches above the waves, boats bob on the swell and a few hawkers wander up and down.

Playa Carrizalillo BEACH

(Map p456) Small Carrizalillo beach, west of the center, is in a cove reached by a stairway of 157 steps. It's good for swimming, bodyboarding and beginner's surfing, and has a line of *palapa* (thatch-roofed) beach bars.

Bahía Puerto Angelito BEACH

The sheltered bay of Puerto Angelito has two smallish beaches with shallow, usually calm waters: the western Playa Angelito and the eastern Playa Manzanillo. Both have lots of seafood *comedores* and are very popular with Mexican families at weekends and on holidays. Manzanillo has the more relaxed vibe and generally more spacious *comedores*. You can rent snorkels for around M$40 at the comedores.

Activities

Surfing

Puerto Escondido has surfable waves most days of the year. The Zicatela **Pipeline** is one of the world's heaviest and scariest beach breaks, normally best in the morning and late afternoon, and at its biggest between May and July. Even when the Pipeline is flat, the point break at **Punta Zicatela** works almost day in, day out. **Playa Carrizalillo** has good beginners' waves. Several annual surf contests are held at Zicatela, usually in August, September and during the November fiestas. An under-18s surf festival at Playa Carrizalillo usually happens in August.

Long or shortboard rental is typically M$100/30 per day/hour; bodyboards are normally M$50/20 per day/hour, plus M$25 for fins. You can buy secondhand boards from around M$1000 at places like Cricket's Surf Shop and Seth Surf Shop at Zicatela.

Numerous surf shops, schools and individuals in Zicatela, Punta Zicatela and Rinconada offer surfing lessons. Lessons normally last 1½ to two hours, and the schools will drive you wherever the waves are most suitable (often Carrizalillo).

Oasis Surf Academy SURFING

(Map p456; ☎954-582-14-45; www.oasissurf-puerto.com; Blvd Juárez 6 , Rinconada; small-group class US$35, 5 classes US$150; ⏰9am-6pm Mon-Sat) Based near Playa Carrizalillo, offering classes with experienced, qualified, bilingual teachers. It's run by local pro surfer and board maker Roger Ramírez, and has apartments for rent, too.

Puerto Surf SURFING

(☎cell phone 954-1096406; www.puertosurf.com.mx; Nayarit s/n, Punta Zicatela; 5-day/6-night surf course & accommodation package s/d M$3600/6400, course only M$1900, individual class M$400) Run by the amiable David Salinas, the youngest of six well-known Puerto surfer brothers, Puerto Surf offers good five-day surf courses (two hours a day plus a two-hour introductory theory session). Shorter courses or single classes are also available. You have the option of staying

SURFING OAXACA

The monster tubes of the Mexican Pipeline off Puerto Escondido's Playa Zicatela rank among the world's top surfing waves, pulling in experienced surfers from around the globe for their thrilling challenge.

But the Oaxaca coast is dotted with dozens of fine surf spots. The best swells generally roll in between March and November and are at their biggest from about May to July. Many breaks are right-hand point breaks, some of them peeling for hundreds of meters.

Toward the west end of the coast, Chacahua (p465) has a good long point break and a scattering of basic *cabaña* accommodations. Puerto Escondido itself has a variety of breaks besides the Pipeline: the left-hand point break of Punta Zicatela (p454) works almost year-round, while the gentler waves of Playa Carrizalillo (p454) are perfect for beginners. The town has numerous surf schools and instructors.

Further east, San Agustinillo (p472) has perfect bodyboarding waves and is another good spot to take classes. The river-mouth right-hander at La Bocana (p479) makes Bahías de Huatulco a worthwhile stop, and the very long point break at the village of Barra de la Cruz (p484), 20km further down the coast, is a popular classic.

The Salina Cruz region at the east end of the coast is the most under-the-radar of Oaxaca's surf zones, with almost no tourism development, but has a couple of dozen top-class point, beach and jetty breaks. Some Salina Cruz–based 'surf camps' have gained a reputation for warning off independent surfers from some spots so that their clients can have the waves to themselves, but only a small handful of breaks still suffer such jealous guardianship now. The village of Concepción Bamba (p486), 40km east of Salina Cruz, has a much more economical and freewheeling surf camp and is the best place for independent surfers to head.

Puerto Escondido

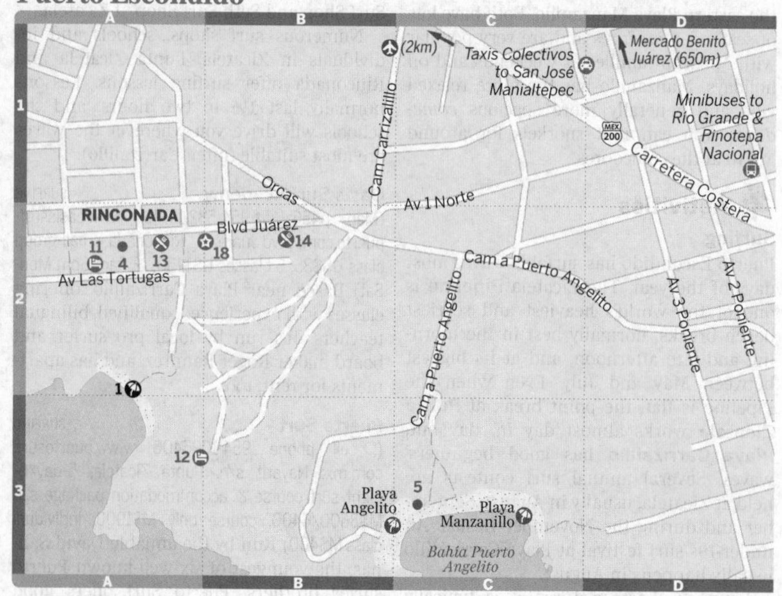

in its comfortable and attractive five-room guesthouse in La Punta.

Central Surf SURFING
(Map p460; ☎954-582-22-85; www.puertoescondidosurfschool.com; Calle del Morro s/n, Zicatela; individual/group class per person M$550/350; ⊙shop 9am-9pm) The team here is led by René Salinas, from a well-known local surfing family. They also offer bodyboard and SUP (stand-up paddleboarding) classes, rent equipment, sell boards and post daily surf reports and plenty of photos and video on partner website http://centralsurf.tv.

Puerto Surf Lessons SURFING
(☎cell phone 954-1010791; www.puertosurflessons.com; Guerrero 4, Punta Zicatela; 1/3/5 classes M$400/1150/1800) This recommended school is headed by lifeguard and highly experienced surfer Celestino.

Wildlife Trips

Sea turtles and dolphins are common in the seas off Puerto, and from around November to April you have a chance of seeing humpback whales, manta rays and even whale sharks. Three-hour trips for small groups are usually M$400 per person – try Omar Ramírez of **Omar's Sportfishing** (Map p456; ☎cell phone 954-5594406; http://tomzap.com/omar.html; Playa Angelito) and dive shop Deep Blue Dive. Local fishers will take groups of up to four out for an hour for around M$450 in their *lanchas* (fast, open, outboard boats): contact the **Sociedad Cooperativa Turística Nueva Punta Escondida** (Map p456; ☎cell phone 954-1188070; Restaurante El Pescador, Marina Nacional) on Bahía Principal.

Diving & Snorkeling

Typical visibility is around 10m, rising to as much as 30m between May and August, when the seas are warmest. The reefs are of volcanic rock, with lots of marine life, including big schools of fish, spotted eagle rays, stingrays and turtles. Most dive sites are within a 15-minute boat ride of town. Both Puerto's dive outfits offer snorkeling and marine-life-spotting trips as well as dives for certified divers and a variety of courses.

Deep Blue Dive DIVING, SNORKELING
(Map p460; ☎cell phone 954-1003071; www.deepbluedivemexico.com; Beach Hotel Inés, Calle del Morro s/n, Zicatela; ⊙9am-2pm & 4:30-8pm) This professional, European-run outfit does one- and two-tank dives for certified divers (M$550 and M$900 respectively), one-morning Discover Scuba sessions (M$800) and a range of PADI courses.

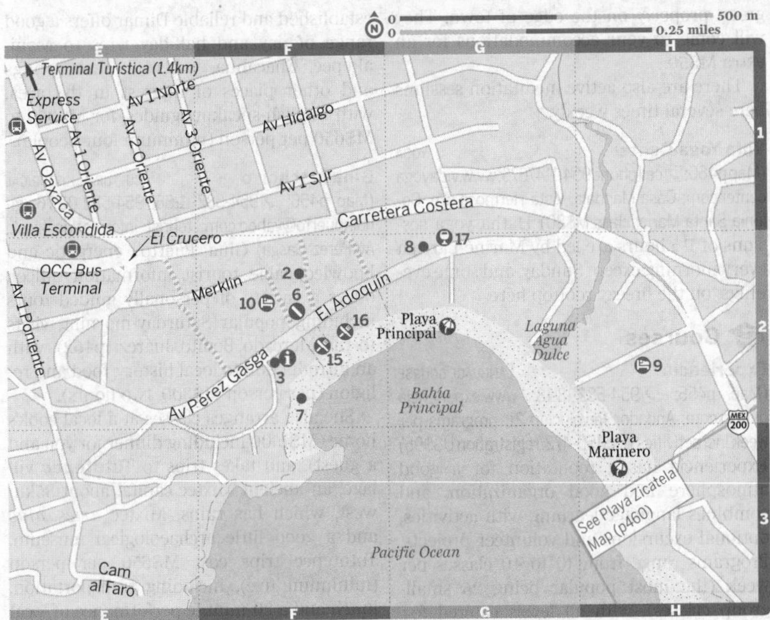

Puerto Dive Center DIVING, SNORKELING
(Map p456; ☎954-582-34-21; www.puertodive-center.com; Andador Libertad s/n; ⏲9am-6pm) PDC does dives for certified divers and beginners, night dives and PADI courses. Owner Sofía Ponce made one of the deepest saltwater dives ever by a woman when she descended to 190m off Puerto in 2010.

Fishing

Local fishers will take two to four people fishing for marlin, sailfish, tuna or smaller inshore fish: a three-hour trip costs around M$1200 to M$1500. Contact Sociedad Cooperativa Turística Nueva Punta Escondida (p456) or Omar's Sportfishing (p456). Catch-and-release is encouraged, but boat owners can also arrange for some of the catch to be cooked for you at one of the town's seafood restaurants.

Yoga & Massage

Temazcalli MASSAGE
(☎954-582-10-23; www.temazcalli.com; Calle Temazcalli, off Av Infraganti, Colonia Lázaro Cárdenas; ⏲9am-6pm) The experts at Temazcalli have been practicing the healing arts in Puerto for 20 years and offer a big range of massages and beauty treatments (M$400 to M$500), plus temascals (traditional indigenous steam baths; M$350), at their peaceful,

Puerto Escondido

Sights
1 Playa Carrizalillo A2

Activities, Courses & Tours
2 Experiencia F2
3 Gina Machorro F2
4 Oasis Surf Academy A2
5 Omar's Sportfishing C3
6 Puerto Dive Center F2
7 Sociedad Cooperativa Turística Nueva Punta Escondida F2
8 Viajes Dimar G2

Sleeping
9 Hotel Flor de María H2
10 Hotel Mayflower F2
11 Hotel Villa Mozart y Macondo A2
12 Villas Carrizalillo A3

Eating
13 El Cafecito A2
14 El Nene B2
15 Pascale F2
16 Restaurante Los Crotos F2

Drinking & Nightlife
17 Congo G2

Entertainment
18 Cinemar B2

green property on the edge of town. They will come to your accommodations for an extra M$50.

There are also active meditation sessions here several times weekly.

Vida Yoga Center YOGA

(Map p460; cell phone 954-1147675; www.vidayogacenter.com; Casa Mandala, Vista Hermosa s/n, Colonia Santa María; class M$80) Hatha yoga sessions of 1½ hours are led by Mariné Larripa every morning except Sunday, and some evenings, on the breezy rooftop here.

Courses

Experiencia LANGUAGE COURSE

(Map p456; 954-582-18-18; www.experienciapuerto.com; Andador Revolución 21; programs per week incl activities US$150-472, registration US$95) Experiencia has a reputation for a good atmosphere and good organization, and combines language learning with activities, optional excursions and volunteer projects. Programs range from 10 to 40 classes per week (the most popular being 25 small-group classes), with all levels catered for. Many students stay either one or four weeks.

Special programs are available for travelers, surfers, retirees and professionals, and there are discounts for walk-ins. The school has spacious, attractive, central premises with wi-fi, a student kitchen, and onsite rooms available (shared/private room per week US$89/170).

Instituto de Lenguajes Puerto Escondido LANGUAGE COURSE

(Map p460; 954-582-20-55; www.puertoschool.com; Carretera Costera, Zicatela; small-group/private classes per person per hr US$8/12) This small school emphasizes both spoken and written Spanish, with a variety of excursions and complementary activities including surfing, cooking, salsa and tai-chi classes available at extra cost. It's set in attractive tropical gardens overlooking Zicatela beach, with wi-fi and student bungalows (per day/week for one or two people US$30/180) available onsite. You can start any day, at any level, for as long as you like.

Tours

Viajes Dimar SIGHTSEEING

(www.viajesdimar.com) **Adoquín** (Map p456; 954-582-15-51; Av Pérez Gasga 905; 8am-9:30pm); **Zicatela** (Map p460; 954-582-23-05; Calle del Morro s/n, Zicatela; 9am-9pm Mon-Fri, 10am-9pm Sat, 10am-3pm Sun) Long-established and reliable Dimar offers a good range of day and half-day trips to Manialtepec, Chacahua, waterfalls, hot springs and other places of interest in the area, with English-speaking guides, for M$350 to M$650 per person (minimum four people).

Gina Machorro CULTURAL, HISTORICAL

(Map p456; 954-582-11-86, 954-582-02-76; ginainpuerto@yahoo.com; tourist information kiosk, Av Pérez Gasga) Gina, Puerto's energetic and knowledgeable tourist information officer, offers a variety of personally guided tours including popular Saturday-morning visits to the Mercado Benito Juárez (p462), with an introduction to local history, food and religion (per person M$300, two hours).

She also arranges classes at a local cook's home (M$1500 including dinner for you and a guest), and takes trips to **Tututepec** village, an ancient Mixtec capital about 85km west, which has ruins, Mixtec *artesanías* and a good little archaeological museum. Tututepec trips cost M$650 per person (minimum five), including transportation, lunch and a 20-minute performance of local dance and music.

Festivals & Events

Puerto Music MUSIC

Some top Canadian and US blues musicians hit Puerto for around eight gigs spread through January and February, playing at the Split Coconut bar on Playa Marinero.

Fiestas de Noviembre CULTURAL, FISHING

(visitapuerto.com/fiestas-de-noviembre) These festivities keep Puerto buzzing through November with many varied events, including the Festival Costeño de la Danza (folk dance), an international sailfish tournament (www.pescadeportivaenpuertoescondido.com), a surfing contest, motocross, food tastings and plenty more.

Sleeping

The two main accommodations zones are Playa Zicatela and the central Adoquín (Avenida Pérez Gasga) area. Zicatela has the most appealing surroundings, with great places to eat as well as sleep. The only drawback is that you can't swim here.

Rates given here are those that commonly apply during the main visitor seasons – roughly mid-December to Easter, and July and August. During the Christmas–New Year and Easter vacations, prices can double or even more, but outside the main seasons many rates drop dramatically. Discounts are widely available for stays of several days or more. In the busy seasons the most popular places often fill up, so it's worth reserving ahead.

Playa Zicatela

Bungalows Puerta del Sol HOTEL $
(Map p460; 954-582-29-22; www.bungalowspuertadelsol.com; Calle del Morro s/n; r M$350, with air-con M$650;) This friendly, helpful and very clean place has a small pool and a communal kitchen either side of a nice green courtyard. The 16 spacious, solid rooms boast cheerful art and, in most cases, balcony and hammock.

Hotel Las Olas HOTEL $
(Map p460; 954-582-09-19; www.hotel-lasolas.com; Calle del Morro s/n; r M$250-300, with air-con M$450-500;) Las Olas has good, clean excellent-value rooms, some with kitchen. Second-floor choices have ocean-view hammocks, and there's a small sundeck.

Hotel Buena Vista HOTEL $
(Map p460; 954-582-14-74; buenavista_97@hotmail.com; Calle del Morro s/n; r M$200, with air-con M$300, with kitchen extra M$50;) The 10 no-frills rooms are big and spotless, with two beds, mosquito screens, hot-water bathroom and breezy balconies. It's good value and would be even better if it had some common areas where guests could socialise.

Ananda GUESTHOUSE $
(Map p460; cell phone 954-1186070; www.anandahotelpuerto.com; Jacarandas 18, Colonia Santa María; r M$150-400;) This friendly, good-value spot is a budget surfers' favorite. There's a kitchen for every two rooms.

Hotel Casa de Dan HOTEL $$
(Map p460; 954-582-27-60; www.facebook.com/hotelcasadan; Jacarandas 14, Colonia Santa María; r M$350-700;) Everything here is set around verdant patios and gardens, and you can enjoy a nice long lap pool as well as a terrace with a perfect Zicatela surf view. The 15 units are of varying size, all with fully equipped kitchens, terraces and attractively tiled bathrooms – and you can walk through to the excellent Dan's Café Deluxe (p461), adjoining. Reservations are advised.

Beach Hotel Inés HOTEL $$
(Map p460; 954-582-07-92; www.hotelines.com; Calle del Morro s/n; r M$350-1400;) German-run Inés has a wide variety of bright, cheerful *cabañas,* rooms, apartments and suites, around a shaded pool area with a cafe serving good Euro/Mexican food. All accommodations have hot water, good mosquito screens and fans, and some come with kitchens or air-con. You can arrange horseback riding, surf lessons, diving and other outings, and security is particularly good here.

Aqua Luna HOTEL $$
(Map p460; 954-582-15-05; www.hotelaqualuna.com; Vista Hermosa s/n; r M$350-900;) An excellent small hotel popular with surfers, Aqua Luna has a panoramic roof deck with a view of the Zicatela Pipeline. The rooms are bright, in a clean, contemporary style, and most are without air-con and in the budget price range. All-day breakfasts and other light dishes (M$30 to M$50) are served at the poolside bar.

It offers big discounts for monthly stays. No under-16s allowed.

Hotelito Swiss Oasis HOTEL $$
(Map p460; 954-582-14-96; www.swissoasis.com; Andador Los Adobes; s/d/tr/q M$500/600/700/800;) This good small hotel provides a guest kitchen with free coffee, tea and purified water, and a pool in the pretty garden, in addition to eight spotless rooms with good beds and attractive color schemes. The well-traveled Swiss owners speak four languages and are very helpful with local information.

Hotel Santa Fe HOTEL $$$
(Map p460; 954-582-01-70; www.hotelsantafe.com.mx; Calle del Morro s/n; r M$1300, ste from M$1800;) A well-run, neocolonial-style hotel set around two good pools in palm-shaded gardens. The 60-plus rooms have attractive tiling and wood furnishings, and some boast original murals. The airy vegetarian-and-seafood restaurant looks out along Zicatela beach.

El Adoquín & Around

Hotel Mayflower HOSTEL, HOTEL $
(Map p456; 954-582-03-67; minnemay7@hotmail.com; Andador Libertad s/n; dm/s/d/tr/q M$100/250/350/450/550;) Clean, popular Mayflower has nine fan-cooled dorms holding four to seven people each (in beds and bunks), and 17 quite attractive private rooms with bathrooms and small balconies. Facilities include a decent guest kitchen,

Playa Zicatela

Top Sights

Activities, Courses & Tours

Sleeping

Eating

Drinking & Nightlife

semi-open sitting areas, lockers and luggage storage.

Hotel Flor de María HOTEL $$
(Map p456; ☎954-582-05-36; www.mexonline.com/flordemaria.htm; 1a Entrada a Playa Marinero; r US$45-65; P ⊖ ☜ ≋ ☺) A popular Canadian-owned hotel with 24 ample rooms sporting good large bathrooms, folksy Mexican decor and pretty wall and door paintings. A highlight is the expansive roof terrace with its fabulous views, bar and small pool. No under-12s here.

Punta Zicatela

La Punta, as it's known, is the far southern end of Playa Zicatela, with a more relaxed, traveler-oriented ambience than the main surfer-focused, Zicatela scene about 2km up the beach.

Cabañas Buena Onda HOSTEL $
(☎954-582-16-63; http://buenaonda.hostei.com; Cárdenas 777; camping/hammock/dm per person M$60/60/110, cabaña M$270; ☜) Popular Buena Onda is set in a shady palm grove, with a beachfront *palapa* hangout area where campers can pitch a tent or sling a hammock. The 10 rustic *cabañas* are clean and equipped with mosquito nets, fans and hammocks, and there are adequate bathrooms and kitchen.

Frutas y Verduras CABAÑAS, ROOMS $
(cell phone 954-1246297; http://frutasyverduras mexico.com; Cárdenas s/n; s M$150-300, d M$250-400, camping s/d M$100/150;) Has a range of smallish but well-kept accommodations –simple *cabañas* with mosquito nets, colorful mosquito-screened rooms – plus good shared bathrooms and kitchen, a decent restaurant, a roof terrace, surfboards for rent and free bicycles for guests.

Osa Mariposa HOSTEL $
(cell phone 954-1108354; http://osamariposa.com; Privada de Cancún, Brisas de Zicatela; dm/d M$100/250, mains M$50-60;) The 'Bear Butterfly' is a relaxed and friendly alternative in Brisas de Zicatela, a little bit north of La Punta. Well-built wooden rooms and dorms, with clean bathrooms, surround a nice tropical garden. Real vegetarian food and plenty of good juices, mezcal and beer are served in the sociable restaurant-and-bar area.

★**Casamar** SUITES $$
(954-582-25-93; www.casamarsuites.com; Puebla 407, Brisas de Zicatela; d and tr US$60-109; groups only May & Nov;) The North American–owned Casamar is a lovely, comfortable vacation retreat. The 15 spacious, air-conditioned rooms are spotless and all have well-equipped kitchens and their own tasteful Mexican art and artisanry, much of it locally made. At the center of things is a large, verdant garden with a sizable pool.

You can join regular yoga and salsa classes (free for guests) onsite, and Monday night cocktails and the Friday night BBQ also help bring guests together. Excellent discounts for stays of six nights or more.

Rinconada & Carrizalillo

Hotel Villa Mozart y Macondo BOUTIQUE HOTEL $$
(Map p456; 954-104-22-95; www.facebook.com/villamozart; Av Las Tortugas 77; r M$400-800;) A short walk from Playa Carrizalillo, Villa Mozart has a personal touch both in its seven individually decorated, very comfortable rooms and apartments (some with kitchens) and in the welcoming attention of its owners. The aesthetic is a lovely contemporary-folksy blend, with some quality original art. Breakfast is available in the sculpture-strewn garden, which is another work of art itself.

Villas Carrizalillo BOUTIQUE HOTEL $$$
(Map p456; 954-582-17-35; www.villascarrizalillo.com; Av Carrizalillo 125; apt US$184-244;) Sublimely perched on the cliffs above Playa Carrizalillo, Villas Carrizalillo has spacious, stylish, air-conditioned apartments from one to three bedrooms, nearly all with kitchens and private terraces. A path goes directly down to the beach, and the hotel has boards, snorkel gear and a kayak for rent, and free bikes. There's a good, breezy in-house restaurant, too. Discounts for cash.

Eating

Puerto's large and varied selection of eateries ranges from solidly satisfying Mexican/international places to some enticing contemporary fusion restaurants. Seafood is plentiful and usually fresh, and there's some good vegetarian fare too.

Playa Zicatela

Dan's Café Deluxe INTERNATIONAL $
(Map p460; www.facebook.com/danscafedeluxe; Jacarandas 14, Colonia Santa María; breakfasts M$40-60, light meals M$40-70; 7am-4pm Mon-Sat, 7am-2pm Sun;) A great spot for hearty, inexpensive, surfer-pleasing breakfasts, and healthy lunch options like salads, whole-wheat sandwiches and vegetable stir-fries.

Restaurante Los Tíos SEAFOOD $
(Map p460; 954-582-28-79; Calle del Morro; mains M$50-100; 8am-10pm Wed-Mon) 'The Uncles' serves great *licuados* (milkshakes) and fresh juices to go with its tasty, well-priced egg dishes, *antojitos* and seafood. It's popular with locals and nicely relaxed.

Portus MEXICAN, INTERNATIONAL $$
(Map p460; Calle del Morro; mains M$70-120; 10am-10pm) Set right over the Zicatela sands, with loungers out front, Portus offers up big fish steaks and generous shrimp, veggie or steak burritos, with daily market-fresh ingredients.

La Hostería Bananas ITALIAN, MEXICAN $$
(Map p460; 954-582-00-05; Calle del Morro s/n; mains M$80-185; 8:30am-12:30am;) The Hostería is an Italian labor of love, from its gleaming kitchen (with computerized wood-fired pizza oven) to the Talavera-tiled bathrooms. A broad selection of tasty dishes, including many veggie and homemade

pasta options, is paired with a great drinks list, good breakfast deals and real coffee.

El Cafecito MEXICAN, INTERNATIONAL **$$**
(breakfast dishes M$45-75, mains M$60-175) It sometimes seems as if half the town descends to the Zicatela Cafecito for breakfast, and with good reason, as the combinations (including a 'Hungry Starving Surfer' offering) are tasty and filling, the service good and the coffee cups bottomless. There are other branches at Zicatela (Map p460; Calle del Morro s/n; 6am-11:30pm;) and Rinconada (Map p456; Blvd Juárez; 6am-10pm;).

Mangos MEXICAN, VEGETARIAN **$$**
(Map p460; Calle del Morro s/n; breakfasts M$35-49, mains M$65-150; 7am-11:30pm;) Mangos might have the best-value breakfast combinations in town, and its tropical-fruit and vegetable juices (M$25 to M$30) are great thirst-killers. It does veggie options like tofu burgers, and good fresh salads, plus plenty of pasta and well-prepared seafood.

Hotel Santa Fe VEGETARIAN, SEAFOOD **$$**
(Map p460; Calle del Morro s/n; mains M$60-180; 8am-10pm;) This airy hotel restaurant looking along Zicatela beach focuses on excellent vegetarian fare and seafood. Vegetarian options include tofu dishes, *antojitos*, and a Mediterranean plate with hummus, tabbouleh, Greek salad and pita bread.

Fish Taco & Beer MEXICAN, INTERNATIONAL **$$**
(Map p460; Calle del Morro s/n; tacos M$25-35, mains M$70-120; 2pm-midnight) The tacos are very salad-heavy, and a 10% tip is obligatory, but this den of long wooden tables and rock music is a big hit with the Zicatela crowd for its festive, sociable atmosphere.

El Adoquín & Around

Pascale MEXICAN, EUROPEAN **$$**
(Map p456; 954-582-10-93; Playa Principal; mains M$85-185; 6-11pm, closed Sep;) Romantically candlelit and right under the palms on the Playa Principal sands, Pascale prepares original and delicious seafood, meat, homemade pasta dishes and French desserts with rare flair. There's a choice of tasty sauces for all pasta dishes, and the seafood is fresh as can be. Service is professional, and there's live music on Fridays.

Restaurante Los Crotos SEAFOOD **$$**
(Map p456; Playa Principal; mains M$115-180; 8am-10:30pm) The best of the local seafooders on Playa Principal, Los Crotos has a neat tiled terrace and will carefully prepare your snapper, shrimps or fish fillet in half a dozen ways from *a la plancha* (straightforward grilled) to *al guajillo* (in a spicy dried-chili sauce).

Other Areas

★**Lychee** THAI **$**
(Cárdenas, Punta Zicatela; mains M$60-90; 5-11pm;) Superb Thai dishes – tom yum soup, red or green curries, tuna summer rolls, chicken satay – are cooked up in the middle of the large, rectangular wooden bar, which has just a handful of alfresco log tables set on the earth around it. Save room for the dessert of caramelized banana on filo pastry with ice cream.

Mercado Benito Juárez MARKET **$**
(Av 8 Norte, btwn Avs 3 & 4 Poniente; mains M$40-100; 8am-7pm) For tasty local flavors and local atmosphere, head to the main market in the upper part of town, where welcoming *comedores* serve up fresh fish and shrimp, soups and *antojitos* at good prices. Wander round the flower, food and craft stalls and try out some of the unusual flavors at the line of juice stalls. 'Mercado' buses (M$5) run up Avenida Oaxaca.

★**El Nene** MEXICAN, FUSION **$$**
(Map p456; Blvd Juárez, Rinconada; mains M$120-150; 2-10pm Mon-Sat) It's worth making a special trip to Rinconada for El Nene's excellent tacos (three for M$40) and Mexican- and international-style fish, shrimp and chicken mains. Fish of the day in white wine or Cajun-style is a good choice, and you could start with a flavorsome Thai or *nopal* soup. The professional service and neat, plant-fringed patio setting add to one of Puerto's best eating experiences.

Drinking & Nightlife

If your dream of Mexico is sitting in a palm-roofed bar, enjoying the crash of waves and an ice-cold beer, you might have to pinch yourself in Puerto Escondido. Numerous establishments along all the beaches are ideal for this purpose. Playa Zicatela has several spots open late with a party scene for its international crowd and regular DJ and live-music nights. The music scene combines the talents of locals and expats playing anything from Latin and jazz to blues and rock, and is busiest from around Christmas to March, when there's at least one gig somewhere almost every night.

★ Playa Kabbalah BAR
(Map p460; Calle del Morro s/n, Zicatela; ⏲8:30am-late) A hip beach bar for nocturnal drinks with a good atmosphere, a Zicatela crowd clustering at the bar or on the loungers on the sands, and mostly electronic dance music playing to flashing fluorescent lights. Frequent DJ nights and the Tuesday and Thursday Ladies' Nights (free cocktails for women from 10pm to midnight) are especially popular.

Casa Babylon BAR
(Map p460; Calle del Morro s/n, Zicatela; ⏲10:30am-late;) Quirky Babylon has a great Mexican mask collection, a big selection of books to exchange, and live music or a DJ some nights. The owner prides herself on her mojitos.

Bar Fly BAR
(Map p460; Calle del Morro s/n, Zicatela; ⏲9pm-late) This open-to-the-stars rooftop bar can get into a good groove especially on its weekend DJ nights.

Congo BAR, DANCING
(Map p456; Av Pérez Gasga; ⏲from 8pm Tue-Sat) Hosts popular live salsa nights every Wednesday.

☆ Entertainment

Cinemar CINEMA
(Map p456; Blvd Juárez, Rinconada; admission M$25; ⏲films 4pm, 6pm & 8pm) This comfortable mini-cinema shows the best Mexican movies and the latest general releases in English. From 9am to 3pm you can choose your own.

ℹ Information

DANGERS & ANNOYANCES

To minimize any risks of robbery or assault, avoid isolated or empty places and stick to well-lit areas (or use taxis) at night. And don't urinate on the beach after nocturnal drinks – cops have pulled people in for this.

INTERNET ACCESS

There are a few internet shops on El Adoquín and Calle del Morro (Zicatela), charging M$10 to M$15 per hour.

MEDICAL SERVICES

Dr Omar López Pérez (☎954-582-04-40; Av Oaxaca 603 Altos; ⏲9am-1pm & 4-7pm Mon-Fri, 9am-1pm Sat) A recommended English-speaking GP.

MONEY

Banks and *casas de cambio* generally exchange cash US dollars and euros. Playa Zicatela has a couple of ATMs but the ones in town work more reliably.

Banamex (Av Pérez Gasga 314; ⏲9am-4pm Mon-Sat) Currency exchange and ATM, up Pérez Gasga from the west end of the pedestrianized strip.

Centro Cambiario Joycy Adoquín (Av Pérez Gasga 905; ⏲10am-9pm Mon-Sat, 3-9pm Sun) Zicatela (Calle del Morro s/n; ⏲10am-9pm Mon-Sat) This *casa de cambio* changes Canadian dollars as well as US dollars and euros.

HSBC (Av 1 Norte, btwn Av 2 Poniente & Carretera Costera) Has a dependable ATM.

TOURIST INFORMATION

Tourist Information Kiosk (Map p456; ☎954-582-11-86; ginainpuerto@yahoo.com; Av Pérez Gasga; ⏲10am-2pm & 4-6pm Mon-Fri, 10am-1pm Sat) Gina Machorro, the energetic, dedicated, multilingual information officer here, happily answers your every question and conducts her own interesting tours.

TRAVEL AGENCIES

You can buy air and bus tickets at reliable, long-established Viajes Dimar (p458).

USEFUL WEBSITES

Head to **Lonely Planet** (www.lonelyplanet.com/mexico/oaxaca-state/puerto-escondido) for planning advice, author recommendations, articles and more.

ℹ Getting There & Away

AIR

Airport (☎954-582-04-91) Three kilometers west of the center on Hwy 200.

Aeromar (www.aeromar.com.mx) Up to three daily flights to/from Mexico City.

Aerotucán (☎954-582-34-61, cell phone 954-5884704; www.aerotucan.com.mx; Airport; ⏲7am-2:30pm Mon-Sat) Flies 13-seat Cessnas daily to/from Oaxaca (M$1940).

VivaAerobus (www.vivaaerobus.com) Budget airline flying daily to/from Mexico City. Flights bought well in advance can cost as little as M$500.

BUS & VAN

OCC Bus Terminal (Map p456; ☎954-582-10-73; Carretera Costera 102) Used by OCC 1st-class and Sur 2nd-class services.

Terminal Turística (Central Camionera; cnr Avs Oaxaca & 4 Poniente) In the upper part of

BUSES FROM PUERTO ESCONDIDO

DESTINATION	FARE (M$)	DURATION	FREQUENCY (DAILY)
Acapulco	380	8-9hr	7 from Terminal Turística
Bahías de Huatulco	64-120	2½hr	25 from OCC terminal
Mexico City (various terminals)	794-1045	12-18hr	6 from Terminal Turística, 2 OCC
Pochutla	40-68	1¼hr	25 from OCC terminal
Salina Cruz	156-256	5hr	12 from OCC terminal
San Cristóbal de las Casas	520	13hr	3 OCC (6:30-9:30pm)

town; used by Altamar (1st- and 2nd-class) and Turistar (deluxe).

Oaxaca

The most convenient way of traveling to Oaxaca is in the comfortable van services via Hwy 131 (seven hours), offered by at least two companies. OCC's 1st-class buses (M$318, 11 hours, three daily) take a much longer route via Salina Cruz and Hwy 190.

Express Service (Map p456; ☎954-582-08-68; Hotel Luz del Ángel, cnr Avs 1 Norte & Oaxaca) Vans depart to Oaxaca hourly from 4am to 5pm, and at 8pm, 10pm, 11pm and 11:30pm, charging M$180.

Villa Escondida (Map p456; Av Hidalgo s/n) Vans to Oaxaca hourly from 3:30am to 9:30pm, and at 11pm, for M$170.

Other Destinations

For Mexico City, the AltaMar and Turistar services from the Terminal Turística go via the outskirts of Acapulco and are much quicker than OCC, which takes a longer route via Salina Cruz.

CAR & MOTORCYCLE

From Oaxaca city, Hwy 131 traverses the lovely scenery of the Sierra Madre del Sur. If you're driving, estimate nine hours for the 254km trip, including a couple of rest stops. It's a winding, often potholed route and service stations are rare, so keep your tank topped up.

Between Puerto Escondido and Acapulco, figure on about seven hours for the 400km drive along Hwy 200, which is well enough surfaced but has a lot of speed bumps.

Los Tres Reyes (☎954-582-33-35; www.lostresreyes.com.mx; cnr Carretera Costera & Belmares, Colonia Santa María; ⊙8am-7pm) Rents out small saloon cars from M$650 per day. The office is on the highway just above Zicatela beach. It has an airport office as well.

ℹ Getting Around

Ticket taxis from the airport will drop you in town for M$35 per person (M$70 to Punta Zicatela). You'll probably find a whole cab for a similar price on the main road outside the airport. Taxi rides within town cost M$25 (M$30 to Punta Zicatela).

Taxis colectivos, local buses and *camionetas* marked 'Zicatela' or 'La Punta' (all M$5) run approximately every 20 minutes to Punta Zicatela from Mercado Benito Juárez up in the north of the town, from sunrise to sunset. They travel down 3 Poniente then east along the Carretera Costera; for the Adoquín or Playa Zicatela you can hop off and walk down in two minutes.

Around Puerto Escondido

Laguna Manialtepec

This 6km-long lagoon, beginning 14km west of Puerto Escondido along Hwy 200, is a paradise for bird enthusiasts and a fascinating place for anyone interested in nature. Ibises, roseate spoonbills, parrots, pelicans, falcons, ospreys, egrets, herons, kingfishers and several types of hawk and iguana call Manialtepec home for at least part of the year. The best months for seeing birds are December to March, and the best time is soon after dawn. The lagoon is mainly surrounded by mangroves, but tropical flowers and palms accent the ocean side, and the channel at the west end winds through to a pristine sandbar beach.

Several operators run three-hour **bird-spotting trips** in motorized *lanchas*, and kayak outings for ambitious paddlers. A magical Manialtepec phenomenon is the *fosforescencia*, when phosphorescent plankton appear for a few days several times a year. At these times nocturnal boat trips are offered, and you can swim or trail your hand in the water to activate the strange phosphorescent glow. The phenomenon can occur between July and August and is best seen on moonless nights.

Tours

Hidden Voyages Ecotours BIRD-WATCHING
(www.hiddenvoyagesecotours.com; Mon-Wed, Fri & Sat mid-Dec–late Mar) *Lancha* trips are led by knowledgeable Canadian ornithologist Michael Malone, and cost M$600 per person including round-trip transportation from your accommodations in Puerto Escondido (departure 7am) and a 45-minute beach break mid-cruise. Binoculars are provided. Book at Viajes Dimar (p458), which itself offers year-round trips (per person M$450) with local bird guides.

Lalo Ecotours BIRD-WATCHING
(cell phone 954-5889164, cell phone 954-1280042; www.lalo-ecotours.com) Lalo's is run by an experienced, English-speaking local bird guide. *Lancha* trips cost M$500 per person including round-trip transportation from your accommodations in Puerto Escondido. Phone or email for reservations.

La Puesta del Sol BIRD-WATCHING
(954-588-90-55, cell phone 954-1328294; restaurant 9am-6pm) This pleasant lakeside restaurant, just off Hwy 200 about 2.5km from the eastern end of the lake, is a good base if you're getting to Manialtepec under your own steam. It has good food (breakfasts M$40 to M$60, mains M$70 to M$120), does boat trips for M$800 for up to five people, and rents out two-person kayaks for around M$120 per hour.

For early-morning lagoon trips, it's a good idea to call the day before. They can speak English on the phone, and English-speaking bird guides are available at no extra cost.

Getting There & Away

From Puerto Escondido, take a *taxi colectivo* bound for San José Manialtepec from Avenida 4 Poniente (M$15, 15 minutes), or a Río Grande–bound minibus (M$20) from Avenida Hidalgo 5, leaving every 15 minutes from 4am to 8pm.

Parque Nacional Lagunas de Chacahua

Heading west toward Acapulco, Hwy 200 wends its way along a coast studded with lagoons, pristine beaches and prolific bird and plant life. Settlements in this region are home to many Afro-Mexicans, descendants of slaves who escaped from the Spanish.

The area around the coastal lagoons of Chacahua and La Pastoría forms the beautiful Parque Nacional Lagunas de Chacahua, which attracts many migratory birds from Alaska and Canada in winter. Mangrove-fringed islands harbor roseate spoonbills, ibises, cormorants, wood storks, herons and egrets, as well as mahogany trees, crocodiles and turtles. El Corral, a mangrove-lined waterway filled with countless birds in winter, connects the two lagoons. The boat trip along the lagoons is fabulous, and at its end Chacahua village sits upon a gorgeous beach curving at least 20km eastward, inviting you to stop for a meal or a night in rustic *cabañas*.

CHACAHUA

Chacahua village straddles the channel that connects the west end of Chacahua lagoon to the ocean. The ocean side of the village, fronting a wonderful beach, is a perfect place to bliss out. The waves here (a very long right-hand point break) can be good for surfers, including beginners, but there are some strong currents; check where it's safe to swim. If you're staying overnight, try a sunset boat trip on Laguna Salina, west of the village (around M$300).

WORTH A TRIP

ATOTONILCO HOT SPRINGS

These mineral-laden springs are a lovely horseback ride of one hour each way along the lushly-vegetated Río Manialtepec, from the village of San José Manialtepec, 23km west of Puerto Escondido. Go between October and March, when the river is not too high, as you crisscross it several times en route to your dip in the hot springs. Viajes Dimar (p458) and Lalo Ecotours (p465) offer trips from Puerto Escondido for around M$500 per person, or you can organize it direct for M$300 with guide **Agileo 'Chucho' Villavicencio** (954-488-18-82; cnr Hidalgo & Porfirio Díaz, San José Manialtepec) in San José. Take some food and drink. *Taxis colectivos* to San José (M$15, 20 minutes) go from Avenida 4 Poniente in Puerto Escondido.

OFF THE BEATEN TRACK

OCHO VENADO

The community ecotourism scheme **Ocho Venado** (☎954-543-82-84; http://ochovenado.wikispaces.com) offers the chance to experience village life in the forested hills behind the Lagunas de Chacahua. It's a rare opportunity to see a little-visited part of the coastal region, take guided walks or horseback rides, eat home-cooked food and join in whatever the villagers are doing when you visit.

The main base, with well-built *cabañas* (M$300 for two people), is Jocotepec village, 700m above sea level, with deer and wild-boar breeding areas, coffee plantations, waterfalls and a hilltop sacred site where locals still go for rain and harvest ceremonies. The Tourist Information Kiosk in Puerto Escondido can help with arrangements.

The beach has a number of simple *comedores,* offering egg, pasta and seafood dishes for around M$35 to M$90. Many of them also have basic, often sand-floored *cabañas* costing around M$150 for two people, with shared bathrooms. You can usually sleep in a hammock or camp for free if you eat at a particular establishment. **Restaurante Siete Mares** (cabañas M$150-400), at the beach's west end (nearest the river), prepares excellent seafood meals and has some of the better *cabañas,* some boasting two double beds, fans, nets, electric light and clean private bathrooms. The *señora* here will lock up your valuables.

Getting There & Away

The starting point for boat trips is the small fishing village of Zapotalito, at the eastern end of Laguna La Pastoría, 70km from Puerto Escondido.

From Puerto Escondido, take a minibus bound for Pinotepa Nacional from Avenida Hidalgo 5 (departures about every 15 minutes, 4am to 8pm) and get out at the Zapotalito turnoff (M$35, 1¼ hours), 58km west of Puerto (and 8km past the town of Río Grande) on Hwy 200. From the turning, *taxis colectivos* will shuttle you the 5km to Zapotalito for a few pesos.

Competing boat cooperatives offer *lancha* services from Zapotalito to Chacahua village, charging M$700/1200 one way/round-trip for up to eight people. The round-trip option lasts about five hours, with about three hours on the beach at Chacahua. When there is sufficient traffic, *colectivo* services run for M$100 per person each way. Check return times before you settle in at Chacahua.

For drivers, a dirt road heads 29km south to Chacahua village from San José del Progreso on Hwy 200, but this is often waterlogged between May and November.

Pochutla

☎958 / POP 14,000

Bustling, sweaty Pochutla is the market town and transportation hub for the central part of the Oaxaca coast, including the nearby beach spots of Puerto Ángel, Zipolite, San Agustinillo and Mazunte.

Hwy 175 from Oaxaca runs through Pochutla as Avenida Lázaro Cárdenas, the narrow, traffic-clogged, north–south main street, and meets the coastal Hwy 200 about 1.5km south of town. The bus and van terminals cluster toward the southern, downhill end of Cárdenas, the main one being the Terminal San Pedro Pochutla on the corner of Constitución.

Sleeping & Eating

One of the best places to eat on the whole Oaxaca coast is just outside of town. If you have to sleep here, **Hotel Izala** (☎958-584-01-15; Av Cárdenas 59; s/d M$200/300, with air-con M$300/450; P❄) and **Hotel San Pedro** (☎958-584-11-23; Av Cárdenas s/n; s/d M$400/500; P❄wifi) are both OK for one night.

★ **Finca de Vaqueros** PARRILLA $$
(☎958-100-43-31; El Colorado village; mains M$130-150; ⏰9am-9pm) This ranch-style eatery with long tables in a large, open-sided barn is worth an expedition from anywhere on the coast for its superb grilled meats. Order some *frijoles charros* (bean soup with bacon bits) and *queso fundido* (melted cheese) to start, followed by some tender *arrachera* (skirt steak) and *chistorra* sausage for a feast you won't forget. El Colorado is on the road to Puerto Ángel, 2km from Pochutla (M$40 by taxi).

There's excellent mezcal and draft Corona Oscura beer, and the *costillas ahumadas* (smoked pork ribs) are another great option. When host Pedro is in the mood, he sings sentimental *ranchera* songs.

Information

Banco Azteca (Av Cárdenas s/n; ⏲9am-9pm) Exchanges cash US dollars and euros; inside the Elektra store 75m south of the main bus station.

Clínica Hospital San Carlos (☎958-584-06-03; Zaragoza 14, Sección 4a; ⏲24hr) A private hospital with good equipment and good specialist doctors; on the hill behind the municipality building.

HSBC ATM (Av Cárdenas 48)

Getting There & Away

OAXACA

Oaxaca is 245km away by the curvy Hwy 175 – six hours in the convenient and fairly comfortable air-conditioned van services (M$150) offered by several companies. Helpfully, drivers will usually stop when you need a bathroom break, or need to vomit, as some people do on this route. OCC runs three daily 1st-class buses to Oaxaca (M$312, 10 hours) from the Terminal San Pedro Pochutla, but they take a much longer and more expensive (though less winding) route via Salina Cruz.

Atlántida (☎958-584-92-39; Hotel Santa Cruz, Av Cárdenas 88) Twelve vans to Oaxaca daily; it's 150m north of the main bus terminal and you can call ahead to reserve a seat.

Líneas Unidas (☎cell phone 958-5841322; Av Cárdenas 94) Just north of the main bus terminal, across the street, with vans to Oaxaca every 45 or 60 minutes from 3:30am to midnight.

OTHER DESTINATIONS

Terminal San Pedro Pochutla (cnr Av Cárdenas & Constitución) The main bus station, entered through a white-grilled doorway toward the south end of Cárdenas. It's used by Turistar (deluxe), OCC and Estrella Blanca (1st-class) and Sur (2nd-class) services. You can also buy OCC and Sur tickets at a separate office about 50m south. For distant destinations with limited service such as San Cristóbal de las Casas and Mexico City, it's advisable to get tickets at least a couple of days in advance.

Transportes Rápidos de Pochutla (TRP; Av Cárdenas) About 30m north of the main terminal; runs 2nd-class buses to Huatulco.

Puerto Ángel

☎958 / POP 2600

The small fishing port and naval town of Puerto Ángel straggles around a pretty little bay between two rocky headlands, surrounded by thickly wooded hills, 13km south of Pochutla. Once the main travelers' base on this coast, the town is now rather drab and shabby and most travelers stay a few kilometers west at Zipolite, San Agustinillo or Mazunte. But Playa La Boquilla, on the eastward coast, makes a lovely outing and has an excellent small hotel. The road from Pochutla winds its way round the back of the bay, passing the fishing pier opposite Calle Vasconcelos, crossing an often-dry *arroyo* (stream) and then heading uphill. It then forks – right to Zipolite and beyond, and left down to Playa del Panteón, a short, shallow beach with some rather overpriced restaurants. The road is called Blvd Uribe as far as the *arroyo*, and then Carretera a Zipolite.

Sights & Activities

Playa La Boquilla BEACH

(P) The coast east of Puerto Ángel is dotted with nice small beaches, none of them very busy. Playa La Boquilla, on a scenic bay about 5km round the coast, is the site of the

BUSES FROM POCHUTLA

DESTINATION	FARE (M$)	DURATION	FREQUENCY (DAILY)
Acapulco	448	9hr	3 Estrella Blanca
Bahías de Huatulco	23-46	1hr	TRP every 20-30min 6:30am-8pm, Sur every 40-60min 7:20am-8:40pm, 9 OCC
Mexico City (Sur) via Acapulco outskirts	900-1025	13½hr	Turistar 5pm, Estrella Blanca 6:20pm
Mexico City (Sur or TAPO) via Salina Cruz	782-796	16½hr	2 OCC
Puerto Escondido	40-68	1¼hr	Sur every 40-60min 6:40am-8pm, 8 OCC
Salina Cruz	160	4hr	8 OCC
San Cristóbal de las Casas	462	11-12hr	2 OCC
Tapachula	512	12hr	OCC 6:50pm

WORTH A TRIP

PLAYA ESCOBILLA

This 15km-long beach, beginning about 30km east of Puerto Escondido, is one of the world's major nesting grounds for the olive ridley turtle (*tortuga golfina* to Mexicans). Up to a million female olive ridleys a year arrive at Escobilla to lay their eggs. Numbers peak at night for a period of about a week around the full moons from May to February, a phenomenon known as an *arribada*. The olive ridley is one of the smaller sea turtles (around 70cm long), but still an impressive animal, especially when seen emerging from the surf at a rate of several thousand per hour, as happens during Escobilla's biggest *arribadas*.

To protect the turtles, there is no general public access to the beach, and this is strictly enforced by the Mexican army. But a community ecotourism cooperative, **Santuario La Escobilla** (958-596-44-08, cell phone 958-5835320; www.ecoturismoenoaxaca.com/laescobilla.html; Hwy 200 Km 180, Escobilla), will take you to see the *arribadas* (per person M$100) and offers canoe trips (M$40) on the local lagoon. Before traveling to Escobilla, you should check first whether an *arribada* is definitely happening. A couple of Puerto Escondido operators make things easier with organized trips: tourist information officer Gina Machorro (p458) takes groups each month (M$500 per person including transportation) on which you'll have the guidance of a resident biologist at Escobilla; Deep Blue Dive (p456) does trips for M$300 per person with a minimum of three people.

You can stay at Escobilla in the cooperative's clean, well-kept **cabañas** (tr/q/f M$250/300/500), which are set in a neat garden and equipped with fans, mosquito nets and hot-water bathrooms. Good meals (M$60 to M$90) are available in its spacious guest *comedor*.

Santuario La Escobilla is beside Hwy 200 on the west side of Escobilla village: look for the 'Centro Ecoturístico La Escobilla' sign on the seaward side of the road. Buses between Puerto Escondido and Pochutla will drop you here (M$24, 45 minutes).

Bahía de la Luna hotel and restaurant, and is good for snorkeling. It's nice to go by boat (M$200/300 each way for two/four people): ask at Puerto Ángel pier or Playa del Panteón.

You can also get here by a 3.5km unpaved road from a turnoff 4km out of Puerto Ángel on the Pochutla road; a taxi from Puerto Ángel costs M$150, from Pochutla M$200, each way.

Azul Profundo WATER SPORTS
(958-584-30-21, cell phone 958-1060420; www.hotelcordelias.com; Playa del Panteón) Enjoyable four-hour, four-beach snorkeling boat trips for M$180 per person, at 10am daily. En route you should see turtles and, with luck, dolphins and even (from December to April) whales. The company can pick up and drop off at its office and internet cafe in Zipolite. Amiable guide Chepe speaks English and German, and sportfishing and diving are also on offer.

The sportfishing is for marlin, swordfish, tuna or *dorado* (dolphinfish): start at 6am and try the local method of trawling with handlines for tuna or *dorado*. A boat for three people, with two lines, costs M$350 per hour (minimum two hours). One-/two-tank dives cost M$750/1000 including a dive guide. The drops and canyons out from Puerto Ángel are thick with fish life and there's an 1870 shipwreck.

Sleeping & Eating

Casa de Huéspedes Gundi y Tomás GUESTHOUSE $
(958-584-30-68; www.puertoangel-hotel.com; s M$250, d M$300-350, s/d without bathroom M$200/250;) This rambling establishment above Blvd Uribe serves up good food with many vegetarian options (mains M$35 to M$85), and offers brightly decorated, basic rooms, with fans, mosquito nets and/or screens, and some offbeat artistic touches. The family speaks English, German and Spanish, and has surf lessons at Zipolite or San Agustinillo. There's a safe for valuables.

Bahía de la Luna HOTEL $$$
(958-589-50-20; www.bahiadelaluna.com; Playa La Boquilla; r M$1350-1500, q M$2100, 4-/7-person house with kitchen M$2900/3900, all incl breakfast; P) This 'rustic chic' hideaway sits

in splendid isolation out at lovely Playa La Boquilla (p468). Its attractive, bright adobe bungalows, on a tree-covered hillside overlooking the beach, have terracotta-tiled floors, fans and attractive craft artifacts. It also offers Mexican/Brazilian/international fusion food (lunch dishes M$50 to M$90, two-course dinner M$200 to M$250), generous margaritas and mezcal from the barrel, served at tables on the sand.

Snorkel gear, kayaks and a paddleboard are free for guests, and there are trails to explore too. Low-season promotions available in May, June, September and October.

Information

Banco Azteca (Blvd Uribe; 8am-8pm) Changes cash US dollars and euros.

Bancomer ATM (cnr Blvd Uribe & Vasconcelos)

Zipolite

958 / POP 1100

The beautiful 1.5km stretch of pale sand called Zipolite, beginning about 2.5km west of Puerto Ángel, moves at a slow pace, withering in the midday heat. This coast's original budget beach-bum magnet, it attracts an international class of sun lovers, shirtless yoga gurus and surfers to its wonderfully elemental surroundings of crashing surf, pounding sun, rocky headlands and tall *palapa* roofs. While there are still plenty of reassuringly rustic budget lodgings and an unmistakable hippie vibe, a number of more comfortable lodgings and classier restaurants at the west end of the village cater to a midrange clientele who also love the Zipolite ambience. There's a certain magic here, and you may postpone departure more than once.

Zipolite has a certain overstated fame as a nudist beach. Total nudity is common only at the western end of the beach and in the small cove called Playa del Amor at the east end, and even there it may meet the raised eyebrows of locals.

The eastern end of Zipolite (nearest Puerto Ángel) is called Colonia Playa del Amor, the middle part is Centro, and the western end, where most of the traveler scene is, is Colonia Roca Blanca. The only street with a commonly used name is Avenida Roca Blanca (also called El Adoquín), a block back from the beach in Colonia Roca Blanca.

Activities

The essence and glory of Zipolite is that organized activity is very minimal. This is a place for hanging out and doing exactly as little as you feel like.

Azul Profundo (p468) provides free transportation from Zipolite for its snorkeling, diving and fishing trips from Puerto Ángel; you can reserve at its office/internet shop on Avenida Roca Blanca.

Piña Palmera VOLUNTEERING
(958-584-31-47; www.pinapalmera.org; Centro; 9am-3pm Mon-Sat) Piña Palmera, a rehabilitation and social integration center for physically and intellectually disabled people from rural communities runs workshops

CENTRAL COAST TRANSPORTATION

There are three ways to travel between transportation hub Pochutla and the beach villages of Puerto Ángel, Zipolite, San Agustinillo and Mazunte: *camioneta* (pickup truck with benches in the back), *taxi colectivo* (shared taxi) and private taxi. One main route heads from Pochutla to Puerto Ángel; the other heads west from Pochutla to San Antonio on Hwy 200, then southeast to Mazunte, San Agustinillo and the west end of Zipolite (Colonia Roca Blanca).

Camionetas and *taxis colectivos* start from the Capilla del Niño Jesús chapel in Pochutla (250m north on Avenida Cárdenas from the main bus station then 150m west along Calle Jamaica). They operate during daylight hours, charging M$10 to M$15 to any of the villages. A private taxi is M$80 to M$120 from Pochutla to the villages, and M$50 from Zipolite to Puerto Ángel, San Agustinillo or Mazunte. Add M$20 or M$30 after about 9pm.

Coming from Puerto Escondido, you can take a 2nd-class Pochutla-bound Sur bus to San Antonio, and switch there to a local *camioneta* (M$10 to Mazunte, San Agustinillo or Zipolite) or a taxi (M$50 to Mazunte or San Agustinillo, M$100 to Zipolite).

A taxi to Huatulco or Puerto Escondido airports from any of the villages should cost M$350 to M$450.

ZIPOLITE PRECAUTIONS

Beware: the Zipolite surf is deadly. It's fraught with riptides, changing currents and a strong undertow. Going in deeper than your knees can be risking your life. Local voluntary lifeguards have rescued many, but people still drown here yearly. The shore break is one only experienced surfers should attempt.

Theft is a potential problem, so it's good to stay where you can lock your valuables in a safe and keep your wits about you when out at night.

and therapies at its beautiful palm-grove site and on village visits. Volunteers should be willing to learn Spanish and (normally) willing to sign on for six months; see the website for details.

Sleeping

The great majority of accommodations are in and around the Roca Blanca area at the west end of Zipolite. Some beach restaurants here and further east along the beach will rent you a hammock for M$40 or so, or let you sling your own hammock or pitch a tent for around M$30. This a great way to save some money and sleep in the breeze; just mind the sand flies and lock away your valuables.

Accommodation rates given here are for the main season, January to Easter. From about September to November and May and June, some places slash prices by as much as half. They may also double them during the Christmas–New Year and Semana Santa vacation periods.

Lo Cósmico CABAÑAS $
(www.locosmico.com; west end Playa Zipolite; hammock M$60, s M$180, d M$250-400; restaurant 8am-4pm Tue-Sun; P) Relaxed Lo Cósmico's conical-roofed *cabañas*, dotted around a tall rock outcrop, offer among the best value on the beach – clean and quite neat, in varying degrees of rusticity. Each has a hammock and mosquito net; the pricier ones have two floors, views and private bathroom. The open-air **restaurant** (dishes M$28-60) serves excellent crepes and salads from an impeccably clean kitchen.

In the dry season (only) you can sleep cheaply on the hammock terrace. A security box is available.

Shambhala GUESTHOUSE $
(Casa de Gloria; cell phone 958-1138033; www.facebook.com/shambhalavision; west end Playa Zipolite; dm M$125-150, camping per person M$50, s M$150-300, d M$200-600; restaurant 8am-10pm; P) This long-established guesthouse ('where the '60s never end') climbs a hill and has great views right along the beach. In part a spiritual retreat, with its own meditation hill and no alcohol or illegal drugs permitted, it's also a tranquil and economical place to stay, with varied, rustic accommodations. The **restaurant** (mains M$50-90) serves no red meat.

Shambhala hosts a big spiritual festival, embracing all beliefs, every New Year's Eve, and is often full over the Christmas–New Year's period.

Hostal El Carrizal HOSTEL $
(958-584-33-38; sylvianelemetais@hotmail.com; Av Roca Blanca; dm/d M$50/100;) Run by a long-time Zipolite resident from France, this is a classic basic backpacker joint with a friendly atmosphere. There are five very simple rooms and cabins, and a five-bed semi-open-air dorm, all with mosquito nets – plus an open-air kitchen.

El Alquimista BUNGALOW $$
(958-587-89-61; www.el-alquimista.com; west end Playa Zipolite; bungalows M$1000-2000; P) A range of excellent accommodations from thatch-roofed bungalows just off the beach (most with double bed, fan, hot-water bathroom and hammocked porch) to big, bright air-con rooms with ample terraces and king-size beds, set back up the luxuriant hillside. Decor is simple and tasteful.

One of Zipolite's best restaurants is here, as are a good pool and spa. Daily hatha yoga sessions (M$100/300 per one/four classes), plus Pilates and meditation, take place in a bright yoga room.

Posada México ROOMS $$
(958-584-31-94; www.posadamexicozipolite.com; Av Roca Blanca; r M$450-750, without bathroom M$350; restaurant 8am-1:30pm & 5-11:30pm; P) This Italian-run joint is on a friendly, personal scale and has the most character among the Roca Blanca beachfront places. The very clean wood-and-palm rooms have good beds, four-poster mosquito nets, fans, safes, ingenious water-saving showers and their own sandy little hammock areas. Best are the two larger, more expensive, beach-facing rooms.

There's a good **cafe-restaurant** (mains M$70-140) too, with enticing seafood creations, wood-oven pizzas and two cocktails for M$50 in the evenings.

Las Casitas BUNGALOW **$$**
(cell phone 958-1009234; www.las-casitas.net; d M$300-800, q M$600-1350; P) Set back on a lane behind the west end of Playa Zipolite, peaceful, pretty Las Casitas enjoys good views from its elevated position. The seven rooms, with tasteful Mexican color schemes and some cute decorative details like the bright Virgin of Guadalupe cushions, are in semi-open-air bungalows scattered around a cute garden. All rooms have private bathrooms and kitchens, and spacious hangout areas.

There's also a larger house for up to four people. A major plus is the onsite restaurant La Providencia.

Casa Sol ROOMS **$$**
(958-1000462; www.casasolzipolite.com; Arco Iris 6; r M$600-1000) Canadian-owned Casa Sol overlooks the small beach of Playa Camarón just west of Zipolite and its three comfortable, spacious, spotless rooms make perfect vacation retreats. No meals are served but rooms have kitchens and there's another kitchen on the large, panoramic terrace. The beach is good for snorkeling when calm (free gear is available for guests).

You can walk to Playa Zipolite in 10 minutes. Vehicle access is by a signposted 400m track off the main road about 1km west of Zipolite.

Heven APARTMENT **$$**
(cell phone 958-1062018; www.hevenresidence.com; Arco Iris 5; r M$600-900) Overlooking picturesque Playa Camarón, a 10-minute walk west from Playa Zipolite, recently-opened Heven features some lovely hand-made Mexican furniture and crafts, including beautiful tilework, in its eight individually-designed apartments and suites and spacious communal areas. Most accommodations have king-size beds.

There's vehicle access from the main road about 1km west of Zipolite.

Posada San Cristóbal HOTEL **$$**
(958-584-30-20; zipol_cristobalaz@hotmail.com; Av Roca Blanca; s M$200-400, d M$250-500; P) Toward the west end of the beach, three-story San Cristóbal has 15 good, large, breezy and bright rooms facing the sea, all with balcony or terrace and tiled floors. The eight cheaper rooms behind are less appealing.

Eating

Eating and drinking in the open air a few steps from the surf is a classic Zipolite experience. Most places serve a mix of Mexican and international fare with a maritime slant.

Piedra de Fuego SEAFOOD **$**
(Mangle, Colonia Roca Blanca; mains M$65-90; 3-11pm) You'll get a generous serving of fresh fish fillet or prawns, accompanied by rice, salad and potatoes, at this superbly simple, very clean, good-value place run by a local family. Good *aguas de frutas,* too.

Orale! Cafe BREAKFAST **$**
(off west end Av Roca Blanca; breakfast dishes M$30-65; 8am-3pm mid-Oct–mid-May) This shady tropical-garden cafe with soothing music is perfect for a relaxed and tasty breakfast.

★**La Providencia** MEXICAN, FUSION **$$**
(cell phone 958-1009234; www.laprovidenciazipolite.com; mains M$110-150; 6-10:30pm Wed-Sun Nov-Apr, Jul & Aug) Zipolite's outstanding dining option, on a lane behind the western end of the beach, combines delicious flavors, artful presentation and a relaxed ambience. You can sip a cocktail in the open-air lounge while you peruse the menu. It's a contemporary Mexican treat, from cold beetroot and ginger soup to beef medallions in smoked-chili sauce or coconut-crusted prawns with mango sauce. Save room for the chocolate mousse!

Reservations are advised during the busy seasons.

El Alquimista INTERNATIONAL **$$**
(954-587-89-61; west end Playa Zipolite; mains M$100-200; 8am-midnight) The classy Alchemist is delightfully sited in a sandy cove, and atmospherically lit by oil lamps and candles at night. Its wide-ranging fare runs from fresh salads to good meat, seafood and pizzas and tempting desserts, complemented by a full bar, and service is attentive.

Pacha Mama ITALIAN, MEXICAN **$$**
(Mangle, Colonia Roca Blanca; mains M$70-130; 6-11pm Fri-Wed) The chef is one of Zipolite's large Italian community, and he turns out very professional steaks, seafood and

home-made pasta with some tasty sauces. With a garden-like setting, this is worth its above-average prices.

Drinking & Nightlife

Zipolite's beachfront restaurant-bars have unbeatable locations for drinks from sunset onward, and beach bonfires provide the focus for informal partying.

Babel Cafe BAR

(Principal, Colonia Roca Blanca; noon-midnight Mon-Sat) Pool table, darts, pizza oven, spacious garden-like setting, well-stocked bar and live music once or twice weekly (rockabilly, reggae, electronic *cumbia*...) make Italian-run Babel a favorite hangout.

Information

The nearest ATM is in Puerto Ángel, but some accommodations may exchange or accept payment in US dollars or euros.

Azul Profundo (958-584-34-37; Av Roca Blanca; internet per hr M$15, wi-fi M$10; 9am-10pm) You can Skype and phone from here, too.

Getting There & Away

After dark, a non-*colectivo* taxi is your only option for getting to Puerto Ángel, San Agustinillo or Mazunte (M$40 to M$50 until around 9pm; M$70 to M$80 after that).

San Agustinillo

958 / POP 290

The tiny, one-street village of San Agustinillo, 4km west of Zipolite by road, centers on a small, curved bay with waves that are perfect for bodyboarding and learning to surf. The swimming is good as well, but avoid the rocks. San Agustinillo's charms have spawned a small bunch of attractive accommodations and good eateries, and an eclectic set of aficionados.

Activities

★Coco Loco Surf Club SURFING, SNORKELING

(www.cocolocosurfclub.com; Calle Principal;) Coco Loco's qualified French surf instructor, David Chouard, gives excellent classes for anyone from five years old upwards (one hour for one/two/four people M$350/650/1000). It also rents out surfboards and boogie boards (per hour/half-day/day M$50/150/200) and snorkel gear (M$30/80/120), and sells surf gear.

Other Coco Loco activities include surf trips to Chacahua and Barra de la Cruz (M$500 per person per day) and an enjoyable three-beach 'discovery trip' combining snorkeling, bodyboarding and a visit to La Ventanilla (p477) for M$280 per person (minimum four people).

★Boat Trips BOAT TOUR

Local fishers will take you on exciting boat trips to look for turtles, dolphins, manta rays and whales (best from November to April for these last two). The cost for three hours is normally M$200 per person (usually with a minimum of four) including a snorkeling stop. Sportfishing trips are usually M$400 to M$500 per hour for up to three people, including equipment (minimum three or four hours). Ask at your accommodations.

Solstice Yoga Center YOGA

(www.solstice-mexico.com) At Solstice Yoga Center, located within Las 3 Marías accommodations on the San Agustinillo hillside, Brigitte Longueville leads 1½-hour restorative hatha yoga classes (M$90) most days at 9am or 5pm. Five-day yoga vacation retreats and teacher trainings are offered here, too. Check the website for the schedule.

Sleeping & Eating

Most places to stay are set right on the beach. Rooms have either mosquito-screened windows or mosquito nets.

Hostal Atrapasueños PENSION $

(cell phone 958-1075050; dm M$170, r without bathroom M$220-320;) It's basic and ramshackle, but the prices are good, you can use the kitchen, and the welcoming owner's quirky sculptures lend this spot some character.

Recinto del Viento GUESTHOUSE $

(cell phone 958-1180300; www.recintodelviento.wordpress.com; s/d without bathroom M$250/300;) Run by a welcoming family, this budget option sits up the hill a bit, with surf views from the hammock-slung terrace. The guest kitchen helps create a sociable, semi-communal atmosphere among guests. The five rooms are smallish but catch the breezes. It's 100m up concrete steps opposite Un Sueño accommodations toward the east end of the main street.

★Punta Placer CABAÑAS $$

(cell phone 958-1096401; www.puntaplacer.com; s/d M$850/1000;) Punta Placer's eight beautiful circular rooms and one large apartment have a fresh, open-air feel thanks to their breezy terraces and wood-slat windows. With welcome touches like good reading lights and stone-lined hot showers with good water pressure, they're a grade above most other San Agustinillo accommodations.

The garden of native plants and stone paving opens directly onto the beach, and there's a great little **restaurant** (mains M$90-125) serving fresh, home-style international dishes with a French touch.

Un Sueño CABAÑAS $$

(cell phone 958-1138749; www.unsueno.com; r/q M$850/1150;) Sueño, toward the east end of the beach, has 16 lovely, good-sized rooms sporting a touch of art and craft from different places around the world, and a semi-open-air feel from bamboo-slat windows and hammock-slung terraces. Also fronting the sands are a breezy hammock area and an excellent restaurant, **Un Secreto**.

The restaurant is open from 8am to 6pm and serves up good breakfasts and, for lunch, *sabores del Pacífico* (flavors of the Pacific) with a touch of French flair. The short but sweet seafood-based menu (mains M$95 to M$120) runs from a delicious foil-wrapped fish with mint to Thai-style shrimp, and you shouldn't miss the lemon pie.

México Lindo y qué Rico! ROOMS $$

(leylabastar8@gmail.com; s/d M$400/500, restaurant mains M$75-120; restaurant 8am-11pm Dec-Easter, Jul & Aug, 8am-6pm May, Jun & Sep-Nov;) Near the west end of the beach, México Lindo has friendly owners and staff, and its five sizable, well-kept rooms feature slatted windows, fans and some bright decor details. Especially good are the two breezy rooms upstairs under the tall *palapa* roof. The food here, served under *palapa* sunshades on the sand, is uncomplicated and among the best in town.

Breakfasts, shrimp tacos and quesadillas, fish fillets, chicken enchiladas and stuffed avocados are carefully prepared and served with a smile, and there's pizza in the evenings.

Rancho Cerro Largo CABAÑAS $$

(rcerrolargo@yahoo.com; Playa Aragón; s M$700-1150, d M$900-1250, incl breakfast & dinner;) With a stunning, secluded position above Playa Aragón, which stretches east from Playa San Agustinillo, Cerro Largo offers comfortable accommodations in nine ocean-view *cabañas,* most constructed of mud and wattle and with private bathrooms. Many have open walls overlooking the crashing coast below. Top-notch, mainly vegetarian meals are taken by all guests together (Cerro Largo makes its own bread, yogurt and granola).

There's also a nice yoga room with 1½-hour morning sessions for all levels daily except Monday (suggested donation: M$50). Access is by a signed driveway from the Zipolite–San Agustinillo road. Book ahead by email in high season.

Bambú CABAÑAS $$

(www.bambuecocabanas.com; d M$750-950, q M$950-1150;) The half-dozen rooms here, toward the beach's east end, are large, attractive, open to as much breeze as possible, and set under high *palapa* roofs. All are cleverly constructed, mainly from bamboo, with pretty tilework, fans and quirky details like seashell shower heads and trees growing inside a couple of rooms.

There's no cafe but there is a guest kitchen with a barbecue grill.

Posada La Mora ROOMS $$

(958-584-64-22; www.lamoraposada.com; r with/without kitchenette M$500/400, apt M$1000;) Friendly, well-kept La Mora makes the most of its little site toward the east end of town. Downstairs, a neat **cafe** (8am-2:30pm year-round, 6:30-10pm Dec-May) serves, among other things, egg dishes, whole-wheat baguettes and organic, fair-trade coffee – and Italian dinners in season. Upstairs are three cheerful rooms in blue, white and yellow, and above them is a bright, spacious apartment that's good for families.

All three floors have terraces that enjoy close-up sea views.

Casa Aamori BOUTIQUE HOTEL $$$

(555-4362538; www.aamoriboutiquehotel.com; r M$1800-2200;) San Agustinillo's newest accommodations are a cut above the rest. Lovingly designed Casa Aamori, toward the east end of town, features original and appealing artisanry from around the world and 10 large, attractive rooms, on themes from Copacabana to Goa to Africa, with floor mosaics and, in most cases, sea views.

The pool-and-restaurant deck gives on to a sandy area overlooking the beach, with hanging beds under the palms, and an airy massage room and a mezcal-and-tapas lounge add to Aamori's appeal. It's for adults only, with a two-night minimum stay.

La Termita ROOMS **$$$**
(☎958-589-30-46; www.posadalatermita.com; d M$1000-1500, q M$1300-1800; P 📶) Roughly in the center of the village, La Termita's flavorsome, wood-oven pizzas (M$85 to M$135) are the best anywhere in the area, and there are good salads to go with them. There are four attractive, sizable rooms with good wood furnishings – two of them are directly over the beach. Restaurant open 8.30am to noon and 6.30pm to 11pm.

Mazunte

☎958 / POP 870

A kilometer west of San Agustinillo, Mazunte has a fine, curving, sandy beach on a scenic bay, an interesting turtle center, and a good variety of basic and fancier places to stay and eat. The village is well known as a travelers' hangout and has a number of foreign residents, attracted by the area's beauty and laid-back atmosphere. There's something of a hippie vibe here. Mazunte's economic mainstays used to be turtle meat and eggs, but after the turtle industry was banned in 1990, it turned to ecotourism.

The main road running through the middle of Mazunte is called Paseo del Mazunte. Four lanes run about 500m from the road to the beach: in east-to-west order they are Andador Golfina, Andador Carey, Andador La Barrita and Calle Rinconcito – this last leading down to the part of the beach called **El Rinconcito**, which is the best bit for swimming. The cape Punta Cometa closes off the west end of the bay. A rough track off Calle Rinconcito heads 750m west to **Playa Mermejita**, a beautiful long, wild beach with a handful of attractive accommodations, some scaling its jungly slopes – unfortunately, tricky currents and strong waves make swimming inadvisable.

> **ETHICS & TURTLE TOURS**
>
> Boat tours to observe turtles, dolphins and other marine life are a popular and exciting activity in several places along the Oaxaca coast. Some guides may jump into the sea and take hold of turtles, so that boat passengers can get a better view or even jump in and hold the animal too. If you are concerned about the stress it could cause the animal, check with boat operators about their policy before embarking.

Sights

★Punta Cometa LOOKOUT, WALKING
This rocky cape, jutting out from the west end of Mazunte beach, is the southernmost point in the state of Oaxaca and a fabulous place to be at sunset, with great long-distance views.

For a beautiful walk to the point, take the lane that heads up toward Playa Mermejita off Calle Rinconcito, and go left up the track passing the entrance to Cabañas Balamjuyuc to reach the community nature reserve entrance after 250m. Here take the path leading down to the right (Sendero Corral de Piedra Poniente), which leads you to the point in 20 to 30 minutes via Cometa's scenic western side. You can return more directly to the reserve entrance by the Sendero Principal path. Total round-trip walking time from Calle Rinconcito (without stops) is about one hour.

Centro Mexicano de la Tortuga AQUARIUM
(☎958-584-33-76; www.centromexicanodelatortuga.org; Paseo del Mazunte; admission M$27; ⏱10am-4:30pm Wed-Sat, 10am-2:30pm Sun; P 👪) 🍃 The much-visited Mexican Turtle Center, at the east end of Mazunte, is an aquarium and research center containing specimens of five of Mexico's seven marine turtle species, plus some freshwater and land varieties. They're on view in fairly large tanks – it's enthralling to get a close-up view of these creatures, some of which are BIG!

Cosméticos Naturales Mazunte HANDICRAFTS
(☎958-587-48-60; www.cosmeticosmazunte.com; Paseo del Mazunte; ⏱9am-4pm Mon-Sat, 10am-2pm Sun) 🍃 This small cooperative, toward the west end of Mazunte, makes and sells products such as shampoo, cosmetics, mosquito repellent, soap and arnica cream, using natural sources like maize, coconut and essential oils. It also sells organic coffee and tahini, and you can have a look at the workshop while here.

Activities

★Boat Trips BOAT TOUR

Local fishers will take three or more people out for exciting three-hour boat trips to snorkel, look for turtles, dolphins and whales, check out some of the beaches along the coast, and fish, if you like. Departure is usually at 8am and the cost around M$200 per person, including snorkel equipment. You can organize this through your accommodations.

Ola Verde Expediciones RAFTING

(cell phone 958-1096751; www.olaverdeexpediciones.com.mx; Calle Rinconcito; office 10am-2pm & 4-9pm) This professional team of adventure-sports enthusiasts takes recommended rafting trips on the Río San Francisco inland from here (Class II to Class III; late July to early October; half-day trip M$500) and the Río Copalita near Huatulco (Class II to Class IV depending on season; late July to January; day trip M$900 to M$1000).

Ola Verde also does a fun half-day river hike on the San Francisco (October to July; adult/child M$450/300), which includes swimming, floating (with life jacket and helmet) and jumping into pools. All its trips take in great tropical scenery and the staff will pick you up anywhere from Puerto Ángel to Mazunte. Minimum numbers range from two to four.

Hridaya Yoga Center YOGA, MEDITATION

(cell phone 958-1008958; hridaya-yoga.com) People come from many countries to this world center of Hridaya yoga, inspired by the teachings of Indian mystic Sri Ramana Maharshi. Three-day tantra workshops, 10-day silent meditation retreats and one-month intensive agama yoga courses are among the regular programs, and visitors can join daily hatha yoga courses at any time (M$50 per class).

The center has a beautiful hilltop location at the far eastern end of Mazunte, with bright, spacious halls and good *cabañas* and dorms, plus vegan meals, for course participants.

Festivals & Events

Festival Internacional de Jazz MUSIC

(www.facebook.com/mazuntejazzbiosferamarina) This festival brings three days of top-quality jazz concerts, workshops and exhibitions to Mazunte around mid-November.

Sleeping

Posada del Arquitecto CABAÑAS $

(www.posadadelarquitecto.com; El Rinconcito; dm M$70, estrella s/d M$90/150, cabañas M$300-750;) Built around the natural features of a small hill by the beach, this popular Italian-owned place provides a variety of airy accommodations. Options range from hilltop open-air hanging beds with mosquito nets, known as *estrellas*, to attractive *cabañas* and casitas (bungalows) built with mostly natural materials. An open-air yoga hall and good beachfront cafe add to the appeal.

Cabañas Balamjuyuc CABAÑAS $

(cell phone 958-5837667; www.balamjuyuc.com.mx; Camino a Punta Cometa; camping per person M$60, tent & bedding rental M$100, cabañas s/d incl breakfast M$250/500; P) Relaxed Balamjuyuc occupies a spacious hilltop site off Calle Rinconcito, with superb coastal views. It has six *cabaña* rooms, some of which are large and airy; all have mosquito nets, fans and clean shared bathrooms. The **restaurant** (mains M$70-100) has many vegetarian options. Also on offer are daily yoga sessions, therapeutic massages, and temascal bath sessions (per person including dinner M$200).

Affable owner Emiliano plans a weekly program of further activities open to all, such as tai chi, Pilates, and sculpture and acupuncture workshops at another property nearby, Tierra Verde.

Hostal La Isla HOSTEL $

(www.facebook.com/laisla.mazunte; off Calle Rinconcito; dm/s/d incl breakfast M$110/180/220;) La Isla is a friendly and sociable budget option with an international crowd and an inexpensive restaurant in its little, hammock-strung garden area, beside a small creek just behind the beach. The dorm offers single mattresses on the floor with mosquito nets, separated by drapes. Rooms are basic and you pay M$30 extra if you want a fan.

★Oceanomar CABAÑAS $$

(cell phone 958-5890376; www.oceanomar.com; Camino a Playa Mermejita; s/d/tr M$800/1000/1200; P) On a lovely and cleverly landscaped hillside site overlooking Playa Mermejita, Italian-owned Oceanomar is a great recent addition to Mazunte's accommodations. It has a gorgeous pool and five spacious, well-built rooms with nice craft details, hammock-slung terraces and good hot-water bathrooms. The **restaurant**

(⏰8-11am & 7:30-10pm; mains M$80-160) is also very good, and features wood-oven pizzas from Thursday to Monday evenings.

Hotel Arigalan HOTEL $$

(📞cell phone 958-1086987; http://arigalan.com; Cerrada del Museo de la Tortuga; cabañas US$35, r US$65-75, ste US$85; P ⊖ ❄ 📶 🏊) This small hotel commands fine coastal views from its site up a steep track at the village's east end, and offers sizable, tastefully furnished rooms and suites with air-con and terraces, plus a few pleasant, fan-cooled *cabañas*. There's a great roof deck, and a path leads directly down to San Agustinillo beach. Breakfast is available on request. No under-18s accepted here.

El Copal CABAÑAS $$

(📞cell phone 555-4079699; www.elcopal.com.mx; Playa Mermejita; d M$1050; P 📶) 🌿 Copal's four *cabañas* of adobe, wood and palm-thatch are spaced around a leafy hillside garden and all contain a double bed on the ground floor and two or three singles above. Their bathrooms are quaint open-air affairs with views. The international fusion **restaurant** (⏰8:30am-10:30pm Thu-Tue, to 2:30pm Wed; mains M$70-120) has beautiful views along the beach.

★ **Casa Pan de Miel** HOTEL $$$

(📞958-584-35-09; www.casapandemiel.com; r US$100-225; P ⊖ ❄ 📶 🏊) This is a place for real relaxation, boasting a lovely infinity pool in front of an inviting large *palapa* area. The nine large, bright, elegant air-conditioned rooms are adorned with varied Mexican art, and all have sea views, kitchen or kitchenette, and terraces with hammocks. Good breakfasts (M$110 to M$170) and snacks are served in the *palapa* area.

It's up a steep track from the main road at the east end of Mazunte and enjoys wonderful views. Children are not accepted because of the cliff-top position.

Celeste del Mar ROOMS $$$

(📞cell phone 958-1075296; www.celestedelmar.com; Playa Mermejita; r M$1000-1500) 🌿 A few steps from Playa Mermejita, Celeste del Mar offers eight carefully designed rooms in two-story *palapa*-roofed cottages with nice contemporary decorative details. The four airy upstairs rooms feature loft areas with big double hammocks. Breakfast and snacks available; no children.

Eating

Chez L'Arquitecto CAFE $

(El Rinconcito; dishes M$50-115; ⏰8am-11pm; 📶) The cafe at the Posada del Arquitecto (p475) has a great position right over Rinconcito beach and serves a fine range of fare from croissants, cakes and tacos to fish/chicken/pasta main dishes.

Fish Taco El Rey TAQUERÍA $

(cnr Paseo del Mazunte & Calle Rinconcito; tacos M$20-25, other dishes M$55-70; ⏰5pm-midnight Wed-Mon) This simple corner place does indeed do tasty and large fish tacos, alongside shrimp, veggie and *arrachera* varieties, and a very good Thai coconut-and-shrimp soup.

Comedor los Traviesos MEXICAN $

(Paseo del Mazunte; mains M$40-110; ⏰8am-11pm) A place to come for traditional Oaxacan and Mexican cooking at decent prices, Los Traviesos does the best *tlayudas* in town. It's just west of the bridge in the middle of town.

La Empanada MEXICAN, ASIAN $

(Paseo del Mazunte; mains M$60-150; ⏰4-11pm; 📶 🖊) Leafy La Empanada, at the west end of town, has a pretty, candlelit atmosphere after dark. The carefully prepared items include curries, sushi, pizzas and very good baked potatoes with different fillings.

Siddhartha INTERNATIONAL $$

(El Rinconcito; dishes M$60-140; ⏰8am-11pm; 📶 🖊) This joint with a view to the beach does tasty Middle Eastern options such as couscous, falafel and hummus as well as seafood and strong coffee. It also has a pool table and excellent bar.

Drinking & Entertainment

You can have drinks in restaurants and cafes while they're open, but the only regular entertainment is live Latin music at Siddhartha or **Estrella Fugaz** next door – there is usually something at least twice a week, most often Friday, Saturday or Sunday from about 8pm.

Information

Internet Dafne (Paseo del Mazunte; internet per hr M$10; ⏰10am-10pm)

Tourist Information Kiosk (Paseo del Mazunte; ⏰2-6pm Wed-Sun) By the roadside at the west end of the village.

La Ventanilla

Some 2.5km along the road west from Mazunte, a sign points to the tiny beach-village of La Ventanilla, 1.2km down a dirt track, where you can take a fascinating boat trip on a crocodile-filled lagoon, go bird-watching or ride a horse along the beach.

Activities

Servicios Ecoturísticos La Ventanilla WILDLIFE-WATCHING

(cell phone 958-1087288; www.facebook.com/laventanilla; 1½hr lagoon tours adult/child M$50/30; tours 8am-5pm) By the roadside as you enter the village, this is Ventanilla's successful ecotourism cooperative, whose work includes a crocodile nursery, mangrove reforestation and turtle protection. Its 12-passenger boat trips on a mangrove-fringed lagoon will show you endangered river crocodiles (there are several hundred in the local protected area), lots of water birds (most prolific from April to July) and a few deer, monkeys and coatis in enclosures.

The cooperative also offers three-hour horseback rides (M$500) and bird-watching tours (per person per hour M$100; best at 6am) – reserve both the day before. On certain days there's the chance to release turtle hatchlings or join night patrols to see turtles laying and help collect their eggs. There are a few clean, very well-built new **cabañas** (s/d M$200/300), with shared showers and compost toilets, plus **rooms** (s/d M$300/400) with private bathroom.

Lagarto Real WILDLIFE-WATCHING

(cell phone 958-5898419; www.facebook.com/lagarto.real; 1½hr lagoon tours adult/child M$50/30; tours 8am-6pm) Somehow this tiny village manages to have two rival boat-tour cooperatives. Lagarto Real, whose members wear red shirts, has its office on the roadside, near the beach. It offers lagoon boat trips (without an island stop), early-morning bird-watching (per person per hour M$100), and nocturnal turtle-nesting observation.

Getting There & Away

Camionetas and *taxis colectivos* on the Pochutla–Mazunte route pass the Ventanilla turnoff, leaving you with the 1.2km walk. A taxi from Mazunte should cost M$50.

Bahías de Huatulco

958 / POP 19,000

Mexico's youngest planned coastal resort lies along a series of beautiful sandy bays (*bahías*) 50km east of Pochutla. This stretch of coast had just one small fishing village until the 1980s. The developers have trodden fairly gently here: pockets of construction are separated by tracts of unspoiled shoreline, the maximum building height is six stories and no sewage goes into the sea. Huatulco (wah-*tool*-koh) is a relaxed, relatively uncrowded resort with a friendly atmosphere – though between October and May an average of four cruise ships a month dock in Bahía de Santa Cruz. The cruise market has helped to spawn all sorts of active pursuits for visitors here.

The Huatulco bays are strung along the coast for 15km west and 10km east from the harbor at Santa Cruz Huatulco. The 'downtown' area, 1km north of Santa Cruz, is called La Crucecita, with a street grid focused on the leafy Plaza Principal. The other main developments are at Chahué and Tangolunda to the east.

Sights

Huatulco's beaches are sandy with clear waters. As in the rest of Mexico, all beaches are under federal control, and anyone can use them, even when hotels appear to treat them as private property. Some have coral offshore and excellent snorkeling.

Some of the western bays and most of the eastern ones are accessible by road, but a boat ride is more fun, if more expensive, than a taxi. *Lanchas* will whisk you out to most beaches from Santa Cruz harbor any time after 8am and return to collect you by dusk. Round-trip rates for up to 10 people: Playa La Entrega M$300, Bahía Maguey M$1000, Bahía Cacaluta M$1200, Playa La India M$1700, Bahía San Agustín M$2500. For beaches west of La Entrega, there's a M$25 fee for entering the **Parque Nacional Huatulco**, also collected at the harbor. Use of nonbiodegradable suntan lotions or sunscreen is prohibited within the national park.

Several operators offer a **seven-bay day tour** in larger boats for M$200 to M$300 per person. You can buy tickets at hotels, agencies and tour kiosks.

Bahías de Huatulco

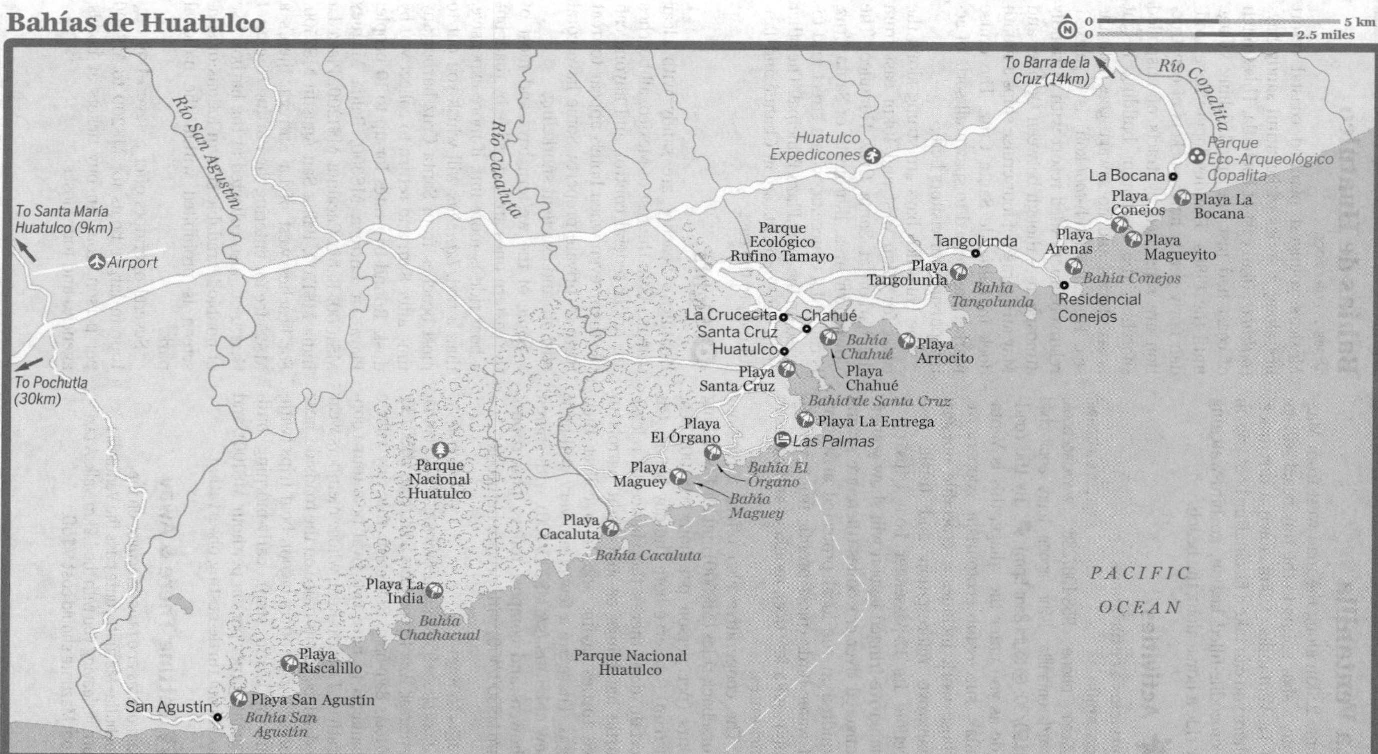

Playa Santa Cruz BEACH

(P) Santa Cruz Huatulco's small beach is easily accessible but often crowded, and its looks are marred by the cruise-ship pier. It has several beach restaurants.

Playa La Entrega BEACH

(P 👪) La Entrega lies toward the outer edge of Bahía de Santa Cruz, a five-minute *lancha* trip or 2.5km drive from Santa Cruz. This 300m beach, backed by a line of seafood *palapas,* can get busy, but it has decent (if sometimes crowded) snorkeling on a coral plate from which boats are cordoned off. Gear is available at **Renta de Snorkel Vicente** (mask & snorkel M$20, fins M$20) at the beach's northern end.

'La Entrega' means 'The Delivery': in 1831, Mexican independence hero Vicente Guerrero was handed over here to his political enemies by a Genoese sea captain. Guerrero was then taken to Cuilapan near Oaxaca and shot.

Bahía Maguey BEACH

(P 👪) Two kilometers west of Santa Cruz, Maguey's fine 400m beach curves around a calm bay between forested headlands. A line of large, family-friendly *palapas* serves fish and seafood dishes for M$100-plus, and there's good snorkeling around the rocks on the east side of the bay. **Escualo** (snorkeling set M$70) rents gear.

Bahía El Órgano BEACH

Just east of Bahía Maguey, this beautiful 250m beach has calm waters good for snorkeling, and no crowds because there's no vehicle access and no *comedores*. You can come by boat, or walk to the beach during dry weather by an unsigned 1km path through the forest.

The path starts about 1.3km back towards Santa Cruz from the Maguey parking lot – 150m before a solitary large tree standing between the road and the concrete sidewalk.

Bahía Cacaluta BEACH

Cacaluta is 1km long and protected by an island, though there can be undertow. Snorkeling is best around the island. Behind the beach is a lagoon with birdlife. There are no services at the beach. *Lancha* is the best way to get here.

Bahía Chachacual BEACH

Inaccessible by land, Chachacual has a headland at each end and two beaches. The easterly **Playa La India** is one of Huatulco's most beautiful beaches and one of the area's best places for snorkeling. No *comedores* here.

Bahía Chahué BEACH

(P) The beach here, 1km east of Santa Cruz Huatulco, is good, though the surf can be surprisingly strong. There's a marina at its east end.

Bahía Tangolunda BEACH

Tangolunda, 5km east of Santa Cruz Huatulco, is the site of the major top-end hotel developments. The sea is sometimes rough: heed the colored-flag safety system.

Bahía Conejos BEACH

Three kilometers east of Tangolunda, Bahía Conejos' long main beach is divided by a small rocky outcrop into the western **Playa Arenas** and the eastern **Playa Punta Arenas**, both reachable by short walks from the paved road. The surf can be strong here. At the east end of the bay is the more sheltered **Playa Conejos**, site of the large Secrets Huatulco Resort. A two-minute walk from Playa Conejos, **Playa Magueyito** is a lovely, 300m-long east-facing beach with rocks offshore.

La Bocana BEACH

(P) About 1.5km east of Playa Conejos, the road runs close to the coast again at La Bocana, at the mouth of the Río Copalita, where you'll find a decent right-hand surf break and a couple of restaurants. Another long beach stretches east from the river mouth.

Parque Eco-Arqueológico Copalita ARCHAEOLOGICAL SITE

(☎958-587-15-91; Blvd Copalita-Tangolunda; Mexican/foreigner M$60/80; ⊙8am-5pm Tue-Sun; P) This pre-Hispanic site 600m north of La Bocana village was opened to visitors in 2010 and is still being excavated. Notable archaeological features revealed so far are limited to a ball court and two fairly modest temples, but an interesting museum, well-made pathways through semitropical forest and a spectacular lookout over the mouth of the Río Copalita add a lot to the appeal.

The site was occupied by different groups between about 500 BC and AD 500, and again from AD 1000 to the 16th century. Visits take one to 1½ hours.

Activities

Diving & Snorkeling

You can rent snorkeling gear, including life jacket and fins, at Santa Cruz harbor for M$100 a day. Renters at one or two beaches have lower rates. The best snorkeling sites include the coral plates at La Entrega, San Agustín and the inshore side of the island at Cacaluta. You can either hire a *lancha* to take you to snorkel sites or take a tour with one of Huatulco's diving outfits.

The Huatulco coast has over 100 **dive sites**, 40 of them marked by buoys. There's a good variety of fish and corals, plus dolphins, turtles and (from about December to March) humpback whales. This is a good place to learn to dive, with warm waters, varied underwater scenery, and calm conditions almost year-round. Visibility averages 10m to 20m. There's a decompression chamber in the local navy hospital.

Hurricane Divers DIVING, SNORKELING
(958-587-11-07; www.hurricanedivers.com; Playa Santa Cruz; 9am-6pm Mon-Fri, 9am-4pm Sat) This very professional international crew is one of Mexico's few PADI 5-Star Dive Resorts. Options include two-tank dives (US$95) and night dives (US$70) for certified divers (US$5 each for BCD, regulator and wetsuit if needed), and PADI Discover Scuba (US$150 for two half-days) for beginners. The popular full-day snorkeling excursion (US$135 per person; minimum two) includes about four stops and a beach lunch. English, French, Dutch and German spoken.

The Hurricane website is an excellent information source on Huatulco diving and snorkeling.

Buceo Sotavento DIVING, SNORKELING
(958-587-21-66, cell phone 958-1095950; www.tomzap.com/sotavento.html; Local 18, Plaza Oaxaca Mall, Plaza Principal, La Crucecita; 9am-9pm) A friendly local outfit offering a range of diving options from a four-hour introduction (M$950) to open-water certification (five days, M$4500). One-/two-tank dives for qualified divers are M$700/950. Sotavento also does four-hour snorkeling trips for M$375 per person (two to seven people), and is certified by the Federación Mexicana de Actividades Subacuáticas (Mexican Underwater Activities Federation).

Fruit & Coffee Plantations

Hagia Sofia FARM, GARDENS
(www.hagiasofia.mx; Apanguito; admission incl round-trip transportation & fruit drinks M$400, with 2 meals M$500;) One of Huatulco's loveliest and most interesting day trips, this 'agro-ecotourism' operation includes a large organic fruit orchard and a gorgeous 500m riverside trail with 60 kinds of tropical flowering plants that attract colorful birds and butterflies. You can have a refreshing dip beneath a waterfall while you're there. It's 9km northwest of Santa María Huatulco and 30km from La Crucecita (a 45-minute drive).

You can visit any day, but reserve the day before through its **office** (958-587-08-71; Local 7, Mitla 402, Santa Cruz Huatulco; 9am-2pm & 4-7pm Mon-Sat). Tours are given in English or Spanish and most people stay about four hours.

Finca La Gloria COFFEE PLANTATION
(day trip per person M$350) This coffee plantation near Llano Grande is a fun trip into the hills, where you are shown the coffee production process, visit a butterfly enclosure, swim in pools below jungle waterfalls and enjoy an excellent lunch. The trip is normally promoted as 'Cascadas Mágicas y Fincas Cafeteleras' (Magical Waterfalls and Coffee Plantations); reserve through agencies, hotels or tour kiosks.

The drive is 1½ hours each way on mostly unpaved roads.

Rafting

Huatulco Expediciones RAFTING
(958-587-21-26; www.huatulcoexpediciones.com; Hwy 200 Km 256, Puente Tangolunda, Comunidad La Jabalina) Well-established Huatulco Expediciones does everything from all-day outings on the Class 3–4 Alemania section of the Copalita (per person M$650 to M$700, minimum two, generally July to December) to a gentler 2½-hour jaunt down the Copalita's final 5km to the sea at La Bocana (per person M$300 to M$350, minimum two people, available all year and suitable for children from 12 years up).

Staff will pick you up from your accommodations for all trips. Rafting trips sold by agencies and kiosks around town are very often with Huatulco Expedicones.

Sleeping

You'll find all budget and many midrange options in La Crucecita. Further midrange possibilities are in Chahué and Santa Cruz.

The top-end resort hotels are at Tangolunda and beyond. Midrange and top-end places tend to raise their rates dramatically for a couple of weeks around Christmas–New Year's and Easter, and from about mid-July to mid-August.

Air-and-lodging package deals are your best bet for a good-value vacation in a top-end Huatulco hotel.

Hotel Jaroje Centro HOTEL **$**

(958-583-48-01; www.hotelhuatulco.com.mx; Bugambilia 304, La Crucecita; d/q M$350/450;) Bright Jaroje, two blocks south of the Plaza Principal, has 13 large, clean, white rooms with mosquito screens, air-con and fine bathrooms. Very good value.

Posada Leo PENSION **$**

(958-587-26-01; posadaleo_hux@hotmail.com; Bugambilia 302, La Crucecita; s/d M$250/300, with air-con M$300/350;) A friendly little budget spot 2½ blocks south of the Plaza Principal. Its six smallish but neat and well-kept rooms all have hot-water bathrooms.

★ **Misión de los Arcos** HOTEL **$$**

(958-587-01-65; www.misiondelosarcos.com; Gardenia 902, La Crucecita; r M$655, ste M$774-893;) This well-run, welcoming hotel, half a block off the Plaza Principal, is embellished by a touch of colonial style and interior greenery. It has big, bright rooms with air-con and very comfortable beds, and most have a balcony. There's walk-through access to the excellent Terra-Cotta restaurant, under the same ownership.

Hotel Posada Edén Costa HOTEL **$$**

(958-587-24-80; www.edencosta.com; Zapoteco 26, Chahué; r/ste incl breakfast M$600/900;) Swiss- and Laotian-owned Edén Costa, 500m inland from Bahía Chahué, has attractive rooms with nice touches including colorful bird murals. Rooms have two double beds, and most overlook the small central pool. Suites have their own kitchens. The attached restaurant, L'échalote, is a big bonus.

Hotel María Mixteca HOTEL **$$**

(958-587-00-60; www.travelbymexico.com/oaxa/mariamixteca; Guamuchil 204, La Crucecita; s/d M$500/550;) María Mixteca offers 14 prettily decorated yellow-and-white rooms on two upper floors around an open patio, with super-comfy beds, air-conditioning, good bathrooms and room safes. It's half a block east of the Plaza Principal.

Hotel Villablanca HOTEL **$$**

(958-587-06-06; www.hotelesvillablanca.com; cnr Blvd Juárez & Zapoteco , Chahué; r from M$728, incl breakfast from M$905;) In a vaguely colonial style, this hotel, 300m from Chahué beach, has helpful staff and a nice large pool. The 61 sizable, attractive white-and-blue rooms all have balconies. The restaurant serves an excellent breakfast and guests have free use of a nearby spa, gym and beach club.

Las Palmas SUITES **$$$**

(cell phone 958-1084265; www.laspalmashuatulco.com; Camino a Playa La Entrega; per night/week casita for up to 4 people US$190/1200, villa for up to 10 US$750/4800;) On a lovely site looking down on little Playa Violín, along the road between Santa Cruz and Playa La Entrega, Las Palmas is an excellent discovery for couples, families or larger groups who have a vehicle and want to self-cater. The three bright, spacious four-bedroom villas boast large sitting/eating areas opening on to their own infinity pools.

The five smaller but also-attractive casitas share a kitchen, pool and large *palapa* dining area. The tilework and crafts are beautiful, kayaks and mountain bikes are provided free, and the whole place has an airy feel.

Camino Real Zaashila LUXURY HOTEL **$$$**

(958-583-03-00; www.caminoreal.com; Blvd Juárez 5 , Tangolunda; r from M$1660, incl breakfast from M$1900;) This attractively landscaped, modern-hacienda-style property has a fabulously enormous pool, 120m long, in lovely gardens giving straight on to the beach. There are 151 rooms, most with sea view and many with their own small pool. Rates can vary wildly with seasons – check the website.

Secrets Huatulco Resort & Spa RESORT **$$$**

(958-583-05-00; www.secretsresorts.com; Blvd Juárez 8, Bahía Conejos; ste incl meals & drinks from US$267;) Opened in 2011, this 399-suite giant is spectacular for its location on a 350m-long sandy beach and its stylishly contemporary design. For adults (18-plus) only, Secrets boasts two vast pools in its beachside gardens, seven à la carte restaurants and a classy spa.

Rates fluctuate wildly with seasons but always include meals, drinks and aquatic activities. Even standard accommodations have features like Jacuzzis on the terrace, hydromassage baths, coffeemakers, and

WORTH A TRIP

BAHÍA SAN AGUSTÍN

The long, sandy beach here, 14km west of Santa Cruz Huatulco, is backed by a fishing village and there is absolutely no resort-type development, but a line of rustic *comedores* stretches along the beach, serving seafood and fish dishes for M$80 to M$130. Usually the waters are calm, and there is coral with very good snorkeling around the rocks in the bay and at Playa Riscalillo round the corner to the east.

San Agustín is in complete contrast to Huatulco's other settlements – it's popular with Mexicans on weekends and vacations but quiet at other times. Some *comedores* rent snorkel gear, and most of them can arrange boats to Riscalillo or Playa La India. Many also have hammocks for rent overnight or tent space; they may let you stay free if you eat with them. **El Tronco** (San Agustín; 2-person tent M$150, hammock per person M$50) toward the north end is run by a friendly family and has a tent to rent as well as hammocks.

You can reach San Agustín by a 13km dirt road heading south from a crossroads on Hwy 200, 1.7km west of the airport. Buses from Huatulco or Pochutla will drop you at the crossroads, where taxis wait to carry people to San Agustín (M$110, or M$22 per person *colectivo*).

magnifying mirrors and plenty of toiletries in the bathroom.

Eating

Antojitos Los Gallos MEXICAN $
(cnr Carrizal & Palma Real, La Crucecita; dishes M$25-70; 2-10:30pm Tue-Sun) This very simple little diner serves super-tasty *antojitos*, soups and meat dishes and is the best place in Huatulco for unadulterated Mexican home-style cooking. You could start with a hearty *caldo tlalpeño* (a soup with chicken, veggies, chili and herbs) followed by a *tlayuda* with *res deshebrada* (shredded beef), or maybe some enchiladas. But really, everything is good here.

It does inventive fruit drinks too, like *agua de pepino y limón* (cucumber and lemon juice).

Casa Mayor CAFE $
(Bugambilia 601, La Crucecita; dishes M$35-135; 9am-midnight Mon-Sat, 4pm-midnight Sun) The best place in town for organic Oaxacan coffee (from Pluma Hidalgo in the mountains behind Huatulco), Casa Mayor serves it almost any way you can think of, including seven varieties of espresso. It overlooks the Plaza Principal and is good for breakfast, baguettes and *antojitos* too.

Terra-Cotta MEXICAN, INTERNATIONAL $$
(958-587-12-28; Gardenia 902, La Crucecita; breakfast dishes M$40-80, mains M$50-150; 7:30am-11:30pm) Highly popular Terra-Cotta, half a block north of the Plaza Principal, has soothing air-con, while good service complements its excellent food: breakfasts, shrimp, steaks, *antojitos*, baguettes and ice cream.

Giordanas ITALIAN $$
(958-583-43-24; cnr Gardenia & Palma Real , La Crucecita; pasta M$85-125; noon-10pm Tue-Sat) The talented Italian chef here makes everything herself, including the pasta. Delicious options include ravioli, fettuccine and meat or vegetarian lasagne. Giordanas also makes a great choice of baguettes with Italian cheeses and salamis.

L'échalote INTERNATIONAL $$
(958-587-24-80; www.edencosta.com; Hotel Posada Edén Costa, Zapoteco 26, Chahué; mains M$95-220; 2-11pm Tue-Sun) The French-Swiss kitchen prepares very tasty French, Italian and Mexican dishes with a few Southeast Asian options. The Thai salad with prawns and bean sprouts is delicious. Main dishes include good fish and steaks and the house specialty fondue. The desserts and French and Italian wines (from M$350) aren't too shabby, either, and you can round things off with a super-smooth Armagnac.

Azul Profundo SEAFOOD, FUSION $$$
(958-583-03-00; Camino Real Zaashila, Blvd Juárez 5, Tangolunda; mains M$210-290; 7-11pm, closed Tue, Thu, Sat & Sun approx May, Jun & Sep-Nov) Tangolunda's big hotels offer a choice of expensive bars, coffee shops and restaurants. For a romantic, no-expense-spared dinner you won't go wrong at the Camino Real's Azul Profundo, right over the beach,

which combines European and Mexican cuisine with a few Asian touches. Reservations required.

 Drinking & Nightlife

La Crema BAR
(☎958-587-07-02; www.lacremahuatulco.com; Gardenia 311, La Crucecita; ⏲7pm-2am) A lively mixed crowd of locals and visitors knocks 'em back at this quirky, dark and spacious rock- and reggae-themed den overlooking the Plaza Principal. La Crema boasts loud tunes, the best cocktail list in town, and terrific wood-oven pizza (medium size MS$90 to M$145). The entrance is just off the plaza on Gardenia.

Paletería Zamora JUICE BAR
(Plaza Principal, La Crucecita; drinks M$15-50; ⏲9am-11pm) Thirst-zapping Zamora blends up a full range of cooling fresh-fruit juices, *licuados*, ice creams and *paletas* (popsicles).

La BiblioT'K LOUNGE
(cnr Gardenia & Palma Real, La Crucecita; ⏲6pm-2am) A *shisha* bar with a vaguely Indian decor, the 'Library' is a popular, often lively spot for cocktails, beers and other beverages at any time of the evening.

Information

Plenty of internet shops, many with options for international phone calls, are around the square in La Crucecita. There are also a few in Tangolunda.

Banorte (Guamuchil 604, La Crucecita; ⏲9am-5pm Mon-Fri) Currency exchange and ATM.

Tourist Information Kiosk (Plaza Principal, La Crucecita; ⏲variable) Has helpful staff.

Getting There & Away

AIR

Huatulco Airport (☎958-581-90-04; www.asur.com.mx) Located 400m north of Hwy 200, 15km west of La Crucecita.

Aeroméxico (☎958-581-91-26; www.aeromexico.com; Airport; ⏲9:30am-6:30pm) Mexico City daily.

Aerotucán (☎958-587-24-27; www.aerotucan.com.mx; Plaza Carmelinas, Blvd Chahué 164, La Crucecita; ⏲9am-8pm Mon-Fri, 9am-6pm Sat) Flies 13-seat Cessnas daily to/from Oaxaca (M$1972).

Air Canada (www.aircanada.com) Weekly flights to/from Toronto from about November to April.

Air Transat (www.airtransat.ca) Weekly flights to/from Edmonton (approximately November to March) and Calgary (January to March).

Frontier Airlines (www.flyfrontier.com) Weekly flights to/from Chicago (November to May) and St Louis (January to March).

Interjet (☎958-105-13-36; www.interjet.com.mx; Plaza Chahué, Blvd Juárez, Chahué; ⏲9am-7pm Mon-Fri, 9am-6pm Sat-Sun) Mexico City at least twice daily.

Magnicharters (☎800-201-14-04; www.magnicharters.com.mx) Mexico City daily except Tuesday.

Sunwing Airlines (www.flysunwing.com) Weekly low-cost flights to and from several Canadian cities from about November to May.

United (www.united.com) To/from Houston, Texas, at least once weekly.

BUSES & VANS FROM BAHÍAS DE HUATULCO

DESTINATION	FARE (M$)	DURATION (HR)	FREQUENCY (DAILY)
Mexico City (Sur) via Puerto Escondido	920-1070	14-15	Turistar 4pm, AltaMar 5:30pm
Mexico City (TAPO) via Salina Cruz	724-942	15	4 from OCC terminal
Oaxaca via Pochutla	180	7	13 Expressos Colombo, 8 Huatulco 2000
Oaxaca via Salina Cruz	302-358	8	4 from OCC terminal
Pochutla	23-27	1	18 from OCC terminal, TRP every 20-30min 6am-7pm
Puerto Escondido	64	2½	18 from OCC terminal
Salina Cruz	71-144	3	17 from OCC terminal
San Cristóbal de las Casas	430	10-11	2 OCC
Tehuantepec	98-160	3½	10 from OCC terminal

BUS, VAN & TAXI COLECTIVO

Some buses to Huatulco are marked 'Santa Cruz Huatulco,' but they still terminate in La Crucecita. Make sure your bus is not headed to Santa María Huatulco, which is some way inland.

Taxis colectivos to Pochutla (M$25, one hour) leave from a lay-by on Blvd Chahué opposite the north end of Bugambilia, 450m north of the Plaza Principal in La Crucecita.

Estrella Blanca Bus Station (Central Camionera; Carpinteros s/n, Sector V) Located 1.2km northwest of central La Crucecita; used by Turistar (deluxe), AltaMar (1st-class) and Transportes Rápidos de Pochutla (TRP; 2nd-class) buses.

Expressos Colombo (cnr Gardenia & Sabalí, La Crucecita) Passenger vans to Oaxaca; the terminal is located 400m north of the Plaza Principal.

Huatulco 2000 (Guamuchil, La Crucecita) Passenger vans to Oaxaca. Located 150m east of the Plaza Principal.

OCC Bus Station (Blvd Chahué, La Crucecita) Located 500m north of the Plaza Principal; used by ADO GL (deluxe), OCC (1st-class) and Sur and AU (2nd-class) buses.

CAR & MOTORCYCLE

Auto-Car Rental Oaxaca (http://oaxacacarrental.com.mx; Centro Comercial Las Conchas, Blvd Juárez, Tangolunda)

Europcar (www.europcar.com.mx) Airport (958-581-90-94; 8:30am-6:30pm); La Crucecita (958-583-47-51; Plaza Carmelinas, Blvd Chahué 164; 8am-6pm) Reasonable rental rates and efficient service.

Getting Around

TO/FROM THE AIRPORT

Authorized Transporte Terrestre vans cost M$100 per person from the airport to La Crucecita, Santa Cruz, Chahué or Tangolunda. Get tickets at airport desks. A whole cab is M$370 to M$570 to Bahías de Huatulco, M$730 to Puerto Ángel or M$940 to Mazunte, but you can usually get one for half those prices, or less, by walking 300m down to Hwy 200, where drivers wait at the airport intersection. Or catch a bus from the same intersection to La Crucecita (M$7) or Pochutla (M$16): they pass about every 15 minutes in both directions from about 6am to 7pm.

Taxis to the airport cost M$150 from La Crucecita.

BUS & TAXI

Blue-and-white local buses run every few minutes during daylight. To Santa Cruz Huatulco (M$4, five minutes) they go from Plaza El Madero mall on Guamuchil, two blocks east of the plaza in La Crucecita. To the Estrella Blanca bus station (M$4, five minutes) they go from Guamuchil one block from the plaza.

Taxis from central La Crucecita cost M$25 to Santa Cruz or the Estrella Blanca Bus Station, M$38 to Tangolunda, M$54 to Playa La Entrega and M$66 to Bahía Maguey.

SCOOTER

Tu Moto (958-587-17-35; Guarumbo 306, La Crucecita; 9:30am-2pm & 4:30-7pm Mon-Sat, 10am-1pm Sun) Zipping around on a scooter can be a fun way to get around Huatulco. Tu Moto rents Japanese makes, with two helmets per bike, from M$450 per day or M$750 for three days. There's generally no insurance available with scooter rental.

Barra de la Cruz

POP 740

This well-tended indigenous Chontal village, about 20km east of Huatulco, offers surfers the chance to catch some amazing waves and everyone the chance to get off the grid and slow right down. The right-hand point break, off the beach 1.5km from the rustic village, gets up to a double overhead and is long and fast. Good swells for experienced surfers are frequent from March to early October and generally at their best in June and July. November to February brings good waves for learners.

There's not much to do except surf and swim, but Barra's beautiful long beach has showers, toilets and a good *comedor* with hammocks and shade. The municipality charges M$20 per person to pass along the road to the beach and imposes an 8pm curfew on it.

You can rent surfboards at El Chontal or Canañas Pepe accommodations. El Chontal's English-speaking owner **Pablo Narváez** (pablo_rafting@yahoo.com; surfboards per day M$100-150, surf classes 3-4hr around M$450, birdwatching tours 3 or 4hr per person M$250) also gives **surf classes** (3-4hr for one or two people M$450), and expertly leads **bird-watching tours** (3 or 4hr per person M$250) around the very varied local habitats.

Sleeping & Eating

A handful of simple accommodations clusters around the entrance to the beach road.

Cabañas Pepe CABAÑAS $
(camping/cabaña per person M$50/100; dishes M$40-60; P) Pepe's has well-built wood-and-palm-thatch cabins with shared toilets and showers, plus a large *palapa comedor* with couches, table tennis and a good selection of dishes.

El Chontal ROOMS $
(☎cell phone 958-1177343; pablo_rafting@yahoo.com; r without/with air-con M$250/350; mains M$65-75; P❄) El Chontal has two quite large, bright and breezy upstairs rooms with shared bathrooms, and serves good chicken, seafood and other dishes under its large *palapa*. It also runs nearby Barradise, where rooms with private bathroom are M$80 to M$90 per person.

Comedor MEXICAN $
(mains M$70-90; ⏰9am-6pm) The community-run beach *comedor* is good for breakfast and lunch. Try its excellent *sopa de mariscos* (seafood soup).

ℹ Getting There & Around

The 2.5km road to Barra de la Cruz heads off Hwy 200 2km east of Puente Zimatán bridge. From the Estrella Blanca Bus Station at Bahías de Huatulco, *taxis colectivos* run to Barra (M$25, 40 minutes) about every half-hour, 7am to 5pm (less often in the middle of the day and on Sunday). They charge an additional M$15 to carry a surfboard. A private taxi costs around M$150 from central La Crucecita or M$300 from Huatulco airport, with or without boards.

ISTHMUS OF TEHUANTEPEC

The southern half of the 200km-wide Isthmus of Tehuantepec (teh-wahn-teh-*pek*), Mexico's narrow waist, forms the flat, hot, humid eastern end of Oaxaca state. Indigenous Zapotec culture is strong here, with its own regional twists. In 1496 the isthmus Zapotecs repulsed the Aztecs from the fortress of Guiengola, near Tehuantepec, and the isthmus never became part of the Aztec empire. An independent spirit pervades the region to this day.

Few travelers linger here, but if you do you'll encounter a lively, friendly populace whose open and confident women take leading roles in business and government. Isthmus people let loose their love of music, dancing and partying in numerous *velas* (fiestas) lasting several days. If you're here for one of these, you'll see women showing off highly colorful *huipiles,* gold and silver jewelry, skirts embroidered with fantastic silk flowers, and a variety of odd headgear. Many fiestas feature the *tirada de frutas,* in which women climb on roofs and throw fruit on the men below!

Of the three main towns, isthmus culture is stronger in Tehuantepec and Juchitán than in Salina Cruz, which is dominated by its oil refinery. All three towns can be uncomfortable in the heat of the day, but evening breezes are deliciously refreshing.

Salina Cruz

This port city of 77,000 bustles with Mexican life, but it's not a pretty place and there's no pressing reason to come here except for transportation connections. The main bus stations are **Estrella Blanca** (cnr Frontera & Tampico), 500m north of the central plaza, with 1st-class Altamar services, and **ADO** (Calle 1º de Mayo), 500m further north, with deluxe, 1st-class and 2nd-class services.

BUSES FROM SALINA CRUZ

DESTINATION	FARE (M$)	DURATION	FREQUENCY (DAILY)
Bahías de Huatulco	108-144	3hr	13 ADO, 4 Altamar
Juchitán	42-58	1hr	33 ADO
Oaxaca	218-260	5-5½hr	9 ADO
Pochutla	138-165	4hr	8 ADO, 4 Altamar
Puerto Escondido	188-254	4-5hr	9 ADO, 4 Altamar
San Cristóbal de las Casas	316	7hr	2 ADO
Tehuantepec	24-38	30min	33 ADO

Tehuantepec

☎971 / POP 42,000

Even though Tehuantepec, some 245km from Oaxaca city, is a friendly town, most travelers blow by here on their way to somewhere else. June and August are the main months for partying in the fiestas of Tehuantepec's 15 barrios (neighborhoods), each of which has its own colonial church. There's a **Tourist Information Office** (Hwy 185; ⏲8am-8pm Mon-Fri, 9am-6pm Sat, 9am-2pm Sun) beside the highway two blocks west from the central plaza; staff are knowledgeable about the area.

Sights

Ex-Convento Rey Cosijopí CULTURAL BUILDING

(☎971-715-01-14; Callejón Rey Cosijopí; ⏲8am-8pm Mon-Fri, 9am-2pm Sat) FREE This former Dominican monastery is now Tehuantepec's **Casa de la Cultura**, where arts and crafts workshops and activities are held. It bears traces of old frescoes, and some rooms hold modest exhibits of traditional dress, archaeological finds and historical photos: ask in the office, upstairs, for them to be opened. The last Zapotec king, Cosijopí, paid for the monastery's construction in the 16th century. It's on a short lane off Guerrero, 400m northeast of the central plaza.

Market MARKET

Tehuantepec's dim, almost medieval indoor market is open daily on the west side of the plaza, and spills out into surrounding streets.

Sleeping & Eating

At night the plaza's east side is lined with tables and chairs beside carts serving cheap tacos and other delights.

Hostal Emilia GUESTHOUSE $

(☎971-715-00-08; h.oasis@hotmail.com; Ocampo 8; r without/with air-con M$300/420; ⊖❄@☎) A block south of the plaza, Emilia has six reasonably comfy rooms, most with shared bathrooms, and a guest kitchen.

OFF THE BEATEN TRACK

CONCEPCIÓN BAMBA

The coast around Salina Cruz has surfers in raptures with its long-peeling, sand-bottom right-hand point breaks and several beach and jetty breaks. La Bamba, as it's known, is a 6km beach with two point breaks in the middle, and stands out because it's home to easily the area's most appealing accommodations. It's 40km west of the city, one of several long, sweeping sandy beaches on a spectacular stretch of coast with monster dunes and forested mountains rising just inland.

There is almost no tourism infrastructure along this coast. A number of 'surf camps' in Salina Cruz itself cater to fly-in surfers willing to spend US$150 to US$300 a night for full-board packages with daily transportation to the surf spots. In the past hackles have been raised over local surf guides stopping independent surfers from surfing in some areas, but this issue now only affects a small handful of spots. The surfing season is from about March to October. Swells don't come every day so check the forecasts.

★ **Cocoleoco Surf Camp** (☎322-221-56-53; www.cabanabambasurfmx.com; cabaña d M$250-400, camping per person M$50; ⏲mid-Mar–mid-Oct; P) at La Bamba is the perfect laid-back surf base, with appealing, rustic *cabañas* equipped with mosquito nets and fans, and good meals available. A dozen good surf spots lie within a 30-minute drive west or east, and local guides here will drive up to five people to the best surf for M$500 per day. Classes are available, and anyone can enjoy horseback riding, kayaking on the lake, or a temascal. Alternative accommodations in the area are not nearly so appealing, so reservations are worthwhile.

The signposted turnoff to Concepción Bamba is at Km 352 on Hwy 200; a 2.5km unpaved road leads to the village, with Cocoleoco on its far side, then it's 800m further to the beach. Buses between Huatulco and Salina Cruz will drop you at the turnoff, from which you'll probably have to walk. Or you can get a *taxi colectivo* to the village from Salina Cruz (M$40, plus M$10 for a surfboard); they leave about hourly from 7am to 7pm, from a lot on Hwy 200 (La Costera) a few steps west of its intersection with Blvd Salina Cruz in the north of town (M$25 by taxi from the town's main bus stations).

BUSES FROM TEHUANTEPEC'S MAIN STATION

DESTINATION	FARE (M$)	DURATION	FREQUENCY (DAILY)
Bahías de Huatulco	122-134	3½hr	6
Mexico City (TAPO)	628-908	11-12hr	8
Oaxaca	130-204	4½-5hr	17
Pochutla	152-172	4½hr	4
Puerto Escondido	200-226	4½-6hr	4

Hotel Calli HOTEL **$$**
(☎971-715-00-85; www.hotelcalli.com; Carretera Cristóbal Colón Km 790; r M$1100, restaurant mains M$75-190; P ❄ @ ☜ ≋) The 100 good-sized, bland modern rooms, designed primarily for bus-tour groups, boast cable TV, air-con and small balconies. Ample common areas include a reasonable restaurant and a pool in grassy gardens. It's beside Hwy 185 on the northeast edge of town.

Pueblo Mío MEXICAN **$**
(Ocampo 8; dishes M$50-100; ⏲9am-9pm Mon-Sat, noon-9pm Sun) Neat, colorful and friendly, Pueblo Mío serves up a range of satisfying fare from *antojitos* and seafood cocktails to fish and meat mains and burgers. Its tasty specialty is *mole de guinado xhuba*, a pre-Hispanic soup made with corn and beef chops.

Getting There & Around

Tehuantepec's main bus station, known as La Terminal, is by Hwy 185, 1.5km northeast of the central plaza. It's shared by deluxe, 1st-class and 2nd-class services of the ADO/OCC group. Second-class Istmeños buses to Juchitán (M$24, 30 minutes) and Salina Cruz (M$18, 30 minutes) depart across the street from La Terminal at least every half-hour during daylight. Taxis to the plaza cost M$15.

Juchitán

☎971 / POP 75,000

Istemeño culture is strong in this friendly town, which is visited by few gringos. About 30 different neighborhood *velas* fill Juchitán's calendar with music, dancing, drinking, eating and fun from mid-April to early September, especially in May. Juchitán is also famed for its *muxes* – openly gay, frequently cross-dressing men, who are fully accepted in local society and hold their own *vela* in November.

Sights

Jardín Juárez PLAZA
Jardín Juárez is a lively central square. In the busy two-story market on its east side you'll find locally made hammocks, isthmus women's costumes, and maybe iguana on the *comedor* menus.

Lidxi Guendabiaani CULTURAL BUILDING
(Casa de la Cultura; ☎971-711-32-08; Belisario Domínguez; ⏲10am-3pm & 5-8pm Mon-Fri, 10am-noon Sat) FREE Beside the San Vicente Ferrer church a block south and west of Jardín Juárez, Lidxi Guendabiaani is set around a big patio. It's used mainly for arts workshops and classes but also has a contemporary art gallery and a small archaeological museum.

Sleeping & Eating

In the evening, plenty of economical open-air *comedores* set up around Jardín Juárez.

Hotel Central HOTEL **$**
(☎971-712-20-19; www.hotelcentral.com.mx; Av Efraín Gómez 30; s M$335-360, d M$390-420; ⊖ ❄ @ ☜) This good-value hotel is 1½ blocks east of the central Jardín Juárez. It offers bare, freshly painted rooms with comfy beds and good-sized bathrooms, though some have little natural light.

Hotel López Lena Palace HOTEL **$$**
(☎971-711-13-88; www.hotellopezlenapalace.com.mx; Av 16 de Septiembre 70; s M$389-497, d M$489-689; P ❄ ☜) Look for the mock-Arabic exterior 600m north of the central Jardín Juárez, halfway to the bus station. The Lena's rooms are cheerful and clean with good air-con and showers. The economical 'minis' are windowless but homey.

La Tossta ITALIAN, MEXICAN **$$**
(Av 16 de Septiembre 37; mains M$80-180; ⏲7am-midnight; ☜) With bright, contemporary ambience and some creative recipe combinations – shrimp in garlic and white wine, beef medallions in port sauce – this is a welcome surprise in Juchitán.

BUSES FROM JUCHITÁN

DESTINATION	FARE (M$)	DURATION	FREQUENCY (DAILY)
Bahías de Huatulco	140-194	3½-4hr	10
Mexico City (TAPO)	610-1282	11-12hr	14
Oaxaca	222-266	5-5½hr	16
Pochutla	170-198	4½-5hr	7
San Cristóbal de las Casas	286	5½-6hr	2
Tapachula	294-398	6-8hr	5

ℹ Getting There & Around

The main **bus station** (Prolongación 16 de Septiembre), used by deluxe, 1st-class and 2nd-class services of ADO/OCC, is 100m south of Hwy 190 on the northern edge of town. Many buses depart inconveniently between 11pm and 7am. 'Terminal-Centro' buses run between the bus station and the central Jardín Juárez. A taxi costs M$25.

Second-class Istmeños buses to Tehuantepec (M$24, 30 minutes) and Salina Cruz (M$36, one hour) leave at least every 30 minutes during daylight, from the next corner south from the main terminal.

Central Pacific Coast

Includes ➡

Best Places to Eat

- Ocean Grill (p526)
- Café des Artistes (p524)
- El Faro de Bucerías (p539)
- Pedro & Lola (p499)
- Mariscos El Aliviane (p536)
- La Alberca (p504)

Best Places to Stay

- Casa Dulce Vida (p522)
- Imanta (p514)
- Hacienda San Angel (p523)
- Mar de Jade (p510)
- Aura del Mar (p551)

Why Go?

Those gigantic aquamarine waves have forever provided that primal, pulsating rhythm that backs any visit to Mexico's Central Pacific Coast, a land of stunning beaches and giant sunsets. Here, you can lounge on the sand and spy humpback whales breaching on the horizon, pelicans flying in formation or a pod of dolphins rising from the waves. Surf world-class breaks, kayak through mangrove-fringed lagoons, munch fresh lobster in ramshackle fishing villages, or hang onto the back of a pickup packed with locals roaring inland toward the blue silhouette of the lofty Sierra Madre. Or switch into lounge mode, margarita in hand, poolside, at a world-class luxury hotel.

Whether you're here for a week of cushy beachfront decadence, or months of down-to-earth exploration on the cheap, the good life on the Pacific coast means finding your own beat.

When to Go

Puerto Vallarta

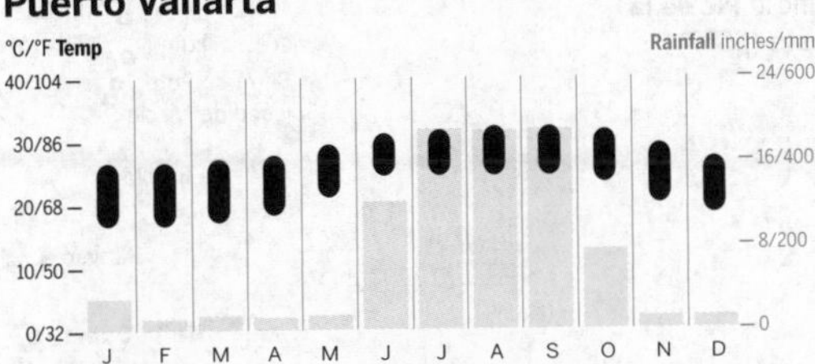

Feb Perfect beach weather. Carnaval reigns in Mazatlán.

Jun–Aug Surf's up and prices are down at Pacific Mexico's prime surfing destinations.

Nov–Dec Puerto Vallarta celebrates everything from gay pride to the Virgin of Guadalupe.

Central Pacific Coast Highlights

1. Take the pulse of the new **Old Mazatlán** (p491) in its renovated historic center
2. People-watch and promenade on the beautiful beachfront *malecón* (oceanfront promenade) in **Puerto Vallarta** (p514)
3. Surf the aggressive barrel swells in **Boca de Pascuales** (p537)
4. Thrill at the fearless finesse of **La Quebrada Clavadistas** (p561) (cliff divers) in Acapulco
5. Soak up the mellow party vibe along the surfer-happy sands and the cafe-encircled plaza in **Sayulita** (p511)
6. Enjoy the easy tempo and local hospitality in charming **Zihuatanejo** (p546)
7. Watch sunrise over the lagoon and sunset over the Pacific in **Pie de la Cuesta** (p557)

History

Archaeologists view pre-Hispanic Mexico's Pacific coast as a unified region, defined by its tradition of shaft or chamber tombs (underground burial chambers at the base of a deep shaft). The ceremonial centers around the tombs suggest a fairly developed spiritual and religious life.

The Spanish arrived in Mexico in 1519 and soon traveled to Acapulco, Zihuatanejo, Puerto Vallarta and Manzanillo. In 1564 conquistador Miguel López de Legazpi and Father Andrés de Urdaneta first sailed from Barra de Navidad to the Philippines and soon after claimed the area for Spain. Acapulco quickly became an established port link in the trade route between Asia and Europe.

It was not until the middle of the 1950s that tourism really hit the coast, starting in Acapulco and Mazatlán, with Puerto Vallarta soon to follow. In recent years more and more foreigners have bought and developed land along the coast, most noticeably around Puerto Vallarta, easily the most thriving and alive of the Pacific beach cities.

Getting There & Away

There are plenty of direct international flights from the US and Canada to Puerto Vallarta, Mazatlán and Zihuatanejo, with a few to Manzanillo and Acapulco. For those traveling by car, the toll roads between the US border and Tepic make for easy sailing, but are pricey. As with elsewhere in Mexico, free roads oscillate between smooth pavement and shock-busting potholes. High-quality bus services connect the resort centers to inland Mexico.

Away from the resorts, coastal Hwy 200 has had an up-and-down safety record, and you'll see convoys of military trucks patrolling the area, especially in the states of Nayarit, Michoacán and Guerrero, which still have a reputation for being unsafe at night.

Getting Around

Bus travel in this region is easy and surprisingly comfortable. Second-class buses serve nearly every community, large or small, while nicer buses – with air-con, comfortable seats, cleanish bathrooms, TVs and other classy comforts – serve bigger towns.

If you're driving, note that nearly everything on coastal Hwy 200 – service stations, stores, tire shops – closes around sundown.

MAZATLÁN

669 / POP 473,000

Thanks to 20km of sandy beaches, Mazatlán became one of Mexico's most alluring and inviting beach destinations in the mid-20th century, before it lurched past its prime and into a midmarket, package-tourist category. Recently, however, Mazatlán's historic core has been restored and peopled by the creative class. The result is a historic city, that eats well, plays hard, and remains just a short walk from those luscious beaches.

To take the pulse of Mazatlán, don't linger too long in the Zona Dorada (Golden Zone), Mazatlán's traditional tourist playground. Instead, head straight for the city's cobblestoned *pueblo viejo* (old town), catch a performance at the wonderful refurbished Teatro Ángela Peralta and then a late-night bite at the atmospheric Plazuela Machado. Step into one of Mazatlán's excellent small museums or go treasure hunting in one of the many new small boutiques. One big attraction is free for all – the daily spectacle of rocky islands silhouetted against the tropical sunset as the fiery red fades into the sea and another starry night begins.

Sights

Old Mazatlán NEIGHBORHOOD

The old town is historical yet progressive, thanks to the university and art students who make it their playground. At its center is the soaring 19th-century **cathedral** (Map p494; cnr Juárez & 21 de Marzo), with its high yellow twin towers and a dramatic interior, located on the Plaza Principal, which attracts legions of old pigeon feeders, plus local families who patronize businesses on the clogged arteries that surround it. Two blocks north, on the corner of Juárez and Valle, is the vibrant local **Centro Mercado** (Central Market; Map p494), full of clothes, housewares, produce, juice stands and shoppers.

A short stroll will bring you to the corner of Avenida Carnaval and Calle Constitución, where you'll find the tree-lined **Plazuela Machado**. The plaza and surrounding streets are abuzz with art galleries, cafes and restaurants.

The center of attention is the **Teatro Ángela Peralta** (Map p494; www.culturamazatlan.com; self-guided tour M$15), half a block south of the plaza. Constructed between 1869 and 1874, the 1366-seat theater was a thriving center of local cultural life for nearly a century, first as an opera house,

Greater Mazatlán

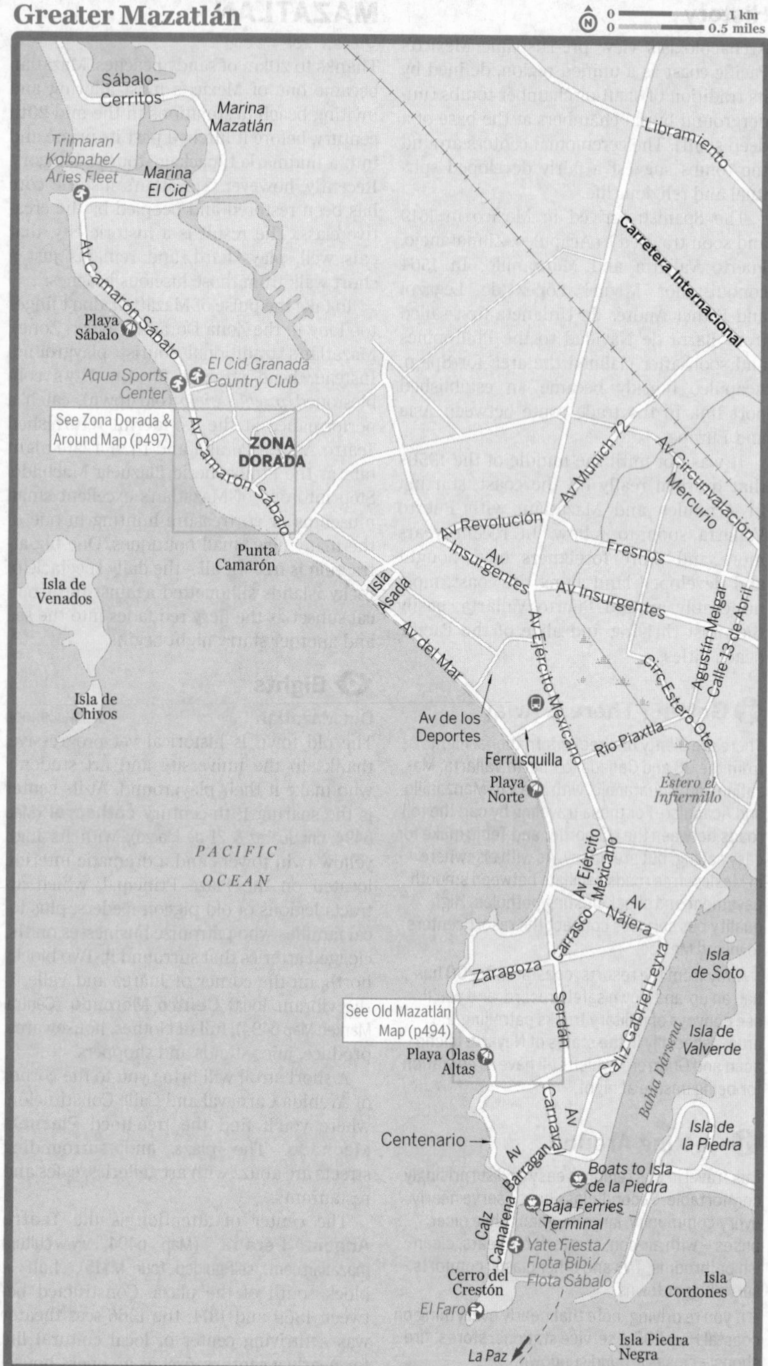

then as a cinema. Abandoned in 1964, and battered by Hurricane Olivia in 1975, it fell into decay and was slated for demolition by the city government before dedicated local citizens came to its rescue in the late 1980s. Declared a national heritage site in 1990 and reopened to the public in 1992, the three-level interior has been restored to its former splendor, and all kinds of cultural events are again staged here, including the annual Festival Cultural Mazatlán (p496).

West of the center is **Playa Olas Altas**, a small beach in a cove. The breezy seafront road, Paseo Olas Altas, strongly evokes 1950s-era Mazatlán, with a couple of faded relic hotels.

Nearby is the platform from which the **clavadistas** (Map p494; Paseo Olas Altas) (cliff divers) cast their bodies into the treacherous ocean swells for your enjoyment. Tip accordingly. You're most likely to see the divers perform around lunchtime on Saturday and Sunday (they won't risk their necks until a crowd has assembled).

At the peninsula's southern end, a prominent rocky outcrop is the base for **El Faro**, which is 135m above sea level and said to be the second-highest lighthouse in the world (after the one in Gibraltar). You can climb up here for a spectacular view of the city and coast.

Isla de la Piedra BEACH

Escape artists love **Isla de la Piedra** (Stone Island), located southeast of Old Mazatlán, for its beautiful, long sandy beach bordered by coconut groves. Surfers come for the waves, and on Sunday afternoons its simple *palapa* (thatched-roof shelter) restaurants draw Mexican families. Most other times you'll have the beach to yourself.

It's a simple matter to get to Isla de Piedra on your own. Take a water taxi (round trip M$30, every 10 minutes from 7am to 6pm) from the Playa Sur *embarcadero* (boat dock) near the Baja Ferries terminal. You'll be dropped off at a jetty just a short walk from the Isla de la Piedra beach. 'Playa Sur' buses leave for the *embarcadero* from the corner of Serdán and Escobedo, two blocks southeast of the Plaza Principal in Old Mazatlán.

Museo Arqueológico MUSEUM

(Map p494; ☎669-981-14-55; Sixto Osuna 76; admission M$35, Sun free; ⏰9am-6pm Tue-Fri, 10am-2pm Sat & Sun) The small but absorbing **Museo Arqueológico** displays pre-Hispanic archeological finds accompanied by fascinating wall texts in Spanish and English.

Museo de Arte MUSEUM

(Map p494; ☎669-985-35-02; cnr Sixto Osuna & Carranza; ⏰10am-2pm & 4-6pm Mon-Sat) FREE This is a small museum in a sprawling colonial courtyard complex, which makes a convincing case for the vitality and innovation of contemporary Mexican art with changing exhibitions of digital works, sculpture, prints and paintings.

Casa Machado MUSEUM

(Map p494; Constitución 77; adult/student M$20/10; ⏰10am-6pm) Worth a peek is the Casa Machado, a restored 19th-century house filled with antique French and Austrian furniture, Carnaval costumes, historic photos and other items. Its 2nd-floor terrace affords a panoramic view over the Plazuela Machado.

Beaches

With over 16km of beaches, it's easy to find a suitable stretch of sand. The following beaches are listed from south to north.

In Old Mazatlán, the crescent-shaped **Playa Olas Altas** is where tourism first flourished in the 1950s, although the pebbly beach is not ideal for swimming.

Flanked by a broad *malecón* popular with joggers and strollers, the golden sands of **Playa Norte** begin just north of Old Mazatlán. The beach arcs toward **Punta Camarón**, a rocky point dominated by the conspicuous castle-like Fiesta Land nightclub complex.

The most luxurious hotels face the fine **Playa Las Gaviotas** and **Playa Sábalo**, the latter extending north of the Zona Dorada. Sheltered by picturesque islands, here the waters are generally calm and ideal for swimming and water sports. Further north, past **Marina El Cid** and the ever-evolving **Marina Mazatlán**, are **Playa Brujas** (Witches Beach), a once-serene beach that has seen a flood of high-rise development in recent years, and **Playa Cerritos**. Both have a smattering of seafood restaurants and decent surf. To reach these northern beaches, catch a 'Cerritos Juárez' bus along Avenida Camarón Sábalo in the Zona Dorada.

Islands

Resembling breaching whales in silhouette, the three photogenic rocks jutting from the sea offshore of the Zona Dorada offer secluded beaches and clear waters ideal for

Old Mazatlán

snorkeling – and great multitudes of seals and marine birds. On the left is **Isla de Chivos** (Goat Island); **Isla de Pájaros** (Bird Island) is on the right. Most visited is the one in the middle, **Isla de Venados** (Deer Island). The islands are part of a wildlife refuge designated to help protect the local birds and marine fauna.

Activities

Surfing

With a season lasting from late March through November, Mazatlán boasts several noteworthy surfing sites. You can rent equipment or take lessons from **Mazatlán Surf Center** (Map p497; ☎669-913-18-21; www.mazatlansurfcenter.com; Av Camarón Sábalo 204; wetsuit/bodyboard/surfboard rental per day US$10/15/25, 2hr lesson incl hotel pickup US$65).

Other Water Sports

The **Aqua Sports Center** (☎669-913-04-51; www.aquasportscenter.com; El Cid Mega Resort, Av Camarón Sábalo s/n) is the place to go for other water sports, including scuba diving (one-/two-tank dive US$70/100), banana-boat rides (per person US$8), waterskiing (per two people US$135) and parasailing (US$40). It also rents out sailboats (per hour US$50), kayaks (per day single/double US$35/50), surfboards (US$40) and snorkeling equipment (per day US$15).

Sportfishing

Handily located at the confluence of the Sea of Cortez and the Pacific Ocean, Mazatlán is world famous for its sportfishing – especially for marlin, swordfish, sailfish, tuna and *dorado* (dolphin fish). It can be an expensive activity (US$350 to US$675 per boat per day, for boats ranging in size from 8m to 11m with four to nine people fishing); fishing from a 7m *super panga* (fiberglass skiff) is less expensive (around US$275 per day with up to four people fishing).

The spiffiest boats leave from Marina El Cid and Marina Mazatlán; for lower prices, try the operators near El Faro on Calz Camarena or negotiate directly with one of the independent fishermen offering half-day *panga* trips along Paseo Claussen near Playa Norte.

Among the recommended operators there is El Cid's **Aries Fleet** (☎669-916-34-68; www.elcid.com/sporting_activities/aries_fleet.cfm; Marina El Cid; per day from US$495), which supports catch-and-release practices; **Flota Bibi** (☎669-913-10-60; www.bibifleet.com; Calz Camarena s/n; charters per day US$399), which operates four boats accommodating four to eight people each, and gives steep discounts

Old Mazatlán

Top Sights
1 Teatro Ángela Peralta D2

Sights
2 Casa Machado C2
3 Cathedral D1
4 Centro Mercado D1
5 Clavadistas A1
6 Museo Arqueológico B3
7 Museo de Arte B3

Sleeping
8 Casa de Leyendas B3
9 Casa Lucila B2
10 Hotel La Siesta B2
11 Hotel Machado C2
12 Hotel Posada Freeman B3
13 Old Mazatlán Condos B1
14 The Jonathon C2

Eating
15 El Fish Market B2
16 Fish Tacos Machado C2
17 Fonda de Chalo B3
18 La Tramoya C2
19 Molika C2
20 Nieves de Garrafa de con Medrano C2
21 Pedro & Lola C2
22 Puerto Viejo B3
23 Topolo D2

Drinking & Nightlife
24 Axesso C2
25 Hotel Belmar Bar B3
26 Looney Bean B3
27 Vitrolas Bar C1

Entertainment
Teatro Ángela Peralta (see 1)

Shopping
28 Casa Etnika C3
29 Gandara Bazaar D2
30 Nidart D2

in the low season; and **Flota Sábalo** (☎669-994-99-14, 669-981-27-61; Calz Camarena s/n; fishing trips from M$6000 for 4-6 people), which offers a wide variety of reasonably priced trips in boats holding four to six people.

Golf

Mazatlán has two renowned championship golf courses. The most striking is the **Estrella del Mar Golf Club** (☎800-727-46-53; www.estrelladelmar.com; green fees 9/18 holes US$76/112), just south of the airport along the coast. **El Cid Granada Country Club** (☎669-989-69-69; www.elcid.com/granada/; Av Camarón Sábalo; 9/18 holes M$780/1040) offers a challenging alternative north of the Zona Dorada.

Tours

★Onca Explorations ECOTOUR
(☎669-913-40-50; www.oncaexplorations.com) Wildlife observation and conservation are the focus of these ecotours, led by marine ecologist Oscar Guzón. Most popular are his Humpback Whale Research Adventure (adult/child US$87/55, December to March) and Wild Dolphin Adventure (per person adult/child US$70/45, year-round) tours, which offer excellent opportunities to observe marine mammals up close.

Other options include an excursion to Las Labradas (adult/child US$70/35), site of the only beachside petroglyphs in the Americas, and custom bird-watching tours to Santa María Bay, Isla Isabel National Park and the Chara Pinta Tufted Jay Preserve.

Trimaran Kolonahe BOAT TOUR
(☎669-916-34-68; www.elcid.com/marinas/marina_tour_mazatlan.cfm; Marina El Cid) The speedy *Trimaran Kolonahe* sets sail for Isla de Venados Tuesday through Sunday at 9:30am. The five-hour cruise costs adult/child US$55/30, including use of kayaks, snorkeling equipment, lunch and drinks.

King David BOAT TOUR
(Map p497; ☎669-914-14-44; www.kingdavid.com.mx; Av Camarón Sábalo 333) Offers boat tours, including a five-hour bird-watching tour (adult/child including lunch US$50/35) into the mangrove-fringed waterways of the Isla de la Piedra wildlife refuge.

Yate Fiesta BOAT TOUR
(☎669-982-31-30; www.yatefiesta.com; Calz Camarena 7) Offers 2½-hour sightseeing tours (M$250) and sunset cruises (including open bar M$300), as well as two-hour cruises to Isla de la Piedra (including lunch and open bar M$350).

Vista Tours TOUR
(Map p497; ☎669-986-86-10; www.vistatours.com.mx; Av Camarón Sábalo 51) Offers a variety of tours in and around Mazatlán, including a colonial tour (US$60) to the foothill towns of Concordia and Copala, and a tequila-factory tour (US$45).

Festivals & Events

Carnaval CARNIVAL

(www.carnavalmazatlan.net) Mazatlán has Mexico's most flamboyant Carnaval celebrations. For the week leading up to Ash Wednesday, the town goes on a nonstop partying spree. Reserve a hotel room in advance.

CineSeptiembre FILM

(☎669-176-46-35; www.cineseptiembre.com; Carnaval Centro) An annual international film festival that has an emphasis on Spanish-language shorts and features, with over 80 films selected for competition each year. Screenings take place in the beautiful Teatro Ángela Peralta (p502).

Festival Cultural Mazatlán ARTS

(www.culturamazatlan.com) If you love the performing arts, plan to visit in November and December and witness captivating theatrical and musical performances in and around the Teatro Ángela Peralta (p502).

First Friday Artwalk ARTS

(www.artwalkmazatlan.com; 4-8pm, 1st Friday of the month, Nov-May) Get a taste of Mazatlán's arts scene through this art walk, held on the first Friday of each month from November through May.

Día de Nuestra Señora de Guadalupe RELIGIOUS

The day of the Virgen de Guadalupe is celebrated on December 12 at the cathedral. Children come in colorful costumes.

Sleeping

Old Mazatlán Condos APARTMENT $$

(Map p494; ☎669-912-29-09, 669-981-43-61; www.oldmazatlancondos.com; Pedregoso 18; studio/1-/2-bedroom apt from M$400-1500;) Perched on a hillside downtown, this tiered brick structure is a dynamite option for longer stays. A labyrinth of comfy studios and one- and two-bedroom apartments – all with wi-fi, well-equipped kitchenettes and individual water heaters – overlooks a central pool and bar area with lounge chairs, gas and charcoal grills, and a shared 'party kitchen.'

The roof terrace has a bird's-eye view of the city and beaches. Book well in advance – snowbirds pack the place from December through April. Rates are slashed in half during the off-season.

Las Girasoles APARTMENTS $$

(Map p497; ☎669-163-99-97, 669-913-52-88; mazatlanrental@hotmail.com; Av Las Gaviotas 709; studios from M$500;) A leafy complex of decent, if dark, apartments and suites on a quiet neighborhood street in the Zona Dorada. Expect red-tiled floors, tinted windows (hence the absence of natural light), a kitchenette, a small sitting room with a futon and a big bedroom with one or two beds. The pool area is terrific. One of the best values in the Golden Zone.

Hotel Machado HOTEL $$

(Map p494; ☎669-669-27-30; www.hotelmachado.com; Sixto Osuna 510A; d incl breakfast from M$650;) The only hotel on gorgeous Plazuela Machado is a mixed bag. Despite the funky charm of its checkerboard floors and wrought-iron beds, the rather basic rooms don't live up to the promise of the lovely facade. The hotel's best feature is the high-ceilinged 2nd-floor *salón social* (sitting room), a delightful place to read or simply gaze out over the square.

Hotel La Siesta HOTEL $$

(Map p494; ☎669-981-26-40; www.lasiesta.com.mx; Paseo Olas Altas 11; interior/ocean-view r M$700/800;) Sitting pretty above Playa Olas Altas, La Siesta is a good option if you can snag one of the choice sea-view rooms. Interior rooms, while spacious and tidy, are less appealing. The pleasant central courtyard and attached restaurant are good places to meet other travelers. Check online for discounts.

Hotel Posada Freeman HOTEL $$

(Map p494; ☎800-614-16-52; www.grupoposadadelrio.com; Paseo Olas Altas 79; r from M$74;) A historic 120-room tower hotel circa 1944, it is the closest thing to a business hotel in the downtown area, with marvelous coastal views, terracotta-tiled floors and satellite TV. It's not luxurious and some rooms feel cramped, but all are recently restored, plenty comfy and offer decent walk-in value. The rooftop pool deck is sweet.

Casa de Leyendas B&B $$

(Map p494; ☎669-981-61-80; www.casadeleyendas.com; Carranza 4; r incl breakfast US$89-125;) Affable expats play host to one of Old Mazatlán's homiest B&Bs. Six comfy rooms, all with coffeemakers, fridges, hairdryers, safes, wi-fi and other nice touches occupy two floors of a sprawling old house near Plazuela Machado and Playa Olas Altas.

Zona Dorada & Around

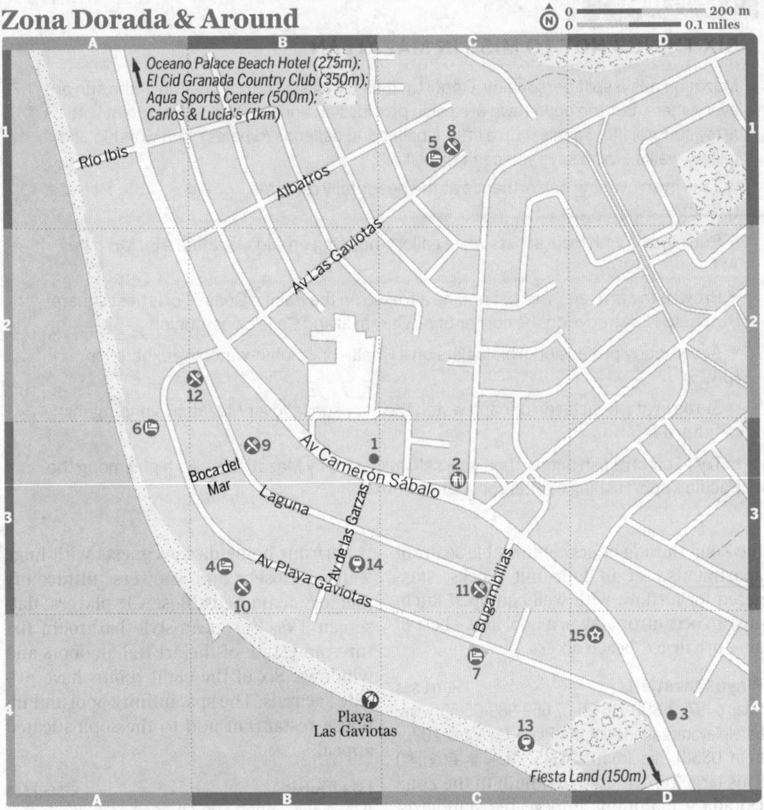

0 200 m
0 0.1 miles

Oceano Palace Beach Hotel (275m); El Cid Granada Country Club (350m); Aqua Sports Center (500m); Carlos & Lucia's (1km)
Río Ibis
Albatros
Av Las Gaviotas
Av Camerón Sábalo
Boca del Mar
Laguna
Av de las Garzas
Av Playa Gaviotas
Bugambilias
Playa Las Gaviotas
Fiesta Land (150m)

Common areas include a library; a lively, well-stocked, reasonably priced bar; a central 'cocktail pool' with Jacuzzi jets; a fully equipped guest kitchen; and two spacious upstairs patios, one with a partial ocean view.

Oceano Palace Beach Hotel HOTEL $$
(☎669-913-06-66; www.oceanopalace.com; Av Camarón Sábalo 2601; r from M$900; P ❄ ☜ ≋) An attractive hotel, with art deco echoes, near the marina. Rooms are among the nicest in Mazatlán, with marble floors in the halls and rooms, terraces overlooking offshore isles, turquoise accent walls and security boxes. Popular among Mexican tourists, there is an inviting pool area overlooking the sea.

Motel Marley MOTEL $$
(Map p497; ☎669-913-55-33; travelbymexico.com/sina/marley; Playa Gaviotas 226; 1-/2-bedroom apt M$1080/1500; P ❄ ☜ ≋) The most atmospheric of the string of low-budget spots in

Zona Dorada & Around

Activities, Courses & Tours
1 King David B3
2 Mazatlán Surf Center C3
3 Vista Tours D4

Sleeping
4 Las Flores B3
5 Las Girasoles C1
6 Motel Marley A3
7 Playa Mazatlán C4

Eating
8 Casa Loma C1
9 La Cocina de Ana B3
10 Pancho's Restaurant B3
11 Pura Vida C3
12 Tomates Verdes B2

Drinking & Nightlife
13 Joe's Oyster Bar C4
14 Pepe Toro B3

Entertainment
15 Cinemas Gaviotas D4

DON'T MISS

SIX THINGS NOT TO MISS IN MAZATLÁN

Mazatlán has a split personality. Opportunities for classic beachside fun in the sun are everywhere, but the downtown area also provides an unexpected counterpoint with its artsy cultural life. So mix it up a little – ballet and *ballenas* (whales), sun worship and gallery walks... Who says you can't have it all?

➡ Take in an evening performance at the beautifully restored **Teatro Ángela Peralta** (p502).

➡ Rub elbows with local artists while gallery-hopping on Old Mazatlán's **First Friday Artwalk** (p496).

➡ Browse the artisans' market or dine alfresco on the Pacific Coast's prettiest square, **Plazuela Machado**, on the corner of Av Carnaval and Calle Constitución.

➡ Accompany professional biologists on a whale- or dolphin-watching expedition (p495).

➡ Settle in at a beachside bar and watch the fiery sunset over Mazatlán's photogenic **offshore islands**.

➡ Try to catch a fish bigger than yourself, and see why Mazatlán ranks high among the Pacific's sportfishing capitals on a **fishing tour**.

the Zona Dorada offers comfortable seafront apartments, set in four-unit blocks, staggered for airflow, with well-equipped kitchens, an oceanfront lawn, a pool and – best of all – privileged beach access.

Playa Mazatlán HOTEL **$$$**
(Map p497; ☎800-716-95-67, 669-989-05-55; www.hotelplayamazatlan.com; Av Playa Gaviotas 202; r from US$81, ste from US$145; P ⊖ ❄ @ ☎ ≋) This large resort – the first built in the Zona Dorada – maintains impeccable standards. Half of the rooms have ocean views, and all come equipped with satellite TV, private terrace and the thoughtful touches that mark a classy operation. Manicured tropical gardens and a breezy oceanside restaurant make this Mazatlán's most stylish large hotel.

The Jonathon BOUTIQUE HOTEL **$$$**
(Map p494; ☎669-915-63-60; www.jonathonhotel.com; Carnaval 1205; s/d M$1100/1309; P ❄ ☎ ≋) A boutique hotel set in a columnar courtyard complex with a modern spiral staircase. Rooms are good sized with soaker tubs, floating beds, built in hardwood closets and shelving, and a flat-screen TV. It's slightly over the top, but it definitely has the most comfortable rooms in the old town, a great location and a rooftop pool with a view.

Casa Lucila BOUTIQUE HOTEL **$$$**
(Map p494; ☎669-982-11-00; www.casalucila.com; Paseo Olas Altas 16; r US$125-295; ❄ ☎ ≋) This boutique hotel in a lavishly restored waterfront home dazzles guests with huge walk-in closets and showers, ultracomfy memory foam beds, Bose CD players, flat-screen TVs, European-style bathroom fixtures and state-of-the-art Italian doors and windows. Six of the eight rooms have private Jacuzzis. The spa, infinity pool and in-house restaurant add to the sophisticated appeal.

Las Flores RESORT **$$$**
(Map p497; ☎800-699-69-00; www.lasflores.com.mx; Av Playa Gaviotas 212; s/d M$1735/2101; P ❄ ☎ ≋) This tower hotel on Playa Gaviotas gravitas offers recently remodeled rooms on 11 floors, a restaurant and bar with a view, and an aging pool area. Some rooms have a new minimalist look, others sport exposed and whitewashed brick, arcing ceilings and turquoise mosaic baths.

If you get a seafront room on the 10th floor, you will be spending an awful lot of time on your balcony enjoying one of the best views in town.

Eating

With all those fishing and shrimping boats heading out to sea every morning, it's no wonder that Mazatlán is famous for fresh seafood. *Pescado sarandeado* is a delicious charcoal-broiled fish stuffed with onion, tomatoes, peppers and spices, beloved from Sinaloa to Jalisco, and the shrimp served here is as sweet as you'll ever taste.

Old Mazatlán

Surrounded by atmospheric eateries, elegant Plazuela Machado is sublime in the evening when jazz musicians descend, kids frolic and the plaza is softly lit to create a very romantic ambience.

Nieves de Garrafa de con Medrano ICE CREAM $
(Map p494; cnr Flores & 5 de Mayo; ice cream M$20; 11am-9pm) A local tradition since 1938, this unpretentious family-run cart opposite Mazatlán's Plaza Principal dishes out delicious homemade ice cream to devoted crowds. Try the vanilla, prune, banana or mandarin flavors.

Fonda de Chalo MEXICAN $
(Map p494; Paseo Olas Altas 166; mains M$33-80; 7am-11pm) This streetfront cafe across from the *malecón* does lunch and dinner too, but it's the breakfasts that are popular with Mazatlán's middle-aged locals. Tables are frequently packed for baskets of *pan dulce* (pastries), *chilaquiles* (tortilla strips drenched in salsa) with *machaca* (spiced, shredded dried beef), and *huevos con nopales* (scrambled eggs with cactus paddles).

Fish Tacos Machado MEXICAN $
(Map p494; 669-981-13-75; Sixto Osuna 34; mains from M$70-120; 7am-11pm) It does shrimp cocktails and whole fish dinners, but its fish taco platters are the thing, though they aren't listed on the menu. Order them anyway. They come three to a plate, stuffed with battered and fried fish and shrimp, and served with a dish of slaw, *pico de gallo* (fresh chopped salsa) and a tasty, smoldering roasted-chili salsa.

Puerto Viejo SEAFOOD $$
(Map p494; 669-982-18-86; Paseo Olas Altas 25; mains M$65-100; 10am-11pm) A classic corner bar that can't be ignored for its popular sundowner location, fresh-as-morning seafood, and the crowd of regulars and *ranchero* troubadours. Locals and tourists alike can't help but be charmed. Daily specials include swordfish, marlin soup and shrimp tacos.

★Pedro & Lola FUSION $$
(Map p494; 669-982-25-89; www.restaurantpedroylola.com; Av Carnaval 1303; mains M$69-182; 6pm-1am) This stylish eatery on Plazuela Machado does outstanding small plates, including delectable shrimp empanadas, pork-shank tacos and lobster burritos. The octopus, sautéed in butter, wine, garlic, olive oil and *poblano* chilis, is a smokier take on the Spanish dish, and is very special.

The tuna tacos aren't seared or raw, but yellowtail cubes charred, seasoned and piled on tacos with the flavor and texture of *carnitas* (braised pork). More tortillas are served on the side, along with searing tomatillo salsa, chopped onions and cilantro. Combine, chomp, enjoy. Live jazz is common and the tables on the plaza are a nice place to listen in.

Molika BAKERY, SANDWICHES $$
(Map p494; Domínguez 1503; mains M$95-135; 9am-11pm Mon-Sat) Exquisite sandwiches, salads, pastas, quiches and homemade breads make this Old Mazatlán's hottest lunch and dinner hangout. The high-ceilinged old building, redone with clean modern lines and designer colors, is also a great place to grab a morning pastry, including the fabulous M$5 madeleines, bursting with orange flavor.

El Fish Market SEAFOOD $$
(Map p494; www.elfishmarket.com.mx; Paseo Olas Altas 3; mains M$100-150; 11am-10pm) OK, that Spanglish name may render it inauthentic, but this polished *cevechería* with the sweet sunset views attracts an upmarket Mexican crowd, and its house special ceviche (seafood marinated in lemon or lime juice, garlic and seasonings) comes with shrimp, scallops and tuna. And it rocks.

La Tramoya MEXICAN $$$
(Map p494; 669-985-50-33; Constitución 509; mains M$80-180; 11am-1am) Hearty Mexican meat and seafood dishes are set out on spacious sidewalk tables on Mazatlán's loveliest square, Plazuela Machado. Unconventional choices include *filete azteca* – a steak stuffed with *huitlacoche* (corn fungus). It also does fusion fajitas and burgers.

Topolo MEXICAN $$$
(Map p494; cell phone 669-1360660; www.topolomaz.com; Constitución 629; mains M$130-220; 3-11pm) For a romantic dinner, step into the softly lit courtyard at this Mexican fusion restaurant and wine bar in a historic building near Plazuela Machado. Waiters prepare salsa fresh at your table, while the chefs cook up seafood specialties such as tequila shrimp or fish in lime-and-cilantro sauce.

Zona Dorada & Around

Pura Vida JUICES, SALADS $
(Map p497; ☎669-916-10-10; Bugambilias 18; juices M$28-39, snacks, salads & sandwiches M$33-65; ⏰8am-10:30pm; ✍) It serves salads, sandwiches, Mexican snacks and vegetarian fair, but it is most sought out for its juices and smoothies. Its menu is packed with creative concoctions blended from all the tropical fruit you love, as well as apples, dates, prunes, wheatgrass, spirulina and strawberries.

La Cocina de Ana BUFFET $
(Map p497; ☎669-916-31-19; Laguna 49; meals from M$35; ⏰noon-4pm Mon-Sat) This homey place offers well-prepared buffet-lunch fare including marlin, meatball soup, *chiles rellenos* (chili stuffed with meat or cheese) and *pollo estofado* (stewed chicken). Everything is sold by the kilo, and the menu changes daily.

Tomates Verdes MEXICAN $
(Map p497; ☎669-913-21-36; Laguna 42; meals M$40; ⏰8am-3pm Mon-Sat) Cozy and unpretentious, this breakfast and lunch spot serves dishes such as *pechuga rellena* (stuffed chicken breast) and flavorful soups such as *nopales con chipotle* (spicy cactus). Meals come with soup, a main dish and rice and beans, and the menu changes daily, but despite the name it's not a friend to vegetarians.

Carlos & Lucía's CUBAN, MEXICAN $$
(☎669-913-56-77; www.carlosandlucias.com; Av Camarón Sábalo 2000; mains M$70-200; ⏰8:30am-10:30pm Mon-Sat) What do you get when you combine the talents of a Mexican named Carlos and a Cuban-born chef named Lucía? A vibrant, colorful little restaurant serving specialties from both countries. Try the *plato Carlos y Lucía:* shrimp or fish cooked in brandy, accompanied by rice, veggies and plantains.

Pancho's Restaurant MEXICAN $$
(Map p497; ☎669-914-09-11; Av Playa Gaviotas 408; mains M$110-210; ⏰7am-11pm) Overlooking Playa Las Gaviotas, this is a good spot to catch the sunset, slurp a monster margarita or devour a huge seafood platter including lobster, shrimp, octopus, a whole red snapper and, for good measure, a pair of frog legs.

Casa Loma INTERNATIONAL $$$
(Map p497; ☎669-913-53-98; www.restaurantcasaloma.com; Av Las Gaviotas 104; mains M$82-368; ⏰1:30-10:30pm) At this genteel eatery, enjoy roast duck *à l'orange* or poached fish *blanca rosa* (with shrimp, asparagus and mushrooms) in the swanky dining room, or outdoors by the burbling fountain.

Drinking & Nightlife

Mazatlán has earned its reputation as a nightlife destination with a great selection of high-energy dance clubs frequented by college students visiting from Guadalajara, Monterrey and Mexico City, lending a Mexican spring-break vibe. Most clubs charge admission in the M$100 to M$200 range; admission generally includes a free drink. The scene starts percolating around 10pm and boils over after midnight. While some clubs close at 2am, several others remain lively until 5am. If you're more partial to sipping and people watching, head to Paseo Olas Altas or deeper into Old Mazatlán and you'll find a home.

★ **Axesso** BAR
(Map p494; ☎669-9910-1717; www.facebook.com/axessosushibar; crnr Domínguez & Escobedo; ⏰1pm-midnight) This hot pink bubble of fun looks like it was seeded here in the '80s, and we can't vouch for the sushi – which is its day job – but when local bands rock, the heads start piling in and it can get wild. It's certainly the best bet for nightlife midweek.

Hotel Belmar Bar BAR
(Map p494; www.hotelbelmar.com.mx; Paseo Olas Altas 166; ⏰11am-2am) One of the two hippest drinking spots for young people on the waterfront at research time. It's steamy *azulejo*-tiled walls, old tile floors and wood paneling practically bead with sweat. So try and grab a sidewalk table where you can sip *ballenas* (1L canons of Pacífico) or buckets of beer to be swilled from, gulp, plastic cups.

Fiesta Land CLUB
(☎669-989-16-00; Av del Mar s/n) That ostentatious white castle on Punta Camarón at the south end of the Zona Dorada is the undisputed epicenter of Mazatlán's nightlife. Inside its walls are a half-dozen clubs, including several of the city's most popular dance spots.

Valentino's draws a mixed crowd to three dance floors throbbing with hip-hop and

WORTH A TRIP

SINALOA'S COLONIAL GEMS

Several small, picturesque colonial towns in the Sierra Madre foothills make pleasant day trips from Mazatlán.

Concordia, founded in 1565, has an 18th-century church with a baroque facade and elaborately decorated columns. The village is known for its manufacture of high-quality pottery and hand-carved furniture. It's about a 45-minute drive east of Mazatlán; head southeast on Hwy 15 for 20km to Villa Unión, turn inland on Hwy 40 (the highway to Durango) and go another 20km.

Also founded in 1565, **Copala**, 40km past Concordia on Hwy 40, was one of Mexico's first mining towns. It still has its colonial church (1748), period houses and cobblestoned streets. It's a 1½-hour drive from Mazatlán.

Rosario, 76km southeast of Mazatlán on Hwy 15, is another colonial mining town. It was founded in 1655 and its most famous feature is the towering gold-leaf-covered altar in its church, Nuestra Señora del Rosario. You can also visit the home of beloved songstress Lola Beltrán, whose long recording career made *ranchera* (Mexico's urban 'country music') popular in the mid-20th century.

In the mountains north of Mazatlán, **Cosalá** is a beautiful colonial mining village that dates from 1550. It has an 18th-century church, a mining museum in a colonial mansion on the plaza, and two simple but clean hotels. To get here, go north on Hwy 15 for 113km to the turnoff (opposite the turnoff for La Cruz de Alota on the coast) and then climb 45km into the mountains.

Latin music; Bora Bora is popular for its open-air dance floor and lax policy on bar-top dancing; and Sumbawa Beach Club is the perfect after-hours spot for dancing in the sand, lounging on an oversized mattress or cooling off in the pool.

Joe's Oyster Bar BAR
(Map p497; ☎669-983-53-33; www.joesoysterbar.com; Av Playa Gaviotas 100; ⏲11am-4am) Part of the Ramada Resort, this popular beachside bar with a neverending two-for-one happy hour is a sports bar by day, and morphs into a DJ-fueled disco that goes ballistic after 11pm, when it's packed with college kids dancing on tables, chairs and each other.

Looney Bean CAFE
(Map p494; ☎669-988-10-39; www.looneybean-maz.jimdo.com; Paseo Olas Altas; coffee drinks M$25-35, pastries M$30; ⏲7:30am-10pm) A terrific local coffee shop on the main seaside drag with strong coffee and espresso drinks and strawberry scones – bigger than your face – that are almost impossible to eat in one sitting, though they are that good you may try.

Pepe Toro GAY
(Map p497; ☎669-914-41-76; www.pepetoro.com; Av de las Garzas 18; ⏲11pm-5am Thu-Sun) This colorful club attracts a fun-loving, mostly gay crowd. On Saturday night there's a drag strip show at 1am.

Vitrolas Bar GAY
(Map p494; ☎669-985-22-21; www.vitrolasbar.com; Frías 1608; ⏲7pm-2am Thu-Sun) This gracious gay bar in a beautifully restored building is romantically lit and, overall, more button-down than mesh muscle shirt. It's also a popular spot for karaoke.

☆ Entertainment

What could be better than a day on a warm beach followed by a night in a town that really knows how to party? Choose from throbbing discos and a much-loved theater. For entertainment listings check **Pacific Pearl** (www.pacificpearl.com), available in hotel lobbies around town and online.

Cinemas Gaviotas CINEMA
(Map p497; ☎669-984-28-48; www.cinemasgaviotas.com.mx; Av Camarón Sábalo 218; admission Thu-Tue M$25, Wed M$20-25) Six screens showing recent releases, including some in English.

★ **Teatro Ángela Peralta** THEATER
(Map p494; ☎ext 103, 669-982-44-47; www.culturamazatlan.com; Av Carnaval 47) To feel the pulse of Mazatlán's burgeoning culture scene, a night at the Peralta is a must. Built in 1860, the theater was lovingly restored over five years to be reopened in 1992. It has an intimate auditorium with three narrow, stacked

balconies. Events of all kinds are presented – movies, concerts, opera, theater and more.

A kiosk on the walkway out front announces current and upcoming events. The schedule is fullest in November and December during the Festival Cultural Mazatlán.

Shopping

The Zona Dorada is replete with tourist-oriented stores that sell clothes, jewelry, pottery and crafts.

Old Mazatlán's Centro Mercado (p491) offers a classic Mexican market experience, complete with vegetable stands, spice dealers, food stalls and shops selling bargain-priced crafts.

Casa Etnika ARTS & CRAFTS
(Map p494; ☎669-136-01-39; www.facebook.com/CASAETNIKA; Sixto Osuna 50; ⏲9am-7pm Mon-Sat) Family-run Casa Etnika offers a small, tasteful inventory of unique objects from Mexico and elsewhere.

Nidart CERAMICS, HANDICRAFTS
(Map p494; ☎669-985-59-91; www.nidart.com; Libertad 45; ⏲10am-6pm Mon-Fri, 10am-2pm Sat) Sells handmade leather masks and ceramics from its in-house studio, and also represents numerous other local artisans.

Gandara Bazaar GIFTS, HANDICRAFTS
(Map p494; ☎669-136-06-65; Constitución 616; ⏲10am-8pm) Enter through the *azulejo*-laid walkway into this wonderful coutryard gallery filled with drums, sculpture, masks, crosses, dolls made from gourds, hearts made from glass... It has a fair amount of mass-produced stuff, but there's some interesting Chinesco ceramic work too.

Information

It's become de rigueur in Mazatlán for hotels and cafes to offer free wi-fi to all.

Banamex Old Mazatlán (Juárez s/n); Zona Dorada (Av Camarón Sábalo) One of many banks near the Plaza Principal and in the Zona Dorada.

Clínica Balboa (☎669-916-79-33; Av Camarón Sábalo 4480; ⏲24hr) Well-regarded, English-speaking walk-in medical clinic.

Emergency (☎060)

Fire (☎669-981-27-69)

Go Mazatlan (Map p494; www.gomazatlan.com) Offers information about Mazatlán and around.

Main Post Office (Map p494; Juárez s/n) On the east side of the Plaza Principal.

Tourist Police (☎669-914-84-44)

Getting There & Away

AIR

General Rafael Buelna International Airport (☎669-982-23-99; www.oma.aero/es/aeropuertos/mazatlan; Carretera Internacional al Sur s/n) is 27km southeast of the Zona Dorada. Carriers servicing the airport include the following:

Aeroméxico (www.aeromexico.com) Zona Dorada (☎669-914-11-11; Av Camarón Sábalo 310); Airport (☎669-982-34-44; Airport) Direct services to Guadalajara and Mexico City.

VivaAerobus (☎Monterrey 81-8215-0150; www.vivaaerobus.com; Airport) Direct services to La Paz (Baja California), Mexico City and Monterrey.

Volaris (☎800-122-80-00; www.volaris.mx; Airport) Direct service to Tijuana.

BUSES FROM MAZATLÁN

DESTINATION	FARE (M$)	DURATION	FREQUENCY (DAILY)
Culiacán	121	2½hr	very frequent
Durango	390-548	7-8hr	7
Guadalajara	355-380	7-8hr	very frequent
Los Mochis	350-400	5-6½hr	hourly
Manzanillo	683-758	12-13hr	10:20pm
Mexicali	1045-1175	24-25hr	frequent
Mexico City (Terminal Norte)	871-986	13-16hr	frequent
Monterrey	1021-1100	14-16hr	2
Puerto Vallarta	450	7-8hr	6
Tepic	230-260	4-5hr	frequent
Tijuana	1159-1310	26-28hr	frequent

BOAT

Baja Ferries (☎800-337-74-37; www.bajaferries.com; seat adult/child one way M$1078/539; ⏰ticket office 8am-4pm Mon-Fri, 8am-3pm Sat, 9am-3pm Sun), with a terminal at the southern end of town, operates ferries between Mazatlán and La Paz in Baja California Sur (actually to the port of Pichilingue, 23km from La Paz). The 16-hour ferry to Pichilingue departs at 4pm (you should be there with ticket in hand at 2pm) on Monday, Wednesday and Friday from the terminal. Strong winter winds may cause delays.

BUS

The full-service **Central de Autobuses** (Main Bus Station; ☎669-982-83-51; Ferrusquilla s/n) is just off Avenida Ejército Mexicano, three blocks inland from the northern end of Playa Norte. All bus lines operate from separate halls in the main terminal.

Local buses to small towns nearby (such as Concordia, Copala and Rosario) operate from a smaller terminal, behind the main one.

CAR & MOTORCYCLE

Local all-inclusive rental rates begin at around M$600 per day during the high season. Online booking is often cheaper.

Alamo (www.alamo.com.mx) Airport (☎669-981-22-66; Airport); Zona Dorada (☎669-913-10-10; Av Camarón Sábalo 410)

Budget (www.budgetmazatlan.com) Airport (☎669-982-12-20; Airport); Zona Dorada (☎669-913-20-00; Av Camarón Sábalo 413)

Europcar (www.europcar.com.mx) Airport (☎669-954-81-15; Airport); Zona Dorada (☎669-913-33-68; Av Camarón Sábalo 357)

Hertz (www.hertz.com) Airport (☎669-985-08-45; Airport); Zona Dorada (☎669-913-60-60; Av Camarón Sábalo 314)

Getting Around

Mazatlán is an easy town to navigate by bicycle, as the *malecón* leads from downtown all the way to the Zona Dorada. You can rent new cruisers, with baskets or baby seats, perfect for the *malecón* from **Baikas** (☎669-910-19-99; bikes per hr/half-day/full day M$70/200/300).

TO/FROM THE AIRPORT

Taxis and *colectivos* (minibuses picking up and dropping off passengers along predetermined routes) operate from the airport to town (27km). Tickets (*colectivo* M$100-150, taxi M$310-350) can be purchased for both at a booth just outside the arrival hall. There is no public bus running between Mazatlán and the airport.

BUS

Local buses run from 6am to 10:30pm. Regular white buses cost M$7; air-con green buses cost M$10.

To get into the city center of Mazatlán from the bus terminal, go to Avenida Ejército Mexicano and catch any bus going south. Alternatively, walk 300m from the bus terminal to the beach and take a Sábalo–Centro bus heading south to the city center.

Major routes:

Route Playa Sur Travels south along Avenida Ejército Mexicano, near the bus terminal and through the city center, passing the Centro Mercado, then to the ferry terminal and El Faro.

Route Sábalo–Centro Travels from the Centro Mercado to Playa Norte via Juárez, then north on Avenida del Mar to the Zona Dorada and further north on Avenida Camarón Sábalo.

TAXI

Mazatlán has a special type of taxi called a *pulmonía*, a small open-air vehicle similar to a golf cart. There are also regular red-and-white and green-and-white taxis. Rates for rides within Mazatlán range from M$50 to M$100, depending on your bargaining skills, the time of day and whether or not there is a cruise ship in port.

MEXCALTITÁN

☎323 / POP 818

This ancient island village, settled some time around the year AD 500, is believed by some experts to be Aztlán, the ancestral homeland that the Aztecs left around AD 1091 to begin their generations-long migration to Tenochtitlán (modern Mexico City). Proponents point to the striking similarities between the cruciform design of Mexcaltitán's streets and the urban layout of early Tenochtitlán. A pre-Hispanic bas-relief in stone found in the area is also provided as evidence – it depicts a heron clutching a snake, an allusion to the sign the Aztecs hoped to find in the promised land.

These days Mexcaltitán is foremost a shrimping town. Men head out into the surrounding wetlands, which are spectacular, in the early evening in small boats, to return just before dawn with their nets bulging. All day long, shrimp are spread out to dry on any available surface in the town, making the prospect of an afternoon stroll a pungent, picturesque proposition.

Tourism has scarcely made a mark here. Mexcaltitán has one hotel, a couple of pleasant waterside restaurants and a small museum, making it a pleasant place to visit for a night.

Sights & Activities

Museo Aztlán del Origen MUSEUM

(admission M$5; 9am-5pm Mon-Sat, to 2pm Sun) This small but enchanting museum, on the northern side of the plaza, offers Spanish-language exhibits explaining the limited collection of basketry and pottery, and larger displays on some of Mexico's most famous Aztec archaeological sites. It also has a reproduction of a fascinating long scroll (the *Códice Ruturini*), telling the story of the Aztec people's travels, with notes in Spanish.

Boat Trips BOAT TOUR

You can arrange boat trips on the lagoon for bird-watching, fishing and sightseeing – every family has one or more boats.

Festivals & Events

Semana Santa RELIGIOUS

Holy Week is celebrated in a big way here. On Good Friday a statue of Christ is put on a cross in the church, then taken down and carried through the streets.

Fiesta de San Pedro Apóstol RELIGIOUS

During this raucous late-June festival, which celebrates the patron saint of fishing, statues of St Peter and St Paul are taken out onto the lagoon in decorated *lanchas* (fast, open motorboats).

Sleeping & Eating

Don't leave town without trying the local specialty of *albóndigas de camarón* (battered-and-fried shrimp balls served with a savory broth) or perhaps a rich *jugo de camarón* (shrimp juice) or *paté de camarón*. The shrimp *tamales* sold in the morning from a wheelbarrow on the streets are another local culinary highlight. Cheery touts in the town square will try to lure you to restaurants they represent, all of which offer similar menus.

Hotel Ruta Azteca HOTEL $

(323-235-60-20; Venecia s/n; r per person M$250-700) The town's only hotel is run by a lovely family. Rooms are simple and clean enough for a night; ask for one out the back that has a view of the lagoon.

Mariscos Kika SEAFOOD $

(323-235-60-54; mains M$70-80; 8am-6pm) For fish, shrimp and octopus cooked a dozen ways, hop on a boat to this family-run place on a small island just across from Mexcaltitán's main dock.

★**La Alberca** SEAFOOD $$

(323-235-60-27; mains M$65-100; 10am-7pm) On the east shore, accessible by a rickety wooden walkway, La Alberca has a great lagoon view and a menu completely devoted to shrimp. Considered by many islanders to be the best, it does shrimp empanadas, shrimp ceviche and shrimp *albóndigas*, which come dry, as an appetizer, or in a chili-inflected shrimp broth, which is wonderful especially when you stir in a dollop of house-made tomatillo salsa! Beers are only M$10.

Getting There & Away

Catch a bus from San Blas (M$50, 1½ hours) or Tepic (M$46, 1½ hours) to the town of Santiago Ixcuintla, 7km west of Hwy 15 and about 70km northwest of Tepic. Once in Santiago, take a *colectivo* (M$25, 40 minutes, four daily) or taxi (M$200) to La Batanga, a small wharf where *lanchas* depart for Mexcaltitán. The arrival and departure times of the *lanchas* are coordinated with the *colectivo* schedule. The boat journey takes 15 minutes and costs M$20 per person. If you miss the *lancha*, you can hire a private one for M$80 per person between 8am and 7pm.

SAN BLAS

323 / POP 8700

The tranquil fishing village of San Blas, 70km northwest of Tepic, has been slated by government tourism officials to become a big resort town for decades. That's not to say it's changed much. It's still a peaceful, drowsy backwater, and therein lies its charm. Visitors come to enjoy isolated beaches, fine surfing, abundant birdlife, and tropical jungles reached by riverboats.

San Blas was an important Spanish port from the late 16th century to the 19th century. The Spanish built a fortress here to protect their trading galleons from marauding British and French pirates. It was also the port from which Junípero Serra, the 'Father' of the California missions, embarked on his northward peregrination. While on either side of the main drag, San Blas is just another cobblestoned backwater, on Avenida Juárez itself, the uniform whitewashed facades lend a dreamy revival quality that is immediately endearing.

Sights & Activities

Life on the water is a recurring theme here, from beaches and offshore islands to boat tours through local estuaries where birds and wildlife abound.

La Contaduría Fort FORTRESS, RUINS

(admission M$10; 8am-7pm) Climb to the top of the Cerro de la Contaduría, and stroll around the ruins of the 18th-century Spanish La Contaduría Fort, where colonial riches were once amassed and counted before being shipped off to Mexico City or the Philippines. The place is still guarded by a collection of corroded cannons.

Nearby are the gorgeous ruins of the **Templo de la Virgen del Rosario** (admission $10), built in 1769. You'll find the road up just west of the bridge over Estuario San Cristóbal.

Beaches

The beach closest to the town is **Playa El Borrego**, at the end of Azueta. It's a wide sweep of grey sand with decent waves. Swimming can be treacherous – beware of rip currents and heed locals' warnings. A handful of old gauchos offer **horse tours** (M$50) on the beach, which last 15 to 30 minutes.

The best beaches are southeast of town around Bahía de Matanchén, starting with **Playa Las Islitas**, 7km from San Blas. To get here, take the main road toward Tepic and turn off to the right after about 4km. This paved road goes east past the village of Matanchén, where a dirt road goes south to Playa Las Islitas and continues on to follow 8km of wonderfully isolated beach. Further down on the paved road, both **Playa Los Cocos** and **Playa Miramar**, also popular for surfing, have *palapas* under which you can lounge and drink fresh coconut milk.

Surfing

Beginner and intermediate surfers choose to hone their skills at San Blas because of its many beach and point breaks. The season starts in May, but the waves are fairly mellow until September and October when the south swell brings long rides. Surf spots include El Borrego, Las Islitas, Second Jetty (adjacent to Stoner's Surf Camp), La Puntilla (by a river mouth south of Playa El Borrego), Stoner's (further south, between San Blas and Las Islitas) and El Mosco (west of San Blas on Isla del Rey).

At Playa El Borrego, **Stoner's Surf Camp** (www.stonerssurfcamp.com; board rental per day M$200, lessons per hr M$200) is the nexus of the scene and offers rentals and lessons. **Natural Surf School** (Playa El Borrego; boards per hour M$50, lessons M$200; Sat & Sun only), a tiny palm-thatched kiosk closer to the breakwater, is the upstart. It rents boards and offer lessons, which include 20 minutes of beach instruction, an hour of instruction in the water and an extra hour to hone your skills on your own.

Tours

A boat trip through the jungle to the freshwater spring of **La Tovara** (324-285-07-21, 323-108-41-74; www.latovara.com) – a federally protected estuary – is a San Blas highlight. Small boats go from the *embarcadero* at the eastern edge of town, or from the main dock 4.5km further east on the road to Matanchén. The three-hour trips go up Estuario San Cristóbal to the spring, passing thick jungle and mangroves. There's a restaurant at La Tovara, where you can stop for lunch, or you can extend the trip to the **Cocodrilario** (Crocodile Nursery), where toothy reptiles are reared in captivity for release in the wild. A group of up to four people costs M$480 to go to La Tovara (two hours round trip) and M$600 to the Cocodrilario (three hours). Each additional person pays M$110 to M$140, depending on the destination.

More boat trips depart from a landing on Estuario El Pozo. They include a trip to **Piedra Blanca** (M$400 for up to six people, one hour) to visit a statue of the Virgin, to **Isla del Rey** (M$15 per person, five minutes) just across from San Blas, and to **Playa del Rey**, a 20km beach on the other side of the Isla del Rey peninsula. Here you can also hire boatmen to take you on bird-watching excursions (M$400 first hour for up to six people, M$300 per hour thereafter).

Isla Isabel makes for an interesting overnight trip. It's a national park and protected ecological preserve three hours northwest of San Blas by boat. The island is a bird-watcher's paradise, but there are no facilities, so be prepared for self-sufficient camping. You can fish your dinner, but tour operators will also help negotiate good prices with local fishermen. Overnight trips generally go for M$8000 for up to six people.

San Blas

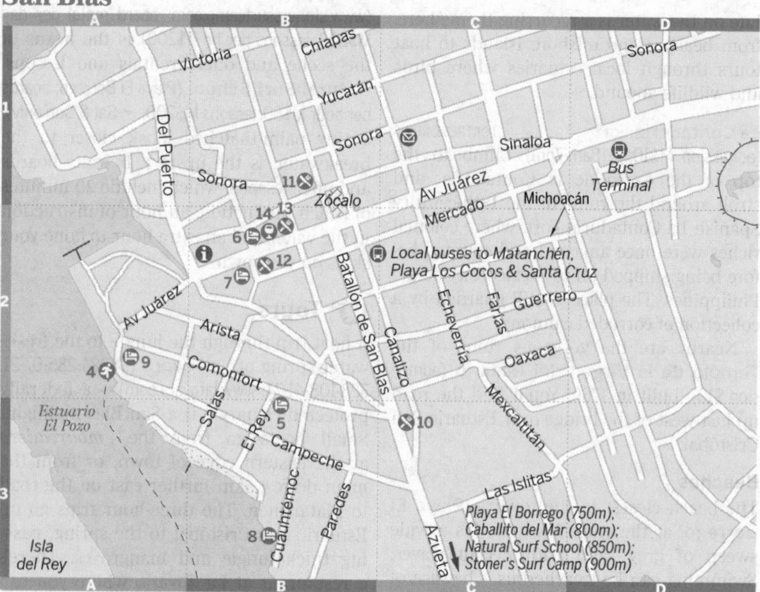

Festivals & Events

Festival Internacional de Aves Migratorias BIRD-WATCHING
(www.avessanblas.uan.mx) Bird-watchers flock to San Blas in late January or early February for the week-long International Migratory Bird Festival. Highlights include tours with English-speaking ornithologists and nightly entertainment in the plaza.

Sleeping

San Blas has plenty of very reasonably priced accommodations.

Estancia Las Flores GUESTHOUSE $
(323-232-30-28; Av Juárez 49; r M$350;) Just four rooms in a budget courtyard hotel on the main drag. The rooms are all cinder-block construction but the tiled floors are clean, the TV has cable, the crochet bedspreads are artful, and so are the baths and wood furnishings.

Stoner's Surf Camp CABAÑAS, CAMPGROUND $
(323-232-22-25; www.stonerssurfcamp.com; Playa El Borrego; campsites per person M$50, cabins M$150-400;) The rustic *cabañas* (cabins) have electricity, mosquito nets and fans at this friendly traveler hangout and surf center. The choicest digs are the rickety, shaggy stilted *cabañas* on the beach. There's space to camp, a communal kitchen, lots of hammocks and a restaurant serving well-prepared fare. Guests in the *cabañas* get free use of bikes plus discounts at the surf center.

Casa Roxanna Bungalows BUNGALOW $$
(323-285-05-73; www.casaroxanna.com; El Rey 1; d M$600-700, q M$700-800;) This refined haven offers eight bungalows of varying sizes; angle for one of the larger upstairs units with full kitchen and screened porch overlooking the pool and manicured grounds. English is spoken and discounts are offered for longer stays.

Hotelito Casa de las Cocadas HOTEL $$
(323-285-90-60; www.lascocadas.sanblasrivieranayarit.com/instalaciones; Av Juárez 145; d M$555;) This small hotel down by the boat docks offers clean, simple yet bright rooms surrounding a central pool, with low-season rates under M$500.

Hotel Marina San Blas HOTEL $$
(323-285-08-12; www.facebook.com/marinasanblas; Cuauhtémoc 197; s/d M$825/970;) Set near the mouth of the river, and within view of the harbor, is this meticulously mantained three-star resort. The grounds are

San Blas

Top Sights

1 La Contaduría Fort E1
2 Templo de la Virgen del Rosario E1

Activities, Courses & Tours

3 Boats to La Tovara & Cocodrilario F1
4 Fishing lanchas & boats to Islands A2

Sleeping

5 Casa Roxanna Bungalows B3
6 Estancia Las Flores B2
7 Hotel Hacienda Flamingos B2
8 Hotel Marina San Blas B3
9 Hotelito Casa de las Cocadas A2

Eating

10 Juan Bananas C3
11 Mercado B1
12 Ofro's B2
13 Wala Wala B2

Drinking & Nightlife

14 Billy Bob's B2

lovely, guests get a free hour's kayak rental, and kitschy marine-themed rooms have lighthouse lamps, and a strange amalgamation of cinder block and tile, but are spotless and comfy with river views and cable TV.

★Hotel Hacienda Flamingos HOTEL $$
(☎323-285-09-30; www.sanblas.com.mx/flamingos; Av Juárez 105; r from M$825, ste from M$970; P ❄ 🛜 🏊) This restored colonial gem provides the classiest accommodations in town. The spacious rooms and courtyard are evocative of old Mexico without even a whiff of kitsch. There's a lounge serving well-crafted cocktails and *botanas* (snacks).

Eating

San Blas is a casual town with casual restaurants and beachfront *palapas,* all serving fresh seafood. Cheaper eats including *tortas* (sandwiches), *jugos* (juices) and *licuados* (milkshakes) can be found at the local **mercado** (cnr Sinaloa & Batallón de San Blas).

Juan Bananas BAKERY $
(Batallón de San Blas 219; banana bread M$45-50; ⏲8am-8pm) For four decades this little bakery has been cranking out some of the world's best banana bread; with any luck, you'll get a loaf hot from the oven. Juan himself is a terrific source of local information.

Ofro's MEXICAN $$
(Av Juárez 64; mains M$50-100; ⏲7am-10pm) A charming high-ceilinged, concrete-floor cafe serving good breakfasts, shrimp, chicken and potato tacos, and *comidas* (lunch main meal) featuring fish and chicken *al gusto.*

Restaurant Alicia SEAFOOD $$
(Playa El Borrego; mains M$70-110, lobster M$220; ⏲8am-7pm) One of the humbler yet more popular of the beachfront *comedores* (food stalls) on Playa El Borrego. The *pescado sarandeado* is delicious and it does all the fried-fish dishes as well as ceviche and *cocteles* (seafood cocktails).

Wala Wala MEXICAN $$
(☎323-285-08-63; Av Juárez 183; mains M$75-140; ⏲7am-10pm Mon-Sat; 🛜) This cheerfully decorated restaurant serves tasty home-style meals, including specialties such as lobster and *pollo con naranja* (chicken with orange). In high season there's live music three nights a week.

Caballito del Mar SEAFOOD $$
(Playa El Borrego; mains M$90-220; ⏲noon-6pm) Under the same management as La Isla, this is among the best of the seafood *enramadas* (thatch-covered, open-air restaurants) lined up along Playa El Borrego.

Drinking & Nightlife

The nightlife in San Blas is unexciting but pleasant enough, with a selection of low-key bars and bar flies.

Cafe Del Mar LOUNGE

(☎323-285-10-81; Av Juárez 5; ⊙6pm-midnight) The coolest and classiest watering hole in town by far, it's set across from the plaza and above a boutique, with whitewashed walls hung with authentic indigenous masks. Jazz, salsa, reggae and rock pours from the sound system, mingling with the tropical breeze.

Billy Bob's BAR

(Av Juárez s/n; ⊙11am-midnight) This popular local dive has sports on TV, loud *ranchero* music from morning til night and two-for-one margaritas at happy hour.

Information

Free municipal wi-fi is available within a 150m radius of the central plaza, and most hotels and restaurants have wi-fi too.

Banamex ATM (Av Juárez s/n)

Cybernet Web On (Canalizo 155B; per hr M$15; ⊙9am-9pm Mon-Sat, 5-9pm Sun) One of several net cafes north of the plaza.

Health Clinic (☎323-285-12-07; cnr Azueta & Campeche; ⊙24hr)

Post Office (cnr Sonora & Echeverría)

Tourist Office (☎323-285-00-73; Av Juárez s/n; ⊙9am-3pm Mon-Fri) This basic tourist office, in the Casa de Cultura, has maps and brochures about the area and the state of Nayarit.

Getting There & Around

The little **bus terminal** (Av Juárez) is served by Norte de Sonora and Estrella Blanca 2nd-class buses. For many destinations to the south and east, it may be quicker to go to Tepic first. For Mazatlán, transfer in Tepic. Daily departures include the following:

Puerto Vallarta (M$162, 3½ hours, 7:30am, 10am, 1:30pm and 4:30pm)

Tepic (M$56, 1½ hours, hourly 6am to 8pm)

Between 7am and 3pm, hourly buses depart the bus station for Playa Las Islitas (M$15), Playa Los Cocos (M$20) and Playa Miramar (M$27). Second-class buses also depart from the corner of Canalizo and Mercado several times a day, serving all the villages and beaches on Bahía de Matanchén.

Taxis will take you around town and to nearby beaches – a good option with two or more people. Rent bicycles from Wala Wala for M$80 per day.

TEPIC

☎311 / POP 336,000 / ELEVATION 920M

Founded by the nephew of Hernán Cortés in 1524, Tepic is the capital of Nayarit state, a predominantly middle-class place with a veritable hum of provincial bustle playing out on its narrow streets. Indigenous Huicholes are often seen here, wearing their colorful traditional clothing, and Huichol artwork is sold on the street and in several shops.

The ornate **cathedral** on **Plaza Principal**, dedicated in 1804, casts a regal eye over the plaza. Opposite the cathedral is the **Palacio Municipal** (City Hall), where you'll often find Huicholes under the arches selling handicrafts at reasonable prices. Residing in a palatial 18th-century neoclassical house, the **Museo Regional de Nayarit** (☎311-212-19-00; Av México Norte 91; admission M$37; ⊙9am-6pm Mon-Fri, to 3pm Sat) presents exhibitions concerned primarily with pre-Hispanic objects, including ancient pottery and tomb artifacts, as well as colonial painting and Huichol culture.

Tepic is a transport hub, but no longer an essential one, and though you can sift through this not-particularly-attractive town, to find its gifts there's no reason to spend the night. If you do find yourself staying in Tepic, check into **Hotel Real de Don Juan** (☎311-216-18-88; www.realdedonjuan.com; cnr Juárez & Av México Sur; r/ste M$1140/1740; P ❄ @ ☎), a

BUSES FROM TEPIC

DESTINATION	FARE (M$)	DURATION	FREQUENCY (DAILY)
Guadalajara	200-224	3½hr	frequent
Mazatlán	230-260	4-5hr	hourly
Mexico City (Terminal Norte)	820-870	10-11hr	hourly
Puerto Vallarta	193-207	3½-4hr	hourly

beautifully done-up old hotel overlooking Plaza Constituyentes. You'll find excellent ceviche and succulent shrimp dishes at **El Marlin de Tepic** (www.marlindetepic.com; Calzada del Panteon 45; mains M$120-300; ⏲11am-10pm), and the scallops and *aguachiles* – soupy, spicy shrimp cocktail full of onions and tomatoes served in a *molcajete* (mortar and pestle) – at **Taquería Fabian** (Av Leon; tostadas M$50, aguachiles M$120; ⏲11am-6pm) earn raves from locals.

Be warned, in recent years Tepic has attained unwelcome fame as the site of some grisly drug-related murders. While tourists are unlikely to be affected by the violence, it's wise to remain vigilant and avoid driving after nightfall.

Information

Banks, internet cafes and *casas de cambio* (money exchanges) line Avenida México between the two plazas.

City Tourist Office (☎311-215-30-01, 311-215-30-02, ext 2000 311-215-30-00; Plaza Principal; ⏲9am-7pm) On the main plaza.

Post Office (cnr Durango Norte & Morelos Poniente)

Getting There & Away

BUS

The main bus station is on the southeastern outskirts of town; local buses marked 'Estación' make frequent trips between the bus station and downtown, stopping at the corner of Amado Nervo and Durango.

TNS operates a small terminal north of the cathedral near the Río Mololoa, with 2nd-class services to San Blas (M$50, 1½ hours, hourly from 5am to 7:15pm).

Getting Around

Local buses (M$6) operate from around 6am to 9pm. Combis (M$6) operate along Avenida México from 6am to midnight. There are also plenty of taxis, and a taxi stand opposite the cathedral.

AROUND TEPIC

Laguna Santa María del Oro

Surrounded by steep, forested mountains, idyllic Laguna Santa María del Oro fills a volcanic crater 2km around and is thought to be over 100m deep. The clear, clean water takes on colors ranging from turquoise to slate-gray. It's a pleasure to walk around the lake and in the surrounding mountains, spotting birds (some 250 species) and butterflies along the way. You can also climb to an abandoned gold mine, cycle, swim, row on the lake, kayak or fish for black bass and perch. A number of small restaurants serve fresh lake fish and seafood.

Koala Bungalows & RV Park (☎cell phone 311-1347178; www.koalabungalows.com; campsite per person US$6, RV site per couple US$15, r/bungalow from US$42/58) is a peaceful park with a restaurant, campsites and well-maintained bungalows sleeping up to 10 people. Turn left at the end of the road that descends to the lake.

If driving, take the Santa María del Oro turnoff about 40km from Tepic along the Guadalajara road; from the turnoff it's about 10km to Santa María del Oro village, then another 8km to the lake. By bus, catch a 'Santa María del Oro' *colectivo* on Avenida México in Tepic, then change to a *colectivo* marked 'Laguna' at Santa María's town square.

Volcán Ceboruco

This active volcano consisting of two calderas and three cinder cones last erupted in 1870, so you'll be safe walking the short trails at the top. The 15km cobblestoned road up the volcano passes lava fields, *fumaroles* (steam vents), and lush vegetation growing on the slopes. The road begins at the village of Jala, 7km off the highway from Tepic to Guadalajara; the turnoff is 76km from Tepic, 12km before you reach Ixtlán del Río. You can also visit as part of a tour; several Puerto Vallarta–based companies include a stop at the volcano as part of their 'tequila tour' itineraries.

CHACALA

☎327 / POP 320

Despite its charm and beauty, the tiny coastal fishing village of Chacala has somehow retained its status as a somewhat-secret paradise. Located 96km north of Puerto Vallarta and 10km west of Las Varas on Hwy 200, it sits pretty along a beautiful little cove backed by verdant green slopes and edged by rugged black rock formations at either end. With just one main, sandy thoroughfare and a few cobbled side streets, it's an ideal place to unwind and contemplate the horizon.

There's no ATM; banking and communication services are readily available in Las Varas. Wi-fi is widely available at hotels and cafes in town.

Activities

The sea provides most of the action. For **small-boat excursions** ask at the **Capitanía del Pueblo**, a small fishing marina located at the northern tip of the shoreline. **Whale-watching** trips cost M$250 per person, with a four-person minimum. **Fishing trips** cost around M$500 per hour, while a **surfing** expedition to the prime spot La Caleta – where a wicked left-breaking point break thrashes the rocky beach – runs M$500 per person, and includes round-trip service. Tell the captain what time to fetch you. Chacala Hostel & Surf Shop (p510) rents boards (per day US$25). The **swimming** in Chacala's luscious bay is safe and tranquil most of the year. You can also **hike** to La Caleta; it's a challenging but rewarding two-hour effort each way.

Sleeping & Eating

Accommodations here range from the simple to the luxurious. For longer stays with a bit more autonomy, **Chacala Villas** (www.chacalavillas.com) offers a variety of rental housing with full kitchens, starting at US$60 per night, including the recommended **Casa Magica** (two people per night US$90).

Chacala Hostel & Surf Shop HOSTEL $
(☎322-191-27-78; www.nayarit4fun.com; dm M$170, s/d M$350/440) This brick townhouse dangling with bougainvillea and topped with a *palapa*-style rooftop deck rents cars, boards and beds. The super-cute hostel, with attractive ceramic-tiled floors and a vaulted brick ceiling is set up downstairs. Dorms have just three beds each, and there is one private room (with private bath) and full kitchen to share.

Techos de México HOMESTAY $
(www.techosdemexico.com; r M$250-750) Travelers interested in befriending the locals should consider this unique organization (inspired by Habitat for Humanity) that helps Chacala residents build good homes with adjacent guest units. Six local families offer lodging through this program, including the well-established **Casa Aurora** (☎327-219-40-27; casaaurora2@hotmail.com; d with kitchenette M$400-600), one block up from the beach. Look for the distinctive Techos signs as you pass through town.

Hotel las Brisas HOTEL $$
(☎327-219-40-15; www.lasbrisaschacala.com; Av Chacalilla 4; d M$500-850; P❄📶) This centrally located, family-run hotel shares beachfront space with one of Chacala's better seafood restaurants (mains M$75 to M$160). Upstairs are nine clean units with satellite TV; downstairs you'll find shrimp and beer. Sweet.

Hotel Mar de Coral HOTEL $$
(☎327-978-20-98, 327-219-41-09; www.hotelmardecoral.com; d M$700, bungalows M$1200) Set in the center of town across the road from the beach, this new build – with a pool in a shady courtyard lobby – offers spacious and tiled rooms with wall-mounted flat-screen TVs, wooden beds and furnishings, and two-tone pastel paint jobs. What it calls bungalows are much larger rooms with an attached kitchen.

★**Mar de Jade** RESORT $$$
(☎327-219-40-00, in the US 800-257-0532; www.mardejade.com; r per person incl yoga classes & 3 meals US$105-150; P❄📶🏊) This idyllic getaway at the far south end of Chacala's beachfront hosts regular yoga, Zen meditation and wellness retreats, but welcomes independent travellers, too. Crashing waves are audible everywhere on the property, from the spacious rooms with deep-tiled bathtubs, to the sauna, Jacuzzi and spa area, and to the sprawling poolside patio where vegetarian-friendly meals (M$140 to M$200) are served.

High-season treats include wood-fired fish and pizza, free yoga classes in the hardwood-floored studios overlooking the palms and ocean, and weekly cultural events including Latin dancing and temascal (pre-Hispanic steam bath) purification ceremonies. Rates are all-inclusive which make them a bargain.

Chac Mool Cafe CAFE $$
(☎327-291-40-37; www.chacmoolcafe.com; Calle Principal; mains M$55-205; ⏰7am-5pm Mon & Tue, to 9pm Wed-Sun; 📶) Open year-round in the village center, here is an inviting spot for coffee, breakfast, nightly dinner specials and free wi-fi with an ocean view. It accepts credit cards.

Getting There & Away

For Chacala, get off a Puerto Vallarta–Tepic bus at Las Varas and take a *colectivo* (M$25) from there. If you're driving, the Hwy 200 turnoff is 1km south of Las Varas.

SAN FRANCISCO

San Francisco, aka San Pancho, is the latest fishing pueblo turned vacation spot, with prettier beaches and a less obvious gringo footprint than what you'll find in Sayulita. There's less action here too, unless you count those real-life gauchos riding horses through the riverbed and along a gorgeous blonde beach, long, wild and driftwood strewn. The last band of the green river reaches the sea at the south end, where the beach begins and palm-dappled hills rise in the background. The sand eventually abuts a headland sprinkled with tiny homes about 1km further north.

Av Tercer Mundo leads from Hwy 200 into town and the beach, where there is an unstaffed lifeguard tower and three *palapa* restaurants serving the usual fish and ceviche dishes and cold beers. Refugio del Sol (p511), a surf shop and guesthouse, offers stand-up paddle (SUP) board rental per hour/day for M$100/300. There's a lone ATM in the beach plaza. It's best to bring cash, lest you pay the extortionate fee. **Paseos a Caballo** (☎322-175-48-26) offers just that: horse tours on mountain trails and back down to that luscious windswept beach. Ask for Rodolfo.

Sleeping & Eating

★Refugio del Sol & Hostal San Pancho HOSTEL, GUESTHOUSE **$**
(☎311-258-41-61; www.hostalsanpancho.com; Av Tercer Mundo; dm M$190, d fan M$500, aircon M$600-700; ❄📶) This tiny Argentine-Mexican-owned guesthouse and hostel is set above and behind its surf shop, just after the entrance to town. It offers super-clean, simple, yet charming rooms and snazzier suites, which are just bigger rooms with splashier baths and a terrace. The attractive dorms and their shared outdoor bathroom are on the ground floor.

There's a groovy common area upstairs where you'll take your free breakfast and surf the wi-fi signal. It also offers free use of bikes, which come in handy as the beach is about 1km away.

Hotel Cielo Rojo BOUTIQUE HOTEL **$$$**
(☎311-258-41-55; www.hotelcielorojo.com; Calle Asia 6; d US$118; ❄📶) The most polished sleep in San Pancho is located a few blocks from the beach. Rooms are simple, comfortable and stylish with terracotta floors and pastel paint jobs. Rates include breakfast and concierge service. Its restaurant, Bistro Orgánico, receives good marks.

La Chalupa MEXICAN **$**
(Calle México; meals M$50-90) It doesn't look like much from the street, but this sweet little *palapa*-style restaurant, owned by a fisherman and his family, does seafood dishes at nearly half the price of the beach restaurants. At lunch, *comidas corridas* (daily specials) are just 50 pesos.

La Perla MEXICAN **$$**
(☎311-258-43-34; Av Tercer Mundo 48; mains M$20-250; ⏰10am-8pm) This charming eatery on the main road was the town's most popular at research time. It offers burgers and fish sandwiches, *tostadas* piled with ceviche, octopus and shrimp, as well as roasted fish dinners and lobster (M$250). Most dishes range from M$20 to $M130.

Getting There & Away

San Franciscois about 49km north of Puerto Vallarta, just west of Hwy 200. It's best to have wheels to access this town, though there is a bus from Puerto Vallarta that makes one or two stops, takes about 45 minutes and costs M$60.

SAYULITA

☎329 / POP 4000

Once upon a time – OK, it was the late 1990s – Sayulita really *was* a tranquil fishing village. Many of the town's *norteamericano* residents still describe it that way, but the truth is that in peak season the place is swarming with gringos, drawn here by the beautiful sandy beach, amiable surfing scene, great restaurants and tasteful B&Bs. Still, if you want a beach-town getaway where you can abandon the car and truly chill out, Sayulita qualifies.

Sights & Activities

You can arrange bicycle hire, boat trips, horseback riding, trekking or kayaking from operators on the main street. One popular nearby destination is **Playa Los Muertos**, where picnics and bodyboarding top the action. It's a 15-minute walk south along the coast road. You can also hire a boat to take your group out to the uninhabited **Islas Marietas** – a protected national park – for picnicking, snorkeling and swimming. Trips cost MS$2450 for up to five people, and include stops on two islands. It takes about 35 minutes to make the crossing.

Surfing

Sayulita is a classic 'boarder' town. Medium-sized waves pour dependably from both the left and the right, so you can practice your well-honed moves or even take up the sport for the first time. Several local surf shops offer rentals and lessons, including the well-established **Lunazul** (☎ 329-291-20-09; www.lunazulsurfing.com; Calle Marlín 4; SUP/surfboard/bodyboard rentals per day M$300/200/150, group/private lessons per 90min US$40/55; ⏲ 8am-5pm).

Stand Up Sayulita STAND UP PADDLE
(☎ 329-291-35-75; www.standupmex.com; Calle Marlín; per hr/half-/full day M$100/300/500, lessons M$500) This is the place to learn how to commandeer a SUP board and ride waves too. Lessons last an hour and include a free 45-minute paddle afterward. Its groovy surf shop has an attached bar, Iguana Gardens, which serves smoothies in the mornings and cold beer on high-season afternoons.

Sleeping

A good selection of private villas can be browsed on the website **Sayulita Life** (www.sayulitalife.com). The following prices are for the winter high season.

Amazing Hostel Sayulita HOSTEL $$
(☎ 329-291-36-88; www.theamazinghostelsayulita.com; Pelicanos 102; dm M$220, d M$800;) Between the plaza and the Puerto Vallarta bus stop (helpful hint: from the plaza, follow the dirt road upriver before crossing the bridge) this somewhat incongruous white concrete-block hostel complex has three dorms with attached bathrooms, along with two air-conditioned private rooms.

The big backyard beckons guests with a 6m-high climbing wall, swimming pool and BBQ, as well as hammocks for lounging under the mango, lemon and tangerine trees. Bikes rent for M$50 per day, kayaks and surfboards for M$200. The friendly, well-traveled owners offer a wealth of local info.

Hotel Sayulita Central HOTEL $$
(☎ 329-291-38-45, in the USA 646-472-5072; www.hotelsayulitacentral.com; Delfín 7; r from US$50;) Ignore the happy scrawlings in the hostel-like lobby and rise up to classy ceramic-tiled rooms, named for rock bands of yesteryear, bright with sun and creativity. All are super clean, have multihued paint jobs and share a sprawling lounge that is a great place to hang.

Bungalows Jaqueline BUNGALOW $$
(☎ 329-291-30-27; www.bungalowsjaqueline.com; Revolucion 52; studios from US$90;) A wonderful rambling complex of 14 spacious studios with full kitchens, ceramic-tiled floors, thick adobe-like walls, pastel paint jobs, brick or ceramic ceilings, surrounding a small shared pool. All are bright and immaculate and a tremendous year-round value. No air-con.

Hotel Hafa BOUTIQUE HOTEL $$
(☎ 329-291-38-06; www.hotelhafasayulita.com; Revolución 55; r US$50-85;) Minimalist cool is yours at this sweet inn just off the plaza. Rooms have concrete floors, ceiling fans, air-con (for a bit extra), and large baths with brass-bowl sinks. Service is *tranquilo* and the downstairs boutique is a gorgeous browse.

★ **Bungalows Aurinko** BUNGALOW $$$
(☎ 329-291-31-50; www.sayulita-vacations.com; Calle Marlín; s/n; 1-bedroom bungalow M$1150-1530, 2-bedroom bungalow M$1920;) There is a wow factor, with bungalows mashed up in a complex of deconstructed houses with indoor/outdoor living rooms and kitchens, and wonderful bedrooms with river-stone floors, accented by tasteful and vibrant modern art. It's steps from the plaza and the beach.

Eating & Drinking

A foodie paradise, Sayulita has a beguiling selection of small, bistro-style cafes, providing agreeable contrast to the inexpensive *palapas* on the beach and the lively taco and hotdog stands that sprout every evening on the streets surrounding the plaza.

★ **Naty's Cocina** TAQUERÍA $
(☎ 329-291-38-18; Calle Marlín 13; tacos M$12; ⏲ 10am-3pm Mon-Sat) A cute and clean taco stand where tortillas are stuffed per your choice with sliced *poblano* chiliss, potatos, beans and mushrooms, beef, smoked marlin, chicken with *mole* (chili sauce), or pork and cactus paddles. Order at the counter and sit at a little drop-down wood bar or on the bench out front. Locals descend en masse for a reason.

Chilly Willy SEAFOOD $

(Calle Manuel Navarrete; dishes M$10-20, meals M$70; ⏲10am-8:30pm) Set on Calle Manuel Navarrete across from the river is this funky, almost disintegrating corner *taquería* popular with locals. Grab a palm-stump bar stool on the sidewalk and munch *tostadas* piled with shrimp and octopus, seafood cocktails and fish tacos. On Saturday and Sunday it does chicken with *mole* and *carne asada* (marinated and grilled steak), both for M$70.

Panino's BAKERY $

(Delfínes 1; pastries, salads & sandwiches M$18-79; ⏲7am-5pm; ✎) Freshly baked, wonderfully crusty European-style bread, salads and *panini* (including vegetarian and vegan options). If it has an apple strudel, get it!

Cafe El Espresso CAFE $$

(Revolución 51; smoothies M$39, mains M$60-80; ⏲6am-10am Mon-Thu, to 2pm Fri-Sun; 📶) It lives up to its name at this corner breakfast spot on the plaza. The coffee is strong and sensational. The Tropical Heaven smoothie blends pineapple, yogurt, honey and papaya or strawberries with basil and coconut cream, and the Mexican breakfasts are dynamite.

Restaurant El Costeno SEAFOOD $$

(Delfínes; tostadas M$20, mains M$70-120; ⏲1-9pm) An old-school beach bar where tables are sunk in the sand beneath a *palapa* roof swinging with rattan lanterns, the shrimp ceviche is fresh, the beer is icy and the sunsets sublime. If all you want is guacamole, an octopus or shrimp cocktail or ceviche *tostadas* and a cold refreshment with a view, this works.

SAYULITA'S CHANGING TIME ZONE

Sayulita's clocks are set to Central time – unlike most of Nayarit state, which still lives on Mountain time. Sayulita made the switch in March 2011, in order to synchronize its clocks with neighboring Puerto Vallarta and Jalisco. Why the big shift? Turns out there was an epidemic of gringos arriving at Vallarta's airport an hour late and missing their homebound flights, either ignorant of the time zone difference or too blissed out by beach life to care!

Don Pedro's INTERNATIONAL $$

(☎329-291-30-90; www.donpedros.com; Marlin 2; appetizers M$100-175, mains M$185-275; ⏲11am-10pm) The snazziest spot on the beach has a gorgeous view of the sea and international dishes including a nice seared ahi. Its appetizers are more ambitious than its mains. Think: Thai ceviche, a scallop cocktail and an octopus carpaccio, but service is superb and the tequila list is terrific.

☆ Entertainment

Bar Don Pato's LIVE MUSIC

(Calle Marlín 10; ⏲8pm-4am) At the sign of the rubber duck, this lively club on the main plaza pumps out live music six nights a week, with an open mic on Tuesdays.

Shopping

Boutiques offering Mexican handicrafts of varying quality abound in Sayulita.

Revolucion del Sueño BOUTIQUE

(☎329-291-38-50; www.revoluciondelsueno.com; Navarrete 55; ⏲10am-6pm) A French-owned brand, it specializes in silkscreened T-shirts and hipster beach bags – we love the mariachi holding a bouquet of flowers. It also has throw pillows, exquisite jewelry, quirky stickers and decorative art pieces, including outstanding papier-mâché skulls.

ℹ Information

There are a few ATMs in town, including one on the plaza and another at the Oxxo convenience store a block away. All of them charge outrageous fees that far exceed what you'll pay in bank-owned ATMs, and therefore should only be used as a last resort. The nearest full-service bank is in Bucerías, 12km to the south on Hwy 200. Smart travelers stock up on cash on the way here. Wi-fi is widely available in hotels and cafes.

Lun@net (Mariscal 5; per hr M$20; ⏲8am-2pm & 4-9pm Mon-Sat) Just off the plaza. Free wi-fi is also available at cafes on the plaza.

ℹ Getting There & Away

Sayulita is about 35km north of Puerto Vallarta, just west of Hwy 200. Buses (M$30, one hour) operate every 15 minutes or so from the stop in front of Puerto Vallarta's Wal-Mart. For a few more pesos, any northbound 2nd-class bus from the Puerto Vallarta bus terminal will drop you at the Sayulita turnoff, leaving you with a 2km walk into town.

PUNTA MITA

Just south of Sayulita, a stunning jungled, mountainous peninsula tumbles into the sea. Much of it has been tamed and groomed into four- and five-star resorts, some are more polished and sterilized than others – we're looking at you, Four Seasons. But there is also a localized beachfront, strung with (arguably overpriced) seafood restaurants that double as tasty day-trip beach hangs for Vallarta families. You can hire boats to Islas Marieta from here, and the beaches from here to Nuevo Vallarta, a stretch known as **Riviera Nayarit**, are some of the best on the Central Pacific Coast. Far from the mocha rivers, here the water is almost always clear and aquamarine, the sand is white and the surf can get fun, too.

Sleeping & Eating

Imanta RESORT **$$$**

(☎329-298-42-42; www.imantaresorts.com; Montenahuac s/n; d from US$450) The domain of the rich, beautiful and famous – foreign and domestic – this is the top five-star resort on the Central Pacific Coast. Set on 100 jungled hectares, which abut a natural reserve, the hotel and villas are made from stone and loom above a private rocky shore.

Even standard rooms are 175-sq-metre suites, with soaker tubs, day beds and walk-in closets, but for the price, why not indulge in a jungle or oceanfront *casa* where you'll find a private infinity pool to call your own.

Rocío SEAFOOD **$$**

(www.insideputamita.com; mains M$120-280; ⏲9am-6pm) One of the best of the beachfront eateries, the ceviche is particularly fresh and tasty, and if you catch them cleaning fresh-caught tuna or *dorado* (dolphin fish), order it grilled.

Getting There & Away

From Puerto Vallarta, take Hwy 200 north through Bucerías, then veer left toward La Cruz de Huanacaxtle to follow the coast toward the namesake penisnsula. You'll be best served with your own wheels.

PUERTO VALLARTA

☎322 / POP 256,000

Puerto Vallarta – referred to simply as 'Vallarta' by its many aficionados – is one of Mexico's liveliest and most sophisticated resort destinations. Stretching around the sparkling blue Bahía de Banderas (Bay of Flags) and backed by lush palm-covered mountains, one couldn't ask for a better place to while away a cosmopolitan vacation. Each year millions come to laze on the dazzling sandy beaches, browse in the quirky shops, nosh in the stylish restaurants and wander through the picturesque cobbled streets or along its enticing *malecón*. If the pretty town beaches aren't enough, you can venture out on cruises, horseback rides, diving trips and day tours – and be back in time for a late dinner and an even later excursion to one of the many sizzling nightspots on offer. Puerto Vallarta is also the gay beach capital of Mexico.

The 'old' town center, called Zona Centro, is the area north of the Río Cuale, with the small Isla Cuale in the middle of the river. The city's two principal thoroughfares are Morelos and Juárez, which sandwich the Plaza Principal. Many fine houses, quite a few owned by foreigners, are found further up the Río Cuale valley, also known as Gringo Gulch.

South of the river, the Zona Romántica is another tourist district with smaller hotels, restaurants and bars. It has the only two beaches downtown – Playa Olas Altas and Playa de los Muertos. We've concentrated most of our listings in these eminently walkable downtown neighborhoods, which remain the heart and soul of Puerto Vallarta.

North of the city is a strip of giant luxury hotels, the Zona Hotelera; Marina Vallarta, a large yacht marina (9km from the city center); the airport (10km); the bus station (12km); and Nuevo Vallarta, a new area of hotel and condominium developments (18km). To the south of the city are a few more large resorts and some of the area's most beautiful beaches.

Sights

The heart of Zona Centro is the **Plaza Principal**, also called Plaza de Armas, just near the sea between Morelos and Juárez. This is where chain-store modernism blends with the old shoeshine days of pueblo yore. Public events such as gaucho parades and mariachi festivals bloom on the sea side of the plaza near an outdoor amphitheater backed by **Los Arcos** (Plaza Morelos), a row of arches that has become a symbol of the city. The wide **malecón** stretches about 10 blocks north from the amphitheater and is dotted with bars, restaurants, nightclubs and a grand collection of public sculptures. Uphill from the plaza, the crown-topped steeple of the **Templo de Guadalupe** (uphill from Plaza Morelos) is another Vallarta icon.

A trip to Vallarta wouldn't be complete without lingering on **Isla Cuale**, where the city's earliest residents built their humble homes. Upstream you'll notice two rickety cable suspension bridges, connecting the island to the Zona Romántica. And when the sun is tolerable find **Calle Cuauhtémoc**, a winding cobblestone street, and follow it to the upper reaches, where views of lush green hills, dotted with gorgeous homes, rise on either side of a river and loom above the bay below.

Or you could just go to the beach. Those on the Bahía de Banderas have many personalities. Some are buzzing with cheerful activity; others are quiet and private. Two, **Playa Olas Altas** and **Playa de los Muertos** (Beach of the Dead), are handy to downtown; both south of the Río Cuale. At the southern end of Playa de los Muertos is the stretch of sand called **Blue Chairs**, one of Mexico's most famous gay beaches.

North of town, in the Zona Hotelera, are **Playa Camarones**, **Playa Las Glorias**, **Playa Los Tules**, **Playa Las Palmas** and **Playa de Oro**. Nuevo Vallarta also has beaches.

Around 3km south of downtown is the beautiful condo enclave of **Playa Conchas Chinas**. It's a tiny cove favored by families for the shallow and sheltered pools created by the burly rock reef further out. That's where the snorkelers and spear fishermen have fun. Although the cove is small, the beach is blond and reasonably wide. It fronts a lineup of resort condo properties, which means lifeguards are on duty.

About 6km south of Zona Centro, **Playa Palmeras** – named not for the nonexistant palms but for the condo complex of the same name – is a narrow but ample stretch of white sand that runs from a clutch of condo high-rises into a rocky cove. These turquoise shallows are favored by locals for swimming as it's far from rivers, which means clear water year-round. Parking is plentiful and free. Look for the beach just after Punta Negra coming from town.

Mismaloya, the location for *The Night of the Iguana,* is about 12km south of town. The tiny scenic cove is dominated by a gargantuan resort. About 4km past Mismaloya, southwest along the coast, is **Boca de Tomatlán**, a seaside village that's less commercialized than Puerto Vallarta. Buses marked 'Boca' stop at both Mismaloya and Boca de Tomatlán (M$7); the 'Mismaloya' bus only goes as far as Mismaloya.

Further around the southern side of the bay are the more isolated beaches, from east to west, of Las Ánimas, Quimixto and Yelapa, all accessible only by boat. **Playa de las Ánimas** (Beach of the Spirits) is a lovely beach with a small fishing village and some *palapa* restaurants offering fresh seafood. **Quimixto**, not far from Las

Greater Puerto Vallarta

Central Puerto Vallarta

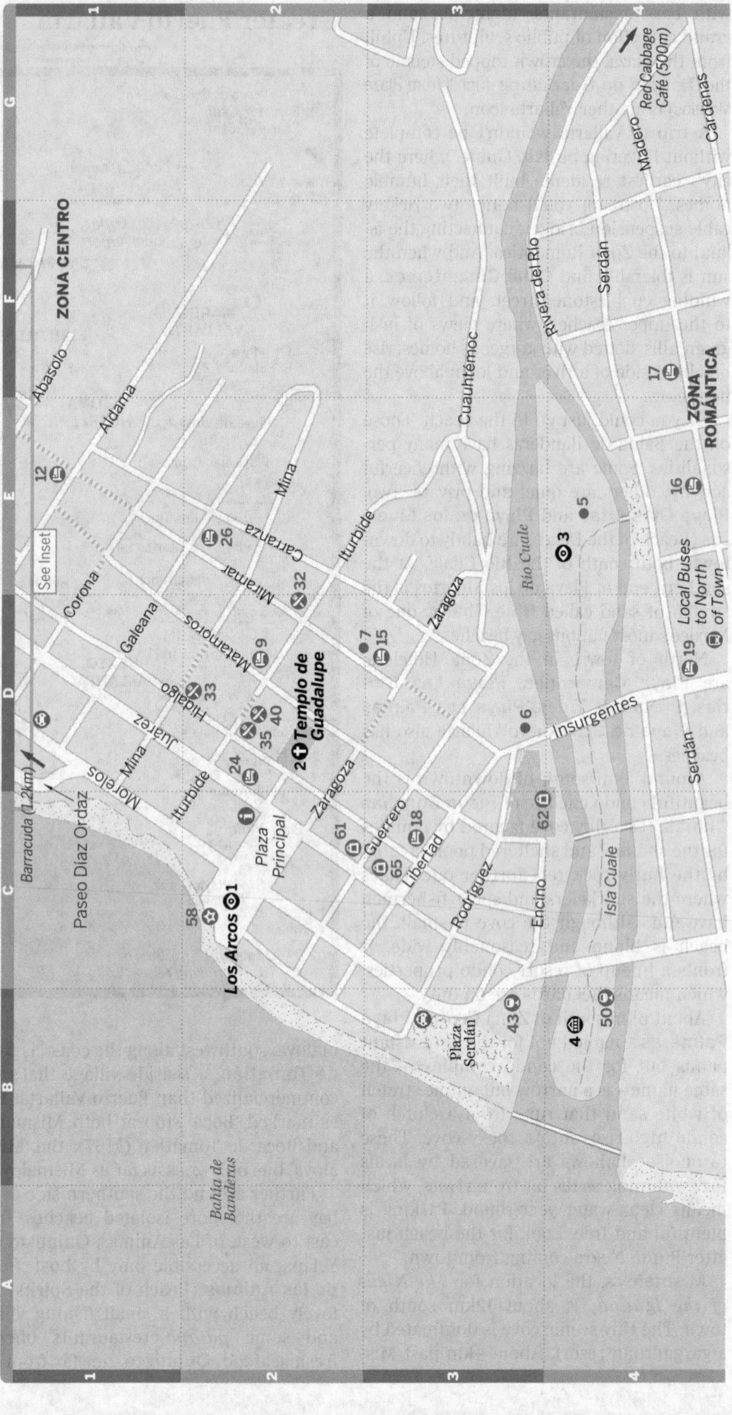

0 200 m
0 0.1 miles

A B C D E F G
1 2 3 4

Barracuda (1.2km)
See Inset
ZONA CENTRO
Paseo Díaz Ordaz
Abasolo
Corona
Aldama
Morelos
Mina
Juárez
Galeana
Iturbide
Hidalgo
Matamoros
Miramar
Carranza
Mina
Bahía de Banderas
Los Arcos 1
58
Plaza Principal
24
35
40
33
9
26
32
2 Templo de Guadalupe
Zaragoza
Iturbide
61
65
Guerrero
7
15
18
Libertad
Zaragoza
Plaza Serdán
Rodríguez
Cuauhtémoc
43
Encino
62
6
Río Cuale
Rivera del Río
3
5
4
50
Isla Cuale
Insurgentes
Serdán
Madero
Red Cabbage Café (500m)
17
16
19
Local Buses to North of Town
Serdán
ZONA ROMÁNTICA
Cárdenas

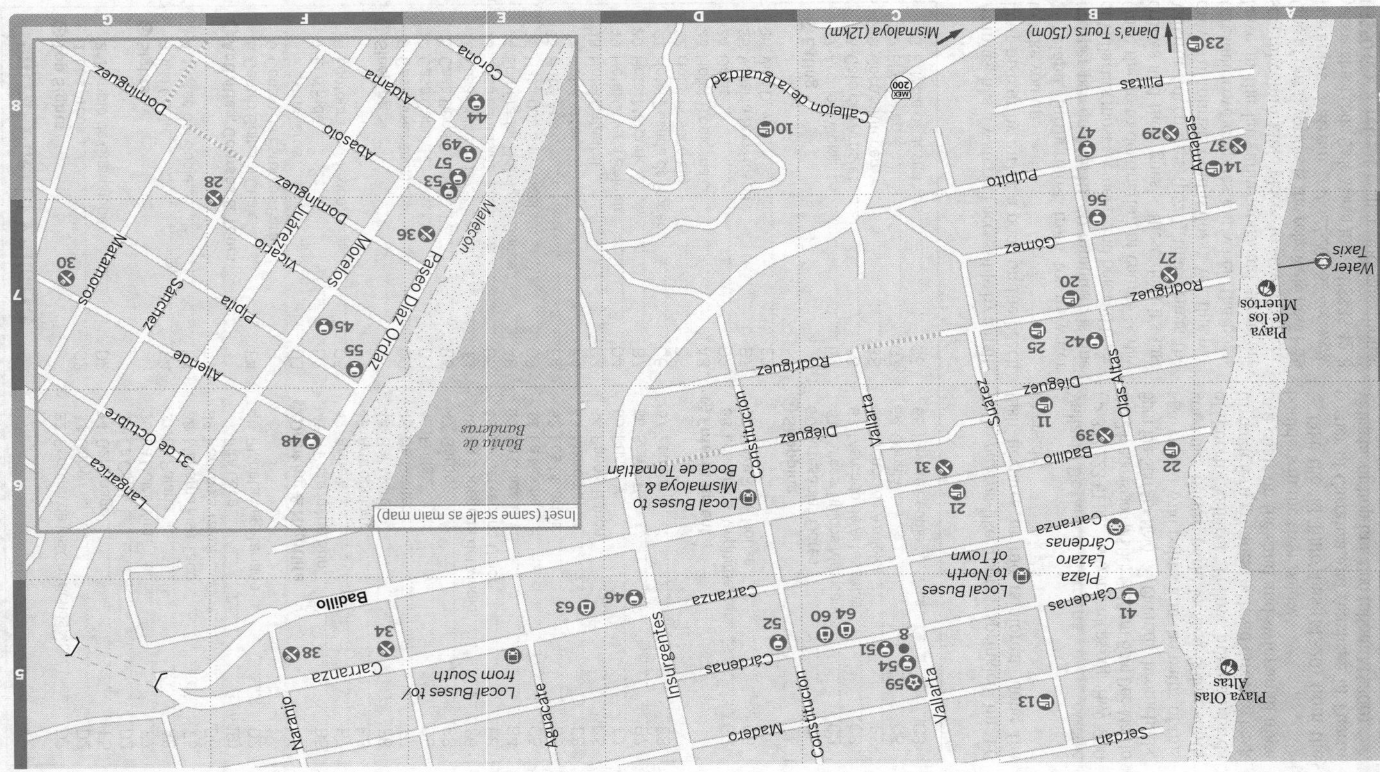
Inset (same scale as main map)
Bahía de Banderas
Langarica
31 de Octubre
Allende
Sánchez
Matamoros
Pípila
Vicario
Juárez
Morelos
Paseo Díaz Ordaz
Malecón
Domínguez
Abasolo
Aldama
Corona
Naranjo
Carranza
Badillo
Local Buses to/ from South
Aguacate
Insurgentes
Madero
Cárdenas
Constitución
Local Buses to Mismaloya & Boca de Tomatlán
Vallarta
Local Buses to North of Town
Plaza Lázaro Cárdenas
Suárez
Diéguez
Rodríguez
Olas Altas
Gómez
Púlpito
Pilitas
Amapas
Serdán
Playa Olas Altas
Playa de los Muertos
Water Taxis
Callejón de la Igualdad
Mismaloya (12km)
Diana's Tours (150m)
MEX 200

Central Puerto Vallarta

Top Sights
1 Los Arcos ... C2
2 Templo de Guadalupe ... D2

Sights
3 Isla Cuale ... E4
4 Museo del Cuale ... B4

Activities, Courses & Tours
5 Centro Cultural Cuale ... E4
6 Centro de Estudios Para Extranjeros ... D3
7 Eco Ride ... D2
8 Ecotours de México ... C5

Sleeping
9 Casa Amorita ... D2
10 Casa Cupula ... D8
11 Casa Dona Susana ... B6
12 Casa Dulce Vida ... E1
13 Casa Fantasia ... B5
14 Emperador Hotel and Suites ... A8
15 Hacienda San Angel ... D3
16 Hotel Ana Liz ... E4
17 Hotel Azteca ... F4
18 Hotel Catedral ... C3
19 Hotel Galería Belmar ... D4
20 Hotel Mercurio ... B7
21 Hotel Posada de Roger ... C6
22 Hotel Posada Lily ... B6
23 Hotel Tropicana ... A8
24 Oasis ... D2
25 Vallarta Sun Hostel ... B7
26 Villa David ... E2

Eating
27 Archie's Wok ... B7
28 Café des Artistes ... F8
29 Coco's Kitchen ... B8
30 El Arrayán ... G7
31 El Mole de Jovita ... C6
32 Esquina de los Caprichos ... D2
33 Gaby's ... D2
34 Garlapago ... F5
35 La Cigale ... D2
36 La Dolce Vita ... E7
37 La Palapa ... A8
38 Marisma Fish Taco ... F5
39 Pancho's Takos ... B6
Pita Loca ... (see 19)
40 Planeta Vegetariano ... D2

Drinking & Nightlife
41 A Page in the Sun ... B5
42 Andale ... B7
43 Antropology ... B3
44 Bar Morelos ... E8
45 De Santos ... F7
46 Frida ... D5
47 Garbo ... B8
48 La Bodeguita del Medio ... F6
49 La Cerveceria Union ... E8
50 La Cuiza ... B4
51 La Noche ... C5
52 Los Muertos ... D5
53 Mandala ... E8
54 Paco's Ranch ... C5
55 Punto V ... F7
56 Sama Bar ... B7
57 Zoo Bar ... E8

Entertainment
58 Los Arcos Amphitheater ... C2
59 Roxy Rock House ... C5

Shopping
60 Artesanías Flores ... C5
61 Dulces Tipicos Mexicanos ... C2
62 Mercado de Artesanías ... C3
63 Mundo de Azulejos ... E5
64 Olinalá ... C5
65 Peyote People ... C3

Ánimas, has a waterfall accessible by a half-hour hike or by hiring a pony on the beach to take you up.

Yelapa, furthermost from town (water taxi per person M$140, 40 minutes), is one of Vallarta's most secluded and beloved bays. Once the go-to destination of countless day cruises and their guests, these days it's just Vallarta Adventures (p520) that brings the droves of tourists (and it does). Yet, this picturesque cove empties out when the boats leave in the late afternoon, and there are several comfortable places to stay the night. One of our favorites is the relatively new **Los Naranjos Retreat** (322-209-52-46; www.yelaparetreat.com; Calle Marlín 100; s US$35-42, d US$50-62), a retreat center and guesthouse with *palapa*-like rooms sprinkled on 1.6 lush hectares in the rainforest along the riverside.

Vallarta Botanical Gardens GARDENS
(322-223-61-82; www.vbgardens.org; Hwy 200 Km 24; admission M$60; 10am-6pm Dec-Mar, to 5pm Tue-Sun Apr-Nov) Orchids, bromeliads, agaves and wild palms line the paths of this gorgeous nature park, located 30km south of Puerto Vallarta. Follow hummingbirds through fern grottoes, or head down to bask in a chair on the sand and swim amid huge boulders in the river below.

Take the 'El Tuito' bus (M$20) from the corner of Carranza and Aguacate in Puerto Vallarta, or hop in a taxi (about M$300).

Museo del Cuale MUSEUM
(Paseo Isla Cuale s/n; ⊙9am-2pm & 3-6pm Tue-Sat) FREE This tiny museum near the western end of Isla Cuale has a small collection of beautiful pottery, grinding stones, clay figurines and other ancient objects.

Activities

Restless souls need not go far to find activities such as swimming with dolphins, bungee jumping, mountain biking and whale-watching. Snorkeling, scuba diving, deep-sea fishing, waterskiing, windsurfing, sailing and parasailing can be arranged on the beaches in front of any of the large hotels or through the tourist office.

Diving & Snorkeling

Below the warm, tranquil waters of the Bahía de Banderas is a world of stingrays, tropical fish and garishly colored corals. Vallarta has several diving operators. Most also offer snorkeling trips, which usually means snorkelers tag along with divers. Dives typically include transportation, gear and light meals.

Banderas Scuba Republic DIVING
(☎322-135-78-84; www.bs-republic.com; Lazaro Cardenas 230; shore/boat dives US$50/85) Maintains a high degree of professionalism with its small-group excursions to lesser-known sites. Private diving tours are also offered.

Deep-Sea Fishing

Deep-sea fishing is popular year-round, with a major international fishing tournament held mid-November every year. Prime catches are sailfish, marlin, tuna, red snapper and sea bass. Fishing trips can be arranged dockside at Marina Vallarta or through the multitude of agencies around town.

Horseback Riding

Vallarta's jungly mountains are wonderful to explore from a horseback perspective.

Rancho El Charro HORSEBACK RIDING
(☎322-294-16-89, 322-224-01-14; www.ranchoelcharro.com; horse rides US$62-120) Rancho El Charro, 12km northeast of downtown Puerto Vallarta, is recommended for its healthy horses and scenic three- to eight-hour trots into the Sierra Madre. Some rides are suitable for kids. Setting it apart from competitors are its multiday tours, including the tempting 'Overnight Lost in the Jungle Ride' (US$350). Transportation is offered from the corner of Proa and Hwy 200 near Marina Vallarta.

Golf

Vallarta's golf courses are north of the city. Most highly acclaimed is the Jack Nicklaus–designed **Pacífico Golf Course** (☎322-291-60-00; www.fourseasons.com/puntamita/golf; Four Seasons Resort, Punta Mita; green fees 9/18 holes US$150/230), where golfers are blissfully distracted from the challenging terrain by the sweeping ocean vistas. Other clubs include **Vista Vallarta Golf Club** (☎322-290-00-30; www.vistavallartagolf.com; Circuito Universidad 653; green fees twilight/daylight US$143/204), 9km east of the airport, which has Nicklaus- and Weiskopf-designed courses side by side, and is one of Mexico's premier golf resorts; **Los Flamingos Golf Club** (☎329-296-50-06; www.flamingosgolf.com.mx; Hwy 200 s/n; green fees twilight/daylight US$90/149), slightly more affordable and 13km north of town; and **Marina Vallarta Golf Club** (☎322-221-00-73;

PUERTO VALLARTA IN FOUR DAYS

Rise and shine! Take a morning dip in the sparkling Bahía de Banderas and a stroll on one of Vallarta's many **beaches**; we like **Playa Palmeras**, which is on the lip of the bay, scanning the horizon for **whales** as you walk. Stop in at the Museo del Cuale or linger beneath the shady rubber trees on Isla Cuale (p515). Join the happy throng on the waterfront **malecón** and enjoy the varied public sculptures. Linger over dinner at one of Vallarta's splendid **restaurants** and then hit one of the sizzling **dance clubs**. If you enjoy salsa dancing, start or end your night at La Bodeguita del Medio (p525).

On day two, get up early (yeah, right) and continue indulging in the pleasures of the city with some **shopping**, or pick one of the many **outdoor adventures**, such as diving, fishing, horseback riding or one of Puerto Vallarta's new **canopy tours**.

On your third day, visit the beautiful Vallarta Botanical Gardens (p519), or hop aboard a boat to an exquisite lunch at Ocean Grill (p526) (make sure to book ahead), then venture further on to the far-flung beaches of **Las Ánimas**, **Quimixto** or **Yelapa**.

For the fourth day, catch a bus to the kick-back town of **Sayulita** for a surfing lesson.

www.marinavallartagolf.com; Paseo de la Marina 430; green fees twilight/daylight US$102/135), an exclusive 18-hole, par-71 course just north of Marina Vallarta.

Cruises

A host of daytime, sunset and evening cruises are available in Vallarta. The most popular ones are the cruises to Yelapa and Las Ánimas beaches; others go to Islas Marietas, further out. Prices are generally negotiable, starting at M$400 for sunset cruises and beach trips; longer trips lasting four to six hours with meals and bottomless cocktails will set you back M$750 to M$1200. Leaflets advertising cruises are available throughout town.

On Thursdays **Diana's Tours** (☎322-222-15-10; www.dianastours.com; cruise M$1050) offers an all-day gay and lesbian cruise, with plenty of food, drink and snorkeling (M$1050). It leaves from Blue Chairs Beach Resort.

Courses

Centro de Estudios Para Extranjeros LANGUAGE COURSE
(CEPE; ☎322-223-20-82; www.cepe.udg.mx; Libertad 105-1) Language courses at this Universidad de Guadalajara–affiliated school range from US$180 for a week of basic tourist Spanish to US$600 for 50-hour intensive courses. Private instruction costs US$35 per hour.

Centro Cultural Cuale ART COURSE
(☎322-222-95-34; www.institutovallartensedecultura.blogspot.com; lessons per person M$100) An arts complex at the easternmost plaza on Isla Cuale, on the more localized hemisphere of the island. Theater productions and battles of the bands bloom in the modest theatre, and that network of storefronts is where locals and tourists alike may take lessons in music, printmaking and painting.

Tours

Nature and outdoor adventure tours are one of Puerto Vallarta's strongest attributes. The following companies tread lightly and follow ecofriendly business practices.

★**Ecotours de México** ECOTOUR
(☎322-209-21-95; www.ecotoursvallarta.com; Vallarta s/n, Marina Vallarta) Run by enthusiastic naturalists, this outfit offers whale-watching (adult/child US$80/65), sea kayaking and snorkeling tours (US$85/65), guided hiking and snorkeling combo tours (US$65/50), bird-watching tours (from US$80/65) and multiday expeditions further afield focusing on sea turtles, monarch butterflies, whale sharks and more.

Eco Ride CYCLING
(☎322-222-79-12; www.ecoridemex.com; Miramar 382; tours M$600-1500) Surrounded by the mountains, jungle and sea, Vallarta offers some truly thrilling mountain biking. This outfit offers guided one-day cycling tours suited for beginners and badasses alike. The most challenging is a 50km expedition from El Tuito (a small town at 1100m) through Chacala and down to the beach in Yelapa.

It also offers hiking tours, including an incredible trip from Boca de Tomatlán to Las Ánimas.

Vallarta Adventures ADVENTURE TOUR
(☎322-297-12-12, in the US 888-526-2238; www.vallarta-adventures.com; Av Las Palmas 39, Nuevo Vallarta) Vallarta's largest adventure tour company, based near Marina Vallarta, offers a dizzying array of options, including whale-watching excursions (adult/child US$85/60), snorkeling and kayaking trips to the Islas Marietas (US$69/45), zip-line canopy tours (US$109/72), sailing trips (US$88) and visits to the colonial mining town of San Sebastián (US$88/60).

Canopy River CANOPY TOUR
(☎322-222-05-60; www.canopyriver.com; Ascencio 1989; adult/child US$64/43) An exhilarating, four-hour canopy tour featuring 12 zip-lines, ranging in height from 4m to 216m above the ground and in length from 44m to a stunning 650m run, that will demand you curl up like a cannonball to reach top speed.

Festivals & Events

Marlin & Sailfish Tournament FISHING
(www.fishvallarta.com) A major international tournament held every November.

Festival Gourmet International FOOD
(www.festivalgourmet.com) Puerto Vallarta's culinary community has hosted this mid-November festival since 1995.

Día de Santa Cecilia MUSIC
On November 22 Vallarta's mariachis jam and sing, honoring their patron saint with an early evening musical procession to the Templo de Guadalupe.

Día de Nuestra Señora de Guadalupe RELIGIOUS

Puerto Vallarta honors Mexico's patron saint with two weeks of celebrations, including processions to the cathedral day and night from November 30 until December 12.

Sleeping

When it comes to accommodations you're spoiled for choice in Puerto Vallarta. Vallarta's cheapest lodgings are south of the Río Cuale. Closer to the ocean, in the Zona Romántica, you'll find several appealing midrange options. The following prices are for the December to April high season; low-season rates can be as much as 20% to 50% lower. Negotiate for discounts if you plan on staying a week or more; monthly rates can cut your rent by half.

Oasis HOSTEL $

(☎322-222-26-36; www.oasishostel.com; Juárez 386; dm M$190, d M$500;) Nestled in the shadow of Templo de Guadalupe just off the plaza are three bright dorms and one simple private room (M$500), which has two beds and a private bathroom. There's a rooftop sun deck with ocean views, free breakfast and lockers to guard your valuables. Management is fabulous.

Vallarta Sun Hostel HOSTEL $

(☎322-223-15-23; www.vallartasunhostel.com; Rodríguez 169; dm/d M$195/550;) This hostel two blocks from Playa de los Muertos is homey with four clean, six-bed dorms, each with its own bathroom and spacious locker facilities. For those seeking a bit more privacy, there's also one double room with shared bathroom.

Hotel Ana Liz HOTEL $

(☎322-779-83-81; Madero 429; s/d M$250/280;) For serious peso-pinchers, Ana Liz' no-frills, fan-cooled rooms are among the cheapest in town. The best rooms are those with small balconies upstairs.

Hotel Azteca HOTEL $

(☎322-222-27-50; Madero 473; d from M$428) A super-clean, terrifically managed budget hotel full of brick arches. Rooms aren't huge or bright as they face an inner courtyard, but they have ceramic-tile floors, satellite TV and enough cute hand-painted touches to make it endearing. Rates drop to M$250 in low season.

Hotel Catedral HOTEL $$

(☎in Canada 877-361-4074, in the USA 877-296-7031, in Mexico 322-222-90-33; www.hotelcatedral-vallarta.com; 166 Hidalgo; d from US$46;) A charming three-star spot, steps from the waterfront and the river. The four floors of rooms surround a courtyard and have Templo de Guadalupe views from the upper reaches. Rooms are clean, if not new, with ceramic tiled floors and flat-screen TVs. The top-floor penthouse has a full kitchen.

Hotel Posada de Roger HOTEL $$

(☎322-222-08-36; www.posadaroger.com; Badillo 237; s/d M$560/630;) Three blocks from the beach, this agreeable travelers' hangout has long been one of Vallarta's most beloved midrange options.

Hotel Galería Belmar HOTEL $$

(☎322-223-18-72; www.belmarvallarta.com; Insurgentes 161; s/d M$600/653;) Brightly painted walls hung with original artwork enliven the tidy, comfortable rooms at this hotel in the heart of the Zona Romántica. Some have kitchenettes (M$100 extra) and many have balconies. Nicest are the top-floor rooms, which get natural light and an ocean breeze.

Hotel Posada Lily HOTEL $$

(☎322-222-00-32; www.facebook.com/HotelPosadalily; Badillo 109; d/tr from M$700/800;) This well-priced option just off the beach offers 18 clean and pleasant rooms, most with good natural light. The largest have three beds and small balconies that overlook the street. Beach chairs and umbrellas are available free to all guests. The only potential downside is noise.

A HOLIDAY FOR WHALES

Like many people reading this guide, during the winter months humpback whales come to the Bahía de Banderas to mate. They leave their feeding grounds in Alaskan waters and show up in Mexico from around November to the end of March. Once they have arrived, they form courtship groups or bear the calves that were conceived the year before. By the end of March the whales' attention turns to the long journey back to their feeding grounds up north. Whale-watching trips operate from December to March.

WORTH A TRIP

HACIENDA EL DIVISADERO

Head for the hills and immerse yourself in rural life at **Hacienda El Divisadero** (cell phone 322-1453455; www.haciendaeldivisadero.com; Camino Tuito–Chacala Km 9, Las Guásimas). This vast ranch 90 minutes south of Puerto Vallarta offers a slew of fun activities in one fantastic day tour (per person US$95). You'll be picked up from Puerto Vallarta at 8am, shuttled to the ranch where you'll enjoy a continental breakfast before your horseback excursions to local petroglyphs, a river swim and a tour of the hacienda's distillery where it produces knock-your-socks-off *raicilla* (a tequila-like distillation of wild agave). Lunch at the onsite restaurant, where you may enjoy melt in your mouth *birria* (spicy-hot soup) and fabulous *mole poblano* (*mole* from the state of Puebla), is included. You'll be dropped off at your hotel at around 5pm. Your price includes everything except beer and tips for the guides (essential).

To get here, drive south of Puerto Vallarta 45km on Hwy 200 to the town of El Tuito, then follow the signs another 10km west to the hacienda. Alternatively, you can visit the ranch on a tour organized by Vallarta Adventures.

★Casa Dulce Vida SUITES $$$

(322-222-10-08; www.dulcevida.com; Aldama 295; ste US$70-250;) With the look and feel of an Italian villa, this collection of seven spacious suites offers graceful accommodations and delicious privacy with more than a touch of *Mad Men* glamour.

Expect a gorgeous red-bottom mosaic pool, leafy gardens, and sumptuous *casas* with ceramic tiled floors, high ceilings, sunny living areas, spectacular wrought-iron doors and windows, well-stocked kitchens, whirring ceiling fans, a roof deck and vibrant sunsets. Most rooms have private terraces and extra beds for groups. Even when the place is fully booked, it retains a quiet and intimate atmosphere. It's a setting that begs for a cocktail and another. Then one more.

Casa Fantasia B&B $$$

(322-223-24-44; www.casafantasia.com; Suárez 203; r M$1200) A lovely B&B a block from the beach with spacious, terracotta tiled rooms with slanted beamed ceilings, flat-screen TVs wired with satellite and a full breakfast every morning in the gorgeous courtyard gushing with fountains, where the popular bar and restaurant is rocking in the high season.

Hotel Tropicana HOTEL $$$

(322-226-96-96; www.tropicanavallarta.com; Amapas 214; d standard/superior M$1050/1200, ste M$1300;) Catering primarily to package-tour groups, this venerable 160-room hotel is showing its age but still offers reasonably priced rooms given its beachside location. The superior rooms are less faded than the standard ones; book ahead for one with an ocean view.

Casa Amorita B&B $$$

(322-222-49-26, in the US 908-955-0720; www.casaamorita.com; Iturbide 309; r incl breakfast US$99-175;) Located on a quiet street above the din of the *malecón*, this small B&B offers four simple but pleasant rooms, complemented by comfortable common areas including a small pool, a massage area, a rooftop terrace with full views of the Templo de Guadalupe, and a fireplace surrounded by couches for reading and lounging.

Casa Doña Susana HOTEL $$$

(322-226-71-01; www.casadonasusana.com; Diéguez 171; d from US$149;) There's old-world elegance in the lobby, plenty of stone and brick arches, and a charming, *azulejo*-studded interior courtyard dripping with plants. Rooms have two-tone paint jobs, terracotta floors and antique wood furnishings, and the roof deck has a pool with mountain and sea views, as well as a chapel where you may count your blessings.

Hacienda San Angel BOUTIQUE HOTEL $$$

(322-222-26-92; www.haciendasanangel.com; Miramar 336; r US$295-325;) The 20 rooms are set in five scattered houses, all exquisitely decorated with fine terracotta floors, antique four-poster beds, *azulejo*-tiled arches and wash basins, knitted together by a fountain-filled courtyard. Two resplendent pool decks offer special city and ocean views and the rooftop restaurant earns repeat customers.

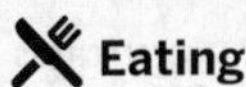

Eating

Foodies are pampered in Puerto Vallarta, and return visitors rate its cuisine scene a prime attraction.

Isla Cuale & South

Some of the tastiest and cheapest food in town comes from the taco stands along Madero and the neighboring Zona Romántica streets in the early evening.

Pancho's Takos TAQUERÍA $
(Badillo 162; tacos M$10; 6pm-2am Mon-Sat) Drawing a regular nighttime crowd, this *taquería* (taco stand) serves delicious *tacos al pastor* (spit-grilled pork, sliced from the spit and served with diced onions, cilantro and a slice of pineapple) until the wee hours.

Marisma Fish Taco TAQUERÍA $
(322-222-13-95; www.marismafishtaco.com; Naranjo 320; tostadas/tacos/quesadillas M$12/16/24; 9am-5pm) Shrimp and smoked marlin are served at this streetside *taquería*. Pull up a stool and watch as the women behind the counter press fresh tortillas and fry up tasty treats from a simple menu weighted heavily toward seafood tacos and quesadillas.

Garlapago TAQUERÍA $
(cnr Carranza & Jacaranda; tacos M$15-25; 9am-4:30pm Tue-Sat) A tiny *taquería* favored by locals for bacon-wrapped fish and shrimp tacos, though you can get them without bacon, too. It also does ceviche tostadas, and octopus quesadillas.

Pita Loca MIDDLE EASTERN $$
(322-888-30-28; www.facebook.com/pitaloca.puertovallarta; Insurgentes 161B; mains M$65-100; 10am-9pm Mon-Thu, to 5pm Fri, to 7pm Sun, closed Sat;) An authentic, Israeli-owned takeout joint that makes its own pita, butchers its own lamb, and makes sensational felafel and *shwarma*. All of it with spices imported from the motherland. Vegetarians rejoice: you have options.

El Mole de Jovita MEXICAN $$
(322-223-30-65; Badillo 220; mains M$60-80; 9am-11pm Mon-Sat) This family-run restaurant specializes in chicken with *mole*, but also serves good breakfasts and reasonably priced Mexican standards.

Coco's Kitchen INTERNATIONAL $$
(322-223-03-73; www.cocoskitchen.net; Púlpito 122; mains M$59-115) The preferred brunch choice south of the river, tables are sprinkled on a ceramic-tiled patio beneath a stilted terracotta roof and in a shady barside garden. Dishes range from *carnitas* and green chili burritos to a range of quesadillas and salads, and some tempting sandwiches like lamb and eggplant.

It does three kinds of gyro, three kinds of eggs Benedict, baskets of biscuits and cornbread, pecan waffles, stuffed French toast, and *huevos rancheros* (fried eggs on a corn tortilla with a tomato, chili and onion sauce served with refried beans) and *chilaquiles*.

Archie's Wok ASIAN $$$
(322-222-04-11; www.archieswok.com; Rodríguez 130; mains M$125-225; 2-11pm Mon-Sat;) The menu may change, but Asian fusion is always served at this elegant, urbane restaurant. Think: savory fish roasted in a banana leaf, and a coconut *poblano* chili soup, which is a nice Thai-inflected take on tortilla soup. The noodle dishes are stellar, the wines are tasty and so are the margaritas.

Red Cabbage Café MEXICAN $$$
(322-223-04-11; www.redcabbagepv.com; Rivera del Río 204A; mains M$120-240; 5-11pm, closed Sep) Though the atmosphere is casual, with eclectic and bohemian artwork, the food is serious and features old recipes and uncommon indigenous sauces. It's a pleasant 10-minute walk from the Zona Romántica; from Cárdenas turn right on Rivero del Río, just before the Río Cuale bridge. No credit cards.

La Palapa SEAFOOD $$$
(322-222-52-25; www.lapalapapv.com; Púlpito 103; mains M$140-340; 8am-11pm) Elegant beach dining at its best. Tables are positioned to take full advantage of the sea views, making it a particularly marvelous spot for breakfast or sunset. Delicacies include pepper-crusted yellow-fin tuna or sherry-and-soy-marinated snapper with asparagus, *chorizo* and shrimp beignets.

North of the Río Cuale

Planeta Vegetariano VEGETARIAN $
(322-222-30-73; www.planetavegetariano.com; Iturbide 270; buffet breakfast/lunch or dinner M$60/85; 8am-10pm Thu-Tue, closed Wed;) This buffet-style place with only 10 tables eschews cheese for fresh, dairy-free dishes such as soy enchiladas, banana lasagna (yes, that's right) and a wide range of creatively conceived salads.

Gaby's MEXICAN $$

(Mina 252; mains M$46-190; ⊙8:30am-10pm Mon-Sat, 10am-10pm Sun) Since 1989, this bright and cheerful family-run place with upstairs seating and a tree-shaded back patio has been serving dependably tasty Mexican classics; it's best at lunchtime, when the daily *comida corrida* (prix-fixe menu; including main dish, soup and *agua fresca*) costs only M$59.

Esquina de los Caprichos SPANISH $$

(☎322-222-09-11; Miramar 402; tapas M$40-85, mains M$85-140; ⊙8:30am-10pm Mon-Sat) This classy little place combines an intimate front room with a Gaudí-inspired back patio full of colorfully painted tables and broken-tile mosaics. Most of the dishes you'd expect to find at a tapas bar in Barcelona – delicious gazpacho, fried calamari, garlic shrimp and paella – are served here on charming handmade plates.

Benitto's Paninoteca Bar DELI $$

(☎322-209-02-87; www.benittos.com; Paseo de la Marina 21; mains M$95-165; ⊙9am-2am; 📶) A terrific gourmet deli in the marina area, popular among upmarket locals for creative *panini*, mixed carpaccios, and imported beers and wines. *Panini* range from a classic French dip to Italian sausage and Dijon to pastrami and goat cheese. It also does main serves of salads, soups and pastas. The kitchen is open until midnight. Drinkers may linger.

La Dolce Vita ITALIAN $$

(☎322-222-38-52; www.dolcevita.com.mx; Paseo Díaz Ordaz 674; mains M$115-168; ⊙noon-2am Mon-Sat, 6pm-midnight Sun) A cheerful, often-crowded spot for good wood-fired pizzas, pastas and people-watching. It's a local expat favorite. Request a table upstairs by the window for great views.

Barracuda SEAFOOD $$

(☎322-222-40-34; www.elbarracuda.com; Paraguay 1290; starters M$89, mains M$148) The only restaurant on the beach north of the river is best known for its grilled-shrimp tacos. Its tuna sashimi garnished with olive and lemon is also good, as is its *mariscos dinamita*, a paella-style dish with shrimp, octopus and fish chunks cooked in rice.

It overlooks a nice slab of beach where turtles still emerge to lay eggs, and whales thrash just offshore all winter long.

La Cigale FRENCH $$$

(www.lacigalebistro.com; Hidalgo 398; mains M$140-250; ⊙5-11:30pm) In the shadow of Templo de Guadalupe, this casual-chic French bistro with chalkboard menus and checkerboard floors serves everything from quiche Lorraine to steak tartare, accompanied by French, Chilean and Argentine wines.

El Arrayán MEXICAN $$$

(☎322-222-71-95; www.elarrayan.com.mx; Allende 344; mains M$150-230; ⊙5:30-11pm Wed-Mon) Owner Carmen Porras takes special pleasure in rescuing old family recipes from obscurity, with an emphasis on fresh local ingredients. Specialties include crispy duck *carnitas* (braised marinated duck) with orange sauce, and rib-eye steak marinated in Mexican spices and tequila. The restaurant, with its open kitchen and romantic courtyard, also serves as a venue for bimonthly cooking classes. It's 10 blocks northeast of the Templo de Guadalupe.

★**Café des Artistes** INTERNATIONAL $$$

(☎322-222-32-28; www.cafedesartistes.com; Sánchez 740; mains M$215-430; ⊙6-10:30pm) Many consider this to be Vallarta's finest restaurant. You're sure to enjoy its romantic ambience and exquisite fusion of French and Mexican influences, and its decor, which ranges from the candlelit garden to modern interior to whimsical castle-like exterior. But the food is the thing.

Fresh catch is sautéed with almonds and radish. Short rib simmers in *chipotle* chilis and is folded into tacos along with softshell crab, and the duck confit *chilaquiles* are a worthy nibble. The service is formal but unobtrusive, and reservations are recommended. It's eight blocks north of the Templo de Guadalupe.

Drinking & Nightlife

It's ridiculously easy to become inebriated in a town where two-for-one happy hours are as reliable as the sunset, margarita glasses look like oversized snifters, and day drinking is an obligation. Coffee shops open about 7am and close around midnight; most bars keep the lime squeezers occupied until well after that. Admission charges are normally waived early in the week; on Friday and Saturday nights they often include one or two drinks.

Along the *malecón* is a bunch of places where teen and 20-something locals and tourists get trashed and dance on tables. On a good night, they all stay open from 11pm until 5am. You can see from the street which one has the most action. Good bets include **Mandala** (www.mandaladisco.com; Paseo Díaz Ordaz 640), **Zoo Bar** (www.facebook.com/zoopuertovallarta; Morelos 630; cover varies; ⌚6am-6pm) and **Punto V** (www.puntovnightclub.com; Paseo Díaz Ordaz 78).

★La Bodeguita del Medio BAR

(☎322-223-15-85; labodeguitadelmedio.com.mx; Paseo Díaz Ordaz 858; ⌚11am-4am) The walls are scrawled with handwritten poetics and inanities in several languages, the bar is blessed with fine rums and tequilas, and the barmen pour a mean mojito, as well as questionable variations. More important, the Cuban bands are authentic, tight and exuberant, and the beautiful salsa dancers span generations. Live music nightly. Salsa lessons are held on Thursday nights.

De Santos BAR

(www.desantos.com.mx; Plaza Peninsula, Blvd Ascensio 2485; ⌚6pm-5am) Candles and strings of vintage lightbulbs create a romantic mood at this terrace bar north of the city center, founded by drummer Alex González from the group Maná. On Fridays and Saturdays there's live jazz funk into the wee hours, plus a great drinks list dominated by mezcal, martinis and the infamous house special *pata salada* – an organically grown, agave-derived local firewater.

La Cuiza BAR

(☎322-223-47-76; www.facebook.com/lacuiza; Isla del Cuale 4; admission varies; ⌚11am-7pm Mon-Wed, to late Thu-Sat, closed Sun; 📶) Set on the west side of the Isla Cuale near the museum, this interesting modern art gallery has colorful canvasses and intriguing original sculpture. There is also a gorgeous bar, a pool table, and a variety of performances – theatrical, musical and otherwise – on weekends. It's also a fabulous place for an afternoon drink.

La Cervecería Union BEER GARDEN

(☎322-223-09-28; Aldama & Paseo Díaz Ordaz; ⌚11am-midnight; 📶) A branch of the Guadalajara beer garden. There's an oyster bar, decent tacos and a sports-bar feel on game days. Along with an ample beer selection that includes a house brew, it has a long tequila list and does tasty *micheladas* (beer cocktails) and *clamatos* – beer cocktails where the beer is mixed with Clamato juice (tomato and clam juice) – with a professional touch.

Los Muertos PUB

(☎322-222-03-08; www.losmuertosbrewing.com; Cárdenas 302; ⌚noon-midnight; 📶) An attractive, brick-arched concrete-floor pub and microbrew. The beer comes in six flavors including an IPA called 'Revenge' and a stout called 'Mc Sanchez.'

A Page in the Sun CAFE

(Cárdenas 179; ⌚7am-11pm summer, to midnight winter; 📶) This friendly and highly recommended cafe doubles as a bookstore and social hangout, with good espresso drinks, comfy couches, regular conversational language groups and Saturday story hour for kids.

Andale's BAR

(☎322-222-10-54; Olas Altas 425; ⌚8am-2am) Party hearty with throngs of young vacationers in this dark den of drink, sports and loud rock music even during the day. This joint has old-school dive bar gravitas and is worthy of a round or two.

Garbo LOUNGE

(☎322-223-57-53; 142 Púlpito; ⌚5pm-2am) If you enjoy jazzy stylings and an excellent martini to go with them, make your way to this concrete-floor habitat. The jazz and torch singing are decent to good, and sing-alongs may happen.

Bar Morelos MEZCALERÍA

(☎322-111-39-40; www.facebook.com/BarMorelosPuertoVallarta; Morelos 589; ⌚7pm-6am) A brand-new (at research time) *mezcalería* that feels much more like the modern, upmarket pub-cum-club that it is rather than the down and dirty mezcal bar of your dreams. Still, it does present fine, brain-twisting mezcal by shot and syringe (no joke) along with a chili-dipped orange slice.

Its tequila list runs deep, the pub grub is decent, there is a DJ at the ready, and there are plenty of cozy (if not quiet) corners to snuggle in the leather booths.

☆ Entertainment

Vallarta's main forms of nighttime entertainment revolve around dancing, drinking and dining. At night everyone and their brother strolls the *malecón,* choosing from a fantastic selection of restaurants, bars and hot night-spots. There's often entertainment in the **Los Arcos Amphitheater** (Malecón) by

DON'T MISS

BITES ABOVE THE BAY

If you like boat rides, rugged tropical shores, jungled mountains and laid-back elegance, not to mention stellar food and excellent drinks, book a lunch at **Ocean Grill** (☎322-223-73-15; www.oceangrillvallarta.com; mains M$140-360; 11am-5pm;), a reservation-only bistro set on a rocky cliff, and a five-minute water-taxi ride from Boca de Tomatlán. Mains range from an olive tapenade–crusted octopus and sensational prawns, to a seasonal 2lb lobster and baby back ribs. It does burgers, chicken and steaks, too. All of it spiced, rubbed and grilled over an open flame and served in a multileveled dining room, its *palapa* roof supported by vine-tangled tree trunks. This is the kind of place you can spend the day, and there are trails from here to Playa de las Ánimas or back to Boca if you want to walk off the feed. Two-hour sittings begin at 11am. The last seating is 3pm. Transfers to and from Boca are included with each reservation.

the sea, opposite the Plaza Principal. Softly lit Isla Cuale is a quiet haven for a romantic promenade in the early evening.

Roxy Rock House LIVE MUSIC
(www.roxyrockhouse.com.mx; Vallarta 217; 8pm-6am) In the heart of the Zona Romántica, this place draws an enthusiastic mixed crowd every Friday and Saturday night, with live rock and blues cover bands and no admission charge.

 Shopping

Vallarta is a haven for shoppers, with many shops and boutiques selling fashionable clothing, beachwear and crafts from all over Mexico. Tequila and Cuban cigars are also big business. Both **Artesanías Flores** (☎322-223-07-73; Cárdenas 282) and **Peyote People** (☎322-222-23-02; www.peyotepeople.com; Juárez 222) sell Huichol beadwork, thread paintings and jewelry.

Mercado de Artesanías HANDICRAFTS
(☎322-223-09-25; Av Rodríguez 260) Straddling the north bank of the Río Cuale, this market sells everything from Taxco silver, serapes (blankets with a head opening, worn as a cloak) and huaraches (woven leather sandals) to wool wall hangings and blown glass. There is a smaller version with similar stalls on the west end of Isla Cuale.

Olinalá ARTS & CRAFTS
(☎322-121-35-76, 322-228-06-59; Cárdenas 274) In business since 1978, this excellent little shop displays authentic Mexican dance masks, folk art and rural-style antiques.

Mundo de Azulejos CERAMICS
(www.talavera-tile.com; Carranza 374; 10am-6pm Mon-Sat) This store offers a vast array of brightly colored Talavera tiles and ceramics.

Dulces Típicos Mexicanos FOOD
(Juárez 1449; 10am-10pm) If you have a sweet tooth, stop by this cute *tienda* (shop) packed with temptation from tamarind chews to exquisite caramels to any number of dried-fruit and sugary-nut concoctions. Be warned, do not venture inside on an empty stomach.

 Information

EMERGENCY

Ambulance (☎322-222-15-33)
Fire (☎322-223-94-76)
Police (☎060, 322-223-25-00)

INTERNET ACCESS

Wi-fi is widely available in restaurants, bars and cafes, and in almost all resorts, hotels and guesthouses listed here.

MEDIA

A pair of English-language print publications – the weekly *Vallarta Tribune* (www.vallartatribune.com) and the biweekly *Bay Vallarta* (www.bayvallarta.com) – offer useful cultural and shopping listings.

MEDICAL SERVICES

San Javier Marina Hospital (☎322-226-10-10; Ascencio 2760) Vallarta's best-equipped hospital.

MONEY

Although most businesses in Vallarta accept US dollars as readily as they accept pesos, their exchange rates are generally abysmal. Several banks around the Plaza Principal have ATMs.

Vallarta has many *casas de cambio;* their rates differ and are slightly less favorable than the banks. Look for them on Insurgentes, Vallarta and the *malecón*. ATMs are the most economical choice.

Banamex (cnr Juárez & Zaragoza) On the southeast corner of the Plaza Principal.

HSBC (cnr Insurgentes & Miramar) Just north of the Río Cuale bridge.

POST

Main Post Office (Colombia 1014)

TELEPHONE & FAX

Pay phones are plentiful everywhere in town, as are *casetas de teléfono* (public telephone call stations). Many internet cafes offer Skype service.

TOURIST INFORMATION

Municipal Tourist Office (☎ext 232, 322-226-80-80; Juárez s/n; ⏲8am-8pm Mon-Sat, 10am-6pm Sun) Vallarta's busy but competent office, in the municipal building at the northeast corner of the Plaza Principal, has free maps, multilingual tourist literature and bilingual staff.

Getting There & Away

AIR

Gustavo Díaz Ordaz International Airport (☎322-221-12-98; wwwww.aeropuertosgap.com.mx/en/puerto-vallarta-3.html; Carretera Tepic Km 7.5; wi-fi) is located 10km north of the city. Airlines servicing the airport include the following:

Aeroméxico (☎322-221-12-04; www.aeromexico.com; Airport) Direct service to Los Angeles, Ciudad Juárez, Guadalajara and Mexico City.

Interjet (☎322-221-32-06; www.interjet.com.mx; Airport) Direct service to Mexico City and Toluca.

VivaAerobus (☎55-4000-0180, 81-8215-0150; www.vivaaerobus.com; Airport) Direct service to Monterrey.

Volaris (☎800-122-80-00; www.volaris.mx; Airport) Direct service to Tijuana and Mexico City.

BUS

Vallarta's long-distance bus terminal is just off Hwy 200, about 10km north of the city center and 2km northeast of the airport, and it has wi-fi.

Primera Plus (Carranza 393) and **ETN** (Cárdenas 268) both have downtown offices south of the Río Cuale where you can buy tickets. If you're heading to Barra de Navidad, Manzanillo or other points south, you can save a trip to the bus terminal by boarding at the corner of Carranza and Aguacate (half a block from the Primera Plus ticket office).

CAR & MOTORCYCLE

Starting at about M$600 per day, on-the-spot car rentals are pricey during the high season; you'll often do better booking online. At other times, deep discounts are offered.

A dozen car-rental agencies maintain adjacent counters in the airport arrivals hall, including the following:

Alamo (☎800-849-8001, 322-221-12-28; www.alamomexico.com.mx)

Avis (☎322-221-16-57; www.avis.mx)

Budget (☎322-221-17-30; www.budget.com.mx)

Europcar (☎322-209-09-21; www.europcar.com)

Hertz (☎999-911-80-40; www.hertz.com)

National (☎322-221-12-26; www.nationalcar.com.mx)

Sixt (☎322-209-06-85; www.sixt.com)

Thrifty (☎322-209-10-05; www.thrifty.com.mx)

Getting Around

TO/FROM THE AIRPORT

The cheapest way to get to/from the airport is on a local bus for M$7. 'Centro' and 'Olas Altas' buses go into town from a stop just outside the arrivals hall. Returning from town, 'Aeropuerto,' 'Juntas' and 'Ixtapa' buses stop at the airport entrance.

BUSES FROM PUERTO VALLARTA

DESTINATION	FARE (M$)	DURATION	FREQUENCY (DAILY)
Barra de Navidad	180-218	3½-4hr	frequent
Guadalajara	354-430	5½hr	very frequent
Manzanillo	230-327	5-5½hr	hourly
Mazatlán	450	8hr	6
Mexico City (Terminal Norte)	948-1025	12hr	7
San Blas	196	3½hr	4
San Patricio-Melaque	247	3½-4hr	frequent
Tepic	193-207	3½-4hr	frequent

GAY & LESBIAN PUERTO VALLARTA

Come on out – the rainbow flag flies high over Puerto Vallarta. An ever-increasing stream of visitors descends on Vallarta annually for its formidable selection of gay bars, nightclubs, restaurants and hotels, as well as its busy annual calendar of gay- and lesbian-themed events. The **Gay Guide Vallarta** (www.gayguidevallarta.com) booklet and website has tons of information and a helpful map for finding gay-friendly businesses.

Clubs & Nightspots

Most dance clubs open from 10pm until at least 4am, and some stay open well past sunrise. For an entertaining introduction to Vallarta's gay nightlife scene, check out the **Old Town Bar Hop** (www.dianastours.com/old_town_bar_hop.php; bar hop US$75; ⏲7:45pm-1am Fri & Sat) offered by Diana's Tours.

The venerable disco/cantina **Paco's Ranch** (☎322-222-18-99; www.pacosranch.com; Vallarta 237; ⏲10pm-6am) stages drag shows Friday through Sunday mornings.

Antropology (www.antropologypv.com; Morelos 101) is a sizzling dance mecca and male-stripper venue with its dark, intimate rooftop patio. Women are unapologetically disallowed.

The Zona Romántica is teeming with atmospheric cocktail bars catering to a gay and lesbian clientele: **La Noche** (Cárdenas 257; ⏲4pm-2am) is well loved for its convivial ambience and buff bartenders; **Sama Bar** (☎322-223-31-82; Olas Altas 510; ⏲4:30pm-2am) is a likable small place with big martinis and tasty margaritas; and **Frida** (www.barfrida.com; Insurgentes 301A; ⏲1pm-2am) is a cozy and sociable cantina featuring enticing drink specials. Exhibit A: margaritas are M$25 on Thursdays.

Resorts & Inns

Hotel Mercurio (☎322-222-47-93, in the US 866-388-2689; www.hotel-mercurio.com; Rodríguez 168; s/d incl breakfast US$98/128; ❄@📶🏊) Less than two blocks from Muertos pier, this three-story hotel features 28 rooms around a pleasant courtyard with a stylish pool and bar. Rooms have fridges, wi-fi, cable TV and double or king-sized beds with fine linens. Gourmet breakfasts, spa packages and free international phone calls are among the other perks on offer. It won the Pink Choice Award in 2013 for excellent service to the gay community.

Blue Chairs Beach Resort (☎322-222-50-40, in the US 888-302-3662; www.bluechairsresort.com; Almendro 4; r US$150-218, ste US$219-265; ❄📶🏊) At the south end of Playa de los Muertos is one of Mexico's most famous gay beaches. The attached beach club is Vallarta's most popular, visible gay beach-bar, with droves of couples enjoying the sun's rays and cool drinks. There's also a raucous nightspot with live entertainment on the roof. The breezy and attractive rooms have cable TV; suites have kitchenettes.

Casa Cúpula (☎322-223-24-84, in the US 866-352-2511; www.casacupula.com; Callejón de la Igualdad 129; r US$185-279, ste US$320-519; ❄@📶🏊) Sophisticated design and luxurious flourishes define this extremely popular resort. Each room is uniquely and tastefully decorated, with amenities ranging from home-theater-sized TVs to private Jacuzzis in some suites. The beach is only a few blocks downhill, although the resort's four pools, gym, onsite restaurant and bar may give you enough incentive to linger here all day.

Villa David (☎322-223-03-15, from the US 877-832-3315; www.villadavidpv.com; Galeana 348; r M$119-139; ❄@📶🏊) Reservations are essential and clothing optional at this swanky, male-only gay retreat in a beautiful hacienda-style mansion. It's the only such B&B in Vallarta's historic district. With gorgeously landscaped grounds and tastefully appointed rooms, this is the perfect choice for a romantic getaway.

Emperador Hotel and Suites (☎322-222-51-43; www.hotelemperadorpv.com; Amapas 114; d/ste M$763/950) A well-located beachside complex where simple but homey rooms have new tiled floors, turquoise accent walls, queen beds and flat screens on the wall. Suites are huge and have full kitchens on the terrace.

From the airport to the city, taxis charge fixed rates ranging from M$180 to M$310, depending on which neighborhood you're traveling to. You can save money by crossing Hwy 200 via the pedestrian bridge outside the arrivals hall and taking a taxi from the opposite side of the street, where drivers are allowed to charge lower fares (M$120 to M$150 per car load). A taxi back to the airport from downtown costs around M$120. A taxi from the bus terminal downtown is M$100.

BOAT

Vallarta's water taxis serve the beautiful beaches on the southern side of the bay, many of which are accessible only by boat. Departing from the Playa de los Muertos pier, they head south around the bay, making stops at Playa Las Ánimas (25 minutes), Quimixto (40 minutes) and Yelapa (55 minutes); the round-trip fare is M$300 for any destination. Boats depart Puerto Vallarta every hour or two between 10am and 4:30pm, returning from Yelapa (the end of the line) with the same frequency between 7:30am and 3:45pm daily.

Private yachts and *lanchas* can be hired from the southern side of the Playa de los Muertos pier, starting from around M$350 per hour. They'll take you to any secluded beach around the bay; most have gear aboard for snorkeling and fishing.

BUS

Blue-and-white local buses operate every five minutes from 5am to 11pm on most routes, and cost M$7. Plaza Lázaro Cárdenas near Playa Olas Altas is a major departure hub. Northbound local buses also stop on Insurgentes near the corner of Madero.

Northbound buses marked 'Aeropuerto,' 'Ixtapa,' 'Mojoneras' and 'Juntas' pass through the city heading north to the airport and Marina Vallarta; the 'Mojoneras' bus also stops at Puerto Vallarta's long-distance bus terminal.

White-and orange 'Boca de Tomatlán' buses (M$7) head south along the coastal highway through Mismaloya (20 minutes) to Boca de Tomatlán (30 minutes). They depart from the corner of Badillo and Constitución every 15 minutes from 5:30am to 11pm.

TAXI

Cab prices are regulated by zones; the cost for a ride is determined by how many zones you cross. A typical trip from downtown to the Zona Hotelera costs M$80; to the airport or the long-distance bus terminal M$120; and to Mismaloya M$130. Always determine the price of the ride before you get in. Hailing a cab is easy in the city center along Morelos. There are several taxi stands, including one on Morelos between Corona and Galeana, one on Morelos at Rodríguez, and one on Carranza at Plaza Lázaro Cárdenas.

COSTALEGRE BEACHES

South of Puerto Vallarta, the stretch of Mexico's Pacific coast from Chamela to Barra de Navidad is blessed with fine beaches. Tourism promoters and developers refer to this shoreline as the 'Costalegre' (Happy Coast). Following are the beaches from north to south (with kilometer numbers measured from the junction of Hwys 80 and 200 just outside San Patricio-Melaque).

Fans of sea turtles (and, really, who isn't in that group?) should stop by the **Majahua Biological Station**, just north of Punta Pérula, where you can camp, and watch the turtles nest with local guides. There's a small hotel here, too. It's become a destination for international students interested in turtles and their habitat.

Playa Pérula (Km 73), a sheltered beach at the northern end of tranquil 11km-long Bahía de Chamela, is great for swimming and extended walks. There are cheap accommodations and a smattering of *palapa* restaurants. You can charter a *panga* (skiff) from here to the **nine islands**.

At Bahía de Chamela, **Playa La Negrita** (Km 64) is an isolated, relaxing beach with a couple of restaurants but no hotels. The nine islands in the expansive bay are beautiful to see in silhouette at sunset.

On the palm-fringed Bahía Tenacatita, **Playa Tenacatita** (Km 28) has clear snorkeling waters and a large mangrove lagoon with good bird-watching. However, there is a land title in dispute here, with a development group in the process of fighting for their rights to build on an otherwise undeveloped beach. You can still visit for now, but camping is no longer allowed. Bring your own food and drinks and enjoy the day. Also on this bay are **Playa Boca de Iguanas** (Km 19) and **Playa La Manzanilla** (Km 13). The shorebreak on Iguanas can be steep and fast, perfect for body boarding. Manzanilla's calm water is ideal for swimming.

BAHÍA DE NAVIDAD

The tight arc of the Bahía de Navidad is practically ringed by deep, honey-colored sand with two resort towns at either end, amiably facing each other. Situated 5km apart, Barra de Navidad and San Patricio-Melaque are siblings with distinct personalities. Barra is beloved for its attractive cobbled streets and aura of good living, while San Patricio-Melaque, which is larger and less quaint, draws budget-minded travelers seeking that beachfront buzz.

San Patricio-Melaque

☎315 / POP 7600

Known by most as Melaque (meh-*lah*-keh), this kick-back beach resort hasn't lost its old Mexico charm. It's a popular vacation destination for Mexican families and a low-key winter hangout for snowbirds (principally Canadians). The main activities are swimming, lazing on the beach, watching pelicans fish at sunrise and sunset, climbing to the *mirador* (lookout point) at the bay's west end, prowling the plaza and public market, or walking the beach to Barra de Navidad.

Tours

The Only Tours TOUR
(☎315-355-67-77; www.theonlytours.com; Las Cabañas 26) Runs full-day tours to Tenacatita (M$450) and Colima (M$850), plus birdwatching and all-terrain-vehicle excursions (M$850) to more remote areas. Also rents out bikes, snorkeling gear and body boards (each M$100 per day).

Festivals & Events

Fiesta de San Patricio TRADITIONAL
Melaque honors its patron saint with a blowout week of festivities, including all-day parties, rodeos, a carnival, music, dances and nightly fireworks, leading up to St Patrick's Day (March 17).

Sleeping

Rates vary greatly depending on the season; the following prices are for the high season (November through May). Discounts are common for longer stays.

Hotel Las Caracoles GUESTHOUSE $
(☎315-355-73-08; www.loscaracoles.com.mx; Gómez Farías 26; s/d M$300/400; wi-fi) Simple and super clean, here are 13 white-tiled, fan-cooled rooms with peach paint jobs and cable TV. Ground-floor rooms don't catch much natural light, but are good value nonetheless.

★ **Posada Pablo de Tarso** HOTEL $$
(☎315-355-57-07; www.posadapablodetarso.com; Gómez Farías 408; r from M$600-1000; P air-con wi-fi pool) One of the more atmospheric places in town, this leafy, brick courtyard hotel with its luscious beachside pool area offers rooms with beamed ceilings, engraved doors, high-end terracotta floors, wooden headboards and built-in vanities at either end. Rooms overlooking the road or the beach are largest.

Las Arenas BUNGALOW $$
(☎315-355-50-97; www.lasarenas.net; Gómez Farías 11; d from M$650, bungalow M$950; air-con wi-fi pool) With umbrellas and chairs on a nice slice of beachfront, the property doesn't have much style, but it is prim and very well maintained. Rooms have queen- or sofa beds, tile floors, flat-screen TVs and wi-fi. The bungalows are simply studios with kitchenettes. The beachfront rooms are only M$100 more and are far bigger and brighter.

Hotel Puesta del Sol HOTEL $$
(☎315-355-57-97; www.melaquepuestadelsol.com; Gómez Farías 31; d M$750; P air-con wi-fi) Set on the main town-center drag, this cozy complex of studios with kitchenettes, granite countertops and high ceilings are artfully tiled, right on the beach, and are solid value.

★ **Villas El Rosario de San Andres** STUDIOS $$
(☎315-355-63-42; www.villaselrosariodesanandres.com; Hidalgo 10; studio M$650-1500; P air-con wi-fi pool) Our favorite sleep in Melaque offers bright, ceramic-tiled studios with attractive kitchenettes, high ceilings and flat-screen TVs. Some sleep up to six, including the huge room with beamed ceilings on the rooftop deck, which is a wonderful common area with special mountain and sea views, but not all rooms have air-con. There is also a small plunge pool.

BUSES FROM SAN PATRICIO-MELAQUE

DESTINATION	FARE (M$)	DURATION	FREQUENCY (DAILY)
Guadalajara	290-359	5½-7hr	hourly
Manzanillo	54-70	1-1½hr	half-hourly
Mexico City (Terminal Norte)	1021	13hr	5:15pm & 7:50pm
Puerto Vallarta	203-259	4-5hr	frequent

La Paloma Oceanfront Retreat APARTMENT $$$
(☎315-355-53-45; www.lapalomamexico.com; Las Cabañas 13; studio US$100-175; P ❄ ☜ ≋) Original art abounds at this unique boutique resort. The 14 singular, comfortable studios have kitchens and terraces with rewarding ocean views. Lush gardens, a 25m beachside swimming pool, a well-stocked library, wi-fi and free breakfast by the poolside in winter make an extended stay here extremely tempting.

From October to April, units rent by the week and advance reservations are essential; per-night rates are sometimes offered during summer.

Eating & Drinking

From 6pm to midnight, food stands serve inexpensive Mexican fare a block east of the plaza along Juárez. A row of pleasant *palapa* restaurants stretches along the beach at the west end of town. Still, the area's best kitchens are in nearby Barra de Navidad.

Lonchería La Central MEXICAN $
(Av Carranza; meals M$35-40; ⏲8am-4pm) A cute diner set across from the Primera Plus station and adjacent to the old terminal, this kitchen is run by two local ladies who offer *comidas* with beef, chicken, pork or *chile relleno,* which come with rice, beans and tortillas. They also do Mexican breakfasts and a nice menu of juices and *licuados*.

Concha del Mar MEXICAN, SEAFOOD $
(Las Palmas 27; mains M$35-105; ⏲noon-11pm) As you stroll 'Palapa Row,' look for the blue archway entrance of this popular beachside eatery. From large breakfasts to Mexican combo plates to shrimp and fish fajitas, the price is right, and the location – with dramatic views of sunset over the rocks offshore – couldn't be better.

Mamitas LOUNGE
(López Mateos 49; ⏲7pm-1am) The choice spot for adult beverages, it's set above the plaza with a false bamboo roof dangling with mosaic lanterns and glass ornaments. There is less trance and more pop music on the stereo than its nearest rival.

Information

Barra de Navidad's tourist office provides basic information on San Patricio-Melaque, including a street map. Internet is widely available in most hotels and restaurants.

Banamex (Gómez Farías s/n) On Melaque's main street. Has an ATM and will change US and Canadian dollars.

Internet El Navegante (Gómez Farías 48; per hr M$10; ⏲9am-9pm Mon-Sat, from 10am Sun) A popular internet cafe just off the plaza.

Post Office (Orozco s/n) Three blocks southeast of the plaza.

Getting There & Away

BUS

Melaque has two bus terminals. Transportes Cihuatlán and Primera Plus/Servicios Coordinados are on opposite sides of Carranza at the corner of Gómez Farías. Both have 1st- and 2nd-class buses and ply similar routes for similar fares.

Local buses to Barra de Navidad (M$11, 15 minutes) leave every 15 minutes from a stop at Juárez and López Mateos, opposite the southwest corner of the plaza.

TAXI

A taxi between Melaque and Barra should cost M$50 to M$60; taxis congregate at the plaza.

Barra de Navidad

☎315 / POP 6300

Barra de Navidad greets you with mellow happiness and easy charm that seeps into your bones. It's a pueblo on both a lagoon and the beach, freckled with clean, cheap sleeps, boasting excellent sportfishing, bird- and crocodile-watching trips, and some succulent seafood. Squeezed onto a sandbar between Bahía de Navidad and the Laguna de Navidad, Barra first came to prominence in 1564 when its shipyards produced the galleons used by conquistador Miguel López de Legazpi and Father Andrés de Urdaneta to conquer the Philippines for King Felipe II of Spain. By 1600, however, most of the conquests were being conducted from Acapulco, and Barra slipped into sleepy obscurity (a state from which it has yet to fully emerge).

In October 2011 Hurricane Jova took a big bite out of Barra's beachfront, leaving a couple of landmark businesses tilting at queasy angles. Rebuilding was complete at research time, and though the town can feel dead during the low season, during winter it is a most charming snowbird paradise.

Activities

Barra's steep and narrow beach is lovely to behold, but conditions are sometimes too rough for swimming. The gentlest conditions are generally in the mornings.

Trips into the Laguna de Navidad are a Barra highlight. The boatmen's cooperative, **Sociedad Cooperativa de Servicios Turísticos** (Veracruz 40; ⏲7am-sunset), books a variety of boat tours ranging from half-hour trips around the lagoon ($300 per boat) to all-day jungle trips to Tenacatita (M$3000 per boat). The waters near Barra are rife with marlin, swordfish, albacore, *dorado,* snapper and other more rarefied catches. Fishing trips on *lanchas* can also be arranged at the cooperative for M$500 per hour or M$3000 per day, including gear; many trips include snorkeling stops. Prices are posted at the open-air lagoonside office.

Golf

Grand Bay Golf Course GOLF
(☎314-331-05-00; Grand Bay Hotel Wyndham Resort, Isla Navidad; green fees 18 holes M$2500) Grand Bay Golf Course is a celebrated 27-hole course with excellent vistas and greens carved into ocean dunes against a backdrop of mountains. Caddies and rental clubs are available.

Courses

Amigas LANGUAGE COURSE
(☎315-107-52-80; www.easyspanish.net; Michoacán 58; lessons per hr private/semiprivate/group US$15/11.50/7.50; ⏲Nov-Mar) This small school aims to make language instruction fun and instantly applicable. Along with basic grammar, you'll learn a thing or two about Mexican slang.

Tours

Experience Mex-ECO Tours ECOTOURS
(☎315-355-70-27; www.mex-ecotours.com; Veracruz 204) This Melaque-based ecotourism company offers fishing charters (per hour from M$500 to M$600), day tours to Tenacatita (per person from M$700), which includes a snorkel over the reef at Playa Mora, and overnight camping trips to the Majahuas Biological Station, where over 3000 turtle nests are collected and protected each year. The Sea Turtle Experience (adult/child M$899/699) is offered three times per year from Melaque, meals included.

Festivals & Events

Torneo Internacional de Pesca FISHING
(☎315-100-41-34) This three-day festival, held around the third week in January, is the most noteworthy of several big-money international fishing tournaments held annually for marlin, sailfish, tuna and *dorado.*

Sleeping

Barra has fewer beachfront rooms than its neighbor Melaque. The prices listed here are for the high season (between November and May), when the wise traveller books well in advance.

Hotel Laguna Luna INN $$
(☎315-355-01-91; www.hotellagunaluna.com; Veracruz 53; r M$550-650; 📶) A family-run three-floor walk-up on the Laguna. Rooms have tiled floors with mosaic accents, porcelain sinks and psychedelic purple, yellow or orange accent walls, high ceilings and cable TV. Pay more for a lagoon view. Interior rooms are a bit dark.

★ **Hotel Delfín** HOTEL $$
(☎315-355-50-68; www.hoteldelfinmx.com; Morelos 23; d/tr/q M$595/695/795; P📶🏊) The homey Delfín is one of Barra's best deals. It has 24 large and pleasant rooms featuring shared balconies, a grassy pool area, an exercise room and a rooftop deck. Factor in excellent management and you have the kind of place you'd rather not leave. Discounts are available for longer stays, but repeat customers fill the place in winter.

Hotel Trivento HOTEL $$
(☎315-355-53-78; www.triventohotel.com; Jalisco 75; d M$795; ❄📶🏊) A family-run inn with small but endearing rooms thanks to creative paint jobs, well-stocked kitchenettes, ceramic tile floors in the rooms and cute tiled baths. The small TV is wired for cable. Prices drop to M$495 in the low season.

Casa Chips HOTEL $$
(☎315-355-55-55; www.casachips.com; Legazpi 198; d US$55-65, ste US$75-110; ❄📶) One of Barra's few beachfront options, Chips is most appealing for its two big ocean-facing suites with terraces, great views, nice tile and brickwork, and kitchenettes. Less welcoming are the interior and street-facing rooms, which can get a bit claustrophobic.

Hotel Barra de Navidad HOTEL $$
(☎315-355-51-22; www.hotelbarradenavidad.com; Legazpi 250; d from M$850-1100; ❄📶🏊)

Providing Barra's best beach access, this white, modern beachside hotel harbors a shaded and intimate courtyard and a small but inviting pool. The most appealing rooms have recently been refurbished with new tile, floating beds, dark-wood desks, fat flat-screen TVs and sweet sea-view terraces.

Eating

Restaurant Ramon's MEXICAN $$
(☎315-355-64-35; Legazpi 260; mains M$96-138; ⏲7am-11pm) This casual and friendly restaurant is justifiably popular for its excellent fish tacos, *chiles rellenos,* and local and gringo favorites such as fish and chips.

Nacho SEAFOOD $$
(Av Legazpi; mains M$70-125, grilled fish per kg M$250 (serves 2-3); ⏲10:30am-9:30pm) It doesn't look like much upon first glance: just little a handful of plastic tables under a stilted *palapa* roof on what feels like a vacant lot spilling out of a ceramic tiled kitchen. Dishes like shrimp empanadas, and that half avocado stuffed with ceviche may be what entices you, but the grilled fish is the deal.

The freshest fish is used, usually *dorado,* coated with spices, and grilled perfectly so it emerges moist and peels off the skin. It comes smothered with raw cucumbers, red onion and grilled bananas. Ask for some of the scintillating house salsa, and order one of the fine *micheladas* to wash it down.

El Manglito SEAFOOD $$
(Av Veracruz; mains M$80-220; ⏲1-9pm) A breezy, leafy and classy restaurant fronting the Laguna next to the boat cooperative offers both ambience and flavor. Grab a table, draped in plaid linens, shaded by colorful parasols, listen to Latin rhythms billow the fern palms and banana trees, and order superlative fresh seafood (this is a great place to splurge for lobster).

It gets creative with shrimp burgers, and stuffed fish fillets, but the ceviche is excellent too. Service could not be better.

Sea Master - Mexico Lindo MEXICAN $$
(☎315-107-08-89; Legazpi 146; mains M$110-195; ⏲noon-midnight) With hip decor, live music and winning sea views, this place scores by merging classic Mexican favorites with *nuovo* Mexican seafood dishes, with delicious results. It's also a fine choice for your sunset happy hour or nightcap. The kitchen stays open late.

Ambar d'Mare EUROPEAN $$$
(☎315-355-81-69; Legazpi 158; mains M$130-350; ⏲5pm-midnight) This romantic spot with a lovely seaside terrace, Ambar d'Mare boasts a good wine and aperitif list and a wide-ranging menu featuring wood-fired pizza, seafood, and French and Italian fare.

Drinking & Nightlife

Toward the pier at the foot of Legazpi, a cluster of bars keeps hopping into the wee hours. Jarro Beach Sports Bar & Disco hosts regular live bands.

Information

All local hotels offer wi-fi in their lobby if not their rooms. Most area restaurants offer wi-fi, as well.

Banamex (Veracruz s/n) One of two ATMs just south of Barra's main plaza.

Cyber Spiaggia (Veracruz s/n; per hr M$15; ⏲9am-10pm) One of several internet places on Barra's main drag.

Post Office (cnr Veracruz & Guanajuato)

Getting There & Around

AIR

Barra de Navidad is served by nearby **Playa de Oro International Airport** (☎315-333-11-19; Carretera Manzanillo–Barra de Navidad Km 42), 26km southeast of Barra on Hwy 200. To get to town from the airport, take a taxi (M$350, 30 minutes).

BOAT

Water taxis operate on demand 24 hours a day from the dock at the southern end of Veracruz, offering service to the Grand Bay Hotel Resort, the marina, the golf course and Colimilla. Round-trip fare to any destination is M$30.

BUS

Some but not all of the long-distance buses stopping at San Patricio-Melaque also stop at Barra de Navidad (15 minutes before or after) at the **Transportes Cihuatlán bus terminal** (Veracruz 228). **Primera Plus** (Veracruz 269) and **ETN** (Veracruz 273) operate from small terminals nearby, on the opposite side of Veracruz. Although Primera Plus buses no longer service Barra directly, you may purchase tickets here for buses that serve Melaque. There are direct buses from Barra to Manzanillo (M$65), Puerto Vallarta (M$207 to M$259) and Guadalajara (M$369).

In addition to the long-distance buses, colorful local buses connect Barra and Melaque (M$11, every 15 minutes, 6am to 9pm), stopping in Barra at the long-distance bus terminals (buses stopping on the southbound side of the road loop round Legazpi and back to Melaque).

TAXI

Catch taxis from one of the official stands (corner of Legazpi and Sinaloa, and corner of Veracruz and Michoacán) to get the best price. A taxi to San Patricio-Melaque costs M$50 to M$60.

MANZANILLO

☎314 / POP 161,000

Manzanillo has a bit of an identity crisis. On the one hand, it's Mexico's busiest commercial seaport, servicing cargo ships, pleasure cruises and naval vessels from around the world. On the other hand, it's a tourist destination, attracting beach lovers to its golden sands (the famous slow-motion scene of Bo Derek running along the beach in Blake Edwards' *10* was filmed here) and anglers to the self-proclaimed 'Sailfish Capital of the World.'

The personalities don't always mesh. Beaches are often streaked with oil that washes up from the busy harbor. And for every ambitious new nightclub or restaurant that opens, another shuts down. The government has poured millions of pesos into renovation projects such as the beautiful downtown *malecón* and the seaside main plaza plus sculpture gardens to attract visitors, but tourism has become an afterthought in Manzanillo. Views from the hills above the bay are still marvelous, though.

Manzanillo extends 16km from northwest to southeast. The resort hotels and finest beaches are concentrated about 10km from downtown on Península de Santiago, a rocky outcrop at the far northwestern edge of Bahía de Manzanillo. Just west of the peninsula, Bahía de Santiago is lined with beaches, as well.

Sights & Activities

Beaches

Playa San Pedrito, 1km northeast of the main plaza, is the closest beach to town, and the dirtiest. The next closest, spacious **Playa Las Brisas**, caters to a few hotels. **Playa Azul** stretches northwest from Las Brisas and curves around to Las Hadas resort and the best beaches in the area: **La Audiencia**, **Santiago**, **Olas Altas** and **Miramar**. Miramar and Olas Altas have decent surfing and bodysurfing. Playa La Audiencia, lining a quiet cove on the west side of the Península de Santiago, has more tranquil water and is popular for motorized water sports. Further west, **Playa La Boquita** is another beach with calm waters at the mouth of a lagoon where fishermen lay out their nets to dry by day, and shove off by night. The beach is lined with seafood restaurants where you can hang for the day. A shipwreck just offshore makes this a popular snorkeling spot.

Diving

The scuba diving around Manzanillo can be interesting, with deep-water pinnacles luring pelagics at **Los Frailes**, and alluring swim-through arches at **Roca Elefante**. **Underworld Scuba** (☎314-333-36-78; www.divemanzanillo.com; Hwy 200 Km 15; ⏲8am-5pm Mon-Sat, 9am-3pm Sun) charges US$95 for two-tank dives, including equipment.

Festivals & Events

Fiestas de Mayo TRADITIONAL

These fiestas celebrate the founding of Manzanillo in 1873. Festivities involve sporting competitions and other events over the first 10 days of May.

Sailfish Tournaments FISHING

(www.torneopescamanzanillo.com) Manzanillo's famous international tournament takes place in November; a smaller national tournament is held in February.

Sleeping

Manzanillo's cheapest hotels are located downtown, in the blocks surrounding the main plaza, and there are several down-on-their-luck three-star habitats on Playa Santiago disguised as proper beach hotels. Top-end places can be found on Playa La Audencia and further north. Prices shown are for high season (December to April) and can drop by 20% outside that period.

Hotel Colonial HOTEL $$

(☎314-332-10-80; hotelcolonialmanzanillo.com; Bocanegra 28; d M$660; P❄📶) One block from Manzanillo's waterfront plaza, this atmospheric old hotel retains the character of a colonial hacienda, with tiled outdoor hallways and a central courtyard. Big rooms are set on four floors surrounding that courtyard and have elegant drapes and wood furnishings, and a huge flat-screen TV. Downstairs rooms absorb a lot of restaurant and bar noise.

Greater Manzanillo

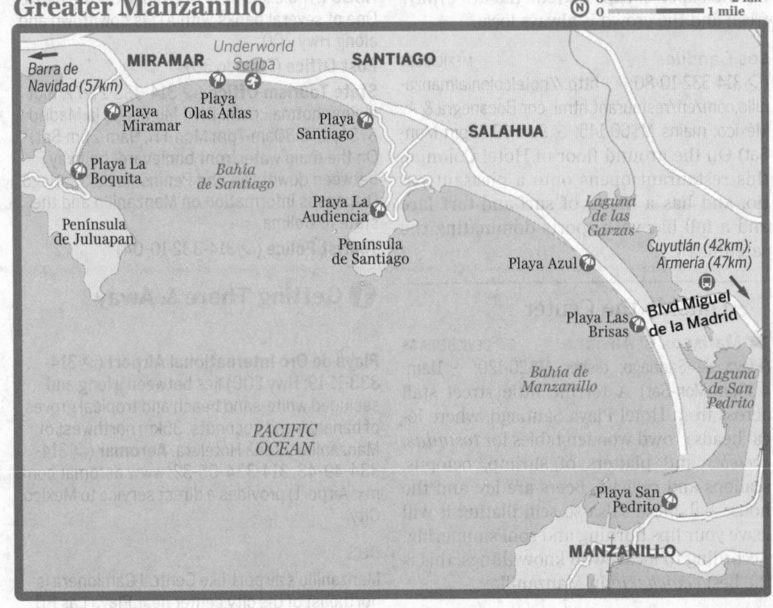

Hotel La Posada HOTEL **$$**
(☎314-333-18-99; www.hotel-la-posada.info; Cárdenas 201; s/d US$58/78; P❄📶🏊) This beachside B&B lures repeat guests with artfully decorated rooms, personalized service and amenities including a library, open-air dining room and honor bar. A small pool overlooks the beach, where you can watch ships – and the occasional whale – trawling the harbor. The location can be challenging for those without a car.

Hotel Real Posada HOTEL **$$**
(☎314-334-12-12; www.realposada.com.mx; Madrid 13801; d from M$750; P❄📶🏊) Set on the main Santiago commercial corridor, the location isn't terrific but it's only a block from Playa Santiago and within walking distance of Playa Las Olas. Just as important, rooms are relatively new and modern with tiled floors, wooden beds, crisp sheets and cable TV.

Hotel Playa de Santiago HOTEL **$$**
(☎314-333-00-55; www.playadesantiago.com; Playa de Santiago; d with fan/air-con M$624/807; P❄📶🏊) The first-ever hotel on Playa de Santiago is showing its age, but though walls may be scruffy, the floors, bathrooms and sheets are clean, there is a pool, it's right on the beach and all rooms have ocean views.

★**Dolphin Cove Inn** HOTEL **$$$**
(☎314-334-15-15; www.dolphincoveinn.com; Av Vista Hermosa s/n; d incl breakfast from M$1400; P⊖❄@📶🏊) This cliffside hotel adjacent to Las Hadas resort has killer views and huge, bright, spacious rooms on tiered floors that cascade to a pretty bayside swimming pool. Units range from basic doubles to two-room suites sleeping four, all with marble floors, kitchens or kitchenettes, vaulted ceilings and sea-view balconies.

Eating

Several good down-to-earth options are near the main plaza, while chain and chainlike spots line Hwy 200 around the bay.

Central Manzanillo

Mercado Francisco Madero MARKET **$**
(cnr Madero & Cuauhtémoc; mains M$30-60; ⊙7am-6pm) Manzanillo's downtown market has a number of inexpensive food stalls to choose from.

Comida Casera Yahualica MEXICAN **$**
(México 310; meals M$35-40; ⊙8am-9pm) A local diner serving everything from *tacos al pastor* to tasty plate lunches and dinners, with a choice of grilled protein, beans and a salad

on the super cheap. Ingredients are always fresh and the crowd is always local.

Los Candiles MEXICAN $$
(☎314-332-10-80; http://hotelcolonialmanzanillo.com/en/restaurant.html; cnr Bocanegra & Av México; mains M$60-145; ⏱8am-10:30pm Mon-Sat) On the ground floor of Hotel Colonial, this restaurant opens onto a pleasant patio, and has a menu of surf-and-turf fare and a full bar with sports dominating the satellite TV.

Outside the Center

★ **Mariscos El Aliviane** CEVICHERIA $$
(Playa de Santiago; dishes M$20-120; ⏱11am-4:30pm Mon-Sat) A terrific little street stall across from Hotel Playa Santiago, where local heads crowd wooden tables for *tostadas, cocteles* and platters of shrimp, octopus, scallops and ceviche. Beers are icy, and the house habanero salsa so scintillating it will leave your lips burning and soul simmering. According to locals who know things, this is the best *cevichería* in Manzanillo.

Paco Pazzo ITALIAN $$
(☎314-336-85-33; www.pocopazzomanzanillo.com; Madrid 923; pastas M$99-163, pizzas M$175-230; ⏱5pm-midnight) Enjoy surprisingly authentic Italian thin-crust pizza, pastas and traditional Italian steaks and seafood dishes on the marina adjacent to Las Hadas resort. Try the fish, baked and piled with clams and mussels, olives and capers, and drizzled with white wine sauce. All the ingredients are fresh, and there is a *gelatería* next door.

Information

Wi-fi is now widely available in hotels, cafes and restaurants throughout Manzanillo.

HSBC (Av México s/n) One block off the plaza. One of several banks with ATMs downtown and along Hwy 200.

Post Office (Galindo 30)

State Tourism Office (☎314-333-22-77; nicteloim@hotmail.com; Blvd Miguel de la Madrid 875A; ⏱8:30am-7pm Mon-Fri, 9am-2pm Sat) On the main waterfront boulevard, halfway between downtown and Península de Santiago. Dispenses information on Manzanillo and the state of Colima.

Tourist Police (☎314-332-10-04)

Getting There & Away

AIR

Playa de Oro International Airport (☎314-333-11-19; Hwy 200) lies between a long and secluded white-sand beach and tropical groves of bananas and coconuts, 35km northwest of Manzanillo's Zona Hotelera. **Aeromar** (☎314-334-49-48, 314-334-05-32; www.aeromar.com.mx; Airport) provides a direct service to Mexico City.

BUS

Manzanillo's airport-like Central Camionera is northeast of the city center near Playa Las Brisas, just off Blvd Miguel de la Madrid (Hwy 200). It's an organized place with tourist information, phones, eateries and left-luggage facilities (M$3 per hour).

CAR & MOTORCYCLE

Renting a car is not only convenient for exploring the Costalegre beaches northwest of Manzanillo's airport, but recommended for getting the most out of Manzanillo in general. Four car-rental agencies are clustered together in the airport arrivals hall:

Alamo (☎314-334-01-24; www.alamo.com.mx)

Budget (☎314-334-22-70; www.budget.com.mx)

Sixt (☎314-333-31-91; www.sixt.com)

Thrifty (☎314-334-32-92; www.thrifty.com)

BUSES FROM MANZANILLO

DESTINATION	FARE (M$)	DURATION	FREQUENCY (DAILY)
Barra de Navidad	38-55	1-1½hr	half-hourly
Colima	102	1½-2hr	half-hourly
Guadalajara	258-354	4½-7hr	hourly
Lázaro Cárdenas	250-283	7hr	hourly
Mexico City (Terminal Norte)	950	12hr	7
Puerto Vallarta	231-333	5-6½hr	frequent
San Patricio-Melaque	55	1-1½hr	half-hourly

Getting Around

There's no bus route to or from the airport, but most resorts have shuttle vans. Fixed-rate taxis from the airport charge M$400 to Península de Santiago or M$450 to downtown Manzanillo. From Manzanillo back to the airport, a taxi costs M$250 to M$350.

Local buses marked 'Santiago,' 'Las Brisas' and 'Miramar' head around the bay to the towns of San Pedrito, Salahua, Santiago, Miramar and beaches along the way. 'Las Hadas' buses take a more circuitous, scenic route down the Península de Santiago. These buses pick up passengers from the corner of Madero and Domínguez; the corner of Juárez and Calle 21 de Marzo near the main plaza; along Avenida Morelos; Avenida Niños Héroes; and from the main bus terminal every 10 minutes from 6am to 11pm. Fares are M$7, depending on how far you're going.

Taxis are plentiful in Manzanillo. From the main bus terminal, a cab fare is around M$45 to the main plaza or Playa Azul, and M$100 to Península de Santiago or Playa Miramar. But you can also grab northbound buses from the Santiago Bus Terminal, which is just a M$35 fare from the Playa Santiago area. Always agree on a price before you get into the taxi.

BOCA DE PASCUALES

Boca de Pascuales is a legendary surf spot that attracts the best boarders from around the world, and is strictly for experienced surfers. Aggressive barrel swells range from 2m to 5m in summer and storm waves occasionally reach 10m. If you have any doubt, don't go out.

Sleeping & Eating

Paco's Hotel HOTEL $$

(cell phone 313-1232027; www.pacoshotel.com; r M$600-800;) Family-run and plastered with autographed photos of famous surfers, Paco's offers simple but comfy rooms, each with a different flower theme lovingly painted by his daughter Lulu. The hotel also has a decent restaurant (mains from M$80).

★ **Las Hamacas del Mayor** SEAFOOD $$

(313-329-19-50; www.lashamacasdelmayor.com.mx; mains M$80-200; 10:30am-6pm;) A local fixture since 1953, Las Hamacas is one of the most famous eateries in Colima state despite its off-the-beaten-path location. The two-level restaurant seats 1000 people and is open every day of the year. Strolling mariachis entertain the crowd, a swimming pool keeps the kids busy, and there are great views of surfers riding the waves just offshore.

Exquisite seafood specialties include fish fillet stuffed with octopus and shrimp, marinated in garlic sauce.

Getting There & Away

To reach Pascuales, first catch a bus from Manzanillo to Tecomán (M$47 to M$60, one hour, every 15 minutes). From here, hourly combis run to Pascuales (M$11, 20 minutes). A taxi from Tecomán is M$80. If driving, follow the sign from downtown Tecomán about 10km to the beach.

MICHOACÁN COAST

Highway 200 hugs the shoreline most of the way along the spectacular 250km coastline of Michoacán, one of Mexico's most beautiful states. The route passes dozens of untouched beaches – some with wide expanses of golden sand, some tucked into tiny rocky coves, some at river mouths where quiet estuaries harbor multitudes of birds. Several have gentle lapping waves that are good for swimming, while others have big breakers suitable for surfing. Many of the beaches are uninhabited, but some shelter communities. Mango, coconut, papaya and banana plantations line the highway, while the green peaks of the Sierra Madre del Sur form a lush backdrop inland. Blue signs along Hwy 200 mark the turnoffs for most beaches. Kilometer markers begin counting down from Km 231 at the state's northern border.

Other beaches of interest beyond those described following are **Ixtapilla** (Km 180), **La Manzanillera** (Km 174), **Motín de Oro** (Km 167), **Zapote de Tizupán** (Km 103), **Pichilinguillo** (Km 95) and **Huahua** (Km 84). It's much easier to explore this stretch of coast, especially the more remote beaches, if you have your own vehicle. However, 2nd-class buses (at least half a dozen daily) along the Manzanillo–Lázaro Cárdenas route will generally drop off and pick up passengers at any town entrance along coastal Hwy 200.

San Juan de Alima

Twenty kilometers south of Boca de Apiza, near where the highway meets the coast, is the cobblestoned town of San Juan de Alima (Km 211). It's seasonally popular with surfers due to its creamy medium-sized breakers

WORTH A TRIP

CUYUTLÁN

With its black-sand beaches, gentle waves and laid-back attitude, Cuyutlán feels a world away from everywhere. Located at the southeastern end of Laguna de Cuyutlán, just 40km southeast of Manzanillo, it's a somewhat depressed beach pueblo that can be popular with Mexican families on weekends

The area's principal attraction is **El Tortugario** (☎313-120-40-80, 313-120-35-12, 313-107-40-69; www.tortugariocuyutlan.com; adult/child M$25/20; ⏲9am-5pm Thu & Fri, Mon & Tue, to 3pm Sat & Sun, closed Wed), a turtle sanctuary located 4km east of Cuyutlán. Since it opened in 1993, conservationists have released two million green, black and leatherback turtle hatchlings into the wild here. The center also has small iguana and crocodile sanctuaries, an education center, swimming pools and a picnic area. Don't miss El Tortugario's lagoon trips on the Palo Verde Estuary, a nature preserve that's home to more than 100 bird species, including 257 migratory birds. *Lanchas* (skiffs) move through mangrove tunnels and past sunbathing crocodiles. The 45-minute ride costs M$40.

Cuyutlán is connected to the world through Armería, a dusty but friendly service center on Hwy 200, 46km southeast of Manzanillo and 55km southwest of Colima. From Armería a 12km paved road heads west past coconut plantations to the coast.

Nuevo Horizonte runs two buses daily between Manzanillo's bus terminal and Cuyutlán (M$42, one hour). Alternatively, catch a bus from Manzanillo to Armería (M$45, 45 minutes, every 15 minutes), then walk two blocks north and one block east to Armería's market and transfer to a local bus to Cuyutlán (M$11, 20 minutes, half-hourly). Returning from Cuyutlán, buses leave from the main plaza a few blocks in from the beach.

Buses also run every 20 minutes between Cuyutlán and Tecomán (M$11, 15 minutes), where you can connect with buses heading southeast on Hwy 200 to Lázaro Cárdenas and elsewhere.

just off the coast. There are several beachfront restaurants and modern hotels.

Hotel Parador (☎313-327-90-21; r M$500-600; P❄🏊) offers a good variety of rooms, some with balconies and views. The hotel's popular restaurant perches directly above the ocean on palm-shaded terraces.

Las Brisas

The cliff-hugging road south of San Juan de Alima climbs above the coast, offering gorgeous views of desolate sandy beaches below. The tiny white strand of Las Brisas (Km 205) is accented by just a few *palapa* restaurants and the comfortable **Hotel Brisas de Verano** (☎313-327-90-55; hotelbrisasdeverano.com; s from M$600, d M$800-900; P❄🏊). Rooms have a kitschy quality with ceramic floors, built-in concrete beds and bench seating, exposed roughly hewn cement walls, and lots of bright oranges and yellows. If you're a bird-watcher, there is a nice mangrove lagoon about 1km south of town. You might also consider this town the southernmost demarcation point of government influence. Which is why the hotel, something of a base camp, is almost always occupied by Federal Police and military personnel. From here they run patrols into cartel territory, which extends from just south of here to Caleta. In otherwords, for the next 150+ kilometres, the cartels own the highway.

Playa La Ticla

A renowned surfing destination, Playa La Ticla (Km 183) is known for its long, left point break and mostly attracts foreign surfers with their own vehicles. The long beach is divided by a swimmable freshwater river.

On the beachfront, a few *enramadas* (thatch-covered, open-air restaurants) serve fresh seafood, and **Parador Turístico La Ticla** (☎313-327-80-86, 424-488-00-25; www.paradoresecoturisticos.blogspot.com/p/parador-turistico-la-ticla_27; d/tr M$440/660, 10-person cabaña M$1650-2200) offers spartan rooms with minimal privacy in handsome, thatched multilevel wooden *cabañas*, with hammocks on the porch, and a circular, thatched common space.

For fine home cooking, head a few blocks inland to **Cabaña de Vicky** (☎313-328-58-23; mains M$50-100; ⏰8am-11pm Mon-Sat), where daily specials (M$50 to M$60) are accompanied by good salsa and fresh tortillas made with corn from Vicky's own backyard.

Faro de Bucerías

Faro de Bucerías (Km 173) is a sheltered crescent beach with clear, pale-blue waters and yellow sand that is perfect for sun worshipping, snorkeling or swimming. The local Nahua community operates a long line of *palapa* seafood restaurants offering plentiful, fat lobsters. The best of the bunch is the **El Faro de Bucerías** (☎313-327-80-96; mains M$100-200; ⏰8am-8pm; 📶) restaurant, where the lobster platters are hard to beat. *Cabañas* are available at the government-subsidized **Centro Ecoturístico** (☎313-322-43-04; cenecoturfaro@hotmail.com; 2-/4-person cabaña M$400/600; 🅿📶), which can also arrange trips to see the turtles in nearby Playa Colola.

Playa Colola

An estimated 70% of the world's population of black sea turtles, along with olive ridley and leatherback turtles, lay their eggs on the long flat sands of Playa Colola (Km 160). And you can see why. Here is a thick and wide slab of creamy sand that runs up against chaparral-coated hills and is framed by two picturesque headlands. This is open ocean, however, not a bay, and though it may look innocent enough there is a shore break here, and an undertow, so swim with caution.

Of course, the main draw are those turtles, and **Sitio Ramsar Playa de Colola** (angel-colola@hotmail.es), established in 2008, monitors the beach, protects the eggs and releases hatchlings. For M$35 visitors can accompany local and international volunteers on their nightly rounds (8pm to 4am). Turtle viewing is best between September and December, when hundreds of turtles nest en masse. Staff hours are variable; contact the site in advance by email to arrange your visit. If you have trouble reaching the center, you may also arrange a visit at the Centro Ecoturístico in Faro de Bucerías.

Playa Maruata

With clear turquoise waters and golden sandy beaches, Playa Maruata (Km 150) is the most beautiful beach in Michoacán. The Nahua fishing village has a bit of a hippie reputation, attracting beach bums from all over. It's a tranquil, friendly place to hang out with your sweetie or a large stack of paperbacks. It's also a prime nesting site for black sea turtles (each night from June to December).

Maruata actually has three beaches, each with its own unique character. The left (eastern) is the longest, a 3km pristine crescent-shaped beach with creamy yellow sand and calm waves perfect for swimming and snorkeling. The small middle arc is OK for strong swimmers. It's sheltered by a climbable rocky headland riddled with caves, tunnels and blow holes, and marked by the unusual **Dedo de Dios** (God's Finger) formation rising from the sea. The far-right (western) beach is known as **Playa de los Muertos** (Beach of the Dead), and for good reason: it has dangerous currents and ferocious waves. During low tide you can scale the rocks on the far right side of Muertos to reach a secluded cove where discreet nude sunbathing is tolerated. But don't get stuck here when the tide comes in. A crucifix on the rocks serves as a stark memorial to the people who have been swallowed by the sea.

This is an extremely poor pueblo, but you'll find a small grocery store and a restaurant near the town's bleak plaza. The *enramadas* on the left beach serve fresh seafood and are also your best bet for camping. Most charge from M$30 per person

MICHOACÁN'S BEACHFRONT PARADORES

Between Km 183 and Km 103 on Hwy 200 you'll see frequent signs for tourist lodgings known as *paradores turísticos* (government-run tourist lodgings); despite mostly wearing the forlorn look of government projects without much local enthusiasm behind them, these offer reasonably priced accommodations right on or just above the beach with killer views. For photos of the various *paradores*, see the Spanish-language website www.paradoreseco turisticos.blogspot.com.

to pitch a tent or rent a hammock. Those who need four semi-solid walls can find a few rustic *cabañas* for M$300 to M$400; alternatively, splurge on one of the 14 tile-floored, *palapa*-roofed units at **Centro Ecoturístico Maruata** (cell phone 315-55150511; 2-/4-person cabaña M$500/1000), on a hillside overlooking the far-right beach.

Barra de Nexpa

753 / POP 100

At Km 55.6, just north of Puente Nexpa bridge, and 1km from the highway down a rough cobbled road, lies the small, laid-back community of Nexpa. It's long been a haven for surfers, attracted to the salt-and-pepper sandbar and long right-hand break at the river mouth, which can rise to double overhead. At its best, rides can last a full kilometer here. Of course, at research time, thanks to Hurricane Manuel and the ensuing floods, the sandbar had been reshaped, altering conditions somewhat.

Jorge & Helen's Tienda (www.surfingrionexpa.com; 9:30am-9:30pm), to the left as you enter town, is a grocery store offering wi-fi (though it was out due to storm damage at research time) and surfboard rentals (per hour/day/week M$70/150/690).

Buses to Nexpa (M$59) depart Lázaro Cárdenas every two hours.

Sleeping & Eating

Several places along the beachfront offer camping from M$30 per person, while a half-dozen *palapas* serve delicious local seafood.

Chicho's GUESTHOUSE $

(cell phone 753-1309236; r M$200-300) One of several *enramadas* lining the beach, Chicho's is a great choice for breakfast, thanks to gargantuan smoothies (M$35) and inspiring views of wave-riding surfers. It also rents out some very basic and very cheap beachfront *cabañas*, featuring hammocks strung upstairs above a cement floor. Meals cost from M$50.

Río Nexpa Rooms GUESTHOUSE $

(cell phone 753-1216501; www.rionexparooms.com; s/d/tr/q M$350/400/450/500) A beautifully crafted Southeast Asian–style *palapa*, about 200m inland along the river, with five comfortable rooms, four with lofts. It has a shared kitchen, a lagoonside garden area and a tranquil communal sitting room.

Jorge and Helen's Place GUESTHOUSE $

(cell phone 753-1160570; www.surfingrionexpa.com; r from M$400; P ❄ wi-fi) There's a handy general store, a surf shop, a wi-fi signal and some sweet, simple, digs. Expect super-clean tiled floors, pastel paint jobs, rain showers and air-con. Easily the most popular choice in Nexpa.

Mar de Noche CABAÑAS, HOTEL $$

(cell phone 753-1183931; www.nexpasurf.jimdo.com; r or cabaña M$800; ❄) The fan-cooled *cabañas* here have comfy beds, hammocks, kitchens and private bathrooms. There's also an adjacent six-room hotel with modern amenities including air-con (if it happens to be working, which is no guarantee). The attached beachfront restaurant, decorated with hand-carved wood columns, serves three meals a day (mains from M$60). Low-season prices plummet to M$300.

Mary Jane INTERNATIONAL $$

(mains M$75-180; 9am-11pm) Stilted above the beach, and the main gathering place for surfers, the Mexican-born owner Martin grew up in the US and he shoots videos of the break each morning to be screened over dinner and drinks each evening. Meals include tasty fish tacos, burgers, pastas and a handful of local delicacies. Bagels are served at breakfast. And about that name...

The Cartel's Coast

Thanks to grisly drug murders – including widely reported beheadings in Morelia and Acapulco – and the systematic targeting of journalists in Ciudad Juárez, you can hardly buy a ticket to anywhere in this great country without triggering uninformed warnings from well-meaning friends about the inherent dangers of travel in a country that by nearly every conceivable measure has thrived and modernized at an enviable pace in the last decade. The fact is, even while travelling through areas where the cartel is endemic, rare is the moment that you'll notice anything out of the ordinary. Except, that is, for this 150km stretch of the Michoacán Coast, where La Familia, perhaps the most notorious of them all, operates and owns the roads.

You might notice young men dressed casually in jeans and T-shirts, with walkie-talkies hooked on their belt loops. Those are foot soldiers who are often recruited as teenagers. They earn approximately US$1000 per month, are on call seven days a week, 24 hours a day, and if they quit or run, they're told they will be hunted and executed. They attend combat training on vast ranches in the mountains, and their prinicipal job is to maintain control of the roads, and watch for federal police or military patrols, which they radio up the chain of command. When 'Wanted' billboards go up on this stretch of highway, they are quickly blotted out, and theft or violence against tourists is not tolerated whatsoever. Once two Canadian surfer girls had an iPhone and iPad stolen from their room in Nexpa by local boys. Reports filtered to folks in charge who sent out the foot soldiers to recover the gear. All was returned safely and with an apology and nobody got hurt. There is (twisted) justice in cartel country.

Caleta de Campos

☎753 / POP 2600

Caleta (Km 50) is a regional service center with all the essentials, including a gas station, a *caseta de teléfono,* late-night *taquerías,* a pharmacy and several grocery stores. It's set up on the bluffs, which open like a clam on either side and taper toward an azure bay where you'll find a nice selection of seafood *enramadas* and a protected cove best suited to novice surfers, if there is any swell at all. On the south side of the bay, stark bluffs tumble to a point. To the north is a decrepit concrete pier and a rock reef that breaches the thrashing sea. There are several large homes up on the bluffs, though most are empty and Caleta does project a ghost-town aura during the off season.

The area's best surf shop, **Surf y Espuma** (☎753-531-5255; surfyespuma@hotmail.com; surfboard rental per day/week US$10/60; ⏲9am-7pm), has two locations, one in town and another (open seasonally) on the beach. The in-town shop washes laundry (M$18 per kg), and the owners also operate the choice hotel in town, **Villa Tropical** (www.caletadecampos.com; r M$450-900;), with barbecues, hammocks, pools and water-sports equipment available to guests.

Parador Turistico (☎753-531-5101; www.partourcaleta.com; Carretera 200 Km 51.25; d/tr M$900/1200;), perched above the beach 1km north of town, has 12 comfortable ocean-view units, with terracotta floors and cable TV surrounding a circular *palapa*-style bar and lounge area. The best suite has a kitchenette, dining room, and private terrace with Jacuzzi.

Hourly buses depart Caleta's main plaza for Lázaro Cárdenas (M$56, 1¼ hours) from 5am to 7pm. A taxi between Caleta de Campos and Barra de Nexpa costs M$50 to M$60.

LÁZARO CÁRDENAS

☎753 / POP 163,000

As an industrial port city, Lázaro Cárdenas has nothing of real touristic interest – but because it's a hub for buses up and down the coast, travelers regularly pass through. Lázaro is also a regional service center where you'll find banks, a post office, pharmacies and Pemex gas stations, but with excellent beaches and waves so near, there is no reason to spend the night.

BUSES FROM LÁZARO CÁRDENAS

DESTINATION	FARE (M$)	DURATION	FREQUENCY (DAILY)
Acapulco	260	6-7hr	6
Barra de Nexpa	56	1 hr	two hourly
Caleta de Campos	59	1hr	two hourly
Guadalajara	524	8hr	4
Manzanillo	283	7hr	hourly
Mexico City (Terminal Norte)	650	8-11hr	7
Morelia	310-550	4-5hr	very frequent
Caleta & Nexpa	56 & 59	1hr	two hourly
Uruapan	210-360	3-4hr	frequent
Zihuatanejo	156	1½-2hr	hourly

Getting There & Away

Lázaro has three bus terminals, all within a few blocks of each other. From the **main bus terminal** (☎753-532-30-06; Lázaro Cárdenas 1810) various operators offer services to Manzanillo, Uruapan, Morelia, Colima, Guadalajara and Mexico City.

From the **Estrella Blanca terminal** (☎753-532-11-71; www.estrellablanca.com.mx; Francisco Villa 65), two blocks west behind the main bus terminal, buses head up the coast to Manzanillo, where you can transfer to a Puerto Vallarta–bound bus; and inland to Uruapan, Morelia and Mexico City.

The **Estrella de Oro terminal** (☎753-532-02-75; www.estrelladeoro.com.mx; Corregidora 318) is one block north and two blocks west of Estrella Blanca and serves Zihuatanejo, Acapulco and Mexico City.

TRONCONES

☎755 / POP 700

Not long ago, Troncones was a poor, sleepy fishing and farming village. That all changed in the mid-1990s when wealthy North Americans arrived and began building luxury beachfront vacation homes and B&Bs. Tourists followed for the beaches, relaxing atmosphere and world-class surfing.

The expat invasion has left an indelible mark: the long strip between Troncones and neighboring Majahua bears more resemblance to a California subdivision than to the traditional Mexican villages at either end, where chickens and *burros* (donkeys) still roam the streets. For entertainment, there's precious little to do aside from catching the waves, relaxing in a hammock and soaking up the sun.

Troncones is located about 25km northwest of Ixtapa, at the end of a 3km paved road from Hwy 200. The paved road ends at a T-intersection, from where a dusty beachfront road continues northwest to the communities of Troncones Point, Manzanillo Bay and Majahua. The majority of tourist attractions are along this beachfront road.

Of the four communities, Troncones is the most built-up. At the T-intersection you'll find a few small grocery stores, a laundry and several cheap food vendors. The surf in Troncones and Troncones Point is rough and geared to experienced surfers. Manzanillo Bay is a sheltered cove more conducive to swimming. Majahua is a traditional fishing village with a few *enramadas* and a mellow beach layered with fine shells for beachcombers. From Majahua, another dirt road (rough in the wet season) leads back out to Hwy 200.

Activities

The **swimming** in the protected cove off Playa Manzanillo is glorious, and on placid days the **snorkeling** is good here too. **Horseback riding** is quite popular; locals stroll the beach with their steeds looking for customers. Other activities that can be arranged through local inns include **mountain biking**, **fishing**, and **spelunking** through the limestone cave system near Majahua.

But surfing rules here and Troncones has several world-class surf spots. The beach breaks can be excellent in summer, but the wave to chase is the left at **Troncones Point**. When it's small, the takeoff is right over the rocks (complete with sea urchins), but when it's big, it's beautiful and beefy and rolls halfway across the bay.

Galería Nuñez SURFING
(☎755-114-35-04, cell phone 755-1030005; www.primesurfboards.net) Just north of the T-intersection, surfer Bruce Grimes offers two-hour lessons (US$60) and board repair (from M$300 to M$500 for a few dings to M$1500 for a broken board). He also designs custom boards (short/long boards US$500/900) and rents out boards (per day/week M$300/1200) and bikes (M$200 per day).

Inn at Manzanillo Bay SURFING
(☎755-553-28-84; www.manzanillobay.com; Playa Manzanillo) Near the point, the Inn at Manzanillo Bay rents out an excellent selection of short and long boards (half-/full day M$200/320), bodyboards (half-/full day M$60/120) and kayaks (half-/full day M$350/650). It also offers surf lessons (M$750).

Tours

Costa Nativa Ecotours ECOTOURS
(☎755-100-74-99; www.tronconesecotours.com) This outfit organizes kayaking, hiking, spelunking, bird-watching and sea-turtle-spotting excursions, ranging in price from M$300 to M$550 per person.

Sleeping

All businesses listed following are along Troncones' main waterfront road. Reservations are advisable during the high season (November through April), when some places require multiple-night stays. During low season, prices can be 25% to 50% less, but be aware that many lodging facilities close during summer. You may also rent one of the many casas and villas available for week-long stays. Check www.vrbo.com for details on the 49 properties available for rent in the area at research time.

Tronco Bay Inn INN $$
(☎755-103-01-10; www.tronco-bay-inn.com; d with garden/sea view M$800/1000) Set at the north end of town on Manzanillo Bay is a new, endearing spot with terrific rooms that sleep up to three, decked out with inlaid tile floors, ceiling fans and wood furnishings set in six split-level duplexes. There's a pool and a sweet slice of beachfront that lures an upmarket local crowd on weekends.

Casa Delfín Sonriente B&B $$
(☎755-553-28-03; www.casadelfinsonriente.com; bungalow/r/ste incl breakfast US$70/85/119; ❄📶🏊) Guests rave about the peaceful, welcoming atmosphere at this B&B, with its good breakfasts, beachfront massage table and pool, hammocks, games and beach toys available to all. If available, grab one of the amazing upstairs suites, which have hanging beds, full kitchens, and a shared rooftop patio and lounge area with insane views of the wild Pacific.

Three rooms have air-con; the rest come with fans.

Inn at Manzanillo Bay BUNGALOW $$$
(☎755-553-28-84; www.manzanillobay.com; Playa Manzanillo; bungalows US$98-138; P❄📶🏊) In a prime setting on Troncones' prettiest beach, this mini-resort has eight thatched-roof bungalows with king-sized beds, canopied mosquito netting, ceiling fans and hammocked terraces surrounding a pool. For an extra dose of creature comforts, you can upgrade to one of the newer terrace suites, which feature air-con and HDTV.

There's also a popular restaurant and bar, a surf shop, and easy access to the primo break at Troncones Point.

Present Moment Retreat BUNGALOW $$$
(☎828-318-39-50; www.presentmomentretreat.com; s/d/tr incl breakfast & 1 class per day US$215/250/345; P🏊🖋) This 'conscious living' spa resort is a haven for the body and mind, specializing in yoga, meditation and massage. The 10 minimalist thatched-roof bungalows all surround a beautiful pool and gardens. The restaurant, on a pretty sea-facing deck, is among the best, healthiest and priciest (mains M$170 to M$400) in town, with dishes for vegetarians and carnivores alike.

It also has a fine tequila list, and who wouldn't Om to that?

Eating & Drinking

Cafe del Mar CAFE
(☎755-103-01-32; mains US$9-15; ⏲8am-5pm Tue-Sat, 8am-3pm Sun) Western breakfasts, smoothies, good coffee and a sunny atmosphere are yours at this cafe on the main road. It's one of the newer shingles in town.

Jardín del Edén FUSION $$
(☎755-103-01-04; www.jardindeleden.com.mx; mains M$120-200; ⏲8am-10pm Nov-May) Just north of Troncones Point, the French chef's fusion menu ranges from Mediterranean to Pacific Rim to traditional Mexican fare. Nightly specials such as pizza, lasagna and *cochinita pibil* (Yucatán-style slow-roasted pork) are cooked on the grill and in the wood-fired oven.

Roberto's Bistro ARGENTINE $$$
(www.robertosbistro.com; mains M$115-250; ⏲8am-10pm) Sizzling steaks and crashing waves create the stereophonic soundtrack at this Argentine-style beachfront grill, 1km south of the T-intersection. From *chorizo* starters to full-on feasts such as the *parrillada argentina* (T-bone, rib-eye and several other cuts grilled together with shrimp), this is carnivore paradise.

Getting There & Away

Driving from Ixtapa or Zihuatanejo, head northwest on Hwy 200 toward Lázaro Cárdenas. Just north of Km 30 you'll see the marked turnoff for Troncones; follow this winding paved road 3km west to the beach.

Second-class buses heading northwest toward Lázaro Cárdenas from Zihuatanejo's long-distance bus terminals will drop you at the turnoff for Troncones (M$35, 45 minutes), if you ask.

White *colectivo* vans shuttle between Hwy 200 and Troncones (M$11) roughly every half-hour; some continue on to Manzanillo Bay (M$16) and Majahua (M$20). Taxis make the same trip for M$50 to M$60.

Taxis de Troncones (☎755-553-29-11) offers service from Troncones to Ixtapa-Zihuatanejo International Airport (M$500), Zihuatanejo (M$350) and Ixtapa (M$300). A taxi *from* Zihuatanejo's airport will set you back about M$750.

IXTAPA

☎755 / POP 6400

Ixtapa was nothing more than a huge coconut plantation until the late 1970s when Fonatur (the Mexican government's tourism development group) decided that the Pacific coast needed a Cancún-like resort. In came the hotel and golf-course developers and up went the high-rises. The result was a planned city with spotless beaches, luxurious hotels, chain restaurants and not a palm tree or blade of grass out of place.

Four decades later, Ixtapa continues to offer a contrived, squeaky-clean version of Mexican beach culture that stands in dramatic contrast to the down-to-earth charms of its sister city, Zihuatanejo. Ixtapa's appeal is best appreciated by families seeking a hassle-free all-inclusive beach getaway, or those who value modern chain-hotel comforts and nightlife over a cultural experience. Plus, when all the Mexico travel warnings went up in response to cartel violence – that, to be fair, never touched Ixtapa – it was this tourism experiment that took the biggest hit. Now, many subdivisions and storefronts are empty and in low season Ixtapa is so empty it feels like a failed tourism state.

Sights

Beaches are the big draw, obviously. **Playa del Palmar** is the longest and broadest stretch of blond sand, that's overrun by parasailing and jet-skiing concessions. The sea takes on an aquamarine sheen in the dry season when it clarifies, which makes it all the more inviting – but take care while swimming, as there can be a vicious shore break and a powerful undertow when the swell comes up. There's aren't many public access points to the beach, thanks to the mega resorts lined up shoulder to shoulder, but you can always cut through a hotel lobby if need be.

Playa Escolleras, at the west end of Playa del Palmar near the entrance to the marina, has a decent break and attracts surfers. Further west, past Punta Ixtapa, **Playa Quieta** and **Playa Linda** are popular with locals, though the water is murky thanks to the nearby rivers and mangroves that nourish and cleanse one another.

Cocodrilario — WILDLIFE RESERVE

FREE Playa Linda has a small *cocodrilario* (crocodile reserve) that is also home to fat iguanas and several bird species. You can watch the hulking crocs from the safety of the well-fenced wooden viewing platform located near the bus stop and extending toward the harbor.

Isla Ixtapa — ISLAND

Isla Ixtapa is a beautiful oasis from the concrete jungle of Ixtapa. The turquoise waters are crystal clear, calm and great for snorkeling (gear rentals cost M$120 per day). **Playa Corales** on the back side of the island is the nicest and quietest beach, with soft white sand, and an offshore coral reef.

Enramada seafood restaurants and massage providers dot the island. Frequent boats to Isla Ixtapa depart from Playa Linda's pier from 9am to 5pm (round trip M$40, five minutes). The island gets mobbed by tourists in high season, and you'll likely have to run the attendant gauntlet of hawkers en route to the pier.

Activities

Cycling

Cycling is a breeze along a 15km *ciclopista* (cycle path) that stretches from Playa Linda, north of Ixtapa, practically into Zihuatanejo.

Ola Rental — CYCLING

(☎755-553-02-59; Centro Comercial Ixpamar; ⏲8am-7pm) Mountain bikes can be rented for M$50/250 per hour/day from Ola Rental.

Surfing

Surfing is good on Playa Linda and Playa Escolleras.

Catcha L'Ola Surf & Stuff — SURFING

(☎755-553-13-84; www.ixtapasurf.com; Centro Comercial Los Patios; board rental per day/week M$200/1000, 3hr lesson M$600; ⏲9am-7pm) You'll find everything you need – rentals, repairs, classes and surfing trips – at Catcha L'Ola Surf & Stuff.

Water Sports

Scuba diving is popular in the warm, clear waters.

Mero Adventure — DIVING

(☎755-101-95-39, cell phone 755-1019672; www.meroaventuras.com/_mero_map__location.7.html; Hotel Pacífica; 1-/2-tank dives US$65/90) Mero Adventure organizes diving, snorkeling, kayaking and fishing trips, as well as swimming with dolphins.

Tours

Adventours ADVENTURE TOUR
(755-553-35-84; www.ixtapa-adventours.com; Centro Comercial Plaza Ambiente, Blvd Ixtapa s/n; tours M$700-950) Adventours offers a variety of guided cycling, kayaking, snorkeling and bird-watching tours around Ixtapa and Zihuatanejo.

Sleeping

With the exception of the campground, Ixtapa's beachfront resorts are all top end. Prices listed here are rack rates for high season, which runs from mid-December to Easter. Prices can drop by 25% or more for the rest of the year. Better rates are often available through package deals or from hotel websites.

Park Royal HOTEL $$$
(755-555-05-50, 755-553-04-38; www.parkroyal.mx/en/park-royal/ixtapa; Blvd Ixtapa s/n; r from M$1550;) An aging four-star resort with a terrific pool area and beachfront catering to a local following. The funky tiled floors are a throwback to the '70s, and well-maintained rooms are all super-clean and bright with small sea-view terraces.

Las Brisas Ixtapa Resort RESORT $$$
(755-553-21-21; www.brisashotelonline.com/ixtapa; d incl breakfast from US$160;) An enormous orange wedge rising from the sands, Las Brisas sits on an isolated stretch of Playa Vista Hermosa south of Ixtapa's main strip. The interior has a contemporary Mexican feel with lots of color and wood throughout. All 416 rooms have extra-large terraces with first-rate ocean views and hammocks. The lobby bar is one of the best in town.

Hotel Presidente Inter-Continental HOTEL $$$
(755-553-00-18, in the US 888-424-6835; www.ihg.com; Blvd Ixtapa s/n; d all-inclusive US$199-279, ste from US$349;) This popular beachfront hotel is first class all the way, with a gym, sauna, tennis courts, seven restaurants and a kids' club with Spanish classes for little ones. The swankiest nest on the beach, bar none.

Sunscape RESORT $$$
(755-553-20-25; www.sunscaperesorts.com; Paseo de Ixtapa s/n; d from $450, all-inclusive, 3-night minimum;) One of Ixtapa's newer properties, rooms are bright, tiled affairs with colorful touches, flat-screen TVs, white-washed wicker furnishings, plush linens and wonderful views from oceanfront rooms. It's all-inclusive, and there are several restaurants on the property to choose from, as well as a full service-spa, activities galore, and an Explorer's Club for kids.

Eating

All the major hotels have their own restaurants. Additional dining options abound in Ixtapa's shopping centers and there are a few at the down-on-its-luck Marina Ixtapa, just northwest of the main hotel strip, where the boats and ships are shiny and the storefronts largely empty.

Captain Meuro MEXICAN $$
(755-555-09-39; mains M$70-170; 8am-11pm) One of the most laid-back and reliably good restaurants in Ixtapa, this spot opposite the Barcelo resort offers *arrachera* (grilled skirt steak) platters, burgers, *chiles rellenos*, tacos, fajitas, tasty octopus and shrimp dishes. It even has a decent smoothie list.

Deli O SEAFOOD $$
(Playa del Palmar; mains M$80-220) One of two restaurant-bars in an accessible slice of beach between the two hotel zones. This is the nicer of the two with lower volume music at midday, zesty *micheladas,* and all the cocktails, ceviches and fish dishes you've come to expect, including a shrimp-stuffed fish fillet (M$220) big enough to share.

Villa de la Selva FUSION $$$
(755-553-03-62; www.villadelaselva.com.mx; Paseo de la Roca; mains M$250-470; 6-11:30pm, closed Sep) This elegant contemporary Mediterranean restaurant was once the home of Mexican president Luis Echeverría. The cliffside villa has superb sunset and ocean views. Offerings include duck tacos, *chipotle*-glazed salmon with couscous, shrimp in tamarind sauce, lobster and an extensive wine list. Reservations are a must.

Drinking & Nightlife

All the big hotels have bars and nightclubs. Many also have discos; in the low season most of these charge less and open fewer nights.

Christine CLUB
(755-553-04-56; www.krystal-hotels.com/ixtapa/english/restaurants-entertainment; Hotel Krystal, Blvd Ixtapa s/n; admission varies; 11pm-4am Fri & Sat) Christine has the sizzling

sound-and-light systems you'd expect from one of the most popular discos in town.

Information

Most information services, such as banks, ATMs, tourist info, a movie theater and a 24-hour pharmacy, are located in the *centro commercial* (shopping center) on Blvd Ixtapa. The nearest post office is in Zihuatanejo. Ixtapa hotels all have wi-fi.

Tourist Office (755-554-20-01; turismozihixt@hotmail.com; Blvd Ixtapa s/n; 10am-5pm) Provides tourist info from a squat orange building in front of Señor Frog's (directly across from Hotel Presidente Inter-Continental).

Getting There & Around

Private taxis (M$365) provide transportation from Ixtapa-Zihuatanejo International Airport to Ixtapa. A taxi from Ixtapa to the airport costs about M$170.

There are bus-ticket offices in the shopping center adjacent to Ixtapa's downtown hotel strip, but very few long-distance buses actually stop here – for most destinations you'll have to go to Zihuatanejo's Central de Autobuses, which services both towns.

Local buses run frequently between Ixtapa and Zihuatanejo from 5:30am to 11pm (M$10, 15 minutes). In Ixtapa, buses stop along the main street in front of all hotels. In Zihuatanejo, buses depart from the corner of Juárez and Morelos. Buses marked 'Zihua–Ixtapa–Playa Linda' run from Zihuatanejo through Ixtapa to Playa Linda. The fare to Playa Linda is M$10/20 from Ixtapa/Zihuatanejo.

A taxi between Zihuatanejo and Ixtapa should be around M$80; always agree on a price before getting into a cab.

ZIHUATANEJO

755 / POP 120,000

The sister cities of Zihuatanejo (see-wah-tah-neh-ho) and Ixtapa could not be more radically different. While Ixtapa is openly a purpose-built, sanitized version of Mexico, Zihuatanejo is the real deal. Zihuatanejo, or Zihua as it's affectionately called, is a Pacific paradise of beautiful beaches, friendly people and an easygoing lifestyle. Until the 1970s, Zihua was a sleepy fishing village best known as a hideaway for pirates, hippies and fictional ex-cons. Tim Robbins and Morgan Freeman escaped here to live out the simple life in *The Shawshank Redemption*. With the construction of Ixtapa next door, Zihua's population and tourism industry boomed practically overnight.

Parts of the city have become quite touristy, especially when cruise ships are in town, and luxury hotels are slowly replacing old family guesthouses. But for the most part, Zihua has retained its historic charm. The narrow cobblestone streets of downtown hide wonderful local restaurants, bars, boutiques and artisan studios. Fishermen still meet every morning on the beach by Paseo del Pescador (Fishermen's Passage) to sell their catch of the day. At night, young lovers and families stroll along the romantic waterfront sidewalk. Zihua is the best of both worlds.

While Zihua's suburbs have spread beyond the bay and into the hills, the city's center remains compressed within a few blocks. It's difficult to get lost; there are only a few streets and they're clearly marked.

Sights

Waves are gentle at all of Bahía de Zihuatanejo's beaches. If you want big ocean waves, head west toward Ixtapa.

Playa Municipal, in front of town, is the least appealing beach on the bay. **Playa Madera** (Wood Beach) is a pleasant five-minute walk east from Playa Municipal along a concrete walkway (popular with young couples in the evening) and around a rocky point.

Over a steep hill from Playa Madera (less than 1km) is the gorgeous broad expanse of **Playa La Ropa** (Clothes Beach), named for a Spanish galleon that was wrecked and had its cargo of silks washed ashore. Bordered by palm trees and seafood restaurants, La Ropa is great for swimming, parasailing, waterskiing and sand-*fútbol* (soccer). You can also rent sailboards and sailboats. It's an enjoyable 20-minute walk from Playa Madera along Carretera Escénica, which follows the clifftops and offers fine views over the water.

Isolated **Playa Las Gatas** (Cat Beach) is named – depending on whose story you believe – for the whiskered nurse sharks that once inhabited the waters or for the wildcats that lurked in the jungles onshore. It's a protected beach, crowded with sunbeds and restaurants. It's good for snorkeling (there's some coral) and as a swimming spot for children, but beware of sea urchins. Beach shacks and restaurants rent out snorkeling gear for around M$100 per day. Boats to Playa Las Gatas depart frequently from

Zihuatanejo's Muelle Municipal (Pier), from 8am to 6pm. Buy tickets (M$40 round trip) at the **Cooperativa Zihuatan** (755-554-85-81) booth at the foot of the pier; one-way tickets can be bought on board.

About 12km south of Zihuatanejo, just before the airport, **Playa Larga** has big surf, beachfront restaurants and horseback riding. This is where Andy Dufrene and Red met up again after their lost years in Shawshank Prison. Nearby **Playa Manzanillo**, a secluded white-sand beach reachable by boat from Zihuatanejo, offers the best snorkeling in the area. To reach Playa Larga, take a 'Coacoyul' combi from Juárez near the corner of González and get off at the turnoff to Playa Larga; another combi will take you from there to the beach.

Museo Arqueológico de la Costa Grande MUSEUM
(755-554-75-52; cnr Plaza Olof Palme & Paseo del Pescador; admission M$10; 10am-6pm Tue-Sun) This small museum houses exhibits on the history, archaeology and culture of the Guerrero coast. Most displays are in Spanish, but gringos can get by with the free English-language handout.

DON'T MISS

EXPLORING ZIHUATANEJO'S GREAT OUTDOORS

Sure, you can spend your whole vacation basking by the pool, but the Zihuatanejo area offers countless other options for getting outdoors. Here are a few ideas to get you started:

- Swim under a waterfall in the Sierra Madre, learn why the tarantula crossed the road and see how many blue morpho butterflies you can count on an ecotour to **Mesas de Bravo**
- Cruise across the bay at sunset on a **catamaran sailing tour**
- Walk barefoot down the entire length of gorgeous **Playa La Ropa** (Clothes Beach)
- Kayak around the lagoon or explore the spectacular Morros de Potosí rocks at **Barra de Potosí** (p556)

Activities

Water Sports

Snorkeling is good at Playa Las Gatas and even better at Playa Manzanillo. Marine life is abundant here due to a convergence of currents, and the visibility can be great – up to 35m in dry months. Migrating humpback whales pass through from December to February.

Carlo Scuba DIVING
(755-554-60-03; www.carloscuba.com; Playa Las Gatas; 1-/2-tank dives US$65/90) Carlo Scuba, run by a third-generation family operation based at Playa Las Gatas, offers dives, snorkeling trips, instruction and PADI certification. Prices include pick-up and drop-off at the Muelle Municipal.

Dive Zihua DIVING
(755-544-66-66; www.divezihuatanejo.com; Álvarez 30; 1-/2-tank dives US$65/90) Offers a variety of dives, plus PADI and DAN courses and certification.

Sportfishing

Sportfishing is very popular in Zihuatanejo. Sailfish are caught here year-round; seasonal fish include blue or black marlin (March to May), roosterfish (September and October), wahoo (October), mahi-mahi (November and December) and Spanish mackerel (December). Deep-sea fishing trips start at around US$180 for a boat holding up to four passengers. Trips run for up to seven hours and usually include equipment.

Two fishing outfits near the Muelle Municipal are **Sociedad Cooperativa José Azueta** (755-554-20-56; Muelle Municipal) and **Sociedad de Servicios Turísticos** (755-554-37-58; Paseo del Pescador 38B).

Yoga & Massage

Zihua Yoga Studio YOGA, MASSAGE
(755-554-22-13; www.zihuatanejoyoga.com; Playa La Ropa; 8-10:45am Mon-Fri, 9-10:15am Sat & Sun) Few yogis can offer the kind of guaranteed enlightenment that comes from gazing through coconut palms into the sun-dappled Pacific from the upstairs terrace of this wonderful studio. Look for it above Paty's Marimar restaurant on Playa La Ropa. Multilevel classes (US$10) are offered daily in high season; Tuesdays and Thursdays in the off season.

Paty also offers 50-minute massages (M$300), manicures (M$150) and pedicures (M$300).

Tours

Picante SAILING
(755-554-82-70, 755-554-26-94; www.picantecruises.com; Muelle Municipal) This 23m

Zihuatanejo

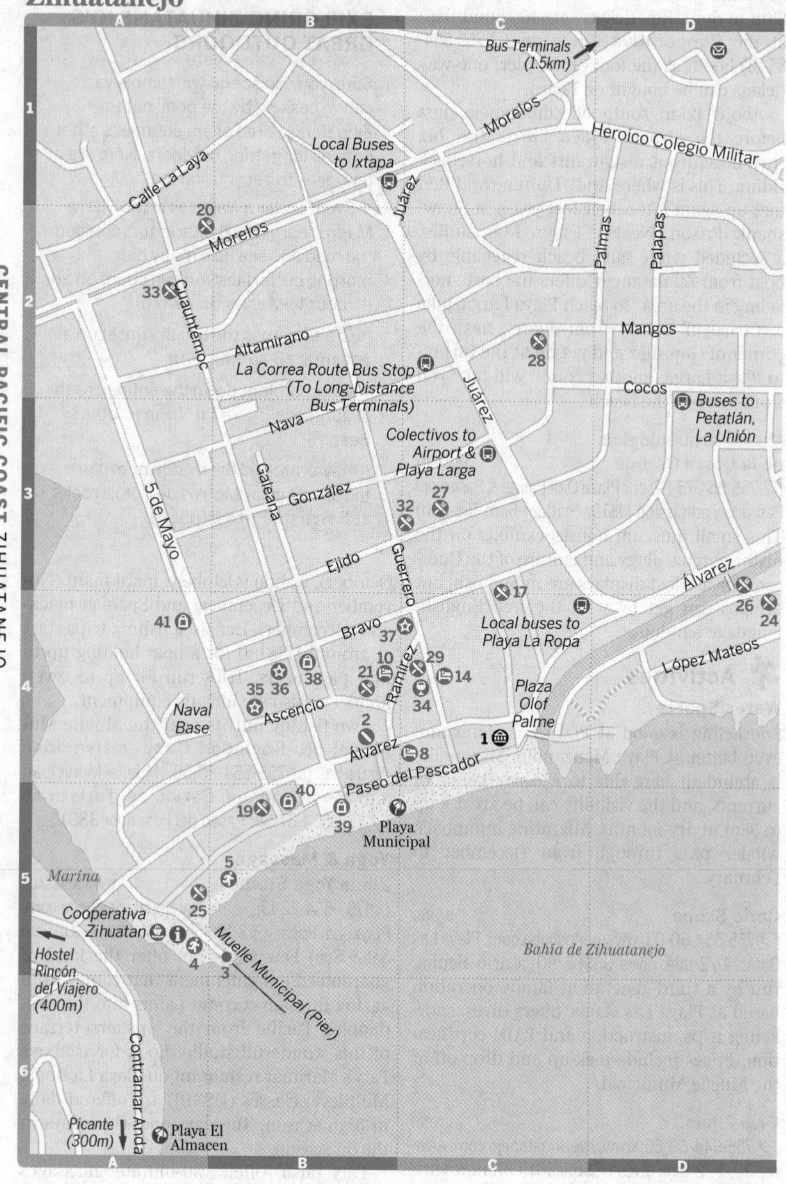

catamaran offers three enjoyable excursions. The 'Sail and Snorkel' trip (US$79 plus US$7 for equipment rental; 10am to 2:30pm) sails south of Zihua to prime snorkeling off Playa Manzanillo. The 'Magical Sunset Cruise' (adult/child US$55/41; 5pm to 7:30pm) heads around the bay and along the coast of Ixtapa. Prices include food and open bar. Reservations are required.

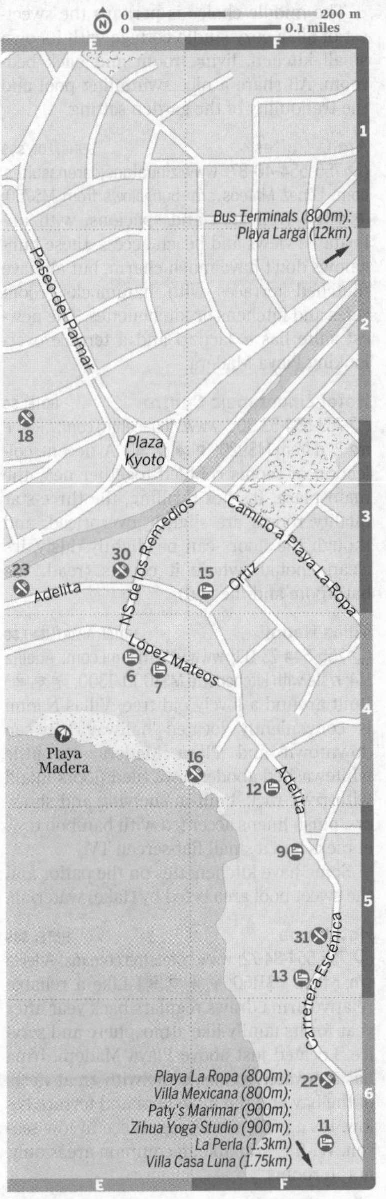

Sleeping

Zihuatanejo has a good selection of hotels for all budgets. Prices listed here are rack rates for high season, which generally runs from December through March. Outside high season, prices drop by up to 20%. You

Zihuatanejo

Sights
1 Museo Arqueológico de la Costa Grande C4

Activities, Courses & Tours
2 Dive Zihua B4
3 Picante B5
4 Sociedad Cooperativa José Azueta A5
5 Sociedad de Servicios Turísticos B5
Zihuatanejo Cooking School .... (see 30)

Sleeping
6 Arena Suites E4
7 Aura del Mar E4
8 Hotel Avila C4
9 Hotel Irma F5
10 Hotel Zuhuatanejo Central B4
11 La Casa Que Canta F6
12 La Quinta de Don Andres F4
13 Mi Casita F5
14 Posada Citlali C4
15 Villas Naomi F3

Eating
16 Bistro del Mar F4
17 Cenaduría Antelia C3
18 Doña Licha E2
19 El Arbolito B5
20 El Gabo A2
21 El Murmullo B4
22 Il Mare F6
23 ITA E3
24 La Gula D4
25 La Sirena Gorda A5
26 Las Adelitas D3
27 Los Braseros C3
28 Mercado C2
29 Panadería Buen Gusto C4
30 Patio Mexica E3
31 Restaurant Kau-Kan F5
32 Restaurante Mexicano Any C3
Rufo's Grill .... (see 30)
33 Yolanda A2

Drinking & Nightlife
34 Andy's C4

Entertainment
35 Bandido's B4
36 Cine Paraíso B4
37 Temptation C4

Shopping
38 Alberto's B4
El Embarcadero .... (see 39)
39 El Jumil B5
40 La Zapoteca B5
41 Mercado Turístico La Marina A4
Pancho's .... (see 36)

can often negotiate lower rates, especially during slow periods or for extended stays.

Hostel Rincón del Viajero HOSTEL $

(☎cell phone 755-1034566; www.hostelzihuatanejo.com; Paseo las Salinas 50, La Noria; dm M$140-160, d/tr M$320/540) Housed in a converted, once-derelict *bodega* (storage room) across the bridge from Zihua's pier, this artsy hostel is the brainchild of local artist and surfer Malinalli. The colorful rooms and common areas are decorated with Mali's original artwork and Mexican handicrafts.

It also has a communal kitchen, rooftop terrace, hammocks, a laundry area, bike rentals and a cafe featuring fruits from the courtyard orchard. Mali speaks several languages and offers airport pick-up in her van, plus surfing trips to local beaches.

Posada Citlali GUESTHOUSE $$

(☎755-554-20-43; Guerrero 4; s/d M$400/550;) Easily the best digs in the town center, this pleasant older posada has clean, simple, cozy tile rooms with queen beds, cable TV, and rockers on a shared patio. Family owned, there's lush garden rising through the courtyard and it's steps from the sea. It can be loud on weekends with Andy's (p554) right across the street.

Mi Casita GUESTHOUSE $$

(☎755-554-45-10; Carretera Escénica s/n; s/d/tr/q M$500/600/700/800;) This humble family-run place perches on the hillside between Playas Madera and La Ropa. The tidy rooms all open onto terraces with hammocks and distant ocean views.

Hotel Avila HOTEL $$

(☎800-832-92-72; www.hotelavila.com.mx; Álvarez 8; d M$500;) Set just off the plaza and the main beach beyond, these older, sizable rooms have pastel-brushed stucco walls, air-con and a pool, but though the price is fair and the location ideal, the property could use some love.

Villa Casa Luna CABAÑAS $$

(☎in the US 310-272-9022; www.villa-casa-luna.com; Playa La Ropa s/n; d US$70, cottage US$120, villa from US$350;) Within this verdant walled compound at the southern end of Playa La Ropa there are three unique living spaces, ranging from the humble 'Cabaña Room' double to a grand villa with multiple bedrooms plus a gorgeously tiled designer kitchen.

The middle choice is perhaps the sweetest of all, a cozy studio cottage with its own small kitchen, living room and back bedroom. All share a nice swimming pool and the tranquility of the garden setting.

Arena Suites BUNGALOW $$$

(☎755-554-40-87; www.zihuatanejoarenasuites.com; López Mateos s/n; bungalows from M$750; P) Well kept and spacious, with unbeatable views and beach access, these bungalows don't have much charm, but all have thatched terraces with hammocks, room safes and kitchens or kitchenettes. The newest suite has a Jacuzzi and a terrace overlooking Playa Madera.

Hotel Zihuatanejo Centro HOTEL $$

(☎755-554-53-30; www.zihuacentro.com; Ramirez 2; d from M$920; P) A decent collection of rooms cobbled together near the main plaza. It's not thrilling, the three-star quality rooms are slightly overpriced, and though the floors can be slightly dusty, it's clean enough where it counts (read: the bathroom and the bed).

Villas Naomi HOTEL, APARTMENT $$

(☎755-544-73-03; www.villasnaomi.com; Adelita 114; r/ste with kitchenette M$1000/1300;) Built around a lovely old tree, Villas Naomi is conveniently located halfway between downtown and Playa Madera. Its little whitewashed abodes have tiled floors inlaid with river rock, built-in shelving and showers, plush linens accented with bamboo towel racks and a small flat-screen TV.

Some have kitchenettes on the patios and the sweet pool area is fed by (fake) waterfall.

Hotel Irma HOTEL $$$

(☎755-554-84-72; www.hotelirma.com.mx; Adelita s/n; r from M$1160; P) Like a reliable relative, Irma draws regulars back year after year for its family-like atmosphere and service. Located just above Playa Madera, Irma has renovated rooms, some with great views of the bay and the huge pool and terrace below. It's a great moderate choice in low season. Wi-fi is available in common areas only, not in rooms.

La Quinta de Don Andrés INN $$$

(☎755-554-37-94; www.laquintadedonandres.com; Adelita 11; r from M$1200;) This burnt orange faux-dobe complex of modern rooms offer terracotta floors, air-con, kitchenettes and a small balcony overlooking the pool and the sea below. It's not fancy but offers fine value.

★ Aura del Mar HOTEL **$$$**
(755-554-21-42; www.hotelauradelmar.com; López Mateos s/n; d incl breakfast from US$147;) A cliff-hugging, red adobe village perched above Playa Madera, Aura del Mar is perfect for a romantic getaway. The spacious rooms and grounds are decorated with traditional Mexican furnishings, tiles and handicrafts. All have private balconies with exquisite ocean views and a hammock. A steep staircase leads to the beach and its Bistro del Mar (p554), one of Zihua's finest restaurants.

Villa Mexicana HOTEL **$$$**
(755-554-78-88; www.hotelvillamexicana.com.mx; Playa La Ropa s/n; r incl breakfast from M$1636;) Its chain-hotel sterility won't inspire much enthusiasm, but you can't argue with the choice location right on Playa La Ropa, at a fraction of the price you'd pay at the luxury resort next door. All 64 tile-and-stucco rooms have cable TV, phone and safe; best of the lot are the 18 front-facing rooms with direct ocean views.

There's also a popular pool and beachside bar and restaurant. Wi-fi is available in the lobby only.

La Casa Que Canta BOUTIQUE HOTEL **$$$**
(800-710-93-45, 755-555-70-00, in the US 888-523-5050; www.lacasaquecanta.com; Carretera Escénica s/n; r US$395, ste US$475-695;) La Casa Que Canta – The House that Sings – is the epitome of luxury and customer service in Zihuatanejo. Perched on the cliffs between Playas Madera and La Ropa, the thatched-roof hotel shelters exquisitely decorated rooms, a restaurant, a spa, a fitness center and two swimming pools.

But perhaps the most valuable amenity is silence: there are no TVs, and children under 16 years are banned.

Amuleto BOUTIQUE HOTEL **$$$**
(755-544-62-22, in the US 213-280-1037; www.amuleto.net; Carretera Escénica 9; r from US$400;) A boutique hotel high in the hills above Playa La Ropa, Amuleto dazzles guests with opulent, earthy rooms decorated in stone, ceramic and wood, plus suites with private swimming pools and scrumptious views. The attached restaurant is equally fabulous. A three-night minimum stay is required.

Eating

Guerrero is famous for its *pozole,* a hearty meat-and-veg soup that's found on most menus in town (especially on Thursday). *Tiritas* (raw fish slivers marinated with red onion, lemon or lime and chili peppers, and served with soda crackers and spicy sauce) are Zihua's specialty, but you won't find them on many menus – look for them at carts near the bus terminals, or request them at any beachfront *enramada.*

Central Zihuatanejo

Seafood here is fresh and delicious. Many popular (if touristy) fish restaurants line Paseo del Pescador, parallel to Playa Municipal; however, the quality-to-price ratio tends to improve as you move inland. A hearty and inexpensive breakfast or lunch is available in the **mercado** (meals M$30-40; 7am-6pm), at the corner of Juárez and González. Late-night taco stands are ubiquitous around town.

Panadería Buen Gusto BAKERY **$**
(Guerrero 11; pastries from M$5; 8:30am-9pm) A good traditional Mexican bakery in the heart of downtown Zihua.

Doña Licha MEXICAN **$**
(755-554-39-33; Cocos 8; mains M$38-85; 8am-6pm) This place near the *mercado* is renowned for its down-home Mexican cooking, casual atmosphere and excellent prices. There are always several *comidas corridas* (prix-fixe menus) to choose from, including a popular roast chicken (M$38) plate; all come with rice, beans and handmade tortillas. Breakfasts are huge.

Cenaduría Antelia MEXICAN **$**
(755-554-30-91; Bravo 14; mains M$35-60; 8am-2pm & 5pm-midnight) Antelia's popular and friendly eatery has been dishing out tasty *antojitos mexicanos* (Mexican snacks) and desserts since 1975. Tuck into a *tamal de pollo en salsa verde* (chicken *tamal* in green sauce) or a bursting bowl of daily *pozole,* and top it off with *calabaza con leche* (squash in milk) for dessert.

El Arbolito MEXICAN **$$**
(755-553-37-00; www.facebook.com/restaurante.elarbolito; Álvarez; mains M$59-169; 2-10pm daily) Fresh yet different dishes are served on the brick promenade. Our favorite was the *pescado al pastor* (M$119). Whether in taco or platter form, the fish comes grilled in *pastor*

DON'T MISS

ZIHUATANEJO COOKING SCHOOL

Ready for a morning of cultural immersion, good eats and just plain fun? Then make a beeline for the **Zihuatanejo Cooking School** (☎755-554-39-49; www.patiomexica.com; cnr Adelita & NS de los Remedios; class 2½hr incl shopping, cooking & eating). Long-time Zihua resident Monica Durán Pérez opens her home kitchen and shares her love of Mexican culinary culture in this wonderful series of classes. Start with a trip to the market to buy ingredients, taste-test fresh cheese, learn about herbs and sample local delicacies that you'd surely miss otherwise. Then return to Monica's backyard, where you grind corn, shape tortillas, pound ingredients in a *molcajete* (traditional mortar and pestle), and cook up one of seven different specialties, depending on the group's interests.

Themes for individual classes include *tamales* (masa mixed with lard, stuffed with stewed meat, fish or vegetables, wrapped and steamed), *pozole* (a soup or thin stew of hominy, meat, vegetables and chilies), ceviche and *tiritas* (raw fish slivers marinated with red onion, lemon or lime and chili peppers, and served with soda crackers and spicy sauce), *mole* (a type of chili sauce), *chiles rellenos* (peppers stuffed with meat or cheese) and Mexican desserts.

sauce, served with greens and dressed with mustard vinaigrette, rice and chunks of grilled pineapple. It also does fresh shrimp stuffed in quesadillas, sautéed in garlic or tossed with pasta, butter, garlic and wine.

La Sirena Gorda SEAFOOD **$$**
(The Fat Mermaid; ☎755-554-26-87; Paseo del Pescador 90; mains M$65-220; ⊙8:30am-10pm Thu-Tue) Close to the pier, this place is a casual and popular open-air restaurant that's good for garlic shrimp, curry tuna and fish tacos, as well as burgers and traditional Mexican dishes.

Restaurante Mexicano Any MEXICAN **$$**
(☎755-554-73-73; Ejido 18; mains M$55-140; ⊙8am-1am) This friendly, if overpriced, place serves traditional Mexican cuisine under its big *palapa* roof. Highlights include to-die-for *tamales* and the sweet, corn-based hot drinks known as *atoles*.

Los Braseros MEXICAN **$$**
(☎755-554-87-36; Ejido 14; mains M$62-197; ⊙8am-1am) With 140 dishes on the menu, this is a wonderful place to sample specialties from all over Mexico. For a quick bite on the go, grab a few *tacos al pastor* (with spit-grilled pork; M$6 each) from the street-facing counter, or sit down and linger awhile over its trademark *alambres* – tasty mixes of grilled fish, meat, veggies and cheese.

Yolanda SEAFOOD **$$**
(cnr Morelos & Cuauhtémoc; mains M$70-120; ⊙10am-8pm) They open oysters with a hammer, and dice and drown ceviche on the street side, where drunk boleros belly up to the sidewalk bar with the boys and sing their unbridled, unrequited romance to one too many beers. And when the choir is breathless, the jukebox picks up the slack. It's known as the Catedral de Mariscos for a reason.

El Gabo SEAFOOD **$$**
(Morelos; mains M$70-275; ⊙11:30am-8pm) A shady hideaway tucked off a major thoroughfare isn't necessarily what you think of as a prime seafood joint, but this one attracts young lovers, happy-hour drifters and post-work professionals. It's an open-sided place with tables scattered beneath a vaulted tiled roof, leather saddle-bar stools, and a menu of lobster brochettes, coconut shrimp, fresh fish done up a half dozen ways, oysters, sashimi, seafood cocktails and ceviche,

El Murmullo FUSION **$$**
(Ascencio; dishes M$80-170; ⊙3-10pm Mon-Sat) An intriguing little bistro with well-dressed candlelit wood tables spilling onto the brick pedestrian street. It serves everything from sashimi to Thai curries to freshly made pastas. It also sautées shrimp in tequila, and does all the traditional Mexican beef, seafood and chicken dishes.

The food is good, not great, but it's a good choice for a change of pace meal, and the service and atmosphere are lovely.

Around the Bay

Pricey restaurants with panoramic views dominate the hilltops, while casual candlelit beachside eateries are the rule on Playa La Ropa. More affordable fare can be found in the burgeoning 'gastronomic ghetto' along Adelita, just inland from Playa Madera.

Las Adelitas MEXICAN $

(☎755-112-18-45; Adelita 6; mains M$35-85; ⏰8am-4:30pm) Set on a sunken plaza along the river, not that you can see it, is this adorable breakfast and lunch cafe with *sarape* tablecloths and a local following thanks to its *chilaquiles* and omelets in the morning and *tortas, chiles rellenos* and fried and grilled fish *comidas* at lunch.

ITA CAFE $

(Adelita 4; mains M$40-110; ⏰7:30am-10:30pm) An atmospheric, locally owned neighborhood cafe, it steams espresso and produces fresh juices and Mexican breakfasts. It also stuffs *chiles rellenos* with shrimp, bathes shrimp in *mole* sauce, rolls burritos with sausage and potatoes, melts fish quesadillas and offers a dozen more interesting options, too.

Patio Mexica BREAKFAST $

(www.patiomexica.com; cnr Adelita & NS de los Remedios; mains M$50-150) Squash blossom omelet and other Mexican delicacies get your day off to a sunny start at this informal breakfast place run by Monica Durán Pérez of the Zihuatanejo Cooking School.

★Paty's Marimar MEXICAN $$

(☎755-544-22-13; www.patys-marymar.com; Playa La Ropa; mains M$60-220; 📶) The best restaurant on Playa La Ropa, it serves everything from grilled octopus and snapper to shrimp sautéed in tequila to fish fajitas, and an array of tasty soups, salads, and omelets. We particularly enjoyed the *tiritas*.

Munch and sip under thatched and linen umbrellas in the sand with rattan lanterns dangling from the palms. Service isn't swift, but you want time to move slow at Paty's.

Rufo's Grill PARRILLA $$

(www.rufosgrill.com; Adelita 1; mains M$90-140; ⏰6-10pm Mon-Sat Sep-May) Tucked onto a concrete patio under a bamboo roof fringed with Christmas lights, this unpretentious corner joint is popular among long-term gringos thanks to its fabulous barbecued meat and shrimp marinated in herbs and olive oil.

Tasty grilled vegetables – red peppers, carrots, zucchini, eggplant and mushrooms – accompany every main course, a welcome alternative to standard rice-and-beans fare, but it's not a local joint.

La Perla MEXICAN $$$

(☎755-554-27-00; www.laperlarestaurant.net; Playa La Ropa; mains M$70-420; ⏰11am-10pm) You name it, they serve it along with an exquisite location on Playa La Ropa. The best dishes include a grilled octopus with garlic butter, tuna steaks seared as rare as you like, fish fillets stuffed with shrimp or steamed in foil, and tacos piled with shrimp, lobster and chicken.

Eat here and hang on the (few) beach lounges as long as you like.

Il Mare ITALIAN, SEAFOOD $$$

(☎755-554-90-67; Carretera Escénica 105; mains M$145-385; ⏰noon-10pm Mon-Sat, 5-10pm Sun) A romantic Italian restaurant with a bird's-eye perspective on the bay, Il Mare is well regarded for its Mediterranean pasta and seafood specialties, including a fresh *insalata di mare* (marinated seafood salad) with squid, octopus and shrimp marinated in olive oil and lime. Pair yours with wine from Spain, Italy, France or Argentina.

La Gula FUSION $$$

(☎755-554-83-96; www.restaurantelagula.com; Adelita 8; mains M$160-230; ⏰5-11pm Mon-Sat) This place wins points for its beautifully presented, creative cuisine. Dishes bear names such as *mosaico mexicano* (tequila, peppercorn and dill-marinated fish carpaccio with avocado mousse) and *eclipse de sol* (shrimp medallions with bacon and *pasilla* chili sauce). The atmosphere, on a breezy upstairs terrace, is nice, though the music can be, well, imposing.

Restaurant Kau-Kan INTERNATIONAL $$$

(☎755-554-84-46; www.casakaukan.com; Carretera Escénica 7; mains M$180-380; ⏰5pm-midnight) High on the cliffs, this renowned gourmet restaurant enjoys stellar views from its candlelit terrace. Menu choices include stingray in black butter sauce, or grilled lamb chops with Dauphinoise potatoes and mint sauce.

Bistro del Mar FUSION $$$

(☎755-554-21-42; www.hotelauradelmar.com/en/bistro.html; Playa Madera s/n; mains M$175-280; ⏰7am-11pm) With its landmark sail roof over candlelit tables and its fusion of Latin, European and Asian flavors, this beachside bistro is a romantic treat. Though its soundtrack may be too sappy for some, the *nuovo* Mexican kitchen will satisfy.

We enjoyed a fresh fillet of snapper topped with *huitlacoche* (a corn fungus that's something of a Mexican delicacy) and fried bananas served on a bed of lentils in a bath of *mole* sauce. Tasty.

Drinking & Entertainment

Downtown Zihua's got the usual slew of bars offering two-for-one beers and margaritas, and you can find some live music and booty-shaking bass on weekends, but in its earthy soul, Zihuatanejo is all about the mellow.

Andy's CANTINA
(Guerrero; ⏲6:30pm-3am Tue-Sun) A groovy new two-room cantina with stone floors, a bar in the front room, and a DJ booth, dance floor and another bar in the rear. There are thick faux-dobe walls, bamboo rafters and lounges aplenty. It gets packed on weekends.

Temptation LIVE MUSIC
(☎755-554-11-29; cnr Bravo & Guerrero; ⏲9:30pm-4am Fri & Sat) The new club (where Black Bull Rodeo used to be) is built like a cruise-ship disco with a raised lit dance floor, handsome center bar, the obligatory disco ball, and red vinyl booths and seats on the main floor and in the mezzanine above. DJs spin *cumbia*, merengue, salsa, electronica and reggae.

Bandido's LIVE MUSIC
(☎755-553-80-72; www.bandidosdezihua.com; 5 de Mayo No 8; ⏲10:30pm-late Fri & Sat) On Thursday, Friday and Saturday nights, this Mexican restaurant, with its blood-red leather chairs ripe for lounging and people-watching, opens its floor for dancing to live salsa and *cumbia*, interspersed with DJ mixes on weekends.

Cine Paraíso CINEMA
(☎755-554-23-18; cnr Cuauhtémoc & Bravo; admission M$40; ⏲films start at 4:40pm, 7pm, 8pm, 9pm & 9:10pm) Screens three films nightly, usually in English with Spanish subtitles.

Shopping

Zihua offers abundant Mexican handicrafts, including ceramics, clothing, leatherwork, Taxco silver, wood carvings and masks from around the state of Guerrero.

A few shops along Cuauhtémoc sell Taxco silver. **Alberto's** (☎755-554-21-61; Cuauhtémoc 12 & 15) and **Pancho's** (☎75-5554-5230; Cuauhtémoc 11) have the best selection of quality pieces.

La Zapoteca HANDICRAFTS
(Paseo del Pescador; ⏲10am-6pm) If you're interested in handwoven anything – *sarapes*, rugs or hammocks (and they have some great ones) – find this emporium, which stands out among the handicraft huddle near the fisherman's marina.

El Jumil HANDICRAFTS
(☎755-554-61-91; Paseo del Pescador 9; ⏲9am-10pm Mon-Sat) This shop specializes in masks – a well-known traditional handicraft of Guerrero state.

El Embarcadero CLOTHING
(Paseo del Pescador 9; ⏲9am-10pm Mon-Sat) Embroidery, textiles and handwoven clothing from Guerrero, Oaxaca, Michoacán and other neighboring states.

Mercado Turístico La Marina MARKET
(5 de Mayo s/n; ⏲8am-9pm) Has many stalls selling clothes, bags and knickknacks.

BUSES FROM ZIHUATANEJO

DESTINATION	FARE (M$)	DURATION	FREQUENCY (DAILY)
Acapulco	182	4-5hr	very frequent EB & EDO
Lázaro Cárdenas	105	1½-2hr	hourly EB & EDO
Manzanillo	561	8-9hr	8:50pm EB
Mexico City (Terminal Sur)	661-675	8-10hr	7:20am EDO, noon EB, frequent night buses EB & EDO
Mexico City (Terminal Norte)	661-675	9-10hr	6:45pm & 11:36pm
Mexico City (Poniente)	661	8-9hr	4 EB
Morelia	390-445	5hr	4-8 EB
Puerto Vallarta	861	13-14hr	8:40pm EB

Information

EMERGENCY

Emergency (☎060)

Hospital (☎755-554-36-50; Morelos) Halfway between the post office and the bus terminal.

Tourist Police (☎755-554-20-40; Álvarez) Next to the basketball court.

INTERNET ACCESS

Zihuatanejo is well stocked with internet cafes and most retaurants and hotels offer free wi-fi.

MONEY

Zihuatanejo has many banks and *casas de cambio* where you can change US dollars; the following banks have ATMs.

Banamex (cnr Ejido & Guerrero)

Bancomer (cnr Juárez & Bravo)

Banorte (cnr Juárez & Ejido)

POST

Post Office (⏲8am-6pm Mon-Fri, 8am-noon Sat) Behind the big yellow Coppel department store off Morelos.

TOURIST INFORMATION

Tourist Office (☎755-554-20-01; turismozihixt@hotmail.com; Pier; ⏲10am-6pm Mon-Fri) This convenient office at the foot of Zihua's pier stocks brochures and maps even when unstaffed in the low season.

Getting There & Away

AIR

The **Ixtapa-Zihuatanejo International Airport** (☎755-554-20-70; www.oma.aero/es/aeropuertos/zihuatanejo; Carretera Nacional) is 13km southeast of Zihuatanejo, a couple of kilometers off Hwy 200 heading toward Acapulco.

The following carriers service the airport:

Aeroméxico (www.aeromexico.com) Airport (☎755-554-26-34, 755-554-22-37; www.aeromexico.com; Airport); Zihuatanejo (☎ext 1, 755-554-20-18; www.aeromexico.com; Álvarez 42) Service to Mexico City, with many onward connections.

Aeromar (☎755-553-70-12; www.aeromar.com.mx; Airport) Direct service to Mexico City.

Interjet (☎755-553-70-02; www.interjet.com.mx; Airport) Direct service to Mexico City and Toluca.

BUS

Both long-distance bus terminals are on Hwy 200 about 2km northeast of the town center (toward the airport): the **Estrella Blanca terminal** (EB), also known as the Central de Autobuses, is a block east of the smaller **Estrella de Oro terminal** (EDO). The former also serves several smaller bus companies including Autovías and Costa Line.

CAR & MOTORCYCLE

There are several car-rental companies at the airport, most with branches in Ixtapa.

Alamo (☎755-553-02-06; www.alamomexico.com.mx) Airport (☎755-554-84-29; Airport); Ixtapa (☎755-553-02-06; Centro Comercial Los Patios)

Europcar (☎755-553-71-58; www.europcar.com.mx) Airport (☎755-553-71-58; Airport); Ixtapa (☎755-544-82-56; Paseo Ixtapa, Local 2)

Green Motion (☎755-553-03-97; www.greenmotion.com) Airport (☎755-554-48-37; Airport); Ixtapa (☎755-553-03-97; Blvd Ixtapa s/n, Plaza Ambientes)

Hertz (☎755-554-29-52; www.hertz.com; Airport)

Thrifty (☎755-553-30-19; www.thrifty.com) Airport (☎755-553-70-20; Airport); Ixtapa (☎755-553-30-19; Hotel Barceló, Blvd Ixtapa)

Getting Around

TO/FROM THE AIRPORT

The cheapest way to get to and from the airport is via a public 'Aeropuerto' *colectivo* van (M$10), departing from Juárez near González between 6am and 10pm and making many stops before dropping you just outside the airport gate. *Colectivo* taxis are a more direct and convenient option for incoming passengers, whisking you from the arrivals area to Ixtapa or Zihua for M$120 per person. Private taxis from the airport into either town cost M$365, although they charge only M$120 or so when returning to the airport.

BUS & COLECTIVO

To reach downtown Zihua or Ixtapa from Zihua's long-distance bus terminals, cross Hwy 200 using the pedestrian overpass directly opposite the Estrella Blanca terminal, then look for signs. Buses for downtown Zihua stop at the foot of the overpass. The stop for Ixtapa is a little further west along Hwy 200.

From downtown Zihua to the bus terminals, catch 'La Correa' route buses (M$6, 10 minutes), which leave regularly from the corner of Juárez and Nava between 5:30am and 9:30pm.

'Playa La Ropa' buses go south on Juárez and out to Playa La Ropa every half-hour from 7am to 8pm (M$7).

'Coacoyul' *colectivos* heading toward Playa Larga depart from Juárez, near the corner of González, every five minutes from 5am to 10pm (M$10, 15 minutes).

TAXI

Cabs are plentiful in Zihuatanejo. Always agree on the fare before getting in. Approximate fares from central Zihua include M$80 to Ixtapa, M$45 to M$50 to Playa La Ropa, M$140 to M$160 to Playa Larga, and M$25 to the Estrella Blanca terminal.

SOUTH OF IXTAPA & ZIHUATANEJO

Barra de Potosí

755 / POP 400

About 26km southeast of Zihuatanejo is the small fishing village of Barra de Potosí, located at the far tip of Playa Larga's seemingly endless, palm-fringed sandy-white beach. It's at the mouth of the brackish **Laguna de Potosí**, a saltwater lagoon about 6.5km long that is home to hundreds of species of birds, including herons, kingfishers, cormorants and pelicans.

Nearly every *enramada,* all of them fishing-family owned, in the pueblo offers 90-minute boat tours of the lagoon, where you can glimpse crocodiles for the standard M$200 price. **Antonio Orregon** (755-557-22-01), based at Restaurante Rosita, is a good choice of guide, and he also offers four-hour snorkeling and fishing trips (M$1500). Trips include a buzz out to the impressive **Morros de Potosí**, a cluster of massive guano-covered rocks about 20 minutes offshore. Boats will circle the Morros, affording views of the many seabirds that nest out here, before heading to nearby **Playa Manzanillo**, where the snorkeling is sublime. The price includes cold drinks, from young coconuts to sodas and beer.

El Refugio de Potosí (755-100-07-43; www.elrefugiodepotosi.org; adult/child M$60/30; 10am-5:30pm Mon, Thu & Sun), a recently opened nature center just inland from the beachfront north of town, rehabilitates injured wildlife, breeds butterflies and parrots, and offers environmental education programs in local schools. A 30-minute guided tour, with excellent bilingual guides, offers opportunities to pet a porcupine, hold snakes and tarantulas, examine whale and crocodile skeletons, and observe a variety of animals, including parrots, hummingbirds, armadillos and a jaguarundi (local wildcat). There's also a 15m observation tower affording dramatic views of lagoons, palm-fringed beaches, the Morros de Potosí and the open ocean beyond. At research time it was closed to prepare new exhibits but will be open by the time you read this.

Sleeping & Eating

A handful of guesthouses are scattered around town, and seafood *enramadas* line the beach.

★ **Casa del Encanto** B&B $$
(cell phone 755-1246122; www.lacasadelencanto.com; d incl breakfast US$70-100;) For bohemian charm and an intimate perspective on the local community, nothing beats this magical space of brilliantly colored open-air rooms, hammocks, fountains and candlelit stairways on a residential street about 300m inland from the beach. Crowing roosters serenade you in the morning, and a nice breakfast is served in the central patio area.

Expat US owner Laura has spent years organizing international volunteers to work with neighborhood school children, and she's a great resource for getting to know the town, finding local guides, discovering late-night backstreet eateries, and timing your visit to coincide with local festivals and events. Her rates are flexible in the off-peak season.

La Condesa SEAFOOD $$
(mains M$80-130; 11am-sunset) Northernmost of the beachfront *enramadas,* this is one of the best. Try its *pescado a la talla* (broiled fish fillets) or *tiritas,* both local specialties, and don't pass up the savory handmade tortillas.

Getting There & Away

By car from Zihuatanejo, drive southeast on Hwy 200 toward Acapulco, take the well-marked turnoff (near Km 225 just south of the Los Achotes bridge) and drive another 9km to Barra de Potosí.

By public transportation, catch a Petatlán-bound bus from either of Zihua's main terminals, or from the stop a couple of blocks east of Zihua's market. Tell the driver to let you off at the Barra de Potosí intersection, where you can catch a *camioneta* (pickup truck) the rest of the way. The total trip takes about 90 minutes and costs about M$35.

Soledad de Maciel

☎755 / POP 380

Known locally as 'La Chole,' the tiny hamlet of Soledad de Maciel sits atop the largest, most important archaeological ruin in Guerrero state. Since excavations began in earnest in 2007, archaeologists have discovered a plaza, a ball court and three pyramids – one crowned by five temples – all constructed by pre-Hispanic cultures including Tepoztecos, Cuitlatecos and Tomiles.

Just inland from the ruins, a **museum** (www.soledaddemaciel.com; ⏲8am-5pm Tue-Sun) FREE houses three rooms full of Spanish-language displays, which place the local archaeological finds in a broader historical context. The most important local artifact is the Chole King, a 1.5m-tall statue depicting deities of life and death, displayed in the courtyard of the village church.

Soledad de Maciel is 33km southeast of Zihuatanejo off Hwy 200. From the well-marked turnoff near Km 214, a very rugged road leads 5km coastwards to the museum, then continues another kilometer to the archaeological site and village. Any bus heading south to Petatlán or Acapulco will get you here; ask to be dropped at the intersection for 'La Chole,' where you can hop on a *camioneta* into town.

PIE DE LA CUESTA

☎744 / POP 820

Just 10km – and 100 years – from Acapulco is the tranquil seaside suburb of Pie de la Cuesta, a rustic beach town occupied by some terrific guesthouses and seafood restaurants. But it's the odd combination of dramatic sunset views from the wide beach and bloody sunrises over the lagoon that have made Pie de la Cuesta famous. See, the town sits on a narrow, 2km strip of land bordered by the Pacific Ocean and the Laguna de Coyuca (where Sylvester Stallone filmed *Rambo: First Blood Part II*). The large freshwater lagoon contains several islands including Isla Pájaros, a bird sanctuary. Pie de la Cuesta is much quieter, cheaper and closer to nature than Acapulco, but still close enough for those who want to enjoy the city's attractions and nightlife.

During the post-Hurricane floods (see the boxed text p570), the local air force base was the only functioning air strip, which served as base of operations for rescue missions, and as an air bridge between Acapulco and Mexico City. At its peak, military choppers airlifted tourists all day long, from the steamy mess of Acapulco's Diamente district, where they'd meet waiting flights out of the Acapulco area.

Activities

The rugged, steep shore break here is better for bodyboarders, but big swells in December get over 10ft and attract surfers. The riptide and strong waves make it somewhat dangerous for swimmers. **Xentral** (☎774-131-30-87; per day SUP/bodyboards & kayaks M$150/200) rents bodyboards, SUP kits and kayaks.

Waterskiing and wakeboarding on the lagoon are both popular pastimes; there are several waterskiing clubs along the main road, all charging around M$700 to M$800 per hour, including **Club de Ski Tres Marías** (☎744-460-00-13, 744-460-00-11; www.tresmariasacapulco.com; Fuerza Aérea 375) and **Club de Ski Chuy** (☎744-460-11-04).

Several establishments offer **boat trips** on the lagoon from M$100 per person, and eager captains await your business along the main road and down by the boat launches at the lagoon's southeast corner.

Horseback riding on the beach costs about M$200 per hour. You may book through your hotel or directly from the galloping gauchos on the sand.

Sleeping

Villa Nirvana HOTEL $$

(☎744-460-16-31; www.lavillanirvana.com; Av de la Fuerza Aérea 302; r M$475-1050; P 📶 🏊) Villa Nirvana's friendly US owners have lovingly landscaped this cheerful property. It has a variety of simple, comfortable accommodations surrounding a central garden and pool area. The priciest rooms upstairs are larger and include sea-view terraces and double hammocks.

Quinta Erika B&B $$

(☎744-444-41-31; www.quintaerika.com; Carretera Barra de Coyuca Km 8.5; s/d incl breakfast US$50/55, 4-person bungalow US$120; P @ 📶 🏊) Quinta Erika is a hidden, jungle-like retreat located 8km northeast of town, 10 minutes on foot from the final bus stop in Playa Luces. The six colorful rooms and one bungalow are tastefully decorated with handmade furniture and traditional Mexican handicrafts.

The estate sits on 2 hectares of lagoonside property, lovingly landscaped with more than 200 palm and tropical fruit trees. Other perks include wonderful breakfasts, kayak rentals, a whimsically decorated pool and outdoor shower, a dock boasting spectacular lagoon views and an upstairs lounge area with hammocks.

Hacienda Vayma Beach Club HOTEL **$$**
(☎744-460-28-82; www.vayma.com.mx; Calz Pie de la Cuesta 378; r M$1050, ste M$2000; P❄📶≋) This relaxing hotel has a fat patch of beach with private *cabañas* and double-width lounge chairs, a big pool with swim-up bar and a choice of room types. 'Rough it' in a smaller budget unit with cold water only, or splurge for a suite with hot water, air-con and Jacuzzi.

Eating

Quinta Rosita MEXICAN, SEAFOOD **$$**
(Playa Pie de la Cuesta; mains M$50-120; ⏲9am-10pm) Treat your tastebuds to shrimp cooked six different ways while basking in the ocean breeze at this beachfront eatery. Sunday specials include paella, Veracruz-style fish and homemade stewed pork.

Restaurant Tres Marías SEAFOOD, MEXICAN **$$**
(Fuerza Aérea s/n; mains M$80-120; ⏲8am-7pm) Facing each other across the main street are these two separate restaurants with identical names and hours, run by a pair of sisters. The one facing the ocean serves fantastic *huachinango al mojo de ajo* (garlicky red snapper) and lets you bring your own drinks if you choose a table on the beach.

Its lagoonside counterpart, underneath a huge thatched roof, is popular for its North American-style breakfasts. Service can be indifferent, either way.

Baxar BISTRO **$$**
(☎744-460-25-02; www.baxar.com.mx; Playa Pie de la Cuesta; mains M$65-159; ⏲8am-8pm) This inn and bistro on the beach, coated in hot pink and exuding barefoot style, serves standards like ceviche and *cocteles*, roasted fish in coconut cream, and folds tasty shrimp tacos with sautéed vegetables into grilled flour *taquitos* – all of it done with flair and flavor.

It also books 21 fabulous little adobe-like suites (M$966 to M$1799), with high-end ceramic tile, sunken sitting area, queen-size beds and tastefully dangling rattan lampshades.

ℹ Information

Pie de la Cuesta's long main road (alternately known as Avenida de la Fuerza Aérea Mexicana and Calzada Pie de la Cuesta) runs through town, past an air force base and on to Playa Luces. Guesthouses all offer wi-fi. The town also has a pharmacy, telephones and a few *minisúper* grocery stores; other services are located in Acapulco.

ℹ Getting There & Away

From Acapulco, catch a 'Pie de la Cuesta' bus on La Costera across the street from the post office. Buses depart every 15 minutes from 6am until around 8pm; the trip costs M$7 and takes 30 to 90 minutes, depending on traffic – on a bad day, it can be total gridlock leaving Acapulco.

Buses from Acapulco marked 'Pie de la Cuesta–San Isidro' or 'Pie de la Cuesta–Pedregoso' stop at the town's arched entryway on Hwy 200, leaving you with a long walk into town; the more convenient 'Pie de la Cuesta–Playa Luces' buses turn off the main highway and follow Pie de la

WHO PUT KETCHUP IN MY CEVICHE?

Strictly speaking, ceviche is a cold salad made with fish, which is sliced then chopped and 'cooked' in lime juice along with red onion, cilantro, chili and salt, among other more proprietary ingredients. Up and down the Pacific Coast you'll catch restaurants advertising shrimp ceviche or a mixed ceviche with scallops, octopus, shrimp and fish. Purists may scoff, but the preparation is roughly the same and the seafood never sees a flame. Whichever way you order it, it will come on your choice of *tostada* (a snack), in a glass to be eaten with a spoon (a light meal), or on a platter served with a side stack of *tostadas* (now that's a meal). But beware, in Guerrero, ceviche is made with a special ingredient known as industrial-grade ketchup. How this isn't seen as sacrilegious and an affront to the seafood that gave its life for the enjoyment of humanity is anybody's guess. But the point is, do not order the ceviche in Guerrero. Order the *tiritas* (spicy, sliced slivers of fish marinated in citrus, chili and onions) instead.

Cuesta's main street 6km through town to Playa Luces, terminating just before Quinta Erika.

Colectivo taxis to Pie de la Cuesta operate 24 hours along La Costera and elsewhere in Acapulco's old town (M$13). A regular taxi from Acapulco costs M$100 to M$150 one way, depending on your haggling skills, the time of day and your point of origin. A taxi to the airport costs M$450 to M$500.

ACAPULCO

744 / POP 780,000

Before Cancún and Ixtapa, Acapulco was Mexico's original party town: it has a stunning topography of soaring cliffs, curling into a series of wide bays and more intimate coves, fringed with pearl beaches, backed by jungle-green hills and crowned with 24-hour nightlife. It was dubbed the 'Pearl of the Pacific' during its heyday when Acapulco was the playground for the rich and famous, including Frank Sinatra, Elvis Presley, Elizabeth Taylor and Judy Garland. John F Kennedy and his wife Jacqueline honeymooned here, and it was immortalized in films such as Elvis' *Fun in Acapulco* and TV's *The Love Boat*.

That topography hasn't changed, and Acapulco remains gorgeous, though overdeveloped. Worse, the city's reputation was tarnished by years of violent battles in Mexico's ongoing drug wars, which spilled into the streets, along with rolling heads (ask any cab driver for details). Tourism was gutted, and countless innocent working people have been affected. But the truth is that the violence is no more and Acapulco is not only safe but offers pockets of calm: romantic cliffside restaurants, the impressive 17th-century fort, a world-class botanical garden and the old town's charming shady *zócalo* (plaza). And when you tire of the crowds, secluded beaches and seaside villages such as Pie de la Cuesta are just a short drive away. Unfortunately, Acapulco remains under a gray cloud. Its latest challenge was Hurricane Manuel and the floods it spawned in September 2013 (see the boxed text p570).

Acapulco borders the 11km shore of the Bahía de Acapulco (Acapulco Bay). Old Acapulco – centered on the cathedral and adjacent *zócalo* – comprises the western part of the city; Acapulco Dorado heads east around the bay from Playa Hornos to Playa Icacos; and Acapulco Diamante is a newer luxury resort area southeast of Acapulco proper, between the Bahía de Acapulco and the airport.

Acapulco's principal bayside avenue, Avenida Costera Miguel Alemán – often called 'La Costera' – hugs the shoreline all the way around the bay. Past the naval base, La Costera becomes Carretera Escénica, which joins Hwy 200 after 9km (at the turnoff to Puerto Marqués). Hwy 200 then leads southeast past ritzy Playa Revolcadero to the airport.

Sights

Most of Acapulco's hotels, restaurants, discos and points of interest are along or near La Costera, especially near its midpoint at **La Diana** (Diana Circle; Map p564) traffic circle. From Playa Caleta on the Península de las Playas, it curves north toward the *zócalo*, then continues east along the beachfront past Parque Papagayo (a large, shady park popular with Mexican families) all the way to Playa Icacos and the naval base at the bay's southeastern edge.

Beaches

Acapulco's beaches top the list of must-dos for most visitors. The beaches heading east around the bay from the *zócalo* – **Playa Hornos**, **Playa Hornitos**, **Playa Condesa** and **Playa Icacos** – are the most popular, though the west end of Hornos sometimes smells of fish from the morning catch. The high-rise hotel district begins on Playa Hornitos, on the east side of Parque Papagayo, and sweeps east. City buses constantly ply La Costera, making it easy to get up and down the long arc of beaches.

Playas Caleta and **Caletilla** are two small, protected beaches blending into each other in a cove on the south side of Península de las Playas. They're both backed by a solid line of seafood *palapa* restaurants. The calm waters here are especially popular with families who have small children, though it is a *panga* harbor so isn't the cleanest. All buses marked 'Caleta' heading down La Costera arrive here. The **Mágico Mundo Marino** (744-483-12-15; adult/child M$60/30; 9am-6pm) aquarium sits on an islet just offshore, forming the imaginary line between the two beaches; boats go regularly from the islet to Isla de la Roqueta.

Playa La Angosta is in a tiny, protected cove on the west side of the peninsula. From the *zócalo* it takes about 20 minutes to walk here. Or you can take any 'Caleta' bus and get off near Hotel Avenida, at the corner of

Greater Acapulco

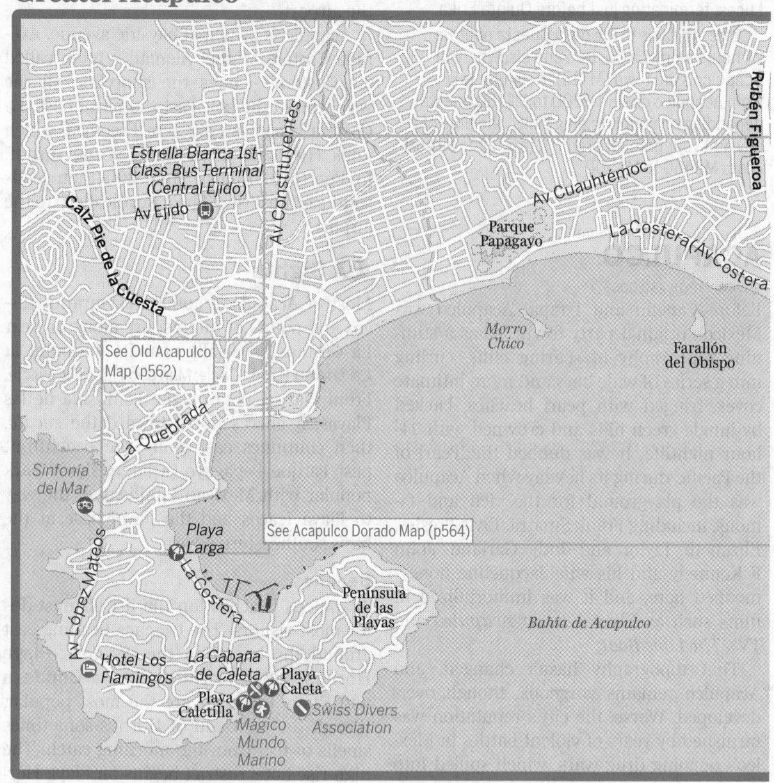

Las Palmas and La Costera, just one short block from the beach.

The beaches on **Bahía Puerto Marqués**, about 18km southeast of the *zócalo,* are very popular, and its calm waters are good for waterskiing and sailing. You get a magnificent view of Bahía de Acapulco as the Carretera Escénica climbs south out of the city. 'Puerto Marqués' buses run here along La Costera every 10 minutes from 5am to 9pm.

Beyond the Puerto Marqués turnoff and before the airport, **Playa Revolcadero** is a long, straight beach that has seen a recent explosion in luxury tourism and residential development. Waves are large and surfing is popular here, especially in summer, but a strong undertow makes swimming dangerous; heed lifeguards' instructions. Horseback riding along the beach is popular.

The two beaches closest to Old Acapulco are **Playa Tlacopanocha**, directly across from the *zócalo,* noteworthy more as a departure point for bay cruises than as a swimming beach; and **Playa Manzanillo**, a small crescent of sand that's popular with locals but not as pristine as the beaches further east.

Isla de la Roqueta ISLAND

This island offers a popular (crowded) beach, and snorkeling and diving possibilities. You can rent snorkeling gear, kayaks and other water-sports equipment on the beach. From Playas Caleta and Caletilla, boats make the eight-minute trip (M$60 round trip) every 20 minutes or so. Alternatively, glass-bottomed boats make a circuitous trip to the island (M$90), departing from the same beaches but traveling via **La Virgen de los Mares** (Virgin of the Seas), a submerged bronze statue of the Virgen of Guadalupe – visibility varies with water conditions. The trip takes about 45 minutes, depending on how many times floating vendors approach your boat.

★La Quebrada Clavadistas CLIFF DIVERS
(Map p562; ☎info 744-483-14-00; Plazoleta La Quebrada; adult/child M$50/10; ⊙shows 12:45pm, 7:30pm, 8:30pm, 9:30pm & 10:30pm) Acapulco's most popular tourist attraction, the famous cliff divers of La Quebrada have been dazzling audiences since 1934, diving with fearless finesse from heights of 25m to 35m into the narrow ocean cove below. The last show usually features divers holding torches. For good road karma, tip the divers when they come through the crowd. Restaurant-Bar La Perla provides a great but pricey view of the divers from above.

Just south of La Quebrada, you'll find the lovely **Sinfonía del Mar** (Symphony of the Sea), an outdoor stepped plaza that occasionally hosts concerts, but mainly serves as an amazing place to view sunsets.

★Fuerte de San Diego FORTRESS
(Map p564; ☎info 744-482-38-28; Hornitos s/n) This beautifully restored pentagonal fort was built in 1616 atop a hill east of the *zócalo*. Its mission was to protect the Spanish *naos* (ships) conducting trade between the Philippines and Mexico from marauding Dutch and English buccaneers. The fort was destroyed in a 1776 earthquake and rebuilt in 1783. It remains basically unchanged today.

The fort is home to the **Museo Histórico de Acapulco** (Map p564; ☎744-482-38-28; www.inah.gob.mx; Hornitos s/n; admission M$46, Sun free; ⊙9am-6pm Tue-Sun), which has fascinating exhibits detailing the city's history, with Spanish and English captions. The fort also puts on regular evening sound-and-light shows, in Spanish and English. Call to confirm times and dates.

★Zócalo PLAZA
(Map p562) Every night Acapulco's leafy old-town *zócalo* comes alive with street performers, mariachis, sidewalk cafes and occasional festivals. It's especially popular on Sunday nights with multiple generations of Mexican families. The **Nuestra Señora de la Soledad cathedral** (Map p562), built in 1930, dominates the square and is unusual for its blue-domed, neo-Byzantine architecture.

Jardín Botánico de Acapulco GARDENS
(☎744-435-04-38; www.acapulcobotanico.org; Av Heróico Colegio Militar s/n; adult/child M$30/free, guided visit per person M$50; ⊙8am-6pm) Located on the campus of Loyola del Pacífico University, these botanical gardens house an impressive collection of flora and fauna. The well-marked footpath climbs from 204m to 411m above sea level through a shaded tropical forest, with plenty of benches to stop and smell the flowers.

La Capilla de la Paz CHAPEL
(Chapel of Peace; Vientos Galernos s/n; ⊙10am-1pm & 4-6pm) Perched on a hilltop high above Acapulco, La Capilla de la Paz is a quiet spot for reflection and meditation. The minimalist, open-air chapel features cascading water, gardens and benches to savor the beautiful view of Acapulco. The chapel's giant white cross is visible from miles across the bay.

Visit during late afternoon, when tourists jockey for positions to capture the sun setting within the sculpture of clasped hands.

Old Acapulco

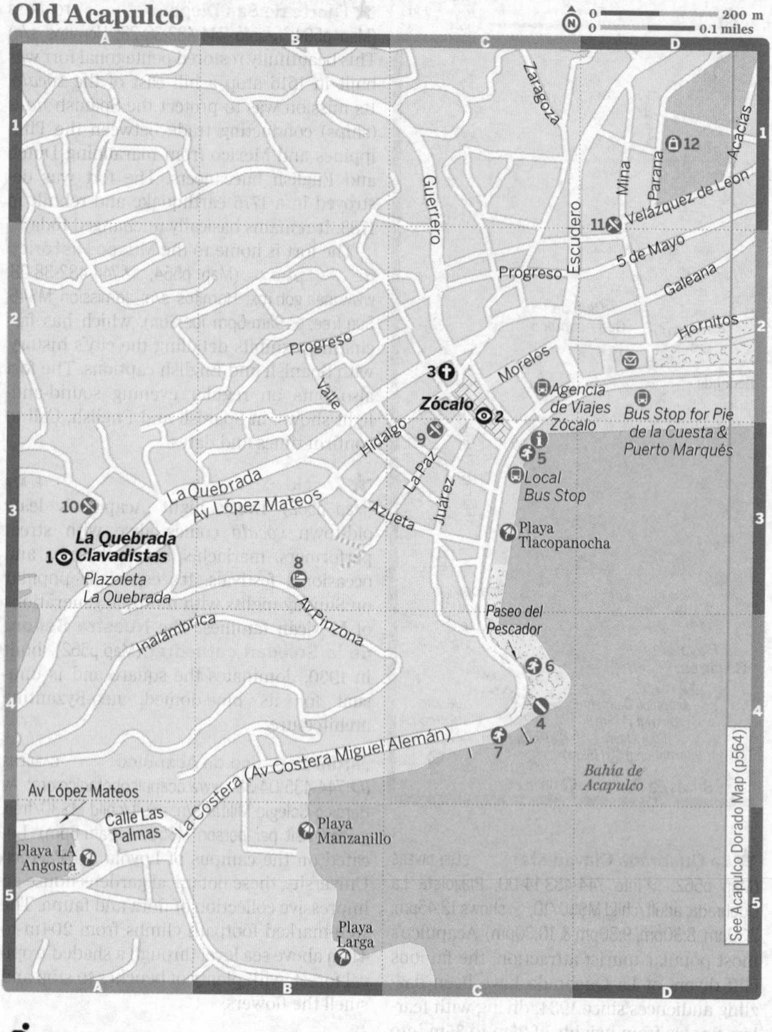

0 — 200 m
0 — 0.1 miles

Zaragoza
Guerrero
Escudero
Mina
Parana
Acacias
12
11
Velázquez de Leon
5 de Mayo
Progreso
Galeana
Hornitos
Progreso
Valle
3
Morelos
Agencia de Viajes Zócalo
Bus Stop for Pie de la Cuesta & Puerto Marqués
Zócalo
2
Hidalgo
9
La Paz
5
Local Bus Stop
La Quebrada
Av López Mateos
Azueta
Juárez
10
Playa Tlacopanocha
La Quebrada Clavadistas
1
Plazoleta La Quebrada
8
Av Pinzona
Paseo del Pescador
Inalámbrica
6
4
7
La Costera (Av Costera Miguel Alemán)
Bahía de Acapulco
Av López Mateos
Calle Las Palmas
Playa Manzanillo
Playa LA Angosta
Playa Larga

See Acapulco Dorado Map (p564)

Activities

Acapulco's activities are largely beach-based.

Water Sports

Just about everything that can be done on or below the water is done in Acapulco. Waterskiing, boating, banana-boating and parasailing are all popular. Outfitters, based in kiosks along the Zona Dorada beaches, charge about M$350 for a five-minute parasailing flight, M$500 for a jet-ski ride and M$800 for one hour of waterskiing or wake-boarding. The smaller Playas Caleta and Caletilla have sailboats, fishing boats, motorboats, pedal boats, canoes, snorkeling gear, inner tubes and water bicycles for rent.

Though Acapulco isn't really a scuba destination, there are some decent dive sites nearby. **Acapulco Scuba Center** (Map p562; ☎744-482-94-74; www.acapulcoscuba.com; Paseo del Pescador 13 & 14; ⏰8am-4pm Wed-Mon) and the **Swiss Divers Association** (☎744-482-13-57; www.swissdivers.com; Hotel Caleta, Cerro San Martín 325; ⏰9am-5pm) both charge US$75 for a two-tank dive trip.

The best **snorkeling** is off small Playa Las Palmitas on Isla de la Roqueta. Unless

Old Acapulco

Top Sights
1 La Quebrada Clavadistas....A3
2 Zócalo....C2

Sights
3 Nuestra Señora de la Soledad Cathedral....C2

Activities, Courses & Tours
4 Acapulco Scuba Center....C4
5 Acarey....C3
6 Fiesta/Bonanza....C4
7 Fish-R-Us....C4

Sleeping
8 Hotel Etel Suites....B3

Eating
9 El Nopalito....C3
10 Restaurant-Bar La Perla....A3
11 Taquería Los Pioneros....D1

Shopping
12 Mercado de Artesanías....D1

you pony up for an organized snorkeling trip, you'll need to scramble over rocks to reach it. You can rent gear on the island or on Playas Caleta and Caletilla, which also have some decent spots. Both Acapulco Scuba Center and the Swiss Divers Association take half-day snorkeling trips for US$38 per person, including boat, guide, gear, food, drink and transportation.

Sportfishing

Fish-R-Us FISHING
(Map p562; 800-347-47-87, 744-482-82-82; www.fish-r-us.com; La Costera 100; 9am-6pm) Fish-R-Us offers half-day fishing trips on 40ft boats, starting around US$450 for up to eight people, including gear and bait. The captain can often combine individual requests into a group large enough to cover the cost of the boat, for M$1000 to M$1500 per person.

Golf

Club de Golf Acapulco GOLF
(Map p564; 744-484-65-83, 744-484-07-81; La Costera s/n; green fees 8am-3pm M$750, after 3pm M$500; 7am-6:30pm) For golfers, Club de Golf Acapulco has a nine-hole course downtown.

Cruises

Various boats and yachts offer cruises, most of which depart from around Playa Tlacopanocha or Playa Manzanillo near the *zócalo*. Cruises are available day and night. They range from glass-bottomed boats to multilevel craft (with blaring salsa music and open bars) to yachts offering quiet sunset cruises around the bay. **Acarey** (Map p562; 744-482-37-63; La Costera s/n; ticket booth 10:30am-1pm & 4:30-10pm) and **Fiesta/Bonanza** (Map p562; 744-483-15-50) are two of the more popular operators; make reservations directly with the eager captains at the marina or through travel agencies and most hotels.

Other Activities

Paradise Bungy BUNGEE JUMPING
(Map p564; 744-484-75-29; La Costera 107; 5pm-1am Sun-Thu, 3pm-3am Fri & Sat) This 50m-high bungee tower is easy to spot on La Costera. For M$800 you can throw yourself (bungee included) from its platform while crowds cheer you from the street.

Festivals & Events

Semana Santa RELIGIOUS
Running from Palm Sunday, this is the busiest time of year for tourism in Acapulco. There's lots of action in the discos, on the beaches and all over town.

Festival Francés CULTURAL
(www.festivalfrances.com) The French Festival, usually held in April, celebrates French food, cinema, music and literature.

Acafest MUSIC
Held for one week in May. Features Mexican and international music stars at venues around town.

Sleeping

Acapulco has more than 30,000 hotel rooms. Rates vary widely by season; peak season is roughly from mid-December to mid-January, Easter Week and during the July and August school holidays. Given the dramatic drop-off in tourism in recent years, you can often bargain for a better rate, especially in low season for extended stays. During Semana Santa or between Christmas and New Year's Day (at which times all bets are off on room prices), it's essential to book ahead. Prices listed here are for high season. Package rates and online bookings can provide substantial savings.

Most of Acapulco's budget hotels are concentrated around the *zócalo* and La Quebrada. The original high-rise zone stretches from the eastern end of Parque Papagayo

Acapulco Dorado

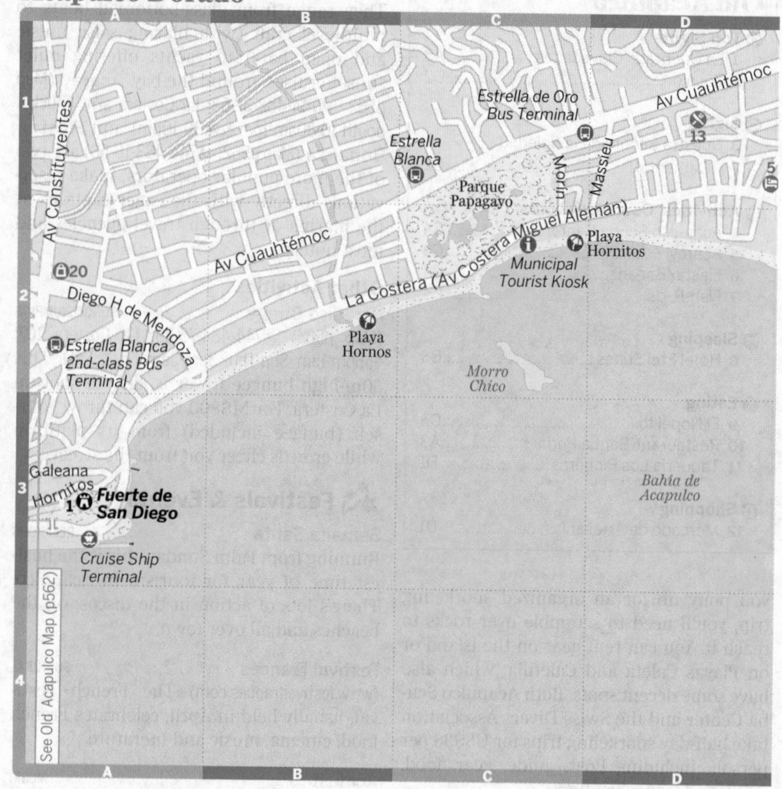

and curves east around the bay; a new luxury 'strip' is springing up on Playa Revolcadero, east of Puerto Marqués.

Hotel Los Flamingos HOTEL **$$**
(☎744-482-06-90; www.hotellosflamingos.com; Av López Mateos s/n; r from US$40; P❄📶🏊) The US$40 hotel with the million dollar view, once owned by Johnny 'Tarzan' Weissmuller, John Wayne and their pals, is a living, hot-pink memory of Acapulco's heyday. Perched on a cliff 135m above the ocean, this classic boasts one of the finest sunset views in town, with hammocks to enjoy them, and a kitschy bar and restaurant.

Images of Hollywood's golden age grace the walls. The rooms are modest, if aged, but comfortable enough.

Hotel Sands Acapulco HOTEL, BUNGALOW **$$**
(Map p564; ☎744-435-08-90; www.sands.com.mx; La Costera 178; bungalow/r M$575/750; P❄📶🏊) An excellent choice for families, Sands is located across the highway from the beach and has a large children's playground, minigolf, pools and a waterslide. Bungalows are small but cozy; the larger rooms sleep up to four people. All have cable TV, air-con and fridge, and there's wi-fi in the common areas. Prices are slashed substantially in the low season.

Bali-Hai MOTEL **$$**
(Map p564; ☎744-485-66-22; www.balihai.com.mx; La Costera 186; r from M$580; P❄📶🏊) This Polynesian-themed motel in the heart of Bahía de Acapulco and across the street from the beach is a good moderate choice, with long rows of spacious 1960s-vintage rooms, with ample wood paneling and natural light flanking a pair of palm-lined pools. Rates jump on holiday long weekends.

Hotel Marzol HOTEL **$$**
(Map p564; ☎744-484-33-96; hotel.marzol@gmail.com; Av Francia 1A; r from M$650) Tucked down

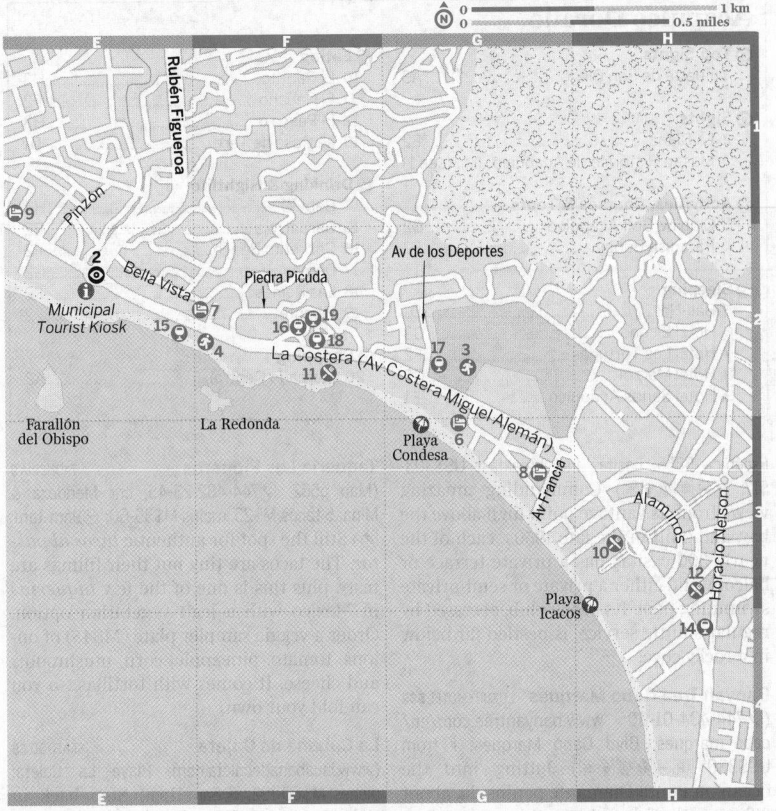

a narrow street leading to the beach, this is a polished if unremarkable three-star boutique high-rise. Rooms have high-end tile floors, high ceilings and beds on the hard side, along with cable TV which makes it a solid-value option.

Hotel Las Tortugas HOTEL **$$**
(Map p564; 744-484-88-89; www.hoteltortugaacapulco.com; La Costera 132; r M$833-2521; P) An aging atrium hotel, dripping with vines and grace, with a turtle pond in the lobby next to the grand piano. Rooms are spread across seven floors and are bright and sizeable with built-in desks and shelving, a funky bubble-glass bathroom divider, cable TV and security boxes. Towels are a touch threadbare, but it's still decent value.

Hotel Etel Suites SUITES **$$**
(Map p562; 744-482-22-40/1; etelste@yahoo.com.mx; Av Pinzona 92; ste with/without terrace M$1000/800, apartments M$1200; P) High above Old Acapulco, with views of both the bay and the Pacific Ocean, rooms need a paint job and some of the bathroom tile is a bit old, but midcentury modernists will love their apartments thanks to dated furnishings and terraces with outrageous city vistas.

Hotel Elcano HOTEL **$$$**
(Map p564; 744-435-15-00; www.hotelelcano.com.mx; La Costera 75; d M$3570; P @) Near the center of Acapulco's crescent of beaches, the Elcano has old-school grace, with groovy art deco tile in the breezy lobby, a sumptuous pool area and a patch of beachfront. Rooms aren't huge but they are bright with marble washbasins, flat-screen TVs and terraces with a commanding view. Low-season discounts make it a steal.

Las Brisas LUXURY HOTEL **$$$**
(744-469-69-00, in the US 866-221-2961; www.brisashotelonline.com/acapulco; Carretera

Acapulco Dorado

Top Sights
1 Fuerte de San Diego ... A3

Sights
2 La Diana ... E2
Museo Histórico de Acapulco ... (see 1)

Activities, Courses & Tours
3 Club de Golf Acapulco ... G2
4 Paradise Bungy ... F2

Sleeping
5 Bali-Hai ... D1
6 Hotel Elcano ... G3
7 Hotel Las Tortugas ... F2
8 Hotel Marzol ... G3
9 Hotel Sands Acapulco ... E1

Eating
10 El Cabrito ... H3
11 El Gaucho ... F2
12 El Pesca'o ... H3
13 La Casa de Tere ... D1

Drinking & Nightlife
14 Baby'O ... H4
15 Barbarroja ... E2
16 Cabretito Beach ... F2
17 Demas ... G2
18 Las Reinas ... F2
19 Picante ... F2

Shopping
20 Mercado Central ... A2

Escénica 5255; casitas incl breakfast US$303-517; P ⊜ ❄ @ ≋ ≋) Commanding amazing views from its vantage point high above the bay, and built in the late 1950s, each of the nearly 300 casitas has a private terrace or balcony and either a private or semi-private swimming pool. Its beach club, accessed by regular shuttle service, is nestled far below in a rocky cove.

Banyan Tree Cabo Marqués LUXURY HOTEL $$$
(☎744-434-01-00; www.banyantree.com/en/cabo_marques; Blvd Cabo Marqués; r from US$330; P ⊜ ❄ @ ≋ ≋) Jutting into the ocean on Punta Diamante peninsula, about 32km south of downtown, this gorgeous resort is Acapulco's most luxurious, dazzling guests with its private pool villas, outdoor massage beds and Asian-themed spa treatments. Enjoy gourmet Thai, Mexican, Italian or Spanish cuisine at the hotel's four restaurants, or opt for 'In-Villa' dining – the ultimate room-service experience.

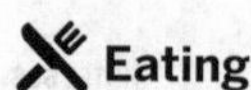

Eating

Old Acapulco

El Nopalito CAFE $
(Map p562; La Paz; mains M$35-48; ⊙8am-8pm) One of several cafes and diners strung along the streets surrounding the *zócalo*. This one attracts people for its daily menu including *mole* and paella on Sundays. Its plate lunches include fruit, juice or coffee and a main like roast chicken, beef enchilada, *carne asada* (marinated grilled beef) or fried fish, served with beans and tortillas.

Taquería Los Pioneros TAQUERÍA $
(Map p562; ☎744-482-23-45; cnr Mendoza & Mina; 5 tacos M$25, mains M$35-60; ⊙9am-1am; ☑) Still the spot for authentic *tacos al pastor*. The tacos are tiny but their fillings are tasty, plus this is one of the few *taquerías* in Mexico with a legit vegetarian option. Order a veggie sampler plate (M$45) of onions, tomato, pineapple, corn, mushrooms and cheese. It comes with tortillas, so you can fold your own.

La Cabaña de Caleta SEAFOOD $$
(www.lacabanadecaleta.com; Playa La Caleta; dishes M$60-192; ⊙8am-11pm) Step back in time and into a slice of traditional Mexican beach life, c 1950, at this venerable, unpretentious seafood shack straddling the sands of Playa La Caleta. Bask under a blue umbrella and gaze at the bay while savoring specialties such as *zarzuela de mariscos* (seafood stew) or *chiles rellenos* stuffed with shrimp, octopus and fish.

Restaurant-Bar La Perla INTERNATIONAL $$$
(Map p562; ☎744-483-11-55; www.miradoracapulco.com/la-perla.asp; Hotel El Mirador, Plazoleta La Quebrada 74; dishes M$115-325; ⊙8am-11pm) Candlelit terraces, sea breezes and first-rate views of the death-defying *clavadistas* almost justify the high price of a meal here; during performances, minimum consumption is M$250 (M$100 at the bar).

Acapulco Dorado

★**La Casa de Tere** MEXICAN $$
(Map p564; Martín 1721; mains M$75-135; ⊙8am-6pm Tue-Sun) This homespun gem near the

Estrella de Oro bus terminal is the place to go for Thursday *pozole* (M$50). Founded on Doña Tere's patio in 1990 using her mother Clarita's traditional recipes, it serves a wide-ranging menu including the sought-after Sunday special: *barbacoa de carnero* (barbecued lamb). All of it comes with house-made tortillas.

El Cabrito MEXICAN $$

(Map p564; ☎744-484-77-11; www.elcabrito-acapulco.com; La Costera 1480; mains M$70-220; ⏲2-10pm) Celebrating nearly 50 years in business, this beloved and brightly decorated restaurant has some of the city's finest traditional Mexican food, such as Oaxaca-style black *mole* made from 32 ingredients. You'd also do quite well with *cabrito al pastor* (roast kid goat; M$220). The shrimp dishes are tasty, so are the house-made tortillas, and the outdoor tables offer prime people-watching.

El Pesca'o SEAFOOD $$

(Map p564; ☎744-481-32-07; www.facebook.com/ElPescaoAcapulco; Maury 1A; mains M$90-250; ⏲1-7:30pm) Tucked down a side street off the La Costera drag is this hopping seafood house, with its intimate palm-leaf interior spilling out onto a pebbled sidewalk. It serves *cocteles* of shrimp, oyster, octopus, scallop and combinations of the same, flays salmon carpaccio, does seafood enchiladas, grills and fries fish a dozen different ways, and has ceviche, of course.

El Gaucho ARGENTINE $$$

(Map p564; ☎744-484-17-00; www.elpresidenteacapulco.com.mx/restaurantes.html; Hotel Presidente, La Costera 8; pasta M$88-115, mains M$205-384; ⏲2:30-11:30pm) Upscale but not stuffy, this glass-box dining room is one of the top spots in town for a steak. All the meat is grilled in true Argentine style, and less carnivorous or extravagant folk can choose from an assortment of pasta dishes. The short but decent wine list includes selections from Mexico, Chile, Spain and Argentina.

Drinking & Nightlife

Most clubs don't get rolling until midnight or later. Admission charges vary by the season, the night and the doorman's mood. Dress to impress; shorts and sneakers are frowned upon.

Acapulco has an active gay scene with several gay bars and clubs, mostly open from 10pm until about 4am.

Demas (Map p564; ☎744-484-18-00; Av de los Deportes 10A; ⏲10pm-7am Wed-Sun) is open only to men and has shows on Friday and Saturday; **Picante** (Map p564; ☎744-484-22-09; Piedra Picuda 16) has a minuscule dance floor, the occasional drag or stripper show, and a mostly male clientele. **Cabaretito Beach** (Map p564; Piedra Picuda 17; no cover; ⏲9pm-noon Wed-Sat) was the most popular gay spot at research time, but was also favored by some straight club kids, too. It has theme parties and drag shows. If karaoke is your thing, **Las Reinas** (Map p564; ☎744-101-02-27; La Costera 74) is the most popular of the three rough-around-the-edges bars serving a mostly gay clientele on La Costera. Acapulco's unofficial gay beach is the rocky section of Playa Condesa by the Fiesta Americana hotel.

★Bar Los Flamingos BAR

(Av López Mateos s/n; ⏲10am-10pm) The clifftop bar of Hotel Los Flamingos is the best sundowner spot in Acapulco, thanks to its famed menu of signature cocktails – such as *cocos locos* (made with rum, tequila, pineapple juice and coconut crème). Its restaurant also serves a tasty, traditional, menu, and service is old-school impeccable.

Barbarroja BAR

(Map p564; ☎744-484-59-32; La Costera 107; ⏲5pm-6am) Ahoy, matey! From a boat-shaped bar to women in pirate costumes dancing on tables, this over-the-top, pirate-themed pub is one of several beachfront bars near the bungee tower. And it's the only one where a 35-year-old can walk in and not feel like the oldest person in the world.

Palladium CLUB

(☎744-446-54-90; www.palladium.com.mx; Carretera Escénica s/n; admission varies; ⏲10:30pm-late Thu-Sat) Hailed by many as the best disco in town, Palladium attracts a young crowd, and offers fabulous bay views from floor-to-ceiling windows, and an international cast of DJs pump out hip-hop, house, trance and techno from an ultraluxe sound system. Dress up, and expect to wait in line.

Baby'O CLUB

(Map p564; ☎744-484-74-74; www.babyo.com.mx; La Costera 22; admission M$100-380; ⏲11pm-5am Thu-Sat) If Barney and Pebbles came of age and wanted to party...in Acapulco, they'd do it here in this Flintstone-esque faux grotto construction that opens up to the thump-thump of unbridled reverie and bad decisions (the fun kind). Translation: it's a popular nightclub among the well heeled with theme nights, and DJs that spin rock, pop, and house.

Entertainment

Bullfights take place at the **Plaza de Toros**, southeast of La Quebrada and northwest of Playas Caleta and Caletilla, every Sunday at 5:30pm from January to March. The 'Caleta' bus passes near the bullring.

Shopping

Mercado Central MARKET
(Map p564; Diego H de Mendoza s/n) This sprawling indoor-outdoor bazaar has everything from *atoles* to *zapatos* (shoes), plus produce, hot food and souvenirs. Any eastbound 'Pie de la Cuesta' or 'Pedregoso' bus will drop you here.

Mercado de Artesanías MARKET
(Map p562; cnr Parana & Velásquez de León) Bargaining is the standard at this leafy and laid-back craft market. Here you'll find better deals on everything that you see in the hotel shops, including hammocks, jewelry, clothing and T-shirts.

Other handicraft markets include the Mercados de Artesanías **Papagayo**, **Noa Noa**, **Dalia** and **La Diana** (all on La Costera), and the **Mercado de Artesanías La Caletilla** at the western end of Playa Caletilla.

Information

DANGERS & ANNOYANCES

Now that the drug violence has evaporated, the main annoyances most visitors will experience are relatively mundane: honking taxis, snarled traffic, crowds and aggressive touts. In high season beaches overflow with a seemingly endless parade of hawkers selling shells, *tamales*, hair braids and temporary tattoos. A simple '*No, gracias*' and smile works wonders. Less common nuisances include petty crime and scams. Always secure your valuables.

EMERGENCY

Ambulance/Fire/Police (☎066)

Locatel (☎744-481-11-00) A 24-hour hotline for all types of emergencies.

Tourist Police (☎744-440-70-24)

INTERNET ACCESS

Acapulco has hundreds of cybercafes, most charging M$8 to M$10 per hour. Most hotels and restaurants offer free wi-fi as well.

MEDICAL SERVICES

Hospital Magallanes (☎744-485-65-44; Massieu 2) A well-established private hospital with English-speaking doctors and staff.

BUSES FROM ACAPULCO

DESTINATION	FARE (M$)	DURATION	FREQUENCY (DAILY)
Chilpancingo	90-110	1¾-3hr	frequent EDO; frequent EB from Central Ejido & 2nd-class terminal
Cuernavaca	380	4-5hr	9 EDO; 5 EB from Central Papagayo
Mexico City (Terminal Norte)	445-600	6hr	frequent EB from Central Papagayo & Central Ejido
Mexico City (Terminal Sur)	445-560	5hr	frequent EDO; frequent EB from Central Papagayo & Central Ejido
Puerto Escondido	500	7-8hr	7 EB from Central Ejido
Puerto Vallarta	1456	17hr	2 EB from Central Ejido, noon from Central Papagayo
Taxco	230-250	4hr	6 EDO
Zihuatanejo	148-190	4-5hr	very frequent EDO; frequent EB from Central Ejido

MONEY

Banks and *casas de cambio* cluster around the *zócalo* and line La Costera. Hotels will also change money, but their rates are usually high.

POST

Main Post Office (Map p562; ☎744-483-53-63; Palacio Federal, La Costera 125; ⊙8am-5pm Mon-Fri, 9am-1pm Sat)

TELEPHONE & FAX

You can make long-distance calls from the many Telmex card and coin phones throughout the city, or from private *casetas* (with signs saying '*larga distancia*').

TOURIST INFORMATION

Municipal Tourist Kiosk (⊙8:30am-8:30pm) La Diana traffic circle (Map p564; ⊙high season only); Marina (Map p562; ⊙year-round); Parque Papagayo (Map p564; ⊙year-round); Playa Caleta (⊙high season only) The city government operates four tourist information kiosks, clearly marked 'Secretaría de Turismo Municipal.' These are located on the marina across from the *zócalo*, at the flagpole across from Parque Papagayo, at La Diana traffic circle and at Playa Caleta.

ℹ Getting There & Away

Acapulco is accessible via Hwy 200 from the east and west, and by Hwy 95 and Hwy 95D from the north. It's 400km south of Mexico City and 235km southeast of Zihuatanejo.

AIR

Acapulco's **Juan Álvarez International Airport** (☎744-435-20-60; www.oma.aero/es/aeropuertos/acapulco; Blvd de las Naciones s/n) has seen a marked decrease in international nonstop flights, although it's still easy to connect through Mexico City (a short hop from Acapulco). All services listed following are direct; some are seasonal.

Aeroméxico (www.aeromexico.com) Airport (☎744-466-91-09; Airport); La Costera (☎744-485-16-00; La Costera 1632) To Mexico City.

Interjet (☎744-466-93-65; www.interjet.com.mx; Airport) To Mexico City.

Volaris (☎800-122-80-00; www.volaris.mx; Airport) To Tijuana.

BUS

Acapulco has two major long-distance bus companies that offer 1st-class services: Estrella de Oro and Estrella Blanca. The modern, air-conditioned **Estrella de Oro bus terminal** (EDO; Map p564; ☎800-900-01-05; www.estrelladeoro.com.mx; Av Cuauhtémoc 1490), just west of Massieu, has free toilets, several ATMs and a ticket machine that accepts bank debit cards; luggage can also be left for M$5 to M$12 per hour, depending on size.

Estrella Blanca (EB; Map p564; www.estrellablanca.com.mx) has two 1st-class terminals: **Central Papagayo** (Av Cuauhtémoc 1605), just north of Parque Papagayo, and **Central Ejido** (☎744-469-20-30, 744-469-20-28; Av Ejido 47). The **Estrella Blanca 2nd-class bus terminal** (Map p564; ☎744-482-21-84; Av Cuauhtémoc 97) sells tickets for all buses, but only has departures to relatively nearby towns. Estrella Blanca tickets are also sold at a few agencies around town, including **Agencia de Viajes Zócalo** (Map p562; ☎744-483-58-88; La Costera 207, Local 18), which offers frequent services to Mexico City, with various levels of luxury.

CAR & MOTORCYCLE

Several car-rental companies have offices at the airport as well as in town; some offer free delivery to you. Shop around to compare prices.

Alamo (www.alamomexico.com.mx) Airport (☎744-466-94-44; Airport); La Costera (☎744-484-33-05; La Costera 34)

Budget (www.budget.com.mx) Airport (☎744-466-90-03; Airport); La Costera (☎744-481-24-33; La Costera 134)

Europcar (☎744-466-93-14; www.europcar.com.mx; Airport)

Hertz (☎744-466-91-72; www.hertz.com; Airport)

ℹ Getting Around

TO/FROM THE AIRPORT

Acapulco's airport is 23km southeast of the *zócalo*, beyond the junction for Puerto Marqués. Arriving by air, you can buy a ticket for transportation into town from the desk at the end of the domestic terminal. Fares are officially regulated: *colectivo* taxis operate whenever there's an incoming flight, charging M$100 per person to any point within Acapulco city limits; private taxis from the airport run constantly, ranging in price from M$150 to M$425, depending on which of the five designated zones you're traveling to (a map of the various zones is posted at the taxi ticket desk).

Leaving Acapulco, taxis from the city center to the airport cost around M$200 to M$300, depending on the distance.

BUS

Acapulco has a good city-bus system (especially good when you get a neon-lit beauty with a bumping sound system). Buses operate from 5am to 11pm and cost M$7 with air-con, M$6 without. Numerous stops are located along La Costera, including one directly opposite the *zócalo*. The bus stop opposite the post office, three blocks east of the *zócalo*, is the beginning

HURRICANE MANUEL

On September 19, 2013, what started out as a tropical storm off Mexico's Pacific Coast morphed into Hurricane Manuel and landed south of Acapulco with vicious force. The storm was relatively slow-moving, gusting sustained winds of 125km/h, which meant rainfall was severe. Rivers swelled high and fast and tore through bridges. Hillsides melted, burying entire neighborhoods. The worst hit area was the village of La Pintada, home to 600 people, where a landslide – which became a wave of mud, water and trees – swept through and destroyed half the town, burying approximately 40 houses and killing 58 people. Acapulco, a geographical marvel in the best of times, was cut off. Road access to Mexico City was no more, bridges north to Zihuatanejo and south toward Oaxaca were washed out. The bays were filled with debris, the airport flooded. For days on end, residents struggled for the basics, finding little food and clean water.

Although Acapulco's town center was only moderately flooded in places for a few days, Acapulco's exclusive Diamante area – where the airport, corporate big-box stores like WalMart and Costco, and the most luxurious hotel and vacation properties are located – was hit hard. And during a simple flyover, it's easy to see why. The entire area was built in a flood plain. In other words, the water went where it was supposed to go, only luxury development and the businesses that fuel them were in the way. Roads became filthy rivers. Residents and tourists alike were completely stranded, and it wasn't long before looting began and the scene turned frightening.

In total, 139 people were killed in the storm, 20,000 wound up living in shelters for weeks and 58,000 tourists were evacuated, some airlifted by military choppers. As a result, Costa Chica was inaccessable to our authors during the research period. We have done the best job possible to update those listings through desk research and through sources on the ground.

of several bus routes (including to Pie de la Cuesta), so you can usually get a seat.

Useful city routes:

Base–Caleta From the Icacos naval base at the southeast end of Acapulco, along La Costera, past the *zócalo* to Playa Caleta.

Base–Cine Río–Caleta From the Icacos naval base, cuts inland from La Costera on Avenida Wilfrido Massieu to Avenida Cuauhtémoc, heads down Avenida Cuauhtémoc through the business district, turning back to La Costera just before reaching the *zócalo*, continuing west to Playa Caleta.

Centro–Puerto Marqués From opposite the post office, along La Costera to Puerto Marqués.

Zócalo–Playa Pie de la Cuesta From opposite the post office to Pie de la Cuesta.

CAR & MOTORCYCLE

Avoid driving in Acapulco if at all possible. The streets are in poor shape and the anarchic traffic is often horribly snarled.

TAXI

Hundreds of zippy blue-and-white VW cabs scurry around Acapulco like cockroaches, maneuvering with an audacity that borders on the comical. Drivers often quote fares higher than the official ones; whenever possible, ask locals what a fair rate is for your destination, and always agree on a price with the driver before getting in.

COSTA CHICA

Guerrero's 'Small Coast,' extending southeast from Acapulco to the Oaxacan border, is much less traveled than its bigger brother to the northwest, but it does have at least one spectacular beach. Afro-Mestizos (people of mixed African, indigenous and European descent) make up a large portion of the population. The region was a safe haven for Africans who escaped slavery, some from the interior, others (it's believed) from a slave ship that sank just off the coast.

From Acapulco, Hwy 200 traverses inland past small villages and farmlands. San Marcos, about 60km east of Acapulco, and Cruz Grande, about 40km further east, are the only two towns of significant size before Cuajinicuilapa near the Oaxaca border. Both provide basic services including banks, gas stations and simple hotels.

Playa Ventura & Around

741 / POP 550

Located 131km southeast of Acapulco, Playa Ventura (labeled Juan Álvarez on most maps) is a pristine beach with soft white-and-gold sands and clear, calm water. The town extends inland for about three blocks and features a small village **museum**, simple seafood restaurants and a few beachfront hotels.

La Caracola (☎cell phone 741-1013047; www.playaventura.com; Ventura 68; s M$385, d M$500-700; P📶❄) is a thatched treehouse on stilts, 1.5km north of the church, which has several rooms with basic beds, mosquito netting, hammocks and fans, and a communal kitchen. Tiny adobe pyramids on the beach house cheaper rooms. The open-air architecture doesn't afford a lot of privacy, but the lovely Venezuelan-born owner makes everyone feel at home. Pets are welcome; kids under 16 years are not.

On the same road as La Caracola, Italian-run **Posada Quintomondo** (☎cell phone 741-1013018; www.posadaquintomondo.info; d M$800; P📶❄) offers beachfront rooms sleeping two to four, along with a great **restaurant** (mains M$90-130) featuring homemade pizzas, pasta and Mediterranean-influenced seafood recipes.

To get here by car, take Hwy 200 to the signposted Playa Ventura turnoff (Km 124), just east of the village of Copala, then continue south 7km to the coast. By bus from Acapulco, take a southeast-bound bus to Copala (M$79, 2¾ hours, 120km). From here, *camionetas* and microbuses depart for Playa Ventura about every half-hour (M$15, 30 minutes, 13km) from just east of the bus stop.

About 13km southeast of the Playa Ventura turnoff on Hwy 200 (Km 137) is the market town of **Marquelia**. The town offers access to an immense stretch of beach backed by coconut palms, which follows the contours of the coastline for many kilometers in either direction. From Marquelia's center you can take a *camioneta* to a section of the beach known as **Playa La Bocana**, where the Río Marquelia meets the sea and forms a lagoon. La Bocana has *cabañas*, a small hotel and some *comedores* with hammocks where you can spend the night.

Cuajinicuilapa

☎741 / POP 26,000

About 200km southeast of Acapulco, Cuajinicuilapa, or Cuaji (*kwah*-hee), is the nucleus of Afro-Mestizo culture on the Costa Chica. The **Museo de las Culturas Afromestizas** (Museum of Afro-Mestizo Cultures; ☎741-414-12-31; www.coax.net/people/lwf/MEX_MAMC.HTM; cnr Manuel Zárate & Av Cuauhtémoc; admission M$10; ⏲10am-2pm & 4-7pm Mon-Fri) is a tribute to the history of African slaves in Mexico and, specifically, to local Afro-Mestizo culture. Behind the museum are three examples of *casas redondas*, the round houses typical of West Africa that were built around Cuaji until as late as the 1960s. The museum is a block inland from the Banamex that's just west of the main plaza.

Buses to Cuajinicuilapa (M$210, 4½ hours) depart Estrella Blanca's Central Ejido bus terminal in Acapulco hourly from 5am, and Estrella Blanca has several buses daily to Cuaji from the town of Pinotepa Nacional (M$42, one hour) in Oaxaca state.

Western Central Highlands

Includes ➡

Best Places to Eat

- Restaurante Lu (p614)
- La Fonda de la Noche (p587)
- Number 4 (p600)
- Lula Bistro (p588)
- Parrilla Libertad (p588)

Best Places to Stay

- Hotel de la Soledad (p613)
- Hotel Morales (p586)
- Casa de las Flores (p586)
- Rancho San Cayetano (p619)

Why Go?

With exquisite colonial architecture, delicious food, butterfly orgies, lonely indigenous pueblos, bustling cities and volcanic calderas, the western central highlands are a wonderland of the urban and the natural. The climate is near perfect and the landscape as diverse as it is mind-blowing. You'll see layered mountains, expansive lakes, thundering rivers and waterfalls, and a tapestry of cornfields, avocado groves, agave plantations and cattle ranches.

However, despite the region's myriad attractions and its easygoing vibe, foreign tourists remain a rare sight throughout much of the region. This means that those who do venture here are certain to be greeted with genuine warmth and friendship at every turn – this is a part of Mexico where locals are likely to accost you in the street to thank you for coming to their town. Perhaps it should be us thanking them for creating a region of such beauty and affection.

When to Go

Guadalajara

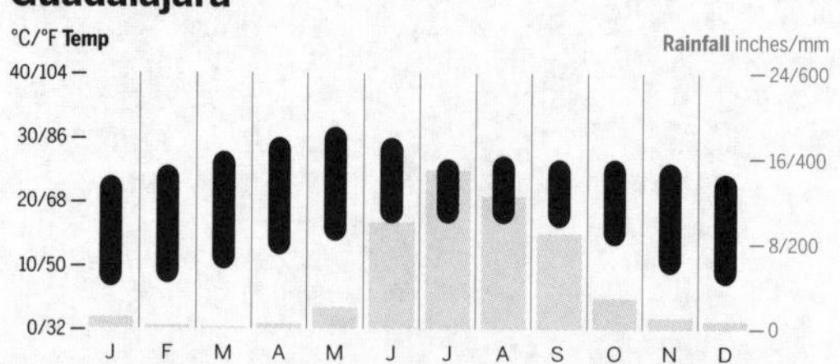

Feb Flutter with the monarch butterflies in the Reserva Mariposa Monarca.

Nov Commune with the dead on Día de Muertos in the villages around Pátzcuaro.

Mar Join the stars of cinema at Guadalajara's Festival Internacional del Cine.

History

The western central highlands were too far from the Maya and Aztecs to fall under their influence, but during the 14th to 16th centuries the Tarascos in northern Michoacán developed a robust pre-Hispanic civilization. When the Aztecs took notice and attacked, the Tarascos held strong thanks to their copper blades. West of the Tarascos was their rival, Chimalhuacán – a confederation of four indigenous kingdoms spread through parts of present-day Jalisco, Colima and Nayarit states. To the north were the Chichimecs.

Colima, the leading Chimalhuacán kingdom, was conquered by the Spanish in 1523. The whole region, however, was not brought under Spanish control until the notorious campaigns of Nuño de Guzmán. Between 1529 and 1536 he tortured, killed and enslaved indigenous people from Michoacán to Sinaloa. His grizzly victories made him rich and famous and won him governorship of his conquered lands, until news of his war crimes leaked out. He was sent back to Spain and imprisoned for life in 1538.

This fertile ranching and agricultural region developed gradually and Guadalajara (established in 1542 and always one of Mexico's biggest cities) became the 'capital of the west.' The church, with help from the enlightened bishop Vasco de Quiroga, fostered small industries and handicraft traditions around the villages of Lago de Pátzcuaro in its effort to ease the continuing poverty of the indigenous people.

In the 1920s the region's two major states, Michoacán and Jalisco, were hotbeds of the Cristero rebellion by Catholics against government antichurch policies. Lázaro Cárdenas of Michoacán, as state governor (1928–32) and then as Mexican president (1934–40), instituted reforms that did much to abate antigovernment sentiments.

Today Jalisco and Michoacán hold many of Mexico's natural resources – especially timber, minerals, livestock and agriculture – and Jalisco has a thriving tech industry. In the past both states have seen large segments of their population head to the USA for work. Michoacán reportedly lost almost half its population to emigrations, and money sent home regularly exceeds US$2 billion. But with the economic slowdown in the USA, the flow north has slowed and these days many have decided to return to Mexico and open up businesses on their home soil.

ℹ Getting There & Around

All major cities in the western central highlands (Guadalajara, Colima, Morelia and Uruapan) are well connected by regional and national bus lines. Guadalajara, Colima and Morelia have regular flights from many other cities in Mexico, as well as from the US.

GUADALAJARA

☎33 / POP 1.5 MILLION / ELEV 1550M

A pueblo (town) of well over a million people, charmingly unself-conscious Guadalajara has somehow, and rather without trying, become Mexico's second city. While often neglected by travelers, the city's charms are distributed equally and liberally throughout its distinct neighborhoods. The city's Centro Histórico (Historic Center) is dotted with proud colonial relics that house museums, government offices, bars and hotels. More modern and spread out Chapultepec is sprinkled with fashionable restaurants, coffeehouses and nightclubs. Mellow suburbs Tlaquepaque (upscale) and Tonalá (grassroots) are a folk-art shopper's dream destinations; and Zapopan has some interesting colonial sites, but is better known as Guadalajara's Beverly Hills. Guadalajara residents (nicknamed *tapatíos,* which also refers to anyone Jalisco-born) are warm and eager to share the essence of their city.

Guadalajara's many contributions to the Mexican lifestyle include tequila, mariachi music, the broad sombrero, *charreadas* (rodeos) and the Mexican Hat Dance, and these days it is also known for its outstanding food. From streetside taco and *torta ahogada* (chili-soaked pork sandwich) stands to neighborhood cafes to fine dining rooms in restored colonial mansions, you're never far from a great meal in joyful Guadalajara.

History

Guadalajara weathered some false starts. In 1532 Nuño de Guzmán and a few dozen Spanish families founded the first Guadalajara near Nochixtlán, naming it after Guzmán's home city in Spain. Water was scarce, the land was dry and unyielding, and the indigenous people were understandably hostile. So, in 1533 the humbled settlers moved to the village of Tonalá (today a part

Western Central Highlands Highlights

1. Get to know spectacular **Morelia** (p608), with its glowing cathedral, animated streets and grandiose architecture
2. Explore charming **Guadalajara** (p573), with its excellent art museums, ancient churches and superb eating possibilities
3. Absorb the beauty of the **Reserva Mariposa Monarca** (p616), the winter retreat for millions of butterflies and an incredible natural phenomenon
4. Peer into the mystical soul of the Purépecha people in tranquil **Pátzcuaro** (p619)
5. Bag two volcanic peaks – the snowy and extinct **Volcán Nevado de Colima** (p606) and young, precocious **Volcán Paricutín** (p631)
6. Hike through the highland forests and pastures that surround the misty, whitewashed town of **Tapalpa** (p601)
7. Travel the Tequila Trail (p598) to see Mexico's most famous drink being made in the distilleries of **Tequila** and other nearby towns

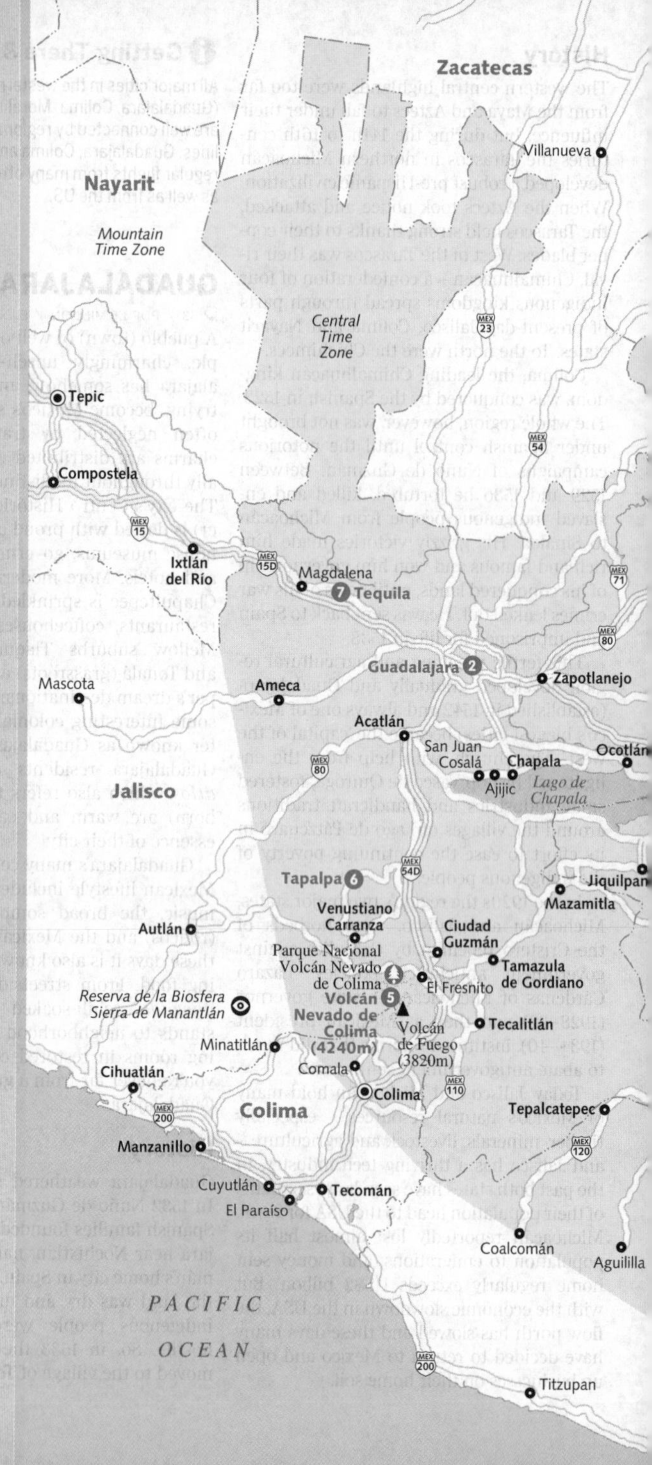

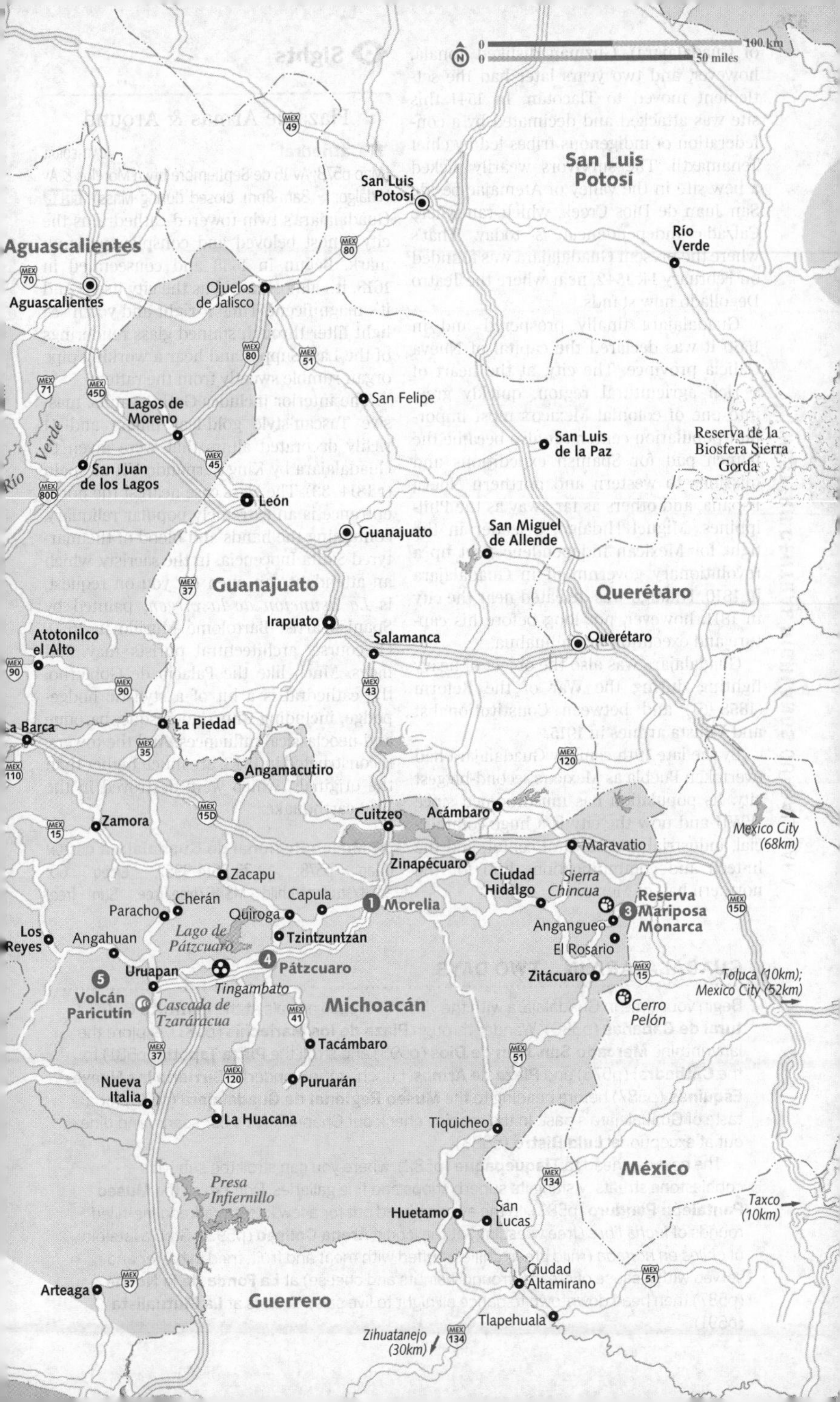
0
0
100 km
50 miles
N
San Luis Potosí
San Luis Potosí
Río Verde
Aguascalientes
Aguascalientes
Ojuelos de Jalisco
San Felipe
Lagos de Moreno
Río Verde
San Juan de los Lagos
León
Guanajuato
San Luis de la Paz
Reserva de la Biosfera Sierra Gorda
San Miguel de Allende
Guanajuato
Querétaro
Irapuato
Salamanca
Querétaro
Atotonilco el Alto
La Barca
La Piedad
Angamacutiro
Zamora
Cuitzeo
Acámbaro
Mexico City (68km)
Maravatio
Zinapécuaro
Zacapu
Ciudad Hidalgo
Sierra Chincua
Cherán
Paracho
Capula
Quiroga
1 Morelia
Reserva Mariposa Monarca
3
Angangueo
El Rosario
Los Reyes
Angahuan
Lago de Pátzcuaro
Tzintzuntzan
4 Pátzcuaro
Uruapan
Tingambato
5 Volcán Paricutín
Cascada de Tzaráracua
Zitácuaro
Toluca (10km); Mexico City (52km)
Cerro Pelón
Michoacán
Tacámbaro
Puruarán
Nueva Italia
La Huacana
Tiquicheo
México
Presa Infiernillo
Huetamo
San Lucas
Taxco (10km)
Ciudad Altamirano
Arteaga
Guerrero
Tlapehuala
Zihuatanejo (30km)
MEX 49
MEX 80
MEX 70
MEX 80
MEX 51
MEX 71
MEX 45D
MEX 45
MEX 80D
MEX 37
MEX 90
MEX 90
MEX 43
MEX 110
MEX 35
MEX 120
MEX 15D
MEX 15
MEX 15D
MEX 15
MEX 41
MEX 37
MEX 51
MEX 120
MEX 134
MEX 37
MEX 51
MEX 134

of Guadalajara). Guzmán disliked Tonalá, however, and two years later had the settlement moved to Tlacotán. In 1541 this site was attacked and decimated by a confederation of indigenous tribes led by chief Tenamaxtli. The survivors wearily picked a new site in the valley of Atemajac beside San Juan de Dios Creek, which ran where Calzada Independencia is today. That's where the present Guadalajara was founded on February 14, 1542, near where the Teatro Degollado now stands.

Guadalajara finally prospered and in 1560 it was declared the capital of Nueva Galicia province. The city, at the heart of a rich agricultural region, quickly grew into one of colonial Mexico's most important population centers. It also became the launch pad for Spanish expeditions and missions to western and northern Nueva España, and others as far away as the Philippines. Miguel Hidalgo, a leader in the fight for Mexican independence, set up a revolutionary government in Guadalajara in 1810. Hidalgo was defeated near the city in 1811, however, not long before his capture and execution in Chihuahua.

Guadalajara was also the object of heavy fighting during the War of the Reform (1858–61) and between Constitutionalist and Villista armies in 1915.

By the late 19th century Guadalajara had overtaken Puebla as Mexico's second-biggest city. Its population has mushroomed since WWII and now the city is a huge commercial, industrial and cultural center, and the hi-tech and communications hub for the northern half of Mexico.

Sights

Plaza de Armas & Around

★Cathedral CATHEDRAL

(Map p578; Av 16 de Septiembre btwn Morelos & Av Hidalgo; 8am-8pm, closed during Mass) FREE Guadalajara's twin-towered cathedral is the city's most beloved and conspicuous landmark. Begun in 1558 and consecrated in 1618, it's almost as old as the city itself. And it's magnificent. Time it right and you'll see light filter through stained glass renderings of the Last Supper and hear a working pipe organ rumble sweetly from the rafters.

The interior includes Gothic vaults, massive Tuscan-style gold-leaf pillars and 11 richly decorated altars that were given to Guadalajara by King Fernando VII of Spain (r 1814–33). The glass case nearest the north entrance is an extremely popular reliquary, containing the hands and blood of the martyred Santa Inocencia. In the sacristy, which an attendant can open for you on request, is *La asunción de la virgen,* painted by Spanish artist Bartolomé Murillo in 1650. Of course, architectural purists may find flaws. Much like the Palacio de Gobierno, the cathedral is a bit of a stylistic hodgepodge, including Churrigueresque, baroque and neoclassical influences. And the towers, reconstructed in 1848, are much higher than the originals, which were destroyed in the 1818 earthquake.

★Museo Regional de Guadalajara MUSEUM

(Map p578; 33-3614-9957; Liceo 60; adult/student/child M$46/free/free, Sun free;

GUADALAJARA IN... TWO DAYS

Begin your time in Guadalajara with the visceral Orozco murals at the **Instituto Cultural de Cabañas** (p580). Wander through **Plaza de los Mariachis** (p581), explore the labyrinthine **Mercado San Juan de Dios** (p593) and stroll the **Plaza Tapatía** (p581) to the **Cathedral** (p576) and **Plaza de Armas**. Lunch at the wonderful **Birriería las Nueve Esquinas** (p587) before heading to the **Museo Regional de Guadalajara** (p576) for a taste of Guadalajara's past. In the evening check out Chapultepec's bar scene, and dine out at exceptional **Lula Bistro** (p588).

The next day head to **Tlaquepaque** (p582), where you can stroll the suburb's cobblestone streets, visiting its superb shops and fine galleries. Don't miss the **Museo Pantaleón Panduro** (p583). In the evening head out for a few kitschy, adrenaline-filled rounds of *lucha libre* (free wrestling) at the iconic **Arena Coliseo** (p592). Grab a late bite of *chiles en nogada* (mild green chilies stuffed with meat and fruit, fried in batter and served with a sauce of cream, ground walnuts and cheese) at **La Fonda de la Noche** (p587) then head downtown to dance all night to live salsa sounds at **La Mutualista** (p591).

Greater Guadalajara

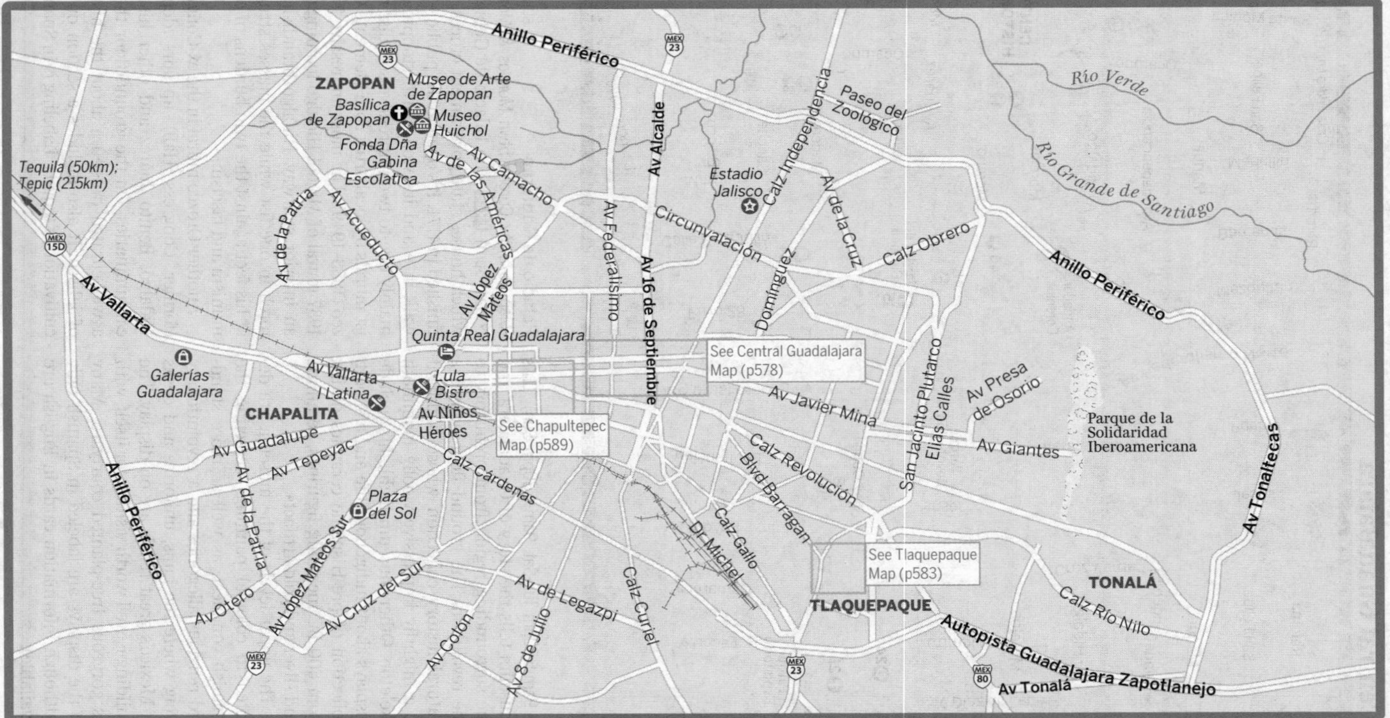

Central Guadalajara

9am-5:30pm Tue-Sat, 9am-4:30pm Sun) This museum tells the story of Guadalajara and the surrounding region from prehistory to the revolution. The ground floor houses a natural history collection whose highlight is a mightily impressive woolly mammoth skeleton. Other museum highlights include displays about indigenous life and a superb collection of pre-Hispanic ceramics dating from 600 BC including figurines, ceramics, and silver and gold artifacts.

The upper levels of the museum are devoted to colonial paintings depicting the Spanish conquest, as well as more standard religious allegories and a revolutionary wing where the guns, uniforms and desks of Mexico's great rebels are on display. The building is well worth visiting for itself, with its gorgeous tree-planted courtyard. Many of the displays are labeled in Spanish only (although information cards in English are available).

Palacio de Gobierno BUILDING
(Map p578; Av Corona btwn Morelos & Moreno; 9am-8pm) FREE The Palacio de Gobierno, which houses state government offices, was finished in 1774. It's open to the public – just walk in – and it's well worth stopping by, mainly due to two impressive socialist realist murals by local artist José Clemente Orozco (1883–1949). The most impressive is the 1937 mural of Miguel Hidalgo looming over an interior stairway. Hidalgo brandishes a torch in one fist while the masses struggle at his feet against the twin burdens of communism and fascism.

Another Orozco mural in the ex-Congreso (former Congress Hall) upstairs depicts Hidalgo, Benito Juárez and other historical luminaries. On the ground floor there's a well-curated **museum** about the history of Jalisco. It also includes a section on the cultivation of tequila. Labeling is in Spanish.

Museo de Arte Sacro de Guadalajara MUSEUM

(Map p578; Av 16 de Septiembre btwn Morelos & Av Hidalgo; adult/child M$10/5; ⏰10am-5pm Tue-Sat, 10am-2pm Sun) Don't miss this museum of sacred art, which quite appropriately sits inside the cathedral (the entrance is on the eastern side). It's filled with dark and brooding 17th- and 18th-century religious art and priceless church treasures.

Teatro Degollado CULTURAL BUILDING

(Map p578; Degollado; viewing admission free; ⏰viewing noon-2pm Mon-Fri) FREE Construction on the neoclassical Teatro Degollado, home of the Guadalajara Philharmonic, was begun in 1856 and completed 30 years later. The five-tiered interior is swathed in red velvet and gold and crowned by a Gerardo Suárez mural based on the fourth canto of Dante's *Divine Comedy*. Over the columns on its front is a frieze depicting Apollo and the Nine Muses.

Plaza Guadalajara PLAZA

(Map p578) Directly west of the cathedral, Plaza Guadalajara is shaded by dozens of laurel trees and has great cathedral views, a few fine cafes and fun people-watching. On its north side is the **Palacio Municipal** (City Hall; Map p578; ⏰10am-7pm Mon-Fri) FREE, which was built between 1949 and 1952 but looks ancient. Above its interior stairway is a dark mural by Gabriel Flores depicting the founding of Guadalajara.

Rotonda de los Jaliscenses Ilustres MONUMENT

(Rotunda of Illustrious Jaliscans; Map p578) Welcome to Jalisco's hall of fame. The plaza on the north side of the cathedral is ringed by 20 bronze sculptures of the state's favorite writers, architects, revolutionaries and a composer. Some of them are actually buried underneath the rotunda, the round-pillared monument in the center.

Central Guadalajara

Top Sights
1 Cathedral ... E2
2 Instituto Cultural de Cabañas ... H2
3 Museo Regional de Guadalajara ... E2

Sights
4 Galería Jorge Martínez ... F1
5 Museo de Arte Sacro de Guadalajara ... E2
Museo de las Artes ... (see 24)
6 Palacio de Gobierno ... E2
7 Palacio de Justicia ... F2
8 Palacio Legislativo ... F2
9 Palacio Municipal ... E2
Paraninfo ... (see 24)
10 Plaza de la Liberación ... E2
11 Plaza de los Mariachis ... G3
12 Plaza Guadalajara ... E2
13 Plaza Tapatía ... G2
14 Rotonda de los Jaliscenses Ilustres ... E2
15 Santuario de Nuestra Señora del Carmen ... C3
16 Teatro Degollado ... F2
17 Templo de Aranzazú ... E4
18 Templo de San Agustín ... F2
19 Templo de San Francisco ... E4
20 Templo de Santa María de Gracia ... F2
21 Templo Expiatorio ... A3
22 Templo Nuestra Señora de las Mercedes ... D2
23 Templo Santa Eduviges ... H3
24 Universidad de Guadalajara ... A3

Activities, Courses & Tours
25 Instituto Mexicano-Americano de Cultura ... D3
Recorridos Turísticos ... (see 9)
26 Tapatío Tour ... E2

Sleeping
27 Casa Vilasanta ... A3
28 Home and Hostel ... B3
29 Hospedarte Downtown ... F3
30 Hostel Plaza Liberación ... E2
31 Hotel Morales ... E3
32 Posada San Pablo ... D3

Eating
33 Birriería las Nueve Esquinas ... D4
34 Café Madrid ... E3
35 La Chata ... E3
36 La Fonda de la Noche ... B1
37 La Fonda de San Miguel Arcángel ... D2

Drinking & Nightlife
38 7 Sins ... D2
39 Café Galería André Breton ... F1
40 California's ... C2
41 Escarabajo Scratch ... C2
42 Hotel Francés ... E2
43 La Fuente ... E2
44 La Mutualista ... C3
45 La Prisciliana ... D3
46 Los Caudillos ... D4

Entertainment
47 Arena Coliseo ... F4
48 Ex-Convento del Carmen ... C3
Instituto Cultural de Cabañas ... (see 2)
Teatro Degollado ... (see 16)

Shopping
49 Mercado Corona ... D2
50 Mercado San Juan de Dios ... H2

Plaza de la Liberación PLAZA
(Map p578) East of the cathedral, this plaza was a 1980s urban planner's dream project and two whole blocks of colonial buildings were eviscerated to make way for this concrete slab.

On the north side of the plaza, next to the Museo Regional de Guadalajara, is the **Palacio Legislativo** (Map p578). Distinguished by thick stone columns in its interior courtyard, this is where the state congress meets. Across the street to the east is the **Palacio de Justicia** (State Courthouse; Map p578). It was built in 1588 and began life as Guadalajara's first nunnery. Duck inside to the interior stairwell and check out the 1965 mural by Guillermo Chávez depicting legendary Mexican lawmakers, including Benito Juárez.

Galería Jorge Martínez GALLERY
(Map p578; ☎33-3613-2362; Belén 120; ⏰10am-7pm) FREE It's worth popping into this interesting modern and conceptual art gallery to see if there's an exhibition showing (there's no permanent collection on display). It's adjacent to, and benefiting, Guadalajara's top art school, Artes Plásticas, which is operated by Universidad de Guadalajara.

East of Plaza de Armas

★**Instituto Cultural de Cabañas** MUSEUM
(Map p578; Cabañas 8; adult/student/child M$70/35/20, Tue free; ⏰10am-6pm Tue-Sun) Standing proudly at the east end of the brilliant Plaza Tapatía is another of Guadalajara's architectural gems. Inside its enchanting neoclassical bones, however, is a most

unexpected series of modernist murals by José Clemente Orozco, which ranks among the city's best sights. The complex also houses a huge collection of Orozco's other work and modern works by the shining lights in Mexico's current art scene.

Between 1938 and 1939 José Clemente Orozco, one of the greatest artists of the Mexican muralist movement, channeled the archetypal struggle for freedom into 57 magnificent murals that now decorate the Capilla Mayor at the center of the complex. Widely regarded as Orozco's finest works, they depict pre-Hispanic Jalisco and the conquest and seethe with dark, unnerving and distinctly modern images of fire, armor, broken chains, blood and prayer. Given the issues of Orozco's era, they almost certainly serve as a warning against fascism and any institution that subverts humanity to cultivate power.

The beautiful building, with masses of hidden arched courtyards, was founded by Bishop don Juan Cruz Ruiz de Cabañas and designed by Spanish architect Manuel Tolsá between 1805 and 1810. It's original purpose was as an orphanage and home for invalids and it remained so for 150 years, housing 500 children at once.Free tours of the institute in English and Spanish are available.

Plaza Tapatía PLAZA

(Map p578) The fabulously wide pedestrian Plaza Tapatía sprawls for more than 500m east from Teatro Degollado. Stroll the plaza on Sundays amid a sea of locals who shop at low-end crafts markets, snack (from both street vendors and cafes), watch street performers and rest on the walls of gurgling fountains. The plaza dead-ends beautifully at the Instituto Cultural de Cabañas.

Plaza de los Mariachis STREET

(Map p578) Just south of Av Javier Mina, this is the birthplace of mariachi music. By day it's just a narrow walking street, flanked by charming old buildings and dotted with a few plastic tables and chairs and the odd uniformed mariachi man chatting on a cell phone. At night it can get lively, when patrons swill beer and listen to bands play requests for about M$100 per song.

West of Plaza de Armas

West of the city center, where Avenidas Juárez and Federalismo meet, is shady **Parque Revolución**, which has become a haven for skaters.

Universidad de Guadalajara UNIVERSITY

(UDG; Map p578) Three blocks west of Parque Revolución is the **Paraninfo** (Theater Hall; Map p578; Av Juárez 975), one of the main buildings of the Universidad de Guadalajara. Inside, the stage backdrop and dome feature large, powerful murals by Orozco. In the back of the same building is the excellent **Museo de las Artes** (Map p578; 33-3134-1664; 10am-6pm Tue-Fri, to 4pm Sat & Sun) FREE, which

COLONIAL CHURCHES

Central Guadalajara has dozens of large and small churches and cathedrals. The following are some of the city's most beautiful and interesting.

The **Santuario de Nuestra Señora del Carmen** (Map p578), facing the small plaza on the corner of Avenida Juárez and Calle 8 de Julio, is lovely with lots of gold leaf, old paintings and murals in the dome. Closer to the city center is the ornate **Templo Nuestra Señora de las Mercedes** (Map p578; cnr Loza & Av Hidalgo), which was built in 1650; inside are several large paintings, crystal chandeliers and more gold leaf. Six blocks further east is the fairly unremarkable **Templo de Santa María de Gracia** (Map p578; cnr Carranza & República), which served as the city's first cathedral (1549–1618). South of the Teatro Degollado is the baroque-style **Templo de San Agustín** (Map p578; Morelos), one of the city's oldest and loveliest churches. The sanctuary at the **Templo Santa Eduviges** (Map p578; Av Javier Mina), built in 1726, is usually packed with worshippers and, during Mass, perfumed with clouds of sandalwood smoke. It's just south of the Mercado San Juan de Dios.

The compact **Templo de Aranzazú** (Map p578; cnr Av 16 de Septiembre & Blanco) is perhaps the city's most beautiful. Built from 1749 to 1752, it has three insanely ornate Churrigueresque golden altars and lovely ceiling detail. Across the road is the larger but less impressive **Templo de San Francisco**, built two centuries earlier. Come at dusk and see the stained glass glow.

houses well-curated temporary exhibitions focusing on contemporary Mexican art.

At the time of research the whole complex was closed for major renovations. It should reopen during the lifetime of this book.

Templo Expiatorio CHURCH
(Map p578; Madero; ⏲7am-11pm) This Gothic temple, dating from 1897, dominates the neighborhood thanks to its enormous stone columns, 15m-high mosaic stained glass windows and a kaleidoscopic steeple. At 9am, noon and 6pm a door in the clock tower opens and the 12 apostles march right out.

Zapopan

The fashionable, middle-class suburb of Zapopan is about 8km from the city center, on the northwestern edge of Guadalajara. There are a few interesting sights around the main plaza, which is in itself a fun place to hang out, with pilgrims coming and going and all sorts of religious tack for sale. After dark the locals get the place back to themselves and the numerous bars and restaurants turn the music up and the beer flows.

To get here from the center of Guadalajara, take any bus marked 'Zapopan' heading north on Avenidas 16 de Septiembre or Alcalde and get off beside the basilica. The trip takes 20 minutes. A taxi from the city center will cost around M$110.

★**Basílica de Zapopan** CATHEDRAL
(Eva Briseño 152) Zapopan's pride and joy, the Basílica de Zapopan, built in 1730, is home to *Nuestra señora de Zapopan,* a petite statue of the Virgin visited by pilgrims year-round. During the Fiestas de Octubre thousands of faithful crawl behind as the statue is carried here from Guadalajara's central cathedral. The kneeling pilgrims then make the final trek up the basilica's aisle to pray for favors at her altar. The Virgin receives a new car each year for the procession, but the engine is never turned on (thus remaining 'virginal') – instead it's hauled by men with ropes.

The early evening, when local families throng the plaza outside and streams of pilgrims, nuns and monks fill the pews, is a magical time to be here.

Museo de Arte de Zapopan MUSEUM
(MAZ; ☎33-3818-2575; www.mazmuseo.com; Andador 20 de Noviembre No 166; adult/student/child M$13/6.50/free, Tue free; ⏲10am-6pm Tue-Sun) One block east of the southeast corner of Plaza de las Américas, MAZ is Guadalajara's best modern art museum. Four sleek minimalist galleries hold temporary exhibits, which have included works by Diego Rivera and Frida Kahlo as well as leading contemporary Mexican artists.

On Sunday the entry fee is halved.

Museo Huichol MUSEUM
(Eva Briseño 152; adult/child M$10/5; ⏲10am-2pm & 3-6pm Mon-Sat, 10am-3pm Sun) The Museo Huichol has a worthwhile display of artifacts from the Huichol people, an indigenous group known for their peyote rituals and bright-colored yarn art. It's just to the right of the Basílica de Zapopan (but inside the basilica grounds).

Tlaquepaque

Though just 7km southeast of downtown Guadalajara, Tlaquepaque resembles your typical *pueblo mágico* (magical village): squint and you could well be in a small colonial town miles from anywhere. But its beauty is not its sole draw: artisans live behind the pastel-colored walls of the abandoned old mansions that line Tlaquepaque's narrow cobblestone streets, and their goods, such as wood carvings, sculpture, furniture, ceramics, jewelry, leather items and candles, are sold in the very chi chi (and yeah OK, expensive) boutiques that keep the shoppers coming all day long.

The plaza, Jardín Hidalgo, is leafy and blooming with flowers, and the benches around the fountain are always packed. The eating is very good and the strolling is even better, especially at sunset when the sky behind the gorgeous, white-domed basilica burns orange and families take to the streets, enjoying the last ticks of daylight.

The Tlaquepaque State Tourist Office offers two- to three-hour **walking tours** (by donation) of the area, which include visits to local workshops and museums and can be given in English or Spanish, but you must reserve ahead.

To get to Tlaquepaque from central Guadalajara, take bus 275 Diagonal, 275B or 647 (M$6). The turquoise TUR bus marked 'Tonalá' has air-con and is more comfortable (M$11). All these buses leave central Guadalajara from Avenida 16 de Septiembre between López Cotilla and Madero; the trip takes about 20 minutes. As you near Tlaquepaque, watch for the brick arch and then a traffic circle, after which you should get off at the next stop. Up the street on the

Tlaquepaque

left is Independencia, which will take you to the heart of Tlaquepaque.

Museo Pantaleón Panduro MUSEUM
(Museo Nacional de la Cerámica; Map p583; ☎33-3639-5646; Sánchez 191; ⏰9am-5pm Mon-Sat, 10am-3pm Sun) This superb collection of local folk art is housed in a converted religious mission and includes miniature figurines, as well as enormous, lightly fired urns and other ceramic crafts from all over the country. Admission is by donation.

Museo Regional de la Cerámica MUSEUM
(Map p583; ☎33-3635-5404; Independencia 237; ⏰10am-6pm Tue-Sat, 10am-4pm Sun) FREE The Museo Regional de la Cerámica is set in a great old adobe building with stone arches and mature trees in the courtyard. It has an impressive collection that exhibits the varied styles and clays used in Jalisco and Michoacán. Explanations are in English and Spanish.

Tlaquepaque

Sights
1 Museo Pantaleón Panduro C1
2 Museo Regional de la Cerámica B2

Sleeping
3 Casa Campos B2
4 Casa de las Flores C4
5 Casa del Retoño C4
6 Quinta Don José C3

Eating
7 Casa Fuerte B2
8 Mariscos Progreso C3
9 The Good Restaurant C2
10 Tortas Ahogadas Chimbombo C2

Entertainment
11 El Parián C2

Shopping
12 Antigua de México B2
13 Orígenes B2
14 Teté, Arte y Diseño C3

Tonalá

This dusty, bustling suburb is about 13km southeast of downtown Guadalajara and home to even more artisans. You can feel Tonalá beginning to take Tlaquepaque's lead with a few airy, inviting showrooms and cafes opening around town, but it remains happily rough around the edges. It's fun to roam through the dark, dusty stores and workshops, browsing glassware, ceramics, furniture, masks, toys, jewelry, handmade soap and more. Anything you can buy in Tlaquepaque you can find here for much less, which is what attracts wholesale buyers from all over the world.

Ask staff at the Tonalá tourist office about two- to three-hour **walking tours** (by donation) of Tonalá's artisan workshops. They're given in English or Spanish, but need to be reserved a couple of days in advance.

To reach Tonalá, take bus 275 Diagonal or 275D (both M$6). The turquoise TUR bus marked 'Tonalá' has air-con and is more comfortable (M$11). All these buses leave Guadalajara from the corner of Avenida 16 de Septiembre and Madero; the trip takes about 45 minutes. As you enter Tonalá, get off on the corner of Avenidas Tonalá and Tonaltecas. The Plaza Principal is three blocks east of Avenida Tonaltecas on Juarez.

Street Market MARKET

On Thursday and Sunday, Tonalá bursts into a huge street market that sprouts on Avenida Tonaltecas and crawls through dozens of streets and alleys and takes hours to explore. With *torta* (sandwich), taco and *michelada* (beer and tomato juice) stands aplenty, the whole area takes on a carnival vibe. The best pieces are usually found at the workshops and warehouses, not on the street.

Courses

Guadalajara is a popular place to study Spanish, with classes available to students of all ages. Prices and curricula vary tremendously.

Centro de Estudios para Extranjeros LANGUAGE COURSE

(CEPE; ☎33-3616-4399; www.udg.mx; Gómez 125) Part of the University of Guadalajara, CEPE offers several levels of intensive two- to five-week Spanish-language courses. Day trips, homestays and longer excursions to other parts of Mexico are available.

Instituto Mexicano-Americano de Cultura LANGUAGE COURSE

(IMAC; Map p578; ☎33-3613-1080; www.spanish-school.com.mx; Guerra 180) Offers courses from one week upwards. Check its website for course fees and homestay options. Music and dance classes are also available.

Tours

GDL Tours TOUR

(☎33-1578-0421; www.gdltours.com) Offers a full menu of English-language guided tours. Options include walking tours of Guadalajara's main sights (from M$390, four hours), trips to the towns of Lago de Chapala (from M$390, six hours) and Tequila Trail tours, which include distillery visits and tastings (from M$390, nine hours). Tour prices drop when there are more participants.

Mexico Cooks! CULINARY

(www.mexicocooks.typepad.com) US-born Cristina Potters, a true expert on Mexican cuisine, gives wonderful personalized foodie tours of Guadalajara (and Morelia), despite now being based in Mexico City. Contact her in advance to arrange a tour of the city.

Tapatío Tour BUS

(Map p578; ☎33-3613-0887; www.tapatiotour.com; tours adult M$110-120, child M$65-70) The ubiquitous double-decker buses of Tapatío Tour ply the city's most popular sights on a circuit track. While the prerecorded narration (in English, Spanish, French, Italian, German and Japanese) is less than inspirational, the tours allow you to hop off and on wherever you wish, making sightseeing a breeze. Buses depart from the Rotonda de los Jaliscenses Ilustres and they operate from 10am to 8pm. Go on a weekday for cheaper rates.

Recorridos Turísticos CITY

(Map p578; Plaza Guadalajara) FREE The city council runs free tours (in Spanish) of central Guadalajara at 9.30am and 7pm. Tours, which leave from the Palacio Municipal, last around an hour and you need to register 15 minutes beforehand. The tourist office can provide further details.

Festivals & Events

Major festivals celebrated in Guadalajara and its suburbs include the following:

Festival Internacional del Cine FILM

(www.ficg.mx) Mexico's most important film festival has been drawing top actors and directors to Guadalajara each March for 25 years. Sidle up to stars such as Gael García Bernal and John Malkovich at screenings and parties across the city.

Feria de Tonalá HANDICRAFTS FAIR
An annual handicrafts fair in Tonalá, specializing in ceramics, is held the weeks before, during and after Semana Santa (Easter week).

Fiestas de Tlaquepaque HANDICRAFTS FAIR
Tlaquepaque's annual fiesta and handicrafts fair takes place from mid-June to the first week of July.

Fiesta Internacional del Mariachi MUSIC
(www.mariachi-jalisco.com.mx) In late August and early September mariachis come from everywhere to jam, battle and enjoy; check the website for more information.

Fiestas de Octubre TRADITIONAL
(www.fiestasdeoctubre.com.mx) Beginning with a parade on the first Sunday in October, these festivities last all month long and are Guadalajara's principal annual fair, with free entertainment, livestock shows, art exhibitions and sporting events.

Feria Internacional del Libro BOOK FAIR
(www.fil.com.mx) This book fair is one of the biggest book promotions in Latin America; held during the last week of November and first week of December, and headlined by major Spanish-language authors.

Sleeping

During holidays (Christmas and Easter) and festivals you *must* reserve ahead. Ask for discounts if you arrive in the low season or will be staying more than a few days.

Central Guadalajara

Southeast of Mercado San Juan de Dios there's a cluster of budget hotels. This part of town is a bit rough, but you can usually find a cheap room here when other places are full. Budget digs can be found around the Antigua Central Camionera (old bus station) as well. The Centro Histórico is full of midrange options, many of which are housed in charming colonial buildings. Top-end accommodations are generally found in Chapultepec and beyond, and are aimed at guests with their own transportation.

Home and Hostel HOSTEL $
(Map p578; ☎33-1522-0834; www.homenhostel.com; Madero 720; dm M$180; wi-fi) This fine hostel is situated in a quiet residential area 15 minutes' walk from the city center. Rooms contain from one to four beds, there are just enough bathrooms to go around and everything is kept very shipshape. There's a sunny courtyard, plenty of travel info, a kitchen for guest use and some cheap places to eat nearby.

Hospedarte Downtown HOSTEL $
(Map p578; ☎33-3562-7520; www.hostelguadalajara.com; Maestranza 147; dm/s/d incl breakfast M$180/350/400; @ wi-fi) One of two Hospedarte hostels now in town, this bright yellow downtown option is popular with a young crowd looking for a good time. The dorms are spacious four-bed rooms with lockers and fans, sharing toilets and showers around a large communal area with a huge kitchen and plenty of activities laid on.

Hospedarte Hostel HOSTEL $
(Map p589; ☎33-3615-4957; www.hospedartehostel.com; Luna 2075; dm/s/d M$180/400/450; @ wi-fi) On a residential side street in Chapultepec, this low-key hostel has pretty much everything a backpacker requires: clean dorms, hammock-filled garden, communal kitchen, free bikes, internet and wi-fi, bars and cheap places to eat within stumbling distance and plenty of traveller-related services.

Discounts for IYHA cardholders.

Hostel Plaza Liberación HOTEL $
(Map p578; ☎33-3614-4504; Morelos 247; dm/d M$150/450; wi-fi) This friendly place has an unbeatable location right in the heart of the Centro Histórico, with many of the 17 rooms overlooking Plaza Liberación. It's a bright and pleasantly furnished hotel and great value, with all rooms having fans and TV.

Posada San Pablo HOTEL $
(Map p578; ☎33-3614-2811; www.posadasanpablo.com; Madero 429; s/d from M$380/450, without bathroom from M$300/380; wi-fi) This very friendly place comes complete with a grassy garden and sunny terrace. Upstairs rooms with balconies are best. There's a communal kitchen and you can even (hand) wash your clothes in the old-fashioned *lavandería* (laundry) out back.

At the time of research it was being renovated so expect it to be even better when it reopens.

★Hotel Morales HOTEL $$
(Map p578; ☎33-3658-5232; www.hotelmorales.com.mx; Av Corona 243; r from M$965; P❄️📶🏊) The towering four-tiered colonial lobby is a suitably impressive entrance to this smart, brilliant-value central hotel. Most of the 94 spacious rooms overlook the elegant central courtyard while others are set around hidden blue-and-white-tiled Andalucían-style courtyards. Do note though that due to the nature of the building some rooms lack natural light. Staff and service are very professional.

Casa Vilasanta HOTEL $$
(Map p578; ☎33-3124-1277; www.vilasanta.com; Rayón 170; dm/r M$200/500; ❄️📶) The bright, pastel-colored rooms of this cheery guest-house are scattered around a cool interior courtyard and decorated with pottery and flowers, and there's a sunny 2nd-floor terrace. The singles can feel cramped, but the doubles are large and all rooms have TV.

There's a shared kitchen and plenty of chill space on both floors. But with just 17 rooms and English-speaking management, this place books up. Reserve ahead! There are a few simple places to eat in the neighbourhood.

Villa Ganz BOUTIQUE HOTEL $$$
(Map p589; ☎33-3120-1416; www.villaganz.com; López Cotilla 1739; r incl breakfast M$2500-3480; P❄️@📶) Very deserving of its reputation as the finest boutique hotel in town, this converted Chapultepec mansion has 10 unique rooms with gorgeous features such as clawfoot tubs, vaulted brick ceilings, rustic wooden furniture and tiled floors throughout. The beautiful garden terrace, with an enormous wood-burning fireplace and too many candles to count, oozes romance.

Children under 12 years old are not admitted.

Casa Pedro Loza BOUTIQUE HOTEL $$$
(☎33-1202-2423; www.casapedroloza.com.mx; Loza 360; r incl breakfast M$1200-2300; ❄️📶) Housed in an impressive colonial mansion in a charming part of the *centro histórico*, this hotel has been lovingly decorated. The 11 rooms are each wildly different; some are stuffed full of beautiful antiques, others are like garish love nests with circular beds and bubbly furnishings. For the novelty value we prefer these!

The retractable roof over the courtyard and the superb roof terrace are other points in the hotel's favor.

Quinta Real Guadalajara LUXURY HOTEL $$$
(☎33-1105-1000; www.quintareal.com; Av México 2727; r from M$2500; P🚭❄️@🏊) There is no denying the beauty of this five-star stay, with its exquisite stone and ivy-covered exterior. The lobby and bar are inviting and stylish, the grounds are impeccably manicured and the service is outstanding. But the rooms are a bit cramped and don't live up to the steep price tag.

Book online for discounts.

Tlaquepaque

Just 15 minutes away by bus or taxi from downtown Guadalajara, Tlaquepaque is an excellent option for those who crave small-town charm but still want to visit the sights of the big city. The shopping is superb, and you won't have to lug your purchases too far.

Casa del Retoño GUESTHOUSE $$
(Map p583; ☎33-3639-6510; www.lacasadelretono.com.mx; Matamoros 182; s/d/tr incl breakfast M$700/850/1100; P📶) The eight rooms in this very pleasant traditional house are all colorfully decorated, share an enormous garden, and boast TVs and good bathrooms. It's a short walk from the main square and run by a friendly local family. It's a good idea to call ahead because the reception isn't always staffed.

★Casa de las Flores B&B $$$
(Map p583; ☎33-3659-3186; www.casadelasflores.com; Degollado 175; r incl breakfast from US$119; 🚭@📶) When you enter this impressive courtyard B&B, you'll be faced with such a swirl of colors that, mouth agape, you'll probably stop dead in your tracks. Every spare centimeter is covered in an incredible collection of Mexican folk art, including some very rare pre-Hispanic pieces. Rooms are all spacious, comfortable and brightly decorated in the same folksy style as the main building.

Out the back there's a blooming subtropical garden and patio patrolled by hummingbirds, and a stocked bar and fireplace in the living room. Breakfasts verge on the ultra-gourmet, especially when co-owner Stan, a former chef at Berkeley's Chez Panisse, is on breakfast duty.

Casa Campos GUESTHOUSE $$$
(Map p583; ☎33-3838-5297; www.casacampos.mx; Miranda 30; s/d incl breakfast M$1012/1190;) This pink and orange converted mansion boasts a gorgeous, flower-filled courtyard, stone columns and sleek wood furnishings. The 11 rooms are spacious, tasteful and well equipped (though bathrooms are nothing special), and it's moments from the best shopping on Independencia.

Quinta Don José BOUTIQUE HOTEL $$$
(Map p583; ☎33-3635-7522; www.quintadonjose.com; Reforma 139; s/d incl breakfast from M$1159/1350;) From the cozy sunken lobby to the sunny, flower-filled pool terrace complete with gurgling fountains, this charming hotel is a great place to escape while remaining in the heart of Tlaquepaque. Sadly the rooms aren't as flamboyant as the gardens but that's a minor niggle.

There's a good in-house Italian restaurant (open to all) and at night you can eat out under twinkling stars and fairy lights.

Eating

Guadalajara is a gourmet's delight; many visitors find that meals here count among the highlights of their stay. A few local specialties to look out for: *birria* (a spicy goat or lamb stew), *carne en su jugo* ('meat in its juice,' a type of beef soup), *tejuino* (a fermented corn drink often sold by street vendors), and, above all, the ubiquitous *torta ahogada* (literally 'drowned sandwich'), a chili sauce–soaked pork roll said to cure everything from hangovers to the flu.

Centro Histórico & Around

Adventurous stomachs can head to the Mercado San Juan de Dios (p593), home to endless food stalls serving the cheapest and some of the tastiest eats in town. The plaza in front of the Templo Expiatorio is a good place to snag late-night tacos, *tortas* and *elote* (grilled corn on the cob).

Café Madrid CAFE $
(Map p578; ☎33-3614-9504; Av Juárez 264; mains M$50-100) The waiters here are dressed in white dinner jackets and the cash register, espresso machines and soda fountains are mint-condition antiques. Come for breakfast: the *huevos rancheros* (fried eggs on a corn tortilla with a tomato, chili and onion sauce served with refried beans) and *chilaquiles* (fried tortilla strips cooked with chili sauce) have been favorites for 50 years.

★**La Fonda de la Noche** MEXICAN $$
(Map p578; ☎33-3827-0917; Jesús 251; mains M$90-120; ⏲7:30pm-midnight Tue-Sun) Set in a rambling art nouveau house this restaurant is a stunner in every way. The cuisine is largely from the Durango region and it would be fair to say that anything that passes by your lips here will taste good, but try the *plato combinado* (combined plate; M$111) – a selection of the chef's four prize dishes.

The menu is simple, and spoken only, so you'll need to speak some Spanish to enjoy it here, although Carlos, the owner, does speak basic English. It's a little hard to find: the door is unmarked and it's in a quiet residential area on the northwest corner of Jesús and Reforma. It's only open in the evenings.

Birriería las Nueve Esquinas MEXICAN $$
(Map p578; ☎33-3613-6260; Av Colón 384; mains M$80-98; ⏲8am-11pm Mon-Sat, 8am-9pm Sun) The gorgeously village-like Nueve Esquinas (Nine Corners) neighborhood specializes in *birria,* meat stewed in its own juices until it's so tender it melts in your mouth. Birriería las Nueve Esquinas, a delightful semi-open-air restaurant covered in blue and white tiles, is renowned far and wide for being the king of *birria.*

The two main offerings here are *birria de chivo* (steamed goat) and *barbacoa de borrego* (baked lamb), although ask the staff and they won't hesitate to tell you that the *chivo* is the best of the two. Both come with a stack of fresh tortillas, pickled onions, cilantro and two salsas – wrap the meat in the tortilla, add various flavors and then dip the tortilla in the meat juice before putting it in your mouth: heavenly.

La Chata MEXICAN $$
(Map p578; ☎33-3613-1315; Av Corona 126; mains M$79-128;) Quality *comida típica* (home-style food), affordable prices and ample portions keep this family diner packed; indeed, demand for a table is so high that queues frequently stretch out the door and down the street. The specialty is the superb *platillo jaliscense* (fried chicken with five sides); it also serves a popular *pozole* (hominy soup).

La Fonda de San Miguel Arcángel MEXICAN $$
(Map p578; ☎33-3613-0809; Guerra 25; mains M$130-200; ⏲8:30am-midnight Tue-Sat,

8:30am-9pm Sun & Mon) A sweet courtyard retreat from the sun where fountains gurgle, an old piano is played, and antique sculpture and birdcages are everywhere. Its specialties are *filete de res oro negro* – beef with *huitlacoche* (corn fungus) sauce – and its famously excellent *molcajete* (a spicy Oaxacan dish served on a sizzlingly hot stone dish with fajitas).

Chapultepec & Around

Chapultepec is home to some of Guadalajara's best cuisine and to all its serious culinary experiences. To get here, catch the westbound Par Vial 400 or 500 bus from Avenidas Independencia and Alcalde. Taxis from the city center cost around M$50.

El Cargol SPANISH **$**
(Map p589; ☎33-3616-6035; López Cotilla 1513; menú del día M$69) El Cargol means snail in Catalan and quite appropriately this is a fine family-run Catalan restaurant that offers really good quality home cooking for a bargain price. In fact, its three-course lunchtime *menú del día* might be one of the best deals in town. Despite the name you should go for the fish dishes.

Karne Garibaldi MEXICAN **$**
(☎33-3826-1286; Garibaldi 1306; mains M$60-100; ⊙noon-midnight) This large and bright cantina is wildly popular with Mexican family groups and has two specialties: *carne en su jugo* and fast service (so speedy it landed in the *Guinness Book of Records* in 1996). The neighborhood is friendly and buzzes at night, and you're almost guaranteed to be the only traveler.

It's a 15-minute walk north of Av Vallarta – stroll there via the back streets and enjoy the colorful houses, quiet streets and little hole-in-the-wall bars on the way.

Tacos Don Luis MEXICAN **$**
(Map p589; cnr Av Chapultepec & Mexicaltzingo; tacos M$9-12; ⊙2pm-late) At night the street outside this garage-like place overflows with hungry club-goers, who crouch on the curb with plastic plates trying not to spill taco fillings on their party dresses and fancy shoes. There are various food stalls in the area, but Don Luis is the oldest and the best.

Tortas Ahogadas César MEXICAN **$**
(Map p589; López Cotilla 1449; tortas M$25; ⊙lunch-late evening) This bare-bones cafe traffics in one thing and one thing only: *tortas ahogadas,* Guadalajara's beloved hangover cure. Baguette-like rolls called *birotes* are filled with chunks of slow-roasted pork and drenched with searing *salsa picante* – ask for yours '*media ahogada*' (half-drowned) for less burn; only die-hard chili-heads should request '*bien ahogada.*'

★ **Parrilla Libertad** MEXICAN **$$**
(Map p589; Libertad 1972; mains M$100-120; ⊙Tues-Sun) This tiny place, with its scattering of tables on the edge of the sidewalk, might be newly opened at the time of research, but its superbly executed dishes are so good we reckon it won't be long until it garners a big following. The house specials are the *costilla* (ribs) and a beef and chorizo *molcajete.*

Most of the ingredients used in the dishes are cooked over a large charcoal barbecue, which sits proudly out the front of the restaurant.

★ **Lula Bistro** INTERNATIONAL **$$$**
(☎33-3647-6432; www.lulabistro.com; San Gabriel 3030; mains from M$250; ⊙2-5pm & 8-11:30pm Tue-Thu, 2-5:30pm & 8pm-midnight Fri & Sat) Guadalajara's most celebrated restaurant is this superchic Chapultepec establishment. Sleek and industrial though the setting is, it's the food people come for, and the long, modern menu, which could best be described as a French-Mexican fusion, is particularly strong on fish and seafood.

It's a couple of kilometers west of the Chapultepec area. Reservations are recommended.

I Latina INTERNATIONAL **$$$**
(☎33-3647-7774; www.ilatinarest.com; Av Inglaterra 3128; mains from M$250; ⊙7:30pm-1am Tue-Sat, 1:30-6pm Sun) This eccentrically decorated place boasts a wall of ceramic pigs, a giant swordfish and lots of kitsch, fun touches. The Asian-leaning international menu is the reason to come, however, and food is excellent. It's hugely popular with a smart and fashionable crowd, and can be loud, so don't come here for a quiet dinner.

It's a couple of kilometers west of Chapultepec. Reservations in the evenings are a good idea.

Cocina 88 MEXICAN **$$$**
(Map p589; ☎33-3827-5996; www.cocina88.com; Av Vallarta 1342; mains M$150-300; ⊙1:30pm-1am Mon-Sat, 2-10pm Sun) Moneyed Guadalajara's restaurant of choice is located in a renovated turn-of-the-20th-century mansion, where

Chapulltepec

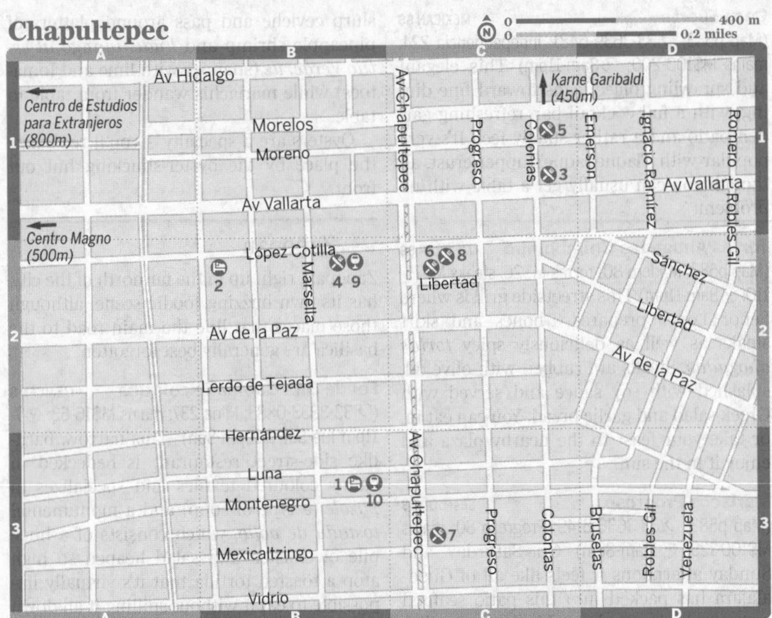

guests choose their cut of beef or fresh seafood from a butcher case and select their wine from the cellar rather than from a list. It's all effortlessly sleek and a great place for a memorable and stylish meal. Reservations are recommended for dinner on Friday and Saturday.

El Sacromonte MEXICAN $$$
(Map p589; ☎33-3825-5447; www.sacromonte.com.mx; Moreno 1398; mains M$180-300; ⊙noon-6pm & 7pm-midnight) Guadalajara's favorite *alta cocina* (gourmet restaurant) establishment serves whimsical takes on classic dishes – think quesadillas sprinkled with rose petals and strawberry sauce, avocado-watermelon soup and giant prawns in lobster sauce with fried spinach. Decor is tastefully arty, with vintage bullfighting posters and folk-art crucifixes. Reservations are recommended.

Chapultepec

Sleeping
1 Hospedarte Hostel B3
2 Villa Ganz B2

Eating
3 Cocina 88 .... C1
4 El Cargol B2
5 El Sacromonte C1
6 Parrilla Libertad C2
7 Tacos Don Luis C3
8 Tortas Ahogadas César C2

Drinking & Nightlife
9 Angels Club B2
10 Santa B3

Tlaquepaque

Tlaquepaque's main plaza overflows with street-food vendors – look for *jericalla* (a flanlike custard), coconut *empanadas* and cups of lime-drenched pomegranate seeds. Just southeast of the plaza, El Parián (p592) is a block of dozens of restaurant-bars with patio tables crowding a leafy inner courtyard. This is where you sit, drink and listen to live mariachi music, especially on Saturday and Sunday, but eat elsewhere.

The Good Restaurant MEXICAN $
(Map p583; Morelos 225; mains M$26-75; ⊙1-9pm) Step away from the pedestrian-only main street, Independencia, with its chi chi boutiques and pricey restaurants, and you'll find much more down-to-earth restaurants including this one, which, with its straw thatch roof and simple, filling home-cooked meals, is as good as the name suggests.

Casa Fuerte MEXICAN $$
(Map p583; ☎33-3639-6481; Independencia 224; mains M$100-200; ⏲8am-11pm) This elegant and sprawling place leans toward fine dining, with a full cocktail bar, refreshing garden patio and a rather stately feel. It's very popular with Tlaquepaque's upper crust, although you can usually get a table with no problem.

Tortas Ahogadas Chimbombo MEXICAN $$
(Map p583; Madero 80; tortas M$26, steaks M$75-110; ⏲8am-11pm) This streetside grill is where Señor Lopez prepares T-bones and skirt steaks as well as deliciously spicy *tortas ahogadas*. Steaks are rubbed with olive oil, splashed with soy sauce and served with Greek salad and garlic bread. You can eat in, or take your feast to the nearby plaza and enjoy it in the sun.

Mariscos Progreso SEAFOOD $$
(Map p583; ☎33-3636-6149; Progreso 80; mains M$100-125; ⏲11am-8pm) On Saturday and Sunday afternoons it feels like all of Guadalajara has packed into this patio seafood restaurant. Dressed-up Mexican families slurp ceviche and pass around platters of pineapple shrimp and *huachinango al estilo Veracruz* (snapper with lime and tomatoes) while mariachis wander from table to table.

Oysters are a specialty – you'll recognize the place by the oyster-shucking hut out front.

Zapopan

Zapopan, right up in the far north of the city, has its own buzzing foodie scene, although those places that line the main road to the basilica are generally best forgotten.

Fonda Dña Gabina Escolatica MEXICAN $
(☎33-3833-0883; Mina 237; mains M$16-62; ⏲7-11pm Tue-Sat, 2-10pm Sun) This narrow, barn-like side-street restaurant is bedecked in sunny coloured textiles and specializes in *pozole* (a type of soup) and a monumental *tostada de pollo*, which consists of a huge pile of chicken and salad heaped so high atop a toasted tortilla that it's virtually impossible to eat it without spilling it all down your front.

GAY & LESBIAN GUADALAJARA

Guadalajara is one of the gayest cities in the country – some call it the San Francisco of Mexico. It's not nearly as open as SF, however, and has a far more dual character: despite a conservative president, mayor and local population, somehow Guadalajara becomes very openly gay after dark. In June everyone gets out and proud when the city hosts one of Latin America's largest gay pride parades.

Guadalajara's so-called 'gay ghetto' radiates out a few blocks from the corner of Ocampo and Sánchez, in the city center, but Avenida Chapultepec, just west of the city center, is starting to see upscale establishments aimed at a gay clientele. The following are some of the busiest bars and clubs in the city. You can read more listings at www.gaymexicomap.com.

California's (Map p578; ☎33-3614-3221; Moreno 652; ⏲8pm-3am Mon-Sat) Attracts a diverse and attractive crowd – everything from cowboys to stockbrokers. It gets packed around 10pm, and Friday and Saturday nights are a madhouse, but there's no dancing – this is the place to start your night before heading to a club.

La Prisciliana (Map p578; ☎33-3562-0725; Sánchez 394; ⏲5pm-1:30am Sun-Tue, to 3am Wed-Sat) Laid-back and stylish, with arched windows, burgundy walls, worn tile floors and an antique wood bar in an old colonial building. It can get wild late and there's a drag show from time to time, but usually things stay chill.

Los Caudillos (Map p578; ☎33-3613-5445; Sánchez 407; admission M$50; ⏲5pm-4am daily, after-party 6-10am Sun) A popular multistory disco, with three dance floors and endless lounges and bars full of gorgeous young things dancing.

7 Sins (Map p578; Moreno 532; admission after midnight M$50; ⏲10pm-4am Fri & Sat) The favorite hangout of the younger section of Guadalajara's gay scene. If you're over 30 you'll feel pretty out of place, but this colonial mansion has a cool staircase and ear-bleeding loud music.

Drinking & Nightlife

The Centro Histórico is fairly quiet at night, though there are several bright spots (if you know where to look) and a thriving gay scene. Chapultepec, however, is always jumping with international-style bars and clubs.

Locals dress up to go out, so try to look the part. Much of the action in the city takes place in its myriad gay clubs, in which straight people are very welcome.

★La Mutualista DANCING

(Map p578; ☎33-3614-2176; Madero 553; ⊙noon-around 2am Mon-Sat) With smoke-yellowed walls and antique chandeliers dangling from high ceilings, this vintage dance hall simmers with the decaying glamour of Old Havana. Thursdays and Saturdays are salsa nights, the real reason to come. A Cuban band kicks off around midnight and the all-ages crowd explodes with eye-popping moves on the dance floor. Prepare to get sweaty.

★Café Galería André Breton BAR

(Map p578; ☎33-3345-2194; Manuel 175; ⊙10am-3am Tue-Sat, 2-8pm Sun) Tucked away on a side street on the eastern side of the Centro Histórico is this charming bar, cafe and live-music venue. As bohemian as its name suggests, this is one of the city's coolest hangouts. Enjoy the French menu (mains M$69), range of artisan beers from around the world and live music (M$40 cover) each evening from 9pm.

La Fuente BAR

(Map p578; Suárez 78; ⊙8:30am-11pm Mon-Thu, to midnight Fri & Sat) La Fuente, set in the old Edison boiler room, is an institution and a perfect example of what a proper Mexican cantina is supposed to be like. It's been open since 1921 and is mostly peopled by regulars who treat newcomers like family and women like queens.

A bass, piano and violin trio sets up and jams from sunset until last call.

Angels Club CLUB

(Map p589; López Cotilla 1495B; ⊙9:30pm-5am Wed-Sat, 6-11pm Sun) Welcome to Guadalajara's megaclub. Sure, it's a gay venue, but straight guys and gals are just as welcome to join the party, which is spread across three dance floors where house, pop and techno reign supreme. Saturday nights get wild. Clubbers often leave for breakfast at around 5am and return for sun-drenched fun after hours.

Santa BAR

(Map p589; ☎33-3616-5251; Luna 2061; ⊙8pm-3am Sun & Tue-Thu, to 4am Fri & Sat) Striking green walls and blinking Señora de Guadalupe pictures sum up the eccentric glam interior at this Chapultepec hot spot. It gets packed on Fridays and Saturdays when DJs take over. During the week well-dressed scenesters sip mezcal (an agave spirit; two for one on Thursday) and listen to lounge music.

Escarabajo Scratch BAR

(Map p578; ☎33-1200-6983; Andador Coronilla 28; ⊙6pm-2:30am Mon-Thu, from 1pm Fri & Sat) This fun hipster bar in the Centro Histórico has elevated the *michelada* (beer and Bloody Mary's lovechild) to fine art and celebrates the days when grunge rock ruled. It also has 11 labels of good tequila.

Hotel Francés BAR

(Map p578; ☎33-3613-1190; Maestranza 35; ⊙noon-midnight) The dark marble courtyard bar encourages you to relax back into another era, where waiters in bow ties treat you like an old friend, happy hour lasts until 8pm and acoustic troubadours strum gorgeous ballads.

☆ Entertainment

Guadalajara is a musical place and live performers can be heard any night of the week at the city's many venues (which include restaurants). Discos and bars are plentiful, but ask around for the newest hot spots – *guadalajarans* love to show off their town.

Several popular venues host a range of drama, dance and music performances. **Teatro Diana** (☎33 3614-7072; www.teatrodiana.com; Av 16 de Septiembre 710) is the current hippest spot. It stages traveling Broadway shows, concerts with local and international artists, and art installations. **Teatro Degollado** (Map p578; ☎33-3613-1115; Degollado) is a downtown cultural center that hosts a range of drama, dance and music performances. **Instituto Cultural de Cabañas** (Map p578; ☎33-3668-1640; Cabañas 8) has occasional drama, dance and music performances. Another downtown venue showcasing theatre and art is the **Ex-Convento del Carmen** (Map p578; ☎33-3030-1385; Av Juárez 638).

Live Music

You can pay your respects to the mariachi tradition in its home city. The Plaza de los Mariachis, just east of the Centro Histórico, is an OK place to sit, drink beer and soak in the serenades of passionate Mexican bands. But you'll be happier at **El Parián** (Map p583), a garden complex in Tlaquepaque made up of dozens of small cantinas that all share one plaza occupied by droves of mariachis. On Saturdays and Sundays the bands battle and jockey for your ears, applause and cash.

State and municipal bands present free concerts of typical *música tapatía* (*guadalajaran* music) in the Plaza de Armas at 6:30pm on most Tuesdays, Thursdays and Sundays and on other days as well during holiday seasons (and especially during the Fiestas de Octubre).

Sports

Charreadas (rodeos) are held at noon most Sundays in the Lienzo Charros de Jalisco ring behind Parque Agua Azul south of the city center. *Charros* (cowboys) come from all over Jalisco and Mexico; *escaramuza* (female stunt riding) teams perform as well.

Fútbol (soccer) flows strongly through *guadalajaran* blood. The city has three local teams in Mexico's top league, the *primera división:* **Guadalajara** (www.chivasdecorazon.com.mx; Las Chivas) – the second-most popular team in the country, **Atlas** (www.atlas.com.mx; Los Zorros) and **Universidad Autónoma de Guadalajara** (www.tecos.com.mx; Los Estudiantes Tecos). The seasons last from July to December and from January to June and teams play at stadiums around the city. You can get an up-to-date season schedule at www.femexfut.org.mx.

Estadio Jalisco STADIUM
(www.estadiojalisco.net; Siete Colinas 1772; admission M$35-100) Just off Calzada Independencia as you head northeast out of Central Guadalajara, this is the main *fútbol* venue (seating around 60,000) in Guadalajara, and it hosted World Cup matches in 1970 and 1986. Check out the website for schedule information. Big games cost more than regular matches. Trolleybus R600 and buses 60 and 62A heading north on Calzada Independencia can drop you off nearby.

★ **Arena Coliseo** MEXICAN WRESTLING
(Map p578; ☎33-3617-3401; Medrano 67; tickets M$50-140; ⏰8.30pm Tue & 6.30pm Sun; 👪) Watching masked *luchadores* (wrestlers) with names like El Terrible and Blue Panther gut-punching each other makes for a memorable night out. Expect scantily clad women, insult-hurling crowds and screaming doughnut vendors: it's all part of the fun of this classic Mexican pastime. The neighborhood surrounding the beloved coliseum can be a bit dodgy – watch your pockets.

Shopping

Guadalajara's wealthiest like to browse at big shopping centers such as **Centro Magno** (☎33-3630-1113; www.centro-magno.com/magno; Av Vallarta 2425), 2km west of the city center, and **Plaza del Sol** (☎33-3121-5750; www.plazadelsol.com; Av López Mateos Sur), 7km southwest of the city center. To reach them, take bus 258 going west from the corner of San Felipe and

SHOPPING IN TLAQUEPAQUE

Tlaquepaque has legendary shopping. Large home-decor boutiques are stocked with ceramics, exquisite light fixtures and handmade wood furniture. Guadalajara's best interior designers are based here and if you take your time you'll discover some rare and creative pieces.

Antigua de México (Map p583; ☎33-3635-2402; www.antiguademexico.com; Independencia 255; ⏰10am-2pm & 3-7pm Mon-Fri, 10am-6pm Sat) Has gorgeous furniture showpieces, such as benches carved from a single tree, which are displayed in expansive, old-world courtyards.

Orígenes (Map p583; ☎33-3563-1041; Independencia 211; ⏰10am-7pm Mon-Fri, 11am-7pm Sat, 11am-6pm Sun) Has a tremendous lighting selection, elegant hammocks and even its own in-house 'Mexican gourmet' restaurant, Casa Luna (mains M$150 to M$250), with tables inside as well as outside in the shade of a tree.

Teté, Arte y Diseño (Map p583; ☎33-3635-7965; www.tetearteydiseno.com; Av Juárez 173; ⏰10am-7:30pm Mon-Sat) Offers massive chandeliers, reproduction antique hardware and one-of-a-kind woodcarvings.

Sebastián Exportaciones (☎33-3124-6560; sebastianexp@prodigy.net.mx; Ejército 45; ⏰9am-2pm & 4-6pm Mon-Fri) Can arrange international shipping (minimum 1 cu meter).

Avenida Alcalde, or TUR 707 going west on Avenida Juárez. The biggest and swankiest mall, **Galerías Guadalajara** (☎33-3777-7880; www.galeriasguadalajara.com; Sanzio 150), is 8km west of downtown, served by bus 25. All malls are open from approximately 10am to 9pm.

Far more appealing to travelers will be the excellent handicrafts from Jalisco, Michoacán and other Mexican states that are available in Guadalajara's many markets. Tlaquepaque and Tonalá, two suburbs less than 15km from Guadalajara's center, are both major producers of handicrafts and furniture – anyone with an interior decorating habit should plan to spend some major quality time in each. You'll find the best value (read: wholesale prices) in Tonalá.

Mercado San Juan de Dios MARKET
(Map p578; cnr Av Javier Mina & Calz Independencia, Mercado Libertad; ⏲10am-9pm) This huge market has three whole floors of stalls offering everything from cowboy boots and DVDs to kitchenware; the salespeople are eager to sell and the food court is outstanding!

Mercado Corona MARKET
(Map p578; cnr Av Hidalgo & Santa Mónica; ⏲9am-8pm) Near downtown is this bustling, block-long market with clothes, household items, knickknacks and food.

Information

EMERGENCY

If you are a victim of crime, you may first want to contact your embassy or consulate and/or the state tourist office.

Ambulance (☎33-3616-9616, 33-3601-3019, 33-3614-5252)

Emergency (☎066, 080)

Fire (☎33-1201-7700)

Police (☎33-3668-0800, 33-3632-0330)

INTERNET ACCESS

Internet cafes (M$10 to M$15 per hour) are scattered around the city but tend to change location frequently. Nearly all hotels and many restaurants, cafes and bars offer free wi-fi.

MEDICAL SERVICES

Farmacia Guadalajara (☎33-3613-7509; Moreno 170; ⏲8am-10pm) Get your first aid, sundry items and prescribed meds here.

Hospital México Americano (☎33-3648-3333, free calls 01-800-462-2238; www.hma.com.mx; Colomos 2110) About 3km northwest of the city center; English-speaking physicians available.

US Consulate (☎33-3268-2200; http://guadalajara.usconsulate.gov/medical2.html) Keeps a regularly updated online list of local English-speaking doctors, including specialists and dentists.

MONEY

Banks are plentiful in Guadalajara and most have ATMs, known as *cajeros*.You can change cash at competitive prices around the clock at one of the eager *casas de cambio* (money changers) on López Cotilla, between Avenida 16 de Septiembre and Corona. Most will also change traveler's checks.

POST

Main Post Office (Map p578; cnr Carranza & Av Independencia; ⏲8am-7pm Mon-Fri, 9am-1pm Sat)

TOURIST INFORMATION

State Tourist Office (Map p578; ☎33-3668-1600; Morelos 102; ⏲9am-7pm Mon-Fri) Enter from either Morelos or Paseo Degollado. English-speaking staff offers information on Guadalajara, the state of Jalisco and the upcoming week's events.

Tlaquepaque State Tourist Office (Map p583; ☎33-3562-7050 ext 2319; www.tlaquepaque.gob.mx; Morelos 88; ⏲9am-3pm Mon-Fri) Upstairs in the Casa del Artesano. There is also a helpful tourist kiosk as you enter the main shopping area of Tlaquepaque on Ejército.

Tonalá Tourist Office (☎33-1200-3912; Zapata 244A; ⏲9am-3pm Mon-Fri) Three blocks west of Avenida Tonaltecas on Zapata.

Tourist Information Booth (Map p578; ⏲9:30am-2:30pm & 5-7:30pm Mon-Fri, 10am-12:30pm Sat & Sun) In the Palacio de Gobierno, just inside the entrance facing the Plaza de Armas. During cultural events and festivals other booths pop up around the city center.

USEFUL WEBSITES

Gobierno de Jalisco (www.visita.jalisco.gob.mx) Official website of Jalisco.

Gobierno Municipal de Tonalá (www.tonala.gob.mx) Official website of Tonalá.

Gobierno Municipal de Zapopan (www.zapopan.gob.mx) Official website of Zapopan.

Tlaquepaque Gobierno Municipal (www.tlaquepaque.gob.mx) Official website of Tlaquepaque.

Vive Guadalajara (vive.guadalajara.gob.mx) Official website of Guadalajara.

Getting There & Away

AIR

Guadalajara's **Aeropuerto Internacional Miguel Hidalgo** (☎33-3688-5248; www.aeropuertosgap.com.mx) is 17km south of downtown, just off the highway to Chapala. Inside are ATMs, money exchange, cafes and car-rental companies. There's also a **tourist office** (8am-6pm).

A multitude of airlines offer direct flights to major cities in Mexico, including the following:

Aeroméxico (800-021-40-00; www.aeromexico.com; Ramón Corona 4386-2, Fraccionamiento Jardín Real, Zapopan) Also offices at airport.

Interjet (800-011-23-45; www.interjet.com.mx; Airport)

Viva Aerobus (33-4000-0180; www.vivaaerobus.com)

Volaris (www.volaris.mx; Airport)

BUS

Guadalajara has two bus terminals. The long-distance bus terminal is the **Nueva Central Camionera** (New Bus Terminal; 33-3600-0135), a large, modern terminal that is split into seven separate *módulos* (miniterminals). Each *módulo* has ticket desks for a number of bus lines, plus restrooms, web cafes and cafeterias. The Nueva Central Camionera is 9km southeast of Guadalajara city center, past Tlaquepaque, just off the motorway to Mexico City.

Buses go to and from just about everywhere in western, central and northern Mexico. Destinations are served by multiple companies, based in the different *módulos,* making price comparisons difficult and time-consuming. The good news is that if you're flexible, you won't have to wait long for a bus (departures at least once an hour for major destinations, fares are for the best buses available; see the table). You can often find cheaper fares by going on slightly less plush buses.

ETN (www.etn.com.mx; Módulo 2) offers a deluxe nonstop ride to many destinations. You'll pay 20% more, but it's more comfortable and faster and some buses even have wi-fi.

Guadalajara's other bus terminal is the **Antigua Central Camionera** (Old Bus Terminal; 33-3650-0479; Dr Michel & Los Angeles), about 1.5km south of the cathedral near Parque Agua Azul. From here 2nd-class buses serve destinations within 75km of Guadalajara. There are two sides to it: Sala A is for destinations to the east and northeast; Sala B is for destinations northwest, southwest and south. There's a M$0.50 charge to enter the terminal, which offers a **left-luggage service** (7.30am-8pm) in Sala B. Bus services run between 6am and 10pm, approximately. Buses leave multiple times an hour for nearby locations, and once an hour or so for longer trips.

CAR & MOTORCYCLE

Guadalajara is 535km northwest of Mexico City and 344km east of Puerto Vallarta. Highways 15, 15D, 23, 54, 54D, 80, 80D and 90 all converge here, combining temporarily to form the Periférico, a ring road around the city.

Guadalajara has many car-rental agencies. All the large international companies are represented, but you may get a cheaper deal from a local company, so it's worth comparing prices and availability online before you travel. Prices start at around M$350 per day for a four-door sedan. And it will cost you (upwards of M$3000) to leave the car in any city other than the one you rented it from.

TRAIN

The only trains serving Guadalajara are the two tourist 'tequila tasting' trains to the nearby towns of Amatitán or Tequila.

Getting Around

TO/FROM THE AIRPORT

The airport is about 17km south of central Guadalajara, just off the highway to Chapala. To get into town on public transportation, exit the airport and head to the bus stop in front of the Hotel Casa Grande, about 50m to the right. Take any bus marked 'Zapote' (M$6) or 'Atasa' (M$12) – both run every 15 minutes from about 5am to 10pm and take 40 minutes to the Antigua Central Camionera, where you can hop on a bus to the city center.

Taxi prices are M$300 to the city center, M$260 to the Nueva Central Camionera and M$220 to Tlaquepaque. Buy fixed-price tickets inside the airport.

To get to the airport from Guadalajara's center, take bus 174 to the Antigua Central Camionera (the stop where you get off is in front of the Gran Hotel Canada) and then get on an 'Aeropuerto' bus (every 20 minutes, 6am to 9pm) from this stop. Metered taxis cost roughly M$250.

TO/FROM THE BUS TERMINALS

To reach the city center from the Nueva Central Camionera, take any bus marked 'Centro' (M$6). You can also catch the more comfortable, turquoise-colored TUR bus (M$11). They should be marked 'Zapopan.' Don't take the ones marked 'Tonalá' or you'll be headed away from Guadalajara's center. Taxis to the city center cost M$121 unless they let the meter tick (some don't use it). A direct taxi from the airport to the Nueva Central Camionera costs M$380.

To get to the Nueva Central Camionera from the city center, take any bus marked 'Nueva Central' – these are frequent and leave from the corner of Avenida 16 de Septiembre and Madero.

To reach the city center from the Antigua Central Camionera, take any bus going north on Calzada Independencia. To return to the Antigua

Central Camionera from the city center, take bus 174 going south on Calzada Independencia. Taxis cost M$40.

Bus 616 (M$6) runs between the two bus terminals.

BUS

Guadalajara has a comprehensive city bus system, but be ready for crowded, rough rides. On major routes, buses run every five minutes or so from 6am to 10pm daily and cost M$6. Many buses pass through the city center, so for a suburban destination you'll have a few stops to choose from. The routes diverge as they get further from the city center and you'll need to know the bus number for the suburb you want. Some bus route numbers are followed by an additional letter indicating which route they take through the suburbs.

The TUR buses, painted a distinctive turquoise color, are a more comfortable alternative. They have air-con and plush seats (M$11). If they roar past without stopping, they're full; this can happen several times in a row during rush hour and may drive you mad.

The tourist office has a list of the complex bus routes in Guadalajara and can help you reach your destination. Following are some common destinations, the buses that go there and a central stop from where you can catch them.

Antigua Central Camionera Bus 174 going south on Calzada Independencia.

Av López Mateos Sur Bus 258 at the corner of San Felipe and Avenida Alcalde, or TUR 707 going west on Avenida Juárez.

Chapultepec Par Vial buses 400 and 500 at Avenidas (not Calz!) Independencia and Alcalde.

Nueva Central Camionera Bus 275B, 275 Diagonal, TUR marked 'Tonalá' or any bus marked 'Nueva Central'; catch them all at the corner of Avenida 16 de Septiembre and Madero.

Parque Agua Azul Any bus marked 'Agua Azul' going south on Calzada Independencia.

Tlaquepaque Bus 275B, 275 Diagonal, 647 or TUR marked 'Tlaquepaque' at Avenida 16 de Septiembre between López Cotilla and Madero.

BUSES FROM GUADALAJARA

From Nueva Central Camionera

DESTINATION	FARE (M$)	DURATION	FREQUENCY (DAILY)
Barra de Navidad	420	5½hr	hourly
Colima	236	3hr	hourly
Guanajuato	420	4hr	every 50min
Manzanillo	425	4hr	hourly
Mexico City (Terminal Norte)	820	7-8hr	every 30min
Morelia	400	4hr	hourly
Pátzcuaro	305	4½hr	hourly
Puerto Vallarta	505	5hr	every 30min
Querétaro	405	5½hr	hourly
San Miguel de Allende	550	5hr	every 2 hr
Tepic	295	3hr	hourly
Uruapan	400	4½hr	hourly
Zacatecas	390	5hr	hourly
Zamora	245	2¼hr	5

From Antigua Central Camionera

DESTINATION	FARE (M$)	DURATION	FREQUENCY (DAILY)
Ajijic	50	1hr	every 15min
Chapala	50	45min	every 15min
Ciudad Guzmán	152	2hr	hourly
Mazamitla	120	3hr	hourly
Tapalpa	106	3hr	10
Tequila	64	1hr	every 30min

Tonalá Bus 275D, 275 Diagonal or TUR marked 'Tonalá' at Avenida 16 de Septiembre and Madero.

Zapopan Bus 275 or TUR marked 'Zapopan' going north on Avenida 16 de Septiembre or Alcalde.

HORSE-DRAWN CARRIAGE

If you fancy trotting around the city in a horse-drawn carriage, reckon on paying M$150 per half-hour or M$200 per hour. There's a carriage stand right at Jardín San Francisco and another in front of the Museo Regional de Guadalajara.

METRO

The subway system has two lines that cross the city. Stops are marked with a 'T.' But the metro isn't tourist friendly because most stops are far from the sights. Línea 1 stretches north–south for 15km all the way from the Periférico Norte to the Periférico Sur. It runs below Federalismo (seven blocks west of the city center) and Avenida Colón: catch it at Parque Revolución, on the corner of Avenida Juárez. Línea 2 runs east–west for 10km below Avenidas Juárez and Mina.

TAXI

Taxis are everywhere in the city center. They have meters, but not all drivers use them. Most would rather quote a flat fee for a trip, especially at night. Generally it's cheaper to go by the meter – if you're quoted a flat fee and think it's inflated, feel free to bargain. From 10pm to 6am a 'night meter' is used and fares rise 25%.

AROUND GUADALAJARA

Beyond Guadalajara's sprawling and seemingly endless suburbs, lonely mountain pueblos and lazy lakeshore towns promise an intoxicating shot of old Mexico. Lago de Chapala, just 45km south of Guadalajara, is Mexico's largest natural lake and offers spectacular scenery, traditional lakeside towns and picturesque pueblos full of retired gringos. Further south and west, Jalisco's Zona de Montaña is home to a string of mountain retreats where horses wander free through dusty streets and there's nothing to do but stroll through the pines and sip *rompope* (a local eggnog-like liquor) by the fire.

This region is also a major producer of tequila: one of the most popular day trips from Guadalajara is to the town of Tequila to see how Mexico's most famous export is made.

Lago de Chapala

Lago de Chapala, Mexico's largest natural lake, lies 45km south of Guadalajara. Surrounded by mountains – some of which tumble dramatically to the shore – its beauty is deep and undeniable. This beauty combined with an addictive climate (always warm during the day and pleasantly cool at night) mean that Chapala continues to lure North American retirees to the area and, at weekends, masses of city folk out for some fresh air and a slap-up fish lunch. For foreign tourists the allure is a little less compelling, although it does still make for a fun excursion from Guadalajara.

Sadly the lake is not as healthy as it is beautiful. Water levels fluctuate due to Guadalajara's and Mexico City's water needs and on-again, off-again drought. Commercial fertilizers washed into the lake have nourished water hyacinth, an invasive plant that clogs the lake's surface and kills aquatic life, which means few people choose to swim here.

Chapala

☎376 / POP 21,000 / ELEV 1550M

With a commanding location on the shores of its namesake lake, Chapala became a well-known resort destination after president Porfirio Díaz vacationed here every year from 1904 to 1909. DH Lawrence and Tennessee Williams were later visitors, sealing the town's literary pedigree, and today Chapala is a simple but charming working-class Mexican town with lovely lakeside walks and a buzzing weekend scene.

Sights

Isla de Mezcala ISLAND

The most interesting island to visit on Lago de Chapala is Isla de Mezcala. Here you'll find a ruined fort where Mexican independence fighters held strong from 1812 to 1816, repulsing several Spanish attacks before earning the respect of, and a full pardon from, their enemies. A 3½-hour round-trip boat ride costs M$1600, for up to eight people.

Isla de los Alacranes ISLAND

A ticket booth at the pier's entrance sells boat tickets to Isla de los Alacranes (Scorpion Island), 6km from Chapala, which has some restaurants and souvenir stalls but is not very captivating. A round trip, with 30 minutes on the island, costs M$350 per boatload; for one hour it's M$420.

Around Guadalajara

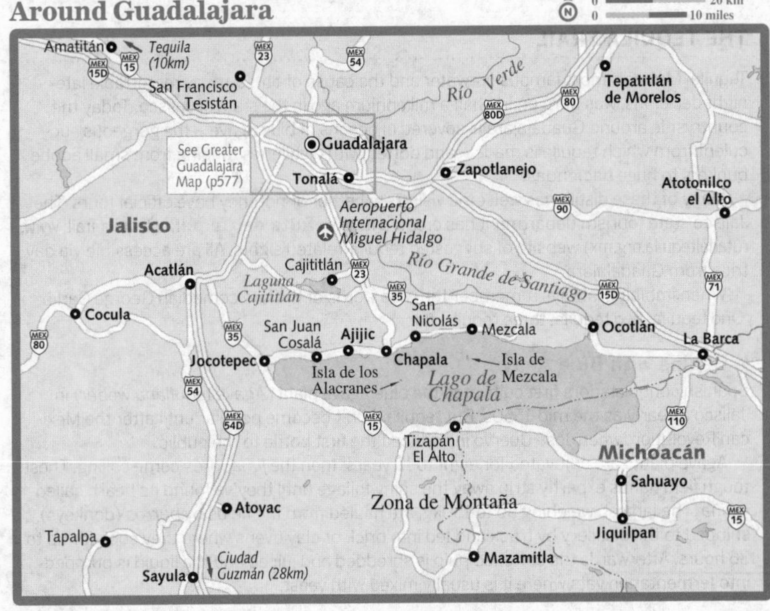

Sleeping

Quinta Quetzalcóatl GUESTHOUSE $$
(376-765-36-53; www.accommodationslakechapala.com; Zaragoza 307; s/d incl breakfast from M$600/800;) Behind the hotel's stone walls are a pool, lush gardens and plenty of private outdoor space. Some rooms are highly eccentric in style (the riding-themed Carriage House is one thing, while the pink bathroom tower in Lady Chatterley's Lover has to be seen to be believed), but the hotel nevertheless attracts many return visitors.

DH Lawrence wrote *The Plumed Serpent* here in 1923, and Lawrence fans can even sleep in the room he lived in. The Australian owners live on-site and are a good source of local information.

Lake Chapala Inn GUESTHOUSE $$$
(376-765-47-86; www.chapalainn.com; Paseo Ramón Corona 23; s/d incl breakfast M$1000/1400;) This imposing white building right on the lakeshore, moments from the town center, enjoys wonderful views over the waters and faraway hills. The furnishings are a little old fashioned, but the views from two of the rooms and the communal terrace are unbeatable. Reductions are available for stays of more than two nights, and the traditional English breakfast is the real deal.

Eating

Seafood joints aimed at tourists can be found all along Paseo Corona (known as the *malecón*); they all have pleasant lake views, although quality can be hit and miss.

La Leña MEXICAN $
(064-22-7813, cell phone 376-7652654; Madero 236; mains M$40-80; noon-midnight) Get away from the rather bland restaurants around the *malecón* and try a slice of local life at this semi-open-air place on Chapala's main street. With a great selection of meaty dishes, the specialty is the fabulous beef *molcajete*.

Chapala's Fonda MEXICAN $
(Paseo de los Ausentes 621; mains M$45-50; 8am-5pm) For something more down to earth than the glossy restaurants around the lake check out the simple restaurants under the *portales* (arcades) of the main plaza. By far the best regarded of these is Chapala's Fonda, where a handful of loose change will get you a fish lunch, a cold beer and a front-row seat on the passing street life.

Getting There & Away

Buses from Guadalajara (M$50, one hour) to Chapala leave from the Antigua Central Camionera multiple times an hour. Buses connect Chapala to Ajijic (M$9, 15 minutes) every 20 minutes.

THE TEQUILA TRAIL

Tequila, Mexico's most famous firewater and the cause of oh-so-many regrettable late-night decisions, was born nearly half a millennium ago in the state of Jalisco. Today the countryside around Guadalajara is covered in oceans of blue agave – the gorgeous succulent from which tequila is made – and dotted with distilleries ranging from small adobe bunkers to huge haciendas.

Many of these distilleries welcome visitors, whether or not they have official tours. The Jalisco state tourism department has created its own **Ruta del Tequila** (Tequila Trail; www.rutadeltequila.org.mx) website of suggested tequila-related sights. All are accessible via day trips from Guadalajara.

When imbibing, always remember the wise words of the late comedian George Carlin: 'One tequila, two tequila, three tequila, floor.'

It Begins with Blue Agave

Spanish conquistadors first cultivated the blue agave plant *(Agave tequilana weber)* in Jalisco as early as the mid-1550s. But tequila didn't become popular until after the Mexican Revolution, when José Cuervo introduced the first bottle to the public.

Agave plants are cultivated for eight to 12 years; then the *jimadores* come calling. These tough field hands expertly strip away the spiny foliage until they've found its heart, called a *piña*. The largest, weighing up to 150kg, are hauled from the fields by *burros* (donkeys), shipped to the distillery by truck and fed into brick or clay ovens where they cook for up to 36 hours. Afterwards the softened pulp is shredded and juiced and the liquid is pumped into fermentation vats where it is usually mixed with yeast.

Five Types of Tequila

Your average cantina tequila is tequila *mixto* (mixed), which can legally contain up to 49% nonagave sugars. The better stuff, which bears the '100% Agave' label, has no additives. Within these two categories, there are five main varieties of tequila.

- *Blanco* or *plata* (white or silver) tequila is relatively unaged, uncolored and has a distinct agave flavor. Best used as a mixer for margaritas or other cocktails.
- *Oro* (gold) tequila is unaged, artificially colored, and best avoided.
- Tequila *reposado* (rested) has been aged from two to nine months in oak barrels and tends to taste sharp and peppery.
- Tequila *añejo* (aged) is aged at least one year in oak barrels. It's sweet and smooth and works best as an after-dinner drink.
- Tequila *extra añejo* (vintage) is aged for at least three years. First sold in 2006, *extra añejo* is the pinnacle of the fast-growing premium tequila market. Sip it neat, of course.

In Mexico you can buy a decent bottle of tequila for M$150, though for something special you'll need to spend over M$300. Treat the good stuff like a bottle of single malt and before you sip it, sniff it a few times to prepare your palate for the heat and it won't taste so harsh.

And don't be looking for a 'special' *gusano* (worm) in each bottle. These are placed in bottles of mezcal (an agave spirit similar to tequila but distilled outside of Jalisco state) as a marketing ploy – and even if you slurp the critter, you won't get any higher.

Touring the Distilleries

The town the spirit is named for, Tequila, has the bulk of the tourist attractions, but there are several other worthwhile tequila-producing pueblos within day-trip distance of Guadalajara.

TEQUILA

There's nothing particularly enchanting about this sun-baked factory town where tequila got its start. Tequila-barrel-shaped trolleys ply the main road looking to whisk visitors to one of several local distilleries.

Right across from the plaza, **Mundo Cuervo** (☎800-006-86-30; www.mundocuervo.com; cnr Corona & José Cuervo; tours M$200-400; ⏰10am-5pm Sun-Fri, to 6pm Sat), which is owned by the José Cuervo distillery, the world's oldest distillery, is a veritable tequila theme park and the biggest game in town. Hourly tours include tastings and a free plastic cup of margarita. The hour-long tour is a bit rushed so it's worth spending a little more on one of the longer and more comprehensive tours.

Five blocks south of Mundo Cuervo, the industrial-looking La Perseverancia distillery **Sauza** (☎374-742-41-40; www.sauzatequila.com; Sauza 80; tours M$100; ⏰11am-4pm Mon-Fri, tours 11am & 2pm Sat) has regular factory tours.

The well-done **Museo Nacional del Tequila** (Corona 34; adult/child M$15/7; ⏰9am-4pm) illustrates the history of tequila-making with photos and distillery apparatus.

AMATITÁN

This lowlands town, 39km northwest of Guadalajara, is the biggest tequila-producing pueblo after Tequila itself. The romantic old hacienda of **Herradura** (☎33-3942-3920; www.herradura.com; Comercio 172; tours M$100; ⏰9am-3pm Mon-Sat, tours 10am, 11am & 3pm Sun) is Mexico's prettiest distillery, with regularly scheduled English-language tours that most people rate as being the best of the various distillery tours. It's this distillery that the much talked about Tequila Express visits. Call ahead for Spanish-language tours at the high-end 100% agave distillery **Tres Mujeres** (☎374-745-08-40, 33-3167-9857; Carretera Guadalajara-Nogales Km 39).

ATOTONILCO EL ALTO

Though not on the official Tequila Trail, this highlands town 80km east of Guadalajara is thought by many to produce the sweetest, smoothest tequila due to a high concentration of iron and other nutrients in the red soil.

Call ahead for free tours at **Siete Leguas** (☎391-917-09-96; Independencia 360; ⏰9am-2pm & 4-7pm Mon-Fri, 9am-2pm Sat), a fine tequila distillery located in a large purple building along the main road into town. After your tour, wander along Independencia for great deals on tequila at various distillery warehouse shops.

Organized Tours

Experience Tequila (☎33-3455-1739; www.experiencetequila.com; 4-day double occupancy packages US$1115) US tequila aficionado Clayton Szczech offers a variety of individualized multiday private tours departing from Guadalajara. Book well in advance.

GDL Tours (p584) This Guadalajara-based day trip features distillery tours and tastings.

Tequila Express (☎33-3880-9090; www.tequilaexpress.com.mx; adult/child M$1200/800) This popular train-trip/fiesta departs every Saturday, Sunday and on holidays from Guadalajara and includes a tour of the Herradura distillery, a mariachi show, lunch and an open bar with *mucho* tequila.

José Cuervo Express (☎800-523-977-377; www.josecuervoexpress.com; adult M$1350-1550, child 13-17yr M$1152, 6-12yr M$912; ⏰Sat & Sun) Ride in elegant train carriages on this high-class train tour to the Mundo Cuervo distillery in Tequila. Prices include transport, distillery tours, meals and a fair bit of tequila. It also runs a Friday-night train tour. It was described to us by tourist board staff as, 'More suitable for mature visitors than the Tequila Express. It's better you go on this one.' Well, thank you.

Ajijic

376 / POP 10,000 / ELEV 1550M

The wonderfully named Ajijic (ah-hee-*heek*) is an outpost of North American retirees and by far the most sophisticated and energetic of the towns that line the north shore of Lago de Chapala. While the gringos may have put Ajijic on the map by opening boutiques, galleries and restaurants galore, much of the town retains its charming, colonial-era vibe, with cobblestone lanes and quiet streets of boldly painted houses. It makes a delightful place to sit back and relax a while, although it's far from the typical Mexico here: English is almost as commonly heard on the streets as Spanish and prices are relatively high.

Sleeping

There is no shortage of B&Bs in Ajijic, with many owned by foreign retirees. Many, however, have minimum stays of several days and don't have permanently staffed reception desks, which can make staying at them problematic if you're looking for a room on the run. The following are operated more like standard hotels.

Casa Mis Amores GUESTHOUSE $$
(376-766-46-40; www.misamores.com; Hidalgo 22B; d incl breakfast Sun-Thu/Fri & Sat M$650/1050; P) Arty without being precious, the town's loveliest guesthouse has a plant-filled courtyard and 12 adobe and tile rooms decorated with local art, Moroccan-style lamps and mosaic-patterned bathrooms.

Casa del Sol B&B $$$
(376-766-00-50; www.casadelsolinn.com; Mina 7; d US$95-110;) Catherine, the Texan owner of this sunny-colored B&B, has won many a fan through her warm welcome, multihued and impeccably kept rooms, easy artistic style and the lush garden, which is home to a swimming pool that's more than just a bit inviting. A solid American-style breakfast is included.

La Nueva Posada GUESTHOUSE $$$
(376-766-14-44; www.hotelnuevaposada.com; Guerra 9; s M$940-1150, d M$1040-1250, incl breakfast; P) This rather grand address right by the lakeside offers a taste of genteel, old-world Mexico. The 19 rooms are spacious, with tasteful furnishings, and some have superb lake views. The garden runs right down to the shore, giving you plenty of space to feel at ease with the world.

Eating & Drinking

El Chile Verde MEXICAN $
(376-766-00-72; Hidalgo 8A; mains M$25-50; 8am-4:30pm) A world away from all the arty expat-style restaurants and cafes, this tiny lime-green place serves up authentic and delicious home-cooked Mexican food which attracts locals and foreigners alike. The lunchtime dish of the day is a bargain-priced M$45.

Ajijic Tango ARGENTINE $$
(376-766-24-58; Morelos 5; mains M$75-185; 12:30-10pm Mon & Wed-Sat, to 6:30pm Sun) Ajijic's most beloved restaurant is never less than packed with locals, tourists and expats alike, all here to enjoy the excellent steaks (it *is* an Argentine restaurant after all). The rest of the food, though, can be rather hit and miss. Reservations on Friday and Saturday nights are recommended.

★ **Number 4** MEDITERRANEAN $$$
(376-766-13-60; Guerra 4; mains M$190-250; dinner Mon & Fri, 2-11pm Sat, 2-8pm Sun) This upscale and highly impressive place has been generating buzz all the way to Guadalajara. Chef Greg Couillard's menu leans toward modern French and includes culinary delights such as an award-winning blackberry and duck confit, and wild-caught salmon.

The open-air dining room, with a high thatched roof, has a theatrical elegance; the attached bar is the area's hippest and there are frequent band nights and special theme evenings. Reservations are recommended.

Getting There & Away

Buses from Guadalajara (M$50, 1¼ hours) to Ajijic leave from the Antigua Central Camionera multiple times an hour and drop you on the highway at Colón. Buses connect Chapala and Ajijic every 20 minutes (M$9, 15 minutes).

Zona de Montaña

South of Lago de Chapala, Jalisco's Zona de Montaña – seemingly endless layered mountains – is an increasingly popular weekend retreat for *guadalajarans,* who come to enjoy the rangeland, the pines, timeless colonial pueblos, local food and the cooler climes.

Tapalpa

☎343 / POP 18,000 / ELEV 2100M

Tapalpa, a labyrinth of whitewashed walls, red-tiled roofs and cobblestoned streets surrounding two impressive 16th-century churches, is one of the most beautiful mountain towns. This beauty hasn't gone unnoticed and at weekends flocks of people flee Guadalajara for the walking, horseback riding and the generally cool and misty climate that Tapalpa offers. During the weekday calm though, when visitors are few in number, Tapalpa retains a country backwater feel; horses clip-clop down the lanes and old men in cowboy hats lounge on benches in the plaza.

Sights & Activities

Perched on the slopes of the Sierra Tapalpa and ringed by a tapestry of pastureland and pine forests threaded with streams, there is good walking in all directions.

Las Piedrotas LANDMARK

Las Piedrotas are a large and impressive set of rock formations set in cow pastures 5km north of town. Most people drive there, but it's an easy and rewarding 2½- to three-hour return walk along a quiet country lane through dark pine forests, past an abandoned old paper mill and up onto a flower-filled plateau grazed by huge horned cattle.

To get there follow Calle Hidalgo westward out of town following the signs for Chiquilistlán (and some signs for Las Piedrotas). Once you've cleared the edge of town just follow the road straight ahead. A taxi costs around M$60.

El Salto WATERFALL

El Salto is a jaw-dropping, 105m-high waterfall about 18km south of town. A taxi costs around M$130.

Sleeping

There are dozens of hotels and guesthouses in town, but you should make reservations for Saturday and Sunday and holidays (when *guadalajarans* stream in).

Casa de Maty HOTEL $$

(☎343-432-01-89; www.lacasadematy.com.mx; Matamoros 69; r from M$850; 📶) It can get mighty cold and damp in these hills at night so you'll want a warm and cozy place to snuggle down. The large rooms with wood-beam ceilings, wooden shutters, excellent beds and open fireplaces tick all the warm and cozy boxes. Casa de Maty overlooks the main plaza.

Hotel Antigua HOTEL $$

(☎343-432-12-28; laantiguahosteria_@hotmail.com; Hidalgo 283; s week/weekend M$500/600, d week/weekend M$800/1000) On the eastern edge of the old town this rambling half-timbered old farmhouse-style building has a warm and snug atmosphere, friendly owners and all up offers easily the best-value cheaper beds in town.

Las Margaritas Posada GUESTHOUSE $$

(☎343-432-07-99; www.tapalpahotelmargaritas.com; 16 de Septiembre 81; d Mon-Thu/Fri & Sat M$500/600; 📶) With bright decorations and wardrobes with carved Chinese-style dragons, this place, which is uphill from the plaza, offers value, comfort and eye-pleasing rooms.

Eating

Local street-food treats include *tamales de acelga* (chard-filled *tamales*) at the cheap food stalls near the church, *rompope* and *ponche* (pomegranate wine).

Los Girasoles MEXICAN $$

(☎343-432-04-58; Obregón 110; mains M$90-110) Tapalpa's classiest restaurant is just off the main plaza and offers quality dishes such as cheese and plantain-stuffed chilies in a coriander sauce. There's a starlit outdoor patio for rare warm nights or those wrapped up well, or you can snuggle in front of the open log fire in the main dining room.

Information

There's an ATM on the plaza.

Tourist Office (☎343-432-06-50; www.tapalpaturistico.com; Plaza; ⏰9am-5pm Mon-Fri, 10am-7pm Sat, 10am-3pm Sun) The tourist office has maps, info and a particularly useful website. Don't, however, ask staff about how long any given walk takes. They only know how long it takes to drive...

Getting There & Away

Ten buses daily travel to Tapalpa, leaving from Guadalajara's Antigua Central Camionera (M$106, three hours); three daily go from the Nueva Central Camionera. There are also four buses a day to/from Ciudad Guzmán (M$77, two hours). Buses in Tapalpa stop at the **Sur de Jalisco bus office** (Ignacio López 10), a block off the plaza.

Mazamitla

382 / POP 8000 / ELEV 2200M

During the week Mazamitla, a simple and charming whitewashed mountain town south of Lago de Chapala and 132km by road from Guadalajara, is seldom fully awake. Shops close at 5pm, restaurants open at 6pm and *abuelas* (grandmothers) dressed in black wander haphazardly through the hilly cobbled roads, stopping traffic. But come the weekend and every man and his sombrero arrives from Guadalajara. Then the town is anything but sleepy; the plaza fills with music and dance, the hotels and restaurants are booked out, and the shops sell an impressive array of tourist tat, but it's all good fun.

Sights & Activities

There's a small but lively **market** (8am-9pm) on Juárez.

Los Cazos PARK
(adult/child M$15/10; 9am-5pm;) About 2km south of town is the leafy park Los Cazos, with the 30m waterfall **El Salto**. You can picnic or hire a **horse** (per hour M$100) and live out your John Wayne fantasies. A taxi here costs M$50 or it's an easy walk.

Sleeping & Eating

There are masses of places to stay in Mazamitla and an equal number of places to eat. Mazamitla sports an interesting take on the Swiss alpine theme and you'll see small storefronts selling fruit preserves, cheeses, *rompope* and *cajeta* (goat's milk and sugar boiled to a paste) around the plaza.

Hostal El Leñador GUESTHOUSE $
(382-538-01-85; www.hostalelenador.com.mx; Netzahualcóyotl 4; r M$450-500;) Stepping through the door of this family-run guesthouse you're likely to be greeted with the words, *'M'i casa es tu casa'* (My house is your house), and with modern, large and very comfortable rooms and staff that welcome you'll probably be glad to call Hostal El Leñador home for a while.

Hotel Cabañas Colina de los Ruiseñores CABAÑAS $
(382-538-03-80; www.mazamitlahotelcabana.com.mx; Allende 50; s/d M$250/400;) Down the hill from the plaza, the Hotel Cabañas Colina de los Ruiseñores is a pleasantly rustic place, with rambling grounds and homey rooms with open log fires.

Posada Alpina HOTEL $$
(382-538-01-04; Reforma 8; s/d from M$310/500;) Right on the plaza, Posada Alpina has a leafy interior courtyard, sweet wooden rooms and outstanding views. It also has a smart restaurant that serves the best *molcajete* (M$105) in town.

Information

There's a bank on the plaza and a **Tourist Office** (382-538-02-30; Portal Degollado 16; 9am-3pm Mon-Fri).

Getting There & Away

Buses to Colima (M$142, 2¾ hours, four daily), Zamora (M$109, 2½ hours, three to four daily), Querétaro (M$345, eight hours, one daily) and Morelia (M$269, five hours, one daily) leave from the Pemex gas station at Galeana and Guerro.

From Guadalajara's Nueva Central Camionera (M$120, three hours) buses arrive at the small bus station at the corner of 16 de Septiembre and Guerro three blocks north of Mazamitla's plaza. The many buses to Ciudad Guzmán (M$107, 2½ hours) arrive and leave from the same place.

Ciudad Guzmán

341 / POP 97,000 / ELEV 1500M

Busy Ciudad Guzmán (Zapotlán El Grande) is no tourist attraction, but it is the closest city to Volcán Nevado de Colima, a majestic volcano about 25km to its southwest.

Guzmán's crowded plaza is surrounded by market stalls and shopping arcades set around two churches: the 17th-century **Sagrado Corazón** and a neoclassical **cathedral**. In its center is a stone gazebo with a homage to famous local-boy muralist José Clemente Orozco – called *Man of Fire* – painted on its ceiling. The original is in the Instituto Cultural de Cabañas in Guadalajara.

The small **Museo Regional de las Culturas de Occidente** (Dr Ángel González 21; admission M$35; 9am-6pm Tue-Sat) is the place to brush up on your history of western Jalisco.

There are numerous hotels surrounding the bustling plaza. **Gran Hotel Zapotlán** (341-412-00-40; Federico del Toro 61; r from M$360;) is set on the plaza with a pretty tiled atrium full of hanging plants, but rooms cannot be described as luxurious. For a quieter night pick a room at the back.

The **tourist office** (341-575-25-27; Colón 63; 8:30am-3pm Mon-Fri) is in the government building on Ciudad Guzmán's plaza. It can help with planning and booking an ascent of the Volcán Nevado de Colima.

Ciudad Guzmán's modern bus terminal is about 3km west of the plaza near the entrance to the city from the Guadalajara–Colima highway. Hop on bus 6 (M$5) to get there and back. Destinations include Guadalajara (M$152, two hours), Colima (M$93, one to two hours), Tapalpa (M$77, two hours), Mazamitla (M$107, two hours), and Zapotitlán, which passes 2km from El Fresnito (M$12, 15 minutes), the closest village to Volcán Nevado de Colima. An alternative way to reach El Fresnito is taking the 1C *urbano* from the Los Mones crossroad in Ciudad Guzmán (M$6, 20 minutes).

INLAND COLIMA STATE

The tiny but ecologically rich and diverse state of Colima (5191 sq km) connects lofty volcanoes in its arid northern highlands to idyllic turquoise lagoons near the hot and humid Pacific coast. This section deals with the state's inland area; the narrow coastal plain is covered in the Central Pacific Coast chapter.

Inland Colima should become Mexico's next great adventure hub. The famous volcanoes in the north – the active, constantly steaming but inaccessible Volcán de Fuego (3820m) and the extinct, snowcapped Volcán Nevado de Colima (4240m) – remain the big draws. But the Reserva de la Biosfera Sierra de Manantlán is a jungle-and-limestone playground in waiting, with single-track mountain biking, exceptional hiking and canyons that see a few canyoneers abseiling, leaping into crystalline streams and bathing in the magical El Salto Falls. Tourism infrastructure hasn't caught up to the area's potential yet, so those who like virgin territory should come now.

History

Pre-Hispanic Colima was remote from the major ancient cultures of Mexico. Seaborne contacts with more distant lands might have been more important: legend says one king of Colima, Ix, had regular treasure-bearing visitors from China. Eventually, northern tribes moved in. The Otomí settled here from about AD 250 to 750, followed by the Toltecs, who flourished between 900 and 1154, and the Chichimecs from 1154 to 1428.

All of them left behind exceptional pottery, which has been found in more than 250 sites, mainly tombs, dating from about 200 BC to AD 800. The pottery includes a variety of comical and expressive figures. The most famous are the plump, hairless dogs known as xoloitzcuintles.

Two Spanish expeditions were defeated and turned back by the Chichimecs before Gonzalo de Sandoval, one of Cortés' lieutenants, conquered them in 1523. That year he founded the town of Colima, the third Spanish settlement in Nueva España, after Veracruz and Mexico City. In 1527 the town moved to its present site from its original lowland location near Tecomán.

Colima

☎312 / POP 137,000 / ELEV 550M

Colima is a laid-back city with blooming subtropical gardens, fine public plazas, a pleasant touch of moisture in the air and the warmest weather in the western central highlands. The city's university attracts students from around the world, while its growing tourism potential derived from nearby canyons, forests and mountains brings in a small but growing number of visitors.

The billowing volcano you see on clear days, Volcán de Fuego – visible 30km to the north – continues to rumble and shake, and the city has been hit by several major quakes over the centuries (the last in January 2003). It's no wonder that Colima has few colonial buildings, despite having been the first Spanish city in western Mexico.

Sights

★Cathedral CATHEDRAL

Light floods the cathedral from the dome windows of this would-be relic on the east side of Plaza Principal. It has been rebuilt several times since the Spanish first erected a cathedral here in 1527, most recently after the 1941 earthquake, so it's too new to offer old-world soul, but it remains a focal point of the community.

Palacio de Gobierno BUILDING

(museum admission free; ⌚10am-6pm Tue-Sun, museum 10am-6pm Tue-Sun) FREE Local artist Jorge Chávez Carrillo painted the stairway murals in the Palacio de Gobierno to celebrate the 200th birthday of independence hero Miguel Hidalgo, who was once parish priest of Colima. The murals honor freedom fighters, indigenous roots and the land of Mexico. There's a great collection of pottery in the 1st-floor museum, including some from 1500 BC.

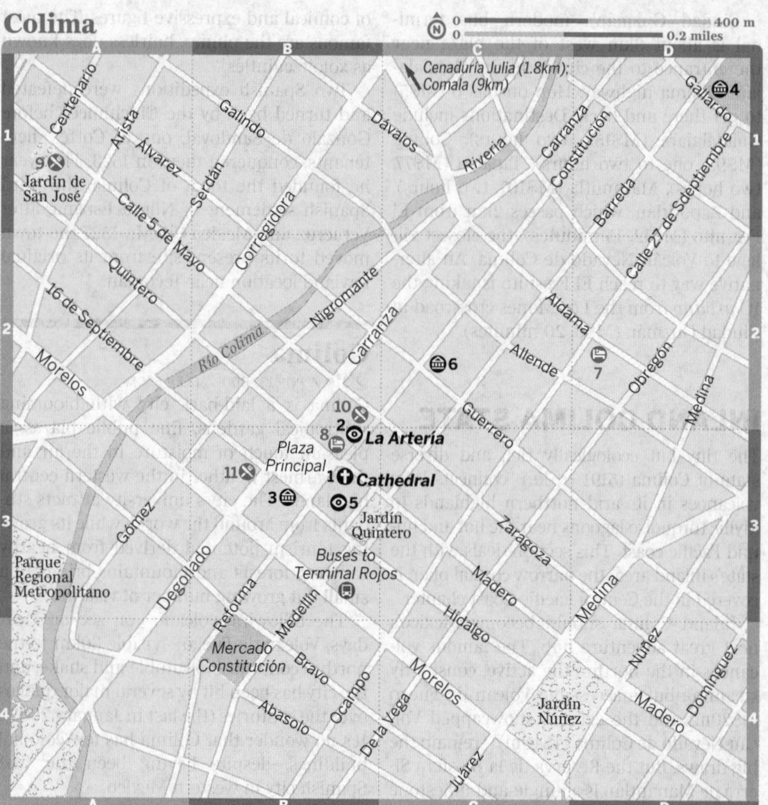

Colima

Top Sights

Sights

Sleeping

Eating

★ La Artería ARTS CENTER

(☎312-312-27-06; www.laarteria.org; Constitución 39) It's worth popping into this new art and culture center in order to see what's going on. Privately run by a group of young artists it has a spontaneous and alternative vibe that few government art centers can match. It's varied calender of events includes art exhibitions, alternative theater, indy music, occasional party nights and even events concerned with indigenous rights.

Museo Regional de Historia de Colima MUSEUM

(☎312-312-92-28; Morelos 1; admission M$46; ⏲9am-6pm Tue-Sat, 5-8pm Sun) This excellent museum has an extensive collection of well-labeled artifacts spanning the region's history, from ancient pottery to conquistadors' armor to a 19th-century horse-drawn carriage. Don't miss the ceramic xoloitzcuintles (Colima dogs) or the walk-through mock tomb excavation.

Museo Universitario de Artes Populares MUSEUM
(University Museum of Popular Arts; cnr Barreda & Gallardo; adult/child & student M$20/10, Sun free; ⏲10am-2pm & 5-8pm Tue-Sat, 10am-1pm Sun) Folk-art lovers will be in heaven at this museum. On display is a stellar collection of masks, *mojigangas* (giant puppets), musical instruments, baskets, and wood and ceramic sculpture from every state in Mexico.

Pinacoteca Universitaria Alfonso Michel MUSEUM
(cnr Guerrero & Constitución; ⏲10am-2pm & 5-8pm Tue-Sat, 10am-1pm Sun) FREE This beautiful museum, in a 19th-century courtyard building, offers four halls filled with surrealist art. Included are a permanent collection of paintings by Colima's Alfonso Michel – whose work has been described as a cross between Picasso and Dalí – as well as works by José Luis Cuevas and Francisco Toledo.

La Campana ARCHAEOLOGICAL SITE
(☎312-313-49-46; Av Tecnológico; admission M$42; ⏲9am-6pm Tue-Sun) The low, pyramid-like structures at this modest archaeological site date from as early as 1500 BC. They have been excavated and restored, along with a small tomb and a ball court (unusual in western Mexico). The structures are oriented due north toward Volcán de Fuego, which makes an impressive backdrop on clear days.

It's about 5km north of Colima city and easily accessible by buses 7 and 22; taxis cost M$42. A word of warning: wear good shoes and socks because there are lots of fire ants – so many that on our last visit we spent more time looking at the ground than the ruins!

Sleeping

Hotel Aldama HOTEL $
(☎312-330-73-07; Aldama 134; s/d M$350/463; ❄📶) A five-minute walk from the central plaza, this new budget hotel kicks way above its weight with rooms that, though small, have had a lot of care put into them: think flowers strewn across the bed sheets, wrought iron and heavy wooden furnishings, and desks to work at. However, there's little soundproofing between rooms.

★**Casa Alvarada** B&B $$
(☎312-315-52-29; www.casaalvarada.com; Obregón 105; r from $650; P❄📶) Not actually in Colima at all but in the outrageously pretty whitewashed village of Comala, 9km northwest of Colima. Casa Alvarada is a homey B&B run by an English-speaking husband-and-wife team. Rooms are decorated with local folk art, breakfasts are family-style, and the patio has a sumptuous hammock bed.

The owners run a whole array of highly recommended local tours, including to the volcanoes, jungle trekking, kayaking, and village and coffee-estate tours.

Hotel Ceballos HOTEL $$
(☎312-316-01-00; www.hotelceballos.com; Portal Medellín 12; r from M$946; P❄@📶🏊) This Best Western property has plenty of charm in its public areas, but its rooms are rather less characterful and a little overpriced. However, some of the better rooms have high ceilings with crown moldings and balconies that overlook Plaza Principal. There's a small gym and tiny rooftop plunge pool, too.

Eating & Drinking

Many small restaurants around Plaza Principal offer decent fare and are good places for people-watching on weekends.

Cenaduría Julia MEXICAN $
(Leandro Valle 80, Villa de Álvarez; mains M$30-45; ⏲6pm-midnight Mon & Wed-Fri, 1:30pm-midnight Sat & Sun; 👪) This institution is Colima's best-loved restaurant. The dishes to have here are the *sopitos* (small circular tortillas topped with meat, spices and tomato sauce; M$35 for eight), as well as the sweet enchiladas (M$30). It doesn't look like much, but at these prices for authentic *cocina colimense* (Colima-style cuisine), it's well worth the short journey here.

It's a M$30 cab ride from the town centre.

1800 INTERNATIONAL $
(Calle 5 de Mayo No 15; mains from M$40; ⏲7pm-2am Tue-Sun) This hip restaurant-lounge attracts a late-coming crowd of uni students for snacks, drinks and, on Thursday nights, live music from around the globe. The menu takes in pizza, sushi, burritos and more, but most people come here to drink and meet friends.

El Trebol MEXICAN $
(☎312-312-29-00; Degollado 59; mains M$25-65; ⏲8am-11pm Sun-Fri) This long-running family restaurant is a great spot for breakfast. The scent of freshly squeezed orange juice perfumes the dining room, and diners devour *huevos a la mexicana* (eggs scrambled with green pepper, onion and tomatoes,

representing the three colors of the Mexican flag) and scrambles with ham, bacon and chorizo.

¡Ah Qué Nanishe! MEXICAN $$
(☎312-314-21-97; Calle 5 de Mayo 267; mains M$95-115; ⊙noon-11pm Tue-Sun) The name of this restaurant means 'How delicious!' and the rich, chocolatey, but not overwhelming *mole* (sauce) is superb. Other don't-miss Oaxacan delicacies available include *chiles rellenos* (stuffed chilis) or, if you're lucky, *chapulines* (crunchy fried grasshoppers).

Half orders of many mains are available for 70% of the full price.

Information

State Tourist Office (☎312-312-43-60; www.visitacolima.com.mx; Palacio de Gobierno; ⊙8am-8pm Mon-Fri, 8am-2pm Sat) Also open on public holidays.

Getting There & Around

Colima's **airport** (☎312-314-41-60; Av Lic Carlos de la Madrid Bejar) is near Cuauhtémoc, 12km northeast of the city center off the highway to Guadalajara (taxis M$140). **Aeromar** (☎312-313-13-40; www.aeromar.com.mx; Airport) flies to Mexico City three times a day.

Colima has two bus terminals. The long-distance terminal is Terminal Foránea, 2km east of the city center at the junction of Avenida Niños Héroes and the city's eastern bypass. There's a **left-luggage facility** (⊙6am-10pm). To reach downtown, hop on a Ruta 4 or 5 bus. For the return trip catch the same buses on Calle 5 de Mayo or Zaragoza. There's a prepay taxi booth at the terminal and the fare to downtown is M$28.

Colima's second bus terminal (serving local towns) is Terminal Rojos, about 7km west of Plaza Principal. Ruta 4 or 6 buses run to Colima's center from this terminal. To get back here, take any bus marked 'Rojos' going north on Morelos.

Taxi fares within town cost M$10 to M$25.

Around Colima

The outlying villages and countryside around Colima are gorgeous and demand exploration. In particular don't miss **Comala**, a 10-minute drive northwest of town, and a picture-perfect village. You can visit most worthy destinations on day trips or by public transportation, but a rental car is liberating.

Parque Nacional Volcán Nevado de Colima

This national park, straddling the Colima-Jalisco border, includes two dramatic volcanoes: the still-active Volcán de Fuego and the inactive Volcán Nevado de Colima. Ciudad Guzmán is the closest city, but, if you have a car and set off early, Colima is a more pleasant base. Contact the state tourist office in Colima for a list of operators offering trips to climb Volcán Nevado de Colima. It can be difficult to find a guide on the fly if you only have a few days, so it's best to organize things in advance.

VOLCÁN DE FUEGO

Overlooking Colima, 30km north of the city, is steaming Volcán de Fuego (3820m), Mexico's most active volcano. It has erupted dozens of times in the past four centuries, with a big eruption about every 70 years. In June 2005 a large explosion sent ash 4.8km into the sky, all the way to Colima. Current information about the volcano is posted on the website of the **Universidad de Colima** (www.ucol.mx/volcan).

VOLCÁN NEVADO DE COLIMA

Higher and more northerly than Volcán de Fuego, Nevado de Colima (4240m) is accessible on foot for most of the year. Patches of pine forest cover Nevado's shoulders, while alpine desert takes over at the highest altitudes.

BUSES FROM COLIMA

DESTINATION	FARE (M$)	DURATION	FREQUENCY (DAILY)
Ciudad Guzmán	93	1-2hr	every 30min
Guadalajara	203-236	3hr	every 30min
Manzanillo	75-102	2hr	every 15min
Mexico City (Terminal Norte)	791-850	10hr	hourly
Morelia	363-456	2hr	6
Uruapan	389	6hr	hourly

WORTH A TRIP

RESERVA DE LA BIOSFERA SIERRA DE MANANTLÁN

A 1396-sq-km swath of the jungle-clad limestone mountains northwest of the city of Colima is protected by Unesco as critical habitat. It's certainly diverse, ranging in elevation from 400m to 2960m, with eight varieties of forest ecosystem – including tropical, cloud, oak and alpine. This land is rich and alive with nearly 2000 varieties of plants, 160 orchid species, 336 bird species (a third of Mexico's bird species can be found here), 60 types of reptile and the two big cats – puma and jaguar. It's also drop-dead gorgeous with spectacular limestone karsts, narrow canyons and powerful waterfalls.

Adventurers will not be bored. There are canyons to explore, 50km of adrenaline-addled downhill single-track for mountain bikers and an abundance of trekking trails. **Fuego Bike** (☎312-119-95-82; www.fuegobike.com) runs adventure trips to the reserve.

Area wildlife includes deer, wild boar, coyote and even a few pumas.

The best months for climbing are the dry months of December through May. But temperatures from December to February often dip below 0°C (32°F) and snow does regularly fall on the upper slopes – *nevado* means 'snow-covered.' Weather changes fast here and lightning strikes the peak in stormy weather, so make sure you keep an eye on the clouds. The park's October to March hours are 6am to 6pm. The summer rainy season is from July to September, when park hours are longer.

To get here on your own from Ciudad Guzmán, take the bus to El Fresnito (M$12), where you can try to hire a driver to take you to La Joya/Puerto Las Cruces (3500m); from there, you can sign in and pay the M$25 park entry fee. Alternatively, you can walk up, and if so, stay on the bus as it covers some of the distance beyond the town. If you choose to walk all the way from the main road or El Fresnito you'll need camping gear and food (and some very warm clothes), because it's impossible to walk there and back in a day. Allow six hours to get to the parking at La Joya/Puerto Las Cruces and then another two hours from there to the summit and about five hours all the way back down again. You can camp at La Joya/Puerto Las Cruces a few kilometers beyond the park gates. If you plan to hitch up, try coming on a Saturday or Sunday, when there is a steady stream of visitors; weekdays can be very quiet.

The *micro-ondas* (radio antennae) are a strenuous 90-minute hike up from the end of the road at La Joya/Puerto Las Cruces. If you want to bag the peak, you'll need another 90 minutes and while the peak is easy to see, you shouldn't go alone. There are many trails up and back and it's very easy to get lost or led to areas with hazardous footing. Going with a guide is highly recommended. A guide for a group of up to five people will be around M$1,200 including transportation from Ciudad Guzmán and entry fees.

The following guides are recommended:

Admire Mexico (☎312-314-54-54; www.admiremexicotours.com; Guillermo Prieto 113, Comala) A highly regarded agency based out of Casa Alvarada in Comala.

Nevado de Colima Tours (☎cell phone 045-3411140004; http://nevadodecolimatours.blogspot.mx) A reliable and experienced agency operating out of Ciudad Guzmán.

Driving up this volcano on the relatively good dirt road means that you'll be ascending to a high altitude very quickly. If you feel lightheaded or dizzy, you may be suffering from altitude sickness. Descend as quickly as possible, as this condition can be fatal.

INLAND MICHOACÁN

Pre-Hispanic traditions and colonial-era architecture meet in Michoacán to dramatic effect. The state is home to three of Mexico's coolest, most under-the-radar cities: the adobe-and-cobblestone town of Pátzcuaro, where Purépecha women sell figs and *tamales* in the shadow of 16th-century churches; the lush agricultural city of Uruapan, gateway to the mythic Paricutín volcano; and the vibrant and cultured colonial city of Morelia, with ancient cathedrals and aqueducts built from rosy pink stone. Michoacán is also gaining renown as a crafts capital – the Purépecha artisans of the state's Cordillera Neovolcánica highlands create wonderful masks, pottery, straw art and stringed instruments – and put on some of the country's best Día de Muertos (Day of the Dead) celebrations. Rich in natural treasures, Michoacán has one of the world's true 'life list'-caliber sights: the annual butterfly migration to the rugged Reserva Mariposa Monarca (Monarch Butterfly Reserve), where millions of mating monarch butterflies cover the grass and trees in a shimmering Aladdin's carpet.

Morelia

☎443 / POP 597,000 / ELEV 1920M

The state capital of Michoacán and its most dynamic and beautiful city, Morelia is an increasingly popular destination, and rightly so: the colonial heart of the city is so well preserved that it was declared a Unesco World Heritage site in 1991, and its cathedral is not just gorgeous – it's inspirational.

Morelia, founded in 1541, was one of the first Spanish cities in Nueva España. The first viceroy, Antonio de Mendoza, named it Valladolid after the Spanish city and he encouraged Spanish nobility to move here with their families. In 1828, after Nueva España had become the Republic of Mexico, the city was renamed Morelia in honor of local hero José María Morelos y Pavón, a key figure in Mexico's independence.

Elegant 16th- and 17th-century stone buildings, baroque facades and archways line the narrow downtown streets, and are home to museums, hotels, restaurants, *chocolaterías* (chocolate shops), sidewalk cafes, a popular university and cheap-and-tasty *taquerías* (taco stalls). There are free public concerts, frequent art installations, and yet so few foreign tourists! Those that do come often extend their stay and enrol in classes to learn how to cook and speak Spanish. Yes, word has started to leak out and more and more internationals are beginning to discover Mexico's best-kept secret.

Sights

★Cathedral CATHEDRAL

(Plaza de Armas; 8am-10pm) Morelia's beautiful cathedral (unforgettable when it's lit up at night) dominates the main city plaza. It took more than a century to build (1640–1744), which explains its combination of Herreresque, baroque and neoclassical styles: the twin 70m-high towers, for instance, have classical Herreresque bases, baroque midsections and multicolumned neoclassical tops. Inside, much of the baroque relief work was replaced in the 19th century with neoclassical pieces.

Fortunately, one of the cathedral's interior highlights was preserved: a sculpture of the Señor de la Sacristía made from dried corn paste and topped with a gold crown from 16th-century Spanish king Felipe II. It also has a working organ with 4600 pipes. Occasional organ recitals take place – a beautiful time to be in the cathedral.

★Museo del Estado MUSEUM

(☎443-313-06-29; Prieto 176; 9am-8pm Mon-Fri, 10am-6pm Sat & Sun) FREE This museum objectively presents the state's history from prehistoric times to first contact with the conquistadors. Pre-Hispanic arrowheads, ceramic figures, bone jewelry and a shimmering quartz skull can be found downstairs. Upstairs are first-person accounts of how force-fed religion coupled with systematic agricultural and economic development tamed the region's indigenous soul. Labeling is in Spanish only.

Museo Regional Michoacano MUSEUM

(☎443-312-04-07; Allende 305, cnr Abasolo; admission M$42, Sun free; 9am-7pm Tue-Sat, until 2pm Sun) This museum is housed in a late-18th-century baroque palace where you can view an impressive variety of pre-Hispanic artifacts, colonial art and relics, including one of the carved stone coyotes from Ihuatzio. There's also an evocative Alfredo Zalce mural, *Cuauhtémoc y la historia*, on the stairway. Labeling is in Spanish only.

Palacio Clavijero MUSEUM

(Galeana) FREE From 1660 to 1767 the Palacio Clavijero, with its awesome main patio, imposing colonnades and pink stonework, was home to the Jesuit school of St Francis Xavier. Today the building houses exhibition spaces showing off high-quality displays of contemporary art, photography and other creative media.

Museo Casa de Morelos MUSEUM

(Morelos House Museum; ☎443-313-26-51; Av Morelos Sur 323; admission M$35, Sun free; 9am-5pm Tue-Sun) In 1801 independence hero José María Morelos bought this Spanish-style house on the corner of Avenida Morelos and Soto y Saldaña. Today it's the definitive museum on Morales and the independence movement. It's very well laid out and displays have good information panels in both Spanish and English.

Fuente Las Tarascas FOUNTAIN

On Plaza Villalongín, this iconic fountain erupts from a fruit tray held by three beautiful, topless Tarascan women. The original vanished mysteriously in 1940 and this reproduction was installed in the 1960s.

El Acueducto AQUEDUCT

Morelia's impressive aqueduct runs for several kilometers along Avenida Acueducto and bends around Plaza Villalongín. It was built between 1785 and 1788 to meet the city's growing water needs. Its 253 arches are gorgeous when illuminated at night.

Palacio de Justicia BUILDING

(Plaza de Armas; museum admission free; ⏲7am-7pm Mon-Sat, museum 10am-2pm & 5-7:30pm) Across from the Museo Regional Michoacano is the Palacio de Justicia, built between 1682 and 1695 to serve as the city hall. Its facade blends French and baroque styles, with stairwell art in the courtyard. An Agustín Cárdenas mural portrays Morelos in action. A small three-room **museum** shares the history of Michoacán's justice system through old photos and papers (look for the grisly cadaver shots).

Palacio de Gobierno BUILDING

(Av Madero Oriente) The 17th-century palace, originally a seminary and now state government offices, has a simple baroque facade and impressive historical murals inside. The murals were commissioned in 1961, painted by Alfredo Zalce and are worth a peek.

Museo Casa Natal de Morelos MUSEUM

(Morelos Birthplace Museum; ☎443-312-27-93; Corregidora 113; ⏲9am-8pm Mon-Fri, to 7pm Sat & Sun) FREE José María Morelos y Pavón, one of the most important heroes in Mexico's struggle for independence, is king in Morelia – after all, the entire city is named after him. He was born in this house on the corner of Calles Corregidora and García Obeso on September 30, 1765. Now home to a museum in his honor, the collection includes photos and documents. An eternal torch burns next to the very spot where he was born.

Colegio de San Nicolás BUILDING

(cnr Av Madero Poniente & Nigromante; ⏲8am-8pm Mon-Sat) Morelos studied here, one block west of the plaza. While not another Morelos museum, it has become a foundation for the Universidad Michoacana. Upstairs, the **Sala de Melchor Ocampo** is a memorial to another Mexican hero, a reformer-governor of Michoacán. Preserved here is Ocampo's library and a copy of the document he signed donating it to the college, just before he was executed by a conservative firing squad on June 3, 1861.

DON'T MISS

BIBLIOTECA PÚBLICA DE LA UNIVERSIDAD MICHOACANA

Town councils of the world take note: if you're going to build a public library (which you should) then please make it look like **Biblioteca Pública de la Universidad Michoacana** (☎443-3125-725; Jardin Igangio Altamirano, cnr Av Madero Poniente & Nigromante; ⏲8am-8pm Mon-Fri). Installed inside the magnificent 16th-century **Ex-Templo de la Compañía de Jesús**, the shelves of the city's breathtaking university library rise up toward the domed ceilings and are crammed from head to toe with thousands (22,901 to be exact) of dusty, antique books recounting the histories of kings and queens, Spain, Europe and the colonies.

Plaza Morelos PLAZA

This conspicuously vacant plaza surrounds the **Estatua Ecuestre al Patriota Morelos** (Plaza Morelos), a majestic statue of Morelos on horseback, sculpted by Italian artist Giuseppe Ingillieri between 1910 and 1913.

Running from here to the Fuente Las Tarascas is the shaded and cobbled **Calzada Fray Antonio de San Miguel**, a wide, romantic pedestrian promenade framed by exquisite old buildings. Branching off its west end, narrow **Callejón del Romance** (Romance Alley) looks like something out of a vintage postcard, all pink stone and trailing vines.

Santuario de Guadalupe CHURCH

On the northeast edge of Plaza Morelos, the pink-and-red walls of this baroque church built from 1708 to 1716 bloom with white flowers and glisten with an abundance of gold leaf. There's so much color, the interior (decorated in 1915) feels not unlike a Hindu temple.

Springing out of all this color are a series of huge paintings depicting the conversion of the indigenous peoples to Christianity. They show scenes such as sacrifical victims about to be beheaded before being saved by the honest, God-fearing folk of Spain. Quite.

Morelia

Beside the church, the much less splashy **Ex-Convento de San Diego** (Plaza Morelos) was built in 1761 as a monastery and now houses the law school of the Universidad Michoacana.

Bosque Cuauhtémoc PARK

Morelia's largest park is favored by families because of its shady trees, amusement park and museums. On its grounds are two worthwhile museums. Housed in a 19th-century building, the **Museo de Arte Contemporáneo Alfredo Zalce** (☎443-312-54-04; Av Acueducto 18; ⏲10am-7:45pm Mon-Fri, to 6pm Sat & Sun) FREE has temporary exhibitions of contemporary art. At the time of research it was closed for renovations. The quirky **Museo de Historia Natural** (☎443-312-00-44; Ventura Puente 23; admission free; ⏲10am-6pm), on the east side of the park, displays stuffed, dissected and skeletal animals and human fetuses.

Courses

Few foreigners and plenty of culture make Morelia an exceptional place to learn how to cook, dance and speak Spanish. Ask for a discount if taking a course for more than two weeks.

Baden-Powell Institute LANGUAGE COURSE

(☎443-312-20-02; www.baden-powell.com; Antonio Alzate 569; private lessons per hr from US$18, group lessons per week from US$180) The small, well-run and affordable Baden-Powell Institute offers courses in Spanish language, as well as Mexican politics, cooking, culture, guitar and salsa dancing. It books homestays (per day US$27) for students.

Centro Cultural de Lenguas LANGUAGE COURSE

(☎443-312-05-89; www.ccl.com.mx; Av Madero Oriente 560; group/private lessons per week US$180/340) Offers Spanish-language classes running from one hour to four weeks, as

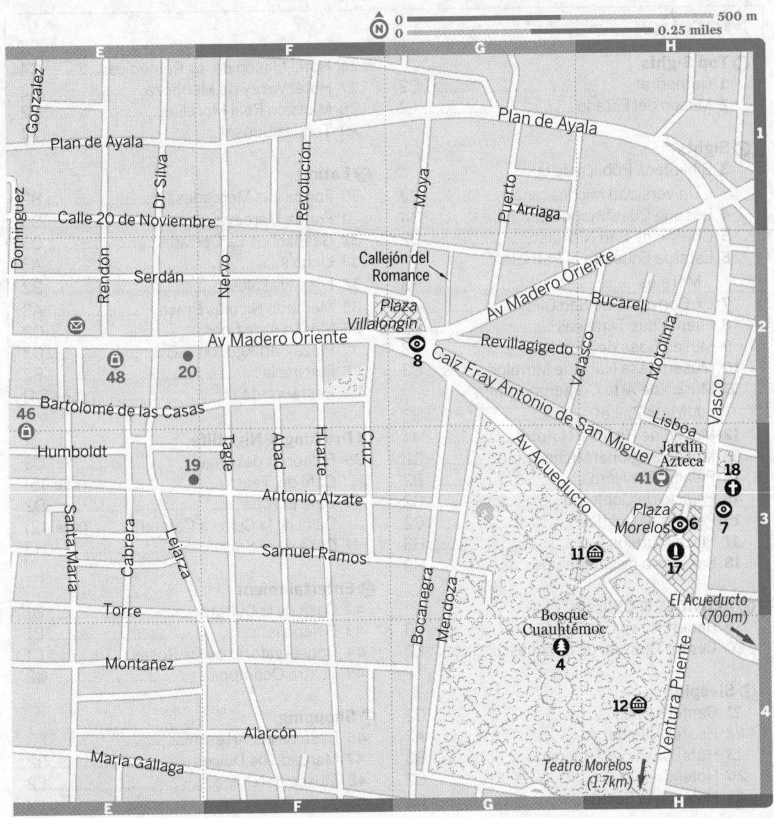

well as music, dance and cooking classes. Homestays (per night from US$25, including meals) are available.

Tours

The tourist office, CAT Centro de Atención al Turista (p616), gives daily city tours at 10am or 4pm. For tours outside the city ask the tourist office for recommendations.

Mexico Cooks! CULINARY
(www.mexicocooks.typepad.com) US-born Cristina Potters, a true expert on Mexican cuisine, gives wonderful personalized foodie tours of Morelia (and Guadalajara), despite now being based in Mexico City. Contact her in advance to arrange a tour of the city.

Festivals & Events

In addition to the usual Mexican celebrations, Morelia's many annual festivals include the following:

Feria de Morelia TRADITIONAL
Morelia's biggest fair, running for three weeks in late April through early May, hosts exhibits of handicrafts, agriculture and livestock, plus regional dances, bullfights and fiestas. May 18 is the city's founding date (1541) and is celebrated with a fireworks show.

Cumpleaños de Morelos FIREWORKS
Morelos' birthday is celebrated on September 30 with a parade and fireworks show.

Festival Internacional de Cine de Morelia FILM
(www.moreliafilmfest.com) This major international exhibition for Mexico's vibrant film industry brings a week of parties and star sightings each October.

Día de Muertos TRADITIONAL
Michoacán's outlying villages and smaller cities are the top attraction in the week of

Morelia

Top Sights
1 Cathedral C2
2 Museo del Estado C1

Sights
3 Biblioteca Pública de la Universidad Michoacana B2
4 Bosque Cuauhtémoc G4
5 Colegio de San Nicolás B2
6 Estatua Ecuestre al Patriota Morelos H3
7 Ex-Convento de San Diego H3
8 Fuente Las Tarascas G2
9 Museo Casa de Morelos D3
10 Museo Casa Natal de Morelos C3
11 Museo de Arte Contemporáneo Alfredo Zalce H3
12 Museo de Historia Natural H4
13 Museo Regional Michoacano C2
14 Palacio Clavijero B2
15 Palacio de Gobierno C2
16 Palacio de Justicia C2
17 Plaza Morelos H3
18 Santuario de Guadalupe H3

Activities & Courses
19 Baden-Powell Institute E3
20 Centro Cultural de Lenguas E2

Sleeping
21 Cantera Diez C2
22 Hostel Allende A2
23 Hotel Casa del Anticuario B3
24 Hotel Casino C2
25 Hotel de la Soledad C2
26 Hotel Mesón de los Remedios C4
27 Hotel Virrey de Mendoza C2
28 Mansión Real Morelia D2
29 Tequila Sunset A1

Eating
30 Fonda Las Mercedes B2
31 Fonda Marceva C3
32 Gaspachos La Cerrada C3
33 Licha's A3
34 Los Mirasoles B2
35 Mercado Nicolás Bravo A3
36 Mesón Agustinos C3
37 Plaza San Agustín C3
38 Pulcinella B2
Restaurante Lu .... (see 24)

Drinking & Nightlife
39 Balcones del Ángel C3
Café del Teatro .... (see 45)
40 Cafe Europa D2
Casa de la Cultura Cafeteria .... (see 42)
41 Casa de la Salsa H3

Entertainment
42 Casa de la Cultura D1
43 Cinépolis B1
44 Conservatorio de las Rosas C1
45 Teatro Ocampo C2

Shopping
46 Casa de las Artesanías E3
47 Mercado de Dulces B2
48 Museo del Dulce E2

November 1, but Morelia hosts free flamenco concerts and stunning art installations in and around Plaza de Armas.

Festival Internacional de Música MUSIC
(www.festivalmorelia.com) The international classical music festival occurs for two weeks in mid-November with orchestras, choirs and quartets giving concerts in churches, plazas and theaters around town.

Día de la Virgen de Guadalupe RELIGIOUS
The Day of the Virgin of Guadalupe is celebrated on December 12 at the Ex-Convento de San Diego; in the preceding weeks a carnival erupts on Calzada Fray Antonio de San Miguel.

Feria Navideña TRADITIONAL
The Christmas Fair, with traditional Christmas items, foods and handicrafts from Michoacán, happens sometime between November and December.

Sleeping

There are a lot of hotels in Morelia and not so many tourists so competition is fierce and, except during rare busy periods, you can be almost certain that all hotels except the very cheapest hostels will offer significant discounts against the rack rates shown here.

Tequila Sunset HOSTEL $
(☎443-313-84-97; www.tequilasunsethostal.com.mx; Tapia 679; dm/r incl breakfast M$180/480; @ 🛜) This friendly and well-run hostel caters to the young and fun, with spotless dorms featuring skylights and groovy graphic murals, a common room stocked with the latest DVDs, and sparkling, sunny bathrooms (although there aren't many of these compared to the number of beds it has).

Staff are eager to please, there's a good shared kitchen, and there are laundry facilities and pleasant outdoor areas.

Hostel Allende HOSTEL $
(☎443-312-22-46; www.hostelallende.com.mx; Allende 843; dm M$215, r M$550-550; @ 📶) A favorite with a mixed-age crowd of international travelers, Hostel Allende has two dorms and 33 private rooms surrounding a leafy courtyard planted with citrus trees. There's also a communal kitchen and a chilled-out vibe.

★Hotel Casa del Anticuario HOTEL $$
(☎443-333-25-21; www.hotelcasadelanticuario.com; Galeana 319; s/d M$650/750; 📶) This luscious yellow guesthouse has rooms with exposed stone walls and wooden roof beams, very helpful staff, piping hot water in the showers, a nice central courtyard and excellent wi-fi reception. In fact, it has everything required to give hotels twice its price a serious run for their money.

Do, however, ask for a room right at the back away from the noisy road.

Hotel Casino HOTEL $$
(☎443-313-13-28; www.hotelcasino.com.mx; Portal Hidalgo 229; r from M$1067; P @ 📶) Set front and center on the plaza, this place has a very chic and inviting lobby area, which contains perhaps Morelia's best restaurant. The rooms themselves are kind of disappointing for a building as stately as this, but its superb location, professional service and frequent significant discounts make it worth a look.

Hotel Mesón de los Remedios HOTEL $$
(☎443-313-88-10; www.hotelmesonremedios.com; Abasolo 556; r from M$990; 📶) Good value, smart and small family-run place on a side street a few minutes' walk from the main plaza. While the rooms are fairly ordinary to look at they are perfectly maintained and there's a pleasing courtyard to relax in.

★Hotel de la Soledad HISTORIC HOTEL $$$
(☎443-312-18-88; www.hsoledad.com; Zaragoza 90; r from M$1770, ste from M$2800, incl breakfast; P 🚭 📶) Wow! Bougainvillea flowers tumble down stone arches, fountains tinkle, classical music wafts on the breeze and palm trees reach for the skies – and that's all just in the central courtyard. The rooms themselves all differ but expect showers made from ancient stone arches, translucent stone basins, hand-carved wooden bedheads and a general sense of utter class.

Cantera Diez BOUTIQUE HOTEL $$$
(☎443-312-54-19; www.canteradiezhotel.com; Juárez 63; r from M$2860; P ❄ 📶) Facing the cathedral is Morelia's slickest boutique hotel. The 11 rooms are all suites, which range from spacious to palatial, all with dark-wood floors, stylish modern furnishings and sumptuous bathrooms you could throw parties in.

Hotel Virrey de Mendoza HISTORIC HOTEL $$$
(☎443-312-00-45; www.hotelvirrey.com; Av Madero Poniente 310; r from M$1600; P ❄ @ 📶) The lobby is drop-dead gorgeous with a spectacular stained-glass atrium that gives the stained-glass windows of the cathedral a run for their money, and the rooms have an aging grace with old, wood floors and high ceilings – ask for a room with plenty of windows, as some can be dark.

The restaurant does Morelia's swankiest Sunday brunch (mains average M$100), complete with made-to-order omelets, platters of fresh tropical fruits and a dessert table with a flowing chocolate fountain.

Mansión Real Morelia BOUTIQUE HOTEL $$$
(☎443-232-02-46; www.mansionrealmorelia.com; Av Madero Oriente 94; r from M$1400; 📶) The rooms might be small but they are crammed with pomp and a sense of royalty, including ceiling-scraping ornate bedheads and quality bathrooms and mattresses (with a ridiculous amount of pillows piled onto them). There's a lovely courtyard bar and restaurant. Front-facing rooms suffer from road noise despite the soundproofing.

Eating

Morelia enjoys some superb eating options to suit all budgets. Street food can be harder to find, but your searching will be well rewarded.

Licha's MEXICAN $
(Corregidora 669; set meals M$40; ⏰1-5pm) One of Morelia's best deals is this superfriendly place, which serves up what it undersells as *cocina económica* (literally 'economic cuisine') to a crowd of loyal locals. The daily changing set meal includes a choice of delicious starters and main courses as well as a drink.

There's no sign and if you were to go past outside the lunchtime period you wouldn't know the place exists.

Fonda Marceva MEXICAN $
(☎443-312-16-66; Abasolo 455; mains M$50-100; ⏰9am-6pm Tue-Sun) Specializing in the cuisine of the *tierra caliente* (hot lands) region of Michoacán's southeast, this lovely courtyard restaurant serves a mindblowing *aporreadillo*

DON'T MISS

MORELIA CAFES

Grand and colonial or modern and young, Morelia has some wonderful cafes. Here are some of our favourites.

Café del Teatro (Café Galería; cnr Ocampo & Prieto; coffee from M$10; ⏲9am-10pm Mon-Sat, 4-10pm Sun) Inside the Teatro Ocampo, this is an elegant 1st-floor cafe with a jazzy soundtrack and pictures of theatre and cinema greats adorning the walls.

Casa de la Cultura Cafeteria (Av Morelos Norte 485; coffee M$10) Sit under the alcoves of this cafe, which is inside the Casa de la Cultura, and listen to the soft notes of live classical music while you sip on a caffeine-infused pick-me-up.

Cafe Europa (www.cafeeuropa.com.mx; Bartolomé de las Casas 97; coffee from M$8; ⏲9am-8.30pm Mon-Sat) Part of a chain of local cafes, this tiny place would be easy to miss were it not for the aroma of roasting coffee beans seeping out of the doorway.

(breakfast stew of eggs, dried beef and chili) and some of the best *frijoles de olla* (beans slow-cooked in a pot) we've ever tasted.

Mesón Agustinos CHURROS $

(Hidalgo 54; churros M$12-13 for 3, mains M$50-90) Although this is one of the few cheap city-centre options where you can get a proper sit-down meal in the evening, it's actually better known for its *churros* and hot chocolate.

Gaspachos La Cerrada SALAD BAR $

(Hidalgo 67; gaspachos M$25; ✎) *Gaspacho* – a salad of diced mango, pineapple and jicama, drowned in orange and lime juice and dashed with salt, chili sauce and cheese (optional) – is a local delicacy served all over town. But according to locals, this place is the best.

Mercado Nicolás Bravo MARKET $

(Mercado Santo Niño, Bravo; snacks M$20-50; ⏲7am-5pm) Here you'll find great food stalls on the 2nd floor. Try stall 127 for Doña Feli's locally famous *birria*.

Plaza San Agustín MEXICAN $

(cnr Abasolo & Corregidora; ⏲1-11pm) A few cheap food stalls with lots of tables can be found under the covered arches here.

★**Restaurante Lu** MEXICAN $$

(☎443-313-13-28; www.lucocinamichoacana.mx; Portal Hidalgo 229; mains M$120-180; ⏲7:30am-10pm Mon-Thu & Sun, to 11pm Fri & Sat) This unassuming restaurant inside Hotel Casino is actually Morelia's most inventive place to dine and one of the best restaurants in the whole region. Talented young chef Lucero Soto Arriaga turns pre-Hispanic ingredients into exquisite gems of *alta cocina,* all beautifully presented. Her four-course tasting menu (with/without wine M$380/285) is well worth dedicating a long lunch to.

Pulcinella ITALIAN $$

(Allende 555; mains M$100-200; ⏲2-10pm Wed-Fri, 2-11pm Sat, 2-7pm Sun) This respected Italian restaurant has a reputation for fresh and delicious fare. Housed in a converted colonial house and run by a charming family, Pulcinella's specialty is its pizzas, but there's a full range of pastas, salads and meat dishes available, too.

Los Mirasoles MEXICAN $$$

(☎443-317-57-75; www.losmirasoles.com; Av Madero Poniente 549; mains M$120-300, tasting menu M$400; ⏲1-11pm Mon-Sat, to 6pm Sun) Authentic Michoacán cooking is served up in the sumptuous premises here – try the four-course tasting menu (M$225) for a culinary tour de force. Specialties include Tarascan soup, *jahuácatas* (triangular unfilled *tamales*) with pork and chili, and a pork shank in pulque sauce. There's also a huge wine list.

Fonda Las Mercedes MEXICAN $$$

(☎443-312-61-13; Guzmán 47; mains M$150-200; ⏲1:30pm-midnight Mon-Sat, noon-8pm Sun) The bar ceiling at this hip, upscale spot is embedded with 200 clay pots, the intimate courtyard dining room is decorated with old stone columns and spheres, and the kitchen serves four cuts of steak 10 different ways.

Drinking & Nightlife

Nightlife is more genteel than rowdy, though a few clubs keep the music pumping into the wee hours. Around the Jardin de las Rosas are masses of bars with terraces that bubble with life in the early evening. Another hot spot is the area around the Fuente Las Tarascas at the eastern end of the city centre. The names of bars and clubs change constantly.

★**Casa de la Salsa** DANCING

(☎443-313-93-62; Plaza Morelos 121; admission free; ⏲2-9pm Mon-Fri, live salsa music & dancing 9:30pm-2:30am Wed-Sat) Locals converge to shake their collective ass to a rocking four-piece band on a raised stage in this dark, cavernous club. Don't worry, this is not one of those snooty, show-off salsa clubs, so feel free to get loose. Tequila and beer are dirt cheap, which makes the atmosphere lots of fun.

Dancing isn't confined to the hours of darkness either. Fancy a whirl at 4pm on a working Tuesday? No problem! If dancing's not your thing, then there's also a bunch of pool tables.

Balcones del Ángel BAR
(443-333-32-33; Garcia Obeso 159; 6pm-midnight Tue-Thu, 6pm-1am Fri & Sat) A hip and beautiful crowd gathers in this open courtyard lounge on the top floor of a 17th-century building just south of the cathedral. The design is seamless, the music bounces between global pop and electronic tunes, and the glowing dome of the cathedral is visible through the open roof.

Entertainment

Being a university town and the capital of one of Mexico's most interesting states, Morelia has a thriving cultural life. Stop by the tourist office or the Casa de la Cultura for *Cartelera Cultural,* a free weekly listing of films and cultural events.

For international films, dance, music and art exhibitions check what's up at the **Casa de la Cultura** (443-313-12-68; Av Morelos Norte 485), a hive of creative energy with music and dance classes and a cool coffeehouse set in an old colonial palace.

For theater experiences visit the **Teatro Ocampo** (443-313-16-79; cnr Ocampo & Prieto) or **Teatro Morelos** (443-314-62-02; www.ceconexpo.com; cnr Camelinas & Ventura Puente); the latter is part of the Centro de Convenciones complex, 1.5km south of the city center. **Cinépolis** (443-312-12-88; www.cinepolis.com; cnr Gómez Farías & Tapia) screens blockbusters in English with subtitles or dubbed Spanish.

Conservatorio de las Rosas (443-312-14-69; www.conservatoriodelasrosas.edu.mx; Tapia 334), the oldest music conservatory in the Americas, has free concerts every Thursday at 8pm. It's pretty cloisters make it worth a look at any time though. The cathedral (p608) has occasional impressive organ recitals.

Shopping

Casa de las Artesanías MARKET
(443-317-25-81; Ex-Convento de San Francisco, Plaza Valladolid; 10am-2pm & 5-7:30pm) If you don't have time to scour the Purépecha pueblos for the perfect folk-art piece, come to the House of Handicrafts, inside the Ex-Convento de San Francisco. It's a cooperative marketplace launched to benefit indigenous craftspeople and arts, and handicrafts from all over Michoacán are displayed and sold here.

SWEETS IN MORELIA

Dulces morelianos – delicious sweets made with ingredients such as fruit, nuts, milk and sugar – are famous throughout the region. They're showcased at Morelia's Mercado de Dulces and at **Museo del Dulce** (Av Madero Oriente 440; sweets from M$5). This old-fashioned *chocolatería* is stacked with truffles, preserves, candied nuts and sugary chunks of candied peaches and pumpkin, and patrolled by women in starched green uniforms.

Watch for these tasty treats.

- *Ate de fruta* – jewel-colored squares or strips of fruit leather, commonly made from guava, mango and quince.
- *Cocadas* – chewy-crunchy pyramids of caramelized coconut.
- *Frutas cubiertas* – chunks of candied fruits such as squash, fig and pineapple.
- *Glorias* – cellophane-wrapped rolls of caramel studded with pecans.
- *Jamoncillo* – fudge-like milk sweets sold in rectangles or molded into shapes like walnuts.
- *Limón con coco* – candied lime halves stuffed with sweetened shredded coconut.
- *Obleas con cajeta* – gooey caramel sandwiched between two thin round wafers.
- *Ollitas de tamarindo* – tiny clay pots filled with sweet-salty-tangy tamarind paste.

Mercado de Dulces MARKET
(Sweets Market; Gómez Farías; ⊙9am-10pm) This seductive market, on the western side of the Palacio Clavijero, deals in the region's famous sweets, including a rainbow selection of *ate de fruta* (fruit leather) in a variety of exotic flavors.

Information

DANGERS & ANNOYANCES

Violent gang warfare has scarred Michoacán for years, most recently following the decline of the La Familia drug cartel, which was quickly replaced by the Caballeros Templarios (Knights Templar), a group of drug-dealing Christian zealots who have killed scores of people around the state. Fortunately, bystanders are very rarely impacted by drug violence in Michoacán. Travelers are unlikely to face anything out of the ordinary except for a higher-than-average army and police presence in some places throughout the state.

MEDICAL SERVICES

Hospital Star Médica (☎443-322-77-00; www.starmedica.com; Virrey de Mendoza 2000)

MONEY

Banks and ATMs are plentiful around the plaza, particularly on and near Avenida Madero.

POST

Main Post Office (Av Madero Oriente 369)

TOURIST INFORMATION

CAT Centro de Atención al Turista (☎443-312-04-14; Portal Hidalgo 245; city tours per person M$150; ⊙9am-9pm) This reasonably helpful tourist office can dole out a few leaflets and offers daily city tours.

Getting There & Around

AIR

The **Francisco J Mújica Airport** (☎443-317-67-80; www.aeropuertosgap.com.mx) is 27km north of Morelia, on the Morelia–Zinapécuaro Hwy. There are no public buses, but taxis to the airport cost M$200. Plenty of flights are available to cities in Mexico and limited flights serve destinations elsewhere in North America.

Airlines servicing Morelia include the following:

Aeromar (☎443-324-67-78; www.aeromar.com.mx; Hotel Fiesta Inn, Pirindas 435)

Volaris (☎800-122-80-00; www.volaris.mx)

BUS & COMBI

Morelia's bus terminal is about 4km northwest of the city center. It's separated into three *módulos,* which correspond to 1st-, 2nd- and 3rd-class buses. To get into town from here take a Roja 1 combi (red) from under the pedestrian bridge, or catch a taxi (M$40). First-class buses depart hourly or more frequently for most destinations.

Around town, small combis and buses operate from 6am until 10pm daily (M$7). Combi routes are designated by the color of their stripe: Ruta Roja (red), Ruta Amarilla (yellow), Ruta Rosa (pink), Ruta Azul (blue), Ruta Verde (green), Ruta Cafe (brown) and so on. Ask at the tourist office for help with bus and combi routes.

Reserva Mariposa Monarca

In the easternmost corner of Michoacán, straddling the border of México state, lies the incredible 563-sq-km **Reserva Mariposa Monarca** (Monarch Butterfly Reserve; adult/child M$45/35; ⊙6am-6pm mid-Nov–Mar). Every autumn, from late October to early November, millions of monarch butterflies flock to these forested Mexican highlands for their winter hibernation, having flown all the way from the Great Lakes region of the US and Canada, some 4500km away. As they close in on their destination they gather in gentle swarms, crossing highways and fluttering up steep mountainsides where they cling together in clusters that weigh down thick branches of the *oyenal* (fir) trees. When the sun rises and warms the forest, they take to the sky in gold and orange flurries, descending to the humid

BUSES FROM MORELIA

DESTINATION	FARE (M$)	DURATION	FREQUENCY (DAILY)
Colima	363	2hr	6
Guadalajara	334	4hr	hourly
Mexico City (Terminal Norte)	360	4¾hr	every 30min
Pátzcuaro	38-53	1hr	every 30min
Uruapan	100-130	2hr	hourly
Zitácuaro	120	3hr	hourly

forest floor for the hottest part of the day. By midafternoon they often carpet the ground brilliantly. The best time to see them is on a warm, sunny afternoon in February – they don't fly as much in cool weather.

In the warm spring temperatures of March the butterflies reach their sexual maturity and the real fun begins – mating. When the vernal equinox strikes (March 20 or 21), pregnant females fly north to the southeastern US, where they lay their eggs in milkweed and die fulfilled. Their eggs hatch into caterpillars that feed on the milkweed, then make cocoons and emerge in late May as new butterflies. These young monarchs flutter back to the Great Lakes, where they breed, so that by mid-August yet another generation is ready to start the long trip south. This is one of the most complex animal migrations on earth and scientists still have no idea how or why they do it.

Though monarch butterflies are not in danger of extinction, the migratory behavior of this particular population is threatened by insecticides and habitat destruction in both Mexico and the US. Some organizations are trying to change these patterns by offering local communities incentives to not only protect their remaining forests, but also to restore habitat via tree-planting projects. For more information check the www.monarchwatch.org website.

The publicly accessible part of the reserve is divided into three areas that are open to visitors from roughly mid-November through March, but exact opening dates depend on weather, temperatures and the butterflies' arrival. El Rosario and Sierra Chincua are the most popular reserve areas. Both are accessible from Angangueo. Angangueo is the closest town to Sierra Chincua (just 8km away) and the best base for this end of the reserve. El Rosario is close to the pueblo of the same name and can be reached from Angangueo via Ocampo. Cerro Pelón is the newest reserve area and has the healthiest habitat. It's best reached from Zitácuaro.

At the beginning or end of the season ask for information on butterfly activity at the Morelia or Mexico City tourist offices before visiting the reserve. However, in the couple of weeks leading up to the official opening of the reserves and the couple of weeks after they close again it's still possible to visit and, hopefully, see plenty of early arriving or late leaving butterflies. Even though the reserves are technically closed at this time the standard entry fees and guiding fees apply. In fact, you can visit the reserves at any time and even though there might not be any butterflies present there are always plenty of birds and other animals. Some people do day trips or tours from Morelia or Mexico City to see the butterflies, but this means more than eight hours of travel in one day. It's better to take your time and enjoy this unique and beautiful region.

The reserve areas are spread out, and most people only visit one. But even though the butterflies look and behave the same in each spot the changing weather does affect the butterflies behavior and the truly interested probably will find a great deal of value in visiting all three reserves on different days.

The daily admission fee for each reserve area is the same and local guides are compulsory (available at entry gates). Note that the length of your hike/horseback ride will be shorter later in the season – the butterflies work their way down as the weather warms up.

HIGH IS WHERE IT HAPPENS

Monarch butterflies like basking at altitude, so getting to them requires hiking (or horseback riding) up to 3000m. Hike slowly, remember to take plenty of breaks (and water) and be aware of the symptoms of altitude sickness.

El Rosario

El Rosario is the most popular area but during the height of butterfly voyeurism (February and March) it gets as many as 8000 visitors a day. It is also the most commercial – souvenir stalls abound on the hillside and the habitat has been severely impacted by illegal logging. El Rosario village and the entrance to the El Rosario reserve area are located about 12km up a good gravel road from the small village of Ocampo. Getting to the butterflies requires a steep hike (or horseback ride) of 2km to 4km from the reserve's parking lot, depending on the time of year. There are a couple of hotels in Ocampo, but it's a far more pleasant experience to stay in the village of Angangueo (just 45 minutes on foot from Ocampo). Guide fees here are M$50 and horses cost M$90.

Sierra Chincua

Sierra Chincua is 8km beyond Angangueo, way up in the mountains. This area has also been damaged by logging, but not as badly as El Rosario. It's a less strenuous hike, so this sanctuary is for those who want an easier walk. Guide fees here are M$50 and horses cost M$90. To get here from Angangueo take the 'Tlalpujahua' bus (M$5) or a taxi (return M$150).

Cerro Pelón

Cerro Pelón, which is actually located in México state, is the newest reserve area and by far the best choice. The mountains rise high (more than 3000m) here, the forest is in great shape and there is barely a trickle of tourism (on its busiest day it may get 80 visitors; you'll usually find yourself all alone on the mountain). Logging has been eliminated and local guides have replanted trees for years to restore habitat. Expect to see huge, cathedral fir trees, moss-covered trunks, wildflowers and incredible canyon views.

Be warned that the climb here is very steep and the relentless ascent takes a good mountain walker at least 1½ to two hours going at a fair pace and without stopping. People not used to mountain walking are likely to struggle. Most people choose to ascend the mountain on horseback (M$200). Camping in a natural meadow just below Cerro Pelón peak, only an hour's hike from where the butterflies gather in the early season, is a terrific option for the self-sufficient (although you will need to go with a guide). Guides will arrange *burros* to haul the heavy stuff up the mountain. Guides charge M$200.

This reserve area is about a 40-minute drive southeast of Zitácuaro, Michoacán's third-largest city, where you can buy necessary food, water and supplies. There are a couple of access points – Macheros and El Capulín. Both are within 1.5km of each other and can be reached by public transportation from outside Zitácuaro's bus terminal (take a bus marked 'Aputzio,' for M$13, which goes as far as the border to México state, then a taxi, which will cost M$20 to M$30). A taxi straight from Zitácuaro to either of the reserve areas costs M$200 to M$250.

Sleeping

JM's B&B B&B $$

(☎726-596-31-17, cell phone 715-1125499; www.jmbutterflybnb.com; Macheros; s/d incl breakfast M$550/600) This newly constructed B&B in the heart of the pretty village of Macheros makes a great overnight base for the Cerro Pelón reserve. Rooms are spacious and have beautiful valley and mountain views. Meals are available and the owner speaks excellent English. It's best to phone in advance.

Angangueo

☎715 / POP 4600 / ELEV 2980M

This drowsy old mining town is the most popular base for butterfly-watchers because it's close to both the Sierra Chincua and the El Rosario sanctuaries. Most services can be found along a single main drag with two names (Nacional and Morelos). There are two attractive churches on Plaza de la Constitución, the center of town, from which Nacional runs down the hill.

Tours

Mario Bernal Martínez TOUR

(☎715-156-03-22; www.marioecotours.com) Knowledgeable and entertaining tours of the butterfly reserves and surrounding region are organised by English-speaking Mario Bernal Martínez for around M$600 per group for the standard butterfly tour.

Sleeping & Eating

Accommodation is fairly basic and be warned that none of the places to stay have any form of heating (except some of the rooms at the Albergue Don Bruno that have wood fires) and it gets very, very cold up here at night. Unless you've just flown in from the Arctic tundra you'll want several layers of thick clothing and you'll probably sleep in them as well! Most guesthouses do food, but there are a couple of taco stands up on the main plaza as well as a restaurant or two.

Hotel Plaza Don Gabino GUESTHOUSE $

(☎715-153-19-26; hotelplazagabino@hotmail.com; Morelos 147; r M$350; P ☰) By far the best of the town's guesthouses, this family-run and exceptionally welcoming place has sparkling clean rooms, hot-water showers (that work!) and a restaurant serving an excellent four-course dinner. It's around a kilometer downhill from the central plaza (ask the bus driver to drop you off here).

Albergue Don Bruno HOTEL $$
(☎715-156-00-26; Morelos 92; s/d from M$550/650; P 📶) The best established hotel in town offers a fairly cold welcome, very cold carpeted rooms (although some have fireplaces – get one!) and an erratic supply of hot water.

Information

Tourist Office (☎715-156-00-44; ⏲8am-8pm Nov-Apr) The small tourist office is just downhill from the plaza.

Getting There & Away

Frequent buses from Morelia go first to Zitácuaro (M$120, three hours), where you'll catch another bus to Angangueo (M$18, 1¼ hours). From Mexico City's Terminal Poniente you can take Autobuses MTZ (M$140, four hours, two hourly) direct to Angangueo; most of the rest of the bus lines go through Zitácuaro.

To reach the El Rosario sanctuary from Angangueo, first take a combi to Ocampo (M$10, 15 minutes, hourly), then another to El Rosario (M$18, 30 minutes, hourly), from the corner of Independencia and Ocampo. In season there are also *camionetas* (pickup trucks) that leave from the *auditorio* (auditorium) in Angangueo, or from outside hotels; these cost about M$600 for around 10 people and take 45 bumpy minutes (via a back road) to reach the sanctuary.

Zitácuaro

☎715 / POP 84,000 / ELEV 1940M

Zitácuaro is Michoacán's third-largest city, but it feels like a provincial working-class town. Known primarily for its baked bread and its trout farms, it's no great looker, but it's a sensible base for visiting the butterflies at Cerro Pelón.

Zitácuaro's bus terminal is 1km from the city center. There are frequent buses to and from Morelia (M$120, three hours), Angangueo (M$18, 1¼ hours) and Mexico City Poniente (M$153 to M$179, two hours), among other destinations.

Sights

Iglesia de San Pancho CHURCH
(⏲9am-2pm & 4-7pm) The Iglesia de San Pancho in the village of San Pancho, just south of Zitácuaro, is a restored 16th-century church that appeared in the great John Huston–Humphrey Bogart film, *The Treasure of the Sierra Madre*, and was visited by Prince Charles in 2002. Come at sunset when light streams through the stained glass. A taxi from town costs M$40.

Sleeping

★**Rancho San Cayetano** HOTEL $$$
(☎715-153-19-26; www.ranchosancayetano.com; Carretera a Huetamo Km 2.3; r from M$1530; P @ 📶 🏊) The best hotel in the entire butterfly region, the Rancho San Cayetano is owned and run by English- and French-speaking Pablo and Lisette. The grounds are huge with stands of pine and fruit trees. Rooms are rustic chic with exposed stone walls and beamed ceilings. And its multi-course, gourmet meals (reserve in advance) are superb.

Pablo is passionate about butterflies and offers detailed maps, driving directions and shows background videos to interested guests. He can also arrange transportation to and from the sanctuaries.

Pátzcuaro

☎434 / POP 55,000 / ELEV 2175M

This small, well-preserved colonial town in the Michoacán highlands is the beating commercial heart of Purépecha country. Indigenous craftspeople from surrounding villages journey here to sell their wares, and their presence, as well as Pátzcuaro's dramatic history and gorgeous architecture, infuses the town with a palpable mystical energy.

Its center is defined by impressive old churches – including a hillside basilica – dusty, cobbled streets, tiled adobe buildings brushed white and reddish-brown, and two bustling plazas: Plaza Vasco de Quiroga (known as Plaza Grande) and the smaller Plaza Gertrudis Bocanegra (popularly known as Plaza Chica).

Just 3km to the north lies scenic Lago de Pátzcuaro, ringed by traditional Purépecha villages and sprinkled with a few islands. Isla Janitzio is Mexico's biggest party magnet during early November's Día de Muertos, when Mexican tourists flock to Pátzcuaro, though plenty also come for Christmas, New Year and Semana Santa. Make advance reservations during holidays and bring warm clothes from November to February – you're at altitude here and it gets frigid.

History

Pátzcuaro was the capital of the Tarasco people (now known as the Purépecha) from about AD 1325 to 1400. After the death of King Tariácuri, the Tarascan state became a three-part league. Comprising Pátzcuaro, Tzintzuntzan and Ihuatzio, the league repulsed repeated Aztec attacks, which may explain why they welcomed the Spanish, who first arrived in 1522. Bad idea. The Spanish returned in 1529 under Nuño de Guzmán, a vicious conquistador.

Guzmán's six-year reign over the indigenous people was brutal, even for those times. The colonial government recalled Guzmán to Spain, where he was arrested and locked up for life, and dispatched Bishop Vasco de Quiroga, a respected judge and cleric from Mexico City, to clean up his mess. Quiroga was an impressively enlightened man. When he arrived in 1536, he established village cooperatives based on the humanitarian ideals of Sir Thomas More's *Utopia*.

To avoid dependence on Spanish mining lords and landowners, Quiroga successfully encouraged education and agricultural self-sufficiency in the Purépecha villages around Lago de Pátzcuaro, with all villagers contributing equally to the community. He also helped each village develop its own craft specialty, from masks to pottery to guitars and violins. The utopian communities declined after his death in 1565, but the crafts traditions continue to this day. Not surprisingly, Tata Vascu, as the Tarascos called Quiroga, has not been forgotten. You'll notice that streets, plazas, restaurants and hotels all over Michoacán are named after him.

Sights

★Plaza Vasco de Quiroga (Plaza Grande) — PLAZA

Pátzcuaro's leafy main plaza is one of Mexico's best hangout spots. It is framed by the 17th-century facades of old mansions that have since been converted to hotels, shops and restaurants, and watched over by a serene **statue of Vasco de Quiroga**, which rises from the central fountain. The arched sides of the plaza are full of food stalls, jewelry and folk-art sellers, and the atmosphere, particularly on the weekend when bands play and street performers entertain, is wonderful.

Museo de Artes Populares — MUSEUM

(☎434-342-10-29; cnr Enseñanza & Alcantarillas; admission M$42; ⏲9am-5pm Tue-Sun) Highlights of this impressive folk-art museum include a room set up as a typical Michoacán kitchen, cases of gorgeous jewelry, and an entire room filled with *retablos* – crudely rendered devotional paintings offering thanks to God for saving the owner from illness or accident.

The museum is housed on the site of the former Colegio de San Nicolás, arguably the Americas' first university, founded by Quiroga in 1540. The building was constructed on pre-Hispanic stone foundations, some of which can be seen behind the museum courtyards.

Plaza Gertrudis Bocanegra (Plaza Chica) — PLAZA

Pátzcuaro's second plaza is named after a local heroine who was shot by firing squad in 1818 for her support of the independence movement. Her statue commands the center of the plaza.

The local **market** on the west side of the plaza is where you can find everything from fruit, vegetables and fresh trout to herbal medicines, crafts and clothing – including the region's distinctive striped shawls and *sarapes*. There's outstanding cheap food, too. A tumbledown **Mercado de Artesanías** operates on the side street adjacent to the library. Wooden masks and pastel crucifixes are among the crafts sold here. The quality varies but prices are low.

Biblioteca Gertrudis Bocanegra — LIBRARY

(☎434-342-54-41; cnr Padre Lloreda & Títere; ⏲9am-7pm Mon-Fri, 10am-1pm Sat) On the north side of Plaza Chica is the town library. Occupying the cavernous interior of the 16th-century San Agustín church, this is the kind of library other libraries dream of imitating. There are oyster-shell skylights and a massive, colorful Juan O'Gorman mural on the rear wall that depicts the history of Michoacán from pre-Hispanic times to the 1910 revolution.

On the west side of the library, the **Teatro Emperador Caltzontzin** was a convent until it was converted into a theater in 1936; it hosts occasional films and performances.

★Basílica de Nuestra Señora de la Salud — CHURCH

(Plaza de la Basílica) This gorgeous church, built on the hill atop a pre-Hispanic

Pátzcuaro

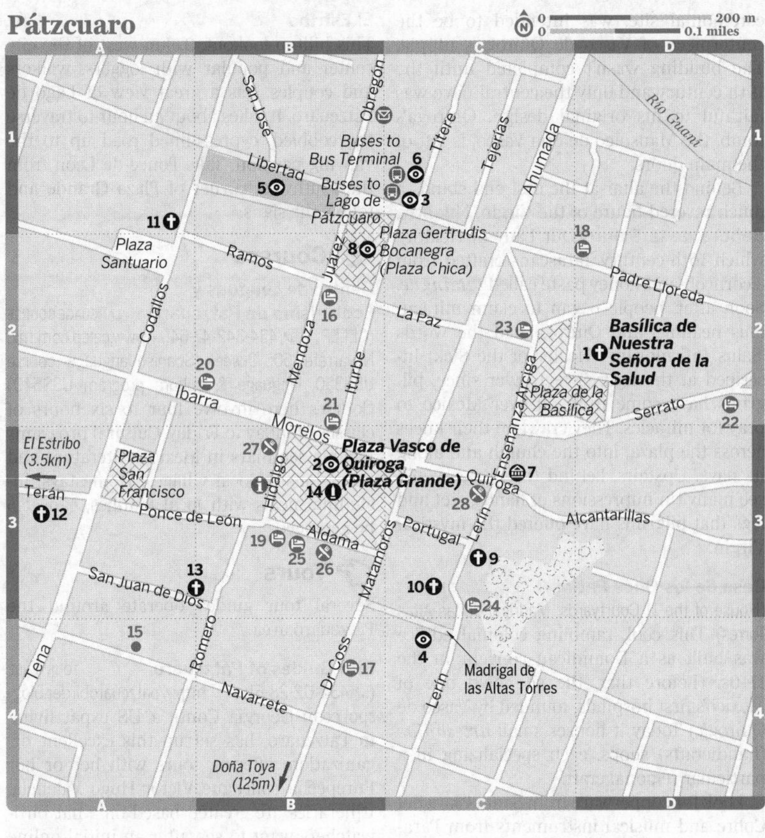

Pátzcuaro

Top Sights
1 Basílica de Nuestra Señora de la Salud D2
2 Plaza Vasco de Quiroga (Plaza Grande) B3

Sights
3 Biblioteca Gertrudis Bocanegra C1
4 Casa de los Once Patios C4
5 Market B1
6 Mercado de Artesanías C1
7 Museo de Artes Populares C3
8 Plaza Gertrudis Bocanegra (Plaza Chica) B2
9 Templo de la Compañía C3
10 Templo del Sagrario C3
11 Templo El Santuario A1
12 Templo San Francisco A3
13 Templo San Juan de Dios B3
14 Vasco de Quiroga Statue B3

Activities, Courses & Tours
15 Centro de Lenguas y Ecoturismo de Pátzcuaro A4

Sleeping
16 Hotel Casa del Refugio B2
17 Hotel Casa Encantada B4
18 Hotel Casa Shanarani D2
19 Hotel Misión San Manuel B3
20 La Mansión de los Sueños B2
21 Mansión Iturbe B2
22 Mesón de San Antonio D2
23 Posada de la Basílica C2
24 Posada Mandala C3
25 Posada San Rafael B3

Eating
26 El Patio B3
27 La Surtidora B3
Priscilla's .... (see 20)
28 Restaurant Lupita C3

ceremonial site, was intended to be the centerpiece of Vasco de Quiroga's utopia. The building wasn't completed until the 19th century and only the central nave was faithful to his original design. Quiroga's tomb, the Mausoleo de don Vasco, is left of the main doors.

Behind the altar at the east end stands a much revered figure of the Virgin, **Nuestra Señora de la Salud** (Our Lady of Health), which 16th-century Tarascans crafted from a corncob-and-honey paste called *tatzingue*. Soon after, people began to claim miraculous healings and Quiroga had the words 'Salus Infirmorum' (Healer of the Sick) inscribed at the figure's feet. Ever since, pilgrims have come from all over Mexico to pray for miracles. They crawl on their knees across the plaza, into the church and along its nave. Upstairs, behind the image, you'll see many tin impressions of hands, feet and legs that pilgrims have offered the mystical Virgin.

Casa de los Once Patios MARKET

(House of the 11 Courtyards; Madrigal de las Altas Torres) This cool, rambling colonial edifice was built as a Dominican convent in the 1740s. (Before that, the site held one of Mexico's first hospitals, founded by Vasco de Quiroga.) Today it houses small *artesanías* (handicrafts) shops, each specializing in a particular regional craft.

Look for copperware from Santa Clara del Cobre and musical instruments from Paracho, as well as lacquerware, hand-painted ceramics and vibrant textiles. Be sure to check out the **Baño Barroco**, a 16th-century bathing room.

Churches CHURCH

Built in the 16th century, the **Templo de la Compañía** (cnr Lerín & Portugal) became a Jesuit training college in the 17th century. The church is still in use and houses some Vasco de Quiroga relics. The adjacent college building fell into ruin after the expulsion of the Jesuits. It is now used for community activities and often has free temporary exhibits.

Pátzcuaro has several other old churches of interest, including the creaky **Templo del Sagrario** (cnr Lerín & Portugal), **Templo San Juan de Dios** (cnr Romero & San Juan de Dios), the pink stone **Templo San Francisco** (Tena) and **Templo El Santuario** (cnr Ramos & Codallos).

El Estribo HILL

This hilltop lookout, 3.5km west of the city center and popular with joggers, walkers and couples, has a great view of Lago de Pátzcuaro. It takes about an hour to traverse the cobbled, cypress-lined road up to the viewing pavilion. Take Ponce de León from the southwest corner of Plaza Grande and follow the signs.

Courses

Centro de Lenguas y Ecoturismo de Pátzcuaro LANGUAGE COURSE

(CELEP; 434-342-47-64; www.celep.com.mx; Navarrete 50; 2-week Spanish-language course US$350, language & culture program US$540) Courses here involve four to six hours of classes Monday to Friday. Cultural programs include seminars in Mexican literature and excursions to local villages. Homestays, including meals with local families, can also be arranged.

Tours

Several tour guides operate around the Pátzcuaro area.

Bird Guides of Pátzcuaro TOUR GUIDE

(434-112-28-61; http://patzcuarobirder.blogspot.com) Georgia Conti, a US expat living in Pátzcuaro, has set up this excellent organization, offering tours with her or her Purépecha colleague Victor Hugo Valencia. Itineraries are created based on what birdwatchers want to see after an initial online chat. Daily rates are from US$60 for two people including transportation, with extras charged for meals and other incidentals. Contact Georgia via her blog to find out what she proposes for you.

Festivals & Events

The villages around Pátzcuaro, most notably Tzintzuntzan and Isla Janitzio, stage the most popular (and crowded!) **Día de Muertos** (Day of the Dead; November 1 & 2) celebrations in Mexico. Parades, crafts markets, dancing, ceremonies, exhibitions and concerts are held in and around Pátzcuaro on the days before and after Día de Muertos. Cemeteries are packed with observants throughout the festivities.

Semana Santa RELIGIOUS

Easter week is full of events in Pátzcuaro and the lakeside villages, including Palm Sunday processions; Viacrucis processions on Good

Friday morning, enacting Christ's journey to Calvary and the crucifixion; candlelit processions in silence on Good Friday evening; and, on Easter Sunday evening, a ceremonial burning of Judas in Plaza Grande.

Nuestra Señora de la Salud RELIGIOUS

On December 8 a colorful procession to the basilica honors Our Lady of Health. Traditional dances are performed, including Los Reboceros, Los Moros, Los Viejitos and Los Panaderos.

Pastorelas RELIGIOUS

These dramatizations of the shepherds' journey to see the infant Jesus are staged in Plaza Grande around Christmas. *Pastorelas indígenas,* on the same theme but including mask dances, enact the struggle of angels against the devils that are trying to hinder the shepherds. These *pastorelas* are held in eight villages around Lago de Pátzcuaro, on different days between December 26 and February 2.

Sleeping

Pátzcuaro has an excellent range of attractive places to stay and caters to all budgets. Despite this, it's usually worth booking ahead for Friday and Saturday nights, and months ahead for Día de Muertos, when the entire town is booked up well in advance. By contrast at all other times you need normally only raise an eyebrow at the more expensive places to see prices tumbling by up to 50% – you're on holiday so indulge in some luxury!

Posada Mandala GUESTHOUSE $

(434-342-41-76; Lerín 14; r M$300-500, without bathroom M$200;) Arty international travelers love this low-profile guesthouse, with six simple, whitewashed rooms surrounding a small plant-filled courtyard. The best rooms are those upstairs, with their own facilities and great views over the rooftops of Pátzcuaro. Weekly pizza nights are held here. Make sure you're a part of it!

Posada San Rafael HOTEL $

(434-342-07-70; Portal Aldama 13; s/d M$300/420; P) The love child of a colonial mission and a US motel, rooms open onto wide verandas overlooking a driveway and parking area filled with plants. Hot water is limited to mornings and evenings, but upstairs rooms are a great deal, with plenty of beautiful details such as columns and beamed ceilings.

Hotel Misión San Manuel HOTEL $

(434-342-10-50; misionsanmanuel5@hotmail.com; Portal Aldama 12; r from M$413;) Behind a startling white exterior is a cheap hotel that stands out for its stone-carved window frames and dramatic columns and arches. Any damsels in distress reading this will be relieved to hear that a knight in armor also awaits them here. The rooms themselves are modern and the bathrooms disappointing.

Hotel Casa del Refugio BOUTIQUE HOTEL $$

(434-342-55-05; www.casadelrefugio.com.mx; Portal Régules 9; d from M$800;) With adobe walls covered in religious motifs and portraits of saints (and possibly a few sinners), a palm-filled atrium with an enormous open fireplace and small, but immaculate rooms, this welcoming hotel might just be the best deal in town. It is sure to put a smile on many a traveller's face.

Mesón de San Antonio GUESTHOUSE $$

(434-342-25-01; www.mesondesanantonio.com; Serrato 33; s/d M$600/750; @) Rooms at this great-value old hacienda-style inn border an impressive colonial courtyard; the beamed overhangs are held up by ancient timbers and the extremely cozy rooms are decorated with fine Purépecha pottery and have wood-burning fireplaces and cable TV. There's also a communal kitchen for self-caterers.

Hotel Casa Encantada B&B $$

(434-342-34-92; www.hotelcasaencantada.com; Dr Coss 15; r incl breakfast M$895-1320; P @) If you are craving affordable luxury, this intimate American-owned B&B offers 12 elegant rooms with local rugs and beautifully tiled bathrooms in a converted 1784 mansion. Many of the rooms are enormous and some come with kitchenettes. Ask for a room at the rear of the property as those at the front suffer from road noise.

Hotel Casa Shanarani BOUTIQUE HOTEL $$$

(434-342-05-12; Padre Lloreda 27; s/d/tr M$1000/1200/1400; P) Beaming angels, walls of candles and old gramophones sit merrily alongside Moroccan lamps at this character-rammed hotel. The small rooms are painted in florid colours, the bathrooms come scattered with beach pebbles and there's a pretty little garden. All up we like this place a lot. Some people might know it by its former name of Hostal Santa Fe.

Mansión Iturbe BOUTIQUE HOTEL $$$
(434-342-03-68; www.mansioniturbe.com; Morelos 59; r incl breakfast M$2800;) Right on the main square, the rooms here are spacious, old-world style and are furnished in heavy dark woods crammed full of antiques, and come with sumptuous bathrooms. There's a wonderful terrace out the back and the feel is one of luxurious sophistication.

The rack rates are steep, but in reality outside of festival periods there are often big discounts of up to 70%, which means it's one of the first places you should head to.

Posada de la Basílica BOUTIQUE HOTEL $$$
(434-342-11-08; Arciga 6; s/d M$1000/1500;) For rustic luxury, consider this boutique hotel with a terracotta rooftop and lake views. The surprisingly bright colonial building contains 12 huge rooms with wood floors and open fireplaces. The master suites are truly special, and the entire place exudes elegance, charm and understatement.

La Mansión de los Sueños BOUTIQUE HOTEL $$$
(434-342-11-03; http://lamansiondelossuenos.com/index-e.html; Ibarra 15; d incl breakfast from M$2712;) This restored mansion built around three adjacent courtyards offers some of the most luxurious accommodations in town. There is art on every wall, coffee machines and minibars in each room, and even fireplaces and lofts in some. To be fair though, the decor in some rooms verges on being tacky so ask to see a few before hopping into bed.

Eating

Pátzcuaro has wonderful street food – look out for *corundas* (triangular *tamales* served with and without fillings), bright green *atole de grano* (an anise-flavored local variant of the popular corn-based drink), *nieve de pasta* (almond and cinnamon ice cream) and chunks of candied squash. Some of the best chow can be found at the food stalls in the open-air market on the northwest corner of the Plaza Chica. If it's *corundas* you're after, head to the basilica in the morning and look for the elderly ladies with baskets.

Most restaurants are attached to hotels and naturally enough most cater primarily for here-today-and-gone-tomorrow tourists and are fussy and mediocre. There are, however, some exceptions. Keep your eyes open for *sopa tarasca,* a rich tomato-based soup with cream, dried chili and bits of crisp tortilla.

★ **Doña Toya** MEXICAN $
(Dr Coss 68; sopes M$8; 7-10:30pm Tue-Sun) At the top of a cobblestone hill and behind an unmarked red door (look for the Coca-Cola sign), Doña Toya serves up the city's finest *sopes* – disks of fried masa (dough) topped with shredded meat, salsa, squeezed lime and fresh cilantro – at little plastic tables in her home's front room. Look no further for a true local dining experience, not to mention one of the best and cheapest meals in town.

La Surtidora MEXICAN $
(434-342-28-35; Hidalgo 71; mains M$30-140; 8am-10pm;) Waiters dress in chef whites and take good care of their clientele at this old-school cafe-cum-deli, which has been operating on Plaza Grande since 1916. The interior is perfumed with roasting coffee, and it serves what are without doubt the best breakfasts in town (you may have to queue for a table) as well as classic Mexican mains.

Restaurant Lupita INTERNATIONAL $$
(434-345-06-59; Quiroga 5; mains M$95-140; 8am-10pm) Yeah OK, so it's aimed very much at tourists but nevertheless the pretty courtyard and craft-covered walls make for a relaxing setting for a meal. If you need a break from the Mexican kitchen, it does a reasonably good array of pasta dishes.

El Patio MEXICAN $$
(Aldama 19; mains M$80-125; 8am-10pm) With much coveted seating on the Plaza Grande, this restaurant attracts as many locals as tourists and is unquestionably a pleasant place for a meal with decent Mexican staples and some well-prepared local dishes.

Priscilla's MEXICAN $$
(tel/info 434-342-57-08; Ibarra 15; mains M$90-140; noon-10:30pm) This smart restaurant inside posh La Mansión de los Sueños makes for a great meal in its charming courtyard setting. Specialties here include seafood, pasta dishes and Mexican *cocina típica.*

Information

Several banks in the city center will change currency; all have ATMs.

La Casa del Té (Portal Morelos 66; per hr M$12; 9am-10pm) Putting the cafe back into internet cafe, this tea shop has a row of computers out the back.

Municipal Tourist Office (434-344-34-86; Portal Hidalgo 1; 9am-8pm)

Post Office (Obregón 13; 9am-4pm Mon-Fri, to 1pm Sat)

Getting There & Around

Pátzcuaro's bus terminal is 1.5km southwest of the city center. It has a cafeteria and left-luggage services.

To catch a bus heading to the city center, walk outside the terminal, turn right and at the corner take any bus marked 'Centro' (M$7). Taxis cost M$25 (with a small surcharge after 11pm).

Buses back to the terminal (marked 'Central') leave from the northeast corner of Plaza Chica. Buses to the boat pier (marked 'Lago'; M$7, five minutes) also leave from here and run from about 6am to 10pm daily.

Common destinations that have multiple daily services include those in the Buses from Pátzcuaro table (prices quoted are for highest and lowest fares when a choice exists).

Around Pátzcuaro

Lago de Pátzcuaro

About 3km north of central Pátzcuaro you will come over a rise to find a lake so blue that its edge blends seamlessly with the sky. Within it are a few populated islands. It is stream fed and natural, and though pollution is a concern, it's still damn beautiful.

To get to the Muelle General, take a bus marked 'Lago' from Pátzcuaro's Plaza Chica (M$7, five minutes). The pier caters to tourists in a profoundly cheesy way – with cheap fish eateries and souvenir shops. The ticket office is about 50m down on the right.

Isla Janitzio is a popular weekend and holiday destination. It's heavily devoted to tourism, with lots of low-end souvenir stalls, fish restaurants and drunk college kids on holiday (OK, it's actually not that nice at all!). But it is car-free and threaded with footpaths that eventually wind their way to the top of the island, where you'll find a 40m-high **statue** (admission M$10) of independence hero José María Morelos y Pavón. Inside the statue are murals depicting Morelos' life. Want a stellar panoramic view? Climb up to his see-through wrist.

Round-trip boat rides to Janitzio cost M$50 (free for children under seven years old) and take 25 minutes each way; they leave when full (about every 30 minutes, quicker on Saturday and Sunday). The last one back is around 8pm.

Lakeside Villages

The villages surrounding Lago de Pátzcuaro make perfect day trips from Pátzcuaro and almost all can be reached by local transportation from Pátzcuaro's bus terminal. Or, to avoid backtracking to the bus terminal, take a 'Lago' bus from Plaza Chica and get off anywhere between the Posada de don Vasco and Hwy 14; then wait by the roadside for a bus heading to your village. Buses to Ihuatzio run directly from Plaza Chica. Frequent combis run between the villages, so you can visit several in one day. Transportation between Quiroga and Erongarícuaro is infrequent, however, so travel between the two may be quicker via Pátzcuaro.

IHUATZIO

Ihuatzio, 14km from Pátzcuaro, was capital of the Tarascan kingdom after Pátzcuaro (but before Tzintzuntzan). Today it's just a slow, dusty village where everyone knows everyone else, until *you* walk into town.

Ihuatzio archaeological site (adult/child M$35/free; 9am-5pm) is a large and partially restored set of pre-Tarascan ruins, some of which date back as far as AD 900. The site lies just over 1km up a cobbled road from the village's small plaza. The ruins' best attraction is an open ceremonial space. It

BUSES FROM PÁTZCUARO

DESTINATION	FARE (M$)	DURATION	FREQUENCY (DAILY)
Erongarícuaro	14	35min	every 15mins
Guadalajara	341	4½hr	hourly
Mexico City (Terminal Norte)	437	5½hr	hourly
Mexico City (Terminal Poniente)	437	5½hr	hourly
Morelia	30-53	1hr	every 30min
Quiroga	18	35min	every 15min
Tzintzuntzan	13	20min	every 15min
Uruapan	58	1hr	hourly

Lago de Pátzcuaro

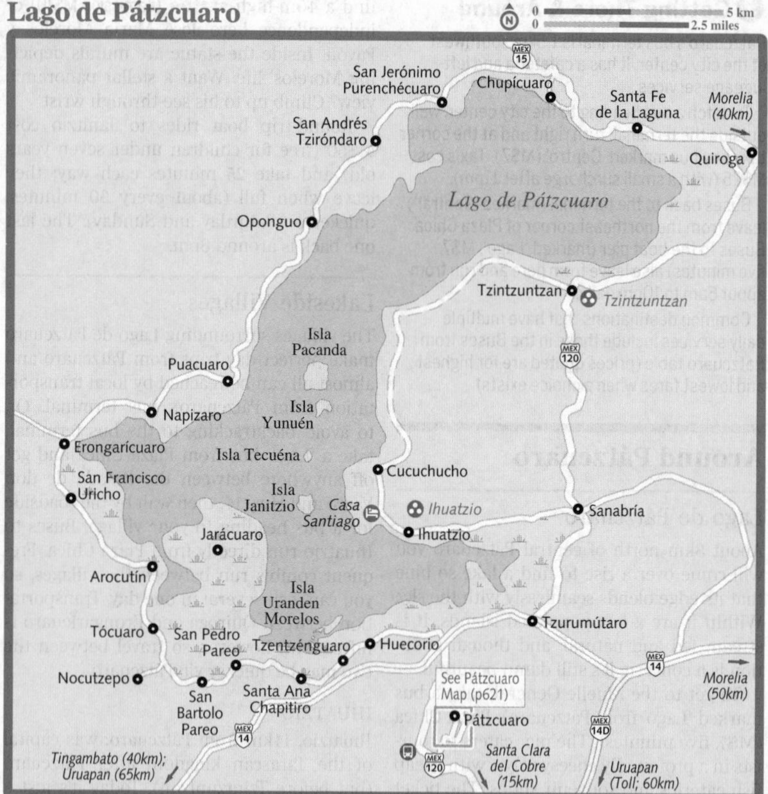

is 200m long and features two pyramid-like structures at its west end. Two carved stone coyotes were found at the site; one is in the National Anthropology Museum in Mexico City, the other can be found at the Museo Regional Michoacano in Morelia.

Casa Santiago (☎434-344-08-80; www.casasantiagomex.com; r incl breakfast M$720-1080; 📶), located 1.5km west of Ihuatzio on the road to Cucuchucho, is a great base from which to experience a night or two in an indigenous pueblo. Rooms are of the rustic-chic kind and the owners, a friendly, knowledgeable US-Purépecha couple, run shopping tours and cook delectable local meals upon request. It's best to let them know in advance that you're coming.

TZINTZUNTZAN

The tiny town of Tzintzuntzan (tseen-*tsoon*-tsahn), about 15km north of Pátzcuaro, was once the Tarascan capital and served as Vasco de Quiroga's first base in the region. It has a beautiful sprawling cemetery that blooms with flowers and crepe paper during heady Día de Muertos celebrations, crumbling Tarascan ruins and some relics from the early Spanish missionary period. The town's pulse comes from its thriving Saturday and Sunday **crafts market**, saintly Quiroga's beloved olive grove and two old churches.

Sights

Ex-Convento de San Francisco CHURCH

On the lake side of Avenida Cárdenas lies the Ex-Convento de San Francisco, a religious compound built partly with stones from the Tarascan site up the hill that the Spanish demolished. This is where Franciscan monks began the Spanish missionary effort in Michoacán in the 16th century. The gnarled, shady olive trees in the churchyard came from seedlings planted by Vasco de

Quiroga; they're believed to be the oldest olive trees in the Americas.

Museo Antiguo Convento Franciscano de Santa Ana (admission M$15; ⏲10am-5pm) is a fascinating museum inside the crumbling, but still-functioning Templo de San Francisco (which is straight ahead as you enter the grounds of the Ex-Convento de San Francisco). The museum showcases Purépecha culture and history, and documents the arrival of the Spanish and the peoples' conversion to Christianity. The building includes a set of faded murals around the galleries and Mudejar-patterned wooden ceiling ornamentation.

Toward the right rear corner of the complex stands the church built for the Purépecha masses, the **Templo de Nuestra Señora de la Salud**. Inside is El Santo Entierro de Tzintzuntzan, a much-revered image of Christ. For most of the year it lies in a *caja de cristal* (glass coffin). During Día de Muertos celebrations it is festooned with fruit and marigolds. On Good Friday, following an elaborate costumed passion play, the image is removed from its coffin and nailed to the large cross; being a Cristo de Goznes (hinged Christ), his arms can be extended and his legs crossed. Afterwards the image is paraded through town until dark, when it is returned to the church. Pilgrims descend from all over, some in chains or carrying crosses, some crawling on their knees.

Tzintzuntzan Archaeological Site RUINS
(Las Yácatas; adult/child M$46/free; ⏲9am-5:30pm) The Tzintzuntzan archaeological site is an impressive group of five round, reconstructed temples known as *yácatas*. They are all that remain of the mighty Tarascan empire. The hillside location offers wonderful views of the town, lake and surrounding mountains, and is interesting to see, as it's still being excavated. At the time of research a **museum** showcasing finds from the site was in the final stages of construction.

TÓCUARO

Some of Mexico's finest mask-makers live in this cobblestoned town surrounded by cornfields, 10km west of Pátzcuaro. But there are no traditional storefronts – just a sign here and there signifying entry into family courtyard compounds with workshops and showrooms.

Prepare to spend. It takes a month or more to produce a fine mask, carved from a single piece of wood. The best ones are wonderfully expressive and surreal and, thanks to a growing legion of global collectors, can cost hundreds of dollars.

Uruapan

452 / POP 264,000 / ELEV 1620M

All praise the thundering Río Cupatitzio. This impressive river begins life underground, then rises sensationally to the surface, feeding a subtropical garden of palms, orchids and massive shade trees in urban Uruapan's Parque Nacional Barranca del Cupatitzio. Without the river, the city would not exist. When Spanish monk Fray Juan de San Miguel arrived here in 1533 he was so taken with his surroundings that he gave the area the Purépecha name, Uruapan (oo-roo-*ah*-pahn), which roughly translates into 'Eternal Spring.' Fray Juan designed a large market square – still a hit with area families on weekends – built a hospital and chapel, and arranged streets into an orderly grid that survives today.

Uruapan quickly grew into a productive agricultural center renowned for macadamias and high-quality *aguacates* (avocados) and still holds the title 'Capital Mundial del Aguacate.' The Feria del Aguacate underlines that point.

Avocados may pay the bills, but the river is king. The city's nicest neighborhoods kiss the riverside. The national park, a 15-minute walk from the city center, is a rush of waterfalls and trickling streams that wind through thick vegetation.

Uruapan is 500m lower than Pátzcuaro and a bit warmer. Don't miss the remarkable Volcán Paricutín, 35km to the west.

Sights

★**Parque Nacional Barranca del Cupatitzio** PARK
(452-524-01-97; Independencia; adult/child M$25/10; ⏲8am-6pm;) This incomparable urban park is just 1km west of the main plaza, but it's another world. Tropical and subtropical foliage is thick and broiling with birds and butterflies. The river bubbles over boulders, cascades down waterfalls and spreads into wide, crystalline pools. Cobbled paths follow the riverbanks from the river's source at the icy-clear **Rodilla del Diablo** pool, near the park's north end, and water from hidden springs peels off the surrounding hillsides before flowing into the great river.

There are a few fruit stands and *taquerías* inside the gardens and there's even a trout farm where you can net your own catch.

Museo de los Cuatro Pueblos Indios MUSEUM

(☎tel/info 452-524-34-34; Portal Mercado; ⏲9:30am-1:30pm & 3:30-6pm Tue-Sun) FREE In the Huatápera, an old colonial courtyard building near the northeast corner of the main plaza, is this three-room museum. Built in the 1530s by Fray Juan de San Miguel, this relic once housed the first hospital in the Americas. The decorations around the doors and windows were carved by Purépecha artisans in a Mudejar style. The museum showcases regional *artesanías,* such as ceramics from Capula and lacquerware from Quiroga.

Fábrica San Pedro TEXTILE FACTORY

(☎452-524-14-63; www.turisticasanpedro.com.mx/quienes.html; Treviño s/n; ⏲tours 9am-6pm Mon-Sat) FREE This great old textile factory from the 19th century is essentially a living museum. Hand-loomed and hand-dyed bedspreads, tablecloths and curtains are made here from pure cotton and wool, and are available for sale. The original machines are more than 100 years old and are still used. Don't miss poking about the abandoned factory below the shop – and try not to let thoughts of ghosts scare you back up the stairs!

You can either wander about on your own or, better, call ahead for a tour and see the entire weaving process from cotton bale to finished tablecloth.

Festivals & Events

Semana Santa RELIGIOUS

Palm Sunday is marked by a procession through the city streets. A major crafts competition takes place on this day, and two weeks after Palm Sunday a week-long exhibition of Michoacán handicrafts fills the plaza.

Día de San Francisco RELIGIOUS

St Francis, the patron saint of Uruapan, is honored with colorful festivities, which are held on October 4.

Festival del Cristo Rey RELIGIOUS

On the last Sunday of October an evening procession parades an image of Christ along the town's winding streets, which are covered in murals made of flower petals or colored sawdust.

Día de Muertos TRADITIONAL

Celebrated across Mexico, the famous Day of the Dead festival happens on November 1 and 2 and brings many visitors to Uruapan for the colorful local celebrations.

Feria del Aguacate FOOD

The Avocado Fair erupts for three weeks in November/December and is celebrated with agricultural, industrial and handicraft exhibitions. Previous years have seen record-setting attempts for the world's largest guacamole.

Festival de Coros y Danzas DANCE

A Purépecha dance and choral contest held December 22.

Sleeping

Reserve a room early for the Día de Muertos (November 1 and 2) and Semana Santa (March/April) festivities.

Hotel Regis HOTEL $

(☎452-523-58-44; www.hotelregis.com.mx; Portal Carrillo 12; s/d/tr M$350/450/550; P 📶) This is the best value among the budget plaza hotels. The public areas are charming in a borderline eccentric manner, and while the rooms are totally average and have poky bathrooms, they are kind of kitsch cool. It's very central.

Hotel del Parque HOTEL $

(☎452-524-38-45; Independencia 124; r M$230; 📶) Of the many bottom-rung places in town, this tidy place, just 70m from the main entrance to the national park, is the pick of the bunch.

★**Casa Chikita** GUESTHOUSE $$

(☎452-524-41-74; www.casachikita.com; Carranza 32; s/d incl breakfast M$450/650; P 📶) This 19th-century house has just four rooms set around a garden decorated with local pottery. The rooms vary quite a bit, but the best are extremely comfortable and decorated with great touches such as granite or wooden counters in the bathroom, tiled floors and local art on the walls.

Homemade breakfasts are sumptuous, the friendly artist owners will make you feel right at home and you're also welcome to use the kitchen to make your own meals. The owners aren't always around so it's best to call in advance and let them know when you'll be arriving.

Mi Solar Bed & Breakfast BOUTIQUE HOTEL **$$**
(452-524-09-12; www.hotelmisolar.com; Delgado 10; r from M$913;) Uruapan's oldest hotel opened in the 1940s to accommodate tourists flooding in to see the newly erupted Volcán Paricutín. Today it's a wholly remodeled boutique place, with 17 spacious rooms on three floors surrounding an atrium bar. Rooms have luscious king beds, high ceilings and hand-carved wooden furniture.

Over the road is a newer annex with larger rooms that are very comfortable but lack the character of the main building. The rack rates shown here only apply in busy periods. Expect a 30% discount at all other times. Despite the name breakfast is not always available.

Hotel Mansión del Cupatitzio HOTEL **$$$**
(452-523-20-60; www.mansiondelcupatitzio.com; Calz Rodilla del Diablo 20; s/d from M$1475/1795;) Enter this beautiful hacienda-style property and you come face-to-face with mounds of flower arrangements, brooding religious art and sparkly balls of roses. It gives off an instant air of calm. This is further enhanced by the carefully tended gardens and beautiful pool. Rooms, though, while perfectly pleasant and comfy, are a bit dowdy in comparison.

It's up by the northern entrance of the Parque Nacional Barranca del Cupatitzio.

Eating & Drinking

La Lucha CAFE **$**
(452-524-03-75; Ortiz 20; coffees M$30; 9am-9pm) The arched interior of this charming cafe makes for a very pleasant place for a coffee, cake or breakfast, with black-and-white photos on the wall and a great little courtyard out the back. Half the town seems to pile in around late afternoon.

Cox-Hanal MEXICAN **$**
(Carranza 31A; mains M$30-80; 11am-9pm) This simple local place serves up delicious *antojitos yucatecos* (dishes from the Yucatán). It's nothing much to look at, but it's always busy and the prices are very reasonable.

Café Tradicional de Uruapan CAFE **$**
(452-523-56-80; Carranza 5B; snacks & breakfast M$35-100; 8am-11pm) It's got burgers, salads, massive platters of *huevos a la mexicana* and all manner of shakes and cakes. Moreover, you can enjoy a very pleasant cafe atmosphere full of locals.

Mole Orapondiro MEXICAN **$**
(Independencia 112; mains M$35-60; 9am-5pm) This sunny cafe specializes in one thing: a rich, thick and chocolatey *mole* sauce. Local ladies smuggle home bottles of it, so they can pass it off as their own. You can have it ladled over chicken, rice and beans and on *tortas*. Get here early because the chicken always sells out.

★**Restaurant Plaza Urani** FISH **$$**
(La Terraza de la Trucha; 452-524-86-98; Calz Rodilla del Diablo 13; mains M$65-120; 9am-6pm) Irresistibly nestled at the north entrance of the national park, you'll find this lazy afternoon restaurant with shady cascade views. Order the trout, of course. Get it grilled, crusted in macadamias or *a la tampiqueña* (with guacamole and beans). It comes with rice and a searing salsa.

At the time of research it was operating under two names but Restaurant Plaza Urani is the new name.

La Casa PIZZERIA **$$**
(452-524-36-11; Revolución 3; mains M$65-200; 2-11pm;) Easily Uruapan's most charming spot with low music, low lighting and folk art scattered within its stone walls. The specialty here is pizza, which, while not particularly great, makes for a welcome change from Mexican fare (be careful, some of the 'gourmet' pizzas are very expensive).

Shopping

Mercado de Antojitos MARKET
(8am-11pm) The Mercado de Antojitos, on the north side of the plaza, is ideal if you're in the market for candy, DVDs, strawberries, bras, cowboy boots or a taco.

Fábrica San Pedro CLOTHING, HOMEWARES
(www.turisticasanpedro.com.mx/quienes.html; Treviño s/n; 9am-6pm) Fábrica San Pedro has exquisite handmade textiles.

Mercado de Artesanías SOUVENIRS
(9am-6pm) Opposite the entrance to the Parque Nacional Barranca del Cupatitzio, the Mercado de Artesanías has local crafts, though mostly of a poor quality.

La Macadamia FOOD
(452-523-82-17; Carranza 21; 9am-2pm & 4-7pm Mon-Sat) La Macadamia sells – you guessed it – products made from local macadamia nuts, from delicious macadamia marzipan to macadamia moisturizer.

Information

Several banks (with ATMs), along with a few *cambios*, are near the central plaza.

Ciber Marvel (Delgado; per hr M$8; ⏲9am-8pm) Internet cafe.

Main Post Office (Jalisco 81; ⏲9am-3pm Mon-Fri, 9am-1pm Sat)

Getting There & Around

Uruapan's bus terminal is 2km northeast of central Uruapan on the highway to Pátzcuaro and Morelia. It has a **left-luggage facility** (⏲7am-11pm) and an internet cafe. For Tingambato (M$15, 30 minutes) take the same bus as those to Pátzcuaro or Morelia. Frequent destinations include those listed in the Buses from Uruapan table (when available we have quoted both the lowest and highest fares depending on bus type; some routes only have one type of bus).

Local buses marked 'Centro' run from just outside the bus terminal to the plaza (M$7). For taxis, buy a ticket inside the bus terminal (M$30). For the return trip catch a 'Central Camionera' bus from the south side of the plaza.

Around Uruapan

Cascada de Tzaráracua

Ten kilometers south of downtown Uruapan, the wild Río Cupatitzio makes its last act count. It pumps hard over the vine-covered, 30m-high red-rock cliffs and crashes into a misty turquoise pool. This is the **Tzaráracua waterfall** (☎452-106-04-41; adult/child M$15/5, car extra M$5; ⏲10am-6pm). On the meandering hike down the 557 slippery steps to the falls you'll see that the raging river has been dammed a few kilometers downstream. The tame lake set against rolling green hills is pretty enough, but it's also a sad fate considering the river's furious beauty.

There's also a 20-minute hike upstream from Tzaráracua to the equally beautiful **Tzararacuita**, a smaller waterfall. This trail is not as well maintained, so bring waterproof sandals. To get here, follow the steep muddy track beyond the Tzaráracua bridge and after about 10 minutes turn right at the stone outcropping.

Hourly buses to Tzaráracua depart from in front of the Hotel Regis, on the south side of Uruapan's main plaza (M$7). Taxis cost M$60.

Tingambato

Stroll through luscious avocado groves to the beautiful **ruins** (admission M$42; ⏲9am-6pm) of this ceremonial site, which predates the Tarascan empire and thrived from about AD 450 to 900. They are located outside of Tingambato village, about 30km from Uruapan on the road to Pátzcuaro. The ruins, which include two plazas, three altars and a ball court (rare in western Mexico), have a Teotihuacán influence. There's also an 8m-high stepped pyramid and an underground tomb where a skeleton and 32 scattered skulls were found – hinting at beheading or trophy-skull rituals.

Buses to Morelia leave from Uruapan's terminal every 20 minutes and stop in Tingambato (M$15, 30 minutes). The ruins are 1.4km downhill on Juárez, the first street on the right as you enter town.

Angahuan

☎452 / POP 5700 / ELEV 2693M

Angahuan, 35km from Uruapan and the nearest town to the incredible Volcán Paricutín, is a typical Purépecha town: there are wooden houses, dusty streets, more horses than cars, women in ankle-length skirts and

BUSES FROM URUAPAN

DESTINATION	FARE (M$)	DURATION	FREQUENCY (DAILY)
Angahuan	20	1hr	half-hourly
Colima	340	6hr	6
Guadalajara	333-400	4½hr	hourly
Mexico City (Terminal Norte)	508-610	7hr	hourly
Morelia	100-165	2hr	hourly
Paracho	20	1hr	every 15min
Pátzcuaro	55	1hr	every 15min

colorful shawls, and loudspeakers booming announcements in the Purépecha tongue.

If you want an early start on climbing the volcano, there are a couple of basic and cheap places to stay and eat.

Sights

★Volcán Paricutín VOLCANO

(admission M$10) The young upstart of Volcán Paricutín (2800m) might be less than 80 years old, but clambering up the volcanic scree slopes to its summit and looking out across blackened, village-engulfing lava fields is a highlight of travel in this part of Mexico.

You can trek to it on horseback or by foot (though the last part is always by foot), but whatever option you choose prepare for a long and rewarding day.

The story behind this volcano is as extraordinary as the views from its summit. On February 20, 1943, Dionisio Pulido, a Purépecha farmer, was plowing his cornfield some 35km west of Uruapan when the ground began to quake and spurt steam, sparks and hot ash. The farmer struggled to cover the blast holes, but he quickly realized his futility and ran. Good thing, because like some Hollywood B-grade movie, a growling volcano began to rise. Within a year it had reached an elevation of 410m above the rolling farmland and its lava had flooded the Purépecha villages of San Salvador Paricutín and San Juan Parangaricutiro. Thankfully, the lava flowed slowly, giving the villagers plenty of time to escape.

The volcano continued to grow until 1952. Today its large black cone whispers warm steam in a few places, but otherwise appears dormant. Near the edge of the 20-sq-km lava field, the top of the ruined **Templo San Juan Parangaricutiro**, San Juan's stone church, protrudes eerily from a sea of black lava. Its tower and altar are the only visible traces of the two buried villages. It's a one-hour walk to the church from Angahuan.

You need to be striding out of Angahuan before 9am if you want to climb Volcán Paricutín. There's no shortage of guides with horses in town offering their services to the ruined church, volcano, or both, and they will meet you at the bus from Uruapan. Horses and a guide should cost around M$650 in total per person per day. The volcano is a 14km or 24km round trip (depending which route you opt for: the shorter route is over sharp lava rock and is slow going so most guides prefer to take the longer but less painful route) that takes up to six hours – of which you'll spend at least four in an unforgiving, wooden saddle – and if you're not used to riding a horse, you're going to end up very sore! You'll have to scramble the last few hundred very steep meters up to the summit. It's a rugged hike up, but you'll get to run, jump and slide down the deep volcanic sand on the descent and visit the San Juan church on the way back. The altar is almost always blessed with colorful offerings of candles and flowers. Close to the church are a number of food stalls serving up fabulously tasty blue-corn quesadillas cooked on old, wood-burning, oil-can skillets. Bring enough water and wear decent shoes.

If wooden saddles intimidate you, or you have energy to burn, you can walk to the volcano, but you'll still need a guide (M$400) as the trail through the pine forest can be hard to find. The long and pretty hike is through avocado groves, agave fields and wildflowers (again it's a 14km or 24km round trip, and again most guides prefer to take the longer route due to the fact that the walking is actually easier). For the longer route you should allow at least eight hours going at a very steady pace, so make sure you set off early.

Iglesia de Santiago Apóstol CHURCH

On the main plaza is the sensational 16th-century Iglesia de Santiago Apóstol. Candles and incense burn, fresh flowers crowd the altar and the detailed doorway was carved by a Moorish stonemason who accompanied the early Spanish missionaries here.

Getting There & Away

Angahuan is 35km from Uruapan. Buses leave the Uruapan bus terminal for Angahuan every 30 minutes from 5am to 7pm (M$20, one hour).

Buses return to Uruapan every 30 minutes until about 8pm and few cabs are available in town, so don't miss that last bus!

Northern Central Highlands

Includes ➡

Best Places to Eat

- Cafe Rama (p666)
- Las Mercedes (p652)
- Los Dorados de Villa (p693)
- El México de Frida (p680)
- San Marcos Merendero (p674)

Best Places to Stay

- Posada Corazón (p664)
- Casa Estrella de la Valenciana (p650)
- Hotel Emporio Zacatecas (p691)
- Community lodges (p642)

Why Go?

From cobbled lanes to pretty plazas, deserts to cloud forest, the northern central highlands region is as varied as its history, cuisine and cultures. It was here that former mineral wealth created colonial cities and revolutionary activity left ghost towns in its wake. Known as the Cuna de la Independencia (Cradle of Independence), the territory is renowned for its part in the country's fight for autonomy.

Particular jewels include silver-ridden Guanajuato and Zacatecas, plaza-filled San Luis Potosí, arty San Miguel de Allende and nature-filled Sierra Gorda. And as for the cuisine... Travel a few kilometers for another take on a trusty tortilla or regional specialty. Culture vultures can feast on pre-Hispanic sites and art museums, concerts, nightlife, festivals and *callejoneadas* – the northern central highlands continues centuries of pomp and ceremony. It sure knows how to put on a good (if noisy) party.

When to Go

Guanajuato

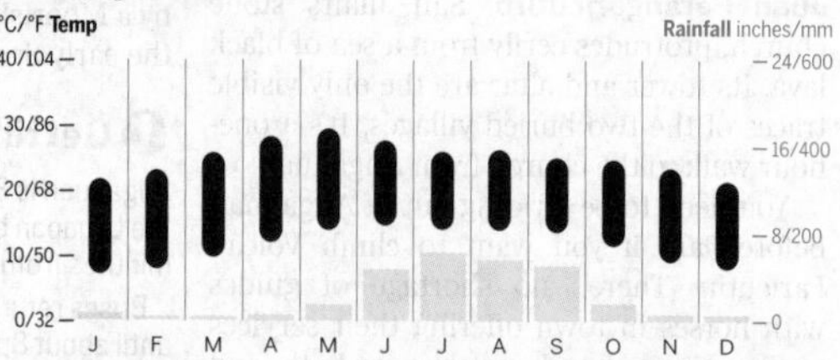

Jul & Aug Days are mild and wildflowers bloom; it's the perfect time for DIY explorations.

Late Oct Villages are abuzz as they prepare for Day of the Dead celebrations (Nov 1 to 2).

Late Mar or Apr Traditional religious festivities abound during Semana Santa (Holy Week).

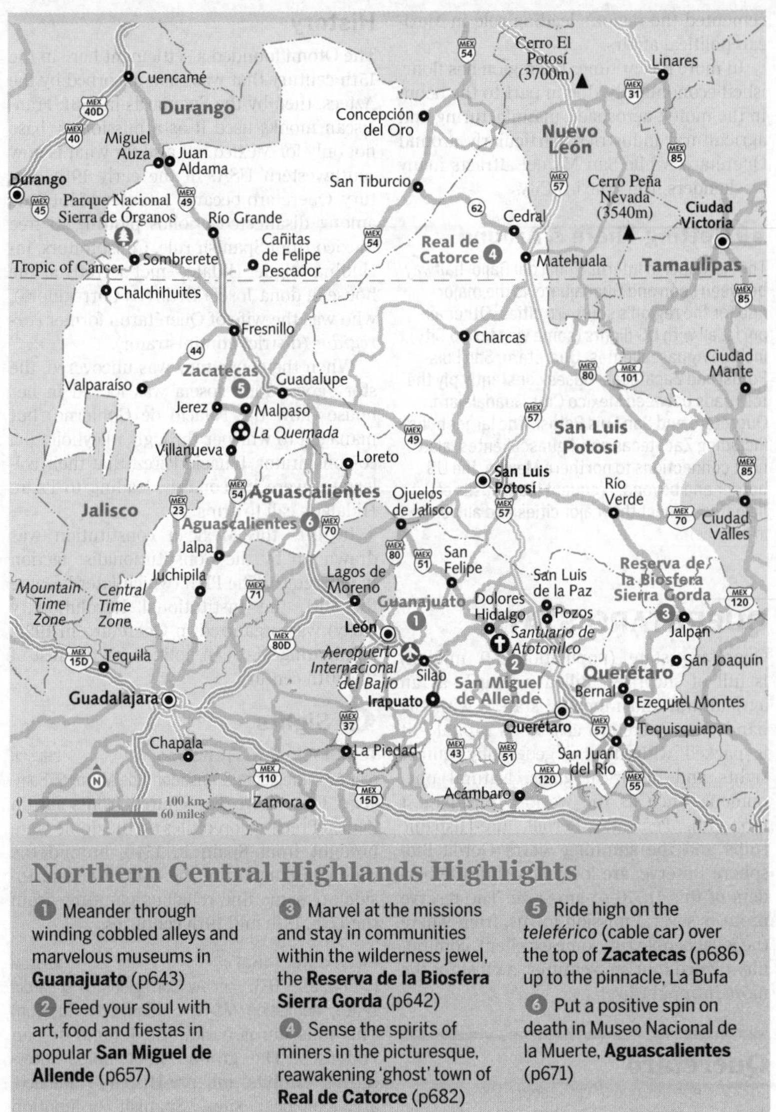

Northern Central Highlands Highlights

1. Meander through winding cobbled alleys and marvelous museums in **Guanajuato** (p643)
2. Feed your soul with art, food and fiestas in popular **San Miguel de Allende** (p657)
3. Marvel at the missions and stay in communities within the wilderness jewel, the **Reserva de la Biosfera Sierra Gorda** (p642)
4. Sense the spirits of miners in the picturesque, reawakening 'ghost' town of **Real de Catorce** (p682)
5. Ride high on the *teleférico* (cable car) over the top of **Zacatecas** (p686) up to the pinnacle, La Bufa
6. Put a positive spin on death in Museo Nacional de la Muerte, **Aguascalientes** (p671)

History

Until the Spanish conquest, the northern central highlands were inhabited by fierce seminomadic tribes known to the Aztecs as Chichimecs. They resisted Spanish expansion longer than other Mexican peoples but were ultimately pacified in the late 16th century. The wealth subsequently amassed by the Spanish was at the cost of many Chichimecs, who were used as slave labor in the mines.

This historically volatile region sparked the criollo fight for independence from Spain, which was plotted in Querétaro and San Miguel de Allende and launched from Dolores Hidalgo in 1810. A century later Francisco Madero released his revolutionary Plan de San Luis Potosí and the 1917 signing of Mexico's constitution in Querétaro cemented the region's leading role in Mexican political affairs.

In more recent times the region has flourished economically, due in part to the boom in the motor, aerospace, manufacturing and agricultural industries, particularly around Querétaro, while San Miguel attracts many weekenders from Mexico City.

Getting There & Around

The Aeropuerto Internacional del Bajío, halfway between León and Guanajuato, is the major hub for the region's southern cities. Other airports, all with US flights (some via Mexico City), include Aguascalientes, Querétaro, San Luis Potosí and Zacatecas. Buses constantly ply the toll roads between Mexico City, Guadalajara, Querétaro and San Luis Potosí. The larger hubs, including Zacatecas and Aguascalientes, also host connections to northern Mexico, the US border and beyond. Frequent local buses efficiently connect the major cities and all points in between.

QUERÉTARO STATE

Querétaro state (population 1.9 million) is full of surprises. Billed primarily as an agricultural and ranching state – with the handsome Querétaro city as its capital – it is packed with diverse geography, quirky sights and historical gems. Natural phenomena, such as the world's third-largest monolith, Peña de Bernal, pre-Hispanic ruins and the stunning Sierra Gorda Biosphere Reserve, are located within the borders of this 11,770-sq-km state. The reserve protects several mission towns, from where the local people run some excellent, community-owned tourism ventures; a must for the more intrepid traveler.

Querétaro

☎442 / POP 805,000 / ELEV 1800M

As far as the silver cities go, Querétaro is sometimes intimated to be the ugly sibling. Indeed, its rather frantic outskirts with its busy freeways can give a misguided first impression. The city's large, historic heart is characterized by charming *andadores* (pedestrian streets, and very clean ones at that), stunning plazas and interesting churches. The sophisticated restaurants serve up quality cuisine and the museums reflect Querétaro's important role in Mexican history.

History

The Otomí founded a settlement here in the 15th century that was soon absorbed by the Aztecs, then by the Spaniards in 1531. Franciscan monks used it as a missionary base not only for Mexico but also for what is now southwestern USA. In the early 19th century, Querétaro became a center of intrigue among disaffected criollos plotting to free Mexico from Spanish rule. Conspirators, including Miguel Hidalgo, met secretly at the house of doña Josefa Ortiz (La Corregidora), who was the wife of Querétaro's former *corregidor* (district administrator).

When the conspiracy was uncovered, the story goes, doña Josefa was locked in her house (now the Palacio de Gobierno) but managed to whisper through a keyhole to a co-conspirator, Ignacio Pérez, that their colleagues were in jeopardy, leading to Padre Hidalgo's call to arms.

In 1917 the Mexican constitution was drawn up by the Constitutionalist faction in Querétaro. The PNR (which later became the PRI, the Institutional Revolutionary Party) was organized in Querétaro in 1929, dominating Mexican politics for the rest of the 20th century.

Sights

Templo de San Francisco CHURCH

(cnr Av Corregidora & Andador 5 de Mayo; 8am-9pm) This impressive church fronts Jardín Zenea. Pretty colored tiles on the dome were brought from Spain in 1540, around the time construction of the church began. Inside are some fine religious paintings from the 17th, 18th and 19th centuries.

Museo Regional MUSEUM

(☎442-212-20-31; cnr Av Corregidora 3 & Jardín Zenea; admission M$41; 10am-6pm Tue-Sun) This museum is beside the Templo de San Francisco. The ground floor holds interesting exhibits on pre-Hispanic Mexico, archaeological sites, Spanish occupation and the state's various indigenous groups. The upstairs exhibits reveal Querétaro's role in the independence movement and post-independence history (plus religious paintings). The table at which the Treaty of Guadalupe Hidalgo was signed in 1848, ending the Mexican–American War, is on display, as is the desk of the tribunal that sentenced Emperor Maximilian to death.

The museum is housed in part of what was once a huge monastery and seminary.

WORTH A TRIP

BERNAL

With a population of 4000, the tiny town of Bernal is quaint, if touristy, and you can cover it in an hour or so. (Note: it comes to life during the weekends; many things are closed from Monday to Thursday). Its drawcard is the 350m-high rock spire, the **Peña de Bernal**, the third-largest monolith in the world and considered mystical by many Mexicans. During the vernal equinox thousands of pilgrims converge on the rock to take in its positive energy. Visitors can climb to the rock's halfway point (allow one hour both ways); only professional rock climbers can climb to its peak.

The town has several **churches** and **El Castillo**, a 16th-century viceregal building. For a more in-depth explanation of the area, friendly **La Peña Tours** (441-296-73-98, cell phone 441-101-48-21; www.lapenatours.com; cnr Independencia & Colon) offers an array of tours (M$150 to M$700) plus climbing sessions on the Peña. For shopping, head to **La Aurora** (Jardín Principal 1; 10am-8pm), an interesting *artesanías* shop; request permission to see the weavers at work at their looms in the attached workshop.

Bernal is also known for its delicious *gorditas*, especially those filled with *nopales en penca* (cheese sauce with nopal cactus). Ask the way to the food market. The **Casa Museo del Dulce** (Bernal; M$40; 10am-6pm Sat & Sun) highlights the town's former factory that produced the caramelised sweets. The M$40 fee includes the entry and samplings plus a short trip on a tranvía.

There are regular buses from/to Querétaro (M$38, 45 minutes). The last return bus to Querétaro departs from the main road around 5pm. For connections to/from Tequisquiapan, change buses at Ezequiel Montes (M$11, 30 minutes).

Begun in 1540, the seminary became the seat of the Franciscan province of San Pedro y San Pablo de Michoacán by 1567. Building continued until at least 1727. Thanks to its high tower, in the 1860s the monastery was used as a fort both by imperialists supporting Maximilian and by the forces who defeated him in 1867.

Templo y Convento de la Santa Cruz NOTABLE BUILDING
(442-212-02-35; Independencia 148 at Felipe Luna; donation requested; 9am-2pm & 4-6pm Tue-Sat, 9am-5:15pm Sun) Ten minutes' walk east of the center of Querétaro is one of the city's most interesting sights. The convent was built between 1654 and about 1815 on the site of a battle in which a supposed miraculous appearance of Santiago (St James) led the Otomí to surrender to the conquistadors and Christianity. Emperor Maximilian had his headquarters here while under siege in Querétaro from March to May 1867. After his surrender and subsequent death sentence, he was jailed here while awaiting the firing squad.

Today it's used as a religious school. Ask at the entrance about visiting with a guide, although an English tour will need to be arranged beforehand (donation requested). The site's main legend is the growth of the Árbol de la Cruz, an ancient tree in the convent's garden whose thorns are in the shape of crosses. This apparent miracle was the result of a walking stick stuck in the earth by a pious friar in 1697.

Museo de Arte de Querétaro MUSEUM
(442-212-23-57; www.museodeartequeretaro.com; Allende Sur 14; admission M$30, Tue free; 10am-6pm Tue-Sun) Adjacent to the Templo de San Agustín, Querétaro's art museum occupies a splendid baroque monastery built between 1731 and 1748. It is worth visiting to see the building alone: angels, quirky gargoyles, statues and other ornamental details abound, particularly around the stunning courtyard.

The ground-floor display of 16th- and 17th-century European paintings traces influences from Flemish to Spanish to Mexican art. Here, too, you'll find 19th- and 20th-century Mexican paintings. The top floor has works from 16th-century Mannerism to 18th-century baroque.

The museum has a good bookstore-cum-gift shop.

Museo de la Ciudad MUSEUM
(442-212-47-02; www.museodelaciudadqro.org; Guerrero Norte 27; admission M$5; 11am-7pm Tue-Sat, to 5pm Sun) Inside the ex-convent and old prison that held Maximilian, the 11-room Museo de la Ciudad has some good alternating contemporary-art exhibits.

Querétaro

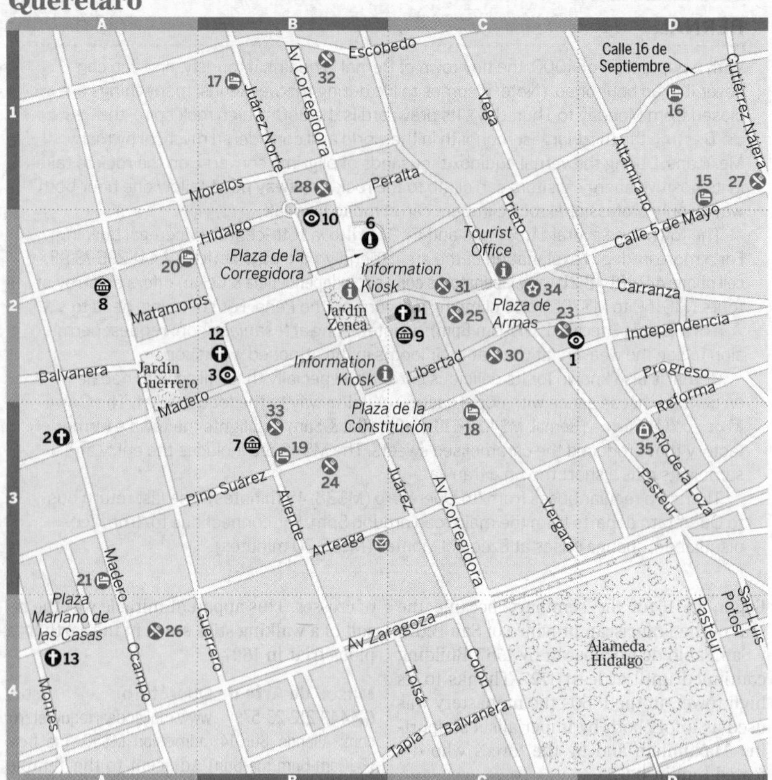

Museo de la Restauración de la República MUSEUM
(☎442-224-30-04; www.queretaro.gob.mx/mrr; Guerrero Norte 23; ⏰9am-5pm Tue-Fri, from 10am Sat & Sun) FREE If you can read Spanish or are a real history buff, this museum may be of interest – it covers Querétaro's role in Mexico's history, particularly the French occupation and the eventual ousting of Emperor Maximilian.

Teatro de la República THEATER
(☎442-212-03-39; cnr Juárez & Peralta; ⏰10am-3pm & 5-8pm) FREE This lovely old and functioning theater, complete with impressive chandeliers, was where a tribunal met in 1867 to decide the fate of Emperor Maximilian. Mexico's constitution was also signed here on January 31, 1917. The stage backdrop lists the names of its signatories and the states they represented. In 1929, politicians met in the theater to organize Mexico's long-time ruling party, the PNR (now the PRI).

Mirador LOOKOUT
Walk east along Independencia past Convento de la Santa Cruz, then fork right along Ejército Republicano, to the **mirador**. There's a fine view of 'Los Arcos,' Querétaro's emblematic 1.28km-long **aqueduct**, with 74 towering sandstone arches built between 1726 and 1738. The aqueduct runs along the center of Avenida Zaragoza.

Mausoleo de la Corregidora MUSEUM
(Ejército Republicano s/n; ⏰9am-6pm) The Mausoleo de la Corregidora, opposite the mirador, is the resting place of doña Josefa Ortiz and her husband, Miguel Domínguez de Alemán.

Casa de la Zacatecana HOUSE
(☎442-224-07-58; www.museolazacatecana.com; Independencia 59; admission M$35; ⏰10am-5:30pm Tue-Sun) This is a finely restored

17th-century home with a lovely collection of 18th- and 19th-century furniture and decorations (and its own murder mystery – skeletons were discovered in the basement).

Monumento a la Corregidora MONUMENT
(cnr Corregidora & Andador 16 de Septiembre) Plaza de la Corregidora is dominated by the Monumento a la Corregidora, a 1910 statue of doña Josefa Ortiz bearing the flame of freedom.

Templo de Santa Clara CHURCH
(cnr Madero & Allende) The 17th-century Templo de Santa Clara has an ornate baroque interior.

Fuente de Neptuno FOUNTAIN
(Neptune's Fountain; cnr Madero & Allende) A block west of Jardín Zenea is the Fuente de Neptuno, designed by noted Mexican neoclassical architect Eduardo Tresguerras in 1797.

Templo de Santa Rosa de Viterbos CHURCH
(cnr Arteaga & Montes) The 18th-century Templo de Santa Rosa de Viterbos is Querétaro's most splendid baroque church, with its pagoda-like bell tower, unusual exterior paintwork, curling buttresses and lavishly gilded and marbled interior. The church also boasts what some say is the earliest four-sided clock in the New World.

Cathedral CATHEDRAL
(cnr Madero & Ocampo) The 18th-century cathedral features both baroque and neoclassical styles, with an emphasis on straight lines (and few curves); it's said that the first mass in the cathedral (then known as San Felipe Neri) was lead by Padre Hidalgo, he of Independence fame (see p655).

Courses

Olé Spanish Language School SPANISH
(☎442-214-40-23; www.ole.edu.mx; Escobedo 32) The Olé Spanish Language School offers a range of courses with homestay options and extracurricular programs. Prices start at around US$15 per hour, and week-long courses range from moderate group classes for 15 hours from US$164 to 35 intensive one-hour private classes for US$577.

Tours

Guided Tours TRAM
(1-/2-hr tours M$80/120) Guided tours of the city center on the Tranvía trolleybus, in Spanish, leave from Plaza de la Constitución. For details, ask at the tourist office or at one of the two information kiosks located in Plaza de la Constitución and in Jardín Zenea.

Night Tours WALKING
(per person around M$120) For Spanish speakers, several different companies run fun night tours. The tours have titles such as Leyendas & Mitos (Myths & Legends) and actors in period costume dramatically reveal the legends and secrets of the dark lanes and buildings. For details, ask at the tourist office (p640).

Festivals & Events

Feria Internacional FAIR
Querétaro's Feria Internacional, one of Mexico's biggest state fairs, happens in the first two weeks of December. It focuses on agriculture but also hosts cultural events.

Querétaro

Sights
1 Casa de la Zacatecana ... C2
2 Cathedral ... A3
3 Fuente de Neptuno ... B2
4 Mausoleo de la Corregidora ... F2
5 Mirador ... F2
6 Monumento a la Corregidora ... B2
7 Museo de Arte de Querétaro ... B3
8 Museo de la Ciudad ... A2
Museo de la Restauración de la República ... (see 8)
9 Museo Regional ... C2
10 Teatro de la República ... B2
11 Templo de San Francisco ... C2
12 Templo de Santa Clara ... B2
13 Templo de Santa Rosa de Viterbos ... A4
14 Templo y Convento de la Santa Cruz ... E2

Sleeping
15 Doña Urraca Hotel & Spa ... D1
16 Home B&B ... D1
17 Hotel Quinta Lucca ... B1
18 Kuku Rukú ... C3
19 La Casa del Atrio ... B3
20 La Casa del Naranjo ... A2
21 MO17 ... A3

Eating
22 Biznarga ... E2
23 Breton ... C2
24 Café del Fondo ... B3
25 Di Vino ... C2
26 Erlum ... A4
La Antojería ... (see 31)
27 La Dolche Vita ... D1
28 La Mariposa ... B1
29 La Vieja Varsovia ... E2
30 Restaurante Bar 1810 ... C2
31 San Miguelito ... C2
32 Sucré Salé ... B1
33 Tikua ... B3

Entertainment
34 Casa de la Cultura ... C2
Teatro de la República ... (see 10)

Shopping
35 Quinto Real ... D3

Sleeping

Kuku Rukú HOTEL, HOSTEL $
(442-245-87-77; www.kukuruku.mx; Vergara 12; dm from M$160; d M$790-1050;) When it comes to hotel-cum-hostels, usually one group of clients gets the better deal. In this funky accommodation hybrid, we think hostel-goers come out on top with clean, modern dorms. The hotel rooms' decor is pretty hip but you'll pay substantially more for the privilege to enjoy it.

It's an attractive joint, with lots of white with paintings and quirky designer touches. A terrace bar is open from 6pm to 11pm Wednesday to Saturday.

Home B&B B&B $$
(442-183-91-39; www.queretarobandb.com; Calle 16 de Septiembre 104; s/d incl breakfast US$45/65;) You can forgive the odd blip in this friendly place, for the helpful and caring Canadian owner. The rooms vary in shape and size, all are light and, true to the accommodations' name, are homey. Breakfasts are very good indeed. Note: by reservation only.

Hotel Quinta Lucca HOTEL $$
(442-340-44-44; www.hotelquintalucca.com; Juárez Norte 119A; r M$960, ste M$1150-1300;) Mexican-modern interiors in neat, clean rooms. Those in the rear are more pleasant; these surround a luscious green courtyard, where a continental breakfast is served.

Doña Urraca Hotel & Spa LUXURY HOTEL $$$
(442-238-54-00, in Mexico 800-021-71-16; www.donaurraca.com.mx; Calle 5 de Mayo 117; ste incl breakfast from M$2965; P) Perfect for people who prefer to be pampered. The 24 spacious suites are lavished with all the right 'fluffy features': bathrobes and handmade herbal soaps plus sound systems and cable TV. It even boasts a wine cellar. Guests have reported that their Sunday brunch has been 'disrupted' by weekend functions here – from kids' parties to other events.

La Casa del Naranjo BOUTIQUE HOTEL $$$
(442-212-76-09; www.lacasadelnaranjo.com; Hidalgo 21; r inc breakfast M$1155-1830; P) The seven rooms in this boutique hotel are decorated in an eclectic but stylish manner. Each room is named after a fruit; the timber from the fruit trees has been incorporated into the design. Downstairs rooms are more cramped than the airier options above, but there are several attractive outdoor lounge areas.

La Casa del Atrio B&B $$$
(442-212-63-14; www.lacasadelatrio.com; Allende Sur 15; r incl breakfast M$1635;) You are paying for the novelty at this one-of-a-kind conceptual space. Accommodations are in-

corporated into a gallery-cum-antique-shop. The six rooms offer nearly-there luxury (the bathrooms are small, and there's little natural light in some, but hey, original sculptures are next to your bed). There's a pretty back garden, and the hotel is also pet friendly.

MO17 BOUTIQUE HOTEL $$$
(442-212-9295; www.mo17hotel.mx; Madero 46; r from M$1800;) This place yells 'notice me!'. One of the city's first design hotels, it is indeed refreshingly different. (Would the words 'Norwegian owner' convince you?) Cutting-edge trendy (think minimalist Scandinavian design), daring limits (open-plan bathrooms with limited ablution privacy) and clever features (such as photo-negative-manipulated visuals).

Eating

★La Mariposa CAFE $
(Peralta 7; snacks M$20-100; 8am-9:30pm) Unchanged since 1940 (as the photos and coffee machine testify), this Querétaro institution is more about the quaint atmosphere than the food. Don't leave without trying the mouthwatering *mantecado* (ice cream made to a special recipe; M$34).

Biznarga CAFE $
(Gutiérrez Najera 17; mains M$38-50; 9am-2pm & 6:30-11:30pm Mon-Sat) Their friends liked their cooking so much they opened their kitchen to the public. And why not? A fun, Rasta experience with graffiti, artwork and memorabilia. Good salads, homemade pizzas, juices and more.

La Antojería MEXICAN $
(mains M$30-80; 10am-10pm;) This family-friendly, fun and Mexican-themed place serves up every style of *antojito* known in Mexico.

Café del Fondo CAFE $
(Pino Suárez 9; everything under M$60; 8am-10pm) This relaxed, rambling alternative hangout is popular with newspaper-reading elder statesmen, chess-heads and chatterboxes. Decent set breakfasts go for just M$35. Snacks and a four-course *comida corrida* (prix-fixe menu) are also available (around M$35).

Erlum INTERNATIONAL $$
(www.erlum.com.mx; Arteaga 55; M$60-150; 1-10pm Tue-Thu, 1-11pm Fri, 10am-11pm Sat, 10am-6pm Sun) This place ticks all the right sustainable/slow food boxes: think homemade condiments, seasonal organic produce; wood-fired breads and pizzas, homemade pastas and microbrewed beers. Then there's the funky recycled paper tablecloths. An excellent and wide-ranging fusion menu. Set lunches available Tuesday to Friday.

San Miguelito MEXICAN $$
(mains M$130-185; 1pm-midnight Tue-Sat, to 6pm Sun) This place is popular for its location near the plaza, its ambience and colorful decor. For a protein kick, don't miss the prime rib – it's a whopping 250g. And that's *after* it's cooked (M$185).

Tikua MEXICAN $$
(Allende Sur 13; M$75-120; 9am-midnight Mon-Sat, 8:30am-9pm Sun) This sprawling spot specializes in Southeastern Mexican cuisine and the dishes – from the *xi'i*, a mushroom salad, to the Oaxacan chorizo recipes – are true to their roots. The *paella del sur-este*, rice with *chapulines* (grasshoppers), *tasajo* (salted beef) and chocolate *mole* (a type of sauce) are especially good.

Di Vino ITALIAN $$$
(Andador 5 de Mayo 12; mains M$145-350; 1pm-midnight Mon-Sat) A stylish, sophisticated Italian restaurant with an upmarket ambience, superb cuisine and an impressive wine cellar. A change from the Mexican theme, and a special experience at that.

Restaurante Bar 1810 MEXICAN $$$
(Libertad 62; mains M$140-320; 8am-11pm Mon-Sat, to 10pm Sun) Covered with fairy lights and situated on the pretty plaza, this is a reliable eatery for excellent steaks and a variety of pastas and seafood dishes. Live crooners complement (or otherwise) your meal.

BAKERIES

Recently, Querétaro has seen an upsurge in excellent contemporary bakeries. Bread and pastry lovers should definitely follow their noses to the following places, some of which double up as cafes: **La Vieja Varsovia** (www.laviejavarsovia.com.mx; Plaza Fundadores; M$40-100; 8:30am-11pm Tue-Sun), **La Dolche Vita** (Calle 5 de Mayo), **Sucré Salé** (Universidade Ote 42; M$25-33; 9am-9:30pm Mon-Sat), and **Breton** (Andador Libertad 82B; 8am-10pm Tue-Sat;).

Drinking & Nightlife

There's a thriving bar scene in Querétaro. Bars and clubs are popping up (and sometimes down) in the historic center and beyond. Calle 5 de Mayo is the fashionable drinking strip in the center; barflies hit these places after 10pm.

Gracias a Dios BAR
(Calle 5 de Mayo; snacks M$55-100; ⏲2pm-1:30am Tue-Sat) One of the many bars near Calle 5 de Mayo, this new place revives – *Gracias a Dios* ('thank God') – traditions of old: a *cantina-botanero* (bar with snacks) complete with barrels and stools and a touch of grunge-and-sticky-bar-syndrome. However, it also has a touch of feminine funk and attracts a young crowd out for whisky, tequila and brandy-fuelled fun.

Entertainment

Querétaro is action-packed with cultural activities. For the latest on what's happening around town, look out for posters on bulletin boards, or ask at the tourist office. On Sunday, free concerts take place in Plaza de Armas at 1pm and in the evenings in Jardín Zenea.

Casa de la Cultura CONCERT VENUE, PERFORMING ARTS
(☎442 212-56-14; Calle 5 de Mayo 40; ⏲9am-2pm & 4-5pm Mon-Fri) Sponsors concerts, dance, theater and art events; stop by to view the bulletin board.

Teatro de la República THEATER
(cnr Juárez & Peralta; tickets M$60-180) Has regular symphony concerts most Fridays.

Shopping

Quinto Real ARTS & CRAFTS
(www.quintoreal.com.mx/english/; Reforma 80; ⏲10am-7pm Mon-Fri, 11am-7pm Sat) This lovely store stocks a huge range of quality Mexican items, from handicrafts to furniture.

Information

There are card phones on Jardín Zenea, Plaza de Armas and elsewhere around the center. There are several banks with ATMs around Jardín Zenea.

Hospital Angeles (☎442-192-3000; www.hospitalangelesqueretaro.com; Bernardo Del Razo No 21, El Ensueño) Southwest of Querétaro's city center, this top-quality, reasonably priced hospital has English-speaking doctors.

Post Office (Arteaga 5)

Tourist Office (☎442-238-50-67, 800-715-17-42; www.queretaro.travel; Pasteur Norte 4; ⏲9am-7pm) Has city maps and brochures (in Spanish), although you might need to ask for both. More helpful kiosks are located on the plazas (open 10am to 6pm daily).

Turismo Beverly (☎442-216-15-00; www.turismobeverly.mx; Tecnológico 118) Travel agent useful for air tickets.

Getting There & Away

AIR

The **Aeropuerto Internacional** (☎442-192-55-00; www.aiq.com.mx), 8km northeast of the center, is around a M$300 taxi ride. Primera Plus also runs from the bus terminal to Mexico City airport (M$315, three hours). **United Airlines** (www.united.com) has flights to various US cities from Querétaro.

BUS

Querétaro is a hub for buses in all directions; the modern Central Camionera is 5km southeast of the center. There's one building for deluxe and 1st class (labeled A), one for 2nd class (B) and another for local buses (C). Facilities include luggage storage.

Primera Plus (www.primeraplus.com.mx) has regular services to Mexico City airport. There is

BUSES FROM QUERÉTARO

DESTINATION	FARE (M$)	DURATION	FREQUENCY (DAILY)
Guadalajara	367-530	4½-5½hr	frequent
Guanajuato	186	2½-3hr	7
Mexico City (Terminal Norte)	187-280	3-4½hr	every 20min 4am-11:30pm
Mexico City Airport	312	3½hr	hourly
Morelia	166-255	3-4hr	frequent
San Luis Potosí	199-260	2½-2¾hr	frequent
San Miguel de Allende	59-90	1-1½hr	every 40min 6am-11pm
Tequisquiapan	45	1hr	every 30min 6:30am-9pm

WORTH A TRIP

HWY 120

Heading north from Tequisquiapan, Hwy 120 provides the most scenic route through the Sierra Gorda. Thirty-eight kilometers from Tequisquiapan, in Cadereyta, signs point to the **Quinta Fernando Schmoll** (☎441-276-10-71; Colegio Militar 1; M$20; ⏰8am-5pm Tue-Sat, 9am-5pm Sun), a beautiful botanic garden with more than 4000 varieties of plants.

Within the magnificent Sierra Gorda Biosphere Reserve, Hwy 120 winds up to a height of 2300m at the pretty town of **Pinal de Amoles** and makes dramatic ups and downs (with many hairpin turns!) before reaching Jalpan at 760m.

one daily service to Xilitla at noon with Primera Plus (M$340).

CAR & MOTORCYCLE

If you want a car to explore the Sierra Gorda, English-speaking **Express Rent-a-Car** (☎442-242-90-28; www.autotodoqueretaro.com; Hotel Real de Minas, Av Constituyentes Poniente 124) has competitive rates.

Getting Around

Once you have reached the city center, you can easily visit most sights on foot. City buses (M$7) run from 6am until 9pm or 10pm. They gather in an area at the end of the bus terminal; turn right from the 2nd-class terminal, or left from the 1st-class side. Several routes go to the center (check as the numbers change). For a taxi, get a ticket first from the bus station booth (M$50 for up to four people).

To get to the bus station from the center, take city bus marked 'Central' (ie Central de Autobuses) from Zaragoza, or any bus labeled 'TAQ' (ie Terminal de Autobuses de Querétaro) or 'Central' heading south on the east side of the Alameda Hidalgo.

Tequisquiapan

☎414 / POP 30,000 / ELEV 1870M

This small town (teh-kees-kee-*ap*-an), 70km southeast of Querétaro, is a quaint weekend retreat from Mexico City or Querétaro. Tequisquiapan used to be known for its thermal springs – Mexican presidents came here to ease their aches and tensions. The town's natural pools may have long-since dried up, but its pretty, bougainvillea-lined streets, colorful colonial buildings and excellent markets make for an enjoyable browse.

Sights & Activities

Plaza Miguel Hidalgo PLAZA

The wide and attractive Plaza Miguel Hidalgo is surrounded by *portales* (arcades), overlooked by the 19th-century neoclassical **La Parroquia de Santa María de la Asunción** (⏰7:30am-8:30pm) with its pink facade and decorated tower.

Horseback Riding HORSEBACK RIDING

(Fray Junípero) Guided trail rides around the surrounding countryside are offered at weekends (M$80 per hour). Guides and their hacks congregate on Fray Junípero, just north of Parque La Pila.

Festivals & Events

Feria Nacional del Queso y del Vino FOOD

The National Wine & Cheese Fair, from late May to early June, includes tastings and music.

Fiesta de la Asunción RELIGIOUS

Commemorates the town's patron saint on August 15.

Sleeping & Eating

The best budget accommodations are the posadas along Moctezuma. Demand is low Monday to Thursday, when you may be able to negotiate a discount. Many restaurants around the plaza offer *comidas corridas* (prix-fixe menus). You'll find *fondas* (food stalls) at Mercado Guadalupana, a block northeast of the plaza.

Posada Tequisquiapan GUESTHOUSE $$

(☎414-273-00-10; Moctezuma 6; s/d M$250/500; P) A kick-back from the '50s, this good-value place offers simple but spacious and clean rooms.

La Granja BOUTIQUE HOTEL $$$

(☎414-273-20-04; www.hotelboutiquelagranja.com; Morelos 12; r from M$1750; P) Located in a pretty part of town, this colonial building has been renovated into a lovely hotel, with spacious and sleek rooms and a large back garden with a pool. Onsite restaurant serves breakfast.

Hotel Hacienda Las Delicias HOTEL $$$
(☎414-273-00-17; www.hotelhaciendalasdelicias.com; Calle 5 de Mayo 1; s/d M$1300/2000; P ≋) A block south of Plaza Principal, this slightly tired hotel is located around a manicured garden with pool. Best (most recently renovated) rooms are numbers 1 to 7 and 26 to 31.

K'puchinos MEXICAN $$
(Independencia 7; mains M$65-180; ⏱8am-10pm Sun-Thu, 8am-noon Sat) Handily located on the plaza, this reliable place caters to hungry souls for any meal of the day.

Shopping

Mercado de Artesanías MARKET
(Carrizal; ⏱8am-7pm) This crafts market is one of three markets including **Vara y Mimbre** (household items) and the **Guadalupana** (for food) found on Carrizal, a block north of Tequisquiapan's main plaza. The main wholesale **Mercado Artesania** is opposite the bus station.

Information

The **tourist office** (☎414-273-08-41; www.tequisquiapanqueretaro.gob.mx; Plaza Miguel Hidalgo; ⏱9am-7pm) has town maps and information on Querétaro state. On the plaza's southeast side, there's a Bancomer ATM.

Getting There & Around

Tequisquiapan is 20km northeast on Hwy 120 from the larger town of San Juan del Río. The bus terminal is around 2km north of the center in the new part of town. Local buses (M$6) from outside the bus station run to the markets on Carrizal, one block northeast of the Plaza Principal.

Flecha Azul runs half-hourly to/from Querétaro between 6:30am and 8pm (M$45, one hour). Buses also run to Ezequiel Montes (change here for Bernal; M$11, 20 minutes). ETN has deluxe buses to/from Mexico City's Terminal Norte (M$225, three hours, eight daily). Coordinados (Flecha Amarilla) and Flecha Roja have 2nd-class services to the same destination (M$182, three hours, regular departures).

Northeast Querétaro State

Those with a love of nature, or hankering to get off the beaten track, should not (again - not) miss the scenic Sierra Gorda, in northeast Querétaro. This area encompasses the incredible Reserva de la Biosfera Sierra Gorda which, thanks to recent ecotourism projects, is becoming increasingly

RESERVA DE LA BIOSFERA SIERRA GORDA

Established in 1997, the **Reserva de la Biosfera Sierra Gorda**, in the rugged Sierra Madre Oriental mountain range, covers the northeastern third of Querétaro state (about 3836 sq km).

Known as the 'green jewel' of central Mexico, the reserve boasts 15 vegetation types, making it the most ecosystem-diverse protected area in the country. Its stunning wilderness areas encompass old-growth cloud forests, semideserts and tropical forests; jaguars, rare orchids and endemic cacti are some of the fauna and flora you might be lucky to spot.

Over the past few years, numerous communities in rural Sierra Gorda have developed sustainable ecotourism projects. Travelers can head into villages with local guides, stay in basic cabins and camping areas, and partake in a range of activities. These include: treks to the Sótano del Barro, the world's second-largest free-fall vertical cave (410m deep), to see resident macaws; hikes to waterfalls including El Chuveje and Puente de Dios; and visits to Cuatro Palos for great views. Many communities have functioning workshops that produce pottery, natural remedies, dried foodstuffs, honey products and embroidery.

The easiest way to arrange overnight community visits is through **Sierra Gorda Eco Tours** (☎441-296-02-42/29; www.sierragordaecotours.com), a not-for-profit organization in Jalpan. Its website lists the current (and growing) list of communities involved, which are based in the municipalities of Jalpan de Serra, Pinal de Amoles, Arroyo Seco, Landa de Matamoros and Peña Miller. Prices vary according to the group number and activity but start at around M$1000 to M$2200 per person (based on a four-person group) – this includes transport (if required), accommodations, meals and activities, a Sierra Gorda Eco Tours guide and community guide (where necessary), plus entrance to attractions. Trips depart from Jalpan; a minimum of four days' notice is required.

accessible to visitors. The only limitation is transport: while it's possible to get to some places on the way by bus, it's much easier and less time consuming if you have your own wheels.

Jalpan

The attractive town of Jalpan centers on the **mission church**, constructed by Franciscan monks and their indigenous converts in the 1750s. It's the gateway to the five missions.

Not surprisingly, given its tropical climate, Jalpan specializes in artesanal – and very delicious – ice creams served in many *heladerías* around town.

Sleeping & Eating

Cabañas Centro Tierra BUNGALOW $
(☎441-296-07-00; www.sierragordaecotours.com; Centro Tierra Sierra Gorda, Av La Presa s/n, Barrio El Panteon; per person M$300) These seven eco-friendly and very comfortable cabins are run by, and situated near, Centro Tierra Sierra Gorda (that handily runs Sierra Gorda Eco Tours, p642). It's a 15-minute walk from the center of Jalpan, near the *presa* (reservoir).

Hotel Misión Jalpan HOTEL $$
(☎441-296-04-45; www.hotelesmision.com; Fray Junípero Serra s/n; r from M$860; P ⊖ ❄ ≋) On the west side of the plaza, the Hotel Misión Jalpan has attractive gardens and a restaurant but rooms are below par for what's generally considered to be the 'top' spot in town. It often offers midweek deals.

Restaurante Carretas MEXICAN $$
(mains M$70-160; ⊙8am-10pm Mon-Sat, to 5:30pm Sun) On the main road, Restaurante Carretas serves up a reasonable feed.

Information

Tourist Office (☎441-296-0243; Plazuel Hidalgo 441; ⊙8am-3:30pm) Housed in the Casa del Artesanía, the office provides basic information and listings and can arrange English-speaking guides to the missions (generally own transport required; around M$1200 to visit five missions).

Sierra Gorda Missions

In the mid-18th century, Franciscans established five beautiful missions in this remote region, including at Jalpan. These were inscribed as a Unesco World Heritage site in 2003. Founder Fray Junípero Serra went on to found the California mission chain. The restored churches are notable for their extraordinary and colorful facades carved with symbolic figures. East from Jalpan on Hwy 120, there are missions at **Landa de Matamoros** (1760–68); **Tilaco** (1754–62), 10km south of the highway; and **Tancoyol** (1753–60), 20km north of the highway. The mission of **Concá** (1754–58) is 35km north of Jalpan on Hwy 69. Generally, you'll need your own transport to get to these places though check with the tourist office in Jalpan or with Sierra Gorda Eco Tours.

GUANAJUATO STATE

The rocky highland state of Guanajuato (population 5.5 million) is full of riches of every kind. In colonial times, mineral resources attracted Spanish prospectors to mine for silver, gold, iron, lead, zinc and tin. For two centuries the state produced enormous wealth, extracting up to 40% of the world's silver. Silver barons in Guanajuato city enjoyed opulent lives at the expense of indigenous people who worked the mines, first as slave labor and then as wage slaves. Eventually, resenting the dominance of Spanish-born colonists, the well-heeled criollo class of Guanajuato and Querétaro states contributed to plans for rebellion.

These days, the state's treasures are the quaint colonial towns of Guanajuato and San Miguel de Allende. The industrial town of León is important economically as a center of leather production. Visitors to this region can enjoy its precious legacies: stunning colonial architecture, established cultural scenes and a stream of never-ending festivals...not to mention friendly, proud locals and a lively university atmosphere.

Guanajuato

☎473 / POP 725,000 / ELEV 2045M

The extraordinary Unesco World Heritage city of Guanajuato was founded in 1559 due to the region's rich silver and gold deposits. Opulent colonial buildings, stunning tree-filled plazas and brightly colored houses are crammed onto the steep slopes of a ravine. Excellent museums, handsome theaters and a fine marketplace punctuate the cobblestone streets. The city's 'main' roads twist around the hillsides and plunge into tunnels, formerly rivers.

Guanajuato

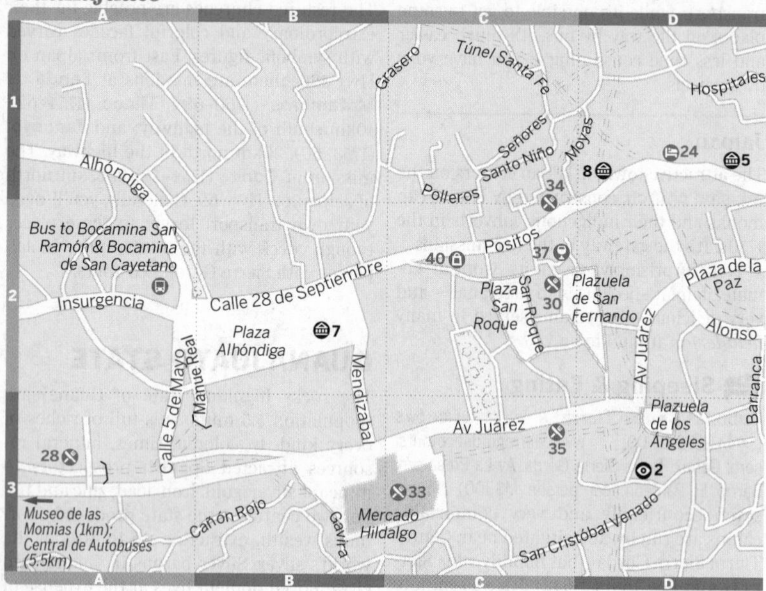

The city is best known globally for its acclaimed annual international arts festival, the Festival Cervantino. Yet this colorful and lively place holds center stage all year long; much of the youthful vibrancy and prolific cultural activities – *callejoneadas*, films, theater and orchestras – can be attributed to the 20,000 students of the city's own University of Guanajuato.

The city usually boasts fine weather during the day, but beware of cold and windy nights in the winter.

History

One of the hemisphere's richest silver veins was uncovered in 1558 at La Valenciana mine; for 250 years the mine produced 20% of the world's silver. Colonial barons benefiting from this mineral treasure were infuriated when King Carlos III of Spain slashed their share of the wealth in 1765. The King's 1767 decree banishing the Jesuits from Spanish dominions further alienated both the wealthy barons and the poor miners, who held allegiance to the Jesuits.

This anger was focused in the War of Independence. In 1810 rebel leader Miguel Hidalgo set off the independence movement with his Grito de Independencia (Cry for Independence) in nearby Dolores (p655). Guanajuato citizens joined the independence fighters and defeated the Spanish and loyalists, seizing the city in the rebellion's first military victory. When the Spaniards eventually retook the city they retaliated by conducting the infamous 'lottery of death,' in which names of Guanajuato citizens were drawn at random and the 'winners' were tortured and hanged.

Independence was eventually won, freeing the silver barons to amass further wealth. From this wealth arose many of the mansions, churches and theaters.

In the late 1990s the state prospered under its PAN (National Action Party) governor, Vicente Fox Quesada, with Mexico's lowest unemployment rate and an export rate three times the national average. Fox was chosen as the PAN candidate for the 2000 presidential election and his popularity sealed the victory (his presidential term ended in 2006).

Sights

Basílica de Nuestra Señora de Guanajuato CHURCH

(Plaza de la Paz s/n) The Basílica de Nuestra Señora de Guanajuato, a block west of Jardín de la Unión, contains a jewel-covered image of the Virgin, patron of Guanajuato.

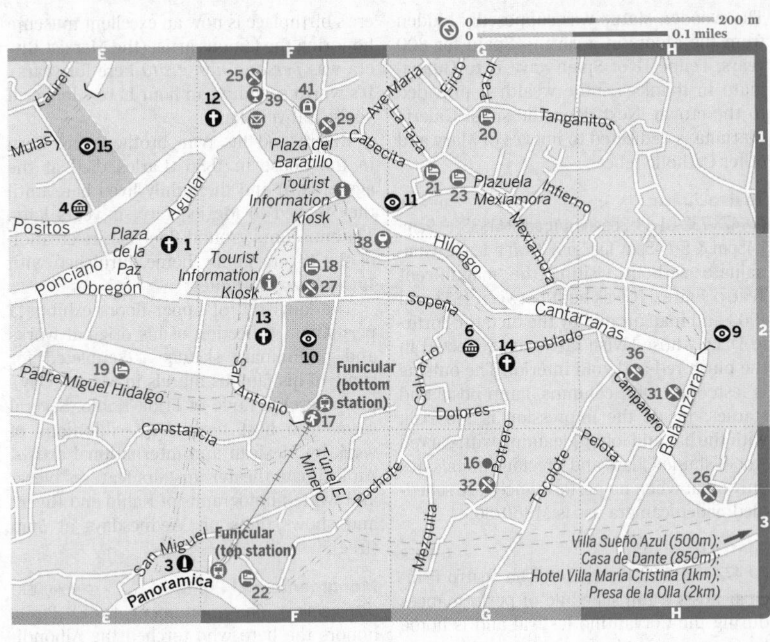

Guanajuato

Sights

1 Basílica de Nuestra Señora de Guanajuato E2
2 Callejón del Beso D3
3 Monumento a El Pípila E3
4 Museo del Pueblo de Guanajuato E1
5 Museo del Siglo XIX D1
6 Museo Iconográfico del Quijote G2
7 Museo Regional de Guanajuato Alhóndiga de Granaditas B2
8 Museo y Casa de Diego Rivera D1
9 Teatro Cervantes H2
10 Teatro Juárez F2
11 Teatro Principal G1
12 Templo de la Compañía de Jesús F1
13 Templo de San Diego F2
14 Templo de San Francisco G2
15 Universidad de Guanajuato E1

Activities, Courses & Tours

16 Escuela Mexicana G3
17 Funicular F2
Plateros Spanish School .... (see 19)

Sleeping

18 1850 Hotel F2
19 Alonso10 Hotel Boutique & Arte E2
20 Casa Bertha G1
21 Casa de Pita G1
22 Casa Zuniga F3
23 El Zopilote Mojado G1
24 Mesón de los Poetas D1

Eating

25 A Punto F1
26 Café Tal H3
27 Casa Valadez F2
28 Central Comercio A3
29 Centro Bharati F1
30 Delica Mitsu C2
31 Habibti H2
32 La Taula G3
33 Mercado Hidalgo C3
34 Meztizo C1
35 Restaurant La Carreta C3
36 Santo Café H2

Drinking & Nightlife

37 Clave Azul C2
38 El Incendio F2
39 El Midi Bistró F1
One Bar & Lounge .... (see 18)

Shopping

40 El Viejo Zaguán C2
41 Xocola-T F1

The wooden statue was supposedly hidden from the Moors in a cave in Spain for 800 years. Felipe II of Spain gave it to Guanajuato in thanks for the wealth it provided to the crown. Next door, the small Galería Mariana is dedicated to images of Mary and other Catholic relics.

Teatro Juárez THEATER
(☎473-732-01-83; Sopeña s/n; adult M$35; ⏲9am-1:45pm & 5-7:45pm Tue-Sun) Don't leave Guanajuato without visiting the magnificent Teatro Juárez. It was built between 1873 and 1903 and inaugurated by the dictator Porfirio Díaz, whose lavish tastes are reflected in the plush red-and-gold interior. The outside is festooned with columns, lamp posts and statues; inside the impression is Moorish, with the bar and lobby gleaming with carved wood, stained glass and precious metals. It's only open when no performances are scheduled; video/camera use is M$60/30.

Teatro Principal THEATER
(☎473-732-15-23; Hidalgo s/n) The Teatro Principal hosts a full schedule of performances during the Cervantino festival and is home to Guanajuato's impressive symphony orchestra. Performances are held most Friday nights (except October and January) at 8:30pm. Tickets cost M$80.

Teatro Cervantes THEATER
(☎473-732-11-69; Plaza Allende s/n) The Teatro Cervantes hosts a full schedule of performances during the Cervantino festival and less-regular shows at other times. Statues of Don Quixote and Sancho Panza grace the small Plaza Allende, in front of its theater.

Museo y Casa de Diego Rivera MUSEUM
(☎473-732-11-97; Positos 47; adult M$20; ⏲10am-6:30pm Tue-Sat, 10am-2:30pm Sun) Diego Rivera's birthplace is now an excellent museum honoring the famous artist (the Marxist Rivera was *persona non grata* here for years). It's worth spending an hour here – longer if you're a Rivera fan.

Rivera and his twin brother were born in the house in 1886 (Carlos died at the age of two) and the family lived here until they moved to Mexico City six years later. The museum's ground floor is a re-creation of the Rivera family home, furnished with 19th-century antiques.

The labyrinth of upper floors exhibits a permanent collection of his original works and preliminary sketches (completed for some of his famous murals in Mexico City), plus there's a nude of Frida Kahlo. Several *salas* also host temporary exhibitions of work by Mexican and international artists. An intimate theater upstairs features black-and white-photographs of Kahlo and Rivera and shows films on Wednesdays at 5pm (free).

Monumento a El Pípila MONUMENT
(Panoramica) The monument to El Pípila honors the hero who torched the Alhóndiga gates on September 28, 1810, enabling Hidalgo's forces to win the first victory of the independence movement. The statue shows El Pípila holding his torch high over the city. On the base is the inscription *Aún hay otras Alhóndigas por incendiar* (There are still other Alhóndigas to burn).

Two routes from the center of town go up steep, picturesque lanes. One goes east on Sopeña from Jardín de la Unión, then turns right on Callejón del Calvario (this becomes Pochote; turn right at Subida San Miguel). Another ascent, unmarked, goes uphill from the small plaza on Alonso. Alternatively, the 'Pípila-ISSSTE' bus heading west on Avenida Juárez will let you off right by the statue, or you can ride up in the funicular.

Museo Regional de Guanajuato Alhóndiga de Granaditas MUSEUM
(☎473-732-11-12; Calle 28 de Septiembre; admission M$49, camera/video use M$30/60; ⏲10am-5:30pm Tue-Sat, 10am-2:30pm Sun) This art and history museum was the site of the first major rebel victory in Mexico's War of Independence. Built between 1798 and 1808 as a grain storehouse, the Alhóndiga became a fortress in 1810 when 300 Spanish troops and loyalist leaders barricaded themselves inside when 20,000 rebels led by Miguel Hidalgo attempted to take Guanajuato. On

COLONIAL CHURCHES

Aside from the Basílica de Nuestra Señora de Guanajuato, other fine colonial churches include the **Templo de San Diego** (Jardín de la Union s/n), opposite the Jardín de la Unión; the **Templo de San Francisco** (Doblado s/n); and the large **Templo de la Compañía de Jesús** (Lascuraín de Retana s/n), which was completed in 1747 for the Jesuit seminary whose buildings are now occupied by the University of Guanajuato.

September 28, 1810, a young miner nicknamed El Pípila tied a stone slab to his back and, thus protected from Spanish bullets, set the entrance ablaze. The rebels moved in and killed everyone inside.

The Alhóndiga was later used as an armory, then a school, before it was a prison for 80 years (1864–1948). It became a museum in 1958. Don't miss José Chávez Morado's dramatic murals of Guanajuato's history on the staircases.

Ex-Hacienda San Gabriel de Barrera MUSEUM, GARDEN

(Camino Antiguo a Marfil, Km 2.5; adult M$22; 9am-6pm) To escape Guanajuato's bustling streets, head 2.5km west to this magnificent colonial home, which is now a museum with tranquil and stunning gardens.

Built at the end of the 17th century, this was the grand hacienda of Captain Gabriel de Barrera, whose family was descended from the first Conde de Rul of the famous La Valenciana mine. Opened as a museum in 1979, the hacienda, with its opulent period European furnishings, provides an insight into the lives of the wealthy of the time.

Take one of the frequent 'Marfil' buses heading west in the subterranean tunnel under Avenida Juárez and ask the driver to drop you at Hotel Misión Guanajuato.

Museo Iconográfico del Quijote MUSEUM

(473-732-33-76; Doblado 1; adult/student M$30/10; 9:30am-6:45pm Tue-Sun) This surprisingly interesting museum is worth half an hour of your time. It fronts the tiny plaza in front of the Templo de San Francisco. Every exhibit relates to Don Quixote de la Mancha, the notorious Spanish literary hero, depicted in numerous different media by different artists in different styles. Paintings, statues, tapestries, even chess sets, clocks and postage stamps all feature the quixotic icon and his bumbling companion Sancho Panza.

Templo La Valenciana CHURCH

(Iglesia de San Cayetano) On a hill overlooking Guanajuato, 5km north of the center, is the magnificent Templo La Valenciana. Its facade is spectacular and its interior dazzles with ornate golden altars, filigree carvings and giant paintings.

One legend says that the Spaniard who started the nearby San Ramón mine promised San Cayetano that if it made him rich, he would build a church to honor the saint. Another says that the silver baron of La Valenciana, Conde de Rul, tried to atone for exploiting the miners by building the ultimate in Churrigueresque churches. Whatever the motive, ground was broken in 1765 and the church was completed in 1788.

Bocamina San Ramón & Bocamina de San Cayetano MINES

(www.bocaminasanramon.com; admission M$35; 10am-6pm) These neighboring mines are part of the famous Valenciana mining district. Silver was discovered here in 1548. At **San Ramón**, you can descend via steps into a mine shaft to a depth of 60m (note: not for claustrophobics). **San Cayetano** has an interesting museum and former miners take you on a brief tour – including a shaft visit. To reach the mines, take a 'Cristo Rey' or 'Valenciana' bus from the bus stop on the corner of Alhóndiga and Calle 28 de Septiembre. Get off at Templo La Valenciana and follow the signs behind the church.

Museo de las Momias MUSEUM

(Museum of the Mummies; 473-732-06-39; Explanada del Pantéon Municipal s/n; adult M$52; 9am-6pm) This famous museum is one of the most bizarre (some might say distasteful) sights at the *panteón* (cemetery). The popular attraction is a quintessential example of Mexico's acceptance of, celebration of and obsession with death; visitors come from all over to see more than 100 disinterred corpses.

While technically these are mummified remains – due to the dry atmosphere in their former crypts – the bodies are not thousands of years old. The first remains were unearthed in 1865 to make room for more bodies in the cemeteries. What the authorities uncovered were not skeletons but flesh mummified (many feature grotesque forms and facial expressions).

The complex is on the western edge of town, a 10-minute ride from Avenida Juárez on any 'Momias' bus (M$5).

Museo del Pueblo de Guanajuato MUSEUM

(473-732-29-90; Positos 7; adult M$20; 10am-6:30pm Tue-Sat, 10am-2:30pm Sun) Located beside the university, this fascinating art museum displays an exquisite collection of Mexican miniatures, and 18th- and 19th-century art with works by Guanajuatan painters Hermenegildo Bustos and José Chávez Morado, plus temporary exhibitions. It occupies the former mansion of the Marqueses de San Juan de Rayas, who owned the San Juan de Rayas mine. The private baroque chapel (built 1696) upstairs in the courtyard contains an interesting three-panelled mural by José Chávez Morado depicting the Spanish colonisation.

Callejón del Beso NOTABLE BUILDING
(The Alley of the Kiss) Narrowest of the many alleyways in Guanajuato's streets is this *callejón*, where the balconies of two houses practically touch. In a local legend, a fine family once lived on this street and their daughter fell in love with a common miner. They were forbidden to see each other, but the miner rented a room opposite and the lovers exchanged furtive *besos* (kisses) from these balconies. Inevitably, the romance was discovered and the couple met a tragic end.

From the Plazuela de los Ángeles on Avenida Juárez, walk about 40m up Callejón del Patrocinio to see the tiny alley on your left.

Casa de Arte Olga Costa-José Chávez Morado MUSEUM
(Pastita 158, Torre del Arco; adult/student M$20/5; ⏲9:30am-4pm Thu-Sat, 10am-3pm Sun) In 1966, artists José Chávez Morado and Olga Costa converted a massive old well into their home and studio; before their deaths, they donated their home and its contents for public use. On display is a small, but fascinating collection of items from the 16th to 18th centuries, including pre-Hispanic and modern ceramics, embroidery, furniture, masks and their own artworks. It's worth heading to the 'suburb' of Pastita to experience a side of Guanajuato you might otherwise miss.

The pretty approach follows the former aqueduct which ends at their house. Take any bus marked 'Pastita' from the eastern end of town.

Universidad de Guanajuato NOTABLE BUILDING
(UGTO; ☎473-732-00-06; www.ugto.mx; Lascuraín de Retana 5) The main building of this university, whose ramparts are visible above much of the city, is one block up the hill from the basilica. The distinctive multistory white-and-blue building with the crenelated pediment dates from the 1950s. The design was (and, some might say, continues to be) controversial as this dominating structure impedes the characteristic, historic cityscape.

Museo del Siglo XIX MUSEUM
(☎473-734-61-93; www.museodelsiglo19.com.mx; Positos 25; admission M$20; ⏲10am-6pm Mon-Sun) Opened in 2010 and housed in a renovated colonial mansion, the seven rooms showcase a private collection of items relating to the history of Guanajuato, from photos, books, paintings and documents of the 19th century, before 1910.

Cristo Rey MONUMENT
Cristo Rey (Christ the King) is a 20m bronze statue of Jesus erected in 1950 on the summit of the Cerro de Cubilete, 15km west of Guanajuato. The location of the statue at the supposed geographical center of the country holds particular significance for Mexican tourists, with impressive views an added draw.

Tour agencies offer 3½-hour trips, but you can go on your own from the center. Buses marked 'Cubilete' or 'Cristo Rey' depart every hour or so from near Alhóndiga (M$38 return).

Funicular FUNICULAR
(Plaza Constancia s/n; one-way/round trip M$15/30; ⏲8am-9:45pm Mon-Fri, 9am-9:45pm Sat, 10am-8:45pm Sun) This incline railway inches up (and down) the slope behind the Teatro Juárez to a terminal near the El Pípila monument. Heading up is fun, but to descend, you can save your pennies by walking down (there are two obvious, well-paved routes).

Courses

Guanajuato is a university town and has an excellent atmosphere for studying Spanish. Group classes average around US$150 to US$210 for 20 lessons (one week's worth) and private lessons average US$17 an hour. Schools can arrange homestays with meals for around US$190 per week. Additional costs may include registration and/or placement test fees, excursions and extracurricular activities. Language schools to consider include **Plateros Spanish School** (☎473-732-99-42; www.platerosspanishschool.com; Alonso 14A), **Adelita** (☎473-100-49-47; www.la-adelita.org; Agua Fuerte 56), **Don Quijote** (☎923-277-200; www.donquijote.org; Calle Pastita 76, Barrio Pastita), and **Escuela Mexicana** (☎473-732-50-05; www.escuelamexicana.com; Potrero 12).

Mika Matsuishi & Felipe Olmos Workshops COURSE
(☎473-120-4299; www.felipeymika.wix.com/mojigangas) Hands-on, fun art workshops for creative souls run by talented artists and *mojiganga* specialists. Materials included; prices vary according to activity.

GUANAJUATO'S PRETTY PLAZAS

A wander around the beautiful main plazas, the bustling hubs of Guanajuato's social life, is a good introduction to Guanajuato's historic center. Pretty **Jardín de la Unión**, surrounded by restaurants and shaded by Indian laurel trees, is the social heart of the city. Here, tourists and locals congregate in the late afternoon, along with buskers, shoe-shiners and mariachis.

The elegant **Teatro Juárez** sits on its southeast corner. Walk west on Obregón to **Plaza de la Paz**, the small triangle beside the basilica, surrounded by the former homes of wealthy silver lords.

Meander west and south along the curving Avenida Juárez to **Plazuela de los Ángeles**, where the steps are popular gathering spots for students. The Callejón del Beso is just a few meters uphill from here.

Continue on Avenida Juárez to three picturesque spaces: the handsome **Jardín de la Reforma**, behind the row of classical columns; **Plaza San Roque**, where *entremeses* (theatrical sketches) are performed during the Cervantino festival; and the pretty, flower-filled **Plazuela de San Fernando** nearby.

Head further west on Avenida Juárez to the bustling area in front of the Mercado Hidalgo. A block north, **Plaza Alhóndiga** has wide steps leading up to the Alhóndiga. From there, wander back east along Calle 28 de Septiembre (which changes names several times), past museums and the university, with a few twists and turns, to **Plaza del Baratillo** with its Florentine fountain. From here you can detour to the tiny **Plazuela Mexiamora** and down again to Baratillo. A right turn and a short block south from there will bring you back to Jardín de la Unión.

Festivals & Events

Baile de las Flores RELIGIOUS

The Flower Dance takes place on the Thursday before Semana Santa. The next day, mines are open to the public for sightseeing and celebrations. Miners decorate altars to La Virgen de los Dolores, a manifestation of the Virgin Mary who looks after miners.

Fiestas de San Juan y Presa de la Olla RELIGIOUS

The festivals of San Juan are celebrated at the Presa de la Olla park in late June. The 24th is the big bash for the saint's day itself, with dances, music, fireworks and picnics. Then on the first Monday in July, everyone comes back to the park for another big party celebrating the opening of the dam's floodgates.

Día de la Cueva RELIGIOUS

Cave Day is a country fair held on July 31, when locals walk to a cave in the nearby hills to honor San Ignacio de Loyola and enjoy a festive picnic.

Fiesta de la Virgen de Guanajuato RELIGIOUS

This festival on August 9 commemorates the date when Felipe II gave the people of Guanajuato the jeweled wooden Virgin that now adorns the basilica.

Festival Internacional Cervantino ARTS

(www.festivalcervantino.gob.mx) Back in the 1950s, the festival merely consisted of *entremeses* from Miguel Cervantes' work performed by students. It has since grown to become one of Latin America's foremost arts events. Music, dance and theater groups from around the world perform diverse works (mostly non-Cervantes-related) for two to three weeks in October at this arts extravaganza.

Tickets for single events range from M$130 to M$650 and should be booked in advance (www.ticketmaster.com.mx) along with hotels. In Guanajuato, tickets are available from a booth by Teatro Juárez two months before the festival.

Sleeping

During October's Festival Internacional Cervantino, Christmas, Semana Santa (and in some cases only, summer holiday periods), prices may be around 20% above the regular rates given here.

Casa Bertha HOSTEL, GUESTHOUSE $

(☎473-732-13-16; Tamboras 9; r per person with/without bathroom from M$190/160, apt per person M$210-260; wifi) This tired, but 'keeps on keeping on' family-run *casa de huéspedes* (guesthouse) is a contemporary version of *The Matrix*. The labyrinth of internal iron staircases leads to various-sized rooms (some with internal-facing windows) and three family-size apartments. The rooftop kitchen/terrace is a bonus. Head up beside Teatro Principal to Plazuela Mexiamora; here, follow the blue 'Casa Bertha' sign.

Casa de Dante HOSTEL $$

(☎ 473-731-09-09; www.casadedante.com; Callejón de Zaragoza 25; dm from M$250, s/d incl breakfast from M$400/800;) 'My family is your family,' greets the owner of this ultrafriendly hostel. You can opt for a dormitory or for a well-kept room (claustrophics note: one private room doesn't have a window). Some rooms have private bathrooms. In addition, there are two kitchens and an outdoor terrace barbecue available for use.

It's a little out of town on the way to La Presa and up 156-plus steps. Head up the *callejón* next to Hotel Independencia on Paseo de la Presa. Prices are considerably lower outside high season and longer-term stays are negotiable.

Casa Zuniga B&B $$

(☎ 473-732-85-46; www.casazunigagto.com; Callejón del Pachote 38; r incl breakfast from M$1100;) This sprawling B&B offers various modern rooms and receives rave reviews for its hospitality extended by the charismatic duo, Carmen and Rick, and its extra generous, carb- and protein-fueled breakfasts. It's located on the hill near El Pípila, to the left of the funicular (as heading uphill), or by car and bus along Panoramica.

Rates include a funicular pass throughout your stay. It's one of the town's few places with a lap pool.

Villa Sueño Azul B&B $$

(☎ 473-731-0157; www.villasuenoazul.com; San Sebastian 88; s M$740-890, d M$940-1290;) Behind a blue facade is this pleasant blue-and-white themed oasis – a secure and tidy B&B with a helpful English-speaking manager, Malí, and ever-so-slightly dated rooms, a lovely sunroom and pot-plant-filled terrace. It's located southeast of, but still within a 10-minute walk to, the hectic downtown area.

It's also on a bus route (read: possible noise in the two front rooms, which cost slightly less as a result. Buses don't run all night, however).

El Zopilote Mojado GUESTHOUSE $$

(☎ 473-732-53-11; www.elzopilotemojado.com; Plazuela Mexiamora 51 & 53; r & apt US$70, 6-person apt US$220;) Six pleasant, rustic rooms are located above Café Zopilote Mojado and in a '70s-style house nearby, where they share a spacious communal kitchen, lounge-dining area and outdoor terraces. Two chic (if dark) apartments and a family apartment are near the plaza. No guests under 14-years-old allowed.

Casa de Pita PENSION $$

(☎ 473-732-15-32; www.casadepita.com; Cabecita 26; s M$300, d M$450-900, apt M$500; @) This secure spot is a literal maze of atmospheric, quirky guest rooms in a centrally located converted house. Lodgings vary in size and facilities – some are apartments and several verge on claustrophic. Best to reserve online.

★ **Casa Estrella de la Valenciana** B&B $$$

(☎ 473-732-17-84; www.mexicaninns.com; Callejon Jalisco 10; r M$2000-2700;) This delightful US-owned abode ticks many boxes: eight unique rooms, some with *boveda* (vaulted) ceilings, private terraces, and stunning, sunny communal areas. Then there's the lovely English-speaking staff, lavish breakfasts and a swimming pool. Perched high above Guanajuato in La Valenciana (around a M$50 taxi ride or M$5 bus ride), it suits those who don't mind being out of the bustle of the city, but you will have to rely on transport to get you to-and-fro.

Hotel Villa María Cristina BOUTIQUE HOTEL $$$

(☎ 473-731-21-82; www.villamariacristina.net; Paseo de la Presa de la Olla 76; ste M$3770-5850;) This stunning converted mansion is scented with expensive perfume. The decor in the spacious rooms features neoclassical French designer furniture, original paintings by local artist Jesús Gallardo, and beds and bathrooms with all the fluffy and puffy trimmings.

Outside, various patios (which are covered in exquisite, original tiles) have everything from fountains and wicker chairs to Jacuzzis plus views of La Bufa. An onsite restaurant is open all day (dinner mains M$195 to M$320). It's in La Presa, a 15-minute walk from the center of Guanajuato.

Alonso10 Hotel Boutique & Arte BOUTIQUE HOTEL $$$

(☎ 473-732-76-57; www.hotelalonso10.com.mx; Alonso 10; ste M$2800-M$3100;) This sleek boutique hotel is located a street away from the centralized chaos. White and taupe hues rule, as do smart rooms with all the trimmings. The front two suites have fabulous balconies with quirky views of the basilica and the back of Teatro Juárez. Downstairs is an elegant restaurant (mains M$100 to M$210).

Mesón de los Poetas HOTEL $$$
(☎473-732-07-05; www.mesondelospoetas.com; Positos 35; r incl breakfast M$1570-2300;) Built against the hillside, this hotel's labyrinth of rooms – each named after a poet – offers, on the whole, comfortable, clean lodgings. You won't wax lyrical about the light (some rooms are dark), but it's worth considering. We like rooms 401, 402 and 403, which share a sunny terrace. Suite 200D is pricier, but recently renovated.

1850 Hotel BOUTIQUE HOTEL $$$
(☎473-732-2795; http://hotel1850.com/index.php/en/; Jardín de la Unión 7; r M$2000-5000;) Snappy and smart and appealing to those who go for Mexican sleek (think: converted mansion with lots of silver and designer trim and, er, dog sculptures). Each room is unique and very, very nice. It's in a marvellous location – right on El Jardin – and the double-glazed windows ensure you don't hear the mariachis in the adjacent plaza. The rooftop bar is unbeatable.

Eating

Eating in Guanajuato won't blow your culinary world apart. Having said that, there are a few exceptions. For fresh produce and cheap snacks and lunches, head to the **Mercado Hidalgo** (Av Juárez), a five-minute walk west of Jardín de la Unión on Avenida Juárez. Another two blocks further down on the right is **Central Comercio** (Av Juárez), with a large supermarket.

Jardín de la Unión & Around

Habibti MIDDLE EASTERN $
(Sostenes Rocha 18B; M$25-110; 9am-11pm Mon-Sat, to 10pm Sunday) This tiny spot is one of the cheapest eats for those on a budget. It's a hole-in-the-wall with a few tables and whips up excellent and oh-so-fresh falafels. Or you can opt for plate combos of tasty morsels – hummus, tabbouleh, dahl and *hojas de parra*.

Santo Café CAFE $
(Puente de Campanero; mains M$45-95; 10am-midnight Mon-Sat, noon-8pm Sun;) Stop by this casual but cozy spot on the quaint Venetian-style bridge and check the latest university vibe. It serves good salads and snacks (the soy burger is great for vegetarians). Some tables overlook the alley below.

Café Tal CAFE $
(Temezcuitate 4; snacks M$23-34; 7am-midnight Mon-Fri, 8am-midnight Sat & Sun;) This spot hasn't changed in the six years we've been coming here; the grungier it gets, the more popular it seems to get. The reason being, it roasts, grinds and serves good coffee plus it's the place for wi-fi seeking students and social expats to meet. Don't miss the *beso negro* (black kiss), ultra-concentrated hot chocolate (M$12).

If you're lucky, Tal the cat might sit on your lap.

La Taula INTERNATIONAL $$
(www.lataula.mx; Callejon del Potrero 2X; M$50-160; noon-midnight Mon-Sat) The idea at this fun spot owned by a charismatic young chef is to share plates – generous portions of *botanas* (snacks). Thursday (supply day) is the day for fish, especially the outstanding salmon carpaccio (M$150), while the *costillas* (ribs) are also a hit at M$65.

Casa Valadez MEXICAN $$$
(☎473-732-11-57; www.casavaladez.com; Jardín de la Unión 3; mains M$100-580; 9am-11pm) This classic place is a smart choice in every respect and attracts a loyal crowd of well-dressed locals. Given its fine location – it faces both the Jardín and Teatro Juaréz – it's reasonable value (make an experience of it). Servings are Mexican (read: generous). Dishes are mainly international with a few Mexican favorites (under 'capriciosos' on the menu) such as *pollo con enchiladas mineras* (enchiladas with chicken and the lot).

Plazuela de San Fernando & Around

★**Delica Mitsu** JAPANESE $
(Cantaritos 37; mains M$40-85; noon-5pm & 7-9pm Mon-Sat) This tiny Japanese-run hole-in-the-wall doesn't have the most salubrious surrounds, but it serves up some of the biggest, freshest and best Japanese flavors around.

Restaurant La Carreta GRILL $
(☎473-732-43-58; Av Juárez 96; mains M$60-150; 10:30am-8:30pm) Follow your nose to La Carreta, a buzzing, unpretentious local

CALLEJONEADAS – THE TRADITIONAL WAY TO PARTY

The *callejoneada* tradition is said to have come from Spain. A group of professional singers and musicians, dressed in traditional costumes, starts up in a central location such as a plaza, a crowd gathers, then the whole mob winds through the alleyways, streets and plazas playing, dancing and singing heartily. In Guanajuato, they are also called *estudiantinas*. Stories and jokes (in Spanish) are told in between songs, often relating to the legends of the alleys. In Zacatecas, there are no stories, but hired bands called *tamboras* (dressed in uniform, not traditional attire) lead dancing revelers. On special occasions a *burro* laden with wine is brought along. Often, strangers are just expected to join the party and the crowd swells. Occasionally, the organizers foot the bill, sometimes you pay a small amount for the wine you drink (or you bring your own). In Guanajuato, the groups themselves or tour companies sell tickets (M$100, 1¼ hours; Tuesday through Sunday) for the *callejoneadas*, and juice (not alcohol) is provided. It's great fun.

eatery lined with wagon wheels, whose street-front grill 'spins' out super-scrumptious *pollo asado con leña* (grilled chicken) and *carne asada* (grilled beef), served with large portions of rice and salad.

Meztizo INTERNATIONAL $$
(Positos 69; mains M$80-135; ⌚1-10pm Tue-Sat, 1-6pm Sun) *Meztizo* means 'mix'; this place is so-called because it houses both a restaurant and gallery (run by the Cabelo father-son team, the fatehr a famous local artist, and his son, a chef). What it lacks in ambience (it's a little dog-eared), it makes up for in its cuisine. While the menu is small, it's big on quality, especially the meat dishes.

Plaza del Baratillo

★ **Centro Bharati** INDIAN, MEXICAN $
(Plaza del Baratillo 11; M$50-90; ⌚8am-7:30pm Tue-Fri, 9am-7:30pm Sat, 1-7:30pm Sun) Tap into your holistic side with flavours of a different kind. This friendly cafe offers a casual eating experience in a colonial building and some of the best-value cuisine around. Plates change daily.

In the mornings from 8am, fresh juices, snacks and bread are available at the front door; everything is made on the premises. A small boutique is upstairs, as is a massage room.

A Punto INTERNATIONAL $$
(Casa Cuatro, San Jose 4; M$150-185; ⌚2-10pm Tue & Wed, 2-11pm Thu-Sun) Among Guanajuato's most cosmopolitan spots, this new place, in the pleasant Casa Cuatro (restored mansion complex) serves up high quality international dishes. Lovely for a long lunch or dinner.

El Midi Bistró MEDITERRANEAN $$
(www.elmidibistro.com; Casa Cuatro, San Jose 4; salads M$17 per 100g; ⌚noon-11pm Wed-Sat & Mon, Sun noon-5pm; 📶) This tastefully decorated part-bistro, part-bar on the top floor serves excellent lunchtime salads (M$17 per 100g), OK dinners and cocktail-fusion fun (see bars). Live music on Thursday evenings and *looong* Sunday brunches make it one of the town's most pleasant places to kick back in. Big magnet for expats, but not exclusively so.

La Presa & Around

México Lindo y Sabroso MEXICAN $$
(☎473-731-05-29; Paseo de la Presa 154; mains M$70-150; ⌚9am-10pm) Tasty Mexican dishes in tasteful and colorful surrounds, including a delightful outdoor veranda. Head up Paseo de la Presa for about 1.4km and it's on the left-hand side. The Sunday brunch buffet attracts hungry locals with big appetites.

San Javier

★ **Las Mercedes** MEXICAN $$$
(☎473-732-73-75; www.guanajuatoesparati.com/lasmercedes; Arriba 6, San Javier; mains M$183-300; ⌚2-10pm Tue-Sat, 2-6pm Sun) In a residential area overlooking the city is Guanajuato's best restaurant. Popular with government and business officials, and for romantic diners, it serves Mexican cuisine *á la abuela* (grandmother's cooking that takes hours to prepare), such as *moles* hand ground in *molcajetes* – with a contemporary twist. Dish presentation is contemporary and stylish. Reservations recommended.

To get there, take a taxi; you'll head down the valley (in a northwesterly direction as though heading to La Valenciana) but will then turn suddenly to head west up a hill.

 Drinking & Nightlife

Every evening, the Jardín de la Unión comes alive with people crowding the outdoor tables, strolling and listening to the street musicians and mariachi bands.

Given the city's immense student population (Thursday is generally their big night out), there's no lack of bars and nightclubs to choose from. Drinking and dancing in Guanajuato generally starts late.

El Midi Bistró BAR

(Casa Cuatro, San Jose 4; cocktails M$50-70; ⏲noon-11pm Wed-Sat & Mon, Sun noon-5pm) When it comes to cocktails at this popular spot, Sam's your man. The chief mixologist and his team blend old-school cocktails with Mexican flavours. Concoctions include daiquiris (with a twist), *ponches* (punch drinks) and a long list of liquid treats infused with everything from basil to lavender. If you're after something more standard, go for the trusty – and very good – margarita.

El Incendio BAR

(Cantarranas 39; ⏲11am-11pm) A former old-school cantina – whose legacy is swinging doors, an open urinal (as per the old cantinas; no longer used) and mural-covered walls – that caters to a fun but rowdy student crowd.

Clave Azul CANTINA

(☎473-732-15-61; Segunda de Cantaritos 31; ⏲1:30-10pm Mon-Thu, 1:30pm-midnight Fri & Sat) It's been around for years but we keep coming back. This artifact-filled cantina offers an authentic Mexican drinking experience with accompanying *botanas* (tapas-like snacks served free with drinks, in this case between 2pm and 5:30pm). It's located up a small alley to the left of Bossanova Café.

One Bar & Lounge BAR

(1850 Hotel, Jardín de la Unión 7; cocktails from M$70; ⏲5pm-midnight Sun-Thu, 5pm-3am Fri & Sat) With views acrosss to Teatro Juarez and Jardín de la Unión below, this ultra-mod bar atop 1850 Hotel is a smart spot for an evening cocktail.

☆ Entertainment

Events include theater (held in one of three fine centrally located theaters), music, opera and dance running from March to December. A monthly listing is available from the tourist kiosks in Jardín de la Unión.

Shopping

El Viejo Zaguán BOOKS

(☎cell phone 7323971; Positos 64; ⏲10:30am-3pm & 5-8pm Tue-Sat, 11am-3pm Sun) Wonderful bilingual publications, art books, gifts and a relaxing coffee stop.

Xocola-T FOOD

(Plazuela del Baratillo 15; Chocolates M$8-12; ⏲9am-9pm Mon-Sat, noon-5pm Sun) This chocoholic's nirvana sells delectable handmade chocolates of pure cocoa with natural flavors and not a trans fat in sight. Quirkier fillings include *chapulines* (grasshoppers), *gusanos* (caterpillars) and *nopal* (cactus).

ℹ Information

INTERNET ACCESS

Many internet places line the streets around the university; most charge M$10 per hour. Several cafes offer wi-fi access. Public wi-fi access is also available in public places (though be careful of flaunting your hardware).

MEDICAL SERVICES

Centro Médico la Presa (☎473-102-31-00; Paseo de la Presa 85)

BUSES FROM GUANAJUATO

DESTINATION	FARE (M$)	DURATION	FREQUENCY (DAILY)
Dolores Hidalgo	60	1½hr	every 30min 5:30am-10:30pm
Guadalajara	269-420	4hr	frequent
León	49-175	1-1¼hr	very frequent
Mexico City (Terminal Norte)	449-540	4½hr	very frequent
Querétaro	178-186	2½hr	8
San Miguel de Allende	87-135	1½-2hr	17

Hospital General (☎473-733-15-73, 473-733-15-76; Carretera a Silao, Km 6.5)

MONEY

Banks along Avenida Juárez change cash and traveler's checks (but some only until 2pm) and have ATMs.

Divisas Dimas (Av Juárez 33A; ⏲10am-8pm Mon-Sat) A *casa de cambio* that even changes traveler's checks (only American Express).

POST

Post Office (Ayuntamiento 25; ⏲8am-4:30pm Mon-Fri, 8am-noon Sat)

TOURIST INFORMATION

Incredibly, the only formal information points in Guanajuato are two small tourist kiosks, located at **Jardín de la Unión** and an extension of this, in **Calle Allende**. Note: do not confuse these with official-looking booths marked 'Information Turística' that are dotted around town. The latter are private companies touting specific hotels and/or other services.

Getting There & Away

AIR

Guanajuato is served by the **Aeropuerto Internacional del Bajío**, which is about 30km west of the city, halfway between Léon and Silao.

BUS

Guanajuato's Central de Autobuses is around 5km southwest of town (confusingly, to get there go northwest out of town along Tepetapa). It has card phones and luggage storage (in the cafe). Deluxe and 1st-class bus tickets (ETN and Primera Plus) can be bought in town at **Viajes Frausto** (☎473-732-35-80; Obregón 10; ⏲9am-2pm & 4:30-7:30pm Mon-Fri, 9am-1:30pm Sat). A handy Venta de Boletos (ticket kiosk) for Primera Plus is located in an arcade opposite Plaza Baratillo.

Ominbus de Mexico has one direct bus to San Luis Potosí (M$225 at 6.45pm; or change in León for frequent connections). Primera Plus and ETN are the main 1st-class operators, while Flecha Amarilla has cheaper services to Dolores Hidalgo, León and San Miguel.

See table of buses from Guanajuato.

Getting Around

A taxi to Aeropuerto Internacional del Bajío will cost about M$400 (there's a set rate of M$450 from the airport; you buy your ticket at a taxi counter inside the airport). A cheaper option from Guanajuato is one of the frequent buses to Silao (M$40; every 20 minutes) and a taxi from there (around M$120). Note: in reverse – from the airport to Silao – the taxi rates are set and cost around 50% more).

Between the bus station and city center, 'Central de Autobuses' buses (M$6) run around the clock. From the center, you can catch them heading west on Avenida Juárez. From the bus terminal, you will enter a tunnel running east under the *centro histórico*. Alight at one of several entry/exit points: Mercado Hidalgo, Plaza de los Ángeles, Jardín de la Unión, Plaza Baratillo/Teatro Principal, Teatro Cervantes or Embajadoras (note: check the destination with the driver). A taxi to/from the bus station costs around M$40.

To get around town keep a look out – local buses display their destination. For the *centro histórico* the rule of thumb is as follows: all buses heading east go via the tunnels *below* Avenida Juárez (for example, if you want to go from the market to the Teatro Principal). Those heading west go *along* Avenida Juárez.

City buses (M$6) run from 7am to 10pm. Taxis are plentiful in the center and charge about M$35 for short trips around town (slightly more if heading uphill to El Pípila and the like).

León

Whether you like it or not, you will probably end up in the industrial city of León, 56km west of Guanajuato, thanks to its importance as a main bus hub within the state of Guanajuato. Also, it's only 20km from Aeropuerto Internacional del Bajío.

It's unlikely you'll need to stay in León; bus connections are plentiful. If you want to fill an hour or two before making a bus connection, it's worth wandering the streets surrounding the bus terminal, known as the Zona Piel, Leather District. (León has a long history of supplying goods: in the 16th

BUSES FROM LEÓN

DESTINATION	FARE (M$)	DURATION	FREQUENCY (DAILY)
Aguascalientes	154-185		frequent
Guanajuato	49-175	¾hr	frequent
Mexico City (Terminal Norte)	449-540	5hr	17 (24 hr)
San Miguel de Allende	173-205	2¼hr	5
Zacatecas	280-334		hourly

century it was the center of Mexico's ranching district, providing meat for the mining towns and processing hides.)

Getting There & Away

Aeropuerto Internacional del Bajío is 20km southeast of León on the Mexico City road. Many US airlines offer flights between US cities and here (often via Mexico City). Unfortunately, no bus service operates between Bajío airport and central León or Guanajuato. A taxi between León and the airport costs around M$400.

The **Central de Autobuses** (Blvd Hilario Medina s/n), just north of Blvd López Mateos 2.5km east of the city center, has a cafeteria, left luggage, money exchange and card phones. There are regular 1st- and 2nd-class services to many places in northern and western Mexico.

Dolores Hidalgo

418 / POP 59,000 / ELEV 1920M

Dolores Hidalgo is a compact town with a pretty, tree-filled plaza, a relaxed ambience and an important history. It has acquired pilgrimage status for Mexicans; the Mexican independence movement began in earnest in this small place. At 5am on September 16, 1810, Miguel Hidalgo, the parish priest, rang the bells to summon people to church earlier than usual and issued the Grito de Dolores, also known as the Grito de Independencia. His precise words have been lost to history but their essence was 'Death to bad government and the *gachupines*!' (*Gachupines*

MIGUEL HIDALGO: ¡VIVA MEXICO!

The balding head of the visionary priest Father Miguel Hidalgo y Costilla is familiar to anyone who has ogled Mexican statues or murals. A genuine rebel idealist, Hidalgo sacrificed his career and risked his life on September 16, 1810, when he launched the independence movement.

Born on May 8, 1753, son of a criollo (Mexican-born person of Spanish parentage) hacienda manager in Guanajuato, he earned a bachelor's degree and, in 1778, was ordained a priest. He returned to teach at his alma mater in Morelia and eventually became rector. But he was no orthodox cleric: Hidalgo questioned many Catholic traditions, read banned books, gambled, danced and had a mistress.

In 1800 he was brought before the Inquisition. Nothing was proven, but a few years later, in 1804, he found himself transferred as priest to the hick town of Dolores.

Hidalgo's years in Dolores show his growing interest in the economic and cultural welfare of the people. He started several new industries: silk was cultivated, olive groves were planted and vineyards established, all in defiance of the Spanish colonial authorities. Earthenware building products were the foundation of the ceramics industry that today produces fine glazed pots and tiles.

When Hidalgo met Ignacio Allende from San Miguel, they shared a criollo discontent with the Spanish stranglehold on Mexico. Hidalgo's standing among the mestizos and indigenous people of his parish was vital in broadening the base of the rebellion that followed.

Shortly after his Grito de Independencia, Hidalgo was formally excommunicated for 'heresy, apostasy and sedition.' He defended his call for Mexican independence and stated furthermore that the Spanish were not truly Catholic in any religious sense of the word but only for political purposes, specifically to rape, pillage and exploit Mexico. A few days later, on October 19, Hidalgo dictated his first edict calling for the abolition of slavery in Mexico.

Hidalgo led his growing forces from Dolores to San Miguel, Celaya and Guanajuato, north to Zacatecas, south almost to Mexico City and west to Guadalajara. But then, pushed northward, their numbers dwindled and on July 30, 1811, having been captured by the Spanish, Hidalgo was shot by a firing squad in Chihuahua. His head was returned to the city of Guanajuato, where it hung in a cage for 10 years on an outer corner of the Alhóndiga de Granaditas, along with the heads of fellow independence leaders Allende, Aldama and Jiménez. Rather than intimidating the people, this lurid display kept the memory, the goal and the example of the heroic martyrs fresh in everyone's mind. After independence the cages were removed, and the skulls (and bodies) of the heroes are now in the Monumento a la Independencia in Mexico City.

was a derisive term for the Spanish-born overlords who ruled Mexico.)

Today, Hidalgo is one of Mexico's most revered heroes. Dolores was renamed in his honor in 1824. Mexicans swarm here for Independence Day (September 16), during which time the price of accommodations can more than double.

The town's *centro histórico* is worth a day visit from San Miguel de Allende, Guanajuato or Querétaro, not only for its interesting independence-themed museums (all of which are within a couple of blocks of the Plaza Principal), but also for its colored Talavera ceramics workshops (several blocks from the plaza) and ice cream (look for the carts on the plaza).

Sights

Parroquia de Nuestra Señora de Dolores — CHURCH

(Plaza Principal) The Parroquia de Nuestra Señora de Dolores is the church where Hidalgo issued the Grito. It has a fine 18th-century Churrigueresque facade. Legends surround his 'cry'; some say that Hidalgo uttered his famous words from the pulpit, others claim that he spoke at the church door to the people gathered outside.

Hidalgo Statue — MONUMENT

(Plaza Principal) The plaza beholds a statue of the man himself, Hidalgo (in Roman garb, on top of a tall column). Here, too, is a tree that, according to the plaque beneath it, was a sapling of the tree of the Noche Triste (Sad Night), under which Cortés is said to have wept when his men were driven out of Tenochtitlán in 1520.

Museo Bicentenario 1810–2010 — MUSEUM

(Casa del Capitán Mariano Abasolo; adult/student M$20/10; ⏲10am-4:45pm Tue-Sun) Adjacent to the church, this museum (previously the Presidencia Municipal) was inaugurated in 2010 for Mexico's bicentennial celebrations. Despite its name, the majority of its seven rooms provide a cultural and historical context of the first 100 years of independence, including mementos produced for the centenary of 1910. Quirkier items include a stunning silk scarf embroidered with hair (depicting the image of Alejandro Zavala Mangas, an architect from Guanajuato city) and the original painted poster promoting the first century of independence. All explanations are in Spanish.

Museo de la Independencia Nacional — MUSEUM

(National Independence Museum; ☎418-182-77-50; Zacatecas 6; adult/student M$15/7.50, Sun free; ⏲10am-5pm) This museum has few relics but plenty of information on the independence movement. The exhibition spans seven rooms and charts the appalling decline in Nueva España's indigenous population between 1519 (an estimated 25 million) and 1605 (1 million), and identifies 23 indigenous rebellions before 1800 as well as several criollo conspiracies in the years leading up to 1810. There are vivid paintings, quotations and details on the heroic last 10 months of Hidalgo's life.

Museo Casa de Hidalgo — MUSEUM

(☎418-182-01-71; cnr Hidalgo & Morelos; admission M$31; ⏲10am-4:30pm Tue-Sun) Miguel Hidalgo lived in this house when he was Dolores' parish priest. It was from here, in the early hours of September 16, 1810, that Hidalgo, Ignacio Allende and Juan de Aldama set off to launch the uprising against colonial rule. The house is now something of a national shrine – think: memorials, replicas of Hidalgo's furniture and independence-movement documents, including the order for Hidalgo's excommunication.

Museo José Alfredo Jiménez — MUSEUM

(www.museojosealfredojimenez.com; Guanajuato 13, cnr Nuevo León; admission M$35; ⏲10am-5pm Tue-Sun) If you don't know of José Alfredo Jiménez before you come to Dolores, you will by the time you leave. (Hint: he's the king of *música ranchera* and beloved by all Mexicans.) Housed in a stunning space – the home where he was born – this new, modern museum cleverly depicts his life through

BUSES FROM DOLORES HIDALGO

DESTINATION	FARE (M$)	DURATION	FREQUENCY (DAILY)
Guanajuato	60	1¼hr	frequent
Mexico City (Terminal Norte) via Querétaro	308-330	5-6hr	frequent
San Miguel de Allende	42	¾hr	frequent

paintings, photos, mementos and recordings (there are hi-tech earphones). The first room features an extraordinary painting by Octavio Ocampo, in which are hidden many figures and symbols.

Festivals & Events

Día de la Independencia HISTORICAL

Dolores is the scene of major Día de la Independencia (September 16) celebrations, when the Mexican president may officiate – according to tradition – in his fifth year of office.

Fiestas Patrias CULTURAL

The dates of the Fiestas Patrias festivities change annually; they run for up to two weeks and always encompass September 16.

Sleeping

Prices can double (even triple) for the independence celebrations in September, and at Easter.

Hotel Hidalgo HOTEL $

(☎418-182-04-77; www.hotelposadahidalgo.com; Hidalgo 15; s/d/tr M$400/475/550; P ⊖ ☎) The reception feels a bit like a doctor's surgery, but this superclean and well-managed place offers a comfortable and '80s-modern' stay. It's conveniently located between the bus stations and the Plaza Principal.

Posada Cocomacán HOTEL $$

(☎418-182-60-86; Plaza Principal 4; s/d M$350/470; ☎) The centrally located and absolutely apricot Cocomacán is an aged, but reliable option. Of the 37 rooms, those on the upper levels, with windows onto the street, are the best. There's also a restaurant (open 8am to 10:30pm).

Eating

Don't leave without sampling a hand-turned ice cream (around M$20) from an ice-cream vendor on the plaza or around town. You can test your taste buds on the flavors: *mole* (chili sauce), *chicharrón* (fried pork skin), avocado, corn, cheese, honey, shrimp, beer, tequila and tropical fruits. The busy market on the corner of Chihuahua and Michoacán serves up some satisfying corn-based snacks.

El Fruty CAFE $

(Hildalgo s/n; M$25-50; ⊙9am-10pm) A cheap and convenient stop for filling sandwiches, natural yogurts and (just) passable coffee.

Restaurant Plaza MEXICAN $$

(☎418-182-02-59; Plaza Principal 17B; mains M$65-205; ⊙8am-10pm; ☎) A central and OK place serving set breakfasts (from M$77) and lunches (M$80), as well as meat dishes, pasta and *antojitos*.

Shopping

Talavera ceramics have been the signature handicraft of Dolores ever since Padre Hidalgo founded the town's first ceramics workshop in the early 19th century. Head to the Zona Artesanal, the workshops along Avenida Jiménez, five blocks west of the plaza, or (by car) to Calzada de los Héroes, the exit road to San Miguel de Allende. Some workshops here make 'antique' colonial-style furniture.

Information

The **tourist office** (☎418-182-11-64; Plaza Principal; ⊙9am-5pm Mon-Fri, 10am-2pm Sat) is on Plaza Principal's southeastern side. The helpful staff provide maps and information. Several banks with ATMs are around the plaza. The **post office** (☎418-182-08-07; ⊙9am-2pm Mon-Sat) is on the corner of Puebla and Veracruz.

Getting There & Away

The **Primera Plus/Coordinados (Flecha Amarilla) bus station** (Hidalgo) is 2½ blocks south of the plaza, near the **Herradura de Plata/Autovías bus station** (cnr Chiapas & Yucatán).

There are regular 2nd-class connections to Querétaro (M$101), León (M$108) and San Luis Potosí (M$159).

San Miguel de Allende

☎415 / POP 70,000 / ELEV 1900M

Many people say that San Miguel is a bit like a Mexican Disneyland for foreign (mainly American) retirees and visiting *chilangos* (those from Mexico City). Indeed, this is a stunning and neat city, with colonial architecture, enchanting cobblestone streets and striking light. Regular festivals, fireworks and parades dominate the local scene.

The town's cosmopolitan panache is reflected in its excellent restaurants and high-class, colonial-style accommodations. Numerous galleries are stocked with some of the best of Mexican *artesanías* (handicrafts) and cultural activities are on tap for residents and visitors. There are few major sights in the compact *centro histórico*: San Miguel *is* the sight. The city – with El Jardín,

San Miguel de Allende

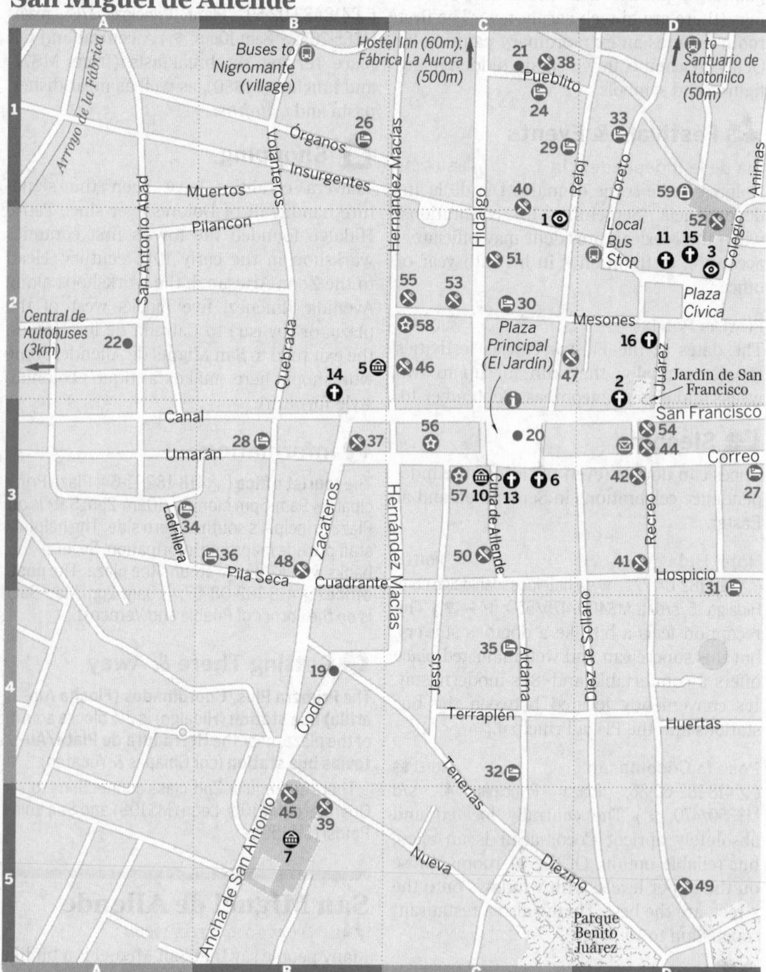

the principal plaza, and the Parroquia, the large church, at its heart – was declared a Unesco World Heritage site in 2008.

Economically speaking, this is no budget destination and is a far cry from the 1940s, when beatniks and artists shacked up here on a shoestring to pursue their creative ventures. While the foreign influence is pervasive (more than 12,000 foreigners are believed to live or have houses here), on the whole the population coexists comfortably.

Beneath the smart B&Bs and fancy shops, another Mexico exists. You only have to laze in the main plaza, visit the food market or interact with the local people to sense a different ambience, color and vibe.

The climate is agreeable: cool and clear in winter and warm and clear in summer, with occasional thunderstorms and heavy rain.

History

The town, so the story goes, owes its founding to a few overheated dogs. These hounds were loved by a Franciscan friar, Juan de San Miguel, who started a mission in 1542 near an often-dry river 5km from the present town. One day the dogs wandered off from the mission; they were found reclining at

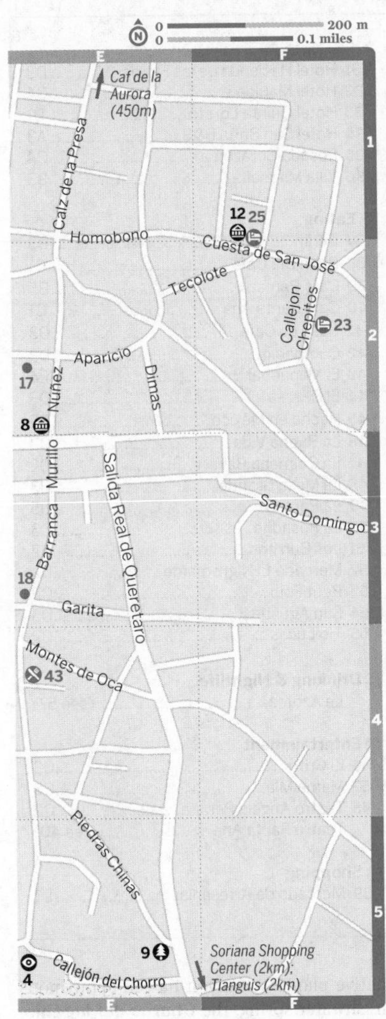

the spring called **El Chorro**. The mission was moved to this superior site.

San Miguel was then central Mexico's most northern Spanish settlement. Tarascan and Tlaxcalan allies of the Spanish were brought to help pacify the local Otomí and Chichimecs. San Miguel was barely surviving the fierce Chichimec resistance, until in 1555 a Spanish garrison was established to protect the new road from Mexico City to the silver center of Zacatecas. Spanish ranchers settled in the area and it grew into a thriving commercial center and home to some of Guanajuato's wealthy silver barons.

San Miguel's favorite son, Ignacio Allende, was born here in 1779. He became a fervent believer in the need for Mexican independence and was a leader of a Querétaro-based conspiracy that set December 8, 1810, as the date for an armed uprising. When the plan was discovered by the authorities in Querétaro on September 13, a messenger rushed to San Miguel and gave the news to Juan de Aldama, another conspirator. Aldama sped north to Dolores where, in the early hours of September 16, he found Allende at the house of the priest Miguel Hidalgo, also one of the coterie. A few hours later Hidalgo proclaimed rebellion from his church. After initial successes Allende, Hidalgo and other rebel leaders were captured in 1811 in Chihuahua. Allende was executed, but on independence in 1821 he was recognized as a martyr and in 1826 the town was renamed San Miguel de Allende.

The Escuela de Bellas Artes was founded in 1938 and the town started to take on its current character when David Alfaro Siqueiros began mural-painting courses attracting artists of every persuasion. The Instituto Allende opened in 1951, also attracting foreign students. Many were US war veterans (who could settle here under the GI Bill); an influx of artists has continued ever since.

⊙ Sights

Parroquia de San Miguel Arcángel CHURCH

The parish church's pink 'wedding cake' towers dominate the Jardín. These strange pinnacles were designed by indigenous stonemason Zeferino Gutiérrez in the late 19th century. He reputedly based the design on a postcard of a Belgian church and instructed builders by scratching plans in the sand with a stick. The rest of the church dates from the late 17th century. In the chapel to the left of the main altar is the much-revered image of the *Cristo de la conquista* (Christ of the Conquest), made in Pátzcuaro from cornstalks and orchid bulbs, probably in the 16th century. The adjacent **Iglesia de San Rafael** (Jardín) was founded in 1742.

La Esquina: Museo del Juguete Popular Mexicano MUSEUM

(www.museolaesquina.org.mx; Núñez 40; admission M$30; ⌚10am-6pm Tue-Sat, 10am-3pm Sun) This bright, modern museum is a must-visit for all kids, big and small. To describe it as exhibiting Mexican toys (the 50-year collection of museum owner, Angélica Tijerina) is to do it a disservice. It is much more. It

San Miguel de Allende

Sights

1 Biblioteca Pública ... C2
2 Capilla de la Tercera Orden ... D2
3 Colegio de Sales ... D2
4 El Chorro ... E5
5 Escuela de Bellas Artes ... B2
6 Iglesia de San Rafael ... C3
7 Instituto Allende ... B5
8 La Esquina: Museo del Juguete Popular Mexicano ... E2
9 Mirador & Parque Benito Juárez ... E5
10 Museo Histórico de San Miguel de Allende ... C3
11 Oratorio de San Felipe Neri ... D2
12 Other Face of Mexico Gallery ... F1
13 Parroquia de San Miguel Arcángel ... C3
14 Templo de la Concepción ... B2
15 Templo de la Salud ... D2
16 Templo de San Francisco ... D2

Activities, Courses & Tours

17 Academia Hispano Americana ... E2
18 Bici-Burro ... E3
19 Bookatour ... B4
Instituto Allende ... (see 7)
20 San Miguel de Allende Walking Tour ... C3
21 The Spanish School ... C1
22 Warren Hardy Spanish ... A2

Sleeping

23 Antigua Capilla ... F2
24 Casa Calderoni B&B ... C1
25 Casa de la Cuesta ... F1
26 Casa de la Noche ... B1
27 Casa Mia ... D3
28 Dos Casas ... B3
29 Hostal Alcatraz ... C1
30 Hostal Punto 79 ... C2
31 Hotel Hacienda de las Flores ... D3
32 Hotel Matilda ... C4
33 Hotel Quinta Loreto ... D1
34 Hotel San Borja B&B ... A3
35 Posada Corazón ... C4
36 Villa Mirasol ... B3

Eating

37 Berlin ... B3
38 Buen Día Café ... C1
39 Café Rama ... B5
40 Café Santa Ana ... C1
41 Casa de Café ... D3
42 Cumpanio ... D3
43 El Manantial ... E4
44 El Pegaso ... D3
45 Hecho en México ... B5
46 La Buena Vida ... C2
47 La Colmena Bakery ... C2
48 La Mesa Grande ... B3
49 La Parada ... D5
50 La Posadita ... C3
51 Los Burritos ... C2
52 Mercado El Nigromante ... D2
53 Petit Four ... C2
54 San Agustín ... D3
55 Tío Lucas ... C2

Drinking & Nightlife

La Azotea ... (see 57)

Entertainment

56 El Grito ... C3
57 Mama Mía ... C3
58 Teatro Ángela Peralta ... C2
Teatro Santa Ana ... (see 40)

Shopping

59 Mercado de Artesanías ... D1

aims to preserve and continue the tradition of toys by showcasing different pieces from the many regions of Mexico. The pieces – divided into three main themed areas – are made from different materials, from wheat to plastic, wood to fabric. Kids will love the interactive games on the computer. A lovely gift shop is attached.

Jardín Botánico El Charco del Ingenio GARDENS

(☎415-154-47-15; www.elcharco.org.mx; off Antiguo Camino Real a Querétaro; admission M$40; ⏱7am-8pm) Northeast of town (1.5km) is the 88-hectare botanic garden, also a wildlife and bird sanctuary, plus recreational and ceremonial space. Pathways head through wetlands and magnificent areas of cacti and native plants. A canyon has an eponymous freshwater spring, the **Charco del Ingenio**. Don't miss the **Conservatory of Mexican Plants**, which houses a wonderful array of cacti and succulent species. Two-hour tours (in English) depart every Tuesday and Thursday at 10am (M$80). Monthly full-moon ceremonies also take place here.

Getting to the garden can seem a slightly prickly business, thanks to new urban development on the town's outskirts that blocks the original route, but it's worth persevering. Walk uphill from Mercado El Nigromante along Homobono and Cuesta de San José. Fork left up Montitlan past a housing development (known as Los Balcones). Continue for another 15 minutes to the main gate. Be sure to keep the garden boundary fence on your left as much as possible. (Occasionally you may have to head around the new houses on sidewalks, after which you head back to the fence.)

Alternatively, a 2km vehicle track leads north from the Soriana shopping center, 2.5km southeast of the center on the Querétaro road. This can be reached on 'Soriana' buses from the bus stop from Mesones, near Plaza Cívica. A taxi to the gardens from the center costs around M$45. Take a 'Soriana' or 'Placita' bus (10 minutes, M$5).

Museo Histórico de San Miguel de Allende MUSEUM
(Museo Casa de Allende; Cuna de Allende 1; admission M$42; ⏲9:30am-4:30pm Tue-Sun) Near the Parroquia de San Miguel Arcángel is the house where Ignacio Allende was born. These days it is home to the Museo Histórico de San Miguel de Allende, which relates the interesting history of the San Miguel area. One of the floors is a reproduction of Allende's home. A Latin inscription on the facade reads *Hic natus ubique notus,* which means 'Born here, known everywhere.'

Mirador & Parque Benito Juárez PARK
One of the best views over the town and surrounding country is from the mirador (overlook) southeast of town. Take Callejón del Chorro, the track leading directly downhill from here, and turn left at the bottom to reach **El Chorro**, the spring where San Miguel was founded (note the fountain and public washing tubs). A path – Paseo del Chorro – zigzags down the hill to the shady **Parque Benito Juárez**, a lovely place to relax and meander through.

Other Face of Mexico Gallery MUSEUM
(www.casadelacuesta.com; Casa de la Cuesta, Cuesta de San José 32; admission M$50) This fascinating private collection of more than 500 masks provides an excellent context of the Mexican mask tradition. It is open by appointment only (call ☎154-43-24). The admission fee goes to charity.

Escuela de Bellas Artes GALLERY
(School of Fine Arts; Centro Cultural Nigromante; ☎415-152-02-89; Hernández Macías 75; ⏲10am-6pm Mon-Sat, 10am-2pm Sun) This beautiful former monastery of La Concepción church was converted into a fine-arts school in 1938 and still offers courses. Don't miss the murals of Pedro Martínez, plus the Siqueiros Room, which features the extraordinary unfinished mural by David Alfaro Siqueiros (it plays with your mind – we won't spoil the surprise). The rest of the gallery holds temporary exhibitions. At the time of research, the wonderful auditorium was about to reopen; ask about performances.

Oratorio de San Felipe Neri CHURCH
(Plaza Cívica) This multi-towered and domed church dating from the 18th century is near the east end of Insurgentes. The pale-pink main facade is baroque with an indigenous influence. A passage to the right of this facade leads to the east wall, where a doorway holds the image of *Nuestra señora de la soledad* (Our Lady of Solitude). You can see into the cloister from this side of the church.

Inside the church are 33 oil paintings showing scenes from the life of San Felipe Neri, the 16th-century Florentine who founded the Oratorio Catholic order. In the east transept is a painting of the Virgin of Guadalupe by leading colonial painter Miguel Cabrera. In the west transept is a lavishly decorated 1735 chapel, the **Santa Casa de Loreto**, a replica of a chapel in Loreto, Italy, legendary home of the Virgin Mary. Behind the altar (although rarely open), the *camarín* (chapel behind the main church) has six elaborately gilded baroque altars. In one is a reclining wax figure of San Columbano; it supposedly contains the saint's bones.

Templo de San Francisco CHURCH
(cnr San Francisco & Juárez) This church has an elaborate late-18th-century Churrigueresque facade. An image of St Francis of Assisi is at the top. Opening hours vary.

Capilla de la Tercera Orden CHAPEL
(Chapel of the Third Order; cnr San Francisco & Juárez) Built in the early 18th century, this chapel, like the Templo de San Francisco, was part of a Franciscan monastery complex. The main facade shows St Francis and symbols of the Franciscan order.

Templo de la Salud CHURCH
(Plaza Cívica) This church, with a dome tiled blue and yellow and a big shell carved above its entrance, is just east of San Felipe Neri. The facade is early Churrigueresque. The church's paintings include one of San Javier by Miguel Cabrera. San Javier (St Francis Xavier; 1506–52) was a founding member of the Jesuits. It was once part of the Colegio de Sales.

Templo de la Concepción CHURCH

(Church of the Conception; cnr Zacateros & Canal) This splendid church has a fine altar and several magnificent old oil paintings. Painted on the interior doorway are a number of wise sayings to give pause to those entering the sanctuary. The church was begun in the mid-18th century; its dome, added in the late 19th century by the versatile Zeferino Gutiérrez, was possibly inspired by pictures of *Les Invalides* in Paris.

Instituto Allende HISTORIC BUILDING

(Ancha de San Antonio 20 & 22) This large 1736 complex, the original home of the Conde Manuel de la Canal, was used as a Carmelite convent, eventually becoming an art and language school in 1951. These days it's split into two – one area of several patios, gardens and an old chapel is used for functions, the other for courses. Above the main entrance is a carving of the Virgin of Loreto, patroness of the Canal family.

Colegio de Sales NOTABLE BUILDING

(Plaza Cívica; ⊙8am-2pm & 5-8pm) Once a college, founded in the mid-18th century by the San Felipe Neri order, the Colegio de Sales has regained its educational status; it currently houses part of the University of León. Many of the 1810 revolutionaries were educated here. Spaniards were locked up here when the rebels took San Miguel.

Biblioteca Pública CULTURAL BUILDING

(☎415-152-02-93; Insurgentes 25; ⊙10am-7pm Mon-Fri, 10am-2pm Sat) As well as housing one of the largest collections of books and magazines in English in Latin America, this excellent public library functions as a cultural center. Its financial enterprises (*Atención San Miguel* newspaper, tours and an onsite cafe) provide for children's scholarships. The library cafe provides a pleasant spot from which to view the cultural action. The tiny Teatro Santa Ana also hosts talks and performances.

Courses

Several institutions offer Spanish courses, with group or private lessons and optional classes in Mexican culture and history. Most private lessons are around US$15 to US$18 an hour; group and long-term rates are much lower. Homestays with Mexican families, including a private room and three daily meals, cost around US$28 per day.

There are also courses in painting, sculpture, ceramics, music and dance. The Escuela de Bellas Artes has courses in art, dance, crafts and music in Spanish and English that cost around US$300 a month, plus materials.

Academia Hispano Americana SPANISH

(☎415-152-03-49; www.ahaspeakspanish.com; Mesones 4) This place, housed in a beautiful colonial building, runs quality courses in the Spanish language and Latin American culture.

Instituto Allende SPANISH

(☎415-152-01-90; www.instituto-allende.edu.mx; Ancha de San Antonio 22) Offers courses in fine arts, crafts and Spanish language. Spanish courses for groups begin every four weeks and range from conversational to intensive.

The Spanish School SPANISH

(☎415-121-25-35; www.liceodelalengua.com; Callejón del Pueblito 5) Small centrally located Spanish school.

Warren Hardy Spanish SPANISH

(☎415-154-40-17; www.warrenhardy.com; San Rafael 6) Offers Spanish instruction. A favorite among local expats.

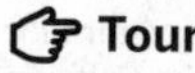

Tours

The tourist office has promotional pamphlets of official English-speaking tour guides who offer both walking and driving tours. See *Atención San Miguel* for the weekly list of tours within San Miguel; most of these support local charities.

Bici-Burro CYCLING

(☎415-152-15-26; www.bici-burro.com; Hospicio 1; trips M$850-1500) Friendly and professional, English-speaking owner Alberto conducts excellent guided mountain-bike tours for groups of two or more. Popular trips include six- or seven-hour excursions to Atotonilco or Pozos and a wonderful 'mezcal' tour that takes in a number of haciendas, one of which produces mezcal (note: for slightly fitter folk). Bike rental also available (M$450 per day).

Bookatour WALKING, CRAFTS

(☎415-152-0198; www.bookatour.mx; Codo 1) This new company offers a range of tours with bilingual guides. Prices are the same for one, two or three people and include transport. These include: walking tours around San Miguel (M$325 per hour); arts and crafts tours (visiting weaving and glass factories and pewter and papier-mâché workshops; M$325 per hour); Independence Route – Dolores and Atotonilco (M$1625, 5 hours); and Guanajuato (M$2080, 8 hours).

San Miguel de Allende Walking Tour WALKING TOUR

This excellent tour takes place every Monday, Wednesday and Friday at 10am, departing from El Jardín (tickets go on sale in El Jardín at 9:45am; M$150). The English-speaking volunteer guides provide a fascinating historical, architectural and cultural commentary on the town's sights.

Coyote Canyon Adventures HORSEBACK RIDING

(☎415-154-41-93; www.coyotecanyonadventures.com; rides per person half-/full-day from M$1,200/M$1,500 (4-person minimum)) The company offers half- and full-day guided horseback tours in a spectacular canyon. **Xotolar Ranch Adventures** (☎415-154-62-75; www.xotolarranch.com; rides from US$85), based on a nearby working ranch, also specializes in canyon trail rides.

Festivals & Events

San Miguel is well endowed with churches and patron saints (it has six) and enjoys a multitude of festivals, many imbued with strong spiritual themes. You'll probably be alerted to a festival event by firework bursts. For programs, ask at the tourist office or check out the website www.visitsanmiguel.travel.

Señor de la Conquista RELIGIOUS

The image of Christ in the Parroquia de San Miguel Arcángel is feted on the first Friday in March, with scores of dancers in elaborate pre-Hispanic costumes and plumed headdresses.

Semana Santa RELIGIOUS

A week of religious activities. Two Sundays before Easter, pilgrims carry an image of the Señor de la Columna from Atotonilco, 11km north, to San Miguel's church of San Juan de Dios, departing at midnight on Saturday. During Semana Santa, the many activities include the solemn Procesión del Santo Entierro on Good Friday and the burning or exploding of Judas effigies on Easter Day.

Fiesta de la Santa Cruz HISTORICAL

This deeply spiritual spring festival has its roots in the 16th century. It happens toward the end of May at Valle del Maíz, 2km from the center of town. Oxen are dressed in lime necklaces and painted tortillas and their yokes festooned with flowers and fruit. A mock battle between 'Indians' and 'Federales' follows. There are *mojigangas*, dancing and musicians, not to mention 96 hours' worth of fireworks.

Fiesta de los Locos RELIGIOUS

Part of the Festividad de San Antonio de Padua in mid-June, the festival of the crazies is a colorful Carnavalesque parade through town with floats, blaring music and costumed dancers throwing out candy to (and sometimes at!) the crowd.

Expresión en Corto FILM

Shared with the city of Guanajuato, this short-film festival in July is internationally recognized.

Chamber Music Festival MUSIC

The Escuela de Bellas Artes sponsors an annual festival of chamber music in the first two weeks of August.

Fiestas Patrias CULTURAL

Two months of cultural programs kick off towards the end of August, incorporating Independence Day. Check with the tourist office for a full event schedule.

San Miguel Arcángel RELIGIOUS

Celebrations honoring the town's chief patron saint are held around the weekend following September 29. The party is celebrated with an *alborada,* an artificial dawn created by thousands of fireworks around the cathedral and turns into an all-night festivity with extraordinary pre-Hispanic dances.

Festival of Jazz & Blues MUSIC

February sees national jazz and blues acts hit town, while November is the month for the international jazz and blues festival.

Sleeping

Accommodations are often full during festivals and high season, so make advance reservations. Thanks to a couple of recent hostel additions, the city now boasts accommodation for all budgets. Midrange options are a bit light on; it's worth loosening the purse strings here. San Miguel is the mecca for good quality luxury B&Bs, boutique hotels and guesthouses.

Hostal Alcatraz HOSTEL $

(☎ 415-152-85-43; Reloj 54; dm from M$150, s without bathroom M$250, d M$400-500; @) One of San Miguel's only hostels is centrally located, with basic dorms and a shared kitchen. The associated **Hostel Inn** (www.hostelinnmx.com; Calzada de La Luz 31A) charges the same prices and is in better condition. Both hostels are a bit short on bathrooms. Owner Luís is helpful.

Hostal Punto 79 HOSTEL $

(☎ 415-121-1034; www.punto79.com; Mesones 79; dm M$190, r with shared bathroom M$250, r M$800;) This centrally located sprawling spot touts itself as a hotel-hostel but the hostel rooms are far more appealing. The dorm rooms are light and pleasant and a good place to bed down, especially if you're on a budget. There's a kitchen (breakfast isn't included).

Hotel San Borja B&B B&B $$

(☎ 415-152-5308; www.hotelsanborja.com; Ladrillera 8; r M$950-1250;) It calls itself a B&B but breakfast is at a nearby cafe. Despite this small shortfall, this lovely mid-range spot is nestled around a secluded garden. Its four rooms are plain (they lack the usual colourful Mexican decor) but they have a hotel quality with a home-style feel. Good for those seeking a bit of quiet.

Villa Mirasol HOTEL $$

(www.villamirasolhotel.com; Pila Seca 35; r from M$1150) This place is a bit like an old aunt – slightly dated, but charming and hospitable. Its bright and airy rooms face on to plant-filled patios. A reliable choice.

Casa de la Noche GUESTHOUSE $$

(☎ 415-152-07-32; www.casadelanoche.com; Organos 19; s M$950, d M$1075-2200;) A bit like the bordello it once was, the place promises big things, especially at the beginning. The refurbished entry and living areas are superb – spacious, stylish and airy – though some of the rooms are a bit cramped and dated. To inflate your enthusiasm, numerous fun nooks and crannies are open for the taking and it's a generally satisfying experience for the price. The friendly artist-owner 'Madame' promotes local talent; artworks prevail.

Hotel Quinta Loreto HOTEL $$

(☎ 415-152-00-42; www.quintaloreto.com.mx; Loreto 15; s/d/tr exc breakfast M$480/600/700;) This dated motel-style place at the back of the artisans' market is spread around large, leafy grounds. One of the better midrange options around, it has a bit of '60s charm. Some of the 28 simple rooms are pleasantly light. The restaurant is open for breakfast and lunch (8am to 5:30pm).

During the day, the gardens serve as a public car park but by the evening it's tranquil. Prices listed here include TV; subtract M$70 for rooms without one.

★ **Posada Corazón** B&B $$$

(☎ 415-152-01-82; www.posadacorazon.com.mx; Aldama 9; d M$2400-2929;) This gorgeous place has a heart, as the name suggests. It's set behind an inconspicuous wall in a delightfully lush plant-and-sculpture garden. The home's spacious open-plan living area (and library) can be shared by guests, and rooms along a deck are light, simple and stylish. Open daily to the public for breakfast (M$165) and afternoon tea (M$65; not Sundays).

★ **Antigua Capilla** BOUTIQUE HOTEL $$$

(☎ 415-152-40-48; www.antiguacapilla.com; Callejon Chepitos 16; r US$149-200;) Constructed around a tiny 17th-century chapel, this utterly stylish, spick-and-span place is hard to fault; it boasts every mod con and service imaginable plus extraordinary breakfasts and a gorgeous plant-lined courtyard. The English- and Spanish-speaking owners are delightful. Access is up a hill but the rooftop terrace affords one of the best views in San Miguel. Excellent price:quality ratio.

Casa Mia APARTMENTS $$$

(☎ 415-152-27-57; www.casamia-sanmiguel.com; Correo 61; apt per night/week from M$1500/5050;) Its tasteful plant-filled courtyard is lined with 10 uniquely decorated apartments, all featuring comfortable hotel-style bedrooms, cable TV, living areas and kitchens. It's better value if you plan to stay for longer than a night or two.

Casa Calderoni B&B B&B $$$

(☎ 415-154-60-05; www.casacalderoni.com; Callejón del Pueblito 4A; r US$120-160;) A very plush, well-managed spot with stylish, artistic rooms, each named after a famous artist (the owner is a painter). We love the Dalí room which is a bit more spacious with good light. Public terraces prevail. It's located in a picturesque *callejón* (small street).

Dos Casas BOUTIQUE HOTEL **$$$**
(☎ 415-154-40-73; www.doscasas.com.mx; Quebrada 101; d M$3500-4900;) This sleek sleep oozes contemporary style with its cream and black hues, fireplaces and private terraces. The restaurant is open to the public and breakfasters can watch the chefs strut their gourmet stuff in the kitchen while sitting at the kitchen bench.

Dos Casas is expanding to a neighboring property, which will see five rooms added to the hotel's current seven.

Hotel Matilda BOUTIQUE HOTEL **$$$**
(☎ 415-152-10-15; www.hotelmatilda.com; Aldama 53; r from US$476;) Dripping in avant-garde elegance, this 'art-boutique' hotel is the most sophisticated sleep in town. Furnished with Egyptian linens, iPod docking stations and soaking tubs, its bright, modern rooms and suites are pure luxury. Works by Spencer Tunick to a copy of Diego Rivera's 1940s portrait of Matilda Stream (the American hotel owner's mother) are displayed throughout the property.

A spa offers wellness experiences (closed Tuesdays) and the public can access the chic bar (3pm to 11pm; closed Mondays) and restaurant (7am to 11pm).

Casa de la Cuesta B&B **$$$**
(☎ 415-154-43-24; www.casadelacuesta.com; Cuesta de San José 32; r US$165;) Perched on a hill behind the Mercado El Nigromante, this ornate, Mexican-themed place has spacious rooms in a decorative colonial mansion, lavish breakfasts and friendly, knowledgeable owners.

Hotel Hacienda de las Flores MOTEL **$$$**
(☎ 415-152-18-59; www.haciendadelasflores.com; Hospicio 16; r M$2370-2640, apt M$2840;) This pleasant spot is less pretentious than other upmarket options and is set within an oasis – a lush garden with swimming pool – which offers a pleasant respite from the busy streets. Rooms are bright (Talvera tiles dominate), if a little dated, and have coffeemakers and microwaves.

Eating

San Miguel's numerous eateries serve a startling variety of quality Mexican and international fine cuisine. Thrifty travelers can enjoy more traditional places catering to loyal crowds of local families. A thriving cafe society prevails, with many serving good local meals at reasonable prices (M$50 to M$150).

Self-caterers are best to head to the supermarkets at Soriana shopping center, 2.5km southeast of the center on the Querétaro road.

For budget bites, on the corner of Ancha de San Antonio and tree-shaded Nueva (near Instituto Allende) are several reliable food stands. They alternate in the mornings and evenings, selling great-tasting juice, *gorditas* (small circles of tortilla dough, fried and topped with meat and/or cheese), burritos and tacos. Reliable juice stands front the small plaza off Insurgentes.

Excellent traditional bakeries include **La Buena Vida** (Hernández Macías 72-14; M$20-60; 8am-4pm Mon-Sat) and **La Colmena Bakery** (Reloj 21; from M$8). For something more contemporary, the trendy *panaderia*, **Cumpanio** (Correo 29; M$20-150; 8am-9pm) is great for takeaway French pastries.

Mercado El Nigromante (Colegio s/n) has good produce stands and market eateries. It's centrally located, but light years away from the gringo scene.

★ **San Agustín** CAFE **$**
(☎ 415-154-91-02; San Francisco 21; snacks M$40-80, mains M$70-165; 8am-11pm Mon-Thu, 9am-midnight Fri & Sat) A 'don't leave San Miguel without...' experience. This sweet tooth's paradise is the best place in Mexico for chocolate and *churros* (doughnut-like fritters; M$40-50).

Buen Día Café CAFE **$**
(Pueblito 3; mains M$55-85; 8am-4pm Tue, 8:30am-4pm Wed-Mon) This simple place, slightly more than a hole-in-the wall, is located in the quaint Callejon Pueblito, opposite Calderoni B&B, and serves up great coffee (complete with latte art) and excellent breakfasts, as well as other snacks.

Petit Four CAFE **$**
(☎ 415-154-40-10; Mesones 99-1; snacks M$10-45; 8am-6pm Tue-Sat, 8am-3pm Sun;) A wonderful place to get your sugar hit: French pastries that you can enjoy in a cozy environment over teas and coffees.

Café de la Aurora CAFE **$**
(☎ 415-154-98-28; Calzada de la Aurora; snacks M$15-60; 8:30am-6pm Mon-Sat, 11am-4pm Sun) Fittingly creative salads, soups and *panini* in a relaxing courtyard setting in the grounds of Fábrica La Aurora.

Café Santa Ana CAFE $
(☎415-152-02-93; Reloj 50A; breakfast M$60-70; ⏲9am-7pm Mon-Fri, 9:30am-2pm Sat; 📶) This relaxing place, in the library annex, is popular with culture vultures.

Casa de Café CAFE $
(☎415-152-01-21; Hospicio 31; snacks M$30-40; ⏲8am-7pm Mon-Sat, to 4pm Sun; 📶) A cute, cozy place with delicious sandwiches, good coffee and freshly baked cakes.

Los Burritos MEXICAN $
(☎415-152-32-22; Hildalgo 23; snacks M$6-35; ⏲10:30am-6pm Mon-Wed, to 10:30pm Thu-Sat, noon-5:30pm Sun) The place for cheap *antojitos* and the mouthwatering, made-to-order *guisados* (fillings) from *mole* to *chipotle* (a type of chili) and potato.

★**Café Rama** BAR, INTERNATIONAL RESTAURANT $$
(www.cafe-rama.com; Calle Nueva 7; mains M$110-200; ⏲8am-midnight Tue-Sun) This cool cafe-bar, near Instituto Allende, has morphed into a fully fledged-restaurant. Its two separate areas are lovingly furnished with antiques and eclectic curios, with cozy couches near the open fireplace. It's changing menu proffers excellent international dishes and is popular with visiting Mexicans and local expats.

El Manantial BAR, CANTINA $$
(Barranca 78; mains M$70-150; ⏲noon-11pm Tue-Sat) Behind the swinging doors of a former saloon, 'The Spring' (whose alter-ego is La Sirena Gorda or 'Fat Mermaid') serves fabulously fresh ceviche. It's got a real buzz, also helped by *jabanero* salsa, the spiciest of chili sauces that will put hair on your chest. Warning: we suggest you don't pile it on like the hardy locals here, a little goes a looong way. Be sure to try one of their ginger margaritas (M$60).

La Parada PERUVIAN $$
(www.laparadasma.com; Recreo 94; ceviche M$90-110; mains M$95-175; ⏲noon-10pm Wed-Sat, to 4pm Sun) This hot spot showcases Peruvian cuisine at its best. Dish presentation is as exquisite as the names ('El Quiquiriquí', aka chicken breast and 'Chino Cochino' pork), but much fancier. And of course, the ubiquitous (and delicious) ceviche. The owners are young, hip and most importantly, trained chefs.

Hecho en México MEXICAN $$
(Ancha de San Antonio 8; mains M$75-140; ⏲lunch & dinner) This isn't the place to come if you want to tune your ear to Spanish – it's a favorite expat hangout. However, for good reason, it seems. The menu is large, varied and very generous. Grab everything from a veggie burger to Mexican fare (plus good value set-lunch menus) and enjoy in a cozy courtyard setting. There's live music every Friday.

Vía Orgánica CAFE $$
(☎415-152-80-42; www.viaorganica.org; Margarito Ledesma 2; snacks M$15-30, mains M$95-150; ⏲8am-9:30pm; 🖉) This casual spot – a cafe and organic vegetable shop – serves minestrone soups, salads and great cakes. Service can be a bit sluggish, but this is a slow-food place, after all. Head north along Hidalgo, veer right onto Calzada de la Aurora, first left into Talavera and first left again.

La Posadita MEXICAN $$
(☎415-154-88-62; Cuna de Allende 13; mains M$110-185; ⏲noon-10pm Thu-Tue) This enjoyable eatery gets five stars for its excellent service, Mexican fare and location near the Parroquia de San Miguel Arcángel. Head up a steep set of stairs to the wonderful rooftop terrace for great vistas. It serves delicious margaritas, enchiladas and meat dishes.

La Mesa Grande BAKERY $$
(www.lamesagrande.com; Zacateros 149; MS$40-100; ⏲8am-5pm Mon-Sat) A contemporary *pandería*-cafe with excellent pastries, great home-baked sourdough loaves, decent snacks, and a large communal table for neighbourly chats. It's open 'til 10pm on Thursdays for oven pizzas.

Berlin INTERNATIONAL $$
(☎415-152-94-32; Umarán 19; mains M$85-190; ⏲4:30pm-midnight) This cool, artsy spot serves up some good international feeds. The bar is great for a tipple.

El Pegaso MEXICAN $$
(☎415-154-76-11; Corregidora 6; mains M$70-170; ⏲8:30am-10pm Mon-Sat) This friendly, colorful and cozy place is a reliable option for meals.

Tío Lucas INTERNATIONAL $$$
(☎415-152-49-96; Mesones 103; mains M$160-300; ⏲noon-midnight) This stylish place with a silver-star-covered courtyard is known for its beef, especially the fillet steak, and for being 'reliable.' Happy hour runs from 6pm to 8pm Monday to Friday, and there's regular live music, from Cuban to guitar and jazz.

Drinking & Nightlife

In San Miguel, drinking and entertainment are often synonymous. Many bars (and restaurants) host live music. Most of the action is on Thursday to Saturday nights, but some places have live music nightly.

La Azotea BAR
(415-152-82-75; Umarán 6) Above the restaurant Pueblo Viejo, this terrace is more of a laid-back lounge and tapas bar, with a smart, gay-friendly crowd and a less touristy vibe.

Mama Mía CLUB
(415-152-20-63; Umarán 8; 8am-midnight Sun-Thu, to late Fri & Sat) This perennially popular place has separate areas for differing entertainment puposes; hit Mama's Bar for live rock/funk on Fridays and Saturdays (or karaoke on weeknights), or join a more sophisticated crowd in the restaurant patio for live folk music (check the changing schedule). Up front, Bar Leonardo's shows big-screen sports and La Terrazza, the terrace bar, offers a fine view of the town.

The joint gets going by 11pm.

El Grito CLUB
(Umarán 15; 10pm-4am Fri & Sat) An oversized face above the doorway of this upscale disco effectively shouts 'high prices' to the fashionable young Mexican crowd queuing outside. Its name loosely translates to 'the cry', after all.

Entertainment

Performing Arts

It's one big cultural party in San Miguel; check out what's on in *Atención San Miguel*. The Escuela de Bellas Artes and the Biblioteca (in the Sala Quetzal) host a variety of cultural events, many in English; check their notice boards for schedules.

Teatro Ángela Peralta THEATER
(415-152-22-00; www.teatroangelaperalta.webpin.com; cnr Calles Mesones & Hernández Macías) Built in 1910, this elegant venue often hosts local productions. The **ticket office** (Hernández Macías 62; 8:30am-4pm Mon-Fri) is around the corner. Tickets cost between M$40 and M$350 depending on the production.

Teatro Santa Ana THEATER
(415-152-02-93; Reloj 50A; tickets M$40-200) This small theater inside the Biblioteca Pública plays host to a good selection of independent and international films, as well as local plays and talks.

Shopping

Be sure to hit the Tianguis (Tuesday market), the biggest weekly outdoor extravaganza, beside the Soriana shopping center, 2.5km southeast of the center on the Querétaro road. Take a 'Soriana' or 'Placita' bus (10 minutes, M$5) from Mesones, near Plaza Cívica.

The local market Mercado El Nigromante (p665) sells fruit, vegetables and assorted goods.

Part of the joy of wandering around San Miguel is to stumble upon the many galleries tucked away in streets around town; there are more commercial galleries than cafes (and perhaps, real estate agents) in San Miguel. The largest concentration of contemporary art galleries and design studios (mainly expatriates' work) is housed in the trendy **Fábrica La Aurora** (415-152-13-12; Aurora s/n; 10am-6pm), a remodeled raw-cotton factory on the north end of town. Many galleries are promoted in local papers, but otherwise be guided by your whim.

San Miguel also has a mind-boggling number of craft shops, selling folk art and handicrafts from all over the country. Local crafts include tinware, wrought iron, silver, brass, leather, glassware, pottery and textiles. Many shops are along Canal, San Francisco, Zacateros and Pila Seca. Price and quality varies widely.

Mercado de Artesanías HANDICRAFTS
(Colegio s/n) A decent collection of handicraft stalls appealing to different tastes (and of varying quality) in the alleyway between Colegio and Loreto.

Information

INTERNET ACCESS

Solutions (415-152-24-97; www.solutions-sanmiguel.com; Mesones 57A; internet per hr M$15; 9am-6:30pm Mon-Fri, to 2pm Sat) Internet access as well as mail-forwarding, fax and shipping services.

MEDIA

Don't contemplate spending time in town without buying the weekly semi-bilingual (English/Spanish) newspaper *Atención San Miguel* (M$10). Published every Friday, it's chock-a-block with what's on for the coming week, including tours, concerts and gallery openings.

It also lists yoga, Spanish, art and dance class schedules. You can buy it at the public library and many cafes or from roaming vendors.

MEDICAL SERVICES

Hospital Tec100 (415-152-22-33; www.medicatec100.com.mx; Libramiento a Dolores Hidalgo 43) This private hospital is located around 3km west of San Miguel's town center.

MONEY

Most banks have their own ATMs and are located on, or within two blocks east of, the Jardín. There are also *casas de cambio* on Correo.

TOURIST INFORMATION

Tourist Office (415-152-09-00; www.visitsanmiguel.travel; Plaza Principal 8; 9am-8pm Mon-Fri, 10am-8pm Sat, 10am-6pm Sun) On the northern side of El Jardín. Good for maps of the town, promotional pamphlets and information on events.

TRAVEL AGENCIES

Viajes Vertiz (415-152-18-56; www.viajesvertiz.com; Hidalgo 1A; 9am-6:30pm Mon-Fri, 10am-2pm Sat) American Express agent (but does not cash traveler's checks); sells domestic and international air tickets.

USEFUL WEBSITES

Atención San Miguel (www.atencionsanmiguel.org) Weekly bilingual newspaper that runs an excellent website.

Visit San Miguel (www.visitsanmiguel.travel) The official, government-run tourism website.

Getting There & Away

AIR

The nearest airport is the **Aeropuerto Internacional del Bajío**, between León and Silao, around 1½ hours away by car. The obvious alternative is Mexico City International Airport.

BUS

The Central de Autobuses is on Canal (Calzada de la Estación), 3km west of the center. Tickets can be purchased at the station. First-class tickets for Primera Plus, ETN and Omnibus de México can also be bought at **Peradora** (415-152-80-11; Cuna de Allende 17).

Second-class services (Coordinados/Flecha Amarilla and Herradura de Plata) also leave from this station. Other 1st-class buses serve Aguascalientes, Monterrey and San Luis Potosí.

CAR & MOTORCYCLE

The only San Miguel-based agency is **San Miguel Rent-a-Car** (415-152-01-98; www.sanmiguelrentacar.com; Codo 1). Prices start at about M$720 per day including insurance.

Getting Around

TO/FROM THE AIRPORT

Many agencies provide shuttle transportation to/from Bajío airport. These include **Viajes Vertiz** (415-152-18-56; www.viajesvertiz.com; Hidalgo 1A; 9am-6:30pm Mon-Fri, 10am-2pm Sat), **Viajes San Miguel** (415-152-25-37; www.viajessanmiguel.com; Diez de Sollano 4-Interior 3; 9am-7pm Mon-Fri, 10am-2pm Sat), **Bajío Go** (415-152-19-99; www.bajiobo.com; Jésus 11; 8am-8pm Mon-Sat, 10am-3pm Sun) and **Peradora**. Alternatively, take a bus to Silao and get a taxi from there to the airport. For Mexico City airport, get a bus to Querétaro and a bus direct to the airport from there.

If heading from the airport to San Miguel by bus, it's easiest to go to León via taxi and take a bus from there. No bus service operates between Bajío airport and central León. A taxi to León costs M$300 to M$415 and to San Miguel M$1200 (for up to four people).

TO/FROM THE BUS STATION

Local buses (M$6) run from 7am to 9pm daily. 'Central' buses run regularly between the bus station and the town center. Coming into town these terminate at the eastern end of Insurgentes after winding through the streets. Heading out of the center, you can pick one up on Canal. A taxi between the center and the bus station costs around M$35; trips around town cost around M$30.

BUSES FROM SAN MIGUEL DE ALLENDE

DESTINATION	FARE (M$)	DURATION	FREQUENCY (DAILY)
Celaya	47	1¾hr	every 15min
Dolores Hidalgo	42	1hr	every 40min 7am-8pm
Guadalajara	367-430	5¼-5½hr	9
Guanajuato	68-196	1-1½hr	19
León	34-160	2¼-2½hr	11
Mexico City (Terminal Norte)	173-285	3½-4¼hr	8
Querétaro	45-80	1-1¼hr	every 40min 7am-8:30pm

WORTH A TRIP

THERMAL SPRING POOLS

The surrounds of San Miguel are blessed with several mineral springs. Some of these have been transformed into commercial *balnearios* (swimming pools) in pretty, landscaped gardens and picnic grounds. The waters are up to 38°C (100°F). Most places are crowded with local families on weekends but *muy tranquilo* (very peaceful) during the week.

The *balnearios* are accessed via the highway north of San Miguel and all are clearly signposted. The most convenient transportation is taxi (around M$150 each way; you can ask the driver to return for you at an appointed time). Alternatively, take a Dolores Hidalgo bus from the San Miguel bus station, or a local bus marked 'Santuario' (hourly) from Calzada de la Luz. These buses will stop out front, or at the turnoffs to some of the *balnearios* from where you'll need to walk (check directions and bus connections with the tourist office). To return to town, it's best to pre-arrange a taxi pick-up, or hail a bus heading along the highway.

Taboada (☎415-152-9250; admission M$100; ⏲9am-5pm Wed-Sun) Olympic-size swimming pool, plus a small pool for children, hot thermal spa and snack kiosk. Hourly 'Nigromante' minibuses, departing from Calzada de la Luz, get you within 1.5km of Taboada.

Balneario Xote (☎415-155-81-87; www.xoteparqueacuatico.com.mx; adult/child M$110/55; ⏲9am-6pm) A family-oriented water park, 3.5km off the highway down the same cobblestone road as Taboada (without transport this is a long, exposed trek).

Escondido Place (☎415-185-20-22; www.escondidoplace.com; admission M$100; ⏲8am-5:30pm) Seven small outdoor pools and three connected indoor pools, each progressively hotter. Set in picturesque grounds, with snack bar.

La Gruta (www.lagrutaspa.com; admission M$90; ⏲7am-5pm) La Gruta is one of the easiest to get to – it's on the Dolores highway, just past Parador del Cortijo at Km 9.5. It's justifiably a favorite among visitors and has three small pools, a tunnel and a cave.

Around San Miguel de Allende

Cañada de la Virgen

Opened in 2011 after many years of archaeological excavation and negotiations with the owner (who donated the ruins and surrounds to the government to allow for public access), the **Cañada de la Virgen** (⏲10am-4pm Tue-Sun) is an intriguing pre-Hispanic pyramid complex and former ritual and ceremonial site located around 25km southeast of San Miguel, dating from around AD 300 to 1050. Bones, believed to be from sacrificial ceremonies, and remnants were discovered here. The most interesting aspects include the alignment of the planets and the main temple and the design of the site (these reflect the surrounding landscape).

A shuttle bus is the compulsory transportation for visitors. It runs between the site office and the site (several kilometers away), departing on the hour between 10am and 4pm and costing M$30. The tours are in Spanish (although are little more than a rote-learned orientation), and you'll be walking on cobbled surfaces and steep steps.

Tours

Coyote Canyon Adventures TOUR
(☎415-154-41-93; www.coyotecanyonadventures.com; 4 people or more M$650 per person, private tour 1/2 person M$1300/1950) Possibly the easiest and most rewarding visit for non-Spanish speakers is to take a tour with Coyote Canyon Adventures. Their guide, English-speaking, Albert Coffee, is an archaeologist who formerly worked on the site. He discusses the site's fascinating cultural and historical context; prices include transport from San Miguel. Lunch at a ranch costs an extra M$100.

Santuario de Atotonilco

The hamlet of Atotonilco, 11km north of San Miguel and 3km west of the Dolores Hidalgo highway, is dominated by an extremely important sanctuary, at least in the eyes of Mexicans. The sanctuary was founded in 1740 as a spiritual retreat, and Ignacio Allende married here in 1802. Eight years later he returned with Miguel Hidalgo and a band of independence rebels en route from Dolores to San Miguel to take the shrine's banner of the Virgin of Guadalupe as their flag.

A journey to Atotonilco is the goal of pilgrims and penitents from all over Mexico, and the starting point of an important and solemn procession two weekends before Easter. Participants carry the image of the Señor de la Columna to the church of San Juan de Dios in San Miguel. Inside, the sanctuary has six chapels and is vibrant with statues, folk murals and paintings. Traditional dances are held here on the third Sunday in July.

From San Miguel, taxis charge around M$150 for a one-way trip. Local buses signed 'Atotonilco' or 'Cruz del Palmar' depart from Calzada de La Luz every hour on the half hour (M$10, 45 minutes).

Pozos

POP 3500 / ELEV 2200M

Less than 100 years ago, Mineral de Pozos was a flourishing silver-mining center of 70,000 people, but with the 1910 Revolution and the flooding of the mines, the population dwindled. Empty houses, a large and unfinished church (note the dome!) and discarded mine workings and shafts were the legacy of abandonment. Today, this tiny place is gradually winning back its place on the map. Visitors can explore the crumbling buildings and tour the fascinating surrounds, including several mine ruins, by mountain bike or horse. Warning: many mine shafts are unfenced and, at 150m deep, are extremely dangerous. A number of expat artists run galleries here and a couple of boutique sleeping options have opened, catering mainly to weekenders from Mexico City.

Be sure to explore beyond the square Jardin Juarez and head up the hill to Plaza Zaragoza and down the hill to Plaza Mineros. Alongside the galleries, many craft shops are dotted around town.

For further information, including local guides, see www.mineraldepozos.com.

Sleeping & Eating

Casa del Venado Azul HOSTEL $

(☎468-688-62-30, cell phone 468-1170387; azulvenado@hotmail.com; Calle Centenario 34; per person M$350) The town's only budget sleep is basic but clean, and run by an English-speaking drummer (that's pre-Hispanic drums) who also arranges temascal (steam) baths.

El Secreto B&B $$

(☎442-293-02-00; www.elsecretomexico.com; Jardín Principal 6; r incl breakfast M$950-1,250; Wi-Fi) On the plaza, this is a tasteful gallery-B&B nestled in a lovely garden (think: cactus and flowers and birds aplenty) with elegant rooms. The English-speaking owners know a lot about the area.

Posada de las Minas BOUTIQUE HOTEL $$$

(☎442-293-02-13; www.posadadelasminas.com; Doblado 1; r from M$1500; Wi-Fi) The restored 19th-century hacienda offers ornate rooms and apartments in a colonial setting. The 'Santa Brigida' room has corner windows with views over town. It's got a bar, and its restaurant (mains M$85 to M$165; open from 8.30am every day) is the best bet in town for meals. There's also an impressive cactus garden.

La Pila Seca MEXICAN $

(Aldama 8; mains M$45-100; 11am-8pm Mon-Thu, to 9pm Fri, 9am-9pm Sat & Sun) The friendly, unpretentious spot offers decent servings of local cuisine. It's the same deal at in-your-face Mexican-themed **Porfirio Díaz**, just a few doors down.

Shopping

The town has a handful of galleries and craft workshops, where community members sell their work. Several workshops make pre-Hispanic musical instruments.

Manos Creativos ARTS & CRAFTS

(Mariscala 2) Manos Creativos, a women's cooperative, produces handmade regional costumes for dolls.

Casa del Venado Azul MUSIC

(☎468-688-62-30; Calle Centenario 34) Among Mexico's folk-instrument makers, shop owner Luis Cruz stands out. The accomplished musician heads his own musical ensemble, which tours internationally. The locaton doubles as a hostel.

Getting There & Away

Pozos is 14km south of San Luis de la Paz, a detour east of Hwy 57. To get here by bus from San Miguel (or Querétaro), go first to Dolores Hidalgo, then to San Luis de la Paz and then take a third bus to Pozos. By car it's about one hour from San Miguel. Bici-Burro (p662) offers fabulous bike tours to the town and mines. Much of the ride is a cross-country trip on tracks across cactus-strewn countryside, via fascinating villages.

AGUASCALIENTES STATE

The state of Aguascalientes (population 1.2 million) is one of Mexico's smallest; its focus is the city of the same name. According to local legend, a kiss planted on the lips of dictator Santa Anna by the wife of a prominent local politician brought about the creation of a separate Aguascalientes state from Zacatecas.

Beyond the museum-rich city formal tourist sites are few, but it's a pleasant enough drive en route to or from Zacatecas, through fertile lands of corn, beans, chilies, fruit and grain.

The state's ranches produce beef cattle as well as bulls, which are sacrificed at bullfights countrywide.

Aguascalientes

☎449 / POP 720,000 / ELEV 1880M

This prosperous industrial city is home to more than half of the state's population. Despite its messy outer (defined by ring roads), at its heart are a fine plaza and handsome colonial buildings. Museums are its strong point: the Museo Nacional de la Muerte justifies a visit, as do those devoted to José Guadalupe Posada and Saturnino Herrán.

History

Before the Spanish arrived, a labyrinth of catacombs was built here; the first Spaniards called it La Ciudad Perforada (The Perforated City). Archaeologists understand little of the tunnels, which are off-limits to visitors.

Conquistador Pedro de Alvarado arrived in 1522 but was driven back by the Chichimecs. A small garrison was founded here in 1575 to protect Zacatecas–Mexico City silver convoys. Eventually, as the Chichimecs were pacified, the region's hot springs sparked the growth of a town; a large tank beside the Ojo Caliente springs helped irrigate local farms that fed hungry mining districts nearby.

Today, the city's industries include textiles, wine, brandy, leather, preserved fruits and car manufacturing.

Sights & Activities

★Museo Nacional de la Muerte MUSEUM
(☎449-139-32-58; www.museonacionaldelamuerte.uaa.mx; Jardín del Estudiante s/n; adult/student M$20/10; ⏰10am-6pm Tue-Sun) This is one 'near death' experience not to be missed. The Museo Nacional de la Muerte exhibits all things relating to Mexico's favorite subject – death – from the skeleton La Catrina to historic artifacts. The contents – over 2500 artifacts, drawings, literature, textiles, toys and miniatures – were donated to the Universidad Autónoma de Aguascalientes by collector and engraver, Octavio Bajonero Gil. Over 1200 are on display. They span several centuries, from Mesoamerican to contemporary artistic interpretations.

In room one, look out for the miniature crystal skull. It's believed to be from Aztec times and there are only two in the world. This wonderful place is far from macabre but a colorful, humorous and insightful encounter.

Museo de Aguascalientes MUSEUM
(☎449-915-90-43; Zaragoza 507; adult/student M$25/free; ⏰11am-6pm Tue-Sun) Housed in a handsome neoclassical building, this museum houses a permanent collection of work by the brilliant Aguascalientes artist Saturnino Herrán (1887–1918), and there are also temporary exhibitions. His works are some of the first to honestly depict the Mexican people. The sensual sculpture *Malgretout* on the patio is a fiberglass copy of the marble original by Jesús Contreras.

Teatro Morelos HISTORIC BUILDING
(Plaza de la Patria) Facing the cathedral's south side is the Teatro Morelos, scene of the 1914 Convention of Aguascalientes, in which revolutionary factions led by Pancho Villa, Venustiano Carranza and Emiliano Zapata attempted unsuccessfully to mend their differences. Busts of these three, plus one of Álvaro Obregón, stand in the foyer and there are a few exhibits upstairs.

Catedral CATHEDRAL
(Plaza de la Patria) The well-restored 18th-century baroque Cathedral, on the plaza's west side, is more magnificent inside than out. Over the altar at the east end of the south aisle is a painting of the Virgin of Guadalupe by Miguel Cabrera. There are more works by Cabrera, colonial Mexico's finest artist, in the cathedral's *pinacoteca* (picture gallery). It's open at Easter only (although if you are lucky, ask a priest and he might let you in).

Palacio de Gobierno HISTORIC BUILDING
(Plaza de la Patria; ⏰8am-8:30pm Mon-Fri, 8am-2pm Sat & Sun) On the south side of Plaza de la Patria, the red-and-pink stone Palacio de Gobierno is Aguascalientes' most noteworthy

colonial building. Once the mansion of colonial baron Marqués de Guadalupe, it dates from 1665 and has a striking courtyard with two levels of murals. including one depicting the 1914 convention by the Chilean artist Osvaldo Barra. Barra, whose mentor was Diego Rivera, also painted the mural on the south wall, a compendium of the economic and historic forces that forged Aguascalientes.

Museo José Guadalupe Posada MUSEUM
(☎449-915-45-56; Jardín El Encino s/n; adult/student M$10/5, Sun free; ⏲11am-6pm Tue-Sun) Aguascalientes native Posada (1852–1913) was in many ways the founder of modern Mexican art. His engravings and satirical cartoons broadened the audience for art in Mexico, highlighted social problems and were a catalyst in the later mural phase, influencing artists like Diego Rivera, José Clemente Orozco and Alfaro David Siqueiros. Posada's hallmark is the *calavera* (skull or skeleton) and many of his *calavera* engravings have been widely reproduced. There's also a permanent exhibition of work by Posada's predecessor Manuel Manilla (1830–90).

Templo del Encino CHURCH
(Jardín El Encino; ⏲7am-1pm & 5-7pm) The Templo del Encino, beside the Posada museum, contains a black statue of Jesus that some believe is growing. When it reaches an adjacent column, a worldwide calamity is anticipated. The huge *Way of the Cross* murals are also noteworthy.

Templo de San Antonio CHURCH
(⏲7am-1pm & 5-7pm) The Templo de San Antonio is a crazy quilt of architectural styles built around 1900 by self-taught architect Refugio Reyes. San Antonio's interior is highly ornate, with huge round paintings and intricate decoration highlighted in gold.

Museo de Arte Contemporáneo MUSEUM
(☎449-915-79-53; cnr Morelos & Primo Verdad; adult/student M$10/5, Sun free; ⏲11am-6pm Tue-Sun) A small, modern museum displaying the work of Enrique Guzmán (1952–86) as well as temporary exhibitions, is well worth visiting.

Museo Regional de Historia MUSEUM
(☎449-916-52-28; Av Carranza 118; adult M$42; ⏲9am-6pm Tue-Sun) This history museum was designed by Refugio Reyes as a family home and features a small chapel. Under new direction, it's been given a new lease of life. Its exhibits run all the way from the big bang to the colonial conquest. It also has a beautiful chapel with ex-voto paintings and works attributed to Correa. Anyone interested in Mexican history will appreciate these displays. For others, the temporary exhibitions can be fascinating; pass by to check what's on.

Expoplaza PLAZA
Half a kilometer southwest of Plaza de la Patria via Avenida Carranza, Expoplaza is a modern shopping and restaurant-bar strip. On the mall's south side, the wide and soulless pedestrian promenade comes alive at night and during the annual Feria de San Marcos. At its west end, the mammoth **Plaza de Toros Monumental** is notable for its modern-colonial treatment of traditional bullring architecture.

On Expoplaza's east side the pedestrian street Pani runs two blocks north to the 18th-century **Templo de San Marcos** (Pani) and the pretty, shady **Jardín de San Marcos**. The **Palenque de Gallos**, in the **Casino de la Feria** building on Pani, is the city's cockfighting arena (only during the feria). Near the northeast corner of Jardín de San Marcos is **Ex-Plaza de Toros San Marcos**, the old bullring (now a bullfighting school).

Baños Termales de Ojocaliente THERMAL BATHS
(☎449-970-07-21; Tecnológico 102; private baths per hr from M$120; ⏲7am-7pm winter, 8am-8pm summer) Despite the city's name, these charming if slightly shabby thermal baths are the only ones near the center. The restored 1808 architecture truly turns back the clock; the waters are said to help all sorts of ailments. Take bus 23 or 25 from Mateos.

Museo del Juguete Tradicional Mexicana MUSEUM
(museodeljuguetetradicional@yahoo.com; Eduardo Correa 246; M$15; ⏲9am-2pm & 4-6pm Tue-Sun) This small and simple museum showcases a range of traditional Mexican toys from all over the country that are made from wood and clay, paper and chewing gum; the Spanish owner talks you through the history of the collection (Spanish only). Most interesting for collectors and anthropologists.

Aguascalientes

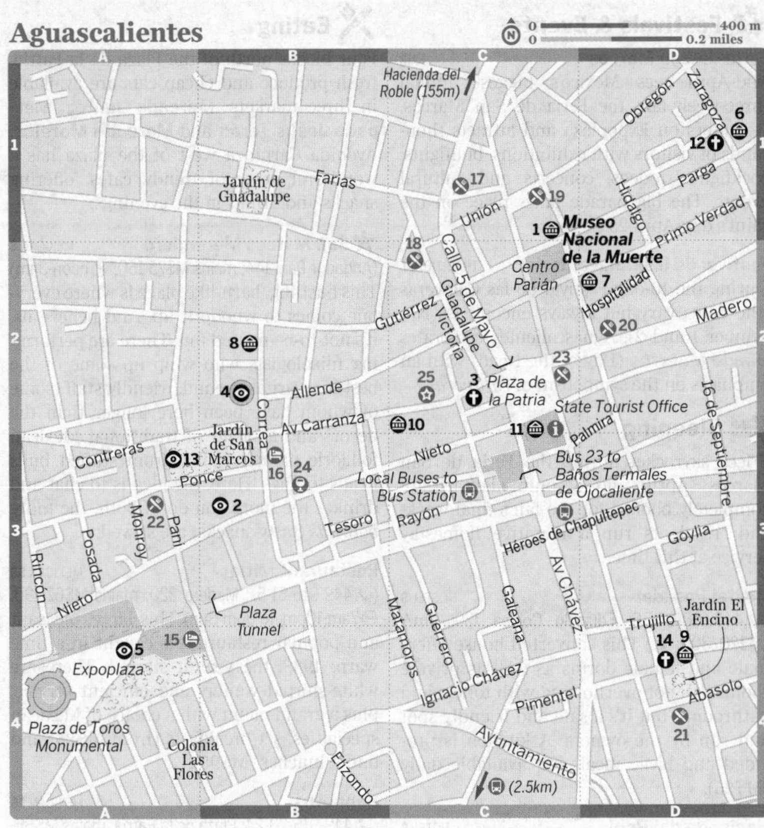

Aguascalientes

Top Sights
1 Museo Nacional de la Muerte....C1

Sights
2 Casino de la Feria....B3
3 Catedral....C2
4 Ex-Plaza de Toros San Marcos....B2
5 Expoplaza....A4
6 Museo de Aguascalientes....D1
7 Museo de Arte Contemporáneo....D2
8 Museo del Juguete Tradicional Mexicana....B2
9 Museo José Guadalupe Posada....D4
10 Museo Regional de Historia....C2
11 Palacio de Gobierno....C2
Teatro Morelos....(see 3)
12 Templo de San Antonio....D1
13 Templo de San Marcos....A3
14 Templo del Encino....D4

Sleeping
15 Fiesta Americana....A4
16 Hostal Posada....B3

Eating
17 Mercado Jesús Terán....C1
18 Mercado Juárez....C2
19 Mercado Morelos....C1
20 Restaurant Mitla....D2
21 Rincón Maya....D4
22 San Marcos Merendero....A3
23 Sanborns....C2

Drinking & Nightlife
24 Pulquería Posada....B3

Entertainment
25 Casa de la Cultura....C2

Festivals & Events

Feria de San Marcos FAIR

Mid-April sees Mexico's biggest annual three-week fair, the Feria de San Marcos. It centers on Expoplaza and attracts thousands of visitors with exhibitions, bullfights, cockfights, rodeos, concerts and cultural events. The big parade takes place on the saint's day, April 25.

Festival de las Calaveras TRADITIONAL

During the 10-day Festival de las Calaveras (the dates vary but always encompass November 1 and 2), Aguascalientes celebrates **Día de Muertos** (Day of the Dead) with an emphasis on the symbolism of *calavera*.

Sleeping

Prices skyrocket during the Feria de San Marcos (April) and accommodations are completely booked for the fair's final weekend; residents run a lucrative homestay service at this time.

Hostal Posada HOSTEL $

(449-918-64-36; Eduardo Correa 139; dm/r M$120/300;) This converted house offers male and female dorms as well as private rooms. It's not overflowing with toilets and bathrooms, but it's a safe and friendly spot and run by the owners. A kitchen is provided and basic meals are available daily (M$25).

Hacienda del Roble HOTEL $

(449-915-39-94; Calle 5 de Mayo 540; s/d M$400/450) This is the best of the limited cheaper choices, with small but modern carpeted rooms, external-facing windows and reasonable bathrooms. The downside is the grittier and noisier location – right on Calle 5 de Mayo – but it's only a 10-minute walk to the plaza.

Fiesta Americana LUXURY HOTEL $$$

(449-910-05-00; www.fiestaamericana.com; Laureles s/n, Colonia Las Flores; r from M$1769;) This luxury chain hotel is a pleasant five-star experience, if slightly pricey; the 192 rooms feature all the amenities and there's a fitness center and an inviting pool. Weekend packages for two cost around M$1500 and include buffet breakfast. Best to check the website for special offers.

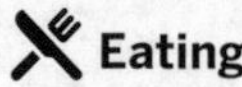

Eating

Four blocks north of the Plaza de la Patria, fresh produce and cheap eats are available in three markets: **Mercado Juárez**, **Mercado Jesús Terán** and **Mercado Morelos**. Avenida Carranza west of the plaza has a wonderful array of trendy cafes, offering snacks and drinks in the evenings.

★ **San Marcos Merendero** MEXICAN $

(Andador Pani 144; mains M$75-150; noon-3am) This bustling, barn-like place is where everyone comes to whoop it up. And believe us, it's not-to-be-missed fun. There are performing mixologists who whip up some of the best margaritas around, friendly staff (some of whom have been here longer than the decor) and a blend of traditional Mexican folkloric paraphernalia, from stuffed bulls heads to flags. Here, the idea is to chat and drink – the more you do of both, the more *botanas* (tasty snacks) are served.

Restaurant Mitla MEXICAN $$

(449-916-61-57; Madero 220; mains M$62-190; 7am-10pm, to 9pm Sun) This large, pleasant and popular restaurant is caught in a time warp: 1938, the year it started. There are white-shirted waiters and efficient service, plus a grand menu with a choice of Mexican specialties, set breakfasts (from M$85) and buffet lunches (M$98).

Sanborns MEXICAN $$

(449-915-20-24; Plaza de la Patria; mains M$65-165; 7am-1am) It may be a chain eatery, but this one is in a glorious, old-fashioned salon with good meals (especially breakfast and afternoon teas) and views over the plaza. Located on the 2nd floor.

Rincón Maya YUCATECAN $$

(449-916-75-74; Abasolo 113; mains M$90-140; 2pm-midnight Mon-Sat, 2-10:30pm Sun) Until lunchtime, this place has service at La Mestiza Yucateca (open 8am to 2pm), its alter ego next door. Both are located in a former hacienda and both serve delectable Yucatecan specialties.

Drinking

Pulquería Posada BAR

(Nieto 445; noon-2am Tue-Sun) Swing by this verging-on-grungy student hangout for the M$18 half-litre *jarras* (jugs) of *pulque* (a traditional Aztec tipple made from fermented agave sap). There's also a good range of mezcals, flavoured with everything from lime to guava.

☆ Entertainment

Pani, the pedestrian street between the Expoplaza and Jardín de San Marcos, is lively most evenings, with a good selection of bars and restaurants.

Casa de la Cultura ARTS CENTER
(☎449-910-20-10; Av Carranza 101) In a fine 17th-century building, the Casa de la Cultura hosts art exhibitions, concerts, theater and dance events. Aguascalientes also has two theaters, **Teatro de AguasCalientes** (☎449-978-54-14; cnr Calles Chávez & Aguascalientes) and Teatro Morelos (p671), that stage a variety of cultural events.

ℹ Information

EMERGENCY

Police (☎080, 066)

INTERNET ACCESS

Most places charge around M$12 per hour.

Café Internet 3W (Centro Parián, Calle Morelos; ⊙9am-9pm Mon-Sat, 11am-6pm Sun)

MEDICAL SERVICES

Several pharmacies in the city center are open 24 hours.

Star Médica (☎449-910-99-00; www.starmedica.com; Universidad 103) Private hospital.

MONEY

Banks with ATMs are common around Plaza de la Patria and Expoplaza. *Casas de cambio* cluster on Hospitalidad, opposite the post office.

TOURIST INFORMATION

State Tourist Office (☎449-915-95-04; www.aguascalientes.gob.mx; Palacio de Gobierno, Plaza de la Patria; ⊙9am-8pm Mon-Sat, 10am-6pm Sun) Free city maps. Ask for *Agenda Cultural*, a monthly what's-on listing.

ℹ Getting There & Away

AIR

Aéropuerto Jesús Terán (☎449-918-28-06) is 26km south of Aguascalientes off the road to Mexico City. **Aeroméxico Connect** (☎449-918-21-27; Madero 474) has flights to Mexico City and Monterrey plus flights via Mexico City to Los Angeles and New York. **Volaris** (www.volaris.mx) serves Los Angeles. American Airlines has regular flights to Houston, Dallas and Los Angeles.

BUS

The **bus station** (Central Camionera; Av Convención) is 2km south of the center. It has card phones, a cafeteria and luggage storage.

Deluxe, 1st- and 2nd-class buses operate to/from Aguascalientes. Deluxe and 1st-class companies include ETN, Primera Plus, Futura and Ómnibus de México. The main 2nd-class line is Coordinados (Flecha Amarilla).

As well as those outlined in the table, frequent services go to Ciudad Juárez, Monterrey, Morelia and Torreón, and one daily bus service to San Miguel de Allende. For Guanajuato, it's easiest to change in León.

ℹ Getting Around

Most places of interest are within easy walking distance of each other. Regular city buses (M$6) run from 6am to 10pm. Buses display route numbers; check which bus heads to the city center as these change regularly. Disembark at the first stop after you go through the town's one tunnel on Calle 5 de Mayo. This is one block from the plaza. From the city center to the bus station, several buses head to the bus station from the corner of Galeana (near Insurgentes).

Taxis charge as per metered fares. Between the bus station and the center the taxi fare is around M$25 to M$30.

BUSES FROM AGUASCALIENTES

DESTINATION	FARE (M$)	DURATION	FREQUENCY (DAILY)
Guadalajara	25-268	2¾-3hr	frequent
Guanajuato	161-214	3hr	7:10am & 7:30pm
León	136-185	2-3½hr	frequent
Mexico City (Terminal Norte)	447-580	6hr	frequent
San Luis Potosí	156-209	3-3½hr	hourly
Zacatecas	136-175	2hr	hourly

SAN LUIS POTOSÍ STATE

The historic state capital city, San Luis Potosí, and the fascinating 'ghost town,' Real de Catorce, are on the high and dry expanses of the state's north and west and are the main reasons visitors come to this region. The pretty tropical, verdant eastern region, the Huasteca, with green valleys and waterfalls, is popular among local tourists.

The state is steeped in history. Before the Spanish conquest, western San Luis Potosí was inhabited by Guachichiles, warlike hunters. In the 18th century the area gained a reputation for maltreatment of indigenous people, partly because the nonmonastic clergy replaced the more compassionate Franciscans.

Today, mining, agriculture, ranching and industry are the economic mainstays of this fairly prosperous state with a population of 2.6 million.

San Luis Potosí

☎444 / POP 736,000 / ELEV 1860M

A grand old dame of colonial cities, San Luis Potosí was once a revolutionary hotbed, an important mining town and seat of government to boot. Today the city has maintained its poise as the prosperous state capital, orderly industrial center and the seat of the university.

A great place to wander through, the city's colonial core is made up of numerous plazas and manicured parks that are linked by attractive pedestrian streets. Although not as striking as Zacatecas or Guanajuato, this lively city's cultural elegance is reflected in its delightful colonial buildings, impressive theater and numerous excellent, museums.

History

Founded in 1592, San Luis is 20km west of the silver deposits in Cerro de San Pedro, and was named Potosí after the immensely rich Bolivian silver town, which the Spanish hoped it would rival. The mines began to decline in the 1620s, but the city was established enough as a ranching center to remain the major city of northeastern Mexico until overtaken by Monterrey at the start of the 20th century.

Known in the 19th century for its lavish houses and imported luxury goods, San Luis was twice the seat of President Benito Juárez's government during the 1860s French intervention. In 1910 in San Luis, the dictatorial president Porfirio Díaz jailed Francisco Madero, his liberal opponent, during the presidential campaign. Freed after the election, Madero hatched his Plan de San Luis Potosí (a strategy to depose Díaz), announcing it in San Antonio, Texas, in October 1910; he declared the election illegal, named himself provisional president and designated November 20 as the day for Mexico to rise in revolt – the start of the Mexican Revolution.

Sights

Museo Federico Silva MUSEUM
(☎444-812-38-48; www.museofedericosilva.org; Obregón 80; adult/student M$30/15; ⏲10am-6pm Wed-Mon, 10am-2pm Sun) This museum should not be missed. The original 17th-century building on the north side of San Luis Potosí's Jardín de San Juan del Dios was once a hospital and later a school under *el porfiriato* (the Porfiriato period). It has been exquisitely transformed into an art museum, ingeniously integrating the building's previous neoclassical finish with the monolithic sculptures of Silva. It hosts temporary exhibitions of international contemporary sculptors.

Museo de Arte Contemporáneo MUSEUM
(MAC; ☎444-814-43-63; Morelos 235; adult/student M$20/10; ⏲10am-6pm Tue-Sat, 10am-2pm Sun) This museum is housed in the city's former post office. These days, the brilliantly transformed space houses temporary art exhibitions that change every three months.

Museo del Centro de las Artes Centenario MUSEUM
(Antigua Penitenciaria; ☎444-137-41-00; Calz de Guadalupe; adult M$15; ⏲10am-2pm & 5-8pm Mon-Fri, 11am-5pm Sat & Sun) Up until 1999, the Museo was a prison, believed to have briefly held Francisco Madero. Ten years later, it was transformed – without losing its fundamental design – into an arts and cultural center. Some of the former cells have been maintained; others have been converted into offices. It's located 12 blocks south of Alameda.

Palacio de Gobierno PALACE
(5 de Mayo) FREE The neoclassical Palacio de Gobierno was built between 1770 and 1816. Its most illustrious lodger was Benito Juárez – first in 1863 when he was fleeing from invading French forces, then in 1867 when

San Luis Potosí

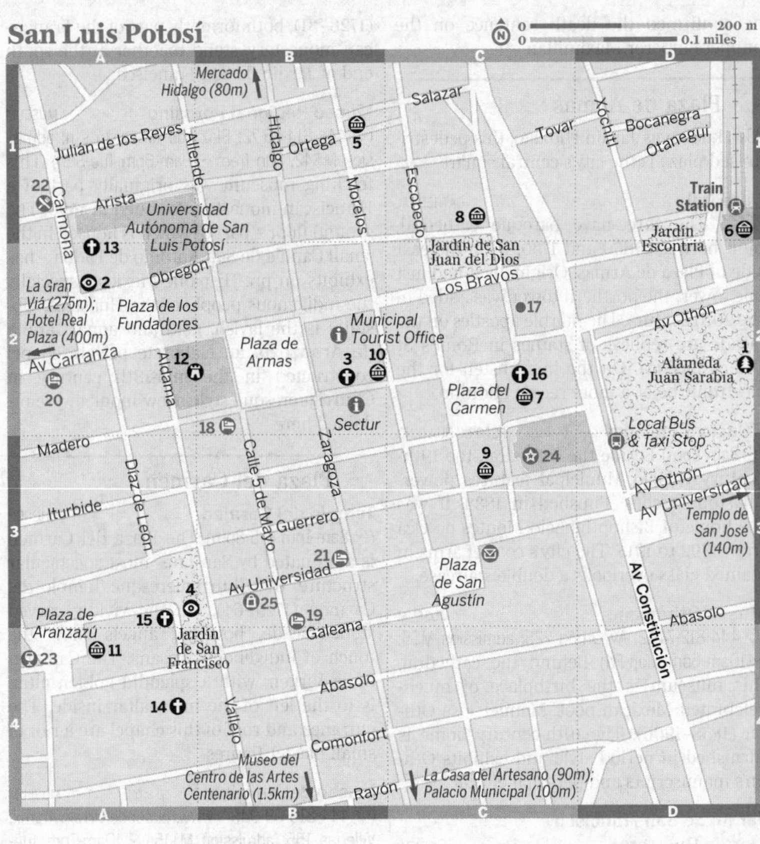

San Luis Potosí

Sights

1 Alameda D2
2 Capilla de Loreto A2
3 Catedral B2
4 Jardín de San Francisco (Jardín Guerrero) A3
5 Museo de Arte Contemporáneo B1
6 Museo del Ferrocarril D1
7 Museo del Virreinato C2
8 Museo Federico Silva C1
9 Museo Nacional de la Máscara C3
10 Museo Othóniano B2
11 Museo Regional Potosino A4
12 Palacio de Gobierno A2
13 Templo de la Compañía A2
14 Templo de la Tercera Orden & Templo del Sagrado Corazón A4
15 Templo de San Francisco A3
16 Templo del Carmen C2

Activities, Courses & Tours

17 Operatour Potosina C2

Sleeping

18 Hotel de Gante B2
19 Hotel Museo Palacio de San Agustín B3
20 Hotel Panorama A2
21 Hotel San Francisco B3

Eating

22 Antojitos El Pozole A1

Drinking & Nightlife

23 La Piqueria Mezcaleria A4

Entertainment

24 Teatro de la Paz C3

Shopping

25 Casa Grande Esencia Artesanal B3

he confirmed the death sentence on the puppet-emperor Maximilian.

Plaza de Armas

Also known as Jardín Hidalgo, this pedestrianized plaza is the city's central square.

Catedral CATHEDRAL

FREE The three-nave baroque cathedral, built between 1660 and 1730, is on the east side of Plaza de Armas. Originally it had just one tower; the northern tower was added in the 20th century. The marble apostles on the facade are replicas of statues in Rome's St Peter's Basilica. On the hour, listen for the electronic bells, a more recent addition.

Palacio Municipal HISTORIC BUILDING

(8am-8pm) Beside the cathedral, the 19th-century Palacio Municipal features powerful stone arches. Finished in 1838, it was the home of Bishop Ignacio Montes de Oca from 1892 to 1915. The city's coat of arms in stained glass overlooks a double staircase.

Museo Othóniano MUSEUM

(444-812-74-12; Av Othón 225; admission M$5; 10am-6pm Mon-Fri) Behind the cathedral, this museum is the birthplace of much-celebrated Mexican poet, Manuel José Othón (1858–1906). The 19th-century home is furnished in period style and exhibits Othón's manuscripts and personal effects.

Jardín de San Francisco (Jardín Guerrero) PLAZA

Dominated by the bulk of the Templo de San Francisco and convent, and with a lovely fountain gracing its interior, this square is one of the city's most fetching.

Templo de San Francisco CHURCH

(Jardín de San Francisco) The altar of the 17th- and 18th-century Templo de San Francisco was remodeled in the 20th century, but the sacristy (the priest's dressing room), reached by a door to the right of the altar, is original and has a fine dome and carved pink stone. The Sala De Profundis, through the arch at the south end of the sacristy, has more paintings and a carved stone fountain. A beautiful crystal ship hangs from the main dome.

Templo de la Tercera Orden & Templo del Sagrado Corazón CHURCH

(Jardín de San Francisco) The small Templo de la Tercera Orden, built in 1694 and restored in 1960, and Templo del Sagrado Corazón (1728–31), both formerly part of the Franciscan monastery, stand together at the south end of Jardín de San Francisco.

Museo Regional Potosino MUSEUM

(444-814-35-72; Plaza de Aranzazú s\n; admission M$42, Sun free; 9am-6pm Tue-Sun) This fetching museum was originally part of a Franciscan monastery founded in 1590. The ground floor – part of which is housed in the small Capilla de San Antonio de Padua – has exhibits on pre-Hispanic Mexico, especially the indigenous people of the Huasteca. Upstairs is the lavish, gold and aqua **Capilla de Aranzazú**, an elaborate private chapel constructed in the mid-18th century in Churrigueresque style. New monks were ordained here.

Plaza del Carmen

Templo del Carmen CHURCH

(8am-1pm & 5-8pm) The Plaza del Carmen is dominated by San Luis' most spectacular structure, the Churrigueresque Templo del Carmen (1749–64). On the vividly carved stone facade, hovering angels show the touch of indigenous artisans. The Camarín de la Virgen, with a splendid golden altar, is to the left of the main altar inside. The entrance and roof of this chapel are a riot of small plaster figures.

Museo del Virreinato MUSEUM

(444-816-09-94; www.museodelvirreinato.mx; Villerías 155; admission M$15; 10am-7pm Tue-Sun) Beside the Templo de Carmen, this museum has a large collection of paintings and artifacts from the Spanish vice-regency. More of interest might be its temporary exhibitions – check what's on.

Museo Nacional de la Máscara MUSEUM

(National Mask Museum; 444-812-30-25; Villerías 2; admission M$15, camera use M$20; 10am-6pm Tue-Fri, to 5pm Sat, 11am-3pm Sun) Displays an interesting collection of ceremonial masks from across Mexico and around the world. There are good descriptions in English and interesting videos of dances performed during festivals in communities.

Plaza de los Fundadores PLAZA

The least pretty of the plazas, Plaza de los Fundadores (Founders' Plaza) is where the city was born. On the north side is a large building constructed in 1653 as a Jesuit college. Today it houses offices of the Universidad Autónoma de San Luis Potosí. It was probably on this site that Diego de la Magdalena, a Franciscan friar, started a small settlement of Guachichiles around 1585.

To the west of these offices is the **Templo de la Compañía** (Plaza de los Fundadores), built by the Jesuits in 1675 with a baroque facade. A little further west is the **Capilla de Loreto** (Plaza de los Fundadores), a Jesuit chapel from 1700 with unusual, twisted pillars.

Alameda PARK

The **Alameda Juan Sarabia** marks the eastern boundary of the downtown area. It used to be the vegetable garden of the monastery attached to the Templo del Carmen. Today it's a large, attractive park with shady paths.

Templo de San José CHURCH

(Alameda Park) Inside the Templo de San José, facing the Alameda's south side, lies the image of El Señor de los Trabajos, a Christ figure attracting pilgrims from near and far. Numerous *retablos* (altarpieces) around the statue testify to prayers answered in finding jobs and other apparent miracles.

Museo del Ferrocarril MUSEUM

(☎444-814-35-89; Av Othón; admission M$15; ⏲10am-6pm Tue-Sun) On the north side of the Alameda, this museum is housed in the city's former train station and very cleverly brings to life its past. The existing building was designed by Manuel Ortiz Monasterio and was constructed in 1936. Exhibits include modern installations relating to train travel plus former locomotive parts.

Tours

Tranvía TOUR

(☎444-814-22-26; www.tranviasanluis.com; 1hr trip M$50) Two *tranvías*, imitations of antique trolleys, do a loop around the historic center starting from in front of the Cathedral on Plaza de Armas. The smaller blue San Luis Rey goes up the narrower streets making for a more interesting ride. Hours change; check with the tourist office.

Operatour Potosina TOUR

(☎444-151-22-01; www.operatourpotosina.com.mx; Sarabia 120) If you want to do a tour, Operatour Potosina is *the* outfit to do it with. The friendly and knowledgeable English-speaking operator, Lori, offers tours around the city, as well as to haciendas, Real de Catorce, Zacatecas and the Huasteca Potosina region (minimum two people). Custom-made tours available, too. The office is located in the Hotel Napoles.

Festivals & Events

Semana Santa RELIGIOUS

Holy Week is celebrated with concerts, exhibitions and other activities; on Good Friday (March/April) at 3pm, Christ's passion is re-enacted in the barrio of San Juan de Guadalupe, followed at 8pm by the Silent Procession through the city center (one of the city's most important events).

Feria Nacional Potosina FAIR

San Luis' National Fair, normally in the last three weeks of August, includes concerts, bullfights, rodeos, cockfights and agricultural shows.

Día de San Luis Rey de Francia RELIGIOUS

On August 25 the city's patron saint, St Louis IX, is honored as the highlight of the Feria Nacional. Events include a parade, concerts and plays.

Festival Internacional de Danza DANCE

This national festival of contemporary dance is held in September and October.

Sleeping

Hotel de Gante PENSION $

(☎444-812-14-92; hotel_degante@hotmail.com; Calle 5 de Mayo 140; s/d/tr M$380/430/490; 📶) In an unbeatable location, near the corner of Plaza de Armas, Gante will please backpackers and budget travelers – old-style, airy rooms with cable TV.

Hotel Panorama BUSINESS HOTEL $$

(☎800-480-01-00, 444-812-17-77; www.hotelpanorama.com.mx; Av Carranza 315; r/ste M$875/1280; P ⊜ ❄ 📶 ≋) It's the best of San Luis' rather average lot of midrange accommodation options and has position going for it – it's opposite Plaza de los Fundadores. Beyond that, it's smart(ish) and all 126 rooms have floor-to-ceiling windows; those on the south side overlook the pool. Popular with business travelers.

Hotel San Francisco HOTEL $$

(www.sanfranciscohotel.mx; Universidad 375; r M$695; P ⊜ ❄ 📶) At last, another decent midrange option in the center. Run by the same crew as Panorama, this recently opened, converted historic building offers modern, business-style rooms. Rooms at the front with external-facing windows are susceptible to traffic noise, while interior rooms don't get the fresh air. But it's a good choice either way.

Hotel Real Plaza HOTEL $$
(444-814-69-69; www.realplaza.com.mx; Carranza 890; s/d M$650/690; P ❄) Despite the rather dark and dull lobby, rooms here are light, clean and neat. Popular with business travelers.

Hotel Museo Palacio de San Agustín HISTORIC HOTEL $$$
(444-144-19-00; www.palaciodesanagustin.com; Galeana 240; r M$4800-5300; P ❄) Warning: this plush 'museum hotel' comes with a snob rating. Formerly a house belonging to the San Agustín monastery, this extraordinary property has been restored to its original condition (think: hand-painted gold-leaf finishes, crystal chandeliers and 700 certified European antiques).

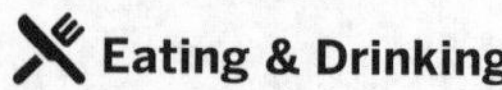

Eating & Drinking

One local specialty is *tacos potosinos* – red, chili-impregnated tacos stuffed with cheese or chicken and topped with chopped potato, carrot, lettuce and loads of *queso blanco* (white cheese).

Antojitos El Pozole MEXICAN $
(cnr Calles Carmona & Arista; mains M$40-70; noon-11:30pm Tue-Sun) The place to try the local *enchiladas potosinas* – the tortilla dough is red (from mild chili). This place was started by a woman selling *antojitos* (Mexican snacks) in her home in the 1980s. Demand for her goods was so high she has since opened several restaurants specializing in what she knows best – *tacos rojos, pozole* and *quesadillas de papa* (potato quesadillas). Yes, they're that good.

★**El México de Frida** MEXICAN $$
(444-811-46-03; www.elmexicodefrida.com; Valentín Gama 646; set meals M$176-284; 1pm-midnight Mon-Sat, 1-6pm Sun) Although it's painted in Kahlo-esque colors, this restaurant is not Frida-kitsch. Rather, the tasteful and tasty menu serves up scrumptious Mexican fare. Try the *chiles ventilla*, chilies with cheese and the most tantalizing creamy sauces. It's 3km along (and just south of) Avenida Carranza.

★**La Gran Vía** SPANISH $$$
(444-812-2899; Carranza 560; mains M$173-350; lunch & dinner Mon-Sat, lunch Sun) Notes of expensive perfume mingle with the aromas of paella, *lechón asado* (roasted piglet) and cod fish – just a few of the dishes on this culinary institution's extensive menu. Great for a special meal out.

La Piqueria Mezcaleria BAR
(Independencia 1190; snacks M$45-70; 5pm-1am Wed-Sat) Another Mexican bar that has re-popularized mezcal and *pulque* drinks. In this case, they're artisanal mezcals, served up with pre-Hispanic *botanos* (snacks, including *chapulines* and quesadillas). There's a fun, buzzy atmosphere.

☆ Entertainment

San Luis has an active cultural scene. Ask in the tourist office about what's on and keep your eye out for posters. The free monthly *Guiarte* booklet and posters detail cultural attractions.

Teatro de la Paz CONCERT VENUE
(444-812-52-09; Villerias 2) This neoclassical theater (1889–94) contains a concert hall with 1500 seats and an exhibition gallery as well as a theater. Posters announce upcoming dance, theater and music events.

Orquesta Sinfónica MUSIC
(444-814-36-01; tickets from M$30) San Luis' own symphony orchestra plays in Teatro de la Paz and other venues; check with the tourist office.

Shopping

La Casa del Artesano HANDICRAFTS
(Jardín Colón 23; 8am-3pm & 5-8pm Mon-Fri, 10am-5pm Sat) For local products, try this shop full of *potosino* pottery, masks, woodwork and canework.

Casa Grande Esencia Artesanal ARTS & CRAFTS
(www.esenciaartesanal.com; Universidad 220; 9am-9pm) Great for gifts that are 100% made in the region of San Luis Potosí.

Information

INTERNET ACCESS

Fox Ciberkafe (Escobedo 315; 9am-9pm) Internet charges are M$15 per hour.

MEDICAL SERVICES

Star Médica (444-100-95-00; Arista 735) Private hospital.

MONEY

Banks with ATMs are scattered around town, including the Plazas de Armas and de los Fundadores. Several *casas de cambio* are along Morelos.

POST

Post Office (444-812-72-86; Av Universidad 526; 8am-3pm Mon-Fri)

TOURIST INFORMATION

Municipal Tourist Office (444-812-27-70; Palacio Municipal; 8am-8pm Mon-Sat, 10am-5pm Sun) On the east side of Plaza de Armas.

Sectur (State tourist office; 800-343-38-87, 444-812-99-39; www.visitasanluispotosi.com; Av Othón; 8am-9pm Mon-Fri, 9am-3pm Sat) Has maps of off-the-beaten-track attractions in San Luis Potosí state.

Getting There & Away

AIR

Aeropuerto Ponciano Arriaga (444-822-00-95; www.oma.aero/en/) is 10km north of the city off Hwy 57. Aeroméxico Connect offers direct service to/from Mexico City and Monterrey with connecting flights to various US cities.

BUS

The **Terminal Terrestre Potosina** (TTP; 444-816-46-02; Carretera 57), 2.5km east of the center, is a busy transportation hub that has deluxe, 1st-class and some 2nd-class bus services. Its facilities include card phones, 24-hour luggage storage and snack places.

First-class companies include ETN, Primera Plus, Transportes del Norte and Futura. The main 2nd-class companies are Coordinados (Flecha Amarilla) and Estrella Blanca.

Daily buses go to Juárez, Chihuahua, Dolores Hidalgo, León, Morelia, Nuevo Laredo, Saltillo, Torreón, and many other destinations.

CAR & MOTORCYCLE

Car-rental prices range from M$1100 to M$1300 per day. Offers week-long packages.

Sixt (444-812-32-29; Obregón 670)

Getting Around

Taxis charge around M$200 to M$220 for the half-hour trip to/from the airport.

To reach the center from the bus station, take any 'Centro' or #46 bus. A convenient place to get off is on the Alameda, outside the former train station. A booth in the bus station sells taxi tickets (M$40 to M$60) to the center. From the center to the bus station, take any 'Central TTP' or bus southbound on Avenida Constitución from the Alameda's west side. City buses run from 6:30am to 10:30pm (M$7). For places along Avenida Carranza, catch a 'Morales' or 'Carranza' bus in front of the train station.

Matehuala

The pleasant but unremarkable town of Matehuala (pop 80,000), between Saltillo and San Luis Potosí on Hwy 57, is the compulsory changing point for buses north to Real de Catorce.

The bus station is just west of the highway, 2km south of the center. From Matehuala, there are daily bus departures to Mexico City Terminal Norte (M$600 to M$775, eight hours, nine 1st-class direct); Monterrey (M$300 to M$336, 4½ hours, hourly 1st class); Saltillo (M$246, 3¼ hours, seven 1st class); San Luis Potosí (M$191 to M$250, 2½ hours, hourly 1st class); Aguascalientes (M$372, 5 hours, one daily); and Querétaro (M$336 to M$406, 4½ hours, seven 1st class).

BUSES FROM SAN LUIS POTOSÍ

DESTINATION	FARE (M$)	DURATION	FREQUENCY (DAILY)
Aguascalientes	155-193	2½-3hr	frequent
Guadalajara	220-515	5-6hr	hourly
Guanajuato	235	3hr	1 direct at 7am
Matehuala	191	2½hr	hourly
Mexico City (Terminal Norte)	398-540	5-6½hr	hourly
Monterrey	675	6hr	5
Querétaro	191-260	2½-4hr	frequent
Xilxitla	340	6hr	4
Zacatecas	170	3hr	frequent

Real de Catorce

488 / POP 1300 / ELEV 2730M

Energy – in a spiritual sense – is a word commonly ascribed to the alluring village of Real de Catorce. This stark, compact and functioning 'ghost town' sits high on the fringes of the magical Sierra Madre Oriental. It was a wealthy silver-mining town of 40,000 people until early last century. Not long ago, it was nearly deserted, its streets lined with crumbling buildings, its mint a ruin and a few hundred people eking out an existence from the annual influx of pilgrims and old mine tailings.

Real has experienced a slight revival; it has attracted investors (including Europeans) who run some of the businesses and smarter hotels in town. Although no longer a 'ghost town', doors do creak in the breeze, dusty cobblestone streets end abruptly and many buildings remain in ruins.

At the time of research, mining concessions had been granted in mines surrounding the town. Many view it as a potential environmental nightmare – having a detrimental affect on water springs in the mountains and age-old Huichol traditions and culture. Others see it as a potential source of employment for many locals, including poorer surrounding communities.

To soak up its magic and unique atmosphere, you need to stay a night here, longer if you wish to explore the surrounding hills on foot or horseback.

History

Real de Catorce translates as 'Royal of 14': the '14' may have been derived from 14 Spanish soldiers killed here by indigenous resistance fighters around 1700. The town was founded in the mid-18th century and the church built between 1790 and 1817.

The town reached its peak in the late 19th century, vying to surpass the famed Valenciana mine of Guanajuato. It had opulent houses, a bullring and shops selling European luxury goods.

Just why Real became a ghost town within three decades is a mystery. Some locals claim (as they do in many ghost towns) that during the Revolution (1910–20) *bandidos* hid out here and scared off other inhabitants. A more plausible explanation is that the price of silver slumped after 1900.

Sights

Templo de la Purísima Concepción CHURCH

(7am-7pm) FREE This charming *parroquia* (parish church) is an impressive neoclassical building. The attraction for thousands of Mexican pilgrims is the reputedly miraculous image of St Francis of Assisi, displayed at the front of the church. A cult has grown up around the statue, whose help is sought in solving problems and cleansing sins.

Walk through the door to the left of the altar to find a roomful of *retablos*, small pictures depicting threatening situations from which St Francis has rescued the victim, with a brief description of the incident – car accidents and medical operations, for example – and some words of gratitude. *Retablos* have become much sought after by collectors and are very occasionally seen in antique shops. Sadly, most of those on sale have been stolen from churches.

Centro Cultural de Real de Catorce NOTABLE BUILDING

(Casa de la Moneda; admission M$10; 10am-7pm Wed-Sun) Opposite the church's facade, the Centro Cultural de Real de Catorce, the old mint, made coins for 14 months (1,489,405 pesos-worth to be exact) in the mid-1860s. This classic monument has been exquisitely restored over the last few years. It now houses a cultural-center-cum-gallery with several levels of temporary exhibitions. The bottom floor has a permanent exhibition showing photos and machinery from the original mint.

Galería Vega m57 GALLERY

(Zaragoza 3; 11am-4pm Sat, to 3pm Sun) FREE Real's only dedicated art gallery hosts exhibitions and installations of contemporary work in a variety of media in a restored colonial building.

Palenque de Gallos MONUMENT

(Xicotencatl s/n; admission free; 9am-5pm) FREE A block northwest of Plaza Hidalgo lies a monument to the town's heyday – the Palenque de Gallos, a cockfighting ring, built like a Roman amphitheater. It was restored in the 1970s and sometimes hosts theater or dance performances.

Capilla de Guadalupe CHURCH, CEMETERY

(8am-5pm) Follow Zaragoza-Libertad north of Real de Catorce to the Capilla de Guadalupe and *panteón* (cemetery). At the

Real de Catorce

Real de Catorce

Sights
1 Centro Cultural de Real de Catorce B2
2 Galería Vega m57 .... A1
3 Palenque de Gallos A1
4 Templo de la Purísima Concepción C2

Sleeping
5 Hotel El Real B2
6 Hotel Real de Álamos B1
7 Hotel Shantiniketan A1
8 Mesón de Abundancia B2
9 Refugio Romano D1

Eating
10 Café Azul B2
Cafe El Real .... (see 5)
Mesón de Abundancia .... (see 8)

Drinking & Nightlife
11 Amor Y Paz C1

time of research the cemetery gate was locked, but it's worth a look around if you can get in. Further along this road you'll hit the remains of the former bullring, **Plaza de Toros** (Zaragoza) FREE.

Activities

Hiking

The ambience of the desert setting makes up for the lack of major sights around town. If you're into walking or horseback riding, there's plenty to keep you occupied here for several days.

If you prefer to do your own hikes, you can head out from Real in almost any direction. The hike closest to home is that up to the **Pueblo Fantasmo** (Ghost Town), on the hill behind – and clearly visible from – the town center. Head along Lanzagorta and stay left (avoid the road that veers right to the car park). The track you follow was the former entrance to town before the tunnel existed. Allow at least one hour to get to the top – there is another section around 100m further on behind the ruins visible from the town. Beware that there are two large shafts (estimated to be hundreds of meters deep) in the ruins.

To extend this hike, head northwest along the ridge to the antennae and to the cross over the town (make sure you note this from the town before you leave, as it becomes obscured when on the ridge). Follow the path behind the cross before you weave your way down to the cemetery (allow three to four hours for the longer hike).

Another shorter hike is to **Socavón de Purísima**, a large chimney of a former mine. Head down Allende and veer right at its end. You are on the road to Estación de Catorce. Follow this road until you reach the chimney (about 45 minutes one way). The road passes through a cut or split rock, the Cerro Trocado. If open, you can enter the mouth of the mine (M$10). To return, it's a longer and harder slog back up the hill

HUICHOL VISIONS

The remote Sierra Madre Occidental, in and around the far north of Jalisco, is the home of the Huicholes, one of Mexico's most distinctive and enduring indigenous groups. Fiercely independent people, they were one of the few indigenous groups not subjugated by the Aztecs.

The arrival of the Spanish had little immediate effect on the Huicholes and it wasn't until the 17th century that the first Catholic missionaries reached the Huichol homelands. Rather than convert to Christianity, the Huicholes incorporated various elements of Christian teachings into their traditional animist belief systems. In Huichol mythology, gods become personalized as plants, totem animal species and natural objects, while their supernatural form is explored in religious rituals.

Every year the Huicholes leave their isolated homeland and make a pilgrimage to the Sierra de Catorce, in northern San Luis Potosí state. In this harsh desert region, they seek out the *mescal* cactus *(Lophophora williamsii)*, known as peyote cactus. The rounded peyote 'buttons' contain a powerful hallucinogenic drug (whose chief element is mescaline) that is central to the Huicholes' rituals and complex spiritual life.

Note: peyote is illegal in Mexico. Under Mexican law, the Huicholes are permitted to use it for their spiritual purposes. For the Huicholes, indiscriminate use is regarded as offensive, even sacrilegious.

Traditionally, the main Huichol art forms were telling stories and making masks and detailed geometric embroidery, or 'yarn pictures.' In the last few decades, brightly colored beads have replaced the yarn. This is painstaking work, where the beads are pressed into a beeswax-covered substrate. This exquisite artwork is sold in craft markets, shops and galleries. Prices are usually fixed and the Huicholes don't like to haggle. To see the best work, visit one of the specialist museums or shops in Zapopan (Guadalajara), Tepic, Puerto Vallarta or Zacatecas.

(one hour one way; on weekends you might be able to grab a lift in a 'Jeep Willys'). Caution: be prepared – tell others where you're headed, and take water, a hat and strong footwear; it's dry and unforgiving country.

Horseback Riding

Ride 'em cowboy! Numerous trails lead out into the dry, stark and fascinating desertscapes – hilly and flat – around Real. The most popular guided trail ride is the three-hour trip to **El Quemado**, the sacred mountain of the Huicholes. Here you'll find expansive views of the high-desert plateau and a small shrine to the sun god.

Horse guides now belong to an association, approved by the municipality; the best of the two is **Caballerangos del Real**. Rates are around M$100 per hour. Note that no protective hats are provided; you clomp off at your own risk.

The horses and guides congregate every morning around Plaza Hidalgo.

Jeep Rides

Trips in 'Jeep Willys' can also be arranged to many of the same locations, mainly on weekends. Ask any of the drivers along Lanzagorta or Allende, or at the tourist office. Rates vary according to the trip and numbers.

Cycling

Lalo Bike CYCLING

(☎ cell phone 488-105-1981; cruz.lalo.bike@gmail.com; 1½ hr rides per person M$100; ⏲ Fri-Sun Nov-Sep) Cyclists of all levels can head out around Real de Catorce on some great-value rides with Lalo (he speaks Spanish only but can arrange an English-speaking guide). Prices include mountain bike, helmet and guide. Spanish speakers can email or ring ahead or, if you are in Real, inquire at Mesón de la Abundancia.

Festivals & Events

Fiesta de San Francisco RELIGIOUS

Between the end of September to the end of October, 150,000 pilgrims pay homage to the figure of St Francis of Assisi in the town's church. Many of them just come for the day, while thousands stay in the town, filling every rentable room and sleeping rough in the plazas. The streets are lined with stalls selling religious souvenirs and food, while many of the town's more upmarket restaurants close for a month.

Note: travelers who desire the tranquil 'ghost-town experience' of Real de Catorce are best staying away during this festival period to avoid disappointment.

Festival del Desierto CULTURAL

The Festival del Desierto cultural festival features folkloric music and dance performances in towns all around the region. Dates vary annually; check before you come.

Sleeping

It can be very cold here in winter in the cheapest digs; bring a sleeping bag or request extra blankets.

Hotel Real de Álamos PENSION $

(Hospedaje Familiar; ☎488-887-50-09; Constitución 21; s/d M$200/350) As basic as they come, the rooms in this hotel are clean and have bathrooms.

★**Mesón de Abundancia** HOTEL $$

(☎488-887-50-44; www.mesonabundancia.com; Lanzagorta 11; d M$850-1250, ste M$1250-1550, f M$1550-1950; 📶) Relive the town's bonanza era on the desert plateau in this delightful stone citadel. The 19th-century former *tesorería* (treasury) building has been renovated into a hotel and restaurant. A massive old-fashioned key lets you in to one of 11 rooms; these are simply and tastefully decorated with local crafts (minus TV) and make a cozy retreat on chilly nights. Rates are significantly lower outside of high season.

Refugio Romano GUESTHOUSE $$

(☎488-111-9353; www.refugioromano.com; Iturbide 38; d M$800-900) 🍃 Yes, keep going... It really is up this rickety laneway. At the end, you'll be rewarded with a true oasis. A lovely green garden of cacti and fruit trees, plus three simple – with a touch of hippy – rooms, each with its quirky idiosyncrasy, from a 'cave' to a terrace. The owners, one an Italian (and a great cook), will whip up organic meals for their clients (mains M$90-139). It follows sustainable practices where possible.

Hotel El Real HOTEL $$

(☎488-887-50-58; www.hotelreal.com.mx; Morelos 20; r M$770-1100; 📶) This historic building with pleasant rooms on three floors around an open courtyard offers some rooms with views over the town and the hills. It also has a cozy cafe-restaurant and a large terrace. Rates are negotiable according to numbers and nights.

Hotel Shantiniketan GUESTHOUSE $$

(Morada de Paz; ☎488-887-50-98; www.shantiniketan.com.mx; cnr Zaragoza & Lerdo; r M$865-1265) There's a definite karma here: the eight rooms are named after Indian spiritual leaders. Each is minimalist and unfussy, although some are a bit dark, and you can't open the windows. The English-speaking owner will open the hotel if you reserve; otherwise the doors – including that of its small cafe – are open weekends only.

Eating & Drinking

Café Azul CAFE $

(☎488-887-5131; Lanzagorta 27; snacks M$25-70; ⏲8am-5pm Thu & Sun-Tue, to 11pm Fri & Sat) Open all day, this airy, Swiss-run spot is perfect for breakfasts, freshly-baked cakes and light meals including excellent crepes. The delightful owners are very helpful with local info.

Cafe El Real INTERNATIONAL $$

(Morelos 20; mains M$145-150; ⏲9am-6pm) This welcoming spot – with sofas and fire – serves up international cuisine from pastas to meats (including wild goat and rabbit dishes). The food won't blow your mind, but it's a reliable choice among the town's limited number of eateries.

Mesón de Abundancia MEXICAN, ITALIAN $$

(☎488-887-50-44; www.mesonabundancia.com; Lanzagorta 11; mains M$90-165; 📶📝) There are several cozy eating areas at the restaurant in this hotel, one with a bar and fireplace. The hearty (read massive) servings of Italian and Mexican dishes are *muy rico* (delicious). It's open all day, every day, including for breakfast.

Amor Y Paz BAR

(cnr Juaréz & Iturbide; ⏲6pm-late Fri & Sat) Real's reputation as a ghost town may in part be due to the fact that its residents and visitors are often all hiding out here at this funky bar, hidden behind the walls of Hotel El Real. It's decked out in antiques (note the amazing wooden bar), retro seating and quirky chandeliers, and serves a range of mezcals and alcoholic tea infusions.

Information

See www.realdecatorce.net for a good overview of the town. Card phones are located around Plaza Hidalgo.

Tourist Office (Palacio Municipal, Constitución s/n; ⌚9am-4pm) Opening hours are a little flexible; simple street maps are available.

Getting There & Away

BUS

Senda runs 1st-class buses from Matehuala's bus station to Real de Catorce (around M$77, 1½ to two hours) at 7:45am, 11:45am, 1:45pm and 5:45pm (with an extra one on Sundays at 9:45am). The bus can be caught 15 minutes later at the Senda office in Matehuala, a little east of and across the street from Hotel Álamo on Méndez. Important: the ticket will show the time the bus leaves from the center, not the bus station (ie 8am, noon, 2pm, 6pm). Don't get caught out; it leaves the main bus station 15 minutes before the times stated.

If you're coming from San Luis Potosí you can buy a one-way (or return; valid for six months) ticket and change in Matehuala (the total cost for two tickets one-way is around M$268).

On arrival in Real, buses park at the east entrance of the Ogarrio tunnel. There, in order to pass through the tunnel, you change to a smaller bus which drops off (or picks up if returning to Matehuala) at the western end of the tunnel, in Real. Confirm the return bus schedule upon arrival. At the time of research, buses from Real to Matehuala (with connections to San Luis Potosí) were at 7:45am, 11:45am, 3:45pm and 5:45pm (M$77, 1½ to two hours). Tickets are purchased at the Senda ticket office, on the edge of the car park at the tunnel's western entrance in Real; if this is not open you can buy them on board the bus.

CAR

If driving from Hwy 57 north of Matehuala, turn off toward Cedral, 20km west. After Cedral, you turn south to reach Catorce on what must be one of the world's longest cobblestone roads. It's a slow but spectacular zigzag drive up a steep mountainside. The 2.3km-long Ogarrio tunnel (M$20 per vehicle) is only wide enough for one vehicle; workers stationed at each end with telephones control traffic flow between 7am and 11pm. If it's really busy, you'll have to leave your car at the eastern tunnel entrance and continue by pick-up or cart. If you drive through, you must leave your car in the parking area to the left of the market.

Vintage 'Jeep Willys' leave Real around noon (and on demand), downhill from the plaza along Allende, for the rough but spectacular descent to the small hamlet of Estación de Catorce (around M$50 per person, one hour). From there, buses head to San Tiburcio, where there are connections for Saltillo and Zacatecas.

> **CASH UP BEFORE YOU COME**
>
> There's one ATM in Real de Catorce, located in the tourist office, but on busy weekends it occasionally runs out of money and is often out of order thanks to electricity cuts and the like. Try to bring cash.

ZACATECAS STATE

The state of Zacatecas (za-ka-*te*-kas) is a dry, rugged, cactus-strewn expanse on the fringe of Mexico's northern semideserts. The state is best known for the wealthy silver city of the same name. Visitors can enjoy the region's historical and natural monuments including the mysterious ruins of La Quemada, a testament to centuries of cultures. The state is one of Mexico's largest in area (73,252 sq km) but smallest in population (1.5 million); it is believed that as many people again (1.5 million) who come from the state currently live in the United States.

Zacatecas

☎492 / POP 138,000 / ELEV 2430M

The most northern of Mexico's fabled silver cities, fascinating Zacatecas – a Unesco World Heritage site – runs along a narrow valley. The large historic center is jam-packed with opulent colonial buildings, a stupendous cathedral (a useful central landmark), magnificent museums and steep, winding streets and alleys. Excellent restaurants and fine hotels make it a very comfortable location for any traveler.

The city has a legacy of historical highs and lows: it was here that Pancho Villa defeated a stronghold of soldiers (today he is still much feted by the locals). Here, too, thousands of indigenous slaves were forced by the Spanish to toil in the mines under terrible conditions. Today, travelers can have their own lofty experiences in a *teleférico* (cable car) to the Cerro de la Bufa, an impressive rock outcrop; the trip affords great views of a collage of church domes and rooftops. Alternatively, you can drop below the surface to tour the infamous Edén mine, or vibrate to the rhythms of its underground disco.

History

Indigenous Zacatecos – one of the Chichimec tribes – mined local mineral deposits for centuries before the Spanish arrived; it's said that the silver rush here was started when a Chichimec gave a piece of the fabled metal to a conquistador. The Spaniards founded a settlement in 1548 and started mining operations that sent caravan after caravan of silver off to Mexico City, creating fabulously wealthy silver barons in Zacatecas.

By the early 18th century, the mines of Zacatecas were producing 20% of Nueva España's silver and the city became an important base for Catholic missionaries.

In the 19th century political instability diminished the flow of silver. Although silver production later improved under Porfirio Díaz, the Revolution disrupted it. In 1914 in Zacatecas, Pancho Villa defeated a stronghold of 12,000 soldiers loyal to President Victoriano Huerta. After the Revolution, Zacatecas continued to thrive on silver.

Sights & Activities

★Museo Rafael Coronel MUSEUM

(☎492-922-81-16; cnr Abasolo & Matamoros; adult/student M$30/15; ⊙10am-5pm Thu-Tue) The amazing Museo Rafael Coronel is not to be missed. Imaginatively housed in the ruins of the lovely 16th-century Ex-Convento de San Francisco, it houses Mexican folk art collected by the Zacatecan artist Rafael Coronel, brother of Pedro Coronel and son-in-law of Diego Rivera. Take your time to wander through the various spaces (follow the arrows; it's easy to miss sections).

The skeleton of the Capilla San Antonio is interesting, though the highlight is the astonishing display of more than 3000 masks (another 8000 are in storage) used in traditional dances and rituals. Also here are pottery, puppets, instruments, pre-Hispanic objects and sketches by Rivera. The grounds and garden are a wonderful place to come and relax.

Museo Pedro Coronel MUSEUM

(☎492-922-80-21; Plaza de Santo Domingo s/n; admission M$30; ⊙10am-5pm Tue-Sun) The extraordinary Museo Pedro Coronel is housed in a 17th-century former Jesuit college and is one of provincial Mexico's best art museums. Pedro Coronel (1923–85) was an affluent Zacatecan artist who bequeathed his collection of art and artifacts from all over the world, as well as his own works. The collection includes 20th-century works by Picasso, Rouault, Chagall, Kandinsky and Miró; and pre-Hispanic Mexican artifacts, masks and other ancient pieces.

Cerro de la Bufa LANDMARK

The most appealing of the many explanations for the name of the hill that dominates Zacatecas is that 'bufa' is an old Basque word for wineskin, which is certainly what the rocky formation looks like. The views from the top are superb and there's an interesting group of monuments, a chapel and a museum. It is also the site of a zip-line, **Tirolesa 840** (☎cell phone 492-946-31-57; www.vivazacatecasadventure.com; rides M$200-250; ⊙10am-6pm), a 1km ride (840m of actual flying) across a former open-pit mine.

The small **Museo de la Toma de Zacatecas** (☎492-922-80-66; adult/student M$20/10; ⊙10am-4:30pm), at the top of the hill, commemorates the 1914 battle fought on the hill's slopes in which the revolutionary División del Norte, led by Pancho Villa and Felipe Ángeles, defeated President Victoriano Huerta's forces. This gave the revolutionaries control of Zacatecas, which was the gateway to Mexico City.

La Capilla de la Virgen del Patrocinio, adjacent to the museum, is named after the patron saint of miners. Above the altar of this 18th-century chapel is an image of the Virgin said to be capable of healing the sick. Thousands of pilgrims flock here each year on September 8, when the image is carried to the cathedral.

Facing the chapel stand three imposing equestrian **statues** of the victors of the battle of Zacatecas – Villa, Ángeles and Pánfilo Natera.

From the right of the statues, a paved path along the foot of the rocky hilltop leads to the **Mausoleo de los Hombres Ilustres de Zacatecas**, with the tombs of Zacatecan heroes from 1841 to the present.

A convenient way to ascend La Bufa (to the church and museum) is by *teleférico*. Alternatively, you can walk up, starting at Calle del Ángel from the cathedral's east end. To reach it by car, take Carretera a la Bufa, which begins at Avenida López Velarde, a couple of kilometers east of the center. A taxi costs around M$55. You can return to town by the *teleférico* or by a footpath leading downhill from the statues.

Zacatecas

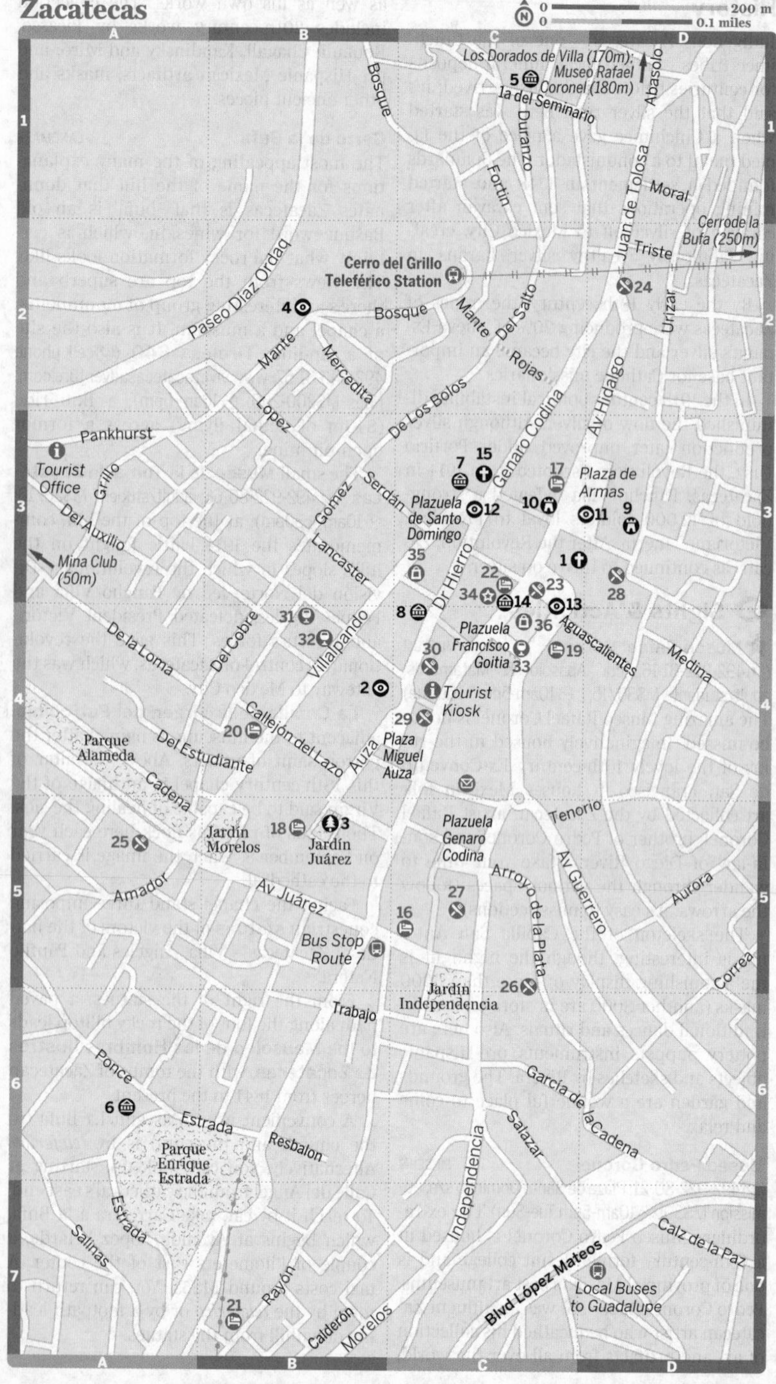

0 200 m
0 0.1 miles
A
B
C
D
1
2
3
4
5
6
7
Los Dorados de Villa (170m); Museo Rafael Coronel (180m)
Cerro de la Bufa (250m)
Mina Club (50m)
Cerro del Grillo Teleférico Station
Tourist Office
Tourist Kiosk
Plazuela de Santo Domingo
Plaza de Armas
Plazuela Francisco Goitia
Plaza Miguel Auza
Plazuela Genaro Codina
Parque Alameda
Jardín Morelos
Jardín Juárez
Jardín Independencia
Parque Enrique Estrada
Bus Stop Route 7
Local Buses to Guadalupe
Paseo Díaz Ordaq
Bosque
Mante
Mercedita
Lopez
De Los Bolos
Pankhurst
Grillo
Del Auxilio
Serdán
Gomez
Lancaster
Villalpando
Dr Hierro
Genaro Codina
Av Hidalgo
Juan de Tolosa
Abasolo
Duranzo
Fortin
Moral
Triste
Urizar
Del Salto
Rojas
la del Seminario
Aguascalientes
Medina
De la Loma
Del Cobre
Callejón del Lazo
Auza
Del Estudiante
Cadena
Amador
Av Juárez
Tenorio
Arroyo de la Plata
Av Guerrero
Aurora
Correa
Trabajo
Ponce
Estrada
Resbalon
Salinas
Rayón
Calderón
Morelos
Independencia
Salazar
García de la Cadena
Calz de la Paz
Blvd López Mateos

Zacatecas

Mina El Edén MINE

(☎492-922-30-02; www.minaeleden.com.mx; tours adult/child M$80/40; ⏲tours every hour 10am-6pm) Visiting one of Mexico's richest mines (worked from 1586 until the 1960s) provides a dramatic insight into the region's source of wealth and the terrible price paid for it. Digging for hoards of silver, gold, iron, copper and zinc, enslaved indigenous people, including children, worked under horrific conditions. Up to five people a day died from accidents or tuberculosis and silicosis.

These days, it's a much safer (read: sanitized) story. An elevator or miniature train takes you inside Cerro del Grillo. Guides (some English-speaking) lead you along floodlit walkways past shafts and over subterranean pools.

The mine has two entrances. To reach the higher one (the east entrance), walk 100m southwest from Cerro del Grillo *teleférico* station; from this entrance, tours start with an elevator descent. To reach the west entrance from the town center, walk west along Avenida Juárez and stay on it after its name changes to Avenida Torreón at the Alameda. Turn right immediately after the IMSS hospital (bus 7 from the corner of Avenida Hidalgo goes up Avenida Juárez and past the hospital) and a short walk will bring you to the mine entrance. Tours begin here with a trip on the narrow-gauge railway (540m), after which you walk another 350m or so.

Museo del Arte Abstracto Manuel Felguérez MUSEUM

(☎492-924-37-05; Ex-Seminario de la Purísima Concepción; adult M$30; ⏲10am-5pm Wed-Mon) This art museum is worth visiting for the building alone; originally a seminary, it was later used as a prison and has been renovated to create some remarkable exhibition spaces, transforming the former dark, depressing cells and steel walkways into a beautiful site. It has a stunning and varied collection of abstract art, particularly the work of Zacatecan artist Manuel Felguérez, and a good book/gift store.

Catedral CATHEDRAL

(Plaza de Armas) Built between 1729 and 1752, the pink-stone cathedral is an ultimate expression of Mexican baroque.

The stupendous main facade is a wall of detailed carvings; this has been interpreted as a giant symbol of the tabernacle. A tiny figure of an angel holding a tabernacle is in the middle of the design, the keystone atop the round central window. Above this, in the third tier, is Christ and above Christ is God. The 12 Apostles are featured, as well as a smaller Virgin figure above the doorway.

The southern facade's central sculpture is of La Virgen de los Zacatecanos, the city's patroness. The north facade shows Christ crucified, attended by the Virgin Mary and St John.

Unveiled in 2010, the grand altar is the work of Mexico's famous artist, Javier Marín. It features 10 large bronze figures and the figure of Christ, arranged on a backdrop of golden blocks.

Museo Zacatecano MUSEUM

(☎492-922-65-80; Dr Hierro 301; adult/student M$30/15; ⊙10am-5pm Wed-Mon) Zacatecas' former mint (Mexico's second-biggest in the 19th century) now houses the wonderful Museo Zacatecano. Spread over a number of rooms, this contemporary museum exhibits a weird mix of all things *zacatecano,* from pre-Hispanic objects to the re-created rooms of a popular composer. Unfortunately, the first few *salas* are text-heavy information boards (in Spanish). The highlight – in the last halls – is the superb collection of Huichol art. Videos (all in Spanish) provide each *sala's* context.

Plaza de Armas PLAZA

The plaza is the open space north of the cathedral. The **Palacio de Gobierno** on the plaza's east side was built in the 18th century for a colonial family. In the turret of its main staircase is a mural of the history of Zacatecas state, painted in 1970 by Antonio Rodríguez.

Across the road, and directly opposite the Palacio, the **Palacio de la Mala Noche** was built in the late 18th century for a mine owner and now houses state-government offices.

Plazuela Francisco Goitia PLAZA

A block south of the cathedral, a broad flight of stairs descends from Avenida Hidalgo to Tacuba, forming a charming open space. The terraces of the *plazuela* (small plaza) are often used as an informal amphitheater by street performers.

Teatro Calderón HISTORIC BUILDING

Opposite the *plazuela* on Avenida Hidalgo, the lovely, renovated 1890s Teatro Calderón dates from the Porfiriato period and holds plays, concerts, films and art exhibitions. Worth a stickybeak even if you don't plan to see a performance.

Plazuela de Santo Domingo PLAZA

A block west of Zacatecas' cathedral, this *plazuela* is dominated by the **Templo de Santo Domingo**. Although the church is done in a more sober baroque style than the cathedral, it has some fine gilded altars and a graceful horseshoe staircase. Built by the Jesuits in the 1740s, the church was taken over by Dominican monks when the Jesuits were expelled in 1767.

Jardín Juárez PARK

Juárez ends at a tiny but charming park of the same name. The Universidad Autónoma de Zacatecas' administrative headquarters are housed in the neoclassical **Rectoría** building on its west side.

Museo Francisco Goitia MUSEUM

(☎492-922-02-11; Estrada 101; adult M$30; ⊙10am-4:45pm Tue-Sun) The Museo Francisco Goitia displays work by several 20th-century Zacatecan artists, including some evocative paintings of indigenous people by Goitia (1882–1960) himself. Other artists represented include Pedro Coronel, Rafael Coronel and Manuel Felguérez. The museum is in a former governor's mansion, above Parque Enrique Estrada, and it is worth visiting for the building and manicured gardens, overlooking the aqueduct.

Ex-Templo de San Agustín NOTABLE BUILDING

(⊙10am-4.30pm Tue-Sun) The Ex-Templo de San Agustín was built for Augustinian monks in the 17th century. During the 19th-century anticlerical movement, the church became a cantina and Masonic lodge. In 1882 it was purchased by American Presbyterian missionaries who destroyed its 'too Catholic' main facade, replacing it with a blank white wall. One surviving feature is the church's plateresque carving of the conversion of St Augustine over the north doorway.

In the 20th century the church returned to the government. Today it hosts art exhibitions plus a multimedia light show (Saturdays at 9pm in summer), when the church's original (and very beautiful) facade is 're-created' in extraordinary 3D scenes.

Teleférico CABLE CAR

(☎492-922-01-70; one way M$40; ⊙10am-6pm) Zacatecas' most exhilarating ride and the easiest way to Cerro de la Bufa's summit is the Swiss-built cable car that crosses high above the city from Cerro del Grillo. It's a short walk east from Mina El Edén (east entrance) to the *teleférico's* Cerro del Grillo station. Alternatively, huff up the steep steps of Callejón de García Rojas, which lead straight to the *teleférico* from Genaro Codina. Cars depart every 15 minutes (except when it's raining or when winds exceed 60km/h) and the trip takes seven minutes.

Festivals & Events

La Morisma RELIGIOUS

Usually held on the last weekend in August. Features a spectacular mock battle commemorating the triumph of the Christians over the Muslims in old Spain. Two rival 'armies' – around 10,000 participants from the barrio of Bracho – parade through the streets in the morning, then, accompanied by bands of musicians, enact two battle sequences that take place between Lomas de Bracho and Cerro de la Bufa.

Feria de Zacatecas TRADITIONAL

Annual fair with a folkloric focus held during the first three weeks in September. Renowned matadors fight famous local bulls. There are also *charreadas* (rodeos), concerts, plays, agricultural and craft shows. On September 8 the image of La Virgen del Patrocinio is carried to the cathedral from its chapel on Cerro de la Bufa.

Festival Internacional de Teatro de Calle THEATER

In mid-October, drama takes to the streets in this vibrant week-long celebration of street theater.

Sleeping

Disappointingly, there are limited budget options in Zacatecas. Midrange and top-end accommodations tend to hike their rates up to double during Zacatecas' high seasons – September's festivals, Christmas and Semana Santa (March/April).

La Terrasse BOUTIQUE HOTEL $$

(☎492-925-53-15; www.terrassehotel.com.mx; Villalpando 209; s/d/tr incl breakfast M$670/780/980;) This small, friendly and centrally located boutique option is run by a proud owner. It has 14 contemporary and slightly sparse rooms but is by far the best midrange option. Back rooms have internal-facing windows which could be claustrophic for some, quiet for others.

Hotel Reyna Soledad HOTEL $$

(☎492-922-07-90; www.hostalreynasoledad.com.mx; Tacuba 170; r M$590-690;) Set in a converted 17th-century convent, the colonial patios of this perfectly located place are tranquil. The rooms are rustic (in a pine-furniture kind of way) but OK if your focus is the city, not the accommodation.

Hotel Condesa HOTEL $$

(☎492-922-11-60; www.hotelcondesa.com.mx; Av Juárez 102; s/d/tr M$450/550/580;) The Condesa's 52 '80s-style modern rooms are a good budget option. The nicest have external-facing windows. An onsite restaurant serves breakfast (M$50 to M$70) and other meals.

★Hotel Emporio Zacatecas LUXURY HOTEL $$$

(☎492-925-65-00, 800-800-61-61; www.hotelesemporio.com; Av Hidalgo 703; r from M$1239;) Zacatecas' central upmarket hotel boasts a superb location, luxurious rooms and delightful terrace areas. Service is professional, the rooms are world class and provide a quiet oasis from external noise. The website sometimes promotes special deals.

Quinta Real Zacatecas LUXURY HOTEL $$$

(☎800-500-40-00, 492-922-91-04; www.quintareal.com; Rayón 434; ste from M$2890;) It's worth seeing red (in terms of your bank balance) to experience this luxury treat. Spectacularly situated around the country's oldest – now retired – bullring and near El Cubo aqueduct, the 49-room hotel is one of Mexico's most contemporary and fetching. The least expensive rooms are spacious, comfortable master suites.

An elegant restaurant, La Plaza, overlooks the ring, and the bar, Botarel, is in the former holding pens.

Santa Rita Hotel BOUTIQUE HOTEL $$$

(☎492-925-41-41, 800-560-81-15; www.hotelsantarita.com; Av Hidalgo 507A; ste M$2184-3404;) A stylish, contemporary and cosmopolitan choice. Disappointingly, some of the 41 suites have internal-facing windows. Prices are significantly lower outside high season.

Hotel Mesón de Jobito HOTEL $$$

(☎492-922-7095; www.mesondejobito.com; Jardín Juárez 143; r M$1000-1670, ste M$1100-1770;) Guests come here to soak up old-fashioned charm and a sense of history. This large place has 53 fine if faded rooms; one restaurant and a bar (plus a slanting balcony, a legacy of its construction 200 years ago). Its Sunday buffet breakfast (M$130) is popular with the public. Often offers deals.

WORTH A TRIP

JEREZ

The delightful country town of Jerez (population 43,000), 30km southwest of Zacatecas, is as Mexican as a tortilla. As such, it's a great place to head for a day to watch the local action. Sundays – market days – are especially fun as you'll see saddle-bound *rancheros* drinking outside the saloons. Jardín Páez, the pretty main plaza, has an old-fashioned gazebo, trees and benches. Here, too, is a **tourist information kiosk** (⌚9am-7pm). Banks (with ATMs) and phones are around the plaza.

Jerez is known for its lively one-week-long Easter fair, featuring, among other activities, *charreadas* (Mexican rodeos) and cockfights.

The town also has some exceptionally fine buildings. The 18th-century **Parroquia de la Inmaculada Concepción** and the 19th-century **Santuario de la Soledad** have lovely stone carvings. Go one block south from Jardín Páez' southeast corner, then one block west for the shrine, or one block east for the church. Just past the shrine, on Jardín Hidalgo's north side, is the not-to-be-missed 19th-century **Teatro Hinojosa** (Reloj Esq Salvador Varela; ⌚8am-7pm Mon-Fri, 11am-5pm Sat & Sun). Head inside to relive theatrical days of the 1870s. The design and decoration reflect the wealth of the times. The **Casa Museo Ramón Lopez Velarde** (De la Parroquia 33; M$20; ⌚10am-5pm Tue-Sun) pays homage to one of Mexico's well-known poets who was born in the house in 1888. It provides insight into life of a middle-class family during the era.

The best option for nosh is the colourful **Hotel Jardín** (☎494-945-20-26; mains M$40-100; ⌚8:30am-10pm), on the plaza.

The Jerez turnoff is near Malpaso, 29km south of Zacatecas on the Zacatecas–Guadalajara road. Ómnibus de México and Estrella Blanca have regular services from Zacatecas's bus station to Jerez (M$50, one hour) as does the slower and cheaper service Linea Zacatecas Jerez (M$44). Jerez's bus station is on the east side of town, 1km from the center along Calzada La Suave Patria. From here, 'Centro' buses (M$6) run to/from the center.

Eating

There are some excellent Mexican and international restaurants serving a range of fare. Local specialties feature ingredients such as *nopal* and pumpkin seeds.

In the morning, look around Avenida Tacuba for *burros* (donkeys) carrying pottery jugs of *aguamiel* (honey water), a nutritional drink derived from the maguey cactus. The two central produce markets are **Mercado El Laberinto** (Plazuela Genaro Codina) and **Mercado Arroyo de la Plata** (Arroyo de la Plata).

San Patrizio Caffé CAFE $
(☎492-922-43-99; Av Hidalgo 403C; drinks & snacks M$50-80; ⌚9am-10pm Mon-Sat, 3-9pm Sun; 📶) Arguably does the best cappuccinos in town and has a relaxing courtyard setting, light snacks, and an array of Italian sodas.

Panificadora Santa Cruz BAKERY $
(☎492-925-48-00; Tacuba 216A; snacks M$8-40; ⌚7am-10:30pm) Almost abutting the cathedral, this reliable bakery/eatery has sinful treats – *pan dulces* (pastries), *tortas* (sandwiches), *tamales* and frappés. Offers set breakfasts (M$58-78).

Acrópolis Café MEXICAN $
(☎492-922-12-84; cnr Av Hidalgo & Plazuela Candelario Huizar; mains M$70-145) Near the cathedral, this Greek-owned cafe has a quirky '50s-style diner feel, and is *the* place to meet for locals and visitors – perhaps more for its location than its meals. It offers light snacks and coffees.

El Pueblito MEXICAN $
(Hidalgo 802; mains M$74-135; ⌚1-10pm Wed-Mon) Furnished in the hues of Mexico – bright purples, yellows, pinks and oranges – this casual spot is the place for Mexican cuisine. Come when the locals eat (afternoon lunches); it can feel a bit barnlike when no-one else is here, but like a party palace when the crowds come to get their mouths around the enchiladas and beyond.

El Recoveco MEXICAN $
(Torreón 513; breakfast buffet M$75, lunch buffet M$85; ⌚8:30am-7pm Mon-Sat, 9am-7pm Sun) 'Cheap and good' is how the locals describe this long-standing place. This means buffet style (as much as you can eat and as many plates as you like) and tasty enough Mexican fare that holds no surprises.

★Los Dorados de Villa MEXICAN $$
(☎492-922-57-22; Plazuela de García 1314; mains M$70-130; ⏲3pm-1am Mon-Sat, 3-11pm Sun) You may have to fight to get into this popular revolutionary-themed restaurant: knock at the door – it's always locked. It's a blast of color and is chock-a-block with atmosphere and relics. Plus it serves up a delicious array of everything – except Pancho Villa himself. Don't miss the *enchiladas valentinas* (M$80).

Trattoria Il Goloso ITALIAN $$
(☎492-123-53-99; Dr Hierro 400; mains M$120-220; ⏲Tue-Thu 2-9:30pm, Fri & Sat 2-11pm, Sun 2-8pm) Trade the tacos for fabulous Italian pasta and other mains in this cozy Sicilian-themed place. It comes complete with enthusiastic, sociable chefs, Aldo and Stefano (an Italian). Aldo's vegetarian lasagne is a standout. It's behind San Patrizio Caffé.

Restaurant La Plaza MEXICAN, INTERNATIONAL $$$
(☎492-922-91-04; Quinta Real Zacatecas, Rayón 434; mains M$100-375) The elegant hotel dining room at the Quinta Real Zacatecas is especially memorable for its outlook to the aqueduct and bullring, as well as for its refined ambience and superb international and Mexican cuisine from different regions. Head here for a Sunday brunch (M$225) or an evening cocktail in the bar, opposite the restaurant on the other side of the ring. Tables in the bar area are nestled in niches, former bull-holding pens (6pm to 1am). Reservations are advisable.

Drinking

Zacatecas has a good late-night scene, especially after 9pm.

Cantina 15 Letras BAR
(☎492-922-01-78; Mártires de Chicago 309; ⏲1pm-3am Mon-Sat) Stop for a drink at this oft-crowded classic, filled with bohemians, drunks and poets. Photos portray Zacatecas of old; the art showcases some well-known local artists.

La Chopería BAR
(☎492-922-61-64; cnr Av Hidalgo & Plazuela Goitia; ⏲2pm-1am) This smart bar in the southwest corner of the Mercado González Ortega attracts a friendly, varied, mostly 30s clientele; it's busiest Thursday through Saturday.

Dalí Café & Bar BAR
(Plaza Miguel Auza 322; snacks M$45-65; ⏲noon-1am Mon-Sat, 5pm-1am Sun; 📶) This sprawling cafe-bar in front of Ex-Templo de San Agustín offers a surreal mix of furniture, cocktails and post-drink munchies (plus good hot chocolate drinks). On Saturday in July and August, reserve a table outside for prime viewing of the multimedia light show (p690).

Mina Club BAR
(☎492-922-30-02; Dovali s/n; cover from M$50; ⏲3-10pm Thu-Sat) Strike it lucky in this unique bar – the tunnel of the Mina El Edén. Check the opening hours as these tend to change (summer hours are longer).

Entertainment

Teatro Calderón THEATER
(☎492-922-81-20; Av Hidalgo s/n; ⏲10am-9pm) This top venue hosts a variety of cultural events including theater, dance and music performances. Check the posters or with the tourist office for current events.

Shopping

Zacatecas is known for silver and leather products and colorful *sarapes*. Try along Arroyo de la Plata (and its indoor market) or at the **Mercado González Ortega** (Plazuela Francisco Goitia).

Centro Platero JEWELRY
(☎492-899-09-94; www.centroplaterodezacatecas.com; ⏲10am-5pm Mon-Fri, 10am-2pm Sat) The Zacatecas silversmith industry lives on in workshops at the Centro Platero, a few kilometers east of town on the road to Guadalupe at the converted 18th-century Ex-Hacienda de Bernardez. Here, young artisans produce various designs, from the traditional to the funky contemporary. To get here, it's easiest to take a taxi (around M$60). Alternatively, shop in its **gallery** (☎492-925-35-50; Villalpando 406; ⏲10am-8pm Mon-Sat, 10am-7pm Sun) in town.

Information

Banks in the center have ATMs and change cash and traveler's checks. Public telephones are at Callejón de las Cuevas, off Avenida Hidalgo. Most internet cafes charge around M$15 per hour for internet access.

Hospital Santa Elena (☎492-924-29-28; Av Guerrero 143)

Post Office (☎492-922-01-96; Allende 111; ⏲8am-4pm Mon-Fri, 8am-2pm Sat)

Tourist Kiosk (www.zacatecastravel.com; Av Hidalgo 403; ⏲9am-9pm) This information kiosk is run by Secturz, the municipal tourist organization, and offers basic maps and information.

Tourist Office (☎492-922-17-57; www.zacatecastravel.com; Av González Ortega s/n; ⏰8:30am-7pm Mon-Fri) The formal headquarters of Secturz, the municipal government's tourism organization, offers maps and information.

Getting There & Away

AIR

Zacatecas' airport is 20km north of the city. **Volaris** (www.volaris.com.mx) has budget flights between Zacatecas and Los Angeles and Chicago.

BUS

Zacatecas' main bus station is on the southwest edge of town, around 3km from the center. Deluxe, 1st- and 2nd-class buses operate to/from here. Deluxe and 1st-class companies include ETN, Ómnibus de México, Futura/Chihuahuenses. The main 2nd-class companies are Transportes de Norte or Zacatecas Jerez (both for Jerez).

Some buses to nearby destinations including Villanueva (for La Quemada) leave from **Plaza del Bicentenario** (Blvd López Mateos).

See the table for daily departures from the main bus terminal. There are also frequent buses to Jerez and Torreón and several a day to places north. For Guanajuato, take a León bus and change there for Guanajuato.

Getting Around

The easiest way to get to/from the airport is by taxi (M$300 to M$350).

Taxis from the bus station to the center of Zacatecas cost around M$40. Bus 8 from the bus station (M$5) runs directly to the cathedral. Heading out of the center, catch a 'route 8' bus heading south on Villalpando.

Around Zacatecas

Guadalupe

☎492 / POP 100,000 / ELEV 2272M

About 10km east of Zacatecas, Guadalupe boasts a fascinating historic former monastery, the **Convento de Guadalupe**. The convento was established by Franciscan monks in the early 18th century as an apostolic college. It developed a strong academic tradition and was a base for missionary work in northern Nueva España until the 1850s. You'll need a couple of hours to wander through the monastery. A quaint plaza, Jardín Juárez, forms a pretty front setting to the convent.

Visitors can enter two parts of the convento: the impressive **church**, that attracts pilgrims to honor the country's beloved Virgin, and the museum, **Museo Virreinal de Guadalupe** (☎492-923-23-86; Jardín Juárez Oriente; admission M$46, Sun free; ⏰9am-6pm Tue-Sun), integral to the convent itself and featureing one of Mexico's best colonial art collections. It houses the building's original religious paintings by Miguel Cabrera, Juan Correa, Antonio Torres and Cristóbal Villalpando. Wandering through the building is a delight; note the extraordinary perspectives in the paintings in the Cloister of San Francisco. Visitors can see part of the library and its 9000 original volumes (the oldest dates to 1529 and thousands are in storage), and step into the stunning choir on the church's upper floor, with its fine carved and painted chairs.

From here, you can peer through a grated window into the gilded and beautifully decorated 19th-century Capilla de Nápoles. The chapel opens for special occasions only.

BUSES FROM ZACATECAS

DESTINATION	FARE (M$)	DURATION	FREQUENCY (DAILY)
Aguascalientes	131-175	2-3hr	hourly
Durango	300-390	4½-7hr	hourly
Guadalajara	390-500	4-7hr	hourly
León	260-335	3-4hr	12
Mexico City (Terminal Norte)	450-835	6-8hr	hourly
Monterrey	455-590	7-8hr	19
Querétaro	411-525	6-6¼hr	14
San Luis Potosí	196-200	3-3½hr	hourly

One room to the right of the museum (the former Museo Regional de Historia) now houses vintage cars.

The museum hosts the **Festival Barroco**, a cultural festival, at the end of September and the town holds an annual fair during the first two weeks of December, focused on the **Día de la Virgen de Guadalupe** (December 12).

Regular Transportes de Guadalupe buses run between Zacatecas and Guadalupe (M$6, 20 minutes); catch one at the bus stop on Blvd López Mateos across from Plaza del Bicentenario. A taxi between Zacatecas and Guadalupe costs around M$60 to M$70.

La Quemada

The impressive **ruins** (admission M$46; ⏲9am-5pm) of La Quemada stand on a hill overlooking a broad valley 45km south of Zacatecas, 2.5km east of the Zacatecas–Guadalajara road. The remote and scenic setting makes the ruins well worth the day trip from Zacatecas. The area is known to have rattlesnakes; keep an eye – and ear! – out.

The exact history and purpose of the site are extremely vague. Many suppositions surround the area – one theory is that it was where the Aztecs halted during their legendary wanderings toward the Valle de México. What is known for sure is that the constructions were destroyed by fire – and thus they came to be called La Quemada (meaning 'burned city').

The modern **site museum** (admission M$10; ⏲9am-5pm) has interesting archaeology exhibits and an excellent video (with English subtitles). It's worth heading here first to contextualize the area and view the museum's miniature site model to get your bearings for your wanderings.

La Quemada was inhabited between about AD 300 and 1200, and it is estimated to have peaked between AD 500 and 900 with as many as 3000 inhabitants. From around AD 400 it was part of a regional trade network linked to Teotihuacán, but fortifications suggest that La Quemada later tried to dominate trade in this region.

Of the main structures, the nearest to the site entrance is the **Salón de las Columnas** (Hall of the Columns), probably a ceremonial hall. Slightly further up the hill are a **ball court**, a steep **offerings pyramid** and an equally steep staircase leading toward the site's upper levels. From the upper levels of the main hill, a path leads westward for about 800m to a spur hilltop (the highest point) with the remains of a cluster of buildings called **La Ciudadela** (the Citadel). To return, follow the defensive wall and path back around to the museum. Take water and a hat; it's mighty exposed out there.

ℹ Getting There & Away

From Zacatecas's Plaza del Bicentenario, board a combi bus for Villanueva (around M$35) and ask beforehand to be let off at *las ruinas*; you'll be deposited at the turnoff, from where it's a 2.5km walk to the site entrance. Returning to Zacatecas, you may have to wait a while for a bus – don't leave the ruins too late.

Baja California

Includes ➡

Best Tours

- ➡ Whale Shark Mexico (p722)
- ➡ Ecocat (p734)
- ➡ Sergio's Sportfishing Center (p707)
- ➡ Malarrimo Eco Tours (p712)
- ➡ Ecoturismo Kuyimá (p715)

Best Places to Stay

- ➡ Bungalows Breakfast Inn (p735)
- ➡ Posada La Poza (p737)
- ➡ Casa Natalia (p730)
- ➡ El Ángel Azul (p725)
- ➡ Palapas Ventana (p728)

Why Go?

Baja is the earth's second-longest peninsula – over 1200km of the mystical, ethereal, majestic and untamed. Those lucky enough to make the full Tijuana to Los Cabos trip will find that the Carretera Transpeninsular (Hwy 1) offers stunning vistas at every turn. The middle of nowhere is more beautiful than you ever imagined, and people are friendly, relaxed and helpful – even in the border towns. Side roads pass through tiny villages and wind drunkenly along the sides of mountains. Condors carve circles into an unblemished blue sky. Some people simply sip drinks and watch the sun disappear into the Pacific. Some choose to feel the rush of adrenaline as they surf that perfect wave. Others walk through sherbet-colored canyons or stare up at the night's canopy of scattered-diamond stars. Whichever way you choose to take it, you'll discover some of Baja's many joys.

When to Go

Cabo San Lucas

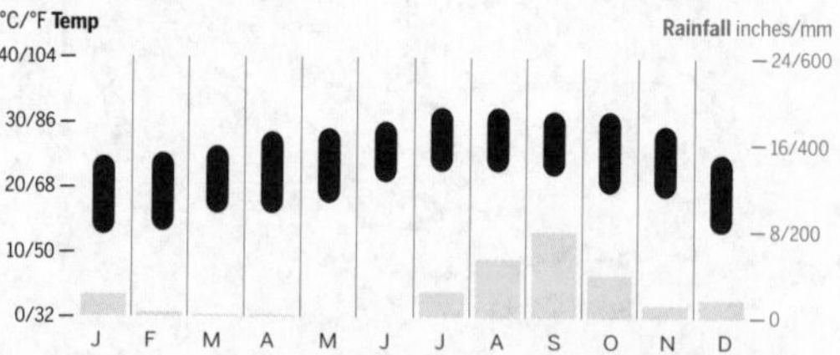

Jan–Mar Flowers bloom, whales and whale sharks play, and big waves delight surfers.

Aug–Sep Beaches all but empty, but it's hot – even in the shade.

Oct–Nov Party-goers, don't miss Sammy Hagar's birthday bash or the Día de Muertos fiesta.

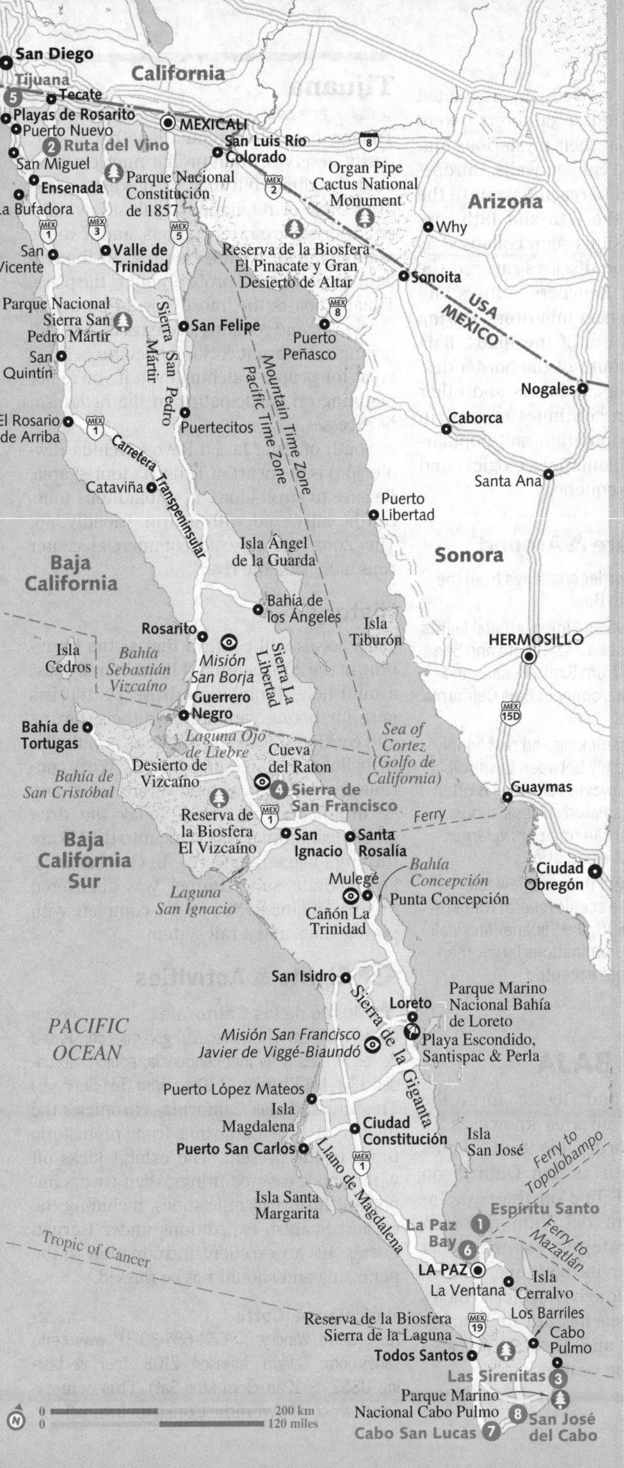

Baja California Highlights

1. Kayak at **Espíritu Santo** (p722) as the big Baja sun drops into the bay
2. Sip, swill and savor the bucolic delights of the **Ruta del Vino** (p703) in northern Baja's unspoiled Valle de Guadalupe
3. Take the plunge at mystical **Las Sirenitas** (p729), in Cabo Pulmo, home to the Sea of Cortez' only living coral reef
4. Marvel at the hundreds of ancient cave paintings at the **Sierra de San Francisco** (p714)
5. Cross the world's most crossed border in **Tijuana** (p698) to eat, drink or shop to your heart's content
6. Get up close to whale sharks in the quiet waters of **La Paz Bay** (p722)
7. Take a sunset cruise in **Cabo San Lucas** (p732) as the sun plunges into the Pacific
8. Peruse the galleries on arty Boulevard Mijares in the heart of **San José del Cabo** (p730)

History

Before Europeans arrived, an estimated 48,000 mobile hunter-gatherers were living in today's Baja; their mysterious murals grace caves and canyon walls. European settlement failed to reach Baja until the Jesuit missions of the 17th and 18th centuries, and the missions soon collapsed as European-introduced diseases ravaged the indigenous people. Ranchers, miners and fishermen were the next inheritors. During the US prohibition era of the 1920s, Baja became a popular south-of-the-border destination for gamblers, drinkers and other 'sinners'. The region continues to grow in economic power, population and popularity, albeit with problematic ecological and environmental consequences.

Getting There & Around

There are six official border crossings from the US state of California to Baja.

Mexican mainland, US and international flights leave from and arrive at La Paz, Loreto and San José del Cabo. Ferries from Santa Rosalía and Pichilingue, near La Paz, connect Baja California to the mainland by sea.

Air-conditioned, nonsmoking and reasonably priced buses operate daily between towns all along the peninsula, however car travel is often the only way to reach isolated villages, mountains and beaches. You can rent cars in larger cities and major tourist destinations.

Highways are good and there are few toll roads. Drivers using the scenic *(cuota)* route to Ensenada will need M$90; the Tijuana–Mexicali route costs M$170. Denominations larger than US$20 or M$200 are not accepted.

NORTHERN BAJA

Tijuana, Mexicali and Tecate form the northern border of an area known as La Frontera (not the border line itself), which extends as far south as San Quintín on the west and San Felipe on the east. Increasingly, the Ruta del Vino (between Ensenada and Tecate) is gaining Napa Valley–like fame for its boutique, award-winning wines. Though northern Baja's border cities and beaches are undeniably hedonistic, Tijuana and Mexicali are also major manufacturing centers.

Tijuana

664 / POP 1.6 MILLION

Tijuana has a bad reputation that it only partly deserves. High-profile murders have made headlines but they are products of the drug trade or retaliations against law officers. Tourists are rarely targets, and if you're not looking for trouble (ie drugs or the red-light district) you'll probably enjoy the place. Tijuana boasts the 'most crossed border in the world,' and remains a remarkably friendly jungle; a vibrant cocktail of cultures that's great for people-watching even if you're not planning on participating in the hedonism or excesses.

South of Calle 1a, La Revo (Avenida Revolución) is the heart of Tijuana's tourist area. Be sure to stroll along it – ubiquitous touts can be answered with a firm, friendly 'no.' The Zona Río upscale commercial center runs alongside the river.

History

Older locals will confirm that at the beginning of the 20th century, TJ was literally 'just a mud hole.' Prohibition drove US tourists here for booze, gambling, brothels, boxing and cockfights, causing Tijuana's population to balloon to 180,000 by 1960. With continued growth have come severe social and environmental problems. Today the drug and illegal-immigrants trade into the US are the city's biggest concerns. In October 2013, an elaborate 'super tunnel' was discovered linking Tijuana to San Diego, complete with power, vents and a rail system.

Sights & Activities

★Museo de las Californias MUSEUM

(664-687-96-41; www.cecut.gob.mx; cnr Paseo de los Héroes & Av Independencia; adult/child under 12yr M$20/free; 10am-6pm Tue-Sun;) The Museo de las Californias chronicles the history of Baja California from prehistoric times to the present. The exhibit kicks off with replica cave paintings, then covers important historical milestones, including the earliest Spanish expeditions under Hernán Cortés. It's an excellent introduction to the peninsula and should not be missed.

Vinícola L.A. Cetto WINERY

(L.A. Cetto Winery; 664-685-30-31; www.cettowines.com; Cañón Johnson 2108; tour & tasting US$2; 10am-5pm Mon-Sat) This winery, southwest of Avenida Constitución, offers tours and tasting. L.A. Cetto produces a range of tasty varietals, as well as sparkling wines and a decent brandy.

Festivals & Events

Tijuana has a busy calendar of annual celebrations and events.

International Craft Beer Festival BEER
(www.facebook.com/TjBeerFest) Taking place during the first week in July, the festival serves some of the best beers, both new and old. Mix with Clamato for the true Mexican experience.

Feria del Platillo Mexicano FOOD
(Mexican Food Festival) Held in September; plates are piled high with goodies – and gobbled down.

Expo Tequila TEQUILA
(Tequila Festival; www.expo-tequila.com) Takes place in mid-October. Tequila in Tijuana? Fits like a hand in a glove.

Festival Hispano-Americano de Guitarra MUSIC
(Hispanic-American Guitar Festival; www.festivalhispanoamericano.com) National guitar graduates and professional players from around the world perform at this guitar festival each November.

Sleeping

The cheapest rooms in Tijuana are sometimes shared with, ahem, hourly rate clientele, so be wary. La Revo can be noisy, so try the side streets or prepare to sleep with a pillow on your head.

Hotel Lafayette HOTEL $
(664-685-39-40; Av Revolución 926; r M$295;) Downtown's most popular budget hotel is run by a welcoming elderly couple. The no-frills rooms have linoleum floors and small bathrooms. If you want a quiet night, request a room at the back.

Hotel Nelson HISTORIC HOTEL $$
(664-685-43-02; www.hotelnelson.com.mx; Av Revolución 721; s/d/tr M$450/530/645; P) The friendly Nelson is a longtime favorite, with high ceilings and 1950s-era touches, such as a real live barbershop of old. The carpeted rooms are slightly scuffed but come with color TV, and some have a view of the (less-than-soothing!) Avenida Revolución.

Hotel La Villa de Zaragoza HOTEL $$
(664-685-18-32; www.hotellavilla.biz; Av Madero 1120; s/d M$580/670; P@) More like a motel, this hotel has rooms set around a central courtyard and carpark. Decor here is business-style bland with a predominantly cream-and-brown color scheme. However, rooms are immaculate and clean, plus there's a restaurant and room service.

Grand Hotel Tijuana LUXURY HOTEL $$$
(664-681-70-00; www.grandhoteltij.com.mx; Blvd Agua Caliente 4500; r from M$1200; P@) Classical music wafts through the lobby and makes for a soothing check-in. Modern rooms in the two 32-story buildings are slick and have panoramic views. The towers also have restaurants and convention facilities.

Eating

Avoid the places with 'free' drink offers. Head to the eateries listed here for great authentic eats.

Tacos Puebla TAQUERÍA $
(Coahuila; tacos M$14; 8am-3pm Mon-Sat) A humble-looking taco stand where you perch on a stool and munch on mouthwatering tacos. Fillings include guacamole, shredded beef and cheese, but they are best enjoyed when joined by crunchy radishes and a jalapeño pepper or two. Owner Pedro is so successful he has put his kids through college in the US on the proceeds.

Tacos El Gordo TAQUERÍA $
(Av Constitución 1342; tacos M$15; 10am-5pm Mon-Sat) Locals in the know flock to this

BAJA SAFETY

In Baja California, basic caution and awareness, such as keeping valuables (including surfboards) out of sight and doors locked, will minimize risk. Most serious crime is not aimed at tourists, and of that, most is crime of opportunity. Border towns such as Tijuana have received awful press due to drug-trade-related killings, but tourists are rarely affected, and Baja California Sur is one of the safest states in all of Mexico.

Sanitation standards in Baja are higher than in other states, and water – even tap water – is usually safe to drink.

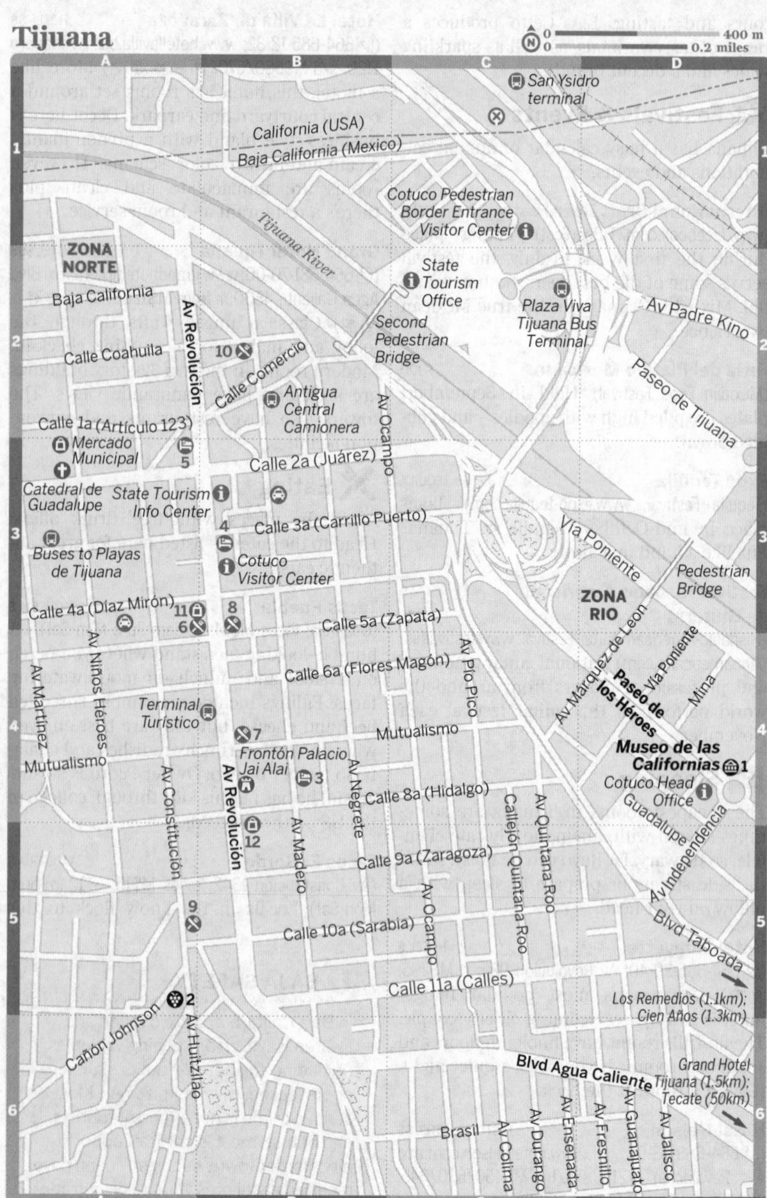

place (which also happens to be across from the best bakery in town – Panadería La Mejor). Tacos, including succulent grilled beef or goat, tossed with cilantro and fried onions, ensure a constant line of salivating customers.

Praga CAFE $

(Av Revolución btwn Calles 4a & 5a; salads M$55, crepes M$58; ⏲8am-11pm Mon-Sat, 9am-9pm Sun; 📶) At last! Somewhere in town that serves seriously good coffee, including cappuccinos, machiatos and espressos. Crepes,

Tijuana

Top Sights

1 Museo de las Californias.................... D4

Sights

2 Vinícola L.A. Cetto A5

Sleeping

3 Hotel La Villa de Zaragoza..................B4

4 Hotel Lafayette.......................................B3

5 Hotel Nelson A3

Eating

6 Caesar's A3

7 Chiki Jai...B4

8 Praga B3

9 Tacos El Gordo.......................................A5

10 Tacos Puebla...B2

Entertainment

Centro Cultural Tijuana................(see 1)

Domo Imax ....(see 1)

Shopping

11 Emporium..A3

12 Sanborns...B5

croissants, sandwiches and some lightweight salads, like spinach with mozzarella, pear and apple, are also served for those suffering from burrito burnout.

★Caesar's ITALIAN $$

(www.caesarstijuana.com; Av Revolución 1927; mains M$110-120; ⌚noon-10:30pm Mon-Wed, to midnight Thu-Sat, to 9pm Sun; P) Step inside and you are transported to the 1950s. Sepia pics line the walls, while the dark wood decor oozes elegance. The Caesar salad (M$90), prepared with panache at your table, was apparently invented here by the restaurant's founder Caesar Cardini, an Italian immigrant from the 1920s. There's an adjacent Spanish-style tapas bar.

Chiki Jai SPANISH $$

(☎664-685-49-55; Av Revolución 1388; mains M$100-150; ⌚11am-10pm Mon-Sat) Tiled walls, a painted ceiling and a mounted *traje de luces* (traditional bullfighter's garb) make this atmospheric and historic restaurant stand out. The cuisine is Spanish, and includes paella, stuffed calamari and that 'other' tortilla (potato-based omelet). Dating from the 1940s, Chiki Jai has illustrious patrons from the past, namely Ernest Hemingway and Anthony Quinn.

Cien Años MEXICAN $$$

(☎664-634-30-39; www.cien.info; Av Velasco 2331; mains M$235-250; ⌚7:30am-11pm Mon-Sat, to 5pm Sun; P 📶) Enjoy delicious and innovative *alta cocina Mexicana* (contemporary Mexican cuisine) as well as traditional dishes like *sopa Azteca* with avocado and tortilla strips, *crepes de huitlacoche* with a creamy pistachio-flavored sauce and *chile relleno* with shrimps and lobster bisque. Ask the waiter to prepare the classic *salsa de molcajete* (roasted salsa made with a traditional Mexican mortar and pestle) at your table.

Drinking

Drinkers in TJ may feel like hounds let loose in a fire-hydrant factory. The bars and clubs off Calle 6a are packed at weekends.

Los Remedios CANTINA

(www.losremedios.mx; Av Rivera 2479; ⌚1:30pm-1:30am) Enjoy fabulous festive decor at this cavernous cantina with its bullfighting posters, classic '50s movie posters, colorful paper flags and ceiling papered with lotto tickets. You can't miss the canary-yellow facade right on the roundabout in Zona Río. Live music at weekends.

Entertainment

If you're in TJ you owe it to yourself to let loose, if only to pay perfectly good money for a photo of yourself on one of the zebra-painted donkeys. Tourist info will have details of current events and performances.

Centro Cultural Tijuana ARTS CENTER

(Cecut; ☎664-687-96-00; www.cecut.gob.mx; cnr Paseo de los Héroes & Av Independencia; ⌚9am-7pm Mon-Fri, 10am-7pm Sat & Sun) Tijuana's sophisticated arts and cultural center would make any comparably sized city north of the border proud. It houses an art gallery, the Museo de las Californias (p698), a theater, and the globular cinema **Domo Imax** (www.cecut.gob.mex; tickets from M$50; ⌚1-11pm Tue-Sun), which shows predominantly art-house movies.

Shopping

Tijuana is great for souvenirs, but be cautious when buying gold and silver as much of it is fake (at those prices it would have to be, right?). You'll note the many drugstores here; they specialize in selling discounted generic pharmaceuticals to US citizens.

Emporium JEWELRY
(☎664-685-13-24; emporium_tj@yahoo.com; Av Revolución 1025; ⏲9am-7pm) This is one of the few places with fair silver prices that are already marked, plus the English-speaking owner is knowledgeable and not too pushy.

Sanborns DEPARTMENT STORE
(☎664-688-14-62; Av Revolución 1102; ⏲7:30am-11pm Sun-Thu, to 1am Fri-Sat) This department store has a decent selection of newspapers and magazines from the USA and Mexico.

Information

DANGERS & ANNOYANCES

If you're street smart and not after trouble then it is unlikely you'll have problems. Touts are sometimes irksome but they deserve a respectful 'no' – they are trying to make a living in a place that has seen a huge downturn in tourism.

Don't drink on the streets. As in any big city, being plastered late at night can invite trouble.

Coyotes and *polleros* (both mean 'people smugglers') congregate along the river west of the San Ysidro crossing. After dark, avoid this area and Colonia Libertad, east of the crossing.

EMERGENCY

Tourist Assistance Hotline (☎078)

MEDICAL SERVICES

Hospital General (☎664-684-00-78; Av Padre Kino, Zona Río) Northwest of the junction with Avenida Rodríguez.

MONEY

Use caution when changing money, especially at night. Everyone accepts US dollars and most banks have ATMs.

TOURIST INFORMATION

Cotuco Visitor Center (☎664-685-31-17; Av Revolución btwn Calle 3a & Calle 4a; ⏲9am-6pm) There is also a visitor center at the border (☎664-607-30-97; pedestrian border entrance visitor center; ⏲9am-6pm Mon-Sat, 9am-3pm Sun) and a head office (☎664-684-05-37; ste 201, Paseo de los Héroes 9365; ⏲9am-6pm Mon-Fri).

State Tourism Office (Secretaría de Turismo del Estado; ☎664-682-33-67; Alarcón 1572, Zona Río; ⏲8am-8pm Mon-Fri, 9am-1pm Sat) There's also an info center (☎664-973-04-24; Av Revolución 842; ⏲8am-8pm Mon-Fri, 9am-1pm Sat) on Avenida Revolución.

USEFUL WEBSITES

See Tijuana (www.seetijuana.com) A Tijuana tourism site.

Tijuana Online (www.tijuanaonline.org) Run by Cotuco.

Getting There & Away

Mexican tourist permits are available 24 hours a day at the San Ysidro–Tijuana border's Mexican **immigration office** (☎664-683-53-49; 720 East San Ysidro Blvd). They are also available, although less dependably, at a small office in the main bus terminal (Central Camionera). **Banjército** (☎664-683-62-44; www.banjercito.com.mx; Calle José María Larroque; ⏲8am-noon) is the only bank in town to process vehicle permit payments.

AIR

Aeroméxico (☎664-683-84-44, 664-684-92-68; www.aeromexico.com; Local A 12-1, Plaza Río Tijuana) Aeroméxico serves many mainland Mexican destinations, and has nonstop flights to La Paz and flights to Tucson and Phoenix in the USA.

Aeropuerto Internacional General Abelardo L Rodríguez (☎664-607-82-00; www.tijuana-aiport.com; Carretera Aeropuerto-Otay Mesa) The airport is in Mesa de Otay, east of downtown.

BUS

The main bus terminal, about 5km southeast of downtown, is the **Central Camionera** (☎664-621-29-82), where **Elite** (www.autobuseselite.com.mx) and **Estrella Blanca** (www.estrellablanca.com.mx) offer 1st-class buses with air-con and toilets. Destinations in mainland Mexico include Guadalajara (M$1617, 36 hours) and

BUSES FROM TIJUANA

DESTINATION	FARE (M$)	DURATION	FREQUENCY (DAILY)
Ensenada	155	1½hr	frequent
Guerrero Negro	1005	12hr	3
La Paz	1940	24hr	3
Loreto	1600	18hr	3
Mexicali	280	2¾hr	frequent
Tecate	98	1hr	frequent

WORTH A TRIP

RUTA DEL VINO & VALLE DE GUADALUPE

You can skip Tijuana's long lines and treat yourself to some beautiful scenery by entering Mexico via Tecate. The border crossing (open 6am to 10pm) is far less congested, and south of Tecate lies the Ruta del Vino in the intoxicatingly beautiful Valle de Guadalupe (Hwy 3). Maps of the wine route (available at local hotels, tourist offices and wineries) will help you locate the vineyards.

Dedicated drinkers should designate a driver first, as 90-plus wineries and one brewery await. If you don't fancy driving, **Baja Wine Tours** (☎664-625-12-40; www.bajawinetours.net; from M$295) is just one of several reputable tour companies that organize day-long wine tours (including lunch) originating from Ensenada or Tijuana. Start at the landmark **Cuauhtémoc Moctezuma Heineken Mexico Brewery** (☎665-654-94-90; www.cuamoc.com; cnr Calles Hidalgo & Obregón, Tecate; ⌚10am-5pm Mon-Fri, to 2pm Sat), which produces Tecate, Dos Equis, Carta Blanca, Bohemia and Sol, among others, and is now under Heineken's umbrella. Tours are run by appointment only at noon and 3pm Monday to Friday, and 11am and 2pm Saturday. Alternatively just order a brew from the bar. The best place to stay in Tecate is the **Estancia Inn Hotel** (☎665-521-30-66; www.estanciainn.com.mx; Encanto Norte s/n; d M$880; P 📶), which has attractive, carpeted rooms with large walk-in showers, and a good restaurant.

From Tecate, head southward, stopping for tours, tastings, lunch and a tipple or two along the way. The vines, planted decades ago, are finally coming into their own, and this gorgeous valley is well on its way to being 'Napa Sur.'

From Tecate, the first winery you come to (albeit after around 70km) is Mexico's largest producer, **L.A. Cetto** (☎646-175-23-63; www.lacetto.com; Carretera Tecate-El Sauzal Km 73.5; tour & tastings M$25; ⌚9am-5pm). It runs tours every half hour, which include the tasting of four wines, one being their highlight cabernet sauvignon. They also offer olive oil, bread and local aged cheese. Further south is one of the most prestigious new wineries in the valley, **El Cielo** (☎646-151-65-15; www.vinoselcielo.com; Carretera Guadalupe-El Tigre Km 118; tastings from US$5-16.50; ⌚noon-8pm). It opened in 2013 and is a gorgeous property encompassing a winery with tasting room, a sophisticated restaurant, and a boutique hotel and spa (the latter was under construction at time of research). Tastings of two to six wines are available. Don't miss the merlot, one of their premium varietals.

Near here is **Bibayoff** (☎646-176-10-08; bibayoff@telnor.net; Carretera Francisco Zarco-El Tigre Km 9.5; tastings US$5; ⌚10am-4pm Tue-Sun), a boutique winery set off the beaten path. Its small museum recounts the fascinating history of the Russians who immigrated here in the early 1900s (the current owner is a descendent). Be sure to ask for a taste of the fruity moscatel.

Right on the highway, **Liceaga** (☎646-155-32-81; www.vinosliceaga.com; Carretera Tecate-San Antonio de las Minas Km 93.5; tastings M$100; ⌚11am-5pm) is a well-established winery with a range of wines and the valley's only true grappa (a strong spirit distilled from grape skins or stems). The tasting fee includes a plate of bread and cheese.

Continuing south, make a stop at the tour center for **Santo Tomás** (☎646-155-31-37; www.santo-tomas.com; Carretera Tecate-El Sauzal Km 73; tour & tastings US$20; ⌚10am-5pm). A 50ft wall of wines backs the sparkling tasting room, where the bar is creatively made from an unused wine press. On the tour note the fermenting tanks that double as chalkboards (listing types of grape, their leaf patterns, wine processes, etc). There's also a video presentation and wine-specific laser show.

For those ready to turn in for the night but not ready to leave the valley, **La Villa del Valle** (☎646-156-80-07; www.lavilladelvalle.com; Carretera Tecate-San Antonio de las Minas Km 88; d from US$215; P ⊖ ❄ 📶 ≋) is a delightful boutique B&B that has a pool, sauna and yoga studio, all with spectacular views of the valley…and they own the **Corazón de Tierra** (☎646-156-80-30; www.corazondetierra.com; Carretera Tecate-San Antonio de las Minas Km 88; menu US$65; ⌚9:30-11:30am & 1-8:30pm), perhaps the finest dining in the Ensenada area. The restaurant looks out over picturesque rolling vineyards and hillsides, and the juxtaposition of rough-hewn timbers and starched tablecloths fits the rustic vineyard motif to a T.

Mexico City (M$1575, 44 hours, 12 daily, hourly). Autotransportes del Pacífico and ABC operate mostly 2nd-class buses to mainland Mexico's Pacific coast and around Baja California. See the table on p702 for destinations served by **ABC** (www.abc.com.mx) buses.

Suburbaja (664-688-00-45) local buses use the handy downtown **Antigua Central Camionera** (cnr Av Madero & Calle 1a), with buses leaving for Tecate (M$42 to M$55, 1½ hours) every 15 minutes.

For border crossings by bus, **Mexicoach** (www.mexicoach.com) runs frequently (US$4 one way, US$6 round trip) from its **San Ysidro terminal** (☎619-428-62-00; 4570 Camino de la Plaza) to Tijuana's **Terminal Turístico** (☎664-685-14-70; Av Revolución 1025) between 8am and 6pm. It also runs Playas de Rosarito–bound shuttles from San Ysidro by reservation (☎619-428-95-17). Returning shuttles leave from the Rosarito Beach Hotel between 8am and 4pm.

Between 5am and 10:55pm, buses leave from the **San Diego Greyhound terminal** (☎800-231-2222, in the US 619-515-1100; www.greyhound.com; 120 West Broadway, San Diego) and stop at **San Ysidro** (☎in the US 619-428-1194; 799 East San Ysidro Blvd) en route to Tijuana's Central Camionera bus terminal or the airport. Fares from San Diego/San Ysidro to the Central Camionera or airport are US$14 one way, US$27 round trip.

CAR & MOTORCYCLE

The San Ysidro border crossing, a 10-minute walk from downtown Tijuana, is open 24 hours, but motorists may find the Mesa de Otay crossing (also open 24 hours) less congested; it's 15km to the east of San Ysidro.

Rental agencies in San Diego are the cheapest option, but most of them only allow journeys as far as Ensenada. Renting a car in Tijuana or taking the bus may be your best option for heading further south.

TROLLEY

San Diego's popular **trolley** (www.sdmts.com) runs from downtown San Diego through to San Ysidro (US$2.50) every 15 minutes from about 5am to midnight. From San Diego's Lindbergh Field airport, city bus 992 (US$2.25) goes to the Plaza America trolley stop in downtown San Diego, across from the Amtrak depot.

Getting Around

For about M$10, local buses go everywhere, but the slightly pricier route taxis are much quicker. To get to the Central Camionera take any 'Buena Vista,' 'Centro' or 'Central Camionera' bus from Calle 2a, east of Avenida Constitución. Alternately, take a gold-and-white 'Mesa de Otay' route taxi from Avenida Madero between Calles 2a and 3a (M$12). Regular taxis will charge about M$75 for rides in and around Avenida Revolucíon or the Zona Río. The airport is about M$150, but always double check first.

Playas de Rosarito

☎661 / POP 91,000

Once a deserted, sandy beach and then a Hollywood film location, Playas de Rosarito is finally coming into its own. Developments and condos are everywhere, but despite the construction clamor, Rosarito is a quieter place to party and is an easy day trip (or overnight trip) from Tijuana or San Diego. **Hotel Rosarito** (now the landmark Rosarito Beach Hotel) and its long, sandy beach pioneered local tourism in the late 1920s. **Fox Studios Baja**, built in 1996 for the filming of *Titanic,* has since served as a primary filming location for *Pearl Harbor, James Bond: Tomorrow Never Dies* and *Master and Commander*.

Despite the studio's influence, in many ways Playas de Rosarito remains a one-horse, one-street town, quiet except for during spring break.

Boulevard Juárez, Rosarito's only major street (and part of the Transpeninsular) has many restaurants, clubs and hotels where the prices balloon to the outrageous during spring break.

Sleeping

Hotel del Sol Inn HOTEL $$

(☎661-612-25-52; www.del-sol-inn.com; Blvd Juárez 32; s/d M$455/585; P ⊖ ❄) The Sol has clean, carpeted rooms with TV, bottled water and simple furniture. Some rooms are reserved for nonsmokers. Note that prices triple during the short spring-break holiday.

Casa Farolito B&B $$$

(☎619-786-80-00; www.casafarolito.com; San Antonio del Mar; s/d incl breakfast from US$90/135; P ⊖ ❄ ᯤ) Located beachside around 5km north of Playas de Rosarito, this place has bucketfuls of charm. Rooms are all different with just enough colorful Mexican pizzazz to avoid a headache coming on. Perks include a welcome margarita, free use of boogie boards, complimentary beach chairs and parasols, and a slap-up breakfast with *huevos rancheros* the specialty.

OFF THE BEATEN TRACK

PUERTO NUEVO

If fresh lobster is your thing, the fishing village of Puerto Nuevo, located just 5km south of Playas de Rosarito, is the dining destination of your dreams. Over 70 no-frills restaurants vigorously compete for punters with prices as low as US$15 for a medium lobster (fried and served in melted butter), plus tortillas, frijoles, Mexican rice, guacamole and even a margarita for good measure. Insist on seeing your live lobster first, however, or you may be palmed off with frozen instead – there is no comparison in taste.

Eating

Tacos El Yaqui TAQUERÍA $
(cnr Palma & Mar del Norte; tacos M$25; 8am-5pm Mon, Tue & Thu, 8am-9:30pm Fri-Sun) This delicious taco stand is so popular that it often closes early when the ingredients run out. Get in line before 4pm if you don't want to risk missing out. It may have expanded its premises to include some sit-down space by the time you read this.

Los Arcos MEXICAN $
(661-612-04-91; Blvd Juárez 29; mains M$65-90; 8am-7pm Mon, Tue, Thu & Fri, 8am-10pm Sat & Sun) For shrimp or fish tacos try this family-owned place. It also has various *antojitos* (typical Mexican snacks), excellent salsa and friendly staff.

El Nido STEAKHOUSE $$$
(www.elnidorosarito.net; Blvd Juárez 67; mains M$170-220; 8am-9:30pm; P) You can't miss the vast rustic frontage of this steakhouse in the center of town. And the atmosphere continues with exposed brick, beams, strings of garlic and a foliage-filled back terrace, complete with aviary. Tortillas are made fresh to order and the menu includes venison, rabbit and chicken, plus the star billing: steak.

Getting There & Around

From downtown Tijuana, *colectivos* (share cars) for Playas de Rosarito (M$15) leave from Avenida Madero between Calles 3a and 4a. Look for a yellow station wagon with a white triangle on the door. You can catch a Mexicoach shuttle (M$150) to Tijuana from the parking lot of the Rosarito Beach Hotel twice daily.

Ensenada

646 / POP 280,000

Ensenada, 108km south of the border, is hedonistic Tijuana's cosmopolitan sister. The city has a quirky mix of just-off-the-boat cruise shippers, drive-by tourists from Cali, visitors from mainland Mexico and seen-it-all locals. In case you've forgotten you're in Mexico (what with all those US dollars and English menus), just look up: a Mexican flag, so large it's probably visible from space, flutters proudly over the tourist zone. Wander Avenida López Mateos (Calle 1a) and you'll find almost anything ranging from tasteful ceramics to tasteless T-shirts. Nearby, Calle 2a – unlit and seedy – is worth avoiding after dark.

Ensenada was the capital of Baja territory from 1882 to 1915, but the capital shifted to Mexicali during the revolution. The city subsequently catered to 'sin' industries until the federal government outlawed gambling in the 1930s...but judging from the strip clubs, peep shows and bars, sin still goes on today as it did in days of old.

Sights

★Riviera del Pacífico HISTORIC BUILDING
(tel/info 646-177-05-94; Blvd Costero) Opened in the early 1930s as Hotel Playa Ensenada, the extravagant Riviera del Pacífico, a Spanish-style former casino, is rumored to have been a regular haunt of Al Capone. It now houses the small **Museo de Historia de Ensenada** (646-177-05-94; Blvd Costero; admission M$10; 10am-5pm Mon-Sat, noon-5pm Sun) and Bar Andaluz (p709), while the **Casa de Cultura** offers classes, retrospective film screenings and art exhibitions.

Museo del Instituto Nacional de Antropología e Historia MUSEUM
(Museo del INAH; 646-178-25-31; Av Ryerson 99; 9am-4pm Mon-Fri) FREE Built in 1886 and once the Aduana Marítima de Ensenada, the city's oldest public building now houses this historical and cultural museum. It has a relatively small but comprehensive collection of artifacts, and discusses (mainly in Spanish) the area's history from prehistoric times.

El Mirador LOOKOUT
Atop the Colinas de Chapultepec, El Mirador offers panoramic views of the city and Bahía de Todos Santos. Climb or drive (note: there's no off-street parking) to this highest

Ensenada

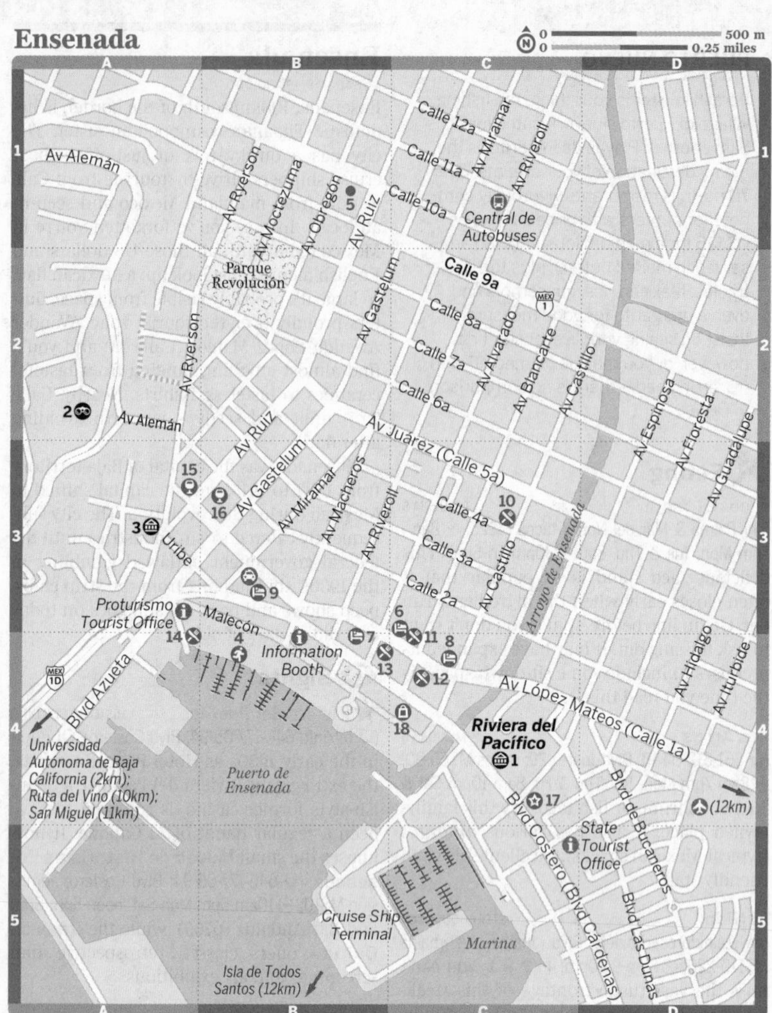

point in town, up Avenida Alemán from the western end of Calle 2a in central Ensenada.

Activities

Surfing

Isla de Todos Santos SURFING

This island off Ensenada's coast (not to be confused with the town near Los Cabos) is where one of the world's top big-wave surfing contests is held each year. **El Martillo** (The Hammer) is legendary, with swells commonly double or triple overhead, even bigger when conditions are right. Boats can be chartered out from the harbor. Prices start at about M$800 per person, four people minimum. Sometimes they can cut you a deal, or you could ask to ride with a fisher.

San Miguel SURFING

(parking M$55) There's not much here but a few campers, a parking lot, and a wonderful point break just offshore. San Miguel was once a hang-out for The Doors legend Jim Morrison. When the waves are big it's an awesome ride.

Fishing & Whale-Watching

Ensenada is known the world over for its excellent sportfishing, though you must have a

Ensenada

Top Sights
1 Riviera del Pacífico C4

Sights
2 El Mirador..A2
Museo de Historia de Ensenada ....(see 1)
3 Museo del Instituto Nacional de Antropología e Historia..A3

Activities, Courses & Tours
4 Sergio's Sportfishing Center B4
5 Spanish School Baja............................ B1

Sleeping
6 Best Western Hotel El Cid C3
7 Hotel Bahía B4
8 Hotel Cortez C4
9 Hotel Santo Tomás...............................B3

Eating
10 El Parián C3
11 El Rey Sol C4
12 Hogaza Hogaza C4
13 La Guerrense.......................................B4
14 Mariscos El Norteño A4

Drinking & Nightlife
Bar Andaluz ....(see 1)
15 Hussong's Cantina...............................A3
16 Ojos Negros...B3

Entertainment
17 Centro Estatal de las Artes................. C4

Shopping
18 Galería Pérez Meillon........................... C4

valid Mexican fishing license (available online at www.bestbajafishing.org) if you want to reel in a live one. Most charter companies also offer whale-watching tours from mid-December to mid-April.

Sergio's Sportfishing Center FISHING
(☎646-178-21-85; www.sergiosfishing.com) Well regarded, Sergio's can be found on the sportfishing pier off El Malecón. Fishing trips include the necessary gear. Day trips per person start at about M$300 and go up to M$5000 or more for private charter trips, depending on the size of the vessel.

Courses

The following language schools offer similar immersion programs that include homestay options.

Universidad Autónoma de Baja California LANGUAGE
(☎646-175-07-40; http://idiomas.ens.uabc.mx/cursos; cnr Blvd Zertuche & Blvd de los Lagos) Has semester-long classes for foreign students.

Spanish School Baja LANGUAGE
(☎646-190-60-49; www.spanishschoolbaja.com; Calle 10 btwn Avs Ruiz & Obregón) Costs start at US$300 for a week.

Festivals & Events

The events listed here constitute a tiny sample of the 70-plus annual sporting, tourist and cultural happenings. Dates change, so contact tourist offices for details.

Carnaval CARNIVAL
(👪) A Mardi Gras–type celebration 40 days before Ash Wednesday, which falls on February 18 in 2015 and February 10 in 2016. The streets flood with floats and dancers.

Fiesta de la Vendimia WINE
(Grape Harvest Festival) Wine harvest, held in the first two weeks of August. Cheers!

International Seafood Fair FOOD
Sample September's scrumptious seafood surprises.

Baja 1000 RACING
Baja's biggest off-road race, held in mid-November. See 'truggies' (truck-buggies) tear up the desert to the cheers of just about everyone. The Baja 500 is in June.

Sleeping

Hotel demand can exceed supply at times, particularly at weekends and in summer.

Hotel Cortez HOTEL $$
(☎646-178-23-07; www.bajainn.com; Av López Mateos 1089; r from M$973; P ⊖ ❄ @ ≋) This is a solid choice in a good location with facilities that include a small gym. The (heated) pool is surrounded by lofty trees. Some of the rooms are a tad dark. If you can, go for the premium rooms, with their chic and contemporary look: all earth colors and plush fabrics.

Hotel Santo Tomás HOTEL $$
(☎646-178-33-11; hst@bajainn.com; Blvd Costero 609; r M$450-590; P ⊖ ❄ @) It's slick and snazzy, with satellite TV in each room. The quirky lobby has a grand sweeping staircase, an elevator with disco mirrors and gold trim, and a fish tank that give it a funky character that other hotels lack. Rates increase on

Friday and Saturday (along with the noise levels outside).

Motel Joya Mar MOTEL $$

(646-176-74-30; Av Veracruz 360; s/d M$500/600;) Across from lovely Playa Hermosa, around 3km north of the center of town, this midrange motel, festooned with a dazzle of bougainvillea, has sizable rooms with tile floors and paisley bedspreads. A communal salon overlooks the sea, while the bar has karaoke and billiards. If you fancy a gallop on the sand, you can rent a horse opposite (US$10 per hour).

Hotel Bahía HOTEL $$

(646-178-21-01; www.hotelbahia.com.mx; Av López Mateos 850; r M$975;) Despite the Stalinist drab exterior, this hotel offers pleasant and spacious carpeted rooms. An attractive pool area with adjacent bar and restaurant, which serve direct to your sunbed, is another perk.

Best Western Hotel El Cid HOTEL $$$

(646-178-24-01; www.hotelelcid.com.mx; Av López Mateos 993; s/d incl breakfast M$960/1327; @) This four-star hotel has comfortable rooms with firm beds, a respected restaurant and a lively bar. Prices include continental breakfast with fresh juice. The bilingual staff are particularly gracious and friendly.

Eating

Ensenada's dining options range from corner taco stands to places serving excellent Mexican and international cuisine.

★La Guerrense TAQUERÍA $

(www.laguerrense.com; cnr Avs Alvarado & Av López Mateos; tacos US$4.50; 10:30am-5pm Wed-Mon) Voted third in the world at the 2013 World Streetfood Congress in Singapore, Sabina Bandera's seafood stand dates from the 1960s and attracts long lines with its outstanding seafood tacos, juicy ceviche and *tostadas*. They also produce their own salsa line (US$5) and there's usually some streetside guitar strumming to add to the atmosphere.

Mariscos El Norteño SEAFOOD $

(Local 4, Fish Market; tacos M$30; 8am-9pm Mon-Sat) You can't go wrong at any of the seafood stalls across from the fish market, but this one has plenty of seating and a superb range of salsas including roasted jalapeños and red chili. Try an original Baja-style taco, which is a deep-fried fish or shrimp taco with shredded cabbage in a creamy white sauce.

El Parián MEXICAN $

(646-128-82-32; cnr Calle 4a & Av Castillo; dinner mains M$50-95; 7:30am-11:30pm) Paper streamers, murals, painted tables and sherbert-colored furniture give a festive atmosphere to enjoying great enchiladas, quesadillas, burritos, *agua de jamaica* (hibiscus water) and friendly service. Flat-screen TVs in every corner mean you (or the wait staff) never have to miss a moment of that cheesy Mexican soap.

Hogaza Hogaza CAFE $$

(Plaza Santo Tomas; bagels from US$4.50; 8am-6pm Mon-Sat;) This artisanal cafe and bakery is located in the smarter end of town. Its peppermint-green facade sets a suitably sweet note for a fabulous array of cakes and pastries, including mini-macaroons. A great spot for breakfast; try the bagels with fillings like cream cheese, capers and onion, or for larger appetites: roast beef with cheese and pesto.

El Rey Sol FRENCH $$$

(www.ensenadaexperience.com; Av López Mateos 1000; mains M$175-250; 7am-10:30pm;) Set within an elegant building's sumptuous interior, replete with flocked wallpaper, chandeliers and stained glass, this landmark restaurant dates from 1947. The cuisine is predominantly French, but also serves Mexican favorites and pasta. This is a dress-for-dinner kind of place – don't arrive in flipflops.

Drinking

On weekends most bars and cantinas along Avenida Ruiz are packed from noon to early morning. If that's not your scene, head for one of the many quality hotels and fine restaurants where you're likely to find a laid-back spot to sip a margarita (said to have been invented here) or sample a top-shelf tequila.

★Hussong's Cantina CANTINA

(Av Ruiz 113; 11am-2am Tue-Sun) The oldest and perhaps liveliest cantina in the Californias has been serving tequila since 1892. A Friday or Saturday night will be packed with locals, a sprinkling of tourists and touting mariachis. The history is fascinating, so request the leaflet (in English and Spanish). The margaritas come warmly recommended as well.

Bar Andaluz BAR

(646-176-43-10; cnr Blvd Costera & Riviera; 10am-midnight Mon-Fri, 9am-1am Sat;) Visit the cultured bar inside the Riviera del Pacífico, where having a drink is an exercise in nostalgia. It's quiet, perfect for a nightcap with that special friend.

Ojos Negros WINE BAR

(Av Ruiz 105; 11am-midnight Tue-Sat, 2-10pm Sun;) Suffering from margarita meltdown? Then head to this relaxed wine bar for a glass of fruity Passion Meritage, an award-winning red from the owners' vineyards: Bodegas San Rafael. Lounge-like seating, chill-out music and burgundy-washed walls set the scene nicely. Nibbles include gourmet flatbread pizzas.

Entertainment

Centro Estatal de las Artes ARTS CENTER

(646-173-43-07; http://cearte.info; cnr Clubrotario & Blvd Costero; 8am-8pm Mon-Sat, noon-7pm Sun, plus event hours in evening) The Centro Estatal de las Artes has shows and exhibits throughout the year.

Shopping

Galería Pérez Meillon HANDICRAFTS

(646-175-78-48; Blvd Costero 1094; 9am-5pm) In the Centro Artesanal de Ensenada, this gallery sells authenticated pottery from the Paipai (one of Baja California's indigenous peoples known for fine craftwork, particularly pottery and baskets) and Mata Ortiz (a major pottery center in central north Mexico). It also sells Kumiai weaving.

Information

EMERGENCY

Municipal Police (066, 646-176-43-43)
State Police (066, 646-172-35-30)
Tourist Assistance (078)

MEDICAL SERVICES

Sanatorio del Carmen (646-178-34-77; cnr Av Obregón & Calle 11a)

TOURIST INFORMATION

Proturismo Tourist Office (646-178-24-11; www.proturismoensenada.org.mx; Blvd Costero 540; 8am-8pm Mon-Fri, 9am-5pm Sat & Sun) Dispenses maps, brochures and current hotel information. There's an information booth (646-178-30-70; Plaza Cívica; Tue-Sun) in the Plaza Cívica.

State Tourist Office (646-172-54-44; Blvd Costero 1477; 8am-6pm Mon-Fri, 9am-1pm Sat & Sun) Carries similar information to the Proturismo office.

USEFUL WEBSITES

Discover Baja California (www.discoverbaja-california.com) The state's tourism site.

Enjoy Ensenada (www.enjoyensenada.com) Ensenada's tourism site.

Getting There & Away

Immigration Office (646-174-01-64; Blvd Azueta 101; document delivery 8am-6pm Mon-Fri, document pickup 1-3pm Mon-Fri) The immigration office sells tourist permits for those arriving in the country by boat.

BUS

Central de Autobuses (Av Riveroll 1075) Ten blocks north of Avenida López Mateos, it hosts Elite (646-178-67-70), which serves mainland Mexican destinations as far as Guadalajara (M$1400, 36 hours) and Mexico City (M$1800, 48 hours) and ABC (646-174-11-77; www.abc.com.mx). The latter, with its subsidiary Aguíla, is the main peninsula carrier.

CAR & MOTORCYCLE

The drive from Tijuana to Ensenada on the scenic (*cuota*) route has three tolls (total M$90) and a military checkpoint.

BUSES FROM ENSENADA

DESTINATION	FARE (M$)	DURATION	FREQUENCY (DAILY)
Guerrero Negro	920	10hr	6
La Paz	1815	22hr	4
Mexicali	315	4hr	4
Playas de Rosarito	125	1hr	frequent
Tecate	164	2hr	frequent
Tijuana	155	1½hr	frequent
Tijuana Airport	280	1¾hr	frequent

Getting Around

The main **taxi stand** is at the corner of Avenidas López Mateos and Miramar; taxis also congregate along Avenida Juárez. Most fares within the city cost from M$50 to M$100.

Surfers can get a trip out to San Miguel and a pickup later in the day for around M$100 in each direction.

La Bufadora

La Bufadora is a popular 'blowhole' (really a notch in the rock that sprays waves upwards) 40km south of Ensenada. If conditions are right it sends a jet of water up to 30m into the sky, drenching cheering onlookers. Conditions aren't always ideal, but if you're up for a gamble you can catch a taxi (M$150 per person round-trip, minimum four persons) or a shuttle tour (M$175), or drive south on the Transpeninsular to the 'Bufadora' sign, then follow the road all the way around to the Pacific side. Parking costs M$20.

Parque Nacional Constitución de 1857

At the end of a challenging unpaved 43km road out of Ojos Negros (east of Ensenada at Km 39 on Hwy 3), Parque Nacional Constitución de 1857 has beautiful conifers, fields of wildflowers and a sometimes-dry lake, **Laguna Hanson** (also known as Laguna Juárez), at an altitude of 1200m. *Cabañas* (cabins; M$550) or campsites (M$130) are available (☎686-554-44-04, 8am to 3pm) but the water may be contaminated by livestock so bring your own.

It's a sublime spot for mountain biking, hiking or just getting away from it all, as long as everyone else isn't getting away at the same time – in peak holiday times it can be busy, but it's a beautiful spot any time of year. The park is also accessible by a steeper road east of Km 55.2, 16km southeast of the Ojos Negros junction.

Mexicali

☎686 / POP 690,000

Mexicali is what Tijuana must have been before the tourist boom – gritty, even scary – and most tourists just head southward. The city offers some decent restaurants and some fun nightlife, but be particularly careful around the border areas after dark.

The Zona Hotelera, far safer at night than the border, is on the east side, along Calzada Juárez from Plaza Azteca to Independencia and beyond. In summer, Mexicali is one of the hottest places on earth – stay away, if possible.

Sights

Plaza Constitución is a good place to hear *banda* (big-band music) groups rehearse in the late afternoon – hence its nickname, Plaza del Mariachi. Most of Mexicali's historic buildings are northeast of Calzada López Mateos.

Catedral de la Virgen de Guadalupe CATHEDRAL
(cnr Av Reforma & Morelos) This cathedral is the city's major religious landmark.

Sleeping

If you don't fancy sleeping in a hotel that has hourly rate customers, you're best off in the pricier Zona Hotelera.

Araiza LUXURY HOTEL $$$
(☎686-564-11-00; www.araizahoteles.com; Calz Juárez 2220, Zona Hotelera; d/ste incl breakfast US$125/150; P⊖❄@🛜🏊) This family-friendly hotel has well-appointed spacious rooms, two excellent restaurants (including Japanese), a bar, tennis courts, a gym and a convention center. For a quieter stay, request a room in the newer executive wing away from the road and pool area.

Eating

Atico Cafe CAFE $
(Zaragoza 1690; snacks from M$45; ⊙10am-11pm; 🔌) Escape the big-city frenzy at this chill-out cafe, with its sink-into sofas, board games, moody lighting and vintage-cum-pop culture decor. Light snacks include salads, crepes and comfortingly homemade-style cakes and desserts. Exotic cocktails are another agreeable specialty.

Petunia 2 JUICE BAR $
(Madero 436; breakfast M$50, lunch M$55; ⊙7am-8pm Mon-Sat, 8am-4pm Sun) Huge *jugos naturales* (freshly squeezed juices) and delicious quesadillas are a great way to start the day. This cheap eatery is close to the border.

Los Arcos SEAFOOD **$$**
(☎686-556-09-03; Calafia 454; dinner mains M$126-290; ⏰11am-10pm) Mexicali's most popular seafood restaurant (even among celebs – note Michael Douglas' pic at the entrance…). The *shrimp culichi* (shrimp in a creamy green chili sauce) is spectacular. Live music brightens the night on Thursday and Friday. Reservations recommended.

ℹ Information

Bancomer (cnr Azueta & Madero; ⏰8:30am-4pm Mon-Fri)

Hospital Hispano-Americano (☎686-552-23-00; Reforma 1000)

State Tourist Office (☎686-566-12-77; Blvd Juárez 1; ⏰8am-6pm Mon-Fri, 9am-1pm Sat) Patient, bilingual staff and plenty of information about regional attractions and events.

Tourist Assistance (☎078)

ℹ Getting There & Away

Mexican tourist permits are available at the main Calexico–Mexicali border crossing 24 hours a day. A second border complex east of downtown is open from 6am to 10pm.

AIR

Aeroméxico (☎686-555-70-47; www.aeromexico.com; Calle México 343) Aeroméxico flies to La Paz, Mexico City, Mazatlán and other mainland points.

Aeropuerto Internacional General Rodolfo Sánchez Taboada (☎686-552-23-17; www.aeropuertosgap.com.mx/es/mexicali.htm; Carretera Mesa de Andrade Km 23.5) The airport is 18km east of town.

BUS

Long-distance/mainland bus companies leave from the **Central de Autobuses** (☎686-557-24-15; Calz Independencia; ⏰24hr), near Calzada López Mateos, and Baja-bound buses leave from the **Terminal Turística** (☎686-552-51-00; Av Mexico 343; ⏰24hr), closer to the border. Autotransportes del Pacífico, Norte de Sonora and Elite serve mainland-Mexican destinations, while ABC serves the Baja Peninsula.

Greyhound (p856) has offices in Mexicali and directly across the border in Calexico. Several departures daily go from Mexicali to Los Angeles (one way US$42.50, round-trip US$78) and four to San Diego (one way US$29.50, round-trip US$55), as well as other destinations in the US.

CAR & MOTORCYCLE

Vehicle permits are available at the border. The main Calexico–Mexicali border crossing is open 24 hours, while the new crossing east of downtown (built to ease congestion) is open from 6am to 10pm.

ℹ Getting Around

Taxis to the airport cost M$175 to M$200, but may be shared. Agree on the price first.

Most city buses start from Avenida Reforma, just west of Calzada López Mateos; check the placard for the destination. Local fares are about M$10.

A taxi to the Centro Cívico-Comercial or Zona Hotelera from the border averages about M$70.

SOUTHERN BAJA

Parts of the state of Baja California Sur (southern Baja) look like a Dr Seuss illustration: no plant more so than the funky *boojum* tree *(cirio)*, which looks like a giant inverted parsnip with some yellow fluff at the top. You can't help but smile. Cardón cacti, ocotillo, cholla and other desert marvels thrive in areas that sometimes don't receive any rain for a decade. Look out for crumbling missions, leafy date palms, coconuts and mangrove swamps as you meander southward.

BUSES FROM MEXICALI

DESTINATION	FARE (M$)	DURATION
Ensenada	315	4hr
Guadalajara	1594	36hr
Guerrero Negro	1275	15hr
La Paz	1859	26hr
Loreto	1805	20hr
Mazatlán	1175	24hr
Mexico City	1800	42hr
Tijuana	280	2¾hr

WORTH A TRIP

PARQUE NACIONAL SIERRA SAN PEDRO MÁRTIR

Bobcats, deer and bighorn sheep await visitors to Parque Nacional San Pedro Mártir, but its real claim to fame isn't what's on the ground but what's in the air: this park is one of only six places in the world where the almost-extinct California Condor is being reintroduced into the wild. At the time of writing around 30 of these majestic birds call this area home and several chicks have been hatched over the past few years, showing promise for a future recovery.

Even if one of the world's largest birds doesn't soar over your head, there are lots of other reasons to make the detour. Conifers scrape the sky, the air is pine scented and clean, and the tortuous drive passes through boulder-studded, ethereal landscapes that seem more Martian than something here on earth.

To reach the park, turn left at the sign at approximately Km 140 on the Transpeninsular, south of Colonet. A 100km paved road climbs to the east through an ever-changing desert landscape, affording satisfying vistas all along the way. Camping is possible (no toilets, bring water) in designated areas, but there are no other facilities.

Observatorio Astronómico Nacional (646-174-45-80; www.astrossp.unam.mx; 10am-1pm) is the country's national observatory, from where it's possible to observe both the Pacific Ocean and the Sea of Cortez. On clear days you can see all the way to the Mexican mainland.

The 25,000-sq-km **Reserva de la Biosfera El Vizcaíno** is one of Latin America's largest single protected areas. It sprawls from the Península Vizcaíno across to the Sea of Cortez and includes the major gray-whale calving areas of Laguna San Ignacio and Laguna Ojo de Liebre, and the Sierra de San Francisco with its stunning pre-Hispanic rock art – more than 60 sites, many of which only archaeologists can view.

The southernmost part of the peninsula contains the cosmopolitan city of La Paz, small seaside towns and villages, and the popular resorts of San José del Cabo and Cabo San Lucas, aka 'Los Cabos.' After the quiet isolation of the state's north, Los Cabos will either be a jarring shock or a welcome relief.

Remember that Baja California Sur state uses Mountain Time, so it is an hour ahead of Pacific time used in northern Baja (Baja California state).

Guerrero Negro

615 / POP 13,000

After the crowds and clamor of the touristy border towns, unassuming Guerrero Negro – a town that sprang up to service the lone salt factory – is a welcome relief. People actually speak Spanish here and nobody's barking out invitations to strip clubs. Though the main tourist draw is the proximity to the seasonal migrations of gray whales, there's also excellent bird-watching in the shallow marshes, and the salt factory's odd white crystalline plains are quite beautiful.

Activities

Guerrero Negro can surprise you. If whales aren't around, try cave-painting viewing in the Sierra de San Francisco, bird-watching or touring the **salt factory**. On the east side of the inlet is a mini-Sahara of 3m to 6m sand dunes made of powdery white sand.

Bird-Watching

Head to the **Old Pier** if you're a bird-watcher, as there is a pleasant 11km drive through prime territory for ducks, coots, eagles, curlews, terns, herons and other birds.

Whale-Watching

During whale-watching season agencies arrange trips on the shallow waters of **Laguna Ojo de Liebre**, where visitors are virtually guaranteed a view of whales in their natural habitat.

Malarrimo Eco Tours WILDLIFE-WATCHING
(615-157-01-00; www.malarrimo.com; Blvd Zapata s/n; adult/child M$50/40) Located at the beginning of the strip, Malarrimo offers four-hour tours.

Other Activities

Salt Factory TOUR
(1-2hr tour M$200 per person) Tours of the salt factory can be arranged via any hotel or tour agency in Guerrero Negro.

Sleeping

The whale-watching season can strain local accommodations; reservations are advisable from January through March.

Hotel Malarrimo MOTEL $

(615-157-01-00; www.malarrimo.com; Blvd Zapata 42; d M$450, campsites M$150, RV sites M$130-200;) Hot, strong showers and a lot more ambience than the other options in town. Whale headboards and a general whale theme make it impossible to forget why you've come here. There is also a small gift shop and excellent restaurant, plus whale-watching tours can be arranged. Campsites and RV hookups available.

Los Caracoles HOTEL $$

(615-157-10-88; www.hotelloscaracoles.com.mx; Calz de la República s/n; r M$590;) This attractive sand-colored hotel blends well with its desert surroundings, as do the modern rooms and, come to that, the bathrooms – all are decorated in tones of yellow and gold. There's a souvenir shop and several computer terminals for the use of guests.

Cowboy Hotel HOTEL $$

(615-157-27-65; hotelcowboy@hotmail.com; Blvd Zapata; s/d/tr M$400/500/600;) On the south side of Zapata, this is one of the latest hotels in town. The rooms (and bathrooms) are more spacious than most, and have shiny tiled floors. There's also a decent restaurant, TVs and off-street parking.

Eating

Caprichos Coffee House CAFE $

(615-157-14-00; Blvd Zapata; coffee M$28-45; 7am-11pm;) Lattes, pies, pastries and occasional impromptu salsa performances make this small cafe well worth a stop.

Santo Remedio MEXICAN $$

(615-157-29-09; www.elsantoremedio.com.mx; Carballo Félix; mains M$120-160; 8am-10pm) One of the fancier Guerrero Negro options, with soft lighting, folk art, ocher-washed walls and a variety of meat and seafood dishes, ranging from T-bone steak to Galician-style octopus.

Information

Nearly all hotels, restaurants and other services are along Blvd Zapata, including an ATM at Banamex.

Clínica Hospital IMSS (615-157-03-33; Blvd Zapata) Guerrero Negro's main medical facility.

Getting There & Away

Guerrero Negro's tiny airport is 2km north of the state border, west of the Transpeninsular.

Aéreo Calafia (615-157-29-99; www.aereocalafia.com.mx; Blvd Zapata; 8am-7pm Mon-Fri, to 4pm Sat) Runs flights to Hermosillo and Isla Cedros, and offers charters.

Aereoservicio Guerrero (624-144-44-43; www.aereoservicioguerrero.com.mx; Blvd Zapata; 7am-7pm Mon-Sat) Runs flights to Hermosillo, Guaymas, Isla Cedros and Ensenada, plus charters.

Bus Station (Blvd Marcello Rubio; 24hr) Served by ABC (www.abc.com.mx) and Autotransportes Águila, one of its subsidiaries.

San Ignacio

615 / POP 720

With its lush, leafy date palms and pretty tranquil lagoon, sleepy San Ignacio is a welcome oasis after the endless Desierto de Vizcaíno. Jesuits located the **Misión San Ignacio de Kadakaamán** here, but Dominicans supervised construction of the striking church (finished in 1786) that still dominates the picturesque, laurel-shaded plaza. With lava-block walls nearly 1.2m thick, and surrounded by bougainvillea, this is one of Baja's most beautiful churches. A small self-guided **museum** (8am-5pm Mon-Fri) FREE offers a glimpse of the area's natural history

BUSES FROM GUERRERO NEGRO

DESTINATION	FARE (M$)	DURATION
Ensenada	920	10hr
La Paz	1275	11hr
Loreto	685	5-6hr
Mulegé	418	4hr
Tijuana	1005	12hr
Mexicali	1275	15hr

CALIFORNIA GRAY WHALES

The migration of gray whales from Siberian and Alaskan waters to the lagoons of Baja is an amazing animal event. In calving grounds of Laguna Ojo de Liebre and Laguna San Ignacio, 700kg calves will draw their first breaths and begin learning the lessons of the sea from their ever-watchful mothers. The season is long but varies due to the fact that some whales arrive early in the Pacific lagoons, while others take weeks or months to round Land's End and find their favorite bays in the Sea of Cortez.

Peak months to see mothers and calves in the lagoons are February to early April, but the official whale-watching season begins December 15 and lasts until April 15.

If you've got *ballena* (whale) fever, one of these destinations will provide a cure:

- Laguna Ojo de Liebre (Scammon's Lagoon; p712)
- Laguna San Ignacio
- Puerto López Mateos (p721)
- Puerto San Carlos (p721)

and also re-creates the famous cave drawings found in the Sierra de San Francisco.

Most services are around the plaza, including public phones, but there is no bank.

Sleeping & Eating

San Ignacio has excellent accommodations tucked away beneath its swaying palms.

The modest cafe-restaurants and kiosks around the plaza are your best best for a quick snack. If you need some energy for the road, dates from the palms cost M$10 to M$30 per bag.

★Ignacio Springs B&B $$
(615-154-03-33; www.ignaciosprings.com; San Ignacio; d from US$87; P ❄) This Canadian-owned B&B comprises eight yurts and three *cabañas*. Idyllically situated fronting the lagoon, the decor ranges from conventional US-style to Aztec ethnic, with brightly colored rugs and ceramics. Breakfast includes homemade breads, preserves and (even) sausages. Kayaks available.

Casa Lereé B&B $$
(615-154-01-58; www.casaleree.com; Morelos 20; r M$520-600; ❄ wi-fi) Part guesthouse, part museum and part bookstore, this beautiful old building sits around a verdant garden with magnificent trees, including a soaring (and shady) *ficus indica*. Rooms are small and simply decorated. The US owner is a wealth of information about the area.

★Tootsie's Bar & Grill INTERNATIONAL $$
(Francisco y Madera 11; mains US$8-13; 1-9pm Tue-Sun, 3-9pm Mon;) Just not what you expect to find tucked away on a back street near the plaza. The Canadian owner-cum-chef is inventive and accomplished. Ask for her recommendations, which could be anything from pasta with homemade pesto to Indian dhal with steaming hot chapatis. An organic herb (and soon to be veg) garden contributes to the fresh-from-the-farm flavors.

Getting There & Away

Bus Station (615-154-04-68) The bus station is near the San Lino junction outside of town. Buses pick up passengers here, arriving about every four hours from 5am to 11pm, both north- and southbound to locations such as Tijuana (M$1125), Mexicali (M$1410), La Paz (M$950) and Cabo San Lucas (M$1130).

Around San Ignacio

Sierra de San Francisco

The sheer quantity of beautiful petroglyphs in this region is impressive, and the ocher, red, black and white paintings remain shrouded in mystery. In recognition of its cultural importance, the Sierra de San Francisco has been declared a Unesco World Heritage site. It is also part of the **Reserva de la Biosfera El Vizcaíno**.

Cueva del Ratón, a cave named for an image of what inhabitants once thought was a rat (or mouse) but is more likely a deer, is the most easily accessible site. Drivers can get there on their own after registering and paying the park entry (M$42) and guide fee (M$80 for two people) at the office of the **Instituto Nacional de Antropología e**

Historia (INAH; ☎615-154-02-22; ⏲8am-5pm Mon-Sat Apr-Oct, daily Nov-Mar), adjacent to the Misión San Ignacio on the plaza in San Ignacio. They can then pick up their guide in the pueblo closest to the paintings. Bringing a camera costs M$45 per day. INAH fees for guides for other trips start at M$200 per day, and each pack animal adds M$150. These are INAH fees only, and guides themselves charge additional (varying) fees.

Those with time should visit the dramatic and well-preserved **Cañón San Pablo**. At **Cueva Pintada**, Cochimí painters decorated 150m of high rock overhangs with vivid red-and-black representations of human figures, bighorn sheep, pumas and deer, as well as more abstract designs. **Cueva de las Flechas**, across Cañón San Pablo, has similar paintings.

The beautiful mule-back descent of Cañón San Pablo requires at least two days, preferably three, and is best done through a tour operator. **Ecoturismo Kuyimá** (☎615-154-00-70; www.kuyima.com; Morelos 23; ⏲9am-3pm Mon-Sat), a cooperative based at the east end of the plaza in San Ignacio, can arrange three-day trips for US$493 per person (four-person minimum). Longer tours also available.

Laguna San Ignacio

Along with Laguna Ojo de Liebre and Bahía Magdalena, Laguna San Ignacio is one of the Pacific coast's major winter whale-watching sites. Plans by Mitsubishi to turn the shores into an industrial site have been thwarted by campaigners and, in 2012, the Mexican government granted an unprecedented level of protection to 199,040 acres of surrounding land. Three-hour whale-watching excursions cost around M$495 per person. Contact Ecoturismo Kuyimá.

Santa Rosalía

☎615 / POP 12,000

Southbound travelers will welcome their first sight of the Sea of Cortez after crossing the Desierto de Vizcaíno. Though the town was devastated by flooding in 2009's Hurricane Jimena, it has repaired and rebounded. Brightly painted clapboard-sided houses, the Iglesia Santa Bárbara, the port, the *malecón* (seaside promenade) and the mining musuem are prime attractions, although they are rivalled by the black-sand beaches, lazy pelicans and great views from the surrounding hills.

The town is poised to become a prosperous mining center once again, with the reopening of the historic El Boleo copper and cobalt opencast mine in 2013 adding around 3800 jobs to the local economy.

OFF THE BEATEN TRACK

MISIÓN SAN BORJA

This well-restored mission is between Rosarito and Bahía de los Ángeles in pristine, spectacular *boojum*-tree-and-cardón desert. The drive alone (though bumpy) makes it worth the trip. A family descended from the original preconquest inhabitants is restoring it by hand and will proudly show you the mission, a freshwater spring, a secret tunnel (now walled up, shucks!) and the old Jesuit ruins. Heading east from Hwy 1, turn right about 45km after leaving the highway.

Sights

Central Santa Rosalía is a cluster of densely packed houses, restaurants, inns and stores. Plaza Benito Juárez, four blocks west of the highway, is the town center.

Museo el Boleo MUSEUM
(☎615-152-29-99; Cousteau 1; admission M$20; ⏲8am-3pm Mon-Fri, 9am-1pm Sat) Built in 1885 by the French to house the offices of the Boleo Company, this mining museum watches over town and the copperworks from its perch on the hill near the Hotel Francés. It's surrounded by cool abandoned locomotives and other pieces of machinery.

Iglesia Santa Bárbara CHURCH
Designed and erected for Paris' 1889 World's Fair, then disassembled and stored in Brussels for shipping to West Africa, Gustave Eiffel's (yes, of Eiffel Tower fame) prefabricated Iglesia Santa Bárbara was, instead, shipped here when a Boleo Company director signed for its delivery to the town in 1895.

Sleeping

Santa Rosalía has a handful of well-priced accommodations.

Hotel Francés HISTORIC HOTEL $$
(☎615-152-20-52; Av Cousteau 15; r M$830; P ⊗ ⊜ ⊠) Overlooking the Sea of Cortez and rusting hulks of mine machinery, the

Hotel Francés is charming and historic. Built in 1886 and originally the dormitory for the 'working girls' of a brothel near the mine, the hotel features beautiful rooms with high ceilings, cloth-covered walls and charming stained-wood details.

Hotel El Morro HOTEL **$$**
(☎615-152-04-14; www.santarosaliaelmorro.com; r from M$480; P❄📶☒) Perched on a cliff 1.5km south of town, the friendly El Morro feels a bit more like it's in Greece than Baja. The view of the Sea of Cortez is enough reason to stay here, but rooms are also spotless, and off-street parking makes for a convenient stay.

Eating

For cheap eats hit one of the taco stands along Avenida Obregón. Most charge M$10 for a tasty fish taco.

Panadería El Boleo BAKERY **$**
(☎615-152-03-10; Av Obregón 30; breads M$5-20; ⏲8am-9pm Mon-Sat, 9am-2pm Sun) Since 1901, this has been an obligatory stop for those in search of good French bread (a rarity in Baja).

El Muelle MEXICAN **$$**
(☎615-152-09-31; cnr Av Constitución & Calle Plaza; mains M$70-135; ⏲8am-11pm) Easy to find in the center of town, the walls here sport everything that is, well, sporty, including cricket bats, ice skates, skis, golf clubs and baseball bats. The menu is less surprising, specializing in sound Mexican fare. Push the boat out with Veracruz-style fish (M$135) and an ice-cold Corona.

Playas Negras MEXICAN, SEAFOOD **$$**
(☎615-152-06-85; Carretera Sur Km 1; mains M$85-135; ⏲8am-11pm; 📶) South of downtown, with a gorgeous view and a funky abalone-shell map of Baja, this waterfront restaurant serves sumptuous seafood, as well as steak, chicken and pizza.

Information

Cafe Internet PC Vision (☎615-152-28-75; cnr Calles 6 & Obregón; per hr M$20; ⏲10am-10pm) Internet access.

Getting There & Away

BOAT

The passenger/auto ferry *Santa Rosalía* sails to Guaymas at 9am Tuesday, Wednesday, Friday and Saturday, and 8pm on Sunday, arriving 10 hours later. Double check in advance as timings may change.

The ticket office is at the **ferry terminal** (☎615-152-12-46; www.ferrysantarosalia.com; ⏲9am-1pm & 3-6pm Mon-Sat, 9am-1pm & 3-8pm Sun) on the highway. Passenger fares are around M$840 (children's tickets are half price). Vehicle rates vary with vehicle length.

BUS

Bus Terminal (☎615-152-14-08; ⏲24hr) Found just south of the entrance to town, in the same building as the ferry terminal.

Mulegé

☎615 / POP 3300

The palm- and mangrove-lined Río Mulegé, with its delta, birds, wildlife and snorkeling and diving opportunities, makes Mulegé a great stop for the outdoorsy or those with kids. Set down in a narrow *arroyo*, Mulegé is prone to flooding in major storms – it was pummeled by hurricanes in 2006, 2009 and 2012. The 18th-century mission and town square give the place a quiet charm that is fast disappearing in other parts of Baja.

BUSES FROM SANTA ROSALÍA

DESTINATION	FARE (M$)	DURATION
Ensenada	1125	13hr
Guerrero Negro	320	3hr
La Paz	815	8hr
Loreto	325	3hr
Mexicali	1560	16hr
Mulegé	120	1hr
San Ignacio	135	1hr
San José del Cabo	1055	12hr
Tijuana	1225	14hr

Sights

Misión Santa Rosalía de Mulegé MISSION

Come to the hilltop Misión Santa Rosalía de Mulegé (founded in 1705, completed in 1766 and abandoned in 1828) for great photos of the site and river valley.

Museo Mulegé MUSEUM

(Barrio Canenea; adult/child under 12yr M$10/free; 9am-2pm Mon-Sat;) The former territorial prison was famed for allowing prisoners to roam free in town during the day. Now the Museo Mulegé, its eclectic collection ranges from fairly mundane prison artifacts to a section of a rocket that plummeted from the sky in the year 2000! Note the blackened cell where a prisoner apparently set fire to himself after hearing his wife was having an affair.

Activities

Diving

Mulegé's best diving spots can be found around the Santa Inés Islands (north of town) and just north of Punta Concepción (south of town).

Dive Mulege DIVING

(615-153-05-00; www.divemulege.com; Moctezuma 75; tank dives from US$100, snorkeling US$55; 8:30am-6pm, dives 24hr;) Offers all levels of diving instruction and other outdoor sports. The tank dives include a captain, dive master, equipment, snacks and drinks.

Kayaking

The beautiful river, the estuary delta and the southern beaches make Mulegé a prime spot for kayaking.

NOLS Mexico KAYAKING

(in the US 307-332-5300, in the US toll-free 800-710-6657; www.nols.edu/courses/locations/mexico/) Runs sea-kayaking, sailing and backpacking courses, and trips out of its sustainable, ecofriendly facility on Coyote Bay, south of Mulegé.

Sleeping

★ **Hotel Las Casitas** HOTEL $

(615-153-00-19; javieraguiarz51@hotmail.com; Madero 50; s/d/tr M$375/425/525;) Perhaps inspired by its beautiful courtyard, fountains, statues and shady garden of tropical plants, beloved Mexican poet Alán Gorosave once inhabited this hotel. The restaurant serves excellent food and has an open-fire grill. The rooms are simple but aesthetically decorated with traditional fabrics and artwork. Owner Javier is a hospitable host.

Hotel Hacienda HISTORIC HOTEL $

(615-153-00-21; www.hotelhaciendamulege.com; Madero 3; r M$400;) The oldest hotel in town, Hacienda has a handsome blue and yellow colonial-style facade. Plain, yet sizable rooms (in need of a little TLC) surround a large courtyard with mature fruit trees and a pool.

Hotel Serenidad HOTEL $$

(615-153-05-30; www.serenidad.com; Mulegé; d M$780, cabañas M$1560;) Dating back to the 1960s, this hotel is a local institution. Plenty of famous folk have flown in here (it has its own 4000-ft paved airstrip!), including John Wayne. The rambling property has carafe-fulls of character, with a vast restaurant, rustic double rooms and small *cabañas*. There's a pig roast every Saturday with live music.

Eating & Drinking

The sidewalks are rolled up pretty early in Mulegé, so dine earlier than usual.

Scott's El Candil BAR $

(Zaragoza s/n; snacks M$50-100; noon-10pm Mon-Sat;) Within an attractive brick building featuring arched windows, this bar looks out onto Zaragoza and back into an open courtyard and large aviary. Snacks are served, including chips with beans and guacamole. True to its sports-bar core, Scott's is open Sundays during the US football season.

DON'T MISS

BEST CLAMS IN BAJA...

Tiny San Quintín is the pismo clam capital, and these mouthwatering morsels are well worth stopping for. Look for 'Almeja Ahumada' signs as you drive southwards and, if time and itinerary permits, stop at one of the roadside stalls for a fire-roasted plate of clams. Restaurant **La Ballena** (with the whale skeleton decorating the frontage) is one of the best. If you're really a do-it-yourselfer, sharpen your clam rake, get a fishing license (available online at www.bestbajafishing.org) and stay a while.

Doney Mely's MEXICAN $$
(615-153-00-95; Moctezuma s/n; mains M$90-125, set menu M$285; 7:30am-10pm Wed-Mon;) A colorfully decorated restaurant with a special weekend menu for two that includes a gut-busting choice of local favorites like *chile rellenos* and *enchiladas verdes*. Breakfasts come plumply recommended as well.

Los Equipales INTERNATIONAL $$$
(615-153-03-30; Moctezuma s/n; mains M$195-285; 8am-10pm) Just west of Zaragoza, this restaurant and bar has gargantuan meals and breezy balcony seating that's perfect for an evening margarita with friends. Lobster salad, T-bone steak and pork ribs are a sampling of the surf-and-turf fare.

Shopping

La Tienda SPORTS
(Martínez s/n; 9am-1pm & 4-6pm Mon-Sat) Sells fishing and diving gear, plus great T-shirts, caps, sandals, local jewelry and books (in English) on the region.

Getting There & Away

Bus Terminal (Transpeninsular Km 132; 8am-11pm) Inconveniently located north of town near the large entry arch. ABC/Águila northbound buses to Santa Rosalía (M$120, one hour) and Tijuana (M$1330, 14 hours) stop six times daily. Southbound buses pass to destinations including Loreto (M$225, two hours) and La Paz (M$815, six hours) five times daily.

Around Mulegé

Cañón La Trinidad

Trinity Canyon is great for bird-watchers, with the chance to see vermilion flycatchers, gila woodpeckers and a host of raptors and buteos. The narrow, sherbet-colored canyon walls and shimmering pools of water are stunning, as are the pre-Hispanic cave paintings. Rendered in shades of ocher and rust, the paintings feature shamans, manta rays, whales and the famous Trinity Deer, leaping gracefully from the walls of the cave as arrows pass harmlessly over its head. You're not allowed to enter by yourself, but Mulegé native Salvador Castro Drew of **Mulegé Tours** (615-161-49-85; mulegetours@hotmail.com; day excursions per person M$450) knows just about everything about the site you'd want to know, including how to avoid the two nasty beehives that 'guard' the paintings. He also does taxi runs to other area sites.

Beaches

As you wind your way south you'll pass some of Baja's most pristine *playas*. You can string up a hammock, pop the top on something frosty and watch the pelicans dive-bomb for fish. Some beaches have bars, restaurants or *cabañas*. **Bahía Concepción**, with its pelican colonies, funky rock formations and milky, blue-green water, remains a top stop for kayakers. **Posada Concepción** (646-151-4838; www.posadaconcepcion.net; Carretera Loreto-Mulegé Km 112; s/d US$24/35) is an inexpensive hotel and restaurant here. **Playa Escondido** (Km 112), **Playa Santispac** (Km 113.5) and **Playa Perla** (Km 91) are just a few of the possible stops along the Transpeninsular on the way. Be extremely cautious about weather alerts – the glassy water here and in Loreto can quickly become dangerous during storms.

Loreto

613 / POP 17,000

Loreto has a lot going for it. It's a very pretty small town with an excellent choice of hotels and restaurants, and a water-sports paradise. It's also home to the magnificent Parque Nacional Bahía de Loreto, where the shoreline, ocean and offshore islands are protected from pollution and uncontrolled fishing.

The Loreto area is also considered by anthropologists to be the oldest human settlement on the Baja Peninsula. Indigenous cultures thrived here due to plentiful water and food. In 1697 Jesuit Juan María Salvatierra established the peninsula's first permanent mission at this modest port some 135km south of Mulegé.

Most hotels and services are near the landmark mission church on Salvatierra, while the attractive *malecón* is ideal for evening strolls.

Sights & Activities

Parque Nacional Bahía de Loreto PARK
This park makes Loreto a world-class destination for all types of outdoor activities. A number of outfitters offer everything from kayaking and diving along the reefs around Islas del Carmen and Coronado to horse-

back riding, hiking and mountain biking in the Sierra de la Giganta. Pay the M$25 to M$50 per-person entrance fee at the park's **office** (613-135-14-29; 8:30am-2pm Mon-Fri, 9am-1pm Sat) in the marina. Staff can advise on water activities.

★ Misión Nuestra Señora de Loreto MISSION

Dating from 1697, this was the first permanent mission in the Californias and was the base for the expansion of Jesuit missions up and down the Baja Peninsula. Alongside the church, the **Museo de las Misiones** (613-135-04-41; Salvatierra 16; admission M$37; 9am-1pm & 1:45-6pm Tue-Sun) chronicles the settlement of Baja California.

Eco Tours WATER SPORTS

(613-135-06-80; www.toursloreto.com; Madero s/n; diving/snorkeling from US$100/65) Loreto is awash with companies offering outdoor sports. This recommended eco-aware place covers a wide range of activities, including diving and snorkeling.

Sleeping

Most of Loreto's accommodations are on or near the *malecón*.

Hotel Posada San Martín HOTEL $

(613-135-11-07; Juárez 4; r with/without kitchenette M$450/350;) Perfectly located a few steps from the plaza, this hotel's large rooms (some with cable TV and small kitchenettes) offer good value despite things looking slightly threadbare. There's a narrow central courtyard for guests.

★ Posada del Cortes BOUTIQUE HOTEL $$

(613-135-02-58; www.posadadelcortes.com; Callejon Pipila 4; r US$60-80;) This elegant small hotel exudes a chic atmosphere with ocher-and-cream paintwork, forest-green tilework, dark-wood furniture and lashings of white linen. There's a small terrace with wrought-iron furniture and a trickling fountain. Rooms include coffeemakers.

La Damiana Inn B&B $$

(613-135-03-56; www.ladamianainn.com; Madero 8; d with breakfast US$60-77;) This historical posada has spacious, individually furnished rooms with decor ranging from brightly colored Baja fabrics, ceramics and artwork to mellow earth tones and Native American pieces. There's a communal kitchen and pretty garden with fruit trees.

Posada de las Flores LUXURY HOTEL $$$

(613-135-11-62; www.posadadelasflores.com; Plaza Cívica; r incl breakfast US$150;) Sitting majestically on the main plaza in town, the interior has a palatial feel due to its stone columns and arches, trickling fountains and an earth-color palette. Rooms are surprisingly small and dark, with curious textured paintwork. Not to worry, the stunning public

ON A MISSION FROM GOD

Baja's missions have a dubious history – built by Jesuits and Dominicans intent on bringing salvation, they instead brought death through introduced European diseases. Many missions were abandoned as populations dropped below sustainable levels. Today however, these beautiful buildings, whether in use or out in the middle of nowhere, make for great photos and fun day trips, and they're an undeniable part of Baja's checkered past. You should not need a 4WD to visit any of those listed here, though the roads can be impressively bad (or impassable) at times.

Misión Nuestra Señora de Loreto The oldest mission, an impressive monument still in use today.

Misión San Borja (p715) Out in the middle of nowhere but well worth the drive. Its treasures include a hot spring and a secret tunnel (now walled up). José Gerardo, a descendant of the original preconquest inhabitants, will show you around.

Misión San Francisco Javier de Viggé-Biaundó (p720) Remote and beautifully preserved; it feels like stepping back in time. The drive here offers awesome vistas and even some cave paintings along the way.

Misión Santa Rosalía de Mulegé (p717) Extremely photogenic. Don't miss the view from behind looking out over the palm-edged river.

Resources for further reading include *Las Misiones Antiguas*, by Edward W Vernon, and www.vivabaja.com/bajamissions; both feature beautiful photos.

spaces extend to a rooftop pool, bar and terrace that has views stretching to the mission.

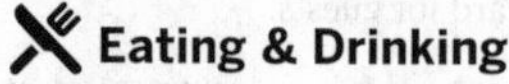

Eating & Drinking

Enjoy the regional standards: excellent seafood with plenty of tasty lime and cilantro, potent margaritas and fruity *aguas frescas* (ice drinks).

Café Olé CAFE, MEXICAN $
(☎613-135-04-96; Madero 14; mains M$35-70; ⏲7am-9:45pm Mon-Sat, to 1pm Sun) This inexpensive cafe has good, basic fare, including great Mexican breakfasts.

Pan Que Pan MEXICAN, ITALIAN $$
(Hidalgo s/n; mains M$50-120; ⏲ 8am-6pm Tue-Sat, to 3pm Sun) Friendly bistro-style restaurant with alfresco dining and a healthy menu of salads, pizza and homemade pasta. Smaller appetites are catered to with half portions available. It doubles as an artisanal bakery.

1697 Restaurant Pub MEXICAN, ITALIAN $$
(Davies 18; mains M$99-160; ⏲6-10pm Tue-Sun) Mexican-Irish-owned (ask how they met, now there's a story!), this pub has cuisine that is fittingly diverse, ranging from creamy pastas to fillet steak and chicken fajitas. Its decor and terrace under the stars make it a good choice for a romantic dinner. Craft beers are also served.

Shopping

The pedestrian mall between Madero and Independencia is best for shopping.

El Caballo Blanco BOOKS
(Hidalgo 19; ⏲10am-5pm Mon-Sat) Probably the most comprehensive collection of books on Baja in the region, plus maps, art materials, pottery and a bottomless coffee pot for browsers.

Silver Desert SILVER
(☎613-135-06-84; Salvatierra 36; ⏲9am-2pm & 3-8pm Mon-Sat, 9am-2pm Sun) Sells good-quality Taxco sterling-silver jewelry. There's a second outlet at Magdalena de Kino 4.

Information

Municipal Department of Tourism (☎613-135-04-11; Plaza Cívica; ⏲8am-3pm Mon-Fri) Has a good selection of brochures.

Getting There & Away

Aeropuerto Internacional de Loreto (☎613-135-04-99; Carretera Transpeninsular Km 7) Served by several airlines, including Aéreo Calafia and Aereoservicio Guerrero.

Bus Station (⏲24hr) Near the convergence of Salvatierra, Paseo de Ugarte and Paseo Tamaral, a 15-minute walk from the town center.

Getting Around

Taxis from the airport, 4km south of Loreto, cost M$160. Groups start at M$70 per person.

Around Loreto

Whale-watching tours are the main tourist draw between Loreto and La Paz, but the wonderful **Misión San Francisco Javier de Viggé-Biaundó** (and the drive to get there) is well worth a daytime detour. The windy road passes minor cliff paintings and some beautiful *arroyos* (streams) before arriving at the mission. Be sure to wander to the back garden to see the 300-year-old olive tree with rope-like bark that looks like something out of a Tolkien fantasy. The mission itself is almost unchanged from its look of three centuries ago. Head south on the Transpeninsular and look for the sign to the right shortly after you leave Loreto.

BUSES FROM LORETO

DESTINATION	FARE (M$)	DURATION
Guerrero Negro	685	6hr
La Paz	590	5hr
Mexicali	1805	20hr
San José del Cabo	840	8hr
Santa Rosalía	325	3hr
Tijuana	1600	18hr

Ciudad Constitución

613 / POP 43,000

Landlocked, and primarily a farming and industrial city, Ciudad Constitución offers little for tourists other than hotels for whale-watching day trips. Transportation to the port cities of López Mateos and San Carlos is infrequent – it's far better to have your own set of wheels.

Sleeping & Eating

Ciudad Constitución's lodgings are limited.

Hotel Conchita HOTEL $
(613-132-02-66; Olachea 180; s/d M$300/340;) Mustard-colored block with clean, if drab, large rooms. Privacy glass obscures any possible views.

Posadas del Ryal MOTEL $$
(613-132-48-00; Victoria s/n; s/d/ste M$410/470/650;) This two-story motel has rooms, decorated in appropriate desert-colored hues, set around a palm-filled courtyard. Bathrooms are small, unless you opt for the spacious 'La Mexicana suite,' which also sports a small terrace.

Asadero 'Tribi' MEXICAN $$
(613-132-73-53; Olachea btwn Madero & Pino Suárez; mains M$95-150; 8am-midnight Mon-Sat) Surround yourself in rustic brick-and-wood decor and enjoy specials such as barbecued ribs, T-bone steak and meat or fish tacos – it's the best restaurant in town.

Getting There & Away

Bus Terminal (613-132-03-76; cnr Juárez & Pino Suárez; 24hr) There are two daily departures for Puerto López Mateos (M$97, 1pm and 8:15pm) and Puerto San Carlos (M$85, 11am and 6pm). Taxis, just outside the station, charge M$800 for a round-trip ride to Puerto López Mateos or Puerto San Carlos.

Puerto López Mateos

613 / POP 2200

Located 58km northwest of Ciudad Constitución, shielded by the offshore barrier of Isla Magdalena, Puerto López Mateos is one of Baja's best whale-watching sites. During the season, the narrow waterway that passes by town becomes a veritable *ballena* cruising strip. Curva del Diablo (Devil's Bend), 27km south of town, is reported to be the best viewing spot. Three-hour *panga* (skiff) excursions from Puerto López Mateos (M$700 per hour for six to eight people, from 7am to 6pm in season) are easy to arrange.

Free camping (bring water), with pit toilets only, is possible at tidy **Playa Boca de la Soledad**, which is near Playa El Faro, 1.6km east of town (turn left at the water tower). Accommodation in Puerto López Mateos is basically left to various locals who hang out signs advertising rooms to rent during the whale-watching season. **Baja Mar** (613-131-51-96; breakfast M$55, mains M$100; 8am-8pm;) offers family-style Mexican dishes.

The bus service to Ciudad Constitución (M$97) leaves at 6am and 4pm from a small ticket office across from the school.

Puerto San Carlos

613 / POP 7000

Puerto San Carlos is a deep-water port and fishing town located 57km west of Ciudad Constitución on Bahía Magdalena. The town turns its attention to whales and travelers when the *ballenas* arrive in January to calve in the warm lagoon. From then until March pangueros take passengers for whale-watching excursions (about M$750 per hour for six people).

Activities

Eco Tours ADVENTURE TOURS
(613-136-00-76; www.villasmaryarena.com; Carretera Federal Km 57; whale-watching per person M$850, fishing trip per person M$3500; Oct-Jun) Whale-watching and fishing trips run from the eco-friendly Hotel Mar y Arena, which is located at the entrance to town.

Sleeping & Eating

Accommodations can be tough to find when the whales are in town.

★**Hotel Mar y Arena** CABAÑAS $$
(613-136-00-76; www.villasmaryarena.com; Carretera Federal Km 57; d US$80-90;) These *palapa*-style *cabañas* have chic earth-toned interiors and luxurious bathrooms. Solar power, desalinated water and a sensitivity to feng shui principles are all part of the local owner's eco-vision.

Hotel Alcatraz HOTEL $$
(613-136-00-17; www.hotelalcatraz.net; Calle San Jose del Cabo s/n; s/d M$450/550;) This rambling hotel has rooms set around a mature leafy courtyard, complete with sunbeds under the trees. Attractive pale-blue tilework

gives the decor a sunny seaside feel. There is a bar and restaurant (mains M$100 to M$250).

Mariscos Los Arcos SEAFOOD **$$**
(Puerto La Paz 170; mains M$80-145; ⏱10am-9pm) A simple place with tables set under the palm fronds, but the seafood dishes are the town's best. Go for one of the nine shrimp dishes.

Getting There & Away

Autotransportes Águila (☎613-136-04-53; Calle Puerto Morelos; ⏱7-7:30am, 11:30am-1:45pm & 6:30-7:30pm) Runs buses at 7:30am and 1:45pm daily to Ciudad Constitución (M$85) and La Paz (M$425), Cabo San Lucas (M$620) and San José del Cabo (M$650). This is the only public transportation from Puerto San Carlos.

La Paz

☎612 / POP 250,000

Cosmopolitan La Paz is a mix of laid-back, old-world beauty and chichi upscale trends. It's surprisingly international – you're as likely to hear French, Portuguese or Italian here as English or Spanish, and yet paradoxically it's the most 'Mexican' city in all of Baja. Its quirky history includes American occupation and even being temporarily declared its own republic. Hernán Cortés established Baja's first European outpost near La Paz, but permanent settlement waited until 1811.

The beachside *malecón*, superb restaurants and funky stores make it a great place to meander, and you can shop uninterrupted by touts' invitations. The city makes a good base for day trips to Cabo Pulmo and Todos Santos, and there's a lively, long-term expat community in and around the marina.

The port of Pichilingue receives ferries from the mainland ports of Topolobampo and Mazatlán, and the airport is served by several US carriers. La Paz' grid street pattern makes basic orientation relatively easy.

Sights

★**Espíritu Santo** ISLAND
A treasure of shallow azure inlets and sorbet-pink cliffs, Espíritu Santo is one of La Paz' gems. It's part of a Unesco World Heritage site comprising 244 Sea of Cortez islands and coastal areas, and a worthy day trip. (It's also part of Parque Nacional Archipiélago Espíritu Santo and Reserva de la Biosfera Islas del Golfo de California.) A number of operators run activities here, including kayaking and snorkeling.

Museo Regional de Antropología e Historia MUSEUM
(cnr 5 de Mayo & Altamirano; adult/child under 12yr M$30/free; ⏱9am-6pm; 👪) This is a large, well-organized museum chronicling the peninsula's history (in Spanish) from prehistory to the revolution of 1910 and its aftermath.

Unidad Cultural Profesor Jesús Castro Agúndez CULTURAL CENTER
(☎612-125-02-07; cnr Gómez Farías & Legaspi; ⏱Cultural Center 8am-2pm & 4-6pm Mon-Fri) The **Teatro de la Ciudad** (☎tel info 612-125-00-04; Altamirano; ⏱hours vary), part of this large cultural center, is the main performance venue in La Paz.

Athough the **Museo Comunitario de la Ballena** (Community Whale Museum; cnr Calles Navarro & Altamirano; ⏱9am-1pm Tue-Sat; 👪) FREE at the periphery of the grounds is small, it holds an impressive 25m-long blue whale skeleton.

Santuario de la Virgen de Guadalupe MONUMENT
(cnr 5 de Febrero & Aquiles Serdán; ⏱7am-6pm) The Santuario de la Virgen de Guadalupe is La Paz' largest religious monument. Its 12m-tall altar is grandiose.

Activities

Whale Shark Mexico WILDLIFE-WATCHING
(☎612-154-98-59; www.whalesharkmexico.com) From October to March you can help researchers study juvenile whale sharks, which congregate in the placid waters of La Paz Bay. Duties vary each trip: you can assist with tagging and even get a chance to name one. These researchers do not rent or provide any gear, and trips must be arranged in advance when the weather conditions are right. Price is currently M$975 per person, and the fees go directly toward the costs of radio tags and other research expenses.

Baja Paradise ADVENTURE SPORTS
(☎612-128-60-97; www.bajaparadiselapaz.com; Madero 23; 👪) Offers guided camping tours on Espíritu Santo, plus many other activities, including snorkeling with whale sharks. The owner is a professor in the local university's ecological tourism program and takes care to make the trips as 'green'

BAJA'S BEST BITES...

(...and we don't mean restaurant reviews.) Some of Baja's coolest creatures are well worth getting to know, but don't get too close – these critters are sporting nature's meanest defenses and an encounter could send you to hospital.

- **Black Widow Spider** This pea-sized black spider packs a potent (though rarely fatal) punch. Look for the crimson hourglass on the underside of the abdomen for positive ID.
- **Portuguese Man O' War** Also known as *agua mala* (bad water), these jellyfish are stunningly pretty, but their bright-blue tentacles can sting long after the animal is dead. Don't pick one up on the beach, and minimize risk when participating in water sports by wearing a full-body rash guard or wetsuit.
- **Scorpion** Glowing under UV light, Baja's scorpions sting, especially if stepped on. Shake your shoes in the morning, use netting at night and look before you sleep.
- **Stingrays** Painfully common in the shallows of many popular beaches, the stingray usually flicks its tail and stabs heels or ankles with a poisonous barb. Minimize risk at beaches by wearing surf booties.

Whether you think they're cool or creepy, these are creatures that will rarely cause you harm if they are left alone. For more information, track down a copy of Roger Tory Peterson's book *A Field Guide to Venomous Animals and Poisonous Plants*.

as possible. Hostel-type accommodation is also available.

Buceo Carey DIVING, SNORKELING
(☎612-128-40-48; www.buceocarey.com; cnr Topete & Legaspi; snorkeling US$85, diving US$125;) A family-run establishment that offers snorkeling, diving, whale-watching, trips to see a sea lion colony and other tours.

Mar y Aventuras KAYAKING
(☎612-122-70-39; www.kayakbaja.com; Topete 564; 8/9 days US$897/1350) Book an eight- or nine-day kayak expedition, or outfit your self-guided trip.

Courses

Buen Provecho COOKING
(☎612-122-64-09; www.buenprovecholapaz.com; Revolución 555; US$65-85; Tue, Thu & Sat) Courses in traditional Mexican cooking ranging from 4½ to six hours. Run by a French Canadian and her Mexican partner. English, French and Spanish spoken.

Se Habla...La Paz LANGUAGE COURSE
(☎612-122-77-63; http://sehablalapaz.com; Madero 540) All levels of Spanish classes, plus an introduction to the culture and cuisine of the country, and homestays arranged, if necessary. Walk-ins welcome, space permitting. Courses cost US$250 per week plus US$75 registration with a maximum of five students in a class.

Festivals & Events

Festivals and other seasonal events often take place at Plaza Constitución, between Revolución and Madero at Calle 5 de Mayo.

La Paz' pre-Lent **Carnaval** is among the country's best. In early May, *paceños* (people from La Paz) celebrate the **Fundación de la Ciudad** (Hernán Cortés' 1535 landing).

Sleeping

Accommodations in La Paz run the gamut from budget digs to swanky hotels. Midrange options are plentiful.

Baja Backpackers HOSTEL $
(info@bajabackpackers.com.mx; cnr Mutualismo & Bravo; 4-bed dm M$250, d without bathroom M$500;) Separate men's and women's dorms, plus a community kitchen, a sitting room, a seaview terrace, and complimentary coffee make this a good choice if you are peso-pinching. It's run by a friendly American-Mexican couple who can advise on all aspects of southern Baja – they also rent snorkeling equipment.

Hacienda Paraiso de La Paz B&B $$
(☎612-122-27-29; www.haciendaparaiso.com; de las Rosas 300; d incl breakfast with/without kitchenettes US$125/95; P) This stunning property, covering some 2500 sq meters, has rooms set among lush gardens and lofty coconut palms. Although a New Yorker, co-owner Richard's passion for Mexico is

La Paz

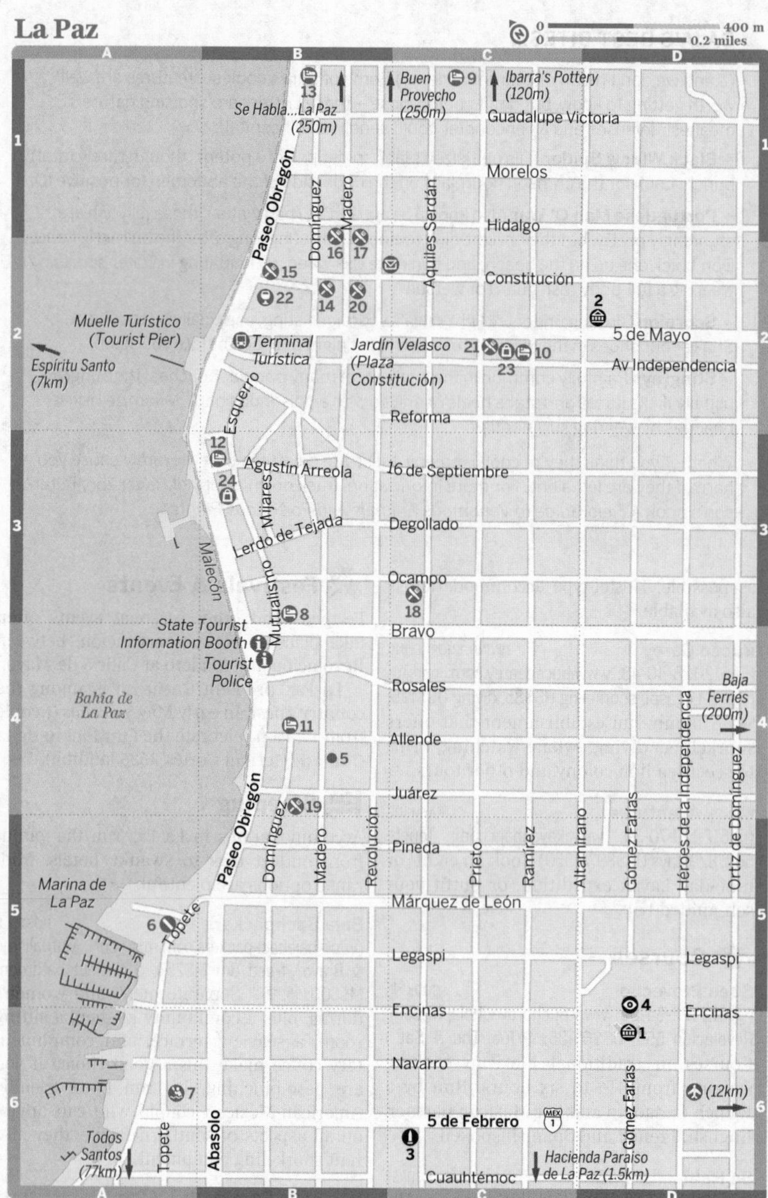

evident in the indigenous artwork, traditional carved furniture, *equipales* chairs and Mexican breakfasts. Facilities include a small gym, sports bar and infinity pool.

Hotel Mediterrane HOTEL **$$**
(612-125-11-95; Allende 36; r M$889-1299; P) Greek-inspired hotel with cool rooms, delicious cafe menu and a rooftop terrace with bay views. Go for the Mykonos

La Paz

room if you can – it has a private terrace and domed roof. Gay friendly.

Hotel Perla HOTEL **$$**
(☎612-122-07-77; www.hotelperlabaja.com; Paseo Obregón 1570; r incl breakfast M$1094; P⊖❄@☎) Pacific-blue fabrics, pine furniture, mosaic-tiled bathrooms and scenic seaview terraces make this family-friendly hotel a good central choice. There are also two Jacuzzis.

★**El Ángel Azul** B&B **$$$**
(☎612-125-51-30; Independencia 518; r incl breakfast US$100-120; P⊖❄☎) Possibly the loveliest of La Paz' lodging options, El Ángel Azul offers simply furnished, pale pastel-washed rooms, which surround a beautiful courtyard that is filled with palms, cacti, birdsong and bougainvillea. There is a colorfully cluttered bar and sitting room, and the multilingual Swiss owner is knowledgeable about all aspects of La Paz.

Casa Tuscany B&B **$$$**
(☎612-128-81-03; www.tuscanybaja.com; Bravo 110; d with breakfast from US$87; ⊖❄☎) Situated a seagull's swoop from the *malecón*, this picturesque B&B has homely rooms decorated with brightly colored paintwork, local rugs and traditional ceramics. Set around a tranquil central courtyard, the rooms vary in size; the most expansive, 'Romeo & Juliet,' has three terraces on several levels with sea views. Breakfast includes *aebleskiver* (Danish pancakes).

Posada de las Flores BOUTIQUE HOTEL **$$$**
(☎612-125-58-71; www.posadadelasflores.com; Paseo Obregón 440; r/ste incl breakfast US$180/290; P⊖❄@☎) Italian-run small hotel. Eight exquisitely decorated rooms and suites with small front terraces. Breakfast on the upper *terazza* offers stunning views of La Paz, as does the second terrace. Shame that there is no bar, so no sundowners.

Eating

La Paz' restaurant scene has become increasingly sophisticated – you'll find the top culinary choices mainly centered around Calles Domínguez and Madero, north of Calle 5 de Mayo. There's also an **organic market** (Madero s/n; ⊙9am-2.30pm Sat).

Tacos El Estadio TAQUERÍA **$**
(cnr Prieto & 5 de Mayo; seafood tacos M$15; ⊙8am-2pm) Join the line. This is where the locals come for their fish tacos. There are a few tables and chairs.

Bagel Shop BAGELS **$**
(Domínguez 291; bagels from M$30; ⊙7:30am-3pm) Owner Fabrizio learned the art of bagel making in the US, and he makes a steaming batch daily. Fillings range from classic lox and cream cheese to smoked marlin with German sausage. Check out the sidewalk tables facing a trendy trio of teashop, juice bar and organic-cum-crafts store.

★**Maria California** MEXICAN **$$**
(www.mariacaliforniarestaurant.com; Juárez 105; breakfast mains M$90-100; ⊙7:30am-2pm Mon-Sat) Great for breakfast with live music

TOP SPOTS FOR FANTASTIC FISH TACOS

Simple and versatile, the humble fish taco is Baja's comfort food. Done right they're magical. These spots are all worth seeking out for a taste of this sublimely delicious snack.

La Guerrense (Ensenada; p708) Good enough to win an international street food competition. Enough said.

El Caballero (Cabo Pulmo; p729) These come with a homemade salsa that's *picante* (spicy) without being smolderingly hot. Perfect after a long, invigorating snorkel.

Los Arcos (Playas de Rosarito; p705) Casual family-run place with guacamole, sour cream and *pico de gallo* (fresh chopped salsa).

Venado (Cabo San Lucas; p735) Flaky, moist morsels of fish on corn or flour. Shrimp tacos are just as good.

Tacos El Estadio (La Paz; p725) Superb seafood tacos and *sopa de mariscos* (seafood soup).

(even) and a fabulous atmosphere throughout the cozy cluttered dining rooms and terraces. Local artwork, photos and brilliant colored paintwork adorn the walls.

Buffalo BBQ STEAKHOUSE $$
(www.buffalolapaz.com; Madero 1145; M$140-160; 2-11pm) Under the mighty mounted buffalo head, eat a carnivorous feast that includes hamburgers, rib-eye steak and grills. Lightweights can opt for the fish of the day. Post dusk, head to the courtyard with its twinkling lights and homespun feel.

Los Tamarindos MEXICAN $$
(cnr Ocampo & Serdan; mains M$69-99; 8am-11pm; P) Right in the bustling center of town, this courtyard restaurant, named after the lofty tamarind trees, provides a romantic setting for dinner for two. Folkloric dances take place at weekends and the menu includes traditional classics like rabbit with *mole* and lobster enchiladas.

Bismarkcito MEXICAN, SEAFOOD $$
(cnr Obregón & Constitución; mains from M$150; 9am-10pm) This seafront restaurant, fronted by its own taco stand, is always packed with locals here for the superb seafood. Consider ordering the lobster chowder. TVs, exposed brick walls and jaunty blue-and-white table linen decorate the huge dining room. Service can be slow.

Las Tres Virgenes INTERNATIONAL $$$
(612-165-62-65; Madero 1130; M$140-185; 1-11pm) An elegant oasis of a restaurant where you can dine in an atmospheric courtyard surrounded by leafy trees and statues. The menu includes both traditional and innovative dishes like seafood risotto, roasted bone marrow, spicy sea snails and a classic Caesar salad made with suitable flourish at your table. Reservations recommended.

Drinking & Nightlife

The highest concentration of bars is between Calles 16 de Septiembre and Agustín Arreola, across from the *malecón*.

Harker Board BAR
(cnr Constitución & Paseo Obregón; 7am-2am;) Head upstairs to the terrace for sweeping views over the bay and a *cerveza*. The local Baja Brewery beer is on tap, and there are 17 more bottled varieties. Pizza also available. This great place doubles as a rental spot for paddle boards (MS$100 per hour).

Club Marlin BAR
(El Centenario; noon-10pm Tue-Sat, 10am-8pm Sun;) Located in El Centenario, around 5km north of the center, this US-owned hotel, bar and restaurant dates from the 1980s and has long served as the resident expat haunt. The views of the bay are sublime and the place (and patrons) have plenty of sunkissed warmth and character. Regular live music.

Shopping

Local stores that cater to tourists have plenty of junk but a smattering of good stuff.

Ibarra's Pottery CERAMICS
(www.ibarraspottery.com; Prieto 625; 9am-3pm Mon-Fri, to 2pm Sat) See potters at work at this ceramics workshop and store that dates back to 1958 – it is famed throughout Baja.

Antigua California CRAFTS
(Paseo Obregón 220; ⏲9:30am-8:30pm) Features a wide selection of crafts from throughout the country.

Allende Books BOOKS
(☎612-125-91-14; www.allendebooks.com; Av Independencia 518; ⏲10am-6pm Mon-Sat) English-language bookstore with a good selection of books on Baja California and mainland Mexico.

Information

The majority of banks (most with ATMs) and *casas de cambio* are on or around Calle 16 de Septiembre.

Hospital Salvatierra (☎612-178-05-01; Av Paseo de los Deportistas 5115; ⏲24hr) The largest hospital in southern Baja, located 4.6km southwest of the centre, via Calles 5 de Febrero and Forjadores de Sudcalifornia.

State Tourist Information Booth (☎612-122-59-39; cnr Paseo Obregón & Bravo; ⏲8am-10pm) Brochures and pamphlets in English.

Tourist Police (☎612-122-59-39, 078; ⏲8am-10pm) Small booth on Paseo Obregón; hours may vary.

Viva La Paz (www.vivalapaz.com) La Paz' official tourism site.

Getting There & Away

AIR

Aeroméxico (☎612-122-00-91; www.aeromexico.com; Paseo Obregón) Has flights every day but Sunday between La Paz and Los Angeles, and daily flights to Tijuana and mainland Mexican cities.

Aeropuerto General Manuel Márquez de León (☎612-124-63-36; www.aeropuertosgap.com.mx; Transpeninsular Km 9) About 9km southwest of the city, it is served by Aeroméxico, Aéreo Calafia and others. The airport has an **immigration office** (☎612-124-63-49; ⏲7am-11pm).

BOAT

Ferries to Mazatlán and Topolobampo leave the ferry terminal at Pichilingue, 23km north of La Paz. Baja Ferries has a **small office** (☎612-125-63-24) at the port and a **larger office** (☎612-123-66-00; www.bajaferries.com; Allende 1025; ⏲8am-5pm Mon-Fri, to 2pm Sat) in town.

Ferries to Mazatlán depart at 6pm Tuesday and Thursday and at 5pm Sunday, arriving 16 to 18 hours later; return ferries leave Mazatlán at 4pm Monday, Wednesday and Friday. Passenger fares in *salón* (numbered seats) are M$1078 per adult and M$539 per child; en-suite cabins with two beds are M$770 extra.

Topolobampo services depart at 2:30pm Monday to Friday and 11pm on Saturday. The return ferry from Topolobampo to La Paz leaves at 11pm Sunday to Friday, arriving in Pichilingue six to seven hours later. Passenger fares in *salón* are M$878 per adult and M$439 per child; cabins for up to four people cost M$770 extra.

Ensure that you arrive at the pier two hours before departure. Vehicle rates vary with vehicle length and destination.

Before shipping any vehicle to the mainland, officials require a vehicle permit. You can obtain one at **Banjército** (www.banjercito.com.mx; ⏲7am-3pm Mon, Wed & Fri-Sun, 7am-7pm Tue & Thu) at the ferry terminal, or from its vehicle permit modules in Mexicali or Tijuana.

There's an **immigration office** (☎612-122-04-29; Paseo Obregón; ⏲8am-8pm Mon-Fri, 9am-3pm Sat) near the center of town.

BUS

Terminal Turística (☎612-122-78-98; cnr malecón & Av Independencia) **ABC** (☎612-122-78-98; www.abc.com.mx) and **Autotransportes**

BUSES FROM LA PAZ

DESTINATION	FARE (M$)	DURATION
Cabo San Lucas	216	3hr
Ciudad Constitución	340	3hr
Ensenada	1815	22hr
Guerrero Negro	1275	11hr
Loreto	590	5hr
Mulegé	815	6hr
San Ignacio	950	9hr
San José del Cabo	250	3½hr
Tijuana	1940	24hr
Todos Santos	90	1½hr

FERRIES FROM LA PAZ

DESTINATION	VEHICLE	FARE (M$)
Mazatlán	car 5m or less/motorcycle/motorhome	2215/1875/15,000
Topolobampo	car 5m or less/motorcycle/motorhome	1082/812/7,700

Águila (612-122-78-98; www.autotransportesaguila.net) both leave from the Terminal Turística along the *malecón.* Autotransportes Águila also operates five daily buses to Playa Tecolote (M$24, 30 minutes) and six to Playa Pichilingue (M$20, 20 minutes) between 10am and 5pm.

Getting Around

Car-rental rates start around M$600 per day.

Budget (612-122-60-40; www.budget.com; cnr Paseo Obregón & Manuel Pineda) One of several agencies with locations both on the *malecón* and at the airport.

Around La Paz

On Península Pichilingue, the beaches nearest to La Paz are **Playa Palmira** (with the Hotel Palmira and a marina), **Playa Coromuel** and **Playa Caimancito** (both with bar-restaurants, toilets and *palapas*). **Playa Tesoro**, the next beach north, has a restaurant. Some 100m north of the ferry terminal is **Playa Pichilingue**, with camping, restaurants, bar, toilets and shade. **Playa Balandra** is a beautiful enclosed cove with shallow azure water, great for paddling toddlers. **Playa Tecolote** has plenty of spots where those with cars could camp, and launches leave from here for Espíritu Santo.

La Ventana

612 / POP 180

Come to this strip of seaside to watch whale sharks, sea lions, whales, sea turtles and a myriad of fish – without the crowds. Diving is best in the summer when the water visibility reaches 25m or 30m (80ft or 100ft). The same winds that made Los Barriles a wind- and-kite-surfing mecca also blow here.

Sleeping & Eating

Baja Joe's HOSTEL $$

(612-114-00-01; www.bajajoe.com; La Ventana; d US$40; P) The hostal rooms here are excellent value with tidy small rooms fronting a communal terrace. The property encompasses a kitesurfing school, a kitchen and Joe's Garage, a popular bar with 10 frothy ales on tap. There are also *cabañas* (US$100 to US$120).

Palapas Ventana CABAÑAS $$$

(612-114-01-98; www.palapasventana.com; La Ventana; cabañas incl breakfast & lunch M$1430-2015; P@) Stay in a delightful *palapa*-style *cabaña* right on the water. Accommodations include a hearty, home-style breakfast and lunch. The more expensive rooms are spacious and have en-suite bathrooms. US owned, Palapas Ventana outfits for diving, snorkeling, windsurfing, kitesurfing, sportfishing, petroglyph hikes and more. It also organizes adventure tours to the Reserva de la Biosfera Sierra de la Laguna (and elsewhere).

Las Palmas MEXICAN $

(El Sargento; mains from M$70; 8am-10pm) Located in El Sargento, a couple of kilometers north of La Ventana, this is a sublime spot overlooking the water and Isla Cerralvo. The Mexican dishes are definitely a notch above the norm; try the *chille relleno* or stuffed clams.

Los Barriles

624 / POP 1200

South of La Paz, the Transpeninsular brushes the gulf at this attractive small town. It is a spectacular spot for wind- and kitesurfing thanks to brisk winter westerlies that average 20 to 25 knots.

Activities

Vela Windsurf WINDSURFING

(www.velawindsurf.com; Hotel Playa del Sol; kitesurfing from US$75; 9am-5pm) One of the longer-established water-sports companies here, it specializes in kitesurfing. The winds die down considerably between April and August, so that is not a good time to take out a board.

Sleeping & Eating

Hotel Los Barriles HOTEL $$

(☎624-141-00-24; www.losbarrileshotel.com; 20 de Noviembre s/n; s/d US$60/73; P❄📶🏊) This hotel has a comfortable laid-back feel. Rooms are set around a pretty lagoon-style pool, complete with outside bar. The owner prides himself on his superior German mattresses and regularly updates the rooms; all have fridges.

Caleb's Cafe CAFE $$

(☎624-141-03-30; Barriles s/n; mains M$60-120; ⏲7:30am-3pm Tue-Sat; P📶👪) Follow the signs from the center of town to arrive at this delightful, American-run cafe, famed for its gooey, buttery sticky buns. Other favorites include zucchini bread and carrot cake, while breakfasts are healthy and hearty (think broccoli scrambled eggs and feta-cheese omelets). There's a small arts and crafts shop here too.

Smokey's Bar & Cantina SEAFOOD $$

(20 de Noviembre s/n; mains M$80-120; ⏲11am-10pm; P) Located next to El Barrelito hotel, this spit-n-sawdust-style place is famed for its smoked fish. Smoked tuna is a good bet, or go for a sampler plate selection of various smoked fish, served with cream cheese, capers and red onions. You can even have your own catch smoked here.

Getting There & Away

Fairly good dirt roads follow the coast south to San José del Cabo. Beyond Cabo Pulmo and Bahía Los Frailes, they are sandy but passable for most vehicles, but are impassable for 4WDs and may be difficult for any vehicles after rainstorms. This road offers awesome glimpses of the coast, Shipwreck Point and the 'green' desertscape. Seven daily buses run to Los Barriles from San José del Cabo (M$90, 1½ hours), en route to La Paz.

Cabo Pulmo

☎624 / POP 50

If you're looking for snorkeling or diving without the crowds, come to Cabo Pulmo, a national marine park that's home to the only Pacific coral reef in the Sea of Cortez. You don't need a 4WD to enjoy the drive out here along the spectacular Eastern Cape (from the south) coastal road or through the Sierra de la Laguna (to the west).

Cabo Pulmo refers to both the park and the tiny village where the following places are located.

Activities

For some of the best snorkeling, head for the beach at **Los Arbolitos**, or follow the shoreline hiking trail to **Las Sirenitas**, where wind and wave erosion has made the rocks look like melting wax sculptures. Eerie and beautiful, they're accessible by boat as well.

Offshore snorkeling, diving and sea-lion colony trips can be booked via several companies that operate out of kiosks down by the water.

Sleeping & Eating

Eco Bungalows CABAÑAS $$

(☎624-158-97-31; www.tourscabopulmo.com; Cabo Pulmo; cabañas with/without bathroom M$600/500; P) These two solar-powered *palapa*-style *cabañas* near the water are plain but pleasantly furnished. The owners organize water sports and whale-watching tours from their Eco Adventures kiosk on the waterfront.

El Caballero MEXICAN $

(Cabo Pulmo; mains M$80; ⏲7am-10pm Fri-Wed) This place serves huge dishes of traditional Mexican cuisine, including superb fish tacos.

Nancy's MEXICAN $$

(☎in the US 617-524-4440; Cabo Pulmo; mains US$10-15; P) Hailing from Illinois and now in her eighties, Nancy gave up her B&B to concentrate on her restaurant (she was fed up with making beds). Sit under the trees on the terrace and try her crab-cake tacos or vegetable enchiladas. There's also a book exchange. A boutique hotel is slated to be built on her land.

Tito's MEXICAN $$

(Cabo Pulmo; buffet US$14; ⏲8am-8pm; P👪) You can't miss this place signposted at the entrance of the village. The well-priced Saturday buffet includes a starter and main of meat, seafood and veg, plus dessert. Have a predining cocktail in the *cabaña* with its seafaring decor of whale bones and fishing pics.

Reserva de la Biosfera Sierra de la Laguna

Hardcore backpackers can strap on their hiking boots, fill their water bottles and head into the uninterrupted wilds of the lush and rugged Sierra de la Laguna biosphere reserve, south of the intersection of the Transpeninsular and Hwy 19. This is not a place for inexperienced hikers, or for anyone unfamiliar with the unique challenges presented by desert trails, but the rewards are great: stunning vistas, close encounters with wildlife, and a unique meadow that was once a lake bed (the feature from which the area gets its name). Hikers are sometimes targets of cougar attacks, so be careful and alert as medical attention is far away. **Baja Sierra Adventures** (☎624-166-87-06; www.bajasierradventures.com), in a tiny ranch called El Chorro, offers a variety of day and overnight trips, biking and trekking through this unique region. Palapas Ventana (p728) is another option for tours to this region.

San José del Cabo

☎624 / POP 70,000

San José del Cabo is like the 'mild' sister of 'wild' Cabo San Lucas, offering quiet shopping, an attractive plaza, a beautiful church and excellent dining opportunities.

The **Fiesta de San José**, on March 19, celebrates the town's patron saint.

Sights & Activities

San José del Cabo consists of San José proper, about 1.5km inland, and a Zona Hotelera with large beachfront hotels, condos and eyesores, er, time-shares. Linking the two areas, Blvd Mijares is a tourist zone of restaurants and art galleries.

The best beaches for swimming are along the road to Cabo San Lucas and include **Playa Santa María** at Km 13.

★Iglesia San José CHURCH

(⌚varies) The colonial-style Iglesia San José, built to replace the 1730 Misión San José del Cabo, faces the spacious Plaza Mijares.

Arroyo San José RIVER

A protected wildlife area replenished by a subterranean spring, Arroyo San José is rumored to have been a refuge for 18th-century pirates between raids on Spanish galleons. A riverside **Paseo del Estero** (Marshland Trail) runs parallel to Blvd Mijares all the way to the Zona Hotelera.

Sleeping

Reserve ahead during the peak winter months.

Hotel Colli HOTEL $$

(☎624-142-07-25; www.hotelcolli.com; Hidalgo s/n; d/tr M$650/850; P ⊖ ❄ 📶) Friendly and family-owned for three generations, the Colli has sunny yellow paintwork in the rooms and is in a great position, only steps away from the plaza and next to the best bakery in town.

Posada Terranova HOTEL $$

(☎624-142-05-34; www.hterranova.com.mx; Degollado s/n; r incl breakfast M$700; P ⊖ ❄ @ 📶) There's art on the walls and views of the pueblo from some of the rooms at this long-standing popular choice. Plus there's a good restaurant and helpful English-speaking staff.

★Casa Natalia BOUTIQUE HOTEL $$$

(☎624-146-71-00; www.casanatalia.com; Blvd Mijares 4; d/ste with spa from US$165/295; ⊖ ❄ 📶 🏊) The fabulous Natalia opens onto San José's plaza and has rooms overlooking a luxurious pool and meandering water feature. The whole place has a sophisticated big-city feel with contemporary furnishings and walk-in bathrooms. The restaurant is superb.

Tropicana Inn HOTEL $$$

(☎624-142-15-80; www.tropicanainn.com.mx; Blvd Mijares 30; s/d incl breakfast M$1584/2376; ❄ 📶 🏊) The spacious rooms are attractively decked out with terracotta tiles and snazzy orange-and-green tiled bathrooms. Perks include satellite TV, a fridge and coffeemaker, while the bucolic courtyard has a huge pool and the squawking parrot 'Paco'.

Eating

French Riviera BAKERY, CAFE $$

(www.frenchrivieraloscabos.com; cnr Hidalgo & Doblado; pastries M$35, mains M$380; ⌚7am-11pm) A French-inspired spot with tasty breads and pastries, gelati that hits the spot on a hot day, and excellent dinners. The continental decor is tasteful and romantic.

Salsitas MEXICAN, BAR $$

(☎624-142-67-87; Obregón 1732; mains M$65-130; ⌚8am-11pm; 📶) An ideal place to beat the heat with a margarita and *antojitos*. The decor is quintessentially Mexican, all hot pinks and reds with oversize pics and traditional leather-backed chairs.

La Ostería MEDITERRANEAN $$

(Obregón 1907; tapas M$90-110, mains from M$140; ⌚11am-9pm) The leafy courtyard setting combined with live music make this an atmospheric venue in which to eat, drink and be merry. Share a tapas plate with 14

San José del Cabo

choices for just M$200 or go for a grilling with steak, chicken or fish.

★Mi Cocina MEXICAN, FUSION $$$
(☎624-146-71-00; Blvd Mijares 4; dinner mains M$190-260; ⏲3:30-10:30pm Wed-Mon; 📶) Set inside the Casa Natalia hotel, Mi Cocina is as classy as dining in San José gets. The decor is artistic, the entrées sublime, and desserts (such as vanilla flan or basil ice cream) are creative culinary masterpieces.

Drinking

Festivals and events are often staged at the plaza; check with your hotel. Head to Cabo San Lucas if you're looking for dusk-to-dawn partying.

Bar La Plaza BAR
(Plaza Mijares 19-20; margaritas M$80; ⏲11am-9pm) This small bar-cum-jewelry-shop offers free, informative tequila tastings with owner Jesus Icaza. He swears that an early morning tequila tipple increases longevity (his wife's grandma does too – she is 112!). The margaritas are also rather good.

Baja Brewing Co BREWERY
(www.bajabrewingcompany.com; Morelos 1227; ⏲noon-1am) A pub-style environment offering local microbrews. Sample 4oz measures of eight different beers for just M$85. Popular choices include the Raspberry Lager and the put-hairs-on-your-chest Peyote Pale Ale.

San José del Cabo

Top Sights
1 Iglesia San José ... C1

Sleeping
2 Casa Natalia ... C1
3 Hotel Colli ... C1
4 Posada Terranova ... B1
5 Tropicana Inn ... C2

Eating
6 French Riviera ... C1
7 La Ostería ... C1
Mi Cocina ... (see 2)
8 Salsitas ... C1

Drinking & Nightlife
9 Baja Brewing Co ... C1
10 Bar La Plaza ... C1

Shopping
11 Cochi Art Gallery ... C1
12 Necri ... C1

Shopping

Boulevard Mijares is the self-proclaimed art district and boasts numerous galleries, studios and stores. The district has an Art Walk on Thursdays from 5pm to 9pm, with open studios, wine tasting and more.

Necri CERAMICS
(www.necri.com.mx; Obregón 17; ⏲10:30am-8pm) One of the longest-established ceramic stores in San José del Cabo, Necri also sells pewter pieces, original Talavera jewelry and mainland crafts.

Cochi Art Gallery GALLERY
(☎624-127-47-02; cnr Obregón & Morelos; ⏲9am-6pm Mon-Sat) Eye-catching paintings and sculpture by an Oaxacan artist.

Information

Several *casas de cambio* here keep long hours.

IMSS Hospital (☎emergency 624-142-01-80, nonemergency 624-142-00-76; cnr Calles Hidalgo & Coronado)

Secretaria Municipal de Turismo (☎ext 150, 624-142-29-60; Transpeninsular; ⏲8am-5pm Mon-Sat) Stocks brochures and maps.

Getting There & Away

AIR

Aéreo Calafia (☎624-143-43-02; www.aereocalafia.com.mx) Flies to Los Mochis, Loreto and Mazatlán.

Aeroméxico (☎624-146-50-98; www.aeromexico.com) Flies daily to many mainland Mexican destinations and Los Angeles. International connections via Mexico City.

Aeropuerto Internacional de Los Cabos (☎624-146-51-11; www.aeropuertosgap.com.mx; Carretera Transpeninsular Km 43.5) The airport, north of San José del Cabo, also serves Cabo San Lucas. All airline offices are found here.

BUS

Main Bus Terminal (☎624-130-73-39; González Conseco s/n) East of the Transpeninsular.

CAR & MOTORCYCLE

The usual agencies rent from the airport. Rates start at about M$600 per day.

Getting Around

Taxi drivers are legally required to display a sanctioned price list. The official government-run company runs bright-yellow taxis and minibuses to the airport for about M$250. Local buses from the main bus terminal to the airport junction cost around M$25, but taking one means a half-hour walk to the air terminal. The toll road from the Transpeninsular to the airport costs M$30.

Los Cabos Corridor

Nowhere in Baja is the desert disappearing faster than in the Los Cabos 'Corridor,' the once-spectacular coastline between San José del Cabo and Cabo San Lucas. In its place: cookie-cutter resorts, American chain stores, aquifer-depleting golf courses and all-inclusive hotels.

Experienced surfers claim that summer reef and point breaks at **Costa Azul** (aka Zippers) match Hawaii's best. The reefs off **Playa Chileno** are excellent for diving. **Playa Santa María**, at Km 13, is one of the best for swimming.

Cabo San Lucas

☎624 / POP 68,500

Come to Cabo expecting to toss your inhibitions to the wind – everyone else does. Where else do clubs round up conga lines so that waiters can pour tequila down dancers' throats? Those moments of absurdity and abandon notwithstanding, Cabo San Lucas has a curious charm. The beaches are protected by beautiful Land's End, and the activities are endless: Jet-Skiing, banana-boating, parasailing, snorkeling, kitesurfing, diving and horseback-riding opportunities can all be done just by walking down to the

BUSES FROM SAN JOSÉ DEL CABO

DESTINATION	FARE (M$)	DURATION
Cabo San Lucas	27	1hr
Ensenada	1705	24hr
La Paz	250	3½hr
Los Barilles	90	1½hr
Tijuana	1850	28hr

Cabo San Lucas

beach. If you rent a car and get outside the city limits, you'll be surrounded by majestic cardón cacti, caracara birds and mystical *arroyos* that will impress you just as much as that crazy club you partied at the night before.

Sights

★Land's End LANDMARK

(M$150) Land's End is by far the most impressive attraction Cabo has to offer. Hop on a *panga* (M$150) and head to **El Arco** (the Arch), a jagged natural feature that partially fills with the tide. Pelicans, sea lions, sea, sky – this is what brought people to Cabo in the first place, and it's still magical, despite the backdrop of cruise ships.

Beaches

For sunbathing and calm waters **Playa Médano**, on the Bahía de Cabo San Lucas, is ideal. **Playa Solmar**, on the Pacific, is pretty but has a reputation for dangerous breakers and riptides. Nearly unspoiled **Playa del Amor** (Lover's Beach; water taxi from Playa Médano or Plaza Las Glorias docks) shouldn't be missed; near Land's End, it is accessible by boat (M$150 round trip). Appropriately,

Cabo San Lucas

Activities, Courses & Tours
1 Ecocat C3
2 La Princesa C2
3 Tio Sports D1

Sleeping
4 Baja's Cactus Hotel & Hostel B3
5 Bungalows Breakfast Inn A2
6 Casa Bella B3
7 Hotel Los Milagros B2
8 Hotel Olas C1

Eating
9 Jo's Garden B3
10 La Fonda A1
11 Mi Casa B3
12 Pancho's B3
13 Venado B2

Drinking & Nightlife
14 Canela B2
15 Slim's Elbow Room B3

Entertainment
16 Cabo Wabo B3
17 Mango Deck D2

Shopping
Mercado Mexicano .... (see 12)

CABO IN...

Two Days

Take a *panga* to **Playa del Amor** (p733) and see **El Arco** (p733) at the same time. Laze for a while or snorkel, then head back for grub or a margarita. Get tipsy on a gorgeous **sunset tour** and then finish the job at **Cabo Wabo** (p735). The next day choose between quiet shopping at **San José del Cabo** or something active: surfing at **Los Cerritos** or diving at **Cabo Pulmo**.

Four Days

Four days gives you all of the above. Or you could rent yourself some wheels and do a loop of the Southern Cape. Start heading east, through **San José del Cabo**, and take in the awesome scenery of the Eastern Cape, one of Baja's best unbeaten paths. Stay in **Cabo Pulmo** for snorkeling and diving, then cruise north on day two to **La Paz**. Hikers will want to see the **Sierra de la Laguna**. Spend day three in the chi-chi galleries and great restaurants of **Todos Santos** or **surfing**. Head back to Cabo San Lucas on day four and end with a fancy meal at **La Fonda** or a relaxing **sunset tour**.

Playa del Divorcio (Divorce Beach) is nearby, across the point on the Pacific side.

Activities

The best diving areas are **Roca Pelícano**, the sea-lion colony off Land's End, and the reef off **Playa Chileno**, at Bahía Chileno east of town. Two-tank dives cost around M$1100 and full-certification courses are M$4000 or higher. **Tio Sports** (☎624-143-33-99; www.tiosports.com; Playa Médano; scuba diving per hr from US$50) at Playa Médano is one of the largest water-sports outfitters, but there are numerous alternatives.

Surprisingly good snorkeling can be done right from Playa del Amor, swimming left, toward the marina. A mask, snorkel and fins should run about M$150 per day. *Panga* rides cost about M$120 for a round trip if you bargain directly with a captain. Tipping is expected.

Tours

Ecocat BOAT

(☎624-157-46-85; www.caboecotours.com; dock N-12; tours per person from US$40) Offers two-hour sunset sailing tours, snorkeling and whale-watching trips, and also plays host to a variety of other options off its giant catamaran.

La Princesa BOAT

(☎624-143-76-76; www.laprincesacharters.com; dock M-O; tours per person from US$49) Located behind Hotel Costa Real, this outfit offers sunset wining and dining trips along with other daytime packages.

Festivals & Events

Fishing Tournaments FISHING

Cabo San Lucas is a popular staging ground for fishing tournaments in October and November. The main events are the **Gold Cup**, **Bisbee's Black & Blue Marlin Jackpot** and the **Cabo Tuna Jackpot**.

Sammy Hagar's Birthday Party DANCE

(Cabo Wabo) Held in early October, this is a major Cabo event with lots of drinking and dancing. Invitations (free) are required – try concierges at the larger hotels or look out for giveaways.

Día de San Lucas RELIGIOUS

A local celebration held on October 18, honoring the town's patron saint, with fireworks, food stalls and a fiesta spirit.

Sleeping

Cabo has plenty of accommodation choice.

Baja's Cactus Hotel & Hostel HOTEL, HOSTEL $

(☎624-105-07-11; www.bajacactushostel.com; cnr Cabo San Lucas & 5 de Mayo; dm incl breakfast M$250, d incl breakfast M$600; P ❄ ☜) This hostel accommodation is the cheapest place in town and has spacious three-bed dorms (no bunks) with tiled floors, en-suite bathrooms and air-conditioning. A large terrace with barbecue and hammocks, and a communal kitchen, mean there is plenty of kick-back space. The doubles are a tad scuffed for the price.

Hotel Olas HOTEL $

(☎624-143-17-80; cnr Revolución & Farias s/n; r M$400; P ❄ ☜) Safe and secure, Hotel Olas' clean and simple rooms are good value for Cabo. The grandfatherly owner is very knowledgeable about Baja and speaks some English. Giant clam shells and other maritime items add to the holiday-by-the-sea decor.

★Bungalows Breakfast Inn B&B $$$
(☎624-143-05-85; www.thebungalowshotel.com; cnr Libertad & Herrera; bungalows incl breakfast US$95-195, ste incl breakfast US$145-210;) Extremely attentive service, delicious breakfasts, tastefully furnished rooms, fragrant palm-thatched *palapas,* hammocks and an expansive swimming pool set this B&B apart. Fresh-fruit smoothies, fruit juices, excellent coffee and warm, welcoming bilingual staff make the bungalows feel like home. Beautiful handmade soaps are one of the many tiny details that makes this *the* place to splurge.

Casa Bella HOTEL $$$
(☎624-143-64-00; www.casabellahotel.com; Hidalgo 10; d from US$160;) Set amid the bustle of terrace restaurants and souvenir shops, this hacienda-style hotel has a real away-from-it-all feel thanks to the juxtaposition of its mature trees and tropical garden with its sunbaked ocher facade. Individually decorated with antiques, rooms have stunning oversized bathrooms.

Hotel Los Milagros HOTEL $$$
(☎624-143-45-66, in USA 718-928-6647; www.losmilagros.com.mx; Matamoros 116; d/ste from US$85/125;) The tranquil courtyard and 12 unique rooms provide a perfect escape from Cabo's excesses. A desert garden (complete with resident iguanas), beautiful deep-blue pool, and friendly, courteous service make a stay here unforgettable.

Eating

Cabo's culinary scene ranges from humble taco stands to gourmet restaurants.

Venado TAQUERÍA $
(☎624-147-69-21; Niños Héroes btwn Zaragoza & Morelos; dinner mains M$50-90; ⌚11am-7am) Open all night and packed from 3am until dawn, Venado has delicious fish tacos, fresh salsas and other *antojitos*. If it's slow, the friendly waitresses might drop a coin in the jukebox and invite you to dance.

Jo's Garden ITALIAN $$
(☎624-157-51-18; cnr Cárdenas & Cabo San Lucas; pizzas M$80-150; ⌚5-10pm Tue-Sun) A rare find in these parts: authentic Italian-style thin-based pizza made in a traditional wood-fired oven. This simple place also sells wonderful rustic pots and decor items. There are a few outside tables and chairs on the terrace. Or opt for takeaway.

Mi Casa MEXICAN $$$
(www.micasarestaurant.com.mx; cnr Cárdenas & Cabo San Lucas; mains M$230-250; ⌚10am-11pm) This place has real wow factor. The courtyard-style interior has rooms on several levels and feels like something out of a 1950s Mexican musical – plants, statues, folksy murals, wicker lights, painted furniture, Día de Muertos figurines and wandering mariachis all set the stage. Try one of the traditional dishes, like *e mole poblano* (chicken with *mole* sauce).

La Fonda MEXICAN $$$
(☎624-143-69-26; cnr Hidalgo & Obregón; dishes M$140-250; ⌚2-10:30pm) Has superb Mexican cuisine that's worlds away from the typical *antojitos* – try the cream of *poblano* soup with pumpkin flowers or the *huitlacoche* (corn mushroom) stuffed chicken. The Don Julio margarita vies for the title of the best in Baja.

Pancho's MEXICAN, BAR $$$
(☎624-143-28-91; www.panchos.com; cnr Hidalgo & Zapata; dinner mains M$220-300, lobster M$420, tequila tasting M$700) Full of festive atmosphere, mariachi band tunes, good food and aromas from the open grill, Pancho's also offers 'all you want to know about tequila.' The tasting is like an intensive tequila class, with inebriation in place of a graduation certificate.

Drinking & Nightlife

Cabo is a proud party town, and alcoholic revelry is encouraged all day long. You have been warned.

Canela BAR
(Plaza del Sol; ⌚8am-11pm) A classier option than most for a Corona or cocktail. Moody lighting, rustic furniture and a curious (and entertaining) Día de Muertos theme.

Cabo Wabo CLUB, MUSIC
(☎624-143-11-88; www.cabowabo.com; cnr Calles Guerrero & Madero) The most famous bar and club in town, established by legendary rocker Sammy Hagar of Van Halen fame.

Slim's Elbow Room BAR
(Blvd Marina s/n; ⌚10am-midnight) In the shadow of Cabo Wabo, this teeny, easy-to-miss

watering hole, wallpapered in dollar bills and clients' signatures, claims to be the world's smallest bar. With four seats inside and two standing spaces, it's a contender for sure. A shot of the vanilla liqueur is well worth the price tag.

Mango Deck CLUB
(☎624-144-49-19; Playa Médano) Great for people-watching and a sunset margarita. And the beach doesn't get any closer. There's even a mechanical bull if you're feeling like a mouthful of sand.

Shopping

Mercado Mexicano MARKET
(cnr Hidalgo & Zapata) This sprawling market, which contains dozens of stalls with crafts from around the country, is Cabo's most comprehensive shopping area.

Information

It's an indication of who calls the shots here that Cabo has no government-sanctioned tourist offices. The 'info' booths you'll see are owned by time-shares, condos and hotels. The staff are friendly and can offer maps and info, but their only pay comes from commissions from selling time-share visits: expect a firm, sometimes desperate, pitch for you to visit model homes. Be warned – the promised freebies are rarely worth wasting precious vacation time on.

Internet cafes abound and many hotels have lobby computers the public can use. Rates are, not surprisingly, cheaper as you go further away from the water.

All About Cabo (www.allaboutcabo.com) A useful site for visitors.

Amerimed American Hospital (☎624-143-96-70; Blvd Cárdenas) Near Paseo de la Marina.

Tourist Assistance (☎078)

Getting There & Away

Immigration Office (☎624-143-01-35; cnr Blvd Cárdenas & Farías; ⊙9am-1pm Mon-Sat) Near the center of Cabo San Lucas.

AIR

The closest airport is at San José del Cabo (p732).

BUS

Buses depart from either the **Águila** (www.autotransportesaguila.net; Hwy 19; ⊙24hr) company, located at the Todos Santos crossroad, north of downtown, or the **bus station**, a 40-minute walk northwest from the tourist zone/waterfront.

CAR & MOTORCYCLE

Numerous car-rental agencies have booths along Paseo de la Marina and elsewhere in town, with prices starting at around M$70 per day.

Getting Around

The **airport shuttle bus** (☎624-146-53-93; per person M$150) leaves every two hours (10am to 4pm) from Plaza Bonita or Plaza Náutica. Cab van fares within town range from M$70 to M$100, and a taxi to the airport is around M$800. The airport shuttle vans (M$150) can drop you off at your hotel. Avoid rides offered by the time-share touts.

Todos Santos

☎612 / POP 5200

Todos Santos is one of the most appealing towns in all of Baja, maybe even all of Mexico. A quirky mix of locals, fishers, surfers and New Age spiritualists, the town of 'All Saints' has thus far escaped the rampant tourism of the other Cape towns, but still has all kinds of things to see and do. Think Taos, New Mexico, before Ansel Adams and Georgia O'Keeffe brought the world there. Be prepared for high prices, however.

Todos Santos' newfound prosperity does not reflect its history. Founded in 1723, but nearly destroyed by the Pericú rebellion in 1734, Misión Santa Rosa de Todos los Santos limped along until its abandonment in 1840. In the late 19th century Todos Santos became a prosperous sugar town with

BUSES FROM CABO SAN LUCAS

DESTINATION	FARE (M$)	DURATION
La Paz	216	3hr
Loreto	810	8¾hr
San José del Cabo	27	1hr
Tijuana	1800	27hr
Todos Santos	110	1hr

several brick *trapiches* (mills), but depleted aquifers have nearly eliminated this thirsty industry. The crumbling, photo-worthy brick structures still remain in several parts of town.

Like many other parts of Baja, Todos Santos is changing. A new four-lane highway has made it easier to zip up from Cabo, and local development is rampant. So come here now before it changes forever.

Sights & Activities

Centro Cultural MUSEUM
(612-145-00-41; Juárez; 8am-8pm Mon-Fri, 9am-4pm Sat & Sun) FREE Housed in a former schoolhouse, the Centro Cultural is home to some interesting nationalist and revolutionary murals dating from 1933. Also on display is an uneven collection of regional artifacts, fascinating old photos and a replica ranch house. Take note of the cradle 'cage' hanging from the ceiling!

Trapiches
Scattered around town are several former *trapiches* (mills), many of which have been repurposed over the years. The restored **Teatro Cine General Manuel Márquez de León** is one – it's on Legaspi, facing the plaza. **Molino El Progreso**, the ruin of what was formerly El Molino restaurant, is another. On Juárez, opposite the hospital, is **Molino de los Santana**.

Surfing
Surfers come here for some of the nicest swells in all of Baja. **San Pedrito** offers Hawaii-like tubes (and Hawaii-like sea urchins if you wipe out). Catch that perfect wave as eagle rays glide below you, or just hang out with the mellow crowd on **Los Cerritos** and watch the coral sun plunge into the Pacific. Boards can be rented for M$150 per day at Pescadero Surf Camp, near the beaches. Mario Beceril's **Mario Surf School** (612-142-61-56; www.mariosurfschool.com; 1-hr surf lessons from US$50;) offers excellent lessons for all levels in the Todos Santos and Pescadero area.

Festivals & Events

Todos Santos' two-day **Festival de Artes** is held in early February. At other times it's possible to visit local artists in their home studios, and there are galleries galore.

WORTH A TRIP

PUNTA LOBOS

This point in Todos Santos, named for its sea-lion colony, is where the fishers launch *pangas*. It's just a sandy beach and a bit out of the way, but anywhere from 1pm to about 3pm you can come and bargain for just-off-the-boat fish to cook at home. Pelicans joust for scraps, and a hiking trail winds up the point to an unparalleled lookout spot.

Sleeping

Pescadero Surf Camp CABAÑAS $
(612-130-30-32; www.pescaderosurf.com; Hwy 19 Km 64; casita M$400-550, penthouse M$750, campsites per person M$120; P@) Friendly, helpful and the only budget place in town, Pescadero Surf Camp has everything a surfer could need – rentals, lessons, advice, a community kitchen and even a BYO swim-up bar.

★ **Posada La Poza** SUITES $$$
(612-145-04-00; www.lapoza.com; Camino a la Poza 282; ste incl breakfast US$210-520; P) Boasting 'Mexican hospitality combined with Swiss quality,' this beautiful boutique retreat is right on the Pacific. A saltwater swimming pool, freshwater lagoon, lush garden and superb restaurant with excellent Mexican wines set it apart. A Mexican sweat lodge and saltwater Jacuzzi offer alternate ways to let stress slip away. No TVs.

Hotel California HOTEL $$$
(612-145-05-25; Juárez s/n; r M$1585;) Although this is the Hotel California that has capitalized on the legendary Eagles song the most, it is more classy sophistication than raucous rock and roll. The public spaces, in particular, are gorgeous, especially around the pool, which is suronded by lush foliage, blood-red hibiscus and lofty palms. There is tasteful artwork throughout and the rooms are traditionally and attractively furnished.

Hotel Casa Tota BOUTIQUE HOTEL $$$
(612-145-05-90; www.hotelcasatota.com; Obregon s/n; r M$1539;) Minimalist decor, earth colours, snazzy abstracts and industrial-chic use of glossed-up concrete give the rooms here a New York–penthouse look. Crisp white linens and beautiful

SURF'S UP

Baja is a prime surfer's paradise with swells coming in off the Pacific that, even on bad days, are challenging and fun. Boards can be rented from surf shops (rental costs around M$250), but use extreme care at all times, as rips, undertow and behemoth waves are dangerous even for experienced surfers. If you're looking for good breaks, check out the following:

➡ **Costa Azul** (p732) Needs southerly swell, but this intermediate break is a whole lot of fun and it's close to either of the Cabos.

➡ **Los Cerritos** (p737) Beautiful sand, good waves, mellow vibe – this is a great beginner beach with a powerful Pacific swell…and eagle rays below.

➡ **San Miguel** (p706) Rocky point break that offers awesome rides when the waves are big. Isla de Todos Santos is another option for the serious.

For more info on surfing, check out the no-nonsense *Surfer's Guide to Baja* by Mike Parise. For surf lessons, contact Mario Surf School (p737).

mosaic-tiled bathrooms complete the look, along with the central pool surrounded by lofty palms, two sun terraces and an excellent restaurant serving arguably the best eggs Benedict in town.

Todos Santos Inn MOTEL **$$$**
(☎612-145-00-40; www.todossantosinn.com; Legaspi 33; d US$125-225;) Fashioned from a restored 19th-century brick building, American-owned Todos Santos Inn has only eight intimate rooms, each with a four-poster bed and a luxurious atmosphere. A tiny swimming pool sits within a verdant tropical courtyard.

Eating

Taco stands along Heróico Colegio Militar offer cheap eats.

★Fonda El Zaguán MEXICAN **$$**
(Juaréz s/n; mains M$125-165; ⏲noon-9pm Mon-Sat;) Good-value prices and creative Mexican cuisine make this one of the most popular places on the main street. Opt for a daily special such as fillet of fish sautéed in a mango *beurre blanc* or organic salad with grilled tofu. And step outside the box with a bitter orange margarita (M$70). Delicious!

Ristorante Tre Galline ITALIAN **$$**
(☎612-145-02-74; cnr Topete & Juaréz; dinner mains M$140-320; ⏲noon-10pm Mon-Sat) This attractive Italian-owned restaurant has tables arranged on descending terraces, which give everyone a little more privacy (candlelight adds to the atmosphere). The seafood platters are particularly scrumptious and the pasta is made fresh daily.

★Café Santa Fe ITALIAN **$$$**
(☎612-145-03-40; Centenario 4; dinner mains M$180-440; ⏲noon-9pm Wed-Mon) The *insalata Mediterranea* (steamed seafood drizzled in lemon juice and oil) will make even seafood haters change their ways. The open-air kitchen, designed by the owner himself, allows you to see the food as it's being prepped. Anything on the menu will delight, surprise and tantalize.

If you need suggestions, however, go for the mussels in wine or any one of the various handmade raviolis: lobster, meat, or spinach and ricotta cheese.

El Gusto! FUSION, MEXICAN **$$$**
(☎612-145-04-00; www.lapoza.com; Posada La Poza, Camino a la Poza 282; mains M$180-240, specials M$350; ⏲noon-3pm & 7-10pm Fri-Wed; P) Reservations are recommended at this beautiful restaurant, which was recently voted a top place to watch a Pacific sunset – sip a margarita on the terrace or in the beautifully decorated dining area. In season, whales head by as you eat. The extensive wine list is made up of Mexico's finest vintages.

Shopping

There are numerous galleries to wander through, especially around the plaza.

Alas y Olas SOUVENIRS
(Juarez 205; ⏲10:30am-5pm Mon-Sat) The American owner here supports women's co-operatives in Chiapas and Guatemala, where many of the finely embroidered clothes and textiles sold here are made.

Agua y Sol Joyeria JEWELRY
(cnr Centenario & Analia Gutiérrez; ⏲10am-5pm) The silver jewelry here is made by local artisans and well priced with some stunning, unusual designs.

Information

Cafélix (☎612-145-05-68; Juárez 4; wi-fi free with purchase; ⏲8am-9pm; 📶) Wi-fi, in addition to great coffee and breakfasts.

El Tecolote (☎612-145-02-95; cnr Juárez & Av Hidalgo) The town lacks an official tourist office, but this English-language bookstore has magazines with town maps and a sketch map of nearby beach areas.

Getting There & Away

Hourly between 6:30am and 10:30pm, buses head to La Paz (M$90, 1½ hours) and to Cabo San Lucas (M$110, one hour) from the **bus stop** (☎612-148-02-89; Heróico Colegio Militar; ⏲7am-10pm) between Zaragoza and Morelos.

Copper Canyon & Northern Mexico

Includes ➡

Best Places to Eat

- Bonifacio's (p752)
- Teresitas (p754)
- La Casa de los Milagros (p776)
- La Galería Café (p795)

Best Places to Stay

- Yeccan (p795)
- Hotel San Felipe El Real (p775)
- Hotel Luz del Sol (p753)
- Riverside Lodge (p771)

Why Go?

Welcome to ultimate frontier land: Mexico's wild north has, for centuries, been frequented by revolutionaries, bandits, law-makers and law-breakers. Landscapes here suit such types: North America's second-largest desert and some of the world's deepest, most spectacular canyons make this perfect territory to hole up in. This is, indeed, quintessential rough-and-ready Wild West: Hollywood filmmakers used dramatic topography here to shoot many fabled Westerns.

Mexico also scatters its paradoxes most thickly in the north. There is the sensational alpine-to-subtropical switch unfolding in the region's set piece, the Copper Canyon, best traversed via Mexico's greatest train ride. The progressive, culturally rich city of Monterrey is here, as are some of its most non-Westernized indigenous peoples. It's a place where you may well find yourself lingering.

When to Go

Chihuahua

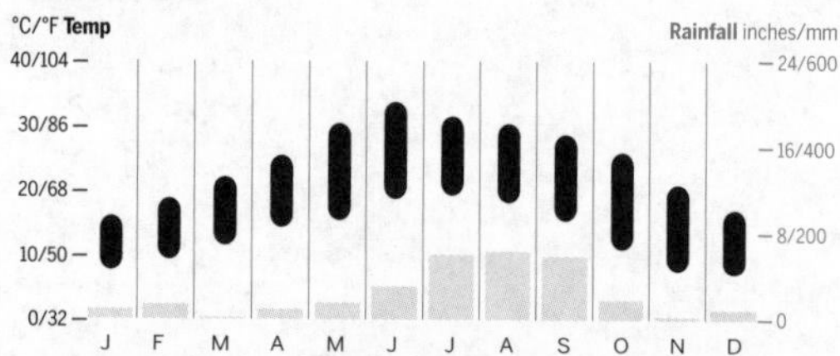

Jun & Jul Heavy rainfall. Key festivals such as Las Jornadas Villistas in Hidalgo del Parral.

Late Sep–Oct Pleasantly hot during the day. Good time to visit blooming Copper Canyon.

Dec & Jan Balmy, dry weather on the Pacific coast makes for a popular winter escape.

History

Pre-Hispanic northern Mexico had more in common with the Anasazi and other cultures of the southwest USA than with central Mexico. The most important town here was Paquimé, a vital trading link between central Mexico and the dry north, before its destruction around AD 1340. Outlying Paquimé settlements such as Cuarenta Casas built their dwellings on cliffsides for protection against attack.

Spanish slavers and explorers, arriving chiefly in search of gold in the 16th century, had mixed fortunes in the north. In the northwest they encountered indigenous peoples including the Opata, Seri, Yaqui and Mayo. Rather than the fabled province of Cíbola with its supposed seven cities of gold, the Spanish found silver and, conscripting indigenous people as slave miners, established prosperous mining cities such as Álamos. Spaniards also soon forged the Camino Real de Tierra Adentro (Royal Road of the Interior): a 2560km trade route from Mexico City to Santa Fe, New Mexico, which helped make towns en route (such as Durango) extremely wealthy. In the northeast, however, harsh conditions and attacks by indigenous Chichimecs and Apaches meant settlement and development came more slowly.

The Spanish never tightened control here sufficiently to quell revolts. In the fight for Mexican Independence (1810), the Mexican-American War of the 1840s and the Mexican Revolution (1910) the northern states necessarily played a key role. Frontiers radically changed with Mexico's loss of Texas and New Mexico (1830s–1850s): the Treaty of Guadalupe Hidalgo (1848) that ended the Mexican–American War established today's frontier of the Río Bravo del Norte (Rio Grande) between the two nations.

Glaring inequities of land ownership between the elite – grown wealthy from the mines – and the impoverished majority contributed to the unrest that made the north a Mexican Revolution hot spot. The revolutionary División del Norte, an army led by legendary Durango-born Pancho Villa, was in the forefront of several major battles. Venustiano Carranza and Álvaro Obregón, other main revolutionary figures, were, respectively, from the northern states of Coahuila and Sonora. All three were initially allies and subsequently enemies in the Revolution, which meant the division of allegiances in the north was acute.

Irrigation programs in the mid-20th century turned Sonora into the granary of Mexico, as well as a cattle-ranching center alongside neighboring Chihuahua. Discovery of petroleum, coal and natural gas and the arrival of the railroad also accelerated development from the late 19th century onward, and the region emerged as an industrial leader.

Today this is the most Americanized part of Mexico, with money and resources surging back and forth across the border and baseball the main sport in many towns. The Texan economy is particularly dependent on Mexican workers, and US investment is behind most *maquiladoras* (assembly-plant operations) that ring all the region's big cities.

Since 2006, drug-cartel violence has plagued northern Mexico as gangs complete for territory. Initially the border cities were worst affected, but the violence has since spread, affecting all the main population centers. Yet despite the headlines, the region's economy remains relatively prosperous, with steady growth rates (except the tourism sector, which has suffered).

ℹ Information

DANGERS & ANNOYANCES

The vast majority of visitors to northern Mexico enjoy a safe, trouble-free trip. That said, the entire region is a transit area for illegal drugs, and narco-related violence is a fact of life.

Most towns and cities are affected to a degree, and trouble erupts as new transport routes are established and turf wars shift. Of the border towns, Ciudad Juárez is particularly notorious and should definitely be avoided. Additionally, Ciudad Acuña, Nuevo Laredo, Reynosa and Matamoros all witnessed violent incidents and gun battles in 2012 and 2013. The security situation in central Monterrey was very grim as recently as 2011, though things had calmed down by 2013. Tampico, Durango and Torreón have also had their share of incidents.

Most violence is gang-on-gang or between the cartels and the security forces. Foreign tourists without such connections are not targeted. There is a risk of being in the wrong place at the wrong time, but the chances of being caught up in a violent incident are actually very slim: tourists are statistically more likely to be involved in a traffic accident than a shoot-out. Consider avoiding bars, nightclubs and casinos in the this part of Mexico, where violent incidents can occur.

Web resources advising on local security situations are rarely that useful. Insight Crime (www.insightcrime.org) provides regular reports

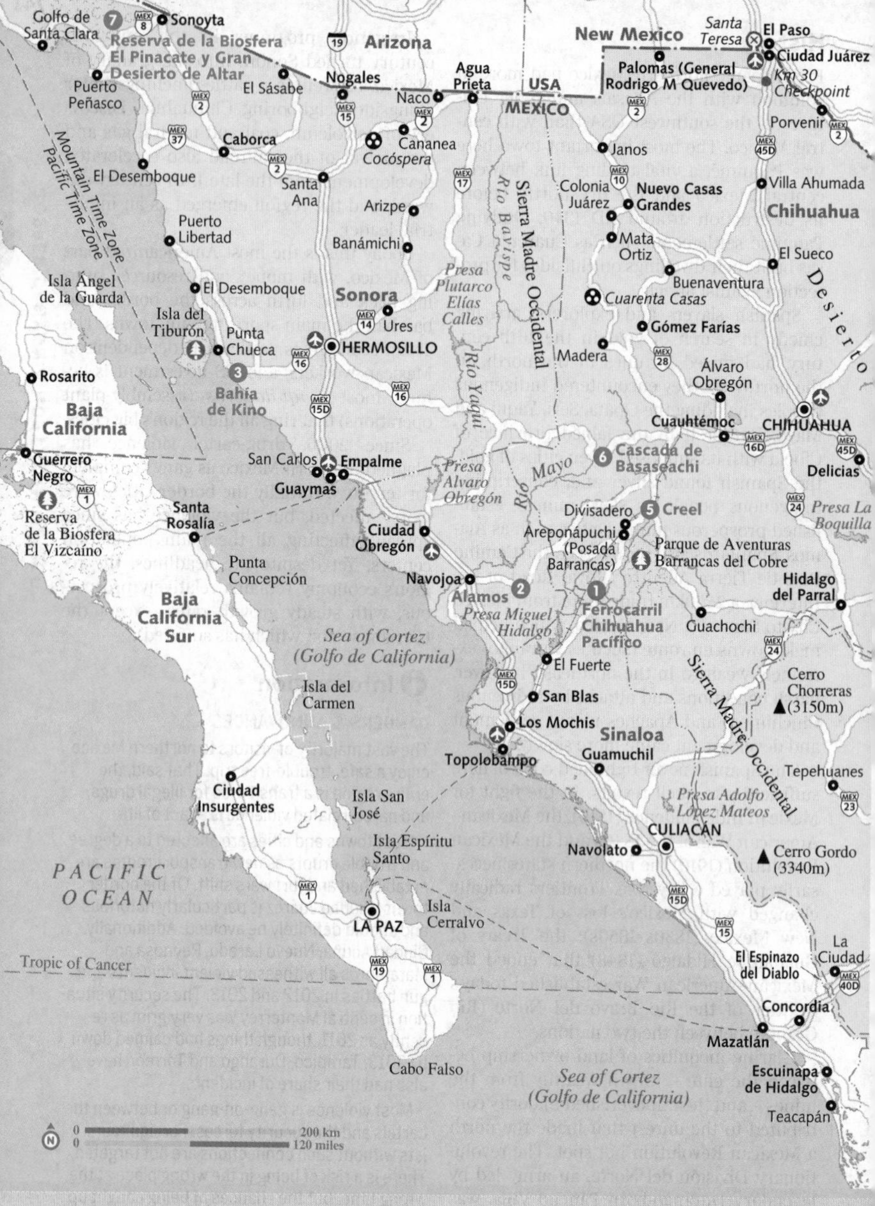

Copper Canyon & Northern Mexico Highlights

1. Ride Mexico's last passenger train through mesmerizing canyon scenery on the **Ferrocarril Chihuahua Pacífico** (p759)
2. Check into a colonial hotel and roll back the years in the exquisite old silver town of **Álamos** (p752)
3. Bask in the balmy beach paradise of **Bahía de Kino** (p749)
4. Be shocked and awed by Monterrey's **Horno3** (p794)

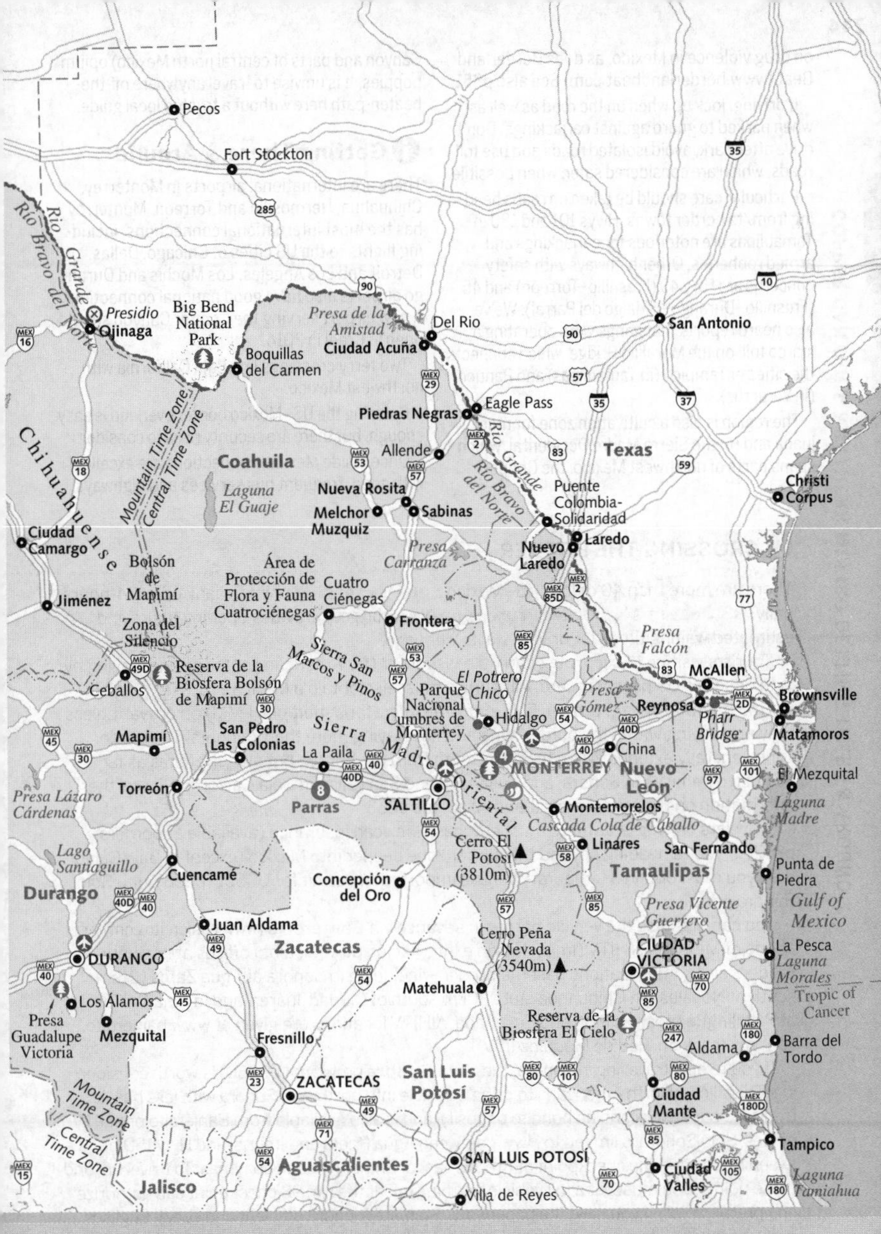

museum, a monument to the town's heavy-metal heritage

5 Explore canyon country on two wheels in mountain-biking heaven around **Creel** (p765)

6 Chill in the plunge pool of Mexico's highest full-time waterfall, **Cascada de Basaseachi** (p770)

7 Experience the lunar landscapes and silence of the desert in the remote **Gran Desierto de Altar** (p748)

8 Enjoy the tranquil ambience and taste fine wines in pretty **Parras** (p788)

on drug violence in Mexico, as does Borderland Beat (www.borderlandbeat.com) See also p851.

If driving, lock up when on the road as well as when parked to guard against carjackings. Don't drive after dark, avoid isolated roads and use toll roads, which are considered safer, when possible.

Particular care should be taken on roads heading from/to border towns. Hwys 101 and 180 in Tamaulipas are notorious for carjackings and armed robberies. Other highways with safety concerns are Hwy 49 (Fresnillo–Torreón) and 45 (Fresnillo–Durango–Hidalgo del Parral). We've also heard reports that gangs were operating a 'narco toll' on the Moralillo Bridge, which connects the cities of Tampico (in Tamaulipas) and Panuco (in Veracruz).

The region is also a cultivation zone for marijuana and (in the Sierra Madre Occidental, which spans parts of northwest Mexico, the Copper Canyon and parts of central north Mexico) opium poppies. It is unwise to travel anywhere off-the-beaten-path here without a trusted local guide.

Getting There & Around

There are international airports in Monterrey, Chihuahua, Hermosillo and Torreón. Monterrey has the most international connections, including flights to the US cities of Chicago, Dallas, Detroit and Los Angeles. Los Mochis and Durango airports also have good national connections. A new airport serving the Copper Canyon should open in Creel in 2014.

Two ferry crossings link Baja California with northwest Mexico.

Crossing the US–Mexico border overland is easy enough, but there are security risks to consider.

Once inside Mexico, connections are excellent, with good, frequent bus services and highways

CROSSING THE BORDER

There are more than 40 official US–Mexico **border crossing** points, many open 24-hours daily. **US Customs & Border Protection** (www.cbp.gov) provides opening hours and estimated waiting times for drivers via its webpage.

Tourists visiting Mexico must carry a passport or (for Americans entering and leaving by land or sea) a US passport card. All tourists must also obtain a Mexican **tourist permit** (*forma migratoria para turista*, FMT, or *forma migratoria múltiple*, FMM) on arrival, unless they are staying within the border zone and not staying more than 72 hours. The border zone generally extends 20km to 30km south from the border, but also stretches as far as Puerto Peñasco in Sonora, and Ensenada and San Felipe in Baja California. For further information on the tourist permit and visas, see p853.

Travelers **taking a vehicle** must purchase Mexican insurance (available at borders; p857). If you're heading beyond the border zone deeper into Mexico (except in Baja California), you must obtain a temporary vehicle importation permit for US$51 (p856), or a Sólo Sonora permit.

You can organise the vehicle permit in advance via **Banjército** (www.banjercito.com) or at one of Mexico's 38 IITV (Importación e Internación de Vehículos) offices at northern borders and some locations past the border – including in Sonora at Agua Zarca (21km south of Nogales), in Chihuahua state 30km south of Ciudad Juárez, and in Baja California at Pichilingue (near La Paz) and Ensenada. All IITV locations are given at www.banjercito.com.mx (click on 'Red de Módulos IITV').

If you're only travelling in Sonora, the **Sólo Sonora** program (US$30) is worth considering. This allows North Americans to bring a vehicle into northwest Sonora with less hassle (reduced paperwork and no bond to deposit), and is also available from Banjército or at IITV offices. Sólo Sonora is limited to Hwy 2 between Agua Prieta and Imuris, and Hwy 15D between Imuris and the checkpoint at Km 98, east of Empalme near Guaymas. To travel beyond these points, you must get a full vehicle permit; staff at the Km 98 checkpoint can authorize one pretty rapidly if you have the paperwork. Staff are friendly, efficient and speak English.

If you take a vehicle into Baja California, and then ship it to mainland Mexico by ferry from Pichilingue, you must get a vehicle permit before embarking your vehicle.

The main border crossings (ordered west to east) are:

Lukeville (Arizona)–Sonoyta (Sonora) (6am-midnight) Best for Puerto Peñasco.

Deconcini crossing (24hr) From Nogales (Arizona)–Nogales (Sonora). Hwy 15/15D is the main highway south.

Santa Teresa crossing (6am-10pm) Some 20km west of Ciudad Juárez in Chihuahua state; good for avoiding security risks near Juárez.

heading south. Better roads are usually toll roads, with tolls between Nogales and Los Mochis, for example, totaling over M$400. It's often remote country, so don't set out beyond major highways without a full tank of gas.

NORTHWEST MEXICO

The magnets for visitors to Mexico's northwest are the inviting beaches of the Sea of Cortez, and the abundant marine life, including some 40 sea-lion colonies and 27 species of whale and dolphin. Tourism here originates largely from Arizona (some towns are so easily reachable from there that they're becoming Mexican-American communities) but the region – encompassing Sonora (by far the safest of Mexico's border states) and northern Sinaloa – still bursts with homespun character. The strains of *norteña* (country) music and the inviting smell of the trademark regional snack, *carne asada* (marinated grilled beef), waft past cowboy-hatted ranchers on the streets.

The perfunctory towns and cities won't detain you long: Los Mochis harbors little interest except as a jumping-off point for the spectacular train ride up the Copper Canyon or for a boat to Baja. The state capital, Hermosillo, has excellent transportation connections but little cultural interest. The glorious exception is delightful Álamos, a colonial jewel surrounded by peaks of the Sierra Madre Occidental that's replete with atmospheric restaurants and cafés and is well worth a diversion off Hwy 15.

El Paso (Texas)–Ciudad Juárez (Chihuahua) Bridge of the Americas (24hr); El Paso St–Av Juárez (24hr); Stanton St–Av Lerdo (24hr) Pedestrian crossings are via the bridges of Stanton St–Avenida Lerdo or El Paso St–Avenida Juárez. To return on foot you must use Avenida Juárez. Access for vehicles is via Bridge of the Americas (Puente Córdova). Tourist permits are available at the end of the Stanton St–Avenida Lerdo bridge and at Bridge of the Americas. Hwy 45D from Juárez is the principal southbound route.

Presidio (Texas)–Ojinaga (Chihuahua) (24hr) From Ojinaga, it's 225km direct to Chihuahua along Hwy 16.

Del Rio (Texas)–Ciudad Acuña (Coahuila) (24hr)

Eagle Pass (Texas)–Piedras Negras (Coahuila) (24hr)

Laredo (Texas)–Nuevo Laredo (Tamaulipas) (24hr) Two main crossings: Puente Internacional No 1 and Puente Internacional No 2. The latter bypasses the city and is the safer option, connecting with Hwy 85D from Nuevo Laredo to Monterrey, from where there are good connections to other destinations in Mexico.

McAllen (Texas)–Reynosa (Tamaulipas) (24hr)

Brownsville (Texas)–Matamoros (Tamaulipas) Puente Nuevo (24hr); Puente Zaragoza (6am-midnight)

There are plenty of cross-border bus services into the region from US cities, most involving a change of buses in a city on the US or Mexican side of the border. Given the time it can take to get through the border, it is often quicker to disembark before the border, make the crossing on foot, and pick up further transportation on the other side.

If you want to avoid staying long in Mexico's border towns, some services will take you directly deeper into Mexico, including Phoenix–Puerto Peñasco via Sonoyta with Transportes Supremo (p747), El Paso–Chihuahua via Juárez with **Autobuses Americanos** (☎ in the US 915-532-1748; www.autobusesamericanos.us; 1007 S Santa Fe St, El Paso) (who have many offices across Texas) and Tufesa (www.tufesa.com.mx), which operates many cross-border buses to California and Arizona.

Many border towns rank among Mexico's most dangerous places. The security situation can change quickly. Ciudad Juárez and Nuevo Laredo are notorious but in 2013 serious violence also erupted in both Matamoros and Reynosa. The Sonoran border crossings were deemed pretty *tranquilo* at the time of research. All border cities mentioned in this chapter have good sleeping and eating facilities if you do choose to spend the night.

Puerto Peñasco

☎638 / POP 57,300

Until the 1920s, 'Rocky Point' (as US citizens affectionately call this Sea of Cortez coastal resort) was just that: a landmark on naval/military maps and no more. Its location alongside one of the driest parts of the Desierto Sonorense (Sonoran Desert) deterred all would-be settlers bar intrepid fishers, until Prohibition gave the fledgling community an unexpected boost. When the global economy nosedived in the 1930s, Puerto Peñasco enjoyed a (very) lengthy siesta, until state investment and a desalination plant kick-started the local economy in the early 1990s. The result has been a boom in development and population, and now this beach town is home to so many non-natives that it has become the seaside destination Arizona never had.

The historic core hugs the rocky point itself while its main waterfront stretch, Sandy Beach, is a sprawling stretch of massive condo-hotel resorts, golf courses carved out the desert, expensive restaurants and minimal Mexican culture.

Travelers without a car, beware: there is no reliable local public transportation. Note that Spring Break is a big deal in Peñasco, and in March the resort is crammed with margarita-chugging US college students.

Sights & Activities

Fishing, snorkeling, diving, kayaking, parasailing and sunset cruises are all popular. There are extensive rock pools to explore at low tide, and trips around the estuary and beyond to the remarkable Reserva El Pinacate y Gran Desierto del Altar can be set up by the likes of CEDO.

Isla San Jorge ISLAND

Also known as Bird Island, Isla San Jorge is one of the best boat excursions in northern Mexico. This rocky island 40km southeast of Peñasco is home to nesting sea birds and also a large community of sea lions (which are curious by nature and will swim alongside boats). To get really up close and personal, book a dive trip. Dolphins are often spotted en route, or if you're really lucky, whales (fin, grey, killer and pilot) are sometimes encountered between October and April.

Several boats at the harbor offer full-day cruises (around US$80) including **Del Mar Charters** (☎638-383-28-02; www.delmarcharters.com; adult US$80). **Sun n' Fun** (☎638-383-54-50; www.sunandfundivers.com; Blvd Benito Juárez btwn Calle 13 & Blvd Fremont; diving/snorkeling M$1500/1000; ⏲9am-5pm Mon-Sat, to 3pm Sun) have Isla San Jorge trips for M$1500 (for two dives) or M$1100 for snorkelers or sightseers.

★CEDO WILDLIFE-WATCHING

(Intercultural Center for the Study of Desert & Oceans; ☎638-382-01-13, in the US 520-320-5473; www.cedointercultural.org; Blvd Las Conchas; ⏲9am-5pm Mon-Sat, 10am-2pm Sun) FREE CEDO is a wonderful place to learn about Rocky Point's fascinating desert-meets-sea ecosystem. Dedicated to the conservation of the upper Gulf of California and surrounding Desierto Sonorense, CEDO has an 'Earthship' visitor center with a good store. There are free natural-history talks in English at 2pm Tuesdays and 4pm Saturdays. CEDO also runs a fascinating program of nature tours, some in collaboration with local cooperatives.

These include tidepool walks (US$15 per person), kayaking on Morúa estuary (US$50), boat trips to Isla San Jorge (US$100) and excursions to El Pinacate Biosphere Reserve with an English-speaking naturalist (US$60).

Tequila Factory DISTILLERY

(www.tequilafactory.mx; cnr Blvd Benito Juárez & Calle 12; ⏲10am-6pm Wed-Mon) FREE This family-owned factory brews artisan tequilas and offers presentations on tequila production as well as tastings. You can also try before you buy in the shop. The oak-aged Añejo and triple-distilled are recommended. It's downstairs from the tourist office.

Sleeping

The Old Port has agreeable down-to-earth options (though it's slim pickings for tight budgets, unless you're in the market for an RV park). All the mega-hotel complexes are at Sandy Beach, to the northwest.

★Posada La Roca HISTORIC HOTEL $

(☎638-383-31-99; www.hotelposadalaroca.blogspot.com; Av Primero de Junio 2; r M$410, without bathroom M$330; P⊖❄🛜) An atmospheric stone structure (built in 1927) in the Old Port that was once a casino/hotel/brothel for US mobsters – including, by all accounts, Al Capone – during Prohibition. The 20 simple, homey rooms are inviting, there's a patio and living room for socializing and the location is convenient.

Dream Weaver Inn APARTMENT $$
(☎638-383-48-05; www.dreamweaverinn.com; Pescadores 3; apt US$45-75; P ⊖ ❄ 📶) Run by Óscar and Lupita, a welcoming couple who run a tight ship, this low-key place has a selection of well-presented apartment-style units, all with cooking facilities and some with sea views. It's very close to the Old Port, shops and restaurants.

Hotel Viña del Mar HOTEL $$
(☎638-383-01-00; www.vinadelmarhotel.com; cnr Av Primero de Junio & Malecón Kino s/n; r M$720-1680; P ⊖ ❄ 📶 🏊) In the Old Port, this motel-style place has spacious rooms with nice beamed ceilings; the best (with kitchens and/or hot tubs) surround the colorful, mosaic pool area right above the rocky shoreline.

Bella Sirena Resort HOTEL $$$
(☎662-219-67-55; www.bellasirenaresort.com; Paseo Costa Diamante; apt US$120-180; P ⊖ ❄ 📶 🏊) Situated on a fine stretch of beach, this large condo complex has selection of attractive apartments all with sea views, good kitchens and modern bathrooms. One of the pools is heated during the winter months and there's two hot tubs and tennis courts.

Eating & Drinking

It takes a little work to find traditional Mexican cuisine between all the sports bars and barbecue joints, but there is some good grub between the cracks.

Kaffee Haus CAFE, EUROPEAN $$
(www.coffeeshaus.com; Blvd Benito Juárez 216B; breakfasts M$85, lunches M$80-135; ⊙7:30-4pm Mon-Sat, 7:30am-2pm Sun; 📶) This bustling cafe-restaurant is famous for its uber-generous European-style breakfasts (try the German Farmer's), excellent coffee and fresh pastries (apple strudel is the house specialty). You'll also find sandwiches (made with homemade bread), great salads and there's always a daily special or two. Portions are huge, so consider sharing a plate.

Aqui es Con Flavio MEXICAN $$
(http://en.aquiesconflavio.com; Malecón Kino; mains M$80-165; ⊙7.30am-11pm) Good Mexican cuisine including lots of seafood (try the garlic-and-butter scallops or a steamed fish fillet) served up alongside occasionally over-exuberant local musicians and by smilingly efficient waiters. Located right on the seafront, in the Old Port district.

Manny's Beach Club BAR, CLUB
(www.mannysbeachclub.com; cnr Matamoros & Arispe; ⊙7am-11pm Sun-Thu, 7am-3am Fri & Sat; 📶) On the 'Strip' east of the Cerro de la Ballena *mirador* (lookout point), this ever-popular place offers beers right on the beach, food (including generous plates of steak and seafood) and live music. There's DJ action on weekends.

JJ's Cantina BAR
(www.jjscantina.com; Cholla Bay; ⊙10am-2am; 📶) There are spectacular views over Cholla Bay, particularly at sunset, from this popular bar-restaurant – an expat favorite – which has live music and pool tables.

Information

There are several ATMs dotted around including **Banamex** (cnr Blvd Benito Juárez & Campeche) near the Old Port. Nearly all hotels have wi-fi.

Rocky Point Tourism & Visitor Assistance (☎638-388-66-24, cell phone 638-386-90-81; www.tourismrockypoint.com; suite 202, cnr Blvd Benito Juárez & Calle 12; ⊙9am-5pm Mon-Fri) offers information, advice and free 24-hour bilingual emergency assistance. It's in the tall blue building on the east side of Juárez.

Getting There & Around

Puerto Peñasco International Airport (Aeropuerto Mar de Cortés; ☎638-383-60-97; www.aeropuertomardecortes.com; Libramiento Caborca-Sonoyta 71) is 3km north of town. There are currently only two connections, both twice-weekly, with **Aeroméxico** (www.aeromexico.com) to Las Vegas and Hermosillo.

Driving south from Arizona, it's about 100km down Hwy 8 from the no-fuss Lukeville–Sonoyta border crossing to Puerto Peñasco. Drivers from California can use the San Luis Río Colorado crossing, south of Yuma in western Arizona, from where average driving time is three hours.

Several shuttle-van services operate between Puerto Peñasco and Arizona, including **Transportes Supremo** (☎638-383-36-40; www.transportesupremo.com; Calle Lázaro Cárdenas) which run to/from Phoenix four times daily (US$47, four hours).

Albatros (☎638-388-08-88; Blvd Benito Juárez btwn Calles 29 & 30) runs 11 daily buses to Hermosillo (M$262, 5½ hours) and five to Nogales (M$265, six hours). **ABC** (☎800-025-02-22; www.abc.com.mx; cnr Calles Constitución & Bravo), one block north of Blvd Benito Juárez, heads to Tijuana (M$529, nine hours) five times daily.

Taxis cost around M$30 for short rides, but around M$60 from the Old Port to Las Conchas or to the Sandy Beach resorts – and can be double that or more coming back.

OFF THE BEATEN TRACK

GRAN DESIERTO DE ALTAR

Northeast of Puerto Peñasco, abutting the US border, are the lunar landscapes of the Gran Desierto de Altar, one of the driest places on earth. Astronauts Neil Armstrong and Buzz Aldrin used this region in the 1960s to prepare themselves for their Apollo 11 moon landing.

Reserva de la Biosfera El Pinacate y Gran Desierto de Altar (El Pinacate Biosphere Reserve; ☎638-105-80-16; http://elpinacate.webbystudio.com; admission M$40; ⌚9am-5pm), a remote, spectacular 7145-sq-km reserve, is a Unesco World Heritage Site. It contains ancient eroded volcanoes, 10 giant craters, 400-plus ash cones and petrified lava flows. Wildlife includes pronghorn antelope (the fastest land mammal in the Americas), bighorn sheep, pumas, amphibians and reptiles, and bountiful birdlife. There's an excellent, highly informative solar-powered visitors center, interpretive hiking trails and two campgrounds.

Over 70km of dirt roads (4WD only in parts) penetrate the reserve. Visitors must register to climb the 1190m Cerro del Pinacate volcano.

The visitors center is about 8km west of Km 72 on Hwy 8 (some 27km from Puerto Peñasco). The craters are accessed by a separate turnoff further north at Km 52 on Hwy 8. CEDO (p746) in Puerto Peñasco organizes excellent tours to the reserve. Good walking shoes are recommended but note that there's no water or electricity available anywhere in the reserve, except at the visitors center.

Hermosillo

☎662 / POP 784,000 / ELEV 238M

Sprawling Hermosillo, Sonora's capital, is no beauty, but it is an important transportation hub and has a decent selection of museums. It's vexingly spread-out, with the often-unbearable afternoon heat garnering it the moniker of Sun City. Central Hermosillo fans out around craggy Cerro de la Campana (Hill of the Bell): the city's aerial-mast-festooned viewpoint.

Sights

MUSAS MUSEUM
(Museo de Arte de Sonora; www.musas.gob.mx; cnr Blvd Vildósola & Av Cultura; M$30; ⌚10am-7pm Mon-Sat, 10am-5pm Sun) This landmark museum, 1.5km south of the center, has edgy displays (there were superb poster art, Sonoran desert and contemporary Mexican art exhibitions when we dropped by), cultural events and films.

Centro Ecológico de Sonora ZOO
(☎662-250-67-68; www.centroecologicodesonora.com; Templo de Tláloc; adult/child M$30/15; ⌚8am-5pm) This lush botanical garden and zoo features an excellent array of plants and wildlife from Sonora's mountains, deserts and prairies, including the endangered, antelope-like Sonoran pronghorn *(berrendo):* North America's fastest-moving land animal.

Sleeping & Eating

Hermosillo has few decent budget options. Most midrange and top-end accommodations are in the Zona Hotelera north of the center – convenient only if you have your own vehicle.

Hotel Washington HOTEL $
(☎662-213-11-83; Noriega 68; r M$260-300; ❄@🛜) The Washington is showing its age, and rooms are perhaps a tad musty, but the friendly staff and central location make it a solid budget choice.

★**Colonial Hotel** MOTEL $$
(☎662-259-00-00; www.hotelescolonial.com; Vado del Río 9; r/ste M$582/747; P⊖❄@🛜≋) The most stylish motel you've ever seen, full of modern art, sleek design touches and artistic flourishes (the lobby Muzak was Miles Davis when we dropped by). Book via their website for special rates.

Mercado Municipal MARKET $
(Matamoros; tacos M$10; ⌚7am-5.30pm) Occupying an entire city block, Hermosillo's historic, bustling covered market hosts dozens of excellent taco stands, and a few cafes and stores selling the *chiltepin* ('bird's eye' minichilis from the Sonoran desert) for which the region is famous.

Restaurante Mochomos FUSION $$$
(www.mochomos.mx; Morelos 701; mains M$110-210; ⌚1pm-midnight Mon-Thu, to 1am Fri & Sat,

to 5pm Sun; [P] [wifi]) In the Zona Hotelera, the intimate Mochomos serves Sonoran fusion cuisine. Try a *brocheta abierta* (beef kebab with chargrilled vegetables) or some seafood.

Information

Hospital San José (Blvd Morelos 340; 24hr) Modern hospital with a 24-hour emergency department.

Tourist Information Kiosk (662-213-55-37; www.gotosonora.com; Plaza Zaragoza; 9am-7pm Mon-Sat) Helpful booth on Plaza Zaragoza with English-speaking staff and information about regional attractions.

Getting There & Away

AIR

Hermosillo Airport (662-261-00-00; www.aeropuertosgap.com.mx; Carretera Bahía de Kino, Km 9.5) has direct flights to airports including Chihuahua, Guadalajara, Los Mochis, Mexico City, Monterrey and San José del Cabo. International connnections include Dallas, Los Angeles and Phoenix.

BUS

Hermosillo's main bus terminal, with frequent services, is the **Central de Autobuses de Hermosillo** (CAH; 662-217-15-22; Blvd Encinas 400), 2km east of the city center. Second-class **Albatros** (Blvd Encinas 354) has another terminal 150m west, and pricier 1st-class **Tufesa** (662-213-04-42; Blvd Encinas btwn Velázquez & Universidad) is a further 400m west.

Second-class buses to Bahía de Kino (M$81 to M$92, two hours, hourly 5:30am to 6:30pm) depart from **AMH & TCH bus terminal** (Sonora btwn González & García) near Jardín Juárez.

Getting Around

City bus 1 (M$7) runs the 2km to the Blvd Encinas bus terminals from the east side of Jardín Juárez. Taxis cost M$50 to M$70 around town or M$180 to/from the airport.

Bahía de Kino

662 / POP 6050

Laid-back Bahía de Kino is a dreamy beach paradise named for Padre Eusebio Kino, who established a small mission here for the indigenous Seri people in the 17th century. The old part, Kino Viejo, is the original settlement. This typical Mexican fishing village fans out along the lengthy main beach, which is perfect for swimming. It's where you'll likely spend most of your time, and also where you'll find the 'snowbirds' (retired North American citizens who head south for the winter). Look out for those hulking RVs. High season is from November to March; at other times, you may find yourself blissfully alone in the hotels here.

Sights & Activities

Punta Chueca INDIGENOUS CULTURE

This village is home to the Seri people, one of Mexico's smallest indigenous groups (less than 1000 people). The Seri are famous for their handicrafts, including their highly regarded baskets and carvings from ironwood. You'll need a 4WD with high clearance to make the journey along the dirt road to the settlement. Punta Chueca is situated 34km north of beach town Bahía de Kino.

Isla del Tiburón ISLAND

(3km offshore from Punta Chueca) Mountainous Isla del Tiburón was once a Seri homeland, but it was depopulated when the island was declared a nature reserve in 1963. Today it's administered by the Seri tribal authorities. An intact desert ecosystem, Tiburón is home to bighorn sheep and large colonies of sea birds. There's good snorkeling around its coast.

You need a permit to visit the island (speak to guides Alfredo López or Ernesto Molina in Punta Chueca) who can set up tours. If you need advice on arrangements try the **Centro de Estudios Culturales y**

BUSES FROM HERMOSILLO

DESTINATION	FARE (M$)	DURATION	FREQUENCY (DAILY)
Guaymas	104-126	2hr	every 30-60min Tufesa, hourly CAH
Los Mochis	342-430	7-9hr	every 30min CAH, every 45 min Tufesa
Mexico City (Terminal Norte)	1465	29-33hr	hourly CAH
Nogales	242-267	3½-4½hr	hourly Tufesa
Phoenix	700-903	8hr	11 Tufesa
Puerto Peñasco	242	5-6hr	12 Albatros

Ecológicos (☎662-242-00-24; www.prescott.edu/kino-bay-center; 151 Calle Cádiz, Kino Nuevo).

Museo de los Seris MUSEUM
(☎662-212-64-19; cnr Av Mar de Cortez & Calle Progreso; admission M$10; ⊙9am-5pm Wed-Sun) Displays include an interesting collection of artifacts and handicrafts, plus panels about Seri history.

Sleeping & Eating

The Kino Nuevo strip has abundant RV parks. Other than the odd low-key bar, there's no nightlife: locals call 9pm 'Kino midnight'.

Apartments Alcatraz Kino Bay APARTMENT $$
(☎662-242-06-93; www.kinoalcatraz.com; Calle Miramar; apt M$500-750;) These good-value apartments offer the best inexpensive lodgings in Kino, each with cooking facilities, fridge and TV/DVD. The tiny pool is for cooling off only (not swimming lengths!). Rates drop the longer you stay. It's located a block back from the shore in Kino Viejo.

Casa Tortuga APARTMENT $$$
(☎662-242-01-22; rentcasatortuga@aol.com; Av Mar de Cortez 2645; apt M$1114-1508;) Beachfront Casa Tortuga has two atmospheric, very comfortable apartments: Pelican, with its stunning ocean-facing, *palapa*-roofed terrace (complete with sunbeds, BBQ and table for outdoor dining) is highly recommended. There are complimentary kayaks, and the owners sometimes take guests out in a boat to Isla Pelícano for bird watching. Prices drop a little in winter.

La Playa Hotel HOTEL $$$
(☎662-242-02-73; www.laplayarvhotel.com; Av Mar de Cortez 101; r/ste M$1200/2100;) Boasting a prime beachside location, this place has well-equipped rooms, featuring two (or three) double beds, mini-kitchens and private terraces with ocean views and suites that can sleep six. The Playa's architecture is reminiscent of the Greek Islands and there's a hot tub in addition to the pool.

Los Náufragos SEAFOOD, MEXICAN $$
(Calle del Muelle; mains M$60-100; ⊙8am-10pm;) This casual beachside place specializes in inexpensive seafood including wonderful *cocteles* (ceviche-style fish, shrimp, squid and octopus), lots of shrimp dishes and snacks including tacos and *tostadas* (M$20 each).

Casablanca NORTH AMERICAN $$
(☎662-242-07-77; www.casablancakinobay.com; cnr Cádiz & Av Mar de Cortez; breakfasts M$60-90, mains M$50-150; ⊙8am-10pm, to midnight Fri & Sat;) This eye-catching restaurant serves tasty Mexican-North American grub, including filling breakfasts, salads and burgers. In the evening the action moves to the upstairs *palapa*-style bar, which has a pool table. Accommodation is also available.

Information

Email **KBnet News** (kbnetnews@aol.com) for the latest Kino news in English on everything from new RV sites to travel warnings.

Cruz Roja (Red Cross; ☎662-242-04-86; cnr Blvr Kino & Av Manzanillo, Kino Viejo) You'll find ATMs at Pemex and at the Cruz Roja, which also provides ambulance and emergency medical services.

Casa del Mar (☎662-242-02-21; cnr Calles Bilbao & Esqueda; ⊙9am-4pm Wed-Sun) FREE This visitors center services the 900-island **Área de Protección de Flora y Fauna Islas del Golfo de California**. It has very informative displays in Spanish and English, and issues permits for visiting the islands (M$40 per person per island per day).

Getting There & Around

Buses to Hermosillo (M$81 to M$92, two hours) run roughly hourly from the bus station about halfway along the strip. You can use these services to get around (local rides cost M$7) as there's no other public transportation. Taxis cost M$50 for a ride of up to 5km, more after dark.

San Carlos

☎622 / POP 2300

With its striking desert-and-bay landscape, the low-key beach retreat of San Carlos feels a universe apart from its gritty port neighbors. It's presided over by some dramatic hills – notably the majestic twin peaks of Cerro Tetakawi – that glow an impressive red-earthed hue as the sun descends.

San Carlos' beaches are a mix of dark sand and pebbles. Head to Playa Algodones (famed for its role in the movie *Catch-22*) for white sand and turquoise seas.

Orientation

San Carlos is not pedestrian friendly, being spread-eagled over some 8km. Most amenities are on the 2.5km stretch of Blvd Beltrones. Head

OFF THE BEATEN TRACK

RÍO DE SONORA VALLEY

North and east of Hermosillo stretches frontier country proper: the mountains and prairies that best convey what life would have been like for Spanish settlers centuries ago. This area is best known for its well-preserved Jesuit missions, many of which were established by famed missionary, Padre Eusebio Kino. Dreamy time-warped colonial towns here also boast beautiful architecture, thermal baths and interesting accommodations. You'll need your own vehicle: public transportation is scarce.

Following Hwy 14 northwest from Hermosillo, it's 80km up to mellow **Ures** with its shady Plaza Zaragoza and shops selling the Sonoran version of tequila, *bacanora*. After another 30km, Hwy 118 branches north to reach **Baviácora**, with one of Sonora's finest cathedrals. **Aconchi**, 15km on, has wonderful thermal baths. A further 22km north is the laid-back colonial town of **Banámichi**, close to good bird-watching and hot springs.

The landscape becomes increasingly eroded with interesting rock formations as you near **Arizpe**, once capital of Nueva España's Provincias Internas (which included California, New Mexico and Texas) in the 18th and 19th centuries. You can loop back to Hermosillo via **Magdalena de Kino**. Padre Kino is buried in the town's mission here, and Magdalena is a great base for visiting surrounding missions such as **Pitiquito** (with outstanding indigenous art on the walls) on the Caborca road, **Tubutama** and the dramatic ruins of **Cocóspera**.

La Posada de Río Sonora (☎623-231-02-59; www.laposadadelriosonora.com; Main plaza; r M$983-1573; ❄📶) One of the best hotels in Banámichi, La Posada de Río Sonora offers home-cooked meals (M$65-130) and horseback riding (M$400), and is a good place to use as a base when exploring and the the Río de Sonora Valley.

right at the intersection by the Oxxo store after the Beltrones strip to get out to Playa Algodones (6km northwest), or straight on for Marina San Carlos (500m west).

Activities

For many, sportfishing tops the list here: April to September are best for big fish; there are seven main annual tournaments. There are coves for diving and snorkeling, as well as some wrecks offshore. At **Isla San Pedro Nolasco**, 35km out to sea, you can snorkel or dive with a sea-lion colony.

★ **Gary's Dive Shop** DIVING
(☎622-226-00-49; www.garysdiveshop.com; Blvd Beltrones Km 10; ⏲7am-5pm) This professional, long-established dive shop and adventure sports center offers fishing excursions and scenic cruises. Dive trips to Isla San Pedro Nolasco (Seal Island) cost US$95 (excluding gear rental). Gary's also rents good-quality snorkeling gear for US$6 a day.

Hattie Sunset Cruises BOAT TRIP
(☎622-197-1351; Marina San Carlos; US$30) Based at the Marina San Carlos, these two-hour sunset cruises offer the possibility of dolphin and whale encounters while guaranteeing spectacular views (and margaritas on tap).

Sleeping

San Carlos is mainly geared to visitors from over the US border, and there are few inexpensive places to stay.

Hotel Creston MOTEL $$
(☎622-226-00-20; Blvd Beltrones Km 10; r M$585-670; P❄📶🏊) OK, it's located very close to busy Blvd Beltrones, but these clean spacious rooms (with satellite TV and good air-con) arranged around a small pool are decent value for San Carlos.

Posada Condominiums & Resort Hotel APARTMENT $$$
(☎622-226-10-31; www.posadacondominiums.com; Blvd Beltrones Km 11.5; apt US$156; P⊜❄📶🏊) Right on the beach (you can hear the waves lapping on the shore at night), these attractive condos all enjoy fine sea vistas from their generous balconies. All boast fully-equipped kitchens, attractive living rooms and TVs with DVD players. They're a short walk from the Marina San Carlos and its restaurants. Rates can drop below US$100 at quiet times of year.

Eating & Drinking

La Palapa Griega MEXICAN, GREEK $$
(Blvd Beltrones Km 11.5; mains M$60-170; ⏲8am-10pm) This beachfront Greek-owned

restaurant offers a memorable setting for a meal. Try a sampler (hummus, taramasalata, baba ghanoush), Greek salad (M$65) or some seafood.

★ **Bonifacio's** FUSION **$$$**
(☎622-227-05-15; www.bonifacios.com; Playa Algodones; mains M$115-350; ⊙11am-11pm Mon-Thu, to 3am Fri & Sat, to 10:30pm Sun;) Perfectly poised on the sands of lovely Playa Algodones, this is one of northwest Mexico's finest restaurants. The place exudes sophistication, from the spacious chandelier-lit, antique-furnished interior to the imaginative Mexican fusion cuisine. Try a *mariscada* – thin small slices of raw fish cured in lime, with *governador* (shrimp) tacos and fish *chicharrón* (fried pork rinds). Doubles as a stylish lounge bar at night.

Information

Banamex (Blvd Beltrones) With two ATMs.
Gary's Dive Shop (☎622-226-00-49; www.garysdiveshop.com; Blvd Beltrones Km 10; ⊙7am-5pm) Has maps and information; there's internet (Mon-Sat; same hours) on the floor above.

Getting There & Around

Buses from Guaymas run as far as Marina San Carlos, and local rides within San Carlos cost M$6. Taxis charge M$50 to M$100 in the San Carlos area.

Long-distance buses will likely drop you at either the **Grupo Estrella Blanca** (Calle 14 No 96) or **Tufesa** (Blvd García López 927) terminals in Guaymas. From Grupo Estrella Blanca, walk north on Calle 14 to Blvd García López and catch the white San Carlos bus (M$12, every 30 minutes). From Tufesa, cross the road to catch the same bus. A taxi from either terminal to San Carlos is M$180.

The **airport** (☎622-221-05-11; www.asa.gob.mx/wb/webasa/guaymas_aeropuertos) is 10km north of Guaymas. **Aéreo Calafia** (www.aereocalafia.com.mx) has flights to Baja California cities including La Paz and Los Cabos.

Álamos & Around

☎647 / POP ÁLAMOS 9300 / ELEV 432M

The most civilized, architecturally rich town in northwest Mexico, Álamos is a cultural oasis and culinary capital. Sheltered in the forested foothills of the Sierra Madre Occidental, its hushed cobblestone streets and imposing colonial buildings hint at a fascinating history, much of it to do with Álamos' role as Mexico's northernmost silver-mining town. The town is both a national historical monument and one of Mexico's *pueblos mágicos* (magical towns).

Álamos' charms have proven irresistible to many US retirees and creative types who, since the '50s, have snapped up decaying colonial buildings to renovate into second homes and hotels. These well-heeled expats comprise a small but influential segment of Álamos' population.

The town's lush surroundings include tropical deciduous forest and mountains covered in pine and oak. The 929-sq-km Sierra de Álamos–Río Cuchujaqui Flora & Fauna Protection Area that almost encircles Álamos has great birding and wonderful walks.

More bizarrely, Álamos and vicinity is where most of the world's jumping beans originate (beans sold as a novelty that 'jump' due to the presence of a larvae inside).

The nicest time to come is between mid-October and mid-April, when the climate is cooler. The biggest number of Mexican tourists come in the rainy months, July to September; at other times, it's far quieter.

History

The area's silver mines were discovered around La Aduana (4km west of Álamos) in the 16th century. Álamos itself was founded in the 1680s, probably as a dormitory suburb for La Aduana's wealthy colonists. Despite hostilities from the indigenous Yaqui and Mayo, Álamos boomed into one of Mexico's principal 18th-century mining centers.

During Mexico's 19th-century turmoils, Álamos was attacked repeatedly, by French invaders, by factions seeking its silver wealth and by the fiercely independent Yaqui. The Mexican Revolution took a further toll and, by the 1920s, most mines were abandoned and Álamos was practically a ghost town.

In 1948, Álamos was reawakened by William Levant Alcorn, a Pennsylvania dairy farmer who bought the Almada mansion on the Plaza de Armas and converted it into Hotel Los Portales. Other *norteamericanos* followed, restoring crumbling mansions to their former glory. Recently they've been joined by wealthy Mexicans, seduced by the relaxed ambience and benign winter climate, creating something of a real estate boom.

Sights

Álamos is ideal for sauntering around and soaking up one of Mexico's most idyllic colonial centers, with perhaps a break at one of the atmospheric restaurants.

The delightful, verdant Plaza de Armas is the setting for **Parroquia de la Purísima Concepción**, a church built between 1786 and 1804. Much of its original interior was fashioned from silver.

El Mirador tops a hill on Álamos' southeastern edge, affording sweeping views of the town and its mountainous surroundings. It's accessible by steps from the Arroyo Agua Escondida two blocks down Obregón from Victoria.

Museo Costumbrista de Sonora MUSEUM
(☎647-428-00-53; Victoria s/n; admission M$10; ⏰9am-6pm Wed-Sun) This well-done museum of Sonoran customs has extensive exhibits (all in Spanish) on the history and traditions of the state. Special attention is paid to the influence of mining on Álamos and the fleeting prosperity it created for the town's well-off, including rooms filled with antiques, period furniture and even a few vintage carriages.

Museo de María Félix MUSEUM
(Linda Vista 6; M$10; ⏰Thu-Sun 9am-4pm; P) Movie star María Félix (known simply as 'La Doña', and often dubbed Mexico's Marilyn Monroe) is the town's most famous daughter, and this museum is dedicated to her. Inside are paintings, photographs and personal effects and an illustration by Diego Rivera. It's on a hillside with great views, a 15-minute walk southwest of the plaza.

Tours

For highly-informative tours around town, English-speaking **Emiliano Graseda** (who can be found at the Álamos tourist office most weekends) charges M$220 per person. Tours take in Álamos' landmarks and private homes, and continue in La Aduana to visit a brick works, *artesanías* workshops and a mission.

Pronatura BIRD-WATCHING
(☎647-428-00-04; Juárez 8; 2hr tour around town per person M$200; ⏰7:30am-7:30pm Mon-Fri) This environmental group is the main contact point for the local guides of bird-watching group **Alas de Álamos** (Wings of Álamos). It also offers day trips further afield.

Solipaso ADVENTURE TOUR
(☎647-428-15-09; www.solipaso.com; El Pedregal, Privada s/n, Barrio el Chalatón) Runs expert bird-watching trips (half-day M$1050) and also superb floating river excursions (per person M$1440, four to 12 people; Nov to Mar) on the Río Mayo northwest of Álamos. You visit ancient petroglyphs, a stone aqueduct, a Mayo village and there's guaranteed to be spectacular coastal and tropical birdlife; river otters and coatimundis are also encountered. Their guides are highly knowledgable. There are no regular office hours; call them directly to book.

Festivals & Events

Festival Alfonso Ortíz Tirado MUSIC
(www.festivalortiztirado.gob.mx) One of northern Mexico's premier cultural events, Álamos' 10-day late-January festival features top-class classical and chamber music, blues, *bossa nova* and *trova* performed by artists from across the globe; there are also events for kids.

Sleeping

Álamos has some of the most atmospheric and attractive accommodations in all of Mexico, many in converted colonial mansions featuring gorgeous interior design. However peso-watchers should beware that budget options are limited.

Such is the summer heat, the cooler months (October to April) are high season in Álamos. However, with northern Mexico's downturn in tourism, discounts are often available at all times of year.

Posada de Don Andrés HOTEL $
(☎647-428-11-10; Rosales; r M$400-600; P❄📶) This decent-value hotel overlooks Plaza Alameda and features two floors of spacious rooms that are comfortable enough but a little on the dark side. Jorge, the owner, is a friendly, welcoming character who makes coffee for his guests in the morning.

★**Hotel Luz del Sol** BOUTIQUE HOTEL $$
(☎647-428-04-66; www.luzdelsolalamos.com; Obregon 3; r incl breakfast M$885; ❄📶) This beautiful, excellent-value hotel has a warm ambience thanks to welcoming staff and the presence of one of the town's best cafes. There are only three rooms, each very spacious with

sultan-sized beds, sumptous furnishings, high ceilings and simply vast adjoining bathrooms with vintage tiling and tubs.

Casa de las Siete Columnas B&B $$
(☎647-428-01-64; www.lassietecolumnas.com; Juárez 36; r incl breakfast M$650-750;) An inviting new Canandian-owned hotel in an imposing centuries-old building – look out for the stunning seven-columned front portico. Rooms are at the rear (around a courtyard and small heated pool) and feature beamed ceilings, fireplaces and tasteful decor. There's a guests' lounge with TV/DVD and pool table. Open October to April only.

Hotel Colonial HOTEL $$$
(☎647-428-13-71; www.alamoshotelcolonial.com; Obregón 4; r incl breakfast M$1680-2650; P) The attention to detail at this incredibly classy historic mansion is highly impressive: it feels more like you are stepping into an Edwardian period drama than it does a Mexican hotel. Ten commodious rooms feature tapestries, oil paintings, antiques and stately fireplaces, and there's a vast roof terrace to enjoy.

El Pedregal LODGE $$$
(☎647-428-15-09; www.elpedregalmexico.com; Privada s/n, Barrio el Chalatón; r incl breakfast M$1300; P@) Lovely adobe and straw-bale cabins with stylish, artistic furnishings and luxury bedding scattered around eight hectares of tropical deciduous forest on the edge of Álamos, 2km from the plaza. The welcoming owners are expert birders and lead tours. Discounts are available between June and August.

Hacienda de los Santos LUXURY HOTEL $$$
(☎647-428-02-22; www.haciendadelossantos.com; Molina 8; r/ste incl breakfast from M$3920/4520; P@) As the name indicates, this is more hacienda than hotel, encompassing five restored colonial houses, three pools, three restaurants, a movie theater, spa, gym, landscaped grounds and a bar (with a 520-strong tequila collection!). Accommodations are astounding, luxurious and highly atmospheric. Rates plummet in the hot months.

Eating

Cenaduría Dõna Lola MEXICAN $
(☎647-428-11-09; Volantín s/n; mains M$40-85; 7am-10pm Mon-Sat, 2-10pm Sun) Down a little lane south of the Plaza de Armas, this unpretentious family-run place offers inexpensive, delicious homemade Mexican food. There's a covered terrace at the rear. It's also known as Koky's.

Los Zarapes MEXICAN $
(Plaza de Armas; meals M$40-70; 7.30am-9.30pm) For traditional Mexican grub (filling breakfasts, *carne asada*, *gorditas* and *enchiladas*) and a fine view of the plaza with its Baroque church, this place is perfect.

★**Teresitas** INTERNATIONAL, BAKERY $$
(www.teresitasalamos.com; Allende 41; mains M$50-135; 8am-9pm Mon-Sat, 9am-6pm Sun;) Simply outstanding bakery-cum-bistro with an open kitchen and tantalising menu:

FERRIES TO BAJA

Two ferry services link mainland northwest Mexico with Baja California. From Topolobampo near Los Mochis, Baja Ferries (p756) leaves at 11:59pm Monday to Friday and 11pm on Sunday for La Paz in Baja; the trip takes around 7 hours. For travel around Semana Santa, Christmas/New Year and in June and July, it's recommended to reserve a month ahead. You can buy tickets in Los Mochis or, on departure day, at the Topolobampo terminal.

The ferry **Santa Rosalía** (www.ferrysantarosalia.com; seating saloon-class M$840, motorcycle/car M$1420/3200) sails from Guaymas for Santa Rosalía, Baja California, at 8pm Monday, Tuesday, Thursday, Friday and Saturday, arriving the next morning around 7am. From mid-November to mid-March, strong winds may cause delays, and the Monday/Tuesday sailings are occasionally canceled in low season. The **ticket office** (☎622-222-02-04; Recinto Portuario Zona Franca s/n, Terminal de Transbordadores, Colonia Punta Arena; 8am-2pm & 3:30-8pm Mon-Sat) is 2km east of Guaymas city center. Reservations are only necessary if you want a cabin or are taking a vehicle (booking three days in advance is sufficient). All passengers and vehicles should be at the terminal by 6:30pm.

it features an excellent salad selection, pasta dishes, crepes, and paninis, as well as amazing cakes and pastries (try the pecan pie). Eat in the fountain-flanked garden or enjoy the comfort of the royal-blue banquette seating inside.

Café Luz del Sol CAFE $$
(647-428-04-66; Obregón 3; mains M$60-115; 7:30am-5pm Mon-Sat;) In a region cruelly deprived of decent coffee shops, this colonial cafe is a better find for caffeine-starved travelers than any silver mine. Devour beautifully prepared breakfasts, Mexican/North American lunches, homemade cakes and, yep, wicked coffee. There's an elegant interior and a small patio.

La Casa Aduana MEXICAN $$$
(647-404-34-73; www.casaladuana.com; Plaza, La Aduana; meals M$170-280; from 1pm Wed-Sun;) In a 1620s customs house, this highly atmospheric restaurant in a country inn offers New Sonoran cuisine such as chicken *cordon verde* with shrimps and *chile poblano*. Book ahead. A taxi from Álamos is around M$170.

Information

Banorte (Madero 37; 9am-4pm Mon-Fri) ATM; money exchange.

Ciber Utopia (Rosales 36; 8am-9pm) This tiny cybercafe just east of Plaza Alameda has moderately-fast connections. No wi-fi.

Hospital General de Álamos (647-428-02-25; Madero s/n; 8am-8pm) Basic local hospital with no emergency services. Some staff speak a little English.

Tourist Office (647-428-04-50; cparra@sonaraturismo.gob.mx; Victoria 5; 8am-6pm Mon-Fri) A helpful information office. On weekends it's usually staffed by local independent guide Emiliano Graseda.

Getting There & Away

Álamos is 53km east of Navojoa, which is 323km southeast of Hermosillo and 156km north of Los Mochis. Second-class buses by **Albatros** (cnr Guerrero & No Reelección, Navojoa) depart Navojoa for Álamos (M$30, one hour) every 30 minutes from 7am to 6:30pm; there's also a bus at 9pm. Over 20 daily 1st-class Albatros and **Tufesa** (642-421-32-10; www.tufesa.com.mx; cnr Hidalgo & No Reelección, Navojoa) buses connect Navojoa with Guaymas and Hermosillo.

Álamos' **Transportes Baldomero Corral terminal** (647-428-00-96; Morelos 7) is on Plaza Alameda. Buses leave for Navojoa (M$30, one hour) every half-hour until 6.30pm.

Los Mochis

668 / POP 256,000

Most travellers don't linger in Los Mochis. Despite being a transportation hub, the climate is perpetually humid and there are no real sights to savor (except an excess of sleazy bars). However if you're venturing to Baja on a boat or up the Ferrocarril Chihuahua Pacífico on a train, you'll find adequate eats and sleeps here.

Sleeping

Hotel Fénix HOTEL $$
(668-812-26-23; Flores 365 Sur; s/d/tr M$455/545/575;) This is the best moderately priced hotel in town, with welcoming staff, a sparkling lobby, an excellent restaurant and renovated rooms that represent good value, all with fast wi-fi and modern furnishings.

Hotel América HOTEL $$
(668-812-35-55; www.losmochishotel.com; Allende 655 Sur; r M$550-680;) It's nothing fancy but this efficiently run hotel has smallish, functional rooms with flat-screen TVs, coffee makers (and some have PCs). The hotel's entire color scheme is a rather unexciting beige-brown.

Best Western Los Mochis HOTEL $$$
(668-816-30-00; www.bestwestern.com; Obregón 691 Poniente; r M$1674;) Enjoying a prime spot overlooking the central plaza, this business-class hotel offers professional staff and service and very comfortable, carpeted rooms with modern bathrooms. The pool is tiny and the small gym has free weights.

Eating

La Cabaña de Doña Chayo TAQUERÍA $
(668-818-54-98; Obregón 99 Poniente; tacos & quesadillas M$23-33; 8am-1am) A simple yet enjoyable place with delectable quesadillas and tacos with *carne asada* or *machaca* (spiced shredded dried beef).

Whimis CAFE, ICE CREAM $
(Leyva 523 Sur; ice cream M$18, coffee M$25; 8am-8pm;) About as fashionable as it gets in Los Mochis, this bright, cheery little place offers an epic selection of ice cream and fruit smoothies, and there's an espresso machine for all your coffee needs.

Los Mochis

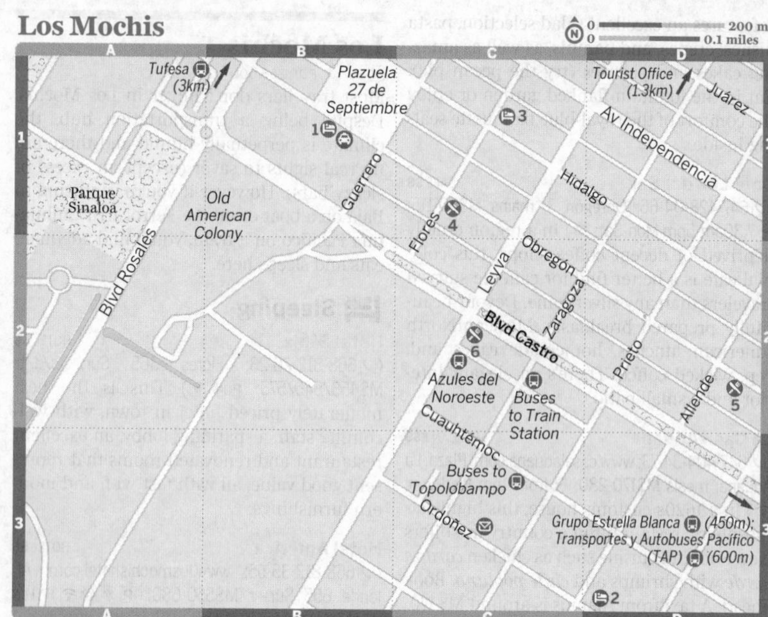

Los Mochis

Sleeping

1 Best Western Los Mochis ... B1
2 Hotel América ... D3
3 Hotel Fénix ... C1

Eating

4 El Farallón ... C1
5 La Cabaña de Doña Chayo ... D2
6 Whimis ... C2

El Farallón SEAFOOD **$$**
(☎668-812-12-73; www.farallon.com.mx; Obregón 499 Poniente; mains M$80-190; ⏰9am-11pm; 📶) Upmarket seafood restaurant with a far-ranging selection of dishes: stick to the tried-and-tested Mexican and Sinaloan dishes (rather than fusion-style sushi rolls and the like) and you won't go wrong. The ceviche and *pescado a la plancha* (grilled fish) are particularly great.

Information

Yinto's Cyberclub (cnr Obregón & Guerrero; ⏰8am-9pm) In addition to internet services, this place offers cheap phone calls and CD-burning.

Getting There & Away

AIR

Los Mochis Airport (☎668-818-68-70; www.aeropuertosgap.com.mx; Carretera Los Mochis–Topolobampo Km 12.5) Los Mochis Airport has daily flights to Mexico City, Hermosillo, Tijuana, Mazatlán and Guadalajara, with airlines including Aeroméxico Connect (☎668-812-02-16; www.aeromexico.com.mx; Obregón 1104 Poniente), **Aéreo Calafia** (www.aereocalafia.com.mx) and **Volaris** (www.volaris.com). Several small airlines fly to Baja California destinations.

BOAT

Baja Ferries (☎668-817-37-52; www.bajaferries.com; Local 5, cnr Blvds Rosales & Centenario; ⏰8am-6pm Mon-Fri, 9am-3pm Sat) This company offers tickets for ferries for Pichilingue, near La Paz in Baja California Sur, leaving from Topolobampo, 24km southwest of Los Mochis. Tickets can be purchased up to two months ahead.

BUS

Los Mochis has a handful of private bus terminals. The main intercity bus stations all have round-the-clock departures.

Azules del Noroeste (☎668-812-34-91; Tenochtitlán 399 Poniente) Second-class buses to El Fuerte (M$72, two hours, 16 times daily).

Grupo Estrella Blanca/Transportes y Autobuses Pacífico (GEB/TAP; Blvd Castro btwn Constitución & Domínguez) Deluxe and 1st-class buses to Mexico City, Nogales and Tijuana.

Tufesa (☎668-818-22-22; www.tufesa.com.mx; Blvd Rosales 2300) First-class buses to Navojoa (for Álamos), Nogales and Phoenix and to Mazatlán and Guadalajara. The terminal is 3km northeast of the center of Los Mochis (M$60 in a taxi).

TRAIN

Los Mochis Train Station (☎668-824-11-51; ⌚5am-5:30pm Mon-Fri, 5-9am & 10:30am-1pm Sat & Sun) The ticket office at Los Mochis train station sells railway tickets up to a month ahead of travel. Opening hours are notoriously unreliable, so be warned. In town, Viajes Flamingo (☎668-812-16-13; www.mexicoscoppercanyon.com; Hotel Santa Anita cnr Leyva & Hidalgo; ⌚8:30am-6pm Mon-Fri, 8:30am-2.30pm Sat) also books tickets in advance.

The station is located 4km southeast of the town center at the end of Bienestar.

Getting Around

Buses 72 'Castro-Chamizal' and 118 'DIF Castro Estación' (M$6) do the 15-minute run to the train station from Blvd Castro, between Zaragoza and Prieto (5:30am to 9pm). They drop you one block before the station. However, as the morning train leaves at 6am, the bus is only useful for reaching the ticket office; you'll need to take a taxi if you want to make the train on time.

Buses to Topolobampo (M$18, every 20 minutes until 7:30pm) leave from the corner of Cuauhtémoc and Prieto for the Baja ferry.

Taxis in town cost M$50, and to the airport/Topolobampo approximately M$160 to M$200. They line up on Obregón, by the Best Western.

THE COPPER CANYON & FERROCARRIL CHIHUAHUA PACÍFICO

The simply breathtaking highland scenery in the Copper Canyon (Barranca del Cobre) region is nature on a very grand scale indeed. Of everything there is to see in northern Mexico, not much comes close to the Copper Canyon, with its astonishing vistas at every turn, towering pine-clad mountains and the fascinating culture of the indigenous Tarahumara people to investigate. This is planet earth on steroids.

A labyrinth of seven main canyons covers an area four times larger than Arizona's Grand Canyon, which are, in several places, considerably deeper (over 1800m). The canyons have been gouged out of the sierra's 25-million-year-old volcanic rock by tectonic movements and rivers. Tropical fruits grow in the canyon bottoms while the high ground is covered in alpine vegetation and, often, winter snows.

Lonely roads do snake into the region, but let the train take the strain: by far the best way to discover canyon country is via the 'Chepe' railway (the Ferrocarril Chihuahua-Pacífico, or Chihuahua-Pacific Railway), perhaps Mexico's greatest feat of engineering. This epic railroad meanders a jaw-dropping journey of over 656km between Los Mochis (near Mexico's Pacific coast) and Chihuahua (on its central high plains).

You *can* ride the train all the way through, or make an overnight stop before heading back the way you came. But the spectacular canyon country deserves much more exploration. The highland village of Creel makes an excellent base near some outrageously

BUSES FROM LOS MOCHIS

DESTINATION	FARE (M$)	DURATION	FREQUENCY (DAILY)
Guadalajara	741-886	13-15hr	half-hourly TAP, 13 Tufesa
Guaymas	286	5-6hr	25 Tufesa
Hermosillo	352-430	6-7hr	half-hourly 1st class GEB, half-hourly Tufesa
Mazatlán	372-428	6-7hr	frequent GEB/TAP, 11 Tufesa
Navojoa	118-146	2hr	frequent 1st class, GEB 32 Tufesa
Nogales	610-731	10-12hr	17 Tufesa
Phoenix	1137-1493	14-16hr	10 Tufesa
Tuscon	879-1174	12-13hr	10 Tufesa

scenic spots. For similar cusp-of-the-canyon experiences you can also stay in the smaller villages of Cerocahui, Areponápuchi or Divisadero, all near the railway. To get a real feel for the canyons, venture right down into them and stay in Urique or Batopilas.

All manner of natural wonders – cliffs, towering rock massifs, rivers, waterfalls, lakes, forests – as well as fascinating indigenous culture, are accessible from all these places by foot, horse and in many cases mountain bike or motor vehicle.

Copper Canyon

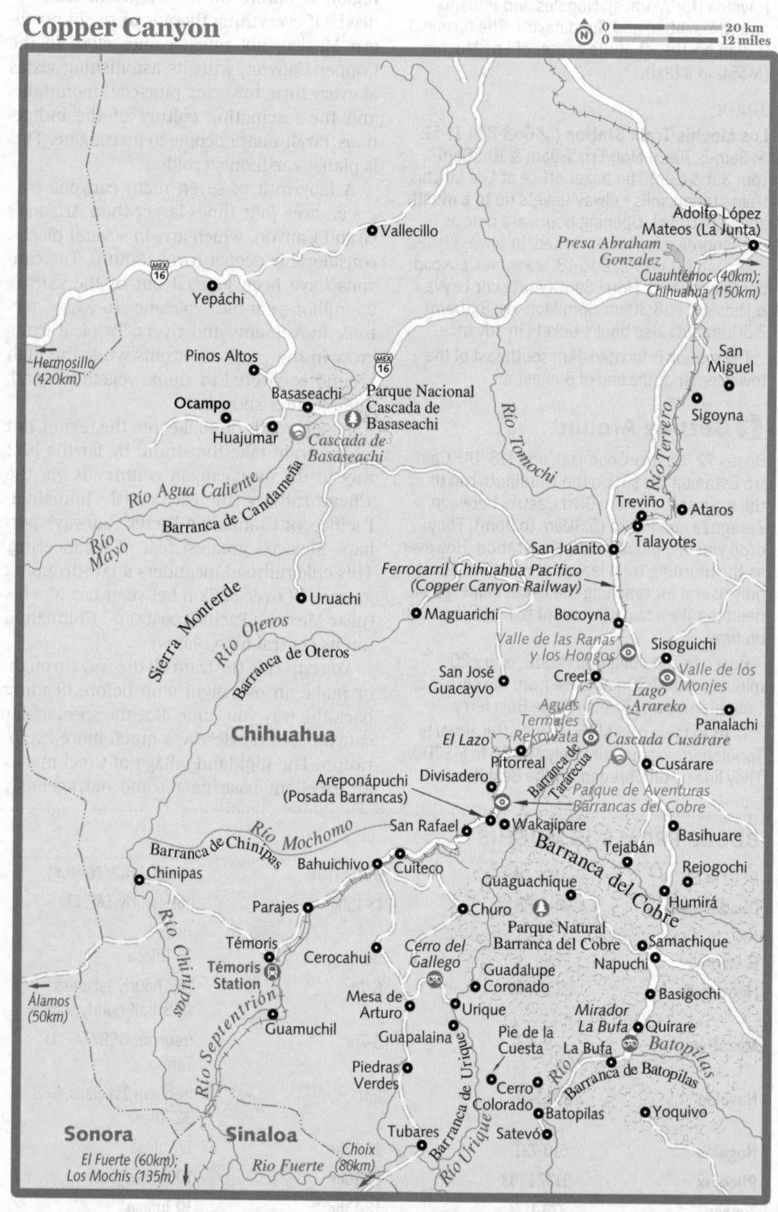

Or for the ultimate buzz, head to the Parque de Aventuras Barrancas del Cobre, where you can soar over death-defying drops on Mexico's most hair-raising ziplines, or by cable car.

Good seasons to visit are spring or autumn, when temperatures are not too hot at the bottom of the canyons nor too cold at the top. A particularly good time to come is between mid-September and November, when vegetation is green after the summer rains (which fall from around late June to late August). Hiking and riding down in the canyons is only really practicable from October to March. May and June are near-unbearable at the bottom of the canyons but OK for activities at the top.

The isolated recesses of this region harbor marijuana and opium plantations, which occasionally provoke bloody incidents involving rival groups and/or the Mexican army. While these narcos are not normally known to target tourists, it's advisable to sound out the situation before venturing to remote areas, and take a trusted local guide if you go anywhere off the beaten track.

The name Copper Canyon, coined by the Spanish when they mistook the greenish glow of lichen for copper, refers specifically to the chasm carved by the upper course of the Río Urique. The canyon's region also forms part of the Sierra Madre Occidental. Apart from the Barranca de Cobre, its other major canyons are the Barrancas de Urique, Sinforosa, Batopilas, Oteros, Chinipas and Candameña. All seven plunge to depths of 1300m or more.

Ferrocarril Chihuahua Pacífico

The stats say everything: 656km of track, 37 bridges, 86 tunnels and more than 60 years in the making. One of the world's most picturesque rail journeys, the **Ferrocarril Chihuahua Pacífico** (Copper Canyon Railway; ☎800-122-43-73, 614-439-72-12, from the US 888-484-1623; www.chepe.com.mx), completed in 1961, is as phenomenal in its engineering prowess as in the canyon views it yields. It connects a town 24km shy of the Pacific coast with the mountainous, arid interior of northern Mexico via tricky canyon gradients which force it to rise up over 2400m. The line is the major link between Chihuahua and the coast, heavily used for freight as well as passengers. The beauty of the landscape it traverses has made it one of Mexico's prime tourist excursions.

Nicknamed 'El Chepe' (using the Spanish initials of 'Chihuahua' and 'Pacífico'), the railway operates one daily train in each direction.

Between Los Mochis and El Fuerte, the train trundles through flat farmland, then begins to climb through hills speckled with dark pillars of cacti. It passes over the long Río Fuerte bridge and through the first of 86 tunnels about four hours after leaving Los Mochis. The train hugs the sides of deepening canyons and makes a spectacular zigzag ascent into a tunnel above Témoris, after which pine trees appear on the hillsides. By the next station, Bahuichivo, you are in the Sierra Madre uplands, with flower-dotted meadows bisecting an entrancing alpine landscape. The biggest highlight of the train ride is stopping at Divisadero, where you get your only glimpse of the actual Copper Canyon (Barranca del Cobre). The train circles back over itself in a complete loop to gain height at El Lazo before chugging on to Creel and Chihuahua.

There's not that much difference between *primera* and *económica* carriages – the former has a dining room the latter a canteen – snacks cost M$20, meals around M$80. Coffee is instant. Frankly, all carriages are aging (dating from the 1980s), and Chepe ticket prices are overpriced given the moderate comfort levels. Both classes have air-conditioning, heating and reclining seats with ample leg room. Cleanliness levels are OK, but certainly not Swiss-clean. The *clase económica* is certainly nice enough for most travelers.

Note that you're not allowed to consume alcohol on any Chepe train. Smoking is tolerated in the open-air gap between carriages. All trains are staffed with machine-gun toting police.

ℹ Information

TICKETS

Outside the peak seasons (Semana Santa, July/August and Christmas/New Year) if there are seats available you can board the train at any station without a ticket and pay the conductor. However it's advisable to reserve/buy tickets a month or more ahead for peak-season travel, and at least a day ahead at other times.

Tickets are sold at Los Mochis station and Chihuahua station for trips starting anywhere along the line. *Primera express* tickets are sold up to a month in advance, and *clase económica* tickets a day in advance. Reservations can be made up to a year in advance by phone (English speakers available) and email. On the *primera express*, you can make stopovers (usually up to three) at no extra cost, if you specify places and dates when you make the booking. For same-day tickets, you should be at Los Mochis or Chihuahua station an hour ahead of departure. Only Los Mochis, Creel, Cuauhtémoc and Chihuahua stations have ticket offices. Agencies such as Viajes Flami (p757) and Rojo y Casavantes (p777) in Chihuahua sell *primera express* tickets at least one day in advance, and any of the area's many **Balderrama Hotels** (www.mexicoscoppercanyon.com) will assist their clients in making reservations.

RAILWAY SCHEDULE– FERROCARRIL CHIHUAHUA PACÍFICO

Eastbound – Los Mochis to Chihuahua

	PRIMERA EXPRESS		CLASE ECONÓMICA	
STATION	ARRIVES (DAILY)	FARE FROM LOS MOCHIS (M$)	ARRIVES (TUE, FRI, SUN)	FARE FROM LOS MOCHIS (M$)
Los Mochis	6am (departs Los Mochis)	–	7am (departs Los Mochis)	
El Fuerte	8:16am	456	9.19am	287
Témoris	11:20am	813	12.24pm	513
Bahuichivo	12:20pm	962	1.24pm	606
San Rafael	1:25pm	1083	2.28pm	683
Posada Barrancas (Areponápuchi)	1:43pm	1121	2.46pm	707
Divisadero	2:22pm	1213	3.14pm	716
Creel	3:44pm	1357	4.39pm	855
Cuauhtémoc	6:37pm	1977	8.07pm	1246
Chihuahua	8:54pm	2482	10.34pm	1564

Westbound – Chihuahua to Los Mochis

	PRIMERA EXPRESS		CLASE ECONÓMICA	
STATION	ARRIVES (DAILY)	FARE FROM CHIHUAHUA (M$)	ARRIVES (MON, THU, SAT)	FARE FROM CHIHUAHUA (M$)
Chihuahua	6am (departs Chihuahua)	–	7am (departs Chihuahua)	
Cuauhtémoc	8:25am	506	9.25am	319
Creel	11:20am	1129	12.47pm	711
Divisadero	1:04pm	1349	2.41pm	850
Posada Barrancas (Areponápuchi)	1:11pm	1365	2.52pm	860
San Rafael	1:37pm	1403	3.16pm	884
Bahuichivo	2:28pm	1524	4.12pm	960
Témoris	3:25pm	1673	5.12pm	1054
El Fuerte	6:23pm	2174	8.19pm	1370
Los Mochis	8:22pm	2482	10.30pm	1564

The *primera express* (1st-class only, and with fewer stops) train runs daily. The *clase económica* (makes more stops, so is slower), runs from Los Mochis to Chihuahua on Tuesday, Friday and Sunday, and from Chihuahua to Los Mochis on Monday, Thursday and Saturday Schedules change and both trains tend to run a little late (by an hour or two), so the timetables comprise just a rough guideline. Check the website, www.chepe.com.mx, for latest details. If you are heading to Los Mochis with hopes of catching the Baja ferry from Topolobampo the same day, don't count on it! There is no time-zone change between Los Mochis and Chihuahua.

El Fuerte

698 / POP 13,000 / ELEV 180M

Clustered around one of the country's most striking plazas, El Fuerte oozes colonial character. For many centuries the most important commercial center in northwestern Mexico due to its proximity to the silver mines in the canyons, this is now a picturesque little town surrounded by one of Latin America's last-standing dry tropical forests.

A preferable starting or ending point for a trip on the Ferrocarril Chihuahua Pacífico, it's worth a stay of more than just a night to take a trip on the Río Fuerte and explore the unique subtropical countryside.

El Fuerte was founded in 1564, and is named for a 17th-century fort built on the distinctive high point of Cerro de las Pilas to protect settlers from indigenous attacks.

Sights & Activities

Bosque Secreto FOREST

(Secret Forest) Five hundred years ago, more than 550,000 sq km of dry tropical forest stretched down the coast from northern Mexico to Panama. Of the 10% that now remains, much is located around El Fuerte, an area known as the Bosque Secreto.

The delightful Río Fuerte, which is incrediby rich with birdlife (including herons, osprey, kingfishers and flycatchers) winds through much of the forest. **Chucho's** (cell phone 698-1069590; alfagu7@hotmail.com; Reforma 100) and Hotel Río Vista both organize kayak or boat trips (M$250 per person) along the river, taking in some 2000-year-old petroglyphs.

A local campaign is seeking to protect this area from rampant deforestation, affecting the 1800 species of native plants and the indigenous Mayo and Yaqui peoples, who depend upon the forest.

Museo Mirador El Fuerte MUSEUM

(698 893-15-01; Montes Claros; admission M$10; 9am-6pm Tue-Sun; P) This museum, built to look like the town's original fort, has a moderate collection of exhibits including ceramics, Mayo handicrafts and information about the Bosque Secreto.

Sleeping

Hotel Guerrero HOTEL $

(698-893-05-24; Juárez 206; r incl breakfast M$280-380;) Excellent budget hotel where the staff go the extra mile to look after guests. The rooms, set around a shady pillared patio, are colorful and the breakfast provided is generous and delicious.

Hotel La Choza HOTEL $$

(698-893-12-74; www.hotellachoza.com; 5 de Mayo 101; r M$740; P) This efficiently run colonial hotel boasts very inviting rooms, all with nice touches such as hand-painted sinks and high, brick-vaulted ceilings around a stunning grassy courtyard. It's excellent value, and the in-house Diligencias restaurant is good bet, too.

Hotel Río Vista HOTEL $$

(698-893-04-13; r M$440-650; P) Located next to the Museo Mirador El Fuerte, this quirky place has been hosting travelers for years. Stylistically it's a bit of a shock to the senses with murals, garish colors and an excess of curios (and the maintenance could be better). But hey, the superb river views compensate. Chal Gámez, the bird-watching owner, offers guided boat tours.

Torres del Fuerte BOUTIQUE HOTEL $$$

(698-893-19-74; www.hotelestorres.com; Robles 102; r M$1270-1760; P) A 400-year-old hacienda that fuses colonial class, rustic elegance and contemporary art, set around gorgeous gardens. All rooms are uniquely themed, many with slate bathrooms and exposed adobe/brick walls. There's also a gourmet restaurant, **Bonifacio's** (mains M$70-300; 7am-10pm).

Posada del Hidalgo RESORT $$$

(698-893-11-94; www.hotelposadadelhidalgo.com; Hidalgo 101; r/ste M$1122/1690; P@) Highly atmospheric hotel offering bundles of classic colonial charm with spacious, elegant rooms grouped around shady garden courtyards. There's a spa, a beautiful open-air restaurant and a popular bar for socializing.

Eating

The wealth of fresh water around El Fuerte produces must-have local specialties such as *cauques* or *langostinos* (freshwater crayfish) and *lobina* (black bass). That said, restaurant choices are very limited.

Restaurante Chayita MEXICAN $
(cnr Juárez & Independencia; meals M$40-60; ⌚7:30am-7pm) Head here for cheap breakfasts, *carne asada* (grilled beef), *tostadas* (crispy corn snack with topping) and *chiles rellenos* (stuffed peppers) in very humble, plastic-chair-fantastic surrounds.

El Mesón del General FISH $$
(☎698 893-02-60; Juárez 202; mains M$95-230; ⌚11am-9:30pm) Traditional, formal restaurant that specialises in fish and seafood, with several styles of *pulpo* (octopus; from M$110) and combo plates of various river delicacies.

Restaurante Diligencias MEXICAN $$
(☎698-893-12-74; 5 de Mayo 101; mains M$68-200; ⌚7am-11pm; 📶) This hotel restaurant is a good choice for breakfasts (around M$50), with lots of international (try the eggs Benedict) and Mexican choices and free coffee refills. Later on, you'll find good steaks and seafood, including shrimp tacos.

Information

Banamex (Juárez 212; ⌚9am-4pm Mon-Fri) ATM.

Cafe Internet (Montesclaros; per hr M$10; ⌚8am-11pm) Internet cafe that also provides tourist information.

Getting There & Around

Buses to Los Mochis (M$72, two hours) depart about every half-hour, 5am to 7:30pm, from Juárez near Calle 16 de Septiembre.

The train station is 6km south of town (M$90 by taxi). Many hotels offer station pickup and drop-off for clients, for which they may or may not charge (up to the taxi rate). If you arrive by train in the evening, awaiting shared taxis charge M$50 per person.

The dirt road to Álamos from here requires 4WD and takes five hours.

Cerocahui

☎635 / POP 1600 / ELEV 1600M

The tiny, attractive village of Cerocahui, dedicated mainly to forestry, sits in the middle of a verdant, vista-laden valley, and is easily reached from Bahuichivo station, 16km away. The canyon country around here sees far fewer tourists than the region near Creel, and the enticing canyon-bottom village of Urique is within striking range.

On the central plaza, Cerocahui's pretty yellow-domed church, **San Francisco Javier de Cerocahui** was founded in 1680.

There's good hiking around Cerocahui, and excursions (offered by all accommodations) to **Cerro del Gallego**, a spectacular lookout over the Barranca de Urique (25km on along the Urique road) are well worth it.

Sleeping & Eating

Hotel & Restaurante Jade HOTEL, MEXICAN $$
(☎635-456-52-75; Parque Central; s/d incl Bahuichivo transfers M$400/600, meals M$60-70; ⌚7am-9.30pm; P ⊖ ❄) This simple place has six, clean functional rooms (each with twin beds) that are the best budget option in town. However, it's the warm welcome from hosts Alberto and María and the outstanding cooking (including homemade bread, fish dishes and veggie options) in the adjacent restaurant that really stand out. Treks and trips to Urique are offered.

Hotel Paraíso del Oso HOTEL $$$
(☎in Chihuahua 614-421-33-72, in the US 800-884-3107; www.mexicohorse.com; campsite/dm/r M$50/150/500, s/d incl 3 meals & Bahuichivo transfers M$1575/2429; P ⊖ @ 📶) This excellent family-owned rural lodge is a great base for bird-watching, hikes, horseback rides and community tourism (the owners have good contacts with the Tarahumara people). The set-up includes spacious, ranch-style rooms overlooking a garden courtyard and a fascinating book collection to browse. It's located 2km north of Cerocahui, on the road to Bahuichivo, though most people arrive by train.

Horseback riding (M$130 per hour) and trekking (from M$40) are offered.

Cabañas San Isidro CABAÑAS $$$
(☎635-456-52-57; www.coppercanyonamigos.com; Carretera a Urique Km 24; s/d/tr incl 3 meals & Bahuichivo transfers M$950/1550/1850; P) High in the hills above Cerocahui, 8km along the road to Urique, this working farm makes a perfect (if isolated) rural base for all kinds of hikes, horseback riding and trips in canyon country. Owners Mario and Tito have excellent links to the Tarahumara community's runner-guides. The cozy adobe-and-wood cabins have wood-burning stoves and the cooking is tasty and plentiful.

Hotel Misión HOTEL $$$
(☎635-456-52-94; www.hotelmision.com; s/d incl 3 meals & Bahuichivo transfers M$1550/2600; P ⊖ @ ≋) This delightful former hacienda

ULTRAMARATHONS IN URIQUE

Held annually in Urique in December or January, the **Ultra Caballo Blanco** (www.ultracb.com) is an 82km ultramarathon on tough canyon trails, at altitude. It was established by Micah True, a legendary American runner who lived for years in the Copper Canyon region and gained international attention when featured in Christopher McDougall's book *Born to Run*.

The ultramarathon pays homage to the native Tarahumara, who have a centuries-old tradition of long-distance running and whose very name means 'the running people'. Their huaraches (sandals with a thin sole usually made from recycled tires) are said to have inspired the barefoot-running method (which tests have shown also reduces energy use) which has now gone global.

The 2013 Ultra Caballo Blanco had almost 600 runners, including 400 Tarahumara and over 100 international athletes. A *caballitos* (kids' race) is also now held the day before the main race. In 2013, around 450 kids from the Sierra area competed.

A second event, Carrera de los Pies Ligeros ('Race of the Light Feet') held each December is a *rarajipari* (essentially a long-distance Tarahumara relay-style running race with two teams kicking a ball along a course). *Rarajipari* are actually much truer to Tarahumara traditions than pure running races. There are two races, one for each sex, each involving two teams (who run with torches at night) over a distance of more than 100km. This race lasts between 12 and 24 hours, and is only open to Tarahumara people.

offers rustic-chic accommodations complete with *chimeneas* (fireplaces), an evocative bar-restaurant, a games room with a pool table and lovely gardens planted with vines. It gets the tour-group action; discounts are often available.

Getting There & Away

Cerocahui hotels will pick you up at Bahuichivo station if you have reserved. If you haven't, you can often catch a ride with one of their vans anyway. A local bus leaves Bahuichivo station for Cerocahui (M$40, 40 minutes) and Urique (M$150, 3½ hours or more), daily after the last train of the day arrives. Returning, it leaves Urique at 7:30am, passes through Cerocahui around 10am to 10:30am, and aims to connect with the bus leaving Bahuichivo for San Rafael (M$80, about one hour) about 11am. From San Rafael there are five daily buses to Areponápuchi (M$15, 15 minutes), Divisadero (M$15, 20 minutes), Creel (M$60, 1½ hours) and Chihuahua (M$295, six to seven hours). A bus back to Bahuichivo leaves San Rafael at 1pm.

There are several intriguing backroads from Cerocahui which look temptingly direct on map but should not be attempted without expert local advice. These roads have tough 4WD-only stretches, traverse isolated lands harboring drug plantations, and parts can be washed out after heavy rains. A track connects Cerocahui to Choix (from where there's a paved road to El Fuerte); and another links Bahuichivo with Álamos via Témoris. Consult the owners of Hotel Paraíso del Oso or Cabañas San Isidro about security and road conditions.

Urique

☎635 / POP 1100 / ELEV 550M

This starry-skied ex-mining village lies at the bottom of the deepest of all the canyons, the spectacular Barranca de Urique (measuring 1870m from rim to river), yet it's by far the easiest canyon-bottom village to access. The village could not be more dramatically situated, scattered along the west bank of the turquoise Río Urique, and is a good hiking base. Getting there is part of the fun: the unpaved road (a 40km trip from Cerocahui) makes a breathtaking descent to the village. Urique is rural – more Tecate beers are passed around here than educations – and marijuana fuels the local economy, so be a little wary about town.

For day hikes you can go up the Río Urique to Guadalupe Coronado village (7km) or downriver to Guapalaina (4km). The two- to three-day trek to Batopilas is a bigger challenge. As robberies have occurred on the route via Cerro Colorado, a more southerly route via Pie de la Cuesta is an alternative. Local guides charge around M$4000 for this trip.

The town hall on the main street has a small, efficient **tourist office** (☎635-456-60-42; turismo.urique@gmail.com; ⏰8am-3pm).

Sleeping & Eating

★Entre Amigos CABAÑAS, CAMPGROUND $

(www.amongamigos.com; campsite per person M$130, dm/r M$200/525; P ⊖ @ ☒) This beautifully designed place has been hosting travelers since 1975. Homey stone cabins, dorms and wonderful campsites are dotted around gorgeous grounds. No meals are offered but there's a good guests' kitchen. Entre Amigos can hook you up with dependable local guides for hiking, camping or fishing and there's an impressive library. It's located near the riverbank, 1km north of Urique town center.

Hotel Estrella del Río HOTEL $

(☎635-456-60-03; Principal; s/d M$250/300; P ⊖ ❄) This two-story hotel on the main drag has 12 very well-kept rooms, with twin or king-size beds, and all with cable TV.

Las Delicias BUNGALOWS $

(☎614-251-00-16; mescaleeramm@gmail.com; camping per person M$50, r M$400; ⊖) Las Delicias is owned by Mike, a friendly gringo who has three spacious bungalows with kitchenettes and two beds. A dorm is planned.

Restaurant Plaza MEXICAN $

(☎635 456-60-03; Principal; meals M$40-100; ⏰6am-9pm) The excellent family-run Restaurant Plaza offers fine food with a real home-cooked flavor. The specialty, *aguachile* (M$80), is a soupy, spicy shrimp cocktail full of onions and tomatoes served in a *molcajete* (pestle and mortar).

Getting There & Away

A bus leaves Bahuichivo train station daily for Urique (M$150, 3½ hours or more) after the last train of the day arrives. Otherwise accommodations can arrange transfers from Bahuichivo for about M$1000. Cerocahui hotels also offer transportation: Cabañas San Isidro charges M$1500 for a return day trip.

Areponápuchi (Posada Barrancas)

☎635 / POP 240 / ELEV 2220M

Right on the lip of the canyon, the tiny settlement of Areponápuchi or 'Arepo' – just a couple of dozen houses, a church and a few hotels – is where it all comes together for the first time, with spectacular, inspirational views over the canyon from several hotels. If you suffer from vertigo, well, this ain't your kind of town.

An easy path with several good viewpoints runs along the canyon edge to the left (north) of Hotel Posada Barrancas Mirador, and several lookouts (as well as the adventure park) lie short distances off the road between here and Divisadero. Local accommodations can organize canyon trips, from hikes along the rim to horseback rides or overnight camping treks right down to the river.

Sleeping & Eating

Cabañas Díaz CABAÑAS $

(☎635-578-30-08; barrancasdelcobre_mexico@yahoo.com.mx; s/d M$280/500, without bathroom M$200/400; P) Family-run lodge known for its rustic cabins (with fireplaces), tasty meals (M$70 to M$80) and great guided hikes and horseback rides (four-hour outing for two by foot/horse M$300/600). The lodge is located along the main road into the village – there is a sign on the right.

Cabañas La Esmeralda GUEST HOUSE $$

(☎cell phone 636-5894088; r M$500; P ⊖ ❄) Inexpensive place with five very well-presented modern rooms, each with two or three beds, that share a communal terrace. No views, but the family owners are friendly and offer home-cooked meals (M$50). It's located on the main road, 600m or so from Posada Barrancas station.

Hotel Mansión Tarahumara HOTEL $$$

(☎635-578-30-30, 800-777-46-68; www.hotelmansiontarahumara.com.mx; s incl 3 meals M$1220-1500, d incl 3 meals M$1720-2240; P ☒) This castle-like hotel (complete with turrets and battlements) offers a variety of accommodations a few minutes' walk from the station. Those on the canyon rim (commanding the highest prices) are the showstoppers, with plush beds and balconies. There's a great rim-poised restaurant (meals M$200) and a wonderful pool and Jacuzzi.

Hotel Posada Barrancas Mirador HOTEL $$$

(☎635-578-30-20, 800-816-81-96; www.mexicoscoppercanyon.com; s/d incl 3 meals M$1975/2985; P ☎) Suspended over the canyon, this hotel's 75 rooms (each with private balcony, beamed ceilings and attractive furnishings) enjoy unbeatable views, as does the restaurant. It's popular with tour groups.

Getting There & Away

Five daily buses operated by Autotransportes Turísticos Noroeste connect Areponápuchi with Creel (M$52, one hour) and San Rafael (M$15, 15 minutes) to the south. Buses drop you at the entrance to the main highway just outside the village. Arepo is within walking distance from Posada Barrancas station.

Parque de Aventuras Barrancas del Cobre

The astonishing Copper Canyon Adventure Park on the canyon rim between Areponápuchi and Divisadero includes Mexico's longest series of *tirolesas* (zip-lines), suspended over some of the world's most profound canyon scenery. The park's **tirolesas** (per person M$600; 9.30am-4.30pm) transport you along seven lines from a height of 2400m to over halfway to the canyon floor. (Currently Line 4 is the most spine-tingling, with over 1km of cable, but a new cable connection under construction which should open by late 2014, will be 2.5km in length, the world's longest).

A couple of heart-in-mouth wobbly bridges help you complete the cross-canyon odyssey. Allow at least an hour to descend to the spectacular viewpoint of Mesón de Bacajípare. This doubles as the lower station for the **teleférico** (cable car; return adult/child under 12 M$250/125; 9am-4:30pm), which you will have to take back up. Or you can skip the zip-lines and head straight down on the cable car (20 minutes each way, plus a 20-minute stop).

The **park center** (689-589-68-05; Piedra Volada; 9am-5:30pm), built over a gobsmacking fissure in the canyon walls also has a restaurant (meals M$70-90) and souvenir shop. Rappelling and rock-climbing, both M$450 per person, can be arranged here. You can also organise **hiking** (M$30 to M$160) and spectacular downhill **mountain biking** (M$350) with Tarahumara guides.

The nearest public transportation is at Areponápuchi or Divisadero, both an easy 1.5km walk away via a great canyon lip-hugging trail. (A smart train station opened in mid-2014 offers even closer access.)

Five direct daily buses from Chihuahua to Areponápuchi pass the park entrance courtesy of **Autotransportes Turísticos Noroeste** (www.turisticosnoroeste.com). Returning, it's not always easy to flag a bus down but it's a pleasant walk to Divisadero/Areponápuchi, or there's also a courtesy mobility vehicle to Divisadero.

Divisadero

ELEV 2240M

Divisadero, a train stop without a village, is your only chance to see into the miraculous canyon if you're just doing the train ride. All trains halt here for 20 minutes, giving you enough time to jump out, gawk, snap some photos at the viewpoint over the road and hop back on. You can just discern a tiny fragment of the Río Urique at the bottom of the actual Copper Canyon. Ration your time carefully, as the station is also a souvenir market and spectacular food court. *Gorditas* (masa cakes, some made with blue corn), burritos and *chiles rellenos,* cooked up in makeshift oil-drum stoves, are worth the stop alone. Gobble it up quickly – the conductors aren't supposed to allow food back onto the train.

All this together with the nearby adventure park 1.5km south means a stay of longer than 20 minutes is a great idea. There's a good choice of places in the nearby village of Areponápuchi, or you'll find **Hotel Divisadero Barrancas** (in Chihuahua 614-415-11-99, in the US 888-232-4219; www.hoteldivisadero.com; standard s/d incl 3 meals M$800/1500, with views 2110/2495; meals M$80-210; P) right by the canyon viewpoint where the standard rooms lack views but the newer rooms (Nos 35 to 52) have astonishing vistas.

Buses serving Areponápuchi, San Rafael and ultimately Bahuichivo also run through Divisadero, stopping below the train station – quicker and cheaper than continuing by train.

Creel

635 / POP 5000 / ELEV 2330M

The Copper Canyon's main tourism center, Creel is actually no more than a low-key highland town strung out along the railway line. It's a very likeable place, surrounded by pine forests and interesting rock formations with good hotels and a few restaurants. The Tarahumara, in their multihued dress, are commonly seen about town. If you meet other travelers anywhere in northern Mexico, it will most probably be here.

Creel can be very cold in winter, even snowy, and it's none too warm at night in autumn. In summer, the alpine air is a wel-

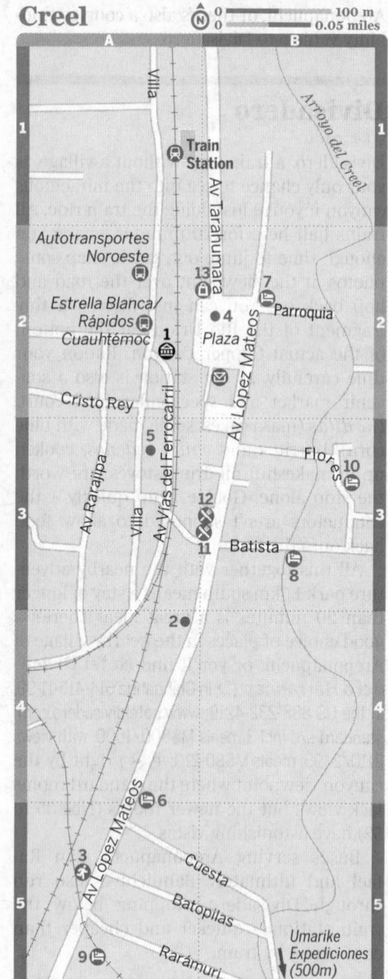

Creel

Sights
1 Museo Casa de las Artesanías del Estado de Chihuahua A2

Activities, Courses & Tours
2 3 Amigos A4
3 El Aventurero A5
4 Tarahumara Tours B2
5 Umarike Expediciones A3

Sleeping
6 Best Western The Lodge at Creel A4
7 Casa Margarita B2
8 Hotel Plaza Mexicana B3
9 Quinta Mision A5
10 Real de Chapultepec Hotel B3

Eating
11 La Cabaña B3
Restaurant Sierra Madre .... (see 6)
12 Restaurant Verónica B3
Rico's .... (see 6)

Shopping
13 Artesanías Misión B2

come relief from Mexico's coastal lowland and desert heat.

Sights

Museo Casa de las Artesanías del Estado de Chihuahua MUSEUM
(☎635 456-00-80; Av Vías del Ferrocarril 178; admission M$10; ⏲9am-5.30pm Mon-Sat, to 1pm Sun; P) Offers excellent exhibits with text in English on local history and Tarahumara culture and crafts. Here you'll see gorgeous woven baskets, traditional clothing, photos and more.

Tours

As soon as you check into a hotel (or even before that), you'll be pushed to sign up for a tour. Standard minivan tours tend to be rushed, ticking off a roster of nearby sights in a short timeframe (most are half-day trips), such as canyons, waterfalls, Tarahumara settlements, hot springs and other places. Themed excursions tend to be more rewarding. Most tours require a minimum number of people, typically four. One popular trip of around five hours covers Cusárare village and waterfall, Lago Arareko and the Valley of Frogs and Mushrooms. Typical prices are M$250 per person for half-day trips and up to M$500 for full-day trips. Other good half- or full-day destinations include Divisadero, the Cascada de Basaseachi and Rekowata hot springs.

Seriously consider exploring the region yourself. This is prime riding country, and many attractions near Creel can be enjoyed on horseback, bicycle or scooter. This is particularly attractive as you can cover terrain the minivans can't manage, and with significantly more peace and quiet. The whole area is a mountain-bike playground: you could just rent a bike and take in all the area's attractions independently.

★3 Amigos
TOUR

(☎635-456-00-36; www.amigos3.com; Av López Mateos 46; ⏰9am-7pm) A very well-informed agency, 3 Amigos has built its reputation on helping you 'be your own guide in the Copper Canyon'; they provide maps to help you negotiate the region's trails. Quality mountain bikes (per four hours/day M$130/200), scooters (per day including fuel M$600) and trucks (double-cab Nissan pickup; per 24 hours M$1300) are for rent. It's also the best source of information in town, and has free maps.

The full-day self-guided mountain-bike route to the Rekowata hot springs and full-day scooter ride to the canyon bottom by the Humira bridge pass through simply mindblowing scenery and are highly recommended. Affiliated company Amigo Trails offers self-guided truck tour packages and customized guided canyon trips.

El Aventurero
HORSEBACK RIDING

(☎635-456-05-57, cell 635-2944585; www.ridemexico.com; Av López Mateos 68; from $100 per hr; ⏰9am-6pm Mon-Fri, 9am-3pm Sat) Superb horseback riding excursions run by Norberto and Susan, a Mexican/US couple who own the ranch. Thrifty backpackers should ask them about their 'bare-bones' riding rates. Rides cost M$100 per hour (minimum two hours and three riders). Accommodation and Spanish lessons are also offered.

Umarike Expediciones
ADVENTURE TOUR

(☎635-456-06-32, cell phone 614-4065464; www.umarike.com.mx) Mountain-biking specialist offering guided bike and hiking adventure trips from one to eight days. Rental bikes (M$250 per day), maps and information are also available.

Tarahumara Tours
GUIDED TOUR

(☎635-456-01-21; Plaza; ⏰9am-7pm) Local driver-guides offering escorted trips, from two hours to two days, at competitive rates.

Sleeping

Casa Margarita
HOSTEL $

(☎635-456-00-45; www.casamargaritacreel.com.mx; Av López Mateos 11; dm/s/d inc breakfast & dinner M$150/400/550; P ⊖ ᯤ) This hostel is a long-running backpackers' stronghold with simple, clean, brightly-colored rooms and bathrooms with Creel's hottest, fastest showers. However it can lack ambience: socializing opportunities are limited now that meals are served in the affiliated Hotel Plaza Mexicana down the road.

Real de Chapultepec Hotel
HOTEL $

(☎635-456-08-94; realdechapultepec@hotmail.com; Flores 260; r M$250; P ᯤ) A good budget place, though it looks a bit scruffy from the street. The units (with hand-carved beds and murals) are grouped around a parking lot. There's a dining room with free wi-fi and they offer good tours.

Hotel Plaza Mexicana
HOTEL $$

(☎635-456-02-45; www.casamargaritacreel.com.mx; Batista s/n; s/d/tr/q incl breakfast & dinner M$500/600/700/800; P ⊖ ᯤ) The friendly staff and attractive layout (comfortable rooms are grouped around a pretty rear courtyard) are plus points at this popular hotel. Rates include good breakfasts (with eggs cooked to order) though dinners can be a little disappointing. It's run by the same family as Casa Margarita.

Best Western The Lodge at Creel
LODGE $$$

(☎635-456-00-71, in the US 800-528-1234; www.thelodgeatcreel.com; Av López Mateos 61; s/d M$1370/1490; P ⊖ @ ᯤ) This very inviting rustic-style lodge has log-cabin-style cabañas with wood-burning stoves and bathtubs, and huge rooms with exposed stone walls and all mod cons. There's a (tiny) fitness center and spa. You won't go hungry or thirsty, as there's a pizzeria with wood-fired oven, a restaurant-bar, and a cafe with espresso machine on the premises. Special deals can drop rates below M$1000.

Quinta Mision
HOTEL $$$

(☎635-456-00-21; http://quintamision.com; Av López Mateos; r M$1200; P ⊖ ❄ ᯤ) 🍃 Probably Mexico's most ecologically senstive hotel, this intriguing new place recycles water and uses wind and solar power. Twenty suite-sized rooms have been created from the shell of an old furniture factory, all with fridge and enough space for a small family.

Eating

Creel has a limited choice of restaurants. For a packed lunch, grocery stores on the main drag sell tasty *queso menonita* (Mennonite cheese) and bread.

Restaurant Verónica
RESTAURANT $$

(☎635-456-06-31; Av López Mateos 33; mains M$50-120; ⏰7:30am-10:30pm; ᯤ) Famous for its huge portions, the signature dish here is

THE TARAHUMARA

A fascinating part of canyon life is the presence of one of Mexico's most distinctive indigenous groups, the Tarahumara, who live in caves and small houses across the countryside here. Most easily identifiable are the women, dressed in colorful skirts and blouses and often carrying infants on their backs. They sell beautiful hand-woven baskets and carved wooden dolls and animals at ridiculously low prices at tourist sites around the sierra. Most men now wear modern clothes like jeans instead of the traditional loincloth, but both sexes still often walk in *huaraches* – sandals hewn from tire tread and strips of leather.

The Tarahumara remain largely an enigma. Even their name is debated (Tarahumara, or Rarámuri?). Many believe it was originally 'ralamuli' which was Hispanicized to 'Rarámuri' and evolved to 'Tarahumara,' the term by which they usually refer to themselves. Contrary to popular belief, the Spanish incursion did not force the Tarahumara into the canyons: they were here when the first Jesuits arrived in 1608. There are two main Tarahumara groups: the Alta (high) and the Baja (low), with whom outside contact was made by Jesuit priests from higher-altitude Hidalgo del Parral and lower-altitude El Fuerte respectively. Culture and language are radically different between the Altas and Bajas, and because of long-term isolation, every community has a slightly different culture and language. No one even knows how many Tarahumara exist. Estimates vary between 50,000 and 120,000.

Rarámuri means 'those who run fast' – and these people are most famous for running long distances swiftly, sometimes up to 20 hours without stopping. They used their aptitude for running to hunt deer by bow and arrow as little as a generation ago. The Copper Canyon area now has its own annual ultramarathon (p763) at Urique.

But a better cultural insight into the Tarahumara is their sense of fairness. 'Korima' is a custom where someone who has a good crop is 'blessed' and obliged to share his good fortune with others. Another tradition is the *tesgüinada*, a raucous social gathering at which Tarahumara relax their natural reserve and celebrate communal work and festivals with plenty of *tesgüino*, a potent corn beer.

Even these traditionally isolated people have been influenced by incomers, and many have adopted a type of Catholicism. However, their take on Christianity and Christian festivals is often idiosyncratic – regularly accompanied by drumming and lots of *tesgüino*.

But the Tarahumara have maintained their lifestyle despite incursions of conquistadors, missionaries, railways, drug gangs and tourism. They have one word to refer all non-Tarahumara people: *chabochi*, which means 'with spider-webbing on the face,' a reference to bearded Spanish colonists. The majority continue to live a subsistence lifestyle in the remote Sierra Madre Occidental countryside.

The Tarahumara are also generally materially poor, and their communities have some serious health problems: there are high rates of infant mortality, malnutrition and teenage pregnancy, with some of the little relief coming from Catholic missions.

el norteño, a cheesy, beefy mess served in a cast-iron skillet that you eat with tortillas.

La Cabaña MEXICAN, INTERNATIONAL **$$**
(Av López Mateos 36; mains M$75-140; 📶) A little pricey but good for a splurge, this orderly Catalan-owned restaurant has flavorsome salads and meat dishes, and always offers a daily special (like local trout stuffed with shrimp).

Rico's CAFE, PIZZA **$$**
(Av López Mateos 61; snacks/meals M$50/90; ⏲9am-10pm; 📶) Located within the Best Western, this likeable place is the only spot in Creel to get a decent espresso (the house coffee is a blend of three high-altitude Chiapan beans). It's a good bet for a panini, homemade cakes, or pizza (try the three-cheese *menonita*) from a wood-fired oven.

Restaurant Sierra Madre MEXICAN, INTERNATIONAL **$$**
(☎635-456-00-71; Av López Mateos 61; mains M$65-190; ⏲noon-9pm; 📶) The Best Western's restaurant is a ranch-style set-up, complete with stone walls, wood beams and plenty of taxidermy. It offers steaks, seafood, pas-

ta and pizza, and less expensive *antojitos* (snacks).

Shopping

Shops in Creel sell Tarahumara handicrafts as well as distinctive Mata Ortiz pottery.

Artesanías Misión HANDICRAFTS
(635-456-00-97; Parroquia 64, Plaza s/n; 9am-1pm & 3-6pm Mon-Sat) Traditional selection of handicrafts: all the store's earnings go to support Creel's Catholic mission hospital, which provides free medical care for the Tarahumara.

Information

Clínica Santa Teresita (635-456-01-05; Parroquia; 24hr) Behind Casa Margarita. Offers basic health-care services.

La Escuelita (Av López Mateos s/n; per hr M$15; 8am-9pm) Tiny internet cafe with a few terminals.

Police Station (635-456-04-50) Just off the plaza.

Post Office (8am-4:30pm Mon-Fri, 8am-noon Sat) On the plaza.

Santander (Av López Mateos 17; 9am-4pm Mon-Fri) Has two ATMs.

Getting There & Around

BUS

Travel between Creel and Chihuahua, and between Creel, Divisadero and Areponápuchi, may be more convenient by bus than train: trips are shorter and more frequent. **Autotransportes Noroeste** (www.turisticosnoroeste.com; Villa) runs buses to Cuauhtémoc (M$160, three hours) and Chihuahua (M$286, 4½ hours) five times daily at 10:30am, 12:30pm, 2:30pm, 4:30pm and 6:30pm. Noroeste also offers buses to Divisadero (M$52, one hour), Areponápuchi (M$52, one hour) and San Rafael (M$64, 1¼ hours) every two hours between 10:30am to 6:30pm. The first bus to San Rafael connects with the 1pm departure from there to Bahuichivo.

Estrella Blanca/Rápidos Cuauhtémoc (635-456-00-73) also has five daily buses to Chihuahua (M$298, 4½ hours).

All buses depart from the main square in Creel.

CAR & MOTORCYCLE

There are paved roads all the way from Chihuahua to Creel and on to Divisadero and Bahuichivo. Another paved road runs southeast to Guachochi, then on to Hidalgo del Parral in southern Chihuahua. Motorbikes and 4WDs can be rented from 3 Amigos (p766).

TRAIN

Tickets for trains are sold at **Creel station** (635-456-00-15; Av Tarahumara) from one hour before trains depart.

Around Creel

The area around Creel is rich in natural wonders, from waterfalls and hot springs to surreal rock formations and expansive parklands, all within a day's hike, ride or drive from town. Local guides offer various tours, or you can go solo on a rented bicycle, scooter or truck. There are some lodging options if you want to stay overnight.

One kilometer southeast of town you enter the Tarahumara *ejido* (communal farming district) of San Ignacio (admission M$20), which spreads over some 200 sq km and is home to about 4000 people living in caves and small houses among farmlands, small canyons and pine forests. The road leads into the **Valle de las Ranas y los Hongos** (Valley of the Frogs and Mushrooms), 2km from the edge of town and named for its respectively fat-and-squashed and thin-but-big-headed rocks. Here you'll find the photogenic, 18th-century **San Ignacio Mission Church** and the **Cueva de Sebastián**, a cave inhabited by 14 Tarahumara people and regularly visited by tourists (donations or craft purchases welcome).

Around 7km further east is the **Valle de los Monjes** (Valley of the Monks) a spectacular outcrop of vertical rock formations that inspire its Tarahumara name Bisabírachi, meaning 'Valley of the Erect Penises.' If you've an hour or so to spare, the countryside around Valle de los Monjes is well worth exploring and less visited than area around the 'frogs' and 'mushrooms'.

Lago Arareko, a twisting, bluish-green lake whose waters reflect the surrounding pines and rocks, sits beside the Cusárare road 8km from Creel. It can be linked with the frogs, mushrooms and monks in a half-to full-day circuit. Rowboats can be rented out for M$50 by the lakeshore.

About 14km on down the road past Arareko is the turning to the Tarahumara village of **Cusárare** (2km), where the 18th-century mission church was restored in the 1970s with striking Tarahumara patterned murals. On Sundays the village is full of life. The **Museo Loyola** (admission M$15) here holds an exceptional collection of colonial religious paintings, but it's now only infrequently open. About 400m past the Cusárare turning, at Km 111 on the highway, a right turn marked 'Cascada de Cusárare' marks the start of a trail that follows a bubbling stream, then passes through a sweeping highland valley to the lovely 30m waterfall **Cascada Cusárare** (admission M$20; ⊙8am-5pm), 3km from the road. If you want to do a little hiking, this section from the road to the falls is shady and very beautiful, offering the chance of a dip along the way.

The lovely **Aguas Termales Rekowata** (Rekowata Hot Springs; admission M$20) are approached from the Divisadero road 7km south of Creel. To get to these hot springs you need to follow a (signposted) dirt road for 11km from the highway to the parking lot. It's then a 3km hike down a rough cobblestone track to the blissfully warm bathing pools into which the springs are channeled. Local Tarahumara also offer transport (M$60 return) in 4WDs from the parking lot. There's also a superb mountain bike trail from Creel to Rekowata. This route initially takes the Cusárare road but then heads offroad down tracks to the right (south) just beyond the outskirts of Creel. You pass through a scenic river valley then an utterly astonishing canyon viewpoint before beginning a steep descent to Rekowata. It's a full-day return-trip ride; 3 Amigos (p766) can provide a map.

With a scooter or car, you've the chance to reach the bottom of the Copper Canyon with your own wheels. Grab a packed lunch in Creel first. The route is very simple: you follow the excellent paved highway southeast of town towards Guachochi. The scenery is staggering, the best section between Km 133 and Km 150 winds around the great ochre walls of the Copper Canyon itself then descends to the Humira bridge beside the foaming waters of the Urique river. It's the same route back, via Cusárare and Lago Arareko. This is another full-day return-trip.

Batopilas

☎649 / POP 1500 / ELEV 460M

Who needs an adventure park? Batopilas citizens could make this argument, as the only road into their splendidly preserved, colonial (former silver-mining) village, deep in canyon country, has more twists, turns and heart-in-mouth vertical drops than any amusement ride.

A delightfully stuck-in-time settlement, Batopilas was founded in 1708, and peaked in prominence in the late-19th century when silver mining boomed. Spread along the canyon floor of the Barranca de Batopilas, the climate is subtropical here year-round.

Batopilas can be slightly rough around the edges. Marijuana fuels the local economy (look out for the state-of-the-art trucks and young men with expensive jewelry). The odd robbery and kidnapping have occurred, and though foreign tourists aren't usually targeted, do take local advice about out-of-town excursions.

Things shut up early here, save for some makeshift bars selling beer from back rooms. However, there are great excursions locally.

Be aware that there are no banks or ATMs in town.

Sights & Activities

Hacienda San Miguel RUIN

(admission M$10; ⊙8am-5pm; P) The monumental, castle-like ruins of the Hacienda San Miguel were built on a very grand scale. They're highly evocative, with bouganvillea tumbling over towers, and roots and shoots reclaiming a once-grand stone structure.

WORTH A TRIP

CASCADA DE BASASEACHI

Few natural sites in Mexico boast the exquisitely pristine beauty of the country's highest full-time waterfalls, **Cascada de Basaseachi** (admission free), where a plume of water tumbles 246m to pools below where you can swim. Basaseachi is 140km northwest of Creel and takes a full day to visit from there (including three hours to walk down to the falls and back). The waterfall is part of the homonymous national park, south of which is the old mining town of Maguarachi, which has delightful **hot springs**. Both sites are accessible via San Juanito, 35km north of Creel. To visit you'll really need your own wheels or a tour with a Creel agency.

Museo de Batopilas MUSEUM
(admission free; ⌚10.30am-4pm & 5-7pm Mon-Sat) FREE Offers a good overview of the town's history, and proprietor Rafael will likely embellish proceedings with his own anecdotes. Tourist information is available here.

Satevó Mission Church Hike HIKING
One of the most popular hikes is to the 18th-century Satevó Mission Church, in a remote spot 8km down Copper Canyon. You can follow the river (the mission suddenly appears, framed in a forested river gorge); it's also possible to drive there.

Ruta de Plata HIKING
(Silver Trail) One of northern Mexico's best treks or horseback rides, the Ruta de Plata (Silver Trail) follows the ancient mule route between Batopilas and Chihuahua.

There is also the challenging, spectacular two- to three-day **Urique trek** (2-4 people 3-day hike with/without mule M$4000/2500), one of the region's very best.

Sleeping & Eating

Casa Monse HOMESTAY $
(Plaza Principal; s/d M$160/220; P ⊜) This great budget place has clean, spartan rooms off a verdant patio. The owner, Monse Alcaraz, who will chat your ear off in presentable English, will fix you Tarahumara cuisine and can help organize a tour with a local guide.

Hotel Juanita's HOTEL $
(☎649-456-90-43; Plaza Principal; s/d M$220/350; ⊜ ❄) Charming, well-kept rooms each get their own crucifix plus a shared river-facing courtyard. Juanita says if you don't like Jesus, you can go elsewhere.

Casa Real de Minas HOTEL $$
(☎649-456-90-45; www.coppercanyonlodges.com; Guerra 1; r M$1017; P ⊜ ❄) Lovely converted townhouse with 10 brightly decorated rooms, a courtyard and two reading areas with antiques and historical photos.

★ **Riverside Lodge** HOTEL $$$
(☎649-488-00-45; www.coppercanyonlodges.com; ⌚s/d incl breakfast M$1453/1890; P ⊜ ❄) For the ultimate hacienda experience check into this stunning colonial mansion, expertly and sympathetically renovated and decorated with lavish murals, oil paintings, rugs and oak furniture. Rooms are all individually furnished and boast en suites with claw-foot bathtubs, and staff are very informative about the region and the town's history. Look out for its trademark blue domes. Located just off the Plaza Principal.

THE CHANGING FACE OF THE CANYONS

The Parque de Aventuras Barrancas del Cobre is the beginning of the redevelopment project known as Megaproyecto Barrancas del Cobre which, depending on your viewpoint, will either revitalize tourism locally or forever tarnish one of nature's greatest wonders. Overall opinion seems to sway towards the former, and the new canyon attractions are far from the mar on the majestic landscape that was feared. Locals generally welcome the prospect of more money and jobs, though two Tarahumara villages have fought attempts to be replacewd by hotels. There also tentative plans for more luxury hotels, an amusement park with canyon-lip roller-coaster and even a canyon-top golf course. But with Copper Canyon tourism in decline it's uncertain how many of these projects will see the light of day. One project that is nearing completion (and should open in late 2014 or 2015) is Creel's new international airport.

Doña Mica MEXICAN $
(Plaza de la Constitución; meals M$60-80; ⌚7am-9pm; ✎) Run by Velia and her husband, this place hits the spot for hearty home-cooked meals. There's usually no menu (just a few choices daily).

Getting There & Away

From Creel, you take the spectacular paved highway south towards Guachochi then turn off at Km 164. The panoramic 65km stretch from here down to Batopilas is slowly but steadily being tarmacked. As work is ongoing, parts of the road are closed (for several hours) each day for roadworks. Check the latest situation with 3 Amigos (p766) in Creel before you set out, so you don't waste your time stuck at the roadside. Work is expected to be finished in 2015.

Public buses (M$260, five hours) leave from **Artesanías el Towi** (Av López Mateos) in Creel daily. Departure times totally depend on when the road is open to traffic so it's impossible to give a timetable, but there should be morning departures most days. Note that the timetable posted at Artesanías el Towi is usually out of date. Return buses, which leave from outside Batopilas church, are subject to the same road restrictions, so check times locally.

Two-day van tours from Creel (normally four-person minimum) cost M$4000 to M$5000). Or you can rent a truck from 3 Amigos in Creel and drive yourself – though the road is steep and narrow, with precipitous drops.

A back road (high clearance 4WD needed), affording canyon-lip views, runs from Batopilas to Urique, fording the Río Urique (passable November to April). Check the security situation before heading out on this route, which is also perfect for mountain biking.

CHIHUAHUA & CENTRAL NORTH MEXICO

Alluringly off the tourist radar, and with an affable frontier feel, central north Mexico is barely known except as a starting or ending point to Copper Canyon excursions (Chihuahua is the eastern terminus for the canyon-traversing Ferrocarril Chihuahua Pacífico train ride). Yet this region offers some of Mexico's most important historic sights across a triptych of colonial cities (Chihuahua, Hidalgo del Parral and Durango) and pretty damned fantastic scenery. The landscape is classic cowboy flick, typified by the starkly beautiful Desierto Chihuahuense (Chihuahuan Desert), which covers most of Mexico's largest state, Chihuahua. While it rises in the west into the fertile folds of the Sierra Madre Occidental, you'll be forgiven wherever you go for thinking you've wandered into a B-grade western (Durango, incidentally, is where many famous westerns *were* filmed). Vast cattle ranches and dudes decked out in big sombreros (hats) are the thing here.

Just as Chihuahua state license plates proclaim, this is very much the 'Tierra del Encuentro' (Land of Discovery). History buffs will delight in compelling museums commemorating famous revolutionaries such as Pancho Villa, while there are also some fascinating archaeological sites.

Tourism has been ravaged by recent upsurges in drug-cartel violence so do not venture anywhere off the beaten track without a guide. The 'Golden Triangle' area – where southern Chihuahua, northwest Durango and northeast Sinaloa converge – is noted for its opium production and particularly high levels of violence. There's some danger of being caught in the wrong place at the wrong time, but perpetrators have not targeted tourists and there have been few incidents involving visitors.

Chihuahua

☎614 / POP 819,000 / ELEV 1440M

Chihuahua, capital of Mexico's biggest state, has more character than any other city in Mexico's north. Many travelers use it only as an overnight stop before or after riding the Ferrocarril Chihuahua Pacífico, but Chihuahua is worth more of your time. The city center combines grand colonial buildings, several beautiful plazas, pedestrianized lanes and a healthy crop of restaurants, cafes and bars. Its museums bear witness to the key episodes of Mexican history that unfolded here. In short, you'll find it an intriguing city with a strong sense of identity.

History

Founded in 1709, Chihuahua soon became the key city of the Nueva España's Provincias Internas (stretching from California to Texas and Sinaloa to Coahuila). The Spanish brought pro-independence rebels including Miguel Hidalgo to be condemned and shot here in 1811. The Porfirio Díaz regime brought railways and helped consolidate the wealth of the area's huge cattle fiefdoms. Luis Terrazas, one-time Chihuahua state governor, held lands nearly the size of Belgium: 'I am not *from* Chihuahua, Chihuahua is mine,' he once said.

After Pancho Villa's forces took Chihuahua in 1913 during the Mexican Revolution, Villa established his headquarters here, arranged various civic projects and soon acquired the status of local hero. Today, the city has one of Mexico's highest living standards, with *maquiladora* (parts factory) jobs contributing significantly to this.

Sights

★Museo Casa de Villa MUSEUM

(Calle 10 No 3010; admission M$10; ⌚9am-7pm Tue-Sat, 10am-4pm Sun) Housed in Quinta Luz, Pancho Villa's 48-room former mansion, this museum is a must-see for anyone who appreciates a made-for-Hollywood story of crime, stakeouts and riches.

The interior is loaded with Villa's personal effects and photographs, and in the back courtyard you'll find the bullet-riddled black Dodge that Villa was driving when he was murdered. Information is in Spanish and English.

After his assassination in 1923, 25 of Villa's 'wives' filed claims for his estate. Government investigations determined that Luz Corral de Villa was the *generalísimo's* legal spouse; the mansion was awarded to her and became known as Quinta Luz. She opened the museum and the army acquired it after her death in 1981.

The rear of the museum concentrates on Mexican revolutionary history.

Casa Chihuahua MUSEUM

(☎614-429-33-00; www.casachihuahua.org.mx; Libertad 901; Museo de Sitio/full admission M$20/40, Sun free; ⏰10am-6pm Wed-Mon) Chihuahua's former Palacio Federal (built 1908–10) is now a cultural center full of good-quality exhibits, with most explanations in English and Spanish. Modern displays concentrate on the culture and history of Chihuahua state with features on Mormons, Mennonites and the Tarahumara. The most famous gallery is the **Calabozo de Hidalgo**, the dungeon where Miguel Hidalgo was held prior to his execution.

The historic dungeon and the church tower above it were preserved within the later buildings erected on the site. A short audiovisual heightens the mournful atmosphere of the dungeon, which contains Hidalgo's bible and crucifix. A plaque outside recalls the verses the revolutionary priest wrote in charcoal on his cell wall in his final hours, thanking his captors for their kindness.

Quinta Gameros GALLERY

(☎614-416-66-84; Paseo Bolívar 401; adult/child & student M$20/10; ⏰11am-2pm & 4-7pm Tue-Sun) Built in an incredibly elaborate Belle Époque architectural style by a wealthy mine owner,

WORTH A TRIP

CUAUHTÉMOC

The small city of Cuauhtémoc, 103km west of Chihuahua, is chief center for Mexico's **Mennonites**. Often blonde-haired and blue-eyed, with men wearing baggy overalls and women wearing long, dark dresses and headscarves, Mennonites speak in a dialect of Low German and trace their origins to Dutchman Menno Simons who founded the sect in the 16th century. Mennonite beliefs (including an extreme pacifism and a refusal to swear oaths of loyalty other than to God) put them at odds with many governments, and thus communities have from time to time moved en masse from one country to another. In the 1920s, around 6000 Mennonites left Canada for northern Mexico and the largest numbers of Mexican Mennonites are today living around Cuauhtémoc.

Indeed, most travelers come to this orderly town, standing in a lush vale of countryside producing most of Mexico's apples, solely to see the Mennonite *campos* (villages). The widely acclaimed movie *Luz silenciosa* (Silent Light), directed by Mexico's Carlos Reygadas – a story of adulterous love in a Mennonite community – was filmed here in 2007. It gave the town unprecedented publicity.

Mennonite *campos* are best visited on a tour (around M$400), which can be set up in Creel, as you will learn far more and visiting the *campos* independently is not always possible. If you haven't pre-arranged a tour, ask at the Museo y Centro Cultural Menonita. It's best to visit during the week (on Saturdays and Sundays Mennonite businesses are partially or fully closed).

Museo y Centro Cultural Menonita (☎625-583-18-95; Carretera Cuauhtémoc–Álvaro Obregón Km 10.5; adult/child M$25/15; ⏰9am-6pm Mon-Sat) is a large museum out in Mennonite country, just north of town, holding tools and other paraphernalia from the early years of Mennonite settlement here. A variety of crafts, cheeses and fruit preserves are sold. On the road out, **Campo 2B** (Carretera Cuauhtémoc–Álvaro Obregón Km 7.5) purportedly has the best *quesería* (cheese factory/shop). A taxi to both the museum and cheese factory from downtown will cost you about M$250 with waiting time.

The train station northeast of the central square, is the last/first stop on the Ferrocarril Chihuahua Pacífico, with daily trains to Chihuahua, and to Los Mochis via Creel.

Estrella Blanca (☎625-582-10-18; cnr Allende & Calle 13), at the east end of town, has buses to Chihuahua (M$102, 1½ hours) every 45 minutes and five buses daily to Creel (M$196, three hours).

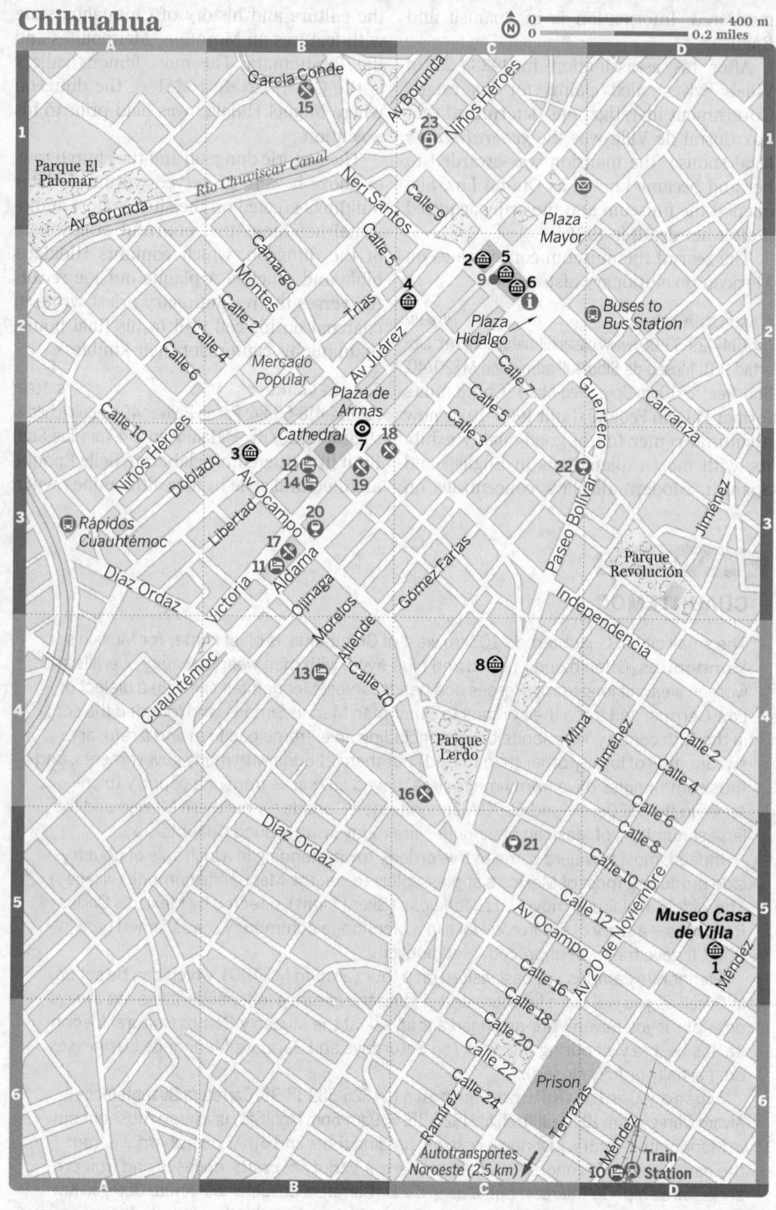

this musuem is filled with a mix of period furnishings and art. Every room is unique and the whole place is a sensuous delight of stained glass, carved wood, and floral and bird motifs.

Manuel Gameros started building Quinta Gameros in 1907 as a wedding present for his much younger fiancée, Elisa Muller. By the time it was finished three years later, she had died, and soon afterwards the Revolution began and the Gameros family fled

Chihuahua

Top Sights
1 Museo Casa de Villa D5

Sights
2 Casa Chihuahua C2
3 Casa Sebastián B3
Galería de Armas .... (see 5)
4 Museo Casa de Juárez C2
5 Museo de Hidalgo C2
6 Palacio de Gobierno C2
7 Plaza de Armas B3
8 Quinta Gameros C4

Activities, Courses & Tours
9 Chihuahua Bárbaro C2

Sleeping
10 Hostal El Chepe D6
11 Hotel Jardín del Centro B3
12 Hotel Plaza B3
13 Hotel San Felipe El Real B4
14 Quality Inn B3

Eating
15 El Papalote B1
16 Encantado C4
17 La Casa de los Milagros B3
18 La Fábrica de Pan y Cafe B3
19 Mesón de Catedral B3

Drinking & Nightlife
20 Café Calicanto B3
21 La Antigua Paz C5
22 Momposina C3

Shopping
23 Casa de las Artesanías del Estado de Chihuahua C1

Mexico. To add yet more color to the story, some guides tell that Elisa fell for Colombian architect Julio Corredor and ran off with him instead.

Plaza de Armas PLAZA
(cathedral 6am-9pm Tue-Sun) Chihuahua's historic heart, with its mass of pigeons, shoeshiners and cowboy-hatted characters, is a simple but pretty place. Its majestic baroque **cathedral**, built between 1725 and 1826, presides over the bustle, still containing the original organ installed in 1796.

Palacio de Gobierno HISTORIC BUILDING
(614-429-35-96; Aldama 901; 8am-8pm) FREE The courtyard of this handsome, 19th-century state-government building features striking 1950s murals by Aarón Piña Mora showing Chihuahua's highly eventful history. You can get a free booklet on the murals in the tourist office.

Hidalgo and the Mexican independence are the subjects of two small museums in the palacio: **Museo de Hidalgo** (9am-5pm Tue-Sun) FREE and **Galería de Armas** (9am-5pm Tue-Sun) FREE.

Museo Casa de Juárez MUSEUM
(Juárez House Museum; 614-410-42-58; Av Juárez 321; adult/child & student M$10/5; 9am-7pm Tue-Sun) President Benito Juárez' residence in this house during the French occupation made Chihuahua the capital of the Mexican republic from 1864 to 1866. Now a museum with the 1860s' feel still intact, it includes documents signed by the great reformer, as well as period exhibits including replicas of his furniture. It's also called the Museo de la Lealtad Republicana (Museum of Republican Loyalty).

Casa Sebastián GALLERY
(614-410-75-06; Av Juárez 601; 10am-1pm & 4-6pm Mon-Fri) FREE This restored 1880s gallery's main draws are the small-scale models of the massive metal sculptures by renowned Chihuahuan artist Sebastián, whose work is seen in cities worldwide. There are several real Sebastianes around Chihuahua, including one just above Parque El Palomar.

Tours

Chihuahua Bárbaro CITY TOUR
(www.chihuahuabarbaro.com; 3hr city tour adult/child M$100/80) This trolleybus offers tours of Chihuahua's main historic sights (narrated in Spanish) and beyond. Its three-hour city tour departs from the Plaza de Armas (where there's a ticket booth) four times daily, and includes the Pancho Villa museum and Quinta Gameros.

Sleeping

Hotel Jardín del Centro HOTEL $
(614-415-18-32; Victoria 818; r M$350-450;) Offering fine value, this pleasant, inviting little hotel has cozy, attractive rooms around a pretty plant-filled courtyard, plus a good little restaurant. Staff are sweet and its location is conveniently close to the center.

Hostal El Chepe HOSTEL $
(614-258-23-40; Méndez 2205;) This simple place enjoys a location just a short stagger with a suitcase from the train station.

Rooms are basic but clean and it's run by a friendly lady.

★ **Hotel San Felipe El Real** BOUTIQUE HOTEL $$
(☎614-437-20-37; www.sanfelipeelreal.com; Allende 1005; r/ste incl breakfast M$950/1150; P ⊖ ❄ @ 📶) In a gorgeous 1880s house with a courtyard with a burbling fountain, this incredibly classy hotel has six uniquely furnished rooms, all with antiques and period furniture. The owners spoil guests, and serve breakfast on one long table in the homey kitchen. Airport and train station pickups are offered.

Hotel Plaza HOTEL $$
(☎614-415-12-12; www.hotelplazachihuahua.com; Cuarta 204; r incl breakfast M$895-1125; P ⊖ ❄ 📶) In design terms, this is about as close as you'll get to a hip hotel in northern Mexico. Sleek, minimalist rooms all boast attractive wooden floors, modish furniture and beds with quality linen. The roof terrace where breakfast is served boasts fine city views, and it could not be more central.

Quality Inn HOTEL $$$
(☎614-439-90-00; www.qualityinnchihuahua.com; Victoria 409; r/ste incl breakfast M$1224/1955; P ⊖ ❄ @ 📶) Geared for business people, this large hotel is perhaps slightly bland, but service is efficient and its location just behind Chihuahua's cathedral is superb for exploring the city's colonial center. The carpeted rooms are spacious and boast multichanneled TV.

Eating

El Papalote BREAKFAST $
(cnr García Conde & Calle 9; breakfasts M$35-45; mains M$60-90; ⏲8am-9pm) Breakfast heartily in this American-style diner among Chihuahua's Mennonite residents. You'll find the city's best choice of egg combinations, and there are abundant *antojitos* (snacks), too.

★ **La Casa de los Milagros** MEXICAN $$
(☎614-437-06-93; Victoria 812; dishes M$55-160; ⏲4pm-1am; 📶) Legend has it that Pancho Villa and his pals hung out in this atmospheric 110-year-old mansion featuring tiled floors, lots of snug little rooms and an airy covered courtyard. The menu has reliable, good-value Mexican classics, *antojitos* (snacks) and grilled meats. There's live music, often *trova* (Latin American folk music), from 9pm Wednesday to Sunday.

La Fábrica de Pan y Cafe CAFE $$
(Independencia 408; 8am-8pm; ⏲ meals M$50-90; 📶) Okay, this cafe has probably taken a little inspiration from the likes of Starbucks, but given the tasty muffins, baguettes, hot cakes and breakfasts (try the *huevos franciscanos* with poached eggs and bacon) we'll forgive them that. All kinds of coffee are available, as well as wine.

Encantado STEAKHOUSE $$
(Av Ocampo 1810; dishes M$35-125; ⏲8am-8pm) A stylish restaurant in a historic building with tables in rooms dotted around a covered patio. The menu is pretty straightforward, with Mexican favorites, salads, filling sandwiches, steaks, burgers and breakfasts.

Mesón de Catedral INTERNATIONAL $$$
(Plaza de Armas; mains M$90-195; ⏲7:30am-midnight Mon-Fri, until 1am Fri & Sat; 📶) Enjoying the best vista in Chihuahua, with a terrace overlooking the city's cathedral, this upmarket place is worth a splurge: try the fish fillet stuffed with peppers and seafood. There's live music on Thursday, Friday and Saturday evenings.

Drinking

★ **Momposina** BAR, CAFE
(Coronado 508; ⏲8am-1am; 📶) Brilliant bohemian bar where creative types gather during the day to lounge on mismatched seats, snack on paninis and sip espressos. Later on, it morphs into a bar and there's often live music featuring Mulata, the Colombian-Mexican owners' band. Beers are inexpensive and the vibe is cool.

La Antigua Paz CANTINA
(Calle 12 No 2203; ⏲noon-1am) This classic Mexican cantina has revolutionary memorabilia on the walls and a good mix of students, 30-somethings and cowboys. It has live music most nights.

Many cantinas can be rough 'n' ready, male-dominated places with extremely local atmospheres. La Antigua Paz, though, is quite female friendly and one of the few cantinas where women are readily accepted.

Café Calicanto BAR
(☎614-410-44-52; Aldama 411; ⏲4pm-1am) Head here for live jazz and *trova* folk music (from 8pm Tuesday to Sunday), luscious cocktails, snacks and meals. Expect a diverse crowd on the tree-lined patio of this intimate cafe.

Shopping

Chihuahua is a big city with very little to recommend it for shoppers. However, the strong cowboy culture here means there are plenty of cowboy-related items to be found for those on the prowl. Cowboy boot-shoppers should make a beeline to Libertad between Independencia and Avenida Ocampo, where lots of boot shops line the street.

Casa de las Artesanías del Estado de Chihuahua HANDICRAFTS
(☎614-410-60-73; Niños Héroes 1101; ⏲9am-5pm Mon-Fri, 10am-5pm Sat) Good selection of *chihuahuense* crafts (including Mata Ortiz pottery) and Mexican foodstuffs such as pecans, oregano oil and *sotol*, a local spirit made from desert spoon plants.

Information

There are lots of banks and ATMs around the Plaza de Armas.

Clínica del Centro (☎614-439-81-00; www.clinicadelcentro.com.mx; Ojinaga 816; ⏲24hr) Has a 24-hour emergency department.

Copy & Print Club (cnr Guerrero & Ojinaga; internet per hr M$12; ⏲8am-8:30pm Mon-Sat, 10am-5:30pm Sun) Internet access.

Post Office (Libertad 1700; ⏲8am-4:30pm Mon-Fri, 8am-noon Sat)

Rojo y Casavantes (☎614-439-58-58; www.rojoycasavantes.com; Guerrero 1207; ⏲9am-7pm Mon-Fri, 9am-3pm Sat) For bus, train and plane tickets.

State Tourist Office (☎800-508-01-11, 614-429-35-96; www.ah-chihuahua.com; Palacio de Gobierno, Aldama; ⏲9am-5pm Mon-Sat) Helpful office that can hook you up with guides for city tours and more.

Getting There & Away

AIR

Chihuahua's **airport** (☎614-420-51-04; www.oma.aero; Blvd Juan Pablo II Km 14) has daily flights to Houston (United Express Airlines) and Dallas (American Eagle). **Aeroméxico** (☎614-201-96-96, 800-262-40-12; www.aeromexico.com; Ortiz Mena 2807, Quintas del Sol, Chihuahua), **Interjet** (☎614-430-25-46; www.interjet.com; Centro Comercial Plaza del Sol, Locales 155/156,Periférico de la Juventud) and **Viva Aerobus** (www.vivaaerobus.com) are among the airlines providing domestic services.

BUS

Chihuahua's main **bus station** (☎614-420-53-98; Blvd Juan Pablo II No 4107), 7km east of the center, has myriad buses including the 1st-class services listed in the table below.

Buses to the US also leave from the main bus station. **Autobuses Americanos** (☎614-429-02-29) runs to destinations including Dallas (M$1320, 17 to 19 hours, one daily) and Los Angeles (M$1275, 22 hours, three daily).

For Cuauhtémoc (M$102, 1½ hours) and Creel (M$294, 4½ hours) **Rápidos Cuauhtémoc** (☎614 416-48-40; Av Borunda) has buses to Cuauhtémoc every 45 minutes, 6am to 10pm, and to Creel at 5:50am and 1:35pm. **Autotransportes Noroeste** (☎614 411-57-83; www.turisticosnoroeste.com; Av Terrazas 7027) also has departures to Cuauhtémoc plus five daily departures (6am to 4pm) to the Copper Canyon hot spots of Creel, Divisadero (5½ hours), San Rafael (six hours) via Parque de Aventuras Barrancas del Cobre.

CAR & MOTORCYCLE

The easiest way out of central Chihuahua to Hwy 45 is northeast along the canal (Avenida Borunda). Heading west out of town, take Cuauhtémoc.

BUSES FROM CHIHUAHUA

DESTINATION	FARE (M$)	DURATION	FREQUENCY (DAILY)
Ciudad Juárez	352-376	5-6hr	every 20min
Durango	615-640	10-13hr	10
Hidalgo del Parral	192	3-5hr	hourly
Madera	296	4½hr	7
Mexico City (Terminal Norte)	1288-1580	19-22hr	16
Monterrey	826-1029	11-12hr	8
Nuevo Casas Grandes	295	4½hr	hourly
Torreón (for Saltillo and Parras)	430	7-8hr	53
Zacatecas	764-822	12-14hr	45

TRAIN

Chihuahua is the northeastern terminus for the Ferrocarril Chihuahua Pacífico, with departures at 6am daily. All trains have first-class carriages, while on Monday, Thursday and Saturday, *clase económica* carriages are coupled on the back. The **station** (☎614-439-72-12; Méndez s/n; ⊙5am-5:30pm Mon-Fri, 9am-12:30pm Sat) is 1.5km south of the Plaza de Armas. It opens from 5am daily for train departures.

Getting Around

To get to the bus station, catch a 'Circunvalación Sur' bus (M$7, 30 to 50 minutes) heading northwest on Carranza, almost opposite Plaza Hidalgo.

Chihuahua is just rolling out a fancy new public transportation network called **Vivebús**, with air-conditioned, wheelchair-friendly buses that run on designated busways (5:30am to 10pm). No cash is accepted, you need a card (M$20), and journeys cost M$6. There's an underground bus stop beneath the Plaza de Armas; the nearest stop for the train station and Museo Casa de Villa is Sagrado Corazón (on Avenida Ocampo). From here it's a short walk past the medieval-looking prison.

Buses do not run to the airport but you can catch a Vivebús to Terminal Sur and then a taxi (around M$75) from there.

From the center, there are taxis to the train station (M$50), bus station (M$100) and airport (M$180). Airport taxis back to town are pricey, around M$285.

Nuevo Casas Grandes & Casas Grandes

☎636 / POP NUEVO CASAS GRANDES 59,300 / ELEV 1463M

Nuevo Casas Grandes, 320km northwest of Chihuahua, is a prosperous but unremarkable country town, with small communities of Mormon and Mennonite settlers. Tourism-wise, its a decent base for the prettier village of Casas Grandes by the pre-Hispanic ruins of Paquimé (7km south) and the pottery center of Mata Ortiz (27km south).

Sights

Paquimé ARCHAEOLOGICAL SITE

(☎636-692-41-40; http://centroculturalpaquime.mex.tl; adult M$46, Sun & child under 13 free; ⊙10am-5pm Tue-Sun) The ruins of Paquimé, in a broad valley with panoramas to distant mountains, contain the mazelike adobe remnants of northern Mexico's most important trading settlement. Paquimé was the center of the Mogollón or Casas Grandes culture, which extended north into New Mexico and Arizona and over most of Chihuahua. The site's impressive, meticulously detailed Museo de las Culturas del Norte (included in the admission) has displays about Paquimé and the linked indigenous cultures of northern Mexico and the southwest USA.

The site was sacked, perhaps by Apaches, around 1340. Excavation and restoration began in the 1950s; Unesco declared it a World Heritage Site in 1998. Plaques, in Spanish and English, discuss Paquimé culture: don't miss the clay macaw cages and the distinctive T-shaped door openings. The Paquimé people revered the scarlet macaw and some structures here represent this beautiful bird, which has never been native to northern Mexico and is evidence of Paquimé's far-reaching trade network.

The Paquimé people were great potters and produced striking cream-colored earthenware with red, brown or black geometric designs; some amazing original examples are on display in the museum, as well as modern reproductions for sale.

Sleeping & Eating

Las Guacamayas B&B B&B $$

(☎636-692-41-44; www.mataortizollas.com; Av 20 de Noviembre, Casas Grandes; s/d incl breakfast US$50/70; P ⊖ ❄ ☎) This adobe-walled place has charming rooms with beamed roofs, all built with recycled materials, and a lovely garden area. Owner Mayte Luján has a world-class collection of Mata Ortiz pottery and is extremely knowledgeable about the region. It is located just a stone's throw from the entrance to the ruins of Paquimé (p778).

Casa de Nopal GUESTHOUSE $$

(☎636-692-44-02; sm@look.net; Av Independencia 81, Casas Grandes; r US$50; P ❄ ☎) This guesthouse boasts huge, artistically presented rooms finished in earthy tones with terracotta floor tiles and decorated with gorgeous hand-woven textiles and sarapes; some also have kitchens. These days, the accommodations are rarely rented on a daily basis, as the owners prefer longer lets, but it's worth a try.

Restaurant Constantino MEXICAN $$

(☎636-694-10-05; cnr Juárez & Minerva; mains M$55-140; ⊙7am-10pm) Ever-popular Constantino offers filling, tasty local food. Try the *enchiladas verdes* (enchiladas in tomatillo sauce).

WORTH A TRIP

MADERA

In pine-covered foothills, the logging town of Madera, with its refreshingly temperate climate, couldn't feel more different from the desert settlements of Nuevo Casas Grandes (M$286, 4½ hours, two buses daily at noon and 10pm) and Chihuahua (M$305, five hours, regular buses). The absorbing archaeological sites nearby, many of which take the form of cliff dwellings, make it a fascinating diversion.

The most impressive cliff dwellings are at **Cuarenta Casas** (9am-5pm) FREE where two dozen adobe homes, probably dating from the 13th century, hug the west cliffside of the dramatic Arroyo Garabato canyon. A round-trip hike takes at least an hour from the small visitors center. The 11:30am bus (M$48, 45 minutes) from Madera's bus station to El Lago goes by the Cuarenta Casas turnoff from which the visitor center is 1.5km. Returning, the bus stops at the turnoff around 4pm. Contact experienced local guide **José Domínguez** (%652-572-22-11), who speaks some English, for tours (M$500, minimum two people) of the area.

In Madera, the good-value **Hotel Parador de la Sierra** (652-572-02-77; cnr Calle 3 & Independencia; s M$270-330, d M$280-350;) near the bus station has spacious, well-presented rooms.

Information

There are several banks with ATMs in town. Check out **Mata Ortiz Calendar** (www.mataortiz calendar.com) for comprehensive information on the Casas Grandes area.

Getting There & Around

In Nuevo Casas Grandes, **Ómnibus de México** (636-694-05-02; www.odm.com.mx; Obregón 312) and **Estrella Blanca/Chihuahuenses** (636-694-07-80; Obregón 308) offer 1st-class buses to Chihuahua (M$335, 4½ hours, hourly), Madera (M$278, 4½ hours, 2am & noon daily), the border at Nogales (M$470, seven hours, seven daily) and Ciudad Juárez (four hours, M$282-313, 15 daily).

To get to Paquimé (p778) from Nuevo Casas Grandes, 'Casas Grandes' buses (M$8, 20 minutes) depart every 40 minutes, northbound from Constitución, just north of Calle 16 de Septiembre. Get off in Casas Grandes' plaza and walk 800m south on Constitución to the ruins. A taxi from Nuevo Casas Grandes to Paquimé is around M$90.

Mata Ortiz

Twenty-seven kilometers south of Casas Grandes, Mata Ortiz, a tiny town of dusty, unpaved streets, loose chickens and unfinished adobe houses, is a major pottery center. Artisans here use materials, techniques and decorative styles inspired by those of the ancient Paquimé culture, and their best pieces of work now sell worldwide for big, big bucks (though you can pick up a nice small one for about M$250).

The well-marked workshop-showroom of Juan Quezada, who revived the tradition in the 1970s, is across from the old train station at the village entrance. Strolling through the village, you'll pass numerous other potteries and will be able to see people working.

Mata Ortiz has no bus service. A taxi from Nuevo Casas Grandes, including a one-hour wait, costs about M$450.

Hidalgo del Parral

627 / POP 107,000 / ELEV 1652M

Easy-going Parral has a big place in Mexican history and some good museums. Its chief claim to fame is that it's where Pancho Villa was murdered on July 20, 1923, and buried – with 30,000 attending his funeral at Parral's Panteón de Dolores cemetery. Three years after his burial, his corpse was dug up and beheaded by persons unknown, and in 1976, his remains were moved to the capital.

Founded as a mining settlement in 1631, throughout the 17th century enslaved indigenous people mined the rich veins of silver and other minerals from Parral's La Prieta mine, which makes a fascinating visit.

If you're anywhere near Parral in mid-July, don't miss the spectacular celebrations to mark Villa's death.

Sights

Museo Francisco Villa MUSEUM
(627-525-32-92; cnr Juárez & Barreda; admission M$10; 10am-5pm Tue-Sun) The building from which Pancho Villa was shot and killed in 1923 houses the Museo Francisco Villa.

It has two floors of interesting photos of Villa the man (fording a river in his beloved Dodge, posing with his gun in mid-conflict, etc), guns and memorabilia. Guided tours (by donation) are available in Spanish (and sometimes English).

The tale guides tell about Villa's body being switched with a decoy after decapitation, and thus not actually being moved to Mexico City, may have credibility.

Mina La Prieta MINE

(Cerro de la Cruz; adult/child M$25/15; 10am-5pm Tue-Sun; P) This mine was the basis of Parral's economy for centuries after it opened in 1629, producing mainly silver but also gold, copper, zinc and lead. Today, it's one of the world's oldest mines still in operation. You can drop down 87m in an original elevator to the second of its 25 levels (the 23 below are now flooded) and walk 250m along a tunnel hand-cut around 1820, with historical displays on mining methods used throughout La Prieta's history.

The mine is still used for malachite extraction, occasionally meaning that it's closed to visitors. On the surface, there is a museum and a *mirador* (lookout) with a big statue of San José. Tours in Spanish (pay by donation) are given about every hour.

Palacio Alvarado PALACE

(627-522-02-90; Riva Palacio 2; adult/child M$25/15; 10am-5pm) Built a century ago in an eclectic European style for silver tycoon Pedro Alvarado, the beautifully restored Palacio Alvarado has pressed aluminum ceilings and plenty of original furnishings and artifacts, including Lady Alvarado's funeral wagon, later used for Pancho Villa. Alvarado was so rich he once offered to pay off Mexico's entire national debt.

Festivals & Events

Las Jornadas Villistas HISTORICAL

For a week leading up to the anniversary of Pancho Villa's death (July 20), Parral goes wild. Thousands of bikers show up and horseback riders make a six-day journey from the north, recalling Villa's epic journeys around northern Mexico. A reenactment of the assassination culminates proceedings.

Sleeping & Eating

Good accommodations are lacking in Parral, but there are one or two options for a decent night's rest. Note that hotels are booked far in advance for the Las Jornadas Villistas festival in mid-July.

Hotel Acosta HOTEL $

(627-522-02-21; Barbachano 3; s/d/tr/q M$290/360/400; @) A quirky time warp of a place which appears little-changed since the 1950s, with fantastic old lobby, original furniture and welcoming staff. Rooms are a bit creaky but comfortable enough and certainly cheap, some with fine city views.

Nueva Vizcaya Suites SUITES $$

(627-525-56-36; Flores Magón 17; s/d M$423/541; P @) A great deal, this efficiently-run suite-hotel has lovely views of the Cerro de la Cruz from some rooms, all with modern bathrooms, cable TV and the suites also with kitchens. There's an attractive bar-restaurant (meals M$50 to M$110) and helpful staff.

Disfruta HEALTH FOOD $

(Domingo Sarmiento 311; snacks & meals M$25-55; 8am-6:30pm;) Yes, northern Mexico is a carnivore's paradise but if you're in need of a fruity pick-me-up head to hip, healthy Disfruta for wonderful fruit cocktails, juices and *licuados* (smoothies), as well as baguettes, salads and crepes.

Al Gusto Restaurante MEXICAN $$

(627-103-19-24; Calle 20 de Noviembre No 5; dishes M$50-120; 8am-10pm) Air-conditioned Al Gusto offers great burgers, salads and filling fajitas.

Micro Cafe BAR

(Independencia 198; 6:30pm-midnight Mon-Sat;) Quite a find in a cowboy town like Parral, this intimate bar has a decidedly boho, artistic vibe with DJs (underground electronica and techno) and live music (indie, acoustic) on Fridays and Saturdays. There's draught beer, hip lighting and a cool crowd.

Information

The helpful **tourist office** (627-525-44-00; 10am-3pm) is at Mina la Prieta (p780). Banks with ATMs are around the Plaza Principal. Many cafes and restaurants have wi-fi.

Getting There & Around

The **Central de Autobuses** (627-523-02-43; Calle de Lille 5) is 2km east from the center along Independencia. It's easiest reached by taxi (M$30). Buses run to Chihuahua (M$205-260, 3-4 hours, hourly), Torreón (M$285-345, 3-4

PANCHO VILLA: BANDIT TURNED REVOLUTIONARY

Macho womanizer, revolutionary, cattle rustler, lover of education, a man of impulsive violence who detested alcohol. No hero in Mexico's history is as colorful or contradictory as Francisco 'Pancho' Villa.

Villa is best known as a leader of the Mexican Revolution, but as much of his adulthood was given over to robbing and chasing women as to any noble cause. Born Doroteo Arango to hacienda workers in northern Durango state in 1878, he turned to banditry by the age of 16, taking the name Francisco Villa (possibly in honor of his grandfather). The story goes that Villa became an outlaw after shooting one of the hacienda-owning family who tried to rape his sister. Between 1894 and 1910, Villa's life veered between spells of banditry and attempts to lead a legitimate existence.

In 1910, amid intensifying opposition to the dictatorial regime of President Porfirio Díaz, Villa was lobbied for support by Abraham González, leader in Chihuahua state of the revolutionary movement headed by Francisco Madero. González knew he needed natural fighting leaders and encouraged Villa to return to marauding. Villa soon raised a fighting force to join the Revolution, which began on November 20, 1910.

When Villa's rebels took Ciudad Juárez in May 1911, Díaz resigned the presidency. Madero was elected president, but in 1913 he was toppled from power by one of his own commanders, General Victoriano Huerta, and subsequently executed. Villa fled across the US border to El Paso, but within a couple of months he was back as one of four revolutionary leaders opposed to Huerta. He quickly raised an army of thousands, the famed División del Norte, and by the end of 1913, with the help of US-supplied guns, he had taken Ciudad Juárez (again) and Chihuahua, installing himself as Chihuahua's state governor for the next two years. He expropriated property and money from rich *hacendados* (landowners), lowered prices of basic necessities and established schools, but favored his troops over noncombatants and tolerated no dissent. His victory over a pro-Huerta army at Zacatecas in June 1914 signaled the end for Huerta's presidency. But the four revolutionary forces soon split into two camps, with liberal leaders Venustiano Carranza and Álvaro Obregón on one side, and the more radical Villa and Emiliano Zapata on the other. Villa was routed by Obregón in the Battle of Celaya (1915) and never recovered his influence.

After the USA recognized Carranza's government in October 1915, Villa decided to simultaneously discredit Carranza and seek revenge on US president Wilson. On March 9, 1916, Villa's men sacked the US town of Columbus, New Mexico, which was home to both a US cavalry garrison and Sam Ravel, who had once cheated Villa on an arms deal. Though as many as half of Villa's 500 militiamen may have died that day (there were 18 US deaths) and Ravel wasn't to be found (he was at the dentist in El Paso), the attack ended up a success for Villa – it drew a US Army punitive expedition into Mexico in his pursuit – and boosted his legend. Villa carried on fighting the Carranza regime, raiding cities and haciendas, but now had to maintain his fighting force by conscription, and sometimes allowed his men to pillage and slaughter.

In 1920 Carranza was deposed by his former ally Obregón, and Villa signed a peace treaty with provisional president Adolfo de la Huerta. Villa pledged to lay down his arms and retire to a hacienda in Canutillo, for which Adolfo de la Huerta's government paid M$636,000. Villa was given money to cover wages owed to his troops and to help the widows and orphans of the División del Norte. He settled 759 of his former troops at Canutillo, setting up a school for them and their children.

For the next three years, Villa led a relatively quiet life. He bought a hotel in Hidalgo del Parral and regularly attended cockfights. He installed one of his many 'wives,' Soledad Seañez, in a Parral apartment, and kept another at Canutillo. Then, one day while he was leaving Parral in his Dodge touring car, a volley of shots rang out and the legendary revolutionary was killed. The light prison sentences the eight-man assassin team received led many to conclude that the execution order came from President Obregón himself, though with all the enemies Villa made over the years, there are many suspects from which to choose.

hours, 7 daily) and Durango (M$345-395, 5-6 hours, 10 daily).

Hwy 45 to Durango is a long, lonely road. Keep a full tank of gas and don't drive it at night. There's also a spectacular back road to the Copper Canyon via Guachochi, which traverses even more remote terrain.

Durango

☎618 / POP 582,000 / ELEV 1912M

Durango state was the birthplace of Mexico's greatest outlaw (Francisco Villa), while Durango city spawned its first president (General Guadalupe Victoria), and the easygoing capital strikes a happy medium between Wild West backwater and sophisticated metropolis.

This is one of Mexico's most isolated cities: you have to travel hours through the desert or the Sierra Madre mountains from here before you'll hit another significant settlement. Yet isolation has fostered distinctive regional traits, from the cuisine through to Durango's celebrated role in the movie business.

Founded in 1563, Durango's early importance was down to nearby iron-ore deposits, along with gold and silver from the Sierra Madre. Today hundreds of *maquiladoras* (assembly plants) dominate the economy. For visitors, the city's striking colonial center commands attention, while good accommodations and restaurants are plentiful.

Note: Durango state's time zone is one hour ahead of Chihuahua and Sinaloa.

Sights

Constitución, pedestrianized between Jardín Hidalgo past the Plaza de Armas to Plazuela Baca Ortiz, is among Mexico's most likeable traffic-free streets, lined with restaurants and cafes, and lively on weekend nights.

Durango

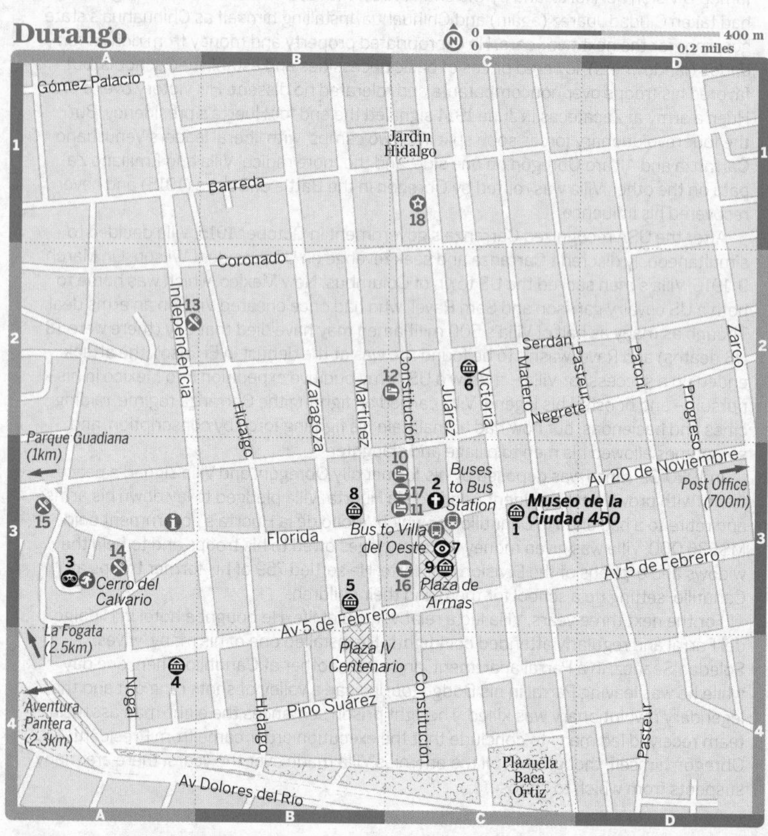

Plaza de Armas PLAZA

The flower- and fountain-filled Plaza de Armas is graced by the handsome baroque **Catedral del Basílica Menor** (⏲8am-9pm). In the plaza's center, you can descend the **Túnel de Minera** (Tunnel of Mining; admission M$20, students free Mon; ⏲10am-10pm), an underground space with displays and audiovisual presentations devoted to the history of mining in Durango.

★**Museo de la Ciudad 450** MUSEUM

(www.museo450.municipiodurango.gob.mx; cnr Av 20 de Noviembre & Calle Victoria; M$20; ⏲9am-5pm Tue-Sun) This impressive museum dedicated to Durango city is housed in a structure that dates back to 1901. The museum's 14 rooms house an impressive permanent collection of interactive exhibits, from pre-Hispanic times through colonization to the present day, and deals the Durango's economy, mining, traditions and culture.

The '450' suffix refers to the years between the city's foundation in 1563 and the museum's reopening in 2013 after a lengthy renovation project.

Cerro de los Remedios LOOKOUT

Durango's best *mirador* is linked by a spectacular, if shortish, **teleférico** (cable car; return M$20; ⏲9:30am-9pm Sun & Tue-Thu, 10am-11pm Fri & Sat), which runs from the Cerro del Calvario. As well as panoramic vistas of the cityscape, the hill is crowned by the church of **Nuestra Señora de los Remedios**. On Friday and Saturday evenings, open-air films are projected onto the church's outer walls.

Museo Nacional Francisco Villa en Durango MUSEUM

(Av 5 de Febrero 97; M$20; ⏲10am-6pm Tue-Sun) The second museum to mark Durango's 450th anniversary deals with that uniquely Mexican hero-rascal, Pancho Villa, and features engaging modern displays and films about the life of the man. It's located in the impressive Palacio de Zambrano building, near the Plaza IV Cenetario.

Museo Regional de Durango MUSEUM

(☎618-813-10-94; http://museo.ujed.mx; Victoria 100 Sur; adult/child M$10/2, Sun free; ⏲9am-4pm Mon-Fri, 10am-3pm Sun) In a palatial French-style, 19th-century mansion, this museum has thorough displays on Durango state's history and culture. Pancho Villa and the area's impressive array of minerals get special attention, and there are paintings by Miguel Cabrera. Most explanations are in English and Spanish.

Museo de las Culturas Populares MUSEUM

(☎618-825-88-27; Av 5 de Febrero 1107 Poniente; admission M$5; ⏲9am-6pm Tue-Fri, 10am-5pm Sat, noon-5pm Sun) Exhibits craftwork from Durango state's indigenous Tepehuán and Huicholes peoples and other artisans, including some hauntingly beautiful masks.

Teatro Ricardo Castro HISTORIC BUILDING

(☎618 811-46-94; cnr Av 20 de Noviembre & Martínez; ⏲9am-2.30pm Mon-Fri) This neoclassical theater, named after the Mexican concert pianist and composer born in Durango, features a large wooden bas-relief in its lobby depicting the founding of Durango.

Durango

MOVIE LOCATIONS

From the 1950s to the 1990s, both Hollywood and the Mexican film industry made hundreds of movies in Durango's unspoiled deserts and mountains. John Wayne, Clark Gable and Steve McQueen spent many hours filming here. *Bandidas* (2006), starring Salma Hayek and Penélope Cruz, was made in the state.

Villa del Oeste (618-112-28-82; Hwy 45; adult/child M$25/15; 11am-7pm) Many of the big-screen cowboys have swaggered through this film set. Today, the set is a souvenir-drenched theme park with gunslingers shooting it out at weekends (2:30pm and 4:30pm on Saturday, 1:30pm, 3:30pm and 5:30pm Sunday), while the rest of the week it's empty. Either way, it's kind of fun.

On weekends, a bus (adult/child M$30/20 including admission) leaves from Durango's Plaza de Armas a half-hour before each show. To get there on weekdays, take any northbound bus (M$10, about every 30 minutes) and remind the driver to drop you there. To get back you'll have to flag down a bus, so expect to stand in the sun for a while.

Chupaderos (www.setchupaderos.com.mx; 10am-6pm) The unfazed residents of Chupaderos have moved right into this former film set. Big-screen-ready cowboys still ride past the village saloon here, but they aren't actors. Big guns battle it out on Saturdays and Sundays (2:30pm and 4:30pm; adult/child M$30/15 entry for the show).

Tours

★Aventura Pantera ADVENTURE TOUR

(618-813-98-75; www.aventurapantera.com.mx; Cerro del Sacrificio 118, Lomas del Parque; 9am-9pm) Aventura Pantera is run by English-speaking Walter Bishop Velarde, one of the pioneers of Mexican ecotourism. He organizes exciting trekking, bird-watching, mountain-biking and camping trips into the Sierra Madre Occidental, Piaxtla Canyon and the wildlife-rich Reserva de la Biosfera Bolsón de Mapimí (north of Durango).

Trips cost from M$1300 per person per day and require at least eight participants, though guaranteed-date trips (listed on the website) go with any number of people.

Festivals

Feria Nacional FAIR

(www.ferianacionaldurango.gob.mx) For three weeks between late June and mid-July, Durango's big annual party remembers its agricultural roots with *charreada* (Mexican rodeos) plus a *duranguense* music-and-culture fest.

Sleeping

Hotel Plaza Catedral HOTEL $

(618-813-24-80; Constitución 216 Sur; r M$280-350; P ❄ ≈) The hotel has tons of history, but unfortunately the rooms are looking a little historic too, with tired-looking carpets and furnishings. That said, the views are unmatched, so try to score a room with a balcony facing the cathedral.

Hotel Posada San Jorge HOTEL $$

(618-813-32-57; www.hotelposadasanjorge.com.mx; Constitución 102 Sur; s/d incl breakfast M675/755; P ⊖ ❄ @ ≈) In an imposing ex-convent with accommodations upstairs around a courtyard, the San Jorge has spacious rooms, each with two beds and some with sofas and small balconies. There's a Brazilian-themed restaurant in the patio below and a good cafe adjoining the hotel.

★Hostal de la Monja HOTEL $$$

(618-837-17-19; www.hostaldelamonja.com.mx; Constitución 214 Sur; r incl breakfast M$1326; P ⊖ ❄ @ ≈) This 19th-century mansion facing the cathedral has been tastefully converted into an atmospheric 20-room hotel and is the best addess in central Durango. The luxurious rooms manage to combine tradition and modern amenities well, and there's a good restaurant, too.

Eating

Specialties in Durango include *caldillo duranguense* (Durango stew), made with *machaca* (dried shredded meat), and *ate* (pronounced '*a*-tay') – a quince paste enjoyed with cheese.

Cremería Wallander DELI $

(618-811-77-05; Independencia 128 Norte; tortas M$35-85; 8:30am-9pm Mon-Sat, 9am-3pm

Sun) Wonderful cafe-deli with a courtyard where you can enjoy healthy breakfasts, and extraordinary *tortas* (sandwiches) made with cold cuts and cheese from the Wallander family farm on fresh-baked rolls.

Los Equipales TAQUERIA $

(Florida 1204; tacos from M$8, mains M$50-105; ⏲1pm-12:30am Sun-Thu, 1pm-1:30am Fri & Sat) In Durango's chic old El Calvario neighborhood, Los Equipales serves up satisfying meaty meals, whether they be tacos, a *gringa* (large tortilla topped with cheese and Durango beef) or a steak. The atmosphere is convivial.

Fonda de la Tía Chona MEXICAN $$

(☎618-812-77-48; Nogal 110; mains M$70-150; ⏲5-11:30pm Mon-Sat, 1-6pm Sun) A Durango institution, this richly atmospheric, venerable place is dedicated to *durangueño* cuisine such as *caldillos* (beef stews) and delicious *chiles en nogadas* (peppers in walnut sauce).

La Fogata MEXICAN $$

(☎618-817-03-47; Cuauhtémoc 200; mains M$60-210; ⏲1pm-midnight; P 📶) The best steakhouse in Durango, with choice cuts of meat served on sizzling hot plates, including a terrific *parrillada* (mixed grilled meats). Also offers salads, and wine. Located 2km northwest of the center, M$50 in a taxi.

Drinking & Entertainment

Bars along Constitución develop a good atmosphere on weekend evenings. While you're in Durango it would be rude not to try a glass of *licor de membrillo*, a special local liquor made from quince.

Da Vinci Café CAFE

(Constitución 310 Sur; coffee M$15-25; ⏲10am-11pm Mon-Sat, 6-11pm Sun; 📶) This cafe boasts great views of Durango's Plaza de Armas and frequently hosts *trova* or acoustic music. It serves nothing stronger than strong coffee drinks – try a frappé.

The Italian Coffee Company CAFE

(Constitución 102 Sur; ⏲8am-8pm; 📶) For all your americano, latte, espresso, cappuccino and mocha needs. Also serves paninis and croissants.

Cineteca Silvestre Revueltas CINEMA

(☎618-811-02-22; Juárez 217 Norte; admission M$15) Cinema that shows art-house films, usually three times daily.

Information

Hospital General (☎618-813-00-11; cnr Av 5 de Febrero & Calle Fuentes; ⏲24hr) For emergencies or walk-in medical care.

HSBC (Constitución s/n; ⏲9am-5pm Mon-Fri) With ATM.

La Chabela (cnr Av 20 de Noviembre & Calle Hidalgo; internet per hr M$12; ⏲8:30am-11pm Mon-Sat, 9am-10pm Sun) Cybercafe with speedy connections.

Post Office (Av 20 de Noviembre 1016 Oriente; ⏲8am-4pm Mon-Fri, 9am-1pm Sat)

Durango State Tourist Office (☎618-811-11-07; www.durango.gob.mx; Florida 1106; ⏲9am-7.30pm Mon-Fri, 10am-5.30pm Sat & Sun) Friendly English-speaking staff.

Getting There & Away

Aeropuerto Guadalupe Victoria (☎618-817-88-98; www.oma.aero; Autopista Gómez Palacios Km 15.5), 15km northeast of town on Hwy 40D is a relatively quiet regional airport. It has a few flights to the USA including **United Express** (www.united.com) to Houston and Los Angeles. Domestic airlines such as **Aeroméxico** (www.aeromexico.com) and **Aeromar** (www.aeromar.com.mx) fly to Mexico City and Tijuana. A taxi here from central Durango is about M$170.

FIRST-CLASS BUSES FROM DURANGO

DESTINATION	FARE (M$)	DURATION	FREQUENCY (DAILY)
Chihuahua	615-640	8½-11hr	11
Hidalgo del Parral	355-395	6hr	9
Mazatlán	410-442	3hr	11
Mexico City (Terminal Norte)	866-1025	11-13hr	13
Monterrey	648-842	8hr	5
Saltillo	395	6½hr	5
Torreón (for Saltillo)	250-270	3-4hr	half-hourly
Zacatecas	260-300	4-5hr	hourly

The **Central de Autobuses** (☎618-818-36-63; Blvd Villa 101), 4km east of the center, has frequent bus departures, including several 1st-class options.

Getting Around

'ISSSTE' or 'Centro' buses (M$6) from the Central de Autobuses parking lot get you to the Plaza de Armas. Metered taxis cost about M$40 to the center.

To reach the Central de Autobuses from downtown, catch 'Camionera' buses along Avenida 20 de Noviembre anywhere near the plaza. Get off before the major intersection with the Pancho Villa equestrian monument and a McDonald's, and walk a short way northeast.

Around Durango

La Ferrería PYRAMID

(9am-5pm) FREE These are the most northerly ancient pyramids in the Americas. On-site is a well-kept museum explaining the culture of the Chalchihuites people who built them. Taxis cost about M$160 one-way from Durango.

NORTHEAST MEXICO

The northeast gets almost totally shunned by tourists these days, which is a mistake. Close to the US, the foreign visitors are mostly North Americans heading south, but the appealing towns and cities here make convenient journey-breakers – when you do stop, you'll be very glad you did. Colonial centers such as Saltillo; modern, culturally vibrant megalopolises like Monterrey and the idyllic wine mecca of Parras are highlights. The northeast also does nature like nowhere else. There's the chance to explore unique desert ecosystems at Cuatro Ciénegas, and to hike or watch wildlife in desert scrub or cloud forest at the Reserva de la Biosfera El Cielo, one of Mexico's most biologically diverse corners.

The region is not without dangers, and has seen some of Mexico's highest increases in drug violence over recent years. In the main border towns (particularly Nuevo 'narco' Laredo, but also Matamoros, Reynosa and Piedras Negras), as well as Monterrey and Torreón, the security situation is tense. Outside Torreón, Coahuila state is far safer, and Parras and Cuatro Ciénegas are *tranquilo* (safe and relaxed).

It's important to stress that tourists are rarely affected by narco-related violence, and the vast majority of visitors experience no trouble and enjoy their time in the northeast.

Saltillo

☎844 / POP 725,000 / ELEV 1600M

Set high in the arid Sierra Madre Oriental, Saltillo is a large and fast-growing city, but the center maintains a relaxed small-town feel. Founded in 1577, it's the northeast's oldest town, boasting fine colonial buildings and cracking cultural surprises (some leading art galleries and museums). Most attractions are conveniently central, and a burgeoning student population adds energy. It's also on the main routes between the northeast border and central Mexico, making it the ideal spot hereabouts to break a journey.

Sights

Saltillo's cultural core around the handsome, expansive Plaza de Armas is replete with historic buildings and ideal for exploring on foot. Alameda Zaragoza, Saltillo's green lung, is six blocks northwest of the plaza.

★ Museo del Desierto MUSEUM

(☎844-986-90-00; www.museodeldesierto.org; Pérez Treviño 3745; adult/child & student M$75/40; 10am-5pm Tue-Sun) Saltillo's top attraction, this no-expense-spared museum is highly enjoyable and informative (even if you don't speak Spanish). Exhibits reveal why sea currents can create deserts and how sand dunes are formed. Children will love the dinosaurs, particularly the Tyrannosaurus rex. There's also a reptile house, prairie dogs and a botanical garden with more than 400 cactus species.

Museo de Sarape MUSEUM

(Hidalgo 305 Sur; 9am-1pm & 3-7pm Mon-Sat) FREE An excellent museum devoted to the Mexican *sarapes* (blankets) that Coahuila is renowned for. There's a priceless collection to admire, and lots of fascinating background information about weaving techniques, looms, natural dyes and regional variations. You'll find very detailed English information in each room and there's a store next door for purchases.

Catedral de Saltillo CHURCH

(Plaza de Armas; 9am-1pm & 4-7:30pm) Built between 1745 and 1800, Saltillo's cathedral has one of Mexico's finest Churrigueresque facades, with columns of elaborately carved pale-gray stone. The central dome features carvings of Quetzalcóatl, the Aztec rain god.

Museo de las Aves de México MUSEUM
(Museum of Mexican Birds; 844-414-01-67; www.museodelasaves.org; cnr Hidalgo & Bolívar; adult/child & student M$10/5; 10am-6pm Tue-Sat, 11am-7pm Sun) Mexico ranks 10th in the world in terms of avian diversity, and this museum displays more than 800 stuffed and mounted species, some in convincing dioramas of their natural habitat. There are special sections on feathers, beaks, migration and similar subjects. Information is only in Spanish.

Instituto Coahuilense de Cultura GALLERY
(844-410-20-33; Juárez 109; 10am-6.30pm Tue-Sun) Saltillo's main cultural center, the beautiful Instituto Coahuilense de Cultura, often features good temporary exhibits by artists from Coahuila and beyond. It also hosts occasional concerts and has a bookstore and cafe.

Casa Purcell GALLERY
(844-414-50-80; Hidalgo 231; 10am-7pm Tue-Sun) This gallery is located in a wonderful English neo-Gothic style 19th-century mansion. Besides temporary art exhibits, Casa Purcell hosts semi-regular rock concerts and art-house films.

Sleeping

★Hotel Rancho el Morillo HISTORIC HOTEL $$
(844-414-40-78; www.ranchoelmorillo.com; Colonia Landín; r M$782; P) Founded in 1934, this highly atmospheric hacienda on the edge of Saltillo is set in very extensive grounds with trails that take in a pine forest, orchard and semi-desert. The family owners are very welcoming and good meals are prepared – after which their homemade *licor de membrillo* (quince liquor) is the perfect digestif.

Hotel Urdiñola HOTEL $$
(844-414-09-40; urdinola@ahg.com.mx; Victoria 251; s/d M$502/552/604; P@) Initial impressions are excellent, what with the stately lobby, sweeping marble stairway and stained glass windows. However the rooms are less impressive, with aging fixtures and fittings, though they're comfortable enough.

Hotel San Jorge HOTEL $$
(844-412-22-22; Acuña 240; s/d M$630/661; P) This slightly bland business-style hotel has neutral, but generously proportioned rooms. It has a (tiny) rooftop pool and a 6th-floor restaurant with panoramic vistas that's great for hearty breakfasts.

Eating & Drinking

Superb *fondas* (family-run eateries) occupy the 2nd floor of Mercado Juárez, by Plaza Acuña.

★Flor y Canela CAFE $
(844-414-31-43; Juárez 257; meals M$60-80; 8:30am-9:30pm Mon-Fri, 9:30am-4:30pm Sat & Sun;) A welcoming cafe with a bohemian ambience it's perfect for breakfast (M$50 to M$68), a good-value set lunch (M$67), paninis or a salad. There's an espresso machine (and organic Chiapas coffee for sale), and lots of *postre* (dessert) action on the menu. Wine and daiquiris are available.

El Tapanco INTERNATIONAL, MEXICAN $$$
(Allende 225; mains M$165-485; noon-11pm Tue-Sun) The most elegant restaurant in town, this classy place has an atmospheric interior and courtyard seating. The menu includes seafood and fish dishes, but (perhaps inevitably in northern Mexico) meat dishes command the most attention. Try the *cabrería azteca* (beef with black mushrooms).

Monster Café BAR
(Mario Escobedo 457; dishes M$100; 4pm-2:30am Mon-Sat;) Half-bar, half-monster museum, this eccentric place somehow works. Sit downstairs surrounded by cobwebs and mini-Frankensteins or enjoy the roof terrace. Tasty food (including homemade burgers) and salads are served.

El Confesionario BAR
(cnr Padre Flores & Abbot; 6pm-midnight Tue-Sat) Saltillo's self-proclaimed 'catedral de rock' hosts local metal, heavy (and just plain hairy) bands on weekend nights. Oh, and indie and punk groups sometimes get a slot ,too. There's a M$30 cover.

Shopping

El Sarape de Saltillo CLOTHING
(844-414-96-34; Hidalgo 305; 9am-1pm & 3-7pm Mon-Sat) This shop sells fine quality, colorful sarapes and other Mexican

artesanías: see wool being dyed and woven on looms inside.

Information

Cyberbase (Padre Flores 159; per hr M$8; ⌚9:30am-10pm Mon-Sat) Internet.

Hospital Universitario de Saltillo (☎844-411-30-00; www.hus.uadec.mx; Madero 1291; ⌚24hr)

HSBC (Allende 203; ⌚8am-7pm Mon-Sat) With ATM.

Post Office (Victoria 203; ⌚9am-4pm Mon-Fri, 9am-1pm Sat)

Getting There & Away

AIR

Saltillo's **Plan de Guadalupe airport** (☎844-488-17-70, 844-488-07-70; Carretera Saltillo–Monterrey Km 13.5) is 15km northeast of town. **Aeromar** (☎844-415-01-93, 844-415-02-67; www.aeromar.com.mx; Europlaza Mall, Carranza 4120) and Aeroméxico Connect have flights to Mexico City. There are buses between Saltillo's bus terminal and Monterrey's airport, which has many more flights.

BUS

The **bus station** (Calle Periférico Echeverría) is on the south side of town 2.5km from the center (a 10-minute bus ride).

Direct departures to destinations in the table below leave at least hourly, except to Durango (it's often quicker to change in Torreón) and Cuatro Ciénegas.

Buses also go to Guadalajara (M$655, nine hours) and Matamoros (M$375, seven hours). **Autobuses Americanos** (☎844-417-04-96; www.autobusesamericanos.com.mx) has services to Chicago, Dallas (US$63, 14 hours) and Houston (US$55, 13 hours).

CAR & MOTORCYCLE

Saltillo is a major road junction. Hwy 40, going northeast to Monterrey, is a good four-lane toll road. Going west to Torreón (262km), Hwy 40D splits off Hwy 40 after 30km, becoming (an overpriced) toll road.

Remote Hwy 57 runs north to Monclova (192km) while Hwy 54 crosses high, dry plains south toward Zacatecas (380km).

Getting Around

Saltillo's airport lies 15km northeast on Hwy 40 and is best reached by taxi (M$130) along Xicoténcatl. To reach the city center from the bus station, take minibus 9 (M$6) from in front of the station. To reach the bus station from the center, catch the returning bus 9 on Aldama, between Zaragoza and Hidalgo. Taxis around town cost M$40.

Parras

☎842 / POP 45,400 / ELEV 1520M

A graceful oasis town in the heart of the Coahuilan desert some 160km west of Saltillo, Parras has a historic center of real colonial character and a delightfully temperate climate, but it's most famous for its wine, with *parras* (grapevines) grown here since the late 16th century. With great places to stay, several enticing bathing pools and all that vino, this is somewhere to soak up and kick back for days – or longer.

Sights & Activities

Attractions around town include several wineries.

Iglesia del Santo Madero CHURCH
(⌚10am-6pm Thu-Tue) The iconic church perched precariously on the rocky outcrop

BUSES FROM SALTILLO

DESTINATION	FARE (M$)	DURATION	FREQUENCY (DAILY)
Chihuahua	674-774	10hr	6
Cuatro Ciénegas	223	5hr	1
Durango	395	6½hr	5
Mexico City (Terminal Norte)	840-905	10hr	12
Monterrey	93-101	1¾hr	every 45min
Nuevo Laredo	341-367	4-5hr	every 45min
Parras	110	2½hr	7
San Luis Potosí	436-471	5hr	hourly
Torreón	290-315	3hr	hourly
Zacatecas	320	4½-5½hr	18

FINE WINE TIME

Parras claims an important place in the history of Mexican wine. A warm climate together with the region's natural irrigation (underground streams from the sierra, which surface hereabouts) meant this part of Coahuila became a principal wine-growing area of Nueva España (New Spain).

Parras valley wines are mostly gutsy, full-bodied reds, although Casa Madero produces a great Cabernet Sauvignon rosé, plus whites made from Chenin Blanc, Chardonnay and Semillon grapes. These, along with local varieties such as San Lorenzo (a white) are available for trying/buying in Parras restaurants and shops, and there's even a **Feria de la Uva** (Grape Fair) every August with its somewhat cacophonous climax at Casa Madero.

Antigua Hacienda de Perote also produces port, vermouth, sherry and melon liquor.

Casa Madero (842 422-00-55; www.madero.com.mx; Carretera 102 La Paila–Parras, Km 18.5; 8am-5:30pm) FREE This, the first winery in the Americas was established at Parras in 1597, a year before the town itself sprang up. It's now an industrial-sized operation exporting vino all over the world. Free half-hour tours take you past winemaking equipment old and new.

You can buy quality wine and brandy onsite, too. From near the main plaza in Parras, catch regular buses (M$20) that pass the winery, just tell your driver where you want off. Or take a taxi (M$90); the winery is 7km north of Parras.

El Vesubio (Madero 36; 9am-1pm & 2-7pm Mon-Fri, 9am-7pm Sat & Sun) Founded in 1891, this quaint winery consists of a few dozen wooden wine barrels and a little shop in front of the family home.

on the south edge of town has, once you've undergone the steep-but-rewarding climb up, some wonderful, expansive views. It's a 30-minute walk from the center, east along Madero then up Benavides.

Museo de los Monos MUSEUM
(842-422-09-38; Madero 37; donations appreciated; 8am-9pm) Utterly kitsch low-budget wax museum with not-even-remotely lifelike figures of Freddy Krueger, Bill Clinton and the like. Far too many of them look like Michael Jackson.

Estanque La Luz SWIMMING
(adult/child M$15/5; 7am-7am) Estanque La Luz is the cleanest and most attractive of the three *estanques* (natural spring-water-fed pools) around town. It's an ideal place to cool off.

Sleeping & Eating

Parras is packed with *dulcerías* (candy stores) selling the region's famous *queso de higo* (fudgy candy with figs).

Hotel Posada Santa Isabel HOTEL $$
(842-422-04-00; Madero 514; s/d M$650/840; P) In a convenient location, this inviting place has well-kept rooms spread out around a fruit-tree-filled courtyard. There's a good in-house restaurant and midweek discounts are usually available.

Hostal El Farol HOTEL $$
(842-422-11-13; www.hostalelfarol.com; Arizpe 301; r M$865-990; P) An atmospheric colonial-style hotel with a lovely central courtyard and restaurant. The 25 spacious rooms have plenty of period character, terracotta floor tiles and attractive wooden furniture. Rates drop from Sunday to Thursday.

Antigua Hacienda de Perote HISTORIC HOTEL $$
(842-422-16-98; www.antiguahaciendadeperote.com; Ramos Arizpe 131; M$900-1500; P) This is a converted hacienda (it's a working pecan farm) on the outskirts of Parras, with spacious accommodation in shady, beautiful gardens that boast two pools (one spring-fed, the other chlorinated). Meals are available and you can tour the *bodegas* (wine cellars) here, too.

Restaurante Chávez MEXICAN $
(Reforma 19; dishes M$30-70; 8am-midnight) A popular simple place, Chávez is renowned for its huge portions of local grub. Try their *caldo de res* (beef soup, served with corn)

or *pollo a la plancha* (grilled chicken). Pizza and burgers are also offered.

Information

Parras Tourist Office (☎842-422-02-59; www.parrascoahuila.com.mx; ⏰10am-2pm & 4-6pm Mon-Fri, 10am-2pm Sat) The main tourist office stocks plenty of brochures and can advise about tours. Some English is spoken.

Getting There & Away

Only 2nd-class buses serve Parras, but most are perfectly comfortable and air-conditioned. There are seven daily to/from Saltillo (M$110, 2½ hours) and five daily to/from Torreón (M$135, three hours). If you want to head to Cuatro Ciénegas without backtracking to Saltillo, catch a bus to San Pedro Las Colonias (M$80, 1½ hours, four daily) and then a bus from there to Cuatro Ciénegas (M$132, two hours, nine daily).

Parras is easily reachable by car; turn off the highway at La Paila and drive 27km south.

Cuatro Ciénegas

☎869 / POP 13,000 / ELEV 747M

The serene town of Cuatro Ciénegas is bespeckled with adobe and colonial buildings and a handful of hotels and restaurants. It's also the perfect base for exploring the Área de Protección de Flora y Fauna Cuatro Ciénegas.

Sights & Activities

Área de Protección de Flora y Fauna Cuatro Ciénegas Park NATURE RESERVE

(admission M$30) With hundreds of shimmering cerulean *pozas* (pools) and streams in the middle of the Desierto Chihuahuense (Chihuahuan Desert), this 843-sq-km nature reserve is a surreal sight. Fed by a network of more than 500 underground springs, it's a desert habitat of extraordinary biological diversity. Cuatro Ciénegas is home to over 75 endemic species, including three kinds of turtles and 11 kinds of fish, as well as primative organisms called *estromatolitos* (stromatolites).

Some pools and the nearby river have been set aside for recreational spots, including swimming.

If you don't have your own transport, exploring the area is tricky, as the desert tracks are not always signposted. Using the services of a guide is wise. Buses to Torreón will drop you at the entrances to sites around the park, but usually won't stop to pick people up.

➡ **Poza Azul Visitors Center**

(⏰10am-6pm Tue-Sun; P) This center has illustrated displays about the reserve's ecology in Spanish and English. The little **Poza Las Tortugas**, a good turtle-spotting pool, is right behind here, while 1.5km further back is aptly named **Poza Azul** (Blue Pond), one of the reserve's most photographed sites.

➡ **Dunas de Yeso**

(Las Arenales; admission M$25; ⏰10:30am-6pm) These blinding-white gypsum sand dunes contrast superbly with the six mountain ranges that ring the valley. To visit you'll need to stop by the visitors center to pay and get the key that opens the gate at the beginning of the track out.

➡ **Río Los Mezquites**

(☎869-696-04-08; admission M$45; ⏰9am-7pm) Swimming with the fish and turtles in this sublime stretch of slow-flowing blue water amid the desert landscape is a surreal, revitalizing experience. There are *palapas* (thatched shelters) for shade.

Casa de Cultura MUSEUM

(☎869-696-05-56; Hidalgo 401 Poniente; adult/child & student M$10/5; ⏰9am-1pm & 3-7pm Mon-Fri, 10am-5.30pm Sat & Sun) Located in the former home of Venustiano Carranza, a revolutionary leader involved in the overthrow of Porfirio Díaz, this museum has a small but interesting display of ancient objects unearthed in the area.

Museo Casa Carranza MUSEUM

(Carranza btwn Juárez & Escobedo; requested donation M$10; ⏰10am-6pm) This museum has audiovisual displays and interesting memorabilia dedicated to Venustiano Carranza, including the revolutionary's suit and his heartfelt correspondence illustrating his ideals.

Tours

Two- or three-day excursions can be organized with guides for about M$1500 per person. Contact him through the travel agency on the plaza (corner of Juárez and Carranza) or the tourist office. These include trips to Valle del Hundido, a magnificent spot to experience the diverse desert ecosystem. Rates include car transportation.

Tours organised by the Hotel Misión Marielena are recommended, with four different options that include the Turtle and Blue Ponds, and a city tour that takes in a winery. Hotel Plaza also offers good tours, including visits to the pools, museum and sights around town. A two-day trip inclusive of accommodation is M$950 (minimum five people).

Sleeping & Eating

Hotel Plaza HOTEL $$
(☎869-696-00-66; www.plazahotel.com.mx; Hidalgo 202 Oriente; s/d incl continental breakfast M$510/695; P ⊖ ❄ @ ☜ ≋) Built in colonial style, this fine-value hotel has very spacious, comfortable rooms with attractive furnishings that all face a grassy patio and that all-important heat-busting pool.

Hotel Misión Marielena HOTEL $$
(☎869-696-11-51; Hidalgo 200 Oriente; s/d incl breakfast M$562/710; P ⊖ ❄ ☜ ≋) This historic hotel has large, well-maintained rooms, all with two double beds. Accommodations are set around two rear courtyards, which have a pool and mountain views. The hotel's restaurant is also decent, with good breakfasts, grilled meats and local wines available.

La Esquina del Marisco SEAFOOD, MEXICAN $$
(Hidalgo 242; meals M$60-130; ⊙9am-7pm) Inexpensive, informal place specializing in fresh seafood, including delicious *cocteles de camarón* (spicy shrimp cocktails served with salty crackers) but also grilled fish and squid. Look out for the garishly-painted green building.

Information

You'll find a **bank** (cnr Zaragoza & Escobedo), with an ATM, one block north of the plaza and a **tourist office** (☎869-696-09-02; Carranza 100; ⊙9:30am-5pm Mon-Fri) in the Presidencia Municipal.

Getting There & Away

The bus terminal occupies the southwest corner of the plaza. First-class buses run to Torreón (M$251, 3½ hours, 8 daily), Saltillo (M$253, five hours, one each morning) and the border at Piedras Negras (M$327, six hours, four daily). Monclova (M$96), two hours away via frequent buses, has more services north and south.

Monterrey

☎81 / POP 4.1 MILLION / ELEV 530M

Cosmopolitan Monterrey is Mexico's third-largest city, second-largest industrial center and *número uno* in per-capita income. This economic powerhouse has a strong entrepreneurial ethos, humming cultural scene, vibrant universities and eclectic cuisine.

With sprawling suburbs of gargantuan air-conditioned malls and manicured housing estates, this is also one of Mexico's most Americanized cities. Boasting world-class museums and a jagged mountain backdrop that offers terrific outdoor adventure sports, the city's attractions are diverse and myriad.

All of this makes Monterrey fiercely independent and very different to any other Mexican metropolis you'll encounter. Sadly, its appeal has recently been compromised by some of Mexico's worst drug violence, much of which was played out in the downtown area in 2011. But by early 2014 the troubles appeared to have eased and cultural life was beginning to return

RECLAIMING THE STREETS

Historically Mexico's most prosperous and progressive city, Monterrey largely avoided the worst narco-troubles during the early drug war years. But in 2011 and 2012, a series of horrific incidents provoked by turf wars spilled into the city's streets, as the Gulf Cartel and the Zetas competed for territory, with 27 killed and eight kidnapped in one attack on a bar just south of the main bus terminal, and 52 (some reports say 61) massacred in an arson attack on a casino.

To reclaim the streets, Nuevo León's governor Rodrigo Medina first purged local police forces, which were deemed to be deeply infiltrated by drug mafias, and 4200 officers were fired or jailed. Then a new state police force, the Fuerza Civil (civil force) was formed, with officers being paid relatively high salaries and given secure compounds to live in.

The stakes are certainly high, with Insight Crime estimating (in 2012) that drug trafficking, extortion and kidnapping is worth up to US$150 million per year in Metropolitan Monterrey. By early 2014 there appeared to be some grounds for optimism, with crime rates falling and local Zeta leaders thought to be largely on the run, in jail or dead. However the factors that created the violence are still undoubtedly present.

Monterrey

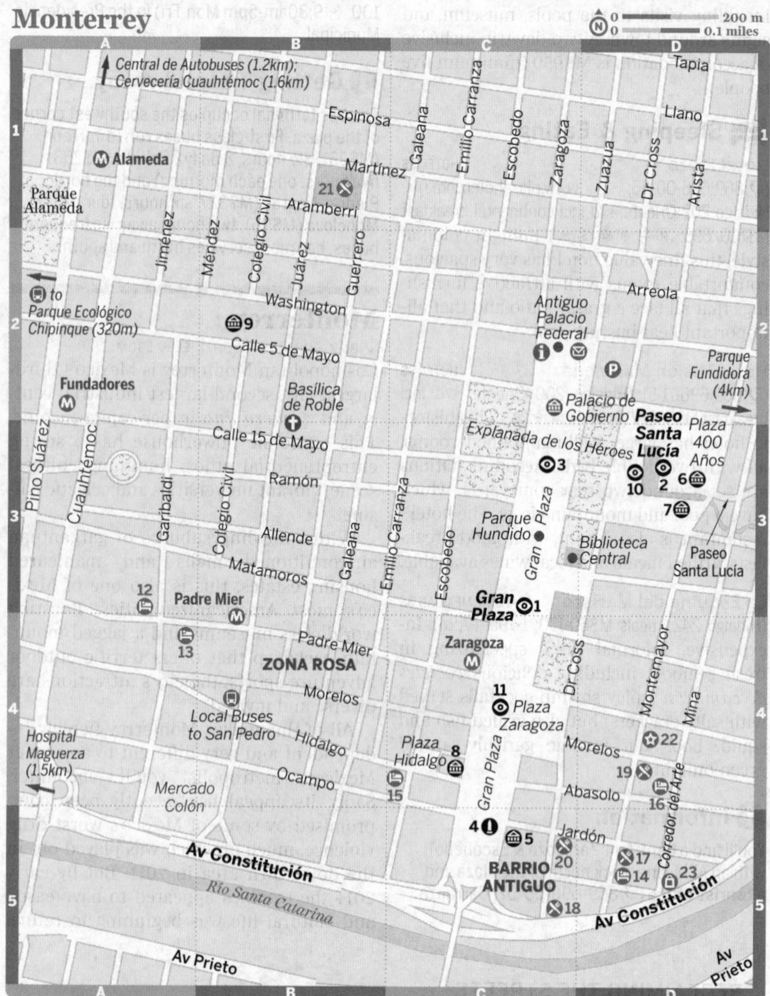

to the heart of the city, with boutiques and bars reopening in the Barrio Antiguo.

If you stay in the center, this historic core is very accessible. Most of Monterrey's main cultural attractions are clustered close by (except the extraordinary Parque Fundidora) and you'll have the Barrio Antiguo on your doorstep. Away from the center, prosperous areas like San Pedro Garza García are dominated by thundering highways so there's little joy exploring them on foot.

History

Dating from 1596, it wasn't until after Mexican independence that the city began to prosper, as proximity to the US gave it advantages in trade and smuggling.

In 1900, the first heavy industry in Latin America, a vast iron and steel works (now the site of the Parque Fundidora) rose to dominate the cityscape. Monterrey soon became dubbed the 'Pittsburgh of Mexico,' and still produces about 25% of Mexico's raw steel. The city also churns out around 60% of the nation's cement and half of its beer.

Sights & Activities

Most major sights are concentrated around the Gran Plaza in the center. East of here is the atmospheric Barrio Antiguo quarter, with low-slung colonial buildings and cobbled streets.

From the Gran Plaza you can jump aboard a metro or catch a boat along a beautiful urban river, the Paseo Santa Lucía, to the city's other main cultural hub: the Parque Fundidora.

Gran Plaza & Around

★ Gran Plaza PLAZA

(Macroplaza; Ⓜ Zaragoza) A monument to Monterrey's ambition, this city-block-wide series of interconnected squares, also known as the **Macroplaza**, was created in the 1980s by the demolition of a prime chunk of city-center real estate. A controversial, but ultimately successful, piece of redevelopment, its charm has increased over the years as once-naked urban space has been softened by parks, trees, fountains and pools.

Said to form the largest public square in the world, it's an intriguing combination of concrete and the neoclassical.

Vistas of the surrounding mountains open up between the roster of iconic edifices – classically designed municipal buildings and cutting-edge modern structures housing some of Mexico's finest museums – that line the Gran Plaza. For visitors, it's a delight to explore on foot, as most traffic is directed away from the heart of the area by underpasses.

At the southern end of the Gran Plaza, the 70m concrete tower **Faro del Comercio** (Lighthouse of Commerce) soars above the city, its green lasers piercing the night sky. The Faro abuts the Baroque form of the **Catedral Metropolitano de Monterrey**, capped by a neon cross. North of here is a shady park, the **Plaza Zaragoza** (Gran Plaza), that's popular with snacking families, smooching lovers and also the venue for open-air concerts and old-school Latin dancing every Sunday.

Monterrey

Top Sights

1 Gran Plaza ... C3
2 Paseo Santa Lucía ... D3

Sights

3 Explanada de los Héroes ... C3
4 Faro del Comercio ... C5
5 Museo de Arte Contemporáneo ... C5
6 Museo de Historia Mexicana ... D3
7 Museo del Noreste ... D3
8 Museo Metropolitano de Monterrey ... C4
9 Pinacoteca de Nuevo León ... B2
10 Plaza 400 Años ... D3
11 Plaza Zaragoza ... C4

Sleeping

12 Hotel Mison ... A3
13 iStay ... A4
14 La Casa del Barrio ... D5
15 Radisson Plaza Gran Hotel Ancira ... C4
16 Yeccan ... D4

Eating

17 El Infinito ... D5
18 El Rey del Cabrito ... C5
19 La Galería Cafe ... D4
20 Madre Oaxaca ... C5
21 Mercado Juárez ... B1

Entertainment

22 Café Iguana ... D4

Shopping

23 Corredor del Arte ... D5

Continuing north, the rest of the Gran Plaza is lined with a succession of concrete municipal structures. If you're a fan of Brutalism, you'll love the **Teatro de la Ciudad** and its architectural cousin, the lofty **Congreso del Estado**. Then down some steps is the **Explanada de los Héroes** (Esplanade of the Heroes; Gran Plaza) lined with statues, and finally the 1908 neoclassical **Palacio de Gobierno**.

Museo de Arte Contemporáneo MUSEUM

(Marco; ☎81-8262-4500, 81-8262-4577; www.marco.org.mx; cnr Zuazua & Jardón; adult/child & student M$70/50, Wed free; ⏲10am-6pm Tue & Thu-Sun, 10am-8pm Wed; Ⓜ Zaragoza) Don't miss the Museo de Arte Contemporáneo, its entrance marked by a gigantic black dove sculpture by Juan Soriano. Inside, its idiosyncratic spaces are filled with water and light and major exhibitions (all temporary, there's no permanent collection) of work by contemporary Mexican and Latin American artists. Call in advance to get a tour in English. Marco also has a fine bookstore and restaurant.

Plaza 400 Años PLAZA
(boat ride adult/child round-trip M$40/20; Ⓜ Zaragoza) This plaza, graced with fountains and pools, forms an impressive approach to the sleek, modernist Museo de Historia Mexicana and the Museo del Noreste. It is the terminus of the lovely Paseo Santa Lucía promenade.

Museo de Historia Mexicana MUSEUM
(☎81-8345-9898; www.museohistoriamexicana.org.mx; adult/child M$40/free, Tue & Sun free; ⏲10am-8pm Tue & Sun, Wed-Sat 10-6pm) This sleek modernist museum presents an extensive but easily manageable chronology of Mexican history. There's also an Earth section full of mounted animals and realistic-looking plants at its heart. All explanations are in Spanish only, but English tours can be arranged by phoning in advance.

Museo del Noreste MUSEUM
(Plaza 400 Años) Technically it's a separate institution from the Museo de Historia Mexicana (p793), but practically speaking its galleries on the culture and history of Nuevo León, Tamaulipas, Coahuila and Texas, packed with video screens and artifacts, function as a new wing of the history museum with one ticket working for both. Begin on the bottom floor to follow the displays chronologically.

★ **Paseo Santa Lucía** RIVER, GARDENS
(⏲24hr) The stunning promenade of Paseo Santa Lucía, which stretches 2.4km, is a world-class example of urban regeneration. This (artificial) river forms a turquoise ribbon through the heart of industrial Monterrey, offering a natural corridor between the Gran Plaza and Parque Fundidora. Take a stroll with the ambling families on this delightful pathway, lined with tropical greenery.

The landscaping is amazing, with lighting illuminating the water at night, striking modernist bridges spanning the water and plenty of seating to take in the views. Boats (M$60 return) also ply the route. There's 24hr security, a few bars and restaurants at its western end and the whole promenade has free public wi-fi. Every city should have one.

Pinacoteca de Nuevo León GALLERY
(☎81-1340-4358; www.conarte.org.mx; cnr Washington & Colegio Civil; ⏲10am-6pm Tue-Sun; Ⓜ Alameda) FREE This art museum, in the gorgeous Colegio Civil building, displays paintings and sculptures from local leading contemporary artists, including Julio Galán (1958–2006), once part of Andy Warhol's circle.

Museo Metropolitano de Monterrey MUSEUM
(☎81-8344-1971; Zaragoza s/n Sur; ⏲10am-6pm Tue-Sun; Ⓜ Zaragoza) FREE This 19th-century structure, the former Palacio Municipal, now houses the Museo Metropolitano de Monterrey. There's a brief, Spanish-only summary of city history on the ground floor and lovely upstairs galleries featuring works by contemporary painters and sculptors.

Outside the Center

★ **Parque Fundidora** PARK
(☎81 8126-8500; www.parquefundidora.org; ⏲6am-11pm; P 👪; Ⓜ Parque Fundidora) Formerly a vast steel-factory complex, this once-blighted industrial zone has been transformed into a huge urban park. Designers cleverly retained the iconic smoke stacks and industrial relics to give a surreal and at times apocalyptic feel, but a vibe very much in keeping with Monterrey's heritage. You can rent bikes, jog the trails, take in a film or browse the photography. Bring the kids. And above all, visit the Horno 3 furnace, for this building is the undoubted star of the show.

Blast Furnace No 3 has been converted into **Horno3** (☎81 8126-1100; www.horno3.org; adult/child & student M$90/55, nocturnal climbs M$40; ⏲10am-6pm Tue-Thu, 11am-7pm Fri-Sun, nocturnal climbs 6-10pm Tue-Thu & Sun, 7-10pm Fri & Sat), an exceptionally impressive high-tech, hands-on museum devoted to Mexico's steel industry, located in the very carcass of the industrial site. Everything about it smacks of class, with no expense spared: from the steaming rocks at the entrance to the to the metal staircase that climbs to the summit. The entire process of steel-making is explained (with some English translations) and its vital relevance to Monterrey and Mexico. Don't miss the dramatic furnace show, beamed from the bulk of Horno 3 itself and ask about nocturnal climbs of the metal tower. Last tickets are sold one hour before closing. There's a good cafe-restaurant here too: El Lingote (p796).

Three other disemboweled redbrick factories compose the **Centro de las Artes** (81-8479-0015; www.conarte.org.mx; film screenings M$45; 10am-9:30pm Tue-Sun) FREE, an arts center with high-class rotating exhibitions that also screens independent/foreign films.

The Fundidora complex also includes the Arena Monterrey used for concerts and basketball, and in the next few years a spectacular new Children's Museum is scheduled to open.

The metro stops within a ten-minute walk of the park, but the best way to get here is to walk along Paseo Santa Lucía from Plaza 400 Años.

Cervecería Cuauhtémoc BREWERY
(brewery tours 81-8328-5355; www.cuamoc.com; Reyes 2202 Norte; brewery tours 9am-4pm Mon-Fri, beer garden 10am-6pm; M General Anaya) FREE Mexico's oldest brewery (established 1890) fills six million bottles of Bohemia, Dos Equis, Tecate and other beers every day. Free **brewery tours** are given about hourly. Reservations are recommended (especially if you'd like a tour in English). Tours start in front of the convivial outdoor **beer garden** where you might get a free mug of Carta Blanca beer.

Festivals & Events

Festival Internacional de Cine en Monterrey FILM
Mexican and international art-house films. Held over two weeks in August.

Aniversario de Independencia TRADITIONAL
Monterrey's biggest celebrations are held on Mexico's Independence Day, September 16, with fireworks, *música norteña* (country ballads) and a parade.

Sleeping

The Barrio Antiguo and Zona Rosa have a few choices and offer the best location. There are also cheap hotels dotted around the bus station.

★ **Yeccan** HOSTEL $
(81-8344-52-65, 81-8340-616-57; yeccan.mty@gmail.com; Abasolo 916A; dm/r M$180/360; M Zaragoza) Unique, outstanding hostel in the Barrio Antiguo, owned by an artistic crew who have created a hip, contemporary look with whitewashed walls and stylish modern furniture. Offers simple, clean and inviting dorms (with lockers and fans) and neat private rooms, a lovely common area with TV and sofas, pool room, guests' kitchen and patio.

La Casa del Barrio HOSTEL $
(81-8344-1800; lacasadelbarrio@gmail.com; Montemayor 1221 Sur; dm M$200, r with/without bathroom M$480/400; M Zaragoza) This hostel seems to covering all its bases, advertising itself as a Spanish School and Waffle Center, too. Offers clean (though hot, there's no air-conditioning) dorms, and the rear garden is pleasant; the private rooms are overpriced.

Hotel Misión HOTEL $$
(81-8150-65-00; www.hotelesmision.com; Padre Mier 201 Pte; r/ste from M$580/1000; M Padre Mier) This hotel sits in a perfunctory (ok, pretty ugly) 1960s block, but its rooms offer good value, all are well-maintained and have a desk and modern bathrooms. The restaurant downstairs serves good buffet breakfasts. It is located just a short stroll from the metro and Macroplaza.

iStay HOTEL $$
(81-8228-51-00; www.mtyhistorico.istay.com.mx; Morelos 191; r M$720; M Padre Mier) A huge concrete hotel that enjoys a great location, backing onto pedestrianized Morelos and close to Monterrey's Gran Plaza. The branding screams 'hip hotel' but iStay's carpeted rooms are actually very standard fare, though comfortable enough and fair value.

Radisson Plaza Gran Hotel Ancira HOTEL $$$
(81-8150-7000; www.hotel-ancira.com; cnr Hidalgo & Escobedo; r/ste incl breakfast M$1288/2352; M Zaragoza) A memorable place to stay, this grand dame of a hotel was built in 1912 in a French Art Nouveau style. The mirror-roofed, gingham-tiled reception-restaurant area is quite something and how many hotels have a live classical pianist at breakfast? Rooms, however, are more standard business class. Look out for promotional rates on their website.

Eating & Drinking

Monterrey's signature dish is *cabrito al pastor* (roast goat). Barrio Antiguo has a good selection of places to eat (and drink), though far fewer than before the troubles which have decimated Monterrey's nightlife.

Mercado Juárez (Av Juárez; 8am-7pm Mon-Sat, to 3pm Sun; M Alameda) has *fondas* (small restaurants) selling tasty, cheap food.

★ **La Galería Café** ITALIAN, LOUNGE **$$**
(Morelos 902; mains M$75-110; 5pm-1am; ; M Zaragoza) Breathing new life into the barrio, this sleek, contemporary restaurant-bar serves suberb pasta (choose from 11 classic sauces) and snacks with electronic mixes in the background. On weekend nights the groovy upstairs terrace comes into its own for neon nightscape gazing and cocktail sipping.

El Infinito CAFE **$$**
(81-8989-5252; Jardón 904; mains M$70-140; 5/6pm-12.30am; ; M Zaragoza) Highly enjoyable culture cafe set inside colonial premises with books to browse and occasional art-house movies and live music. Offers filling soups, sandwiches, cheese plates, fruit frappés, mango martinis and properly made espresso.

El Rey del Cabrito MEXICAN **$$**
(81-8345-3292, 81-8345-3352; www.elreydelcabrito.com.mx; cnr Dr Coss & Av Constitución; mains M$100-250; 11am-midnight; M Zaragoza) Famous for its goat, this landmark restaurant has a hunting-lodge-kitsch interior and the signature *cabritos* slow-roasting over charcoal in its window. Dishes arrive still sizzling on a bed of onions, with a large salad and tortillas.

Madre Oaxaca MEXICAN **$$$**
(Jardón 814; mains M$135-220; 1-11pm Mon-Sat; M Zaragoza) This lovely restaurant set in a historic building has real atmosphere with its original floor tiles, quirky curios (check out that mad mushroom) and intimate dining rooms. The menu is loaded with authentic Oaxacan dishes using rich *moles* – try a mixed *tlayuda oaxaqueña* (huge flat bread with toppings) – and there's a good wine selection.

El Lingote MEXICAN, INTERNATIONAL **$$$**
(www.ellingoterestaurante.com; Horno 3, Parque Fundidora; mains M$140-280; 1pm-midnight Tue-Sun; P) This smart, expensive amazing-looking restaurant is worth a splurge. The cooking puts a modern twist on Mexican classics such as tacos and empanadas or tuck into a rib-eye steak or some pasta. Portions are not huge but the setting is superb (and even the menu is made of steel).

☆ Entertainment

Monterrey has numerous cinemas and an active cultural life. The best sources of what is happening are the daily Gente and Vida sections of *El Norte* newspaper, and *Agenda Cultura*, which is free from the tourist office and some museums.

The Barrio Antiguo bars/clubs frequented by Monterrey's affluent younger set include fashionable live-music venues such as **Café Iguana** (81-8343-0822; Montemayor 927 Sur; 9pm-3:30am Thu-Sat; underground rail Zaragoza) on Montemayor. However, many venues have closed down here because of drug cartel violence nearby. Things were picking up again a little in early 2014, but be careful if out and about at night.

Shopping

Try the main downtown market, Mercado Juárez (p795), for everyday items.

Corredor del Arte CRAFTS MARKET
(Art Corridor; 10am-6pm Sun; M Zaragoza) Calle Mina in the Barrio Antiguo becomes the Corredor del Arte, a combination arts/crafts/flea market, on Sundays. Bands play, too.

Information

DANGERS & ANNOYANCES

Monterrey developed a reputation as one of Mexico's most dangerous cities after gang violence spilled into the city, reaching a peak in 2011. Today the situation is calmer, and the numbers of armed robberies, gun battles and carjackings has dropped considerably. However you should exercise caution, particularly if out after dark.

Upmarket San Pedro Garza García in the southwest of the city is considered safe, as is the Zona Rosa area on the west side of the Gran Plaza. Incidents in the Barrio Antiguo (where things got bad in 2011) have dropped markedly and people and nightlife are returning to this historic district, too.

However, south of here, across the Río Santa Catarina, the crime-plagued barrio of Colonia Independencia is still affected by narco gangs and should not be entered day or night.

INTERNET ACCESS

El Rincón Zapatista (www.rznuevoleon.ideosferas.org; Tapia 1538; per hr M$8; 2-8pm

Tue-Sun; Ⓜ Alameda) Cool cafe with internet access and film screenings.

MONEY

Banks and/or ATMs abound on nearly every block of the Zona Rosa.

MEDICAL SERVICES

Hospital Muguerza (☎81-8399-3400; www.christusmuguerza.com.mx; Hidalgo 2525 Poniente; ⏲24hr; Ⓜ Hospital)

POST

Post Office (Washington 648 Oriente; ⏲8am-4:30 Mon-Fri, 8am-12:30pm Sat; Ⓜ Zaragoza)

TOURIST INFORMATION

Infotur (☎81-2020-6789, in the US 866-238-3866; Antiguo Palacio Federal, Washington 648; ⏲9am-6:30pm Mon-Fri, to 5pm Sat & Sun) Friendly, English-speaking staff at this information center have plentiful information (much published in English with some in French) about sights/events across Nuevo León. There's a kiosk at the bus station, too.

TRAVEL AGENCIES

BCD Travel (☎81-8133-5160; www.bcdtravel.com.mx; Vasconcelos 158 Ote, San Pedro Garza García) Books flights for a small commission.

Getting There & Away

AIR

There are direct flights to all of Mexico's major cities, plus direct international flights to Houston, Dallas, Detroit, Los Angeles, Las Vegas, Atlanta and Chicago.

Viva Aerobus (☎81-8215-0150; www.vivaaerobus.com; Av Eugenio Garza Sada 2132) Flies to cities including Chihuahua.

Aeroméxico (☎800-021-40-00; www.aeromexico.com; Av Eugenio Garza Sada 3551) Destinations include Las Vegas, Chicago and many regional cities in Mexico.

BUS

Monterrey's colossal bus station, **Central de Autobuses** (Av Colón; Ⓜ Cuauhtémoc), is busy 24/7 with departures and arrivals from across Mexico. Use the official taxi desk inside the station, the fare is M$50 to most central locations.

Getting Around

TO/FROM THE AIRPORT

Noreste (www.noreste.com.mx) runs 11 daily buses (M$65, 45 min) from the airport to the main bus terminal. A taxi to/from the center is around M$275.

BUS

Frequent buses (M$7 to M$9) get you most places you can't reach by metro. One note-

BUSES FROM MONTERREY

Prices are for 1st-class buses unless stated.

DESTINATION	FARE (M$)	DURATION	FREQUENCY (DAILY)
Chihuahua	826-1029	9-11hr	11
Dallas, US	1022-1107	12hr	3 direct (or change at Nuevo Laredo)
Durango	648-842	8-9hr	14
Houston, US	940	11hr	4 direct (plus 7 changing at Nuevo Laredo)
Mexico City (Terminal Norte)	930-1005	11hr	31
Nuevo Laredo	271-301	3hr	every 20 min
Piedras Negras	580-755	5-7hr	9
Reynosa	256	3hr	every 30 min
Saltillo	93-101	1¾hr	every 45 min
San Luis Potosí	521-561	6½hr	every 45 min
Zacatecas	461-473	6½-7hr	every 45 min

worthy bus is Ruta 130, which goes from the corner of Juárez and Hidalgo in Zona Rosa through San Pedro, heading west along Avenida Vasconcelos.

CAR & MOTORCYCLE

Budget (☎81-8340-4100; www.budget.com; Hotel Misión Monterrey, Padre Mier 201; Ⓜ Padre Mier) Also has a desk at the airport.

METRO

Metrorrey (single trip M$4.50; ⏰5am-midnight) Monterrey's modern, efficient metro system, consists of two lines. Elevated Línea 1 runs from the northwest of the city to the eastern suburbs, passing the Parque Fundidora. Línea 2 begins underground at the Gran Plaza and runs north past Parque Niños Héroes up into the northern suburbs. The two lines cross right by the bus station at Cuauhtémoc station.

Several metro stations are connected with metrobuses (specialized buses with set stops) to outlying areas. Construction has also has started on Línea 3, which will connect Zaragoza station by the Gran Plaza to the northeastern suburbs. Work is expected to be completed in 2015.

TAXI

Taxis (all have meters) are ubiquitous in Monterrey and reasonably priced. From the Zona Rosa to the bus terminal or to Parque Fundidora is usually about M$35. Call 8372-8800 or 8130-0600 for radio-taxi service.

Around Monterrey

Part of Monterrey's charm has always been the awe-inspiring nearby scenery, although the threat of drug-related violence has made the area less safe: be sure to check the local security situation before embarking on a trip.

Right outside town is a stunning mountainside section of the Parque Nacional Cumbres de Monterrey, **Parque Ecológico Chipinque** (☎81-8303-5575; www.chipinque.org.mx; pedestrian/cyclist/vehicle M$20/35/35; ⏰6am-8pm). It's incredible that such a wild locale can exist so close to such a large city. There's great hiking and mountain-biking on trails through dense forest, and up to rocky peaks including high point **Copete de Águilas** (2200m). Maps, snacks, trail advice and permits for those heading into the park are available at the visitor center located near the entrance, a 15-minute drive southwest of central Monterrey via Avenida Gómez Morín in the San Pedro neighborhood.

Free Saturday/Sunday and holiday buses to Chipinque leave from the southwest corner of Parque Alameda at 8am, 10am and noon; be sure to ask when the last bus returns. Alternatively use bus 130 from San Pedro Garza García area (from the junction of Vasconcelos and Gómez).

There are more natural wonders in the vicinity. Six kilometers uphill from El Cercado, a village 35km south of Monterrey on Hwy 85, pretty **Cascada Cola de Caballo** (Horsetail Falls; ☎8347-1533; adult/child M$35/20; ⏰9am-7pm May-Oct, to 6pm Nov-Apr) has Mexico's highest (70m) **bungee jump** (☎81-8369-6640; www.coladecaballo.com; jump M$360; ⏰3-8pm Fri, 11am-8pm Sat & Sun), as well as a 200ft **canopy tour**.

The towering limestone walls of **El Potrero Chico** (http://potrerochico.org), about 45 minutes northwest of Monterrey near the town of Hidalgo, are home to world-class rock climbing, with more than 600 routes. **El Potrero Chico Climbing School** (www.elpotrerochico.com.mx) charges a whopping M$2150 per day for two people (not including shoe rental, food or water). You can rent climbing gear, or hire mountain bikes, from the same people.

In Monterrey, Autobuses Mina (M$28, 1½ hours) run to Hidalgo. From Hidalgo's central plaza the canyon is a M$60 taxi ride. If you're driving, go to the cement factory in central Hidalgo, then follow signs.

There are decent accommodations at both Cascada Cola de Caballo and El Potrero Chico.

Understand Mexico

Mexico Today

When Enrique Peña Nieto of the PRI (Institutional Revolutionary Party) began his six-year presidential term in December 2012, he promptly struck a 'Pact for Mexico' with the two main opposition parties to enable important reforms to pass through congress. There was much talk of this being 'Mexico's moment' – a chance, with political infighting laid aside for the moment, for the country finally to make good on its economic potential and relieve some of its glaring social problems.

Best on Film

Amores Perros (Love's a Bitch; 2000) Gritty groundbreaker that set director Alejandro González Iñárritu and actor Gael García Bernal on the path to stardom.

Y Tu Mamá También (And Your Mother Too; 2001) Classic 'growing up' road movie about two privileged Mexico City teenagers (Gael García Bernal and Diego Luna).

Heli (2013) Amat Escalante won the Cannes best-director garland for this tale of a young couple caught up in the drugs war.

Rudo y Cursi (2008) Story of two brothers' comic climb to professional soccer success.

Best in Print

God's Middle Finger Richard Grant investigates the narco-riddled Sierra Madre Occidental (called *Bandit Roads* in the UK).

Pedro Páramo The ultimate Mexican novel, by Juan Rulfo.

El Narco Author Ioan Grillo spent more than a decade covering the drugs war in some of Mexico's most dangerous territories.

Under the Volcano British consul drinks himself to death in Cuernavaca in Malcolm Lowry's 1938 classic.

Diluting Pemex

The economy has, overall, grown nicely since 2010 but could do much better. Top of Peña Nieto's list was ending the debilitating monopoly of the state oil and gas company Pemex. Mexico is the world's 10th biggest crude oil producer, and Pemex provides one-third of the government's income, but oil output has fallen by a quarter since 2004, and the country imports nearly half its gasoline. Constitutional changes passed in December 2013 now allow private companies to explore and drill for new oil fields and invest in refineries, which Pemex could not afford to do. Opposition to the reform from the left-of-center Democratic Revolution Party (PRD) fractured the Pact for Mexico, but the prospect is that within a few years Mexico will be producing more oil, enjoying cheaper energy and attracting more foreign investment, and the government will have more money to spend.

Testing the Teachers

On the social front, the big issue is improving standards in education, which are a long way short of developed-world standards. Peña Nieto introduced tests for teachers and banned them from selling their jobs or passing them on to family members (both surprisingly common practices). In part, the government was trying to break the grip of the 1.5 million-member National Education Workers' Union. Teachers' protests disrupted Mexican life for months (they blockaded the national congress and Mexico City International Airport), and seemed likely to rumble on, especially in the southern states of Oaxaca, Chiapas and Michoacán, after the government declared in December 2012 that it would no longer pay teachers who had refused to take part in a census of the school system.

Combating Crime

Then there's the drugs war. Peña Nieto's predecessor, Felipe Calderón, had declared war on the country's frighteningly powerful drug gangs, who ship US$13 billion worth of cocaine, marijuana and methamphetamines into the US each year. The conflict saw an estimated 60,000 people murdered between 2006 and 2012, nearly all in turf wars between rival gangs or in confrontations with the security forces. Within a year of taking office, Peña Nieto was announcing that organized-crime-related murders had fallen by 20%. Some observers questioned his statistics, but there was hope that his new approach would reap dividends: among other things, the government stepped up efforts to tackle underlying causes by channeling money to jobs, schools, parks and cultural activities in the country's 220 most violent neighborhoods. But security remained Mexicans' gravest concern. Even if drug-related murder rates are declining, there has been a frightening increase in kidnappings (a staggering 106,000 of these in 2012, according the national statistics institute, Inegi) and extortion.

Despite all the dreadful publicity, the drugs war has had surprisingly little overall effect on tourism, with annual tourist arrivals hovering around the 23 million level, thanks in part to deep discounting on vacation packages. The reality is that drug violence is nearly all localized in specific areas and rarely affects tourists.

On the Lighter Side...

Mexicans may get a little slimmer after the government slapped taxes of one peso per liter on fizzy drinks and 8% on junk food (foods high in salt, sugar and saturated fats) in 2013. Mexicans' love for *refrescos* (sodas) and salty, fatty snacks has given them an unenviable adult obesity rate of 33% (similar to the US). Public-health officials calculate the cost of obesity will exceed M$130 billion (US$10 billion) a year by 2017, and diabetes, an obesity-related disease, afflicts about one in 10 adults, making it one of the country's two biggest causes of death (the other is heart disease). As the new taxes were passed into law, President Peña Nieto urged Mexicans to adopt healthier lifestyles and take an hour's exercise a day.

POPULATION: **116 MILLION**

AREA: **1.9 MILLION SQ KM**

GDP PER CAPITA: **US$11,830**

INFLATION: **3.4%**

RECOGNIZED NATIONAL LANGUAGES: **69**

if Mexico were 100 people

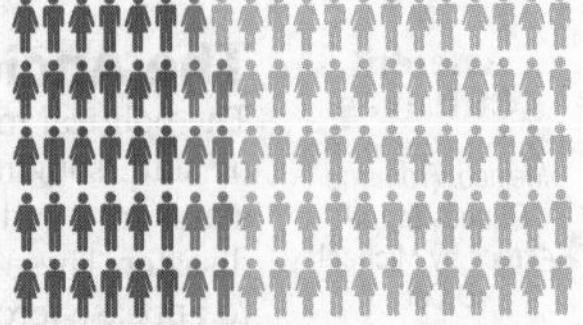

30 would have predominantly indigenous ancestry

9 would have predominantly European ancestry

61 would have mixed ancestry

Note: Figures are estimates; official figures do not use these classifications.

belief systems

(% of population)

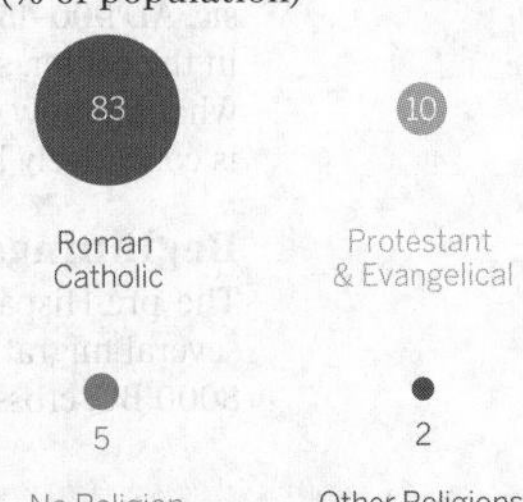

population per sq km

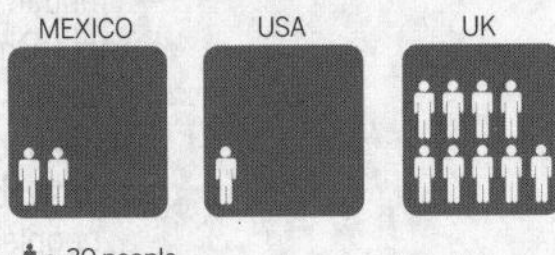

History

Mexico's story is always extraordinary and at times barely credible. How could a 2700-year tradition of sophisticated indigenous civilization crumble in two short years at the hands of a few hundred adventurers from Spain? How could Mexico's 11-year war for independence from Spain lead to three decades of dictatorship under Porfirio Díaz? How could the people's revolution that ended that dictatorship yield 80 years of one-party rule? Mexico's past is present everywhere you go, and is key to any understanding of Mexico today.

Ancient Cultures

Mexico: From the Olmecs to the Aztecs by Michael D Coe

The Aztecs by Richard F Townsend

Foundation for Advancement of Mesoamerican Studies (www.famsi.org)

The Ancient Civilizations

The political map of ancient Mexico shifted constantly as one city, town or state sought domination over another, and a sequence of powerful states rose and fell through invasion, internal conflict or environmental disaster. These diverse cultures had much in common. Human sacrifice to appease ferocious gods was practiced by many societies; observation of the heavens was developed to predict the future and determine propitious times for important events like harvests; society was heavily stratified and dominated by priestly male ruling classes. Versions of a ritual ball game were played almost everywhere and seem to have always involved two teams trying to keep a rubber ball off the ground by flicking it with various parts of the body. The game sometimes served as an oracle, and could also involve the sacrifice of some players.

A common framework divides the pre-Hispanic era into three main periods: pre-Classic, before AD 250; Classic, AD 250–900; and post-Classic, AD 900–1521. The most advanced cultures in Mexico emerged chiefly in the center, south and east of the country. Together with Maya lands in what are now Guatemala, Belize and a small part of Honduras, this zone is collectively known to historians and archaeologists as Mesoamerica.

Beginnings

The pre-Hispanic inhabitants of the Americas arrived from Siberia, in several migrations during the last Ice Age, between perhaps 60,000 and 8000 BC, crossing land now submerged beneath the Bering Strait. Early

TIMELINE

8000–3000 BC

Agriculture develops in places such as the Tehuacán valley and Yagul. Chili seeds and squashes are planted; later corn and beans are cultivated, enabling people to live semi-permanently in villages.

1200–400 BC

Mexico's 'mother culture' (the Olmecs) flourishes on the Gulf coast at San Lorenzo and La Venta. Jade, a favorite pre-Hispanic material, appears in a tomb at La Venta.

AD 0–150

A huge planned city is laid out in a grid arrangement at Teotihuacán in central Mexico, and the 70m-high Pyramid of the Sun is constructed there.

Mexicans hunted big animal herds in the grasslands of the highland valleys. When temperatures rose at the end of the last Ice Age, the valleys became drier, ceasing to support such animal life and forcing the people to derive more food from plants. In central Mexico's Tehuacán Valley and at Yagul near Oaxaca, archaeologists have traced the slow beginnings of agriculture between about 8000 and 3000 BC.

The Olmecs

Mexico's 'mother culture' was the mysterious Olmec civilization, which appeared in the humid lowlands of Veracruz and Tabasco. The evidence of the masterly stone sculptures they left behind indicates that Olmec civilization was well organized and able to support talented artisans, but lived in thrall to fearsome deities. Its best known artifacts are the awe-inspiring 'Olmec heads,' stone sculptures up to 3m high with grim, pug-nosed faces that wear curious helmets. Far-flung Olmec sites in central and western Mexico may have been trading posts or garrisons to ensure the supply of jade, obsidian and other luxuries for the Olmec elite.

Olmec art, religion and society had a profound influence on later Mexican civilizations. Olmec gods, such as the feathered serpent, persisted right through the pre-Hispanic era.

Teotihuacán

The first great civilization in central Mexico arose in a valley about 50km northeast of the middle of modern Mexico City. The grid plan of the magnificent city of Teotihuacán was laid out in the 1st century AD. It was the basis for the famous Pyramids of the Sun and Moon as well as avenues, palaces and temples that were added during the next 600 years. The city grew to a population of about 125,000 and became the center of the biggest pre-Hispanic Mexican empire, stretching as far south as modern El Salvador. It may have had some control over the Zapotecs of Oaxaca, whose capital, Monte Albán, grew into a magnificent city in its own right between AD 300 and 600. Teotihuacán's advanced civilization – including writing, and a calendar system with a 260-day 'sacred year' composed of 13 periods of 20 days – spread far from its original heartland.

Teotihuacán was eventually burned, plundered and abandoned in the 8th century. But many Teotihuacán gods, such as the feathered serpent Quetzalcóatl (an all-important symbol of fertility and life) and Tláloc (the rain and water deity), were still being worshipped by the Aztecs a millennium later.

The Classic Maya

The Classic Maya, in the view of many experts the most brilliant civilization of pre-Hispanic America, flowered over a large area extending from

Virtual Visits

Colecciones Especiales Street View (Google Street View for 30 archaeological sites; www.inah.gob.mx/especial-street-view)

Museo Nacional de Antropología (Mexico City; www.inah.gob.mx/paseos/mna)

Teotihuacán (www.inah.gob.mx/paseos/sitioteotihuacan)

Templo Mayor (Mexico City; www.templomayor.inah.gob.mx)

250–600
Teotihuacán grows into a city of an estimated 125,000 people, the Pyramid of the Moon is built, and the civilization comes to control the biggest of Mexico's pre-Hispanic empires.

250–900
The brilliant Classic Maya civilization flowers in southeast Mexico, Guatemala, Belize and parts of Honduras and El Salvador.

695
The great Maya city of Tikal (in modern-day Guatemala) conquers Maya rival Calakmul (in Mexico), but is unable to exert unified control over Calakmul's subjects.

750–900
Maya civilization in the central Maya heartland – Chiapas (southeast Mexico), El Petén (northern Guatemala) and Belize – collapses, probably because of prolonged severe droughts.

the Yucatán Peninsula through Guatemala to Honduras and into Belize and the lowlands of Chiapas (Mexico). The Maya attained heights of artistic and architectural expression, and of learning in fields like astronomy, mathematics and astrology, that were not surpassed by any other pre-Hispanic civilization.

The Mel Gibson–directed *Apocalypto* (2006), a violent tale of a young man trying to escape becoming a human sacrifice, gives some idea of what ancient Maya life might sometimes have been like.

Politically, the Classic Maya were divided among many independent city-states, often at war with each other. In the first part of the Classic period most of these appear to have been grouped into two loose military alliances, centered on Tikal (Guatemala) and Calakmul (in the south of the Yucatán Peninsula).

Calakmul lies in a now-remote area which was one of the four main zones of Classic Maya concentration in Mexico. The area is known as the Río Bec zone and is typified by long, low buildings decorated with serpent or monster masks and with towers at their corners. A second main Classic Maya zone was the Chenes area in northeastern Campeche state, with similar architecture except for the towers. A third area was the Puuc zone, south of Mérida, characterized by buildings with intricate stone mosaics, often incorporating faces of the hook-nosed rain god Chac. The most important Puuc city was Uxmal. The fourth zone was lowland Chiapas, with the cities of Palenque (for many people the most beautiful of all Maya sites), Yaxchilán and Tonin.

A typical Maya city functioned as the religious, political and market hub for surrounding farming hamlets. Its ceremonial center focused on plazas surrounded by tall temple pyramids (usually the tombs of rulers, who were believed to be descended from the gods). Stone causeways called *sacbeob*, which were probably for ceremonial use, led out from the plazas, sometimes for many kilometers.

Maya Websites

Mesoweb (www.mesoweb.com)

Maya Exploration Center (www.mayaexploration.org)

Mundo Maya Online (www.mayadiscovery.com)

The Classic Maya Collapse

In the second half of the 8th century, conflict between Maya city-states started to increase, and by the early 10th century, the several million inhabitants of the flourishing central Maya heartland in Chiapas, northern Guatemala's Petén region and Belize had virtually disappeared. The Classic era was at an end. A series of droughts combined with population pressure is thought to have brought about this cataclysm. Many Maya probably migrated to the Yucatán Peninsula or the highlands of Chiapas, where their descendants live on today. The jungle reclaimed the ancient lowland cities.

The Toltecs

In central Mexico, for centuries after the fall of Teotihuacán, power was divided between varying locally important cities, including Xochicalco, south of Mexico City, Cacaxtla and Cantona to the east, and Tula to the

c 1000

Chichén Itzá, an abandoned Maya city on the Yucatán Peninsula, is reoccupied, developing into one of Mexico's most magnificent ancient cities, in a fusion of Maya and central Mexican styles.

1325

The Aztecs settle at Tenochtitlán, on the site of present-day Mexico City. Over the next two centuries they come to rule an empire extending over nearly all of central Mexico.

1487

Twenty thousand human captives are sacrificed over a period of four days for the rededication of Tenochtitlán's Templo Mayor after a major reconstruction.

1519–20

A Spanish expedition from Cuba, under Hernán Cortés, reaches Tenochtitlán. Initially well received, the Spaniards are attacked and driven out on the Noche Triste (Sad Night), June 30, 1520.

ANCIENT RELIGION & BELIEF

The Maya developed a complex writing system, partly pictorial, partly phonetic, with 300 to 500 symbols. They also refined a calendar used by other pre-Hispanic peoples into a tool for the exact recording and forecasting of earthly and heavenly events. Temples were aligned to enhance observation of the heavens, helping the Maya predict solar eclipses and movements of the moon and Venus. The Maya measured time in various interlocking cycles, ranging from 13-day 'weeks' to the 1,872,000-day 'Great Cycle.' They believed the current world to be just one of a succession of worlds, and this cyclical nature of things enabled the future to be predicted by looking at the past.

To win the gods' favors they carried out elaborate rituals involving dances, feasts, sacrifices, consumption of the alcoholic drink *balche*, and bloodletting from ears, tongues or penises. The Classic Maya seem to have practiced human sacrifice on a small scale, the later post-Classic Maya on a larger scale.

The Maya universe had a center and four directions, each with a color: the center was green; east was red; north, white; west, black; and south, yellow. The heavens had 13 layers, and Xibalbá, the underworld to which the dead descended, had nine. The earth was the back of a giant reptile floating on a pond.

The later Aztecs, similarly, observed the heavens for astrological purposes and also saw the world as having four directions, 13 heavens and nine hells. Those who died by drowning, leprosy, lightning, gout, dropsy or lung disease went to the paradisiacal gardens of Tláloc, the rain god, who had killed them. Warriors who were sacrificed or died in battle, merchants killed while traveling far away, and women who died giving birth to their first child all went to heaven as companions of the sun. Everyone else traveled for four years under the northern deserts in the abode of the death god Mictlantecuhtli, before reaching the ninth hell, where – tough luck – they vanished altogether.

The Aztecs believed they lived in the 'fifth world,' whose four predecessors had each been destroyed by the death of the sun and of humanity. Aztec human sacrifices were designed to keep the sun alive.

north. The cult of Quetzalcóatl remained widespread, society in at least some places became more militarized, and mass human sacrifice may have started here in this period. The Quetzalcóatl cult and large-scale human sacrifice both reached the Yucatán Peninsula, where they're most evident at the city of Chichén Itzá.

Central Mexican culture in the early post-Classic period is often given the name Toltec (Artificers), a name coined by the later Aztecs, who looked back to the Toltec rulers with awe.

The Aztecs

The Aztecs' legends related that they were the chosen people of the hummingbird deity Huitzilopochtli. Originally nomads from somewhere in

1521

The Spanish, with 100,000 native Mexican allies, capture Tenochtitlán, razing it building by building. They then rename it 'México' and go on to rebuild it as the capital of Nueva España (New Spain).

1524

Virtually all the Aztec empire, plus other Mexican regions such as Colima, the Huasteca and the Isthmus of Tehuantepec, have been brought under Spanish control.

1534–92

The Spanish find huge lodes of silver at Pachuca, Zacatecas, Guanajuato and San Luis Potosí, all north of Mexico City.

1540s

The Yucatán Peninsula is brought under Spanish control by three (related) conquistadors all named Francisco de Montejo. Nueva España's northern border runs roughly from modern Tampico to Guadalajara.

western or northern Mexico, they were led by their priests to the Valle de México, the site of modern Mexico City, where they settled on islands in the valley's lakes. By the 15th century the Aztecs (also known as the Mexica) had fought their way up to become the most powerful group in the valley, with their capital at Tenochtitlán (where downtown Mexico City stands today).

Find out all about Maya time, what your birth day signifies, and what you should do each day of the 20-day week with the iPhone app Maya Calendar (www.mayan-calendar.com).

The Aztecs formed the Triple Alliance with two other valley states, Texcoco and Tlacopan, to wage war against Tlaxcala and Huejotzingo, east of the valley. The prisoners they took became the diet of sacrificed warriors that voracious Huitzilopochtli (no sweet hummingbird himself) demanded to keep the sun rising every day.

The Triple Alliance brought most of central Mexico, from the Gulf coast to the Pacific, under its control. This was an empire of 38 provinces and about five million people, geared to extracting tribute (tax in kind) of resources absent from the heartland – items like jade, turquoise, cotton, tobacco, rubber, fruits, vegetables, cacao and precious feathers, all needed for the glorification of the Aztec elite and to support their war-oriented state.

Aztec Society

Tenochtitlán and the adjoining Aztec city of Tlatelolco grew to house more than 200,000 people. The Valle de México as a whole had more than a million people. They were supported by a variety of intensive farming methods based on irrigation, terracing and swamp reclamation.

The Aztec emperor held absolute power. Celibate priests performed cycles of great ceremonies, typically including sacrifices and masked dances or processions enacting myths. Military leaders were usually elite professional soldiers known as *tecuhtli*. Another special group was the *pochteca* – militarized merchants who helped extend the empire, brought goods to the capital and organized the large daily markets in big towns. At the bottom of society were pawns (paupers who could sell themselves for a specified period), serfs and slaves.

Today the Aztecs' eagle-snake-cactus emblem sits in the cener of the Mexican flag.

Other Post-Classic Civilizations

On the eve of the Spanish conquest, most Mexican civilizations shared deep similarities. Each was politically centralized and divided into classes, with many people occupied in specialist tasks, including professional priests. Agriculture was productive, despite the lack of draft animals, metal tools and the wheel. Corn tortillas, *pozol* (corn gruel) and beans were staple foods, and many other crops, such as squash, tomatoes, chilies, avocados, peanuts, papayas and pineapples, were grown in various regions. Luxury foods for the elite included turkey, domesticated hairless dog, game and chocolate drinks. War was widespread, and often

1605
Mexico's indigenous population has declined from an estimated 25 million at the time of the Spanish conquest to little over a million, mainly because of introduced diseases.

1767
The Jesuits, important missionaries and educators in Nueva España and many of them criollos (Mexican-born people of Spanish ancestry), are expelled from all Spanish dominions, unsettling criollos in the colony.

1795
José Guadalupe Cuervo, owner of land rich in agave plants in Jalisco, receives from King Carlos IV of Spain the first official concession to market *vino mezcal* (tequila).

1810
On September 16 priest Miguel Hidalgo launches Mexico's War of Independence with his Grito de Dolores (Cry of Dolores), a call to rebellion in the town of Dolores.

connected with the need for a supply of prisoners to sacrifice to a variety of gods.

Several important regional cultures arose in the post-Classic period:

➡ **Michoacán** The Tarasco people, who were skilled artisans and jewelers, ruled Michoacán from their base around the Lago de Pátzcuaro. They were one group that managed to avoid conquest by the Aztecs.

➡ **Oaxaca** After 1200 the Zapotecs were increasingly dominated by the Mixtecs, skilled metalsmiths and potters from the uplands around the Oaxaca–Puebla border. Much of Oaxaca fell to the Aztecs in the 15th and 16th centuries.

➡ **Yucatán Peninsula** The city of Mayapán dominated most of the Yucatán after the 'Toltec' phase at Chichén Itzá ended around 1200. Mayapán's hold dissolved from about 1440, and the Yucatán became a quarreling ground for many city-states.

Legend tells that the Aztecs built their capital at Tenochtitlán because there they witnessed an eagle on a cactus, devouring a snake – a sign, their prophecies told, that they should stop their wanderings. The temple they built on the spot (the Templo Mayor) was considered the center of the universe.

The Spanish Arrive

Ancient Mexican civilization, nearly 3000 years old, was shattered in two short years by a tiny group of invaders. They destroyed the Aztec empire, brought a new religion, and reduced the native people to second-class citizens and slaves. Rarely in history has a thriving society undergone such a transformation so fast. So alien to each other were the newcomers and the indigenous Mexicans that each doubted whether the other was human (Pope Paul III declared indigenous Mexicans to be human in 1537). Yet from their traumatic encounter arose modern Mexico. Most Mexicans today are mestizo, of mixed indigenous and European blood, and thus descendants of both cultures.

The Spanish Background

In 1492, the year Christopher Columbus arrived in the Caribbean, Spain was an aggressively expanding state, fresh from completing the 700-year Reconquista (Reconquest) in which Christian armies had gradually recovered the Spanish mainland from Islamic rule. With their mix of brutality and bravery, gold lust and piety, the Spanish conquistadors of the Americas were the natural successors to the crusading knights of the Reconquista.

Seeking new westward trade routes to the spice-rich Orient, Spanish explorers and soldiers landed first in the Caribbean, establishing colonies on the islands of Hispaniola and Cuba. They then began seeking a passage through the land mass to the west, and soon became distracted by tales of gold, silver and a wealthy empire there. Spain's governor on Cuba, Diego Velázquez, asked a colonist named Hernán Cortés to lead one such expedition westward. As Cortés gathered ships and men, Velázquez became uneasy about the costs and about Cortés' loyalty, and

General History Resources

A History of Mexico by Lynn V Foster

Mexico Online (www.mexonline.com)

Mexconnect (www.mexconnect.com)

1811

After initial victories, the rebels' numbers shrink and their leaders, including Hidalgo, are captured and executed in Chihuahua. José María Morelos y Pavón, another priest, assumes the rebel leadership.

1813

Morelos' forces blockade Mexico City for several months. A congress at Chilpancingo adopts principles for the independence movement, but Morelos is captured and executed two years later.

1821

Rebel leaders Vicente Guerrero and Agustín de Iturbide devise the Plan de Iguala, for an independent Mexico with constitutional monarchy and Catholic religious supremacy.

1821–22

The Plan de Iguala wins over all influential sections of society, and the Spanish viceroy agrees to Mexican independence. Iturbide takes the new Mexican throne as Emperor Agustín I.

tried to cancel the expedition. But Cortés, sensing a once-in-history opportunity, ignored him and set sail on February 15, 1519, with 11 ships, 550 men and 16 horses.

The Conquest

The Cortés expedition landed first at Isla Cozumel, then sailed around the coast to Tabasco. They defeated inhospitable locals in the Battle of Centla near modern-day Frontera, where the enemy fled in terror from Spanish horsemen, thinking horse and rider to be a single, fearsome beast. Afterward the locals gave Cortés 20 maidens, among them Doña Marina (La Malinche), who became his indispensable interpreter, aide and lover.

Resentful Aztec subject towns on the Gulf coast, such as Zempoala, welcomed the Spaniards. And as the Spaniards moved inland toward Tenochtitlán, they made allies of the Aztecs' longtime enemies, the Tlaxcalans.

Aztec legends and superstitions, and the indecisiveness of Emperor Moctezuma II Xocoyotzin, also worked to the Spaniards' advantage. According to the Aztec calendar, 1519 would see the legendary Toltec god-king Quetzalcóatl return from banishment in the east. Was Cortés actually Quetzalcóatl? Omens proliferated: lightning struck a temple, a comet sailed through the night skies and a bird 'with a mirror in its head' was brought to Moctezuma, who saw warriors in it.

The Spaniards, with 6000 indigenous allies, were invited to enter Tenochtitlán, a city bigger than any in Spain, on November 8, 1519. Aztec nobles carried Moctezuma out to meet Cortés on a litter with a canopy of feathers and gold, and the Spaniards were lodged, as befitted gods, in the palace of Moctezuma's father, Axayácatl.

Though entertained in luxury, the Spaniards were trapped. Unsure of Moctezuma's intentions, they took him hostage. Believing Cortés a god, Moctezuma told his people he went willingly, but tensions rose in the city. Eventually, after six or seven months, some of the Spaniards killed about 200 Aztec nobles in an intended pre-emptive strike. Cortés persuaded Moctezuma to try to pacify his people. According to one version of events, the emperor tried to address the crowds from the roof of Axayácatl's palace, but was killed by missiles; other versions say it was the Spaniards who killed him.

The Spaniards fled, losing several hundred of their own and thousands of indigenous allies on what's known as the Noche Triste (Sad Night). They retreated to Tlaxcala, where they built boats in sections, then carried them across the mountains for a waterborne assault on Tenochtitlán. When the 900 Spaniards re-entered the Valle de México in May 1521, they were accompanied by some 100,000 indigenous allies. The defenders resisted fiercely, but after three months the city had been

Spanish Conquest: First-Hand Accounts

The Broken Spears: The Aztec Account of the Conquest of Mexico by Miguel Leon-Portilla

History of the Conquest of New Spain by Bernal Díaz del Castillo

Anna Lanyon's *The New World of Martín Cortés* tells the fascinating and poignant story of the first mestizo, the son of Hernán Cortés and La Malinche.

1824

A new constitution establishes a federal Mexican republic of 19 states and four territories. Guadalupe Victoria, a former independence fighter, becomes its first president.

1836

US settlers in the Mexican territory of Texas declare independence. Mexican forces under President Santa Anna wipe out the defenders of the Alamo mission, but are routed on the San Jacinto River.

1845–48

US Congress votes to annex Texas, sparking the Mexican-American War (1846–48). US troops occupy Mexico City. Mexico cedes Texas, California, Utah, Colorado and most of New Mexico and Arizona.

1847–48

The Maya people of the Yucatán Peninsula rise up against their criollo overlords in the 'War of the Castes' and narrowly fail to drive them off the peninsula.

THE TRAGICOMEDY OF SANTA ANNA

Intervention in politics by ambitious soldiers plagued Mexico throughout the 19th century. Antonio López de Santa Anna first hit the limelight by deposing Emperor Agustín I in 1823. He also overthrew President Anastasio Bustamante in 1831, then was himself elected president in 1833, the first of 11 terms he served in 22 chaotic years. Above all, Mexicans remember Santa Anna for losing large chunks of Mexican territory to the US. After his 1836 post-Alamo defeat in Texas and his disastrous territorial losses in the Mexican-American War of 1846–48, a Santa Anna government sold Mexico's last remaining areas of New Mexico and Arizona to the US for US$10 million in 1853.

razed and the new emperor, Cuauhtémoc, was captured. Cuauhtémoc asked Cortés to kill him, but he was kept alive as a hostage until 1525, undergoing occasional foot-burning torture as the Spanish tried to force him to reveal the whereabouts of Aztec treasure.

Mexico as a Colony

Spain's policy toward all its conquests in the Americas can be summed up in one word: exploitation. The Spanish crown saw the New World as a silver cow to be milked to finance its endless wars in Europe, a life of luxury for its nobility, and a deluge of new churches, palaces and monasteries that were erected around Spain. The crown was entitled to one-fifth of all bullion sent back from the New World (the *quinto real,* or royal fifth). Conquistadors and colonists saw the American empire as a chance to get rich themselves. Cortés granted his soldiers *encomiendas,* which were rights to the labor or tribute of groups of indigenous people. Spain asserted its authority through viceroys, the crown's personal representatives in Mexico.

The populations of the conquered peoples of Nueva España (New Spain), as the Spanish named their Mexican colony, declined disastrously, mainly from new diseases introduced by the invaders. The indigenous peoples' only real allies were some of the monks who started arriving in 1523. The monks' missionary work helped extend Spanish control over Mexico – by 1560 they had converted millions of people and built more than 100 monasteries – but many of them also protected local people from the colonists' worst excesses.

Northern Mexico remained beyond Spanish control until big finds of silver at Zacatecas, Guanajuato and elsewhere spurred efforts to subdue the territory. The northern borders were slowly extended by missionaries and a few settlers, and by the early 19th century Nueva España included (albeit loosely) most of the modern US states of Texas, New Mexico, Arizona, California, Utah and Colorado.

Santa Anna had a leg amputated after being wounded by French forces in 1838. He later had the leg buried with military honors in Mexico City. Its whereabouts are now unknown but its prosthetic replacement was captured by Americans in 1847 and now resides in the Illinois State Military Museum.

1858–61

Liberal government laws requiring the church to sell property precipitate the War of the Reform: Mexico's liberals (with their 'capital' at Veracruz) defeat the conservatives (based in Mexico City).

1861–63

Benito Juárez becomes Mexico's first indigenous president, but Mexico suffers the French Intervention: France invades Mexico, taking Mexico City in 1863 despite a defeat at Puebla on May 5, 1862.

1864–67

Napoleon III sends Maximilian of Hapsburg over as emperor in 1864, but starts to withdraw his troops in 1866. Maximilian is executed by Juárez's forces in 1867.

1876–1911

The Porfiriato: Mexico is ruled by conservative Porfirio Díaz, who brings stability but curbs civil liberties and democratic rights, and concentrates wealth in the hands of a small minority.

Colonial Society

A person's place in colonial Mexican society was determined by skin color, parentage and birthplace. At the top of the tree, however humble their origins in Spain, were Spanish-born colonists. Known as *peninsulares,* they were a minuscule part of the population of Nueva España, but were considered nobility.

Next on the ladder were the criollos, people of Spanish ancestry born in the colony. As the decades passed, the criollos began to develop a distinct identity, and some of them came to possess enormous estates (haciendas) and amass huge fortunes from mining, commerce or agriculture. Not surprisingly, criollos sought political power commensurate with their wealth and grew to resent Spanish authority.

Below the criollos were the mestizos (people of mixed ancestry), and at the bottom of the pile were the indigenous people and African slaves. Though the poor were paid for their labor by the 18th century, they were paid very little. Many were *peones* (bonded laborers tied by debt to their employers), and indigenous people still had to pay tribute to the Spanish crown.

Social stratification follows similar patterns in Mexico today with, broadly speaking, the 'pure-blood' descendants of Spaniards at the top of the tree, the mestizos in the middle and the indigenous people at the bottom.

Mexico as a Republic

Criollo discontent with Spanish rule really began to stir following the expulsion of the Jesuits (many of whom were criollos) from the Spanish empire in 1767. The catalyst for rebellion came in 1808 when Napoléon Bonaparte occupied Spain, and direct Spanish control over Nueva España evaporated. The city of Querétaro, north of Mexico City, became a hotbed of intrigue among disaffected criollos who were plotting rebellion against Spanish rule. The rebellion was finally launched on September 16, 1810, by Padre Miguel Hidalgo in his parish of Dolores (now Dolores Hidalgo). The path to independence was a hard one, involving almost 11 years of fighting between rebels and loyalist forces, and the deaths of Hidalgo and several other rebel leaders. But eventually rebel general Agustín de Iturbide sat down with Spanish viceroy Juan O'Donojú in Veracruz in 1821 and agreed on terms for Mexico's independence.

Mexico's first century as a free nation started with a period of chronic political instability and wound up with a period of stability so repressive that it triggered a social revolution. A consistent thread throughout was the opposition between liberals, who favored a measure of social reform,

Independence Sites

- *Alhóndiga de Granaditas (Guanajuato)*
- *Dolores Hidalgo (Guanajuato)*
- *Calabozo de Hidalgo, Casa Chihuahua (Chihuahua)*
- *Ex-Hotel Zevallos (Córdoba)*
- *Museo Casa de Morelos (Morelia)*

1910–11

The Revolution starts when Mexico rises against the Díaz regime on November 20, 1910. Díaz resigns in May 1911, and reformist Francisco Madero is elected president in November.

1913–14

Madero is deposed and executed by conservative rebel Victoriano Huerta. Northern revolutionary leaders unite against Huerta. Huerta's troops terrorize the countryside, but he is forced to resign in July 1914.

1917

Reformists emerge victorious over radicals in the revolutionary conflict and a new reformist constitution, still largely in force today, is enacted at Querétaro.

1920–24

President Álvaro Obregón turns to post-Revolution reconstruction. More than a thousand rural schools are built, some land is redistributed from big landowners to peasants.

SOME WE LOVE, SOME WE LOVE TO HATE

Mexicans have strong opinions about some of their historical characters. Some are immortalized by statues and street names all over the country. Others, just as influential, are considered objects of shame and ridicule.

Heroes

Cuauhtémoc Aztec leader who resisted the Spanish invaders.

Benito Juárez Reforming, liberal, indigenous president who fought off French occupiers.

Miguel Hidalgo Priest who launched the War for Independence.

Pancho Villa Larger-than-life revolutionary.

Villains

Hernán Cortés The original evil Spanish conqueror.

Carlos Salinas de Gortari President from 1988 to 1994, blamed for the drugs trade, corruption, peso crisis, Nafta, you name it.

General Santa Anna Winner at the Alamo, but loser of Texas, California, Arizona, Utah, Colorado and New Mexico.

La Malinche Doña Marina, Hernán Cortés' indigenous translator and lover.

and conservatives, who didn't. Between 1821 and the mid-1860s, the young Mexican nation was invaded by three different countries (Spain, the USA and France), lost large chunks of its territory to the US, and underwent nearly 50 changes of head of state.

It was an indigenous Zapotec from Oaxaca who played the lead role in Mexican affairs for two tumultuous decades after the halfway point of the century. Lawyer Benito Juárez was a key member of the new liberal government in 1855, which ushered in the era known as the Reform, in which the liberals set about dismantling the conservative state that had developed in Mexico. Juárez became president in 1861. With the French Intervention almost immediately afterward, his government was forced into exile in provincial Mexico, eventually to regain control in 1866. Juárez set an agenda of economic and social reform. Schooling was made mandatory, a railway was built between Mexico City and Veracruz, and a rural police force, the *rurales*, was organized to secure the transportation of cargo through Mexico. Juárez died in 1872 and remains one of the few Mexican historical figures with a completely unsullied reputation.

1926

President Plutarco Elías Calles closes monasteries, outlaws religious orders and bans religious processions, precipitating the Cristero Rebellion by Catholics (until 1929).

1929

Elías Calles founds the Partido Nacional Revolucionario: it and its later mutations, the Partido de la Revolución Mexicana and the Partido Revolucionario Institucional (PRI), will rule Mexico until 2000.

1934–40

President Lázaro Cárdenas redistributes 200,000 sq km of land and expropriates foreign oil operations, forming the state oil company Petróleos Mexicanos (Pemex). Foreign investors avoid Mexico.

1940s & '50s

The Mexican economy expands, helped by growth during WWII, major infrastructure projects and the development of tourism. The population almost doubles in two decades, and millions migrate to urban areas.

A rather different Oaxacan, Porfirio Díaz, ruled as president for 31 of the following 39 years, a period known as the Porfiriato. Díaz brought Mexico into the industrial age, stringing telephone, telegraph and railway lines and launching public works projects. He kept Mexico free of civil wars – but political opposition, free elections and a free press were banned. Peasants were cheated out of their land by new laws, workers suffered appalling conditions, and land and wealth became concentrated in the hands of a small minority. All this led, in 1910, to the Mexican Revolution.

The best movie about the Mexican Revolution is Elia Kazan's *Viva Zapata!* (1952), starring Marlon Brando. John Steinbeck's script is historically sound up to the 1914 meeting between Pancho Villa and Emiliano Zapata in Mexico City. Beyond that point it flounders until Zapata is assassinated.

The Mexican Revolution

The Revolution was a tortured 10-year period of shifting conflicts and allegiances between forces and leaders of all political stripes. The conservatives were pushed aside fairly early on, but the reformers and revolutionaries who had lined up against them could not agree among themselves. Successive attempts to create stable governments were wrecked by new outbreaks of devastating fighting. All told, one in eight Mexicans lost their lives in the Revolution.

Francisco Madero, a wealthy liberal from Coahuila, would probably have won the presidential election in 1910 if Porfirio Díaz hadn't jailed him. On his release, Madero called successfully for the nation to revolt, an uprising which spread quickly across the country. Díaz resigned in May 1911, and Madero was elected president six months later. But Madero could not contain the diverse factions that were now fighting for power throughout Mexico. The basic divide was between liberal reformers like Madero and more radical leaders such as Emiliano Zapata, who was fighting for the transfer of hacienda land to the peasants, with the cry of '*¡Tierra y libertad!*' (Land and freedom!).

In 1913 Madero was deposed, executed and replaced as president by one of his own top generals, Victoriano Huerta, who had defected to conservative rebels. The revolutionary forces united (temporarily) in opposition to Huerta. Three main leaders in the north banded together under the Plan de Guadalupe: Venustiano Carranza, a Madero supporter, in Coahuila; Francisco 'Pancho' Villa in Chihuahua; and Álvaro Obregón in Sonora. Zapata also fought against Huerta.

But fighting then broke out again between the victorious factions, with Carranza and Obregón (the 'Constitutionalists,' with their capital at Veracruz) pitted against the radical Zapata and the populist Villa. Zapata and Villa never formed a serious alliance, and it was Carranza who emerged the victor. He had Zapata assassinated in 1919, only to be liquidated himself the following year on the orders of his former ally Obregón. Pancho Villa was killed in 1923.

Revolution Sites

- *Museo Casa de Villa (Chihuahua)*
- *Museo Francisco Villa (Hidalgo del Parral)*
- *Cuartel General de Zapata (Tlaltizapán, Morelos)*
- *Museo de la Revolución (Puebla)*
- *Museo Casa Carranza (Cuatro Ciénegas)*

1964–70

President Gustavo Díaz Ordaz resists democratizing the PRI. During demonstrations against one-party rule before the 1968 Olympics, an estimated 400 protestors are massacred at Tlatelolco, Mexico City.

1970

Construction starts on the first hotel at Isla Cancún, a coconut plantation with no permanent inhabitants on the Yucatán Peninsula's Caribbean coast.

1970s

Mexico enjoys an economic boom thanks to a jump in world oil prices. On the strength of the country's vast oil reserves, international institutions begin lending Mexico billions of dollars.

1980s

Oil prices plunge and Mexico suffers its worst recession in decades. Amid economic helplessness and rampant corruption, dissent and protests increase, even inside the PRI.

Mexico as a One-Party Democracy

From 1920 to 2000, Mexico was ruled by the reformists who emerged victorious from the Revolution and their successors in the political party they set up, which since the 1940s has borne the name Partido Revolucionario Institucional (Institutional Revolutionary Party), or PRI as it's universally known. Starting out with some genuinely radical social policies, these governments became steadily more conservative, corrupt, repressive and self-interested as the 20th century wore on. Mexico ended the century with a bigger middle class but still with a yawning wealth gap between the prosperous few and the vast numbers of poor.

The problem of land ownership was addressed by redistributing more than 400,000 sq km from large estates to peasants and small farmers between the 1920s and '60s. Nearly half the population received land, mainly in the form of *ejidos* (communal landholdings).

Meanwhile, Mexico developed a worrying economic dependence on its large oil reserves in the Gulf of Mexico. The 1970s and '80s saw the country veer from oil-engendered boom to oil-engendered slump as world oil prices swung rapidly up then just as suddenly down. The huge government-owned oil company Pemex was just one face of a massive state-controlled economic behemoth that was established as the PRI sought control over all important facets of Mexican life.

The PRI was discredited forever in the minds of many Mexicans by the Tlatelolco Massacre of 1968, in which an estimated 400 civil-liberties protestors were shot dead. The PRI came to depend increasingly on strong-arm tactics and fraud to win elections.

Mexicans' cynicism about their leaders reached a crescendo with the 1988–94 presidency of Carlos Salinas de Gortari, who won the presidential election only after a mysterious computer failure had halted vote-tallying at a crucial stage. During Salinas' term, drug trafficking grew into a huge business in Mexico, and mysterious assassinations proliferated. Salinas did take steps to liberalize the monolithic state-dominated economy. The apex of his program, the North American Free Trade Agreement (Nafta), boosted exports and industry, but was unpopular with subsistence farmers and small businesses threatened by imports from the US. The last year of Salinas' presidency, 1994, began with the left-wing Zapatista uprising in Mexico's southernmost state, Chiapas, and shortly before Salinas left office he spent nearly all of Mexico's foreign-exchange reserves in a futile attempt to support the peso, engendering a slump that he left his successor, Ernesto Zedillo, to deal with.

It was also left to Zedillo to respond to the rising clamor for democratic change in Mexico. He established a new, independently supervised

In the 1920s outstanding Mexican artists such as Diego Rivera were commissioned to decorate important public buildings with large, vivid murals on historical and social themes. Many of these can be seen in Mexico City.

Between 1940 and 1980 Mexico's population more than trebled from 20 million to 67 million, and Mexico City's population multiplied tenfold.

1985

On September 19 a massive earthquake, with a magnitude of 8.1 on the Richter scale, strikes Mexico City. At least 10,000 people are killed.

1988–94

The PRI's Carlos Salinas de Gortari narrowly defeats left-of-center Cuauhtémoc Cárdenas in a disputed presidential election. Salinas reforms Mexico's economy toward private enterprise and free trade.

1994

Nafta, the North American Free Trade Agreement, takes effect. The Zapatista uprising in Chiapas begins. Luis Donaldo Colosio, Salinas' chosen successor as PRI presidential candidate, is assassinated.

1994–2000

Under President Ernesto Zedillo, Mexico emerges from a recession triggered by a currency collapse days after he took office. Crime and emigration to the US increase.

electoral system that opened the way for the country's first-ever peaceful change of regime at the end of his term in 2000, when Vicente Fox of the business-oriented Partido Acción Nacional (PAN) won the presidential election.

Mexican migration to the USA fell from 3 million people a year in the late 1990s (with 700,000 returning annually), to 1.4 million by 2010, with the same number coming back home. Some 12 million Mexican citizens still live (legally or illegally) in the US.

PAN Rule & the Drugs War

Vicente Fox's election itself – a non-PRI president after 80 years of rule by that party and its predecessors – was really the biggest news about his six-year term. He entered office backed by much goodwill. In the end, his presidency was considered a disappointment by most. Lacking a majority in Mexico's Congress, Fox was unable to push through reforms that he believed were key to stirring Mexico's slumbering economy.

Fox was succeeded in 2006 by another PAN president, Felipe Calderón. During Calderón's term Mexico's economy sprang back surprisingly fast after the recession of 2009, and Mexico became something of a global environmental champion when it enshrined its carbon-emissions targets in law in 2012. But Calderón's presidency will be remembered far more for its war on drugs. Presidents Zedillo and Fox had already deployed the armed forces against the violent mobs running the multi-billion-dollar business of shipping illegal drugs into the USA, but had failed to rein in their violence or their power to corrupt. By 2006 over 2000 people a year were already dying in violence engendered chiefly by brutal turf wars between rival gangs.

Calderón declared war on the drug cartels and put 50,000 troops plus naval forces and several police forces into the field against them, predominantly in cities along the US border. Some top gang leaders were killed or arrested, and drug seizures reached record levels, but so did the killings – an estimated 60,000 in the six years of Calderón's presidency. The gangs' methods grew ever more shocking, with street gun-battles, gruesome beheadings, torture and even, allegedly, human sacrifices. The northern city of Ciudad Juárez, with over 3100 killings in 2010, became the world's murder capital. Cities such as Monterrey, Nuevo Laredo, Acapulco and Veracruz saw violence spike when local turf wars erupted. When the total number of killings finally started to fall at the end of Calderón's presidency, many people believed this was simply because the two most powerful cartels – the Sinaloa cartel in the northwest of Mexico and Los Zetas in the northeast – had effectively wiped out their weaker rivals.

The Mesoamerican Ballgame (www.ballgame.org) is an interesting website about the indigenous ball game, past and present, with video of a modern contest in action.

Against this background, the PRI managed to convince enough Mexicans that it had cleaned up its act for them to vote it back into power, in the shape of its candidate Enrique Peña Nieto, in the presidential election of 2012.

2000

Mexico's first-ever peaceful change of regime: Vicente Fox of the right-of-center Partido Acción Nacional (PAN) wins the presidential election under a new, transparent electoral system set up by Zedillo.

2006

The PAN's Felipe Calderón narrowly defeats Andrés Manuel López Obrador of the left-of-center Party of the Democratic Revolution (PRD) in the presidential election, and declares war on Mexico's drug cartels.

2006–12

In the six years of Calderón's war on drugs, 50,000 troops are deployed around the country and some 60,000 people are killed, most of them in inter-gang turf wars.

2012

The PRI returns to power as Enrique Peña Nieto wins the presidential election, promising reforms to propel the economy forward. López Obrador of the PRD again comes a close second.

The Mexican Way of Life

Any travels in Mexico quickly reveal that Mexicans are a vastly diverse bunch, from the industrial workers of Monterrey to the rich sophisticates and bohemian counterculture of Mexico City and indigenous villagers eking out subsistence in the southern mountains. But certain common threads run through almost everyone here – among them a deep vein of spirituality, a respect for the family, and a simultaneous pride and frustration about Mexico itself.

Life, Death & the Family

One thing you can never do with Mexicans is encapsulate them in simple formulas. They adore fun, music and a fiesta, yet in many ways are deeply serious. They work hard, but enjoy life to the full. They're hospitable, warm and courteous to guests, yet are most truly themselves within their family group. They will laugh at death, but have a profound vein of spirituality. They love the new and modern, while remaining traditional in essence.

Most Mexicans, however contemporary and globalized they may appear, still inhabit a world in which omens, coincidences and curious resemblances take on great importance. When sick, many people still prefer to visit a traditional *curandero* – a kind of cross between a naturopath and a witch doctor – rather than resort to a modern *médico*. The ancient belief in the cyclical, repetitive nature of time persists, too, in the Mexican subconscious.

On a more mundane level, most Mexicans are chiefly concerned with earning a crust for themselves and their strongly knit families – but also with enjoying the leisurely side of life, whether partying at clubs or fiestas, or relaxing over an extended-family Sunday lunch at a restaurant. Holidays for religious festivals and patriotic anniversaries are essential to the rhythm of life, ensuring that people get a break every few weeks and bringing them together for the same processions and rituals year after year.

Mexicans may despair of their country ever being governed well, but at the same time they are fiercely proud of it. Mexicans naturally absorb a certain amount of US culture and consciousness, but they also strongly value what's different about Mexican life – its more humane pace, its strong sense of community and family, its unique food and drinks, and the thriving, multifaceted national culture.

Nobel Prize–winning Mexican writer Octavio Paz argues in *The Labyrinth of Solitude* that Mexicans' love of noise, music and crowds is just a temporary escape from personal isolation and gloom. Make your own judgment!

The Great Divides

Fly into Mexico City and you'll get a bird's-eye view of just how little space is not occupied by buildings or roads. Around the edges of the city, new streets climb the steep slopes of extinct volcanoes, while shacks on the city's fringes, made from a few concrete blocks or sheets of tin, 'house' the poorest. More affluent neighborhoods have blocks of relatively spacious apartments. In the wealthiest quarters, imposing

Around 10% of Mexicans adhere to non-Catholic varieties of Christianity. Some are members of Protestant churches set up by US missionaries in the 19th century. Millions of others, especially among the indigenous rural poor of southeast Mexico, have been converted since the 1970s by a wave of American Pentecostal, Evangelical, Mormon, Seventh-Day Adventist and Jehovah's Witness missionaries.

detached houses with well-tended gardens sit behind high walls with strong security gates.

One in every two Mexicans now lives in a city or conurbation of more than a million people. A quarter of them live in smaller cities and towns, and another quarter in villages. The number of urban dwellers continues to rise as rural folk are sucked into cities.

Out in the villages and small towns, people still work the land and members of an extended family often live in yards with separate small buildings, of adobe, wood or concrete, often with earth floors. Inside these homes are few possessions – beds, a cooking area, a table with a few chairs and a few aging photos of departed relatives. Few villagers own cars.

Mexico's eternal wealth gap yawns as wide as ever. The world's richest man, entrepreneur Carlos Slim Helú, is a Mexican. His net worth was estimated at US$73 billion by *Forbes* magazine in 2013. At the other extreme, the poorest city dwellers barely scrape an existence as street hawkers, buskers or home workers in the 'informal economy,' rarely earning more than M$50 (US$4) a day.

While rich kids go clubbing in flashy cars and attend private schools (often in the US), and the bohemian urban counterculture enjoys its mezcal bars, state-funded universities and underground dance clubs, poor villagers may dance only at local fiestas and often leave school well before they reach 15.

Land of Many Peoples

Mexico's ethnic diversity is one of the most fascinating aspects of traveling around the country. The major distinction is between mestizos – people of mixed ancestry (mostly Spanish and indigenous) – and the *indígenas*, the indigenous descendants of Mexico's pre-Hispanic inhabitants. Mestizos are in the great majority and hold most positions of power and influence, but the *indígenas*, while mostly materially poor, are often culturally rich. Approximately 60 Mexican indigenous peoples survive, each with their own language and, often, unique costumes, and their way of life is still imbued with communal customs, beliefs and rituals bound up with nature. By official figures approximately 15 million people in Mexico (13% of the population) are indigenous. The biggest group is the Nahua, descendants of the ancient Aztecs, nearly three million of whom are spread around central Mexico. The approximately two million Yucatec Maya on the Yucatán Peninsula are direct descendants of the ancient Maya, as (probably) are the Tzotziles and Tzeltales of Chiapas (totaling about one million). Also directly descended from well-known pre-Hispanic peoples are the estimated one million Zapotecs and 800,000 Mixtecs, mainly in Oaxaca; the 400,000 Totonacs in Veracruz; and the 200,000 Purépecha (Tarasco people) in Michoacán.

The Spiritual Dimension

Yoga, the temascal (indigenous cleansing steam bath) and new-age cosmic energies may mean more to some Mexicans today than traditional Roman Catholicism, but a spiritual dimension of some kind or other remains important in most Mexicans' lives.

Roman Catholicism

About 85% of Mexicans profess Roman Catholicism, making this the world's second-biggest Catholic country after Brazil. Almost half of Mexican Catholics attend church weekly. Though church and state have a history of rocky relations, Catholicism remains very much part of the nation's established fabric. Most Mexican fiestas are built around local

COMMUNING WITH DEPARTED SOULS

Perhaps no other festival reveals more about Mexican spirituality than the Día de Muertos (Day of the Dead), the happy-sad remembrance of departed loved ones at the beginning of November. The Día de Muertos originated in colonial times, when the Catholic Church fused indigenous rites honoring and communing with the dead with its own celebrations of All Saints' Day (November 1) and All Souls' Day (November 2).

Today Muertos is a national phenomenon, with people everywhere cleaning graves and decorating them with flowers, holding graveyard vigils and building elaborate altars to welcome back their loved ones. For the mestizo (mixed ancestry) majority, it's more of a popular folk festival and family occasion. The Catholic belief is that departed souls are in heaven or in purgatory, not actually back on a visit to Earth. Nevertheless, many find comfort in a sense that lost loved ones are somehow more present at this time. Among many indigenous communities, Muertos is still very much a religious and spiritual event. For them, the observance might more appropriately be called Noche de Muertos (Night of the Dead), because families actually spend whole nights at the graveyard communing with the dead.

Sugar skulls, chocolate coffins and toy skeletons are sold in markets everywhere, both as Muertos gifts for children and graveyard decorations; this tradition derives in great measure from the work of artist José Guadalupe Posada (1852–1913), renowned for his satirical figures of a skeletal Death cheerfully engaging in everyday life, working, dancing, courting, drinking and riding horses into battle.

saints' days, and pilgrimages to important shrines are a big feature of the calendar.

The church's most binding symbol is Nuestra Señora de Guadalupe, the dark-skinned manifestation of the Virgin Mary who appeared to an Aztec potter, Juan Diego, in 1531 on Cerro del Tepeyac hill in what's now northern Mexico City. A crucial link between Catholic and indigenous spirituality, the Virgin of Guadalupe is now the country's religious patron, an archetypal mother whose blue-cloaked image is ubiquitous and whose name is invoked in political speeches and literature as well as religious ceremonies. December 12, her feast day, sees large-scale celebrations and pilgrimages all over the country, biggest of all in Mexico City.

Though some church figures have supported causes such as indigenous rights, the Mexican Catholic Church is a socially conservative body. It has alienated some sectors of the population by its strong opposition to Mexico City's legalization of abortion and to the gay marriages or civil unions which are now legal in Mexico City and the states of Colima, Quintana Roo and Coahuila.

The secrets of physical and spiritual health of a Nahua *curandera* (literally 'curer') are revealed in *Woman Who Glows in the Dark* by Elena Ávila.

Indigenous Religion

The Spanish missionaries of the 16th and 17th centuries won indigenous Mexicans over to Catholicism by grafting it onto pre-Hispanic religions. Old gods were renamed as Christian saints, old festivals were melded with Christian feast days. Indigenous Christianity is still fused with ancient beliefs today. Jalisco's Huichol people have two Christs, but Nakawé, the fertility goddess, is a more important deity. In the Catholic church at the Tzotzil Maya town of San Juan Chamula, you may see chanting *curanderos* (healers) carrying out shamanistic rites. In the traditional indigenous world almost everything has a spiritual dimension – trees, rivers, hills, wind, rain and sun have their own gods or spirits, and illness may be seen as a 'loss of soul' resulting from wrongdoing or from the malign influence of someone with magical powers.

SANTA MUERTE

A bizarre and growing challenge to mainstream religion comes from the cult of Santa Muerte (Saint Death), which was condemned as blasphemous by the Vatican in 2013 but by some estimates now has eight million followers in Mexico. Many Mexicans who feel that the traditional Catholic Trinity and saints are not answering their prayers are now praying and making offerings to cloaked, scythe-wielding skeleton images in private and public sanctuaries. Drug gangs are notoriously among the cult's most loyal followers, and there have even been reports of alleged human sacrifices to Santa Muerte. The best known **Santa Muerte Altar** (Alfarería, north of Mineros; Ⓜ Tepito) is in Mexico City's crime-ridden Tepito neighborhood.

Letting off Steam

Mexicans have many ways of releasing their emotional and physical energy. Religion (p816), artistic expression (p819) and the countless fiestas (p30) are among them. So are sports.

The 2008 film *Rudo y Cursi* tells the (fictional) tale of two brothers from a poor Mexican village rising to professional playing success in a corrupt Mexican *fútbol* (soccer) world. It's a comical and lovable movie that stars two of the country's top actors, Gael García Bernal and Diego Luna.

Fútbol

No sport ignites Mexicans' passions more than *fútbol* (soccer). Games in the 18-team Liga MX, the national First Division, are played at weekends almost year-round before crowds averaging 25,000 and followed by millions on TV. Attending a game is fun, and rivalry between opposing fans is generally good-humored. Tickets are sold at the entrance for anything from M$50 to M$650, depending on the stadium, game and seat. For *fútbol* fixtures and results, check espnfc.com.

The two most popular teams with large followings everywhere are América, of Mexico City, known as the Águilas (Eagles), and Guadalajara, called Chivas (Goats). Matches between the two, known as Los Clásicos, are the biggest games of the year. Other leading clubs include Cruz Azul and UNAM (Pumas) of Mexico City, Monterrey and UANL (Los Tigres) from Monterrey, Santos Laguna from Torreón, and Toluca.

Bullfights

Bullfighting arouses strong passions in many Mexicans. While the activity has many fans, there is also a strong anti-bullfighting movement spearheaded by groups such as Mexican Animal Rights Association (AMEDEA) and AnimaNaturalis. Bullfights are now banned in the state of Sonora and eight other cities and towns.

Bullfights usually take place on Sunday afternoons or during local festivals, chiefly in the larger cities. In northern Mexico the season generally runs from March or April to August or September. In central and southern Mexico, including Mexico City's monumental Plaza México, one of the world's biggest bullrings, the main season is from about October to February.

Mexico has produced many world champions in boxing. The legendary Julio César Chávez won five world titles at three different weights, and achieved an amazing 90 consecutive wins after turning pro in 1980.

Other Sports

The highly popular *lucha libre* (Mexican wrestling) is more showbiz than sport. Participants in this pantomime-like activity give themselves names like Último Guerrero (Last Warrior), Rey Escorpión (Scorpion King) and Blue Panther, then clown around in Day-Glo tights and lurid masks. For the audience it provides a welcome change from real life because the good guys normally win. Mexico City's 17,000-seat **Arena México** (☎55-5588-0266; www.arenamexico.com.mx; Dr Lavista 197, Colonia Doctores; ⏱7:30pm Tue & 8:30pm Fri; 🚌Cuauhtémoc) is the big temple of this activity.

Charreadas (rodeos) are popular events, particularly in the northern half of Mexico, during fiestas and at regular venues often called *lienzos charros*. **Decharros** (www.decharros.com) has plenty of information.

The Arts

Mexicans are an obsessively creative people. Wherever you go in their country you'll be amazed by the marvelous artistic expression on display. Colorful painting, stunning architecture and beautiful crafts are everywhere, Aztec dancers vibrate in the very heart of Mexico City, musicians strike up on the streets and in bars and buses. This is a country that has given the world some of its finest painting, music, movies and writing.

Architecture

Mexico's priceless architectural heritage from pre-Hispanic and colonial times is one of its greatest treasures.

Pre-Hispanic

At places like Teotihuacán, Monte Albán, Chichén Itzá, Uxmal and Palenque you can still see fairly intact, spectacular pre-Hispanic cities. Their grand ceremonial centers were designed to impress, with great stone pyramids (topped by shrines), palaces and ritual ball courts – all built without metal tools, pack animals or wheels. While the architecture of Teotihuacán, Monte Albán and later Aztecs was intended to awe with its grand scale, the Maya of Chichén Itzá, Uxmal, Palenque and countless other sites paid more attention to aesthetics, with intricately patterned facades, delicate stone 'combs' on temple roofs, and sinuous carvings, producing some of the most beautiful human creations in the Americas. The technical hallmark of Maya buildings is the corbeled vault, a version of the arch: two stone walls leaning toward one another, nearly meeting at the top and surmounted by a capstone. Teotihuacán architecture is characterized by the *talud-tablero* style of stepped buildings, in which height is achieved by alternating upright *(tablero)* sections with sloping *(talud)* ones.

The 2012 documentary *Hecho en México* is a fascinating and colorful look at contemporary Mexican life and arts, and had the participation of many of the country's top musicians, actors and writers. It's directed by Duncan Bridgeman.

Colonial Period

The Spaniards destroyed indigenous temples and built churches and monasteries in their place, and laid out new towns with handsome plazas and grids of streets lined by fine stone edifices – contributing much to Mexico's beauty today. Building was in Spanish styles, with some unique local variations. Renaissance style, based on ancient Greek and Roman ideals of harmony and proportion, with shapes such as the square and the circle, dominated in the 16th and early 17th centuries. Mérida's cathedral and Casa de Montejo are outstanding Renaissance buildings, while Mexico City and Puebla cathedrals mingle Renaissance and baroque styles.

Baroque, which reached Mexico in the early 17th century, layered new dramatic effects – curves, color, increasingly elaborate decoration – onto a Renaissance base. Painting and sculpture were integrated with architecture, notably in ornate, enormous *retablos* (altarpieces). Mexico's finest baroque buildings include Zacatecas cathedral and the churches of Santo Domingo in Mexico City and Oaxaca. Between 1730 and 1780 Mexi-

Mexico's Biggest Pyramids

- *Pirámide Tepanapa (Cholula)*
- *Pirámide del Sol (Pyramid of the Sun; Teotihuacán)*
- *Pirámide de la Luna (Pyramid of the Moon; Teotihuacán)*

can baroque reached its final, spectacularly out-of-control form known as Churrigueresque, with riotous ornamentation.

Indigenous artisans added profuse sculpture in stone and colored stucco to many baroque buildings, such as the Rosary Chapels in the Templos de Santo Domingo at Puebla and Oaxaca. Spanish Islamic influence showed in the popularity of *azulejos* (colored tiles) on the outside of buildings, notably on Mexico City's Casa de Azulejos and many buildings in Puebla.

Neoclassical style, another return to sober Greek and Roman ideals, dominated from about 1780 to 1830. Outstanding buildings include the Palacio de Minería in Mexico City, designed by Mexico's leading architect of the time, Manuel Tolsá.

Churrigueresque Architecture

- *Sagrario Metropolitano (Mexico City)*
- *Santuario de la Virgen de Ocotlán (Tlaxcala)*
- *Capilla Doméstica (Tepotzotlán)*
- *Templo de Santa Prisca (Taxco)*

Nineteenth to 21st Centuries

Independent Mexico in the 19th and early 20th centuries saw revivals of colonial styles as well as imitations of contemporary French or Italian styles. Mexico City's semi-art-nouveau Palacio de Bellas Artes is one of the most spectacular buildings from this era.

After the 1910–20 Revolution came 'Toltecism,' an effort to return to pre-Hispanic roots in the search for a national identity. This culminated in the 1950s with the Ciudad Universitaria campus in Mexico City, where many buildings are covered with colorful murals.

The great icon of more recent architecture is Luis Barragán (1902–88), a modernist who exhibited a strong Mexican strain in his use of vivid colors, space and light. His oeuvre includes a set of wacky colored skyscraper sculptures in Ciudad Satélite, a Mexico City suburb. Another modernist, Pedro Ramírez Vázquez (1919-2013), designed three vast public buildings in Mexico City: the 1960s Estadio Azteca and Museo Nacional de Antropología and the 1970s Basílica de Guadalupe. But the talk of the town lately has been the capital's new Museo Soumaya Plaza Carso, designed by Fernando Romero for the art collection of his father-in-law Carlos Slim, the world's richest man. It's a love-it-or-hate-it six-story construction that might be described as resembling a giant, twisted blacksmith's anvil covered in 16,000 honeycomb-shaped aluminium plates.

Check out the good and the bad of what's going up in Mexico's cities (and the rest of the world) at www.skyscrapercity.com.

Painting & Sculpture

Since the earliest times Mexicans have exhibited a love of color and form, and an exciting talent for painting and sculpture. The wealth of art in mural form and in Mexico's many galleries is a highlight of the country.

Pre-Hispanic

Mexico's first identified civilization, the Olmecs of the Gulf coast, produced remarkable stone sculptures depicting deities, animals and wonderfully lifelike human forms. Most awesome are the huge Olmec heads, which combine the features of human babies and jaguars.

The Classic Maya of southeast Mexico between about AD 250 and 800 were perhaps ancient Mexico's most artistically gifted people. They left countless beautiful stone sculptures, complicated in design but possessing great delicacy of touch.

Top Ancient Mural Sites

- *Palacio de Tepantitla (Teotihuacán)*
- *Cacaxtla*
- *Bonampak*

Colonial & Independence Eras

Mexican art during Spanish rule was heavily Spanish-influenced and chiefly religious in subject, though portraiture advanced under wealthy patrons. Miguel Cabrera (1695–1768), from Oaxaca, is widely considered the most talented painter of the era.

The years before the 1910 Revolution finally saw a breaking away from European traditions. Mexican slums, brothels and indigenous poverty began to appear on canvases. José Guadalupe Posada (1852–1913), with his characteristic *calavera* (skull) motif, satirized the injustices of the Porfiriato period, launching a tradition of political and social subversion in Mexican art.

The Muralists

In the 1920s, immediately following the Mexican Revolution, education minister José Vasconcelos commissioned young artists to paint a series of public murals to spread a sense of Mexican history and culture and of the need for social and technological change. The trio of great muralists – all great painters in smaller scales, too – were Diego Rivera (1886–1957), José Clemente Orozco (1883–1949) and David Alfaro Siqueiros (1896–1974).

Rivera's work carried a left-wing message, emphasizing past oppression of indigenous people and peasants. His art, found in many locations in and around Mexico City, pulled Mexico's indigenous and Spanish roots together in colorful, crowded tableaus depicting historical people and events, with a simple moral message.

Siqueiros, who fought in the Revolution on the Constitutionalist (liberal) side, remained a political activist afterward and his murals convey a clear Marxist message through dramatic, symbolic depictions of the oppressed and grotesque caricatures of the oppressors. Some of his best works are at the Palacio de Bellas Artes, the Castillo de Chapultepec and Ciudad Universitaria, all in Mexico City.

Orozco, from Jalisco, focused more on the universal human condition than on historical specifics. He conveyed emotion, character and atmosphere. His work was at its peak in Guadalajara between 1936 and 1939, particularly in the 50-odd frescoes in the Instituto Cultural de Cabañas.

Other 20th-Century Artists

Frida Kahlo (1907–54), physically crippled by a road accident and mentally tormented in her tempestuous marriage to Diego Rivera, painted anguished self-portraits and grotesque, surreal images that expressed her left-wing views and externalized her inner tumult. Kahlo's work suddenly seemed to strike an international chord in the 1980s and '90s. She's now better known worldwide than any other Mexican artist, and her Mexico City home, the Museo Frida Kahlo, is a don't-miss for any art lover.

Rufino Tamayo (1899–1991) from Oaxaca is sometimes thought of as the fourth major muralist, but he was a great artist at other scales too, absorbed by abstract and mythological images and the effects of color. After WWII, the young Mexican artists of La Ruptura (the Rupture), led by José Luis Cuevas (b 1934), reacted against the muralist movement,

Top Art Museums

Museo Frida Kahlo (Mexico City)

Museo Jumex (Mexico City)

Museo Nacional de Arte (Mexico City)

Museo Dolores Olmedo Patiño (Mexico City)

Museo de Arte de Tlaxcala (Tlaxcala)

Museo Pedro Coronel (Zacatecas)

Mexico City's annual contemporary art fair, Zona Maco (www.zonamaco.com), held over five days every February, pulls in artists, galleries, dealers and cognoscenti from around the world.

2501 MIGRANTS

Alejandro Santiago (1964–2013) created a stir with his 2007 installation *2501 Migrantes*, comprising 2501 large, all-different human figures sculpted in clay, representing all the people who had had to migrate for economic reasons from his home village of Teococuilco, Oaxaca. The work was first exhibited at Monterrey's Universal Forum of Cultures in 2007, and later in front of Oaxaca's Santo Domingo church. It's the subject of a fascinating documentary film directed by Yolanda Cruz, *2501 Migrants: A Journey*.

which they saw as too obsessed with *mexicanidad* (Mexicanness). They opened Mexico up to world trends such as abstract expressionism and pop art. Other fine 20th-century artists include the Oaxacans Francisco Toledo (b 1940) and Rodolfo Morales (1925–2001), whose visions draw on pre-Hispanic roots. Sculptor Sebastián (b 1947), from Chihuahua, is famed for his large, mathematics-inspired sculptures that adorn cities around the world.

Art Books

The Art of Mesoamerica by Mary Ellen Miller

Mexican Muralists by Desmond Rochfort

Contemporary Art

Today, thanks to dynamic artists, galleries and patrons and the globalization of the world art scene, new Mexican art is reaching galleries the world over. Mexico City has become an international art hot spot, while other cities such as Monterrey, Oaxaca, Mazatlán and Guadalajara also have thriving art scenes. Mexican artists attempt to interpret the uncertainties of the 21st century in diverse ways. The pendulum has swung away from abstraction to hyper-representation, photorealism, installations and video. Rocío Maldonado (b 1951), Rafael Cauduro (b 1950) and Roberto Cortázar (b 1962) all paint classically depicted figures against amorphous, bleak backgrounds. Check out Cauduro's murals on state-sponsored crime in Mexico City's Suprema Corte de Justicia. Leading contemporary lights such as Miguel Calderón (b 1971) and Gabriel Orozco (b 1962) spread their talents across many media, always challenging the spectator's preconceptions.

Modern Art Websites

Arte Mexico (www.artemexico.org)

Galería Nina Menocal (www.ninamenocal.com)

Kurimanzutto (www.kurimanzutto.com)

LatinAmericanArt.com (www.latinamericanart.com)

Museo Colección Andrés Blaisten (www.museoblaisten.com)

Music

Music is everywhere in Mexico. It comes booming out of sound systems in markets and passing automobiles, and live musicians may start up at any time, on plazas, in buses or the Mexico City metro. These performers are playing for a living and range from marimba (wooden xylophone) teams and mariachi bands (trumpeters, violinists, guitarists and a singer, all dressed in smart Wild West–style costumes) to ragged lone buskers with out-of-tune guitars. Mariachi music, perhaps the most 'typical' Mexican music, originated in the Guadalajara area but is played nationwide. Marimbas are particularly popular in the southeast and on the Gulf coast.

Rock & Hip-Hop

So close to the big US Spanish-speaking market, Mexico can claim to be the most important hub of *rock en español*. Talented Mexico City bands such as Café Tacuba and Maldita Vecindad emerged in the 1990s and took the genre to new heights and new audiences (well beyond Mexico), mixing influences from rock, hip-hop and ska to traditional Mexican *son* (folk music) or mariachi. Café Tacuba's albums *Re* (1994), *Avalancha de éxitos* (1996), *Tiempo transcurrido* (2001) and *Sino* (2007) are all full of great songs. Also still popular are the Monterrey rap-metal band Molotov, who have upset just about everyone with their expletive-laced lyrics. Mexico's 21st-century indie wave threw up still highly successful bands such as Zoé from Mexico City, who are popular throughout the Spanish-speaking world, and Monterrey's Kinky, who have a strong electronic/house leaning.

Powerful, colorful Alejandra Guzmán is known as La Reina del Rock (Queen of Rock) and has sold 15 million discs in a two-decade career.

The Mexican band most famous outside Mexico is undoubtedly Guadalajara's Maná, an unashamedly commercial outfit reminiscent of The Police. El Tri, the grandfathers of Mexican rock, are still pumping out energetic rock 'n' roll after more than four decades.

LILA DOWNS

Singer Lila Downs, who has an American father and a Oaxacan mother, is gaining an international name with her passionate and original versions of Mexican folk songs today, often with a jazz influence. If you saw the 2002 movie *Frida*, you heard Lila on the soundtrack. Her best albums include *La sandunga* (1997), *Border* (*La línea*; 2001) and *Pecados y milagros* (2011).

Pop

Paulina Rubio is Mexico's answer to Shakira. She has also starred in several Mexican films and TV series, and has lately turned to judging for TV talent shows. Natalia Lafourcade, a talented singer-songwriter who mixes pop and *bossa nova* rhythms, won a 2013 Latin Grammy with her album *Mujer Divina – Homenaje a Agustín Lara*.

Balladeer Luis Miguel is Mexico's Julio Iglesias and incredibly popular, as is Juan Gabriel, who has sold millions of his own albums and written dozens of hit songs for others.

Ranchera & Norteño – Mexico's 'Country Music'

Ranchera is Mexico's urban 'country music' – mostly melodramatic stuff with a nostalgia for rural roots, sometimes with a mariachi backing. The hugely popular Vicente Fernández, Juan Gabriel and Alejandro Fernández (Vicente's son) are among the leading *ranchera* artists.

Norteño or *norteña* is country ballad and dance music, originating in northern Mexico but nationwide in popularity. Its roots are in *corridos,* heroic ballads with the rhythms of European dances such as waltz or polka. Originally the songs were tales of Latino-Anglo strife in the borderlands or themes from the Mexican Revolution. Modern *narcocorridos* started out dealing with drug runners and other small-time crooks trying to survive amid big-time corruption and crime, but in recent years some have told of exploits of major Mexican drug gangs. Some gangs even commission *narcocorridos* about themselves.

Norteño groups *(conjuntos)* go for 10-gallon hats, with backing centered on the accordion and the *bajo sexto* (a 12-string guitar), along with bass and drums. *Norteño's* superstars are Los Tigres del Norte, originally from Sinaloa but now based in California. They play to huge audiences on both sides of the frontier, with some *narcocorridos* in their repertoire. Other top stars include Los Huracanes del Norte, Los Tucanes de Tijuana and accordionist/vocalist Ramón Ayala.

The Tijuana-based Nortec Collective melds traditional Mexican music with electronica into a fun genre known as Nortec. Look for their *Tijuana Sessions* and *Tijuana Sound Machine* albums. Big electronica events with top Mexican or international DJs are frequent in or around the big cities: www.kinetik.tv has details.

Son – Mexico's Folk Roots

Son (literally 'sound') is a broad term covering Mexican country styles that grew out of the fusion of Spanish, indigenous and African music. Guitars or similar instruments (such as the small *jarana*) lay down a strong rhythm, with harp or violin providing the melody. *Son* is often played for a foot-stomping dance audience, with witty, sometimes improvised, lyrics. There are several regional variants. *Son huasteco* (or *huapango*), from the Huasteca area inland from Tampico, features falsetto vocals between soaring violin passages. Keep an eye open for top group Los Camperos de Valles. The exciting *son jarocho,* from the Veracruz area, is particularly African-influenced: Grupo Mono Blanco have led a revival of the genre with contemporary lyrics, and the music has even begun to gain a following in the USA. The famous 'La Bamba' is a *son jarocho!*

MÚSICA TROPICAL

Although their origins lie in the Caribbean and South America, several brands of percussion-heavy, infectiously rhythmic *música tropical* are highly popular in Mexico. Mexico City, in particular, has numerous clubs and large dance halls devoted to this scene, often hosting international bands.

Two kinds of dance music – *danzón,* originally from Cuba, and *cumbia,* from Colombia – both took deeper root in Mexico than in their original homelands. The elegant, old-fashioned *danzón* is strongly associated with the port city of Veracruz but is currently enjoying quite a revival in Mexico City and elsewhere, too. The livelier, more flirtatious *cumbia* has its adopted home in Mexico City. It rests on thumping bass lines with brass, guitars, mandolins and sometimes marimbas. *Cumbia* has spawned its own contemporary sub-varieties: *cumbia sonidera* is basically electronic *cumbia* played by DJs, while 'psychedelic *cumbia*' actually harks back to Peruvian *cumbia* of the 1970s. Listen out for the psychedelic album *Cumbia Salvaje* by Mexico City's Sonido Gallo Negro.

Almost every town in Mexico has some place where you can dance (and often learn) salsa, which originated in New York when jazz met *son,* cha-cha and rumba from Cuba and Puerto Rico. Musically it boils down to brass (with trumpet solos), piano, percussion, singer and chorus – the dance is a hot one with a lot of exciting turns. *Merengue,* mainly from the Dominican Republic, is a blend of *cumbia* and salsa.

Trova

This popular genre of troubadour-type folk music, typically performed by solo singer-songwriters *(cantautores)* with a guitar, has roots in 1960s and '70s folk and protest songs. Many *trova* singers are strongly inspired by Cuban political musician Silvio Rodríguez.

Cinema

Mexican cinema has made a resounding comeback since the start of the 21st century, after decades in the doldrums. A clutch of fine, gritty movies by young Mexican directors has won commercial success as well as critical acclaim; government support for the film industry has climbed; the number of Mexican productions has risen to about 70 a year; and several places including Morelia, Guadalajara, Oaxaca, Monterrey, Los Cabos and the Riviera Maya now stage successful annual film festivals.

The new Mexican films confront the ugly, tragic and absurd in Mexican life as well as the beautiful and comical. The first to really catch the world's eye was *Amores perros* (Love's a Bitch; 2000), directed by Alejandro González Iñárritu and starring Gael García Bernal, who have since both become international celebrities. Set in contemporary Mexico City, with three plots connected by one traffic accident, it's a raw, honest movie with its quota of blood, violence and sex as well as ironic humor.

Y tu mamá también (And Your Mother Too), Alfonso Cuarón's 2001 'growing up' road movie about two privileged Mexico City teenagers (Gael García Bernal and Diego Luna), was at the time the biggest grossing Mexican film ever, netting more than US$25 million. Carlos Carrera's *El Crimen del Padre Amaro* (The Crime of Father Amaro; 2003), again starring Gael García Bernal, painted an ugly picture of church corruption in a small town.

Success has spirited some of these talents away from Mexico. González Iñárritu moved to Hollywood to direct two more great movies with interconnected multiple plots and a theme of death – *21 Grams* (2003) and *Babel* (2006). In 2010 he returned with the stunning *Biutiful*, a joint Mexican-Spanish production starring Javier Bardem in a harrowing 'down and out in Barcelona' tale. Alfonso Cuarón moved on to *Harry Potter and the Prisoner of Azkaban* (2004) and the multi-Oscar-winning (including for best director) science-fiction epic *Gravity* (2013).

But back home, less mainstream Mexican directors have been making films that rake in awards at the Cannes Festival. The claustrophobic, sexually explicit *Año bisiesto* (Leap Year), directed by Mexico-resident Australian Michael Rowe, with a great performance by Mónica del Carmen, won the 2010 Cannes prize for best new director. Carlos Reygadas took the best director award for *Post tenebras lux*, a confusing mix of fantasy and reality, dream and documentary, about a middle-class family living in the countryside, which divides audiences and critics alike. Amat Escalante was Cannes' best director in 2013 with *Heli*, about a young couple caught in Mexico's violent drugs war. Other top 2013 movies on tough topics were Diego Quemada-Diez's *La jaula de oro* (The Golden Cage), about young Central American migrants trying to get to the USA through Mexico, and *Workers*, directed by José Luis Valle, a moving, sometimes humorous film about two elderly working people struggling for their rights. Meanwhile another film addressing class divisions, but this time in a comic way, Gary Alazraki's *Nosotros los nobles* (We The Nobles), became the all-time biggest-grossing Mexican film in Mexican cinemas, with 3.3 million viewers.

The historical golden age of Mexican movie-making was the 1940s, when the country was creating up to 200 films a year – typically epic, melodramatic productions. The four big stars were Dolores del Río, María Félix, Mario Moreno ('Cantinflas') and Pedro Infante. Then Hollywood reasserted itself, and Mexican filmmakers struggled for funding for decades. Today Mexico has the world's fifth-biggest cinema audience, but more than 90% of box-office takings are still for US films.

Frida & Diego Books

Frida Kahlo and Diego Rivera by Isabel Alcántara and Sandra Egnolff

Kahlo by Andrea Kettenmann

Frida by Hayden Herrera

Rivera by Andrea Kettenmann

Literature

Mexicans such as Carlos Fuentes, Juan Rulfo and Octavio Paz have written some of the great Spanish-language literature.

Fuentes (1928–2012), a prolific novelist and commentator, is probably Mexico's best known writer internationally. Perhaps his most famous novel, *The Death of Artemio Cruz* (1962) takes a critical look at Mexico's postrevolutionary era through the eyes of a dying, corrupted press baron and landowner.

In Mexico, Juan Rulfo (1918–86) is widely regarded as the supreme novelist. His *Pedro Páramo* (1955), about a young man's search for his lost father among ghostlike villages in western Mexico, is a scary, desolate work with confusing shifts of time – a kind of Mexican *Wuthering Heights* with a spooky, magical-realist twist.

Octavio Paz (1914–98), poet, essayist and winner of the 1990 Nobel Prize for Literature, wrote a probing, intellectually acrobatic analysis of Mexico's myths and the national character in *The Labyrinth of Solitude* (1950).

Of a whole school of novels inspired by the Mexican Revolution, the classic is *The Underdogs*, the story of a peasant who becomes a general, by Mariano Azuela (1873–1952). More recently, Laura Esquivel (b 1950) made her name with *Like Water for Chocolate* (1989), a Revolution-era rural love story interwoven with both fantasy and recipes.

In poetry, the great names are Octavio Paz and a reclusive figure from Chiapas, Jaime Sabines (1925–99), who both treated themes of love and death with stark, vivid imagery.

Mexico in Others' Words

The Power and the Glory by Graham Greene

Under the Volcano by Malcolm Lowry

The Treasure of the Sierra Madre and *The Rebellion of the Hanged* by B Traven

Queer by William Burroughs

On the Road by Jack Kerouac

All the Pretty Horses by Cormac McCarthy

Folk Art

Mexicans' skill with their hands and their love of color, fun and tradition find expression everywhere in their appealing *artesanías* (handicrafts). Crafts such as weaving, pottery, leatherwork, copperwork, hat-making and basketry still fulfil key functions in daily life as well as yielding souvenirs and collectibles. Many craft techniques and designs in use today have pre-Hispanic origins, and it's Mexico's indigenous peoples, the direct inheritors of pre-Hispanic culture, who lead the way in *artesanía* production.

Traditional Textiles

The 'yarn paintings' of the indigenous Huichol people – created by pressing strands of yarn onto a wax-covered board – depict scenes resembling visions experienced under the influence of the drug *peyote,* which is central to Huichol culture.

In some of Mexico's indigenous villages you'll be stunned by the variety of colorful, intricately decorated attire, differing from area to area and often from village to village. Traditional costume – more widely worn by women than men – serves as a mark of the community to which a person belongs. The woven or embroidered patterns of some garments can take months to complete.

Three main types of women's garments have been in use since long before the Spanish conquest:

- *huipil* – a long, sleeveless tunic, found mainly in the southern half of the country
- *quechquémitl* – a shoulder cape with an opening for the head, found mainly in central and northern Mexico
- *enredo* – a wraparound skirt

Spanish missionaries introduced blouses, now often also embroidered with great care and detail.

The primary materials of indigenous weaving are cotton and wool, though synthetic fibers are also common. Natural dyes have been revived – deep blues from the indigo plant, reds and browns from various woods, and reds and purples from the cochineal insect.

The basic indigenous weavers' tool, used only by women, is the backstrap loom *(telar de cintura)* on which the warp (long) threads are stretched between two horizontal bars, one of which is fixed to a post or tree, while the other is attached to a strap around the weaver's lower back; the weft (cross) threads are then intricately woven in, producing some amazing patterns. Backstrap-loom *huipiles* from the southern states of Oaxaca and Chiapas are among Mexico's most eye-catching garments.

Diamond shapes on some *huipiles* from San Andrés Larráinzar, in Chiapas, represent the universe of the villagers' Maya ancestors, who believed the earth was a cube and the sky had four corners.

Treadle looms, operated by foot pedals (usually by men) can weave wider cloth than the backstrap loom and tend to be used for rugs, *rebozos* (shawls), *sarapes* (blankets with an opening for the head) and skirt material. Mexico's most famous rug-weaving village is Teotitlán del Valle, Oaxaca.

Ceramics

Many small-scale potters' workshops turn out everything from plain cooking pots to elaborate works of art. One highly attractive pottery variety is Talavera, made chiefly in Puebla and Dolores Hidalgo, and characterized by bright colors (blue and yellow are prominent) and floral designs. The Guadalajara suburbs of Tonalá and Tlaquepaque produce a wide variety of ceramics. In northern Mexico the villagers of Mata Ortiz make a range of beautiful earthenware, drawing on the techniques and designs of pre-Hispanic Paquimé, similar to some of the native American pottery of the US southwest. Another distinctive Mexican ceramic form is the *árbol de la vida* (tree of life). These elaborate, candelabra-like objects are molded by hand and decorated with numerous tiny figures of people, animals, plants and so on. Some of the best are made in Metepec in the state of México, which is also the source of colorful clay suns.

Masks

For millennia Mexicans have worn masks in dances, ceremonies and shamanistic rites: the wearer temporarily becomes the creature, person or deity represented by the mask. You can admire mask artistry at museums in cities such as San Luis Potosí, Zacatecas and Colima, and at shops and markets around the country. The southern state of Guerrero has probably the broadest range of fine masks.

Wood is the basic material of most masks, but papier-mâché, clay, wax and leather are also used. Mask-makers often paint or embellish their masks with real teeth, hair, feathers or other adornments. Common masks include animals, birds, Christ, devils, and Spaniards with comically pale, wide-eyed features.

Lacquerware & Woodwork

Gourds, the hard shells of certain squash-type fruits, have been used in Mexico since antiquity as bowls, cups and small storage vessels. The most eye-catching decoration technique is lacquering, in which the gourd is coated with paste or paint and then varnished, producing a nonporous and, to some extent, heat-resistant, vessel. Lacquering is also used to decorate wooden boxes, trays and furniture, with a lot of the most appealing ware coming from remote Olinalá in Guerrero: artisans create patterns using the *rayado* method of scraping off part of the top coat of paint to expose a different-colored layer below.

The Seri people of Sonora work hard ironwood into dramatic human, animal and sea-creature shapes. Villagers around Oaxaca city produce brightly painted imaginary beasts carved from copal wood, known as *alebrijes*.

Crafts Books

The Crafts of Mexico by Margarita de Orellana and Alberto Ruy Sánchez

Arts and Crafts of Mexico by Chloë Sayer

Mexican Textiles by Masako Takahashi

Mexconnect (www.mexconnect.com) features a wealth of articles and links on Mexican arts.

The Mexican Kitchen

by Mauricio Velázquez de León

In Mexico we love food, especially our own. Ask a group of Mexicans where to find, say, the best *carnitas* (braised pork) in Mexico City, and you're launching a passionate, well-informed, lengthy debate. Visiting Mexico, you'll find out why. The food will be fresh, often locally grown, and enormously varied from one place to another, a far cry from the 'Mexican' fare served in restaurants outside the country. If you want to know Mexico and its people, you must try our food.

This chapter was written by Mauricio Velázquez de León. Born in Mexico City, his food writing has been widely published in Mexico and the US. He is the author (under the name Puck) of *My Foodie ABC: A Little Gourmet's Guide* (duopress, 2010). Additional research by John Noble.

What's on the Menu?

A Mexican menu will vary with the region you are visiting, but in most cases you can find food that is made with a few staples: corn, an array of dry and fresh chilies, and beans. Contrary to popular belief, not all food in Mexico is spicy, at least not for the regular palate. Chilies are used as flavoring ingredients and to provide intensity in sauces, *moles* and *pipiáns,* and many appreciate their depth over their piquancy. But beware; some dishes do indeed have a kick, reaching daredevil levels in a few cases. The *habanero* chili in the Yucatán is the spiciest pepper in the world, and the *chile de árbol* can be terribly fierce. A good rule of thumb is that when chilies are cooked and incorporated into the dishes as sauces they tend to be on the mild side, but when they are prepared for salsas (relishes or sauces) they can be really hot.

There are other staples that give Mexican food its classic flavoring. Among them are spices like cinnamon, clove and cumin, and herbs such as thyme, oregano and, most importantly, cilantro (coriander) and *epazote. Epazote* may be the unsung hero of Mexican cooking. This pungent-smelling herb (called pigweed or Jerusalem oak in the US) is used for flavoring beans, soups, stews and certain *moles.*

Eating as a Whim

Antojitos are at the center of Mexican cooking. The word *antojo* translates as 'a whim, a sudden craving,' so an *antojito* is a little whim, but as any Mexican will quickly point out, it is not just a snack. You can have them as an entire meal, or have a couple as appetizers, or yes, eat one as a *tentempié* (quick bite) before hopping in the metro.

Markets are perfect places to munch on some really good *antojitos.* In the gargantuan Mercado de la Merced in Mexico City the best *antojito* may be the *huarache,* a 30cm-long tortilla shaped like the shoe for which it is named, grilled and topped with salsa, onions, cheese and a choice of *chorizo* sausage, steak, squash blossoms and more. The *huarache* competitor can be found in the markets of Oaxaca City, where large flat tortillas called *tlayudas* are spread with refried beans and topped with Oaxacan string cheese, salsa and pork strips.

American award-winning chef and Mexican food expert Rick Bayless has a great way to define *antojitos* by grouping them according to the one component present in all: corn masa (dough). Using this criterion we can say that there are eight types of *antojitos*:

➡ **Tacos** The quintessential culinary fare in Mexico can be made of any cooked meat, fish or vegetable wrapped in a tortilla, with a dash of salsa and garnished with onion and cilantro. Soft corn tortillas are used to wrap grilled meats in *tacos al carbón*, an array of stews in *tacos de guisado* or with griddle-cooked meats and vegetables in *tacos a la plancha*. When tacos are lightly fried they are called *tacos dorados*. If you are in northern Mexico, chances are you will find tacos with flour tortillas *(tortillas de harina)* and the fillings will be more meat-based than vegetarian.

➡ **Quesadillas** Fold a tortilla with cheese, heat it on a griddle and you have a quesadilla. (*Queso* means cheese, hence the name.) But real quesadillas are much more than that. In restaurants and street stalls quesadillas are stuffed pockets made with raw corn masa that is lightly fried or griddled until crisp. They can be stuffed with *chorizo* and cheese, squash blossoms, mushrooms with garlic, *chicharrón* (fried pork fat), beans, stewed chicken or meat.

➡ **Enchiladas** In Spanish *enchilar* means to put chili over something, so enchiladas are a group of three or four lightly fried tortillas filled with chicken, cheese or eggs and covered with a cooked salsa. Enchiladas are usually a main dish, and can also be baked, like the famous *enchiladas suizas* (Swiss-style enchiladas).

➡ **Tostadas** Tortillas that have been baked or fried until they get crisp and are then cooled. In this state they can hold a variety of toppings. *Tostadas de pollo* are a beautiful layering of beans, chicken, cream, shredded lettuce, onion, avocado and *queso fresco* (a fresh cheese).

➡ **Sopes** Small masa shells, 5cm to 7.5cm in diameter, that are shaped by hand and cooked on a griddle with a thin layer of beans, salsa and cheese. *Chorizo* is also a common topping for *sopes*.

➡ **Gorditas** Round masa cakes that are baked until they puff. Sometimes *gorditas* are filled with a thin layer of fried black or pinto beans, or even fava beans.

➡ **Chilaquiles** Typically served as breakfast. Corn tortillas are cut in triangles and fried until crispy. At this point they are indeed tortilla chips *(totopos)*. When cooked in a tomatillo sauce (for *chilaquiles verdes*) or tomato sauce *(chilaquiles rojos)* they become soft and then are topped with shredded cheese, sliced onions and Mexican *crema*.

➡ **Tamales** Made with masa mixed with lard, stuffed with stewed meat, fish or vegetables, wrapped and steamed. Every Mexican region has its own, the most famous being the Oaxacan-style *tamales* with *mole* and wrapped in banana leaves, the Mexico City *tamales* with chicken and green tomatillo sauce wrapped in corn husks, and the Yucatecan style, made with chicken marinated in *achiote* (annatto paste) and wrapped in banana leaves.

Josefina Velázquez de León is considered the mother of Mexican cuisine. She ran a successful culinary school and wrote more than 140 cookbooks, the most ambitious being *Platillos Regionales de la República Mexicana*, considered to be the first book to collect Mexico's regional cuisine in one volume.

MULLI (MOLE)

Mexican chef and author Zarela Martínez once told me that in *mole* the sauce is the dish. What she meant was that when we eat *mole* we eat it because we want the sauce. The meat – whether it be chicken, turkey or pork – plays a secondary role. A complex sauce made with nuts, chilies and spices, *mole* defines Mexican cuisine. Although *mole* is often called chocolate sauce, only a very small percentage of *moles* include this ingredient. The confusion is somewhat understandable since the recipe for *mole poblano* (*mole* from the state of Puebla), the most widely known *mole* in the country, includes a small amount of chocolate. But most Mexicans would agree that when it comes to *mole*, Oaxaca is the place to go. It's known as 'The Land of Seven *Moles*'. See p434 for more on Oaxaca *moles*.

A Day of Eating: From Sunrise to Sunset & Beyond!

It's easy to find a place to eat in Mexico. From an early *antojito* at a small *puesto* (street or market stall) to a lavish late dinner at a fine restaurant, food seems to always be available. One thing you should know, though, is that mealtimes in Mexico are different from what you might be used to.

➡ **Desayuno** (breakfast) Usually served in restaurants and *cafeterías* from 8:30am to 11am, and it tends to be on the heavy side. Egg dishes are popular morning fare. *Huevos rancheros*, two fried eggs atop lightly fried tortillas with a layer of black beans and topped with a chunky tomato, onion and chili salsa, are widely served. If you are in the Yucatán region, you will find *huevos motuleños*, a similar preparation that also includes diced ham, peas and plantains. Many *cafeterías* offer a bread basket at breakfast with an array of *pan de dulce* (sweet breads). These bakery goods are great company for a cup of coffee or tea, and their names will draw a smile on your face: *bigotes* (mustaches), *conchas* (shells), *besos* (kisses) and *orejas* (ears) are only a few names for these treats.

➡ **Almuerzo** Those who have a light breakfast or skip it altogether can have an *almuerzo* (a mid-morning snack) or an *antojito* or other quick bite. *Taquerías* (places specializing in tacos), *torterías* (small establishments selling *tortas*) and *loncherías* (places that serve light meals) are good options for *almuerzo*.

➡ **Comida** This is the main meal in Mexico. It is usually served from 2pm to 4:30pm in homes, restaurants and cafes. Places called *fondas* are small, family-run eateries that serve *comida corrida*, an inexpensive fixed-price menu that includes soup, rice, a main dish, beverage and dessert. In many big cities it's common to see people enjoying long, relaxed business lunches or friend gatherings where food, conversation and drinks mingle for a couple of hours. Popular *comida* fares are soups, such as *sopa de fideo* (vermicelli noodles in a soupy tomato broth), or *sopa de frijol* (bean soup), while well-liked main dishes include *guisados* (stews) such as slowed-braised meats and vegetables in cooked *chipotle*, tomatillo or tomato salsas.

➡ **Cena** Frequently dinner is not served until 9pm and it is usually light when eaten at home. In restaurants, however, dinner is often a social gathering where eaters share a complete meal that can last until midnight.

➡ **And...** When people go to a bar, a club or a late movie, they often stop off for a quick taco before returning home. Many famous *taquerías* cater to hungry insomniacs and don't close until the wee hours. On Fridays and Saturdays so many customers visit these places that sometimes you have to wait for a table at 3am!

Top Mexican Cookbooks

Authentic Mexican, 20th Anniversary Edition: Regional Cooking from the Heart of Mexico by Rick Bayless

The Essential Cuisines of Mexico by Diana Kennedy

The Food and Life of Oaxaca: Traditional Recipes from Mexico's Heart by Zarela Martínez

THE NEW BREED OF CHEFS

The typical Mexican kitchen is very much a matriarchal place where the country's culinary traditions are preserved and practiced year in, year out. But it's mostly the male of the species who are garnering celebrity status from the new wave of creative contemporary restaurants that meld the traditional and the innovative in ingredients and recipes with a flair for presentation. Mexico City is the epicenter of this movement and Enrique Olvera of the famed Pujol is often considered the father of new Mexican cuisine. He has been mentor to other leading lights in the capital like Eduardo García of Maximo Bistrot Local. Ricardo Muñoz is famed for his reinventions of traditional recipes at Azul y Oro, while Mónica Patiño keeps the flag flying for women with her seafood creations at Taberna del León. Chefs like José Manuel Baños at Oaxaca's Pitiona, and Diego Hernández Baquedano at Corazón de Tierra in Baja California's Valle de Guadalupe wine region, are spreading the word to the regions.

VEGETARIANS & VEGANS

In Guadalajara's market there is a large sign for an eatery named Restaurante Vegetariano (Vegetarian Restaurant) listing some menu items underneath. It has salads, rice, beans, grilled chicken and fish in garlic sauce. This sign shows one of the problems for vegetarians and vegans in Mexico: the concept is not always fully understood. Many Mexicans think of a vegetarian as a person who doesn't eat meat, and by 'meat' they mean red meat. Many more have never even heard the word *veganista,* the Spanish term for vegan. The good news is that almost every city, large or small, has real vegetarian restaurants, and their popularity is increasing. Also, many traditional Mexican dishes are vegetarian: *ensalada de nopales* (cactus-leaf salad); quesadillas made with mushrooms, cheeses and even flowers like zucchini flowers; *chiles rellenos de queso* (cheese-stuffed poblano chilies); and *arroz a la mexicana* (Mexican-style rice). Be warned, however, that many dishes are prepared using chicken or beef broth, or some kind of animal fat, such as *manteca* (lard).

Have You Heard the Word 'Fiesta'?

Food and fiestas go hand-to-hand in Mexico. They can be national holidays, religious festivals, local fiestas or personal celebrations, but chances are you will get caught in one of them during your visit. During national holidays food's always present, but toasting with tequila is a prerequisite, especially during Día de la Independencia (September 16), which celebrates independence from Spain. The largest religious festivity is the Día de Nuestra Señora de Guadalupe (December 12), where *tamales, mole* and an array of *antojitos* are traditional fare. During Lent, meatless dishes such as *romeritos* (a wild plant that resembles rosemary served with dried shrimp, potatoes and *mole*) show up on most menus. On the Día de los Santos Reyes (Three Kings Day; January 6) we celebrate by eating *rosca de reyes,* a large oval sweetbread decorated with candied fruit. The *rosca* is served with corn *tamales* and hot chocolate. During Christmas, a traditional Mexican menu includes turkey, *bacalao* (dry codfish cooked with olives, capers, onions and tomatoes) and *romeritos*.

There is no celebration in Mexico with more mystique than the Día de Muertos (Day of the Dead; November 2). Its origins date back to pre-Hispanic times and it commemorates lost relatives and loved ones. By celebrating death we salute life and we do it the way we celebrate everything else, with food, drinks and music. An altar to the dead is set up in a house, or, as some families prefer, in the graveyard. It is decorated with bright *cempasúchil* (marigold) flowers, plates of *tamales,* sugar-shaped skulls and *pan de muerto* (bread of the dead; a loaf made with egg yolks, mezcal and dried fruits), and the favorite foods of the deceased are laid out so that they feel welcomed upon their return.

Under the Jaguar Sun by Italian writer Italo Calvino is a compelling account of a husband and wife discovering Mexico and its cuisine. The couple in the story becomes so enamored of the cuisine that their passion is transferred from the bedroom to the dining table.

¡Salud!

Tequila

In Mexico we love tequila. We drink it on large and small national holidays, at funerals and anniversaries, at casual lunches, and at dinner and in bars with friends. Legally, tequila is our champagne. All tequila has to come from the state of Jalisco and is protected with a Designation of Origin (DO) by the Consejo Regulador del Tequila (Tequila Regulatory Council). This organization ensures that all tequila sold throughout the world comes from this state in western Mexico. This arid area with highland soil creates the perfect conditions for the blue agave, the plant from which tequila is distilled, to grow. No tequila made in China (or elsewhere), *por favor*. We drink it because we are proud of its Mexican provenance, and because we really like its taste.

Taste is a key word when it comes to tequila. Tequila has become more and more sophisticated and today is considered a refined drink that rivals an imported single-malt whiskey or a quality cognac – not only in price but in its smooth, warm taste. Today's finest tequilas are meant to be enjoyed in a small glass, with pleasure, in tiny sips.

The process of making tequila starts by removing the *piña* (heart) of the blue agave plant. This *piña* is then steamed for up to 36 hours, a process that softens the fibers and releases the *aguamiel* (honey water). This liquid is funneled into large tanks where it is fermented. Fermentation determines whether the final product will be 100% agave or *mixto* (mixed). The highest-quality tequila is made from fermenting and then distilling only *aguamiel* mixed with some water. In tequilas *mixtos* the *aguamiel* is mixed with other sugars, usually cane sugar with water. When tequila is 100% agave it will say so on the label: otherwise, it is a *mixto*.

English sailors coined the term 'cocktail' upon discovering that their drinks in the Yucatán port of Campeche were stirred with the thin, dried roots of a plant called *cola de gallo*, which translates as 'cock's tail.'

The next step in the tequila-making process is to distill the *aguamiel* and store it in barrels for aging. The aging is important, especially for today's fancier tequilas, because it determines the color, taste, quality and price. Silver or *blanco* (white) is clear and is aged for no more than 60 days. Tequila *blanco* is used primarily for mixing and blends particularly well into fruit-based drinks. Tequila *reposado* (rested) is aged from two to nine months. It has a smooth taste and light gold color. Tequila *añejo* (old) is aged in wooden barrels for a minimum of 12 months. The best-quality *añejos* are aged up to four years. Tequila *añejo* has a velvety flavor and a deep dark color. These three kinds of tequilas are equally popular in Mexico, and it is entirely a matter of personal taste that determines which one to drink.

Mezcal

Mezcal is tequila's brother and it is currently experiencing a boom with people who believe tequila has gone too mainstream (and expensive!). Like tequila, mezcal is distilled from agave plants, but mezcal doesn't have to come from blue agave, or from the tequila-producing areas of Jalisco. In other words, all tequila is mezcal, but not all mezcal is tequila. Since mezcal can be made with any type of agave plant, it can also be produced throughout the country, where it's sometimes known by other names, such as *bacanora* in Sonora state or *sotol* in Chihuahua. For more on mezcal, see p437.

Pulque

If tequila and mezcal are brothers, then *pulque* would be the father of Mexican spirits. Two thousand years ago ancient Mexicans started to extract the juice of agave plants to produce a milky, slightly alcoholic drink that the Aztecs called *octli poliqhui*. When the Spanish arrived in Mexico they started to call the drink *pulque*. Even though pulque has a lower alcohol content than tequila or mezcal, it is much harder on the palate. Because it is not distilled, it retains an earthy, vegetal taste and has

CANTINAS

Cantinas are the traditional Mexican watering holes. Until not long ago, women, military personnel and children were not allowed in cantinas, and some cantinas still have a rusted sign stating this rule. Today everybody is allowed, although the more traditional establishments retain a macho edge. Beer, tequila and *cubas* (rum and coke) are served at square tables where patrons play dominos and watch *fútbol* (soccer) games on large TV screens. Cantinas are famous for serving *botanas* (appetizers) like *quesadillas de papa con guacamole* (potato quesadillas with guacamole) or snails in *chipotle* sauce.

a thick, foamy consistency that some people find unpleasant. In some places it is mixed with fruit juices such as mango or strawberry to make it more palatable. When pulque is mixed with juices it is called *curado*.

Beer

For some visitors, '*Una cerveza, por favor*' is their most commonly used Spanish phrase while in Mexico. This makes sense. Mexican *cerveza* is big, and it's a great match with, well, Mexican food! Most Mexican brands are light and quench beautifully the spiciness of a plate of enchiladas. Beers are also a great companion for the thousands of *fútbol* matches that we follow in this country with religious zeal.

Two major breweries dominate the Mexican market. Grupo Modelo, based in Mexico City and Guadalajara and now owned by Belgium-based AB InBev, makes 12 brands, among them Corona, Victoria, Modelo Especial, Pacífico, Montejo and Negra Modelo. Although Corona is one of the world's best-selling beers, beer aficionados regard Negra Modelo, a darker beer, as the brewery's jewel. In the industrial city of Monterrey, Cervecería Cuauhtémoc Moctezuma (now a subsidiary of Heineken International) produces Sol, Carta Blanca, Dos Equis, Superior, Tecate and Bohemia, among others. The original early-20th-century version of Dos Equis, the darker and fuller-bodied Dos Equis Ámbar, is enjoying a resurgence in popularity today. Another recent development in the Mexican beer world is microbrews *(cervezas artesanales)*, mostly ales, which are increasingly on offer in the better restaurants and bars. The array of Mexican beer allows for drinking them in many different environments. A day on the beach calls for a Corona, a Superior or a Pacífico. Victoria and Montejo are good matches for seafood; Modelo Especial and Carta Blanca go really well with meat; and a Bohemia or Negra Modelo would pair perfectly with a very good, decadent dinner.

Micheladas are prepared chilled beers ranging from simple drinks to complex cocktails. The basic *michelada* is a mix of the juice of one or two key limes in a previously chilled mug, a few ice cubes, a dash of salt and a Mexican cold beer. They are often served with a few drops of hot sauce, Worcestershire sauce and Maggi seasoning.

Wine

Now may be the right time to expand your Spanish vocabulary to include '*Una copa de vino, por favor*.' Although the wine industry is still much smaller than that of tequila or beer, Mexican wines are leaping forward at a great rate. Since the 1990s, challenged in part by the success of Californian, Chilean and Argentine wines, Mexican producers began yielding good wines in nine regions, from Querétaro to Sonora, with the best coming from the north of Baja California. The two larger wineries in Mexico, Pedro Domecq and LA Cetto, offer solid table wines and some premium labels like Chateau Domecq and Private Reserve Nebbiolo. 'Boutique wineries' with names like Monte Xanic, Casa de Piedra and Casa Valmar are also producing great wine in smaller quantities.

In Tenochtitlán (present-day Mexico City) chocolate was considered the 'drink of the gods' and it was called *tlaquetzalli* (precious thing) in the Náhuatl language. Chocolate was so valued by the Aztecs that the cacao bean, from which chocolate is derived, was also used as a form of currency.

Nonalcoholic Drinks

The great variety of fruits, plants and herbs that grow in this country are a perfect fit for the kind of nonalcoholic drinks Mexicans love. All over the country you will find classic *juguerías,* street stalls or small establishments selling all kinds of fresh-squeezed orange, tangerine, strawberry, papaya or carrot juices. These places also sell *licuados,* a Mexican version of a milkshake that normally includes banana, milk, honey and fruit. There are some incredibly creative combinations too, with ingredients such as *nopal* (cactus leaves), pineapple, lemon and orange, or vanilla, banana and avocado.

In *taquerías* and *fondas* you will find *aguas frescas,* juices diluted with water and sugar. Some of them resemble iced teas. In *agua de tamarindo* the tamarind pods are boiled and then mixed with sugar before being chilled, while *agua de jamaica* is made with dried hibiscus leaves. Others like *horchata* are made with melon seeds and/or rice.

Landscapes & Wildlife

One of the thrills of travel in Mexico is the incredible, ever-changing landscape. From the cactus-strewn northern deserts and the snowcapped volcanoes of central Mexico to the tropical forests and wildlife-rich lagoons of the south, there's rarely a dull moment for the eye. Nature lovers will revel in this country which, thanks to its location straddling temperate and tropical regions, is one of the most biologically diverse on earth.

In all its 1400km length, the Sierra Madre Occidental is crossed by only one railway and two paved roads: the Ferrocarril Chihuahua Pacífico (Copper Canyon Railway) from Los Mochis to Chihuahua; Hwy 16, from Hermosillo to Chihuahua; and the dramatic Espinazo del Diablo (Devil's Backbone) route, Hwy 40, from Mazatlán to Durango.

The Land

Nearly two million sq km in area, Mexico is the world's 14th-biggest country. With 10,000km of coastline and half its land above 1000m in elevation, the country has a spectacularly diverse and rugged topography. Almost anywhere you go, except the Yucatán Peninsula, there'll be a range of mountains in sight, close or distant.

Central Volcanic Belt

The Cordillera Neovolcánica, the spectacular volcanic belt running east-west across the middle of Mexico, includes the classic active cones of Popocatépetl (5452m), 70km southeast of Mexico City, and Volcán de Fuego de Colima (3820m), 30km north of Colima. Some 30 million people live within the area that could be directly affected should smoking 'Popo' erupt in a big way. Also in the volcanic belt, but dormant, are Mexico's highest peak, Pico de Orizaba (5611m), and the third-highest peak, Popo's 'sister' Iztaccíhuatl (5220m). Mexico's youngest volcano and the easiest to get to the top of, Paricutín (2800m) only popped up in 1943 near the Michoacán village of Angahuan.

The upland valleys between the volcanoes have always been among the most habitable areas of Mexico. It's here – the Valle de México (a 60km-wide basin at an elevation of 2200m) – that the country's capital, Mexico City, with its 20 million people, sits ringed by volcanic ranges.

Northern Plains & Sierras

A string of broad plateaus, the Altiplano Central, runs down the middle of the northern half of Mexico, fringed by two long mountain chains – the Sierra Madre Occidental in the west and Sierra Madre Oriental in the east. The *altiplano* and the two *sierras madre* end where they run into the Cordillera Neovolcánica.

The *altiplano* is crisscrossed by minor mountain ranges, and rises from an average elevation of about 1000m in the north to more than 2000m toward the center of the country. Most of the northern *altiplano* is occupied by the sparsely vegetated Desierto Chihuahuense (Chihuahuan Desert), which extends north into Texas and New Mexico. The landscape here is one of long-distance vistas across dusty brown plains to distant mountains, with eagles and vultures circling the skies. The southern *altiplano* is mostly rolling hills and broad valleys, and includes some of the best Mexican farming and ranching land in the area known as El Bajío, between the cities of Querétaro, Guanajuato and Morelia.

The rugged Sierra Madre Occidental is fissured by many spectacularly deep canyons, including the famous Barranca del Cobre (Copper Canyon) and its 1870m-deep continuation, the Barranca de Urique.

The Sierra Madre Oriental includes peaks as high as 3700m but has semitropical zones on its lower, eastern slopes.

Baja California

Baja California, one of the world's longest peninsulas, runs down the northwest coast, separated from 'mainland' Mexico by the Sea of Cortez (Golfo de California). Baja is 1300km of starkly beautiful deserts, plains and beaches with a mountainous spine that reaches up to 3100m at Picacho del Diablo in the Sierra San Pedro Mártir.

Coastal Plains

Coastal plains stretch down Mexico's Pacific coast and as far as the Tabasco lowlands on the Gulf coast. Both coasts are strung with lagoons, estuaries and wetlands, making them important wildlife habitats.

On the Pacific side a dry, wide plain stretches south from the US border almost to Tepic, in Nayarit state. As they continue south to the Guatemalan border, the Pacific lowlands narrow to a thin strip and become increasingly tropical. The Gulf coast plain, an extension of a similar plain in Texas, is crossed by many rivers flowing down from the Sierra Madre Oriental. In the northeast the plain is wide, with some good ranchland, but is semimarshy near the coast. It narrows as it nears Veracruz.

The South

Yet another rugged, complicated mountain chain, the Sierra Madre del Sur stretches across the states of Guerrero and Oaxaca, roughly paralleling the Cordillera Neovolcánica, from which it's divided by the broiling hot Río Balsas basin. The Sierra Madre del Sur ends at the low-lying Isthmus of Tehuantepec, Mexico's narrow 'waist' which is just 220km wide. The north side of the isthmus is a wide, hot, humid plain strewn with wetlands and meandering rivers.

In the southernmost state of Chiapas, the Pacific lowlands are backed by the Sierra Madre de Chiapas. Dormant Volcán Tacaná, whose 4110m cone rises on the Mexico–Guatemala border, is the westernmost of a string of volcanoes that stretch across Guatemala. Behind the Sierra Madre de Chiapas are the Río Grijalva basin and then the Chiapas highlands. Past these highlands, the land sinks to the lowlands of the Lacandón Jungle and the flat, low expanse of the Yucatán Peninsula.

Volcano Activity Check

Popocatépetl (www.cenapred.gob.mx, in Spanish, with webcam images)

Volcán de Fuego de Colima (www.ucol.mx/volcan)

SACRED WATERS

There are over 6000 cenotes (natural sinkholes) around the Yucatán Peninsula and debate continues as to why there are so many in the area. What is generally agreed is that cenotes are formed when the limestone bedrock forming the roof of an underground cavern collapses, exposing the groundwater underneath.

Cenotes are usually connected to the network of underground rivers that runs beneath the entire peninsula. An entire industry has grown around cenote diving and, alongside dinosaur and human remains, divers have discovered many valuable items from Maya times. It's believed they were cast into cenotes in rituals to appease the gods (most probably the rain god, Chac). There's also evidence suggesting that cenotes were used for human sacrifice. Caves had a special meaning as they were believed to be the gateway to Xibalbá, the underworld.

History and geology aside, cenotes also make for fantastic swimming holes. There's nothing like slipping into those cool, crystal-clear waters in the middle of the jungle on a steamy Yucatán day. However, note that cenotes close to large cities are often polluted.

Wildlife

From the whales, sea lions and giant cacti of Baja California to the big cats, howler monkeys and cloud forests of the southeast, Mexico's fauna and flora are exotic and fascinating. Getting out among it all is becoming steadily easier as growing numbers of local outfits offer trips to see birds, butterflies, whales, dolphins, sea turtles and much more.

Bird Books

Mexican Birds by Roger Tory Peterson and Edward L Chalif

Birds of Mexico and Central America by Ber van Perlo

A Guide to the Birds of Mexico and Northern Central America by Steve NG Howell and Sophie Webb

Those That Walk

The surviving tropical forests of the southeast still harbor five species of large cat (jaguar, puma, ocelot, jaguarundi and margay) in isolated pockets, plus spider and howler monkeys, tapirs, anteaters and some mean reptiles, including a few boa constrictors. Small jaguar populations are scattered as far north as the northern Sierra Madre Occidental, just 200km from the US border, and the Sierra Gorda in the Sierra Madre Oriental. You may well see howler monkeys – or at least hear their eerie growls – near the Maya ruins at Palenque and Yaxchilán.

In the north, urban growth, ranching and agriculture have pushed the larger wild beasts – such as the puma (mountain lion), wolf, bobcat, bighorn sheep, pronghorn, coyote and deer – into isolated, often mountainous pockets. Raccoons, armadillos and skunks are still fairly common – the last two in much of the rest of Mexico, too.

In all warm parts of Mexico you'll encounter two harmless, though sometimes surprising, reptiles: the iguana, a lizard that can grow a meter or so long and comes in many different colors; and the gecko, a tiny, usually green lizard that may shoot out from behind a curtain or cupboard when disturbed. Geckos might make you jump but they're good news – they eat mosquitoes.

Those That Swim

Baja California is famous for whale-watching in the early months of the year. Gray whales swim 10,000km from the Arctic to calve in its coastal waters. Between Baja and the mainland, the Sea of Cortez hosts more than a third of all the world's marine mammals, including sea lions, fur and elephant seals, and four species of whale. Humpback whales follow plankton-bearing currents right down the Pacific coast between December and March, and, like dolphins and sea turtles, are commonly seen on boat trips from coastal towns.

Mexico's coasts, from Baja to Chiapas and from the northeast to the Yucatán Peninsula, are among the world's chief nesting grounds for sea turtles. Seven of the world's eight species are found in Mexican waters. Some female turtles swim unbelievable distances (right across the Pacific Ocean in the case of some loggerhead turtles) to lay eggs on the beaches where they were born. Killing sea turtles or taking their eggs is illegal in Mexico, and there are more than 100 protected nesting beaches.

Dolphins play along the Pacific and Gulf coasts, while many coastal wetlands, especially in the south of the country, harbor crocodiles. Underwater life is richest of all on the coral reefs off the Yucatán Peninsula's Caribbean coast, where there's world-class diving and snorkeling. Near Isla Contoy, off the Yucatán's northeast tip, you can snorkel with whale sharks, the world's biggest fishes.

Spectacular Birds

Scarlet macaw (Las Guacamayas, Chiapas)

Resplendent quetzal (Reserva de la Biosfera El Triunfo, Chiapas)

California condor (Parque Nacional Sierra San Pedro Mártir, Baja California)

Those That Fly

All of coastal Mexico is a fantastic bird habitat, especially its estuaries, lagoons and islands. An estimated three billion migrating birds pass by or over the Yucatán Peninsula each year. Inland Mexico abounds with eagles, hawks and buzzards, and innumerable ducks and geese winter in the northern Sierra Madre Occidental. Tropical species such as trogons,

GREAT DIVERSITY

One of the top five most biologically diverse countries on earth, Mexico is home to over 1000 bird species, more than 500 mammals, over 1100 amphibians and reptiles, about 2000 butterflies and about 26,000 plants – for each of these groups, that's about 10% of the total number of species on the planet, on just 1.4% of the earth's land. The southern state of Chiapas alone, thanks largely to its Lacandón Jungle, has some 10,000 plant species, more than 600 bird species (twice as many as the USA) and 1200 species of butterflies.

hummingbirds, parrots and tanagers start to appear south of Tampico in the east of the country and from around Mazatlán in the west. The southeastern jungles and cloud forests are home to colorful macaws, toucans, guans and even a few quetzals. Yucatán has spectacular flamingo colonies at Celestún and Río Lagartos. Dozens of local operators around the country, especially along the coasts, offer bird-watching trips.

Mexico's most unforgettable insect marvel is Michoacán's Reserva Mariposa Monarca, where the trees and earth turn orange when millions of monarch butterflies arrive every winter.

Endangered Species

According to Mexico's National Biodiversity Commission (CONABIO) over 270 animal species are in in danger of disappearing from Mexico. Many of these exist nowhere else, including the jaguar, ocelot, northern tamandua (an anteater), pronghorn, Central American (Baird's) tapir, resplendent quetzal, scarlet macaw, Cozumel curassow, sea otter, Guadalupe fur seal, four types of parrot, and both spider and howler monkeys. The Margarita Island kangaroo rat and Hubbs freshwater snail may be less glamorous, but their disappearance will forever affect the other plants and animals around them. As they're endemic to Mexico, once gone from here, they're gone from the universe. A host of factors contribute to these creatures' endangered status, including deforestation and other habitat loss, species trafficking and illegal hunting.

The country's main tools for trying to save endangered species is its network of national parks and biosphere reserves, which covers 13% of the national territory, and a 'priority species' program which focuses on 52 emblematic and important creatures, including the jaguar, golden eagle, Mexican wolf, harbor porpoise and leatherback sea turtle. Government programs are supplemented by the work of local and international conservation groups, but progress is slowed down by large gaps in the protected areas network, patchy enforcement and limited funding.

Plants

Northern Mexico's deserts, though sparsely vegetated with cacti, agaves, yucca, scrub and short grasses, are the world's most biodiverse deserts. Most of the planet's 1000 or so cactus species are found in Mexico, including more than 400 in the Desierto Chihuahuense alone. Isolated Baja California has a rather specialized and diverse flora, from the 20m-high cardón (the world's tallest cactus) to the bizarre *boojum tree*, which looks like an inverted carrot with fluff at the top.

Mexico's great mountain chains have big expanses of pine (with half the world's pine species) and, at lower elevations, oak (135 types). In the southern half of the country, high-altitude pine forests are often covered in clouds, turning them into cloud forests with lush, damp vegetation, many colorful wildflowers, and epiphytes growing on tree branches.

More Books

Animals & Plants of the Ancient Maya by Victoria Schlesinger

Southern Mexico (Travellers' Wildlife Guides) by Les Beletsky

The natural vegetation of the low-lying areas of southeast Mexico is predominantly evergreen tropical forest (rainforest in parts). This is dense and diverse, with ferns, epiphytes, palms, tropical hardwoods such as mahogany, and fruit trees such as the mamey and the chicozapote (sapodilla), which yields chicle (natural chewing gum). Despite ongoing destruction, the Selva Lacandona (Lacandón Jungle) in Chiapas is Mexico's largest remaining tropical forest, containing a significant number of Chiapas' 10,000 plant species.

The Yucatán Peninsula changes from rainforest in the south to tropical dry forest and savanna in the north, with thorny bushes and small trees (including many acacias), resembling the drier parts of the Pacific coastal plain.

TOP PARKS & RESERVES

PARK/RESERVE	FEATURES	ACTIVITIES	BEST TIME TO VISIT
Parque Marino Nacional Bahía de Loreto (p718)	islands, shores & waters of the Sea of Cortez	snorkeling, kayaking, diving	year-round
Parque Nacional Archipiélago Espíritu Santo (p722)	waters around Espíritu Santo & neighboring islands in the Sea of Cortez	kayaking with whale sharks, snorkeling with sea lions, sailing	year-round
Parque Nacional Iztaccíhuatl-Popocatépetl (p165)	live & extinct volcanic giants on rim of Valle de México	hiking, climbing	Nov-Feb
Parque Nacional Lagunas de Chacahua (p465)	Oaxacan coastal lagoons; beach	boat trips, bird-watching, surfing	year-round
Parque Nacional Volcán Nevado de Colima (p606)	live & extinct volcanoes; pumas; coyotes; pine forests	volcano hiking	Dec-May
Reserva de la Biosfera Banco Chinchorro (p295)	largest coral atoll in northern hemisphere	diving, snorkeling	Dec-May
Reserva de la Biosfera Calakmul (p341)	rainforest with major Maya ruins	visiting ruins, wildlife-spotting	year-round
Reserva de la Biosfera El Vizcaíno (p712)	coastal lagoons where gray whales calve; deserts	whale-watching, hikes to ancient rock art	Dec-Apr
Reserva de la Biosfera Montes Azules (p396)	tropical jungle; lakes; rivers	jungle hikes, canoeing, rafting, bird-watching, boat trips, wildlife-watching	year-round
Reserva de la Biosfera Ría Celestún (p318)	estuary & mangroves with plentiful bird life, incl flamingos	bird-watching, boat trips	Mar-Sep
Reserva de la Biosfera Ría Lagartos (p331)	mangrove-lined estuary full of bird life, incl flamingoes	bird-, crocodile- and turtle-watching	Apr-Jul
Reserva de la Biosfera Sian Ka'an (p294)	Caribbean coastal jungle, wetlands & islands with incredibly diverse wildlife	bird-watching, snorkeling & nature tours, mostly by boat	year-round
Reserva de la Biosfera Sierra Gorda (p642)	transition zone from semi-desert to cloud forest	hiking, bird-watching, colonial missions	year-round
Reserva Mariposa Monarca (p616)	forests festooned with millions of monarch butterflies	butterfly observation, hiking	Nov-Mar

Parks & Reserves

Mexico has spectacular national parks and other protected areas – nearly 13% of its territory (254,000 sq km) is under some kind of federal environmental protection. Governments never have enough money for protection of these areas, but gradually, with some help from conservation organizations, more 'paper parks' are becoming real ones.

National Parks

Mexico's 67 *parques nacionales* (national parks) cover 14,453 sq km of territory. Many are tiny (smaller than 10 sq km), and around half of them were created in the 1930s for their archaeological, historical or recreational value rather than for ecological reasons. Several recently created parks protect coastal areas, offshore islands or coral reefs. Despite illegal logging, hunting and grazing, national parks have succeeded in protecting large tracts of forest, especially the central Mexico coniferous forests.

WWF's Wildfinder (worldwildlife.org/science/wildfinder) is a database of over 26,000 animal species, searchable by species or place. For each of 23 Mexican ecoregions, it will give a list of hundreds of species with their names in English and Latin, their threatened status, and often pictures.

Biosphere Reserves

Reservas de la biosfera (biosphere reserves) are based on the recognition that it is impracticable to put a complete stop to human exploitation of many ecologically important areas. Instead, these reserves encourage sustainable local economic activities within their territory. Today Mexico has 56 Unesco-protected and/or national biosphere reserves, covering some 142,000 sq km. They protect some of the country's most beautiful and biologically fascinating areas, focusing on whole ecosystems with biodiversity. Sustainable, community-based tourism is an important source of support for several of them, and successful visitor programs are in place in reserves like Calakmul, Sierra Gorda, Montes Azules, Mariposa Monarca, La Encrucijada and Sian Ka'an.

Ramsar Sites

Over 89,000 sq km of Mexican landmass and coastal waters are protected as 138 Wetlands of International Importance, known as Ramsar sites for the Iranian town where the 1971 Convention on Wetlands of International Importance was signed. Nearly all designated in the last decade, they include whale-calving grounds, turtle-nesting beaches, coral reefs, and coastal lagoons and mangrove forests that are of crucial importance for birds and many marine creatures.

Environmental Issues

Mexico achieved the status of a global standard-bearer on climate change in 2012 when it became only the second country (after the UK) to enshrine carbon-emission commitments into law. The climate-change law, which passed through Mexico's congress with all-party support, commits the country – currently the world's 11th biggest carbon emitter – to be producing 35% of its electricity from renewable energy by 2024, and to cut its carbon emissions by 50% from previously expected levels by 2050. Subsidies on fossil fuels for electricity and transportation – currently worth over US$22 billion a year by some estimates – will be phased out. Self-interest doubtless played a part in what was one of several environment-friendly initiatives taken during the presidency of Felipe Calderón (2006–12). While Mexico is the world's sixth-biggest exporter of crude oil, it has to import nearly half of its gasoline because it is short on refineries. Replacing such costly imports with homegrown renewable energy makes much economic sense. With its limitless supplies of sunshine Mexico has plenty of potential for solar power, and already 13% of its electricity come from hydro sources and 3% from wind and geothermal. Unfortunately, the law still has hurdles to jump if it is to be successfully implemented, as much of its funding is slated to come from the Green Climate Fund, established at the 2010 UN Climate Change Conference in Cancún, Mexico. Intended to support sustainable-energy initiatives in the developing world, the Green Climate Fund still has question marks over exactly who will be providing its money.

The Nature Conservancy (www.nature.org), Conservation International (www.conservation.org) and WWF (wwf.panda.org; www.wwf.org.mx) all provide lots of information on the Mexican environment, including on their programs in the country.

Water & Forests

When Enrique Peña Nieto became president at the end of 2012 he focused on accelerating economic growth and reinvigorating Mexico's crude oil exports, at the expense of environmental initiatives. His six-year national development plan, announced in 2013, did at least prioritize the crucial issue of water sustainability – a key question in a nation where the south has 70% of the water, but the north and center have 75% of the people, and around 10% of the population still lacks access to clean drinking water and drainage systems. A new water law was expected to focus on ensuring water supplies to urban areas (especially Mexico City) and economically productive sectors, modernizing irrigation technology and increasing desalination efforts on the Pacific coast.

One area where Mexico has already achieved some success is forest conservation. Mexico has lost about three-quarters of the forests it had in pre-Hispanic times, as all types of forest from cool pine-clad highlands to tropical jungles have been cleared for grazing, logging and farming. Today only about 17% of the land is covered in primary forest, though a further 16% has regenerated or replanted forest. The good news is that deforestation rates have declined from about 3500 sq km a year in the 1990s to under 1600 sq km a year today.

Environmental awareness has certainly made great progress in Mexico, not only in government but also at a local level. The country has no large-scale environmental movement, but it does have plenty of smaller organizations working on local issues. Probably the most influential national group is **Pronatura** (www.pronatura.org.mx), which works chiefly on climate-change projects, protecting priority species, water issues and the conservation of ecosystems.

Urban Problems

Mexico Sustainable (www.mexico-sustainable.com) has some useful information on sustainable tourism projects and programs around the country.

Mexico City is a megalopolis surrounded by a ring of mountains that traps polluted air in the city. In an effort to limit pollution levels, many vehicles are banned from the roads on a rotational basis one day a week. The capital consumes over half of Mexico's electricity and pumps a quarter of its water needs from outside the Valle de México. These problems of water supply, sewage treatment, overcrowding and traffic pollution are mirrored on a smaller scale in most of Mexico's faster-growing cities.

Tourism, a key sector of Mexico's economy, can bring its own set of environmental problems when development is on a large scale. After several years of environmental opposition to the planned large-scale Cabo Cortés tourism development in Baja California, President Calderón canceled plans for the project in 2012 because its developers had failed to show that it would be environmentally sustainable. This delighted campaigners who had argued strongly that the project would seriously damage the Parque Marino Nacional Cabo Pulmo, part of a Unesco World Heritage site.

On the Caribbean coast's Riviera Maya, organizations such as **Centro Ecológico Akumal** (www.ceakumal.org) and **Salvamento Akumal de Vida Ecológica** (SAVE; saverivieramaya.org) campaign to limit damage from reckless tourism development to coral reefs, turtle-nesting beaches, mangrove systems and even the water in the area's famed cenotes (limestone sinkholes). A slowly growing number of hotels and resorts in the region are adopting green policies.

Survival Guide

Directory A–Z

Accommodations

Accommodations in Mexico range from hammocks and huts to hotels of every imaginable standard, including superluxury resorts. In popular destinations at busy times, it's best to reserve a room in advance or go early in the day to secure a room.

Price Categories

Many midrange and top-end establishments in tourist destinations raise their rates during short 'extra' seasons such as the Semana Santa (Easter), Christmas–New Year's holiday periods or local festival times, and cut them during low seasons. Budget accommodations are more likely to keep the same rates all year.

Budget ($) Most cities popular with international budget travelers now have at least one travelers' hostel, often several, typically charging M$150 to M$200 for a dorm bed. Every Mexican town also has its cheap hotels. There are clean, friendly, secure ones, and there are dark, dirty ones where you may not feel your belongings are safe. Adequate rooms with private bathroom are available for under M$400 in most of the country. Budget accommodations also include campgrounds, hammocks, *cabañas* (cabins) and guesthouses. Recommended accommodations in this range will be simple and without frills but generally clean.

Midrange ($$) Mexico specializes in good midrange accommodations. The more you pay, the more facilities, comfort and style the place is likely to have, but in some places even M$500 can get you an attractive room in a friendly small hotel. Many midrange places have a restaurant and a bar, almost all have wi-fi and quite a lot have swimming pools. Many of the country's most appealing and memorable lodgings are in the midrange bracket, including many old mansions and inns turned into hotels. These can be wonderfully atmospheric, with fountains gurgling in flower-decked, stone-pillared courtyards or verdant gardens. You'll also find some B&Bs, apartments, bungalows and more comfortable *cabañas* in the midrange bracket.

Top end ($$$) Accommodations in this category offer the expected levels of luxury – pools, gyms, bars, restaurants, design, professional service – at prices that are sometimes agreeably modest, and sometimes not. They range in style from converted haciendas or small, chic boutique hotels to expansive modern resorts and spas. If you like to stay in luxury but also enjoy saving some money, look for deals on hotel websites or phone up and ask how to obtain the best price. Good news for families and other small groups: many hotels have rooms for three, four or five people that cost not much more than a double.

BOOK YOUR STAY ONLINE

For more accommodations reviews by Lonely Planet authors, check out http://lonelyplanet.com/mexico/hotels. You'll find independent reviews, as well as recommendations on the best places to stay. Best of all, you can book online.

Symbols & Abbreviations

In this guide 'single' (abbreviated to 's') means a room for one person, and 'double' ('d') means a room for two people. Mexicans sometimes use the phrase *cuarto sencillo* (single room) to mean a room with one bed, which may be a *cama matrimonial* (double bed); a *cuarto doble* often means a room with two beds, which may both be *camas matrimoniales*.

The air-con icon (❄) and nonsmoking icon (⊖) mean that the establishment offers at least some air-conditioned and nonsmoking rooms, respectively.

Taxes

The price of accommodations in Mexico is subject to two taxes:

IVA (value-added tax; 16%)

ISH (lodging tax; 2% or 3% depending on the state)

Many of the less expensive establishments only charge you these taxes if you require a receipt, and they quote room rates accordingly (ie not including taxes). Generally, though, IVA and ISH are included in quoted prices. Prices given in this guide are those you are most likely to be charged at each place.

SLEEPING PRICE RANGES

The following price ranges refer to accommodations for two people in high season, including any taxes charged.

$ less than M$460

$$ M$460–1150

$$$ more than M$1150

Types of Accommodations

Apartments In some resort towns you can find tourist apartments with fully equipped kitchens. They can be good value for three or four people, especially if you're staying more than a few days. The internet, local ads and agencies, and tourist offices are good sources of information on these.

B&Bs Mexican B&Bs are usually small, comfortable, midrange or top-end guesthouses, often beautifully designed and offering friendly, personal attention. Many of them are effectively boutique hotels.

Cabañas *Cabañas* are cabins or huts (of wood, brick, adobe or stone), often with a palm-thatched roof, and are most often found at beach destinations. The most basic have dirt floors and nothing inside but a bed, and you provide the padlock for the door. At the other extreme, some *cabañas* are positively deluxe, with electric lights, mosquito nets, large comfy beds, bathrooms, hammock-strung decks and even air-con and a kitchen – though they'll usually still have an agreeably rustic, close-to-nature ambience. The most expensive *cabañas* are on the Caribbean, where some luxury units can cost over M$2000.

Campgrounds & Trailer Parks Most organized campgrounds are actually trailer parks set up for RVs (recreational vehicles, campers) and trailers (caravans) that are also open to tent campers at lower rates. Some are basic, others quite luxurious. Some restaurants and guesthouses in beach spots or country areas will let you pitch a tent on their patch for around M$50 per person.

Hammocks Hammock space is available in many of the more low-key beach spots. A hammock can be a very comfortable, not to mention cheap, place to sleep in hot areas (keep mosquito repel-

SAFETY GUIDELINES FOR DIVING

Before embarking on a scuba-diving, skin-diving or snorkeling trip, carefully consider the following points to ensure a safe and enjoyable experience:

- Possess a current diving-certification card from a recognized scuba-diving instruction agency (if scuba diving).
- Be sure you are healthy and feel comfortable diving.
- If you don't have your own equipment, ask to see the dive shop's before you commit. And make sure you feel comfortable with your dive master: after all, it's your life.
- Obtain reliable information about physical and environmental conditions at the dive site from a reputable local dive operation, and ask how local trained divers deal with these considerations.
- Be aware of local laws, regulations and etiquette about marine life and the environment.
- Dive only at sites within your level of experience; if available, engage the services of a competent, professionally trained dive instructor or dive master.
- Ensure that your dive shop has up-to-date certification from **PADI** (www.padi.com), **NAUI** (www.naui.org) or the internationally recognized Mexican diving organization **FMAS** (www.fmas.com.mx).
- Know the locations of the nearest decompression chambers and the local emergency telephone numbers.
- Avoid diving less than 18 hours before a high-altitude flight.

lent handy). Some places have hammocks to rent for anywhere between M$40 and M$100. It's easy to buy hammocks in Mexico, especially in Oaxaca and Chiapas states and on the Yucatán Peninsula.

Hostels There are traveler hostels in most places where budget travelers congregate. They provide dormitory accommodations typically from M$150 to M$200 per person, plus communal kitchens, bathrooms, living space, nearly always wi-fi, and often private double rooms too for a bit more than the price of two dorm beds. Some of the best hostels have pools, bars, gardens, sundecks and even design and charm. Cleanliness and security do vary, but popular hostels are great places for meeting fellow travelers. International hostel websites such as **Hostelworld** (www.hostelworld.com) provide plentiful listings and online reservations.

Posadas & Casas de Huéspedes Posadas are inns, meaning anything from basic budget hotels to tastefully designed, small, midrange places. A *casa de huéspedes* is a guesthouse, a home converted into simple, inexpensive guest lodgings, usually family run and often with a relaxed, friendly atmosphere.

Activities

Further information about specific activities can be found in the If You Like... chapter (p25).

If you're planning to fly to Mexico with a surfboard, check with the airline first: most of them charge US$50 or more (each way) to carry boards, and some won't carry them at all to some destinations or at some times of year.

Resources

AMTAVE (www.amtave.org) The Mexican Adventure Tourism & Ecotourism Association, with over 90 member organizations.

WannaSurf (www.wannasurf.com) The Mexico section gives data on over 300 surf spots.

Planeta.com (www.planeta.com) Good resource on active and responsible tourism.

Mexonline.com (www.mexonline.com) Includes listings of activities providers.

Customs Regulations

You may bring the following into Mexico duty-free:

- two cameras
- three cell phones or other portable wireless network devices
- one laptop, notebook or similar
- three surfboards
- two musical instruments
- medicine for personal use, with prescription in the case of psychotropic drugs.

See www.aduanas.gob.mx for further details.

The normal routine at customs when you enter Mexico is to complete a declaration form (which lists duty-free allowances), and then place it in a machine. If the machine shows a green light, you pass without inspection. If a red light shows, your baggage will be searched.

Discount Cards

For reduced-price air tickets at student- and youth-oriented travel agencies, the following cards are widely recognized:

- ISIC student card
- IYTC (under 26 years) card
- ITIC card for teachers

Reduced prices for students and seniors on Mexican buses and at museums and archaeological sites are usually only for those with Mexican residence or education credentials, but the ISIC, IYTC and ITIC will sometimes get you a reduction. The ISIC is the most widely recognized.

Electricity

Embassies & Consulates

If you're having trouble locating your nearest Mexican embassy or consulate, check the website of Mexico's foreign ministry, the **Secretaría de Relaciones Exteriores** (www.sre.gob.mx), which has links to the websites of all Mexican diplomatic missions, including the 50 consulates in US cities. Some of these sites have useful information on visas and similar matters.

Embassy websites usually link to consulates' websites (where they exist) and often have much other useful information about Mexico.

Australian Embassy (☎55-1101-2200; www.mexico.embassy.gov.au; Rubén Darío 55, Mexico City)

Belizean Embassy (☎55-5520-1274; www.mfa.gov.bz; Bernardo de Gálvez 215, Lomas de Chapultepec, Mexico City); Consulate (☎983-285-35-11; Génova 369, Colonia Benito Juárez, Chetumal)

Canadian Embassy (www.canadainternational.gc.ca/mexico-mexique) Embassy (☎55-5724-7900; Schiller 529, Polanco, Mexico City); Consulate (☎744-484-13-05; Pasaje Diana, La Costera 121, L-16, Fraccionamiento Magallanes, Acapulco); Consulate (☎624-142-43-33; Local 82, Plaza San Lucas, Carretera Transpeninsular Km 0.5, Colonia El Tezal, Cabo San Lucas); Consulate (☎998-883-33-60; Oficina E7, Centro Empresarial, Blvd Kukulcán Km 12, Zona Hotelera, Cancún); Consulate (☎33-3671-4740; Piso 8, Torre Pacífico, World Trade Center, Av Otero 1249, Colonia Rinconada del Bosque, Guadalajara); Consulate (☎669-913-73-20; Office 41, Centro Comercial La Marina Business Life, Blvd Marina Mazatlán 2302, Colonia Marina Mazatlán, Mazatlán); Consulate (☎81-8378-0240; Suite 404, Torre Gómez Morín 955, Av Gómez Morín 955, San Pedro Garza García, Monterrey); Consulate (☎951-513-37-77; Local 11B, Pino Suárez 700, Oaxaca); Consulate (☎322-293-00-98; Local Sub F, Plaza Península, Blvd Medina Ascencio 2485, Zona Hotelera Norte, Puerto Vallarta); Consulate (☎664-684-04-61; Condominio del Parque, Gedovius 10411-101, Zona Río, Tijuana)

French Embassy (☎55-9171-9700; www.ambafrance-mx.org; Campos Elíseos 339, Polanco, Mexico City); Consulate (☎33-3616-5516; López Mateos Norte 484, Colonia Ladrón de Guevara, Guadalajara); Consulate (☎999-930-15-00; Calle 60, No 385, Mérida); Consulate (☎55-9171-9700; Lafontaine 32, Polanco, Mexico City); Consulate; (☎951-515-21-84; Planta Baja, 3a Privada de J López Alavez 5, San Felipe del Agua, Oaxaca) Consulate (☎cell phone 984-1123472; Local C6, Plaza Paraíso, 10 Av, Playa del Carmen)

German Embassy (☎55-5283-2200; www.mexiko.diplo.de; Horacio 1506, Los Morales, Mexico City); Honorary Consulate (☎998-884-15-98; Punta Conoco 36, SM24, Cancún); Honorary Consulate (☎33-3810-2146; Calle 7, No 319, Colonia Ferrocarril, Guadalajara); Honorary Consulate (☎999-944-32-52; Calle 49 No 212, Mérida)

Guatemalan Embassy (☎55-5520-6680; embajada guatemalamx.mex.tl; Av Explanada 1025, Lomas de Chapultepec, Mexico City); Consulate (☎963-110-68-16; 1a Calle Sur Pte 35, Comitán); Consulate (☎962-626-12-52; cnr Calle Central Pte & 14a Av Sur, Tapachula)

Irish Embassy (☎55-5520-5803; www.irishembassy.com.mx; Cerrada Blvd Ávila Camacho 76-3, Lomas de Chapultepec, Mexico City); Honorary Consulate (☎998-112-54-36; Av Coba 15, MZ 8, SM 22, Cancún)

Italian Embassy (☎55-5596-3655; www.ambcitta delmessico.esteri.it; Paseo de las Palmas 1994, Lomas de Chapultepec, Mexico City); Consulate (☎33-3616-1700; 1st fl, Av López Mateos Norte 790, Fraccionamiento Ladrón de Guevara, Guadalajara); Honorary Consulate (☎984-803-47-14; Av 10 btwn Calles 12 & 14, Playa del Carmen)

Netherlands Embassy (☎55-1105-6550; mexico.nlambassade.org; 7th fl, Edificio Calakmul, Av Vasco de Quiroga 3000, Santa Fe, Mexico City); Consulate (☎998-884-86-72; Pabellón Caribe, Av Nichupté, Lote 22, MZ 2, SM 19, Cancún); Consulate (☎33-1655-0269; Condominio Santa Anita, Paseo del Bosque 203, Tlajomulco de Zúñiga, Guadalajara); Consulate (☎999-924-31-22; Calle 64 No 418, Mérida)

New Zealand Embassy (☎55-5283-9460; www.nzembassy.com/mexico; Level 4, Jaime Balmes 8, Los Morales, Mexico City)

Spanish Embassy (☎55-5282-2982; www.maec.es; Galileo 114, Polanco, Mexico City); Consulate (☎998-848-99-18; Edificio Oasis, cnr Blvds Kukulcán & Cenzontle, Zona Hotelera, Cancún); Consulate (☎33-3630-0450; Mezzanine Izquierdo, Torre Sterling, Quevedo 117, Colonia Arcos Vallarta, Guadalajara)

UK Embassy (ukinmexico.fco.gov.uk) Embassy (☎55-1670-3200; Río Lerma 71, Colonia Cuauhtémoc, Mexico City); Consulate (☎998-881-01-00; Royal Sands, Blvd Kukulcán Km 13.5, Zona Hotelera, Cancún); Consulate (☎55-1670-3200; Río Usumacinta 30, Mexico City); Consulate (☎664-686-53-20; Blvd Salinas 1500, Fraccionamiento Aviación, Tijuana)

US Embassy (☎55-5080-2000; mexico.usembassy.gov; Paseo de la Reforma 305, Mexico City); Consulate (☎998-883-02-72; Despacho 301, Torre La Europea, Blvd Kukulcán Km 13, Zona Hotelera, Cancún); Consulate (☎656-227-30-00; Paseo de la Victoria 3650, Fraccionamiento Partido Senecú, Ciudad Juárez); Consulate (☎33-3268-2100; Progreso 175, Colonia Americana, Guadalajara); Consulate (☎669-916-58-89; Hotel Playa Mazatlán, Playa Gaviotas 202, Zona Dorada, Mazatlán); Consulate (☎999-942-5700; Calle 60 No 338K, btwn Calles 29 & 31, Mérida); Consulate (☎81-8047-3100; Av Constitución 411 Pte, Monterrey); Consulate (☎951-514-30-54; Office 20, Plaza Santo Domingo, Alcalá 407, Oaxaca); Consulate (☎322-222-00-69; Paradise Plaza, Paseo de los Cocoteros 85 Sur, Nuevo Vallarta); Consulate (☎624-143-35-66; Local B221, Tiendas de Palmilla,

EATING PRICE RANGES

The following price ranges refer to prices of typical main dishes, including value-added tax (IVA).

$ less than M$80

$$ M$80–160

$$$ more than M$160

Carretera Transpeninsular Km 27.5, San José del Cabo); Consulate (☎415-152-23-57; Locales 4 & 5, Plaza La Luciérnaga, Libramiento Zavala 165, Colonia La Luciérnaga, San Miguel de Allende); Consulate (☎664-977-20-00; Paseo de las Culturas s/n, Mesa de Otay, Tijuana)

Food

For information on eating in Mexico, see p42 and p828.

There is a 16% value-added tax (IVA) on restaurant prices, and this is nearly always included in the menu prices.

Gay & Lesbian Travelers

Mexico is increasingly broad-minded about sexuality, although the conservative influence of the Catholic Church remains strong. Gays and lesbians don't generally adopt a high profile, but rarely attract open discrimination or violence. The legalization of gay marriages in Mexico City has energized gay life in the capital, which has a hip, international bar and club scene. Puerto Vallarta is the gay beach capital of Mexico. There are also lively scenes in places like Guadalajara, Veracruz, Cancún, Mazatlán, Mérida and Acapulco. Gay marriages or civil unions are now also legal in the states of Colima, Quintana Roo and Coahuila.

Gay Mexico (www.gaymexico.com.mx) has a clickable map linking to gay guides for many cities. **Gay Mexico Map** (www.gaymexicomap.com) also has listings of accommodations, bars and clubs in many cities, and **GayCities** (www.gaycities.com) is good on Mexico City, Guadalajara, Puerto Vallarta and Cancún. Also well worth checking out are the **International Gay & Lesbian Travel Association** (www.iglta.org), with worldwide information on travel providers in the gay sector, and **Out Traveler** (www.outtraveler.com).

Health

Travelers to Mexico need to guard chiefly against food- and mosquito-borne diseases. Besides getting the proper vaccinations, carry a good insect repellent and exercise care in what you eat and drink.

Private hospitals generally provide better care than public ones, but are more expensive: the best are in Mexico City. Your country's embassy or consulates in Mexico and the national tourism secretariat **Sectur** (☎078, 800-903-92-00, 55-5250-0151, in the US 800-482-9832; www.visitmexico.com) can usually give information on local hospitals, and some consulates provide it on their websites. You should have travel insurance that covers the cost of air evacuation to another country should you develop a life-threatening condition.

Recommended Vaccinations

Make sure all routine vaccinations are up to date and check whether all vaccines are suitable for children and pregnant women.

Hepatitis A All travelers (except children less than one year old).

Hepatitis B Long-term travelers in close contact with local population (requires three doses over a six-month period).

Rabies For travelers who may have contact with animals and may not have access to medical care.

Typhoid All travelers.

Internet Resources

MD Travel Health (www.mdtravelhealth.com) Complete travel health recommendations for every country.

Centers for Disease Control & Prevention (wwwnc.cdc.gov/travel) Comprehensive official US website.

Health Hazards in Mexico

Altitude Sickness May develop in travelers who ascend rapidly to altitudes greater than 2500m. Symptoms may include headaches, nausea, vomiting, dizziness, malaise, insomnia and loss of appetite. Severe cases can lead to death. To lessen the chance of altitude sickness, ascend gradually to higher altitudes, avoid overexertion, eat light meals and avoid alcohol. People showing any symptoms of altitude sickness should not ascend higher until the symptoms have cleared. If the symptoms become worse or if someone shows signs of fluid in the lungs (high-altitude pulmonary edema) or swelling of the brain (high-altitude cerebral edema), such as trouble breathing or mental confusion, descend immediately to a lower altitude. Descent of 500m to 1000m is generally adequate except in cases of cerebral edema.

Dengue Fever A viral infection transmitted by aedes mosquitoes, which usually bite during the day. Usually causes flu-like symptoms. There is no vaccine and no treatment except analgesics.

Malaria Transmitted by mosquito bites, usually between dusk and dawn. The main symptom is high spiking fevers. Malaria pills are recommended when visiting Chiapas or rural areas in Oaxaca, Sinaloa, Nayarit and parts of Sonora, Chihuahua and Durango states. The first-choice malaria pill is chloroquine. Protecting yourself against mosquito bites is just as important as taking malaria pills.

Snake & Scorpion Bites In the event of a venomous snake bite or scorpion bite, keep the bitten area immobilized, and move the victim immediately to the nearest medical facility. For scorpion stings, immediately apply ice or cold packs.

Precautions

Mosquito Bites Wear long sleeves, long pants, hats and shoes. Don't sleep with windows open unless there is a screen. Use a good insect repellent, preferably one containing DEET, but don't use DEET-containing compounds on children under age two. If sleeping outdoors or in accommodations that allow entry of mosquitoes, use a mosquito coil, or a bed net treated with permethrin.

Sun Stay out of the midday sun, wear sunglasses and a wide-brimmed hat, and apply sunscreen with SPF 15 or higher. Drink plenty of fluids and avoid strenuous exercise when the temperature is high.

Water Tap water in Mexico is often not safe to drink. Purified water in plastic bottles is sold everywhere and is also available from large dispensers in some accommodations, which allows you to refill bottles. The most effective means of water purification is vigorous boiling for one minute (three minutes at altitudes over 2000m). Another option is a **SteriPen** (www.steripen.com), which kills bacteria and viruses with ultraviolet light. Pregnant women and those with a history of thyroid disease should not drink iodinated water.

Insurance

A travel-insurance policy to cover theft, loss and medical problems is a very good idea. Some policies specifically exclude dangerous activities such as scuba diving, motorcycling and even trekking.

You may prefer a policy that pays doctors or hospitals directly rather than you having to pay on the spot and claim later. If you have to claim later, ensure that you keep all documentation. Check that the policy covers ambulances or an emergency flight home.

Worldwide travel insurance is available at www.lonelyplanet.com/travel_services. You can buy, extend and claim online anytime – even if you're already on the road.

Internet Access

Wi-fi *(internet inalámbrico)* is common in Mexican accommodations and also available in some cafes, bars, airports and city plazas; in this guide the wi-fi icon (wi-fi icon) means that wi-fi is available in at least some part of the premises. The internet icon (@) means that the establishment has internet-enabled computers for guests to use. These services may or may not be free of charge.

Mexico also has thousands of internet cafes, typically charging M$10 to M$20 per hour. Many of them are equipped with webcams, headphones, Skype and so on.

Language Courses

Mexico has many professional, experienced Spanish schools, offering everything from short courses for beginners with empasis on the spoken language, to longer courses for serious students of the language. Many schools are located in Mexico's most attractive and interesting cities, such as Oaxaca, Guanajuato, San Cristóbal de las Casas, Mérida, Cuernavaca, Morelia and Guadalajara. They present a great opportunity to get an inside experience of Mexican life, with plenty of extracurricular activities like dance, cooking, music, excursions and volunteering usually available.

Some courses are geared mainly to college students wanting credits for courses back home, but other schools focus more on travelers or independent language students. Some Mexican universities have special departments with tailor-made courses for foreigners (usually lasting between one month and one semester). Private schools typically offer shorter courses, from a few days to three months, with more flexible schedules and, often, smaller classes.

123 Teach Me (www.123teachme.com) offers listings of over 70 language schools in Mexico.

The **National Registration Center for Study Abroad** (www.nrcsa.com), **CIEE** (www.ciee.org), **AmeriSpan** (www.amerispan.com) and **Spanish Abroad** (spanishabroad.com) are among US-based organizations offering a range of study programs in Mexico.

Costs

- A typical rate for group classes in private schools is US$10 per hour.
- Most schools offer a choice of living options including homestays and apartments, and their own student accommodations. Homestays are often the cheapest option (typically around US$150 per week for your own room in a family's home and two meals a day).
- All up, 25 hours of classes per week, plus homestay accommodation and meals, averages around US$400.
- Some schools charge extra for enrolment/registration and/or materials.

Legal Matters

Mexican Law

Mexican law is based on the Roman and Napoleonic

codes, presuming an accused person guilty until proven innocent.

A law passed in 2009 determined that possession of small amounts of certain drugs for personal use – including marijuana (up to 5g), cocaine (500mg), heroin (50mg) and methamphetamine (40mg) – would not incur legal proceedings against first-time offenders. But people found in possession of small amounts may still have to appear before a prosecutor to determine whether they are for personal use. The easiest way to avoid any problems related to these drugs is certainly not to use or carry them.

It's against Mexican law to take any firearm or ammunition into the country (even unintentionally).

Useful warnings on Mexican law are found on the website of the **US State Department** (travel.state.gov).

See p857 for information on the legal aspects of road accidents.

Getting Legal Help

If a foreigner is arrested in Mexico, the Mexican authorities are supposed (according to international law) to promptly contact the person's consulate or embassy if asked to do so. They may not. If they do, consular officials can tell you your rights, provide lists of lawyers, monitor your case, try to make sure you are treated humanely, and notify your relatives or friends – but they can't get you out of jail. By Mexican law, the longest a person can be detained without a specific accusation after arrest is 48 hours (though official arrest may not take place until after a period of initial questioning).

Tourist offices in Mexico, especially those run by state governments, can often help you with legal problems such as complaints and reporting crimes or lost articles. The national tourism ministry, **Sectur** (☎078, 55-5250-0151, US 800-482-9832; www.sectur.gob.mx), has a toll-free number offering 24-hour telephone advice.

If you are the victim of a crime, your embassy or consulate, or Sectur or state tourist offices, can give advice. In some cases, there may be little to gain by going to the police, unless you need a statement to present to your insurance company. If you go to the police, take your passport and tourist permit, if you still have them. If you just want to report a theft for insurance purposes, say you want to '*poner un acta de un robo*' (make a record of a robbery). This should make it clear that you merely want a piece of paper, and you should get it without too much trouble.

Maps

Nelles, ITM and Michelin all produce good country maps of Mexico that are suitable for travel planning. ITM also publishes good larger-scale maps of many Mexican regions.

Tourist offices in Mexico provide free city, town and regional maps of varying quality. Bookstores and newsstands sell commercially published ones, including Guía Roji's recommended all-Mexico road atlas, *Por Las Carreteras de México*.

Inegi (Instituto Nacional de Estadística, Geografía e Informática; www.inegi.org.mx) Sells large-scale 1:50,000 and 1:250,000 topographical maps at its Centros de Información in every Mexican state capital (detailed on the website), subject to availability.

Money

Mexico's currency is the peso, usually denoted by the 'M$' sign. Any prices quoted in US dollars will normally be written 'US$5' or '5 USD' to avoid misunderstanding. The peso is divided into 100 centavos.

The most convenient form of money in Mexico is a major international credit or debit card – preferably two cards. With these you can obtain cash easily from ATMs. Visa, MasterCard and American Express are accepted for payment by most airlines and car-rental companies, plus many upper midrange and top-end hotels, and some restaurants and stores. Occasionally there's a surcharge for paying by card, or a discount for paying cash. Buying by credit card normally gives you a similar exchange rate to ATM withdrawals. In both cases you'll normally have to pay your card issuer a foreign-exchange transaction fee of around 2.5%.

As a backup to cards, it's a good idea to take a little cash – best in US dollars, which are easily the most exchangeable foreign currency in Mexico, though euros and Canadian dollars are also widely exchangeable. In tourist resorts and many Mexican cities along the US border, you can make some purchases in US dollars, though the exchange rate will probably not be in your favor.

ATMs

ATMs (*cajero automático* or *caja permanente*) are plentiful. You can use major credit cards and some bank cards, such as those on the Maestro, Cirrus and Plus systems, to withdraw pesos from ATMs. The exchange rate you'll get is normally better than the 'tourist rate' for currency exchange at banks and *casas de cambio* (exchange offices), though that advantage may be negated by the M$25 to M$70 fee the ATM company charges as well as any foreign-transaction fees that may be levied by your card company.

For maximum security, use ATMs during daylight hours and in secure indoor locations, not those in standalone booths or on the street.

Banks & Casas de Cambio

You can exchange cash at *casas de cambio* and some banks. *Casas de cambio* exist in just about every large town and in many smaller ones. They are quick and often open evenings or weekends, and usually offer similar exchange rates to banks. Banks go through more time-consuming procedures, and usually have shorter exchange hours (typically 9am to 4pm Monday to Friday and 9am to 1pm Saturday).

Taxes

Mexico's *impuesto al valor agregado* (IVA; value-added tax) is 16%. By law the tax must be included in virtually any price quoted to you, and should not be added afterward. Notices in stores and on restaurant menus often state '*IVA incluido*.'

Hotel rooms are also subject to the *impuesto sobre hospedaje* (ISH; lodging tax) of 2% or 3%, depending on which Mexican state they're in.

Tipping & Bargaining

Tourism and hospitality workers often depend on tips to supplement miserable basic wages. Normal tips:

Restaurants About 10% to 15%, unless service is included in the check.

Hotels From 5% to 10% of your room costs for the staff, especially if you stay a few days.

Taxis No tip expected unless some special, extra service is provided.

Airport & hotel porters From M$50 to M$100.

Gas-station & car-parking attendants Tip M$5 or M$10.

Room rates are pretty firm, though it can be worth asking if any discounts are available, especially if it's low season or you are going to stay a few nights. In markets a little haggling is expected. You should also haggle with drivers of unmetered taxis.

PRACTICALITIES

- Mexico uses the metric system for weights and measures.
- Mexican law does not allow smoking in indoor public spaces, except in specially designated smoking areas. It also requires at least 75% of a hotel's rooms to be nonsmoking. Enforcement, however, is very patchy.
- Mexico's only English-language daily newspaper (actually, Monday to Friday) is the *News* (www.thenews.com.mx). Distribution is very patchy outside Mexico City. The best and most independent-minded Spanish-language national newspapers include *Reforma* and the left-wing *La Jornada*.

Opening Hours

Typical hours are as follows, though variations are manifold:

Banks 9am to 4pm Monday to Friday, 9am to 1pm Saturday; banks in smaller towns may close earlier and not open Saturday.

Bars 1pm to midnight

Cafes 8am to 10pm

Restaurants 9am to 11pm

Stores/Shops 9am to 8pm Monday to Saturday; in the south, some shops close 2pm to 4pm. Supermarkets and department stores usually open from 9am or 10am to 10pm every day.

Photography

Normal courtesies apply: it's polite to ask before taking photos of people. Some indigenous people can be especially sensitive about this.

Lonely Planet's *Travel Photography* is a comprehensive, jargon-free guide to getting the best shots from your travels.

Special permits are required for any photography or filming with 'special or professional equipment' (which includes all tripods but not amateur video cameras) at any of the 187 archaeological sites or 129 museums administered by INAH, the National Archaeology and History Institute. Permits cost M$4464 per day for still photography and M$8927 per day for movie or video filming, and must be applied for at least two weeks in advance. You can apply by email: details are given in Spanish at www.tramites.inah.gob.mx.

Post

Mail to the US or Canada typically takes between four and 10 days to arrive. Mail to Europe averages one to two weeks.If you're sending a package internationally from Mexico, be prepared to open it for customs inspection at the post office; it's better to take packing materials with you, or not seal it until you get there. For assured and speedy delivery, you can use one of the more expensive international courier services, such as **UPS** (www.ups.com), **FedEx** (www.fedex.com) or Mexico's **Estafeta** (☎800-903-3500; www.estafeta.com). A 1kg package typically costs around M$500 to M$600 to the US or Canada, or M$750 to Europe.

Public Holidays

On official national holidays, banks, post offices, government offices and many other offices and shops close throughout Mexico.

Año Nuevo (New Year's Day) January 1

Día de la Constitución (Constitution Day) February 5 (observed on first Monday of February)

Día de Nacimiento de Benito Juárez (anniversary of Benito Juárez's birth) March 21 (observed on third Monday of March)

Día del Trabajo (Labor Day) May 1

Día de la Independencia (Independence Day) September 16

Día de la Revolución (Revolution Day) November 20 (observed on third Monday of November)

Día de Navidad (Christmas Day) December 25

National holidays that fall on Saturday or Sunday are often switched to the nearest Friday or Monday.

In addition, many offices and businesses close on the following optional holidays:

Día de los Santos Reyes (Three Kings' Day, Epiphany) January 6

Día de la Bandera (Day of the National Flag) February 24

Viernes Santo (Good Friday) Two days before Easter Sunday; March or April

Cinco de Mayo (anniversary of Mexico's victory over the French at Puebla) May 5

Día de la Madre (Mother's Day) May 10

Día de la Raza (commemoration of Columbus' arrival in the New World) October 12

Día de Muertos (Day of the Dead) November 2

Día de Nuestra Señora de Guadalupe (Day of Our Lady of Guadalupe) December 12

Safe Travel

Mexico's drugs war is undeniably horrific and frightening. However, the violence is almost exclusively an internal matter between the drug gangs and people involved with them, or between the gangs and the Mexican security forces. Tourists have rarely been victims.

Mexico's main visitor destinations are by and large pretty safe places, and your main security precautions should just be those you would take in any unfamiliar place. Enjoy yourself along the coasts, but beware of undertows and riptides on ocean beaches, and don't leave your belongings unattended while you swim.

See p858 and p860 for some safety tips for car and bus travel.

Theft & Robbery

Pocket-picking and bag-snatching are risks on crowded buses and metro trains, at bus stops, bus terminals, airports, markets and in packed streets and plazas, especially in large cities. Pickpockets often work in teams, crowding their victims and trying to distract them; for example, by grabbing hold of your bag or camera while an accomplice picks your pocket.

Mugging is less common but more serious: these robbers may force you to remove your money belt, watch, rings etc. Do not resist, as resistance may be met with violence, and assailants may be armed.

The following precautions will minimize risks:

- Avoid places where there are few other people, such as empty streets, empty metro carriages at night, little-used pedestrian underpasses and isolated beaches.
- Use taxis instead of walking in potentially dodgy areas. In Mexico City, make sure you take the right kind of cab (see p138).
- Be alert to the people around you.
- Leave valuables in a safe at your accommodations unless you have immediate need of them. If no safe is available, divide valuables into different stashes secreted in your room or a locker.
- Carry just enough cash for your immediate needs in a pocket. Avoid having bulging pockets. If you do have to carry valuables, use a money belt, shoulder wallet or pouch *underneath* your clothing.
- Don't keep cash, credit cards, purses, cameras and electronic gadgets in open view any longer than necessary. At ticket counters in bus terminals and airports, keep your bag between your feet.
- Go easy on alcohol – drunkenness makes you an easier victim.
- Use ATMs in secure indoor locations, preferably during daylight.

If you do become a crime victim, report the incident to a tourist office, the police or your country's nearest consulate, which should be able to offer useful advice.

GOVERNMENT TRAVEL ADVICE

These government websites have information on potential danger areas and general safety tips:

Australia (www.smartraveller.gov.au)

Canada (travel.gc.ca)

Germany (www.auswaertiges-amt.de)

Netherlands (www.rijksoverheid.nl)

New Zealand (www.safetravel.govt.nz)

UK (www.fco.gov.uk)

USA (travel.state.gov)

THE DRUGS WAR

By most estimates, since 2007 in Mexico an average of about 10,000 people a year have died in violence involving the gangs who traffick some US$13 billion worth of illegal drugs to US drug users each year. The great majority of the violence happens in a relatively small number of areas.

➡ Hot spots come and go as intergang turf wars flare, but cities along the US border (from Tijuana to Matamoros), and areas south from the border as far as Culiacán, Durango, Torreón, Monterrey and Tampico have always been among the worst hit.

➡ Further south, the states of Michoacán and Guerrero have also seen some of the highest organized-crime-related murder rates.

➡ Within each of these regions, violence occurs mostly in certain specific areas.

➡ Two of Mexico's most visited regions, the Yucatán Peninsula and Baja California Sur, have seen minimal drug-related violence. It's a similar story in other attractive areas such as the states of Oaxaca, Chiapas, Guanajuato, Querétaro and Puebla.

➡ Major coastal tourism destinations generally see little violence, although Acapulco suffered a temporary spike in 2011–12.

You can obtain information on drug-violence blackspots from government foreign affairs departments and from websites of embassies and consulates in Mexico. But the drugs war is a shifting phenomenon, so it's a good idea to keep an eye on the media and ask local advice as you travel. Two well-informed websites are **InSight Crime** (www.insightcrime.org) and **Justice in Mexico Project** (justiceinmexico.org). See p741 for a summary of the situation in the north of the country.

Kidnapping and extortion are other prevalent crimes practiced by the drug gangs and others, including 'virtual kidnapping' in which the villains attempt to convince victims by telephone that they are under threat and must pay ransoms. Again, tourists are rarely victims.

Telephone

Cell (Mobile) Phones & Smartphones

Mexico's main cell-phone *(teléfono celular)* companies include **Telcel** (www.telcel.com), **Movistar** (www.movistar.com.mx) and **IUSACell** (www.iusacell.com.mx). Telcel has the most widespread coverage (almost everywhere there are people) and dominates the market with ubiquitous sales outlets. Movistar can be cheaper but its coverage can be poor outside cities. Government moves to bring more competition into the telecommunication industry may see newcomers like Virgin Mobile enter the field (and, hopefully, may result in lower prices for cell-phone users).

➡ Roaming in Mexico with your own phone from home is possible if you have a GSM or 3G phone, but can be extremely expensive unless you organize a travel plan with your phone company. **Roaming Zone** (www.roamingzone.com) is a useful source on roaming arrangements.

➡ Much cheaper is to put a Mexican SIM card ('chip') into your phone, but your phone needs to be unlocked for international use. If it isn't already unlocked, many Mexican cell-phone stores, often with names like 'Hospital del Celular,' can unlock it for M$200 to M$300.

➡ SIMs are available from countless phone stores, often for M$50 or less. A bewildering array of plans and offers is available for prepaid smartphone usage (www.mexicoguru.com/articles/phones-in-mexico.php has some useful tips). To take one example, a Movistar SIM used by one of our authors while researching this guide cost M$300 per month with unlimited calls, texts, Facebook, Twitter and email access and 250MB of downloads.

➡ For around M$300 you can buy a new, basic, no-frills Mexican cell phone with a chip and some call credit included. New smartphones start around M$1500, plus M$300 to M$500 a month for calling and data credit. Sales staff are likely to give you more help in setting everything up if you buy a phone rather than just a chip. Make sure you take your passport for ID with you when you go to buy a chip or phone; you may also have to provide a local address and postcode.

➡ You can buy new credit at many places including convenience stores, newsstands, pharmacies, groceries or department stores.

CALLING CODES & COSTS

Like Mexican landlines, every Mexican SIM card has an area code. The area code and the phone's number total 10 digits.

- From cell phone to cell phone, just dial the 10-digit number.
- From cell phone to landline, dial the landline's area code and number (also a total of 10 digits).
- From landline to cell phone, dial 044 before the 10 digits if the cell phone's area code is the same as the area code you are dialing from, or 045 if the cell phone has a different area code.
- From another country to a Mexican cell phone, dial your international access code, then the Mexican country code (52), then 1, then the 10-digit number.

Credit of M$100 on a basic cell phone normally enables you to make about 20 minutes of calls within the card's area code, but once you are outside that area code calls generally cost more. At the time of buying your chip you can choose your area code. So if you're in Mexico City for a few days and buying a chip there, but will be staying two months in Palenque, it works out better to ask for a Palenque area code. There are also plans available where you pay a (slightly higher) flat rate per minute wherever you are in Mexico.

Collect Calls

A *llamada por cobrar* (collect call) can cost the receiving party much more than if they call you, so you may prefer to arrange for the other party to call you. You can make collect calls from public card phones without a card. Call an operator on ☎020 for domestic calls, or ☎090 for international calls.

Some call offices and hotels will make collect calls for you, but they usually charge for the service.

Landlines

Mexican landlines *(teléfonos fijos)* have two- or three-digit area codes, which are listed under city and town headings throughout this guide.

- From a landline to another landline in the same town, just dial the local number (seven or eight digits).
- From a landline to a landline in a different Mexican town, dial the long-distance prefix 01, then the area code, then the local number.
- To make an international call, dial the international prefix 00, then the country code (1 for the US or Canada, 44 for the UK etc), area code and local number.
- To call a Mexican landline from another country, dial your international access code, then the Mexico country code 52, then the area code and number.

Operator & Toll-Free Numbers

Domestic operator ☎020

Emergency ☎066, ☎088

International operator ☎090

Mexican toll-free numbers 800 followed by seven digits; always require the 01 long-distance prefix

Public Card Phones

These are common in towns and cities, and you'll usually find some at airports and bus terminals. The most abundant are those of the country's main phone company, **Telmex** (www.telmex.com). To use a Telmex card phone you need a phone card known as a *tarjeta Ladatel*, sold at kiosks and shops everywhere in denominations of M$30, M$50 and M$100. You insert the card into the phone while you make the call. Calls cost M$3 for unlimited time for local calls (M$1.50 per minute to local cell phones); M$2.50 per minute long distance within Mexico (M$3 to cells); M$5 per minute to the US (except Alaska and Hawaii), Canada and Central America; and M$10 per minute anywhere else.

SMARTPHONE TIPS

- Turn off mobile data in the phone's settings to avoid background apps swallowing up your phone credit in minutes (you can still use wi-fi if you do this).
- Before signing up for a data package, check that your smartphone itself is compatible with data systems in Mexico: some travelers with non-American iPhones, for example, have found that they could not get data even with a Mexican SIM installed.
- Instant-messaging apps such as Whatsapp and Viber are widely used in Mexico. When adding a phone contact, be sure to add +521 before the Mexican cell-phone number, or else the contact may not show in the apps.

Time

Time Zones

Hora del Centro The same as CST (US Central Time; GMT minus six hours in winter, and GMT minus five hours during daylight saving), this time zone applies to most of Mexico.

Hora de las Montañas The same as MST (US Mountain Time; GMT minus seven hours in winter, GMT minus six hours during daylight saving), this time zone applies to five northern and western states in Mexico – Chihuahua, Nayarit, Sinaloa, Sonora and Baja California Sur.

Hora del Pacífico The same as PST (US Pacific Time; GMT minus eight hours in winter, GMT minus seven hours during daylight saving), this time zone applies to Baja California (Norte).

Daylight Saving

Daylight saving time (*horario de verano;* summer time) in nearly all of Mexico runs from the first Sunday in April to the last Sunday in October. Clocks go forward one hour in April and back one hour in October. Exceptions to the general rule:

- The northwestern state of Sonora ignores daylight saving, so remains on MST all year.
- Daylight saving is also ignored by a few remote rural zones elsewhere.
- Ten cities on or near the US border – Ciudad Acuña, Ciudad Anáhuac, Ciudad Juárez, Matamoros, Mexicali, Nuevo Laredo, Ojinaga, Piedras Negras, Reynosa and Tijuana – change their clocks on the second Sunday in March and the first Sunday in November to synchronize with US daylight-saving periods.

Tourist Information

Just about every town of interest to tourists in Mexico has a state or municipal tourist office. These are generally helpful with maps, brochures and questions, and usually some staff members speak English.

You can call the Mexico City office of the national tourism secretariat **Sectur** (☎078, 800-903-92-00, 55-5250-0151, in the US 800-482-9832; www.visitmexico.com) 24 hours a day, seven days a week, for information or help in English or Spanish. You'll find links to tourism websites of each Mexican state at www.sectur.gob.mx.

Travelers with Disabilities

A gradually growing number of hotels, restaurants, public buildings and archaeological sites provide wheelchair access, but sidewalks with wheelchair ramps are still uncommon. Mobility is easiest in major tourist resorts and the more expensive hotels. Bus transportation can be difficult; flying or taking a taxi is easier. The absence of formal facilities is partly compensated by Mexicans' helpful attitudes, and special arrangements are gladly improvised. The following websites have useful information for disabled travelers:

Access-able Travel Source (www.access-able.com)

Mobility International USA (www.miusa.org)

MossRehab ResourceNet (www.mossresourcenet.org)

Visas & Tourist Permits

Every tourist must have a Mexican-government tourist permit, easily obtained on arrival. Some nationalities also need visas. Citizens of the US, Canada, EU countries, Argentina, Australia, Brazil, Israel, Japan, New Zealand, Norway and Switzerland are among those who do not need visas to enter Mexico as tourists. Chinese, Indians, Russians and South Africans are among those who do need a visa. Mexican visas are not required for people of any nationality who hold a valid visa for the USA.

If the purpose of your visit is to work (even as a volunteer), report, study or participate in humanitarian aid or human-rights observation, you may well need a visa whatever your nationality. Visa procedures might take a few weeks and you may be required to apply in your country of residence or citizenship.

The Mexican regulations sometimes change: it's wise to confirm them with a Mexican embassy or consulate. The websites of some Mexican consulates, including the **London consulate** (consulmex.sre.gob.mx/reinounido) and **Washington consulate** (consulmex.sre.gob.mx/washington), give useful information on visas and similar matters. The rules are also summarized on the website of Mexico's **Instituto Nacional de Migración** (INM, National Migration Institute; www.inm.gob.mx).

Non-US citizens passing (even in transit) through the US on the way to or from Mexico should check well in advance on the US's complicated visa rules. Consult a US consulate or the **US State Department** (travel.state.gov) or **Customs and Border Protection** (www.cbp.gov) websites.

Tourist Permit & Fee

The Mexican tourist permit (tourist card; officially the *Forma migratoria múltiple* or FMM) is a brief paper document that you must fill out and get stamped by Mexican immigration when you enter Mexico, and keep till you leave. It's available at official border crossings, international airports and ports, and often from airlines, travel agencies and Mexican consulates. At land borders you won't usually be given one automatically – you have to ask for it.

The length of your permitted stay in Mexico is written on the card by the immigration officer. Normally they will put down the maximum (180 days), but they may sometimes put a lower number (even as little as 15 or 30 days) unless you tell them specifically what you need.

The fee for the tourist permit, called the DNR (*Derecho para no remunerado;* fee for visitors without permission for paid activities) is M$295, but it's free for people entering by land who stay less than seven days. If you enter Mexico by air, the fee is included in your airfare. If you enter Mexico by land, you must pay the fee at a bank in Mexico at any time before you reenter the border zone to leave Mexico (or before you check in at an airport to fly out of Mexico). The border zone is the territory between the border itself and the INM's control points on highways leading into the Mexican interior (usually 20km to 30km from the border).

Most Mexican border posts have on-the-spot bank offices where you can pay the DNR fee immediately on arrival in Mexico. Your tourist permit will be stamped to prove that you have paid.

Look after your tourist permit because you need to hand it in when leaving the country. You can be fined for not having it.

Tourist permits (and fees) are not necessary for visits shorter than 72 hours within the border zones.

EXTENSIONS & LOST PERMITS

If the number of days given on your tourist permit is fewer than 180, its validity may be extended, one or more times, up to this maximum. To get a permit extended, you have to apply to the INM, which has offices in many towns and cities: they're listed on the **INM website** (www.inm.gob.mx): click 'Contact Us' then select 'Oficinas y Horarios' from the 'Contacto' box). The procedure costs around M$300 and should only take half an hour or so. You'll need your passport, tourist permit, photocopies of them and, at some offices, evidence of 'sufficient funds' (a major credit card is usually OK). Most INM offices will not extend a permit until a few days before it is due to expire.

If you lose your permit, contact your nearest tourist office, which should be able to give you an official note to take to your local INM office, which will issue a replacement for about M$300.

Volunteering

A great way to engage with Mexican communities and contribute something other than tourist dollars is to do some volunteer work. Many organizations can use your services for periods from a few hours to a year or more. Work ranges from protecting sea turtles to helping disadvantaged children. Some organizations are looking for people with relevant experience and/or Spanish-language skills; others can use almost any willing hand.

Many language schools offer part-time local volunteering opportunities to complement the classes you take.

Volunteer Directories

Go Abroad (www.goabroad.com)

Go Overseas (www.gooverseas.com)

Go Voluntouring (www.govoluntouring.com)

Idealist.org (www.idealist.org)

The Mexico Report (themexicoreport.com/non-profits-in-mexico)

Transitions Abroad (www.transitionsabroad.com)

Mexico-Based Programs

SOCIAL PROGRAMS

Casa de los Amigos (www.casadelosamigos.org) Mexico City-based, with volunteer programs to assist refugees and migrants (see p103).

Centro de Esperanza Infantil (www.oaxacastreetchildrengrassroots.org) Center for street kids in Oaxaca (see p426).

Fundación En Vía (www.envia.org) Oaxaca-based nonprofit organization providing microfinance loans to help village women develop small businesses (see p429).

Junax (www.junax.org.mx) Offers information and lodging in San Cristóbal de las Casas for people wanting to volunteer with indigenous communities in Chiapas; Spanish-language skills needed.

Misión México (www.lovelifehope.com) A children's refuge and surf school in Tapachula (see p407).

Piña Palmera (www.pinapalmera.org) Work with physically and intellectually disabled people at Zipolite on the Oaxaca coast (see p470).

ENVIRONMENTAL PROGRAMS

Centro Ecológico Akumal (www.ceakumal.org) Environmental work including turtle protection (see p285).

Grupo Ecologista Vida Milenaria (www.vidamilenaria.org.mx) Excellent turtle project at Tecolutla (see p242).

Natatè (www.natate.org) Turtle conservation and other projects in Chiapas and elsewhere (see p284).

Organizations Based Outside Mexico

Global Vision International (www.gviusa.com)

Los Médicos Voladores (www.flyingdocs.org)

Projects Abroad (www.projects-abroad.org)

Women Travelers

Women usually have a great time in Mexico whether traveling with companions or solo. Gender equality has come a long way, and Mexicans are generally a very polite people, but lone women may still be subject to some whistles, loud comments and attempts to chat them up.

Don't put yourself in peril by doing things that Mexican women would not do, such as drinking alone in a cantina, hitchhiking, walking alone through empty streets at night, or going alone to isolated places. Keep a clear head.

On the streets of cities and towns and local transportation you'll notice that women cover up and don't display too much leg, midriff or even arm. This also makes it easier to keep valuables out of sight.

Transportation

GETTING THERE & AWAY

As well as flying in, you can enter Mexico by car or bus from the USA, Guatemala or Belize. Flights, tours and rail tickets can be booked online at www.lonelyplanet.com/bookings.

Entering the Country

US citizens traveling by land or sea can enter Mexico and return to the US with a passport card, but if traveling by air will need a passport. Citizens of other countries need their passport to enter Mexico. Some nationalities also need a visa (see p853).

Land

Belize

Frequent buses run between Chetumal in Mexico and and Belize City (M$180, three to four hours), via the Belizean towns of Corozal (M$30, one hour) and Orange Walk (M$35 to M$50, 2¼ hours). For more information see p300.

Guatemala

The road borders at Ciudad Cuauhtémoc/La Mesilla, Ciudad Hidalgo/Ciudad Tecún Umán and Talismán/El Carmen are all linked to Guatemala City, and nearby cities within Guatemala and Mexico, by plentiful buses and/or combis.

These companies run a few daily buses the whole way between Tapachula, Chiapas and Guatemala City (five to six hours):

Línea Dorada (www.lineadorada.com.gt; fare M$220)

Tica Bus (www.ticabus.com; fare M$247)

Trans Galgos Inter (www.transgalgosinter.com.gt; fare M$305)

Between Chetumal and Flores, Línea Dorada runs one daily bus each way (M$430 or Q250, eight hours), via Belize City.

For the Río Usumacinta route between Palenque, Mexico, and Flores, there are vans between Palenque and Frontera Corozal (M$100, 2½ to three hours), from where it's a 40-minute boat trip to Bethel, Guatemala (M$75 to M$400 per person depending on numbers). From Bethel hourly 2nd-class buses run to Flores (4½ hours) until 4pm.

Travel agencies in Palenque and Flores offer bus/boat/bus packages between the two places for M$350 to M$450, but if you're traveling this route it's well worth taking the time to visit the outstanding Maya ruins at Yaxchilán, near Frontera Corozal.

Another possible route between Mexico and Flores is via the border at El Ceibo, near Tenosique, Tabasco. Vans,

CLIMATE CHANGE & TRAVEL

Every form of transport that relies on carbon-based fuel generates CO_2, the main cause of human-induced climate change. Modern travel is dependent on airplanes, which might use less fuel per kilometer per person than most cars but travel much greater distances. The altitude at which aircraft emit gases (including CO_2) and particles also contributes to their climate change impact. Many websites offer 'carbon calculators' that allow people to estimate the carbon emissions generated by their journey and, for those who wish to do so, to offset the impact of the greenhouse gases emitted with contributions to portfolios of climate-friendly initiatives throughout the world. Lonely Planet offsets the carbon footprint of all staff and author travel.

buses and taxis run between Tenosique and El Ceibo, and there are vans between the border and Flores.

USA

There are over 40 official crossing points on the US–Mexico border. Some Mexican cities on the border and elsewhere in northern Mexico are affected by drug-gang violence, so it's advisable to check travel warnings (p850) and the media if you are thinking of crossing this border. See the boxed texts on p745 and p741 for more information. The road between Matamoros and Tampico was certainly one to avoid at the time of writing.

BUS

Cross-border bus services link many US and Mexican cities. On most trips you will transfer between a US and a Mexican bus on the US or Mexican side of the border, although you can usually buy a ticket right through to your final destination thanks to affiliations between different bus lines.

Autobuses Americanos (www.autobusesamericanos.com.mx) From Chicago and cities across the southern half of the USA to northeast, central north and central Mexico.

Greyhound (☎558-79-95, 760-357-18-95; www.greyhound.com; Calexico 123 East 1st St; Mexicali 1244 Centro Cívico-Comercial; ⏰5:30am-11:30pm) From California, Arizona and Texas to border cities, with onward transfers into northwest Mexico.

Ómnibus Mexicanos (www.omnibusmexicanos.com.mx) From Texas and the southeastern USA to northeast, central north and central Mexico.

Transporte Supremo (www.transportesupremo.com) Shuttle-van service between Phoenix and Puerto Peñasco.

Tufesa (www.tufesa.com.mx) From many cities in the US southwest and California to northwest Mexico, Mazatlán and Guadalajara.

Turimex Internacional (www.gruposenda.com) From Chicago, Texas and southeastern USA to northeast, central north and central Mexico.

Most routes are covered by several buses daily.

You can (often as quickly) go to the border on one bus (or train – see www.amtrak.com), cross it on foot or by local bus, then catch an onward bus on the other side. Greyhound serves many US border cities.

CAR & MOTORCYCLE

The rules for taking a vehicle into Mexico change from time to time. You can check with a Mexican consulate, **Sanborn's** (www.sanbornsinsurance.com) or, in the US, or the free **Mexican tourist information number** (☎800-482-9832).

Driving into Mexico is most useful for travelers who have plenty of time; like independence; have surfboards, diving equipment or other cumbersome luggage; and/or will be traveling with at least one companion. Drivers should know at least a little Spanish and have basic mechanical knowledge. A sedan with a trunk (boot) provides safer storage than a station wagon or hatchback.

Mexican mechanics are resourceful, but it pays to take as many spare parts as you can manage (spare fuel filters are very useful). Tires (including spare), shock absorbers and suspension should be in good condition. For security, have something to immobilize the steering wheel, and consider getting a kill switch installed.

Motorcycling in Mexico is not for the fainthearted. Roads and traffic can be rough, and parts and mechanics hard to come by. The parts you'll most easily find will be for Kawasaki, Honda and Suzuki bikes.

VEHICLE PERMIT

You will need a *permiso de importación temporal de vehículo* (temporary vehicle import permit), costing US$51 (including IVA), if you want to take a vehicle into Mexico beyond the border zone. This extends 20km to 30km into Mexico along the US frontier and up to 70km from the Guatemalan and Belizean frontiers. The only exceptions to this are the Baja California peninsula, where the permit is not needed, and Sonora state as far south as Guaymas, which offers a cheaper, simplified procedure (p745) – but you will need a permit if you embark a vehicle at Pichilingue (La Paz) in Baja California, on a ferry to 'mainland' Mexico.

The vehicle permits are issued by offices at border crossings or (in some cases) at posts a few kilometers into Mexico, and also at Ensenada port and Pichilingue ferry terminal in Baja California. Details of all these locations, including their opening hours (which can be shorter than those of the border crossings themselves), are given on the

SOME CROSS-BORDER BUS SERVICES

ROUTE	FARE (US$)	DURATION (HR)
Dallas–Monterrey	77	12
Houston–Mexico City	140	25
LA–Guadalajara	240	36
Phoenix–Guaymas	64	10

website of **Banjército** (www.banjercito.com.mx), the bank that deals with vehicle-import procedures – click on 'Red de Módulos IITV.' US and Canadian residents can also apply for the permit online at www.banjercito.com.mx ('Application for Temporary Import Permit for Vehicles'), in which case it will be delivered to you by courier. The online procedure also involves obtaining electronic pre-authorization for your Mexican tourist permit.

The person importing the vehicle will need to carry the original and one or two photocopies of each of the following documents, which as a rule must all be in his/her own name (except that you can bring in your spouse's, parent's or child's vehicle if you can show a marriage or birth certificate proving your relationship):

➡ tourist permit (FMM): at the border go to *migración* before you process your vehicle permit

➡ certificate of title or registration certificate for the vehicle (note that you should have both of these if you plan to drive through Mexico into either Guatemala or Belize)

➡ a Visa or MasterCard credit or debit card issued outside Mexico, or a cash deposit of between US$200 and US$400 (depending on how old the car is); your card details or deposit serve as a guarantee that you'll take the car out of Mexico before your FMM expires

➡ passport or US passport card

➡ if the vehicle is not fully paid for, a credit contract, or invoice letter not more than three months old, from the financing institution

➡ for a leased or rented vehicle, the contract, in the name of the person importing the vehicle

➡ for a company car, proof of employment by the company as well as proof of the company's ownership of the vehicle.

With the permit you will be given a hologram sticker for you to display on your windshield.

When you leave Mexico, you must have the import permit canceled by the Mexican authorities. An official may do this as you enter the border zone, usually 20km to 30km before the border itself. If not, you'll have to find the right official at the border crossing. If you leave Mexico without having the permit canceled, the authorities may assume you've left the vehicle in the country illegally and decide to keep your deposit, charge a fine to your credit card, or deny you permission to bring a vehicle into the country next time.

INSURANCE

It is essential to have Mexican liability insurance. If you are involved in an accident in Mexico, you can be jailed and have your vehicle impounded while responsibility is assessed. If you are to blame for an accident causing injury or death, you may be detained until you guarantee restitution to the victims and payment of any fines. Adequate Mexican insurance coverage is the only real protection: it is regarded as a guarantee that restitution will be paid.

Mexican law recognizes only Mexican motor insurance *(seguro)*, so a US or Canadian policy, even if it provides coverage, is not acceptable to Mexican officialdom. You can buy Mexican motor insurance online through the long-established **Sanborn's** (www.sanbornsinsurance.com) and other companies. Mexican insurance is also sold in border towns in the US and at some border points. At the busiest border crossings there are insurance offices open 24 hours a day. Some deals are better than others.

Short-term insurance is about US$15 a day for full coverage on a car worth under US$10,000; for periods longer than two weeks, it's often cheaper to get a semi-annual or annual policy. Liability-only insurance costs around half the full coverage cost.

Sea

Daily boats sail between Chetumal and San Pedro (US$42.50) and Caye Caulker (US$45) in Belize.

GETTING AROUND

Air

Over 60 Mexican cities have airports with scheduled passenger services. Depending on the fare you get, flying can be good value on longer journeys, especially considering the long bus trip that is probably the alternative.

Aeroméxico (including its subsidiary Aeroméxico Connect) has the biggest network, but Interjet, Volaris and VivaAerobus serve many cities and often with lower

DEPARTURE TAX

The airport departure tax Tarifa de Uso de Aeropuerto TUA (TUA) is almost always included in your ticket cost, but if it isn't, you must pay in cash during airport check-in. It varies from airport to airport and costs US$20 to US$35 for international flights, and a little less for domestic flights. This tax is separate from the fee for your tourist permit, which is always included in airfares.

MEXICAN DOMESTIC AIRLINES

AIRLINE	WEBSITE	AREAS SERVED
Aéreo Calafia	www.aereocalafia.com.mx	Baja California, northwest, Puerto Vallarta
Aeromar	www.aeromar.com.mx	central Mexico, west, northeast, Gulf coast, Pacific coast
Aeroméxico	www.aeromexico.com	over 40 cities nationwide
Interjet	www.interjet.com.mx	32 cities nationwide
Magnicharters	www.magnicharters.com	Mexico City, Guadalajara, León, Mérida, coastal resorts
Mayair	www.mayair.com.mx	Yucatán Peninsula, Veracruz
VivaAerobus	www.vivaaerobus.com	27 cities nationwide
Volaris	www.volaris.com	33 cities nationwide

fares. VivaAerobus offers some particularly low fares but its website does not accept all foreign credit or bank cards – you may have to buy through a travel agent.

Bicycle

Cycling is not a common way to tour Mexico. The size of the country, poor road surfaces, careless motorists and other road hazards are deterrents. If you're up for the challenge, take the mountainous topography and hot climate into account when planning your route. All cities have bicycle stores: a decent mountain bike suitable for a few weeks' touring costs around M$5000.

Consider the bring-your-own-bike tours of southern Mexico and the central volcano country offered by the fun and friendly **iEl Tour** (www.bikemexico.com).

Boat

Vehicle and passenger ferries connecting Baja California with the Mexican mainland sail between Santa Rosalía and Guaymas; La Paz and Mazatlán; and La Paz and Topolobampo. One-way passenger seat fares are from M$840 to M$1078 depending on the route; a car up to 5.4m in length costs M$1900 to M$3200.

Bus

Mexico has a good road network, and comfortable, frequent, reasonably priced bus services connect all cities. Most cities and towns have one main bus terminal where all long-distance buses arrive and depart. It may be called the Terminal de Autobuses, Central de Autobuses, Central Camionera or simply La Central (not to be confused with *el centro*, downtown).

Classes

Mexico's buses offer the following classes.

DELUXE & EXECUTIVE

De lujo services, and the even more comfortable *ejecutivo* (executive) buses, run mainly on the busier intercity routes. They are swift and comfortable, with reclining seats, plenty of legroom, air-conditioning, movies on video screens, few or no stops, toilets on board, and sometimes drinks, snacks and even wi-fi. They use toll roads wherever available.

FIRST CLASS

Primera (1a) clase buses have a comfortable numbered seat for each passenger. All sizable towns are served by 1st-class buses. Standards of comfort are adequate at the very least. The buses have air-conditioning and a toilet, and they stop infrequently. They show movies on video on TV screens.

PRACTICAL TIPS

➡ Buses do occasionally get held up and robbed. Traveling by day and on deluxe or 1st-class buses, which use toll highways where possible, minimizes any risk.

➡ Baggage is safe if stowed in the bus' baggage hold: get a receipt for it when you hand it over. Keep your most valuable documents (passport, money etc) in the cabin with you.

➡ Air-conditioned buses can get cold, so wear long pants or a skirt and take a sweater or jacket and maybe a blanket on board. Eyepads and earplugs can be handy if you don't want to watch videos the entire trip!

They also use toll roads where possible.

SECOND CLASS

Segunda (2a) clase or *'económico'* buses serve small towns and villages, and provide cheaper, slower travel on some intercity routes. A few are almost as quick, comfortable and direct as 1st-class buses. Others are old, slow and shabby. These buses tend to take non-toll roads and will stop anywhere to pick up passengers: if you board midroute you might make some of the trip standing. In remoter areas, they are often the only buses available.

Companies

Mexico has hundreds of bus companies. Many of the major ones belong to large groups that dominate bus transportation in different parts of the country. Their websites have schedule information.

ETN Turistar (www.etn.com.mx) Comprises two good executive lines, ETN and Turistar, covering the center, north and west of Mexico and as far down the Pacific coast as Puerto Escondido.

Grupo ADO (boletotal.mx) Connects Mexico City and the east, south and southeast of the country; companies include ADO Platino (deluxe), ADO GL (deluxe/1st class) and ADO and OCC (1st class).

Grupo Estrella Blanca (www.estrellablanca.com.mx) Focuses on Mexico City and the center, north and west of Mexico; includes Futura Select (deluxe), and Futura, Elite, Oriente and Transportes Chihuahuenses (1st class).

Primera Plus (www.primeraplus.com.mx) This 1st-class company provides frequent service around the center of the country.

Costs

First-class buses typically cost around M$1 per kilometer and travel 70km to 80km in an hour. Deluxe buses cost about 20% more than 1st class; executive services can be 50% more. Second-class buses cost about 20% less than 1st class.

HOW MANY STOPS?

It's useful to understand the difference between the types of bus service on offer:

Sin escalas Nonstop

Directo Very few stops

Ordinario Stops wherever passengers want to get on or off the bus; deluxe and 1st-class buses are never *ordinario*

Express Nonstop on short- to medium-length trips; very few stops on long trips

Local Bus that starts its journey at the bus station you're in and usually leaves on time; *local* service is preferable to *de paso*

De paso Bus that started its journey somewhere else; you may have to wait until it arrives before any tickets are sold, and if it's full, you have to wait for the next one

Vía corta Short route

Vía cuota By toll road

Viaje redondo Round trip

Reservations

For 1st-class, deluxe and executive buses, you buy your ticket in the bus terminal before the trip. For trips of up to four or five hours on routes with frequent service, you can usually just go to the bus terminal, buy a ticket and head out without much delay. For longer trips, or routes with infrequent service, or for any trip at busy holiday times, it's best to buy a ticket a day or more in advance. You can usually select your seat when you buy your ticket. Try to avoid the back of the bus, which is where the toilets are and also tends to give a bumpier ride.

Many 2nd-class services have no ticket office; you just pay your fare to the conductor.

In some cities you can buy bus tickets from downtown agencies in order to avoid an extra trip to the bus terminal. **Boletotal** (boletotal.mx) has dozens of ticket offices for Grupo ADO buses, in around 20 cities right around the country.

Car & Motorcycle

Having a vehicle in Mexico gives you a whole lot of flexibility and freedom, and with a little adaptation to local road conditions is no more difficult than in most other countries. See p856 for information on bringing your own vehicle into Mexico.

Driver's License

To drive a motor vehicle in Mexico, you need a valid driver's license from your home country.

Fuel

All *gasolina* (gasoline) and diesel fuel in Mexico is sold by the government's monopoly, Pemex (Petróleos Mexicanos). Most towns, even small ones, have a Pemex station, and the stations are pretty common on most major roads. In remote areas, fill up whenever you can. Gasoline is all *sin plomo* (unleaded). There are two varieties:

Magna (87 octane) Roughly equivalent to US regular unleaded, costing about M$11.80 per liter (US$3.40 per US gallon).

Premium (91 octane and lower in sulfur content) Roughly equivalent to US super unleaded, costing about M$12.40.

Diesel fuel is widely available at around M$12 per liter. Regular Mexican diesel has a higher sulfur content than US diesel, but a *bajo azufre* (low sulfur) variety has started to become available in Mexico City and some nearby areas. Gas stations have pump attendants (who appreciate a tip of around M$5).

Rental

Auto rental in Mexico can be expensive by US or European standards but is not hard to organize. Many major international rental firms have offices throughout the country.

Renters must provide a valid driver's license (your home license is OK), passport and major credit card, and are usually required to be at least 21 (sometimes 25, or if you're aged 21 to 24 you may have to pay a surcharge). Read the small print of the rental agreement. In addition to the basic rental rate, there will be tax and insurance costs. Comprehensive insurance can more than double the basic cost quoted in some online bookings: you'll usually have the option of liability-only insurance at a lower rate. Ask exactly what the insurance options cover: theft and damage insurance may only cover a percentage of costs, or the insurance might not be valid for travel on rough country tracks. It's best to have plenty of liability coverage.

Rental rates typically start around M$500 a day including unlimited kilometers, basic insurance and tax. In some beach resorts you may pay as little as M$350. If you rent by the week or month, per-day costs come down. The extra charge for drop-off in another city, when available, is usually about M$4 per kilometer.

Motorbikes or scooters can be rented in a few tourist centers. You're usually required to have a driver's license and a credit card. Many renters do not offer any insurance, however.

Road Conditions & Hazards

➡ Mexico's highways are serviceable and fairly fast when traffic is not heavy. There are more than 6000km of toll highways *(autopistas)*, which are generally good, four-lane roads: tolls vary from M$0.50 to M$1.50 per kilometer.

➡ Driving at night is best avoided, since unlit vehicles, hard-to-see speed bumps, rocks, pedestrians and animals on the roads are common and drunken drivers are more numerous – and general highway security is better by day.

➡ Some hijackings, holdups and illegal roadblocks connected with drug-gang activities occur, mainly in the north. The northeastern states of Tamaulipas and Nuevo León are especially notorious – above all, the Tampico–Matamoros road. In this part of the country especially, it is best to stick to toll highways, drive only by day, and keep doors locked and windows closed when driving through cities. Check travel warnings (p850) and seek local advice. If you do become a victim, do not try to resist.

➡ There are also some perfectly genuine military or police roadblocks, which are generally looking for illegal weapons, drugs, migrants or contraband. They are unlikely to give tourists a hard time, and are no cause for alarm.

➡ It's best to leave vehicles in secure lock-up parking lots overnight – these are fairly common in cities and hotels can tell you where they are if they don't have their own secure parking.

➡ About 14 of every 100,000 Mexicans die in road accidents each year – more than double the rate of most Western countries. Driving under the influence of alcohol and nonuse of seat belts are more prevalent here, but otherwise Mexicans seem to drive as cautiously and sensibly as people anywhere. Traffic density, poor surfaces, speed bumps, animals, bicycles and pedestrians all help to keep speeds down.

➡ Be wary of 'Alto' (Stop) signs, *topes* (speed bumps) and holes in the road. They are often not where you'd expect, and missing one can cost you in traffic fines or car damage. 'Tope' or 'Vibradores' signs warn you of many speed bumps: the deadly ones are the ones with no warning signs!

➡ There is always the chance that you will be pulled over by traffic police. If this happens,

THE GREEN ANGELS

The Mexican tourism secretariat, Sectur, maintains a network of Ángeles Verdes (Green Angels) – bilingual mechanics in green uniforms and green trucks who patrol 60,000km of major highways throughout the country daily from 8am to 6pm looking for tourists in trouble. They can give you directions, make minor repairs, change tires, provide fuel and oil, and arrange towing and other assistance if necessary. Service is free; parts, gasoline and oil are provided at cost. If you have access to a telephone, you can call the **hotline** (☎078).

stay calm and polite. If you don't think you have committed an infraction, you don't have to pay a bribe, and acting dumb may eventually make the cop give up. You can also ask to see the officer's identification, and documentation about the law you have supposedly broken, ask to speak to a superior, and note the officer's name, badge number, vehicle number and department (federal, state or municipal). Make clear that you want to pay any fines at a police station and get a receipt, then if you wish to make a complaint head for a state tourist office.

Road Rules

- Drive on the right-hand side of the road.
- Speed limits range between 80km and 120km per hour on open highways (less when highways pass through built-up areas), and between 30km and 50km per hour in towns and cities.
- One-way streets are the rule in cities.
- Legal blood alcohol limits for drivers range from 0.5g/L to 0.8g/L – roughly two or three beers or tequilas.
- Antipollution rules in Mexico City ban most vehicles from the city's roads on one day each week, on a rotation system (see p137).

Colectivos, Combis & Other Vehicles

In some areas a variety of small vehicles provide alternatives to buses. *Taxis colectivos* (shared taxis, usually carrying four passengers who each pay a quarter of the full cab fare), Volkswagen minibuses (combis) and more comfortable passenger-carrying vans operate services between some towns. Fares are typically a little less than 1st-class buses. *Microbuses* or '*micros*' are small, usually fairly new, 2nd-class buses with around 25 seats, usually running short routes between nearby towns. More primitive are passenger-carrying *camionetas* (pickups) and *camiones* (trucks), with fares similar to 2nd-class bus fares. Standing in the back of a lurching truck full of *campesinos* (land workers) and their machetes and animals is always an experience.

Local Transportation

Bicycle

Bicycle culture is on the up in Mexican cities. Most of them are flat enough to make cycling an option and some city authorities are starting to accommodate cyclists. Mexico City offers free bike rental and at least three dedicated bike routes. You can rent bikes in several other towns for M$150 to M$250 per day. Seek out the less traffic-infested routes and you should enjoy it. Mass Sunday rides are a growing phenomenon.

Bus

Generally known as *camiones*, local buses are usually the cheapest way to get around cities and out to nearby towns and villages. They run frequently and fares in cities are just a few pesos. In many cities, fleets of small, modern *microbuses* have replaced the noisy, older buses.

Buses usually halt only at fixed *paradas* (bus stops), though in some places you can hold your hand out to stop one at any street corner.

Colectivo, Combi, Minibus & Pesero

These are all names for vehicles that function as something between a taxi and a bus, running along fixed urban routes usually displayed on the windshield. They're cheaper than taxis and quicker than buses. They will pick you up or drop you off on any corner along their route: to stop one, go to the curb and wave your hand. Tell the driver where you want to go. Usually, you pay at the end of the trip and the fare (a little higher than a bus fare) depends on how far you go.

Metro

Mexico City, Guadalajara and Monterrey all have metro (subway, underground railway) systems. Mexico City's, in particular, is a quick, cheap and useful way of getting around. With 195 stations and over four million passengers every weekday, it's the world's third-busiest metro system.

Taxi

Taxis are common in towns and cities, and surprisingly economical. City rides cost around M$10 to M$15 per kilometer. If a taxi has a meter, you can ask the driver if it's working *('¿Funciona el taxímetro?')*. If the taxi doesn't have a functioning meter, establish the price of the ride before getting in (this may involve a bit of haggling).

Many airports and some big bus terminals have a system of authorized ticket-taxis: you buy a fixed-price ticket to your destination from a special *taquilla* (ticket window) and then hand it to the driver instead of paying cash. This saves haggling and major rip-offs, but fares are usually higher than you could get on the street.

Renting a taxi for a day-long out-of-town jaunt generally costs something similar to a cheap rental car – M$500 or M$600.

Train

The spectacular Ferrocarril Chihuahua Pacífico (Copper Canyon Railway: p759), running through the Sierra Madre Occidental between Los Mochis and Chihuahua, is one of the highlights of travel in Mexico. All the rest of Mexico's regular passenger-train system died after the railroads were privatized in the 1990s.

Language

Mexican Spanish pronunciation is easy, as most sounds have equivalents in English. Also, Spanish spelling is phonetically consistent, meaning that there's a clear and consistent relationship between what you see in writing and how it's pronounced. Note that kh is a throaty sound (like the 'ch' in the Scottish *loch*), v and b are like a soft English 'v' (between a 'v' and a 'b'), and r is strongly rolled. There are also some variations in spoken Spanish across Latin America, the most notable being the pronunciation of the letters *ll* and *y*. In some parts of Mexico they are pronounced like the 'll' in 'million', but in most areas they are pronounced like the 'y' in 'yes', and this is how they are represented in our pronunciation guides. In other Latin American countries you might also hear them pronounced like the 's' in 'measure', the 'sh' in 'shut' or the 'dg' in 'judge'. The stressed syllables are indicated with italics in our pronunciation guides. Bearing these few things in mind and reading our coloured pronunciation guides as if they were English, you should be understood just fine.

The polite form is used in this chapter; where both polite and informal options are given, they are indicated by the abbreviations 'pol' and 'inf'. Where necessary, both masculine and feminine forms of words are included, separated by a slash and with the masculine form first, eg *perdido/a* (m/f).

BASICS

Hello.	*Hola.*	o·la
Goodbye.	*Adiós.*	a·*dyos*

WANT MORE?

For in-depth language information and handy phrases, check out Lonely Planet's *Mexican Spanish Phrasebook*. You'll find it at **shop.lonelyplanet.com**, or you can buy Lonely Planet's iPhone phrasebooks at the Apple App Store.

How are you?	*¿Qué tal?*	ke tal
Fine, thanks.	*Bien, gracias.*	byen *gra*·syas
Excuse me.	*Perdón.*	per·*don*
Sorry.	*Lo siento.*	lo *syen*·to
Please.	*Por favor.*	por fa·*vor*
Thank you.	*Gracias.*	*gra*·syas
You're welcome.	*De nada.*	de *na*·da
Yes.	*Sí.*	see
No.	*No.*	no

My name is ...
Me llamo ... me *ya*·mo ...

What's your name?
¿Cómo se llama Usted? ko·mo se *ya*·ma oo·*ste* (pol)
¿Cómo te llamas? ko·mo te *ya*·mas (inf)

Do you speak English?
¿Habla inglés? a·bla een·*gles* (pol)
¿Hablas inglés? a·blas een·*gles* (inf)

I don't understand.
Yo no entiendo. yo no en·*tyen*·do

ACCOMMODATIONS

I'd like a ... room.	*Quisiera una habitación ...*	kee·*sye*·ra *oo*·na a·bee·ta·*syon* ...
single	*individual*	een·dee·vee·*dwal*
double	*doble*	*do*·ble

How much is it per night/person?
¿Cuánto cuesta por noche/persona? *kwan*·to *kwes*·ta por *no*·che/per·*so*·na

Does it include breakfast?
¿Incluye el desayuno? een·*kloo*·ye el de·sa·*yoo*·no

campsite	*terreno de cámping*	te·*re*·no de *kam*·peeng
hotel	*hotel*	o·*tel*
guesthouse	*pensión*	pen·*syon*

KEY PATTERNS

To get by in Spanish, mix and match these simple patterns with words of your choice:

When's (the next flight)?
¿Cuándo sale (el próximo vuelo)? — kwan·do sa·le (el *prok*·see·mo *vwe*·lo)

Where's (the station)?
¿Dónde está (la estación)? — don·de es·*ta* (la es·ta·*syon*)

Where can I (buy a ticket)?
¿Dónde puedo (comprar un billete)? — don·de *pwe*·do (kom·*prar* oon bee·*ye*·te)

Do you have (a map)?
¿Tiene (un mapa)? — *tye*·ne (oon *ma*·pa)

Is there (a toilet)?
¿Hay (servicios)? — ai (ser·*vee*·syos)

I'd like (a coffee).
Quisiera (un café). — kee·*sye*·ra (oon ka·*fe*)

I'd like (to hire a car).
Quisiera (alquilar un coche). — kee·*sye*·ra (al·kee·*lar* oon *ko*·che)

Can I (enter)?
¿Se puede (entrar)? — se *pwe*·de (en·*trar*)

Could you please (help me)?
¿Puede (ayudarme), por favor? — *pwe*·de (a·yoo·*dar*·me) por fa·*vor*

Do I have to (get a visa)?
¿Necesito (obtener un visado)? — ne·se·*see*·to (ob·te·*ner* oon vee·*sa*·do)

youth hostel	*albergue juvenil*	al·*ber*·ge khoo·ve·*neel*
air-con	*aire acondicionado*	*ai*·re a·kon·dee·syo·*na*·do
bathroom	*baño*	*ba*·nyo
bed	*cama*	*ka*·ma
window	*ventana*	ven·*ta*·na

DIRECTIONS

Where's ...?
¿Dónde está ...? — don·de es·*ta* ...

What's the address?
¿Cuál es la dirección? — kwal es la dee·rek·*syon*

Could you please write it down?
¿Puede escribirlo, por favor? — *pwe*·de es·kree·*beer*·lo por fa·*vor*

Can you show me (on the map)?
¿Me lo puede indicar (en el mapa)? — me lo *pwe*·de een·dee·*kar* (en el *ma*·pa)

at the corner	*en la esquina*	en la es·*kee*·na
at the traffic lights	*en el semáforo*	en el se·*ma*·fo·ro
behind ...	*detrás de ...*	de·*tras* de ...
far	*lejos*	*le*·khos
in front of ...	*enfrente de ...*	en·*fren*·te de ...
left	*izquierda*	ees·*kyer*·da
near	*cerca*	*ser*·ka
next to ...	*al lado de ...*	al *la*·do de ...
opposite ...	*frente a ...*	*fren*·te a ...
right	*derecha*	de·*re*·cha
straight ahead	*todo recto*	*to*·do *rek*·to

EATING & DRINKING

Can I see the menu, please?
¿Puedo ver el menú, por favor? — *pwe*·do ver el me·*noo* por fa·*vor*

What would you recommend?
¿Qué recomienda? — ke re·ko·*myen*·da

Do you have vegetarian food?
¿Tienen comida vegetariana? — *tye*·nen ko·*mee*·da ve·khe·ta·*rya*·na

I don't eat (meat).
No como (carne). — no *ko*·mo (*kar*·ne)

That was delicious!
¡Estaba buenísimo! — es·*ta*·ba bwe·*nee*·see·mo

Cheers!
¡Salud! — sa·*loo*

The bill, please.
La cuenta, por favor. — la *kwen*·ta por fa·*vor*

I'd like a table for ...	*Quisiera una mesa para ...*	kee·*sye*·ra *oo*·na *me*·sa *pa*·ra ...
(eight) o'clock	*las (ocho)*	las (*o*·cho)
(two) people	*(dos) personas*	(dos) per·*so*·nas

Key Words

bottle	*botella*	bo·*te*·ya
breakfast	*desayuno*	de·sa·*yoo*·no
cold	*frío*	*free*·o
dessert	*postre*	*pos*·tre
dinner	*cena*	*se*·na
fork	*tenedor*	te·ne·*dor*
glass	*vaso*	*va*·so
hot (warm)	*caliente*	kal·*yen*·te
knife	*cuchillo*	koo·*chee*·yo
lunch	*comida*	ko·*mee*·da
plate	*plato*	*pla*·to
restaurant	*restaurante*	res·tow·*ran*·te
spoon	*cuchara*	koo·*cha*·ra

Meat & Fish

bacon	*tocino*	to·*see*·no
beef	*carne de vaca*	*kar*·ne de *va*·ka
chicken	*pollo*	*po*·yo
crab	*cangrejo*	kan·*gre*·kho
duck	*pato*	*pa*·to
goat	*cabra*	*ka*·bra
ham	*jamón*	kha·*mon*
lamb	*cordero*	kor·*de*·ro
lobster	*langosta*	lan·*gos*·ta
mutton	*carnero*	kar·*ne*·ro
octopus	*pulpo*	*pool*·po
oysters	*ostras*	*os*·tras
pork	*cerdo*	*ser*·do
shrimp	*camarones*	ka·ma·*ro*·nes
squid	*calamar*	ka·la·*mar*
turkey	*pavo*	*pa*·vo
veal	*ternera*	ter·*ne*·ra
venison	*venado*	ve·*na*·do

Fruit & Vegetables

apple	*manzana*	man·*sa*·na
apricot	*albaricoque*	al·ba·ree·*ko*·ke
banana	*plátano*	*pla*·ta·no
beans	*frijoles*	free·*kho*·les
cabbage	*col*	kol
cactus fruit	*tuna*	*too*·na
carrot	*zanahoria*	sa·na·o·rya
cherry	*cereza*	se·*re*·sa
corn	*maíz*	ma·ees
corn (fresh)	*elote*	e·*lo*·te
cucumber	*pepino*	pe·*pee*·no
grape	*uvas*	*oo*·vas
grapefruit	*toronja*	to·*ron*·kha
lentils	*lentejas*	len·*te*·khas
lettuce	*lechuga*	le·*choo*·ga
mushroom	*champiñón*	cham·pee·*nyon*
nuts	*nueces*	*nwe*·ses
onion	*cebolla*	se·*bo*·ya
orange	*naranja*	na·*ran*·kha
peach	*melocotón*	me·lo·ko·*ton*
peas	*guisantes*	gee·*san*·tes
pepper	*pimiento*	pee·*myen*·to
pineapple	*piña*	*pee*·nya
plantain	*plátano macho*	*pla*·ta·no *ma*·cho
plum	*ciruela*	seer·*we*·la
potato	*patata*	pa·*ta*·ta
pumpkin	*calabaza*	ka·la·*ba*·sa
spinach	*espinacas*	es·pee·*na*·kas
strawberry	*fresa*	*fre*·sa
(red) tomato	*(ji)tomate*	(khee·)to·*ma*·te
watermelon	*sandía*	san·*dee*·a

Other

bread	*pan*	pan
butter	*mantequilla*	man·te·*kee*·ya
cake	*pastel*	pas·*tel*
cheese	*queso*	*ke*·so
cookie	*galleta*	ga·*ye*·ta
(fried) eggs	*huevos (fritos)*	*we*·vos (*free*·tos)
French fries	*papas fritas*	*pa*·pas *free*·tas
honey	*miel*	myel
ice cream	*helado*	e·*la*·do
jam	*mermelada*	mer·me·*la*·da
pepper	*pimienta*	pee·*myen*·ta
rice	*arroz*	a·*ros*
salad	*ensalada*	en·sa·*la*·da
salt	*sal*	sal
soup	*caldo/sopa*	*kal*·do/*so*·pa
sugar	*azúcar*	a·*soo*·kar

Drinks

beer	*cerveza*	ser·*ve*·sa
coffee	*café*	ka·*fe*
juice	*zumo*	*soo*·mo
milk	*leche*	*le*·che
smoothie	*licuado*	lee·*kwa*·do
sorbet	*nieve*	*nye*·ve
(black) tea	*té (negro)*	te (*ne*·gro)
(mineral) water	*agua (mineral)*	*a*·gwa (mee·ne·*ral*)
(red/white) wine	*vino (tinto/blanco)*	*vee*·no (*teen*·to/*blan*·ko)

Signs

Abierto	Open
Cerrado	Closed
Entrada	Entrance
Hombres/Varones	Men
Mujeres/Damas	Women
Prohibido	Prohibited
Salida	Exit
Servicios/Baños	Toilets

EMERGENCIES

Help!	*¡Socorro!*	so·*ko*·ro
Go away!	*¡Vete!*	*ve*·te
Call ...!	*¡Llame a ...!*	*ya*·me a ...
a doctor	*un médico*	oon *me*·dee·ko
the police	*la policía*	la po·lee·*see*·a

I'm lost.
Estoy perdido/a. es·*toy* per·*dee*·do/a (m/f)

I'm ill.
Estoy enfermo/a. es·*toy* en·*fer*·mo/a (m/f)

It hurts here.
Me duele aquí. me *dwe*·le a·*kee*

I'm allergic to (antibiotics).
Soy alérgico/a a (los antibióticos). soy a·*ler*·khee·ko/a a (los an·tee·*byo*·tee·kos) (m/f)

Where are the toilets?
¿Dónde están los baños? *don*·de es·*tan* los *ba*·nyos

SHOPPING & SERVICES

I'd like to buy ...
Quisiera comprar ... kee·*sye*·ra kom·*prar* ...

I'm just looking.
Sólo estoy mirando. *so*·lo es·*toy* mee·*ran*·do

Can I look at it?
¿Puedo verlo? *pwe*·do *ver*·lo

I don't like it.
No me gusta. no me *goos*·ta

How much is it?
¿Cuánto cuesta? *kwan*·to *kwes*·ta

That's too expensive.
Es muy caro. es mooy *ka*·ro

Can you lower the price?
¿Podría bajar un poco el precio? po·*dree*·a ba·*khar* oon *po*·ko el *pre*·syo

There's a mistake in the bill.
Hay un error en la cuenta. ai oon e·*ror* en la *kwen*·ta

ATM	*cajero automático*	ka·*khe*·ro ow·to·*ma*·tee·ko
credit card	*tarjeta de crédito*	tar·*khe*·ta de *kre*·dee·to
internet cafe	*cibercafé*	see·ber·ka·*fe*
market	*mercado*	mer·*ka*·do
post office	*correos*	ko·*re*·os

Question Words

How?	*¿Cómo?*	*ko*·mo
What?	*¿Qué?*	ke
When?	*¿Cuándo?*	*kwan*·do
Where?	*¿Dónde?*	*don*·de
Who?	*¿Quién?*	kyen
Why?	*¿Por qué?*	por *ke*

tourist office	*oficina de turismo*	o·fee·*see*·na de too·*rees*·mo

TIME & DATES

What time is it?	*¿Qué hora es?*	ke *o*·ra es
It's (10) o'clock.	*Son (las diez).*	son (las dyes)
It's half past (one).	*Es (la una) y media.*	es (la *oo*·na) ee *me*·dya
morning	*mañana*	ma·*nya*·na
afternoon	*tarde*	*tar*·de
evening	*noche*	*no*·che
yesterday	*ayer*	a·*yer*
today	*hoy*	oy
tomorrow	*mañana*	ma·*nya*·na
Monday	*lunes*	*loo*·nes
Tuesday	*martes*	*mar*·tes
Wednesday	*miércoles*	*myer*·ko·les
Thursday	*jueves*	*khwe*·ves
Friday	*viernes*	*vyer*·nes
Saturday	*sábado*	*sa*·ba·do
Sunday	*domingo*	do·*meen*·go
January	*enero*	e·*ne*·ro
February	*febrero*	fe·*bre*·ro
March	*marzo*	*mar*·so
April	*abril*	a·*breel*
May	*mayo*	*ma*·yo
June	*junio*	*khoon*·yo
July	*julio*	*khool*·yo
August	*agosto*	a·*gos*·to
September	*septiembre*	sep·*tyem*·bre
October	*octubre*	ok·*too*·bre
November	*noviembre*	no·*vyem*·bre
December	*diciembre*	dee·*syem*·bre

TRANSPORTATION

boat	*barco*	*bar*·ko
bus	*autobús*	ow·to·*boos*
plane	*avión*	a·*vyon*
train	*tren*	tren
first	*primero*	pree·*me*·ro
last	*último*	*ool*·tee·mo
next	*próximo*	*prok*·see·mo
A ... ticket, please.	*Un billete de ..., por favor.*	oon bee·*ye*·te de ... por fa·*vor*
1st-class	*primera clase*	pree·*me*·ra *kla*·se

2nd-class	*segunda clase*	se·*goon*·da *kla*·se
one-way	*ida*	ee·da
return	*ida y vuelta*	ee·da ee *vwel*·ta

I want to go to ...
Quisiera ir a ... kee·*sye*·ra eer a ...

Does it stop at ...?
¿Para en ...? *pa*·ra en ...

What stop is this?
¿Cuál es esta parada? kwal es *es*·ta pa·*ra*·da

What time does it arrive/leave?
¿A qué hora llega/ sale? a ke *o*·ra *ye*·ga/ *sa*·le

Please tell me when we get to ...
¿Puede avisarme cuando lleguemos a ...? *pwe*·de a·vee·*sar*·me *kwan*·do ye·*ge*·mos a ...

I want to get off here.
Quiero bajarme aquí. *kye*·ro ba·*khar*·me a·*kee*

airport	*aeropuerto*	a·e·ro·*pwer*·to
aisle seat	*asiento de pasillo*	a·*syen*·to de pa·*see*·yo
bus stop	*parada de autobuses*	pa·*ra*·da de ow·to·*boo*·ses
cancelled	*cancelado*	kan·se·*la*·do
delayed	*retrasado*	re·tra·*sa*·do
platform	*plataforma*	pla·ta·*for*·ma
ticket office	*taquilla*	ta·*kee*·ya
timetable	*horario*	o·*ra*·ryo
train station	*estación de trenes*	es·ta·*syon* de *tre*·nes
window seat	*asiento junto a la ventana*	a·*syen*·to *khoon*·to a la ven·*ta*·na

I'd like to hire a ...	*Quisiera alquilar ...*	kee·*sye*·ra al·kee·*lar* ...
4WD	*un todo-terreno*	oon to·do·te·*re*·no
bicycle	*una bicicleta*	*oo*·na bee·see·*kle*·ta
car	*un coche*	oon *ko*·che
motorcycle	*una moto*	*oo*·na *mo*·to
child seat	*asiento de seguridad para niños*	a·*syen*·to de se·goo·ree·*da* *pa*·ra *nee*·nyos
diesel	*petróleo*	pet·*ro*·le·o
helmet	*casco*	*kas*·ko
hitchhike	*hacer botella*	a·*ser* bo·*te*·ya
mechanic	*mecánico*	me·*ka*·nee·ko

Numbers

1	*uno*	*oo*·no
2	*dos*	dos
3	*tres*	tres
4	*cuatro*	*kwa*·tro
5	*cinco*	*seen*·ko
6	*seis*	seys
7	*siete*	*sye*·te
8	*ocho*	*o*·cho
9	*nueve*	*nwe*·ve
10	*diez*	dyes
20	*veinte*	*veyn*·te
30	*treinta*	*treyn*·ta
40	*cuarenta*	kwa·*ren*·ta
50	*cincuenta*	seen·*kwen*·ta
60	*sesenta*	se·*sen*·ta
70	*setenta*	se·*ten*·ta
80	*ochenta*	o·*chen*·ta
90	*noventa*	no·*ven*·ta
100	*cien*	syen
1000	*mil*	meel

petrol/gas	*gasolina*	ga·so·*lee*·na
service station	*gasolinera*	ga·so·lee·*ne*·ra
truck	*camion*	ka·*myon*

Is this the road to ...?
¿Se va a ... por esta carretera? se va a ... por *es*·ta ka·re·*te*·ra

(How long) Can I park here?
¿(Cuánto tiempo) Puedo aparcar aquí? (*kwan*·to *tyem*·po) *pwe*·do a·par·*kar* a·*kee*

The car has broken down (at ...).
El coche se ha averiado (en ...). el *ko*·che se a a·ve·*rya*·do (en ...)

I had an accident.
He tenido un accidente. e te·*nee*·do oon ak·see·*den*·te

I've run out of petrol.
Me he quedado sin gasolina. me e ke·*da*·do seen ga·so·*lee*·na

I have a flat tyre.
Tengo un pinchazo. *ten*·go oon peen·*cha*·so

MEXICAN SLANG

Pepper your conversations with a few slang expressions! You'll hear many of the following expressions all around Mexico, but some are particular to Mexico City.

¿Qué onda?
What's up?/What's happening?

¿Qué pasión? (Mexico City)
What's up?/What's going on?

¡Qué padre!
How cool!

fregón
really good at something/way cool/awesome

Este club está fregón.
This club is way cool.

El cantante es un fregón.
The singer is really awesome.

ser muy buena onda
to be really cool/nice

Mi novio es muy buena onda.
My boyfriend is really cool.

Eres muy buena onda.
You're really cool.

pisto (in the north)
booze

alipús
booze

echarse un alipús/trago
to go get a drink

Echamos un alipús/trago.
Let's go have a drink.

tirar la onda
try to pick someone up/flirt

ligar
to flirt

irse de reventón
go partying

¡Vámonos de reventón!
Let's go party!

reven
a 'rave' (huge party with loud music and a wild atmosphere)

un desmadre
a mess

Simón.
Yes.

Nel.
No.

No hay tos.
No problem. (literally: 'there's no cough')

¡Órale! (positive)
Sounds great! (when responding to an invitation)

¡Órale! (negative)
What the ...? (taunting exclamation)

¡Caray!
Shit!

¿Te cae?
Are you serious?

Me late.
Sounds really good to me.

Me vale.
I don't care./Whatever.

Sale y vale.
I agree./Sounds good.

¡Paso sin ver!
I can't stand it!/No, thank you!

¡Guácatelas!/¡Guácala!
How gross!/That's disgusting!

¡Bájale!
Don't exaggerate!/Come on!

¡¿Chale?! (Mexico City)
No way!?

¡Te pasas!
That's it! You've gone too far!

¡No manches!
Get outta here!/You must be kidding!

un resto
a lot

lana
money/dough

carnal
brother

cuate/cuaderno
buddy

chavo
guy/dude

chava
girl/gal

jefe
father

jefa
mother

la tira/julia
the police

la chota (Mexico City)
the police

GLOSSARY

(m) indicates masculine gender, (f) feminine gender, (sg) singular and (pl) plural

adobe – sun-dried mud brick used for building

agave – family of plants with thick, fleshy, usually pointed leaves, from which tequila, mezcal and *pulque* are produced (see also *maguey*)

Alameda – name of formal parks in some Mexican cities

alebrije – colorful wooden animal figure

Ángeles Verdes – Green Angels; government-funded mechanics who patrol Mexico's major highways in green vehicles; they help stranded motorists with fuel and spare parts

arroyo – brook, stream

artesanías – handicrafts, folk arts

atlas (sg), atlantes (pl) – sculpted male figure(s) used instead of a pillar to support a roof or frieze; a telamon

autopista – expressway, dual carriageway

azulejo – painted ceramic tile

bahía – bay

balneario – bathing place; often a natural hot spring

baluarte – bulwark, defensive wall

barrio – neighborhood of a town or city

boleto – ticket

brujo/a (m/f) – witch doctor, shaman; similar to *curandero/a*

burro – donkey

cabaña – cabin, simple shelter

cabina – Baja Californian term for a public telephone call station

cacique – regional warlord; political strongman

calle – street

callejón – alley

calzada – grand boulevard or avenue

camioneta – pickup truck

campesino/a (m/f) – country person, peasant

capilla abierta – open chapel; used in early Mexican monasteries for preaching to large crowds of indigenous people

casa de cambio – exchange house, place where currency is exchanged; faster to use than a bank

casa de huéspedes – cheap and congenial accommodations; often a home converted into simple guest lodgings

caseta de teléfono, caseta telefónica – public telephone call station

cenote – a limestone sinkhole filled with rainwater; often used in Yucatán as a reservoir

central camionera – bus terminal

cerro – hill

Chac – Maya rain god

chac-mool – pre-Hispanic stone sculpture of a hunched-up figure; the stomach may have been used as a sacrificial altar

charreada – Mexican rodeo

charro – Mexican cowboy

chilango/a (m/f) – person from Mexico City

chinampa – Aztec garden built from lake mud and vegetation; versions still exist at Xochimilco, Mexico City

chultún – cistern found in the Chenes region, in the Puuc hills south of Mérida

Churrigueresque – Spanish late-baroque architectural style; found on many Mexican churches

clavadistas – cliff divers of Acapulco and Mazatlán

colectivo – minibus or car that picks up and drops off passengers along a predetermined route; can also refer to other types of transportation, such as boats, where passengers share the total fare

colonia – neighborhood of a city, often a wealthy residential area

combi – minibus

comedor – food stall

comida corrida – set lunch

completo – no vacancy (literally 'full up'); a sign you may see at hotel desks

conde – count (nobleman)

conquistador – early Spanish explorer-conqueror

cordillera – mountain range

criollo – Mexican-born person of Spanish parentage; in colonial times considered inferior by *peninsulares*

cuota – toll; a *vía cuota* is a toll road

curandero/a (m/f) – literally 'curer'; a medicine man or woman who uses herbal and/or magical methods and often emphasizes spiritual aspects of disease

de paso – a bus that began its route somewhere else, but stops to let passengers on or off at various points

DF – Distrito Federal (Federal District); about half of Mexico City lies in DF

edificio – building

ejido – communal landholding

embarcadero – jetty, boat landing

entremeses – hors d'oeuvres; also theatrical sketches such as those performed during the Cervantino festival in Guanajuato

escuela – school

esq – abbreviation of *esquina* (corner) in addresses

ex-convento – former convent or monastery

feria – fair or carnival, typically occurring during a religious holiday

ferrocarril – railway

fonda – inn; small, family-run eatery

fraccionamiento – subdivision, housing development; similar to a *colonia*, often modern

gringo/a (m/f) – US or Canadian (or other Western) visitor to Latin America; can be used derogatorily

grito – literally 'shout'; the Grito de Dolores was the 1810 call to independence by priest Miguel Hidalgo, sparking the struggle for independence from Spain

gruta – cave, grotto

guayabera – man's shirt with pockets and appliquéd designs up the front, over the shoulders and down the back; worn in hot regions in place of a jacket and tie

hacha – ax; in archaeological contexts, a flat, carved-stone object connected with the ritual ball game

hacienda – estate; Hacienda (capitalized) is the Treasury Department

henequén – *agave* fiber used to make sisal rope; grown particularly around Mérida

hostal – small hotel or budget hostel

huarache – woven leather sandal, often with tire tread as the sole

huevos – eggs; also slang for testicles

huipil (sg), huipiles (pl) – indigenous woman's sleeveless tunic(s), usually highly decorated; can be thigh-length or reach the ankles

Huizilopochtli – Aztec tribal god

iglesia – church

INAH – Instituto Nacional de Antropología e Historia; the body in charge of most ancient sites and some museums

indígena – indigenous, pertaining to the original inhabitants of Latin America; can also refer to the people themselves

isla – island

IVA – *impuesto de valor agregado*, or 'ee-vah'; a sales tax added to the price of many items (16% on hotel rooms)

jai alai – the Basque game *pelota*, brought to Mexico by the Spanish; a bit like squash, played on a long court with curved baskets attached to the arm

jardín – garden

Kukulcán – Maya name for the plumed serpent god *Quetzalcóatl*

lancha – fast, open, outboard boat

larga distancia – long-distance; usually refers to telephone calls

local – refers to premises, such as a numbered shop or office; a *local* bus is one whose route starts from the bus station you are in

maguey – *agave*; sometimes refers specifically to *Agave americana*, from which *pulque* is made

malecón – waterfront boulevard or promenade

maquiladora – assembly-plant operation importing equipment, raw materials and parts for assembly or processing in Mexico, then exporting the products

mariachi – small ensemble of street musicians playing traditional ballads on guitars and trumpets

marimba – wooden xylophone-like instrument popular in southeastern Mexico

mercado – market; often a building near the center of a town, with shops and open-air stalls in the surrounding streets

Mesoamerica – historical and archaeological name for central, southern, eastern and southeastern Mexico, Guatemala, Belize and the small ancient Maya area in Honduras

mestizo – person of mixed (usually indigenous and Spanish) ancestry

Mexican Revolution – 1910 revolution that ended the *Porfiriato*

milpa – peasant's small cornfield, often cultivated using the slash-and-burn method

mirador (sg), miradores (pl) – lookout point(s)

Mudejar – Moorish architectural style imported to Mexico by the Spanish

municipio – small local government area; Mexico is divided into 2394 of them

Nafta – North American Free Trade Agreement

Náhuatl – language of the Nahua people, descendants of the Aztecs

nao – Spanish trading galleon

norteamericano – North American; someone from north of the US–Mexican border

Nte – abbreviation for *norte* (north); used in street names

Ote – abbreviation for *oriente* (east); used in street names

palacio de gobierno – state capitol, state government headquarters

palacio municipal – town or city hall, headquarters of the municipal corporation

palapa – thatched-roof shelter, usually on a beach

PAN – Partido Acción Nacional (National Action Party); the political party of Felipe Calderón and his predecessor Vicente Fox

panga – fiberglass skiff for fishing or whale-watching in Baja California

parada – bus stop, usually for city buses

parque nacional – national park; an environmentally protected area in which human exploitation is banned or restricted

parroquia – parish church

paseo – boulevard, walkway or pedestrian street; the tradition of strolling around the plaza in the evening, men and women moving in opposite directions

Pemex – government-owned petroleum extraction, refining and retailing monopoly

peninsulares – those born in Spain and sent by the Spanish government to rule the colony in Mexico

periférico – ring road

pesero – Mexico City's word for *colectivo;* can mean 'bus' in the northeast

peyote – a hallucinogenic cactus

pinacoteca – art gallery

piñata – clay pot or papier-mâché mold decorated to resemble an animal, pineapple, star, etc and filled with sweets and gifts, then smashed open at fiestas

pirata – literally 'pirate'; used to describe passenger-carrying pickup trucks in some parts of Mexico

playa – beach

plaza de toros – bullring

plazuela – small plaza

poblano/a (m/f) – person from Puebla; something in the style of Puebla

Porfiriato – reign of Porfirio Díaz as president-dictator of Mexico for 30 years until the 1910 *Mexican Revolution*

portales – arcades

posada – inn

PRI – Partido Revolucionario Institucional (Institutional Revolutionary Party); the political party that ruled Mexico for most of the 20th century

Pte – abbreviation for *poniente* (west), used in street names

puerto – port

pulque – milky, low-alcohol brew made from the *maguey* plant

quetzal – crested bird with brilliant green, red and white plumage native to southern Mexico, Central America and northern South America; quetzal feathers were highly prized in pre-Hispanic Mexico

Quetzalcóatl – plumed serpent god of pre-Hispanic Mexico

rebozo – long woolen or linen shawl covering women's head or shoulders

refugio – a very basic cabin for shelter in the mountains

reserva de la biosfera – biosphere reserve; an environmentally protected area where human exploitation is steered toward sustainable activities

retablo – altarpiece, or small painting placed in a church as thanks for miracles, answered prayers etc

río – river

s/n – *sin número* (without number); used in addresses

sacbé (sg), sacbeob (pl) – ceremonial avenue(s) between great Maya cities

sanatorio – hospital, particularly a small private one

sarape – blanket with opening for the head; worn as a cloak

Semana Santa – Holy Week – the week from Palm Sunday to Easter Sunday; Mexico's major holiday period when accommodations and transportation get very busy

sierra – mountain range

sitio – taxi service

stela/stele (sg), stelae/steles (pl) – standing stone monument, usually carved

sur – south; often seen in street names

taller – shop or workshop; a *taller mecánico* is a mechanic's shop, usually for cars; a *taller de llantas* is a tire-repair shop

talud-tablero – stepped building style typical of Teotihuacán, with alternating vertical *(tablero)* and sloping *(talud)* sections

taquilla – ticket window

telamon – statue of a male figure, used instead of a pillar to hold up the roof of a temple; an *atlas*

teleférico – cable car

teléfono (celular) – (cell/mobile) telephone

temascal – pre-Hispanic–style steam bath, often used for curative purposes; sometimes spelt *temazcal*

templo – church; anything from a chapel to a cathedral

teocalli – Aztec sacred precinct

Tezcatlipoca – multifaceted pre-Hispanic god; lord of life and death and protector of warriors; as a smoking mirror he could see into hearts; as the sun god he needed the blood of sacrificed warriors to ensure he would rise again

tezontle – light red, porous volcanic rock used for buildings by the Aztecs and *conquistadores*

tianguis – indigenous people's market

tienda – store

típico/a (m/f) – characteristic of a region; used to describe food in particular

Tláloc – pre-Hispanic rain and water god

tope – speed bump; found on the outskirts of towns and villages; they are only sometimes marked by signs

trapiche – mill; in Baja California usually a sugar mill

UNAM – Universidad Nacional Autónoma de México (National Autonomous University of Mexico)

universidad – university

voladores – literally 'fliers'; Totonac ritual in which men, suspended by their ankles, whirl around a tall pole

War of Independence – war for Mexican independence from Spain (from 1810 to 1821), ending three centuries of Spanish rule

War of the Castes – 19th-century Maya uprising in the Yucatán Peninsula

zócalo – literally 'plinth'; used in some Mexican towns for the main plaza or square

FOOD GLOSSARY

For basic food terms, see p863
For basic menu terms, see p47

adobada – marinated with adobo (chili sauce)
al albañil – 'bricklayer style' ie served with a hot chili sauce
al mojo de ajo – with garlic sauce
al pastor – cooked on a pit, shepherd's style
albóndigas – meatballs
antojitos – 'little whims': tortilla-based snacks like tacos and enchiladas
arroz mexicana – pilaf-style rice with a tomato base
atole – gruel made with ground corn
avena – oatmeal

barbacoa – pit-smoked barbecue
bolillo – French-style roll
brocheta – shishkabob
burrito – filling in a large flour tortilla

cajeta – goat's milk and sugar boiled to a paste
calabacita – squash
carnitas – pork simmered in lard
cecina – thin cut of meat, flavored with chili and sautéed or grilled
chicharrones – fried pork skins
chile relleno – chili stuffed with meat or cheese, usually fried with egg batter
chiles en nogada – mild green chilies stuffed with meat and fruit, fried in batter and served with a sauce of cream, ground walnuts and cheese
chorizo – Mexican-style bulk sausage made with chili and vinegar
chuleta de puerco – pork chop
churros – doughnut-like fritters
cochinita pibil – pork, marinated in chilies, wrapped in banana leaves, and pit-cooked or baked
coctel de frutas – fruit cocktail
costillas de res – beef ribs
crepas – crepes or thin pancakes

empanada – pastry turnover filled with meat, cheese or fruits

filete a la tampiqueña – Tampico-style steak: a thin tenderloin, grilled and served with chili strips and onion, a quesadilla and enchilada
flor de calabaza – squash blossom
frijoles a la charra – beans cooked with tomatoes, chilies and onions (also called *frijoles rancheros*)

guacamole – mashed avocado, often with lime juice, onion, tomato and chili

horchata – soft drink made with melon seeds
huachinango veracruzana – Veracruz-style red snapper with a sauce of tomatoes, olives, vinegar and capers
huevos motuleños – fried eggs sandwiched between corn tortillas, and topped with peas, tomato, ham and cheese
huevos rancheros – fried eggs served on a corn tortilla, topped with a sauce of tomato, chilies, and onions, and served with refried beans
huevos revueltos – scrambled eggs
huitlacoche – a much esteemed fungus that grows on corn

lomo de cerdo – pork loin

machacado – pulverized jerky, often scrambled with eggs
menudo – tripe stew
milanesa – thin slices of beef or pork, breaded and fried
mixiote – chili-seasoned lamb steamed in agave membranes or parchment
mole negro – chicken or pork in a very dark sauce of chilies, fruits, nuts, spices and chocolate
mole poblano – chicken or turkey in a sauce of chilies, fruits, nuts, spices and chocolate

nopalitos – sliced cactus paddles, sautéed or grilled

picadillo – ground beef filling that often includes fruit and nuts
pipián verde – stew of chicken, with ground squash seeds, chilies and tomatillos
pozole – soup or thin stew of hominy, meat, vegetables and chilies

queso fundido – cheese melted, often with chorizo or mushrooms, and served as an appetizer with tortillas

rajas – strips of mild green chili, often fried with onions

tinga poblana – stew of pork, vegetables and chilies

Behind the Scenes

SEND US YOUR FEEDBACK

We love to hear from travelers – your comments keep us on our toes and help make our books better. Our well-traveled team reads every word on what you loved or loathed about this book. Although we cannot reply individually to postal submissions, we always guarantee that your feedback goes straight to the appropriate authors, in time for the next edition. Each person who sends us information is thanked in the next edition – the most useful submissions are rewarded with a selection of digital PDF chapters.

Visit **lonelyplanet.com/contact** to submit your updates and suggestions or to ask for help. Our award-winning website also features inspirational travel stories, news and discussions.

Note: We may edit, reproduce and incorporate your comments in Lonely Planet products such as guidebooks, websites and digital products, so let us know if you don't want your comments reproduced or your name acknowledged. For a copy of our privacy policy visit lonelyplanet.com/privacy.

OUR READERS

Many thanks to the travelers who used the last edition and wrote to us with helpful hints, useful advice and interesting anecdotes:

Anders Rehle, Annette Hill, Arthur Baars, Asim Sheikh, Bertrand Lavallee, Bob Broughton, Cailin Rogers, Caroline Edwards, Caryn Wolfe, Catherine Gordon, Clayton Szczech, Daniela Zuegel, David Tobias, Eugenio Cortes, Geraldine Aguilar Shields, Glenn Bernard, Guillermo Loam, Hank Raymond, Héctor Lara, Jack Benjamin, James Varney, Jeff Randall, John Malone, Jón Bergamann Maronsson, Klara Prinz-Prueller, Laura Gonzalez Arriaga, Lee Doan, Liz Montes, Manuel Rueda, Manuela Arigoni, Marianne Kerrebrouck, Mark Broadhead, Miguel Yapur, Mogens Ditlev, Nicole Samaha, Peter Mifsud, Peter van der Kroon, Phyllis Cooper, Rachel Van Ness, Ramona Scheurer, Ricarda Krumbiegel , Sabrina Bernhardt, Sharon Keld, Silvia Naylor, Suzanne Fee, Suzanne Millward, Theresa Michaelis, Tuuli Nummi, Yossi Margoninsky.

AUTHOR THANKS

John Noble

I dedicate my part in this book to Catherine Craddock-Carrillo, who commissioned this and the previous three editions of Lonely Planet *Mexico*, and who has always been the perfect colleague; among other things supportive, inspirational, reliable, fair, reasonable...Mexico isn't the same without you Cat! Extra special thanks also to Fausto Jasso, Leyla Bastar, Julien Pardinilla, John and Maria Taylor, Gina Machorro, Maria Crespo, Ron Mader, Carlos Gross, Claudia Schurr and the wonderful, super-professional team of authors!

Kate Armstrong

Muchas gracias como siempre: Angel Pineda in Querétaro, Thomas Peter and Brigitte Sigrist in Real de Catorce, Cesar Arias and Roz Colley in San Miguel. A huge cheer to the ever-reliable John Noble and the Mexico team, plus Cat Craddock, former (and much missed) CE extraordinaire. Finally in print: massive *gracias* to the wonderful, professional former CEs and editors. You are gurus. Lastly, thanks to Chris: ever-patient about my itinerant LP lifestyle... and the world's best chef.

Stuart Butler

First and foremost I must, once again, thank my wife, Heather, for putting up with my extended periods away whilst working on this project, and coping so admirably with two small children on her own. And, thank you to Jake and Grace for also putting up with their daddy disappearing off again. In Colima thanks to Jupiter Rivera, Lety Zepeda and Sofia de Alva, in Ciudad Guzmán thanks to Gerardo R Bernabe Aguayo and in Angangueo thanks to Mario Bernal Martinez. Finally, I'd like to thank the truck driver who decided to redesign the back of my hire car by driving into it. It looked so much better after that...

John Hecht

Many thanks to all my good friends in Mexico City for the helpful recommendations, and my gratitude to coordinating author John Noble and the book's previous and current cowriters. A very special shout-out to commissioning editor Catherine Craddock-Carrillo – I miss you Cat! As always, a big hug for Lau.

Beth Kohn

Thanks so much to Cat Craddock-Carrillo – you were (and will be) greatly missed! Fernando Mérida (Palenque) and Ricardo López Vassallo (Tonalá) offered their expertise in those regions, and the Zap-Castillo clan made San Cristóbal my cushy second home once again. Stalwart John Noble helped out as always, and made sure his fellow scribes weren't subsumed by rising floodwaters. Love to Claudio.

Tom Masters

Many thanks to all those who helped me on my travels through Veracruz, the staff at the various tourist offices throughout the state, the guys in Fortín who helped me find a mechanic on a Sunday when my car broke down, and all the kind hoteliers who shared their local knowledge and tips with me. Special thanks to Diego Cantu Llorens, Enrique Perosi, Alain Garcia, William Van Meter and Mario Gosha.

Josephine Quintero

I would like to thank coordinating author John Noble for his suggestions and support. *Gracias* also to Sally Harrison for her good humor, great map-reading skills and adventurous spirit on the road. I would also like to thank my supportive Quintero family in San Diego and La Paz, plus numerous other old and new friends, including Robin Chapman, Yvonne Chastang, José Guttierez, Luis Barrio Ruiz and all the helpful folk at various tourist information offices and tour companies.

Adam Skolnick

As is always the case for me in Mexico, I received far too many friendly smiles and welcome insights to thank everyone appropriately. So allow me to give one giant hug to this wild, spicy and soothing country that is so very easy to adore. I'd also like to thank Audrey, Lee & Chawnalee and Christian Kohl in PV, Eugenia Michel Gomez in Melaque, John Hecht in Mexico City, Lia Barrett and Claudia Wilcher, Cat Craddock-Carrillo, John Noble, Bruce Evans and the entire Lonely Planet team.

Iain Stewart

Thanks to Cat Craddock-Carrillo for inviting me on board again and all the staff in Melbourne and beyond; John Noble for his advice; and my family for putting up with another extended absence. On the road I was greatly assisted by Miguel in Durango, Ivan in Creel, Mario and Tito in Cerocahui, Perry in Kino, and Chal in Fuerte.

Phillip Tang

Muchísimas gracias to Ernesto for sharing and creating an amazing journey with me on and off the road. *Gracias* to Sr and Sra Alanis for the hospitality, route planning and *panques*. Thanks Vek for getting me hooked again on Mexico's one-horse towns, and thanks Abeyami for a sense of home and dressing for the Kennedys. Hooray to my adventuring sister Lisa, Anna – the face :-O, and Slayer Jack for safe harbour in London.

Lucas Vidgen

Thanks first and foremost to the Mexicans in general for making a country that's such a joy to travel and work in. Vanessa Hines, Bea and Mario were a huge help in Playa del Carmen and Cancún, and Donard was a fantastic source of information for Mérida and surrounds. As always, thanks to América, Sofía and Teresa for being there, and for being there when I got back.

ACKNOWLEDGMENTS

Climate map data adapted from Peel MC, Finlayson BL & McMahon TA (2007) 'Updated World Map of the Köppen-Geiger Climate Classification', *Hydrology and Earth System Sciences*, 11, 163344.

Chichén Itzá illustration pp324-5 by Michael Weldon.

Cover photograph: Taxco, Guerrero, David Bank/AWL.

THIS BOOK

This 14th edition of Lonely Planet's *Mexico* guidebook was researched and written by John Noble (coordinating author), Kate Armstrong, Stuart Butler, John Hecht, Beth Kohn, Tom Masters, Josephine Quintero, Adam Skolnick, Iain Stewart, Phillip Tang and Lucas Vidgen. The essay 'The Mexican Kitchen' was written by Mauricio Velázquez de León. This guidebook was commissioned in Lonely Planet's Oakland office, and produced by the following:

Commissioning Editor Catherine Craddock-Carrillo

Destination Editor Clifton Wilkinson

Product Editor Tracy Whitmey

Senior Cartographer Mark Griffiths

Book Designer Lauren Egan

Assisting Editors Michelle Bennett, Joe Bindloss, Nigel Chin, Megan Eaves, Gemma Graham, Jodie Matire, Kristin Odijk, Susan Paterson, Matt Phillips, Sarah Reid, James Smart, Anna Tyler

Assisting Cartographers Jeff Cameron, Corey Hutchison, Valentina Kremenchutskaya, Alison Lyall

Cover Researcher Naomi Parker

Language Content Branislava Vladisavljevic

Thanks to Anita Banh, Imogen Bannister, Kate Chapman, Ryan Evans, Larissa Frost, Genesys India, Briohny Hooper, Kate James, Elizabeth Jones, Jouve India, Kate Mathews, Claire Naylor, Karyn Noble, Katie O'Connell, Martine Power, Ross Taylor, Angela Tinson

Index

Map Pages **000**
Photo Pages **000**

Map Pages **000**
Photo Pages **000**

Map Pages **000**
Photo Pages **000**

Map Pages **000**
Photo Pages **000**

Map Pages **000**
Photo Pages **000**

Map Legend

Sights
- Beach
- Bird Sanctuary
- Buddhist
- Castle/Palace
- Christian
- Confucian
- Hindu
- Islamic
- Jain
- Jewish
- Monument
- Museum/Gallery/Historic Building
- Ruin
- Sento Hot Baths/Onsen
- Shinto
- Sikh
- Taoist
- Winery/Vineyard
- Zoo/Wildlife Sanctuary
- Other Sight

Activities, Courses & Tours
- Bodysurfing
- Diving
- Canoeing/Kayaking
- Course/Tour
- Skiing
- Snorkeling
- Surfing
- Swimming/Pool
- Walking
- Windsurfing
- Other Activity

Sleeping
- Sleeping
- Camping

Eating
- Eating

Drinking & Nightlife
- Drinking & Nightlife
- Cafe

Entertainment
- Entertainment

Shopping
- Shopping

Information
- Bank
- Embassy/Consulate
- Hospital/Medical
- Internet
- Police
- Post Office
- Telephone
- Toilet
- Tourist Information
- Other Information

Geographic
- Beach
- Hut/Shelter
- Lighthouse
- Lookout
- Mountain/Volcano
- Oasis
- Park
- Pass
- Picnic Area
- Waterfall

Population
- Capital (National)
- Capital (State/Province)
- City/Large Town
- Town/Village

Transport
- Airport
- BART station
- Border crossing
- Boston T station
- Bus
- Cable car/Funicular
- Cycling
- Ferry
- Metro/Muni station
- Monorail
- Parking
- Petrol station
- Subway/SkyTrain station
- Taxi
- Train station/Railway
- Tram
- Underground station
- Other Transport

Note: Not all symbols displayed above appear on the maps in this book

Routes
- Tollway
- Freeway
- Primary
- Secondary
- Tertiary
- Lane
- Unsealed road
- Road under construction
- Plaza/Mall
- Steps
- Tunnel
- Pedestrian overpass
- Walking Tour
- Walking Tour detour
- Path/Walking Trail

Boundaries
- International
- State/Province
- Disputed
- Regional/Suburb
- Marine Park
- Cliff
- Wall

Hydrography
- River, Creek
- Intermittent River
- Canal
- Water
- Dry/Salt/Intermittent Lake
- Reef

Areas
- Airport/Runway
- Beach/Desert
- Cemetery (Christian)
- Cemetery (Other)
- Glacier
- Mudflat
- Park/Forest
- Sight (Building)
- Sportsground
- Swamp/Mangrove

Beth Kohn

Chiapas & Tabasco Beth has been sojourning in Mexico for more than 30 years, and this was her fourth whirl through Chiapas and Tabasco for the *Mexico* guide. This time around, she waited patiently at highway mudslides, cavorted with fireflies in the Lacandón Jungle and absorbed untold miles of spine-adjusting *terracería*. A thankful resident of San Francisco, she's also co-authored Lonely Planet's *California*, *South America* and *Yosemite, Sequoia & Kings Canyon National Parks* guides. You can see more of her work at www.bethkohn.com.

Tom Masters

Veracruz Tom is a travel writer based in Berlin. His first experience of Mexico was in the jungle of Chiapas filming at Palenque, which led to repeat visits and a stint of living in Mexico City. Having previously authored the Around Mexico City and Western Central Highlands chapters of this book, this time Tom covered the much overlooked state of Veracruz. He can be found online at www.tommasters.net.

Josephine Quintero

Baja California Josephine was married for many years to a Mexican American with a large extended family, leading to a healthy exposure to mariachi music and margaritas. She made frequent trips over the border from her home in San Diego and continues to be enthralled by the heady mix of vibrant culture, wonderful people, fabulous food and all that history. Now living in Andalucía, Spain, Josephine was thrilled to have the opportunity to revisit Baja California, one of her favorite regions in Mexico.

Read more about Josephine at:
lonelyplanet.com/members/josephinequintero

Adam Skolnick

Central Pacific Coast Adam has written about travel, culture, health, sports, human rights and the environment for *Lonely Planet*, the *New York Times*, *Outside*, *Men's Health*, *Travel & Leisure*, *Salon.com*, *BBC.com* and *ESPN.com*. He has authored or coauthored 25 Lonely Planet guidebooks. His debut novel, *Middle of Somewhere*, is set to publish in 2014. You can read more of his work at www.adamskolnick.com. Find him on Twitter and Instagram (@adamskolnick).

Iain Stewart

Copper Canyon & Northern Mexico Iain first travelled through Mexico in 1993, journeying between Nogales and Chetumal by road and rail. He's returned regularly and authored several chapters for Lonely Planet guidebooks over the years. On this trip he was humbled by the majesty of the Copper Canyon and the silence of the desert, and impressed by some superb museums. Iain has written guidebooks for destinations as diverse as Ibiza and Indonesia. He lives close to the beach in Brighton, UK.

Phillip Tang

Around Mexico City Phillip first visited Mexico in 2002 and keeps being summoned back. He falls in love with the country again with every *comida corrida*, candy-coloured wall, and *calavera*. He is now accidentally living in Mexico City en route between his other homes of London and Sydney. On the road for this guide, he created animated gifs (tacotrauma.tumblr.com), Instagrammed (@mrtangtangtang) and tweeted (@philliptang). More of his travel writing can be found at philliptang.co.uk.

Lucas Vidgen

Yucatán Peninsula Lucas first visited the Yucatán in 2002, breezing through long enough to be captivated by the lush scenery, irresistible beaches and delicious food. He now lives in Guatemala and makes it a point to pop over the border whenever he can to munch down on *pibil* and splash around in cenotes. Lucas has contributed to a variety of Lonely Planet's Latin American titles. Back home he publishes – and occasionally works on – Quetzaltenango's leading nightlife and culture magazine, *XelaWho* (www.xelawho.com).

OUR STORY

A beat-up old car, a few dollars in the pocket and a sense of adventure. In 1972 that's all Tony and Maureen Wheeler needed for the trip of a lifetime – across Europe and Asia overland to Australia. It took several months, and at the end – broke but inspired – they sat at their kitchen table writing and stapling together their first travel guide, *Across Asia on the Cheap*. Within a week they'd sold 1500 copies. Lonely Planet was born.

Today, Lonely Planet has offices in Melbourne, London and Oakland, with more than 600 staff and writers. We share Tony's belief that 'a great guidebook should do three things: inform, educate and amuse'.

OUR WRITERS

John Noble

Coordinating Author, Oaxaca John has been making extended trips to Mexico for over three decades and coordinated every edition of this guide since 1994, wandering from Tijuana to Chetumal and many, many places in between. He's climbed volcanoes, boated down jungle rivers, explored the barrios of Mexico City and understood why Oaxacans revere mezcal. Mexico's food, drinks, landscapes, arts, history and, above all, the warmth of the Mexicans themselves always have him looking forward to the next trip. Originally from England's Ribble Valley, John has lived for 20 years in the land of Mexico's old colonial masters, Spain.

Read more about John at:
lonelyplanet.com/members/ewoodrover

Kate Armstrong

Northern Central Highlands An Australian by birth but a Latina (she believes) in a former life, Kate visits Mexico regularly. This is the fourth time she's covered the silver cities for Lonely Planet. On this trip she embraced the country's patriotic Independence Day celebrations, partied at village festivals, ate her way through kilos of street foods (*gorditas* are her favorite), and danced her way through the magic of Mexico. Kate's other freelance writing adventures appear at www.katearmstrong.com.au and @nomaditis.

Read more about Kate at:
lonelyplanet.com/members/kate_armstrong

Stuart Butler

Western Central Highlands Stuart first traveled to Mexico in the late 1990s as part of a longer trip through Latin America. Mexico stood out for him thanks to its heady mix of beaches, wildlife, surf, mountains and rich culture, and he has since made a number of repeat visits. Hailing from southwest England, Stuart now lives on the beautiful beaches of southwest France, close to the Spanish border, with his wife and young son and daughter. He is also the coauthor of many Spain-based Lonely Planet books.

John Hecht

Mexico City John has lived in Mexico for two decades now. He spent the early years in Guadalajara studying Spanish and practicing his new language skills in the neighborhood cantinas. Several years later he moved to Mexico City and turned freelance writer. Working on the Mexico City chapter reminded him of everything he loves about his adopted city, especially the mezcal and taco crawls. He's worked on five Lonely Planet *Mexico* books.

Read more about John at:
lonelyplanet.com/members/johnhecht

OVER PAGE MORE WRITERS

Published by Lonely Planet Publications Pty Ltd
ABN 36 005 607 983
14th edition – Sep 2014
ISBN 978 1 7422 0806 0

10 9 8 7 6 5 4 3 2 1
Printed in Singapore